Stories Old and New

古今小説
（喻世明言）

Stories Old and New

A MING DYNASTY COLLECTION

Compiled by Feng Menglong (1574–1646)

Translated by Shuhui Yang and Yunqin Yang

UNIVERSITY OF WASHINGTON PRESS

SEATTLE AND LONDON

The publication of *Stories Old and New* was generously supported by grants from the Chiang Ching-Kuo Foundation for International Scholarly Exchange, from the Pacific Cultural Foundation, and from Bates College.

Library of Congress Cataloging-in-Publication Data
Feng, Meng-lung, 1574–1646.
[Ku chin hsiao shuo. English]
Stories old and new : a Ming dynasty collection / compiled by Feng Menglong (1574–1646) : translated by Shuhui Yang and Yunqin Yang. p. cm.
Includes bibliographical references.
ISBN 0-295-97843-0 (alk. paper).—ISBN 0-295-97844-9 (pbk. : alk. paper)
1. Feng, Meng-lung, 1574–1646 Translations into English.
I. Yang, Shuhui. II. Yang, Yunqin. III. Title.
PL2698.F4K7813 2000
895.1'346—dc21
99-28753
CIP

The paper used in this publication is acid-free and recycled from 10 percent post-consumer and at least 50 percent pre-consumer waste. It meets the minimum requirements of American National Standard for Information Sciences—Permanence of Paper for Printed Library Materials, ANSI Z39.48–1984. ∞

To our parents and sisters

Contents

Selected Illustrations from the 1620 Edition

Acknowledgments

This translation benefited greatly from the help of Prof. Robert E. Hegel and Prof. David Rolston, to whom we wish to express our profound gratitude. Prof. Hegel has, from the very conception of this project, given us enthusiastic encouragement and unfailing support. Both professors read the entire manuscript, compared it with the original, pointed out omissions, corrected errors, and made many valuable suggestions for improvement. We also owe Prof. Hegel a debt of gratitude for having obtained for us reproducible copies of a selection of illustrations from the 1620 Chinese edition of *Stories Old and New*. Our thanks go as well to the Imperial Diet Library of Japan for permitting us to reproduce these illustrations from Nagasawa Kikuya's volume *Mindai sōzubon zuroku: Naikaku bunko shozō tanpen shōsetsu nobu* (Tokyo: Nihon Shoshigakkai, 1962). We are very grateful to our editor, Lorri Hagman, for her enthusiasm for the project, her expertise in preparing the book for press, and her sharp eye for detecting errors and inconsistencies. Needless to say, any errors and infelicities that remain are solely ours.

Introduction

In Chinese literary studies, the second half of the Ming dynasty (1368–1644) is customarily regarded as the golden age of vernacular fiction, an age that witnessed the emergence of the well-known "four masterworks of the Chinese novel": *The Romance of the Three Kingdoms* (Sanguo zhi yanyi), *Outlaws of the Marsh* (Shuihu zhuan), *Journey to the West* (Xiyou ji), and *The Plum in the Golden Vase* (Jin ping mei). Toward the end of this period, there appeared three collections of short stories that represent the most important milestone in the development of the Chinese vernacular story.

Stories Old and New (Gujin xiaoshuo) was the first of these three collections, published in Suzhou (Soochow) in 1620. Perhaps as a result of its instant success, the other two soon followed as its sequels: *Comprehensive Words to Warn the World* (Jingshi tongyan) in 1624 and *Constant Words to Awaken the World* (Xingshi hengyan) in 1627. Each collection contains forty stories, and since *Stories Old and New* is also known as *Illustrious Words to Instruct the World* (Yushi mingyan), they are most often referred to collectively as the *Sanyan* (lit., *Three Words*), from the common Chinese character with which each title ends.

The *Sanyan* collections were edited by Feng Menglong (1574–1646), the most knowledgeable connoisseur of popular literature of his time. He came from a well-to-do, educated family in the exceptionally prosperous Suzhou Prefecture, one of the great cultural centers of Ming China. His father was closely associated with a few distinguished scholar-official families in the area, including that of Wang Jingchen (1513–1595), a renowned orthodox Confucian scholar. Feng Menglong was the second of three talented brothers known as the Three Fengs of the Wu Area. His older brother Menggui was an accomplished artist and his younger brother Mengxiong a highly regarded poet. Feng Menglong himself acquired the preliminary academic degree of *shengyuan* around the age of twenty and was greatly admired by his friends and school-mates as a brilliant and widely read scholar.[1]

But this talented young man also had a propensity for things unconventional and "heterodox." Not only did he avidly study and openly advocate the unorthodox theories of Li Zhi (1527–1602), but he also frequented gambling houses and courtesans' quarters. Of the gambling guides he compiled, two are still extant: *Classic of Cards* (Pai jing), in thirteen *juan* (sections), and *Rules of the Madiao Games* (Madiao jiaoli), in ten *juan*, *madiao* being a card game Feng is said to have invented.[2] The latter work was long held as a classic among card players in the Qing dynasty (1644–1911).[3] Feng's popularity with the Suzhou courtesans was also something he was proud of. In a note to a popular song in *Guazhir*, a book of songs to the tune "Guazhir," he says he was often showered with gifts from courtesans.[4] He was deeply involved in romantic affairs with at least two of them (including Hou Huiqing, who finally, much to Feng's grief, married someone else) and helped compile *The Hundred Beauties of Nanjing* (Jinling baimei), a book that ranks and evaluates the hundred most beautiful and accomplished courtesans in Nanjing.[5] He also wrote individual courtesans' biographies, at least three of which are extant.[6] We get a glimpse of the kind of romance he had with courtesans in story 12, "The Courtesans Mourn Liu the Seventh in the Spring Breeze," in this volume if we read the main character Liu Yong (d. ca. 1053), a famous Song dynasty *ci* (lyric) poet, as Feng Menglong's self projection. Feng's philogynous reputation was so widespread that other writers' books about women were sometimes attributed to him in order to promote sales.[7]

Feng's involvement with courtesans indeed helped his writing career. He published a collection of his own art songs, *Songs of Charm and Harmony* (Wanzhuan ge), and reprinted sixteen sets in an art-song anthology, *Celestial Songs Played Anew* (Taixia xin zou) many years later. Although *Songs of Charm and Harmony* is lost, we can see clearly that all of the extant sixteen sets are about his relationships with courtesans, with as many as six relating to his loss of Hong Huiqing.[8] And it is reasonable to assume that some of the songs in *Celestial Songs Played Anew* were performed in pleasure houses before Feng collected and published them,[9] as is the case with many folk songs Feng published in his *Guazhir* and *Hill Songs* (Shange).[10] Feng mentions that one song in *Guazhir* was "provided by Feng Xisheng, a famous courtesan."[11]

As can be expected, Feng's bohemian way of life invited criticism from conservative moralists. Feng responded by defending Liu Yong's liaisons with courtesans (and indirectly, his own) in a note in story 12 in *Stories Old and New*: "Lord Guo [Ziyi] and Prime Minister Wen [Tianxiang] were also self-indulgent men who frequented courtesan quarters, but, once charged with important missions, they dedicated themselves to the nation to the neglect of their self interests. What does a pedantic Confucian moralist know!" This note, however, reveals another side of Feng's personality—a strong sense of social responsibility along with ambition to hold office himself. He spent more than twenty years, as his younger brother tells us, studying *The Spring and Autumn Annals* (Chunqiu), which he chose as his civil service examination specialty.[12] He made two long trips to the Macheng area in Hubei Province,

the center of scholarship on the *Annals,* in order to study the classic in a special study group, the first time between 1612 and 1617 and the second in 1620.[13]

As a result, three of his examination handbooks on the *Annals* were pub-
lished within a few years: *Guide to the Spring and Autumn Annals* (Linjing
zhiyue), 1620; *New Light on the Central Ideas of the Spring and Autumn Annals*
(Chunqiu dingzhi canxin), ca. 1623; and *A Spring and Autumn Annals The-
saurus* (Chunqiu hengku), 1625, also known as *An Alternative Edition of the
Complete Guide to the Spring and Autumn Annals* (Beiben Chunqiu daquan).[14]
In 1630 he published another examination handbook, *Guide to the Four Books*
(Sishu zhi yue). These handbooks seem to have sold fast; the gazetteer of
Feng's hometown, *Suzhou fu zhi,* even mentioned *Guide to the Spring and
Autumn Annals* and *A Spring and Autumn Annals Thesaurus* as the two most
important guidebooks for civil service examination candidates specializing
in the *Annals.*[15] The *Thesaurus* became a standard work for much of the Qing
dynasty.[16]

Ironically, Feng himself never passed the provincial-level civil service examinations, in spite of his sustained effort, his erudition, and the market success
of his examination handbooks, which must have benefited other candidates.
His continuous bad luck in the examinations, however, turned out to be bliss
for the reading public. Unencumbered by official duties, Feng was able to
devote more time to his publishing career. During the ten years between 1620
and 1630, he produced so much at his desk that he "must surely have been
making his living by writing."[17] Apart from the four handbooks on Confucian
classics mentioned above, he published at least another nine titles during the
decade, including the three famous *Sanyan* collections; *The Quelling of the
Demons* (Ping yao zhuan), 1920, Feng's first vernacular novel; *Talks Old and
New* (Gujin tangai), 1920, an anthology of classical-language anecdotes and
tales; *Selections from the Grand Gleanings of the Taiping Period* (Taiping guangji
chao), 1926, a drastic revision of the Song dynasty encyclopedic anthology of
anecdotes and tales *Taiping guangji; Sack of Wisdom* (Zhi nang), 1626, a joke
book with comments; *History of Love* (Qing shi), after 1628, a classical-language
anthology of more than 850 tales and anecdotes on love and compassion, also
called *A Classified Outline of the History of Love* (Qingshi leilüe); and *Celestial
Songs Played Anew* (1628). *A New History of the States* (Xin leiguo zhi), Feng's
first attempt at fictionalized history, may have been published in 1628 or after.

In 1630, at the age of fifty-six, Feng Menglong seems to have lost hope
in passing the examinations and decided, instead, to take the alternative route
to office by accepting the status of tribute student. He then served one term
as assistant instructor in Dantu County (about ninety miles northwest of
Suzhou), probably from 1631 to 1634,[18] before he was promoted to a minor
official position as magistrate of Shouning County, Fujian. He held this office

for four years and proved himself to be an honest, caring, and efficient administrator, as is registered in *County History of Shouning* (Shouning xian zhi), compiled in the early Qing period, which also tells us that Feng "venerated literary studies more than anything else" (*shou shang wenxue*) during his service.[19] This means Feng kept on writing when he was off duty, although he published far less than before. He finished compiling *Supplement to "Sack of Wisdom"* (Zhi nang bu) in 1634 and most probably completed his play *Perfect Satisfaction* (Wanshi zu), one of the sixteen extant plays he wrote, adapted, or edited, in 1635.[20] As county magistrate, he published in 1637 a local history with the unusual title *A Provisional History of Shouning* (Shouning dai zhi), which suggests, according to Patrick Hanan, Feng's "personal approach to the impersonal face of local history."[21]

Feng's last political involvement, toward the end of his life, was his association with the Southern Ming government in its desperate resistance against the crushing forces of the Manchus. Shortly after the fall of Beijing and the suicide of the emperor in 1644, he compiled *Veritable Records of the National Resurgence* (Zhongxing shilu), in which he both records the disastrous events and makes plans of action to handle the crisis. A few months later this book was incorporated into his larger compilation *Records of the Year Jiashen, 1644* (Jiashen jishi). In the middle of 1645, *Veritable Records* was reissued as *Grand Designs of the National Resurgence* (Zhongxing weilüe), with some revision and a new preface by Feng. He died soon afterward in 1646 at the age of seventy-two, without finishing his *Ink Crazy Studio's New Song Manual* (Mohan zhai xinding cipu).

Feng Menglong was one of the most prolific writers of his time. The books he published could literally be "piled up to reach his own height" (*zhuzuo dengshen,* a phrase traditionally used by critics to praise exceptionally productive writers),[22] and they covered such a wide range of interests and literary genres that Feng has been described as "presenting himself in two distinct personae, or . . . in a range of personae between two extremes."[23] At one extreme, he appears in some of his works as the wit, the ribald humorist, the bohemian, the drinker, the romantic lover. This is the Feng Menglong who compiled *Treasury of Jokes* (Xiaofu; date unknown), who published two volumes of folk songs (*Guazhir* and *Hill Songs*), mostly on erotic or ribald themes, and whose passionate love affair with the famous Suzhou courtesan Hou Huiqing is revealed in some of his poems. At the other extreme is Feng Menglong the patriot, the orthodox scholar, and the ardent examination candidate, who authored at least three handbooks on the Confucian classic *The Spring and Autumn Annals,* who wrote a similar handbook on the Four Books, and who published many patriotic tracts as a consequence of his participation in Southern Ming resistance activities. These two personae may seem to be mutually exclusive, yet in his fiction as well as his plays, Feng Menglong often reveals elements of both in a single text.[24]

Modern scholars generally agree, however, that Feng Menglong's greatest contribution to literature was in the field of vernacular fiction, particularly his collecting and editing of the three *Sanyan* collections of 120 vernacular short stories. This genre, known as *huaben,* is believed to have developed, along with the vernacular novel, during the Song and Yuan dynasties and reached maturity in the late Ming. Two social factors are considered to have played a crucial role in the rise of this literary genre: the success of the publishing industry as a result of economic progress and educational expansion, and the increasingly difficult competition for examination degrees. The former offered job opportunities and the chance to pursue private interests to examination candidates before they were granted official positions, if ever; the latter guaranteed a sufficient supply of highly qualified writers and editors, as well as readers.

The Publishing Industry and the Civil Service Examinations

The Song and Yuan dynasties (960–1279, 1260–1368) witnessed the first rapid growth of the publishing industry in the Jianyang area of Fujian Province, on the southeast coast of China. But the economic boom of the sixteenth century as a result of monetization of silver[25] moved the center of the book publishing trade to the lower Yangzi region, the most developed and urbanized area in late Ming China. Suzhou, Feng Menglong's hometown, was the site of most printing houses for which location can be ascertained, followed by Hangzhou and Nanjing.[26]

Recent scholarship has shown that publishing houses during the late Ming were of several types: official (supported by branches of the central government in Beijing and Nanjing), commercial (book dealers), private (collectors and scholars), and academic (private academies). Although book dealers were most prolific in number of titles and volume of production, "the finest books were produced by scholarly collector-printers who catered to the refined tastes of others of their class."[27]

Ironically, the economic boom that contributed to the development of the publishing industry also stimulated expansion of the school system and thus increased the number of examination candidates competing for degrees.[28] The civil service examination system, the best-known political institution of imperial China, consisted of examinations at three levels: district (prefectural), provincial, and national (metropolitan). Successful candidates on the first level received a *shengyuan* degree, on the second a *juren* degree, and on the third, the highest degree of *jinshi*. Normally *shengyuan* degree holders were not appointed to official positions. From the late fourteenth century to 1600 (when Feng Menglong was a young man of twenty-six), the number of recipients of this lowest degree increased by twentyfold, but the bureaucracy did not grow accordingly.[29] Consequently, the highest barrier was in the provincial examination; only one out of one hundred candidates could pass.[30] The competition in the lower Yangzi region was even more intense, for the quotas the government imposed on the numbers of successful candidates favored culturally less-developed areas. What is worse, the officials who administered the examinations under such circumstances "had to think more about how to eliminate candidates than about how to select the best scholars, and they devised various complicated formal requirements that in the end destroyed the true purpose of the whole system."[31] Not surprisingly, as Robert E. Hegel points out, it was in that area at that time that Chinese vernacular fiction reached maturity, for many writers were from precisely this large and disgruntled group of *shengyuan* holders in the lower Yangzi region.[32] Feng Menglong was a case in point. All of his vernacular fiction—two novels and three collections of short stories—was published in his most productive (and perhaps most frustrated) ten years before he was appointed assistant instructor in Dantu at the age of fifty-six or fifty-seven. It is therefore not surprising that he expressed time and again in the *Sanyan* collections his anxiety over the examination system. For example, story 31, "Sima Mao Disrupts Order in the Underworld and Sits in Judgment," is about a talented and erudite examination candidate who continues to fail the examinations even after the age of fifty. When he finds himself led to the underworld, he confronts and criticizes King Yama vehemently for such unjust treatment to the talented and virtuous in the human world. To this Feng Menglong added a marginal note: "He says everything I wanted to say to unburden myself of all my complaints."

The Sanyan *and the Vernacular Story*

Feng Menglong can be considered the most important figure in the development of the vernacular story; he almost single-handedly established this genre with *Stories Old and New* and his other two collections of stories. As a passionate champion of popular literature, he managed to rescue from oblivion a significant proportion of the early *huaben* stories by making them available to the public again. But preservation of existing stories was by no means Feng Menglong's only concern—he probably was more interested in giving prestige to this new literary genre and establishing it socially. In the Preface to *Stories Old and New*, he places vernacular fiction on a par with the highly esteemed classical tales of the Tang Dynasty:

> *Literature and the arts have been so vigorously advanced by the imperial court of this Ming dynasty that each and every school is flourishing; in vernacular fiction*

*alone, there is no lack of writings of a quality far above those of the Song. It is a
mistake to believe, as some do, that such works lack the charm of those of the
Tang. One who has a love for the peach need not forsake the apricot. Fine linen,
silk gauze, plush, brocade—each has its proper occasion for wear.*

In order to elevate the status of the vernacular story, Feng Menglong also
claims, in the same Preface, that the origin of all fiction is the grand tradition
of historiography, and he ascribes to the *huaben* story more educational and
moral power than to *The Analects of Confucius* (Lunyu).[33] To substantiate
such claims, not surprisingly, Feng is believed to have extensively modified
some of the stories he had collected and to have incorporated many of his
own stories and some of his friends' into the *Sanyan* collections, although he
makes no acknowledgment of authorship whatsoever in the Preface.[34] According to Patrick Hanan, who applied rigorous stylistic criteria in his studies of
the dating and authorship of Chinese vernacular stories, Feng Menglong is
the probable author of nineteen stories in *Stories Old and New,* sixteen in the
second collection, and one or two in the third.[35]

PAIRED STORIES

A less drastic but more obvious aspect of Feng's "editing" is his rearrangement
of the stories in the three collections into pairs. The thematically and gram-
matically parallel pairs of titles may be an attempt to parody the parallelism
of classical poetry and belles lettres prose (the two most honored literary
genres of Feng's time),[36] or may simply represent his effort to elevate the vernacular short story. However, on the textual level, it is clear that stories were
composed with their pairs in mind.[37] The paired stories often share common
features in subject matter or plot line, and occasionally they contrast or comment on each other.

Stories 7–8 and 15–16 in *Stories Old and New* can serve as examples of
Feng's pairing practice. Story 7, "Yang Jiao'ai Lays Down His Life for the Sake
of Friendship," and story 8, "Wu Bao'an Abandons His Family to Ransom
His Friend," share the theme of friendship, one of Feng's most highly regarded
virtues. But the relationship between paired stories may involve more than a
shared theme or subject matter. Margaret L. John has demonstrated that the
self-sacrifice described in the second story is "unequivocally superior to those
of either of the friends in the first story": Wu Bao'an of the second story is willing to undergo tremendous hardship for the sake of a friend he has never even
met, and the events in "Yang Jiao'ai" take place in less than a week, whereas Wu
and Guo show their loyalty to each other over years. What is more impressive
for the family-centered Chinese reader is Wu Bao'an's abandoning his family

for ten years in an effort to ransom his friend Guo. By comparison it seems "easy enough" for Yang Jiao'ai and his friend Zuo Botao to die for each other, because "they had no families for whom they were responsible."[38]

This argument can be pursued further if we look into the unique publication history involving the pairing of two other stories. "Yang Jiao'ai" was taken from *Sixty Stories* (Liushijia xiaoshuo), the earliest surviving anthology of vernacular short stories, published in 1550, where it was originally paired with "The Chicken-and-Millet Dinner of Fan and Zhang in Life and Death" (which appears as story 16 in *Stories Old and New*). This original pairing reflects the "almost perfect identity of structure and theme. Both present high-minded individuals entering . . . into a bond of friendship for which each eventually offers up his life."[39] If similarity in subject or structure was Feng Menglong's main concern in pairing stories, one would expect these stories to remain paired in the *Sanyan*. That each is paired with a different story in *Stories Old and New* suggests that Feng may have had other concerns in mind.

Although he has made stylistic improvements in "Yang Jiao'ai," by retaining its original title in a note, Feng makes it clear that the story appears as a reprint from an earlier anthology. Feng has also left an anachronism unchanged in the text—a glaring mistake that Feng could have easily corrected, had he wished to: the famous assassin Jing Ke (who was already dead in the story) actually was born toward the end of Warring States period (475–221 B.C.E.), a few hundred years after the death of the two friends. Instead, Feng added an explanatory note. To pair such a story with one written by himself may suggest that not only is the friendship represented in "Wu Bao'an" unequivocally superior to that of the two friends in "Yang Jiao'ai," but in artistic quality the second story is itself far superior to the first. Feng may have deliberately crafted "Wu Bao'an" in the pair to not merely echo or resonate with "Yang Jiao'ai," but to overshadow or outshine it.

On the other hand, "The Chicken-and-Millet Dinner of Fan and Zhang," the original companion story to "Yang Jiao'ai" in *Sixty Stories,* is included without any indication of its origin in *Stories Old and New,* where it appears as the companion story to story 15, "The Dragon-and-Tiger Reunion of Shi Hongzhao the Minister and His Friend the King." The two seem to share almost nothing in common. One describes a future emperor and a general at the beginning of their careers as ruffians and thieves; the other is about two scholar friends who kill themselves for each other. There is conceivably irony in the first story (but none in the second): on the one hand the narrator constantly speaks of his protagonists as "destined to rise to the highest dignities," but on the other hand portrays them simply as "loafers and social outcasts."[40] Therefore it seems likely that the second story, with its lofty theme of self-sacrifice and noble friendship, is set purposefully to contrast the future rulers' abject behavior in stark relief—an indirect criticism of the ruling class or of a specific Ming ruler and his ministers.[41]

THE STORYTELLER'S RHETORIC

One of the most interesting and controversial characteristics of Chinese vernacular fiction is its "storyteller's rhetoric." This is part of what Patrick Hanan refers to as the "simulated context," or "the context of situation in which a piece of fiction claims to be transmitted."[42] In the *Sanyan* stories (and in other Chinese vernacular fiction as well), this simulacrum almost always takes the form of a professional oral storyteller addressing his audience. The storyteller-narrator asks questions of his simulated audience, converses with them, makes explicit reference to his own stories, and intersperses his narrative with verses and poems. Usually the narrator begins his talk with one or more prologue stories or poems, which supposedly allows his audience time to gather before the main piece in his performance is presented.

Hanan explains these peculiar formal features of Chinese vernacular fiction as parts of a "three mode schema": commentary (including the introductory remarks or prologue, explanations, comments, and summaries by the narrator); description (stoptime description of characters or settings, usually in parallel prose or poetry); and presentation (dialogue and narrated action).[43] The story is told through the use of all three modes, but commentary and description are separated from presentation. One of the main functions of the storyteller-narrator is to "guide the reader through the transitions from one mode to the next"[44] by using "storyteller phrases," such as *yuanlai* ("It so happened that . . ." or "As a matter of fact . . .") to turn to the mode of commentary; *danjian* and *zhijian* ("Behold!" or "There, for all to see, was . . .") to description; and *huashuo* ("The story goes that . . ." or "The story is about . . ."), or *qieshuo* or *queshuo* ("To get on with our story . . ." or "Let me now turn to . . .") to presentation.

Of course, in written literature, this storyteller's pose is only a pretense in which "the author and reader happily acquiesce in order that the fiction can be communicated."[45] It was a way to "naturalize, by reference to the familiar situation of hearing stories told in the vernacular by professional storytellers, the unfamiliar process of writing and reading fiction in vernacular Chinese."[46] But this formal feature, plus a misunderstanding of the term *huaben*, led many scholars of Chinese literature to subscribe, until a couple of decades ago, to the "prompt-book" theory, which held that the Chinese vernacular story developed directly from the prompt-books of marketplace storytellers in the Song dynasty, and that the pre-*Sanyan* texts were no less than genuine prompt-books written for performance in the Song and Yuan or early Ming periods.[47] W. L. Idema, however, argues that the storyteller's manner was deliberately developed in literati imitations by Feng Menglong and others. According to Idema, the conspicuous use of this rhetorical stance in the *Sanyan* collections was "a consequence mainly of Feng Menglong's reinterpretation of the genre and due to his overall rewritings."[48] In other words, Feng's editing of his collections included a systematic elaboration of this storyteller rhetoric, which became a hallmark of the *huaben* story he envisioned.

But this is not to deny the presence of elements of oral folk literature in the *Sanyan* stories. Most contain anecdotes or episodes known even to the illiterate, which suggests that the editor looked to storytelling for raw materials as well as for rhetorical formulas. And we may assume that traces of the marketplace storyteller and the values he represented would unavoidably have remained in these *huaben* stories in spite of Feng Menglong's often meticulous editing. Idema argues that professional storytelling was but one of the many factors that helped to shape traditional Chinese fiction.[49] Sources for these vernacular stories can be traced to many other forms of narrative, such as drama, historiography (both official and unofficial), and classical tales. The fact that the publication dates of *Talks Old and New, Sack of Wisdom, Selections from the Grand Gleanings of the Taiping Period, History of Love,* and *Supplement to "Sack of Wisdom"* coincide roughly with the *Sanyan* suggests that they could have been compiled as aids for the preparation of the *Sanyan*.[50] Small wonder that the *Sanyan* collections provide for us such a vivid panoramic view of the bustling world of imperial China before the end of Ming: not only do we see scholars, emperors, ministers, and generals, but also a gallery of ordinary men and women in their everyday surroundings—merchants and artisans, prostitutes and courtesans, matchmakers and fortune-tellers, monks and nuns, servants and maids, thieves and impostors. We learn about their joys and sorrows, likes and dislikes, their views of life and death, and even their visions of the underworld and the supernatural. We see the noble friendship of ancient scholars in the Spring and Autumn period (770–476 B.C.E.) in story 7, a late Ming triangular love relationship of merchants and their wives in story 1; instances of Buddhist reincarnation in stories 29 and 30, Taoist magic and long-term "hibernation" in stories 13 and 14; the fall of a tragic hero in story 39, the rise of rude men of violence in story 15; fidelity in love during the Jurchen invasion of the Song in story 17, family reunion after the Japanese pirate raids in the Ming in story 18; frustrated scholars touring the underworld in stories 31 and 32, men and women predestined to live in heaven as immortals in story 33; a naive man who almost dies from excessive sex with a prostitute in story 3, and women who are superior to men in both talent and integrity in story 28.

Thus the *Sanyan* stories are necessarily overdetermined texts, historically, ideologically, and formally. They can be justifiably taken as an intersection of complex cultural determinations, with generic mixture and multiple voices making different and sometimes conflicting claims. This complexity of multiple voices in *Stories Old and New* has never been fully presented to the English reader before. Of the forty stories in this collection, until now only seventeen have been published in English translation, and they appeared separately in journals and anthologies of Chinese literature, never arranged in pairs and in the original sequence. Even when stories have been presented individually, the storyteller's rhetoric, the verses, and the prologue stories often have been deleted.[51] The interlinear and marginal comments, generally believed to have been made by Feng Menglong himself,[52] are omitted even in modern Chinese editions of the collection. This volume represents the first effort to translate this seventeenth-century collection in its entirety, an effort not only to provide for the English reader a fuller picture of the bustling world of imperial China, but, more importantly, also to show the intricate interactions among different voices in the texts, especially between the voice of the conventional storyteller narrator and that of the literati editor Feng Menglong.

THE EFFECT OF THE *SANYAN* ON LATER FICTION WRITERS

The two most important vernacular story writers after Feng Menglong were Ling Mengchu (1580–1644), who published two collections, *Slapping the Table in Amazement* (Pai'an jingqi; 1628) and *Slapping the Table in Amazement, Second Collection* (Erke Pai'an jingqi; 1632); and Li Yu (1611–80), who published three, *Silent Operas* (Wusheng xi; 1655/56), *Silent Operas, Second Collection* (Wusheng xi erji; ca. 1656), and *Twelve Towers* (Shi'er lou; 1658). Unlike Feng, Ling wrote all of the nearly eighty stories himself and made no attempt to hide his authorship. This can been seen as a sign that by Ling's time, the vernacular story as a genre was firmly established due to Feng's success. In his preface to his first collection of stories, Ling states that since Feng Menglong had already exhausted all the old texts, he could only take "those miscellaneous and scattered pieces of the past and present that could refresh one's views and understanding . . . and expand and elaborate them into a number of stories."[53] The narrator in Ling's stories appears to have a single, fairly consistent personality, and is often found "equating himself with the author, in the sort of comment we might expect to find in a preface or in the author's own editorial notes."[54]

If Ling Mengchu was still dependent on preexisting anecdotes for his stories, Li Yu insisted on the value of originality in literature. Of the stories in the three collections he published, none is clearly based on any previous source material,[55] and all distinctly bear his own individual stamp. One of the most striking features of his stories is that the traditional storyteller is replaced by a literati persona, who often sounds "like a vernacular version of Li Yu the essayist . . . sly, mocking, ingenious, self-congratulatory—and even self-contradictory."[56]

After reaching maturity in the late Ming, the simulated context of the oral storyteller developed, as David Rolston observes, along two lines. One was "for the marks of the presence of the narrator as storyteller to drop away to a minimum," and the other was "to bring the storyteller persona even more into the foreground, dramatizing the storytelling process . . . or personalizing the narrator."[57] Both Ling Mengchu and Li Yu seem to have taken the second course, with Li Yu even further personalized. Neither Ling nor Li was much interested in Feng's arrangement of paired stories; instead, each chose to write a parallel couplet as the title for each story.[58]

These short-story writers' reasons for not following Feng's literary techniques were necessarily complex. On the social level, the changed cultural environment with an ever-increasing literati concern for declining morals may have compelled Ling to speak more directly, and the fall of the Ming and the vicissitudes of his own life may have made Li Yu more cynical about human follies. On the personal level, however, it is possible that in the face of Feng's great literary achievement, these latecomers in the field of vernacular short-story writing also suffered from "the anxiety of precedents."[59] Refusing to directly imitate Feng's specific techniques may have been their strategy for claiming "new territory" for themselves. Perhaps, in their eyes, the once frustrated Feng Menglong was not a victim of the civil service examination system anymore, but had become a formidable literary giant in their field, due to the success of his *Sanyan* collections.

Shuhui Yang

Translators' Note

This translation follows the text of the 1620 *Tianxuzhai* edition of *Gujin xiaoshuo* as reprinted in the 1987 facsimile edition by Shanghai Guji Chubanshe. The interlinear and marginal comments in the original text appear in italic within parentheses in this translation.

Chinese proper names are rendered in the *pinyin* system, the only exception being "Taoism" (*pinyin:* Daoism). For the convenience of those readers who are more accustomed to the Wade-Giles system of romanization, we have provided the following short list of difficult consonants:

$$c = ts'$$
$$q = ch'$$
$$x = hs$$
$$z = tz$$
$$zh = ch$$

Information about previous translations (in varying degrees of completeness and accuracy) of stories in this collection is provided in the endnotes for individual stories.

Names of people in the border states are rendered following the spelling system used in *The Cambridge History of China,* vol. 6, ed. Denis Twitchett and John K. Fairbank (Cambridge: Cambridge University Press, 1994).

Frequently Encountered Chinese Terms

chi, a unit of measurement, translated as "foot"

jin, translated as "catty," equals one-half of a kilogram

jinshi, one who had passed the imperial civil service examinations at the metropolitan level

li, approximately one-third of a mile

liang, translated as "tael," equals one-sixteenth of a *jin*

shi, a married woman known by her maiden name, e.g., Wang-shi

xiucai, translated as "scholar," a successful candidate at the local level

zhuangyuan, a *jinshi* who ranked first in the palace examination

zi, translated as "courtesy name," the name by which an educated person was addressed by people of his/her own generation probably more often than by his/her official name

Among the reference works we have consulted are:

Bishop, John L., ed. *Studies of Government Institutions in Chinese.* Cambridge, Mass.: Harvard University Press, 1968.

Chen Xizhong, ed. *Yushi mingyan: Xinzhu quanben.* Beijing: Beijing Shiyue Wenyi Chubanshe, 1994.

Cihai. Shanghai: Shanghai Cishu Chubanshe, 1989.

Ciyuan. Beijing: Shangwu Yinshuguan, 1989.

Hanyu da cidian. Shanghai: Hanyu Da Cidian Chubanshe, 1994.

Ho, Ping-ti. *The Ladder of Success in Imperial China: Aspects of Social Mobility, 1368–1911.* New York and London: Columbia University Press, 1962.

Hucker, Charles O. *A Dictionary of Official Titles in Imperial China.* Stanford: Stanford University Press, 1985.

Soothill, W. E., and Lewis Hodous. *A Dictionary of Chinese Buddhist Terms, with Sanskrit and English Equivalents and a Sanskrit-Pali Index.* Delhi: Motilal Banarsidass, 1987.

Chronology of Chinese Dynasties

Xia	ca. 2100–ca. 1600 B.C.E.
Shang (Yin)	ca. 1600–ca. 1028 B.C.E.
Zhou	ca. 1027–256 B.C.E.
Western Zhou	ca. 1027–771 B.C.E.
Eastern Zhou	770–256 B.C.E.
Spring and Autumn	770–476 B.C.E.
Warring States	475–221 B.C.E.
Qin	221–207 B.C.E.
Han	206 B.C.E.–C.E. 220
Western Han	206 B.C.E.–C.E. 8
Xin	9–25
Eastern Han	25–220
Three Kingdoms	220–265
Wei	220–265
Shu	221–263
Wu	222–280
Six Dynasties (Wu, Eastern Jin, Former Song, Southern Qi, Southern Liang, and Southern Chen)	222–589
Jin	265–420
Western Jin	265–316
Eastern Jin	317–420
Southern and Northern Dynasties	420–589
Southern Dynasties	
Former Song	420–479
Southern Qi	479–502
Southern Liang	502–557
Southern Chen	557–589
Northern Dynasties	
Northern Wei	386–534
Eastern Wei	534–550
Western Wei	535–556
Northern Qi	550–577
Northern Zhou	557–581

Sui	581–618
Tang	618–907
Five Dynasties and Ten	
Kingdoms	907–979
Five Dynasties	
Later Liang	907–923
Later Tang	923–936
Later Jin	936–946
Later Han	947–950
Later Zhou	951–960
Ten Kingdoms	907–979
Liao (Khitan)	916–1125
Song	960–1279
Northern Song	960–1126
Southern Song	1127–1279
Xixia (Tangut)	1038–1227
Jin (Jurchen)	1115–1234
Yuan (Mongol)	1260–1368
Ming	1368–1644
Qing (Manchu)	1644–1911

Stories Old and New

古今小説

（喻世明言）

Stories Old and New

WITH FULL ILLUSTRATIONS*

Works such as *Romance of the Three Kingdoms* and *Outlaws of the Marsh* are indeed great landmarks of fiction. However, those works that evolve around one character in one action also provide entertainment and therefore should not be slighted, just as is the case with the variety show in relation to the romance drama.[1] This studio has purchased one hundred twenty stories collected by men of distinction, past and present, and hereby presents one third of them as the first collection.

Heavenly Promise Studio

*[See p. xi for a list of the selected illustrations reproduced in this translation.]

Preface [to the 1620 edition]

Fiction began to rise when the tradition of historiography showed signs of decline. With Han Fei [ca. 280–233 B.C.E.] and Lie Yukou [ca. 450–375 B.C.E.] as its progenitors, it started to take shape toward the end of the Zhou dynasty [ca. 1027–256 B.C.E.], flourished in the Tang dynasty [C.E. 618–907], and became widespread in the Song dynasty [960–1279]. Although the *Spring and Autumn Annals of Wu and Yue* [Wu Yue chunqiu] appeared during the Han dynasty [206 B.C.E.–C.E. 220], in general few works [of fiction] were produced after the book burning of the Qin dynasty [221–206 B.C.E.] until the Kaiyuan reign period [C.E. 713–42], when men of letters turned with enthusiasm to the writing of fiction. As for the colloquial novel [*yanyi*], little is known about how it came into being. What *is* known, however, is that affiliated with the Bureau of Court Services of the Southern Song dynasty [1127–1279] were storytellers, not unlike the marketplace storytellers of our day, whose language was simple and easy to understand, though the authorship of the stories is untraceable.

After the Song emperor Gaozong yielded the throne to his son [in 1163] to enjoy the support of all under heaven in the later years of his long life of virtue, he took delight in reading *huaben* stories in his hours of leisure. He had the eunuchs find him a new story every day, and if the story was to his liking, the person who provided it would be richly rewarded with cash. Hence the eunuchs searched high and low for strange tales of former days and for the idle talk of the streets and alleys. They would then have the material elaborated into stories to be presented to the emperor for his pleasure. But once read, the stories were cast aside and most ended up in the interior quarters of the palace; not more than one or two out of ten ever came to circulate among the people. Yet some of them, such as "Wanjiang Tower" and "The Double-Fish Pendants" are so shallow and vulgar that they provide no delectation. In the Yuan dynasty [1260–1368] both Shi Nai'an and Luo Guanzhong promoted [vernacular fiction], and works such as *Romance of the Three Kingdoms, Outlaws of the Marsh,* and *The Quelling of the Demons* attained substantial length and became great landmarks of fiction. In general, it was not as a hobby in times of peace, but to keep their distance from the controversies of the day and to while away their time, that they composed their works, which, like jade hidden in rocks, did not receive the amount of attention they deserved.

Literature and the arts have been so vigorously advanced by the imperial court of this Ming dynasty that each and every school is flourishing; in vernacular fiction alone, there is no lack of writings of a quality far above those of the Song. It is a mistake to believe, as some do, that such works lack the charm of those of the Tang. One who has a love for the peach need not forsake the apricot. Fine linen, silk gauze, plush, brocade—each has its proper occasion for wear. To measure Song writing by Tang standards is like measuring the Tang by Han standards, and measuring the Han in turn by those of the Spring and Autumn and Warring States periods [770–221 B.C.E.]. By such logic, even the divine Fuxi's[2] strokes of the Trigrams would also be deprived of all their worth. That is an absurd proposition indeed.

For the most part, Tang writers preferred an elegant style that appealed to literary minds. Song writers used the colloquial attuned to the common ear. Now common ears outnumber literary minds in our world, and fiction draws less from the elegant than from the colloquial style. Just ask the storytellers to demonstrate in public their art of description: they will gladden you, astonish you, move you to sad tears, rouse you to song and dance; they will prompt you to draw a sword, bow in reverence, cut off a head, or donate money. The faint-hearted will be made brave, the debauched chaste, the unkind compassionate, the obtuse ashamed. One may well intone the *Classic of Filial Piety* [Xiaojing] and the *Analects of Confucius* every day,[3] yet he will not be moved so quickly nor so profoundly as by these storytellers. Can anything less accessible achieve such effect? The Heretical Historiographer of Maoyuan[4] has amassed quite a collection of popular stories old and new. Upon the request of a merchant, he selected for publication a volume of forty stories that may appeal to the common ear. I was so delighted upon reading them that I picked up my brush pen and wrote this preface.

Inscribed by
the Master of the Green Sky Studio[5]

Winter ends, but not the sorrows.
Spring returns, but not the traveler.
Lamenting her loneliness as the day dawns,
She refuses to try on her New Year's clothes.

Jiang Xingge Reencounters His Pearl Shirt

Wealth and rank are of no account,
And all too few live past seventy.
Can worldly fame last beyond the grave?
All in life is but an empty game.
Indulge not in youthful follies;
Nor with wine and women dally.
Break free from quarrels and worries;
Be content and enjoy a life of ease.

The above lyric poem to the tune of "The Moon over the West River" advises all to take life as it comes, to find delight in whatever lies in your lot, and not to let "drink," "lust," "wealth," and "wrath" consume your energies and compromise your integrity. Joy may turn out to be sorrow, and a gain may turn out to be a loss. But of the four vices cited above, "lust" is by far the most ruinous. The eyes are the go-between of love; the heart is the seed of desire. At the beginning, you will suffer from pangs of longing. By the end, your soul will take leave of your body. An occasional affair on the spur of the moment with some "wayside flower and willow" brings little harm, but never hatch deliberate plans against all sense of decency to seek some momentary gratification at the expense of the long-standing marriage of others. How would you feel if your own dear wife or beloved concubine were to fall a victim to another man's seduction? There is an ancient quatrain that puts it well:

The human heart may be blinded,
But the will of heaven never errs.
If I debauch not other men's wives,
Other men will not debauch mine.

Dear audience, now hear me tell the story of "The Pearl Shirt" as an illustration of the never-failing retribution of heaven to serve as a lesson for all young men.

The story is about a man named Jiang De, also known as Jiang Xingge, a native of Zaoyang County in Xiangyang Prefecture, Huguang Province.[1] His father, Jiang Shize, was a merchant who began traveling extensively in Guangdong at an early age. Shize's wife Luo-shi, now deceased, had left him with an only child, Xingge, who was nine years old at the time of her death. Jiang Shize could not bear the thought of parting with the child, yet neither could he afford to give up his Guangdong business as a means of livelihood. After giving much thought to the matter, he found no alternative but to take the nine-year-old along as a travel companion and teach the boy some worldly wisdom. Young as the boy was, he had

Trim brows and bright eyes,
White teeth and red lips.
He moved with grace
And spoke with ease.
In intellect he surpassed the well-read.
In cleverness he was equal to grown men.
Everyone called him the darling boy;
All praised him as a priceless gem.

Wary of stirring up envious feelings, Jiang Shize presented the boy, throughout their journeys, not as his son but as Young Master Luo, his wife's nephew. As a matter of fact, the Luo family was also engaged in business in the Guangdong region. Whereas the Jiang family had been in the Guangdong business for one generation only, the Luo family had been in it for three. The innkeepers and brokers there knew all three generations of the Luos and treated them as their own kith and kin. Indeed, it was through the initiation of his father-in-law, Mr. Luo, that Jiang Shize had first become a traveling merchant. However, due to straitened circumstances that resulted from a succession of unjust lawsuits against them, the Luos had not visited the area in the last several years. The innkeepers and brokers missed them so much that at the sight of Jiang Shize, everyone asked after the Luo family. When learning upon inquiry that the boy with him, with refined looks and a ready tongue, was from the Luo family, all rejoiced, for their friendship with the last three generations of the Luo family was now continuing into the fourth.

Not to encumber our story with unnecessary chatter, let us speak of Jiang Xingge, who, after traveling a few times with his father, learned, to his father's immense delight, to handle all business matters with adroitness and competence. It turned out, in a way no one would have expected, that when he was seventeen years old, his father died of a sudden illness. Luckily, he died at home instead of ending up a ghost on the road. After shedding some bitter tears, Xingge could not help but wipe his eyes dry and set about making arrangements for the funeral. Apart from the mortuary rites, he also had Buddhist prayers chanted to ensure that his father's spirit be spared the torments of hell, but that needs no more description here.

During the forty-nine days of mourning, all kith and kin on both sides of the family came to offer their condolences. A Mr. Wang of the same county, father of Xingge's newly betrothed fiancée, was among the visitors. Naturally, members of the Jiang clan engaged him in conversation as a courtesy. As the conversation turned to how mature Xingge was for his age in so ably handling such important matters all by himself, someone urged him, "Kinsman Wang, now that your daughter has come of age, why don't you marry them to offset the sadness of the occasion? Life will be easier for the couple when they have each other for company." That day Mr. Wang left without giving his consent.

After the burial rites were over, the relatives tried the proposition on Xingge. The young man also refused at first, but, after much persuasion, considerations about his lonely status prompted him to give in. The original matchmaker was sent to speak to the Wang family, but Mr. Wang declined, saying, "Our family needs to prepare a modest dowry, and it's not something to be had at a moment's notice. Moreover, to hold a wedding before the year of mourning is over would be against the rules of propriety. If there is to be a wedding, we'd better wait until after the first anniversary of the death." When the matchmaker brought back this reply, Xingge did not press the point, for he knew Mr. Wang to be right.

Time sped by like an arrow. Before they realized it, the anniversary was upon them. After offering oblations to his father's spirit tablet and taking off his garments of mourning made of coarse hemp, Xingge again asked the matchmaker to speak to the Wang family. This time, the proposal was accepted. Within several days, the six preliminaries[2] were completed, and the bride was brought over the threshold, as is attested by the following lyric poem to the tune of "The Moon over the West River":

> Red curtains replaced the white of mourning;
> Hemp gave way to colorful clothing.
> The festooned halls aglow with candles;
> The nuptial wine and wedding feast all set out.
> Why envy the splendor of a dowry?
> Harder to come by is beauty.
> Tonight, the pleasure of clouds and rain;[3]
> Tomorrow, visitors with wishes of joy.

The bride was Mr. Wang's youngest daughter, nicknamed Number Three. Because she was born on the seventh day of the seventh month, she was also known as Sanqiao.[4] The two older married daughters of the family were also of remarkable beauty. Within the county of Zaoyang there circulated a four-line song that voiced the admiration for the Wang girls held by all and sundry:

> *Women in the world are many;*
> *Those with the Wangs' beauty are few.*
> *He who takes a Wang girl as wife*
> *Is better off than the emperor's son-in-law.*

As the proverb says, "Failure to make a business deal is a matter of the moment; failure to marry the right wife is a woe of a lifetime." In selecting daughters-in-law, some families of distinction seek only a matching family background or rich dowry and arrange the betrothal with never a thought about other considerations. Later, when the grotesquely ugly bride is brought into the family and called upon to greet the members of the clan, imagine what poor figures the parents-in-law cut! Moreover, the discontented husband can hardly resist the temptation of illicit affairs. Yet, it so happens that ugly wives are best at bossing their husbands. If the husband reacts in the same way, he invites marital strife, but if he yields to her a couple of times out of face-saving considerations, she starts to put on airs. It was to avoid such unpleasant situations that Jiang Shize, upon learning that Mr. Wang was prone to producing beautiful daughters, had sent over betrothal gifts early on to commit Mr. Wang's youngest girl to his son, both of whom were then at a tender age. Now that Sanqiao had crossed the threshold of the Jiang house, she was perceived to be as full of grace and charm as expected. In fact, she was twice as beautiful as her two older sisters. Truly,

> *Xishi of Wu⁵ did not measure up to her.*
> *Nanwei of Chu⁶ was hardly her match.*
> *Should she take the Bodhisattva's place,⁷*
> *Just as much homage would she be paid.*

The handsome Jiang Xingge and his newly wedded beautiful wife were like a pair of exquisite jade statues from the hands of a master sculptor, and ten times more loving than the average married couple. After the third day, Xingge changed back into clothes of lighter colors and, declining all dealings with the outside world on the pretext of being still in mourning, stayed upstairs with his wife, enjoying every moment of the days and nights that went by. Indeed, they were never apart, whether in motion or at rest; even in their dreams they kept each other company. It has always been said that hard days pass slowly, whereas happy moments flit by all too quickly. With the passage of summers and winters, the mourning period came to an end. The spirit tablet for the deceased was removed, and the mourning clothes were taken off, but of this, we shall speak no further.

One day, it occurred to Xingge that his father's Guangdong business had been unattended to for over three years. Revenues from many accounts remained uncollected. In the evening, he said to his wife that he wished to make a trip there. At first, she agreed that he should go, but later, as she learned the distance of the journey, tears fell involuntarily from her eyes, for how could such a loving couple bear to part with each other? Nor did Xingge feel ready to leave her. After some sad laments, the matter was dropped. This happened more than once. (*Good description.*)

Time went by. Before they noticed it, another two years had elapsed. Xingge made up his mind to go. He did his packing away from home, without his wife's knowledge. It was not until five days before the auspicious day chosen for his departure that he said to her, "As the proverb says, 'He who sits idle will eat away a mountain of a fortune.' If the two of us are to start a family and build a career, we can't very well afford to give up this source of income, can we? It being now the second month of the year, with the weather neither cold nor hot, what better time than this to start on the road?"

Realizing that she would not be able to keep him home any longer, she asked only, "When are you coming back?"

Xingge replied, "I have no other choice but to take this trip, but I'll be back in one year's time no matter what. I'll just stay longer the second time around, if that's what it takes."

Pointing at the toon tree in front of the house, she said, "Next year when this tree begins budding, I'll be expecting you back." With these words, tears fell like rain from her eyes. As he wiped away her tears with his sleeves, Xingge felt tears on his own cheeks as well. A few words hardly suffice for an adequate description of their grief at parting and their deep affection for each other.

Five days later, the night before the scheduled departure, the couple sobbingly talked the whole night through, with no wish to go to sleep. At the fifth watch, Xingge rose to get ready for the journey. He handed over to his wife all his inherited pearls and other valuables, taking along for himself only enough silver to serve as business capital, the original copies of the account books, some clothes, and bedding. Gifts to be offered to business associates had also been packed in good order. Of the two male servants, the younger one was to follow him. The older and more mature one was to stay behind to serve the mistress, run errands, and attend to the daily needs of the household, whereas two waiting women were charged with kitchen duties. There were also two maids, one called Clear Cloud, the other Warm Snow, whose job it was to serve the mistress in her private chamber, with orders not to wander too far away. Having thus assigned all the duties to the servants, Xingge turned to his wife: "Pass your time in patience. There is no lack of frivolous young men in the neighborhood. Being as pretty as you are, you'd better not look out the front door, so as not to attract undue attention." (*These words will turn out to be prophetic.*)

"Don't worry. Go quickly now and come back early."

They took a tearful leave of each other. Truly,

> *The myriad sorrows of this world*
> *All stem from parting, in life or by death.*

For whole days on the road, all of Xingge's thoughts were with his wife, to the exclusion of everything else. Some time later, he arrived in Guangdong and found lodgings in an inn. Old acquaintances came to greet him, and he, in his turn, offered them gifts and went from household to household, enjoying their hospitality in his honor. Thus, he had not a moment of rest for fifteen to twenty days in a row. He had already depleted his energy at home. The tribulations of the journey plus the now-excessive wining and dining brought on an attack of malaria, which lasted throughout the summer and turned to dysentery with the onset of autumn. With a physician checking his pulse and administering medicine every day, he finally recovered toward the end of autumn. In the meantime, his business was left unattended. It looked like he would not be able to return home in one year's time. Truly,

> *For profits the size of a fly's head,*
> *He abandoned his love nest.*

Homesick though he was, with the passage of time, he felt he might as well put aside such thoughts.

We shall leave Xingge to his travels and return to his wife, Sanqiao, who, just as her husband instructed on the day of his departure, did not look out the window or take a step down the stairs for quite a few months. Time sped by like an arrow. All too soon, the year was drawing to a close. Every household noisily lit bonfires of pine branches in the courtyard, set off firecrackers, and gathered together merrily for family feasts and games. The sight of such festivities made Sanqiao miss her husband even more. What a miserable night it was! Just as an ancient quatrain put it,

> *Winter ends, but not the sorrows.*
> *Spring returns, but not the traveler.*
> *Lamenting her loneliness as the day dawns,*
> *She refuses to try on her New Year's clothes.*

The following day was the first day of the first month of the year. In the morning, Clear Cloud and Warm Snow did all they could to urge their mistress to go to the front of the house to watch the goings-on in the street. As a matter of fact, the Jiang residence consisted of two interconnected wings that ran parallel to each other. The bedchamber was in the back wing behind the one that looked out onto the street. As a rule, Sanqiao used only the back wing. That day, unable to resist the maids' urging, she went to the front wing through a passageway. With the windows pushed open and the curtains let down, the three of them looked out from behind the curtains. That day, the street was a scene of hustle and bustle. Sanqiao remarked, "Of all these people coming and going, why isn't there a fortune-teller? If there is one, I'll be glad to have him come here so I can ask him for news about my husband."

Clear Cloud said, "New Year's Day is for everybody to relax and have fun. Who would want to be out telling fortunes?"

Warm Snow said loudly, "Ma'am, just leave it to the two of us. Within five days, we'll surely get you one."

After breakfast on the fourth day of the month, Warm Snow was downstairs relieving herself when she heard a clanging sound in the street. It came from the device called "announcer" that blind fortune-tellers use to attract attention. Before she was through with what she was doing, she hastily pulled up her pants, ran out the door, and stopped the blind man. She then turned around and ran up the stairs in one breath to report to her mistress. Sanqiao instructed her to have him sit and wait in the reception hall downstairs. Having flipped a coin and said her prayers, Sanqiao descended the stairs to listen to what he had to say. The blind man picked a trigram and asked what the divination was for. The two kitchen maids who came over at the commotion answered for the mistress, "It's to ask about a traveler on the road."

"Is it a wife wishing to ask about her husband?" the fortune-teller demanded to know.

"Exactly," said the maids.

And this was what the fortune-teller said: "With the green dragon in a reigning position, the wealth star is set in motion. If this is a case of a wife inquiring about her husband, the traveler is on his way home, laden with a thousand cases of treasure, and safe from the slightest hint of a storm. (*Fortune-tellers can be quite misleading.*) The green dragon being of the wood phase of the five phases and spring being the thriving season for wood, the traveler started on his way back around the time of the spring equinox and will surely be at home by the end of this month or the beginning of the next, bringing much wealth with him."

Sanqiao had the male servant give the fortune-teller three tenths of a mace of silver,[8] and, having thus sent the man on his way, she merrily went up to her room. As the proverbs go, she was "slaking thirst by looking at plums" and "allaying hunger by drawing cakes."

In most situations, if you don't get your hopes up too high, your peace of mind is not likely to be disturbed. Once you do, you indulge in wishful thinking that makes every moment of your life miserable. Believing the fortune-teller's words, Sanqiao had no other thoughts but of her husband's return. From then on, she often went to the front wing of the house and peered out onto the street from behind the curtains. The days went by, and there still was no sign of his return when the toon tree began budding at the beginning of the second month, reminding her of her husband's promise. All the more anxious, she looked out the window several times a day. Then, as if something was destined to happen, her eyes came to rest upon a handsome young man. Truly,

> *Those with predestined bonds will meet,*
> *However far apart they are.*
> *Those without will never meet,*
> *Face to face though they may be.*

Who might this handsome young man be? He was not a local resident but a native of Xin'an [New Peace] County in Huizhou. Chen Shang by name, he was also known familiarly as Daxige [Big Happy Brother], which was later changed to Dalang [Big Fellow]. At twenty-four years of age, he was a strikingly handsome young man, not any less so than Song Yu[9] and Pan An.[10] As was the case with Jiang Xingge, Dalang had also lost both parents. Having scraped together two to three thousand taels in cash as capital, he had gone into the rice and bean business, making yearly trips to Xiangyang to ply his trade. He stayed outside the city, but that day he happened to be in town to check at Squire Wang's pawnshop on Great Market Street for letters from home. The pawnshop being right opposite the Jiang residence, his steps took him past Sanqiao's window. How, you may ask, was he dressed? He was wearing, just as Jiang Xingge usually did, a Suzhou-style bell-shaped hat made of coir and a Huzhou silk robe of a fish-belly-white shade. Looking from afar, Sanqiao mistook him for her husband. She lifted the curtains and fixed her eyes upon him. When Chen Dalang raised his head and saw a beautiful young woman gazing at him from an upper window, he thought the woman had taken a fancy to him, and he also threw a significant glance at her. But in fact, it was a misunderstanding on both sides. Realizing that the man was not her husband, Sanqiao flushed crimson with embarrassment. Hastily closing the window, she ran to the back wing of the house and sank down on the edge of her bed, her heart pounding violently. (*Just like that debauched woman[11] when she first started out.*) In the meantime, Chen Dalang's soul had been snatched away by her gaze.

After he returned to his lodgings, his mind was still with the woman. He thought to himself, "My wife at home is not unattractive, but she's not nearly half as pretty as that woman. (*A foreshadowing.*) How I wish I could have some way to approach her! If I could just spend one night with her, I would not have lived in vain, even if it cost me all of my business capital." After a few sighs, he suddenly remembered that he had done some business with a Granny Xue, vendor of pearls, who lived on East Lane off Great Market Street. With a gift of the gab and a propensity for dropping by people's houses from street to street, she should know everyone in town and, if consulted, would surely come up with a good suggestion.

He tossed and turned all through that wakeful night to rise at the first light of dawn. Saying he had business to attend to, he asked for some cold water, washed and combed, and went to town posthaste, carrying with him a hundred taels of silver and two large ingots of gold. This is indeed a case of

> You need to work yourself to death,
> To find some enjoyment in life.

Once in town, Chen Dalang headed straight for East Lane off Great Market Street and knocked at Granny Xue's door. Her hair disheveled, Granny Xue was sorting out her pearls in the courtyard when she heard the knocking. While putting away her bags of pearls, she asked, "Who is it?" At the first few words of reply announcing that he was Mr. Chen of Huizhou, she hastened to open the door and invite him in, saying, "I haven't done my toilette yet, so I won't stand on ceremony with you. How early you are! Might I ask what brought you here?"

"I'm here specially to see you. I was afraid I might not find you at home if I came later."

"Are you here to buy jewelry from me?"

"Yes, but apart from buying pearls, I also have a big job for you."

"But I know little about things other than my own line."

"Can we talk here?" asked Chen Dalang, whereupon Granny Xue closed the door and took him into a small room.

"What can I do for you, sir?"

Seeing no one around, Dalang drew out some silver from his sleeve, untied the cloth parcel, laid the contents on the table, and said, "I'll tell you, Godmother, only if you accept them." Not knowing what he had come for, she stoutly refused to take the hundred taels of silver.

"Maybe that's not enough?" asked Dalang. He quickly added two ingots of shining gold to the silver on the table, saying, "Please also accept these ten taels of gold. If you still refuse, I'll take that to mean you are turning me down. It is I who am asking a favor from you, and not the other way around. I have come to you because no one but you can pull off this big job. Even if it can't be done, the gold and silver will still be yours to keep. I won't ever come to claim them back. Who knows if we won't meet again later in life? I, Chen Shang, am not a petty sort!"

Dear audience, is there any procuress who does not covet money? How could the sight of so much gold and silver have failed to stir her greed? At that moment, her face breaking into a wide smile, Granny Xue said, "Please don't get me wrong. I have never, in my whole life, taken any money, not even a fraction of a penny, from any source that was not well accounted for. However, I shall respect your wish and keep the money for the time being. If I cannot be of service, I will return everything to you." So saying, she put the ingots of gold into the parcel of silver, wrapped them up together, and, exclaiming, "If I may be so bold," she excused herself and put the parcel away in her bedchamber. In a trice, she reemerged to say, "Sir, I won't presume to thank you yet, but you must tell me what this big job is that you have for me."

"I desperately need a treasure with life-saving magic powers. It's nowhere to be found except in one particular household on Great Market Street. Please, Godmother, do me the favor of going there to borrow it for me." (*A godmother doubling as a life-saving go-between.*)

The woman burst into laughter. "What a funny thing you said!" she exclaimed. "I have been living here in this alley for over twenty years without ever hearing anything about any life-saving magic thing. Tell me, which household is it?"

"The two-story house opposite my fellow townsman Squire Wang's pawnshop. Who lives there?"

After a moment of reflection, the woman said, "That's the house of Jiang Xingge of this town. He's been traveling away from home for over a year now. There's only his wife in the house."

Dalang said, "It's precisely from her that I would like to borrow the lifesaving magic thing." He pulled his chair up closer to the woman and poured out his secret to her. Barely had he finished than the woman shook her head and said, "This can hardly be done! Jiang Xingge has had this wife for less than four years, and the couple have been as inseparable as fish and water. Now that the man's had to go away, the young lady never even takes a step down the stairs—so chaste is she! Because Xingge is of a somewhat unpredictable nature and easily finds fault with people (*He is certainly not to blame for doing so*), I have never seen the inside of his house. I don't even have any idea what the young woman looks like. This job is beyond me. What you gave me is not destined for me to enjoy, after all."

At these words, Chen Dalang fell to his knees. When the woman tried to raise him, he grabbed her by her sleeves and held her so firmly on the chair that she could not budge. He said, "My life is in your hands, Godmother. To save my life, you've got to think of some ingenious way for me to get to know her. If you pull this off, I'll reward you with another hundred taels of silver. If you decline, I'll have to kill myself right now."

The woman was so alarmed that, at a loss what to do, she relented, saying, "All right! All right! Don't put me on such a spot. Please get up and listen to me."

Only then did Chen Dalang rise to his feet. With folded hands, he said, "Please tell me what good plans you have in mind."

"You'll have to give me some time," said she. "If you want it to work out, don't set a time limit. I can't possibly do it for you if you give me a deadline."

Chen Dalang said, "As long as it'll work out, I don't mind waiting a few days. But what do you propose to do?"

"Tomorrow, meet me in Squire Wang's pawnshop after breakfast, not too early or too late. Bring a lot of cash and just say that you have a business deal to make with me. That'll be part of my plan, you see. If I can manage to cross the threshold of the Jiang house (*Of first importance*), you'll be in luck. You should then quickly go back to your lodgings. Don't loiter around that house, for if your intentions are seen through, that'll be the end of it all. When I see a chance, I'll come back to let you know."

"I'll do whatever you say." With a deep bow, he happily opened the door and went on his way. Truly,

Before Xiang Yu's defeat and Liu Bang's rise,
A platform was built to honor the Marshal.[12]

Of the events of the rest of the day, there is no more to tell. On the following day, a neatly attired Chen Dalang betook himself to the Wang pawnshop on Great Market Street, followed by a page boy carrying a big leather case containing three to four hundred taels of silver. He cast a glance at the upper windows of the house opposite and took the tightly shut windows to mean that the woman was not in the front wing. Saluting the pawnshop clerk with folded hands, he asked for a wooden bench and sat down at the door, looking eastward. Before long, Granny Xue came into sight, holding a wicker box in her arms. Chen Dalang stopped her and asked, "What do you have in the box?"

"Pearls and other pieces of jewelry. Would you have any use for them, sir?"

"The very things I want to buy."

Granny Xue stepped into the pawnshop, greeted the clerk, and, with a polite word or two, opened the box. There were, in the box, about ten packets of pearls as well as a few small boxes containing fashionable ornaments in the shape of flower clusters, with kingfisher-feather inlay. The designs were most exquisite and the luster dazzled the eyes. Chen Dalang picked a few strings of extremely large white pearls and put them in a pile along with some hairpins and earrings, saying, "I'll take all of these."

Giving him a meaningful look, the old woman said, "You may use them if you want, sir, but I'm afraid you might not be ready to pay the stiff price."

Taking her hint, Chen Dalang opened his leather case, spread the silver on the table in a dazzling display (*Showing off his wealth*), and yelled at the top of his voice, "Don't tell me that with all this silver I can't afford those things of yours!"

By this time, seven or eight idle onlookers from the neighborhood had already gathered at the door. The old woman said, "I was only joking. How could I dream of taking you for less than you are? You'd better be careful with your silver. Please put it away. I'll be happy as long as we strike a fair deal."

And so the bargaining began, one asking for a high price and the other countering with a small offer, with the distance of heaven from earth between the sums. While the woman held her ground firmly, Chen Dalang picked up the pearls, and, refusing to put them down or raise his offer, he deliberately stepped out of the shop. Turning each piece over and over for a good look, he commented on which ones were genuine and which ones fake, and appraised their value while all the time letting them sparkle in the sunlight. He soon attracted a large crowd, which frequently burst into cheer.

The old woman shouted, "Buy them if you want. If not, that'll be that. Why do you have to waste my time like this!"

Chen Dalang retorted, "How do you know I'm not buying?" And the haggling started all over again. Truly,

> The haggle over the price
> Caught the beauty's eye.

Hearing the commotion opposite her house, Wang Sanqiao stepped, without realizing she was doing so, to the front wing of the house and pushed open the windows for a glimpse. There, for all to see, was the lovely sight of pearls sparkling in all their splendor. As the old woman and the customer were still locked in a haggle over price, she told her maid to have the woman come over and show her the merchandise. (*No sight, no desire. She cannot but fall into the crafty old woman's trap.*) Thus instructed, Clear Cloud walked across the street and, with a tug at Granny Xue's sleeve, said, "My mistress would like to see you."

The old woman asked deliberately, "Which family might that be?"

"The Jiang family across the street."

With one sweep of her hand, the old woman whisked away all the pearls, wrapped them up in haste, and said, "I can't afford to be held up by you like this!"

Chen Dalang insisted, "I'll add some more and we can close the deal!"

"No, I'm not selling. At your price, I could have sold them a long time ago." While saying this, she put her jewels into the box, locked it as before, and carried it away.

"Let me carry it for you," said Clear Cloud.

"No, I can manage." With never a look back, she headed straight for the house across the street. Filled with inward joy, Chen Dalang also gathered up his silver, took leave of the pawnshop clerk, and returned to his lodgings. Indeed,

> His eyes look for the victory flag;
> His ears listen for glad tidings.

Clear Cloud led Granny Xue upstairs to meet Sanqiao. At the sight of the young woman, Xue thought to herself, "What a heavenly beauty! No wonder Chen Dalang is so infatuated. If I were a man, I'd also lose my head." Aloud, she said, "I have long heard about your virtues. I regret that I haven't had a chance earlier to make your acquaintance."

"What is your honorable name, may I ask?"

"My surname is Xue. I live right near here on East Lane. In fact, I am a neighbor of yours."

"Why did you say you weren't selling these things?"

The old woman said with a laugh, "If they were not for sale, I wouldn't have taken them out. I'm just amused that the traveler, however handsome and smart he looked, knew nothing about the value of my goods." (*Clever remark.*) Having said these words, she opened the box, took out a few hairpins and earrings, and handed them to the young lady for her to look at. "Madam," she exclaimed. "You can well imagine how much it costs just to make such fine jewelry. At his ridiculous price, how am I to go back and report the loss to my employer?" She then lifted a few strings of pearls and continued, "Such top quality! He must have been dreaming!"

Sanqiao asked about the amount and remarked, "That's truly unfair to you."

"Being from a genteel family, you have seen a lot, after all. Your judgment is ten times better than a man's."

Sanqiao told her maid to serve tea, but the old woman said, "I'm not going to trouble you for tea. I need to go to West Lane for some important business. That man wasted too much of my time. This is truly a case of 'a deal that fails to go through holding up all your work.' May I leave this box here in your care, lock and all? I'll be back soon." With these words, she took her leave. Sanqiao had Clear Cloud see her down the stairs. She then went out the door and set off in a westerly direction.

Much taken with the pieces of jewelry, Sanqiao waited eagerly for the old woman to come back to talk about prices. Five days went by without the

woman's making an appearance. (*The delaying tactics of a master strategist.*)
In the afternoon of the sixth day, a sudden rainstorm sprang up. Before the
sound of the rain had subsided, there came knocks at the door. Sanqiao had
a maid open the door, and who should walk in but Granny Xue with her
clothes half drenched. Carrying a broken umbrella, she chanted,

> *You don't go out when the weather is fine,*
> *But wait till raindrops pour down your head.*

She put the umbrella by the stairs and went up to the second floor. With a
bow of greeting, she said, "Madam, sorry I didn't keep my word the other day."

Sanqiao hastened to return her greeting and asked, "Where have you been
the last few days?"

"I went to see my daughter's new baby son and stayed there for a couple
of days. I didn't get back until this morning. It started to rain when I was halfway here, so I borrowed an umbrella from a friend, but it turned out to be
broken. What bad luck!"

"How many children do you have?"

"I have only one son who is already married. As to daughters, I have four.
The one I went to see is the youngest. She is married as a concubine to Squire
Zhu of Huizhou, who owns a salt shop outside the north city gate."

"You have too many daughters to care if they get the best deals. There's no
lack of men in this area who'd take her as wife, not as concubine. How could
you have married off your daughter to an outsider as a concubine?"

"You might not know that, in fact, people from other places are more
gracious. My daughter may be a concubine, but the first wife only stays at
home. It's my daughter who orders the maids about in the shop just as a wife
would do. Every time I go there, he treats me with all the respect that an elder
deserves, without the slightest neglect. Now that she's given him a son, things
are even better." (*Another clever remark.*)

"You're lucky to have married off your daughter so well."

At this moment, Clear Cloud brought in tea. After the two of them drank
their tea, Granny Xue said, "There being nothing to do on such a rainy day,
may I make so bold as to ask for a look at your jewelry? It would be helpful if
I could keep in mind some exquisite designs."

"Mine are nothing fancy. Please don't laugh." So saying, Sanqiao opened
her caskets with a key and, little by little, took out quite a number of hairpins,
filigrees, tassels, and the like. Granny Xue was profuse with praises. "With such
a collection of treasures, I would expect you to turn up your nose at those few
items of mine."

"It's kind of you to say so, but I was just going to ask you for prices."

"You are a good judge of quality," said the old woman. "Why waste my breath?"

Sanqiao put away her things and placed Granny Xue's wicker box on the table. Handing the key to Granny Xue, she said, "Please open it and see if everything is intact."

"You don't have to be so discreet." The old woman opened the box and took out the items one by one for Sanqiao's appraisal. The prices Sanqiao offered were all close to what Granny Xue would have asked. Without any objections, the old woman said cheerfully, "That'll be a fair deal. I'll be happy even if I make a few strings of cash less."

"But there's one problem. Right now, I'm not able to pay more than half of the total sum. I'll have to wait for my husband to come home to pay off the balance. He should be back in a couple of days."

"A few days won't make any difference. It's just that because I've made quite a concession on the price, I'd like to have the silver in the finest quality."

"That can be easily done." So saying, Sanqiao picked out pieces of jewelry and pearls that she liked most. She then called Clear Cloud to serve some wine for Granny Xue to stay a little longer. "How can I disturb you like this?" said the old woman.

"I have little to do most of the time," said Sanqiao. "It's so seldom that you are here to chat with me and keep me company. If you don't mind my not being a good hostess, please come visit me often."

"Thank you for such kindness, which I hardly deserve. My house is unbearably noisy, but your house is indeed too quiet."

"What line of business is your son in?"

"He does nothing more than receive jewelry dealers at home. I can't stand their daily requests for wine and soup. Thanks to the need to visit different households on business, I don't stay at home a lot, so it's all right. If I had to be cooped up in those six feet of space at home, I'd be annoyed to death."

"Our house being so close to yours, do come over for a chat whenever you need a break." (*Falling into the trap.*)

"But I wouldn't presume to disturb you too often."

"What kind of talk is this!" exclaimed Sanqiao.

In the meantime, the two maidservants were busily going back and forth setting the table, laying out two sets of cups and chopsticks, two bowls each of smoked chicken and meat, fresh fish, and ten dishes of vegetables and fruits, bringing the total number of dishes to sixteen. "What a fine spread!" said Granny Xue.

"These are just what we have at the moment. Please don't think ill of me for not being a good hostess." Having said this, Sanqiao poured out wine for the old woman and handed her the cup. The latter offered a toast, and the two sat down across the table from each other and fell to drinking. As it was, Sanqiao had a good capacity for wine, and Granny Xue was a veritable wine jug. As they drank, the two felt even more drawn to each other than before and wished they had gotten to know each other sooner. They drank until evening set in. As the rain had stopped, Granny Xue said her thanks and wanted to leave, but Sanqiao took out a large silver wine vessel, urged her to drink more, and, after a few more vessels, they ate dinner together. Sanqiao pleaded, "Stay around some more before I let you go with half the money I owe you."

"It's getting late," said Granny Xue. "Take your time. One night doesn't make any difference. I'll come to get it tomorrow. I'll leave the wicker box here, also, for the road will be too muddy and slippery for me to carry anything." (*Delaying tactics again.*)

"I'll be expecting you tomorrow," said Sanqiao. The old woman took her leave, went down the stairs, picked up her broken umbrella, and went out the door. Truly,

> Goodness knows how many people
> Fall for a wicked crone's talk.

In the meantime, Chen Dalang was waiting in his lodgings for news. Several days went by without any word from Granny Xue. Convinced that the old woman should be at home that rainy day, he headed into town through the rain and the mud to ask her for news, only to learn that she was not at home. He went into a wineshop, where he had three drinks and ate some refreshments before returning to Granny Xue's door, but she had not come back. As he waited, afternoon dimmed into evening, and he was on the point of turning back when Granny Xue walked into the alley with a limp, her face flushed with wine. Chen Dalang took a few steps forward, greeted her with a bow, and asked, "How is your plan coming along?"

The woman shook her hand in a gesture of negation and said, "There's still a long way to go. I've just sown the seeds. The shoots haven't come up yet. You won't get a taste until five or six years later when they blossom and bear fruit. Don't you stick your nose in here. Your old mother is not the kind that meddles in other people's affairs."

Seeing that she was addled with wine, Chen Dalang could do no more than return to his lodgings.

The following day, Granny Xue bought some fresh fruit, chicken, fish, pork, and the like, and had a cook prepare them. She then packed the food up in two boxes, and bought a jar of the best wine. With the boy from next door carrying the load, she betook herself to the Jiang residence. Sanqiao was expecting Granny Xue's visit that day. On her instruction, Clear Cloud was on the point of opening the door to take a look around for Granny Xue when whom should she see but the old woman herself. Granny Xue told the boy to put the load down by the stairs and sent him on his way. In the meantime, Clear Cloud announced the visitor to her mistress. Treating Granny Xue as an honored guest, Sanqiao went as far as the stairway to greet her and invite her up. With profuse words of thanks, the old woman bent her knees slightly in a gesture of greeting and said, "I happen to have some watery wine today and brought it along for your enjoyment."

"I shouldn't have put you to such expense," said Sanqiao. The old woman asked the two maids to bring up the food and wine, and a fine spread they made.

Sanqiao said, "You really shouldn't be so extravagant."

Granny Xue replied with a smile, "A humble household like mine has nothing fancy to offer. Just take this as a cup of tea." Clear Cloud went to fetch cups and chopsticks, while Warm Snow started lighting the portable brazier. When the wine was warm enough a moment later, Granny Xue said, "This is my treat, so would you please sit in the guest seat?"

"I am indeed much obliged," said Sanqiao, "but this being my humble house, how can I presume to accept that honor?"

After much arguing, each trying to yield the seat of honor to the other, it was Granny Xue who ended up taking the guest's seat. This being the third time they were together, they felt even more at ease in each other's company.

In the midst of their drinking, Granny Xue commented, "Your husband has been away a long time now. How can he abandon his wife like this!"

Sanqiao said, "You're right. He said he would be back in one year. I wonder what's keeping him."

The old woman pressed her point: "The way I see it, even making piles of gold and jade does not justify abandoning such a beautiful wife." She continued, "As a rule, traveling merchants take the inn as home and treat their home as an inn. Take my fourth son-in-law, Squire Zhu, for example. Ever since he's had my daughter as a concubine, he's been enjoying her from morning to night, with never a thought of the family he left behind! He goes home only once every three or four years and comes back after staying for no more than a couple of months. His first wife is virtually a widow taking care of the orphans, not knowing what he is up to behind her back." (*Convincing argument.*)

"My husband is not that kind," said Sanqiao.

Granny Xue conceded, "I was only saying that for the sake of conversation. How would I dream of comparing earth with heaven?" (*Good retreat.*) They went on to play games of riddle-guessing and dice-throwing and did not take leave of each other until they were tipsy with wine.

Two days later, the old woman came again, this time with the boy to take back her things as well as to collect payment for half of the purchase. Sanqiao kept her again for some refreshments.

Henceforth, Granny Xue frequented the Jiang residence, ostensibly to ask about Xingge, using the unpaid half of the money as a pretext. With her glib tongue and her playful ways with the maids (*Behavior befitting the character*), she won the heart of everyone in the household, high and low, so much so that Sanqiao would feel lonely if a single day went by without the old woman making an appearance. She had an old servant find out where Granny Xue lived, and, with constant invitations, visits from Granny Xue grew all the more frequent. (*Falling into the trap.*)

There are, in this world, four kinds of people with whom it would be wise not to get involved, for once you do, you'll never be able to free yourself from them. Who are these people? They are traveling monks and Taoists, beggars, vagrants, and go-betweens. The first three kinds are more tolerable than the last one, for go-betweens have access to private chambers. In moments of loneliness, nine women out of ten welcome their visits. Now, Granny Xue was not the kind-hearted sort by nature. Her sweet tongue made Sanqiao so attached to her that the latter could hardly do without her, not even for a moment. Truly,

> You may draw the skin of a tiger, but not its bones.
> You may know the face of a man, but not his heart.

More than once, Chen Dalang tried to get information out of her, but Granny Xue always put him off, saying it was not yet time. It being the middle of the fifth month, with the weather turning hot, the woman casually mentioned to Sanqiao that her home was most unfit for summer living, for it was as small as a snail's shell, with western exposure, and was far less spacious and airy than the latter's two-story house. Sanqiao said, "If you don't mind, you may sleep here at night." (*Falling into the trap.*)

"That would be nice, but what if your husband comes back?"

"Even if he does, it won't be in the middle of the night."

"Since you don't mind my intruding—and I *am* the kind to impose myself on others, I'll bring over my bedding this very evening to keep you company. How about that?"

"I have extra bedding. You don't have to bring yours. Just tell your folks that you are staying here for the whole summer. How would you like that?"

The old woman did indeed tell her son and daughter-in-law so, and brought over nothing more than a box of toilet articles. Sanqiao said, "You didn't even have to do that! You don't really think there's a lack of combs in this house, do you?"

"My biggest fear in life is of sharing other people's combs and face-washing water. Plus, I'm afraid your combs are too nice for me. Nor would I use the maids' combs. It's better to bring my own. (*Even such trivial details are interesting.*) But, tell me, which room is for me?"

Pointing at a small rattan couch by her own bed, Sanqiao said, "I've got everything done. By staying closer, we can chat at night when sleep doesn't come to us." (*Falling into the trap.*) So saying, she took out a green gauze bed-curtain and had Granny Xue hang it up herself. The two had a drink before they retired. The two maids used to sleep at the foot of Sanqiao's bed to keep her company, but, now that Granny Xue had moved in, they were sent off to the next room.

From then on Granny Xue would return to the Jiang residence after a day of peddling her merchandise from door to door, and the Jiang residence came alive with frequent merry drinking. The bed and the couch being arranged in a "T" shape, the two women lay as close to each other as if they were side by side, though separated as they were by a curtain. At night they would chitchat, and, with one asking questions and the other answering, their gossip included all of the sordid details about happenings in the neighborhood. (*Closing in on her, step by step. A most credible detail.*) Sometimes the old woman would feign drunkenness and talk about her clandestine love affairs in her younger days, to stir up Sanqiao's amorous thoughts, and, indeed, the color came and went on the latter's fair-skinned and delicate cheeks. (*Most cunning.*) Granny Xue realized that the lewd stories were working, but found it awkward to bring up the real subject yet.

Time sped by. In no time, the seventh day of the seventh month rolled around. As it happened to be Sanqiao's birthday, Granny Xue rose bright and early and prepared two boxes of birthday presents to celebrate the occasion. Sanqiao said her thanks and asked Xue to stay for the birthday noodles. Granny Xue said, "I have a busy day ahead of me. I'll come in the evening to keep you company, and we'll watch the Herdboy and Weaving Maiden get together." (*Every word is significant.*) Having said these words, she went off.

Barely had she walked down the steps than she ran into Chen Dalang. As they could not very well talk on the street, Chen Dalang followed her into a secluded alley. Wearing a frown, he grumbled, "Mother, how you've been dragging your feet! Spring is gone, summer is behind us, and autumn is here. Day after day, you say nothing but that it's not yet time, it's not yet time, but do you know that, for me, a day is as long as a year? A few more days and her husband will be back and the whole thing will be off! Won't you be killing me? Just remember: I'll haunt you from the netherworld to make you pay me back with your life."

"Don't carry on like that. I was just on my way to invite you, and here you are. Whether the whole thing can be pulled off or not will depend on tonight. You'll have to do as I say." And she went on to instruct him to do thus and so. "Everything has to be done quietly. You must not get me into any trouble."

Chen Dalang said with a nod, "A wonderful plan! Wonderful! I'll have a handsome reward for you if it works." With that, he went merrily on his way. Truly,

> The trap was laid to capture the beauty;
> Brains were racked to play at clouds and rain.

To get on with our story, Granny Xue promised Chen Dalang that action was to be taken that very night. After a misty drizzle all afternoon, night fell with a darkness unrelieved by any glimmer of star or moonlight. In the inky darkness, Granny Xue took Chen Dalang to the left of the house door, where she told him to hide while she herself went to knock at the door. A paper lantern in hand, Clear Cloud opened the door. Granny Xue deliberately groped in her own sleeves and said, "I lost my Linqing[13] handkerchief. Would you be so kind as to look for it for me, dear?"

While Clear Cloud was tricked into turning her lantern toward the street, the old woman motioned Chen Dalang over, and the two slipped through the door. Having led him to hide behind the staircase (*With such meticulous planning for every move, Granny Xue could very well be a military strategist*), Granny Xue cried out, "I've found it! You don't have to look anymore."

Clear Cloud said, "My lantern happened to go out, too. Let me light up another one for you."

"I know my way about by now," said the woman. "I don't need a light." With the door closed behind them, Granny Xue and Clear Cloud groped their way up the stairs.

"What was it you dropped?" asked Sanqiao.

Pulling out a small handkerchief from her sleeve, the old woman answered, "It was this cursed thing. It's not worth much, but it's a gift from a traveler from Beijing. Isn't it true that 'the gift is trifling but it's the thought that counts'?"

Sanqiao said teasingly, "Could it be a keepsake from some old flame?"

The old woman laughed. "That wouldn't be too far from the truth." Merrily, they fell to drinking. The old woman suggested, "There being so much food and wine, why don't you offer some to the servants in the kitchen? Let them also have some fun on this night of celebration." Accordingly, Sanqiao told the maid to take four dishes and two jugs of wine downstairs. The three servants in the kitchen—two women and a man—consumed the food and wine and withdrew to their own quarters. And there we shall leave them.

In the meantime, Granny Xue asked in the midst of the drinking, "Why isn't your husband back yet?"

"It's been a year and a half now," said Sanqiao.

"Even the Herdboy and the Weaving Maiden meet once a year. And here you are, beating them by half a year. It's often said, 'In status, traveling merchants come second only to officials.' Where can't travelers find romance? It's their wives at home who suffer." (*Most cunning.*)

With a sigh, Sanqiao hung her head and fell silent. The old woman said, "Well, I shouldn't be shooting off my mouth like that. Tonight, the Herdboy meets the Weaving Maiden. It's an occasion that calls for wine and merrymaking. Let me say nothing that saddens the heart." (*These are nothing less than words that sadden the heart.*) So saying, she poured Sanqiao a cup of wine.

When they were well warmed with wine, Granny Xue offered some to the two maids, saying, "This is in celebration of the tryst between the Herdboy and the Weaving Maiden. Drink your fill. I hope you will marry loving husbands who stay with you every moment of your lives."

Unable to fight her off, the two maids reluctantly drank the wine. The effect of the wine soon made them sway and tumble every which way. Sanqiao ordered them to close the staircase door and go to sleep (*Falling deeper into the trap*), whereas she and Granny Xue continued to drink at their ease.

While drinking, the old woman kept up a steady stream of chatter. "How old were you when you married?" she asked. (*There she goes.*)

"Seventeen," answered Sanqiao.

"It's not such a bad deal if you did the thing late. As for me, I lost my virginity at the age of thirteen."

"You married that early?"

"If you're talking about marriage, I married when I was eighteen. I might as well tell you, I was learning to sew in a neighbor's house when the young master seduced me. I fell for his good looks and gave in to him. At first, the pain was excruciating, but after doing it two or three times, I came to like it a lot. Was it the same case with you?"

Sanqiao giggled without answering. Granny Xue continued, "It would be better had I not experienced what it's like. Once you've had the experience, you can't get it out of your mind, and you get an itch for it from time to time. It's better during the day, but nighttime is most dreadful."

"You must have known a lot of men before marriage. How did you manage to pass yourself off as a virgin when you got married?"

"My mother was afraid of a scandal because she had some idea of what was going on. So she gave me a prescription for restoring virginity. The thing tightened up after being washed with pomegranate skin and alum. I made a great fuss about the pain and so I passed."

"But before you married, didn't you have to sleep by yourself at night?"

"I remember that before I married, I used to sleep in the same bed with my sister-in-law, head to head, foot to foot, when my brother was away. We took turns playing the man's part on each other's belly."

"What's the good of two women sleeping together?"

The old woman walked over, sat down by her side, and said, "You may not know this, but, as long as both know how to do it, it's just as much fun and provides just as much relief."

Sanqiao gave the woman a playful slap on the shoulder and said, "I don't believe this. You're lying." (*She takes the bait.*)

Seeing that Sanqiao's desires had been stirred up, the woman continued to work on her: "I am fifty-two years old, but at night, I still often have maddening fits of desire that I can hardly fight off. You are lucky to be able to stay calm, young as you are."

"You don't mean you'll have an affair with some man when your desire gets the better of you?"

"I am a withered flower, a dried-up willow tree. Who wants me anymore? I might as well tell you: I know a way to give myself pleasure, an 'emergency relief measure.'"

"You are lying. What is it?"

"I'll tell you everything about it when we get to bed in a moment," said the old woman.

At this juncture, a moth was seen fluttering over the lamp. Granny Xue swatted at it with a fan, deliberately putting the lamp out. (*The woman's craftiness is frightening.*) "Aya!" she cried. "Let me go and get another light." With that, she left to open the staircase door. In the meantime, Chen Dalang had already mounted the stairs and had been hiding by the door for some time now. This was all part of Granny Xue's scheme. "I forgot to bring a match with me," Granny Xue called out. So she retraced her steps and led Chen Dalang to lie down on her own couch, while she herself went downstairs and came up again a moment later, saying, "It's so late now that the pilot fire in the kitchen has gone out. What's to be done?"

"I'm used to sleeping with a light on," said Sanqiao. "This darkness is scary!"

"Shall I sleep in the same bed with you to keep you company?"

Wishing to ask her about the "emergency relief measure," Sanqiao said, "That'll be fine."

"You can go to bed first," said Granny Xue. "I'll join you after I close the door."

Sanqiao undressed first and got into bed, saying, "Please come quickly."

"Coming!" said Granny Xue, while dragging Chen Dalang, all naked, from the couch into Sanqiao's bed. Sanqiao touched his body and said, "For a woman of your age, what smooth skin you have!" Without a word of reply (*He can't very well talk, can he?*), the man slipped under the quilt, embraced her, and kissed her on the mouth. Still thinking it was the old woman, she put her arms around him. Suddenly, the man mounted her and started to do the real thing. Partly because she was tipsy with wine and partly because her amorous desires had been roused by the old woman, she let him have his way without bothering to find out who he was.

> One was a young wife in seclusion longing for love,
> The other a traveler craving romance.
> She, after many agonizing nights,
> Was like Wenjun when first seeing Xiangru.[14]
> He, after waiting so long,
> Was like Bizheng upon meeting Miaochang.[15]
> A welcome rain after a long drought
> Brings more joy than old friends meeting in a distant land.

Being an old hand in the world of love, Chen Dalang played the game of clouds and rain so well that the woman was brought into raptures.

After their passion had abated, Sanqiao asked, "Who are you?" Chen Dalang gave a full account of how he had seen her from the street, how he had fallen in love, and how he had pleaded hard with Granny Xue for a way to see her. "Now that I have fulfilled the dream of my life, I'll have no regrets when I die."

At this moment, Granny Xue approached the bed and said, "It's not that I was impertinent, but I thought it a shame that a young woman like you should be living all alone. I also wanted to save his life. As a matter of fact, the two of you are drawn together by a predestined bond. I had nothing to do with it."

Sanqiao said, "Now that things have come to this, what's to be done if my husband gets to hear about this?"

The old woman said, "This is a secret between us. If we bribe Clear Cloud and Warm Snow and tell them not to shoot their mouths off, who else will let on anything? Leave this to me, and I'll guarantee that you can enjoy yourselves every night without a worry. Just don't forget me in the future."

Sanqiao was in no mood at this time to concern herself with too many things, and the two resumed their amorous sport. They were still loath to part when daybreak drew near after the drum of the fifth watch. It was at Granny Xue's urging that Chen Dalang rose and went out the door in Xue's company.

Henceforth, they did not miss a single night. He came either alone or in Granny Xue's company. The latter used honeyed words and dark threats alternately on the two maids and had their mistress reward them with clothes. The man, for his part, also tipped them from time to time with a few pieces of loose silver for them to buy sweets with. The two maids were so delighted that they willingly became accomplices, greeting the visitor at night and sending him off in the morning with never an obstacle in the way. The couple came to be as inseparable as glue and lacquer, and more loving than the average lawfully wedded man and wife. With his mind set on binding the woman more securely to him, Chen Dalang showered her with nice clothes and fine jewelry and paid on her behalf all the money she owed Granny Xue. As a token of his gratitude, he gave the old woman another hundred taels of silver. In a little more than six months since he had first come to know Sanqiao, he spent nearly a thousand taels of gold. Sanqiao also gave Granny Xue gifts worth over thirty taels of silver. It was for the sake of such ill-gotten gains that the old woman agreed to be a procuress, but this is of no concern to us here.

The ancients said, "No feast does not come to an end."

> The Lantern Festival had just gone by
> When the Clear and Bright Festival rolled around.[16]

Uneasy over the thought of having neglected his business for too long, Chen Dalang now wished to return to his hometown. One night, he brought up the subject to Sanqiao, but, both being as deeply attached to each other as they were, neither could bear the thought of separation. The woman would have gladly packed up her personal belongings, eloped with the man, and lived with him ever after as his wife, but Chen Dalang objected: "This won't do. Granny Xue knows about our relationship all too well. My landlord Mr. Lü must also have his suspicions as to where I'm off to every night. What's more, there'll be a lot of travelers on the boat. Whom do you think we can fool? Nor can we bring along the two maids. When your husband comes back and finds out everything, he's not going to let the matter rest. Be patient. At this time next year, I'll come again and quietly send you a message from some secluded lodgings so that the two of us can slip away, unbeknownst to god or ghost. Wouldn't that be safer?"

"What if you don't show up by that time?" asked the woman, whereupon Chen Dalang pledged a vow. "Since you do mean it," said Sanqiao, "I will not fail you, either, whatever happens. When you get home, please send a message to Granny Xue by anyone who happens to come this way, so as to put my mind at ease."

Chen Dalang promised, "I'll surely do that. Don't worry."

A few days later, Chen Dalang hired a boat, and, after his provisions had been loaded, he went to bid Sanqiao farewell. That night they were doubly tender to each other, talking, weeping, and indulging in their desires by turns, without so much as a wink of sleep throughout the night. They rose at the fifth watch, and the woman opened a trunk, from which she took out a prized possession called the "pearl shirt." Handing it over to Chen Dalang, she said, "This shirt is a Jiang family heirloom that has a wonderful cooling effect on the body in summertime. You'll need it because the weather is getting warm. This will be a keepsake from me. To wear this shirt is to feel my body." Chen Dalang was so choked with sobs that he felt himself go limp and was unable to utter a single word. Sanqiao put the shirt on him, had a maid open the door, and saw him off as far as the door, where they took leave of each other with much emotion. As the poem says,

> *In tears, she saw off her husband years before.*
> *Today she weeps, bidding her lover farewell.*
> *Alas! Many a woman, fickle as water,*
> *Attracts wild birds to replace her drake.*

Our story forks at this point. After he came into possession of the pearl shirt, Chen Dalang wore it every day next to his skin. When he had to take it off before sleep every night, he put it under his quilt, and never, for a moment, did he part with the shirt. All along the journey, the boat was sailing with the wind. Within two months, he reached Maple Bridge in Suzhou Prefecture. There being in the neighborhood a trading center for brokers in rice and fuel, Chen Dalang naturally went to look for a buyer for his goods, but let us speak no more of this.

One day, at a fellow townsman's party, he met a merchant from Xiangyang. This man was in fact none other than Jiang Xingge. What had happened was that after having done some trading in pearls, tortoiseshell, sappanwood, aloeswood, and the like in Guangdong, Xingge had set off together with some fellow merchants. As his fellow travelers suggested going to Suzhou to sell their goods, Xingge agreed, recalling the saying "Above, there is paradise; below, there are Suzhou and Hangzhou." A trip to such a big port would be worthwhile for some more business deals before returning home. He had arrived in Suzhou in the middle of the tenth month of the previous year. As Jiang was known in business circles as Mr. Luo, Chen Dalang had no inkling as to his true identity. At such a chance meeting, the two men, being of about the same age and similar physical appearance, came to respect and admire each other in the course of their conversation. At the dinner table, they asked for the location of each other's lodgings, and thus started a close friendship and a stream of frequent mutual visits.

After having taken care of his accounts, Xingge went to Chen Dalang's lodgings to bid the latter farewell, for he was now ready to be on his way. Dalang set out some wine, and the two fell into a most pleasant conversation.

33

The weather being hot, for it was drawing near the end of the fifth month, they took off their outer garments as they drank. As Chen Dalang did so, the pearl shirt was exposed to full view before Xingge's eyes. However astonished he was, Xingge could not very well claim the shirt as his. Instead, he confined himself to commenting that it was a nice shirt indeed. Believing he had a friend to confide in, Dalang asked, "Do you, Brother Luo, happen to know a Jiang Xingge who lives on Great Market Street in your county?"

Being the discreet man he was, Xingge replied, "I've been away for too long. I've heard of such a man, but I don't know him personally. Why do you ask, Brother Chen?"

"To tell you the truth, my brother, I've come to be connected with him in a way." Whereupon he supplied a full account of his affair with Sanqiao. Pulling at his shirt, he said, his eyes brimming over with tears, "This shirt is a gift from her. Now that you are leaving for home, please do me the favor of delivering a letter for me. I will send the letter to your place first thing tomorrow morning."

While he gave his promise, Xingge thought to himself, "How extraordinary! With the pearl shirt as evidence, his story must be true." Feeling as if being stabbed by needles in the stomach, on some pretext he declined more offers of wine and hastened to leave. Back in his lodgings, he sank into reflection for one moment and grew fretful the next. How he wished he could learn some magic trick to shrink the distance and be home in a trice! He packed up all of his belongings before the night was out and embarked on the boat early in the morning, ready to be on his way.

At this juncture, a man ran up to the boat, panting for breath. It was Chen Dalang. He handed over to Xingge a large package, reminding him to be sure to deliver it. Xingge's face turned ashen with rage. Speech failed him, as did his will to live or to die. It was not until Chen Dalang had left that he took a look at the envelope. It bore the line "Please be kind enough to deliver the letter to Granny Xue's house in East Lane off Great Market Street."

Angrily, Xingge ripped open the package with a single swipe of his hand, revealing a peach-pink gauze scarf more than two yards in length. There was also an oblong paper box containing a phoenix hairpin of fine white jade and a note saying, "Godmother, please do me the favor of delivering these two small gifts to my beloved Sanqiao as a token of my love. I will certainly see her next spring. Tell her to take good care of herself." In a rush of rage, Xingge tore the letter to pieces and tossed them into the river. Next, he picked up the jade hairpin and threw it onto the deck, where it broke in two. Then an idea occurred to him: "What a fool I am!" he said to himself. "Why don't I keep them as evidence?" He picked up the pieces of the hairpin, wrapped them up with the scarf, put the package away, and urged the boatman to get under way. All through the journey home he was gripped by intense anxiety.

As his house came into sight, tears fell from his eyes in spite of himself. (*Pitiable.*) "What a loving couple we used to be!" he thought. "It's my foolish pursuit of profits the size of a fly's head that made her a virtual widow in the prime of her youth and caused such a scandal. Regrets are too late now!" While on the way, he had been only too anxious to reach home, but now that he found himself approaching the house, feelings of pain and regret overcame him. His pace slackened. (*How realistic!*) As he crossed the threshold, he was obliged to curb his anger and force himself to greet his wife, though he had hardly a word to say. Sanqiao, for her part, felt so ill at ease that, with shame written all over her face, she did not presume to step forward and strike up an affectionate conversation. After he finished moving his baggage into the house, Xingge said he wanted to pay a visit to his parents-in-law, but, in fact, he spent the night on the boat.

The following morning, he went back home and said to Sanqiao, "Your parents are both gravely ill. That's why I had to stay with them for the night to take care of them. They miss you very much and wish to see you. I have hired a sedan-chair, which is waiting at the door. You may go quickly. I will follow soon."

Sanqiao had grown apprehensive about her husband's absence for the night and readily believed this story about her parents' illness. Filled with alarm, she hurriedly handed the trunk keys to her husband and mounted the sedan-chair, taking a waiting woman with her. Xingge stopped the waiting woman, gave her a letter that he took out from his sleeve, and told her to deliver it to Mr. Wang. "After giving him the letter," he continued, "you may return by the same sedan-chair."

Upon arrival, Sanqiao was surprised to find both parents in good health. Mr. Wang also gasped with astonishment at his daughter's unannounced return. As he took the letter from the waiting woman, he found, upon opening, that it was a statement of divorce that read,

> *This is a statement of divorce by Jiang De, a native of Zaoyang County in the Prefecture of Xiangyang, betrothed at an early age through a matchmaker to the Wang family's daughter. Little did I expect that once married, the said woman would be guilty, as she is, of some of the seven offenses[17] that constitute grounds for divorce. Out of consideration for my sentiments for her, I cannot bring myself to reveal the details but would fain return her to her parents. She is free to remarry without any objections from me. This statement of divorce is written on this ———— day of the ———— month of the second year [1466] of the Chenghua reign period.*
>
> *(palm print)*

In the envelope was also a peach-colored scarf and a broken jade phoenix hairpin. In great alarm, Mr. Wang called forth his daughter for questioning. Hearing that her husband had divorced her, Sanqiao broke down into sobs without saying a word. In a huff, Mr. Wang stormed through the streets and into his son-in-law's house. Jiang Xingge hurriedly stepped forward with a bow of greeting. Mr. Wang returned the greeting and said, "My good son-in-law, my daughter was a pure and innocent girl when she married you. What did she do wrong to make you divorce her? You owe me an explanation."

"I can't very well tell you. Ask your daughter and you'll know."

"She keeps crying without saying a word. I'm all in the dark! My daughter has always been a sensible girl, and I don't think she would be guilty of something like adultery or theft. If it's just some minor misdemeanor, please forgive her for my sake. The two of you were betrothed when you were seven or eight years old, and you have never had a harsh word for each other in your peaceful married life. You haven't even been home for more than a day since you came back from your travels. What could you have found wrong? Such heartlessness on your part will hold you up for ridicule for being a most unkind man." (*The very thing a father-in-law is likely to say under the circumstances.*)

"I will not venture to say too much to you, my father-in-law, but you may ask your daughter if she still has the pearl shirt, an heirloom of my family, that was entrusted to her care. If she still has it, well and good. If not, do not blame me for what I did."

Mr. Wang made haste to return home and asked his daughter, "Your husband is only asking you for a pearl shirt. Now tell me, whom did you give it to?" The woman flushed crimson with shame, for these words struck right on her sore point. Without knowing what to say, she burst into loud wails of grief. Mr. Wang was so disconcerted that he was at a loss what to do. In an attempt to placate her, Mrs. Wang said, "Don't keep crying like that. Tell Mom and Dad the truth, so we can help you sort things out." The daughter firmly refused to tell them anything. Instead, she kept weeping bitterly. Mr. Wang could do nothing more than hand over to his wife the divorce statement, the scarf, and the hairpin and tell her to be gentle with their daughter and gradually get the truth out of her.

The much-bewildered Mr. Wang went to a neighbor's house for some idle talk. Observing that her daughter's eyes were all red and swollen from crying, Mrs. Wang came to fear that her health would break down. After a few soothing words, she went to the kitchen to warm some wine to cheer up her daughter with.

Sitting all by herself in her room, Sanqiao began to wonder how the secret of the pearl shirt could have been divulged and where the scarf and hairpin had come from. After some moments of reflection, she said to herself, "I see. The broken hairpin means the marriage is at an end, just as a broken mirror symbolizes a broken marriage. The scarf is obviously for me to hang myself with. (*Even a guess sounds so real.*) Considering his feelings for me, he chose not to say it in so many words, so as to let me keep my good name. How sad it is that four years of a happy marriage are so suddenly brought to an end. It's all my fault, for I betrayed my husband's love. I suppose I will know no more happiness if I live on. I'd better hang myself and be done with it." At this point, she broke down in another fit of weeping. She put something under a stool to raise it, threw the scarf over a rafter, and proceeded to hang herself. However, she was not destined to die yet.

With the door left ajar, Mrs. Wang walked in with a flask of fine, heated wine. The sight of her daughter getting ready to hang herself threw her into such panic that, without stopping to put down the flask, she rushed forward to pull her daughter away. In the confusion, she kicked over the stool, and she and her daughter fell in a heap on the floor amid spilled wine. Mrs. Wang scrambled to her feet and helped her daughter up, saying, "How foolish you are! You are only in your twenties, like a flower not yet in full bloom. How could you have done such a thing! Even if your husband won't change his mind and goes through with the divorce, you, with your looks, won't have to worry about any lack of marriage proposals. You can well afford to pick a good husband and enjoy the marriage the rest of your life. Just relax and get on with your life. Forget all worries."

After he returned home and learned about his daughter's suicide attempt, Mr. Wang also tried to comfort her with some soothing words. At the same time, he told his wife to be on alert and watch their daughter closely. A few days later, Sanqiao gave up the thought, as she saw the futility of any more such attempts. Truly,

> Husband and wife were birds in the same woods,
> But flew apart at the destined hour.

Let us come back to Jiang Xingge. He tied up Clear Cloud and Warm Snow with rope and beat them to make them confess. At first, they denied any knowledge of the affair, but later, unable to withstand the pain, they finally confessed all the details from beginning to end. It was thus made clear that no one else was to blame but Granny Xue, who had single-handedly pulled off the whole thing. The following morning, Xingge led a group of men to Granny Xue's house and smashed everything into pieces the size of snowflakes, falling just short of tearing the house down. Well aware that she was in the wrong, Granny Xue slipped out of the way, and no one dared to step forward to say anything. This lack of protest made Xingge feel vindicated. Upon returning home, he summoned a go-between and sold the two maids. As for the sixteen trunks of various sizes stored upstairs, he did not open any of them but wrote thirty-two sealing strips and sealed them in crisscross fashion, two to each trunk. Why did he do so? It was because, as a matter of fact, Jiang Xingge had been deeply in love with his wife. True, he had divorced her in a moment of anger, but his heart was twisted with pain. He could hardly bear the sight of anything that would remind him of her.

Let us pick up another thread of the story and tell of a man with a *jinshi* degree by the name of Wu Jie, a native of Nanjing, who was passing by Xiangyang in a boat on his way to Chaoyang County, Guangdong, to assume his newly assigned post of county magistrate. He did not bring his wife and children, and had a mind to find himself a beautiful concubine. None of the many women he saw along the way struck his fancy. Having heard that the daughter of Mr. Wang of Zaoyang County was known throughout the county for her beauty, he sought the services of a go-between and made a marriage proposal along with an offer of fifty taels of gold as a gift. Mr. Wang would have gladly accepted the proposal, but, afraid that his former son-in-law would be against the idea, he went to the Jiang household and acquainted Xingge with the fact. Xingge raised no objections.

On the eve of the wedding, Xingge hired some help and had the still-sealed and untouched sixteen trunks delivered, along with the keys, as the bride's dowry onto Magistrate Wu's boat to be handed over to Sanqiao. (*An act of kindness.*) She was overwhelmed with the sense that she did not deserve such generosity. When the story got around, some praised Xingge for his kindness, some laughed and called him a fool, and there were also those who despised him for his softness. So different indeed are human hearts.

Let us get on with our story. Chen Dalang, after having disposed of all of his merchandise in Suzhou, returned to Xin'an County, his mind still filled with thoughts about Sanqiao. The sight of the pearl shirt morning and night prompted him to sigh with emotion. Her suspicions aroused, his wife Ping-shi quietly took it away while he was asleep and hid it above the ceiling. When he rose in the morning without being able to find the shirt that he wanted to put on, he asked his wife for it, but she stoutly denied any knowledge of it. He flew into a rage and ransacked all boxes and chests. When the search proved to be futile, he let loose a torrent of angry words at his wife, who tearfully answered back, and the quarrel lasted for two to three days. Finally, in agitation, he hurriedly put together some money and, taking a page boy with him, set out on a journey back to Xiangyang.

When approaching Zaoyang, he ran into a gang of robbers, who not only made off with all of his capital, but also killed the page boy. Being keen of eye, Chen Dalang hid himself behind the rudder at the stern of the boat and was thus able to survive. Now that he could not afford the journey home, he planned to stay in the inn where he had stayed before, ask for a loan from Sanqiao, and start building his business anew. With a sigh, he stepped off the boat and went ashore.

To Mr. Lü, his landlord, who lived outside the Zaoyang city gate, he gave an account of what had happened and said that he wanted to ask Granny Xue, who was in the pearl business, to borrow some money on his behalf from some acquaintances. "You may not have heard about it," said Mr. Lü, "but that old woman caused a scandal by corrupting Jiang Xingge's wife. Last year when Xingge returned home, he asked his wife for some sort of pearl shirt, but she could not come up with an answer because she had, in fact, given it away to some lover of hers. Xingge divorced her then and there and sent her back to her parents. She has now remarried and is the second wife of *jinshi* Wu of Nanjing. As for the old woman, Jiang Xingge had her house smashed so badly that not a piece of roof tile was spared. Knowing that she would be given no peace, the old woman has moved to a neighboring county."

Chen Dalang was so shocked by these words that he felt as if a bucketful of icy water had been dumped on his head. That night, he fell ill with bouts of heat and cold. Brought on partly by depression, partly by lovesickness, and partly by the shock, the illness, with some symptoms of consumption, kept him confined to bed for over two months, with frequent improvements and relapses. With full recovery beyond sight, even the landlord's page boy attending to his needs ran out of patience. Feeling apologetic, Chen Dalang mustered enough strength to write a letter home. He then asked his landlord to find someone who happened to be available to deliver the letter and bring him back some traveling money along with a kinsman to take care of him. This was exactly what Mr. Lü wanted to hear. It so happened that there was an official courier, an acquaintance of Mr. Lü's, who was passing by Zaoyang on his way by land as well as water routes to the Huizhou and Ningzhou region to deliver official documents. To have mail delivered by him would be as quick as could be. Mr. Lü took Chen Dalang's letter and gave it to the courier, along with half a tael of silver on Dalang's behalf, asking him to deliver the letter at his convenience. Indeed, as the saying goes, "A lone traveler goes at his own pace; a courier goes with the speed of fire." In a matter of days, the courier arrived in Xin'an County and asked his way to Chen Dalang's house. After delivering the letter, he mounted his horse and galloped away. Truly,

> A precious letter home
> Led to another marriage.

When Ping-shi opened the letter, she recognized the handwriting to be her husband's. The letter said,

Greetings from Chen Shang to my good wife Ping-shi: After I left home, I ran into robbers in Xiangyang. My money was taken away and my page boy killed. The shock made me fall ill. I have been confined to bed in my old lodgings at Mr. Lü's for over two months now, without any sign of recovery. Upon receipt of this letter, please quickly send a trusted relative to see me, bringing along as much money for traveling expenses as possible. Written in haste, leaning on my pillow.

Ping-shi did not quite believe it. She thought to herself, "The last time he came back, he claimed to have lost as much capital as a thousand taels of gold. That pearl shirt must have been acquired by some improper means. And now he has come up with this story of a robbery to ask for as much travel money as possible. He must be lying." Then another thought struck her: "If he wants some trusted relative to go quickly to see him, he must be gravely ill. That part might be the truth, for all I know. Now, of whom can I ask the favor?" She kept turning the matter over and over in her mind, but, unable to put her mind at ease, she took the counsel of her father, Squire Ping. Then she put together some valuables, took with her the servant Chen Wang and his wife, and, in the company of her father, hired a boat and headed for Xiangyang to see her husband for herself. When they reached Jingkou,[18] Squire Ping suffered an attack of bronchitis and was escorted back home. Ping-shi and the Chen couple continued on the journey upstream.

Before many days had passed, they arrived at the city gate of Zaoyang and asked their way to Mr. Lü's house. It turned out that Chen Dalang had died ten days before. With a little of his own money, Mr. Lü had perfunctorily put the body in a coffin. Ping-shi cried until she collapsed to the ground, and remained unconscious for a considerable while. Upon coming to, she made haste to change into mourning clothes and repeatedly pleaded with Mr. Lü to open the coffin for her to see her husband once more and to transfer the body into a better coffin. Mr. Lü would not hear of it. Left with no alternative, Ping-shi could do no more than buy some boards to serve as an outer shell of the coffin. She also engaged some monks for a sutra-chanting service and burned an abundance of paper money for the benefit of the deceased. Having already obtained from her twenty taels of silver as a token of gratitude for his help, Mr. Lü said nothing to all this ado.

More than a month later, Ping-shi announced that she would like to select a propitious day and escort the coffin back home. Believing that the woman was too young, attractive, and well-provided-for to remain a widow for the rest of her life, Mr. Lü had a mind to keep her as wife for his yet-unbetrothed son Lü Er. Wouldn't that be lovely on both counts? He bought some wine, treated Chen Wang to a drink, and asked Chen Wang's wife, with promises of a handsome reward, to put the proposal tactfully to Ping-shi. Being a stupid woman, Chen Wang's wife thoughtlessly blurted out everything to her mistress. After all, what did she know about tact? Ping-shi was incensed. She gave the woman a tongue-lashing and a few slaps on the face. Even Mr. Lü was not spared a few scathing remarks from her. The humiliation reduced Mr. Lü to a resentful silence. Truly,

> *The mutton bun escaped his lips;*
> *He had but the foul smell all over his body.*

As a consequence, Mr. Lü urged Chen Wang to run away. For his part, Chen Wang also thought that to stay on would not be to his advantage any more. He took counsel with his wife. Under his instructions and with his collaboration, she stole all of Ping-shi's money and jewelry, and then the couple slipped away under cover of night. Knowing full well what had happened, Mr. Lü turned around and blamed Ping-shi for having brought along such scoundrels. "Luckily," he went on to say, "they stole only from their mistress. Wouldn't it look bad if they had stolen from someone else!" Then, complaining that the coffin was scaring his customers away, he told Ping-shi to have it removed as soon as possible. He added that, this being the wrong place for a young widow to stay, she would do well to leave. Under such pressure, Ping-shi resignedly rented a room elsewhere and hired some men to move the coffin there. Her plight hardly needs further description here.

Next door to her lived a Seventh Aunt Zhang, who was quite a sociable woman. Ping-shi's sobs frequently drew her over to offer words of comfort. She also often did Ping-shi the favor of pawning some of the latter's clothes in exchange for daily expenses, for which Ping-shi was deeply grateful. In a matter of a few months, all of her clothes had been pawned. Being good at sewing, a skill that she had acquired at an early age, Ping-shi began to consider making a living by teaching sewing skills to rich men's daughters before deciding what to do next. When she asked Seventh Aunt Zhang for advice, the latter said, "I don't know how to put this, but a rich man's house is not the best place for a young woman like you. The dead are dead and gone, which is too bad for them, but the living need to get on with their lives. You have a good part of your life ahead of you. You can't be a seamstress for some rich household until the end of your days, can you? It's such a lowly position that you'll be looked down upon. Also, what are you going to do about the coffin? That's another important thing you need to take care of. Even if you go on paying rent for it, that's no solution in the long run."

"I have also thought about all this," said Ping-shi, "but I can't come up with a better idea."

"I have an idea," said Seventh Aunt Zhang. "Don't take offense if I say so, but, for a penniless lonely widow a thousand li from home, to escort the coffin back is nothing but a lot of wishful thinking. Widowhood won't be easily maintained when daily subsistence is uncertain. But even if you do hold out for some time, what good will it do to you? As I see it, the best thing to do is to find a good match while your youth and good looks last, and give yourself up to him. Betrothal gifts can be used for their cash value to buy a piece of land to bury your husband in. Thus your future will be secure, and you'll have no regrets, dead or alive."

Convinced by her reasoning, Ping-shi reflected for some time before she answered with a sigh, "Oh well, to sell myself in order to bury my husband shouldn't be cause for ridicule."

"If you've made up your mind, I do happen to have someone for you. He's about your age. A decent man, and quite wealthy, too."

"If he's that wealthy, I'm afraid he won't take someone who's been married before."

"He's also been married before. He told me that he doesn't mind if the woman is marrying for the first time or not, as long as she is of uncommon beauty. Your looks should be attractive enough to impress him."

As a matter of fact, Jiang Xingge had indeed asked Seventh Aunt Zhang to find him a good match. As his ex-wife was a ravishing beauty, he was looking for someone as pretty. Ping-shi might not have been as beautiful as Sanqiao but was the better of the two when it came to matters of the mind and the finger.

The following day, Seventh Aunt Zhang went into town and told Jiang Xingge about the matter. Upon learning that Ping-shi was from the lower reaches of the Yangzi River, Xingge was all the more delighted. For a wedding gift Ping-shi wanted only what was necessary for the purchase of a nice plot of land for the burial of her husband. After Seventh Aunt Zhang shuttled back and forth quite a few times, both sides agreed to the deal.

To make a long story short, Ping-shi watched the lowering of the coffin into the pit, and, after the funeral, she shed bitter tears, removed Chen Dalang's spirit tablet, and took off her mourning clothes. As the wedding day drew near, Jiang Xingge sent over clothes and jewelry and redeemed all the clothes that she had pawned. On their wedding night, as was usual with wedding festivities, candles decorated with designs of dragons and phoenixes were lit in the bridal chamber amid the musical fanfare of a band. Truly,

> *Though the rites had been gone through before,*
> *More loving were they than newlywed couples.*

Ping-shi's gentle manners won much respect from Jiang Xingge. One day, returning home from outside, he found Ping-shi sorting out a trunk of clothes.

Among the clothes, he recognized the pearl shirt. In astonishment, he asked, "Where did you get this shirt?"

"There's something strange about it." She then launched into an account of how her ex-husband had carried on about it, and how they had parted in anger after many harsh words. She continued, "When I was hard up some time ago, I thought several times of pawning it, but I was afraid of bringing it into the open, because its questionable origin might have gotten me into trouble. To this day, I have no idea where it came from."

"Was your ex-husband Chen Dalang, also called Chen Shang? Did he have a fair complexion? No beard? Long fingernails on his left hand?"

"Exactly."

Sticking out his tongue, Jiang Xingge joined his palms and looked up to the sky. "It's all too clear that heavenly principles have been at work," he exclaimed. "How fearsome!" Ping-shi asked why he said such a thing. "This pearl shirt," he explained, "was an heirloom of my family. Your husband seduced my wife and got the shirt from her as a keepsake. I didn't know anything about the affair until I saw the shirt when I met him in Suzhou. I divorced Wang-shi as soon as I returned home. Who would have foreseen that your husband would die on the road? When I remarried, I heard only that you were the ex-wife of a Mr. Chen, a merchant of Huizhou. Who would have guessed that he was none other than Chen Shang! Isn't this a heavenly retribution?"

These words made Ping-shi's hair stand on end, as a sense of awe swept over her. Henceforth, they grew even fonder of each other. This, then, is what basically constitutes our story "Jiang Xingge Reencounters His Pearl Shirt." As the poem says,

> The ways of heaven are not to be slighted;
> To whose advantage is the exchange of wives?
> Interest must be paid on any debt incurred;
> The marriage bond is but briefly suspended.

But the story continues. With a wife to take care of the household, Jiang Xingge set off a year later for Guangdong again on another business journey. This was one of those occasions when something was destined to happen. One day when he was in Hepu County[19] trading in pearls, a deal had already been struck when his client, an old man, stole a pearl of enormous size and refused to admit the theft. In anger, Xingge grabbed him by his sleeves in an attempt to search him, but the sheer force of the move brought the old man down to the ground. As the old man lay there without making a sound, Xingge hurried to help him up, only to find him dead. The old man's family and close neighbors rushed over, some weeping, some screaming, and seized Xingge. Without allowing a word of explanation, they gave him a sound beating and locked him up in an empty room. That very night, they wrote an official complaint and, after daybreak, took the defendant as well as the letter of complaint to the county magistrate's morning court session. The magistrate accepted the case, but, as there was other official business at hand, he had the accused locked up to await trial the next day.

Who, you may ask, was this county magistrate? Named Wu Jie, he was a *jinshi* of the greater Nanjing area. He was none other than Sanqiao's second husband. He originally had been assigned to a post in Chaoyang, but, as his superiors found him free from corruption, he was transferred, as a promotion, to the pearl-producing region of Hepu County. That night, Wu Jie was carefully reading by lamplight the accepted letter of complaint when Sanqiao, looking idly over his shoulders, happened to see these words: "The homicide case of Song Fu against Luo De, merchant of Zaoyang." Who could this Luo De be but Jiang Xingge? As memories of the happy marriage came flooding back to her, she appealed to her husband tearfully, her heart stricken with pain: "This Luo De is my older brother, who was brought up by my maternal uncle of the Luo family. I little expected that he would commit such a major crime while traveling on the road. For my sake, please spare his life and let him go back home."

"That'll have to depend on how the trial goes. If he is indeed guilty of murder, I can't be lenient with him."

Her eyes brimming over with tears, Sanqiao fell to her knees and pleaded piteously on behalf of the accused.

"Don't be so upset yet," said the magistrate. "I know what to do."

The following morning, as he was about to go to his court session, Sanqiao again grabbed him by his sleeve and said sobbingly, "If my brother's life is not spared, I will surely kill myself. You won't see me again."

That day when the county magistrate assumed the bench in his court, the first case he took up was the one involving Jiang Xingge. The brothers Song Fu and Song Shou tearfully pleaded that the murderer of their father should pay with his life. "Our father," they said, "was struck unconscious by the defendant in a dispute about some pearls and fell dead on the spot. Please do right by us, Your Honor." As the county magistrate took testimony from witnesses, some said the old man was knocked down and others said he fell when pushed. Jiang Xingge said in defense of himself, "Their father stole a pearl from me. I got into an argument with him in anger. Being an old man, he was not too steady of foot and fell to his own death. I had nothing to do with it."

The magistrate asked Song Fu, "How old was your father?"

"Sixty-seven."

"Elderly people faint easily without necessarily having to be hit," said the magistrate.

Song Fu and Song Shou insisted that their father was killed by the blow from Jiang Xingge.

"Whether there are injuries or not needs to be verified by a postmortem. Since you insist that he was killed, the corpse shall be sent away to the county mortuary and judgment will be made during the evening session of the court."

As a matter of fact, the Songs were a prominent and respected family. The sons could hardly allow the body of their father, once a neighborhood alderman, to be exposed for autopsy in a mortuary. They pleaded while kowtowing, "There are many witnesses to our father's death. We request that the postmortem be done in our home rather than in a public place."

The magistrate said, "Without evidence of injuries to the bones, the accused will hardly admit to his crime, will he? Without duly filled-out forms of postmortem results, I can't report to my superiors, can I?" As the two brothers continued their entreaties, the county magistrate flew into a rage. "If you refuse to have a postmortem done, I can hardly try this case."

In panic, the brothers kowtowed repeatedly and said, "We will go by whatever ruling you make, Your Honor."

"For a sexagenarian," said the magistrate, "death is only to be expected. Suppose he did not die from a blow and an innocent man is wrongly accused. That would only serve to add to the sins of the dead. Your father lived to a venerable old age, something that you, as sons, had hoped for. Now, you wouldn't want to give him the bad reputation of having died a violent death, would you? However, though your father was not killed intentionally, he was indeed pushed. If Luo De is not severely punished, you would hardly feel avenged. Therefore, my judgment is for him to put on mourning clothes, observe the rituals in a manner befitting a son, and defray all expenses for the funeral. Will you be content with that?"

"We will not presume to be otherwise, Your Honor," said the brothers.

Xingge was overjoyed at the unexpectedly forthright verdict reached without resorting to corporeal punishment. The defendant as well as the plaintiffs kowtowed in gratitude. The county magistrate went on, "Nor will I commit my judgment to paper. I will have the defendant escorted out of the court by lictors who will report back to me after what needs to be done is done. At that time, I will remove the original complaint from the file." Truly,

> Easy it is for a judge to commit karmic sin,
> Nor is it hard for him to get hidden merit.
> Observe how this Magistrate Wu of our times
> Rights the wrong and absolves guilt, to both parties' joy.

While her husband was in court, Sanqiao was as anxious as if she were on pins and needles. No sooner had she heard that the court session was over than she stepped forward to ask about what had transpired. The county magistrate said, "I made such-and-such a verdict. For your sake, I didn't put him to even one stroke of the rod."

Profuse with thanks, Sanqiao said, "After such a long separation, I am dying to see my brother to ask him how my parents are. I would be greatly obliged if you could be so kind as to arrange for us to meet."

"That can be easily done."

Dear audience, you may well ask how come Sanqiao was still so full of affection for Jiang Xingge, when she should have severed all emotional ties with the man who divorced her. The truth is that the couple had been as loving as could be. It was because of Sanqiao's misdemeanor that Xingge divorced her against his inclinations. In fact, he felt so sorry that he gave her back all the sixteen trunks intact on the night of her second wedding. Just this gesture alone was enough to melt Sanqiao's heart. Now that she was living in the midst of wealth and honor, and he was in distress, she could hardly do anything else than extend a helping hand. This is a case of returning kindness for kindness.

Now, Jiang Xingge followed the county magistrate's judgment and carefully fulfilled the ceremonial requirements asked of him, sparing no expense. The Song brothers found themselves without cause for complaint. After the funeral was over, Jiang Xingge returned under guard to the magistrate's court for a report. The county magistrate summoned him into the private quarters of his yamen, granted him a seat, and said, "My brother-in-law, I might have treated you unfairly in the lawsuit if your younger sister had not pleaded hard for you." With no inkling as to what he was talking about, Xingge was at a loss for an answer.

A moment later when they finished their tea, the county magistrate invited him into the study in the inner quarters of the yamen and called forth his concubine to greet the guest. This all too unexpected reunion was indeed as unreal as a dream. Without a salute or a word, the two of them fell into a tight embrace with loud sobs that were more heartrending than those ever heard at the funeral of a father or a mother. Overcome with pity, the county magistrate, who was standing on one side, said, "Please do not grieve so. I don't think you look like brother and sister. Tell me the truth; I'll help you out."

The two of them were so shaken by the violent shudders of weeping that neither was ready to speak. However, under the county magistrate's pressing questions, Sanqiao had no other choice but to fall on her knees to say, "I deserve to die ten thousand times for my sins, for this man is, in fact, my ex-husband."

Knowing that the truth was not to be concealed any longer, Jiang Xingge also dropped to his knees and gave a full account of their loving marriage, the divorce, and the remarrying on both sides. Having poured out the story, the two of them again fell into a tearful embrace. Even County Magistrate Wu found his own tears streaming down. "How can I bring myself to separate such a loving couple?" he said. "Luckily, no child was born during these three years. You may go together this very moment and resume your marriage." The couple took deep bows in gratitude.

With all speed, the county magistrate hired a small sedan-chair and saw Sanqiao out of the yamen. He then had some laborers carry all the sixteen trunks of dowry over to Jiang Xingge and sent a subordinate official to escort the couple out of the county. Such was the immense kindness of County Magistrate Wu. Verily,

> The Hepu pearls glowed with greater luster.[20]
> The Fengcheng swords shone in greater splendor.[21]
> Mr. Wu's kindness was admired by all.
> Wealth and beauty he coveted none.

He had never had a son, but, later, after his transfer to the Ministry of Personnel, he took a concubine who bore him three sons in succession. All three were successful in the imperial examinations. This was believed to be a blessing for the good deeds he had done. But this is no immediate concern of ours here.

Let us return to Jiang Xingge, who took Sanqiao back home and introduced her to Ping-shi. If the first marriage were taken into consideration, Sanqiao would have taken precedence over Ping-shi. However, she had been divorced, whereas Ping-shi was married to Jiang Xingge through the mediation of a go-between, as required by proper etiquette. Moreover, Ping-shi was one year older. Therefore, Ping-shi took the position of first wife and Sanqiao became the second wife. With the two women addressing each other as "Sister," the threesome lived happily ever after, as this poem attests:

> Loving though they were for the rest of their lives,
> How shameful that she fell from wife to concubine.
> How true that one's deeds are repaid for ill or fair;
> Heaven above weighs the scales; you need not seek far.

Censor Chen Ingeniously Solves the Case of the Gold Hairpins and Brooches

The affairs of the world spin like wheels;
The woe and weal of the moment may not be real.
Watch how in the end man is fairly judged.
When has heaven ever failed the good at heart?

I have heard elders in my story-telling profession tell the tale of a man by the name of Jin Xiao [Gold Filiality], whose native place has slipped my memory. A middle-aged bachelor who lived alone with his mother, he peddled oil for a living. One day, carrying his load of oil on a pole across his shoulders, he was walking down the road when he suddenly felt the need to relieve himself and went into a latrine. There he found a cloth belt containing a packet of approximately thirty taels of silver. Beside himself with joy, he returned home and said to his mother, "Today's my lucky day! I found a lot of silver!"

The old lady was startled at the sight of the silver. "You didn't steal it, did you?" she demanded.

Jin Xiao said, "How can you say such a thing! When did I ever become a thief? Luckily the neighbors didn't hear you. Someone dropped this belt by the edge of the latrine pit. It was my good fortune to have been the first one to see it and pick it up. Such windfalls don't often come the way of petty peddlers like me. Tomorrow, I'll make an offering of burnt paper money to the god of fortune. The silver can be used as the capital for setting up my own oil business. Wouldn't that be better than selling on credit?"

"My son," admonished his mother, "as the saying goes, 'Wealth and poverty are all a matter of fate.' If you are predestined for a life of comfort, you would not have been born into an oil-peddler's family. As I see it, even though you didn't get the silver by deception of any kind, you didn't earn it by the sweat of your brow, either. What I fear is that undeserved gain will only bring pain. Who knows if this silver belongs to someone local or some traveler from another town? Nor do we know if it's the man's own money or borrowed. Its loss must be causing the man considerable distress. It may even have cost a life, for all we know. I've heard tell of a man named Pei Du in ancient times who earned merit in the underworld by returning to the owner some jade belts that he found in a temple.[1] You should go back to the place where you found the silver. If somebody goes there to look for it, bring him here to claim what rightfully belongs to him. This will earn you merit in the underworld. Heaven will certainly not fail you."

Humbled by his mother's lecture, Jin Xiao, being the prudent law-abiding person that he was, said over and over, "Yes, yes! How right you are! How right you are!" (*What a filial son!*) He put down the silver-filled belt and ran back to the latrine. There, a clamoring crowd was gathered around a man in a fit of rage crying out to heaven and earth. Jin Xiao went up and asked what all this commotion was about. It turned out that this man, a traveler from another town, could not find the silver that he believed had fallen into the latrine pit when he loosened his belt to relieve himself. He wanted to have the frame of the latrine pit removed, and the several ruffians whom he had gathered together were about to go down for a retrieval attempt under the eyes of the idle spectators.

"How much silver did you have?" Jin Xiao asked the traveler, who answered offhand, "About forty or fifty taels."

Being the honest man that he was, Jin Xiao blurted out, "Was there a white cotton belt?"

"Yes!" The man grabbed Jin Xiao. "Give it back to me if you have found it. I will gladly pay you a reward."

Some busybody in the crowd commented, "By rights, even a fifty-fifty split wouldn't be unreasonable."

Jin Xiao said, "I did find it. It's at my house. Just follow me home and get it." The onlookers, amazed that a finder of lost property would seek out the owner to return the money instead of secretly keeping it for himself, followed them to Jin's house.

Upon arrival at home, Jin Xiao handed over the belt with both hands to the man, who, after examining the silver packet, realized that it was intact. Out of fear that Jin Xiao would demand a reward and that the onlookers would suggest a fifty-fifty split, he hit upon a wicked idea and accused Jin Xiao instead. "I should have forty to fifty taels of silver," he bluffed. "How come this is all that's left! Give me back the other half that you kept for yourself!"

"As soon as I stepped into the house with the silver, my mother drove me out to look for the owner and give it back to him. How could I have taken even a cent of it?"

As the traveler insisted that part of his silver was missing, Jin Xiao felt so injured that, in a mad rage, he charged headlong at the man. The traveler, being the stronger of the two, grabbed him by his hair, lifted him up, and hurled him to the ground as he would a chicken. His brandishing fists were about to land upon Jin Xiao (*Such an evil and shameless man deserves a death sentence*) when Jin's seventy-year-old mother rushed out the door, crying out Jin's innocence. All of the onlookers, wrought up by the injustice done to Jin Xiao, began shouting as if throwing themselves into a battle.

It so happened that the county magistrate was passing by and heard the clamor. He called his sedan-chair carriers to a halt and sent some runners to bring the men over for questioning. Afraid of being implicated, most of the crowd scattered in all directions. The more venturesome ones stood by, wishing to see how the magistrate would handle the case.

Now, having been led by the runners into the presence of the county magistrate, the traveler, Jin, and his mother all dropped to their knees right there in the street to plead their cases. The traveler said, "He found my silver and kept half of it for himself."

Jin countered, "I followed my mother's advice and returned the silver to him in good faith, but he turned around and is trying to frame me."

The magistrate turned to the onlookers: "Are there witnesses?" They all stepped forward and said, "The traveler was looking for his lost silver in the latrine when Jin Xiao voluntarily walked up and said that he had found it and took the man home to claim it. We witnessed everything with our own eyes, only we have no idea how much silver there was." (*The truth can hardly be covered up or falsified.*)

"There is no need for further argument between you two," the magistrate said. "I have a solution." So saying, he had the runners bring the whole crowd to the county court. There he assumed the bench, and all the others fell to their knees. The magistrate ordered that the belt and the silver be brought up to him. Then he ordered the treasury clerks to weigh the silver and report to him.

"Thirty taels," they reported.

The magistrate asked the traveler, "How much silver did you have?" (*Good question.*)

"Fifty taels."

"Did you see him pick the silver up, or did he tell you about it?"

"He told me about it himself."

"If he wanted to cheat you out of your silver, he could have kept all of it," the magistrate said. "Why would he hide half of it and then tell you about the rest out of his own free will? How could you have known, if he had not told you? Therefore, it is evident that he had no intention of cheating you out of your silver. What you lost was fifty taels, but what he found was thirty taels. This silver does not belong to you, but to someone else." (*How decisive the man handling the case!*)

"The silver is indeed mine. I'll be content with claiming no more than the thirty taels."

"The sums do not match. How can you lay false claim to something that is not yours? My judgment is for Jin Xiao to keep all of the silver to support his mother. As for the fifty taels that you lost, go and look for it on your own."

With the silver now in his possession, Jin Xiao thanked the magistrate profusely before he left the court, supporting his aged mother. How dare the traveler contest the judgment of the court? With tears in his eyes, he went away, swallowing his shame, much to the amusement of the crowd. Truly,

> He who preys upon a fellow man
> Ends up a victim to his own plan.
> To himself he brings disgrace,
> For others he provides amusement.

Dear audience, let me now tell the extraordinary story "The Golden Hairpins and Brooches," in which a married man loses his wife and a bachelor gains one, just as the traveler who plotted to get extra silver lost his own, but Jin Xiao, who wanted none of it, received the full amount. Though the details differ, the heavenly principle is the same.

There lived a certain Investigation Commissioner Lu in Shicheng [Stone Wall] County of Ganzhou Prefecture of Jiangxi Province. He was called by all and sundry Pure Water Lu because his reputation as an official was untarnished by greed. The Lu family and the family of Inspector Gu of the same county had been friends for generations. As Inspector Gu's daughter Axiu was betrothed to Commissioner Lu's son Lu Xuezeng, the two families had long been accustomed to addressing each other as in-laws. After his wife died from an illness, Commissioner Lu took his son with him to his post and kept putting off the wedding. Quite unexpectedly, the commissioner died from sudden illness during his term of office. After bringing the coffin home, Lu Xuezeng the son observed three years of mourning, as was the rule. The family fortune further deteriorated until all that remained was a dilapidated house. Even daily subsistence became uncertain.

Inspector Gu, witnessing the reduced circumstances of his prospective son-in-law, began to regret having made the betrothal. In a discussion with his wife, Lady Meng, he said, "It looks like that penniless Lu will not be able to complete the 'six preliminaries,'[2] and the wedding will have to be postponed indefinitely. It would be best for us to look around for another match rather than compromise our daughter's lifelong happiness."

"True, the Lu family has fallen on hard times," admitted his wife, "but what excuse can we use for breaking off this engagement pledged since childhood?"

"We can send someone to say that as the betrothed are not getting any younger, the wedding ceremony should be held as soon as possible. As both families are of distinguished background and share the same values on the importance of decency and propriety, for him to admit the lack of means is unthinkable. He has to conduct the wedding with all proper decorum. That beggar, knowing that it's beyond his means to do that, will undoubtedly agree to withdraw from the engagement. With a written statement from him declaring the betrothal null and void, won't we have severed all ties with him?" (*A fine plan indeed!*)

Lady Meng hesitated. "Our Axiu is a little unpredictable. I'm afraid she might not agree."

"A woman is supposed to obey her father before she gets married. This matter is not for her to decide. You just try to patiently talk her into it."

Without letting a moment slip by, Lady Meng went into her daughter's room and communicated her father's wish to her. Axiu protested, "A virtuous woman serves only one man until her death. To be only concerned over money in a marriage is nothing less than barbarous. Such snobbishness on Father's part is absolutely immoral. I will never obey." (*A virtuous woman serves only one man until her death. A worthy young woman she truly is!*)

"Your father is going to urge him to hold the wedding ceremony. If he can't afford it and would rather call off the engagement, it'll be pointless for you to insist."

"What kind of talk is this!" snapped Axiu. "If Lu is too poor to afford the marriage expenses, I would just as soon remain unmarried to the end of my life. Qian Yulian of ancient times threw herself into the river to preserve her chastity. Her good name will never fade.[3] If father pushes me too hard, what's to stop me from taking my own life?"

Lady Meng bemoaned her daughter's stubbornness, but, at the same time, her heart was filled with pity. An idea suddenly occurred to her: "Why don't I secretly send for Young Master Lu without my husband's knowledge and give the young man whatever is necessary for a wedding ceremony as soon as possible? Only thus would the match be brought off."

One day, Inspector Gu left for his holdings in the East Farmstead to collect rent and was expected to stay there for quite a number of days. Lady Meng, after confiding in her daughter, sent for the gardener, Old Ou, and told him to ask young Master Lu to come. He was to meet the young master at the back gate and do thus-and-so. "Don't let a word of this leak out. I'll have a handsome reward for you."

As ordered, the old gardener came to the door of the Lu residence, where he saw

> *The gate like that of a crumbling temple,*
> *The house like a tumbledown kiln.*
> *The windows, all broken and decayed,*

Opened and closed whichever way the wind blew.
The kitchen cold and desolate,
Without a wisp of smoke or steam.
The cracked walls and leaking roof
Could hardly withstand a rainfall.
The chairs and beds, worn and torn,
Could barely serve as firewood.
All talk of the decline of the powerful,
But who pities an honest official's orphan?
(Such are the lamentable ways of the world, which breed corrupt
    officials generation after generation.)

Indeed, words are inadequate to describe the poverty of the Lu household.

Let us now retrace our steps. Lu Xuezeng had an aunt who was married to the family of Liang, living about ten li away. The husband had died, leaving behind only a son, Liang Shangbin, who lived comfortably with his mother and his newly wedded wife, a good and worthy woman.

On the day the old gardener called, young Mr. Lu happened to be away on a trip to his aunt's house to borrow some rice. The old gardener, finding no one at home but a white-haired old woman-servant attending to the kitchen fire, had no other choice but to convey Lady Meng's message to her, adding that she should get the young man back without delay. "This is a special favor from Lady Meng," said the old man. "She will be expecting Mr. Lu in the next few days while my master is away. Mr. Lu must not fail her." With these words, he took himself off.

The old woman realized that this matter was of a nature not to brook any delay, nor could it be entrusted to anyone else. She had once joined the now deceased Mrs. Lu on a trip to her sister's house and still had a vague memory of the directions. Without a moment of delay, she asked a neighbor to watch the house for her, and she stumbled and fumbled her way, with the help of a few inquiries, to the Liang residence, where Mr. Lu was having a meal at his aunt's invitation. After the greetings, the old woman repeated the old servant's message in full.

"Isn't that nice!" exclaimed Lu's aunt, and she urged the young man to go at once.

Elated though he was, Mr. Lu would rather not let his mother-in-law see him in his shabby clothes. He turned to his cousin Liang Shangbin for the loan of a gown. (*Cause of all the troubles to come.*)

Now this Liang Shangbin was a scoundrel not content with a law-abiding life. With an evil scheme taking shape in his mind, he said, "I do have a gown for you, but it's now too late in the day to go to town. You have no idea how things are in an official's residence. Although there is this message from your mother-in-law, the servants may not necessarily know about your visit. You need to watch out when you go. Believe me, it would be better if you spent one more night here, and when you go tomorrow, set out in the morning, not in the evening." (*The villain couches his lies in sensible words.*)

"As you say, brother," Mr. Lu agreed.

Liang Shangbin continued, "I need to go to see a family in East Village to attend to a trifling matter. Please excuse my absence." To his mother, he said, "Put the old woman up for the night, too. She must be tired from so much walking. She can leave tomorrow."

Mrs. Liang, attributing good intentions to his suggestion, accordingly lodged both guests for the night. As it turned out, this was all part of his treacherous plan. He was afraid that should the old woman go back and the gardener come again to repeat the invitation, they would notice Mr. Lu's absence, and his chances of passing himself off as Mr. Lu would be foiled. Truly,

> He deceives heaven, unbeknownst to men.
> He sets traps on earth, undetected by ghosts.

Without Mr. Lu's knowledge, Liang Shangbin changed into a new outfit, sneaked out of the house, and made his way to the Gu residence in town.

In the meantime, the old gardener was waiting for young Master Lu by the open gate, as instructed by Lady Meng. After the sun had sunk below the western hills, there emerged in the darkness a well-dressed but nervous young man who hesitated at the gate. "Might you be young Master Lu?" asked the old gardener.

Liang Shangbin answered with an eager bow, "Yes! I am here at the request of the lady of the house. Please be so kind as to announce my arrival."

The gardener promptly led the guest into an arbor to wait. He himself went with all speed to the interior of the house to report to Lady Meng, whereupon the housekeeper was sent out to invite the young man to the inner chamber. Barely had he stepped out of the arbor than two maids, each carrying a gauze lantern, came up to meet him. After winding their way past chamber after chamber, they finally came upon an elaborately ornamented, vermilion hall, where, with candles lit and the vermilion curtain raised, Lady Meng was already waiting in her private chamber.

Liang Shangbin, being of humble background, had never seen such wealth and style. Besides, he was a rustic with little education. All this, added to his consciousness of being an impostor, made him feel ill at ease. As he greeted Lady Meng and answered her questions, his uncouth manners and dull speech caused her to wonder, "How strange! He is not at all like the son of an official."

But then, another thought struck her. "It's often said that a man in poverty is short on intelligence. How can I blame him for his lack of composure, when he is in such straitened circumstances?" At this second thought, greater compassion welled up in her heart. (*A mistake.*)

After tea, Lady Meng ordered dinner preparations started and then called her daughter to come forward and be presented to the guest. Reluctant at first, Axiu yielded after her mother's persistent urging.

"If father does carry out his wish of breaking off the engagement," she thought to herself, "tonight is the time for bidding farewell. I will die content if I get to see my intended husband, even if only once." (*Poor thing.*) With these thoughts on her mind, she bashfully stepped out of her boudoir.

"My child, come over here and greet young Master Lu," bade Lady Meng. "Just a small curtsy will do."

The impostor bowed twice with folded hands. Before Axiu could withdraw after returning the greeting with two curtsies, Lady Meng stopped her. "Since you will be husband and wife, there's nothing improper in sitting together." She bade her daughter sit by her side. The impostor kept ogling her and melted with desire at the sight of her elegant beauty. Feeling never a doubt that it was her future husband in front of her, the young lady, silent and overcome with grief, kept her head down and could barely refrain from breaking down in tears. Truly,

Worlds apart are the feelings of the real and the fake.

Food and wine were presently brought in. Two tables were laid out at Lady Meng's order, with the guest taking the table of honor, while the mother and daughter sat at the table by the side. Lady Meng said apologetically, "It is in order to help you financially with the wedding ceremony that I invited you at such short notice. Please excuse me for the lack of propriety." Scarcely had he managed to utter a couple of polite words in response than the impostor flushed crimson with nervousness.

During the dinner, Lady Meng mentioned briefly her daughter's wish not to marry another man. She took the man's evasiveness as totally justifiable modesty. Feeling awkward at the dinner table, the imposter, who actually had a large capacity for liquor, declined offers of wine, claiming that he was not much of a drinker, nor did Lady Meng insist. After a few more moments, she gave orders that bedding be prepared in the east chamber for the man to stay overnight. (*Wrong move on Lady Meng's part.*) The impostor feigned readiness to take his leave, only to be detained by Lady Meng. "Why stand on ceremony with your own family? My daughter and I have more to confide to you." The imposter showed no outward indication of his delight.

A maid came in to report that the east chamber was now ready for him to retire to. With a bow of gratitude for the dinner, the impostor followed the lantern-bearing maid into the east chamber.

Lady Meng beckoned her daughter into her room, dismissed the maids, and took out of a chest eighty taels of silver from her private savings, as well as two pairs of silver cups and sixteen pieces of jewelry worth about a hundred taels of gold. Handing them over to her daughter, she said, "This is all your mother has. Take them to young Master Lu for the marriage expenses." (*Another wrong move.*)

"I am too embarrassed to go," said Axiu.

"My child," exhorted Lady Meng. "Just as some rituals are immutable, whereas others are adaptable to suit contingencies, so are there matters that need different treatment in order of priority. At this delicate moment, if you don't personally go to him and move him with wifely love, how will he have the motivation to exert himself? Poverty-stricken young men like him tend to lack wisdom in worldly affairs. If he consults someone outside the family circle, he might be tricked into squandering all the money away. If that happens, all the pains I've gone through would be to no purpose. By then, regrets would be too late! Now stuff these things into your sleeves and make sure no one sees them."

When Axiu heard this argument, she was obliged to comply. "But mother, I can't very well go to him all by myself," she said.

"I'll have the housekeeper go with you." At once, she summoned the housekeeper and told her to escort the young mistress under the cover of night to the east chamber for a talk with young Master Lu. She added in a whisper, "After escorting her there, you just wait outside the door to be out of their way so that they can talk freely." (*Both mother and daughter are at fault.*) The woman understood.

The impostor, in the meantime, was sitting alone in the east chamber, determined not to go to sleep yet, for he had a hunch that something was afoot. Just as he expected, some time after the first watch of the night sounded, the housekeeper pushed open his door and announced, "The young lady is here to see you." The impostor rose with alacrity and offered his greetings for a second time. Something unimaginable happened: the impostor, who had been tongued-tied in the presence of Lady Meng, turned into a glib talker, pouring out tender words to the young lady, who, at first coy and demure, became more self-assured now that her mother was not with her. (*This stands to reason. Nothing out of the ordinary.*) Questions and answers went back and forth for a considerable time. As Axiu was speaking in all sincerity, tears streamed down her cheeks before she knew it. The impostor, on the other hand, put on a disgusting display of grief, beating his chest, heaving sigh upon sigh while dabbing at his eyes and blowing his nose. Under the pretense of comforting her, he gathered her in his arms and fondled her to his heart's content. (*What a good play for the stage!*)

The housekeeper standing outside the door was moved to tears upon hearing the heart-rending sobs. Little did she realize that of the two, one meant every word she said, whereas the other was but faking it all. How Axiu drew from her sleeves the silver and jewelry and handed them to the impostor with many words of admonishment is needless to narrate here.

The money now in his possession, the impostor blew out the lamp and, with an arm around the young lady, pleaded piteously for intimacy. Out of fear that her plans would be thwarted if the maids heard the commotion of a struggle, Axiu saw no other way but to give her reluctant consent. (*She lacks good sense.*)

There was someone who wrote a lyric to the tune of "As in a Dream: A Song":

> *Alas! A precious flower in her boudoir*
> *Is ravished by a savage bee*
> *Ere comes the rightful one she awaits.*
> *What a grievous mistake it was*
> *To do as the east wind bade.*

As the proverb has it, "If you act before much thought, in regret you will surely be caught." In surreptitiously providing the young man with gifts so that he could afford the wedding, Lady Meng was full of the best intentions, but, for a matter of such momentous importance, how could she have failed to instruct the old gardener to meet young Master Lu face to face? Even after the impostor presented himself, nothing would have gone wrong had she asked the gardener to escort the young man back immediately after giving him the gifts and the words of advice. The very last thing she should have done was to have her daughter come out to greet the man and, later, go to his room all alone for a private talk. By so doing, Lady Meng was, to all intents and purposes, paving the way for the man to exceed the bounds of propriety. Even Mr. Lu himself should not have been allowed such freedom, let alone an impostor! A fine subject for gossip and criticism she became for the rest of her life! This is, alas, a case of a mother's excessive indulgence causing her daughter irreparable harm. (*It is all Lady Meng's fault.*)

But enough idle comments. Our story relates further that the impostor, having gotten what he wanted from the young mistress, let her go. At the sound of the fifth watch, Lady Meng dispatched a maid to wake him up to wash and dress, and have some tea and refreshments. She exhorted him, "My husband will be back soon. It would be best if my good son-in-law could make preparations without delay. Don't be remiss in this." Taking leave of her, the impostor left by the backyard gate.

"What a great stroke of luck!" he thought to himself as he went along. "I had my way with an official's daughter at no expense to myself and walked off with a bundle of valuables, without ever giving myself away! The only thing that will spoil the otherwise perfect pleasure is that Mr. Lu himself will be coming today. Since Inspector Gu will be back soon, why don't I detain Lu until tomorrow? He won't dare to go once the inspector is back, and I'll get away clean!" (*What a schemer!*) With his mind thus made up, he walked into a wineshop, where he drank three cups of wine by himself and ate his fill. It was not until afternoon that he finally returned home.

Mr. Lu was, in the meantime, still waiting in great vexation, but unable to leave for lack of presentable clothes. His aunt, also restless, sent a farmhand to look for her son in East Village, but the latter was nowhere to be seen. She then went to her daughter-in-law's room. "Do you know if he has any clothes for Master Lu?" she asked.

Liang's wife, Tian-shi, answered, "He keeps them all locked up in his trunk and doesn't leave out the key." Tian-shi, originally from East Village, was the daughter of Mr. Tian, a tribute student[4] at the National University. She was as fair to look upon as she was well-versed in scholarship and decorum. Mr. Tian used to be known in Shicheng County for his chivalrous acts. When a certain official who bore him grudges sought to ruin him, Liang Shangbin's father told his brother-in-law, Commissioner Lu, about the case. The latter, who had long held Mr. Tian in high esteem, pleaded his case to the best of his ability and got Mr. Tian out of trouble, whereupon Mr. Tian married his daughter into the Liang family as a token of his gratitude. Now Tian-shi was a woman who had more than a trace of her father's chivalry. Disgruntled with her oaf of a husband who was given to misconduct, she called him "the Bumpkin" out of scorn. As there was no love lost between the couple, the wife never bothered to help the husband in anything, not even in taking care of his clothes.

Now let me return to Mr. Lu and his aunt, who were consumed with anxiety when whom did they see but Liang Shangbin stepping into the house, his face flushed with wine.

His mother exploded. "Your cousin has been here waiting for your clothes while you were out drinking the whole night! And we had no idea where to look for you!" Without a word in reply, Liang Shangbin headed straight to his own room, where he hid the valuables that were stuffed in his sleeves before emerging out of the room to address Mr. Lu: "I was detained by a trifling matter that came up unexpectedly, and I apologize for having held you up for one day. As it is getting late, you'd better go tomorrow."

His mother snapped, "Just lend some clothes to your cousin, and let him do what he is supposed to do! Never you mind whether he goes today or tomorrow!"

Mr. Lu said, "I'll have to borrow not only the clothes, but shoes and socks as well."

"I do have a pair of black satin shoes for you, but they are with the cobbler next door. The soles need fixing. I'll tell him to rush the job this evening so that you can have them tomorrow morning." Mr. Lu could do no more than stay another night.

The following morning, Liang Shangbin feigned a headache and slept until the sun was well up in the sky. It wasn't until breakfast was over that he rose and took out the robe, shoes, and socks with deliberate slowness, for no other purpose than to delay Lu's departure as much as possible to ruin his chances.

Mr. Lu could not bring himself to put on the fine clothes right away. Instead, he borrowed a piece of cloth, wrapped up his outfit, and gave the parcel to the old woman-servant for her to carry. His aunt, in the meantime, put together a bag of rice and vegetables and had a farmhand escort Mr. Lu back. She reminded her nephew, "Do let me know when the wedding is settled, to spare me from worrying."

Mr. Lu bowed and turned around to leave. At this moment, Liang Shangbin stepped forward to see him off. "Watch out for yourself," he advised. "Beware of any evil intentions and false pretenses. As I see it, the best course is to hold up your head and try the front gate. They can't drive out their would-be son-in-law, can they? Besides, you're not throwing yourself cheaply upon them but are invited, through the gardener, and that's ample evidence. If they mean well, they'll naturally let you in. If they give you a hard time, don't be afraid to reason with them, and be sure to make the neighbors hear you. If you go to the back gate through the yard where there's no one around, there will be no one to turn to for help if they trick you."

"Surely you're right," Mr. Lu said. Truly,

> He stabs him in the back
> But feigns concern to his face.
> One harbors a wicked mind;
> The other detects no evil.

Back at home, Mr. Lu put on the gown, socks, and shoes. The one thing he did not borrow was a cap because of the difference in size. He took down his old one, rinsed it with clean water, had the old woman borrow an iron from a neighbor, lit a fire to heat the iron, and pressed out all the wrinkles on the cap. He then applied some grains of cooked rice to the frayed spots to fill them up nice and hard, and, lastly, painted the cap black with ink. All this work and the repeated fittings to get it to look just right took over two hours. (*As is often the case with poverty-stricken scholars. Pitiable.*) After getting approval of his appearance from the old woman-servant, he directed his steps to the Gu residence.

Never having seen him before, the gatekeeper said, "The master went to the East Farmstead."

Mr. Lu had, after all, been well brought up in an official's family. He replied in great composure, "Kindly announce to the lady of the house that Mr. Lu is here." Only then did the gatekeeper realize who he was, but, having no inkling as to the purpose of the visit, he did not relent: "As the master is not at home, I dare not make unauthorized announcements."

Mr. Lu tried again: "I am here at the bidding of the lady of the house. You will know once you make the announcement. You will not be blamed for anything."

The gatekeeper did go in, saying, "Young Master Lu is at the gate, asking to see you, madam. Should I let him in or turn him away?"

Lady Meng was taken aback. She thought to herself, "He left only yesterday. Why is he back again?" Thereupon she ordered to have him admitted into the main hall. She then sent the housekeeper to go and ask him what he had come for. Scarcely had the woman stepped out and taken a look than she rushed back to Lady Meng. "This young Master Lu is an impostor. (*If she took the fake to be the real, it follows that she now takes the real to be the fake.*) He is not the one who came the other night. That one was fat with a dark complexion, but this one is thin with fair skin."

Lady Meng could not believe what she heard. "How can that be?" She went to the back of the main hall and peeked from behind the screen. Sure enough, this was not the one who had come before. At a loss what to do, she sent the housekeeper into the hall to cross-examine the young man about his family background. His answers were correct to the last detail. Suspicions had lurked at the back of her mind when Lady Meng had first laid eyes upon the previous alleged young Master Lu. The young man she was looking at now had the grace and the elegant speech of a true young Master Lu. When asked the purpose of his visit, he explained, "I am here at the invitation transmitted by the old gardener. I happened to be away in the country at the time and did not return until this morning. Then I hastened here to pay the call. Please forgive me for the delay."

Lady Meng was convinced. "So this is what happened," she said to herself. "But who was that cursed man who came the night before last?" She quickly rushed to her daughter's room and explained the situation to her. "It is your father's lack of moral sense that landed you in this mess," she added. (*True, true.*) "Regrets are too late now. Luckily, no one knows about this, and let's not remind ourselves of what has gone by. Now that my future son-in-law is in our house at my special invitation, I have nothing to offer him. What am I to do?" Truly,

One false move can cost the whole game.

Axiu was at a loss for words for a considerable time. There swept over her a wave of mixed emotions that defies description: it was panic, shame, chagrin, and agony, and yet it was none of these. It was as if, being stuck with needles all over, she could hardly distinguish where she felt a pinch and where a pain. (*Good description.*) To her credit, she had more fortitude than the average person and soon came up with a plan. "Mother," she said, "why don't you go out to the hall and meet him. I know what to do."

Lady Meng did as her daughter said and entered the main hall to greet Master Lu. The young man grabbed a chair and set it at a spot usually reserved for the most honored seat in the hall. "Mother-in-law," said he, "please take the seat of honor and allow me, your humble future son-in-law, to pay my respects."

After a few polite words declining the honor, Lady Meng stood by the side of the chair and, after the young man had made two bows in a kneeling position, asked the housekeeper to raise him to his feet and help him take a seat.

"My straitened circumstances have caused me to be remiss in my observance of proper etiquette," said Mr. Lu. "But you have not rejected me. In this life and beyond, I will never forget your great kindness."

Lady Meng, overcome with shame, found no words for a reply. Instead, she instructed the housekeeper to shut the door of the main hall and ask the young mistress to come forth and greet young Master Lu.

Axiu went as far as the screen and refused to move another step. From there, behind the screen, she asked the housekeeper to relay these words: "Young Master Lu should not have tarried in the country. He ruined the best plans my mother and I had for him."

Mr. Lu equivocated: "I tarried because I took ill in the country. But I am here now. How did I ruin anything?"

Axiu replied from behind the screen, "Three days ago, this body of mine was yours, but now, for fear of sullying your good name, I am not worthy to serve you and accomplish my wifely duties. Nor am I able to help you materially other than with two gold hairpins and a pair of gold brooches that I still have. These I now give to you as a small token of my sentiment. I advise you to find yourself another match and put me out of your thoughts."

Taking these words to be a hint of a renouncement of the marriage, Mr. Lu grimly refused to accept the jewelry that the housekeeper now presented to him.

"Please keep them," added Axiu. "You will know why soon enough. Now please go away. It will not be to your advantage to remain in this place." With these words, she turned and sobbed her way back. (*Pitiable.*)

All the more suspicious, Lu Xuezeng unleashed on Lady Meng an explosion of angry words: "Poor as I am, I came not for a few pieces of jewelry. Why didn't you say anything when your daughter was giving that speech, dropping hints about breaking off the engagement? Did you summon me here just to treat me like this?"

"My daughter and I have no wish to back out of our commitment. She is upset because she believes that your procrastination shows that you do not take this betrothal seriously enough. Don't be overly suspicious."

Lu Xuezeng was not convinced. Instead, he started recounting the mutual affection between the two families before his father's death. "How could you turn against me just because my father is gone and I am reduced to poverty, whereas your family is intact and rich! I had no one else but you, Mother-in-law, to stand up for me. How could *you* also abandon me, over a matter of a three-day delay!" And so the tirade went on. Lady Meng could hardly cut in with a word in defense of herself, nor was she able to get away from his presence.

Suddenly, a commotion broke out in the inner quarters of the house. A maid ran up, gasping for breath: "Madam! It's horrible! Come save the young mistress!" Lady Meng broke into a cold sweat. How she wished she could have two more legs to get her there faster! Supported by the housekeeper on her left side, she ran into her daughter's room only to find the girl dead, having hanged herself with a length of silk over her bed. Frantically they tried to save her, but the breath of life had already left her. For all their calling of her name, she did not come to. Everyone in the room broke down in tears.

When Mr. Lu overheard that the young mistress was dead, he took it to be just another trick to drive him out of the house, and he started shouting in the hall all by himself, until Lady Meng, in spite of the pain in her heart, sent for him. What confronted his eyes upon his arrival in the boudoir was the body of the dead girl lying stiff on the brocade quilt of the ivory bed.

"My good son-in-law," said Lady Meng between sobs, "come and meet your betrothed." (*Sad words.*) At this point, he burst into loud sobs, his heart aching as if pierced by ten thousand arrows.

"My good son-in-law," admonished Lady Meng, "this is not a place for you to stay on any longer. I fear that trouble will fall upon you if you do. Please go home at once." She told the housekeeper to stuff the pieces of jewelry into his sleeves and escort him out.

Seeing that there was nothing else to be done, Mr. Lu choked back his tears and went away.

While busying herself over arrangements to have her daughter's body encoffined, Lady Meng sent for her husband, who was still away at the East Farmstead, saying nothing more than that their daughter had committed suicide as a protest to the breaking off of the betrothal. Stricken with remorse, Mr. Gu wept bitterly. The funeral was held, but we need not go into details about that. A poet of later times wrote these lines in praise of Axiu:

> The pledge was worth a thousand pieces of gold,
> But none foresaw the deceit most foul.
> With three feet of red gauze, she repaid her betrothed.
> Defiled though her body was, unsullied remained her soul.

Let us now return to Mr. Lu. Back at home, he cried and sighed over the gold hairpins and brooches, now taken by suspicion, now attempting to probe for an explanation. As no amount of thinking provided an answer, he was reduced to accepting his ill fate with resignation.

The following day, he wrapped up his borrowed outfit in the same way as before and betook himself to his aunt's house to return the parcel. When he heard that Mr. Lu had come, Liang Shangbin slunk away. As Mr. Lu told his aunt about the girl's suicide, the old lady heaved sigh upon sigh. She kept Mr. Lu until after he had taken some wine and a meal.

Liang Shangbin asked upon returning, "Did my cousin say when he was here a moment ago whether he had paid the Gu family a visit?"

Liang's mother replied, "He went yesterday, but for some reason, the young lady blamed him for being three days too late and then hanged herself to death."

Forgetting himself, Liang Shangbin blurted out, "Good grief! A most beautiful girl, too!" (*Most clever choice of words. Gives the story a nice twist.*)

"You have seen her? Where?" asked his mother.

Knowing that he would not be able to lie his way out of this, Liang Shangbin told his mother about his adventure as an impostor.

The old lady was aghast. "You cursed beast!" she lashed out. "What an evil thing you've done! You owe your marriage to your uncle, and now you return his kindness with this vicious act, breaking up your cousin's betrothal and killing Miss Gu! How can you rest at ease with your conscience!" Repeatedly calling him a beast, she gave him such a heated lecture that he could hardly wedge in a word. As he approached his own room, he was greeted by another torrent of tongue-lashing from his wife, Tian-shi, from behind the closed door. "You scoundrel! Heaven will soon judge you! You'll end up in a violent death! From now on, I won't have anything to do with you. Don't you drag me into your evil doings!"

Liang Shangbin happened to be looking for a vent for his pent-up rage, and at this volley of curses from his wife, he broke into the room with a savage kick at the door and, grabbing her hair with one hand, began to rain blows upon her. His mother had to rush over and order him out of the room. Amid wails of grief and beatings on her chest, Tian-shi said she would be better off dead than alive. Unable to calm her down, Liang's mother called a sedan-chair and sent her back to her parents' home.

The shock, the indignation, the pain of it all, and the fear that the treachery would come to light kept the old lady awake throughout the night. Rushes of heat and chill ran through her alternately. She died after seven days of illness.

When she learned of her mother-in-law's death, Tian-shi returned for the funeral and put on mourning clothes. Liang Shangbin snapped at her, his anger still smoldering, "You slut! I thought you were going to spend the rest of your life at your parents' home. What brought you back, may I ask?" Another altercation followed.

"You did that evil thing, then drove your mother to her grave, and now it's my turn, isn't it! If it hadn't been for Mother-in-law's sake, I'd never have come back to see this bumpkin face of yours!"

Liang Shangbin shot back, "Do you think I can't get a wife elsewhere? Would I want a shrew like you to come back? I'm throwing you out this minute with a written statement of divorce, and don't you ever come back!"

"I'd rather be single till I die than follow a filthy villain like you. A divorce couldn't suit me better! It's something worthy of an offering of incense as soon as I get back."[5] (*Tian-shi is indeed a woman of bold spirit.*)

There being no predestined bond between this couple, these impetuous words about divorce led to action. In a fit of rage, Liang Shangbin wrote a statement of divorce bearing his thumb print and handed it to Tian-shi. She took a tearful farewell of her mother-in-law's spirit tablet and left the house. Truly,

> *He seduced another man's betrothed,*
> *But failed to keep his own wife.*
> *What an injustice to the good Miss Tian,*
> *To be thrown out after a domestic fight.*

Let us follow another thread of the story and describe how, in the midst of Lady Meng's daily weeping in memory of her daughter, a thought came to her mind: it was Old Ou who had sent the message and the same Ou who had brought back the dark, fat man. It followed, therefore, that either Ou himself was an accomplice or he had leaked out the secret. While her husband was away paying a social call, she summoned the old gardener to the main hall and cross-examined him.

The truth was that Old Ou had not breathed a word to anyone. It was Lu Xuezeng who had, by borrowing clothes—something he should not have done—made the treacherous deed possible. Lady Meng knew that there were two different men, one of whom, the impostor, had come that very night after the message was sent, and the other one, the true young Master Lu, three days later. But the gardener believed the two were one and the same man. However hard he pleaded his case, it was to no avail. Lady Meng flew into such a towering rage that she ordered her men to hold him to the ground and give him thirty strokes with bamboo poles till his skin split and his blood spurted out.

One day, chance brought Inspector Gu into the garden, and, as he tried to summon the old gardener to have the place cleaned, he was told that the old man was so severely wounded from the beating done at Lady Meng's order that any movement was beyond him. The inspector had the old man brought to him. Under questioning as to the reason for the beating, Old Ou gave a detailed account of how he had been sent by Lady Meng for Mr. Lu and how the young couple met that night in the chambers.

Mr. Gu exploded with rage. "So, that's what happened!" Promptly, he called a sedan-chair and went straight to the county yamen, where he stated the case to the county magistrate and demanded that Lu Xuezeng pay with his life. The magistrate asked for a written complaint and, having obtained that, sent runners to bring Lu Xuezeng to court for an interrogation.

Being the honest man that he was, Lu told of every detail, adding, "The gold hairpins and brooches that you see are gifts from her, but the alleged private meeting with her through the rear gate did not happen." When the county magistrate called Old Ou the gardener out to counter his testimony, the old man firmly hung on to his belief that the man was none other than the accused. The truth was that the old gardener was of failing eyesight and had not seen the impostor clearly in the darkness of the night. Moreover, he was now under instructions from his master to hold Mr. Lu responsible. The magistrate, too, was under Mr. Gu's influence. Accordingly, he submitted Lu to torture. When the pain became unendurable, Mr. Lu offered a confession: "Mrs. Gu kindly summoned me and gave me the gold jewelry for the marriage expenses. When I noticed Axiu's beauty, lust got the better of me and I forced myself upon her, which was a thing I shouldn't have done. On the third day, I paid another visit, which was again wrong, and caused Axiu to kill herself out of shame." The deposition was duly recorded. The verdict was that as Lu Xuezeng and Axiu were not yet husband and wife, for lack of a formal ceremony (in spite of a verbal commitment), Lu was to be sentenced to death by hanging for the crime of rape, which had led to suicide. Having issued the order to throw Lu into the prison cell designated for convicts awaiting execution, the magistrate then wrote a detailed report for submission to his superior.

Lady Meng was horrified when she got wind of this. She also learned that the only occupant of his house, the old woman-servant, was now ill from the shock and was unavailable for sending Lu food. "Mr. Lu had nothing to do with Axiu's death," she thought to herself. "It was I who brought him into this mess." She then entrusted her housekeeper with some silver for delivery, through the right person, to bribe the prison wardens. At the same time, she repeatedly pleaded with her husband to spare Lu's life, but her pleas only served to aggravate Mr. Gu further. The story soon spread throughout the streets and alleys of the whole county. Truly,

> Good news stays within closed doors;
> Scandal travels far and wide.

The stigma thus connected with his name strengthened Mr. Gu's determination to be satisfied with nothing less than Lu Xuezeng's death.

Let me now tell of an imperial censor named Chen Lian, a native of Huguang, whose father's name had appeared on the same honor roll for recipients of *jinshi* degrees as Inspector Gu. Therefore, he was, to Mr. Gu, a nonconsanguineous nephew. The young man had a sharp intelligence and a perceptive eye and, in order to redress injustices, took the most delight in analyzing cases of trumped-up charges. Now, this Mr. Chen happened to be in Jiangxi as he made his rounds throughout the country under imperial orders. Before Censor Chen even stepped onto Jiangxi territory, Mr. Gu had already sent word regarding this case. Censor Chen agreed verbally to give the case his attention, but did not think much of the matter. On the third day of his stay in Jiangxi, he sent notice to Ganzhou to announce his upcoming visit. The news scared the staff in the prefectural administration out of their wits.

On the day that the review of criminal cases started, convicted prisoners from all the counties in the prefecture were brought to court. When Lu Xuezeng's case came up, Censor Chen read the confession, examined the jewelry, and called in Lu Xuezeng. "Were these pieces of jewelry given to you on your first visit?" he asked.

"I went only once. There was no second visit."

"Then why did you say in the confession that you went again in three days? How do you explain that?"

Lu exclaimed in an outburst, "I am innocent! I am innocent!" and went on to say, "My father, now deceased, had arranged for my betrothal to Mr. Gu's daughter. My father being a clean, incorrupt official, our family was reduced to poverty after his death, and I could not afford the marriage preliminaries.

Inspector Gu wanted to break off the betrothal, but my mother-in-law refused and secretly had the old gardener send for me with promises of offers of gold and silk. But as I was detained in the country, I did not go until three days later. I met only my mother-in-law. I never even laid eyes on Miss Gu, and the confession of rape was made under torture."

"If you didn't see Miss Gu, who gave you the gold hairpins and brooches?"

"The young mistress was standing behind the screen, blaming me for having ruined everything by not coming on time, and saying that the marriage was off, let alone the promises of gold and silk. The gold hairpins and brooches were meant to be keepsakes. Taking her words as a hint to break off the engagement, I got into an argument with her mother, without knowing that she would hang herself in her room. To this day, I still have no inkling as to the cause."

"So you did not go to the back garden that night."

"Truthfully, I did not."

The imperial censor fell into a thoughtful silence. He said to himself, "If Lu was sent for, it must have been for more than an offer of hairpins and brooches. The bitterness in Axiu's tone suggested that there must have been someone who went before Lu did, laid false claim to the valuables, and went as far as taking advantage of her. The shame of it would explain her suicide." At this point in his thoughts, he had Old Ou brought in and asked, "Did you see Lu Xuezeng when you went to the Lu residence?"

"I did not."

"If you did not, how did you know the one who came at night was Mr. Lu and not anyone else?"

"He said that he was young Master Lu calling at an invitation. I showed him in at Lady Meng's order. How can he deny that?"

"When did he leave after the visit?" asked Mr. Chen.

"I heard that Madam asked him to stay for some wine and offered him many gifts. He left at about the fifth watch."

Lu Xuezeng started protesting again, but the imperial censor stopped him.

"Did you usher Lu Xuezeng in the second time he came?" (*Good question.*)

"The second time around, he came in by the front gate. I had nothing to do with it."

"But why did he forsake the front gate the first time and go to the back-yard to look for you?"

"That's because Madam told me to have him take the back gate."

The censor turned to Lu Xuezeng. "Since your mother-in-law wanted you to use the back gate, why did you go to the front?"

"As I was not sure about the true intentions of the invitation, I was afraid of being tricked in that deserted patch of land at the back of the house. That's why I made straight for the front gate."

Upon reflection, the censor concluded that behind the discrepancies in their accounts lay the key to the mystery. Pointing at Lu Xuezeng, he asked Old Ou, "Are you sure he is the one who came by the back gate? Don't say yes too readily."

"I didn't really see very clearly in the darkness of the night, but the features did look like his."

"To whom did you give the message when Lu Xuezeng was not at home?"

"To an old woman, the only person in the house. There was no one else around."

"Are you sure you told no one else?" the censor snapped.

"Absolutely," replied the old man.

The censor paused for a good while. "If I cannot get to the bottom of this," he thought to himself, "how am I going to convict the man? What should I say to Mr. Gu?"

He turned to Lu Xuezeng again. "You said you were in the country, but how far is it from the town? And when did the message reach you?"

"The village is only ten li north of the town, and I got the message on the very same day."

"Lu Xuezeng!" thundered the censor with a fierce slap on the table. "You lied when you said you went to the Gu residence three days later! You should have been only too happy at the invitation. It doesn't stand to reason for you to have waited for three days when you were only such a short distance away!"

"Please don't be angry with me, sir," pleaded Lu Xuezeng, "and let me explain. Being as poor as I am, I went to my aunt's house in the country to borrow rice. I was indeed eager to leave for town as soon as I received the message. However, as I was in rags, my cousin agreed to lend me his clothes, but as it happened, he had some business to attend to elsewhere and did not return until the following night. In the meantime, I was there waiting for the clothes. That accounts for the delay."

"Did your cousin know why you wished to borrow his clothes?" asked the censor.

"Yes, he did."

"What does your cousin do? What's his name?"

"He is Liang Shangbin. He has a farm."

At this point, the censor dismissed the hearing, saying that the session would be resumed the next day. Truly,

> *The mighty pen should not be wielded lightly;*
> *The Buddha-like kind heart allows no oversight.*

Rarely do past verdicts get overturned;
There's no lack of hidden injustices.
(The bright mirror of justice hangs high.)

The following day, the gate of the censor's tribunal opened just wide enough to hang out a placard on which was written, "His Honor the censor is indisposed. All officials are hereby instructed to wait until further notice for official business. Dated: this —— day of this month." How the officials of the prefecture expressed concern for his health twice a day is no concern of ours here.

Let us pick up another thread of the story and come to Liang Shangbin, who felt much relieved when he got word of Mr. Lu's death sentence. One day, he heard a commotion outside the door. Peeping out through a crack, he saw that it was a traveling fabric merchant trying to make a sale. Wearing a new mourning-cap and an old white cotton robe, the merchant claimed, in a Jiangxi accent, to be a native of Nanchang who was anxious to dispose of his hundreds of bolts of fabric at a bargain so that he could return home before the night was out, because he had just received news that his father had died. But he turned down all offers for only one bolt or two or three bolts. "I won't be free to go if I sell at retail. If only a rich man will come along and buy all this stuff wholesale, I'll give him a good price."

After listening for some time, Liang Shangbin emerged from behind the door and asked, "How many bolts do you have? How much did you pay for them?"

"I have more than four hundred bolts, for which I paid two hundred taels of silver."

"How can you find a buyer on such short notice? You'll have to be willing to suffer a little loss before someone will come to take advantage of the good deal," said Liang.

"I don't mind if I lose around ten taels (*Tempting him with monetary gains*), as long as the deal is done fast, so that I can be free to be on my way."

After examining the samples, Liang Shangbin also stepped into the merchant's boat carrying the fabric to rummage through the bolts in stock, all the while exclaiming, "Good stuff! Good stuff!"

"If you are not buying," complained the merchant, "at least have the goodness not to mess up my stock and disrupt my business." (*Leading him on with challenging words.*)

"How do you know I'm not buying?" said Liang Shangbin.

"If you are," challenged the merchant, "show me the silver."

"Should you be willing to take a twenty-percent loss," bargained Liang, "I'll pay you eighty taels of silver for half of what you have." (*That's the eighty taels he had just laid his hands on.*)

"What nonsense is this!" exclaimed the merchant. "What broker can afford a twenty-percent loss! And I'll get rid of only half the stock, too. What am I going to do with the other half? Much good that does me! Didn't I say you don't look like a buyer?" He continued with a sardonic smile, "Of so many households this side of the north gate, none is rich enough to afford a mere four hundred bolts of fabric! Oh well, I'll just have to go over to the east gate to find a buyer." (*Leading him on nicely with another challenge.*)

Liang Shangbin bristled at these words. Moreover, he could not let go of an opportunity to make a profit out of such attractive prices. He said, "What a bully you are! I'm taking all of it. Now what do you say to that?"

"If you mean what you say," replied the merchant, "I'll knock off twenty taels." (*Working on him with greater temptation.*)

Liang Shangbin insisted on making it forty taels, but the merchant held his ground. The onlookers said to the merchant, "Since you're anxious to get rid of the stuff and this Mr. Liang enjoys gaining petty advantages, why don't the two of you strike a compromise and close off the deal at one hundred seventy taels?"

The merchant was still unwilling, but gave way at the urging of the crowd. "Oh, very well," he conceded, "It's only out of respect for all of you present that I'm giving up the ten taels. But hand over the silver quickly so I can be on my way."

"I don't have that much silver," said Liang Shangbin, "but I do have some pieces of jewelry. Will you take them instead?"

"Jewelry is just as good as silver," said the merchant, "as long as the appraisal is fair."

Liang invited him into his parlor. Some silver and two pairs of silver cups were worth one hundred taels altogether. Then he took out the jewelry, which was estimated by the crowd of onlookers to be worth seventy taels in total. The silver, jewelry, and the bolts of fabric changed hands, much to the delight of Liang Shangbin, who congratulated himself upon this good deal. Truly,

> *Like a snake trying to swallow an elephant,*
> *His greed knew no bounds.*
> *Like a mantis catching a cicada,*
> *His victory might just be his doom.*

If the truth be told, this fabric merchant was none other than Imperial Censor Chen in disguise. Having closed his tribunal pleading illness, he had traveled incognito with his gatekeeper to Shicheng County, where a boat was already in waiting, loaded as it was with bolts of fabric that Battalion Commander Nie had obtained at his secret order. Commander Nie then followed him as his valet, leaving the gatekeeper to keep watch on the boat. No one saw through the plot (*The truth is hardly to be covered up*), such was the ingenuity of the censor.

Now, scarcely had Censor Chen stepped off the boat than he wrote Liang Shangbin's name on an arrest warrant that he had brought with him for the purpose and told Commander Nie to bring the man to him quietly. Then he sent an invitation for Mr. Gu to come for a meeting. (*This is the day of reckoning.*) By the time the censor returned to his tribunal, claiming that he had recovered from the illness, Liang Shangbin had already been brought there and Inspector Gu had also arrived. The censor hastened to have wine set out in Mr. Gu's honor in the chamber behind the main hall and asked Mr. Gu to stay for a light meal.

In the course of their conversation, Inspector Gu again brought up the case of Lu Xuezeng. The censor said with a smile, "Uncle, it is exactly in order to get to the bottom of this case that I invited you here." With these words, he told his gatekeeper to open a box, from which he took out two silver cups and an abundance of jewelry for the inspector to take a look at.

Recognizing them as his family possessions, the inspector asked in astonishment, "Where did you get these?"

The censor said, "They are the clues to your daughter's death. Please wait while I call the court to session to conduct the interrogation and solve the mystery for you."

He went into the front hall and started the court session by calling forth Lu Xuezeng, who was then led to one side of the hall. As Liang Shangbin was brought out, the censor thundered, "Liang Shangbin! A fine thing you did at Inspector Gu's residence!" This came as a bolt out of the blue for Liang. He was just about to say something in brazen defense of himself when the censor had the gatekeeper bring out the silver cups and the jewelry as evidence of his crime. "Where did you get these things?" asked the censor. Liang was aghast with horror when he raised his eyes and saw that the censor was none other than the fabric merchant. All the words that he managed to utter were "I deserve to die."

"I will spare you the ankle-squeezer," said the censor. "Just write me a truthful confession."

Knowing that he would not be able to deny anything, Liang had no alternative but to confess. How, you may ask, was the confession written? There are two lyric poems to the tune of "Suo Nan Zhi" that bear witness:

> Writing this confession is Liang Shangbin.
> It all started with my cousin Lu Xuezeng.
> His mother-in-law knows him to be poor,
> And offered him money for the wedding.

> *This I came to know,*
> *For he wished to borrow my clothes.*
> *I resorted to cheating*
> *To keep him from leaving.*
>
> *Under cover of the dark night,*
> *I passed myself off as the invited.*
> *The gardener led me to the chamber,*
> *Where Lady Meng gave me all the treasure.*
> *I was asked to stay overnight,*
> *And the girl I did defile.*
> *Lu's visit three days later*
> *Made the girl hang herself in shame.*

Having put away the confession, the censor called forth Old Ou the gardener. "Look carefully," said the censor. "Was it this man who claimed to be young Master Lu that night in the back garden?"

His eyes wide open, Old Ou scrutinized the man and said, "Yes, Your Honor, it was him," whereupon the censor ordered that Liang Shangbin be given eighty strokes of the rod. The cangue was taken off Lu Xuezeng and put on Liang Shangbin. (*How efficient!*) The crime of rape being punishable by death, Liang was sent to the county prison to await execution. The four hundred bolts of fabric were recovered and returned to the warehouses they had come from. The silver and jewelry were given back to the Gu family through Old Ou. Lu Xuezeng got back the gold hairpins and brooches and was discharged, a free man, but he did not set out for home without first making kowtows of gratitude to the censor for having saved his life. Truly,

> *The crime came to light;*
> *The wrong was set to right.*
> *The inspector's divine wisdom*
> *Ensured that justice was done.*

Meanwhile, in the rear chamber, Inspector Gu heard the trial out and was astounded. He waited until the censor dismissed the court to greet him with a profusion of words of gratitude. "If it were not for your divine wisdom, the wrong done to my daughter would not have been redressed. But how did Your Honor get hold of all the silver and jewelry?" The censor told him the whole story in a whisper.

"How ingenious!" exclaimed Mr. Gu. "May I add that Liang Shangbin's wife must be a party to the conspiracy and might still be keeping a few pieces of the jewelry that belong to my family? Please apprehend her, also."

"That can be easily done," promised the censor, who proceeded to issue the necessary documents empowering Shicheng County officials to apprehend Liang's wife for a rigorous interrogation and to confiscate whatever loot remained in her possession. Inspector Gu then took leave of the censor and returned home.

Upon receipt of the decree from the censor, the magistrate of Shicheng County summoned Liang Shangbin from prison. "What is your wife's surname?" he asked. "Was she part of this?"

Out of spite for his wife, Liang answered, "My wife Tian-shi, driven by her greed for the valuables, was part of the conspiracy," whereupon the magistrate immediately sent lictors to bring Tian-shi to court.

Let us now go back to Tian-shi, who, now living with her brother and his wife after her parents' death, made a living by sewing. On the particular day of which we speak, her brother Tian Zhongwen happened to be present at the magistrate's court. No sooner had he heard that his sister was wanted by the court than he rushed back home to tell her about it. "Don't panic, my brother," she said. "I know what to do." In no time at all, she mounted a sedan-chair and, carrying the divorce statement with her, made straight for the Gu residence and asked to see Lady Meng. For a moment, Lady Meng's vision turned blurry, and whom did she see walking in but her daughter Axiu! It wasn't until the visitor drew near that she realized with a start that she was looking at a beautiful woman she had never seen before. "Who are you?" she asked.

Prostrating herself on the ground, Tian-shi said, "I was Liang Shangbin's wife, already divorced before his arrest, because I was afraid of implication in the evil doings of that vile husband of mine. As your husband does not know this, I am here to beseech you to intercede and save my life." With these words, she presented Lady Meng with the divorce statement.

Lady Meng was reading the statement when, all of a sudden, Tian-shi pulled at her sleeves and wailed, "Mother, my father has done such harm to me!" *(How extraordinary!)*

Recognizing Axiu's voice, Lady Meng also wept. "My child! What do you want to tell me?"

Her eyes tightly closed, Tian-shi said between bitter sobs, "A momentary slip on my part made me lose my virginity to that wicked man. Too ashamed to face my husband-to-be, I took my own life to preserve my virtuous name. To my dismay, Father failed to make a thorough investigation. His rashness almost cost young Master Lu his life. Luckily, the case is now solved, but through the fault of you, Mother, and me, he has lost a wife. If you care for me, please advise Father to take care of this matter so as not to sever the marriage bond between the two families. If so, in the netherworld I will have no regrets." And with that, she fell to the ground. *(Extraordinary. Pitiable.)* Lady Meng also fainted from too much crying.

The housekeeper, the maids, and the waiting women all gathered around and awoke the two. Still in a daze, Tian-shi sat on the floor, unable to answer any questions about what had happened. The sight of Tian-shi reminded Lady Meng of her daughter, and Lady Meng began another fit of crying, but the maids around her managed to calm her down. Overcome with grief, she asked Tian-shi, "Are your parents still alive?"

"No," Tian-shi answered.

"Now that I am childless, you are no less dear to me than my own daughter. Would you be willing to be my adopted daughter?"

Tian-shi said with a bow, "It would be an honor to serve you, madam." Immensely pleased, Lady Meng kept her in the house.

Inspector Gu, now back at home, learned that Tian-shi was not involved in the foul deed, her divorce having preceded Liang's arrest, whereupon he sent a letter, with the divorce statement attached, to the county magistrate, pleading that the magistrate withdraw the warrant for Tian-shi's arrest and forward the letter to the censor.

Impressed by Tian-shi's virtue and intelligence, he gave consent to his wife's wish to adopt her as a daughter. Lady Meng described to him how their daughter Axiu had attached her soul to the body of Tian-shi, insisting that the marriage bond with the Lu family not be severed. "Since Tian-shi is young and beautiful," she went on to suggest, "why not have Mr. Lu marry into our family to fulfill the marriage bond?" *(A wonderful twist to the story.)*

Suffering as he was from pangs of conscience for having afflicted anguish on Lu Xuezeng for something he was innocent of, Inspector Gu was all too ready to support his wife's proposal. Afraid that Mr. Lu would be suspicious of the move, he paid Lu a visit to apologize for his behavior before bringing up the subject of marriage. Mr. Lu repeatedly declined the proposal but finally gave in after much persuasion. An auspicious day was selected for the wedding, with the gold hairpins and brooches as the betrothal presents.

As it happened, when speaking to Mr. Lu, Inspector Gu had referred to Tian-shi only as an adopted distant niece, and, to Tian-shi, Lady Meng had mentioned that the bridegroom was a scholar, without giving away his name. *(It would be embarrassing to give out the name.)* It was not until after the wedding ceremony that they came to know each other's identity. From then on, the couple lived in domestic peace and were as dutiful to their elders as could be. Since Inspector Gu was without male issue, Mr. Lu became heir to the family fortune and devoted his efforts to studying for the imperial examinations. In due course, he was sent to the National University by Inspector Gu, who believed that Lu was now ready for all three sections of the examinations. Later, he did indeed pass the examinations at all levels. His two sons were given the surnames of Lu and Gu respectively to carry on the names of both families, whereas Liang Shangbin's family line terminated. *(Neat ending.)* There is a poem that says,

> *One night of pleasure ruined his life;*
> *A blissful marriage he yielded to another.*
> *All seducers who resort to intrigue,*
> *Take warning from Liang's sorry fate!*

3

Han the Fifth Sells Her Charms in New Bridge Town

To please the pampered beauty deprived of freedom,
Beacon fires were lit on Mount Li to fool the lords.
That one laugh from her toppled the empire,
And filled jade towers with dust from enemy horses.

This quatrain, quoted from *Poems on Historical Events* by Hu Zeng,[1] relates how King You [r. 781–771 B.C.E.] of the Zhou dynasty showered favors on his favorite concubine, Baosi, and how he tried by every conceivable means to please her. In order to win a smile from her, he lit the beacon fires on Mount Li that were signals of distress to the feudal lords. Believing the king to be in danger, the lords came rushing over with their troops to the rescue, only to find, upon arrival at the king's halls, that nothing was amiss. Baosi exploded with mirth. Later, when western tribes raised armies and invaded the empire, none of the lords bothered to come to the king's aid, and King You perished at the barbarians' hands at the foot of Mount Li.

Again, in the Spring and Autumn period, there was a Duke Ling of the state of Chen who had an illicit relationship with Lady Xia, mother of Xia Zhengshu, and, with his retainers Kong Ning and Yi Xingfu, spent his days and nights at her home drinking and making merry. Out of shame and spite, Zhengshu shot the duke to death with an arrow.

Later, in the Six Dynasties period [222–589], the king of Chen was so enamored of Zhang Lihua and Lady Kong that he composed the song "Jade Tree and Flowers of the Rear Court" in praise of their beauty and wallowed in lecherous pleasures to the neglect of affairs of government. When pursued by Sui soldiers, he had nowhere to hide and threw himself, together with his two concubines, into a well, but they were captured by the Sui general Han Qinhu. Thus, his kingdom perished. (*Lust leads to ruin of oneself as well as the kingdom. How fearsome! How dreadful! How infuriating!*) As the poem says,

Midst pleasure, disaster struck in the Xia stable;[2]
In the dry well was heard the "Jade Tree" song.[3]

Witness how the two Chens shared the same fate;
Many are women who bring kingdoms to ruin.

Emperor Yang [r. 605–17] of the Sui dynasty was infatuated, in the same fashion, with Consort Xiao. In order to view the scenery of Yangzhou, he conscripted a million laborers with Ma Shudu as overseer and dredged the Bian River for over a thousand li.[4] Numerous laborers died in the process. He also built phoenix ships and dragon boats and made palace maids pull them along the river amidst music that could be heard a hundred li away from both shores. Later, Yuwen Huaji[5] rose in rebellion at Jiangdu and killed Emperor Yang at the foot of Wugong Terrace. His empire also came to an end. There is a poem in evidence:

When the thousand-li canal was opened,
Waves to destroy Sui surged in from heaven.
War came before the brocade sails were furled,
Nor did the dragon boats ever turn back.

In the Tang dynasty, Emperor Minghuang doted on the beautiful Consort Yang, spending his springs in outings with her and his nights cavorting with her alone, little knowing that she was, in the meantime, having an illicit affair with An Lushan, who was known to the public as her adopted son. One day, Emperor Minghuang ran into her when she had just finished a game of clouds and rain with An Lushan, her hairpin out of place, her hair in disarray. Though she got by with some excuse or other, the emperor grew suspicious from then on and sent An Lushan away to Yuyang as a regional commander. Still longing for Consort Yang, An Lushan raised an army in rebellion. Truly,

The Yuyang drums advanced with earth-shaking beats,
Drowning the melody "Rainbow Skirt and Feathered Robe."

Emperor Minghuang could do no better than lead the assembly of officials in fleeing from the capital. At the foot of the Mawei Hills, his troops mutinied and demanded Consort Yang's death. Emperor Minghuang continued on to Western Shu. It was not until General Guo Ziyi [697–781] fought with all his might for several years that the two capitals[6] were recovered.

It was the lust for feminine beauty that caused all the rulers I have cited above to lose their kingdoms and bring about their own undoing. How can the benighted man of the street not take warning and guard against his lust?

Storyteller, why all this talk about guarding against one's lust?

Well, let me now tell of a young man who, instead of heeding the warning, got himself involved with a woman, nearly wrecked his own body, ruined his family's prosperous business, and caused quite a sensation in the town of New Bridge. The affair has been made into a romantic story to

Use mistakes of the past
To warn generations to come.

As the story goes, in the Song dynasty, ten li outside the prefecture of Lin'an was the town of Lake Villa, and another five li away was the town of New Bridge, in which there lived a rich man, Squire Wu, whose wife Pan-shi bore him an only son called Wu Shan. Wu Shan later married, and his wife Yu-shi bore him a child who was now four years old. What with the silk-floss shop in the front portion of his house, his money-lending business, and his speculations in grain, Squire Wu amassed a sizable fortune and filled his trunks with gold and silver and his granaries with rice and grain. He built another house in the town of Gray Bridge five li away and had his son Wu Shan take care of a new shop, with the help of a manager. The shipments of silk floss he received at home were forwarded to the new shop to be sold to local weavers. Wu Shan being a clever and handsome man with some rudimentary knowledge about decorum and a practical turn of mind averse to frivolity, Squire Wu knew he had nothing to worry about, for his son was not the kind to get himself into trouble.

Wu Shan would start his day in the shop early in the morning and return home after night fell. With the shop occupying only the front section of the house, the rest of the house was empty. One day, Wu Shan was detained at home and did not arrive at the shop until high noon. Upon entering, what did he see but four or five men moving into the empty quarters of the house trunks, baskets, tables, benches, and other pieces of furniture from two barges that were moored in the river behind the house. From the barges also emerged a middle-aged fat woman, an old woman, and a young woman, all of whom walked right into the house, an event that was destined to cause Wu Shan to be

Weak as the waning moon at the fifth watch,
Feeble as the spent oil lamp before dawn.

Wu Shan asked the manager, "Who are these people moving into my house like this without permission?"

The manager replied, "They came from the city. Because the men of the family were called away to serve the yamen, the women cannot find a place to stay on such short notice and have asked Old Fan next door to plead on their behalf so that they can stay here for just two or three days. I was about to report to you when you came in."

Wu Shan was about to lose his temper when he saw the young woman adjust her sleeves and step forward with a deep bow of greeting. "Please do not be angry, sir," she said. "This has nothing to do with the manager. It was I who made bold to come here without any prior notice, because of the lack of time to do otherwise. Please forgive us and let us stay for three or four days until we have found a house to move into. Rent will be paid according to established practice."

Wu Shan's expression softened. "In that case," said he, "I don't mind if you stay longer. Please make yourselves comfortable," whereupon the young woman went to busy herself with the trunks and baskets. Itching with the desire to help, Wu Shan also went to carry a few pieces of the household effects.

Storyteller, didn't you say that Wu Shan was a down-to-earth kind of man not given to frivolity? If so, why did his anger turn to joy at the sight of this woman, so much so that he even gave her a helping hand?

Well, you must realize that when he was at home, he was under the strict control of his parents, who forbade him to get near any place that was less than decent. Being a clever, good-looking, and energetic man, he was not as unexcitable as a piece of wood. Now, when his parents were not around, how could he, a man in the prime of youth, not be aroused at the sight of such an attractive woman right in his shop?

Both the fat woman and the young woman said, "Please don't exert yourself like this, sir."

Wu Shan replied, to the joy of everyone present, "Since you'll be staying here, we're like family. Why stand on ceremony?"

When night fell, Wu Shan returned home, but not without first telling the manager to draw up a lease with the new tenants. The manager promised to do as he was told, but of this, we shall speak no further.

Let us resume our story. Wu Shan returned home, but he did not tell his parents about the new tenants. That night, all his thoughts were with the young woman. The following morning, he rose bright and early, and, after he was properly done up, he called his page boy Shoutong to follow him and swaggered his way to the shop. Truly,

> The unlucky drink on credit;
> The ill-fated run into lovers.

After Wu Shan arrived in the shop and made some sales, the servant of the new tenants came in with an invitation to tea, for they were ready to give him the lease. Wu Shan had been hoping for a chance to enter their quarters of the house, and, rejoicing at the well-timed invitation, he got up and went in. Radiant with smiles, the young woman stepped out to greet him. "Please come in and have a seat," said she. Wu Shan sat down in the middle hall. The old woman and the fat one also came in to greet him, and so, there he was, in the company of three women.

Wu Shan asked, "May I ask your surname? Why don't I see a man in your family?" (*How is he to know that this is not a decent family?*)

"My unworthy husband is named Han," said the fat woman. "He and our son are footmen in the yamen. They leave home early and come back late. Official business keeps them away from home."

After a while, Wu Shan lowered his head and threw a furtive glance at the young woman. With her flirtatious eyes fixed on Wu Shan, the young woman asked, "May I make so bold as to ask how old you are, sir?"

"I have frittered away twenty-four years. May I ask your age?"

"There must be a predestined bond between us. I'm also twenty-four. I moved out of the city only to meet you, who happen to be my age! This bears out the saying 'Those destined for each other will meet, however great the distance.'"

At such a turn of the conversation, the old woman and the fat one stood up and departed on some excuse, leaving the young woman making suggestive remarks to Wu Shan as the two sat facing each other. Wu Shan had thought that she was from a good family and had decided to let her stay, with no more intention than to be able to flirt with her. Little did he expect her to try to seduce him when they were hardly acquainted. Realizing that the woman was not a decent sort, he was about to leave, when she drew nearer to sit by his side. Coquettishly, she said, "Show me the gold hairpin on your head, sir." Wu Shan took off his cap and was on the point of removing the hairpin, when the young woman held his hair knot with one hand and, with the other, pulled out the hairpin. Rising, she said, "Let's go upstairs. I have something to say to you." So saying, she mounted the stairs. Wu Shan followed up the stairs to get his hairpin back. Indeed,

> You may be as smart as a demon,
> But you still have to drink water she washed her feet with.

Wu Shan went up the stairs and cried, "Young lady, please give me back my hairpin. I need to go back home now to take care of some business."

"You and I have a predestined marriage bond. Don't you give me any more of your false pretenses. Come and enjoy the bed with me."

Wu Shan protested, "That can't be done! It won't look good if people find out. Besides, there are too many curious eyes and ears around here."

Before he could go down, the woman, exhibiting all her charms, put her arms around him, pressed herself against him, and pulled his pants down with her slender and soft fingers. Unable to curb his passion, which was rising like a flame, he went to bed with her, hand in hand, and the two plunged into a game of clouds and rain. After the intimacy was over, they sat up, holding each other in an embrace. Wu Shan asked in a pleasantly surprised tone, "Sister, what's your name?"

"I am the fifth child in the family. The name I was given at birth is Saijin [Good as Gold]. When I was older, my parents came to call me Jinnu [Gold Maid]. May I make so bold as to ask what your seniority is among your siblings and what business you are in?"

"I am the only child. My family is in the silk and money-lending business. We are quite well known in the town of New Bridge for our wealth. This shop here is my own." (*It is understandable to boast of one's wealth to someone inferior, but little did he know that these words would make him a patron of that family.*)

Jinnu was inwardly delighted. "To be able to get myself such a rich man is not a bad deal at all," she thought to herself.

The truth of the matter is that the woman was an unlicensed prostitute, a so-called "private nest" not openly in business. She provided the only source of income for the household. The old woman was the fat woman's mother, and Jinnu was the fat one's daughter. The fat woman came from a decent family and got into this line of business only because her husband, a good-for-nothing, could hardly eke out a living on his own. Jinnu, being a pretty girl with some rudimentary education, had been married off but was sent back to her parents because of her illicit affairs with other men. As coincidence would have it, the fat woman, by this time, was approaching the age of fifty, and her clients had been dwindling in number. With her daughter to replace her, the business not only went on but expanded in a big way. However, someone reported them to the authorities, and, in panic, they left the town where they lived and moved to this place to flee from trouble. Their path, alas, crossed that of Wu Shan, whom they lured right into their well-laid trap. Why was there no man in the family? As a matter of fact, the father and son had developed the habit of slipping away whenever they saw a client coming. Whoever took a fancy to Jinnu would fall into her trap, and Wu Shan was not the only one.

Let us come back to our story. Jinnu said, "We moved here on short notice in great haste and are therefore short of money. Would you lend us five taels of silver? Please don't turn me down."

Wu Shan gave his consent, rose, and adjusted his clothes and cap. Jinnu gave his gold hairpin back to him. The two of them went downstairs and resumed their seats in the main hall. Wu Shan thought to himself, "I've been here for quite some time now. I'm afraid the neighbors will start to talk." Another cup of tea later, Jinnu invited him to stay for lunch, an offer that he declined. "I've stayed for too long," said he. "I can't stay for lunch, but I'll send over the money shortly."

"This afternoon, I'll get some food and wine ready for you. Do come!" After these words, Wu Shan went out into the shop.

It so happened that a neighbor had seen Wu Shan enter the interior of the house. It was a two-story house with two six-room sections, one of which was occupied by Jinnu and the other by the silk shop, but the story above the shop was empty. This busybody, wondering what could be keeping Wu Shan for so long inside, had sneaked into that empty room and, crouching by the partition, saw everything that happened.

When Wu Shan returned to his seat in the shop, several neighbors came in and said to him, "Congratulations! Young Master Wu!" Wu Shan already had a suspicion that he had been somehow found out, and now that he was being laughed at, he countered, his face flushed crimson, "What nonsense is this? What's there to congratulate me about?" Thereupon, the one who had seen the goings-on, Shen Erlang, owner of the general store across the street, said, "Why bother to deny it! After the gold hairpin was taken out, what did you go up for?" As the words struck him right on his sore spot, Wu Shan rose to go under some excuse, without being able to come up with a reply. The neighbors blocked his way. "We'll put some silver together for a celebration!" Ignoring their remarks, Wu Shan left in a huff, heading in a westerly direction.

He walked to his maternal uncle's house, the Pan household, and asked for lunch there. In no hurry, he paced to the door, borrowed a small scale from a shop, weighed out two taels of silver from the amount he had on him for buying silk, and tucked away the two taels in his sleeve. He hung idly about and did not return to the shop until late afternoon.

"The new tenants are inviting you for a drink, sir," said the manager.

At this point, the old servant appeared to say, "Where have you been, sir? I couldn't find you anywhere. We've prepared some food and wine for you. There are no other guests, besides the manager."

Wu Shan and the manager thus went to the room where the dinner table was already all laid out with the usual fare of fish, meat, wine, and fruit. With Wu Shan in the seat of honor, Jinnu sitting opposite, and the manager on the side, the servant started serving the wine. A few cups later, the manager, well aware of what was afoot, said he needed to close the shop and left.

Without much capacity for wine, Wu Shan drank to his heart's content with Jinnu after the manager was gone but, after more than ten cups, began to feel the effects of the wine. Giving Jinnu the silver that he had in his sleeve, he rose and said to her, taking her hand, "I have something to say to you. This thing is not all that appropriate. The neighbors all know about it and have been making fun of me. Should my parents get wind of this, what's to be done? There are too many curious eyes and wicked, unforgiving tongues around here. Some might be so resentful as to spread vicious lies around and make life hard for us. Sister, as I see it, it would be best for you to find a more quiet place. I'll often come to see you."

"You are right. Let me talk it over with my mother."

At this moment, the old servant brought in two cups of tea. After the tea, the two again indulged in some amorous sport. As Wu Shan got ready to leave, he reminded her, "I won't come again, to avoid gossip. After you've found another place, have the servant tell me so that I can come and see you off." Having said this, Wu Shan went back into the shop, gave some instructions to the manager, and returned home, and there we shall leave him.

It being dark after she saw Wu Shan off, Jinnu remounted the stairs, washed off her heavy makeup, and went down again for supper, after which she related to her parents everything Wu Shan had said about the necessity of moving. They then retired for the night.

The following morning, the fat woman told the servant to find out quietly what the neighbors were talking about. Accordingly, the old man stood outside the door for a while and then sat idly for a while in front of Zhang Dalang's rice shop next door. All he heard was gossip by the neighbors about Wu Shan's affair with the woman. Upon returning home, the old man said to the fat woman, "All those wagging tongues around here don't make this the best neighborhood to live in."

"We moved here," said the fat woman, "because of harassment in the city, hoping to find a nice place to live in permanently. Who would have thought we would run into such neighbors again!" With a sigh, she told her husband to go and look for another house while she kept watch on the neighbors' reaction, before deciding on the next thing to do.

To come back to Wu Shan, after he returned home that day, he pleaded illness to his parents and, without telling them the real reason, stopped going to the shop, for fear of incurring further gossip. The manager took care of the shop all by himself.

Jinnu was not used to such peace and quiet in the house. Therefore, the old servant again set about inviting former clients, and the business resumed. (*Of course.*) At first, the neighbors had been aware only of Wu Shan's visits, but later, at the sight of the busy traffic, they realized this was a veritable business establishment. Some busybody said, "Ours is a decent neighborhood. How can we tolerate such filth among us? It is often said that 'fornication leads to murder.' Fights of jealousy can end up in killing, and we the neighbors would all be implicated." Before the words were quite out of their mouths, the old servant had already gone home to report what the neighbors were saying again today. The fat woman, with no one to vent her spleen on, lashed out at the old woman: "Who are you afraid of, at your rotten old age? Why don't you go out to get at those cursed tongue-wagging bastards?"

So the old woman got up and went out the door. "Which cursed tongue-wagging bastards are farting again?" she screamed. "If you dare to take me on, I'll have it out with you even if I have to die for it! Which family doesn't have visits from relatives?"

When the neighbors heard her, they said, "What a shameless old bitch! She's hurling abuses at us neighbors when she should have apologized for the naughty things they do at home!"

Shen Erlang, the general-store owner, was about to take the old woman on when someone who was not given to meddling in other people's affairs stopped him with these words: "Let her be. Don't argue with this half-dead old thing. Just drive them away and that'll be that."

Having cursed unchallenged for some time, the old woman went back into the house.

The neighbors went to the manager and said to him, "You should have known better than to allow such unsavory characters to live here. Instead of apologizing for their own behavior, they sent the old woman to curse us. You must have heard her. If we report the matter to Squire Wu, your boss, it won't reflect too well on you."

The manager said, "Please don't be angry, my good neighbors. You don't have to say another word. I'll tell them to move as soon as possible."

Having said what they had come to say, the neighbors went off. The manager immediately stepped inside and said to the fat woman, "You must quickly find a place and move out of here. Don't drag me into any of this. With things the way they are, you'll know no peace if you stay."

"Say no more," the fat woman replied. "My husband is already looking for a house in the city. We'll be out of here anytime now." At this, the manager went off.

The fat woman said to Jinnu, "We'll be moving into the city tomorrow morning. We can send the old man quietly to Young Master Wu to tell him about this, but his parents must not know."

With these instructions, the old servant betook himself to Squire Wu's silk shop in New Bridge Town, but, without the courage to go straight in, he stood under the eaves of a house across the street while keeping an eye on the shop. Before long, Wu Shan was seen emerging from the house at a leisurely pace. At the sight of the old servant, he hurried over and led the old man away from his own door to a silk weaver's house, where they sat down. "What message do you bring?" asked Wu Shan.

"I am sent here to let you know that Fifth Sister is moving into the city tomorrow, just as you told her to."

"That's the best way out," said Wu Shan. "But where in the city exactly are you moving to?"

"To Cross Bridge Street, south of the Patrol Battalion's Wool Camp." Wu Shan took out a piece of silver of about two mace's[7] worth and said, handing it to the old man, "Go ahead and buy yourself a cup of wine with this. Tomorrow at noon, I'll come to see the family off." The old man tucked away the silver, said his thanks, and returned home.

At about nine the following morning, Wu Shan had Shoutong follow him to a grocery store by Brocade Bridge, where he bought two packages of dried fruit. With the page boy carrying the packages, the two wended their way to the shop in Gray Bridge. After the greetings, Wu Shan went over with the manager the daily sales accounts. Wu Shan then rose and went inside to see Jinnu and her mother. The initial amenities over, he took the dried fruit from the page boy and produced a packet of silver from his gown, saying, "The two packages of dried fruit are for Sister to make tea with. The three taels of silver are to help you toward the moving expenses. I'll come to see you after you've settled down."

Jinnu took the dried fruit and the silver, and rose with her mother from their seats to thank him, saying, "How can we deserve such a great favor?"

"Don't thank me. We'll be seeing more of each other." So saying, he got up and looked around, and saw that all the trunks, baskets, and furniture had already been carried down onto the boats.

"When will you come to see me again?" asked Jinnu.

"In three to five days at most."

After bidding Wu Shan adieu, Jinnu and her family moved into the city that very day. Indeed,

> If this place will not keep them,
> There are places that will.

Wu Shan was prone to suffer from summer sickness. When the full heat of summer came on, he would feel tired, and his body would grow emaciated. As it was the beginning of the sixth month, he engaged the services of an acupuncturist to give him moxibustion treatments on his back. Since he needed to be nursed back to health, he stopped going to the shop. His thoughts were constantly with Jinnu, but the pain of the moxibustion kept him indoors.

Let us retrace our steps and turn our attention to Jinnu, who moved to Cross Bridge Street on the seventeenth day of the fifth month. That street happened to be inhabited mostly by soldiers' families averse to her profession. Moreover, it was a secluded street with hardly any traffic. (*Moved to the wrong place again.*) The fat woman said to her, "Mr. Wu promised us that day that he would come within three to five days of our move. It's been one month now. Why hasn't he shown up? If he comes this way, he'll surely drop in to see us."

Jinnu suggested, "Why don't we send the servant to the shop at Gray Bridge to see him?"

Accordingly, the old man went out Mount Gen Gate[8] to the silk shop in Gray Bridge to see the manager. After the greetings, the manager said, "What brings you here, Grandfather?"

"I'm here to see Young Master Wu."

"He's having moxibustion treatments at home. He hasn't recovered, so he hasn't been here for a long time."

"When you go back, please send him a message and let him know that I've been here to see him."

Without delay, the old servant took leave of the manager and returned home for a report to Jinnu.

"I see. So he's having moxibustion treatments at home," said Jinnu. "That's why he hasn't come."

That day, after consulting her mother, Jinnu had the servant buy two pieces of pig maw and clean them. She then stuffed them with sweet rice and lotus seeds and cooked them until tender. The following morning, she prepared some ink and, spreading out a piece of colored stationery, wrote a letter with her brush-pen:

> *Saijin humbly bows to her beloved Young Master Wu:*
>
> *Since I saw you last, my heart has been with you all the time. As you were so good as to have made a promise to see me, I have been leaning against the door, expecting your visit, but to no avail. Yesterday, I sent the servant to send you my greetings, but he returned without seeing you. I have been most lonely since moving here. Word about the pain you suffer from the moxibustion makes me too worried to sit or sleep in peace. While I fret in vain, how I wish I could take your place in the suffering! I have cooked two pieces of pig maw as a way to express my wishes for your recovery. Please kindly accept this small gift. My feelings need not be dwelt on.*
>
> *With love and another bow,*
> *Saijin*
> *on this twenty-first day of the second month of summer*

Upon finishing the letter, she folded it and sealed it with a piece of paper. After packing the pig maw into a box and wrapping it up with a piece of cloth, she handed the letter and the box to the servant, saying, "Be sure to deliver it into Young Master Wu's hands when you get to his house."

With the box in his hand and the letter in his bosom, the old man went out of the house, down the street, out Wulin Gate, and into the town of New Bridge, where he sat down on a curbstone by the door of Squire Wu's house. The page boy Shoutong, who happened to come out, saw the old man. "Grandpa, where did you just come from? Why are you sitting here?"

The old man pulled the boy to a quiet, secluded place and said, "I'm here to speak to your master. I'll be waiting here. You tell him I'm here."

Promptly Shoutong turned around, and before he had gone for long, Wu Shan walked slowly out. The old man made haste to greet him with a bow. "Master, I'm glad you look fine."

"Well, Grandpa," said Wu Shan. "What is it you've got in the box?"

"Fifth Sister is concerned about your moxibustion treatments and cooked two pieces of pig maw for you, for lack of anything better."

Wu Shan led the old man to a wineshop and asked, after they had taken their seats upstairs, "How's the new place?"

The old man replied, "It's miserable." So saying, he handed the letter over to Wu Shan, who opened it and, after reading it, folded it as before and put it in his sleeve. Then he opened the box, took out one piece of maw and told the waiter to put it on a plate, cut it up, and serve it with two flasks of warmed wine.

"Grandpa, please help yourself to the food and wine while I go home to write a reply for you to take back."

"Please go ahead," said the old man.

Wu Shan went back to his own bedroom, wrote the reply surreptitiously, and weighed out five taels of silver. He then returned to the wineshop and had a few drinks with the old servant.

"Thank you very much for the good wine," said the old man, "but I can't have any more." As he rose to go, Wu Shan gave him the silver and the letter of reply, saying, "The five taels of silver are to help the family with daily expenses. Please tell Fifth Sister that I will surely come to pay her a visit in two or three days." The old man tucked away the silver and the letter and went downstairs. Wu Shan saw him out of the wineshop.

Evening had set in when the old man got home and gave Jinnu the silver and the letter of reply. She opened the letter and read it by the lamp. It said,

Shan humbly bows to his beloved Fifth Sister Han:

I am much obliged to you for your great kindness to me at our previous meetings. Your loving tenderness at the pillow has never been absent from my memory. I have disappointed you, but I would have kept my promise of visiting you had I not been inconvenienced by the moxibustion treatment. I am most grateful to you for having sent your servant to visit me and for the delicacies you kindly prepared. (Delicacies that are going to take away his life.) *I will certainly see you within two or three days. Please accept the enclosed five taels of silver as a token of my sentiments.*

Wu Shan bows again

Jinnu and her mother were happy beyond measure with the silver, but, of this, no more need be said.

Wu Shan stayed around in the wineshop until evening. Taking the other piece of pig maw with him, he returned quietly to his own bedroom and said to his wife, "An acquaintance of mine, a weaver, heard that I was under moxibustion treatments and kindly gave me two cooked pieces of pig maw. I ate one with a friend before I came back. This one I brought home for you."

His wife said, "Then you must reciprocate tomorrow." That evening, Wu Shan ate the piece of maw with his wife in their own room, unbeknownst to his parents.

Two days went by. On the third day, the twenty-fourth day of the sixth month, Wu Shan rose bright and early and said to his parents, "I have been absent from the shop for quite some time. Luckily I have recovered now and feel ready to go today. I also need to collect money from some weavers in Shrine Lane in the city. I'll be back soon."

"Go ahead, but don't overtax yourself," said his father.

Wu Shan took leave of his father, asked for a sedan-chair, and went on his way, followed by the page boy Shoutong holding an open umbrella. As it turned out, Jinnu almost took away Wu Shan's life on this visit. Indeed,

> *Tied to the body of the sixteen-year-old beauty*
> *Is a sword to cut down stupid men.*
> *Though no head is seen to roll to the ground,*
> *She secretly makes your bone marrow run dry.*

Wu Shan mounted the sedan-chair and, before he knew it, found himself in the town of Gray Bridge. He alit from the sedan-chair and greeted the manager. With his thoughts obsessed with Jinnu, he sat for only a short while before he rose and told the manager, "I am going into the city to settle some weavers' accounts. We'll go over your daily accounts when I come back."

Well aware of where he was heading, the manager did not presume to stop him but confined himself to this advice: "Having just recovered, you can't afford to walk around too much, for you'll only bring on the pain again." Wu Shan ignored him and mounted the sedan-chair. The carriers, as previously instructed, headed straight for Mount Gen Gate. They then wound their way to South Cross Bridge near Wool Camp and asked for the Han family from the town of Lake Villa. Someone said, pointing at a house, "It's the door next to the medicine shop." After Wu Shan got down from the sedan chair, Shou-tong knocked at the door. The old servant opened the door and, at the sight of Wu Shan, hurried inside to make the announcement. As Wu Shan walked in, the mother and daughter greeted him with ingratiating smiles, saying, "It's so seldom that we have such a distinguished guest! What wind brought you here today?"

After the necessary amenities with the mother and daughter, he was led inside to sit down for a cup of tea. "I'll show you my room," Jinnu said and took him upstairs to her own room. Indeed,

> Real friends never tire of each other;
> Soul mates, when chatting, find themselves well matched.

Upstairs in Jinnu's room, Jinnu and Wu Shan were as happy as fish in water and as inseparable as lacquer and glue. They poured into each other's ears the usual words of tender love. The occasion naturally called for a feast. The old servant carried the dishes upstairs, moved the mirror stand, and set the dishes on the dressing table. The old man then went down and did not dare to go up again until Jinnu asked him for more wine. As the two of them sat side by side, Jinnu poured out a cup of wine and offered it to Wu Shan with both hands, saying as she did so, "You were never absent from my thoughts while you were undergoing moxibustion treatments."

Wu Shan took over the cup and replied, "I failed to keep my promise because of the moxibustion treatments." After he downed the wine, he filled a cup to offer to Jinnu in return. More than ten cups later, their passion was aroused, and, amid reminiscences of the old days, they experienced the very height and fulfillment of their love. After the intimacy was over, they rose, washed their hands, and started another bout of drinking. Though their eyes were bleary with wine, they were still burning with lingering desires. Wu Shan had abstained from sex for a month while undergoing the moxibustion treatments. Now that he was with Jinnu, how could he be content with only one round? (*Only he who can manage to stay unperturbed at such a moment is a worthy man. Someone counters, "A worthy man doesn't get himself into such a fix." I reply with a smile, "That's not the way it is."*) He should have been a dead man by now, for Jinnu had thrown his soul and his spirit into confusion. He plunged into another round with rekindled passion. Truly,

> Too much good food leads to illness.
> Too much pleasure leads to disaster.

Afterward, Wu Shan found himself fighting a losing battle against fatigue and mental confusion. Without eating anything, he lay down on the bed and went to sleep. Seeing him sleeping, Jinnu walked downstairs and told the sedan-chair carriers waiting outside, "The master had a few cups of wine and is now asleep upstairs. You two gentlemen please wait for a while. Do not rush him."

"We wouldn't dare," they said.

Jinnu went back upstairs and lay down by Wu Shan's side.

In the meantime, Wu Shan had barely closed his eyes before he heard someone cry out, "How nicely you sleep, Young Master Wu!" After a few more repetitions, Wu Shan saw, through his wine-sodden eyes, a big fat monk in a worn-out monk's robe, a pair of monk's shoes on his bare feet, and a yellow silk sash around his waist, signaling a greeting to him. Wu Shan jumped up from bed and returned the greeting, saying, "Master, which monastery are you from? Why are you calling my name?"

"I am the abbot of Water and Moon Monastery at Mulberry Garden. My disciple having died, I am here to recruit you because, judging from your physiognomy, I believe you are not richly blessed by fate. Glory and splendor being out of reach, you might as well opt for a life of austerity, renounce the world, and become a disciple of mine."

"What a senseless monk you are!" said Wu Shan. "My parents are in their fifties, and I am their only son, with the responsibility to continue the family line and family tradition. How can I become a monk?"

"But that is your only choice," said the monk. "If you still want to seek glory and splendor, you'll die in no time. Do as I say and come with me."

"What nonsense is this?" asked Wu Shan. "This is a woman's boudoir. What are you, a monk, doing here?"

Opening his eyes wide, the monk cried, "Are you coming or not?"

"You unreasonable bald ass! Why are you pestering me like this!"

In a rage, the monk dragged Wu Shan off. When reaching the staircase, Wu Shan cried out in protest. At a violent push from the monk, he tumbled downstairs, head first. (*These are all meant to be scenes in a dream.*) He woke up in a start with cold sweat all over his body. When he opened his eyes, he found Jinnu still asleep. So it had been nothing but a dream. In something of a trance, he sat up in bed and for quite some time stared blankly into the air. Jinnu also woke up and said to him, "How well you slept! It's so seldom that you come. Rest now. Don't leave until tomorrow morning."

"But my parents must be worried about me. I have to go now. I'll be back to see you again some other day."

Jinnu rose to see about the serving of some refreshments. Wu Shan stopped her, saying, "I don't feel well enough to eat anything." Noticing that he did look ill, Jinnu dared not insist. After adjusting his clothes and cap, Wu Shan went downstairs, took leave of Jinnu and her mother, and hastily mounted the sedan-chair.

In the darkness of the evening, Wu Shan thought to himself in the sedan-

chair, "What a strange dream I had, and it was broad daylight, too!" Seized
with alarm and worry, he felt a stomachache coming on, but, being in the
sedan-chair, there was nothing he could do. Wishing he could be home sooner,
he told the sedan-chair carriers to move faster. By the time he arrived home at
last, the pain was overwhelming. He jumped off the sedan-chair, rushed into
the house and up the stairs, and sank down on the night-stool. Each spasm
of pain was followed by a fit of diarrhea, discharging nothing but blood-red
water. (*Illness that he brings upon himself.*) Only a considerable while later did
he throw himself into bed, his head in a whirl, his eyes blurred, his limbs
weary, and his bones aching all over. As a matter of fact, the excessive indulgence in lust was too much for his weak constitution not richly endowed with
life's vital force.

Having noticed his son's greenish complexion, Squire Wu ran up the stairs
and stood aghast. "You look awful, Son!" he said.

"I had too many drinks at a client's house and took a nap there," Wu Shan
tried to explain. "When I woke up hot and thirsty, I drank a bowl of cold
water, which gave me cramps, and now it's diarrhea." Before the words were
quite out of his mouth, he gnashed his teeth as a shiver ran through him. A
cold sweat broke out, but his body felt as hot as burning charcoal. Squire Wu
rushed downstairs and called a doctor.

"The pulse is almost gone," said the doctor. "This case is beyond me."

After much piteous pleading for him to do whatever he could to save Wu
Shan, the doctor said, "This is not diarrhea but something caused by excessive
indulgence in sex, which depleted his vital force. Such cases of the loss of yang
are usually hopeless. I will now prescribe a dose of medicine to help restore
his vital force. If, after he takes the medicine, his fever subsides and his pulse
comes back, he may have a chance." (*Medicine can't kill.*) The doctor got together a prescription for Wu Shan and left. To his parents' repeated questions,
Wu Shan shook his head and remained silent.

At about the first watch of the night, Wu Shan took the medicine and lay
down on his pillow. Suddenly the monk appeared to him again. Standing by
the bedside, he said, "Wu Shan! Why are you trying so hard to hang on to
life? You'd do well to go with me." (*The Buddha seeks out only those predestined
to join the order.*)

"Go away! Leave me alone!" Before Wu Shan could say another word, the
monk tied his yellow silk sash around Wu Shan's neck and pulled him along.
(*Unmistakably a dream.*) Holding on to the bed frame, Wu Shan gave a shout
and woke up with a start, only to realize that it was again a dream. When he
opened his eyes, he saw in front of him his parents and his wife.

"What did you see that made you wake up in alarm?" asked his parents.

Feeling disconcerted, Wu Shan knew that he would not be able to hold out any longer, and he told his parents everything about his affair with Jinnu and his dreams about the monk. As he broke down in sobs, his parents and his wife were also reduced to tears. His son being so critically ill, Squire Wu saw fit not to scold him but to comfort him with solacing words.

After the confession, Wu Shan fainted several times. Upon regaining consciousness, he said to his wife tearfully, "Serve my parents well and take good care of our son. The revenues of the silk shop should be enough for daily expenses."

His wife replied between sobs, "Just relax and get well. Don't worry about anything for now."

With a sigh, Wu Shan had a maid help him sit up and said to his parents, "I am dying. You brought up this unfilial son in vain. Perhaps it is dictated by my ill fate that I should run into my nemesis at this time of my life. Regrets are too late now! (*Too late indeed.*) Please warn other young men not to follow in my footsteps and do something that should not be done, for they'll only end up losing their lives. A man's life is precious. Those who fall easily for feminine charms should take this lesson from my experience. After I die, please throw my body into the river. That'll be my way of apologizing for having neglected my wife and son and failed to support my parents." Barely had he closed his eyes after saying these words than the monk appeared to him again. Wu Shan pleaded with him, "My master, what have I done to you to make you haunt me like this?"

"This poor monk died in the place where you were because I violated the commandment forbidding lust. I have been stranded in hell ever since without being able to extricate myself. The other day, when I happened to see you in the act of love-making in broad daylight, my heart gave a leap and I wanted to have you as a companion in the underworld." Having said this, he disappeared.

Upon waking up, Wu Shan told his parents about the dream. Squire Wu said, "So it was an aggrieved soul pestering you." In haste, he went out the door into the street, where he lit incense and candles, laid out some food offerings, and prayed to heaven, "Please show compassion and spare my son's life. I will go to the place where you died and hold a prayer service for you." Having said this prayer, he burned some paper money.

Squire Wu returned upstairs after evening had set in and saw Wu Shan sleeping on the bed with his face turned toward the wall. All of a sudden, he sat up and said with his eyes wide open, "Squire, I violated Tathagata Buddha's commandment against lust and committed suicide at Wool Camp. When your son also went there to indulge in his lust, I could hardly avoid recalling what I had done. I wanted to have him replace me or ask him to hold a service for my salvation. Your offerings of food and paper money as well as your promises of a service for me have made me decide to let go of your son and stop haunting him. I will now go back to Wool Camp to wait for your prayer service, and if I get reincarnated, I will never come again." Barely were the words out of his mouth than Wu Shan joined his palms in a salute and woke up. His face regained its former color. His wife felt his body and found that the fever had gone. He rose from bed to relieve himself and realized that the diarrhea had also stopped. The entire family rejoiced and summoned the same physician they had engaged before. "His six pulses[9] are back," said the doctor. "He'll pull through." (*Lucky man.*) After taking for several days the herb medicine prescribed by the doctor, Wu Shan gradually recovered.

Squire Wu engaged some monks and held a service in Jinnu's house for an entire day and night. Jinnu's family dreamt that a fat monk walked away with his staff.

After resting for six months, Wu Shan went back to his business in New Bridge Town. One day, his conversation with the manager turned to the subject of what had happened to him. He said remorsefully, "People of this world must, by all accounts, guard against unconscionable behavior, for it is true that reprobation comes both from fellow men and ghosts of the netherworld, and I almost lost my life for having failed to take heed." Henceforth, he mended his ways and never paid Jinnu another visit. (*An atonement for his misconduct.*) None of the relatives and neighbors aware of the situation did not hold him in respect. Verily,

> *A fool falls for every woman he sees;*
> *An impassive eye finds fault with them all.*
> *Once you gain enlightenment, you'll find your lust gone,*
> *And you'll have a lifetime of peace and quiet.*

4

Ruan San Redeems His Debt
in Leisurely Clouds Nunnery

When good marriage affinities go awry,
Blame not the gods or fellow men.
Just marry your children early, like Xiang Ziping,[1]
And live the rest of your life in peace and quiet.

The above quatrain exhorts parents to settle their debts with their children early. As the saying goes, "A grown son should take a wife; a grown daughter should have a husband. If no marriage takes place, scandals will bring you disgrace." Goodness knows how many parents have unduly delayed their daughter's matrimony by being too fastidious in picking the right son-in-law from the right family. How can youngsters who have been awakened to love withstand their desires? In the case of a young man, he would turn to clandestine love affairs or visit houses of ill repute. A young woman, if unanchored in a betrothal, is also likely to go astray, and by that time, regrets will be too late!

Let me now tell of a prominent official, Chen Taichang by name, who lived in Tuyan Lane, off Wutong Street, in the [Song dynasty's] Western Capital,[2] Henan Prefecture. Of humble origin, he worked his way up the echelons of officialdom till he attained the post of marshal of the palace guards. In his late forties, he took a concubine who bore him no son but only a daughter, whom they named Yulan [Jade Magnolia]. By the time she reached sixteen, this young lady of noble birth raised in the depths of her boudoir was as fresh as a flower and as fair as the moon, and accomplished in the arts of embroidery, sewing, musical instruments, chess, calligraphy, and painting. Chen Taichang often commented to his wife, "If no worthy husband is found for our talented and beautiful only daughter, my position as a minister in the imperial court as well as my immense wealth would all be to no avail." He therefore summoned a registered matchmaker and gave her these instructions: "Our daughter is now of age for marriage. Don't come back to me until you have found an eligible candidate with all of the following three qualities: first, he must be the son of an incumbent official in the imperial court; second, his looks and talents must match those of our daughter; third, he must have a *jinshi* degree. Only one who meets all three conditions will qualify for marriage into our family. He who lacks one of the three qualities is not even worth considering." Candidates in the subsequent search were found to be either qualified scholars but of humble origin, or of eminent family background but with no scholarly achievements, or to be satisfactory in both of these qualities but too distant in age. Therefore, the matter was put off year after year. Time sped by like an arrow, and, before they knew it, Yulan was nineteen but not yet betrothed.

It was now the Lantern Festival of the second year of the [Song dynasty's] Zhenghe reign period [C.E. 1112], and there was to be a joyous celebration as decreed by the imperial court. A host of colored lanterns were piled up in the shape of a hill in front of the Gate of Five Phoenixes. The streets were ablaze with bright lanterns, and the air was filled with the sound of gongs and drums. The curfew in the capital was lifted from the fifth through the twentieth of the first month, and the imperial court rejoiced with the populace. How do we know this? There is a lyric poem to the tune of "Auspicious Crane Fairy" depicting the festive scene:

> *An auspicious mist floats over the palace;*
> *Spring descends upon the vermilion gate.*
> *It is the middle of the first month when*
> *The moon waxes to its fullest.*
> *Streets sparkle with hibiscus flowers.*
> *Seen from the Dragon Towers, the city*
> *Is aglow with candles and lanterns.*
> *Where curtains of beads are raised high,*
> *Songs and music last all day long,*
> *And precious hairpins and bracelets gather.*
> *An enviable sight! What better time*
> *To be among the silks and the perfumes!*
> *In the gentle breezes of the warm night,*
> *Midst flowers and cheerful laughter,*
> *Hair ornaments twirl around with the hats*
> *In clusters all over the place.*
> *How wonderful! The capital's old glory*
> *Shines again in these times of peace!*

Everywhere were people out to view the lanterns, and every household indulged in fun and frolic. All this merriment brought about the romance that makes up our story.

It is said that in Tuyan Lane there lived a talented young man by the name of Ruan Hua. Being the third son of the family, he was known as Ruan Sanlang

[Ruan the Third Young Master]. His eldest brother, Ruan Da, was a merchant who constantly traveled with their father, as they plied their trade between the Western Capital and the Eastern Capital.[3] The second son was in charge of the household. The third, Ruan San, was an eighteen-year-old, refined and graceful in bearing, well versed in poetry of every style, and a virtuoso in the playing of the *xiao*.[4] In the company of several sons of the wealthy, he sought pleasure every day in song-houses and brothels. On this night of the Lantern Festival, he invited several friends to his home and, while admiring the lanterns, sang and played the *sheng*[5] and the *xiao* until the third watch of the night. When bidding his friends good-bye at the gate, Ruan San saw that all was quiet, with few pedestrians about, and that the moonlight was as bright as day. "How can we go to sleep and miss out on such a beautiful night?" he exclaimed. "Why don't we play one more song?" They agreed and sat down right on the stone curb facing the moon, took out their *sheng, xiao,* and ivory clappers and started the music and the singing again. Truly,

> *If walls have ears,*
> *How can windows have no eyes?*

The Ruan house was right across from Marshal Chen's residence. After some fun at the festival, the young lady Yulan was about to retire for the night when she heard, from the street, music that seemed to resound all the way up to the clouds. Thinking that the other members of the house had already gone to sleep by this time of night, she called a maid and, gently directing her steps to the gate, listened for a while. Her emotions stirred up by the music, she told Green Cloud, a trusted maid, in a low voice, "Go out for me and find out who they are." Only too eager to be of service to her mistress, the maid readily obliged and walked cautiously to the street. Upon recognizing the young master of the residence opposite, she hurried back and reported, "It's Ruan San of the house across the street, playing and singing at his gate with some friends."

The young lady, without saying anything out loud for quite some time, thought to herself, "This must be the Ruan San that Father mentioned a few days ago. Father said he was a candidate for the emperor's son-in-law but was rejected and sent back home because of his lack of connections. His talents and looks would naturally be out of the ordinary." After she listened for nearly two more hours, all went back to their separate quarters, and she also retired to her boudoir, but she could not sleep a wink the whole night through. All her thoughts were with Ruan San: "Married life would be worthwhile if I could have such a handsome man for a husband. How can I arrange to meet him, if only a single time?" Indeed,

The neighbor girl fixed on Song Yu her furtive gaze;[6]
Wenjun's mind strayed away from the musical notes.[7]

To resume our story, at dawn the following day, Ruan San and his friends went to amuse themselves at the Monastery of Eternal Bliss. Amorous thoughts rose in his mind at the sight of the endless stream of beautiful women making offerings of incense. Back at home that evening, he again gathered the same group of friends to amuse themselves with their own music. This went on every night until that of the twentieth, when his friends, for various reasons, failed to show up at his home. In a small room next to the gate facing the street, a bored Ruan San took a purple bamboo *xiao* down from the wall and, playing the five notes of the musical scale, began a popular new tune. He was barely halfway through the tune when, suddenly, a maid pushed open the door and entered with a deep curtsy. Ruan San stopped his playing and asked, "Which family are you from?"

"I am Green Cloud, personal maid of the daughter of Mr. Chen of the residence across the street. My mistress secretly admires you and told me to ask for a date with you."

Ruan San thought to himself, "That's an official's residence with no lack of watchful eyes. Going in would be easy, but coming out would be a problem. What am I supposed to say if asked questions when I'm seen? Wouldn't I be humiliated for nothing?" With these thoughts in mind, he replied, "Please tell your mistress that it would be inconvenient for me to enter and leave her house, so I can't very well comply with her wish," whereupon Green Cloud turned back and relayed the message to her mistress.

Recalling the charm of the music that she heard nightly, the young lady was overcome by a wave of passion. She took off from her finger a gem-inlaid gold ring and handed it to Green Cloud. "Take this to Ruan Sanlang and bring him to me. Assure him that absolutely no harm will come to him." The ring in hand, her heart anxious as a flying arrow, her feet moving as if on wings, Green Cloud scurried to Ruan San's small room.

When Green Cloud produced the ring and conveyed the mistress's message, Ruan San thought, without saying a word, "Since I have this thing as evidence and the maid as a guide, what do I have to fear?" Thereupon, he followed Green Cloud to the side gate of the Chen residence, where the young lady was already waiting. She stared in fascination at him, and he also fixed his gaze on her. They were on the point of exchanging words when a cry came from outside the gate: "The marshal has returned to the residence!" The young lady hastened back to her room, and Ruan Sanlang also ran home as fast as his legs could carry him.

Thereafter, he wore the ring tightly on a finger of his left hand. Memory of the young lady filled him with tender longing, which was all the more tormenting because of the virtual impossibility of communicating with her, secluded as she was in the depths of her boudoir. Wherever he was, whether at home or away, the sight of the ring brought pain to his heart. Having no grounds for another date, he was left with only his memory to cherish. Though inferior in status to sons of highly placed officials, Ruan San was nonetheless a talented and quick-witted young man from an affluent family. But as the days wore on, the lovelorn Ruan San gradually grew emaciated from insomnia and loss of appetite. In less than three months, he became a very sick man. However relentlessly his parents questioned him, he refused to say a word. Truly,

> *Like a mute tasting bitterness,*
> *He suffered alone in silence.*

There was a young man named Zhang Yuan, from a family as rich as the Ruans, who had a long-standing friendship with Ruan San. Worried upon hearing about Ruan San's prolonged illness, he came one morning to the Ruan residence for a visit. Lying in bed, Ruan San heard a voice in the hall that sounded like Zhang Yuan's, whereupon he summoned a servant to invite the visitor into his room. The sight of a sallow and gaunt Ruan San coughing up phlegm filled Zhang's heart with grief. He sat down on the bed and heaved sigh after sigh. "Elder Brother," he said, "it's been just a few days since I saw you last. What brought about such ill luck? What illness is this?"

Ruan San shook his head but remained silent. "Elder Brother," continued Zhang Yuan, "give me your hand and let me feel your pulse." Forgetting himself, Ruan San raised his left hand for Zhang Yuan. As he pressed his hand on Ruan's wrist, Zhang Yuan's eyes chanced to rest upon the gem-inlaid gold ring on the sick man's finger. Without uttering a word, Zhang thought to himself, "As gravely ill as he is, he's still holding on to this thing. What's more, it's not what a man would normally wear. It must be a keepsake from a woman. I suppose that's the root cause of the illness." Instead of talking about Ruan San's pulse, he asked, "Elder Brother, where did the ring on your finger come from? Such illness should not be taken lightly. You are so good as to have treated me as a friend for all these years. Since we have shared the innermost secrets in our daily lives and understand each other's mind, why don't you tell me what really happened?"

Seeing that Zhang Yuan had already guessed eighty to ninety percent of the story and was a trusted friend after all, Ruan San felt obliged to tell him everything. Zhang Yuan reasoned, "Elder Brother, even though she's from an official's family, without this keepsake, you wouldn't know if she were willing even if you met her face to face. But this keepsake makes all the difference.

After you have recovered your health, count on me to come up with a plan to fulfill your wish."

"This is exactly what caused my illness," Ruan San professed. "The only way to cure me is to work out something as soon as possible." He then withdrew from beneath his pillow two ingots of silver and, handing them to Zhang Yuan, said, "Don't spare this trivial sum if there's a need for it." Zhang Yuan took the silver and promised, "Give me some time. I'll let you know as soon as there's good news. In the meantime, rest easy and take care!"

After taking leave of his friend, Zhang Yuan dallied for about four hours in front of the Chen residence. As he did not see any acquaintances among the many people who entered and left the house, he went home with a heavy heart.

The following day, he went again to look for an opportunity but found none. (*Willing to go to such trouble, he is a loyal friend indeed.*) He thought to himself, "It would be hard to bring the matter up with anyone else but Green Cloud, if and when she comes out." It was already late in the day when he saw a man leave the house with two porcelain jars, crying, "Where's the errand boy of the house frittering away his time? The mistress wants you to send these two jars of vegetables to Reverend Mother Wang of Leisurely Clouds Nunnery." (*Good twist in the plot.*)

As he heard this, Zhang Yuan thought, "Why, I know Wang the nun of Leisurely Clouds Nunnery! Since the mistress of the house sends her food, she must be quite close to the family. Someone like her who has access to the residence could serve as an excellent messenger. Why don't I go and talk with her?"

Another night went by. The following morning, equipped with the two ingots of silver, he proceeded to Leisurely Clouds Nunnery. Though small, the nunnery was tastefully laid out. How do we know this? There is a poem that bears witness:

> A short fence-wall and a small pavilion,
> With bamboo leaves rustling over half the eaves.
> The heart is calm where no mortal dust falls;
> Nothing but a wisp of incense and two sutra texts.

The nun, named Wang Shouchang, had been a woman of easy virtue before converting to Buddhism. As her mentor had only recently left the world, she had not yet acquired any disciples except for the two maids responsible for burning incense and attending the stoves. The nun sought alms only from the affluent. Of the three new statues of Guanyin [the bodhisattva Avalokitesvara], Manjusri, and Samantabhadra at the back of the nunnery, the middle one, Guanyin, was gilded thanks to a kind donation from Mrs. Chen. The other two images were still without a benefactor. On this particular day, the nun was just leaving the nunnery gate when she ran into Zhang Yuan. "Where might Master Zhang be heading?" she asked.

"I am here to see you," was the reply.

The nun turned back and invited him to take a seat in the main hall.

"Where were you going, Reverend Mother?" asked Zhang Yuan after tea.

"Thanks to the munificence of Madame Chen, the holy statue of Guanyin has been completed, but I haven't thanked her for it. Yesterday she was again kind enough to have sent me some vegetables. So, I was thinking of preparing some small gifts to take to her residence tomorrow as a token of gratitude. Her generosity is still needed for the other two statues. As I am short of people to run errands for me, I have to do things myself, even if it's just to buy a few trifles."

"What a good opportunity!" Zhang Yuan thought to himself. He then said to the nun, "Reverend Mother, I have a bosom friend from a rich family. It won't be a problem to ask him to take care of the other two holy statues all by himself, except that a favor needs to be asked of you." He took out the two ingots of silver from his sleeves, put them on the incense table, and continued, "This much silver is but a start. After the job is done, you can build nunneries and temples to your heart's content."

The nun was a greedy soul. Radiant with smiles at the sight of the silver, which was of the finest quality, she asked, "Who is this person you know? What can I do for him?"

Zhang Yuan said, "This is strictly confidential. Only you can pull it off. If convenient, let's go to a room where we will not be overheard." He then stuffed the two ingots of silver into the nun's sleeves. It was not without some initial show of reluctance that the nun accepted. (*Don't do what Pan Bizheng and Chen Miaochang did.*)[8] The two entered a small room and sat down in front of a bamboo couch.

"That bosom friend of mine, Mr. Ruan San," explained Zhang, "received through a maid a keepsake from Marshal Chen's daughter. That happened in the first month of this year, but so far they have had no chance for a date. Since you are going to see the lady of the Chen residence tomorrow, you'll be doing him a favor if you could take the opportunity to go to the daughter's room and find an excuse for her to set up a date with him in your nunnery."

After a few moments of reflection, she said, "I won't presume to make casual promises. Let me think about what to do after I meet the young lady and observe her reaction. What did you just say about a keepsake?"

"It's a gold ring inlaid with a gem," said Zhang Yuan.

"I'd like to borrow it for the time being. I will try to work out something."

Zhang was elated that the nun accepted the silver without much demur.

After taking leave of her, he went to Ruan San, asked for his gold ring, and delivered it to the nun before the night was out.

Our story now goes back to the nun. Having turned the matter over in her mind for half the night, she rose at daybreak and, after finishing her toilette, put the ring on her left finger and, with a maid carrying the gift box on a pole, wended her way to the Chen residence. They headed straight for the back chamber, where they sat down for a rest.

No sooner had she caught sight of them than Madam Chen exclaimed, "How could a nun be made to go to such expense?"

With a bow, the nun said, "Thanks to your generosity, the holy statue of Guanyin has been completed. Blessed are the gates of the nunnery! This poor nun was just about to come to offer you thanks when I was again overwhelmed with another benefaction yesterday. My gratitude is boundless."

The lady said, "I remember you said that you had no good dishes to go with porridge. It so happened that a man from south of the Yangzi River sent us a few jars of squash and other vegetables, and I gave you two. Why thank me for such trifles?"

Joining her palms, the nun said, "Amitabha Buddha! Even a drop of water shouldn't be easily wiped off. Though we nuns live off alms from everywhere, we find it hard to take things for granted."

The lady said, "The statues as a group would look better with the middle one gilded. I will certainly also help you with the other two statues."

"I am most indebted to you for you benefaction. Your wealth in this life is the result of charity in your previous life. More gifts of charity will ensure you prosperity and affluence in your next life as well."

Madam Chen had a maid put away the gift box and told the kitchen staff to prepare a vegetarian lunch for the nun.

In a short while, Madam Chen partook of the vegetarian meal with the nun, her daughter sitting by their side. After lunch, the nun pronounced, "This humble nun will now venture to extend an invitation. Since the holy statue at the nunnery has now been completed, I have picked the eighth day of the fourth month, the birthday of the Buddha, for a ceremony to paint the eyes on the holy statue. Madam and the young lady are invited to honor us with your presence on the occasion."

"I will certainly come for the worship of Buddha," said Madam Chen, "but my daughter can't very well come."

The nun knitted her brows, and a plan came to her mind. "I had a bout of diarrhea the day before yesterday that has not quite gone yet. May I use your lavatory?"

The young mistress, still yearning for Ruan San, was in low spirits.

Without anything to do to take her mind off her misery, she was overjoyed at the nun's invitation and was on the point of saying something when she heard her mother voice her disapproval. Now that the nun wanted to relieve herself, Yulan saw her chance for a private talk with the nun. "I'll take you there," she offered, whereupon the two made straight for the young lady's boudoir. Verily,

> Evil comes out of talks on the sly;
> Furtive dealings breed nothing but vice.

Sitting on the nightstool, the nun said, "Would you be willing to come with your mother on the eighth of the month to my nunnery?"

"How I wish I could come! Only my parents might not allow me to."

"If you insist," advised the nun, "your mother might concede, and if she approves, you'll have nothing to fear from the marshal." As she spoke, the nun reached out for toilet paper and in doing so, deliberately displayed the gold ring on her finger.

Startled at the sight, the young lady asked, "Where did you get this ring?"

The nun replied, "Two months ago, a refined-looking young man who came into the nunnery to look at the statue of Guanyin took off this ring from his finger, put it on the boddhisattva's finger, and offered this prayer: 'If I cannot have my wish granted in this life, I pray that I will meet her in my next one.' There he stood tearfully in front of the statue for a long time. It was after I pressed him for an answer that he said, 'I will tell you only if you will find the other ring that forms a pair with this one.'" (*There she goes with the tricks of a procuress.*)

The young lady blushed deeply at this mention of her secret. After a while, unable to contain herself, she asked again, "What's the name of the young man? Does he often go to your nunnery?"

"His name is Ruan," replied the nun. "He comes to the nunnery from time to time to look around."

The young lady said, "I have a ring that happens to form a pair with his." She opened a jewel box, took out a ring inlaid with gems, and handed it over to the nun, who compared the two and broke out into laughter upon finding them identical.

"Why do you laugh?"

"I'm laughing at the young man," said the nun. "There he was, obsessed with the desire to find the other ring, and now that it has been found, I wonder what he'll say."

The young lady said, "Reverend Mother, I would like to—" She caught herself without finishing the sentence.

"The first and foremost virtue of us nuns is discretion," said the nun. "Whatever you say will be safe with me."

"I would like to see him. Would that be possible?"

"So, his prayers to Buddha must have been for your sake," exclaimed the nun. "That can be easily done. You will surely meet him on the eighth day of the fourth month."

"How do I get away from my mother, even if my parents allow me to go?" asked the young lady.

"On the day you come to the nunnery," whispered the nun into her ear, "when relaxing after lunch, just say that you need a nap, and the rest will work out."

The young lady nodded in understanding and gave the nun her ring as a donation.

"The gold," said the nun, "can be used to gild the statues. I guarantee that everything will turn out as you wish." With these words, the two emerged from the room.

Mrs. Chen, upon seeing them, asked, "You were in the room for a long time. What were you talking about?"

The much-startled nun hastened to answer, her heart pounding, "The young lady asked me about the origin of the custom of washing the Buddha's statue upon his birthday, and my explanation is what took so long." She added, "As the young lady also wishes to pay her respects to the holy statues, please inform the marshal so that she can come with you." Mrs. Chen escorted her out of the hall, and the nun, with a deep curtsy of gratitude, bade the mistress goodbye. Verily, she was

> An old hand at employing sure-fire plots
> To pair off young couples.

After leaving the Chen residence with the gold ring that the young lady had given her, the nun betook herself to Zhang Yuan's home. Zhang had been waiting for her at the door for a long time. Seeing her from a distance, he thought to himself without saying anything out loud, "We can't very well bring up this matter here, in the presence of so many people," whereupon he took a few hurried steps in her direction, saying, "Please be so kind as to return to the nunnery, Reverend Mother. I'll join you there immediately." The nun thus turned back into another lane. After having threaded his way through the alleys, Zhang Yuan met the nun at the nunnery and was invited into a room, where the nun gave him a full account of all of the details and handed the pair of rings to him.

"If it weren't for you, this would not have been possible," said Zhang Yuan. "Master Ruan San will surely repay you handsomely." Zhang Yuan went straight to report to Ruan San. The latter's happiness when putting this second ring on the other hand goes without saying.

On the seventh day of the fourth month, the nun again went to the Chen residence to repeat the invitation: "Because of the visit of Madam and the young lady, this poor nun has declined all other benefactors. There will be no other visitors tomorrow. Please be sure to come early."

Pestered by her daughter from morning to night with her pleas to worship Buddha, Mrs. Chen had no alternative but to give her consent. That evening, Zhang Yuan proceeded first to Ruan San's place. In the quiet of the evening, a woman's sedan-chair was carried surreptitiously into the nunnery. The nun ushered them in and put Ruan San up for the night in a secluded room. Indeed,

> *Like pigs and sheep on their way to the butcher's,*
> *With each step they went nearer to their death.*

The nun rose at the fifth watch and woke up the maid. Incense was burned, candles were lit in front of the statues of the Buddha, and breakfast preparations got under way. At the break of day, she summoned a painter to paint the eyes on the holy statue and, for the convenience of the female visitors, sent him away by breakfast time. Only nuns were allowed into the hall for sutra-chanting sessions.

Mrs. Chen and the young lady came by sedan-chair at about nine in the morning. The nun hastened to greet them, and led them into the hall. After tea was over, they went to the front and the back of the nunnery for incense burning and worshipping Buddha. Mrs. Chen was pleased that there were no other visitors. The nun invited the whole entourage to sit in a small room, assigning each a seat. She then took Mrs. Chen and the young lady on a walking tour of the temple before returning for lunch. Noticing that her daughter ate little and looked drowsy after lunch, Mrs. Chen said, "Child, you must have gotten up too early this morning."

"Madam," said the nun with great alacrity, "this nunnery is absolutely free of unauthorized people. Even well-behaved women are not allowed into my private chamber. The young lady can take a nap in my room in all privacy with the door bolted while Madam can take a leisurely walk. Since it's so seldom that you come, please do make yourselves comfortable!"

"Child, how sleepy you look! It would indeed be better if you go and take a nap in the Reverend Mother's chamber."

Complying with her mother's order, the young lady walked into the room. No sooner had she bolted the door than she saw Ruan San emerge from behind the bed, saying with a deep bow, "Sister, I have been waiting for you for quite some time."

Waving her hand in alarm, the young lady said under her breath, "Not so loud!" Ruan San took a few steps back while the young lady advanced until they held each other's hands. Then the two went around the bed and, through

a side door, entered another room, where there was a small and exquisite lac-
quered table and a wicker bed, safe from any peeping eyes. They embraced.
After a few tender words, both loosened their clothes and, as eager as thirsty
dragons at the sight of water, fulfilled their desires to the utmost, as attested
by a lyric poem to the tune of "The Moon over the West River":

> She recalled the delightful xiao music;
> He was filled with gratitude for the ring.
> Both suffered from longing for half a year,
> And rejoiced at the meeting.
> He was weak from his illness,
> She ready to lose her virginity.
> The groans at the pillow did not cease,
> But the ecstasy ended all too soon.

As it was, Ruan San was afflicted with a prolonged illness brought on by
his yearning for this girl. At the rendezvous, he was so overcome by desire that
his life was put in jeopardy. As for the woman, tormented as she had been by
the lack of a chance to meet him, she now did the best she could to please him
and experienced the very height of love. Little did they know that their ecstasy
was to end in sorrow. He lost his yang, his life force. In a moment, he ceased
to breathe. His seven earthly souls scattered, and his spiritual souls returned
to the netherworld. (*Ruan San is meant to die at this moment, and the death is
worthwhile, too. If Yulan could have died with him, he would have been able to
find greater peace in death.*) This truly bears out the saying

> In nature there are unexpected storms;
> In life, there are unforeseen vicissitudes.

When she felt Ruan San lying motionless on top of her, she put her arms
tightly around his waist and stuck her tongue into his mouth, only to find
that his teeth were tightly clenched and his body icy cold all over. The young
lady wallowing in pleasure a moment ago was now overcome by panic from
head to toe. She turned the body over, pushed it to the other side of the bed
against the wall, hurriedly got dressed, and went into the antechamber, closing
the side door after her. Still panting in great agitation and afraid that her mother
might come for her, she started redoing her makeup in front of the dresser
mirror. She had barely finished when her mother's voice came from outside.
Without a moment's delay, she pulled the door open.

"Child," said Mrs. Chen, "the sutra-chanting session in the hall is over.
Did you just wake up?"

"I slept for a while and was just adjusting my hairpins to get ready to
return home with you."

"The sedan-chair carriers have been waiting for a long time," said Mrs. Chen.

The young lady and her mother thanked the nun, mounted the sedan-chair, and went back home, and there I shall leave them.

Let me now turn to Wang Shouchang the nun, who, after seeing the visitors off, returned to the nunnery, washed the dishes and utensils in the kitchen, and put away the incense and offerings. After everything had been put in order, Zhang Yuan and Ruan Er [Second Brother Ruan] entered the nunnery and thanked the nun profusely. "Where's my brother?" asked Ruan Er.

"Still sleeping in my room." So saying, the nun led Ruan Er and Zhang Yuan to her room, opened the side door, and called out, "Third Brother! How well you sleep!" There was no answer to the repeated cries. Ruan Er pushed the body with his hand, but there was no motion. No breath was coming out from the nose and the mouth. Upon a closer look, they realized that he was dead. Ruan Er cried in horror, "Reverend Mother, why is my brother dead? You're going to hear more from me!"

In panic, the nun explained, "The young lady said she needed a nap after lunch and entered this room, where she stayed for a few hours. She left just a while ago when the old lady woke her up after the sutra-chanting session was over in the hall. I thought they were asleep. How could I have known that such a thing had happened!"

"You may very well say so, but what's to be done?" asked Ruan Er.

"Master Ruan Er," said the nun. "Luckily, Master Zhang is here with us. It was in accordance with Master Zhang's instructions that I planned the whole thing, hoping that your family's generosity would benefit this nunnery. You can't accuse me of murdering your brother. Master Zhang, what happened today all started from your coming to ask me for a favor, and not the other way around. If this goes to court, both you and I will be hurt. Of the two ingots of silver you gave me, I spent one. The remaining one I dare not keep. It can be used toward buying a coffin for the funeral. Just say that he was recuperating from his illness in the nunnery but died unexpectedly." So saying, she took out the ingot of silver and laid it on the table. "The two of you are free to do whatever you want with it."

The two men were at a loss for words. After some moments of silence, Ruan Er said, "Let's first buy a coffin before we talk about the next thing to do." Zhang Yuan took the silver and, with Ruan Er at his side, walked out of the nunnery into the winding alleys. "Second Brother, the nun is not to blame for this," said Zhang Yuan to Ruan Er. "Brother San was of weak constitution and must have overexerted himself with the woman. Loss of yang would naturally lead to death. I had to do this for him out of our friendship, because there was no way I could resist his pleading when I was at his bedside the other day."

Ruan Er replied, "As I see it, in all fairness, neither you nor the Reverend Mother is to blame. It's my brother's fate and the doings of the gods that he should end like this. I am quite reconciled to it. My only fear is that my father and my elder brother might make a fuss when they come back."

Before the night was out, the two of them bought a coffin, carried it to the nunnery, put the body in it, and placed it in the west corridor so that Squire Ruan and the eldest brother could make a final decision upon their return. Truly,

A feast about to end loses its fun;
A man of ill fate does nothing but sigh.

There came the day when Squire Ruan and the eldest son returned from their business trip. The whole family rejoiced when the two met with the lady of the house. At the father's inquiry about the third son's illness, Ruan Er had no choice but to give a detailed account of the whole incident. The father wailed with grief upon hearing of his son's death and wanted to write a complaint to the court to have Chen's daughter pay for the young man's death. "It's that cheap hussy who seduced my son!" he cried.

The two brothers tried to pacify him: "Father, if we think about it, it's our brother's own fault that he lost his life. If you sue the Chen family, we are no match for them in terms of power and influence on the one hand, and, on the other hand, this really does not concern the marshal." Under their persuasion, Squire Ruan relented. On a chosen date, the funeral was held in the nunnery and the body was sent outside the city for burial.

Let me now describe how, more than a month after her return from Leisurely Clouds Nunnery, Miss Chen began to experience nausea, fatigue, and a craving for pickles. Three months went by without menstruation. The doctor's prescriptions on regulation of menstrual functions had no effect.

"Child," asked the mother discreetly, "Did you do anything improper? Tell me the truth."

Realizing that she could not keep it a secret any longer, the young lady had no other recourse but to tell her mother what had really happened.

The mother was aghast. "Your father meant to get you an honorable and talented man, so as to rely upon you to provide for him in his old age until he dies. What's to be done now that you've caused such a scandal? What will happen if your father finds out about this?"

"Mother, now that things have come to this, I have no other way out but to die."

Mrs. Chen's heart twinged with pain.

When he returned home that night, the marshal saw that his wife looked distressed. "What's bothering you today?" he asked.

"There's one thing that's preying on my mind."

"What is it?"

Seeing that she would not be able to ward off his questions, Mrs. Chen told him everything. All would have been well if Mr. Chen had not heard of this, but as it was, he boiled with rage. "If you, as a mother, can't keep an eye on the child, what good are you?" Reduced to tears, she dared not retort.

After a sleepless night turning the matter over and over in his mind, Mr. Chen left at daybreak to attend to some business. Upon returning home, he consulted his wife. "We have to work out something today. A lawsuit would bring shame on our girl and tarnish the reputation of the family. We'll have to talk it over with the girl."

The daughter hung her head in silence, tears streaming down her cheeks. After a while, she pulled her mother to a quiet and secluded place, saying, "It was my fault that Ruan Sanlang died. I would have killed myself if I had not been three months pregnant with his child, and yet, if I don't take my own life, I will be held up for ridicule." She continued between sobs, "A better option is to carry the child to full term, be it a boy or a girl, so that Ruan San will have someone to carry on his name. I owe him this for the sake of our love. A woman should remain faithful to one man until death. However brief, it was a moment of married life. I will never marry another man. Should heaven take pity on me and let me have a son, I will bring him up and give him back to the Ruan family when he is of age so as to acquit myself of my obligation as a wife. I will then take my own life as a punishment for the disgrace that I've brought to my parents." (*Pitiable.*)

Mrs. Chen repeated these words to the marshal, who only heaved a helpless sigh. However, he quietly sent for Squire Ruan to come to his home for a discussion of the situation. He said, "It was because I did not discipline my daughter strictly enough that she did such a shocking thing behind our backs and took your son's life, but I won't dwell more on this. Now, my daughter is three months pregnant with his child. What is to be done? We'll just say that my daughter was betrothed to your son. Upon meeting each other in Leisurely Clouds Nunnery, they consummated their love because the young man had already been pining away for her love and was almost on the verge of death. Thus, with a legitimate betrothal, the birth of a child will be less of a scandal." (*A proposal made in desperation, but a reasonable one, nonetheless.*) Squire Ruan agreed, and from then on, the two families began to pay mutual visits.

When the pregnancy reached its full term in the tenth month, Squire Ruan sent over gifts to give blessing to the birth. Sure enough, a boy was born. When the boy reached three years of age, the young lady told her mother of her wish to take the child to pay their respects to her parents-in-law and visit Ruan San's grave. Mrs. Chen conveyed the request to her husband, who gave his consent. An auspicious day was chosen for the visit. The young lady pre-pared some gifts and went to pay her respects to Mr. and Mrs. Ruan. On the following day, she tearfully made offerings at Ruan San's grave and then, to honor the memory of her deceased husband, took out some silver and hired eminent priests for a grand prayer service for all dead souls on land and in water. That night, Ruan San appeared to her in a dream.

"Do you know that there was a predestined reason for what happened?" asked he. "In our previous existence, you were a courtesan in Yangzhou and I was a native of Jinling visiting relatives there. I fell deeply in love with you and promised to return in one year to take you as my wife. After going back home, however, I made no mention of my intention to my father, for fear of his anger, and married another woman instead, thereby doing you great harm. You waited in vain day and night for my return and eventually died of a bro-ken heart. Since our predestined relationship was not severed, our brief meet-ing at Leisurely Clouds Nunnery rekindled our love. It was with the intention of demanding payment for the injustice you suffered in your previous exis-tence that you went to the nunnery. My immediate death evened our score. Thanks to your sincere commemoration, I have found a good family to be reborn into. It was with high aspirations and moral integrity that you ended your previous life. You are therefore entitled to glory and wealth in this one. Your child is bound to be a prominent figure in the future. Raise him well. From now on, think no more of me." In her dream, the young lady Yulan grabbed Ruan San, but before she could ask him where he was going to be reincarnated, Ruan San had pushed her away. She woke up with a start and sighed in wonderment at the knowledge that life, death, and love were all decided by debts in one's previous life.

From that time on, the young lady thought no more of her love but devoted her whole heart to the raising of her son. Time shot by like an arrow. Before one realized it, the boy was already six years old. He was as handsome as Ruan San and was also endowed with intelligence. Marshal Chen cherished him as he would a lustrous pearl in his palm. Using his own surname, he gave the boy the name of Chen Zongruan[9] and hired a tutor for him. By age six-teen, as was expected, the boy was already an erudite scholar. The books he had studied could fill up five wagons and the caves of the two You Mountains.[10] At age nineteen, he sat for the imperial examinations and won first honor as a zhuangyuan. By order of the emperor, he returned to his hometown to take a wife. The Chen and Ruan families vied with each other in welcoming him to their homes, which were filled with guests and friends. They took turns hold-ing celebration feasts in his honor. At the time when he was born, those neigh-bors who had heard something had wagged their tongues and mocked the family behind their backs. But now that the boy Chen Zongruan had achieved instant fame, they turned around and praised Yulan for her chastity, wisdom, her good upbringing of her now-famous son, and her other virtues. Such are the ways of the world that people are judged mostly by their success or failure. When promoted to the post of acting minister of personnel, Chen Zongruan composed a memorial to the emperor, in which he commended his mother for having maintained widowhood since the age of nineteen and for having brought up her son who had now risen to fame. He also requested the erection of a memorial archway in her honor. (*True virtue, indeed.*) This is truly a case of "A poor family can do nothing, but a rich family can make the demons grind its mill." Even though this is true, Miss Chen did preserve her chastity, which sufficiently covered up her disgrace with a "brocade quilt." Her story is still being told with admiration in Henan even to this day. There is a poem that bears witness:

> *In Tuyan Lane, he fell sick with love;*
> *At Leisurely Clouds, he paid off his debt.*
> *Her virtue alone made it all end well*
> *And covered up the disgrace with a brocade quilt.*

世人尚口我尚足
口易必波瀾能涉陸
重下不傾千至萬
遞勞重賞薄寡言迎
奉酬之以酒慰爾懷

Worldly men venerate the mouth;
I alone revere the feet.
The mouth stirs up waves;
The feet tread solid ground.
Lowly as they are, they never fail me,

But carry me over thousands of li.
For such service, they get little reward;
With no complaint, they endure the abuse.
With wine I thank you
For all that you've gone through.

Penniless Ma Zhou Meets His Opportunity through a Woman Selling Pancakes

The future is a mystery hidden from view.
Autumn moon and spring flower, each has its season.
Just submit yourself to the word of heaven.
Why bustle around, night and day?

Our story takes place after Emperor Taizong of the great Tang dynasty ascended the throne and changed the reign title to Zhenguan [627–49]. The emperor, a benevolent and enlightened ruler, enlisted worthy men to serve in his imperial court. A veritable galaxy of talents it was, with the eighteen academicians of the civil administration[1] and the eighteen regional military commanders.[2] All men with ability and wisdom throughout the land gained office through recommendation and achieved their aspirations to the full. As a result, peace reigned in the empire and the populace lived in contentment.

Of all these men, our story is about a certain Ma Zhou, courtesy name Binwang. He was a native of Chiping in Bozhou Prefecture. Bereaved of both his parents, he was a penniless bachelor in his thirties, living all by himself. Well versed from an early age in the classics and histories, he was an erudite scholar with the highest aspirations and unparalleled knowledge about strategies. His poverty and lack of friends were the only reasons he received no recommendations for office. Indeed, he was not unlike a divine dragon bogged down in mud, unable to soar into the air. (*How sad that such is the common fate of all too many worthy men, past and present!*) Watching those with far less talent rise to prominence and wealth, he brooded over his failure to gain recognition and sighed every day to himself, "It is all a matter of timing, luck, and fate." Having a large capacity for wine throughout the years, he spent his hours of depression drinking, stopping only when he had drunk himself into a stupor. He did not mind the uncertainty of his daily meals—wine was the one thing he could not do without. At times when he ran out of money for wine, he would find out which neighbors had wine and go there for a free drink. In his flamboyant and careless way, after drinking he would rant and rave like a demented man. (*The wise pity him for his lack of better things to do. The undiscerning question his morals.*) None of the neighbors could stand such outbursts of madness and the streams of curses. Behind his back, they called him Penniless Ma Zhou and "the drunkard," but he did not take these sobriquets to heart in the slightest when they did reach his ears. Truly,

> Before the dragon met the tiger,[3]
> He ignored what horses and oxen called him.

Now, the prefect of Bozhou, named Da Xi, having long heard of Ma Zhou's reputation as a fine scholar, employed him as prefectural instructor. (*This prefect qualifies as one who does not resent the talented.*) On the day he arrived to assume the post, as the scholars brought wine for a celebration, Ma Zhou unwittingly took a drop too much. The following day, the prefect made a personal appearance at the college to ask for instruction, only to find him in an inebriated state, unable to stand up on his feet. The prefect stormed out in a rage. Upon waking up and learning that the prefect had been there, Ma Zhou went to the prefectural yamen to apologize. As the prefect lectured him long and hard, Ma Zhou humbly uttered promises to change his ways—promises that he failed to keep. Every time a student came along to ask him questions about the classics, Ma Zhou would keep him for a drink. Even though all of his salary was spent in the wineshops, he still could not have enough and reverted to his old habit of freeloading. Now it was his students whom he imposed himself upon.

One day, tipsy with wine and supported on both sides by two students, he sang all the way back home. (*A vivid scene.*) By coincidence, halfway down the road, they ran into the procession of the prefect and his entourage. The advance guards sharply ordered him to get out of the way, but he would not hear of it. With dilated eyes, he shot back angry words, only to bring on another burst of rage from the prefect right there on the street. Ma Zhou was too drunk to be aware of much that happened, but after he woke up the following day, his students came to advise him to apologize to the prefect. With a sigh, he said, "Poor and friendless as I am, I submitted myself to the will of others out of wishes for advancement. (*Speaking the truth.*) Now that I have been humiliated time and again by the prefect for my excessive drinking, how can I face him again and bow deeply to ask for mercy? A worthy man in olden times refused to stoop low for the sake of five piculs of rice,[4] nor will this position as prefectural instructor hold me here for the rest of my life." So saying, he handed his robe of office over to the student for him to give it back to the prefect. Then he threw back his head and gave a hearty guffaw before he went out the door. (*Like a true hero.*) Truly,

He left to find better use for his tongue;
To return would be to lose all dignity.

As the ancients said, "It is the rapids that make water surge; it is insults that arouse men to action." Humiliation from the prefect over his drinking made Ma Zhou leave his residence with a sigh. He went to a certain place where he met someone through whose good offices he rose to be the minister of personnel, but this happened later.

To come back to our story, where was he to go? He dismissed the thought of roaming around the country, for lack of opportunities of advancement. The best course of action was to go to Chang'an, capital of the empire, where, among the multitudes of dukes and princes, there might be someone like Prime Minister Xiao He[5] or Wei Wuzhi,[6] known for his readiness to recognize and recommend talent. Only then could he be pulled out of his misery and realize the dream of his life. He headed for the west and, before many days had passed, arrived in Xinfeng.

The city of Xinfeng [New Feng] was founded by Emperor Gaozu,[7] who, a native of Feng, had led an armed uprising, overthrew the Qin empire, conquered Xiang Yu [another contender for the throne], and became the Son of Heaven of the Han dynasty. While living in Chang'an the emperor's father, honored as the Imperial Patriarch, grew nostalgic for the scenes of his native place. Consequently, the emperor ordered skilled craftsmen to build a new city modeled on Feng and relocated Feng residents to the new city, where the layout of all the streets, marketplaces, and houses was identical to that of Feng, so that even all the chickens and dogs, if left on the streets, could still find their way home. The Imperial Patriarch was immensely delighted and named the city Xinfeng. Chang'an having resumed its status as the capital of the empire in the new dynasty of Tang, Xinfeng also came to life as a bustling and prosperous city this side of the Pass, with goodness knows how many inns and hostels for traveling merchants.

By the time Ma Zhou arrived in Xinfeng, dusk had already set in. He picked a large inn and entered at a leisurely pace. There, for all to see, was a stream of horse carriages stirring up clouds of dust. A great many merchants with boxes of merchandise on their shoulders followed upon each other's heels into the inn. Mr. Wang the innkeeper greeted his guests, busily assigned them to their rooms, and directed the traffic of luggage carriers while the guests found their way to their seats at the tables. The waiters ran around with their orders for food and wine, as busy as horses on a revolving lantern. Ma Zhou sat all alone by himself, without getting the slightest attention. (*Such are the snobbish ways of the world.*) In anger, he slapped the table and thundered, "Innkeeper! This is unfair! Am I not also a guest? Why am I not being served?"

Hearing this outburst of anger, Mr. Wang came over to placate him, saying, "Honorable guest, please do not be angry. I had to take care of the big party over there, thinking that since you are all by yourself, your needs should be easily accommodated. Now please tell me what you need for dinner."

"I haven't washed my feet all along the way," said Ma Zhou. "Bring me some clean warm water."

Mr. Wang said, "The pots are all being used. You'll have to wait a while for warm water."

"In that case, bring me some wine first."

"How much wine?"

Pointing at the party gathered around a large table across from him, Ma Zhou said, "Give me the same amount they ordered."

"There are five of them, with one jar of fine wine for each."

"That's not even enough to get me half drunk. But since I'm cutting down on wine while traveling, just give me five jars, and bring me as many nice dishes as you can carry."

Mr. Wang had the waiter put on the table five jars of warmed wine, a large porcelain bowl, and several dishes of meat and vegetables. Ma Zhou raised the bowl and drank as if there were no one else present.

After downing three jars of wine, he asked for a washbowl to bathe his feet in and poured into it all the wine that was left. Then, he kicked off his boots, put his feet into the wine, and washed them (*Extraordinary*), much to the amazement of all the other guests who witnessed the scene. Mr. Wang secretly marveled at the sight and knew that the man was by no means a common sort. A contemporary, Cen Wenben, did a painting titled *Ma Zhou Washing His Feet*. Zhang Zhihe, a Tang poet who called himself Angler on the Misty Waters, inscribed onto the painting a poem of praise:

> *Worldly men venerate the mouth;*
> *I alone revere the feet.*
> *The mouth stirs up waves;*
> *The feet tread solid ground.*
> *Lowly as they are, they never fail me,*
> *But carry me over thousands of li.*
> *For such service, they get little reward;*
> *With no complaint, they endure the abuse.*
> *With wine I thank you*
> *For all that you've gone through.*
> *For you to forget your cares is better*
> *Than for my stomach to be full.*
> *Witnesses marvel at the sight:*

So free of worldly restraints is the man.
(These words of praise are just as extraordinary.)

That night, he retired to his room without further ado. The following day, Mr. Wang rose bright and early, settled accounts with guests, and sent them on their way. With no money or other valuables about him, Ma Zhou took off his fox-fur coat, for the weather was getting warm, and gave it to Mr. Wang as payment for the wine and food. Impressed by his generosity and overwhelmed by the value of the coat, Mr. Wang adamantly refused to take it, whereupon Ma Zhou asked for a brush-pen and wrote the following poem on the wall:

> *In return for the favor of one meal,*
> *The ancients would give a thousand in gold,[8]*
> *Not so much for the food itself,*
> *But for the value of friendship.*
> *Here I am, drinking Xinfeng wine,*
> *Without having to pay with my coat.*
> *A worthy man is my host,*
> *Of nobler spirit than the common run.*

He finished by signing his name: "Ma Zhou of Chiping." The poem as well as the calligraphy filled Mr. Wang with admiration and respect. "Where are you going from here, Mr. Ma?" he asked.

"To Chang'an to make a name for myself."

Mr. Wang asked further, "Do you have any place there to stay?"

"No."

"With your talent," continued Mr. Wang, "you will surely be blessed with wealth and rank. But Chang'an is a place where rice costs as much as pearls, and firewood is as expensive as cinnamon. Since you have already exhausted your means, how are you going to support yourself? I have a niece who lives on Longevity Street in Chang'an. She is married to Zhao Sanlang, who sells pancakes. I will write them a letter so that you can stay with them. That would be more convenient than for you to go to other places. I also have here a tael of silver for you to use on the road. Please accept this small offer."

Ma Zhou accepted the silver with gratitude. Mr. Wang wrote the letter and handed it to Ma Zhou, who thankfully bade him farewell with the promise "I will never forget your graciousness should I ever rise in the world, however insignificantly."

He made his way to Chang'an and found it to be indeed a bustling, prosperous place of a different order than Xinfeng. He headed straight for the Zhao residence on Longevity Street and presented Mr. Wang's letter. As it turned

out, Zhao Sanlang, whose family had been in the pancake business for generations, had died two years before, leaving the store to his widow, who was none
other than the niece of Mr. Wang of Xinfeng. Though already in her thirties,
she remained a striking beauty, known by local residents as the Pancake Lady.
Earlier, when she had just started selling pancakes in the store, Yuan Tiangang
the Divine Fortune-Teller had exclaimed in astonishment upon first laying
eyes on her, "This woman, with a face like the full moon, lips like red lotus-
petals, a clear voice, a refined look, and a straight nose, is meant for a life of
distinguished eminence as the wife of an official of the highest rank. Why is
she here in this humble place?" By chance, he mentioned this woman one day
to Commandant Chang He, who, with deep faith in Yuan Tiangang's predictions, ordered his valet to visit the store every day under the pretext of buying
pancakes and to persuade the woman to be the commandant's concubine.
Madam Wang responded with only a dry smile. Never once did she give any
promise. Truly,

> *Marriages are predetermined by fate.*
> *Seek not what is not ordained in your lot.*

The night before Ma Zhou's arrival, Madam Wang had a strange dream
in which a white horse approached her from the east and, in one gulp, ate up
all of the pancakes. A whip in hand, she ran after it, but, soon enough, she
found herself rising onto the back of the horse, which then changed into a
fiery dragon and flew heavenward. Upon waking up in a rush of heat, she
wondered at the extraordinary dream.

That same day, she received the letter from her maternal uncle Mr. Wang
introducing Ma Zhou. She was intrigued by the fact that the guest was named
Ma [horse] and was dressed in white. She kept him in the house and diligently
served him three meals a day. Ma Zhou, for his part, took the attentiveness for
granted. Not for a moment did he show any appreciation, but Madam Wang
did not slacken the slightest bit in her services. However, there were among
her neighbors some young rakes who, coveting the pretty widow, would often
loiter around her door and make lewd and provocative remarks. Madam
Wang never paid them any attention, winning much admiration from all and
sundry for her sense of honor. Now that a bachelor from afar was staying with
her, rumors started to float around. Being an observant person, Madam Wang
was well aware of the gossip. She said to Ma Zhou, "I wish I could keep you
longer, but, being a widow, I will incur gossip by doing so. You, sir, have a
bright future ahead of you. You'd better look for a place more helpful to your
career. It would be a shame for your talent to be wasted here." (*What a sensible
woman!*)

Ma Zhou replied, "I am more than willing to be of service to someone, only I have nowhere to go."

Before the words were quite out of his mouth, Commandant Chang's valet appeared again for pancakes. Madam Wang thought that, being a military official, Chang He must be in need of some assistance from scholars. She therefore asked the valet, "I have a relative named Ma, a truly learned scholar, who is looking for a place to serve. Would your master find some use for him?"

The valet said, "That would be good."

It so happened that, at the time, a drought was plaguing the empire, and Emperor Taizong had instructed all officials above the fifth rank to submit their opinions and well-considered proposals to remedy the situation. As he was among those solicited for such a memorial, Chang He was about to look for someone of wisdom and knowledge to write it for him. Madam Wang's recommendation of Scholar Ma was as timely as food for the hungry and drink for the thirsty. It scratched him where he itched, so to speak. At the valet's report, a greatly delighted Chang He immediately had his men prepare a horse to bring Ma Zhou to him. Thus, Ma Zhou took leave of Madam Wang and went to the residence of Commandant Chang. Ma's air of distinction filled the commandant with admiration and respect. Wine was set out and the study cleaned up for Ma Zhou to sleep in.

The following day, Chang He went personally into the study and presented him with a gift of twenty taels of silver and ten bolts of colored silk. The commandant then sought his counsel about the emperor's decree soliciting advice. Ma Zhou asked for a brush-pen and an ink slab and, spreading out a roll of white paper, wrote twenty proposals without so much as a moment's pause. Chang He heaved sigh upon sigh in admiration. Before the night was out, the text was copied in neat, fine penmanship for submission to the emperor at the court session the following morning. Emperor Taizong found every one of the proposals to his liking and asked Chang He, "Such insightful comments are beyond your capabilities. How did you come by them?"

Chang He threw himself onto the ground and exclaimed, "What I have done is punishable by death! These twenty proposals are indeed beyond the capabilities of an ignorant man like me. They are in fact written by my house guest Ma Zhou." (*Taking no credit for another man's work, this Chang He is also a man of integrity.*)

"Where is this Ma Zhou?" asked the emperor. "Bring him to me quickly."

Thus ordered, the custodian of the palace gate went straight to Commandant Chang's residence and summoned Ma Zhou, but he failed to wake the latter up from his wine-induced morning nap. Another imperial decree followed. When the third decree came, Chang He made a personal appearance.

From this can be seen how Emperor Taizong valued men of talent. There is a poem by a historian that says,

Three summons came one after another,
Such was the emperor's love for men of worth.
If every court treats men in the same way,
No talent will suffer in obscurity.

As he stepped into the study, Chang He had a houseboy raise Ma Zhou to his feet and spray cold water on his face. Only then did Ma Zhou wake up. Upon learning about the imperial decrees, he mounted the horse in great haste. Chang He led him to the golden palace and into the presence of the emperor.

After Ma Zhou finished with his obeisance, the emperor asked, "Where are you from? Have you ever held office?"

Ma Zhou answered, "I am a native of Chiping County. I used to be a prefectural instructor in Bozhou. As the job was beneath my capabilities, I resigned and came here for a tour of the capital. It is indeed my great fortune to be able to see Your Royal Countenance."

Immensely pleased, Emperor Taizong granted him there and then the title of investigating censor and a robe, a tablet, and a belt befitting his official status. In his new attire, Ma Zhou thanked the emperor for his grace and returned to Chang He's residence to thank him for his recommendation. Chang He had another banquet laid out and served wine in celebration of the occasion.

By night, when the banquet was over, Chang He did not presume to make Ma Zhou, now a man of exalted status, stay overnight in his study. Instead, Chang He had a sedan-chair prepared to send him back to "your relative, Madam Wang's house."

Ma Zhou said, "Madam Wang is not related to me in any way. I was staying in her house just as a guest."

In great astonishment, Chang He asked, "Is the investigating censor not married?"

"No, I'm ashamed to say that I've been too poor to marry."

Chang He said, "Mr. Yuan Tiangang the fortune-teller once predicted that Madam Wang was destined to be the wife of an official of the first rank. I was afraid that she might be your kith and kin, which would be quite an inconvenience. But, since you are not related in any way, you are indeed meant by divine will to be husband and wife. Should it be agreeable to you, I will be most happy to be of service as a go-between."

Ma Zhou, grateful for Madam Wang's solicitude, was likewise inclined. "If you could bring about this union," said he, "I would be most obliged." That night, Ma Zhou stayed in the Chang residence as before.

The following morning, Ma Zhou and Chang He went again into the presence of the emperor, who was in the very process of dispatching four commanders to lead an army to suppress an uprising by Tartars and Turks. Asked for suggestions as to how best to crush the rebellion, Ma Zhou burst into a flow of eloquence. Nothing he said did not find favor with the emperor (*That is because he is in luck*), who then promoted him to the position of supervising secretary. Chang He was also rewarded for his recommendation with a hundred bolts of silk.

Chang He left the court after expressing his gratitude to the emperor, and then he ordered his attendants to lead him directly to the pancake shop. There, he asked to see Madam Wang. Believing that the commandant had come to take her by force, Madam Wang hastily hid herself and refused to come out on any account. (*Good detail.*) Chang He took a seat in the store and sent his valet to find an elderly female neighbor who could pass to Madam Wang a message to the effect that Commandant Chang was there for the sole purpose of serving as a matchmaker for her and Investigating Censor Ma. Madam Wang learned, after some inquiries, that Investigating Censor Ma was none other than Ma Zhou. Her dream about a white horse changing into a dragon had now come true. Such a marriage bond preordained by heaven was not to be resisted. Upon learning that Madam Wang had given her consent, Chang He offered as betrothal gifts on Ma Zhou's behalf the bolts of silk that the emperor had bestowed upon him. He also rented an empty house for Ma Zhou. The wedding ceremony was held on a chosen auspicious day with the entire assembly of court officials attending and offering congratulations. Indeed,

> A humble scholar in dire poverty
> Became overnight an honored guest at court.

After the wedding, Madam Wang brought all her belongings to the Ma residence, much to the envy of her neighbors, but this is no concern of ours here.

Let us come back to Ma Zhou, who, since his first audience with Emperor Taizong, kept offering advice and suggestions, which were all adopted without exception. Within three years' time, he attained the position of minister of personnel, and Madam Wang was granted the title of Lady.

Having heard about Ma Zhou's rise to fortune and eminence, Mr. Wang, innkeeper of Xinfeng, made a special trip to Chang'an to visit him as well as his niece. When he came to Longevity Street, he failed to find the pancake shop and assumed that she must have moved away. It was after making inquiries of the neighbors that he learned that his niece had been widowed and had just married Minister Ma. The news sent Mr. Wang into raptures. He betook himself to the minister's residence, saw Ma Zhou and his wife, and the three of them reminisced about the old days. After staying with the couple for over a month, Mr. Wang took leave of them, whereupon Ma Zhou offered him a thousand pieces of gold, a gift that Mr. Wang adamantly declined. Ma Zhou said, "The poem that I wrote is still on your wall. How can I ever forget the meal you offered me, which was worth a thousand pieces of gold?" (*At this point, this extraordinary story comes to an end.*) Only then did Mr. Wang thankfully accept the gift. He returned to Xinfeng a wealthy man. This is a case of "giving a melon and receiving jade" and "repaying kindness with kindness," but, of this, no more need be said.

Let us turn our attention back to Prefect Da Xi, who had gone back to his native place to mourn the death of one of his parents. Upon returning to the capital after the expiration of the three-year mourning period and learning that Ma Zhou was now the minister of personnel, he was seized with fear, for he had given the new minister offense. So frightened was he that he dared not report to the ministry for reappointment. Aware of Da Xi's predicament, Ma Zhou repeatedly issued invitations to him. Prostrating himself on the floor, Da Xi said, "My eyes failed to recognize Mount Tai. Please forgive me."

Ma Zhou hastened to raise him to his feet and said, "An instructor in the employment of the prefect should be a paragon of virtue and an example for the students. I was wrong to engage in excessive drinking and wild ranting. You, sir, were not to blame." That very day, he recommended that Da Xi be made magistrate of the capital. All of the officials in the capital were, to a man, impressed with Ma Zhou's magnanimity.

Ma Zhou enjoyed wealth and eminence for the rest of his long life, in the companionship of Madam Wang. A later poet had this to say:

> A great statesman rose from among drunkards.
> Neither was the pancake woman the common sort.
> Men of the times had no Persian eyes,[9]
> And allowed bright pearls to be buried in dust.

6

Lord Ge Gives Away Pearl Maiden

King Zhuang of the five great leaders of the time
Not only was stronger than the others.
A woman's charm has toppled many a state,
But he, in the helmet case, showed himself without equal.

During the Spring and Autumn Period [770–476 B.C.E.], there was a King Zhuang, Mi Lü by name, of the state of Chu, who was one of the five great leaders of the time. Once, he treated his ministers to a grand banquet in the private quarters of his palace, with court ladies in attendance. When a sudden gust of wind blew out the candles, one of the guests took advantage of the darkness and tugged at a court lady's clothes. The woman snapped off the strap of his helmet and complained to King Zhuang, asking for investigation and punishment of the culprit. The king thought to himself, "It is only natural to forget one's manners under the influence of wine. How can I give out punishment just for a woman's sake, at the risk of becoming a laughing stock? It is shameful to value feminine beauty over the merits of a worthy man." So he ordered, "Let all those present break off their helmet straps in celebration of this joyous occasion." By the time the candles were relit, all the helmet straps had been taken off. There was no way of finding out who had flirted with the woman. Later, in a battle with the state of Jin, King Zhuang found himself besieged by Jin soldiers. He was in critical danger when a warrior fought his way through the tight encirclement and rescued him. Once out of danger, King Zhuang asked, "Who are you, savior of my life?"

Prostrating himself on the ground, the warrior said, "I am the one whose helmet strap was snapped off. Since you did me the great kindness of covering for me instead of punishing me, I am more than willing to die for you in payment of my debt of gratitude."

King Zhuang was most pleased. "If I had listened to that woman," said he, "I would have lost a brave warrior."

The Jin army was later put to rout. All the lords of other states abandoned Jin and swore allegiance to Chu, which rose to be the greatest power of the time. There is a poem in evidence:

She snapped off the strap to no avail.
How could the king choose her over a brave subject?
Blame not King Zhuang for his martial spirit;
Remember who played with fire on Mount Li.[1]

The average man in this world is narrow-minded and mean, and takes delight in digging up dirt in other people's pasts in order to show his own shrewdness. If he does succeed in discovering some wrongdoing, do not expect him to show mercy! Such people harbor no benevolence in their hearts but only meanness. If it so happens that they fall into a desperate situation, no one will be there to share their worries and lend them a helping hand. In contrast, King Zhuang of Chu forgave a petty misdemeanor and, as a result, accomplished his goal. This was truly a heroic action, rare in times past and present.

Storyteller, is there really not even one other man like him?

Dear audience, let me tell of another one. Of what dynasty was this man? He was a man of the Five Dynasties [907–60], at the end of the Tang dynasty. What were the Five Dynasties? Namely, the Later Liang [907–23], founded by Zhu Wen; the Later Tang [923–36], founded by Li Cunxu; the Later Jin [936–46], founded by Shi Jingtang; the Later Han [947–50], founded by Liu Zhiyuan; and the Later Zhou [951–60], founded by Guo Wei. Our story is about a valiant commander in the court of the Later Liang dynasty by the name of Ge Zhou, a man of a magnanimous mind and high aspirations. A battle-tested warrior, he had the strength to fight ten thousand men at once. He started his career with Zhu Wen at Mount Mangdang. After Zhu Wen received the imperial power from the Tang and established himself as emperor of the Later Liang, Ge Zhou was granted the posts of commander-in-chief and regional commander and ordered to defend Yanzhou in Shandong. Yanzhou was near Hebei, which was the territory of Li Keyong of the Later Tang dynasty. That was precisely the reason why the Liang emperor sent his trusted subordinate Ge Zhou to that strategic area with the mission of guarding Shandong while preparing for an invasion of Hebei. The mere mention of Ge Zhou's name struck such awe in the people of Hebei that a two-line song began to spread throughout the region:

Touch that Shandong vine,
And you lay your life on the line.[2]

Henceforth, he came to be called Lord Ge. That he had under him a hundred thousand fearless soldiers and a galaxy of valiant generals need not be described further.

Of all his subordinates, our story will now focus on a certain Shentu Tai, a native of Sishui, seven feet in height, handsome in appearance, and skilled in swordsmanship and archery. Before his time had come, he was nothing more than one of Lord Ge's bodyguards. During one of Ge's hunting expeditions on Mount Zeng, Shentu Tai shot down a deer. The army martial arts instructor came up to claim the deer, but Shentu easily overpowered him. With the dead deer in hand, he went to Lord Ge to ask for forgiveness. The latter was so impressed by his bravery that, instead of reproaching the man, he had a mind to promote him. The following day, during martial arts practice on the drill ground, Lord Ge praised him for his archery and horsemanship and promoted him to the position of captain, to be at the commander's service at all times. He was also entrusted with all important military matters. Without the where-withal for marriage, Shentu took up residence in a small room by the side of the central chamber in Lord Ge's mansion. As all the guards of the mansion called him Chamber Chief, he came to be known to all and sundry, superiors and subordinates alike, as Chamber Chief. Truly,

> *Xiao He was once but a prison warden,*[3]
> *Han Xin no more than a palace guardsman.*[4]
> *To be worm or dragon is all in one's fate.*
> *Of what account is a man's family origin?*

Our story branches at this point. As he had more concubines than could be comfortably accommodated in his present residence, Lord Ge had a geomancer study the topography and started building a magnificent mansion on an auspicious site to the southeast of the old residence. The construction was to be finished within a year. The Chamber Chief was given the mission of inspecting the site twice a day.

It was the Clear and Bright Festival.[5] Everywhere were men and women out to enjoy the spring and the lush green grass. Lord Ge had a feast arranged in Yueyun Tower, the highest point in the city of Yanzhou. He led his entourage of concubines up the tower for a view of the panorama. Among the multitude of his concubines, only one, Pearl Maiden, had great beauty. How did she look?

> *Her eyes bright like pools of autumn waters,*
> *Her brows like the contours of distant hills.*
> *Her tiny mouth as red as a cherry,*
> *Her lithe waist as supple as a willow.*
> *No less bewitching than Lady Yang,*[6]
> *More light and lissome than Zhao Feiyan.*[7]
> *Could she be a fairy maiden from heaven?*
> *For her Xishi*[8] *and Nanwei*[9] *are no match.*

Lord Ge showered favors on her and kept her by his side day and night. Within the mansion she came to be called Madam Pearl. On the day of which I speak, she was with Lord Ge in Yueyun Tower, enjoying the pleasures of wine.

After having made his rounds of inspection at the construction site, Shentu Tai proceeded to the tower to report on the work. Lord Ge summoned him upstairs and rewarded him with fine wine served in big golden vessels shaped like lotus flowers. After three servings, Shentu Tai bowed in acknowledgement of his gratitude and rose to stand at one side. When he raised his head, his eyes chanced to rest upon a radiant beauty with bright eyes and white teeth standing by the side of Lord Ge. "Could she be of this mortal world? Or is she a fairy from heaven?" he wondered. Being in the prime of his life, he was at the age when desire for women is strongest. Moreover, he was still a bachelor. He had heard that Lord Ge had a most attractive concubine called Madam Pearl and was annoyed at the lack of opportunity to lay his eyes upon her. Now, he was convinced that this was none other than Madam Pearl. So entranced was he that he kept his eyes fixed on her as if he would never get tired of the sight. (*When down on their luck, gallant heroes tend to find sustenance in wine and feminine beauty. Ma Zhou[10] and Shentu Tai are no exceptions.*) Quite unexpectedly, Lord Ge directed a question at him: "Chamber Chief, when will the construction be finished? Hey! Shentu Tai, Shentu Tai! I am asking you when the construction will be finished!"

The repeated questions failed to solicit a single response from the man. As the proverb has it, one mind cannot be used for two purposes. It so happened that as his mind was all set upon the woman, Shentu Tai did not hear a thing. Seeing that Shentu could not take his eyes off the woman, Lord Ge ordered, with an understanding smile, that the banquet table be cleared. He did not address any more remarks to Shentu Tai, nor did he give any indication that he knew what the latter was preoccupied with.

The guardsmen present at the time were breathless with alarm when Lord Ge got no response from Shentu Tai. Relieved that no word of reprobation came his way, they also wondered why and told Shentu what had happened. Shentu was mortified. "I am as good as dead," he told himself. "It's only a matter of time." Fear for his life kept him awake all night. Verily,

> Troubles only from idle words arise;
> Anxiety visits none but the young and unwise.

The following day, while Lord Ge held court, Shentu Tai stood at a far distance from him without even once daring to raise his head. His only wish was for the session to be dismissed early so that another day would pass without mishap. For several days in succession, he was absent-minded and restless, knowing no peace sitting or lying down. Aware of his distress, Lord Ge sent him some kind words to comfort him and ordered him to the construction site, where he was to devote all his time supervising the project. He was as relieved to leave Lord Ge's presence as if he had gained a new life. Hardly had any peace of mind set in than uneasiness grew again for fear that Lord Ge would still inflict punishment by finding fault with him in this new job. Therefore, he went about his mission gingerly, working long hours from morning till night and sparing no pains to acquit himself well.

One day, Lord Ge sent a certain Officer Xu Gao to replace Shentu Tai, who was to return to the mansion. The news again filled him with apprehension. In great trepidation, he left the construction site and requested an audience with Lord Ge. "For what assignment did you summon me, sir?" he asked.

"His Majesty suffered a setback in the battle at Jiazhai, and Tang soldiers are coming in by different roads. Li Cunzhang of Tang and his troops are advancing upon our border with Shandong. As local troops have been sending in urgent requests for immediate help, I am preparing to go to the front line and push back the enemy. Because there is no one else here worthy enough, I would like you to go with me."

"I will certainly obey your order," said Shentu Tai.

He was then presented with a suit of bronze armor taken out from the arsenal. Shentu Tai bowed in gratitude, but his feelings were mixed. He was glad at the opportunity to follow Lord Ge to the battlefield and prove his worth but was also worried that a minor slip could lead to punishment for the previous misdemeanor as well. Truly,

> When a green dragon and a white tiger go together,[11]
> There's no knowing if what follows is joy or sorrow.

Let me now turn to Lord Ge, who selected his generals and soldiers and, that very day, led the troops on their way. It was truly an awe-inspiring sight, with banners and flags blocking out the sky, and the sound of gongs and drums shaking the earth. General Li Cunzhang of Tang was about to storm the city of Tancheng when he heard about the imminent arrival of troops from Yanzhou. He then seized a high vantage point on Langya Hill as a preemptive step and pitched three camps of varying sizes. Upon reaching the city and realizing that they had lost the advantage in terrain, Ge Zhou's forces retreated thirty li and pitched camp there to avoid confrontation. For four or five days in succession, Ge Zhou's men went forward to challenge the Tang troops to a battle, but Li Cunzhang firmly held his ground and paid no heed to the taunting remarks. On the seventh day, Ge Zhou's troops broke camp and marched straight up to Li's main camp to dare him to come out to battle. Li Cunzhang was well prepared. He put his troops into a square formation at the foot of the hill so as to be able to engage the enemy on all four sides. Within the formation were hidden archers shooting at all who tried to break up the array. Lord Ge personally led some of his men to the battlefront and, at the sight of the orderly ranks as impregnable as a mountain, said with a sigh, "I have heard about Li Cunzhang's famous battle at Baixiang.[12] This array truly convinces me of his talent as a great general. This battle array is the formation of Nine Palaces and the Eight Trigrams, which helped Fu Chai, King of Wu, in ancient times defeat the King of Jin at Huangchi. The only way to breach the formation is to wait and attack when the soldiers are tired and begin to show signs of disorder. Otherwise, throwing such a formation into disarray is a formidable task." Lord Ge promptly ordered his troops to refrain from rash actions and just stand in combat readiness.

At around three in the afternoon, Lord Ge saw that his men were fidgeting from hunger and thirst. He was inclined to beat a retreat but hesitated for fear that the Tang forces would sweep forward in pursuit, riding on the crest of their victory. He suddenly caught sight of Shentu Tai at his side. "Chamber Chief, what advice do you have?"

Shentu Tai replied, "In my humble opinion, though their army is still in good shape, the soldiers must be as tired as we are. I suggest that several daring men who are ready to risk their lives charge at the enemy in a surprise attack. If they can break up the array, the main troops can then follow, and victory will be at hand."

Stroking his back, Lord Ge said, "I've always known you to be a brave man. Will you do this for me?"

Without letting a moment slip by, Shentu Tai mounted his horse, sword in hand, shouting, "Those who are brave enough, follow me and crush the enemy!" No one moved. Without even a look back, he galloped toward the enemy battle array.

In great alarm, Ge Zhou quickly led several generals in charging forward to provide cover for Shentu Tai. Behold! There he was, his horse galloping with the speed of lightning, his sword slashing about like a wind-driven wheel, with never a moment of pause. Recklessly, he rode straight into the enemy ranks. It so happened that the Tang troops did not take this lone rider seriously at the beginning. To their dismay, this daredevil man charged back and forth in the array as if he were in no man's land, wielding his sword with supernatural swiftness, hacking men down as if chopping gourds or vegetables. Chancing upon Shen Xiang, the vanguard, he knocked him down from his horse after only one exchange of blows and, jumping down to the ground, decapitated him. Shentu Tai then remounted his horse and rode out of the enemy lines, encountering no resistance. By this time, Ge Zhou's troops had arrived. "The Tang troops are in disarray! All those who want to kill the devils, follow me!" So exclaiming, Shentu Tai threw Shen Xiang's head before Ge Zhou's horse and turned back into the enemy ranks.

At the waving of Ge Zhou's insignia banner, Ge's troops marched as one man and pushed deep into the enemy lines, driving them into great disorder. Unable to control his men, Li Cunzhang spurred on his horse and took flight before all others did. The Tang troops were driven in all directions by the Liang army. The swift of foot survived. Those less swift became ghosts of the battlefield. Li Cunzhang, the renowned general of Tang, met a crushing defeat. His men fled pellmell at the mere sight of the enemy, leaving behind more weapons and horses than could be counted. It was a total victory for the Liang army. Lord Ge said to Shentu Tai, "All the credit for today's victory goes to you."

With a deep bow, Shentu Tai replied, "What ability do I have? It was entirely due to your awe-inspiring might that the battle was won!"

Overjoyed, Lord Ge wrote a report to the imperial court and issued orders that the soldiers be rewarded with bounties. After three days of rest, the victorious army returned to Yanzhou. Truly,

> Cheerfully they rap their stirrups with whips;
> Joyfully they return with songs of triumph.

Upon Lord Ge's return to his residence, all the concubines and the staff greeted him with words of felicitation. Smilingly, he said, "To a general, defeating enemies in battles is all in a day's work. What is there to congratulate me for?" Pointing at Madam Pearl, he continued to all the other women, "It is she you should congratulate."

The women said, "The imperial court will certainly reward you for having beaten the enemies and saved the territory. All of us in your service feel honored as well. Why is Madam Pearl alone to be congratulated?"

"The victory is entirely due to one man who put up a hard fight. Having nothing to reward him with, I will give her to him as his wife. Isn't it to be rejoiced that she will enjoy a blissful marriage for the rest of her life?"

Secure in the knowledge that she was his favorite, Madam Pearl did not believe what she heard. "Don't you tease me," she grinned.

"I never tease people. I have already withdrawn from the treasury six hundred thousand in cash to buy a dowry for you. You will sleep tonight by yourself in the west chamber, and I will not trouble you with service at dinner." (*A clean break, like the man of action that he is.*)

Madam Pearl was so startled that tears streamed down her cheeks and she dropped to her knees, begging, "Since I started serving you years ago, I have never displeased you. Now that you have thrown me out to another man, I would rather die than obey your order."

He roared with laughter. "Silly girl! I am not made of wood or stone. How can I not have any feelings for you? But the other day at our feast in Yueyun Tower, I noticed that this man couldn't take his eyes off you. I could tell that he had fallen in love with you. He is a young bachelor who just did me outstanding service. Only you can please him most."

Pulling at his sleeves, Madam Pearl pouted and sulked coquettishly, saying she would never comply with the order.

"This matter is not up to you to decide," said Lord Ge. "It is better to be a wife than a concubine. Consider it your good fortune that this man's future status will not be any lower than mine. I am not doing you any harm. Why do you lament so?" He told the other concubines to help her to her feet and make her stop crying. The other women all loathed Madam Pearl for her monopoly over the master and were only too anxious to be rid of her. Her marriage could not have been better news for them. Now, swarming forward, they helped her up and dragged her along to the west chamber, all the while trying to pacify her with soothing words. By this time, Madam Pearl was resigned to the situation and just heaved a sigh upon realizing that the commander's lofty mind rose above his affection for women. From that day onward, Lord Ge sent two different concubines every night to eat and sleep with Madam Pearl, and never did he ask for her again. There is a poem that bears witness:

> She was his most beloved woman,
> But no longer is she summoned.
> It is not that he loves her any less,
> But that he fears the consequences more.

Now I come to Shentu Tai. After his return from Tancheng, Shentu Tai reported to Lord Ge without any mention of his merit in the battle, and resumed his job as supervisor of the construction of Lord Ge's new mansion. It so happened that on the day the construction was completed, the treasury clerk came to report, "Items of the dowry worth six hundred thousand in cash are now ready, and we await further instructions."

Lord Ge said, "Keep them where they are until I settle down in the new residence." He then had a fortune-teller select an auspicious day, and the whole family moved to the new mansion, leaving behind only Madam Pearl and tens of waiting women. Upon the orders of Lord Ge, the treasury officials moved all of the dowry items to the old residence and furnished the whole mansion in grand style. General speculations were that the decoration was done because Lord Ge wanted to have the old residence as a second home. Who could have guessed the real reason!

On this particular day, Shentu Tai was offering congratulations with other military officers in the new mansion when Lord Ge called him forth and said, "Reward for your service at Tancheng is long overdue. Since I heard that you are still a bachelor, I now give you as your bride my beautiful concubine. I have prepared a meager dowry, which is in the old residence. Today being an auspicious day, you may hold your wedding right away, and I offer you and your wife my former residence."

Shentu Tai turned pale with fright. He kept bowing and was only able to come up with the words "How dare I!" So mortified was he that speech was beyond him.

Lord Ge said again, "A true gentleman would offer his head, let alone a concubine, out of loyalty for a friend. My mind is made up. Do not refuse me."

While Shentu Tai was still voicing protests, Lord Ge had the other officers put flowers and a red cape on him, and the band struck up music. The officers thundered, "Shentu Tai! Make a bow and thank his lordship!"

As if in a dream, Shentu Tai made a few bows and was involuntarily pushed by the crowd out of the house onto a horse and straight to the old residence, led all along the way by the band. All the former guardsmen of the residence, having received orders ahead of time, were already there to greet him. The whole mansion was decked out with flowers and multicolored festoons. As the maids and waiting women brought out the bride for the ceremony, music from the band resounded to the skies, and tables were set for the wedding banquet. Fixing his eyes upon the bride, Shentu recognized the very woman whom he took to be a heavenly maiden when he first laid eyes on her in Yueyun Tower. His fixed gaze on her had almost brought upon him trouble serious enough to cost him his life. Who would have foreseen that on this day, he would be joined with her in matrimony when least expecting it. What a stroke of luck that was! When he walked into the mansion, what met his eyes were all kinds of brand new furniture and housewares. At the thought of being provided with such a comfortable nest, he was overwhelmed with a sense of unworthiness in the face of such generosity. That night, the couple took up their quarters in the west chamber. Their happiness goes without saying.

The following day, the couple made their way to the new mansion to thank Lord Ge, but the latter had ordered that a sign saying that he was not seeing anyone be posted on the gate. Soon after they returned home, it was announced that his lordship himself was at their door. Shentu rushed out and sank to his knees in front of Lord Ge's horse. Lord Ge dismounted, raised Shentu to his feet, and headed straight for the hall, where he took out a letter of appointment and promoted Shentu to be chief of staff. In those days, regional commanders usually kept blank forms of imperial appointments and could, on their own authority, fill out the forms if they saw suitable candidates in the army. Only then would they submit the forms to the imperial court, which never failed to approve such requests. Besides, Shentu Tai did indeed have a fine record of service. The court would naturally grant the application priority consideration and give its approval. Lord Ge had a belt of office put on Shentu Tai and acknowledged Shentu's new status with proper decorum. Shentu's heart overflowed with gratitude to him for having removed for good the nickname Chamber Chief.

One day, in a casual conversation with his wife, he asked her how Lord Ge could have brought himself to part with her, his favorite concubine, whereupon Madam Pearl told him how his eyes were seen glued upon her in Yueyun Tower. (*Recalling the past.*) "Lord Ge said that you were in love with me and gave me, his favorite concubine, to you as a gift."

Shentu Tai now came to appreciate fully what a noble mind it took to understand human nature so much as to value merit in a subordinate more than love for a woman. As the story spread, no one in the army failed to praise Lord Ge for his magnanimity, and all were ready to serve him to the best of their ability, even at the cost of their lives. For the rest of his life, he was held in high esteem by the populace, and the area under his jurisdiction enjoyed peace and security. A poem written in later times had this to say of him:

> *Few value merit over beauty;*
> *Fewer yet turn rancor to amity.*
> *Reading Yanzhou's glorious record of old,*
> *We see a fair lady on the platform of gold.*[13]

7

Yang Jiao'ai Lays Down His Life for the Sake of Friendship

Friends one moment and enemies the next,
All too many know no fidelity.
The friendship of Guan and Bao in poverty
Is scorned as dust by men of today.

In olden times, there lived in the state of Qi two men, Guan Zhong, courtesy name Yiwu, and Bao Shu, courtesy name Xuanzi, who fostered a friendship from an early age, when both were in straitened and humble circumstances. Later in their lives, Bao Shu preceded Guan Zhong in rising to prominence in the service of Duke Huan of Qi. As a trusted subordinate of the duke, he recommended that Guan Zhong be prime minister, a position higher than his own. The two men assisted their sovereign in governing the state with one heart and mind from beginning to end. Guan Zhong had said, "Three times I joined in battles and each time was put to flight, but Bao Shu did not take me as a coward, for he knew that I had my aged mother to look after. Three times I took office and each time was expelled, but Bao Shu did not take me as a worthless man, for he knew that my time had not yet come. I have given him counsel that made matters worse, but he did not take me to be an ignorant man, for he knew that there were moments less lucky than others. I have engaged in business dealings with him and taken the larger share of the profits, but he did not take me to be a greedy man, for he knew I was poor. It was my parents who gave me my life, but it is Bao Shu who truly understands me." Henceforth, all deeply devoted friendships have invariably been referred to as Guan-Bao relationships. I shall now tell of two friends who pledged brotherhood upon a chance encounter and laid down their lives for each other. Their names will be passed on through the ages.

During the Spring and Autumn period, King Yuan [unknown] of Chu had the highest regard for scholars and Confucian moral principles and sought worthy men to enter into his service. As the word spread, numerous men throughout the empire converged to offer their allegiance.

In the Piled Rock Mountain region of Western Qiang[1] there lived a worthy man by the name of Zuo Botao, whose parents had died when he was still at a tender age. He applied himself to his studies with assiduity and acquired learning sufficient to enable him to bring prosperity to the land and peace to the populace. In his late thirties he still had not yet attained any office, for, at a time when the feudal lords were constantly warring upon one another, ruthless despots far outnumbered benevolent sovereigns. As word came to him that King Yuan of Chu, out of admiration for virtue and honor, was seeking worthy men from all quarters, he took leave of his neighbors and friends and, bringing along a sack of books, set out on a journey to the kingdom of Chu. It was then the depth of winter. In the region of Yong he was caught in a raging rainstorm. There is a lyric poem to the tune of "The Moon over the West River" that describes a rainy winter scene:

> *A bitter wind lashes the face,*
> *An insistent drizzle soaks the clothes,*
> *Bringing on the chill of ice and snow.*
> *Gone is their gentle tone of kinder times.*
> *The hills are shrouded in gloom;*
> *Sunlight is rare and dim.*
> *Wayfarers wish they were at home;*
> *Travelers regret they are out in the cold.*

Braving the wind and the rain, Zuo Botao traveled on the road the whole day. At dusk, his clothes all wet, he came to a village, where he looked for a place to stay for the night. At some distance ahead of him, lamplight shone through a broken window in the midst of a bamboo grove. Upon drawing nearer, he saw that it was a thatched hut surrounded by a low latticed fence. He pushed open the gate and knocked gently on the crude-looking door. A man opened the door and stepped out. Standing under the eaves, Zuo Botao eagerly saluted the man and said, "I am Zuo Botao, native of Western Qiang. I was on my way to Chu when I was caught in the rain. There being no inns in the neighborhood, may I have your permission to stay here for the night and leave early tomorrow morning?"

The man hastily returned the salutation and invited him into the hut, which, as Botao saw when he entered, contained no furniture except a couch, on which was nothing but a pile of books. Since his host was evidently a scholar, Botao was about to drop to his knees for an obeisance when his host said, "This is no time for ceremony. Let me make a fire to dry your clothes before we talk."

After lighting some bamboo sticks to make a fire for Botao to dry his clothes, the man cordially set out wine and food to offer to Botao. When asked his name, the man said, "I am Yang Jiao'ai. My parents having died when I was small, I live here by myself. I am so devoted to learning that my farm has gone to waste. I am honored that a gentleman has come here from afar, but, there being nothing in this humble home of mine to offer to you, I beg your forgiveness."

"To offer me a shelter in this dismal rain is already an act of kindness, not to mention serving wine and food. How could I ever forget such hospitality!"

That night, the two of them slept in the same bed, head to foot and foot to head, and talked all through the night about subjects of scholarly concern.

When the day broke, it was still drizzling. Jiao'ai kept Botao in his hut and treated his guest to everything he had. They swore brotherhood, with Botao, five years the senior of Jiao'ai, honored as the elder brother. It was not until three days later that the rain finally stopped and the road dried out.

"My brother," said Botao, "you have the ability and aspirations to assist the sovereign in governing the land. It is a sheer waste of talent for you to live out your life in contentment among the woods and streams without making any attempt to seek lasting fame."

Jiao'ai rejoined, "It is not that I have no wish to seek office, but no opportunity has ever come my way."

Botao suggested, "The King of Chu is sincerely seeking men of talent. If such is your intention, why don't you go with me?"

"I will do as my brother says."

Thereupon, they put together some money for travel expenses and some provisions, left the hut, and set out on their southbound journey.

Two days had not quite gone by before a dismal rain started again. Forced to put themselves up at a roadside inn, they found that their travel funds were quickly exhausted. Left with nothing more than a bag of food, they sallied out into the rain, carrying the bag by turns. Before the rain had subsided, a strong wind sprang up, bringing on a blinding snowstorm. How bad was the storm? Behold:

> The wind adds chill to the snow;
> The snow gives a sharper bite to the wind.
> Like willow catkins, the snowflakes spin around,
> Dancing wildly like so many goose feathers.
> Churning and swirling,
> They make one lose one's bearings.
> Blotting out the earth and the sky,
> They drain everything of its color.
> Poets seeking plum blossoms revel at the sight,
> But travelers on the road are sick at heart.

Having passed Qiyang, the two men found themselves in the Liang Mountains.[2] To their inquiries, woodchoppers all advised them not to advance farther, for stretching ahead was about one hundred li of wilderness infested with tigers and wolves, with no human habitation. Botao asked Jiao'ai, "What does my good brother think?"

Jiao'ai said, "As the ancients say, 'Life or death is all a matter of fate.' Since we've come this far, why don't we go on? Let's not think of quitting." So, on they went for another day and stayed for the night in an ancient tomb. Their thin clothes provided poor protection against the bone-chilling winds.

The following day, the snow came down thicker, and soon the mountain was covered by a foot-thick blanket of snow.

Unable to hold out any longer against the cold, Botao said, "This is what I think: There is not a single house for the next hundred li, and we don't have enough food or clothes. If one of us goes alone, he will be able to make it to the kingdom of Chu. If both of us try together, we will surely die of hunger on the way, if not of cold. What good is there in rotting away with the grass and trees? I am going to take off my clothes and put them on you so that you can take along all the food and struggle your way ahead. I have no more strength left in me to walk another step. I would rather die in this spot. I'm sure you'll be given a high position once you meet the king of Chu. It won't be too late to come back to bury me then." (*The words of a hero and also the best way out in a desperate situation.*)

Jiao'ai objected, "What nonsense is this! Though we were not born of the same parents, we are closer to each other than brothers of flesh and blood. How can I bear the thought of going alone to seek advancement for myself?" He would not hear of Botao's suggestion but, instead, supported Botao and moved farther down the road. Less than ten li later, Botao said, "The snow-storm is getting worse. We can't go any farther. Let us find a place to rest by the roadside." They saw a withered mulberry tree that could provide quite a shelter from the snow. As the tree could accommodate only one man, Jiao'ai placed Botao at its foot. Botao told Jiao'ai to strike rocks to ignite a fire and to gather some dry branches to feed the fire for protection against the cold. By the time Jiao'ai came back with some firewood, Botao had already taken off all his clothes and put them in a pile on the ground. (*He sent Jiao'ai away so that he could take his clothes off. There was no other way to make Jiao'ai give up all hope.*) Jiao'ai was aghast. "Why did my brother do this?"

Botao replied, "I couldn't think of a better way out. My good brother, please don't ruin your own chance. Quickly put on these clothes, take the parcel of food, and be on your way. I will stay here until I die."

Putting his arms around Botao, Jiao'ai burst into loud sobs. "You and I will be with each other, dead or alive," he declared. "How can I leave you?"

"Should both of us die of hunger, who is to bury our bones?"

Jiao'ai rejoined, "In that case, I would be most happy to have you put on my clothes, take the food, and go. Let me die here."

Botao protested, "I am of weak constitution, whereas you are so much younger and stronger. What is more, you are also a better scholar. If you can get to see the king of Chu, you will certainly rise to prominence. My death is of no consequence. Do not linger here too long. Go, quickly!"

Jiao'ai was adamant: "If you starve to death under this mulberry tree while I rise to fame and fortune, I would be committing an act of betrayal, and that's something I will never do."

"After I left the Piled Rock Mountain, I met you for the first time and yet felt that I had known you as an old friend. Impressed by your remarkable talent, I urged you to seek office. It is my misfortune that the elements are against me, which means that my allotted life span is coming to an end. It will be my fault should you also perish here." With these words, Botao tried to get up and throw himself into the ravine in front of them, but Jiao'ai pulled him back. Weeping bitterly, Jiao'ai wrapped him up in the clothes and brought him back to the mulberry tree, but Botao cast off the clothes again. Jiao'ai was about to bend forward and try once more to talk him over, when he noticed a change in Botao's complexion. His limbs getting cold, Botao waved his hand for Jiao'ai to go, without being able to utter a word. (*According to Guang Yu Ji*[3] *Zuo Botao died in Heyang County, Xi'an Prefecture, Shaanxi, but the Liang mountains lie by the Qi Mountains in Qianzhou.*) Jiao'ai thought to himself, "If I stay longer, I, too, will die from the cold, and who will bury my brother?" Thereupon, he bowed to Botao in the snow and said between sobs, "Your unworthy younger brother will now leave you, counting on your help from the netherworld. As soon as I make a name, however modest, for myself, I will certainly come back and give you a proper burial." Botao nodded feebly by way of reply. Jiao'ai took the clothes and the food and left in tears. Botao died under the mulberry tree. A later poet had this to say in praise:

> With the cold came three feet of snow.
> The travelers went on a thousand li journey.
> What a trial it was—trudging through the snow,
> With little stock of food within their bag!
> Not to share the food would let one of them survive;
> For both to go on would mean death for both.
> For both to die, what good would that bring?
> One life saved was better than none.
> Zuo Botao, what a noble soul!
> He gave his life so that another could live.

Cold and famished, Jiao'ai arrived in the kingdom of Chu and found lodging at an inn. The following day, he headed toward the capital city and asked where to go to answer the king's call for worthy men. He was told that by the side of the palace gate was a guesthouse where Pei Zhong, the senior grand master, was receiving all applicants. It so happened that just as Jiao'ai was approaching the guesthouse, Pei Zhong alighted from his carriage. Jiao'ai stepped forward and made a bow.

Seeing such a distinguished-looking man in rags, Pei Zhong promptly returned the salute and asked, "Where are you from, my good man?"

Jiao'ai answered, "My name is Yang Jiao'ai. I am a native of Yongzhou, here to answer the king's call for worthy men to enter into his service."

Pei Zhong invited him into the guesthouse, served him wine and food, and lodged him in the house.

The following day Pei Zhong betook himself to the guesthouse and, by way of testing Jiao'ai's knowledge, asked him questions that had been puzzling his mind. To each and every question, Jiao'ai had an immediate reply. So eloquent was he that a delighted Pei Zhong reported the matter to the king, who immediately summoned him and sought his opinions on ways to increase the wealth of the kingdom and to build up its military power. Jiao'ai submitted ten proposals, which were, one and all, applicable to matters that needed the most urgent attention. Immensely pleased, the king treated him to a royal banquet, honored him as ordinary grand master,[4] and bestowed on him one hundred taels of gold and one hundred bolts of colored silk. As he bowed again and again, Jiao'ai burst into tears. The king asked in alarm, "Why are you in tears?" Whereupon Jiao'ai gave a detailed account of how Zuo Botao had taken off his clothes and offered his food. The king was moved by the story and so were all the ministers present.

"What are you planning to do?" asked the king.

"I wish to ask for leave so that I can go give Botao a proper burial before I come back to serve Your Majesty." The king then conferred upon the deceased Botao the posthumous title of ordinary grand master, granted a generous amount of money for his funeral, and sent a carriage and a retinue of men to escort Jiao'ai to the mountains.

After taking leave of the king, Jiao'ai set out straight for the Liang Mountains. As he approached the mulberry tree, he saw, just as he expected, Botao's body still lying there, his complexion the same as before he died. Jiao'ai bowed and wept. He had his followers summon some elderly men in the area and, by divination, chose a burial lot on the plains of Putang. With a large stream in front, a high cliff at the back, and a range of mountains on its left and right, the burial spot thus chosen was a blessed place with the best geomantic features. Botao's body was bathed in perfumed water and, complete with a ministerial robe and cap, was encoffined and buried in a grave. All around the grave, a wall was erected and trees were planted. About thirty steps from the grave was built an altar hall with an image of Botao in it. In front of the altar stood ornamental columns, on which were hung an inscribed board. By the side of the wall a tile-roofed hut was built for the caretaker. After the work was done, a tearful sacrificial ceremony was held in the altar hall. Every single one of the local attendees and Jiao'ai's followers shed tears. The ceremony over, all dispersed and went their separate ways.

That night, Jiao'ai sat by a brightly lit lamp, sighing with emotion in memory of his friend. All of a sudden, a chilly wind sprang up, extinguishing the candle. When the candle flickered back into flame again, Jiao'ai saw that there was, in the candlelight, a man who kept stepping back and forth, sobbing gently as he did so. Jiao'ai cried out, "Who goes there? How dare you barge in at this time of the night?" No answer came from the man. Jiao'ai rose and saw that it was Botao. In astonishment, Jiao'ai said, "Your soul being nearby, there must be a reason for your visit."

Botao explained in these words: "I am grateful to you, my good brother, for having remembered to seek the king's approval for burying me as soon as you gained office. A royal title, a coffin, and fine burial clothes are all that could ever be asked for. However, my grave happens to be near the grave of Jing Ke,[5] the one who was killed for a failed attempt on the First Emperor's life and was buried in this place by Gao Jianli. A most arrogant man, he comes every night with his sword to curse at me, saying, 'You died but an insignificant death from cold and hunger. How dare you build a grave in a position above mine to take away my geomantic advantage? If you don't move elsewhere, I will break open your grave and throw your body into the wilderness!' Now my good brother, I have come to you at this moment of crisis in the hope of being moved somewhere else so that such a horrible thing won't happen."

Before Jiao'ai could ask him anything, Botao disappeared suddenly in a puff of wind. With a start, Jiao'ai woke from his dream, still remembering all that had occurred in it.

At the break of day, he called the village elders together once more and asked if there were other graves in the neighborhood. He was told that in the shade of the pine trees lay Jing Ke's grave, with a temple in front.

"That man," said Jiao'ai, "was killed for a failed assassination attempt against the First Emperor of Qin. Why is his grave here?"

The village elders replied, "A native of these parts called Gao Jianli heard that Jing Ke's body was abandoned in the wilderness, and so he stole the corpse and buried it here. Many a time has the deceased manifested his supernatural power. The local residents built a temple here and offered seasonal sacrifices to ask for his blessing."

These words convinced Jiao'ai of the truth of the dream. He led some followers, rushed to the temple of Jing Ke, and lashed out at the latter's image: "You were but a worthless man from the state of Yan supported by the Prince of Yan, who showered upon you treasures and beauties, but, instead of devising a good plan worthy of the trust placed in you, you ventured into the state of Qin for the assassination attempt that not only ended your life but also jeopardized the well-being of your country. And now, here you are, intimidating the local people and demanding sacrificial offerings! (*[Illegible] Jing Ke [illegible].*) How dare you bully my brother Zuo Botao, a reputed scholar of our age and a paragon of virtue! If you don't change your ways, I will smash your temple, dig up your grave, and destroy, once and for all, the root of your existence!" Then he went to Botao's grave and said, "Should Jing Ke come to harass you again tonight, pray do not fail to let me know."

He returned to the altar hall and sat by candlelight, waiting. Just as he expected, Botao appeared to him and said between sobs, "I am grateful to you for having done what you did. However, Jing Ke has a large following of retainers offered up to him by the local residents. What you can do is to make some straw effigies, put colored clothing on them, attach weapons to their hands, and then burn them in front of my grave. If I have them to help me, Jing Ke can do me no harm." With these words he disappeared from view. Before the night was out, Jiao'ai did as he was told. A few scores of straw effigies, complete with colored clothing, swords, spears, and other weapons, were planted by the side of the grave and burned. Jiao'ai prayed, "If this works, please also let me know."

During the course of the night, he heard a storm that resembled the sounds of a battle. Stepping out the door to take a look, he saw Botao running toward him, saying, "The men you burned are not of much use, whereas Jing Ke has the support of Gao Jianli. My body will be cast out in no time. (*A complication in the plot.*) Please move me quickly to some other place of burial before the terrible thing happens."

Jiao'ai was indignant. "How dare that man bully my brother like this! I will certainly help you fight it out."

"You are a mortal being, whereas we are ghosts in the netherworld. However valiant, a living man cannot cross into the netherworld and fight ghosts. The straw men can do nothing more than utter battle cries. Driving away such a powerful presence is beyond them."

"You may go now," said Jiao'ai. "I will find a way tomorrow."

The following day, Jiao'ai went again into Jing Ke's temple and, with a stream of curses, smashed Jing Ke's image. He was about to set the temple on fire when there came to him several village elders pleading over and over, "This is the only temple in the area. Should any harm come to it, the local residents' lives might be jeopardized." In a trice, a crowd of natives gathered to plead with Jiao'ai. Failing to win the argument, Jiao'ai had to give up.

After returning to the altar hall, he wrote a memorial to the king of Chu to acknowledge his gratitude, saying, "It was thanks to Botao, who gave me his food, that I lived on to meet Your Majesty. Receiving a noble title from you leaves me with no more desires for the rest of my life. Please allow me to repay your kindness with all my heart in my next life." The words were filled with emotion. He gave the memorial to a valet for delivery and went to Botao's grave, where he burst into wails of grief. Turning to his followers, he said, "I cannot bear the thought that my brother is to be displaced by Jing Ke's insolent spirit. I would have burnt the temple and destroyed Jing Ke's grave if not for fear of offending the local inhabitants. It is better for me, therefore, to be a ghost under the Nine Springs, so as to help my brother fight that bully. You may bury my corpse to the right of this grave, so that I shall be with my brother in death, as I was with him in life, to repay him his kindness in offering me his ration. When you report the matter to the king of Chu, be sure to plead with him to follow my advice to make his state last forever." With these words, he pulled out the sword that hung at his waist and plunged it into himself. His followers hastened to try to save his life, but were too late. Promptly, they prepared his burial clothes and a coffin and buried him next to Botao's grave.

At the second watch of the night, there came on a furious storm with driving rain amid peals of thunder and flashes of lightning. Battle cries could be heard tens of li away. By early dawn, there, for all to see, were heaps of white bones scattered all over Jing Ke's grave, which had burst open as if by some explosion. The pines and cypresses around the grave had been uprooted. A fire blazed up in the temple and burned it to the ground. Greatly alarmed, the village elders hurried to the graves of Yang and Zuo and paid homage to them with offerings of incense.

When Yang's followers returned to Chu and reported the matter to the king, the latter, moved by Yang's loyalty, sent officials to build a temple in front of his grave. Yang Jiao'ai was also posthumously granted the title of senior grand master, and on the temple was hung a horizontal board bearing the inscription "Temple of Loyalty and Honor." With a stone tablet erected to commemorate the event, the temple has never been short of worshippers making offerings of incense. Henceforth, Jing Ke's spirit ceased to manifest itself. (*According to* The Biography, *after reaching Chu and becoming senior grand master, Jiao'ai buried Botao with rituals befitting a minister and then killed himself to be with Botao. No mention is made of his fight against Jing Ke. Moreover, Jiao'ai died before Jing Ke and Gao Jianli. The author is using Jiao'ai to humiliate Jing Ke out of indignation at the latter for letting Prince Dan down.)* The prayers of the local people in their seasonal sacrificial ceremonies were readily answered. There is an ancient poem that says,

> *Virtue that pervades the sky and the earth*
> *Dwells in the confines of the human heart.*
> *In this temple in calm autumn weather,*
> *Lit by the soft moon, are two noble souls.*

8

Wu Bao'an Abandons His Family to Ransom His Friend

Men of old made friends of the heart;
Men of today know friends but by face.
Friends of the heart share life and death;
Friends by face share not poverty.
The thoroughfares teem with men on horses;
Social visits go on with never a pause.
The host brings out his wife to the guests;[1]
Toasts go around with brotherly goodwill.
But a clash of interests, let alone true peril,
Suffices to turn friendships sour.
Consider instead Yang and Zuo[2] *of yore,*
Still praised in the annals, friends unto death.

The above lyric poem, titled "On Friendship," laments modern men's treachery and the lack of the true spirit of friendship. When passing around the wine cups, they can be as cordial as brothers, but, at the slightest conflict of interests, they turn their backs on each other. Truly, wine-and-meat brothers are to be had in the thousands; a true friend in distress is nowhere to be found. (*This is particularly true of Suzhou natives. How detestable! How absurd!*) There are also those who are brothers in the morning but enemies by evening. Scarcely have they put down their wine cups and walked out the door before they turn toward each other with bow and arrow drawn. Tao Yuanming's expressed wish to break off all friendships,[3] Ji Shuye's letter rejecting a friendly offer,[4] and Liu Xiaobiao's essay "On the Severing of All Relationships"[5] all were prompted by indignation at the deplorable morals of their times. I shall now propose to tell of two friends who, never having seen each other but drawn together by a similar sense of loyalty, went to each other's rescue in adversity in both life and death, proving themselves to be true friends of the heart. Indeed, it was just as

When Gong Yu dusted his cap, ready to go,[6]
Or when Jing Ke drew his sword for the thrust.[7]

Our story takes place in the Kaiyuan reign period [713–41] during the Tang dynasty. The prime minister and duke of Dai, named Guo Zhen, with the courtesy name Yuanzhen, a native of Wuyang, Hebei (*Wuyang is present-day Daming County in Daming Prefecture*), had a nephew, Guo Zhongxiang, who, despite his talent in both the civil as well as military arts, had received no recommendation for office, because his chivalrous spirit was often at odds with conventional codes of behavior. Anxious that he had not amounted to anything by this age, his father wrote a letter for him to take to his uncle Guo Yuanzhen in the capital, asking that he be given a start in his career. Yuanzhen said to him, "If a worthy man cannot establish a career for himself by taking the first honors in the imperial examinations, he should at least try to attain wealth and rank by proving his worth in foreign lands, as Ban Chao[8] and Fu Jiezi[9] did. If your ambition is to rise through family connections, how far do you expect to get?" Zhongxiang humbly voiced his agreement.

About this time, reports from the frontier to the capital said that the cave-dwelling barbarians in the south were in rebellion. The fact was that after Empress Wu Zetian[10] assumed power, she gave small bounties every year and big ones every three years to the barbarians in the Nine Ravines and Eighteen Caves in a bid to bribe them into submission. This system was abolished upon Emperor Xuanzong's ascension to the throne. The barbarians, therefore, rose in revolt and raided counties and prefectures. The imperial court dispatched Li Meng as governor-general of Yaozhou (*Present-day Dali and Yao'an in Yunnan were part of Yaozhou in Tang times*) to lead an expedition against the rebels. Thus authorized by imperial decree, Li Meng made a special trip, before his departure, to the prime minister's residence to bid him adieu as well as to solicit advice. Guo Yuanzhen said, "In olden times, Zhuge Liang captured Meng Huo[11] seven times but released him each time, in order that the barbarian should sincerely acknowledge his defeat rather than grudgingly submit to Zhuge's power. If you act with caution, victory will certainly be yours. My nephew Guo Zhongxiang is a capable man. I will have him follow you on this expedition, so that when you have defeated the barbarians and proven your worth, he can benefit from some of your glory and make a name for himself." Thereupon he called Zhongxiang to come forth and be introduced to Li Meng. Li Meng was impressed by Zhongxiang's air of distinction. Moreover, the young man was the nephew of the incumbent prime minister, who was personally asking him to take the young man on board. He could hardly dare to decline. Then and there, he granted Zhongxiang the post of aide-de-camp. Zhongxiang took leave of his uncle and set out with Li Meng.

When they came to the area south of the Jian Mountains,[12] Zhongxiang received a letter, delivered by a messenger on horseback, from a certain Wu

Bao'an, courtesy name Yonggu, who was sheriff of nearby Fangyi County
in the prefecture of Suizhou in eastern Sichuan. Being a native of the same
district that Zhongxiang was from, Wu Bao'an had long heard about Zhongxiang's loyalty to friends and his readiness to help others, though the two men
had never met. Zhongxiang opened the letter, which read,

> I, Wu Bao'an, am an unworthy man, but it is my great fortune to be from the
> same district as you are. I have long held you in high esteem, though I have
> neglected to pay my respects to you. With an immensely talented man like you
> as aide to General Li on this expedition against some minor bandits, victory is
> close at hand. I have applied myself assiduously in my study over the years but
> have gained no higher post than that of county sheriff in this remote place beyond
> the Jian Mountains, with my home far beyond reach except in dreams. Moreover,
> with my term of office expiring, I feel uncertain about my next appointment, for
> the regulations of the Ministry of Personnel may not be favorable to me. I have
> heard that you, sir, like the ancients, have great compassion for people in distress.
> With your mighty army on the march, this is a time of need for men. I wish you
> would, in consideration of our same place of origin, grant me an insignificant
> post in order that I may be of service to the expedition. I shall never forget to
> repay this kindness.

After a moment of reflection on the letter, Zhongxiang sighed, "This man has
never seen me, but he turns to me for help in his hour of need. He is indeed
someone who truly understands me. Isn't it shameful if a worthy man cannot
do anything for a trusting friend?" (*The man is asked a favor by someone he has
never met, and yet, strangely enough, his heart exults. Who can understand this?*)
Thereupon he praised Wu Bao'an's abilities to Li Meng and asked that Wu be
recruited into the army. Governor-General Li accepted the recommendation
and issued an order to be delivered to Suizhou, appointing Sheriff Wu Bao'an
as a clerk for the army.

No sooner had the messenger been sent on his way than some scouts
came back to report that the barbarian troops were fiercely pushing deeper
into the interior. Governor-General Li ordered the army to march posthaste
under cover of night. Upon reaching Yaozhou, they encountered barbarian
troops on a looting spree. The barbarian soldiers were caught off guard by the
sweeping army and ran pellmell everywhere in total defeat. Emboldened by
the victory, Governor-General Li led the mighty army in pursuit for a good
fifty li. When night fell, they pitched camp, and Guo Zhongxiang offered this
advice: "The barbarians are extremely cunning people. Now that they have
fled far away and your awe-inspiring name has been established, it would be
best for us to return to the prefectural seat while, at the same time, dispatching messengers to spread word about your power and benevolence so as to

induce them to surrender. To give further pursuit now is to get ourselves deeper into their terrain and risk falling into their traps."

Li Meng snapped hotly, "The barbarians are terror-stricken. If we don't take this opportunity to sweep their caves clean, when will we have another chance? Say no more! Just watch me crush them!"

The following day, they broke camp. After marching for several days, they reached the territory of the Wuman tribes,[13] where all that met their eyes were vast stretches of green wooded mountains, with no indication of a road. Growing apprehensive, Li Meng ordered the troops to withdraw, for the time being, to some open and flat land to pitch camp while, at the same time, looking for local residents to ask for directions. Suddenly, from amidst the valleys, all around them broke out the sounds of gongs and drums. Barbarian soldiers swept down the hills and descended upon the government troops from all directions. Their chief, Meng Xinuluo (*According to* The History of the Tang Dynasty, *Yaozhou was in Meng's possession after the Tianbao reign period, whereas Xinuluo was the ancestor of the six Wuman tribes. The story just borrows the latter's name*), never missing a shot with his wooden crossbow and poisoned arrows, led all the tribal chieftains in running through the woods and over the hills. They moved as fast and as effortlessly as flying birds and galloping beasts. The Tang army, caught in an ambush, tired and knowing nothing about the terrain, was in no position to fight back. However brave he was, there was nothing the governor-general could do to save the day. Seeing that he had few men left, he sighed, "If I had not ignored Aide-de-camp Guo's advice, I wouldn't have ended up humiliated by these dogs and sheep." He drew a dagger from his boot and cut his own throat. (*Li Meng is also a true hero.*) His entire army perished in the barbarian land. A later poet had this to say:

> Ma Yuan's[14] bronze pillars stand through the ages;
> Zhuge Liang's flag tower marks the Nine Ravines' defeat.
> What made an entire Tang army perish?
> Ill-starred indeed, the general named Li.

Another poem blames Governor-General Li for having courted defeat by ignoring Guo Zhongxiang's advice. The poem says,

> Ill-starred the general was not;
> To advance so deep is to risk danger.
> Had he followed the advice to retreat,
> The barbarians would have held him in fear.

Guo Zhongxiang was among the captured. Xinuluo was impressed by his distinguished looks, and when it was found out, after interrogation, that

the young man was Guo Yuanzhen's nephew, the barbarian chief gave him
to Wuluo, chieftain of his own cave. As a matter of fact, the southern barbarians had no greater ambition than to lay their hands on Chinese goods. The
Chinese captives were shared among the various cave chieftains. Those with
greater battle honor were given more; those with less received fewer. All of the
captives, regardless of their varying degrees of intelligence and worth, were
treated as slaves to chop firewood, feed horses, and herd sheep at the bidding
of the barbarians. Chieftains who had more slaves could trade those they did
not need. Nine out of ten Chinese who ended up there would rather die than
live, but, with barbarians watching them, they could not find ways to die—
such was their misery. In the last battle, a great number of Chinese were captured, among whom were many of high rank. When their background was
found out during interrogation, the barbarian chieftains made them write letters home to ask their relatives in China to ransom them at high prices. Now
who in such circumstances would not want to return home? Such a policy
prompted all captives, rich and poor alike, to write letters home. Those families that had far too little means to afford the ransom had to give up the idea,
but those that did have kith and kin to borrow from tried their best to scrape
together enough money for the ransom. For even a penniless bachelor, the
heartless and greedy barbarian chieftains sought as many as thirty bolts of fine
silk. For those of high rank, the ransom could be exorbitant. Having learned
that Guo Zhongxiang was the nephew of the incumbent prime minister,
Wuluo asked for the high price of a thousand bolts of silk.

Zhongxiang thought to himself, "Only my uncle can afford to produce a
thousand bolts of silk. But how am I to send a letter to him over such a great
distance?" Suddenly, a thought struck him: "Wu Bao'an is a friend who truly
understands me. I recommended him strongly to Governor-General Li for
the post of clerk on the basis of a few lines from him, without ever having
seen him. He must be appreciative of what I had done for him. Luckily, he
set out late and has been spared this misery. He should have arrived in Yaozhou by now. It shouldn't be too hard for him to deliver a message for me to
Chang'an." So he wrote a letter to Bao'an, describing in detail the plight he
was in as well as the ransom sought by Wuluo. The letter also said, "Please be
kind enough to convey a message to my uncle for him to deliver the ransom
as soon as possible, so that I might return alive. Could you, Yonggu, bear the
thought of letting me live as a captive slave and die as a ghost in a barbarian
land?" Yonggu was the courtesy name of Bao'an. At the end of the letter he
added the following lines:

Like Ji Zi,[15] *I'm a slave in an alien land;*
As Su Wu,[16] *I've fallen into barbarian hands.*

A righteous man of deep compassion,
You'll come to the rescue, as the ancients would do.

After he finished the letter, it so happened that an official from Yaozhou in charge of grain transport was released upon ransom. Zhongxiang entrusted the man with the letter and, before he realized it, burst into tears, for he felt as if his heart were stabbed by ten thousand arrows at the thought that others were being released, whereas he was left behind, unable to spread his wings. Truly,

He watched other birds fly high in the sky,
But remained stuck in his cage, freedom denied.

We shall now leave Guo Zhongxiang in the barbarian land but turn our attention to Wu Bao'an, who, having received Governor-General Li's letter and learned about Guo Zhongxiang's recommendation, left his wife, Zhang-shi, and their newborn child in Suizhou and, followed by a servant, traveled to Yaozhou with all speed to assume his post. The news about General Li's death in battle came to him as a shock. Not hearing anything about Zhong-xiang, he decided to stay on to learn what he could of the matter. It so happened that the official in charge of grain transport returned at that moment from the barbarian land, bringing with him the letter. Wu Bao'an opened and read the letter and was overcome with grief. He wrote a reply, assuring Zhongxiang that the ransom would be paid. He left the letter with the official and asked him to have someone send it to the barbarian land at his earliest convenience, to put Zhongxiang's mind at ease. He himself made haste to pack, and, in no time, he set off for Chang'an. It was more than three thousand li from Yaozhou to Chang'an through eastern Sichuan. Bao'an did not return home but went directly to the capital, Chang'an, and asked for an audience with Prime Minister Guo Yuanzhen. But, in fact, Yuanzhen had died a month before and his entire family had escorted the coffin back to their native place.

All his hopes dashed, all his travel money spent to the last penny, Wu Bao'an had no choice but to sell his servant and his horse to meet his immediate needs. Upon returning home to Suizhou and seeing his wife, Zhang-shi, and his child, he broke down in unrestrained sobs. To Zhang-shi's inquiries, he gave an account of Zhongxiang's captivity in the barbarian land and said, "I must ransom him, but, since I don't have the means, I'm making him wait in vain in that wretched place. How can I be at peace with myself?" The tears started flowing again.

Zhang-shi tried to stop him by saying, "It is often said that 'The cleverest housewife can't prepare porridge without rice.' Since you don't have the means to do as you wish, you'll have to give up the idea."

Bao'an shook his head. "I wrote to him before and he kindly recommended me for office. Now that he has entrusted me with his life at a time of great peril, how can I let him down? I swear not to live on if I fail to get him back."

And so he sold all his family possessions, which came to no more than the equivalent of two hundred bolts of silk. He left his wife and child and went out as a traveling merchant. However, afraid that more letters from the barbarian land might be delivered to him, he limited his routes to the greater Yaozhou area. From morning till night he traveled about in all directions, wearing tattered clothes and eating the coarsest food. Every penny, every grain of rice was saved toward the purchase of silk. When he bought one bolt, he set his mind on ten. Having bought ten, he set his mind on a hundred. When he got a hundred bolts, he deposited them in the prefectural treasury of Yaozhou. In his dreams, all that filled his mind was the name Guo Zhongxiang. Even his wife and child faded from his memory. A full ten years he spent on the road (*Who else would be willing to do this? Who else?*) and all he had accumulated came to barely seven hundred bolts of silk, still three hundred short of the amount required. Verily,

> *A thousand li from home he sought small gains,*
> *All for the sake of a true friendship.*
> *With the debt still unpaid after ten years,*
> *When was he to bring comfort to his friend?*

To pick up another thread of our story, we shall now tell of Wu Bao'an's wife, Zhang-shi, and their child, who stayed on in Suizhou, forlorn and desolate. In the beginning, there were people who helped them out in small ways out of regard for the former sheriff, but, as the years went by without any word from the husband, they gradually turned away from the woman and child. Nor did Zhang-shi have any savings to fall back on. After ten years, she found it impossible to go on living without enough food and clothing. She put together her few pieces of old and broken household goods and sold them in exchange for some traveling money. Taking along her eleven-year-old son, she asked for directions and set out on a journey to Yaozhou to look for her husband, Wu Bao'an. Traveling by day and resting by night, they could cover no more than thirty to forty li per day.

By the time they reached the borders of Rongzhou, all their traveling money had been exhausted. At her wits' end, Zhang-shi thought of begging her way along but, never having done this before, was too embarrassed to do it now. Lamenting over her tragic fate, she thought she would be better off dead, but she could ill bear to part with her eleven-year-old son. (*Someone said, "Wu Bao'an abandoned his family and spent ten years trying to ransom a friend he had* never even seen. Isn't this a bit unwise?" Yu Zhongxiang[17] commented, "A gentleman can leave this world without regrets if he has found himself one truly trusting friend." Precisely what Bao'an had in mind.) While she turned her thoughts this way and that, evening had set in. Sitting in the foothills of the Wumeng Mountains, she burst into loud wails of grief. Her crying alarmed an official who happened to be passing by. Named Yang Anju, the official was on his way to assume office as governor-general of Yaozhou to fill the vacancy left by Li Meng's death. He started his journey from Chang'an and was passing by the foothills of the Wumeng Mountains when he heard the woman's heart-rending cries. He called his horse carriage to a halt and asked the woman to step forward and tell him what the matter was. Taking her eleven-year-old son by the hand, Zhang-shi went over and said tearfully, "I am the wife of Wu Bao'an, sheriff of Suizhou. This child is my son. In order to have a thousand bolts of silk to ransom his friend Guo Zhongxiang from the barbarians, he left us to go to Yaozhou, and I haven't heard anything from him for ten years. I am now on my way to look for him because I have no one to turn to for help in my poverty. But it's still a long way ahead, and there's no more food left. That's why I was crying."

Anju marveled inwardly, "What a man of honor! What a pity I haven't had the good fortune to get acquainted with him!" To Zhang-shi, he said, "Don't worry, madam. I am the new governor-general of Yaozhou. As soon as I arrive in Yaozhou, I will send someone out to look for your worthy husband. I will take care of all your traveling expenses. Please go to the courier station further down the road. I will arrange lodging for you."

Zhang-shi restrained her tears and bowed in gratitude, although still not without some apprehension. Governor-General Yang's carriage left with the speed of wind.

Zhang-shi and her son supported each other and, step by step, made their way to the courier station. Governor-General Yang having already given instructions to the officer in command, the mother and son were led into a vacant room and served food after they were questioned as to their identity. At the fifth watch the following morning, Governor-General Yang took his departure. Acting on the governor-general's orders, the officer in command provided Zhang-shi with ten thousand in cash for traveling expenses as well as a carriage and some of his men to escort them all the way to the Pupeng courier station in Yaozhou. Zhang-shi's heart overflowed with gratitude. Truly,

> The good will be aided by the good,
> The evil tormented by the evil.

No sooner had he arrived in Yaozhou than Yang Anju set lictors out in every direction to find Wu Bao'an. Within three or four days, they found him. Anju invited him to the governor-general's residence, went down the front steps to greet him and, taking him by the hand, led him into the main hall and offered him kind words. (*Where can you find a man nowadays with Mr. Yang's respect for worthy men?*) "I have often heard," said the governor-general, "that the ancients were wont to form friendships that remained true through life and death, and now I see such an example in you. Your wife and son have come a long distance to look for you and are now at the courier station. Please go to see them and fill each other in on what happened in these ten years. I will take care of the bolts of silk that you need."

"It is only my duty to serve my friend as best I can," said Bao'an. "How can I presume to get you involved?"

"I just want to help you fulfill your wish out of my admiration for your spirit of loyalty."

Bao'an replied with a kowtow, "I will not presume to decline your most kind offer. I do still need one third of the total ransom. If I could have the entire sum now, I would go to the barbarians and redeem my friend. It won't be too late for me to see my wife and child after that."

Being new in his post, Anju had to borrow four hundred bolts of silk from the government treasury plus a fully saddled horse to give to Bao'an. Immensely delighted, Bao'an took the four hundred bolts as well as the seven hundred bolts that he already had and, equipped with all one thousand one hundred bolts, he set out on horseback for the southern barbarian land. Upon arrival, he found a Chinese-speaking barbarian and told him to convey his message to the other barbarians. To this man he gave the extra one hundred bolts for his expenses. He would be perfectly content if only Zhongxiang could be released. Truly,

> To see him at the hour of his release
> Is worth more than all the gold in Yueyang.

To retrace our steps, Guo Zhongxiang, under Wuluo, was treated well and amply provided with food and drink in the beginning because Wuluo was hoping to get a heavy ransom for him. But, after more than a year went by without any ransom-offering Chinese showing up, Wuluo was displeased and reduced Zhongxiang's rations to only one meal a day and made him herd the battle elephants. Unable to stand the misery, Zhongxiang was so consumed with homesickness that one day, when Wuluo was away on a hunting expedition, he escaped in a northerly direction. After he walked for a day and a night on dangerous mountain paths, the soles of his feet were all lacerated. Barbarians who herded the battle elephants ran after him with the speed of wind, caught up with him, and took him back. Wuluo was so incensed that he sold Zhongxiang as a slave to Xinding, chieftain of a southern cave two hundred li away from Wuluo's territory.

Now this Xinding was a most cruel man. Whenever a job displeased him in the slightest, he would flog Zhongxiang a hundred strokes with a leather whip until he was swollen and bruised all over his back. This happened more than once. The pain being too much for him, Zhongxiang escaped at the next chance that presented itself. However, as he was not familiar with the terrain, he ended up going in circles in the mountain valleys and was captured again by the local barbarians, who took him to Xinding. Xinding did not want him any more and sold him to another southern cave, and thus he was taken further south. This new chieftain, the Wild Bodhisattva, was even more merciless. Learning that Guo Zhongxiang had repeatedly tried to escape, he made Zhongxiang stand on two wooden boards, each five to six feet long and three to four inches thick, and drove iron nails through his feet into the wood. During the day, the wooden boards encumbered his movements, nor could he turn the slightest fraction of an inch at night as he slept in a pit covered by thick wooden boards, on which barbarians of the cave slept to keep watch over him. With pus and blood often oozing out from the wounds on his feet, the suffering was no less than the torments of hell. There is a poem in evidence:

> Sold farther and farther south by the southerners,
> He lived in a pit, nailed to wooden boards.
> For ten years no word from the central plains,[18]
> He saw his friend in dreams but dared not say a word.

Now, the Chinese-speaking barbarian went to see Wuluo with Wu Bao'an's message. Wuluo could hardly contain his joy at the prospect of a thousand bolts of silk. He sent a messenger down south to buy Guo Zhongxiang back. Xinding, the chieftain of the southern cave, led the messenger to the Wild Boddhisattva, and, as the ransom exchanged hands, iron pincers were put to work to pull out the nails from Zhongxiang's feet. Having been in the flesh for a long time, the nails were like part of the flesh after the pus had dried up. Now that they were being drawn out, the pain was more insufferable than when they were first driven in. Zhongxiang fell unconscious in a pool of blood. When he came to a considerable while later, he found himself unable to move so much as a step. There was no choice but to put him in a leather bag so that two barbarians could carry him to Wuluo. With the silk now in his possession, Wuluo could not have cared less whether Zhongxiang was dead or alive but handed him over to the Chinese-speaking barbarian, who then brought him to Wu Bao'an.

Wu Bao'an greeted him as he would his own flesh and blood. This being the first time the two friends met, they took a good look at each other before they found their voices. Then they fell upon each other's shoulders and wept, both wondering if they were meeting in a dream. That Guo Zhongxiang was grateful to Wu Bao'an goes without saying. Saddened by Zhongxiang's ghostly, emaciated look and his inability to use his feet, Bao'an gave his friend his horse while he himself followed behind on foot, traveling back to Yaozhou to report to Governor-General Yang.

As a matter of fact, Yang Anju had once been Guo Yuanzhen's subordinate. Though he had never seen Guo Zhongxiang before, he considered himself connected with the Guo family. Moreover, being a man of integrity, he did not base his regard for others on their change of status. The sight of Zhongxiang greatly delighted him. He had Zhongxiang take a bath and change into new clothes and bade an army physician attend to the wounds in his feet. With good nutrition and careful nursing, Zhongxiang recovered within a month.

Let us come back to Wu Bao'an. It was not until after he returned from the barbarian land that he went to the Pupeng courier station to see his wife and son. Still in swaddling clothes when they had parted, the boy was now eleven years of age. Bao'an could not help feeling sad at the quick passage of time. For his great loyalty, Yang Anju held him in the utmost esteem. Not only did the governor-general praise Bao'an to everyone he met, but he also wrote letters to highly placed officials in Chang'an, the capital, describing how Bao'an had ransomed a friend at the sacrifice of the well-being of his own family. Then he sent Bao'an off with lavish gifts and substantial provisions to go to the capital to get a new appointment. Impressed by the governor-general's treatment of him, all of the officials of Yaozhou showered gifts upon Bao'an as well. Zhongxiang was kept in the yamen as the governor-general's aide-de-camp. Wu Bao'an shared half of all the presents he received with Zhongxiang, over the latter's repeated objections. After expressing his gratitude to the governor-general, Wu Bao'an left for Chang'an with his family. Zhongxiang accompanied them beyond the Yaozhou border, and there they parted with bitter tears. Bao'an left his family in Suizhou and went alone to the capital, where he was promoted to be assistant magistrate of Pengshan County, Jiazhou Prefecture (*Present-day Pengshan County, Meizhou*). Jiazhou being within the borders of Sichuan, a location to which he could conveniently bring his family, Bao'an went merrily on his way to take up his post. Of this, no more need be said.

Let us now come back to Guo Zhongxiang, who, after all those years among barbarians, had gained a substantial knowledge of their way of life. Their women were quite beautiful but fetched lower prices than men. During the three years of his term of office, Zhongxiang repeatedly sent men to the caves to purchase beautiful young girls. Altogether he bought ten, whom he then personally taught to sing and dance, decked out in beautiful clothes and jewelry, and offered as a present to Yang Anju in acknowledgment of his gratitude. Anju said with a laugh, "I took pleasure in helping you out because I value the spirit of loyalty. If you repay me for what I did, won't you be treating me like a merchant?" (*Mr. Yang is no less a worthy man than Wu and Guo. How extraordinary to meet three such men at once. Too bad I never met one.*)

"It is your kindness that gave me new life. I am offering these girls to you as an all too slight token of my gratitude. Should you decline the gift, I shall not find peace even in death."

Impressed by his sincerity, Anju said, "I have a daughter whom I dote on. I'll keep only one of these girls, as a companion for her. The rest I would not presume to accept." Zhongxiang gave the remaining nine girls to nine trusted officers under Governor-General Yang so as to make manifest Mr. Yang's benevolence. (*Good thing to do.*)

The imperial court was, at the time, enlisting the service of the sons and nephews of the late Prime Minister Guo as a tribute to his distinguished military achievements. Yang Anju submitted a memorial that read,

> *Guo Zhongxiang, nephew of the late Prime Minister Guo Zhen, offered advice to General Li Meng while in his service, predicting the outcome of the campaigns against the barbarians. Later, he fell into the hands of the barbarians but remained a staunchly faithful subject of the empire. Ten years elapsed before he returned from the barbarian land. For three years now he has been in the service of your humble servant. While rewards are to be granted to the descendants of those with distinguished service to the empire, the recipients' own merits should also be recognized.*

Thus it came about that Guo Zhongxiang was granted the post of inspector of Weizhou. During the fifteen years of his absence, his father and his wife had learned nothing more than that he had fallen captive to the barbarians. They had long given him up for dead, but unexpectedly they received a letter from him in his own hand, saying that he would take the family to Weizhou, where he was to assume office. The joy of the entire family knew no bounds.

Zhongxiang made quite a name for himself during his two years as an official in Weizhou and was promoted to be the adjutant comptroller of revenue of Daizhou. Three years later, his father died of illness. He escorted the coffin back to Hebei. After the funeral was over, he heaved a sudden sigh and said, "I owe my life to Mr. Wu's ransom efforts. With my elderly father to support, I did not have time to consider repaying him for his kindness. Now that my father has passed away and the funeral rites are over, how can I forget about my benefactor?" After inquiries, he learned that Wu Bao'an had not returned from his place of office and went to Pengshan County in Jiazhou to pay him a visit.

Little did he know that Bao'an, upon expiration of his term of office, had been too poor to afford the journey to the capital to await reappointment, but had stayed behind in Pengshan and had died six years before of a plague that also claimed the life of his wife. Their bodies had been perfunctorily buried in a vacant lot behind the Yellow Dragon Temple. His son Wu Tianyou, whom his wife had taught to read and write at an early age, made a living by tutoring beginners in the same county. Upon learning this, Zhongxiang burst into inconsolable wails of grief. Putting on mourning clothes made of sackcloth, with a white hemp belt around his waist, he went, staff in hand, to the Yellow Dragon Temple, where he made offerings and poured libations at the graves, amid violent sobs. Thereafter, he sought out Wu Tianyou, put his own clothes on the young man, and called him his younger brother. He then consulted Tianyou about plans to take his parents' remains to their native place for a proper burial. He composed a prayer dedicated to Bao'an's spirit and dug open the makeshift grave, revealing two dried-up skeletons. Zhongxiang broke down in a flood of tears. Nor was there a dry eye among the onlookers.

Zhongxiang had prepared two silk bags for the bones of Bao'an and his wife. Afraid that the bones would be mixed up and difficult to rearrange into the right order for the burial, he made ink marks on the bones before he put them into the silk bags, which he then deposited into a bamboo basket. This done, he set off on the journey, carrying the basket over his shoulder. Wu Tianyou tried to snatch away the bamboo basket, claiming that his parents' bones should, by rights, be carried by him, but Zhongxiang would not hear of it. Tearfully, he said, "Yonggu devoted ten years of his life to my ransom. By carrying his bones for a little while, I am doing what little I can to show my gratitude." He wept as he went along. Each time he stopped at an inn, he would put the bamboo basket in the seat of honor and make offerings of wine and food to the spirits of the deceased before starting a meal with Tianyou. At night, he would also make sure to put the basket in a proper place before going to bed. The distance of thousands of li from Jiazhou to Wei County was to be covered by foot. Though the wounds on his feet—wounds from being nailed to the boards—had healed over, the blood vessels had been injured. The several days of walking hurt his feet, which became all purple and swollen. Soon he would no longer be able to walk, but he still pushed ahead, determined not to accept help with the load. There is a poem in evidence:

> *Too late to pay his debt, he hastened to the funeral.*
> *The bones on his back, he forged ahead day and night.*

With Yangping[19] still thousands of li away,
How long before he could reach their native place?

Zhongxiang thought to himself, "With so much more distance to cover, what shall I do?" At nightfall, when he stopped at an inn, he placed wine and food in front of the basket and, in tears, made repeated bows, praying piously, "May the spirits of Wu Yonggu and his wife show their power and relieve Zhongxiang of what ails his feet so that he can reach Wuyang County[20] unencumbered and in good time for the burial." Wu Tianyou, on one side, joined in the prayers. The following morning, as soon as he got up, Zhongxiang felt himself light and strong in the foot, and he experienced no more pain all the way to Wuyang County. It was not only Wu Bao'an's spirit, but also heaven that was at work protecting a good man.

After arrival at home, Zhongxiang kept Wu Tianyou with him and cleaned up the main hall, where he set up shrines for Wu Bao'an and his wife. He also bought coffins and funeral clothes for a reburial. Wearing mourning clothes, he kept vigil at the grave with Wu Tianyou, and together they received mourners and hired some men to build a grave mound. Everything was done in exactly the same way as he had buried his own father. A stone tablet was also raised on which was recorded the story of how Bao'an ransomed his friend through sacrificing the well-being of his family, so that all who stopped to read the inscriptions would learn about the good deed. Zhongxiang observed mourning for three years, living with Wu Tianyou in a hut beside the grave mound. In the course of the three years, he taught Tianyou to read the classics, so that the young man could be enough of a scholar to take up office. At the end of the three-year period, when he was ready to return to Chang'an to seek reappointment, he chose from among his nieces in the Guo clan a girl of virtue and married her to Wu Tianyou, for he was a bachelor with no family. Not only did Zhongxiang give Tianyou the eastern half of his residence for the young couple to live in, but he also presented Tianyou with half of all his property. (*Bao'an's kindness is unprecedented, and so is Zhongxiang's return of the kindness.*) Indeed,

He once left his wife and child for a friend;
Now his orphan enjoys the benefit.
Truly, "The gift of a papaya was repaid in jade."[21]
A good man will not fail the good at heart.

Zhongxiang went to the capital after the mourning period was over and was given the post of administrator of Lanzhou as well as the honorary title of Grand Master for Closing Court. His thoughts still on Bao'an, he wrote a memorial to the emperor, the gist of which was

Your servant understands that encouraging virtue is the canon of the empire and that repaying kindnesses is the duty of even the humblest of men. Some years ago, your servant followed the late Li Meng, governor-general of Yaozhou, on an expedition against the barbarians. After victory was won in the first battle, your servant advised caution against penetration into enemy terrain, but the governor-general ignored the advice, and, as a consequence, the entire army perished. Descendant of a distinguished family honored in China throughout the generations, your servant was taken captive in the poverty-stricken remote land. The greedy barbarians demanded ransoms of silk for the captives and asked from your servant, as nephew of the prime minister, a thousand bolts of silk. There being no means of communication at my disposal to notify my family ten thousand li away, I suffered misery of every description for ten years. My body was tortured; my tears never ceased flowing. I had the resolve of Su Wu but had little chance of having the letter-carrying wild goose shot down.[22]

Wu Bao'an, sheriff of Fangyi County in Suizhou Prefecture, who happened to be in Yaozhou at the time, did his best as a loyal friend to secure my ransom without ever having met me, though we were from the same native place. To raise the ransom, he undertook various endeavors away from his home for many years, to the detriment of his own health and the well-being of his wife and son. But he died suddenly before I could repay his great kindness to me in saving me from the brink of death and giving me a new life. It is a source of shame to me that while I am now enjoying favors from the imperial court, Bao'an's son Tianyou is suffering in dire poverty. Tianyou, being a fine young scholar, is fully qualified for office. I would fain cede my post to Tianyou, a move that would not only be of benefit to the empire through the encouragement of the good, but also relieve me of my debt of gratitude. I would be content with life in retirement till the end of my days. (The other sacrificed himself and his family. What's an official title in comparison? After all, Zhongxiang comes off better than Bao'an does.) *With great reverence I submit this memorial, risking death by boldly making my wish known.*

It was the twelfth year of the Tianbao reign period [753]. When the memorial was sent to the Ministry of Rites for deliberation, it caused quite a stir among the entire assembly of court officials. Granted that Bao'an's good turn happened first, Guo Zhongxiang's loyalty was also unusual. They were indeed friends in both life and death. The Ministry of Rites submitted a memorial to the throne in praise of Guo Zhongxiang's fine qualities, suggesting, at the same time, that an exception be made in this case as an example to the populace and that Wu Tianyou be granted the post of marshal of Langu County, while Zhongxiang should remain in his present position. In choosing Langu County, which was adjacent to Lanzhou, the Ministry of Rites officials were acting out of consideration for the two men's wish to see each other often.

After the imperial court granted the request, Zhongxiang gratefully left the capital with Wu Tianyou's letter of appointment and returned to Wuyang County, where he handed the letter to Tianyou. Offerings and libations were made at the graves of both families. On an auspicious day, the two families set off together for the Western Capital to report for duty.

This extraordinary story came to be spread far and wide, causing people to declare that the Wu-Guo friendship surpassed the Guan-Bao and Yang-Zuo relationships of ancient times. Later, Guo Zhongxiang in Lanzhou and Wu Tianyou in Langu County proved to be such good administrators that both received promotions to other places. In respectful commemoration of the event, the people of Lanzhou built a temple, which they named the Temple of Double Loyalty, in honor of Wu Bao'an and Guo Zhongxiang. All local residents who had pledges of friendship to make said their prayers in the temple, which, to this day, has never been short of worshippers. There is a poem in evidence:

> *Frequent handshakes may not mean much.*
> *Only in disaster is friendship shown.*
> *The true friendship between Guo and Wu*
> *Is far above the common run.*

9

Duke Pei of Jin Returns a Concubine
to Her Rightful Husband

However great your wealth, however high your rank,
Hoary age sets in before they are enjoyed.
Only kind deeds and good works
Live forever in people's hearts.

Back in the days of Emperor Wen [r. 179–156 B.C.E.] of the Han dynasty, there was a court minister named Deng Tong who stood high in the emperor's favor. Such was the emperor's fondness for him that he was always at the emperor's side, in the traveling retinue as well as on the royal bed. There was a physiognomist of divine talent by the name of Xu Fu, who, judging from the two vertical lines that extended from both sides of Deng Tong's nose down to his upper lip, predicted that he was to die of hunger and poverty. The emperor exploded with rage when he heard of this: "It is up to me alone to decide who is to gain wealth and who is not. Who then, may I ask, can reduce Deng Tong to poverty?" He thereupon gave Deng Tong a copper mine in Sichuan so that he could have copper coins minted for his own use. Thus it came about that the land was flooded with coins produced by Deng, whose wealth matched that of the whole empire.

One day, Emperor Wen found himself in unbearable pain from a running sore, whereupon Deng Tong fell to his knees and sucked out the pus and blood. Much relieved of the pain, the emperor asked, "What kind of people in the whole world love each other the most?"

Deng Tong replied, "No love is deeper than that between father and son."

It so happened that the crown prince stepped into the palace at that moment to inquire after his father's health, only to be told by the emperor to suck at the sore.

The crown prince declined, saying, "As I have just eaten fresh meat, I am afraid that it would be inadvisable for me to be near what ails you."

The emperor sighed after the crown prince had left. "Even my son," said he, "whose love for me should be surpassed by none, refuses to do what Deng Tong did for me. Indeed, Deng Tong loves me more than my son does."

Favors were further bestowed upon Deng Tong. When the emperor's remarks reached the ears of the crown prince, hatred burned in him against Deng Tong for his sucking of the sore. In due course, the emperor died, and the crown prince ascended the throne as Emperor Jing [156–140 B.C.E.]. He set about inflicting punishment upon Deng Tong under charges that Deng had ingratiated himself with the deceased emperor by sucking at his sore and that he had disrupted the empire's monetary laws. All of Deng Tong's assets were registered onto imperial ledgers and confiscated. Deng himself was thrown into an empty cell and denied food and water until he starved to death.

Later, also during the reign of Emperor Jing, Prime Minister Zhou Yafu, with similar vertical lines from his nose to his upper lip, was cast into prison on some trumped-up charges by the emperor out of jealousy of his prestige. He died while on a hunger strike as a statement of his indignation. These are two instances of men of immense wealth and the highest rank who died of unnatural causes because of the hunger lines on their faces.

However that may be, there is also the argument that physiognomy is less important than personal character. Among those with the most propitious physiognomic features, some lost their moral credit in the otherworld by committing evil deeds and were, therefore, condemned to a miserable end. By the same token, among those with features that portend calamity, some have turned doom into bliss by grace of their personal integrity and good deeds that earned them merit in the otherworld. I am not saying that physiognomy is unreliable but that human effort can indeed prevail over predestined fate.

Now I come to a certain Pei Du of the Tang dynasty, who had been poverty-stricken in his youth before his time had come. A physiognomist said that he was to die of hunger, because he had lines that ran from both sides of his nose down to his upper lip. Later, when touring Fragrant Hill Temple, he found three jeweled belts on the balustrade of a pavilion over a well. Pei Du thought to himself, "Someone must have left them behind inadvertently. I should not benefit myself at the expense of others. That would be an unconscionable thing to do." So, he sat down and waited for the owner to come.

Before long, a woman came into view, saying tearfully, "My father is in jail. I borrowed three jeweled belts to redeem him. But I lost them when I stopped at this temple to wash my hands before burning incense. Should any one have found them, please have pity on me and return them to me so that my father's life can be spared."

Pei Du promptly handed the three belts to her. She bowed with gratitude and went on her way.

Shortly thereafter, he met the physiognomist again. Agape with astonishment, the latter said, "Your physiognomy has totally changed," he said. "You are no longer the man in whom I saw hunger. You must have done some good deed that earned you merit in the netherworld."

Pei Du denied this, but the physiognomist insisted, "Try to think back. You must have done something like saving a person from drowning or putting out a fire," whereupon Pei Du told him about the returning of the belts.

"This is a major merit," said the physiognomist. "Please accept my congratulations in advance, for you will gain both riches and honor."

As it turned out, Pei Du passed the imperial examinations later on, rose to be the prime minister of the empire, and lived to a ripe old age. Truly,

> *Fate is determined more by heart than face;*
> *All must earn merit by doing good deeds.*
> *If one's fate allows not the slightest change,*
> *How could one doomed to hunger rise to wealth?*

Storyteller, you have told how Duke Pei of Jin gained wealth and honor through good deeds, but do you also know that his good deeds were even more numerous after he achieved wealth and rank?

Well, then, listen while I tell of how he returned a concubine to her rightful husband, and a remarkable story it is.

It is said that in the thirteenth year of the Yuanhe reign period [818], under Emperor Xianzong of the Tang dynasty, Pei Du led the imperial troops in defeating the rebel Wu Yuanji of the Huaixi region. Upon returning to the imperial court, he was made prime minister as well as duke of Jin. Two other commanders long in rebellion, who controlled strategically positioned outlying prefectures, submitted a memorial to the throne out of fear of Pei Du's awe-inspiring might, stating their willingness to yield land in redemption of their offense. Wang Chengzong, regional commander of Heng and Ji,[1] conceded the two prefectures of De and Li. Li Shidao, regional commander of Zi and Qing,[2] conceded the three prefectures of Yi, Mi, and Hai.

Seeing that the rebellions had been subdued and all was well with the empire, Emperor Xianzong started a grand-scale construction project, renovating the Hall of the Virtue of the Dragon, dredging Dragon-Head Lake, and building the Hall of Brightness. Under the influence of a Taoist hermit by the name of Liu Mi, the emperor tried his hand at concocting an elixir of longevity, turning a deaf ear to Pei Du's repeated remonstrations.

There were then two evil ministers in the court. One was Huangfu Bo, director of the Bureau of General Accounts, and the other was Cheng Yi, Salt Monopoly commissioner. Together, they did nothing but extort from the people money that they called a "surplus" tax for use in times of peace. This pleased the emperor immensely. The two sycophants were made joint managers of state affairs with the Secretariat and the Chancellery.

Ashamed to be associated with such people, Pei Du petitioned to be allowed to retire. However, instead of granting the request, the emperor accused him of trying to form factions. Thus it was that he came to be distrusted and resented by the emperor. Realizing that his fame and merit were too great for his own good, Pei Du detached himself from affairs of the court in order to avoid invoking the emperor's anger any further. Instead, he indulged in the pleasures of wine and women to provide himself with some amusement in his declining years. (*[Illegible] How sad!*) Officials all over the land offered him singers and dancers. It was not that he sought any such offers, but those ingratiating officials, in trying to curry favor with the prime minister, laid hold of the girls either by purchasing them at high prices or by sheer force. Falsely presented as domestic women of pleasure or as maid-servants, the beautifully dressed girls were eagerly sent to the prime minister. Duke Pei, for his part, felt obliged to accept whatever came his way.

There lived a certain Tang Bi, courtesy name Guobao, in Wanquan [Ten Thousand Springs] County in Jinzhou Prefecture. He had started his career from the post of county marshal of Longzong County in Kuozhou, a position he had acquired through recommendations on the merit of his filial piety, and was now magistrate of Kuaiji³ of Yuezhou. Before he started his official career, he was betrothed to a Huang Xiao'e, daughter of Imperial Student Huang of the same district, but at the time Xiao'e was too young to marry. When she was of age, Tang Bi had left for the south, where his official duties for his two successive posts took him. Thus, the wedding was put off from year to year.

Now eighteen years of age, Xiao'e had a face as fair as a flower and a figure as graceful as a carved jade statue. Her beauty was no less striking than her talent in music. As for the vertical bamboo flute, the pipe, the *pipa* [four-stringed lute], and the like, there was none that she could not play well. As it happened, the prefect of Jinzhou was selecting from the region beautiful singing girls to be offered to Pei Du, the duke of Jin, to please the latter. The group of five that had already been assembled still needed a girl of outstanding talent to be their leader. Huang Xiao'e's fame reached the ears of the prefect, and he bade the magistrate of Wanquan County to approach the girl with an offer of no less than thirty thousand in cash to be paid by the prefect, because the daughter of a member of the National University was not to be short-changed. The magistrate, all too eager, in his turn, to ingratiate himself with the prefect (*Evil is bred in the continuous chain of attempts to ingratiate oneself with one's superiors*), dispatched a messenger to the Huang residence, only to be told by Mr. Huang that his daughter was already betrothed and that he therefore had to decline the offer with regret. To the magistrate's repeated commands Mr. Huang turned a deaf ear.

While all this was going on, the Clear and Bright Festival⁴ came around. The entire Huang family went out to sweep the ancestral graves, leaving Xiao'e at home all by herself. When the magistrate learned of this, he went in person to the Huang residence, where he found Xiao'e after a search and had her carried away in a sedan-chair. In the company of two women attendants, she was brought immediately to the prefect's tribunal. The three hundred thousand in cash was thrown down in the Huang residence as the price for the girl.

Upon returning and learning that his daughter had been kidnapped by the county magistrate, Mr. Huang hurried with all speed to the county tribunal, but was told that his daughter had already been sent to the prefectural tribunal, whereupon he went to Jinzhou and appealed to the prefect's sympathy.

The prefect said, "With her remarkable beauty and talent, your daughter will surely gain favor with the prime minister. Wouldn't that be better than marrying some common man and busying herself with household chores? What's more, you have already pocketed six hundred thousand in cash. Why don't you give the money to the man your daughter is betrothed to so that he can get himself another wife?"

Mr. Huang countered, "I did not take the money in the county magistrate's presence. It was left in my house while I was away paying respects to my ancestors' graves. I brought with me the entire amount, which is no more than three hundred thousand, for what I want is my daughter, not the money."

With a slap on the table, the prefect roared in a towering rage, "You sold your daughter for a price that you claim to be three hundred thousand less than what it was, and now you are here pestering me with your endless harangue. What kind of behavior is this! Your daughter, I tell you, is already in the prime minister's mansion. You can go there to claim her instead of wasting your time with me."

Seeing that the infuriated prefect was resorting to brazen lies, Mr. Huang did not venture to say anything further but left the place with tears in his eyes. He stayed in Jinzhou for several days in the vain hope of seeing his daughter, if only once. As nothing came of his waiting, he could not do otherwise but return home, and that he did with a sigh.

Meanwhile, the prefect lavished a thousand pieces of gold on fancy costumes and fine jewelry for the six girls, until they looked no different than fairy maidens from heaven. From morning till night, they practiced in the tribunal on a whole range of musical instruments until, finally, the duke of Jin's birthday drew near, and the group was escorted to his mansion as his birthday present. The prefect had spared neither pain nor money in his attempt to impress the prime minister. As it turned out, however, the prime minister's mansion was already teeming with numerous singers and dancers and beauties offered by local officials from all quarters of the land. The addition of this group of six was hardly enough to impress the prime minister. (*How sad it is that girls as pretty as flowers are reduced to nothing more than Liaodong pigs!*)[5] This is usually what happens to sycophants, who not only gain nothing for their pains but also have to sustain losses. (*The small-minded would gladly sustain such losses.*) There is a poem that bears witness:

> To please the duke, they could cut their own flesh;
> To pick singers, they used thousands in cash.
> Unimpressed the duke turned out to be,
> Much to the sycophants' burning shame.

Let us follow another thread of the story and turn to Tang Bi, who was due for a promotion and a reappointment to another location, his term of office at Kuaiji having just expired. Since Huang Xiao'e should by now be old enough to marry, he decided to return to his native town to hold the wedding before going to the capital to receive his next appointment. Consequently, he packed up the belongings acquired during his term of office and set out in the direction of Wanquan County. The very day after his arrival, he paid a visit to Mr. Huang, who guessed what he came for and, before he raised the subject, gave him a full account of how the young lady had been kidnapped. Tang Bi was struck speechless. It was a good while before he said bitterly, between clenched teeth, "What is there to live for if a worthy man drifting around as a petty official cannot even protect his wife?"

Mr. Huang tried to comfort him with these words: "My good son-in-law, being as young and talented as you are, you will surely be blessed with a good marriage. It is my daughter's misfortune to have been taken by force away from you. Please do not let excessive grief jeopardize your future."

But Tang Bi was not to be placated. He talked instead of fighting it out with the prefect and the county magistrate.

Mr. Huang tried again: "With her already gone, what's the good of more arguing? Moreover, you'll be standing in the way of Prime Minister Pei, who is now second only to the emperor in the whole empire. Your career will be at stake if you incur his ill feelings." Having spoken these words, he ordered that the three hundred thousand in cash left behind by the magistrate be brought out. When handing the money over to Tang Bi, he said, "This is to help you find another match. My daughter is wearing your betrothal gift of carved green jade, and therefore I cannot return it to you. Please put your own future before everything else. Do not let a small setback compromise your career."

With tears streaming down his cheeks, Tang Bi said, "For a man approaching thirty years of age, the loss of such a good fiancée means the end of all hopes of marriage. Nor will I ever seek advancement in career again, for the pursuit of some meager fame and fortune does nothing but ruin a man." With these words, he gave way to his emotion and so did Mr. Huang. The two cried their hearts out before Tang Bi took his leave, but nothing could make him take the money. He returned empty-handed.

The following day, Mr. Huang called upon Tang Bi and repeatedly urged him to go without delay to the capital for reappointment and, thereafter, to start looking for a good match. Tang Bi would hear nothing of it at first, but, unable to withstand any longer Mr. Huang's persistent nagging for several days on end, he conceded, thinking that rather than brooding at home, he might as well take a trip to Chang'an to take his mind off his troubles. Much against his inclinations, he selected a propitious day and engaged a boat for the purpose. Mr. Huang slipped the three hundred thousand onto the boat and quietly instructed Tang's men in these words: "Do not tell your master about the money until two days after the boat sets out. It's for him to use in the capital and get himself a good post."

The sight of the money sent another wave of grief over Tang Bi. He said to his servants, "This is money given in exchange for Mr. Huang's daughter. Not a cent is to be touched." (*How sad!*)

Upon arriving in Chang'an after a few days, he hired some men to carry the baggage on their shoulder-poles and found lodging in an inn near the east side of Prime Minister Pei's mansion, the more convenient for him to make frequent inquiries about Xiao'e. (*He still has his heart set on finding out about her.*) The following morning, he reported to the Ministry of Personnel and had his credentials examined. Then he returned to the inn and, immediately after lunch, went to stand at the entrance of the mansion. At least ten times each day he went there, but a month went by without his getting half a word in. Officials going in and out of the mansion looked as busy as ants. Who would dare go up to them with some woeful tale? Truly,

> Once she entered the depths of the yamen,
> He became nothing more than a stranger.

One day, on the list of imperial appointments publicized by the Ministry of Personnel, Tang Bi found his own name. He was to assume the post of administrative supervisor in the prefecture of Huzhou, in the south. Being familiar with the area, Tang Bi was delighted. When the appointment letter came, he packed up his belongings and hired a boat for the journey out of the capital. When he came upon the area of Tongjin, the boat was attacked by a gang of robbers. As the ancient proverb has it, "To put off hiding your money is to invite thieves." The three hundred thousand cash that Tang Bi took with him wherever he went had somehow caught the greedy eye of some miscreants, who had banded together for action. They followed him from the capital all the way to Tongjin and, having reached an understanding with the boatman, waited for night to fall before they struck. Tang Bi, however, was not destined to die that night. He was relieving himself on the bow of the boat when the commotion started. Without a moment's delay, he threw himself overboard into the river, scrambled ashore, and heard the robbers pole the boat away after all the racket died down. Wondering whether his servant was dead or alive, he stood there all by himself, with nothing left in his possession but the clothes on his back. Truly,

> An all-night rain wrecks a hut already leaking;
> A head wind thwarts a boat already slow.

The three hundred thousand cash and his personal belongings were trifles compared with the loss of his certificates of office and the appointment letter, which were the identification papers for his new post. With those went all his hopes of holding office. At his wit's end, he took stock of the situation: "As ill luck would have it, I now have nothing to my name. To return home would be too much of a disgrace. To go to the capital and seek help from the Ministry of Personnel would be out of the question without a penny of traveling money. There is no acquaintance of mine in these parts whom I can ask for a loan. Am I to be reduced to begging?" The thought of drowning himself in the river crossed his mind, but he told himself, "Surely this is no end for a worthy man." He sat by the side of the road and broke down in tears. The crying started him off on a new train of thought, only to bring on another burst of sobs. He ran his mind over various plans but found none that would do him any good. And so he wept from midnight to daybreak.

Luckily, rescue came in the form of an old man with a staff, moving toward him. "Why are you weeping, sir?" asked he, whereupon Tang Bi gave an account of how he was robbed while on his way to assume a new post.

"Pray forgive me for not recognizing a man of distinction," exclaimed the old man. "Please follow me to my humble house a short distance away." He led Tang Bi to his home about one li away and went through the proper salutations. "My surname is Su," said he. "My son, Su Fenghua, being the county marshal of Wuyuan in Huzhou Prefecture, is actually a subordinate of yours. (*A good opportunity presents itself.*) I will be all too happy to be of service to you for your journey to the capital." So saying, he hastened to set out wine and food, and had Tang Bi change into a new outfit. He also presented Tang Bi with twenty taels of silver for his traveling expenses.

With profuse thanks, Tang Bi took leave of Mr. Su and went on his way all by himself. Upon reaching the capital, he took his lodging in the same inn where he had stayed before. The innkeeper's heart went out to him at hearing about his misfortune. When Tang Bi sorrowfully reported the case to the Ministry of Personnel, he was told that since he had no identification papers whatsoever, there was no way to decide as to the truth of his statement. Five days of pleading produced no effect, although he had exhausted all the silver he had to satisfy employees of the yamen.

Back at the inn, as he sat there with tears in his eyes, brooding over his anxieties and lamenting his ill fate, there stepped in from the outside a man of an age past the prime of his life, looking like a lower-ranking officer wearing a gauze hat with soft flaps, a purple outfit, a leather belt, and a pair of black boots. As his eyes came to rest upon Tang Bi, he sat down with a bow opposite him and asked, "Where, may I ask, are you from, and what brought you here?"

Tang Bi replied, "Don't ask me, for I'm afraid the story of my misery will take a considerable time to tell." Before the words were quite out of his mouth, the tears came streaming down.

"Pray let me hear what is troubling you," said the man in purple. "Please tell me everything. I might be able to help."

"My name is Tang Bi. I am a native of Wanquan County of Jinzhou. I was on my way to my new post as administrative supervisor of Huzhou when, in the area of Tongjin, I came upon a group of robbers, who took away everything I had, including my certificates of office and the appointment letter, thus making it impossible for me to assume office."

"It is not your fault that you ran into robbers. Why didn't you report to the Ministry of Personnel to apply for a reissuance of the appointment letter? What kept you from doing that?"

"I did plead several times, but to no avail. And now, without anyone to turn to for help, I can't leave the city any more than I can stay."

"The incumbent prime minister, Duke Pei of Jin, is a compassionate man most inclined toward helping those in distress. Why don't you go to see him?"

That remark plunged Tang Bi into deeper despair. "Please don't mention that man," he said between louder sobs. "That very name stabs me to the heart." (*Good twist in the plot.*)

The man in purple was astounded. "Why do you say so?"

Tang Bi explained, "As I have held office in different places in the south, I have not been able to marry my prospective wife betrothed to me from early childhood. The prefect and the county magistrate kidnapped her to make her join a band of female musicians that they then offered to the duke of Jin. That is how I, a man in the prime of life, have come to remain a bachelor. Although the duke had no hand in the kidnapping, he is not any less to blame, because it is his willingness to accept bribery that encourages the local officials to scramble for his favor. How can I bear the sight of that man?"

"What is the name of your betrothed?" asked the man in purple. "What betrothal gifts was she given?"

"Her name is Huang Xiao'e. The betrothal gift of a piece of carved green jade is still with her, I believe."

"As I happen to be a personal bodyguard of the duke," declared the man in purple, "I have the privilege of access to his private quarters. I will gladly make some inquiries on your behalf."

"Now that she has entered that mansion, there is no hope of our seeing each other again. If you would be kind enough to get a word in and let her know my feelings, I shall die contented."

"By this time tomorrow, I will certainly bring you good news." With these words, the man in purple folded his hands in front of him and stepped out of the inn.

As Tang Bi thought about what had just occurred, regrets began to set in: "That officer in purple must have been a trusted follower of the duke and sent out as a spy. I shouldn't have made those accusing remarks. If those words get into the duke's ears and stir his anger, much trouble will be in store for me." And thus he fretted all through the wakeful night.

When daylight finally came, he washed and dressed and went to the Pei mansion for a look. Word got out that the duke had excused himself from public appearance for the day. Even so, the traffic of messengers in and out of the mansion kept flowing, but the man in purple was nowhere to be seen. After having waited for a long time, Tang Bi returned to the inn for lunch and then came back to the mansion, but still had no luck. As the day was drawing to a close, that the man in purple had broken his promise became a certainty. With sigh after sigh, the dejected Tang Bi dragged himself back to the inn.

He was about to light the lamp when he caught sight of two men looking like runners from the court entering the inn in great haste, asking, "Who is Administrative Supervisor Tang Bi?" So frightened was he that he hid himself around a corner without daring to reply. (*A wonderful story.*)

The innkeeper approached them with the question "Who might you be?"

"We are runners from the Pei mansion. We are here at the bidding of the duke to invite Administrative Supervisor Tang to the mansion for a talk."

The innkeeper said with a point of his finger, "He's right there."

Tang Bi had no alternative but to step forward and present himself, saying, "I am a perfect stranger to the duke. Why this sudden invitation? Besides, I am not appropriately dressed for the occasion. I wouldn't dream of being amiss in decorum."

The runners insisted, "The duke is waiting. Please do not decline, sir."

Supported on both sides, he was brought to the mansion with the speed of wind. Once inside the main hall, the two men went into the inner quarters after telling him, "Please be seated, sir. After reporting to the duke, we will be back in a moment to usher you in." Presently, hurried footsteps were heard . before the two men reappeared with the words "The duke is inside, being on leave today, and invites you in." They wound their way through the mansion grounds, which were lit as bright as day. The two men, one in front and the other behind, escorted Tang Bi into a small room lined with two rows of gauze lamps. The duke, wearing casual clothes and a cap with pointed corners, was already standing there waiting, his hands folded in front of his chest in a gesture of respect. A consternated Tang Bi broke into a sweat and fell prostrate on the ground, without daring to venture a glance upward. The duke ordered that he be helped to his feet, saying, "Please do not stand on ceremony. This is but a private meeting." He then bade Tang Bi sit down. Tang Bi did so by the duke's side only after a few moments of customary demur. He stole a glance at the duke and found the latter to be none other than the very man in purple he had met at the inn. He broke into a sweat and went breathless with fear, keeping his head down all the time.

What had happened was that Pei, in his moments of leisure, was given to traveling incognito for his own amusement. The day before, a whim took him to the inn, where he met Tang Bi. After returning to the mansion, he checked the register for the name of Huang Xiao'e and called her into his presence. Much impressed by her beauty, he questioned her about her personal history and found that her account tallied with Tang Bi's version. When he asked to see the carved green jade, he saw that the piece of jade was worn tight and secure on her arm. Overcome by sympathy, the duke said, "Your prospective husband is here. Do you wish to see him?"

With tears in her eyes, Xiao'e answered, "A pretty woman is doomed to a sorry fate. I don't expect to see him again. It is up to the duke to decide whether I should see him. I wouldn't dream of taking the decision upon myself." (*Good answer.*)

The duke nodded and told her to withdraw for the moment. Secretly he instructed his attendants to get ready gifts worth a thousand strings of cash and had a messenger send to the Ministry of Personnel an appointment form on which he had filled in Tang Bi's name. It was an authorization for checking his background and issuing another copy of the letter appointing him as administrative supervisor of Huzhou Prefecture. It was not until after all this had been done that he sent for Tang Bi (*One needs to be thorough in dealing with relationships. I wish I could meet such people!*), who, in his state of fright, had no inkling of the duke's good intentions.

The duke addressed him as follows: "From what you told me yesterday, I learned of the pain deep in your heart. I plead guilty to failing to stem the flow of presents, thus separating you from your wife."

Tang Bi rose from his seat and fell to his knees, saying, "In my confused state yesterday brought on by the series of mishaps that befell me, I made some affronting remarks punishable by death. I humbly beg for your magnanimous forgiveness."

The duke bade him rise. "Today is an auspicious day," he said. "I have taken it upon myself to preside over the wedding ceremony for you. I have about a thousand strings of cash to offer as a humble wedding present, in atonement for the wrong I did you. As soon as the wedding is over, you may go to your new post with your wife."

Tang Bi thanked him profusely but did not muster up enough courage to ask about the new post. A musical fanfare was heard coming from the private quarters, then there appeared several pairs of red lanterns, a band of female musicians, and some matrons of honor and waiting women, all of whom ushered in Huang Xiao'e, fresh as a flower and fair as jade. Before Tang Bi could dodge to one side, one of the matrons said, "Bride and bridegroom, please salute each other."

As the waiting women spread out the red carpet, Huang Xiao'e and Tang Bi stepped on it and made four bows skyward, to which the duke bowed back from his position to one side. Sedan-chair carriers who had long been waiting for the bride outside the room now carried her all the way to the inn. Tang Bi, too, was enjoined by the duke to return there without delay. As he approached the inn, he heard a clamor of voices. There for all to see were chests of silk and caskets of gold and cash watched over by the two runners, who were waiting to deliver the goods to Tang Bi in person. There was a small box sealed by a strip of paper bearing the duke's handwriting. On opening it, Tang Bi found, to his immense delight, a reissued letter of appointment for the position of inspector of Huzhou. That night, the room in the inn served as their bridal chamber. Their joy knew no bounds, far exceeding that of average couples at the consummation of their marriages. Truly,

> When your time goes, ill luck follows your heels.[6]
> When your time comes, good luck falls in your lap.[7]
> Endowed with wife and post as he is now,
> Gone are the sorrows that darkened his brow.

Thus it came about that Tang Bi was blessed now with a wife, a career, and a fortune worth a thousand in cash, a change of luck no less remarkable than that of a wretched soul condemned to the eighteenth tier of hell rising to the thirty-third circle of heaven. Such bliss would not have been possible without Pei's gracious kindness.

The following day, Tang Bi paid the duke another visit to express his gratitude, only to be turned away by the gatekeeper, who had been so instructed by the duke. Back at the inn, Tang Bi packed his clothes for the journey and, before setting out, hired several servants, who followed the couple back to their native village. The reunion with Mr. Huang, father of the bride, was filled with joy, as if spring had come to a withered tree or a broken string on a lute had been joined together again. A few days later, the couple went on their way to Huzhou for Tang Bi to take up his new post. Out of gratitude toward Duke Pei, they had a statuette of him carved out of agalloch eagle-wood, to which they offered prayers morning and night for his well-being and longevity. Indeed, the duke lived to be over eighty years of age, with a growing and flourishing clan of descendants, a blessing that was attributed to his good deeds, which earned him merit in the netherworld. As the poem says,

> *With no wife or post, his grief knew no bounds*
> *Till a kind hand turned his fortune around.*
> *Those who are given to generous deeds,*
> *Well blessed may they and their offspring be.*

Magistrate Teng Settles the Case of Inheritance with Ghostly Cleverness

> *Like the Xie brothers of jade-tree fame,*
> *And the three Tians under the redbud twigs,*[1]
> *Brothers who live in harmony*
> *Fill their parents' hearts with delight.*
> *All too many fight over property*
> *And torment siblings who share the same root.*
> *When the snipe and the clam grapple,*
> *They benefit none but the fisherman.*

The above lyric poem to the tune of "The Moon over the West River" urges brothers to live in harmony. All of the classics and scriptures of the three teachings of our time serve the same purpose of exhorting people to virtue. Confucianism has the Thirteen Classics, the Six Classics, and the Five Classics; Buddhism has the many volumes of the *Tripitaka;* and Taoism has the *Zhuangzi,* the *Liezi,* and so forth. However, all of these volumes that fill up trunks and clutter desks are in fact quite superfluous, for, as I see it, only two words suffice to make a good person: *xiao* and *ti*—filial piety and fraternal love. Again, of these two, just *xiao,* "filial piety," would suffice.

Those who show filial piety to their parents and love and honor whatever their parents love and honor will, for the sake of the parents, extend such feelings to their brothers, who are like branches on the same tree. Thus, how can there be any lack of harmony? As far as family estates are concerned, since they were all acquired by the same parents, why divide them up into what is "yours" and what is "mine," what is fertile and what is barren? If you were born into a poor family without a penny to inherit, you would naturally have to earn a living, however hard it might be, by the sweat of your brow. As for those with land and property to inherit, if they fight over the size of their portions and all too readily accuse their parents of favoritism and lack of fairness, in the Nine Springs of the netherworld the parents would surely be saddened, something that filial sons should never allow to happen. (*Well said.*)

Therefore, it is as the ancients said so well: "Brothers are hard to come by, but land is easy to acquire." Why are brothers hard to come by? Well, for everyone in this world, parents are the people dearest to you, but, at the time you were born, your parents should have at least reached a mature age and will therefore die before you do. They can be with you for no more than half of your life. As for a married couple whose love for each other has no equal, they may enjoy each other's company to a hoary old age, and yet, before they were married, they lived in separate households, under different family names, in childhoods that they did not share. Only brothers, born in the same family and as close to one another as hands and feet, can be with each other all their lives, consulting each other and helping each other out in times of need. How deep the bonds are! Fertile lands and wealth, if lost, can be won back some day, but loss of a brother is no less than loss of a hand or a foot that would leave you maimed for the rest of your life. Is it not true, then, that "brothers are hard to come by but land is easy to acquire?" Rather than fall out for the sake of a piece of land, it would be better that brothers be penniless with nothing to inherit, for they could at least be spared involvement in disputes.

I now propose to tell a story that took place in our dynasty [the Ming], a story titled "Magistrate Teng Settles the Case of Inheritance with Ghostly Cleverness." It exhorts people to value morality over money and not to forget "filial piety and fraternal love." Dear audience, whether you have brothers or not is none of my business. What matters is that everyone should follow his conscience and learn to be a good person. Truly,

> *A good person takes this advice to heart;*
> *An evil one lets it go past his ear.*

As our story has it, during the Yongle reign period [1403–24] of the current dynasty, there lived, in Xianghe [Fragrant River] County in Shuntian Prefecture under the direct jurisdiction of Beijing, a certain Prefect Ni, whose given name was Shouqian and courtesy name Yizhi. He was in possession of immense wealth, fertile lands, and fine houses. His wife Chen-shi had given birth to an only son named Shanji but died after he had grown up and married. Prefect Ni resigned from his post and lived the life of a widower. Advanced in years though he was, he remained active and healthy and, instead of enjoying a life of leisure, kept himself busy attending to all matters relating to the collection of rents and loans of money.

When he was seventy-nine years old, his son Ni Shanji said to him, "As the saying goes, 'Rare are those who live to be seventy.' Being seventy-nine going on eighty next year, why don't you turn the family business over to me?

Wouldn't it be nice to have everything done for you so that you can just enjoy life?"

The old man shook his head and said,

> *"I'll be in charge every day that I live.*
> *Let me work for you to share a living.*
> *When I give up the ghost, my feet stretched stiff,*
> *That'll be the day my cares come to a stop."*

Every year in the tenth month, Prefect Ni would go in person to his farms to collect rent and stay out for the entire month. His tenant farmers would treat him royally to their fattest chickens and the finest wine. This year, he went again and stayed several days. When taking a leisurely walk around the village one afternoon, viewing the bucolic scenery, he suddenly saw a girl and a white-haired old woman pounding clothes on a rock by the stream. In spite of her rustic country attire, the girl was quite attractive:

> *Her hair black as lacquer,*
> *Her eyes bright as sparkling water,*
> *Her fingers slender as scallions,*
> *Her curving eyebrows black as if painted.*
> *Her shapely body in plain cotton clothes*
> *Had more grace than in silk and satin.*
> *Like wild flowers in a rustic scene,*
> *Her beauty needed no jewelry.*
> *Her petite figure full of charm,*
> *At sixteen, she was in the bloom of youth.*

In spite of his age, Prefect Ni found himself in raptures at the sight. After she finished the laundry, the girl left with the old woman. The old man kept his eyes on her and saw that, after passing several houses, she went through a small white latticed gate. He hurriedly turned back, summoned the manager of the farmstead, described to him what he had seen, and told him to find out about the girl's background and whether or not she was betrothed. "If she is not," said he, "I would like to take her as my concubine. I wonder if she would be willing."

All too eager to please his master, the manager set to work immediately. As it turned out, the girl, with the family name of Mei, was the daughter of a scholar but living now with her maternal grandmother, both of her parents having died when she was young. Seventeen years of age now, she remained unbetrothed.

Having thus established the facts, the manager said to the old woman, "My master is impressed with your granddaughter's looks and wants to take her as his concubine. Although a concubine, she'll have no one above her to order her about, because the first wife died long ago. Once she is married, not only will she be richly provided for, which is a matter of course, but you, Granny, will also be well taken care of in terms of clothes, tea, and rice, not to speak of a decent funeral when you pass away. I wonder if such good fortune is in your stars."

These sweet words were so persuasive that the old woman gave her consent right away. In fact, it was because the marriage was predestined that the match was so easily made. At the manager's report, Prefect Ni was immensely delighted. The betrothal gifts were decided upon, and an auspicious day for the wedding was chosen after consulting the imperial calendar.[2] Afraid that his son might raise objections, he presented the gifts and held the wedding ceremony right there at the farmstead. What a handsome wedded couple they made, with one so old and the other so young! There is in evidence a lyric poem to the tune of "The Moon over the West River":

> He with dark gauze cap over his white hair,
> She with black locks over her bridal gown,
> They stood like a girl and her grandfather,
> A withered vine around a tender bud.
> She was filled with dismay;
> He was all in jitters,
> Fearing that thing of his
> Might not be up to the job.

That night, Prefect Ni mustered up his vital force and fulfilled what was expected of a bridegroom. Truly,

> Forget not this night of married love.
> His vigor was equal to his days of youth.

Three days later, he called a sedan-chair and brought Mei-shi back to his home, where she was presented to his son and daughter-in-law. All the men and women of the household came to kowtow to her, addressing her as "Young Mistress." Prefect Ni distributed gifts of cotton and silk, to the delight of all and sundry except Ni Shanji. Displeased, he said nothing in public, but privately he complained to his wife, "What a dirty old man! At his age, when he's like a candle in the wind, he should have enough sense to know that with at most five to ten years to live, he shouldn't be doing such a stupid thing. He needs to have enough stamina to deal with such a flower of a girl. He can't very well leave her alone and make her a wife in name only. Also, goodness knows how many old men's young wives, when left unsatisfied, have illicit affairs and bring disgrace to the family. What's more, for a young woman, living with an old man is like living out a year of famine away from home. When the crops are ripe and the famine is over, she'll be gone. While married, she'll steal from here and there to fatten her own private savings, which she'll hide in different places, but, at the same time, she'll use her charms to have the old man buy her clothes and jewelry. When the tree falls and the birds fly away, so to speak, she'll marry someone else and take all her booty with her to enjoy her new life. She's like a worm in the wood and a maggot in the grain. Nothing does a family more harm than having such a woman in its midst!"

He continued, "This woman, with her coquettish ways, looks like a prostitute, with none of the good manners of someone from a decent family. She seems to be an expert in putting on airs and an old hand at capturing husbands. She should be more of a maidservant than a concubine for our father. If we call her 'Sister,' we'd be leaving some room for ourselves in the future. It's laughable that our father is so muddle-headed that he wants everyone to call her 'Young Mistress.' He can hardly expect us to call her 'Mom'! We'd better not humor her too much, lest all the fawning and cringing make her think too much of her importance and turn around to bully us."

The couple's whisperings went on without stop. Some eavesdroppers quickly set their tongues wagging. When word got to his ears, Prefect Ni kept his displeasure to himself. Fortunately, Mei-shi was of a gentle disposition and treated people nicely regardless of status, so that all lived in peace.

Two months later, Mei-shi found herself pregnant, but kept the news from all except her husband. One day stretched to three days and three stretched to nine until, in the tenth month, when the pregnancy was carried to full term, a son was born, to the amazement of the entire family. That day being the ninth of the ninth month, the boy was given the pet name Double Ninth. On the eleventh day of the same month, which happened to be Prefect Ni's eightieth birthday, a steady flow of visitors came to offer their congratulations. Prefect Ni held a feast in celebration partly of his birthday and partly of the boy's third day after birth.

The guests said, "To have a son at your advanced age, sir, is a sign that, with your vigor, you should have a great many more years ahead of you." The prefect was greatly delighted.

Ni Shanji, however, commented again behind his father's back, "A man stops producing sperm at the age of sixty. He's already eighty. Has anyone seen a withered tree bursting into blossom? This boy is definitely not of my father's blood but a bastard from who knows where. I'll never acknowledge him as a brother." Again, these words came to the ears of his father, who, as before, kept the knowledge to himself.

Time sped by like an arrow. Quite unnoticeably, another year passed by.

To mark the boy's first birthday, a tray containing various objects was prepared for a test of the boy's disposition.[3] Members of the clan, close and distant, came again to offer their congratulations. Ni Shanji, however, went out, although he should have stayed to entertain the guests. The prefect knew what was on his mind, but, instead of calling him back, took it upon himself to drink with the clansmen for the whole day. Though he said nothing, he was none too pleased. As the ancients put it, "A filial son brings the father peace of mind." But Ni Shanji was a greedy and ruthless soul obsessed by the fear that the boy would grow up to take away a share of the family property. That was why he refused to acknowledge the boy as a brother and spread around malicious rumors so that, in the future, he could keep the mother and son under his thumb.

Prefect Ni, being a man who had attained office through assiduous studies, was smart enough to have seen through his son's designs. His only regret was that at his age, he could hardly afford to antagonize his older son, because he was too old to see Double Ninth grow up and the boy would most likely have to depend on his brother for a living. There was no alternative for him but to put up with the insolence. The sight of the little baby and his youthful wife filled his heart with pain. All too often, such thoughts plunged him into shifting moods of depression, anguish, and remorse.

Four years later, when the boy had grown to be a smart and active five-year-old, the prefect wished for him to start schooling and gave him the school name Shanshu, after his brother Shanji.[4] An auspicious day was chosen, on which he prepared some fruits and wine and took the boy to pay his respects to the teacher. The teacher being the same one whom Prefect Ni had engaged at home to teach his grandson, it was a most convenient arrangement for the little uncle and nephew to go to the same class. But Ni Shanji had other ideas. He was annoyed that the boy was named Shanshu, which meant that he and the boy were of the same generation. And now that the boy was to go to the same class with his son, he thought it best to call his son back and find him another teacher, for he was afraid that if his son got used to calling the boy "Uncle," his son would be bullied by the latter in the future. That very day, he called his son out and, pleading illness, kept him from class for several days in a row. At first, Prefect Ni thought his grandson was indeed taken ill, but, a few days later, the teacher said to him, "Your son engaged another teacher to set up a separate class. I wonder why he did that."

It would have been well if Prefect Ni had not heard about this, but when he did, he smoldered with rage in spite of himself. He was about to summon his older son and ask him a few questions when he thought, "Being born to be such an unfilial sort, he won't listen to reason. I'd better let him be." In low spirits, he returned to his room but accidentally tripped over the threshold and fell. Mei-shi hastened to raise him to his feet and helped him sit down in a recliner. By this time, he had already lost consciousness. Without a moment of delay, she called a doctor, who said it was a stroke. After having been revived by some ginger soup forced down his throat, he was helped to bed. Though his mind was clear, he was paralysed all over, unable to move an inch. Mei-shi sat at the head of the bed preparing herbal medicine and attending devotedly to his needs, but several doses of the medicine in succession proved to be totally ineffectual. The doctor said after feeling his pulse, "He is beyond hope of a full recovery. He'll linger for some days at best." Upon hearing this, Ni Shanji also came for a few visits. Realizing that his father was too gravely ill to ever rise again, he started throwing his weight about, beating and scolding servants as if he already were master of the house. Such behavior vexed his father even more. Mei-shi could do nothing but weep. The little boy stopped his lessons and stayed in the room to keep his father company.

Well aware of the gravity of his illness, Prefect Ni called his older son to him and took out an account book with records of all the family's lands, houses, and accounts to be collected. He said, "Shanshu being only five years old, he needs all the help he can get. Mei-shi is also too young to manage a household. Since it will not be of any use to give them any share of the family estate, I have decided to bequeath everything to you. After Shanshu grows up, please, for my sake, find him a wife and give him a small house and about fifty or sixty *mu*⁵ of good land so that he won't go cold or hungry. What I have just said has already been written in the family account book for you to keep as a guideline when dividing up the family property. Whatever Mei-shi wishes to do, either to remarry or to stay with her son, let her have her way. You'll have been a filial son if, after I die, you do everything as I just said, and I'll be able to rest content at the Nine Springs."

Ni Shanji opened the account book and found that, sure enough, everything was written clearly, in a most detailed fashion. All smiles, he promised readily, "Don't worry, Father, I'll surely do as you say." With that, he went off merrily, clutching the account book in his arms.

Seeing that he was a safe distance away, Mei-shi said tearfully, pointing at the boy, "Isn't this little one also of your own flesh and blood? Now that you have given the older son everything, what will my son and I live on?"

"You may not know it," said Prefect Ni, "but I believe Shanji is not a kind man. If the family estate were divided equally, this little one's life would be put in jeopardy. The best thing to do is to give Shanji everything to his satisfaction so that he won't have grounds for jealousy." (*None knows a man better than his father. This old man has good sense.*)

Mei-shi rejoined tearfully, "You may very well say so, but, as the ancients put it, 'All sons, by whichever wife, are sons no less.' Such unfairness will make you a laughing stock."

"I can't afford to concern myself with that," said Prefect Ni. "You are still young. I entrusted the boy to Shanji while I am still alive so that after I die, you may, in one year's time at most and half a year's time at least, pick a good husband and enjoy the rest of your life without having to subject yourself to their bullying."

"What kind of talk is this!" protested Mei-shi. "I am also from a Confucian scholar's family. A woman should follow her one and only husband to the end of her life. Moreover, how can I bear the thought of parting with my son? Whatever happens, I'll be at his side."

"Will you indeed maintain widowhood for the rest of your life? Won't you regret it later on?"

Thereupon Mei-shi took a solemn oath.

"If you are indeed determined to do so," said the prefect, "you don't have to worry that you and the boy will have nothing to live on." So saying, he groped around his pillows and produced something, which he handed over to her. At first, Mei-shi thought it was another family account book, but she found it to be a scroll one foot wide by three feet long.

"Why would I need a scroll?"

"This is a portrait of me," answered the prefect. "There's more to it than what you see now. Put it away in a safe place and don't show it to anyone until the boy is grown up. Keep your feelings to yourself even if Shanji refuses to take care of him. Wait until a wise judge appears before you go to him for justice. Take this scroll, tell him about my will, and ask him to reflect well upon the case. He will surely come up with a settlement that will give you and the boy enough to live on." Mei-shi accordingly put the scroll away.

To make a long story short, Prefect Ni lingered on for a few more days. Then one night he choked on some phlegm and failed to wake up to callings of his name. He died at the age of eighty-four. Truly,

> As long as the three inches of breath remains,
> It can be used in a thousand ways.
> Once you breathe your last,
> All things come to an end.
> Had you known you could take nothing to the grave,
> Why would you have worked so hard to feather your nest?

In the meantime, with the family account book now in his possession, Ni Shanji obtained keys to the various storehouses and busied himself every day with checking family possessions in money as well as in kind. How could he spare a moment for a visit to his father? It was not until Mei-shi sent a maid to inform him of his father's death that he and his wife showed up with a few wails of grief. Within a couple of hours, they were off again, leaving Mei-shi to keep vigil over the body. Fortunately, the burial clothes and the coffin had been prepared beforehand. There was no need for Shanji to be bothered about anything.

After the body had been encoffined and the mourning clothes put on, Mei-shi and her son kept vigil in the hall of mourning. Weeping from morning to night, they stayed with the coffin with never a step away from the room, whereas Shanji occupied himself only with receiving visitors and registering their names, without any indication of grief or pain. Before the customary forty-nine days of mourning were over, a day was chosen for the burial.

On the night the soul of the deceased was supposed to return home,[6] Shanji and his wife went to Mei-shi's room and rummaged through the trunks and boxes in search of any private savings that his father might have put away. Afraid that they might take the prefect's portrait, Mei-shi, being the sensible woman she was, voluntarily opened the two trunks that she had brought with her as a bride and took out some old clothes for Shanji and his wife to examine. (*Mei-shi, with her wisdom and virtues, is the only possible protection for the fatherless child.*) Seeing that she was so obliging, Shanji changed his mind and turned his eyes away from the trunks. After creating quite a mess, Shanji and his wife went away. Mei-shi gave way to her grief and burst into loud sobs. The sight so disturbed the little boy that he, too, started weeping. At such a scene,

> *A man of clay would shed tears;*
> *A man of iron would break down in grief.*

The following morning, Shanji called in a builder to remodel the house, for his son was about to be married. Mei-shi and her son were moved into three storage rooms in the backyard and were given nothing more than a small four-legged bed and a few coarse tables and stools. There was not even a decent piece of furniture. Of her two maids, they took away the older one, leaving only the eleven- or twelve-year-old maid. The mother and son's daily provisions had to be brought over from Shanji's kitchen, and no one cared whether there was food for them. Vexed at the inconvenience, Mei-shi asked for some rice and did her own cooking on a makeshift earthen stove. By doing some sewing morning and evening, she made enough money to be able to afford provisions for a simple life. She also paid for her son's lessons at a neighbor's house.

More than once, Shanji sent his wife to persuade Mei-shi to remarry and sought the services of matchmakers, but they gave up the idea when Mei-shi swore that she would rather die than submit. As Mei-shi was as forbearing as could be and never had a word of complaint, Shanji, for all his maliciousness, put the mother and son out of his mind.

Time shot by like an arrow. Quite unnoticeably, Shanshu had grown to be fourteen years old. Being discreet by nature, Mei-shi had never told the boy a word about the past, for fear that he might not know how to guard his tongue. Should he say something that would lead to trouble, he would only be hurting their own chances. Now that he was a fourteen-year-old capable of figuring things out for himself, he could not be kept in the dark any longer.

One day, he asked his mother to buy him a new silk gown. As Mei-shi answered that she could not afford it, Shanshu said, "My father was a prefect and had only two sons. Why is my brother so rich, whereas I can't even have a new gown? Since you don't have the money, Mother, I'll go and ask my brother for some." With those words, he turned to go.

Mei-shi grabbed him and said, "My son, a silk gown is not important enough for you to go beg for it. It is often said, 'Those who count their blessings will have more coming their way,' and 'Those who wear coarse cotton when young will wear silk when they grow up.' If you wear silk now when you're young, you won't even have coarse cotton to wear later. In a few more years' time, after you've made progress in your studies, I would go so far as to sell myself to buy clothes for you. Your brother is not one to provoke. Why bother him?"

"You're right, Mother." While saying so, he thought differently to himself: "My father's immense wealth should, by rights, be divided between us two brothers. I am not a stepson brought here from a previous marriage. Why doesn't my brother take the least care of me? And what strange things Mother says! Am I to understand that the only way I can have some lousy silk is for my mother to sell herself? My brother is not some man-eating tiger. Why should I be afraid of him?" He struck upon a plan. Unbeknownst to his mother, he headed straight for the great house and sought out his brother. When he said his greetings to his older brother, the latter was taken by surprise and asked him what he had come for.

"I am an official's son," said Shanshu, "but my tattered clothes are a subject of ridicule. I am here to ask you for some silk to make a gown with."

"You should ask your mother for that," said Shanji.

"Father's family property is in your care, not Mother's."

At the mention of the words "family property," which signified awareness of a larger issue, Shanji reddened. "Who made you say this?" he demanded. "Are you here today to ask for clothes or to fight over family property?"

Shanshu said, "We can hardly avoid dividing the inheritance some day, can we? But I'm here today just to ask for some clothes to look more decent."

"What do you care about decency, you bastard! Even if Father did leave property worth ten thousand strings of cash, there is the legitimate son, and the legitimate grandson as well. What business is it of yours, bastard! Whose evil words sent you here to ask for what's more than your share? Don't you provoke me, or else you and your mother will have no roof over your heads!"

"Both of us are Father's sons. How come I am a bastard? What if I do provoke you? Don't tell me you'll bump off my mother and me and keep the entire inheritance for yourself!"

Shanji flew into a rage. "You little beast! How dare you contradict me!" He grabbed the boy by his sleeve and hit him on the head with his fist seven or eight times, until the boy's head was all bruised and swollen. Then Shanshu tore himself free and dashed off like a streak of vapor. Weepingly he went to his mother and told her everything. Mei-shi scolded, "I told you not to stir up trouble. It served you right for not listening to me!" For all the harshness of her words, she was reduced to tears as she used her blue cotton blouse to rub the bruises on his head. There is a poem in evidence:

> The young widow and her fatherless child
> Lived on little food and thin clothing.
> For lack of filial regard in the family,
> On one branch of the tree, part thrived, part withered.

After giving much thought to the matter, Mei-shi sent her maid to Shanji, for fear that the latter might be unforgiving, to apologize for her son's offense against his older brother, saying that the boy was too young to know much about the proper codes of behavior. But Shanji's anger remained unassuaged.

Early the following morning, Shanji invited a few clansmen, took out his father's handwritten instructions for the division of family property, and summoned Mei-shi and her son. After showing the document to all present, he said, "As you, my venerable elders, are witnesses, it is not that I refuse to support the mother and son and want to drive them out, but yesterday Shanshu quarreled with me over the family property and said words that he shouldn't have said. I'm afraid that when he grows up, he might have much more to say. Therefore I am sending them out of this house to live at the East Farmstead in a house with fifty-eight *mu* of land. This is in strict accordance with father's will. Not in the least would I ever dream of making arbitrary decisions on my own. That is why I humbly ask that you, my elders, serve as witnesses."

The clansmen knew all too well what a ruthless man Shanji was. With the father's will in front of their eyes, who would venture to speak out of turn and antagonize him unnecessarily? All of them said only things that would please his ears. Those bent on currying favor with him said, "'A dead man's handwritten will is worth more than a thousand pieces of gold.' The inheritance being divided in accordance with the will, there is no more to be said." Even those in sympathy with Shanshu and his mother said only, "'A man shouldn't live on the rice he inherits; a woman should not go on wearing her dowry clothes.' Goodness knows how many people have built themselves a fortune from nothing. Now that you have a house to live in and land to till, you can't say you don't have anything to start with. One needs to work one's way up. Don't complain that the porridge you get is too thin. Everyone has his own fate."

Mei-shi knew that the rooms in the backyard were not meant to be a permanent abode for them. So she had no other choice but to do as she was bid. With her son, she thanked the elders of the clan, took respectful leave of the ancestral shrine, bade farewell to Shanji and his wife, took a few pieces of old furniture along with the two trunks that she had brought with her as a bride, and went on the back of a hired beast to the East Farmstead. It was a dilapidated house grievously out of repair, and the land was overgrown with weeds. With many tiles missing, the leaky roof made the house too damp for it to be inhabitable. Making the best of the situation, she cleaned a couple of rooms and put the beds in place. When she called in some tenants for information, she was told that the fifty-eight *mu* of land could not be any poorer, yielding less than half of a crop in a good year. In a bad year, just to put in the seeds was to suffer a loss. Mei-shi could only bemoan their bitter fate.

It was her son who had the good sense to say to her, "My brother and I being sons born of the same father, why was our father so partial when it came to inheritance? There must be a reason behind it. Could it be that the will was not in my father's handwriting? It is said since ancient times, 'Family property should be divided equally, regardless of status.' Mother, why don't you bring the matter to court? We'll go by the judge's ruling."

Now that the boy had raised the matter, Mei-shi told him all that she had kept from his knowledge for over ten years. "My son," said she, "there is nothing suspicious about the will. It is indeed in your father's handwriting. He was afraid that because you were so young, you might be cheated by your brother. That's why all the property was left to your brother to put his mind at ease. Before your father passed away, he gave me a scroll with his portrait on it, saying repeatedly that there was a riddle to it and that if I could wait until an upright and wise judge came to this place and submit the case to him, you and I would be free from poverty."

"Why didn't you tell me earlier about all this? Where's the portrait? Show it to me quickly."

Mei-shi opened a trunk and took out a cloth-wrapped parcel. After removing the cloth, she came upon a layer of oilpaper that was bound and sealed. When the seal was broken, they saw a scroll one foot wide by three feet long. They spread it out, hung it on a chair, and kowtowed to it. Mei-shi pleaded to the portrait, "Please forgive us for any lack of propriety, but incense and candles are hard to come by in these rustic quarters."

After the kowtows, Shanshu rose and took a closer look at the portrait. It was a most lifelike portrait of the prefect seated in a chair with an official's black gauze cap over his white hair. Holding an infant to his bosom, he was pointing to the ground with one hand. As no amount of thinking yielded the slightest clue, Shanshu could do no better than wrap up the scroll and put it back in the parcel as before, his mind deeply disturbed.

A few days later, Shanshu went to a neighboring village to find someone who could shed light on this mystery. As he chanced to pass by the Lord Guan Temple,[7] there came into view some villagers carrying over their shoulders a pig and a sheep in a sacrificial rite to honor Lord Guan. As Shanshu stopped in his tracks to take a look, an old man passing by also stopped and leaned on his bamboo staff to watch. "What's the sacrifice for?" asked the old man.

"We were wrongly accused in a court case. Luckily, we had a wise magistrate who saw that justice was done. As we had made promises to the gods to repay them if we won the case, we are here today to give votive offerings."

"How were you wrongly accused?" asked the old man. "And how was the case settled?"

One man in the crowd said, "In this county, as is ordered by the authorities, ten households constitute one security unit. I am Cheng Da, the unit headman. In our unit, there is a master tailor named Zhao who often worked nights in clients' houses and would stay away from home for days at a time. One day, he left home again, and, after an absence of over a month, his wife, Liu-shi, sought help from us to search high and low for him, but not a trace of him was found.

"A few days later, a corpse with a crushed head floated up in the river. After the local headman reported to the authorities, the clothes were identified as belonging to Tailor Zhao.

"The day before Tailor Zhao left home, he and I had some angry words after drinking. In a rage, I charged into his home and smashed a few things. That did happen. But, as it turned out, his wife brought the case to court and charged me with murder. Mr. Qi, the county magistrate at the time, believed her story and sentenced me to death. My neighbors in the same security unit were also implicated because they would not inform against me. I had nowhere to go for vindication and stayed in prison for three years.

"Luckily, the new magistrate named Teng is a very wise man, though he has no more than a *juren* degree. When it came time at the height of summer for the annual review of cases of the convicted, I presented my case to him with tearful pleas for justice. He was also perplexed and said, 'A drunken brawl is not some major feud that involves killing.' He accepted my petition and issued warrants to bring witnesses to court for a review of the case.

"Upon first sight of Tailor Zhao's wife, Magistrate Teng asked, of all things, if she had remarried. Liu-shi said, 'I have, because it was too hard to maintain widowhood in my poverty.' When asked who her new husband was, she replied, 'It's Tailor Shen Bahan.' Magistrate Teng immediately had Shen Bahan brought to court and asked him, 'When did you marry this woman?' The man said, 'I didn't marry her until more than a month after her husband's death.' The magistrate asked, 'Who was the matchmaker? What betrothal gifts did you give?' The man replied, 'The now deceased Tailor Zhao had borrowed seven or eight taels of silver from me. When I heard about his death, I went to his house to ask what had happened and to press for the return of the money. Liu-shi had nothing to pay me back with but agreed to marry me to offset the debt. We didn't have a matchmaker.' The magistrate asked again, 'Being someone who works with his hands, where did you get all that silver?' The tailor replied, 'That was the total sum of small loans over a period of time.'

"The magistrate gave him paper and pen to write a detailed list of the loans. According to Bahan's list, there were altogether thirteen loans in rice or in cash, totaling seven taels and eight mace of silver. After reading the list, the magistrate roared, 'It was you who beat Tailor Zhao to death. How dare you falsely accuse an honest man?' The ankle-squeezer was applied to him, but he still refused to confess. The magistrate said, 'Let me give you the facts of the case, and you'll have to acknowledge the truth. If you were in the money-lending business, why were all loans given out to Tailor Zhao only? It must be because you had an affair with his wife and, since Zhao had designs on your wealth, he looked the other way. Later, you murdered him in order to join his wife in a legitimate marriage. Then you had the woman press charges against Cheng Da. Your handwriting on this list of loans matches the handwriting on the accusation paper. Who can the murderer be if not you?' (*Good reasoning.*)

"He ordered that the finger-squeezer be applied to the woman to make her confess. When she heard the magistrate's account, accurate to the last detail, she was frightened out of her wits by the power of his mind, which was clearly on a par with that of Master Guigu.[8] How could she dare deny anything? She confessed as soon as the finger-squeezers were put on. Bahan was also obliged to confess.

"As a matter of fact, when Bahan had first begun his clandestine affair with Liu-shi, no one knew about it. Later, when they started seeing each other more and more often, Tailor Zhao was afraid that others might notice, and he tried to put an end to the relationship. Bahan consulted Liu-shi about murdering Zhao and marrying her, but Liu-shi objected. When Zhao came back one night from his work at a client's house, Bahan coaxed him into a wineshop, where he made Zhao drink himself into a stupor. When they left the wineshop and went to the river's edge, Bahan knocked him to the ground, smashed his head with a rock, and tossed him into the river. Then he waited for the excitement to cool down before he married the woman.

"Later, the body floated up and was identified. Bahan knew that I had once had a fight with Zhao, and he urged the woman to press charges against me. It was after she was remarried that the woman learned about the murder. Since she was already his wife, she kept quiet. Magistrate Teng, having established the truth, punished the couple and set me free. I feel much obliged to my neighbors for having pooled money for this sacrificial ceremony. Sir, won't you agree that there isn't a worse case of injustice?"

The old man remarked, "Such a wise official is truly hard to come by! The people of this county are fortunate indeed!"

Having heard these words, Ni Shanshu returned home and repeated everything to his mother. "With such a good magistrate, what better time than this to take the portrait to him?"

The mother and son thus made up their minds, and, having learned the day on which the magistrate was to take up cases of complaint, Mei-shi rose before dawn that day and, carrying the scroll, took her fourteen-year-old son to the county yamen and cried out her grievances.

The magistrate was puzzled at the sight of a single small scroll instead of any formal written complaint. When asked, Mei-shi gave a full account of Ni Shanji's behavior and the deceased prefect's last words to her before he died. Magistrate Teng put away the scroll and told her to go home for the moment, for he would need to go back to his private quarters and examine it closely. Truly,

> There was a riddle hidden in a portrait;
> Immense treasures were waiting to be found.
> For the woes of a widow and her son,
> The magistrate set his sharp mind to work.

We will not follow Mei-shi and her son home but focus our attention on Magistrate Teng, who, after his business of the day was over, returned to his private quarters and spread out the scroll. He pondered for a considerable while over the portrait of Prefect Ni, who held an infant in one arm and pointed to the ground with the other hand. He thought to himself, "Needless to say, this infant is Ni Shanshu. By pointing to the ground, did he mean to tell whoever takes up the case to do their best out of regard for his soul in the underworld? Then again, since he had written a will with his own hand, the authorities can hardly judge otherwise. But if he said there was a riddle to the portrait, there must be something more to it than meets the eye. If I fail to come to the bottom of this, my long-standing reputation for brilliance will be put in jeopardy." Every day, after he retired from the court, he took out the portrait and gave himself up to thought. Several days went by, but he was still nowhere nearer to an answer.

The mystery, however, was destined to be solved, and an opportunity did present itself one day after lunch, when Magistrate Teng was studying the scroll again. The maid came in to serve tea. As he reached out for the tea cup, he accidentally spilled some tea on the scroll. He put down the cup, went out to the terrace, and spread the scroll with both hands to dry it in the sun. In the sunlight he suddenly caught sight of traces of characters inside the scroll. Growing apprehensive, he peeled off the surface layer and saw that mounted underneath the portrait was another sheet of paper, on which was written in Prefect Ni's handwriting,

> *I, a prefect at the advanced age of over eighty, when death is only to be expected at any moment, should have no regrets upon leaving this world. However, Shanshu, my son by the concubine, being only one year old, will not be able to make a living for himself for quite some time to come and may, in future, be ill treated by Shanji, my older son by the first wife, a man lacking in the feelings of filial love. I hereby bequeath to Shanji the two newly acquired mansions and all of my land. To Shanshu, I bequeath the small old house on the left side of the estate. Though small, the house contains, under its left wall, five thousand taels of silver in five jars and, under its right wall, a thousand taels of gold and another five thousand taels of silver in six jars, the total amount being the equivalent of the value of the landed estate I bequeathed to Shanji. To whichever official settles this case in his wisdom, my son Shanshu shall present a reward of three hundred taels of silver.*
> *The above is written in my own handwriting.*
> *Signed on this ——— day of the ——— month of the ——— year*
> *by Ni Shouqian, eighty-one years of age*

As a matter of fact, this portrait had been done during the celebration of the baby's first birthday, when Prefect Ni was eighty-one years old. This indeed bears out the old saying "None knows a son better than the father."

Magistrate Teng was a most shrewd man. His greed was stirred by the mention of so much gold and silver. He knitted his brows and hit upon a plan. He sent quietly for Ni Shanji for a talk.

In the meantime, Ni Shanji, fully content with his possession of the entire family property, made merry at home every day. All of a sudden, a messenger from the prefectural yamen appeared with a summons in the magistrate's handwriting. Unable to decline, since the messenger would not allow him a single moment of delay, Shanji had no choice but to follow him to the yamen.

The magistrate happened to be in the middle of a court session. At the messenger's announcement that Ni Shanji was there, the magistrate called him forth and asked, "Are you Prefect Ni's older son?"

"Yes, I am."

"Your step-mother, Mei-shi, lodged a complaint against you, saying that you drove her and your younger brother out and seized all of the property and estate. Is this true?"

"My step-brother Shanshu grew up under my care. Recently, he and his mother declared their wish to move out. I did not drive them out. As regards the family property, everything was done in accordance with Father's will written in his own hand. I wouldn't dream of doing otherwise."

"Where is your father's handwritten will?"

"It is at home. Please allow me to get it and present it to you."

"According to the complaint, the case involves an immense inheritance. This is hardly a trivial matter. The authenticity of the will remains to be established. Out of consideration for your gentry class background, I will not make things difficult for you for the moment, but tomorrow I will summon Mei-shi and her son to your house. I will personally come to your house to check the status of the family property. If the division of the inheritance is indeed unfair, justice will prevail over personal considerations." With these words, he had runners escort Shanji out of the court before summoning Mei-shi and her son for the hearing the next day. The runners accepted some bribes from Shanji and let him return home by himself. They then headed for the East Farmstead for Mei-shi and her son.

Now, Shanji was much frightened by the harsh tone of the magistrate because it was true that the inheritance had not been divided at all. With nothing but his father's will to vouch for him, he also needed the testimony of members of the clan to make his actions assume full force. That very night, he distributed silver among the Ni clan as well as relatives on his mother's and wife's sides of the family, asking them to assemble in his house the next morning and support him with one voice in the investigation into the will.

Since Prefect Ni died, none of those relatives had ever received any gift from Shanji, nor had the latter bothered to invite them for a drink on festive occasions. And now he was giving away large chunks of silver. Truly, "He burns no incense when everything goes well, but is quick to embrace the Buddha's feet in a moment of need." They laughed in their sleeves and readily accepted the silver for some extra indulgence in food. As for the hearing to be held the next day, they would see how things went before saying anything. A contemporary had this to say:

Blame not the step-mother for bringing charges;
The brother was overly greedy indeed.
Now he bribes clansmen with so much silver,
When he could have just given the child a little silk.

At the summons from the runners, Mei-shi knew that the magistrate had taken up her case. Early next morning, the mother and son went straight to the county yamen to see Magistrate Teng.

"I will naturally take the side of a widow and a fatherless child," said the magistrate, "but as far as I know, Shanji acted in accordance with his deceased father's will. What's to be done about that?"

"There is indeed such a will," conceded Mei-shi. "However, it was written not as an expression of my deceased husband's true wishes but for the sake of protecting the child. Your Honor will understand if you examine the amounts specified in the family account book."

Magistrate Teng replied, "As the saying goes, 'Even the most unbiased judge finds it hard to settle a family dispute.' I will try to let you and your son have enough to live on for the rest of your lives. Don't get your hopes too high." (*Do not get the hopes too high, lest they be more easily dashed. Magistrate Teng is preparing her for his settlement.*)

Mei-shi said gratefully, "I'll be more than content to be free from hunger and cold. I wouldn't presume to be as rich as Shanji."

Magistrate Teng instructed Mei-shi and her son to go to Shanji's house and wait for him there. Shanji had already cleaned the main hall, placed in it an armchair covered with a tiger's skin, and lit some fine incense. At the same time, he urged the relatives to come early and await the arrival of the magistrate. At the sight of so many members of the clan, Mei-shi and Shanshu said their greetings and could hardly fail to ask the relatives to put in a good word for them. For all his pent-up fury, Shanji could not very well flare up on such an occasion. Each quietly prepared words to say to the magistrate.

Before long, there came into hearing from afar shouts to clear the way. Realizing that the county magistrate was approaching, Shanji adjusted his clothes and cap and went to welcome him. The older and wiser among the clan members also made ready to step forward and greet him, while the younger and more timid peeped out from behind the screen wall in front of the house to find out what was going on. Behold: Under the blue silk canopy behind the two rows of guards of honor was the wise Magistrate Teng himself.

Upon reaching the Ni residence, the guards dropped to their knees and gave a shout. Mei-shi and the Ni brothers also knelt down in a gesture of welcome. As a retainer shouted, "All rise!" a sedan-chair was set down and Magistrate Teng, all calm and composed, alighted from it. Just as he was about to enter the house, he suddenly made a succession of bows to the sky and said things as if in reply to the greetings of his host. All those present stood watching in amazement.

Magistrate Teng then bowed his way into the main hall, never failing to yield the right of way to the unseen host. While bowing, he kept up a stream of polite words of greeting. After saluting the south-facing tiger-skin chair as if he were being offered that seat, he turned hastily, pulled up another chair, which he placed facing north as if for the host, and did not take his seat of honor until he bowed a few more times to the air. Awestruck by the sight of someone who appeared to have seen a god or a ghost, the gaping crowd stood on two sides, with no one daring to take a step forward.

From his seat, Magistrate Teng made another bow and said, "Your wife lodged a complaint with me about the inheritance. Could you tell me what it is all about?" Having said that, he assumed the posture of someone listening intently. After a considerable while, he stuck out his tongue and commented, shaking his head, "Your older son is not an honorable man." After listening quietly for a few more moments, he asked, "What is the younger son to live on?" A little later, he spoke again, "What is there in the small house on the right?" Then he said, "I see, I see." After another pause, he continued, "I will do as you say and give that to the younger son as well." A moment later, he said with a bow, "How would I presume to accept such a great favor?" After much demurring, he said, "Since you are so insistent, I will accept it against my better judgment and give a receipt to your younger son." (*What audacity on the part of the magistrate! But at least he does this without risk of compromising his merit in the netherworld, for this is better than accepting filthy bribes.*) With that, he rose and said with a few more bows, "I shall go there right now." Everyone present was aghast.

Magistrate Teng stood up, looked around, and asked, "Where has Prefect Ni gone?"

The retainers replied, "We haven't seen any Prefect Ni."

"How extraordinary!" exclaimed the magistrate. He summoned Shanji and said to him, "Your father personally greeted me outside the door. Everyone must have heard what your father said to me all this time."

"I did not hear what he said," said Shanji.

"Was Prefect Ni a tall man with a thin face, high cheekbones, narrow eyes, long eyebrows, big ears, three strands of silvery beard, a gauze cap, black boots, a red robe, and a golden waistband?"

Breaking into a cold sweat, everyone knelt down in awe and said, "That's exactly how he looked."

"Why did he suddenly disappear?" said the magistrate. "He said that in addition to the two big houses, there is also a small house to the east. Is that indeed the case?"

Shanji dared not hide the truth, and admitted, "Yes, that is indeed true."

"We shall now go to the small house on the east side," said the magistrate. "I shall have something to say."

Having witnessed the magistrate talking to himself and describing Prefect Ni's looks with such accuracy, everyone believed that the prefect had indeed made an appearance. There was not a tongue that did not hang out, nor a heart that did not beat fast. Little did they know that Magistrate Teng was faking it all. His descriptions of the prefect were based on his memory of the portrait. Everything else he said was sheer fabrication. (*How ingenious!*) There is a poem that bears witness:

> *Saints and sages are topics harmless enough,*
> *But ghosts and spirits are not to be provoked.*
> *Had the magistrate not put on a show,*
> *The unfilial son would not have succumbed.*

With Ni Shanji leading the way, the whole crowd went with the magistrate to the old house on the east side. Originally inhabited by Prefect Ni before he passed the examinations and built the big houses, it had later become a granary for rice and wheat. A servant and his family lived there. After walking all around the house, the magistrate took a seat in the main hall and said to Shanji, "Your father's spirit, for that's what it was, gave me a detailed account of the concerns of the family and instructed me to give this old house to Shanshu. What do you say to that?"

Shanji said with a bow, "I will go by any ruling of yours, Your Honor."

The magistrate asked for the family account book, read it closely, and said time and again, "What a large family estate!" When he came to the will at the end of the account book, he burst into laughter. "So, the old gentleman wrote all this himself, and yet, a moment ago, he said to me many bitter words against Shanji. He wasn't a man with a determined mind of his own, was he?" Thereupon the magistrate called forth Shanji and announced, "Since the will spelled out everything clearly, the lands and the accounts are therefore bequeathed to you alone. Shanshu is not to raise any contest."

Lamenting to herself at such a turn of events, Mei-shi was about to step forward and make her pleas, when the magistrate resumed, "This old house is bequeathed to Shanshu. Nor is Shanji to lay any claim to anything found in the house."

Shanji thought to himself, "The broken furniture in this house is not worth anything. Even though there is still some rice and wheat left, the amount is insignificant because I sold seventy to eighty percent of the stock a month ago. I'm getting a good deal." Thereupon he said eagerly, "Your Honor, your ruling is most wise."

The magistrate declared, "That's settled then. Neither of you should go back on your word. Since all of you present are members of the family, I invite you to be witnesses. Mr. Ni Senior told me just now, face to face, 'Buried under the left wall of this house are five jars of silver, five thousand taels in total, which I bequeath to my younger son.'"

In disbelief, Shanji said, "If this is true, my brother may have ten thousand taels of gold without a word of objection from me."

The magistrate said, "I will not allow any objections from you." So saying, he ordered his men to ask for hoes and shovels, and, with Mei-shi and her son leading the way, they went with some able-bodied locals to the east wall. When the ground under the wall was dug open, sure enough, there came into view five big jars, which, when lifted out, were revealed to be filled to the brim with silver. When one of the jars was weighed on the scale, it was found that the silver amounted to sixty-two and a half catties, the exact equivalent of a thousand taels. Everyone stood aghast. Shanji was now convinced that if his father's spirit had not appeared and told the magistrate about the hidden silver, the latter would not have known something that even the family had no knowledge of.

Magistrate Teng had the five jars of silver laid out in a straight row in front of himself and turned to Mei-shi with these words: "There are another five jars under the wall on the right, which contain another five thousand taels. In addition, there is a jar of gold, which Mr. Ni Senior wishes to give to me as a reward. I did not think it proper to accept it, but he was so insistent that I had to comply."

Mei-shi and Shanshu said while kowtowing, "The five thousand under the left wall is already more than we could ever hope for. If there is another five thousand under the right wall, we will certainly not fail to follow the orders of the deceased."

"I learned about this through Prefect Ni himself," said the magistrate. "I don't think he would be making it up." At his orders, the men started digging under the western wall, and, sure enough, there were six big jars, five with silver and one with gold.

His eyes bloodshot at the sight of so much gold and silver, how Shanji wished he could grab an ingot or two! However, he dared not utter a word, for he had given his promise. (*To the indescribable joy of Shanshu, dismay of the jealous Shanji, amazement of the awestruck spectators, and gratification of the magistrate.*)

Magistrate Teng drew up a document and gave it to Shanshu. The family that was taking care of the house was also given to Shanshu and his mother.

Beside themselves with joy, Mei-shi and Shanshu kowtowed in gratitude. For all his mortification, Shanji felt obliged to make a couple of bows and force himself to say, "Thank you, Your Honor, for your judgment."

With the jar of gold sealed up with paper strips, the magistrate had it carried in front of his sedan-chair to his yamen for his personal enjoyment.

Believing that Prefect Ni had indeed promised the magistrate the jar of gold as payment for his services, the onlookers thought it only right that the magistrate did what he did. No one presumed to raise a word of objection. This is indeed a case of "When the snipe and the clam grapple, it's the fisherman who gets the benefit." Had Ni Shanji been a kind man enjoying a harmonious relationship with his brother and willing to divide the inheritance equally, the thousand taels of gold would have been shared between the brothers, five hundred taels each. They never would have ended up in Magistrate Teng's hands. With not the least gain to himself, Shanji brought wealth to another man. What he got in return was nothing but mortification and notoriety as an unfilial son and unloving brother. However calculating he was, he ended up a victim of his own schemes.

Let us not encumber our story with more of such idle comments but turn our attention to Mei-shi and her son, who paid Magistrate Teng a visit the following day to express their gratitude. The magistrate had already removed the will from the scroll and had the portrait remounted. It was not until he gave the portrait back to Mei-shi that she and her son came to realize that by pointing to the ground, the prefect in the portrait was pointing at the hidden treasure. With the ten jars of silver, they bought land and became rich. Later, Shanshu married and had three sons in succession, all of whom won fame through their assiduous studies. Of the Ni clan, Shanshu's branch was the most prosperous. Shanji's two sons, on the other hand, were given to loafing and frittered away their inheritance. After Shanji's death, the two big houses were sold to Uncle Shanshu. None of those who were acquainted with the Ni family story did not take that as an example of heavenly retribution. As the poem says,

> The way of heaven has never been unfair.
> Brother Ni's greed was truly laughable.
> As the prime heir, he bullied his step-mother,
> Only to be outwitted by his dead father.
> The words inside the scroll were there by design;
> The gold under the wall now belongs to the judge.
> Wouldn't it be better to be fair and just
> And be free from disputes and legal suits?

Zhao Bosheng Meets with Emperor Renzong in a Teahouse

A three-inch tongue can be a sword to bring peace to the land;
A five-character poem can be a ladder to the sky.
Those so destined will reach the blue clouds[1] in the end,
With vows not to turn back without honors on the exams.

The story goes that during the reign of Song Emperor Renzong [1023–63], there lived a scholar by the name of Zhao Xu, courtesy name Bosheng, in the prefecture of Chengdu in Sichuan. He started studying classical texts at an early age and, after only one glance at *The Book of Songs* [Shijing], *The Book of History* [Shujing], *The Book of Rites* [Liji], and *The Book of Music* [Yuejing], was able to write essays as fast as his brush-pen could go. An erudite scholar, he learned, to his great joy, that the imperial examinations were soon to be held in the Eastern Capital [present-day Kaifeng]. He went to the main hall of the house and informed his parents of his wish to take the examinations. Both his father, Zhao Lun, courtesy name Wenbao, and his mother, Liu-shi, were from genteel families of long standing and readily gave their consent to his journey to the capital. On the day chosen for his departure, Zhao Xu was getting ready to be on his way, when his father gave him a poem that read,

May you read more classics to fill your mind,
Rather than succumb to the lure of wine.
In spring next year at the peach blossom tide,[2]
Win first honors and return in triumph.

His mother, Liu-shi, also said to him, "May you win first place in the examinations and fulfill the ambition befitting a worthy man."

Zhao Xu respectfully took leave of his parents, and, carrying his zither, sword, and cases of books and followed by a servant, he set off for the Eastern Capital. To relatives and friends who accompanied him as far as the south gate of the city, he intoned a poem that he improvised to the tune of "Song of the River Goddess":

Who in the wineshop is chanting "Weicheng"?[3]
Thoughts of parting fill my heart with sorrow.
The boat lies at the deserted ferry,
Bestrewn with broken willow branches.[4]
As you fade into the hazy distance,
The sight of the green mountains pains my heart.
The autumn dew on the lotus petals
Washes off their rouge.
The chill of the doleful wind
Brings on morning frost.
My sword is cold as the autumn waters;
The sadness of parting bedims its rainbow light.
My robe stained with a thousand drops of tears,
When, I ask, will they ever cease to flow?

With that, Zhao Xu took leave of his relatives and friends and set out on his journey, traveling by day and resting by night, stopping only for food and drink when he felt the need. Before many days had passed, he arrived in the Eastern Capital. As he toured the city, what met his eyes were fine houses and stylishly dressed people. It was indeed a thriving and prosperous place. He made his way to the section of town where candidates for the imperial examinations stayed, and found lodging at an inn, where he waited for the examination day. When that day finally came, he duly proceeded to the examination grounds. The three sessions of the examination over, he returned to the inn to await the pronouncement of the list of successful candidates. "I will surely be on the list," he thought joyfully to himself.

After breakfast the following morning, he went to the teahouse across the street for a cup of tea with some friends who were staying in the same inn. As his eyes fell upon some wooden tablets provided for patrons to write poems on, he took a brush-pen and wrote a lyric poem on the white-washed wall:

With my feet on the ladder to the clouds,
My hands gripping the celestial laurels,
I find my name on the list of honor.
As I approach on horseback high,
My name as zhuangyuan *the heralds announce*
To rows of jade belts and golden saddles.
The feast[5] over, I stroll all over town,
The ambition of a worthy man now fulfilled.
To the one in the phoenix tower[6]
A much sought-after husband I will be.

Great was his delight when he finished the poem. He and his friends then parted company and returned to their rooms, and there we shall leave them for now.

By the time all the examination papers had been graded, the full assembly of examination officials reported to Emperor Renzong at the morning court session. The emperor said, "As a rule, three candidates are selected to top the list. Who are the top three this year?" Thereupon an examiner presented to him the examination papers of the top three for his inspection.

After reading the first one, the emperor smiled and said to the examiner, "This is an excellent piece of work. What a pity there is a wrongly written character."

Prostrating himself on the ground, the examiner asked the emperor which character it was.

The emperor continued with a smile, "It is the character *wei* 唯. Its left radical should be *kou* 口, but it is written here as *si* 厶."

The examiner kowtowed again before he said, "The two radicals are interchangeable."

"What is this man's name?" asked the emperor. "Where does he come from?" Thereupon the seal over the personal identification section of the paper was removed to reveal that the candidate was Zhao Xu, a native of Chengdu Prefecture of Sichuan, now lodging in the candidates' quarters of the city. The emperor dispatched a messenger to send for him with all speed.

At the summons, Zhao Xu hastened from the inn and followed the messenger to the court, where he borrowed the blue robe and wooden tablet for officials of the lowest rank before he was led into the presence of the emperor.

After having made his obeisance, he heard the emperor ask, "Where are you from?"

With a kowtow, Zhao Xu answered, "I am from Chengdu Prefecture in Sichuan. I started studying the civil arts at an early age and am now in the capital for the imperial examinations. Fortunate indeed I am at finding myself in Your Majesty's august presence."

The emperor continued, "What topic were you given for your composition? How long did you write? How many characters were there?"

With another kowtow, Zhao Xu answered the questions in an orderly fashion, with never a stumble. The emperor secretly marveled at the way the words came trippingly off his tongue like a stream of water. It was too bad, he thought, that such a man should have written a wrong character. He said, "You wrote one character incorrectly in your paper."

A consternated Zhao Xu threw himself upon the ground and asked, "Which character, may I venture to ask?"

"It is the character *wei* 唯. Why did you write the radical *kou* 口 as *si* ㄙ?"

Zhao Xu answered with another kowtow, "The two radicals are interchangeable."

The emperor was displeased. Using the four treasures of the scholar's study[7] on his desk, he wrote eight characters. Handing the paper to Zhao Xu, he said, "Take a look. What I wrote are the characters 单單，去吉，吴矣，吕台. If you say those two radicals are interchangeable, explain to me how the radicals are interchangeable in each of the four pairs."

Zhao Xu stared at the note for a considerable time without being able to come up with an answer.

"You may now withdraw and go back to your studies," said the emperor.

A shamefaced Zhao Xu left the imperial court and returned to the inn in great distress.

His friends came to see him and said, "You must be thrilled!" When Zhao Xu told them of what had happened, everyone was aghast. They invited him to the teahouse, hoping to cheer him up over a cup of tea. Suddenly he caught sight of the poem that he had written on the wall the other day. Heaving sigh upon sigh, he took up the four treasures of the scholar's study and wrote another lyric poem:

> *My wings were almost ready,*
> *Honors were almost in hand.*
> *My life's ambition was all but achieved.*
> *The god of spring brought word to the peony,*
> *But for others the royal feast was held.*
> *Because of a single character,*
> *I lost my chance for fame and fortune,*
> *All my hopes dashed by the will of heaven.*
> *For return, I look back to my hometown,*
> *Beyond vast waters and distant hills, three thousand li away.*

When the list of successful candidates was posted, he had someone take a look and was told, just as he had expected, that his name was not there. Amid sighs and tears, he decided to stay on in the capital instead of returning home in shame. "Another three years of study would not be to no avail," he thought. In low spirits, he wrote four lines on the wall of his room:

> *Song Yu[8] was weighed down with grief,*
> *Jiang Yan[9] consumed with resentment.*
> *Han Yu[10] was thrown into exile,*
> *Su Qin[11] shunned in isolation.*

To relieve his depression and boredom, he went on to compose another poem. It was a lyric poem to the tune of "Sand of the Silk-Washing Stream":

> *Autumn leaves float about in the cold air;*
> *Insects chirp in the boredom of the night.*
> *The sun sets, a man's shadow across the bridge.*
> *The chrysanthemums still in full bloom*
> *Will soon be crushed by the wintry frost.*
> *This morning's rainstorm will return as night falls.*

Thoughts about his home and his ill-fated search for fame and fortune kept him tossing and turning throughout a wakeful night. He rose and wrote another lyric poem to the tune of "Manifold Little Hills":

> *Alone and sleepless I sit by the cold lamp,*
> *Grieving over thoughts of home far away.*
> *Mandarin ducks by the lotus flowers*
> *Bewail their parting in the autumn rain*
> *And shed tears of blood in the evening wind.*
> *Lifting my eyes, I see wild geese flying*
> *And have them send word to the ends of the earth.*
> *Here I am, resolved to stay till next year.*
> *The sorrow of waiting too deep to bear,*
> *The blue carpet is soon drenched with my tears.*

Thus he stayed on in the capital. By late autumn, his servant refused to work for him any longer and went home without notifying him. Left all by himself with no money at his disposal, Zhao Xu eked out a living by offering his services as a scribe to passersby on the street. Feeling miserable in his thin, tattered clothes made of yellow grass,[12] which provided poor protection against the bitter west wind, he wrote a lyric poem to the tune of "Partridge Sky":

> *Yellow grass clothes can hardly ward off the cold;*
> *Old and worn out, they are the color of ash.*
> *Frayed at the shoulders, tattered at the sleeves,*
> *They cannot stand the nonstop autumn wind.*
> *Barely covered in these tear-stained rags,*
> *I fear the sight of old acquaintances.*
> *Softly the neighbor woman asked me,*
> *"May I have your clothes to make shoe soles with?"*

One rainy autumn day, Zhao Xu was sitting in the inn. The clerk offered him these words of advice: "Scholar, being as poor as you are, why don't you go across the street to the teahouse and play your flute in exchange for some money? You can make a living that way." Greatly vexed at this suggestion, Zhao Xu wrote another poem:

A lonesome soul desolate in an inn,
I gather wild herbs for my daily meals.
The bumpkin sees not a great man's worth,
But asks if I can play the flute.

Time flashed by. At around the third watch one night more than a year later, Emperor Renzong dreamt of a god in a gold cuirass heading straight for the inner quarters of the palace in a cart loaded with nine red suns. He woke up with a start and realized that it was nothing but a dream. The next morning, after the assembly of civil and military officials had withdrawn from the court following the usual ceremonies, the emperor asked Eunuch Miao, director of the Imperial Observatory, "I saw in a dream last night a god in a gold cuirass sitting in a cart that was loaded with nine red suns. What do you make of this dream?"

"Nine suns make up the character *xu*,"[13] said Eunuch Miao. "It is most likely a personal name or the name of some prefecture or county."

"If it is a personal name," said the emperor, "I would like to see the man. But how do I go about it? Do a divination for me."

Eunuch Miao had learned from a man with supernatural powers a most quick and accurate method of divination attributed to Zhuge Liang of the Three Kingdoms period. Right away he did as the emperor bade and said, "Your Majesty will see him today, but only if Your Majesty and I go out into the streets, disguised as plain-robed scholars."

Accordingly, the emperor took off his royal robe and jade waistband, dressed himself as a white-robed scholar, and, together with Eunuch Miao clad in the same manner, stepped out of the palace and into the streets reserved for the emperor as well as other lanes and alleys of the city.

Before long, there came into view a most impressive multistory wineshop. It was the famous Fan Tower by the east gate of the Eastern Capital. There is a lyric poem to the tune of "Partridge Sky" that bears witness:

The high tower reaches into the sky,
Filled with rare delicacies most divine.
Dismounting, patrons get drunk from the mere aroma,
And lavish fortunes on a single drink.
To attract noble guests and worthy men,
Singing and music add charm to the place.
The tables are spread with delicacies;
Painted eaves stretch over the railings.

Emperor Renzong and Eunuch Miao ascended the stairs to drink some wine and sat down, with the emperor taking the seat of honor. It being the height of summer, the emperor fanned himself with a jade-handled round fan the color of white pears. As he watched the street down below, he rapped the handle of the fan against the railing and accidentally dropped the fan down onto the street. A hurried search on the street turned up nothing. The emperor had Eunuch Miao do another divination and got the answer "The fan will reappear today." The two finished their wine, paid their bill, and went down the stairs and out onto the streets again.

Their steps took them to the examination candidates' quarters, where they caught sight of a teahouse. The emperor suggested going in for a cup of tea. They entered and had just sat down when they saw two poems on the white wall written in elegant diction and vigorous calligraphy. Noticing the signature "Zhao Xu, Scholar of Chengdu," the emperor exclaimed with a start, "This must be our man!" Thereupon Eunuch Miao summoned a waiter and asked, "Who wrote the poems on the wall?"

"It's a scholar who failed the examinations," said the waiter. "He's stranded here because he's too ashamed to return home."

Eunuch Miao asked further, "Where is he from? Where is he staying now?"

"He is a native of Chengdu Prefecture in Sichuan and is now lodged at an inn across the street in the examination candidates' quarters. He makes a living by offering writing services while waiting for the next round of examinations."

These words reminded the emperor of what had happened before. He said to Eunuch Miao under his breath, "This man scored first place in the last examination. He has great literary talent but wrote a wrong character. I was annoyed at his refusal to admit his mistake and struck him off the list of successful candidates. I had no idea he would be stranded here like this." (*Those who refuse to admit mistakes can hardly amount to anything, because knowledge is accumulated only through the admission of mistakes.*) He then instructed the waiter, "Go and find him for me. I need him to write something for me. I'll give you a reward when you bring him here."

The waiter went out, but Zhao Xu was nowhere to be found. The waiter said to himself with a sigh, "This scholar is indeed out of luck. Where on earth can he be?" He returned to the teahouse and reported to the two patrons, "Gentlemen, I can't find him."

"We'll stay a little longer," said the emperor. "Give us some more tea." While having tea, they sent the waiter out again to look for the man. The waiter searched the inn and all the wineshops in the neighborhood but to no avail. "This scholar is indeed destined to be poor!" he thought to himself.

"He could have made some money from these two gentlemen. Too bad for him!" He went back to the teahouse with the same answer: "I can't find him."

The two patrons paid their bill and were about to rise and leave, when the waiter exclaimed, pointing, "There he is!"

"Where?" asked Eunuch Miao.

The waiter pointed at a man in a tattered blue robe approaching the teahouse. Eunuch Miao had the waiter invite him in. The waiter went out and addressed the man, "Scholar Zhao, there are two gentlemen in the teahouse waiting for you. I looked for you twice, but you were nowhere to be found." With hurried steps, Zhao Xu entered the teahouse.

After an exchange of greetings, he sat down next to Eunuch Miao and the three began drinking tea together.

"Did you write the poems on the wall?"

Zhao Xu answered, "They're just ridiculous nonsense from this unworthy student."

"What are you, a native of Chengdu, doing here?" asked the emperor.

"I am too ashamed to return home," replied Zhao Xu, "because, as bad luck would have it, I failed the examinations." As he spoke, he began searching in his sleeves.

Eunuch Miao remarked, "What is it in your sleeves, scholar?"

Instead of answering, Zhao Xu took out a white-pear-colored round fan with a jade handle. With both hands, he respectfully showed them the fan. Upon a closer look, Eunuch Miao saw a poem newly written on it:

> Boughs twisted, the tree stands in verdant grandeur;
> Unknown, the dragon hides itself in the dirt.
> Some day, with the advent of the wind and clouds[14]
> A jade beam it will be to support the sky.

"Where did you get this fan?" asked Eunuch Miao.

"I was passing by under the Fan Tower," answered Zhao Xu, "when it fell from upstairs and planted itself right on my tattered sleeve. As I was called to Prime Minister Wang's residence to write poems about pine trees, I also wrote this poem on the fan."

"This fan," said Eunuch Miao, "belongs to this Mr. Zhao,[15] who dropped it while having a drink in the tower."

"In that case, I'll be happy to give the fan back to you."

Immensely pleased, the emperor proceeded to ask why Zhao Xu had failed the examinations, whereupon Zhao answered, "I did pass all three sessions of the examinations, but as it turned out, the emperor read my papers and found one wrongly written character. That is how I ended up here."

The emperor remarked, "His Majesty lacks good sense."

"That is not true," protested Zhao Xu.

"Which character did you write wrong?" asked the emperor.

"It was the character *wei* 唯. I wrote the radical *kou* 口 as *si* ム. The emperor, with his great learning, pointed out my mistake. I said that the two radicals were interchangeable, whereupon His Majesty wrote the eight characters 单罩, 去吉, 吴矣, 吕台 and told me to explain how the radicals were interchangeable in these four pairs. I failed to come up with an answer, and that is how I failed the examinations and came to be stranded here. I have only myself to blame, because I should have known better than to make that mistake. It was not the emperor's fault." (*Now he's talking!*)

Emperor Renzong then asked, "Since you are from Sichuan, do you happen to know Commissioner Wang?"

"I know him, but he doesn't know me."

The emperor continued, "He's a nephew of mine. I'll write a letter to him and have someone take you to him to seek a position and get a start in your career. What do you say to that?"

Zhao Xu dropped to his knees and said with deep bows, "If I should indeed receive such help from you two gentlemen, I will never forget your kindness."

Eunuch Miao suggested, "Why don't you write a poem as a token of gratitude for Mr. Zhao's favor?"

Zhao Xu readily consented and wrote these lines:

> *Jade was hidden in the rock;*
> *Gold was buried in the mud.*
> *A helping hand pulled me up*
> *Onto the ladder leading to the sky.*

The emperor was delighted. "Why do you say so?" he asked. "You don't know yet if my recommendation will work. Let me also write a poem in return." And this is what he wrote:

> *He failed the exam over one character,*
> *Became stranded here, his plans disrupted.*
> *A letter from me to the Sichuan region*
> *Will work better than pleas at court.*

Zhao Xu's heart overflowed with gratitude at these lines. Eunuch Miao put in, "Now that Mr. Zhao has written, it is my turn to write you a few lines." And this is what he wrote:

> *Your presence here bore out heavenly signs;*
> *But for one word, you'd have won first honors.*

This letter sent to Commissioner Wang
Will bring glory to the clan of Zhao.

Eunuch Miao then said, "You may now go back to the inn. Tomorrow morning, I will remind Mr. Zhao to have someone send over the letter and traveling money to you and to accompany you on your journey."

"Could you tell me where you live so that I can come to express my gratitude?" asked Zhao Xu.

Eunuch Miao declined: "It's too far from here. Please do not take the trouble."

Zhao Xu had to content himself with repeated bows of gratitude in the teahouse. The three of them then left the premises and took leave of each other.

The following morning, Zhao Xu rose bright and early and waited until he saw, indeed, the beardless plain-robed scholar coming toward the inn. Following him was an officer carrying a trunk and a parcel, but Mr. Zhao was not with them. Zhao Xu went out of the inn to meet them. After the exchange of greetings, Eunuch Miao said, "Last night, Mr. Zhao followed my advice and entrusted this man with the letter and an ingot of silver worth fifty taels. He is to accompany you on your journey back to Chengdu. The letter is with him. Take good care on the journey."

Zhao Xu thanked him profusely and asked, "May I ask your name?"

"My name is Miao Xiu. I am a retainer of Mr. Zhao's. You will find out all the details when you see Commissioner Wang."

"Should this trip bring me what I seek," said Zhao Xu, "I will not forget to repay you," whereupon he intoned a poem and wrote it on a piece of white paper as a souvenir:

> *I sat for the exam last year but failed;*
> *Next time, my efforts will not be in vain.*
> *Pleas to the prime minister unavailing,*
> *A teahouse chance meeting was a blessing.*
> *A fan from the sky that stuck in my sleeve*
> *Inspired the poem I left in the mansion.*
> *Filled with gratitude for the kind letter,*
> *I depart to serve the commissioner.*

Eunuch Miao took the poem, bade him farewell, and returned to where he had come from. Zhao Xu chiseled the ingot of silver into smaller pieces, paid his inn bills, and packed his belongings. Three days later, he set out on his journey.

On the way, they traveled by day and rested by night, stopping only for food and drink when they felt the need. After some days, they found themselves about one hundred li outside Chengdu Prefecture. Word got to them that there was quite a bustling crowd of military men and civilians ahead waiting to greet the new commissioner. Runners had been dispatched to meet him midway. Zhao Xu was alarmed at the news. "I am here to see Commissioner Wang, but he has apparently left his post. Woe is me! What is to be done?" Thereupon he intoned another poem:

> Here I am in Sichuan, letter in hand,
> But the long journey to find a patron is all in vain.
> What a poor return for His Honor's kindness!
> Though nearer to home, I yield to despair.

The officer offered this advice: "Do not despair yet. Let us first find out what's really happening." Zhao Xu dragged his reluctant feet over another twenty-five li until they came upon the pavilion, located about ten li from the city, built for holding ceremonies of greeting or sending off officials. The noisy crowd gathered there, officials included, were complaining about the failure of the new commissioner to show up, even though they had been waiting for three days. The officer accompanying Zhao Xu said, "Scholar, let us go to the pavilion to take a look."

Zhao Xu declined, "No! I will have no one to turn to if I make a wrong move."

Over his protests, the officer walked straight up to the pavilion, still carrying the suitcase and the parcels. "Why are you officials still waiting?" he shouted. "The new commissioner is here!"

Much startled, the assembly of officials gathered there exclaimed, "But we don't see him!" From the parcel, the officer took out an envelope, tore it open and announced, "The new commissioner is none other than this scholar."

Zhao Xu was also astounded. The officer opened the trunk, from which he extracted a purple robe, a golden belt, an ivory tablet, and a pair of black boots and, putting a gauze cap on himself, began to read aloud the imperial edict. Zhao Xu bowed in gratitude for the imperial edict that granted him the post of commissioner of the fifty-four prefectures of Sichuan.

After the assembly of officials came forward and exchanged greetings with him, he sent someone to look for a comfortable place to stay while waiting for an auspicious day to assume office. Thinking back over what had led to this, he said to himself, "I almost won first honors but for one wrong character. Who would have thought that I was indeed destined to achieve fame and fortune? So the Mr. Zhao I met in the teahouse was, in fact, Emperor Renzong himself." Truly,

Flowers wither when given too much care;
Willows flourish when left unattended.

Zhao Xu asked the officer, "Who is the plain-robed man who saw me off?"

"That's Eunuch Miao, director of the Imperial Observatory. It was he who told me to accompany you here."

Zhao Xu said to himself, "My undiscerning eyes failed to see Mount Tai!"

On the day chosen for assuming office, he mounted a fine steed with a decorated saddle and, under a three-tiered canopy, set off for his new mansion, preceded by an orderly procession and followed by a retinue of officials. It was indeed a grand sight to see. The ceremony over, he returned home to pay respects to his parents, who went out of the house in great agitation to greet their son amid the bustling commotion. Zhao Xu dismounted the horse, entered the hall, and, in his purple robe, golden belt, and black boots, bowed to his parents, his ivory tablet in hand. His parents asked, "Didn't you fail the examinations and get stranded in the capital? Why have you been assigned this post? And in your native town, too!"

At Zhao Xu's account of the whole story, his parents raised their hands to their foreheads in a gesture of joy and said, "By the radiance of the sun and the moon, may you serve the emperor loyally to repay your debt of gratitude." Zhao Xu wrote a poem to mark the occasion:

Honor and success I should both have won
If not for the sake of a single word.
Hating the surging waves at the Dragon Gate,
Suddenly I hear a bolt of thunder.

His parents were immensely pleased. The entire family rejoiced while friends and relatives came to offer their congratulations. They feasted for quite a few days. The servant who had abandoned him was now accepted back, his disloyalty forgiven. Zhao Xu also wrote a memorial to the court to acknowledge his gratitude for the benevolence of the emperor. From then on, he attended to his duties and responsibilities over all the civilians as well as the military in Sichuan while supporting his parents, who lived with him in his yamen. Indeed, this bears out the saying "When a son is favored by the emperor, the whole family benefits." There is a poem in evidence:

Xiangru stopped by Shu on his way to his post[16]
Su Qin passed by Luoyang, loaded with gold.[17]
There have always been men who return to hometowns in glory,
But none can match him who met the emperor in a teahouse.

Like clouds the courtesans swarmed to Leyou
To pay respects to Liu's grave of romance.
How absurd that men of high offices
Had less love for talent than did those in skirts.

The Courtesans Mourn Liu the Seventh
in the Spring Breeze

> To the court I offer not my poems,
> But return to my hut on South Mountain.[1]
> Untalented, I am forsaken by the wise ruler;
> In ill health, I am deserted by old friends.
> My graying hair quickens my decline;
> The approaching spring sends away another year.[2]
> Sleepless with unending sorrows on my mind,
> I watch through my lonesome window the moonlit pines.

The above poem is by Meng Haoran[3] of the Tang dynasty, the most famous poet from the region of Xiangyang. During a sojourn in the Eastern Capital,[4] he developed a close friendship with Zhang Yue, the prime minister, who was an ardent admirer of his talent.

One day Zhang Yue was on duty in the Imperial Secretariat, trying to compose a poem by order of the emperor. Frustrated at not being able to come up with good lines however hard he tried, he quietly sent for Meng Haoran to ask for his counsel on a couplet. With tea brewing in the pot, they were deep in their discussion when Emperor Minghuang suddenly made his appearance. Caught off guard, Meng Haoran ducked behind the bed without, however, escaping the emperor's notice.

"Who is the man trying to hide himself from me?" he asked Zhang Yue.

"He is Meng Haoran, a poet from Xiangyang and an old friend of mine, who happened to come by," explained Zhang. "As he is but a commoner, he dares not show himself in Your Majesty's presence."

The emperor said, "We have long heard of this man. I do not mind meeting him." (*A saintly ruler appreciative of talents.*)

Meng Haoran was thus obliged to emerge from his hiding place. Prostrating himself upon the floor, he begged for forgiveness for an offense that was punishable by death. The emperor said to him, "We have long heard that you are a good poet. Recite for me a poem that you yourself are most proud of." Thereupon, Meng Haoran recited the poem quoted above at the beginning of our story. The emperor remarked, "You are not among the untalented, nor am I a wise ruler, but abandon you I did not, for you never even presented yourself to me." Displeased, the emperor rose and left.

The following day, while at court, Zhang Yue offered apologies to the emperor, but, at the same time, he did his best to recommend that Meng Haoran be granted office on the merit of his talent.

The emperor replied, "I know these lines by Meng Haoran: 'Flickering stars bedim the Milky Way;⁵ / Sprinkling raindrops bedew the *wutong* trees.' What exquisite lines! I also know another couplet by him: 'The mist moistens the Yun Meng Marshes; / The ripples shake Yueyang Tower.'⁶ What a magnificent couplet! And yet, of all his verses, he picked a most dull and bitter poem for me to hear yesterday. Such a rancorous man is by no means fit to hold office. It would be best to let him have his way and return to South Mountain, since that appears to be the ambition of his life!" That is how Meng Haoran came to be known until this day as Meng the Man of the Mountain, who never attained any office to the end of his days. A poet of later times had this to say of him:

> To the emperor he presents a new poem;
> Hopes for fame and fortune change to obscurity.
> Neither "untalented" nor "forsaken by the wise ruler,"
> To be rich or poor is all in one's fate.

Among the ancients, there were men who rose to be prime ministers by virtue of nothing more than a single brilliant remark or a poem. Is it not, then, a matter of predetermined fate that Meng Haoran lost favor with the emperor over eight lines that happened not to strike the latter's fancy?

Let me now tell of another famous man of talent who lost his chance at fame and fortune for the sake of a *ci* [lyric] poem but, after a lifetime of frustrations, came to enjoy a reputation far and wide as a romantic lover. Who was this man? As our story has it, he was Liu Yong [d. ca. 1053], courtesy name Qiqing, who lived during the reign of Emperor Renzong [1023–63]⁷ of the Song dynasty. Originally a native of Chong'an County in Jianning Prefecture, he followed his father to the capital upon the latter's appointment as a court official and came to be stranded there. Being the seventh child of the family, he was called by all and sundry Young Master Liu the Seventh. At twenty-five years of age, he was as graceful in bearing as he was talented in the arts of music, chess, calligraphy, and painting. He was at his best in the writing of poetry and was a true master of *ci* poetry.

What, you may ask, is a *ci* poem? Li Bai's "Remembering the Lady of Qin" and "Deva-like Barbarian," and Wang Wei's "Yu lun pao," for example, are *ci* poems, or lyrics composed to given tunes. Also known as expanded *shi* poetry, *ci* poems were used extensively for singing by celebrated courtesans of the Tang dynasty. By Song times, the officials of the Imperial Bureau of Music had collected large numbers of tune patterns and had written verses to fit the tunes and offered the resulting *ci* poems to the emperor. The *ci* poem is, therefore, marked by its definite tonal and metrical arrangements as dictated by the restrictions of the music. The lines vary in length in accordance with a fixed tonal sequence. In composing a *ci* poem, one needs to observe strictly the rules of prosody and, with the utmost care, match the words with the musical notes. This, then, is how *ci* poems are written.

Being an unsurpassed expert in the music of these tunes, Liu the Seventh added new tunes to those collected and standardized by the Bureau of Music, bringing the total number of tunes to over two hundred. Unabashedly proud of his own matchless talent, he held everyone else in contempt and thought it beneath his dignity to cultivate friendships with the local gentry or fellow scholars. Instead, he spent his days frequenting only houses of pleasure. Of the numerous courtesans in the Eastern Capital, none did not admire him and take it as an honor to see him. Any girl who did not know Liu the Seventh was laughed at as being unworthy of the company of courtesans. There came to be circulated among courtesans' quarters these catchy phrases:

> I'd rather have Brother Liu than satins.
> I'd rather be called by Liu than by kings.
> I'd rather possess Liu's heart than riches.
> I'd rather see Liu's face than deities.

There was indeed not a morning or a night that Liu the Seventh did not spend in a house of pleasure. He was particularly taken with three famous courtesans of the highest class: Chen Shishi, Zhao Xiangxiang, and Xu Dongdong, who vied with one another in providing for Liu the Seventh out of their own pockets. How do we know this? There is a *ci* poem called "In Jest" to the tune of "The Moon over the West River" that bears witness:

> For flirtation, Shishi is the best;
> For furtive love, Xiangxiang has no equal;
> But, for a soul mate, I turn to Dongdong.
> All three of them I keep for myself.
> Offices, I hold none,
> Leisure, I have to spare.
> How delicious to be among three women
> Who make up the character "adultery"![8]

Liu's brilliance as a poet outshone that of all the officials in the imperial court. Therefore, for all his arrogance, those near the emperor still held him in some admiration. As it was a time when peace reigned in the land, all men with talent were sought out for office. As recommendations of Liu Yong met with support in the imperial court, Liu was thus granted the office of magistrate of the county of Yuhang in Zhejiang. Though not satisfied with the assignment, Liu accepted it as a stepping-stone toward further promotions in his future career. His only regret was to have to tear himself away from the three courtesans. As he made ready for his departure toward the end of spring, he wrote a *ci* poem to the tune of "The Moon over the West River" to express his sorrow at the parting:

> *Phoenix embroidered curtains are rolled up high;*
> *Beast shaped knockers on red doors swing without stop.*
> *The late morning spring sun shines atop the flowers,*
> *But languidly I stay in my bed.*
> *My happy dreams are gone with the willow catkin,*
> *My sorrows thicker than the finest wine.*
> *With no night rain and morning clouds,*
> *The finest hours go by, unenjoyed!*

Upon hearing that Brother Liu was leaving for a post in Zhejiang, the three courtesans came for a farewell dinner that turned out to be well attended by courtesans from all quarters. In the course of the feast, Liu the Seventh intoned a *ci* to the tune of "As in a Dream: A Song":

> *The thousand li of green country*
> *Sets off the ten rows of red skirts.*
> *The waiting carriages bid us to hurry*
> *And cut short the tender words of farewell.*
> *Many a furtive tear I shed;*
> *If only I could multiply myself to be with you!*

Liu the Seventh thus took leave of the courtesans and went on his way, dressed like a scholar on a study tour, carrying his zither, sword, and cases of books. Enjoying the scenery all along the way, he stopped at Jiangzhou, where, upon making inquiries about local courtesans, he was told that the one most outstanding in both beauty and talent was called Xie Yuying. Having obtained her address, he went for a visit. Yuying greeted him and was so impressed by his refined manners that she led him into her small study. A look around the room convinced Liu of her exquisite taste. He saw

> *A clean table by a bright window,*
> *A tea stove by a bamboo couch.*
> *A priceless zither above the bed,*

An antique painting on the wall.
An undying fragrance:
An incense burner never short of sandalwood.
A cool, soothing breeze:
A flower vase never out of fresh water.
Ten thousand books for leisurely reading,
A chess board for many a pleasant game.

Liu's eyes fell on a book lying on the table with the inscription *Recent* Ci *Poems by Liu the Seventh*. Flipping through the pages, he found that the volume was a collection of his lyrics handwritten in fine penmanship.

"Where did you get these poems?" asked Liu the Seventh.

Yuying explained, "These are poems by the gifted scholar Liu the Seventh of the Eastern Capital. I am a great admirer of his poems. Every time I hear his works read out loud, I write them down and bind the pages into volumes." (*Similar to Qin Shaoyou's⁹ wonderful experience.*)

Liu asked further, "Of so many *ci* poets in the land, why do you favor him?"

"He is most expressive and accurate in depicting scenery and describing feelings. For example, at the end of the poem 'Thoughts on an Autumn Day,' he says, 'Looking at each other in sorrow amid the cries of a lonely goose, / Standing till the westering sun sinks below the horizon.' In the poem titled 'Parting on an Autumn Day,' there are these lines: 'Where will I wake up after tonight's wine? / The willow-lined bank, the dawn breeze, the waning moon.' These are lines no one else is capable of. Every time I read his poetry, I can't bring myself to stop. How I wish I could meet him in person!"

"So you want to make his acquaintance? You are looking at him this very moment."

Much startled, Yuying asked him about his background. After being assured that he was indeed Liu the Seventh himself on his way to Yuhang to assume his post, Yuying fell on her knees, crying, "Please forgive me, a mortal being, for failing to recognize a deity." She then set out wine and, in all sincerity, urged him to stay for the night.

Deeply moved by her devotion, Liu stayed on. However, after several days, he felt obliged to take his leave, for fear of missing the assigned date for the assumption of his post. Yuying had come to be so attached to him that she made a solemn pledge to follow him and serve him as a wife. Liu declined: "It is not appropriate for you to follow me on this trip. If you really mean what you say, wait for me until my term of office expires, and we will go to Chang'an¹⁰ together."

Yuying agreed: "Since you deign to favor me with such great kindness, I shall, as of today, turn away all patrons and wait only for you. Please do not, on any account, abandon me and leave me to 'heave sighs over my graying hair,' as the poem goes." Liu asked for a piece of paper and wrote a *ci* to the tune of "The Fairy Maiden and Her Jingling Jade Pendants":

> *The fairy maiden from the pearl palace*
> *Returns not to her heavenly abode.*
> *As a commoner she dresses and speaks,*
> *But all the more striking is her beauty.*
> *I'd fain liken her to a priceless flower,*
> *But others might call this a vain attempt.*
> *I came to see, as I reflect deeper,*
> *That however precious flowers may be,*
> *They, in their few colors of red or white,*
> *Pale when compared with this lovely maiden,*
> *With her thousand ways to please a man's heart.*
>
> *In her ornate room, moonlit and breezy,*
> *I willingly squander away my time.*
> *Seldom have men of talent ever had*
> *Mates with as much matching youthful beauty.*
> *Nestling in my tender embrace,*
> *She holds dear my richly endowed talent.*
> *In admiration of her qualities,*
> *I swear by the side of the pillow,*
> *Never to give her cause for sorrow.*

With this poem, Liu took leave of Yuying and went on his way. Before many days had passed, he came upon the Suzhou area. Much taken by the picturesque scenery, he stepped into a tavern by the roadside and ordered three cups of wine. A sudden boom of drumbeats drew him to the window, where he saw a group of children on small boats in the lake playing with the water and picking lotus flowers. They were singing a song in the style of the Wu area:

> *The lotus-picking girls vie for beauty,*
> *Like red lotus blossoms against the white.*
> *Proud of their color though the red ones are,*
> *The white ones claim to have a sweeter smell.*
> *([Illegible] good.)*
> *Fragrant, fragrant they are indeed.*
> *Flower-lovers fight for them on first sight.*
> *The red ones are priced too high,*

> *And the white ones none too cheap.*
> *He who at the market loses the deal*
> *Tries a settlement in private.*
> *No one sees, underneath the spreading leaves,*
> *The tendrils of the lotus roots that grow apace.*

Having heard them out, Liu the Seventh took out a pen and wrote these lines on the wall in the same style:

> *Of ten miles of lotuses, nine are red.*
> *Fluffy white is the one in the middle.*
> *The white ones are best for the roots that grow below;*
> *The red ones best for their seedpods galore.*
> *Best for their seedpods they are indeed,*
> *And how delicate the seedpods look!*
> *What is most clear and refreshing inside*
> *Is wrapped up heavily on the outside.*
> *He who takes a bite for the taste*
> *Is caught unawares in his haste.*
> *Expecting nothing but sweetness,*
> *How would he know the bitterness in my heart?*
> *The flowering and the seeding*
> *Have left me empty inside.*
> (This is almost a prophecy poem.)

This song is still sung in the Wu region to this day.

After passing the Suzhou region, Liu the Seventh arrived in the county of Yuhang to take up his post, and he turned out to be an upright official whose rule of justice reduced the number of court cases. What leisure time he spared from office he spent climbing Mount Dadie, Mount Tianzhu, and Mount Youquan to view the scenery while reveling in poetry and wine. In Yuhang County there were also courtesans affiliated with the Ministry of Music who served him by turns, and he would turn down all court cases involving courtesans as defendants. (*Courtesans all too often get involved in court cases.*) Among the courtesans was a Zhou Yuexian, a woman of remarkable beauty as well as learning. One day, she was singing and serving wine at the yamen when County Magistrate Liu noticed her sadness and asked for an explanation. Yuexian hung her head and remained silent, but tears were seen gushing from her eyes. It was only at the insistence of the county magistrate that she came out with her story.

It so happened that Yuexian was deeply in love with a local scholar named Huang and had her heart set on marrying him, but the scholar was too poor to afford the necessary wedding gifts. Out of faithfulness to him, Yuexian was unswervingly determined not to take any more patrons, in spite of all the pressure from the procuress, who, being her own mother, could not very well do anything to her. Scholar Huang's school being on the other side of the river, Yuexian took the ferry every evening to spend the night with him and returned to her own quarters in the morning. There was a Squire Liu the Second in the same county, who, coveting Yuexian's beauty, asked for a rendezvous, only to be turned down firmly by her with the quatrain

> I am not a fickle roadside willow,
> But an orchid in a quiet valley.
> A roaming bee in his search for conquests
> Had best not take me for a wildflower.

Squire Liu, however, hit upon a plan. He instructed a boatman to go to a deserted place at night with his ferryboat while Yuexian was on it, rape her, and return with evidence of the deed so as to claim a handsome reward. (*What a villain, Squire Liu!*) Prompted by his avarice, the boatman went ahead to do as he was told. As soon as Yuexian stepped onto his boat, he started poling away from the usual route. Noticing that the boat was not headed where she should be going, Yuexian told the boatman to stop, but he turned a deaf ear and did not stop until they came to a deserted place deep in the tall reeds. He moored the boat, walked into the cabin, and, grabbing Yuexian's arms, tried to force himself upon her. Knowing that she had not a chance to free herself from the man's grip, Yuexian had no choice but to submit. After the clouds and rain[11] were over, she ruefully intoned a poem:

> How I loathe being a courtesan
> Who has to keep insults to herself.
> In shame, I return to the moonlit ferry;
> In disgust, I embark the flower boat.

That night, Yuexian stayed with Mr. Huang as usual, but dared not mention the incident. She returned home in the morning. The boatman, who had memorized her poem, repeated it to Squire Liu, who duly rewarded him with an ingot of silver. He then sent someone to summon Yuexian to serve him with wine at his residence. When he was well warmed with wine, he made advances again to Yuexian, only to be pushed away as before, whereupon he produced a fan and made her read the quatrain inscribed on it. Yuexian was struck speechless in shock upon realizing that these were the very lines she had intoned on the ferryboat. Squire Liu sneered, "Wouldn't the ivory bed and brocade quilts here be preferable to the reeds and the moon? Don't give me any more of your demure pretensions." Yuexian was so overcome with shame that she was reduced to submission. Henceforth, Squire Liu kept her exclusively to himself and allowed her no time for Mr. Huang. (*This differs from what appears in "Story of the Wanjiang Tower" [Wanjianglou ji], where Magistrate Liu is said to have lusted after Yuexian and had the boatman trick her, an allegation quite damaging to his reputation as a man of good taste and refinement. The account given here should naturally be taken as the more authentic one.*)

As the saying goes, "The girls love a good-looking face; the madam loves the sight of cash." A fine scholar Mr. Huang might be, but how was he to compete with a man loaded with money? The madam was much delighted, but Yuexian, aching for Mr. Huang, was consumed with sorrow. Now, at the insistence of the county magistrate, she poured out her whole story. Being an old hand in the world of love, Liu the Seventh felt deeply for the girl. There and then, he summoned the madam and redeemed Yuexian with eighty thousand in cash. He then invited Mr. Huang to come and take Yuexian home as his lawfully wedded wife. (*Lovers commiserate with lovers, just as talents appreciate other talents. Those who feel not the least bit of concern for each other do not belong to the same kind of people.*) Mr. Huang and Yuexian were grateful beyond words. Truly,

> *One romantic soul pities another;*
> *One true lover encounters another.*

Liu's three-year term of office in Yuhang expired. He was on his way back to the capital when he recalled Xie Yuying's pledge and made a stopover at Jiangzhou. As it happened, after Liu's departure, Xie Yuying did, as she had promised, turn away all patrons, but after a year had elapsed without any word from Liu, a grudge against him grew in her heart. For one thing, she had no more income for her daily expenses; for another, it was no easy job turning away all who lined up at her door in their carriages day after day. Moreover, how was she to know if Liu meant what he said after they had been together for only five nights? Therefore, at the urging of some busybody, she changed her mind and resumed her old profession. There came along a Squire Sun, an immensely rich merchant from Xin'an and a man not without some literary taste, who lavished more than a thousand taels of silver on her over a year's time. Upon arrival at Yuying's door, Liu the Seventh was told that she was out with Squire Sun viewing boats on the lake. Realizing that the absent Yuying had gone back on her word, he became so sick at heart that he took a sheet of flowered notepaper and wrote a *ci* poem to the tune of "Tapping the *Wutong* Tree":

> *With lovely dimples and bewitching charm,*
> *Bestowed by heaven a beauty divine,*

Tenderly she attended to my needs,
Using her artful ways to win my heart.
On parting, she promised to meet again,
And pledged to me the rest of her life.
That such fragile feelings might vanish
Has ever since been preying on my mind.

Now here I am, but the house is empty,[12]
Without a sincere word of love.
Goaded by evil counsel,
She broke her word of honor.
I ask of Song Yu of Lantai,
Fine poet and man of many talents:
Where is one to turn now
For more clouds and rain?

By way of finishing, he added the line "Written by Liu Yong of the Eastern Capital on the occasion of a failed attempt to see Yuying." After reading the poem over again, he posted it on the wall and left in a huff, with a flick of his sleeves. Back in the Eastern Capital, he was promoted, after repeated recommendations, to the post of vice-director of the Bureau of State Farms. His interchanges of visits with the courtesans of the city resumed. In the courtesans' quarters he spent all his salary and the gifts he received in exchange for poems. (*Zhang Youyu,[13] a native of the Wu region, had the same way of living.*)

One day he was sporting with Xu Dongdong in her residence when a messenger sent by Prime Minister Lü Yijian found his way in and announced, "In preparing for celebrating the sixtieth birthday of Prime Minister Lü, the girls of the house find themselves short of a new song to dedicate to him and sent me to request an impromptu song from you for them to practice. Two bolts of Sichuan brocade and four bolts of Wu silk are respectfully offered as compensation."

Liu the Seventh accepted the offer and kept the messenger for some food and drink downstairs. He then asked Xu Dongdong for some paper of good quality, whereupon she took two rolls of fine paper from a casket and laid them out on the table. Liu rubbed his ink-stick against the ink-stone until the ink was ready, dipped his brush-pen well into the ink, and, spreading out a scroll, wrote a lyric to the tune of "A Thousand Years" without even bothering with a first draft:

With peace reigning throughout the vast land,
Great men appeared on the scene again.
With no beacon-fires in sight,

Comets are seen shining bright.
Of venerable age and virtue,
He assists the emperor in the court
And wins battles while feasting at the table.
His good fortune boundless, his fame timeless,
He preserves eternal youth.

Fishing at Wei many a year ago,
Lü Wang became the power of the land
And fulfilled the flying bear prophecy.[14]
Of the same surname, the Lü of today
Won eminence much younger.
His black gauze cap over hair not yet white,
From the gold vessel he gaily pours wine.
Much to the envy of all and sundry,
In high office forever he shall be.[15]

Still in a poetic mood, on the remaining scroll he wrote another *ci* poem to the tune of "The Moon over the West River":

Born with shining literary talent,
I find my pen flowing like the Yangzi.
Though each word costs more than a bolt of silk,
I never stoop to haggle over price.
I bow to no one for fame and riches;
Others make bows to me for my poems.
A dashing poet unexcelled in ci,
A minister in a commoner's robe.

He was laying the finished poems out on the table when a maid sent by Chen Shishi, another courtesan, entered to announce, "A beautiful lady who refuses to reveal her name has come all the way from the south to see you. She is now waiting at our residence. Please be so kind as to come at once." Liu hastily sealed up what he had written and, sending the messenger away, set off for Chen Shishi's residence. The sight of that woman staggered him. Who, you may ask, was she? Truly,

She's nowhere to be found when looked for,
But here she comes of her own accord.

That woman was none other than Xie Yuying of Jiangzhou. After returning from the lake where she had been viewing ships, she had seen the poem "Tapping the *Wutong* Tree" on the wall and, after reading it over and over again, was overcome with shame at the realization that Liu, true lover that he was, had come back to her in fulfillment of his promise. Without telling Squire Sun a word, she packed up her belongings and hired a boat for a journey to the Eastern Capital. Upon arrival, she was told, after inquiries, that Master Liu the Seventh had an intimate relationship with Chen Shishi. She therefore presented herself to Chen Shishi and asked for an introduction to Liu. She was beside herself with joy at the reunion. This was nothing less than a case of a cut flower being rejoined and a waning moon waxing full once more. After learning all the details, Chen Shishi asked Xie Yuying to live with her. But, not wishing to inconvenience Shishi, Yuying asked to have the eastern wing as her private quarters. After her arrival in the Eastern Capital, she never took customers but served Liu exclusively in a wifely manner, nor did she attempt to stop Liu from visiting other courtesans. Her generosity was much admired.

To pick up another thread of the story, I now return to Liu. In haste—which inevitably breeds mistakes—he sealed up both poems in a momentary lapse of attention and handed them to the messenger. After breaking the seal, Prime Minister Lü read the birthday poem first and was delighted. Then, as he saw the other one to the tune of "The Moon over the West River," he naturally read on. When he came to the line "Though each word costs more than a bolt of silk, I never stoop to haggle over price," he sneered, saying, "When Pei Du, the duke of Jin,[16] requested a poem from Huangfu Ti to embellish the newly built Monastery of the Light of Bliss, Huangfu Ti demanded three bolts of silk for each character. So this man is complaining about the amount I pay." At the lines "I bow to no one for fame and riches; / Others make bows to me for my poems," rage seized him. "What impudence! I bow to him, he says!" Henceforth, his heart was set against Liu, whereas the latter, whose mind was well above petty grudges, had forgotten all about that poem.

A few days later, the minister of personnel recommended to the emperor that Liu Yong be appointed to fill a vacancy in the Hanlin Academy. Emperor Renzong, much impressed by Liu's work for the Imperial Bureau of Music in standardizing and expanding the collection of tunes for *ci* poems, asked Lü Yijian, the prime minister, "Do you know this Liu Yong? I have a mind to make him a member of the Hanlin Academy."

Lü Yijian answered, "I grant him his talent, but the man is too arrogant and has no regard whatsoever for the honor of his position as vice-director of the Bureau of State Farms. His all-too-frequent visits to the houses of ill fame are greatly detrimental to the respectability of all officials. Should he be given an important post, I am afraid that officials' morality in general would never be the same again." (*Lord Guo[17] and Prime Minister Wen[18] were also self-indulgent men who frequented courtesan quarters, but, once charged with important missions, they dedicated themselves to the nation to the neglect of their self interests. What does a pedantic Confucian moralist know!*) Then he proceeded to recite Liu's poem to the tune of "The Moon over the West River." The emperor nodded. Some officials in the Bureau of Remonstrance[19] had long been informed of Prime Minister Lü's anger toward Liu Yong and now seized the opportunity to ingratiate themselves with the prime minister by supporting the removal of Liu from his current post. The emperor took up his brush-pen and wrote the following quatrain:

> *For riches and honor Liu Yong makes no bow;*
> *Nor will riches and honor go his way.*
> *A commoner's robe he shall wear,*
> *To write poems in moonlight and breeze.*[20]

At the news of his dismissal, Liu burst into a roar of laughter. "All those holding office nowadays are nothing more than benighted illiterates," he said. "How can such men be expected to tolerate a gifted poet like me?" He thereupon changed his name to Liu of Three Changes. To his bewildered friends, he explained, "When I was a most brilliant student in my younger days, I had hopes of attaining instant fame so as to offer my contribution to the imperial court. However, repeated failures at the examinations changed me into a grumpy and frustrated poet. My talent should have been more than enough for eternal fame, but, all too unexpectedly, I was recommended for office, and there I was, a poet changed into an official complete with hat and belt. Yet, descent to the lowly level of a bureaucrat was by no means what my heart was after. Hence the third change: released by imperial edict, I am now as carefree as an immortal being."

From that time on, he grew even more dissolute in his ways and went so far as to take up residence in the courtesans' quarters. On a tablet of the kind that was held by officials, he wrote, "Liu of Three Changes, Imperial Poet Designate." Before he called on a courtesan, he would first send over this tablet and she would then prepare wine and dishes and bedding for the night. (*What a carefree life! This is better than serving as an official.*) The following day, he would visit another courtesan and repeat the same process. For every poem he wrote, however trivial, he would add the words "Written by order of the emperor," much to the amusement of all and sundry.

Several years went by in this way. One day he was taking a nap in Zhao Xiangxiang's residence when a yellow-robed messenger from heaven appeared to him in a dream, saying, "By a decree from the Jade Emperor,[21] the tune 'Song of the Rainbow and Feather Clothes' is dated and needs to be rewritten by you with your divine talent. Please follow me without delay." Liu the Seventh woke up and asked for a bath in perfumed water. To Zhao Xiangxiang he said, "The Lord on High has just summoned me. I will be gone in a moment. You may send a message to all the sisters and tell them that I will not be able to see them any more." So saying, he sat down and closed his eyes. Xiangxiang took a good look and saw that he was already dead. (*This is a man who rises well above mundane concerns. Who says he yearns for nothing but wine and women? Such gross injustice done to a true man is enough cause for eternal sorrow.*) With great alacrity, she sent word to Xie Yuying, who hastened to the scene, so consumed with grief that she had to drag herself along every step of the way. Chen Shishi and Xu Dongdong arrived shortly thereafter. Several other courtesans who had known him also came upon hearing the news.

The truth of the matter was that Liu the Seventh had absolutely no possessions of any value, even though he had served two terms of office. (*This fact alone makes him tens of thousands of times superior to others.*) Yuying, supposedly the woman to depend upon him for a living, had, on the contrary, brought her own belongings, costing him not a penny. Paying their last respects to him now were Xie Yuying as his wife and the other courtesans as his relatives. With Chen Shishi taking charge, they collected enough money and silk from other local courtesans to buy a coffin and burial clothing in preparation for the funeral ceremony to be held at the Zhao residence. In her mourning clothes, Xie Yuying officiated at the funeral. The other three leading courtesans, also in mourning, gathered together and kept vigil over the coffin. In the meantime, they bought a vacant lot on the Leyou Plains, had a grave dug on the site, and chose a propitious day for the burial. (*Is this understood at all? Could a mere rake have brought all this about?*) On the grave was erected a small stone tablet with the inscription "Tomb of Liu of Three Changes, Imperial Poet Designate," in imitation of his own style. On the day of the burial, some officeholding acquaintances of his also came to attend. There, for all to see, was nothing but white silk all over the place, for no courtesan over the length and breadth of the city was not there. Their wailing made the earth tremble. The officials felt so ashamed of themselves that they covered their faces and slunk away.

In less than two months' time, Xie Yuying died of an illness caused by excessive grief and was buried next to Liu's grave. Such a virtuous courtesan is indeed hard to come by, but of her, no more.

Since Liu's burial, every year around the time of the Clear and Bright Festival[22] celebrated courtesans would, by no prior agreement, gather at his grave and, in the soft breeze of spring, lay out their sacrificial offerings and burn paper money in a ceremony that came to be known as "visiting the grave of Liu the Seventh" or "visiting the grave of romance." Those who had not attended the ceremony dared not set foot on the Leyou Plains. This annual ritual gradually became a tradition and did not come to an end until after Emperor Gaozong's court moved south. A later poet had this to say about Liu's grave:

> *Like clouds the courtesans swarmed to Leyou*
> *To pay respects to Liu's grave of romance.*
> *How absurd that men of high offices*
> *Had less love for talent than did those in skirts.*

13

Zhang Daoling Tests Zhao Sheng Seven Times

They are said to have risen to the skies,
But no one sees them come back down to earth.
Should the sky be torn asunder some day,
The air will resound with cries of pain.

The above light-hearted quatrain should not be taken seriously, for it was written by Scholar Tang[1] of the present dynasty [Ming] in playful derision of immortal beings. Ever since the beginning of the universe, three religions have been in existence: the Supreme Ultimate Lord Lao [Lao Zi] founded Taoism [Daoism], Sakyamuni founded Buddhism, and Confucius Confucianism. Confucianism has produced sages and people of virtue, Buddhism has produced Bodhisattvas and Taoism immortals. Of all the followers of the three religions, Confucians lead prosaic and dull lives, and Buddhists live stoically in self-denial. Only the Taoists, in their quest for immortality and bodily transformation, are carefree and unrestrained.

Dear audience, the story that I shall now tell is about how Zhang Daoling tested Zhao Sheng seven times, Zhang Daoling being no less than the very first patriarch of the generations of Taoist celestial masters living on Dragon and Tiger Mountain, and Zhao Sheng his disciple. There is a poem in evidence:

Jade is revealed only when hard rocks are split open;
Gold is seen only when mud and sand are washed away.
Not that the earthbound lack divine aura,
But immortals are different at heart.

As the story goes, Zhang Daoling, with the courtesy name Fuhan, the first to hold the title of Celestial Master, was a native of the state of Pei and an eighth generation descendant of Zhang Zifang.[2] He was born in the tenth year of the Jianwu reign period [C.E. 34] during the rule of Emperor Guangwu of the Han dynasty. Before conceiving him, his mother saw in a dream that the seventh star of the Big Dipper fell from the sky and changed into a man over ten feet tall, who held in his palm a magic pill the size of a chicken egg with a fragrance that assailed her nostrils. She took the pill and swallowed it. When she woke up, she felt a fiery warmth in her abdomen, and her room was permeated with an extraordinary fragrance that lingered for months. This was how she became pregnant. In the tenth month, when the pregnancy reached its full term, Daoling was born in the midst of a dazzling light that suddenly lit up the room in the middle of the night. When seven years old, he could already explicate the *Daode jing*[3] and knew all there was to know about Fuxi's[4] eight trigrams and books on divination. By the time he reached sixteen, he had mastered all of the Five Classics. Nine feet two inches in height, he had an awe-inspiring appearance with his thick eyebrows, broad forehead, ruddy neck, green eyes, high-bridged nose, square jaws, prominent bony ridge extending from between his eyebrows to the top of his head, arms reaching below his kneecaps,[5] and a demeanor that was as imposing as that of a dragon or a tiger. He was recommended to the National University for his worthiness and moral integrity. One day he sighed to himself, saying, "A hundred years fly by in an instant like lightning. What if I do attain the highest office there is? It does nothing to prolong life!" Henceforth, he devoted himself to the cultivation of the Tao [Dao; Way] as well as to alchemical experiments in search of an elixir of immortality. Among his fellow students was a Wang Chang, who, deeply convinced of the truth in Daoling's words, honored Daoling as his mentor and joined him in his journeys to famous mountains in search of the Tao.

When they approached Yuzhang Prefecture they came upon a boy in embroidered clothes, who asked them, "What are you two gentlemen's plans, that you've come such a long way to arrive here at this late hour?" Much taken aback, Daoling realized that this boy was no common sort and told him about their wish to seek the Tao. The boy said, "Mortal beings talk all too flippantly about Taoism. In fact, only by following the Yellow Emperor's nine-crucible method of preparing the elixir of immortality will one be able to achieve ascension to heaven." Upon the two travelers' request for advice, the boy intoned the following two lines:

> *Dragon on the left, tiger on the right;*
> *In the middle lies the celestial abode.*

With this, he disappeared into thin air. Daoling made a mental note of the two lines, without understanding their meaning.

One day, when the onward journey took them to Dragon and Tiger Mountain, Daoling's heart gave a leap. "'Dragon on the left, tiger on the right' could very well be a reference to this place," he said to Wang Chang. "The 'celestial abode' could be a place where secret books are hidden."

When they climbed to the top of the mountain, there came into sight a stone cave called Bilu Cave. They entered the cave and, following a partly lit winding path, they came upon a double door made of stone. "This door surely leads to a residence of immortals," thought Daoling to himself. He and his follower Wang Chang then solemnly sat down by the door. On the seventh day, the stone door suddenly swung wide open, revealing stone stools and a stone table with nothing on it but a book. When they took up the book and examined it, they found that it was *The Classic of the Yellow Emperor's Nine-Crucible Divine Elixir*. Lifting his hand to his forehead, Daoling exclaimed, "What a stroke of luck!" The two men's joy knew no bounds. They studied the book day and night and learned everything there was to learn about the method. However, they lacked the means to meet the lavish expenses that would be involved in the purchasing of the ingredients and the crucibles, and keeping a fire going under the latter. Daoling had, in earlier years, learned to cure illness by using holy water. People of the Shu [Sichuan] region being known for their innocence and honesty, Daoling headed there and, together with Wang Chang, settled down on Crane Cry [Heming] Mountain, where, calling himself a patriarch, he started using holy water to cure illness. As the holy water proved to be most effective, he began to attract more patients as well as disciples who wished to learn how to use holy water.

Encouraged by the faith and trust that he had inspired, the patriarch laid down some rules. Patients had to write truthful accounts of all the ill deeds that they had done since they were born. The patriarch would then write down their confessions and cast the confessions into the pond in front of the patriarch's house. The patients would then vow to the gods not to repeat their sins, on pain of instant death. Only after taking such a vow would they be allowed to drink the holy water. After recovery, they were to pay for the service with five bushels of rice. The patriarch's disciples spread out to different areas to pursue the same practice. They dedicated to the gods all the rice and silk they received, keeping not the slightest speck of anything for themselves. Thus it came about that people attributed all minor ailments to punishment by the gods and willingly made a clean breast of their sins. After recovery, they were so ashamed of their previous behavior that they changed their ways and dared not commit further sins. (*If this practice gains popularity throughout the land, how can there be no peace?*)

After several years had gone by in this way, Daoling amassed a sizable fortune, which he spent on ingredients for the immortality elixir. He then retired with Wang Chang into a private room, and their project of producing Dragon and Tiger pills got under way. It took three years before the pills of immortality were ready. After taking the pills, the sexagenarian patriarch rejuvenated till he looked like a young man of thirty. Henceforth, he could be in more than one location at the same time, touring the east and west streams on a small boat while, at the same time, intoning the scriptures in the hall with never a pause. When visited by guests, his multiple manifestations would greet them and send them off or engage them in games of chess over cups of wine. Unable to tell which manifestation of the patriarch was the true one, witnesses all marveled at the wondrous ways of the immortals.

One day, a Taoist priest came to say that in the western section of the city, there was a white tiger spirit that was addicted to the drinking of human blood. A local resident was killed every year to be offered to the spirit as sacrifice. It pained the patriarch's heart to hear of such a practice, and he made a personal appearance there when the day for the sacrifice was drawing near. He did indeed witness the local people tie up a man and, led by a band of musicians, send the man into the temple dedicated to the spirit of the white tiger. Upon inquiry, the patriarch received answers that tallied with the Taoist priest's account. Should they fail to offer human sacrifices, a raging rainstorm would sweep over the region and wipe out all crops, seedlings, and animals. Out of fear, the local community would buy a man at a high price every year and send him, all stripped and trussed up, into the temple for the spirit to suck his blood in the middle of the night. This had become a tradition that the authorities found impossible to abolish.

"Why don't you release this man," said the patriarch, "and put me there instead?"

The local residents replied, "This poverty-stricken fellow with no one to turn to for help is willing to forsake his life as human sacrifice. The fifty thousand in cash that he received from us has already been spent to the last penny on the funeral service for his father and the wedding of his younger sister. For him, to die is to fulfill his obligation. Why should you offer to die for him?"

"I just don't believe that a supernatural being would take human lives," replied the patriarch. "Should this turn out to be true, I shall assume full responsibility for myself and die with no regrets."

In discussing the matter among themselves, the locals said, "It's none of our business that he doesn't believe a bit of this. A human life needs to be offered—it doesn't matter whose it is." Accordingly, the man bound in ropes was set free, as the patriarch suggested. Having regained his life, the man bowed in gratitude and left. As the locals pressed forward to bind him up, the patriarch stopped them, saying, "Being a volunteer, I will certainly not try to escape. Why do I need to be tied up?" Everyone agreed.

As the patriarch stepped into the temple, what met his eyes were swirling wisps of incense amid fearsome-looking clay figures of gods brightly lit by lamps and candles. On the altar were already laid out a host of sacrificial offerings. After paying homage to the spirit and saying the prayer, the locals locked the patriarch up in the temple and sealed the door. Motionless, he sat with closed eyes, waiting for the spirit to appear.

In the depth of the night, a gust of fierce wind brought the white tiger spirit into the presence of the sage. At the very moment the spirit reached out for him, rays of red light flashed forth from the patriarch's mouth, ears, eyes, and nose by the power of the immortality elixir and fixed the white tiger spirit in their web.

"Who are you?" asked the spirit in consternation.

"By order of the Lord on High," replied the patriarch, "I, with jurisdiction over all gods of the four seas and five mountains, am conducting an investigation in different places in multiple physical manifestations of myself. What accursed vermin are you to dare to bring devastation to human lives here? So heinous is your crime that your destruction by heaven is inevitable!"

Before the white tiger spirit could rise to his own defense, he found himself surrounded on all sides by multiple manifestations of the patriarch emitting red light from head to toe. The white tiger spirit was so dazzled that he could not so much as open an eye and had to kowtow to ask for mercy. The white tiger spirit had been, in fact, the god of metal. After the five strong men dug a tunnel through the Shu Mountains,[6] the metal essence in the mountains leaked out and was transformed into a white tiger that haunted the region, wreaking havoc on the local residents. It was not until after the local people erected a temple and promised to offer annual human sacrifices to him that the harassments stopped. Now, the patriarch, with his experience with alchemy, had come to be a true master of the element of fire. Fire being the element that overcomes metal, the patriarch's victory was a matter of course. There and then, he subdued the white tiger spirit and made him pledge to stop destroying human lives. Thus warned, the white tiger spirit went away.

Early the following morning, local residents were shocked to find the patriarch still in the temple, safe and sound. To their questions, he gave a full account of what had happened and assured them that the spirit would not come again to prey on human lives and do harm. As the locals reverently asked for his name, he replied, "I am Zhang Daoling of Crane Cry Mountain." With these words, he left with light and airy steps. In front of the White Tiger Temple, the local people built three additional front halls to hold images of Patriarch Zhang. The practice of human sacrifice was thus brought to an end. There is a poem in evidence:

> An immortal he later came to be,
> Less through the elixir than his good deeds.
> By saving lives and subduing evil,
> He gained himself credit in the next world.

In the Green Rock Mountains in Guanghan, there was a giant python that preyed upon human lives. A whiff of the poisonous breath that the python puffed during the daytime was enough to send wayfarers to their deaths. Again, the patriarch offered his services and got rid of the poisonous python so that the local people could walk during the daytime in the mountains again without fear.

On the fifteenth night of the first month of the first year of the Han'an reign period [C.E. 142] under Emperor Shun, the patriarch was sitting by himself in his abode on Crane Cry Mountain when he heard celestial music wafting faintly toward him from the east. As the sounds of a divine chariot drew near, he stepped out into the yard for a look and saw a white chariot descending slowly from a purple cloud to the east. In the chariot, amid a halo of a dazzling brilliance too bright for the eyes to look upon, sat a dignified god with a complexion as fair as jade and as clear as ice. Standing in front of the chariot was none other than the boy in embroidered clothes whom Daoling had encountered in Yuzhang Prefecture.

"Fear not," said the boy. "This is the Supreme Ultimate Lord Lao Zi himself." The patriarch hastened to make his obeisance.

Lao Zi addressed him in these words: "It pained me deeply to see many demons wreaking havoc recently in the Shu region. Your assistance in subduing them for me in the interests of the local people was an act of boundless beneficence and will surely earn you a place on the Red Terrace."[7] So saying, he handed to the patriarch *The Auspicious Alliance Registers of the Orthodox Unity* [Zhengyi mengwei milu], nine hundred and thirty volumes of scriptures of the Three Pure Ones; seventy-two books on talismanic registers, alchemy, and secret formulas; a pair of male and female swords; and a seal for the Surveyor of Merit. He then reminded the patriarch, "I will see you in the abode of the immortals in a thousand days." The patriarch bowed in acknowledgement before Lao Zi rose in the air and floated away on a cloud.

Henceforth the patriarch pored over the books every day and cultivated his nature in accordance with the instructions. Word came to him that millions of demon soldiers under the command of eight demon generals were ravaging the region of Yizhou and killing numerous people. With a mandate from Lao Zi, the patriarch brought along *The Auspicious Alliance Registers* and headed for Green City Mountain, where he set up a glazed altar with a tablet for the Celestial Honored Primordial on the left and thirty-six volumes of the scriptures on the right. He also erected ten talismanic banners and set up platforms all around him. Striking the bells and chimes, he gathered together celestial troops and deployed them for the capture of the demon generals. In the meantime, the demon generals and their demon soldiers, armed with knives, arrows, and stones, charged at him. He raised a finger on his left hand, and that finger changed into a great lotus flower with dense foliage impenetrable by any weapon. The demons then lit over a thousand torches in an attempt to burn him to death. At a flick of his sleeve, the fire turned back onto the demons.

Calling out from afar, the demons demanded, "Why does the master, a resident of Crane Cry Mountain, come to harass us in our territory?"

The patriarch replied, "Your heinous crimes against humanity have become known to heaven. I am here by order of the Venerable Lao Zi to punish you. Should you plead guilty, you will come to no harm if you quickly leave for the barren western region and stop plaguing the people. The moment you resume your old ways, you will perish along with all your offspring."

The following day, the demon generals, still defiant, sought the help of six demon kings, who led millions of demon troops on an expedition against the patriarch. After they had pitched camp, the patriarch suggested, in a bid to convince them of his power, "Let all of us show the best of our magic powers and see who will come out the winner." The six demon kings agreed.

The patriarch had Wang Chang pile up some wood and light a fire. No sooner had the patriarch thrown himself into the raging flames than a green lotus flower appeared under his feet and raised him out of the fire.

The six demon kings laughed. "That's a cheap trick," they said. Parting the flames with their hands, two of the demon kings took the plunge, only to reemerge with singed beards and eyebrows. Flinching with pain, they scurried back to their previous positions. The other four dared not even budge an inch.

The patriarch then threw himself into the water but just as soon rose to the surface on the back of a yellow dragon, without even a wet spot on his clothes.

The six demon kings laughed again. "Fire is indeed formidable, but what can water do to us?" With a splash, all six of them jumped in, but they rolled head over heels several times in the water before they could get out, choking with enough swallowed water to fill their bellies.

Next, the patriarch threw himself onto a rock, which, at this very juncture, split open, letting him come out at the back.

The six demon kings again roared with laughter. "With our strength, we can get through mountains, not to mention this little rock!" With shoulders thrust forward, they did push themselves into the rock, but, at the chanting of some incantation by the patriarch, all six got stuck midway. Unable to extricate themselves, they wailed with grief. Fuming with anger, the eight demon generals changed themselves into eight slant-eyed tigers. Baring their fangs and brandishing their claws, they charged at the patriarch, who, in the twinkling of an eye, changed into a lion to chase after them. The demon generals now changed into eight giant dragons to clutch at the lion, which, in its turn, changed into a roc with golden wings. Opening wide its huge beak, it was on the point of pecking out the dragons' eyeballs when the demons changed again into multicolored clouds and mist that darkened heaven and earth, whereupon the patriarch transformed himself into a red sun that rose into the high heavens and dispelled the clouds and mist with its piercing rays.

With the demon generals at their wits' end, the patriarch picked up a stone and tossed it toward heaven. In a trice, it changed into a huge boulder the size of a small hill, hanging over the demons' camp by a thread as thin as lotus-root fibre. On top of the rock were two mice fighting to be the first one to gnaw through the thread. At this critical juncture, the demon kings and the demon generals, witnessing the whole scene from a vantage point up on high, were seized with the fear that all their offspring were to perish. With one accord, they begged pitiably for mercy, pledging that they would move to the kingdom of Sala[8] in the West rather than ever even think of molesting the people of China again. Consequently, the patriarch ordered that the six demon kings return to the northern section of hell and the eight demon generals move to the West.

Now that the demon kings were freed from the boulder, they ganged up with the demon generals and showed no eagerness to go. Since demons, as the patriarch knew, could not be sent away with too much civility, he intoned a divine incantation that rose into the high heavens. The very next moment, Wind Uncle stirred up the winds, Rain Master unleashed the rain, Thunder God started the thunders rolling and Lightning Mother shot bolts of lightning. The celestial generals and soldiers assembled and, wielding their various weapons, fought the demons till none remained in sight. Not until then did the patriarch call off his magic. "From now on," he said to Wang Chang, "the people of Shu can sleep in peace." There is in evidence a lyric poem to the tune of "The Moon over the West River":

> The demon generals played tricks in vain;
> The kings flaunted their strength to no avail.
> They little knew that the Tao master's might
> Was to transcend all natural elements,
> Be it blazing fire or chilling water,
> Or hard rock that he threw himself into.
> The tempest that wiped out all the demons
> Was proof of his heaven-endowed powers.

The patriarch turned to Wang Chang again: "My time to ascend to heaven is near. Let's not forget Bilu Cave, where I first entered the Taoist order." Thereupon, they returned to Yuzhang and settled down again on Dragon and Tiger Mountain, where they continued to devote themselves to making the elixir of immortality with the nine cycles and seven returns method.[9]

One day, the tinkling celestial music of the kind he had heard before at Crane Cry Mountain again fell on the patriarch's ears. Hastily he adjusted his clothes and dropped to his knees in front of the steps. Up there, moving back and forth without attempting to descend, was Lao Zi himself with an entourage of thousands of celestial beings on chariots and horses. At another bow from the patriarch, Lao Zi sent a messenger to address him in these words: "Your accomplishments have earned you a place among the celestial beings. I sent you into the Shu region to separate demons from humans, so as to purify the air. However, you killed an excessive number of demons, presumptuously summoned wind and rain, and called into service enough celestial soldiers to darken the sky and fill the canopy of the heavens with the reek of killing. All of this runs counter to heaven's love for life. The Lord on High is taking you to task and that is why I cannot get near you today. You are now to retire into a life of seclusion and to cultivate your inner nature assiduously. There will be two other people to ascend to heaven with you at the same time. When that time comes, I will be waiting for you in the Eight Scenes Palace in the Realm of Exalted Purity." After this was said, the divine chariot returned the way it had come. In sincere repentance, the patriarch went back to Crane Cry Mountain with Wang Chang.

There was much discontented talk among his disciples on the mountain that the patriarch, with his infinite powers, was showing favoritism and a reluctance to share his knowledge, for he limited his teaching to Wang Chang only. The patriarch said to them, "How can you rise above the mortals when you have not yet discarded your worldly ways? What you can get from me will be nothing but some techniques of sexual hygiene, or the taking of herbs to prolong your life span. At noon on the seventh day of the first month next year, a man of short stature with a square face, wearing a sable coat and a brocade jacket, will come from the east. He will be no less a true Taoist than Wang Chang." The disciples were not sure if they were to believe him.

At noon on the seventh day of the first month of the following year, the patriarch said to Wang Chang, "Your junior fellow apprentice is here." He then gave Wang Chang a series of instructions as to what to do. Thus instructed, Wang Chang stepped out of the temple, and, lo and behold, to the inward amazement of all the disciples, there was indeed a man coming from an easterly direction with his attire and physical features exactly fitting the patriarch's descriptions. Wang Chang said under his breath to the other disciples, "Our master is going to pass on all his knowledge to this man. When he comes to the gate, do not announce his arrival. You can insult him and deny him admittance. He will certainly give up and go on his way." Throwing glances at each other, the disciples thought this was a good idea. (*Wang Chang is acting on secret instructions from the master. The other disciples are being used without realizing it.*)

When the man came to the gate, calling himself Zhao Sheng, a native of Wu Prefecture, and saying that he was there to pay his respects to the venerable

Taoist master, the disciples countered, "The master is away on a journey. We dare not admit you on our own authority." Leaving Zhao Sheng standing there with his hands respectfully clasped in front of his chest, the disciples went their separate ways. The man was not let in even after nightfall, and so he spent the night outside the gate without a roof over his head.

The following day, the disciples opened the gate, only to find Zhao Sheng still standing with his hands clasped and still asking to see the master. The disciples said, "Our master is a most narrow-minded man who has taught us absolutely nothing over the tens of years we have been serving him. What do you think you can get from him?"

Zhao Sheng replied, "To teach or not to teach is entirely the master's decision. I have come over such a long distance for no greater wish than to see him, if only once, so that I would not have admired him in vain all my life."

"We would gladly comply with your wish," said the disciples, "but our master is indeed away and we have no idea when he is coming back. Please do not stay around so stubbornly, for you will only be compromising your future."

"It is out of heartfelt sincerity that I have come all the way here," said Zhao Sheng. "Should the patriarch be away for ten days, I will wait for ten days, or a hundred days for that matter."

After several days passed without a sign of Zhao Sheng's even turning his back, the disciples' detest of him intensified. Gradually, they began to hurl insulting words at him. So insolent did they become that they eventually even treated him like a beggar and used foul language to pour scorn upon him. Zhao Sheng, on his part, became even more pleasant in his manner and did not mind the abuse in the slightest. (*An indication of his unusual qualities.*) Every day he went to the village before noon to buy his one meal of the day and, after eating, returned to the gate to resume his wait. By night, he slept at the foot of the steps by the gate, as no one would let him in. After more than forty days went by in this way (*Who else would be willing to do that?*), the disciples told each other, "Even though we can't get rid of him, we have luckily kept the whole thing from the master, who is still in the dark after so many days." Hardly were these words out of their mouths than the patriarch sounded the bell in the hall and assembled the disciples for the following announcement: "The young man by the name of Zhao has suffered enough humiliation over the last forty days and more. He may be summoned in today."

The disciples were dumbfounded. Not until then did they realize the full extent of their master's prophetic power. Wang Chang, thus ordered by the master, went to call Zhao Sheng in.

At the sight of the patriarch, Zhao Sheng made obeisance amid tears and sobs and asked to be accepted as a disciple. The patriarch knew he was sincere in seeking the Tao, but he nevertheless wanted to test the man further. After a few days, he ordered Zhao Sheng to go to a farmhouse to keep watch over millet crops.

Zhao Sheng accordingly made his way to the fields. There was only one small thatched hut out there all by itself, though there was no lack of wild beasts running around. From morning to night, Zhao assiduously drove away the beasts, with never a lapse of attention. On one glorious moonlit night, Zhao Sheng was sitting alone in the hut when a strikingly beautiful woman came to him and said with a deep bow, "I am a farmer's daughter living in West Village. I was out on an excursion with friends to admire the moon when I went into a field to relieve myself and lost sight of my friends. I tried to find them but lost my bearings and ended up here. My feet are so sore that I can't move another step. I would be deeply grateful if you, sir, could kindly let me spend the night here." Before Zhao Sheng could object, the woman had already lain down on his bed with flirtatious moans of pain. Without suspecting anything, Zhao Sheng could not do otherwise than let her have the bed. He himself spread some hay on the ground as bedding and slept in his clothes all night. The following day, the woman again pleaded sore feet and deliberately refused to move a step. Coquettishly, she asked Zhao Sheng to serve her tea and meals, which Zhao Sheng resignedly did. She then set out to seduce him with suggestive remarks and, at nighttime, went so far as to take off her clothes, get into bed, and ask Chao Sheng to get her a quilt and put some clothes on her. As unperturbed as iron and stone at the woman's lecherous advances, Zhao Sheng did not so much as even step into the hut again and sat by the field all through the night until daybreak. On the fourth day, the woman disappeared from sight. There on the earthen wall for him to see was a quatrain that read,

> Beauty wins the hearts of all men,
> Except yours of iron and stone.
> Forsaking the pleasures of youth,
> You let your life go by in vain.

The ink of the delicate and coquettish calligraphy was still fresh. With a hearty laugh, Zhao Sheng exclaimed, "How long can the pleasures of youth last?" He then took off a shoe and wiped the writing away with it. (*None but honorable men are allowed to take up the Taoist order.*) Verily,

> The flowers fall into the water, seeking love,
> But the water does not love them in return.

Time flashed by. Before one knew it, spring had gone and autumn came. By order of the patriarch, Zhao Sheng took up his axe and set off for the far side of the mountain to chop firewood. At his powerful stroke, a withered pine tree yielded to his axe with a whish, exposing the roots to view. When he pulled up the roots for a look, his eyes came upon a shining pot of gold underneath. A voice in the sky said, "This is a gift to Zhao Sheng from heaven."

Zhao Sheng thought to himself, "What do I, a man who has renounced the world, need gold for? What's more, I have done nothing to deserve any gift from heaven," whereupon he covered the gold with dirt. Having gathered together his load of firewood, he felt a fatigue stealing over him and sat down for a rest, leaning against a rock. All of a sudden, a fierce wind sprang up and three tigers with brown spots leaped out of the valley. Zhao Sheng remained where he was, undisturbed. The three tigers descended upon Zhao Sheng, gnawing his clothes but otherwise doing him no physical harm. Without showing the slightest fear, Zhao Sheng said to the tigers, "I, Zhao Sheng, have never done anything against my conscience. Having renounced the world and entered the Taoist order, I have traveled a distance of a thousand li to search for an enlightened master who can show me the way to immortality. If I owed you a debt in my previous life, I will not recoil from serving as your meal. If not, I advise you to leave this place quickly and stop harassing me." Thus admonished, the three tigers left with ears drooped and heads lowered. Zhao Sheng said, "They must have been sent by the mountain god to test me. Life or death is all a matter of fate. What do I have to fear?" That day, he returned with his load of firewood, without mentioning to any of the other disciples his adventures with the gold and the tigers. (*He thinks nothing of what others marvel at.*)

Another day, the patriarch sent Zhao Sheng to the marketplace to buy ten bolts of silk. After paying for it, Zhao Sheng took the silk and started on his way back. He had gone only part of the way when a shout came from behind: "Stop thief!" He looked back and saw the man who had just sold him the silk, running swiftly toward him. The man grabbed Zhao Sheng and said, "How could you have taken my silk without paying a cent! Give me back the silk, or you'll know no peace!"

Zhao Sheng said not a word in defense of himself. "My master needs the silk," he thought to himself. "If I give the silk back to this man, what shall I say to my master?" Thereupon, he took off his own sable coat and gave it to the man as payment for the silk. But the man was not satisfied until Zhao Sheng added his brocade jacket. Only then did the man turn away.

When presented with the silk, the patriarch asked Zhao Sheng, "Where have your clothes gone?" Zhao Sheng replied, "I happened to have a rush of heat. So I took them off."

The patriarch said with a sigh, "He does not begrudge his possessions, nor does he pass judgment on others' wrongdoing. Such a man is indeed hard to come by." Thereupon he gave Zhao Sheng a cotton robe, which the latter joyfully put on himself.

On another occasion, Zhao Sheng and the other disciples were harvesting crops in the fields when a man was suddenly spotted by the side of the road, bowing and begging for food. This man in rags was covered with dust and grime and gave off a repelling stench from the sores and pus all over his body. He could not walk, for both of his feet were festering. Zhao Sheng's peers covered their noses and sharply ordered the man to go away. Zhao Sheng was the only one who had compassion. He helped the man sit down in the hut and attended to his needs, serving him food that he spared from his own portion. He boiled a bucketful of hot water and washed his festering sores clean. When the man complained of coldness and asked for clothes, Zhao Sheng unbuttoned his cotton robe and took off his shirt to provide the man with some protection against the cold. When night fell, Zhao Sheng kept him company lest he be too lonely. When, in the middle of the night, the man called out for help to relieve himself, Zhao Sheng hastily rose to help him go outside to do his business and then helped him back into the hut. By day, he fed the man with what he spared from his own food, while he himself went half-starved. By night, he also took good care of him. More than ten days went by in this way without any slackening of effort on his part. His sores having gradually healed, the man suddenly took his departure one day without even a word of farewell, but Zhao Sheng harbored no grudge against him. A later poet had this to say in his praise:

> To those in need, do lend a helping hand.
> Only a small mind expects to be paid.
> Begrudge not good deeds, expect no reward,
> And the glow of spring will fill up the earth.

One day early in summer, the patriarch assembled his students for a climb to the crest of Heavenly Pillar Peak. Situated to the left of Crane Cry Mountain, it had cliffs on three sides in the shape of a city fortress. The patriarch led his disciples to the very top, where they looked down and saw a peach tree standing out horizontally from the cliff like an outstretched arm above an abyss of unfathomable depth. The branches of the tree were laden with appealingly ripe peaches. The patriarch said to his students, "I will teach the essence of Taoist magic to whoever can get the peaches." The two hundred thirty-four disciples, excluding Wang Chang and Zhao Sheng, had scarcely taken a quick look than they were, to a man, so overwhelmed by dizziness that, shaking all over in cold sweat, they recoiled with great haste lest they should fall. The only one who remained undaunted was Zhao Sheng. Stepping forward to face the assembly of fellow disciples, he declared, "Since our master orders that the peaches be picked, there will surely be a way to get them. Our master's presence here also ensures that I will be protected by the spirits and gods from meeting my death in the deep valley." So saying, he measured the distance to the tree with his eyes and jumped. (*What thorough understanding and good reasoning!*) What a marvel it was that he landed, with his legs stretched apart, right on the peach tree. With the peaches within easy reach, he looked up and saw that over the twenty to thirty feet of distance from the tree to the edge of the cliff, there was nothing whatsoever for him to hang on to for an upward climb, so he tossed up the peaches he had picked for the sage to catch. Then followed another round of picking, tossing, and catching, and so it went on until the tree was stripped of all its fruit. Having caught all of the peaches, the patriarch ate one. Wang Chang also ate one. With one kept for Zhao Sheng, there remained two hundred thirty-four to be distributed among the disciples, with not a peach too many or too few. (*Could this peach have been produced by magic as well?*)

The patriarch asked the disciples which one of them could bring Zhao Sheng up. Looking at each other in dismay, they dared not venture a response. The patriarch himself went to the edge of the cliff and stretched out an arm toward Zhao Sheng. In a twinkling, the arm grew until it was twenty to thirty feet long and reached Zhao Sheng, who then climbed up the arm. The disciples were dumbfounded, one and all. The patriarch handed over to Zhao Sheng the peach that was left for him and announced with a smile, "It is because of Zhao Sheng's pure heart that he could land right on the tree without a single false move. Now I would like to take the plunge to test if my heart is pure. If so, I should be able to come back up with a giant peach."

The disciples remonstrated with him: "A true master of Taoist magic though you are, how can you jump down into the unfathomably deep abyss just to see what will happen? Zhang Sheng had you to help him. If you fall, who is there to help you? You cannot do this on any account." Several of the disciples grabbed the master by his gown and pleaded with him not to go. Only Wang Chang and Zhao Sheng uttered not a word. Ignoring all the remonstrations, the patriarch threw himself over the cliff. The crowd looked at the peach tree, but the patriarch was not there. With no way of knowing whether the master was dead or alive now that he had disappeared into the abyss, inaccessible by any means, the stunned disciples let out wails of grief.

Zhao Sheng said to Wang Chang, "Our master is like our father. Now that he has thrown himself over the cliff, what peace of mind can there be for us? We might as well also jump down and see what will happen," whereupon Zhao Sheng and Wang Chang gave a mighty leap and landed right in front of the patriarch, who was sitting safe and sound on a rock. At the sight of Zhao and Wang, the patriarch laughed out loud. "I just knew the two of you would come," he said. These episodes have been told by storytellers as "The Seven Tests of Zhao Sheng." Which seven?

The first test:	Humiliation and abuses that failed to turn him away.
The second test:	Feminine seduction that failed to stir him.
The third test:	The allure of gold that failed to interest him.
The fourth test:	Tigers that failed to frighten him.
The fifth test:	The silk transaction when he did not begrudge his possessions or defend himself when wrongly accused.
The sixth test:	His sincerity in doing charitable deeds.
The seventh test:	His willingness to rescue his master at the risk of his own life.

As a matter of fact, it was the patriarch who was the mastermind behind all seven tests. The gold, the woman, the tiger, and the beggar were all transformations of spirits who assumed these shapes at his command. The silk vender was not any more real. This was a case of testing the real with the unreal.

All those who wish to enter the Taoist order must, before all else, rid themselves of the seven emotions. What are the seven emotions? They are joy, anger, worry, fear, love, hate, and desire. This is what the patriarch meant when he said to his disciples, "How can you rise above the mortals when you have not discarded your worldly ways?" But the contemporary men of the world are so wrapped up in their own self-importance that they bristle with resentment at the slightest reproachful tone from their teacher. How can they be expected to suffer humiliation, much less the misery of forty days and forty nights in open air, for the sake of seeking out a teacher?

As for the element of lust that everyone is born in and eventually dies of, who can claim not to be under its spell? Dear audience, let us suppose that you are living alone with much leisure time on your hands. Wouldn't you be in raptures at the most welcome sight of a woman, unattractive though she might be? Now if it were a woman of striking beauty who set out to use her charms on you, wouldn't you be seized with desire? Among the ancients, Liuxia Hui[10] was, in all likelihood, the one and only man ever to have resisted such temptations.

In our own times, for the sake of a few strings of cash, brothers can fall out with each other, friends can turn against each other. Finding a penny by the roadside is enough to make one beam with joy and thank his lucky star. Who would not be stirred at the sight of an unclaimed pot of gold that is to be had for the taking?

An approaching fierce-looking dog, let alone tigers, can send shivers down one's spine, but Zhao Sheng was not any less fearless than even Master Lü Chunyang,[11] who fed himself to hungry tigers.

As regards the episode of buying silk, wouldn't you agree that in buying or selling, people nowadays revel in gaining even a penny's worth of advantage over the other party but burst out into curses at the slightest unfairness? Who would pay twice for the same thing? What a magnanimous mind it took to give his own clothes up without a grudge, in spite of the gross injustice done to him!

As for serving parents bedridden with some foul disease, those offspring less than totally filial would be filled with disgust, though they make no such remarks in public. Now, attending to the needs of a roadside beggar at Zhao's own expense was by no means an unworthy deed.

Finally, jumping twice from the cliff was evidence of his unshakable devotion to his master, for whose sake he would have died with no regrets. All seven tests proved that Zhao Sheng had rid himself totally of all attachments to the seven worldly emotions and was ready to achieve the Tao. (*These are well-chosen words that lay bare the ugly side of life.*) Indeed,

> *The stronger the will to seek the Tao,*
> *The fewer mundane emotions remain.*
> *Only when vulgar desires are purged clean*
> *Can one's destiny with the Tao be fulfilled.*

Let us not encumber our story with more of such idle comments. Impressed by the unflinching faith of Zhao Sheng and Wang Chang in Taoism, the patriarch passed on to them all the secrets he had learned, down to the last detail. After three days and three nights of such sessions, the two of them learned all there was to learn. When the patriarch flew up the cliff, the two followed him up. Their fellow disciples were astounded at their return.

One day, upon waking up from a nap he took while seated, the patriarch said to Wang Chang and Zhao Sheng, "The county of Badong is plagued by demons. Let us go together and get rid of them." Thereupon the three of them, the master and the disciples, set out for the region. Upon arriving, they were met by twelve fairy maidens in front of the mountain, welcoming them with smiles. The patriarch asked, "Where is the saline spring of this region?" The fairy maidens answered, "It is the large pond right ahead of you. Recently it has been occupied by a poisonous dragon and the water is now contaminated."

The patriarch drew a magic figure and tossed it into the sky. It flew round and round before changing suddenly into a golden-winged roc that wheeled back and forth over the pond. Greatly alarmed, the poisonous dragon left the pond. No sooner had it gone than the turbid water became clear and limpid again. Each of the twelve fairy maidens offered the patriarch a jade ring that she took out from her bosom. "We have long been admiring you," they said. "We will be only too happy to offer you wifely services."

The patriarch took their rings and, with a twist of his hand, merged the twelve rings into one and threw it into a well. "Whoever gets this ring," said he to the fairy maidens, "is the one destined for me, and I will marry her accordingly."

In a bid to be the first one to snatch the ring, the twelve fairy maidens took off their clothes and jumped into the well. The patriarch drew another magic figure and threw it into the well, saying as he did so, "You will be goddesses of the well to the end of time." He called the local residents together to draw water from the well—water that, after much boiling and simmering, produced salt. He reminded all who planned to get salt this way in the future to make sacrificial offerings to the twelve fairy maidens, who were, in fact, evil spirits that had bewitched men and wreaked havoc in the region. However, subdued by the patriarch with his magic figures and content with the sacrificial offerings, the evil spirits never appeared again. Henceforth, the inhabitants of the region lived under no threat from the fairy maidens but gained profit from the salt-producing well.

Having subdued the evil spirits, the patriarch returned to Crane Cry Mountain. Around noon one day, a man in a black cap and a silk gown with a sword hanging from his waist and a jade casket in his hands appeared before him and said, "Your Reverence is summoned by a holy decree from the divine realm to tour the celestial gardens." In a trice, there came a purple chariot driven by a black dragon. Ushered by two celestial maidens, the patriarch mounted the chariot and went straight to the golden palace. The assembly of celestial beings announced to him, "You may now proceed to see the Celestial Honored Primordial." Two celestial boys dressed in red and carrying scarlet staffs led him into a jade hall with gold steps. The patriarch adjusted his gown and went in. After he had made his bows in the hall, the celestial boys, holding the celestial register books, bestowed upon the patriarch the title First Celestial Master. By the authority of *The Auspicious Alliance Registers of the Orthodox Unity*, he was empowered to declare that all his descendants from generation to generation would inherit the title of Celestial Master and guide the unenlightened mind. The date of his ascension to heaven was also secretly revealed to him.

Back on the mountain, the patriarch gathered *The Auspicious Alliance Registers*, *The Surveyor of Merit Credentials* and other scriptures, the two demon-subduing swords, the celestial volumes, and the jade seals together into a sealed package and declared to his disciples, "Before long, I will rise to heaven. Whoever among you can lift this package will be my successor." With great alacrity, the disciples came forward to try to lift the package, but it was far too heavy for any one of them to move so much as a fraction of an inch. The patriarch said, "Three days after I am gone, my successor of lineal descent will be here to be your master."

When his time came, the patriarch summoned Wang Chang and Zhao Sheng. "The two of you are true masters of the Tao by now," he said to them. "I still have some immortality elixir left after several attempts to fly. You may take it and follow me up to heaven today." At noon, celestial immortals and their retinue descended for the occasion, and, with celestial music leading the way, the patriarch in the company of Wang Chang and Zhao Sheng rose to heaven from Crane Cry Mountain in broad daylight. With their faces turned toward the sky, the disciples watched the clouds for a considerable time until the three men totally disappeared from view. This happened on the ninth day of the ninth month in the first year of the Yongshou reign period under Emperor Heng [C.E. 155], when the patriarch was already one hundred twenty-three years of age.

Three days after the patriarch's ascension to heaven, his oldest son, Zhang Heng, arrived from Dragon and Tiger Mountain. It was not until then that the disciples came to understand what the patriarch had said about a successor of lineal descent. They showed Zhang Heng the sealed package and related to him the patriarch's instructions. Gently, Zhang Heng raised it and broke the seal. He then made obeisance to the sky in acknowledgment of the receipt of the sacred scriptures and the jade seal. Henceforth, he dedicated himself to the study of the scriptures and successfully applied his knowledge to the slaying and suppression of demons and evil spirits. Until this day, all his descendants have inherited generation after generation the title of Celestial Master. A later poet wrote these lines about the seven tests of Zhao Sheng:

> *Though immortals are on everyone's lips,*
> *Who has ever seen one rise to heaven?*
> *It is not that immortals are frauds,*
> *But devoted Taoists are far too few.*

Chen Xiyi Rejects Four Appointments
from the Imperial Court

All speak of leisure with delight,
Yet who would fain have leisure for life?
Not that leisure is hard to attain,
But true leisure is beyond the common lot.

The written character for "leisure" is so structured that the "moon" is contained within a "door." Busy as the moon is going through doors and windows, its light stays as serene and dispassionate as ever in its place in the sky. Only if one learns to be like the moon and find tranquility amidst the hustle and bustle of life can one attain true leisure. Some say that human life in this world is divided equally between the activities of the day and the leisurely slumber of the night. Little do they know that the spirits of those with much to occupy themselves with during the day are so disturbed that what engages their minds during the day recurs at night in their dreams. When even the sleeping soul knows no peace, what leisure is there to speak of? In olden times, there was a venerable immortal named Zhuang Zhou who dreamed that he had changed into a butterfly fluttering joyfully about. Upon waking up, he still thought he was an incarnation of the butterfly. It was his carefree and unfettered mind that produced the dream. Otherwise, how do we account for the fact that never has there been another man to claim such a dream among goodness knows how many people with a love for the pillow? Thus it will be apparent that even in sleep, there are those who fret and those who truly enjoy leisure. Run-of-the-mill daily activities aside, once you are afflicted with the obsession for fame and gain, a full night's sleep may become a thing of the past. Therefore, there is an ancient poem that says,

For morning court sessions, ministers brave the cold.
To cross passes, generals march in the night.
But in temples, monks sleep till the sun is high.
Indeed, leisure is worth more than fame and gain.

As is said in Chen Tuan's[1] *Workings of the Heart,* "A worthy man indeed is he who falls asleep the moment he lies down in bed; a man of leisure he is not who stays awake on his pillow." So preoccupied are men of modern times with fame and gain that though they may lie in bed, their myriad thoughts keep them from getting to sleep. Hardly have they drifted into sleep than they wake up again with a start. Those who do indeed sleep endlessly in torpor, confusing days with nights, do so mostly because they wear themselves out by overindulging themselves in wine and sex, or because their minds are overly disturbed by harrowing thoughts. In all of these cases, sleeping is devoid of true enjoyment.

Now let me tell of Mr. Chen Tuan, who was matchless in the enjoyment of sleep. How do we know this? There is a poem as testimony:

> *His slumber lasted days and nights,*
> *Through summers, winters, and years on end.*
> *Peng Zu's life of eight hundred years[2]*
> *Was hardly longer than Chen Tuan's sleep.*

Legend has it that Chen Tuan slept for eight hundred years at one stretch. But this is sheer exaggeration, for, granted that he did become an immortal in the end, how could he have slept for eight hundred years when he lived for only one hundred eighteen years? From this legend, we do get the idea, however, that he was more often asleep than awake. He twice retired to live the life of a recluse in famous mountains and four times rejected appointments of office from the imperial court. Throughout his life, he kept his distance from women and avoided the entanglements of human relationships. That was why he enjoyed true leisure and peace of mind. His sleep was not easily imitable, for it was induced by a breathing method unique to Taoists. Storyteller, what are the two mountains he lived on as a recluse? Which imperial appointments did he reject? Here is a poem as testimony:

> *The Five Dynasties were an age of war.*
> *The Tang and Zhou flew by, the Song came along.*
> *To the royal cage swarmed colored birds,*
> *But not the celestial crane in the clouds.*

As the story goes, Chen Tuan, courtesy name Tu'nan, nicknamed Fuyaozi and a native of Zhenyuan in Bozhou Prefecture, was known in his childhood as "the Mute," for he had still not learned to talk by the time he was five or six years old. One day he was playing at the water's edge when a woman in blue calling herself "the Hairy Maiden" carried him into a mountain, where she fed him ambrosia. Chen Tuan started to talk, and his mind was awakened. The

Hairy Maiden stuffed a book into his upper garment and taught him the
following quatrain:

> *My basket not yet filled with herbs,*
> *I climb farther up the steep cliff.*
> *Turning, I point at the road of return,*
> *But into the green clouds I go on my way.*

Upon returning home, Chen Tuan suddenly chanted these four lines,
to the great astonishment of his parents. "Who taught you these lines?" they
asked. (*The celestial qualities of an immortal come with birth.*) While relating
the whole story, Chen Tuan took out the book, which was recognized to be
a copy of *The Book of Changes* [Yi jing], whereupon he began reading it aloud
and gained a substantial understanding of the eight trigrams. Henceforth,
he read every book that came to hand, but it was *The Book of Changes* that
he kept with him at all times, sitting or sleeping. His other favorite books
included *The Yellow Court Canon* and *Lao Zi,*[3] which filled him with the wish
to renounce the mortal world.

At the age of eighteen, when both of his parents died, he distributed all
the family wealth among relatives and neighbors (*Who else would be willing
to do that?*), keeping for himself only a stone tripod that he took with him to
Mount Yin in his home county to live the life of a recluse. In his dreams, the
Hairy Maiden taught him ways to cultivate his inner nature until his mind
and spirit merged with the spirit of the universe. So devoted was he to this
endeavor that he kept away from cities and towns altogether. In admiration
for Mr. Chen's fame as a man with the qualities of a celestial being, scholar-
officials of the Later Liang and Later Tang dynasties tried to meet him, but to
no avail. To visitors, the venerable Mr. Chen turned his back, refusing to rise
from bed to offer greetings. Amid his snores, the visitors would sigh and take
their leave.

During the Changxing reign period [930–33] under Emperor Mingzong
in the Later Tang dynasty, the venerable name of Chen Tuan reached the
emperor, who took up his brush-pen and wrote an imperial decree summoning him to court to assume an official post. A stream of messengers were sent
to Chen Tuan, who, finding that he could not very well disobey an imperial
decree, could do nothing other than follow the messengers to Luoyang, the
capital of the empire. Once in the presence of the Son of Heaven, he clasped
his hands in front of his chest in a gesture of greeting without prostrating
himself upon the ground, to the great consternation of the entire assembly
of civil and military officials. The emperor, however, did not take it amiss.
Supporting Chen Tuan with his hands, he made the guest sit on a brocade
stool and said, "I am so glad that you have come here over such a great

distance. The good fortune of being in your illustrious presence would last me for three lifetimes."

Chen Tuan replied, "I am nothing but a lowly rustic, no more useful to the world than a piece of rotten wood. Being unworthy of the great honor Your Majesty has done to me by summoning me for an official post, I humbly request that I be released back to the mountains to live the life that befits a rustic like me."

"Since you are so good as to have come here," the emperor insisted, "how can you leave right away, before I benefit from your teachings?"

Chen Tuan did not respond but closed his eyes and drifted off to sleep.

The emperor said with a sigh, "Such a venerable sage is not to be treated in conventional ways." Thereupon, Chen Tuan was escorted to a guesthouse reserved for the most honorable visitors, where he was given the most elaborate service. Using none of the many pieces of fancy furniture provided, the venerable sage sat in lotus position all day long on a straw mat in meditation. The emperor paid him visits in the guesthouse, but there were several times when he happened to be asleep. On such occasions, the emperor simply turned away without venturing to wake him up. Convinced that this was by no means an ordinary man, the emperor showed him even greater respect and wished to bestow upon him a high post, an offer that Chen Tuan adamantly declined.

Feng Dao, the prime minister, proposed, "To my knowledge, of the seven human emotions,[4] none is stronger than love. Of the six desires,[5] none is stronger than that for sex. In the wintry rain and snow that are assailing us, Chen Tuan must be cold sitting all by himself on his straw mat. Your Majesty can have someone send him a jar of fine wine and select three beautiful women to see to it that he drinks the wine as well as warms his feet. If he does drink the wine and keep the women, Your Majesty can rest assured that he will accept the offer of an official title."

Following this advice, the emperor selected from the palace three sixteen-year-old girls of matchless beauty who looked doubly striking when dressed up in finery. A court attendant was also sent to present Chen Tuan with a jar of fine wine brewed specially for the emperor. Announcing the imperial favors, the court attendant said, "The emperor is sending you fine wine and beautiful women to provide you with some protection against the unusually cold weather. Please do not decline the offer on any account."

Without hesitation, Chen Tuan opened the jar and drank up the wine in one gulp. Nor did he reject the women. The court attendant's report greatly pleased the emperor.

On the following day, after the morning court session was over, the emperor sent Prime Minister Feng to the guesthouse to invite Chen Tuan to see the emperor at court and to receive his titles. Thus instructed, Prime Minister Feng mounted his horse and went on his way. Do you think Chen Tuan would follow him to the court? Truly,

> *A divine dragon covets not a bait, however fragrant;*
> *A sacred phoenix enters not a cage, however ornate.*

When the prime minister arrived at the guesthouse, all he found were the three women in an empty room. Chen Tuan was nowhere to be seen. "Where is the sage Mr. Chen?" he asked.

The women replied, "After drinking the wine sent by the emperor, Mr. Chen fell asleep on the straw mat. We waited and waited until he woke up at the fifth watch and said to us, 'I regret to have no gift for you in compensation for having waited all through the night.' Then he wrote a poem, and, after telling us to give it to the emperor, he put us in this room and went off. We have no idea where he is."

Taking the three women with him, Prime Minister Feng returned to court to report to the emperor, who asked to see the poem. This is how the poem read:

> *Bodies white as snow, faces fair as jade;*
> *Grateful I am for the emperor's gifts.*
> *The hermit dreams not of clouds and rain;*
> *The fairy maidens descended in vain.*

The emperor heaved sigh upon sigh after reading the poem. He sent messengers to look for Chen Tuan in all directions, but no trace of him was found, not even in his former abode on Mount Yin, but of this, no more need be said.

Meanwhile, Chen Tuan had made his way to Mount Wudang in Junzhou Prefecture. Originally called Taiyue or Taihe, the mountain had as many as twenty-seven peaks, thirty-six cliffs, and twenty-four ravines and was the place where Zhenwu[6] perfected his inner nature and ascended to heaven in broad daylight. People of later times changed the name of the mountain to Mount Wudang, which meant that no one but Zhenwu could accomplish such a deed. It was on Nine Rock Cliff on this mountain that Chen Tuan now started anew his life as a recluse.

One day, there came to him five white-bearded old men, who asked for his interpretation of the meaning of the eight trigrams in *The Book of Changes.* While expounding the text in detail, Chen Tuan marveled at the five old men's ruddy complexion and asked how they had kept themselves in such good shape. They told him they used the hibernation method. What was this method? Well, in winter, with heaven holding its breath, all tortoises and snakes hibernate without taking in any food.[7] There was once a man who used a tortoise to replace a broken bed-leg and ten years later, upon moving the bed, found the tortoise still alive, thanks to the way it held its breath. Having now acquired the hibernation method, Chen Tuan was able to abstain from food and to sleep for several months at one stretch. If it were not for the hibernation method, the pangs of hunger would have awoken him from his dreams.

Now a septuagenarian after having lived for over twenty years on Mount Wudang, he was visited again one day by the five old men, who said to him, "The five of us are actually five dragons from Sun and Moon Pool. This is not the place for you. Having benefited from your teachings, we are now here to escort you to a place more worthy of you." Asking Chen Tuan to close his eyes, they carried him off. Chen Tuan felt that he was airborne, the whistle of wind and rain filling his ears. After a little while, he landed on the ground, heels first. When he opened his eyes, the five old men were nowhere to be seen. All he saw were five dragons disappearing into the sky. The divine dragons, with their magic power, had in fact whisked him over a great expanse of land to Mount Hua in the West.

Thus it was that Chen Tuan came to live on Mount Hua. Thinking it most extraordinary that there was no stove or pots and pans in Chen's abode, Taoists on the mountain secretly kept him under observation and found that he did nothing but sleep.

One day, Chen Tuan went down Nine Rock Cliff and was not seen for several months. The same Taoists thought that he had moved away. Later, in the firewood storage shed was spotted an object which, upon a closer look, turned out to be none other than Chen Tuan. Nor did anyone know how long he had been sleeping there, for no one had seen him until the pile of firewood was substantially reduced.

On another occasion, a woodcutter was cutting grass at the foot of the mountain when he came upon a dust-covered corpse lying in a gully. Touched with compassion, the woodcutter decided to give it a burial. As he lifted the body, whom did he recognize but Chen Tuan! "Why, it's the venerable Mr. Chen!" he exclaimed. "I wonder how he ended up dying in this place." (*This is exactly what is meant by Zhuang Zi when he said, "The body is a dead tree, the heart a heap of cold ashes."*)

Hardly had he finished before Chen Tuan straightened his back, opened his eyes, and said, "Who woke me up from my happy sleep?" The woodcutter roared with laughter.

Wang Mu, the prefect of Huayin Prefecture, personally went to Mount Hua to visit Chen Tuan. When he reached Nine Rock Cliff, all that met his eyes were bare rocks with not even a semblance of a hut anywhere within sight.

"Where do you sleep?" he asked. Chen Tuan gave a great guffaw and, by way of a reply, intoned a poem that said,

> *The peak of the hill is my palace;*
> *The morning wind is my chariot.*
> *I need no gold padlocks for my doors,*
> *Sealed as they are by the white clouds.*

Wang Mu offered to cut trees and build him a temple, but he turned a deaf ear. This took place during the Xiande reign period [954–60] under Emperor Shizong of the Later Zhou dynasty. Upon hearing of the above quatrain, the emperor realized that the poet was nothing less than a sage and summoned him for inquiries about the future of the empire. The following quatrain was what Chen Tuan offered as an answer:

> *A fine piece of wood,*
> *Matchless in rich foliage.*
> *To stand the test of time,*
> *It needs a canopy on top.*

Emperor Shizong was named Chai Rong. As Chai meant "firewood" and Rong meant "luxuriant plant growth," he took the first two lines of the quatrain to be a fitting description of himself. The phrase "stand the test of time" seemed to him to be also an auspicious prediction, only he did not realize that if the character "wood" were topped by a canopy, the new combination would form the character "Song," which was to stand for the Song dynasty, to be founded by Emperor Taizu in replacement of the Zhou dynasty. Chen Tuan had the foresight to know that the Song dynasty was to last long.

Chen Tuan declined Emperor Shizong's offer of the highest official rank and insisted on being permitted to return to the mountains. Taking the line "Sealed as they are by the white clouds," the emperor conferred upon him the title Sage of the White Clouds. Later, at the Chen Bridge mutiny, Zhao Kuangyin[8] assumed the throne by letting his men throw the yellow robe on him. When the sage learned of this while riding to Huayin County on the back of a mule (*Where does the mule come from?*), he clapped his hands and indulged in hearty laughter. When asked the reason for this outburst of mirth, he answered, "What a great stroke of luck for you people! The empire is now blessed with a new ruler who will bring peace to the land."

Sometime before, Chen Tuan had been walking leisurely down the road one day, shortly before the demise of the Later Tang dynasty, when he noticed, amid the crowd of civilians fleeing from the oncoming Khitan[9] troops, a woman carrying two children in a bamboo basket that was hanging from her shoulder. Chen Tuan intoned two lines that said,

Say not that emperors are too few;
Here in a basket come a pair.

Who do you suppose the two children were? Well, the older boy was Zhao Kuangyin, the future first emperor of the Song dynasty, and the younger boy was Zhao Kuangyi, later to be Emperor Taizong. The woman was to be Queen Mother Du. As early as twenty-five or twenty-six years ahead of time, Chen Tuan recognized the future Song emperors with true mandates from heaven.

On another day years later, Chen Tuan was touring the city of Chang'an when he encountered the Zhao brothers and Zhao Pu drinking in a wineshop. As he also entered the wineshop to buy some wine, he saw Zhao Pu sitting on the righthand side of the Zhao brothers. Pushing Zhao Pu away from the table, he said, "You are but a minor star near the Polar Star. How dare you occupy this seat of honor?"

Zhao Kuangyin marveled at these remarks. Someone who knew Chen Tuan said, pointing a finger at Chen, "This is Chen Tuan, Sage of the White Clouds."

To Zhao Kuangyin's questions about the future, Chen Tuan said, "The stars that represent you and your brother are much larger than the one that represents him."

Henceforth, Zhao Kuangyin's confidence in himself grew. Later, when he became ruler of the empire, he sent messengers several times to offer Chen Tuan a post in the imperial court—offers that Chen Tuan declined. When Emperor Taizu wrote a decree in his own handwriting to force the matter, Chen Tuan explained to the messenger, "It is imperative that the founder of an imperial dynasty demonstrate to the world his adherence to the rules of propriety. I am but a worthless man of the mountains. To prostrate myself when in the emperor's presence is against my nature, but to refrain from prostrating is an affront to His Majesty. This is why I would not presume to comply with the decree." Thereupon he wrote a quatrain at the end of the decree:

Ask not the red phoenix to bring me
Decrees from the ninth heaven.
The heart of the man of the mountains
Is where the white clouds are.

At the messenger's report, Emperor Taizu laughed and put the matter aside.

After his succession to the throne upon Taizu's death, Emperor Taizong, remembering the encounter in the wineshop, also summoned Chen Tuan for an audience for old time's sake, with the promise of exempting him from standard etiquette. The emperor also gave him a poem that read,

You were called Sage of the White Clouds
But were never heard from since.
Should you deign to comply with my summons,
The three peaks of Mount Hua will be yours.

Having read these lines, Chen Tuan put on a Taoist cap, a cotton gown, and a pair of straw sandals, and made his way to the Eastern Capital, where he was granted an audience with the emperor in a side hall. With nothing more than a greeting with his hands clasped in front of his chest, he said, "Being an unworthy rustic, isolated from the world, I am not used to the custom of kneeling. Please forgive me, Your Majesty."

The emperor asked him to take a seat and asked him about ways to achieve the Tao. Chen Tuan answered as follows: "An emperor's first concern should be the well-being of the whole empire. What good would you do your subjects if you achieve immortality and ascend to heaven? With a sagacious emperor and virtuous ministers attending so assiduously to the affairs of the empire and cultivating good morals, blessed indeed are all corners of the land. Your good name will live for a hundred generations to come. To achieve the Tao is to do no more than this." (*Too bad neither the First Emperor of Qin nor Emperor Wudi of Han heard these words of wisdom.*)

Emperor Taizong nodded in appreciation of these words. His respect for Chen Tuan grew deeper. "Please tell me if there is anything that you wish for," he said.

"I have no other wish than to have a quiet room."

Thereupon, the emperor granted him the privilege of taking up residence in Jianlong Taoist Temple.

At the outset of an expedition against inhabitants of the region east of the Yellow River, Emperor Taizong sent a messenger to ask Chen Tuan about his chances of victory. Mr. Chen wrote the character "desist" on the messenger's palm. The emperor was displeased but, as the army was already on its way, did nothing to halt the expedition. When a second messenger was sent to Chen Tuan, Chen was found soundly asleep, his snoring audible outside the door. The following day, he was found to be in the same slumberous state and remained so for a total of three months. As was expected, the commanders and soldiers of the expeditionary force returned with no victory to their credit. The emperor was sighing over this when whom should he see but Chen Tuan in a Taoist cap and casual clothes, sailing nonchalantly up the steps of Gold Bell Palace. The emperor was greatly astonished at this self-invited visit. Chen Tuan declared, "I am here to bid Your Majesty farewell, for I am returning to the mountains today."

Struck with a sense of loss by this announcement, the emperor offered to confer upon him the title of Imperial Taoist Master and to build him a hall so as to give the emperor easy access whenever the need arose to seek his advice. Chen Tuan, however, was unyielding in his refusal to accept the offer. He presented to the emperor a poem which read,

> *Into the wilds came the emperor's call*
> *For Chen Tuan, styled Tunan,*
> *A man of leisure for a thousand years,*
> *Over the three peaks and the four seas.*
> *Never kind are the ways of the world.*
> *In poetry lies the real.*
> *As free of will as a deer,*
> *Where can I not serve you?*

He continued, "I will come to see Your Majesty in twenty years' time."

Knowing that Chen Tuan was not to be detained, the emperor held a grand banquet, to which were invited the prime minister as well as the officials of the Hanlin Academy. Every guest composed a farewell poem to mark the occasion of Chen Tuan's departure. All of Mount Hua was granted by imperial decree to Chen Tuan exclusively for his cultivation of the Tao, free from intrusion by outsiders. With the titles Sage Xiyi [Tranquility and Nonaction] and Master of the White Cloud Cave, he was released to go off into the mountains. This took place in the first year of Emperor Taizong's Taipingxingguo reign period [976].

By the fifth year of the Duangong reign period [988–89],[10] Emperor Taizong, who ruled the empire for twenty years, had not yet designated a crown prince. His eldest son, Yuanzuo, prince of Chu, burned the palace to vent his anger at not being invited to an imperial family reunion feast on the ninth day of the ninth month. In a towering rage, the emperor disowned him, reducing him to the status of a commoner. The emperor's favorite was his third son, Yuankan, prince of Xiang. Wishing to know what was in store for his third son, he thought to himself without saying anything out loud, "Chen Tuan, the sage Xiyi, is the best physiognomist there is. Many years ago, in a wineshop, he predicted that my brother and I were destined to be emperors and Zhao Pu to be a prime minister. I wish I could have him come to help me make a decision." He had hardly finished this train of thought when a court attendant appeared to report, "Chen Tuan, hermit of Mount Hua, is at the palace gate requesting an audience."

Much startled, the emperor summoned him in and asked, "What is the purpose of your visit?"

"I am here to dispel any doubt you may have in your mind."

With hearty laughter, the emperor said, "I always knew you to be a prophet, and indeed you are! I have not yet decided on the successor to my throne. Yuankan, prince of Xiang, being blessed with a magnanimous and benevolent nature, has the qualifications of an emperor, but I do not know if he is destined to be one. Please do me the favor of taking a look at him in his residence."

Accordingly, Chen Tuan proceeded to the prince of Xiang's residence, but he had barely reached the gate before he turned back.

The emperor said, "I asked you the favor of taking a look at the physiognomy of the prince of Xiang at his residence. Why are you back here so soon?"

"I have already been there," said Chen Tuan. "All the men leaving and entering the residence carrying out orders have the looks of future generals and ministers. What need is there for me to look at the prince himself?"

Consequently, the emperor's mind was made up. On that very day, he issued an edict declaring the prince of Xiang to be the crown prince. He later became Emperor Zhenzong. Chen Tuan stayed in the capital for one more month before taking his leave suddenly one day and returning to Nine Rock Cliff.

Upwards of a hundred of his followers, including Mu Bochang and Zhong Fang, built their abodes at the foot of Mount Hua, where they listened to his lectures day and night. The only thing he held back from passing on to his students was the hibernation method he had acquired from the five dragons. One day, he sent some followers to cut a stone chamber into the highest cliff hanging over the Zhangchao Valley (*Named after Zhang Kai, courtesy name Gongchao, of the Southern Han dynasty, who lived a hermit's life on Mount Hua*) to the northeast of Hairy Maiden Peak on Mount Hua. The men did not dare disobey. Upon completion of the stone chamber, Chen Tuan and his followers went for a look. Standing on that highest rock, Chen Tuan said, pointing at the greenish clouds down below, "This is what the Hairy Maiden meant when she said, 'Into the green clouds I go on my way.' And so in this very spot shall I depart this life." His words were still ringing in the air when he sat down in a lotus position, waved the followers off, closed his eyes, and, with his right hand supporting his cheek, breathed his last at one hundred eighteen years of age. The followers gathered in a circle around the body and kept vigil for seven days, during which time his complexion was as when he was alive and his body and limbs remained warm and soft, emitting an extraordinary fragrance. They then made a stone casket to encase the body. Covered with a stone lid, the casket was bound with iron chains tens of feet in length and placed in the stone chamber. After the departure of the followers, the rock split into two precipitous cliffs with multicolored clouds lingering around the opening for months. This place came to be known later as Xiyi Gorge.

During the Xuanhe reign period [1119–25] under Emperor Huizong, there was a Taoist from Fujian Province by the name of Xu Zhichang who was touring Mount Hua when he caught sight of some iron chains hanging down from the cliff. He climbed up the cliff by the chains and came upon the stone chamber, where he saw a casket with its lid out of place. He raised the lid and saw, lying in the casket, the remains of an immortal with a ruddy complexion and a sharp fragrance that assailed his nostrils. With two bows, Xu Zhichang put the lid back into place (*Surely the stone lid does not need help from human hands. It's just that Zhichang is the one predestined to be there*) and climbed down the cliff again. As he happened to be in Emperor Huizong's favor and held the exalted office of minister in charge of Taoist affairs, Xu Zhichang reported his findings to the emperor, who sent him to Xiyi Gorge again with an offering of imperial incense to bring the remains back for enshrinement within the palace walls. When he reached the edge of the gorge, the iron chains were nowhere to be seen. All that he saw was a heavy shroud of mist and clouds over precipitous cliffs. With a sigh, he went back the way he had come. To this day, Sage Xiyi's remains still lie in the Zhangchao Valley, hidden from all human eyes, as these lines attest:

> Scholars of all times seek name and fame.
> Who but Xiyi enjoyed lifelong leisure?
> Twice he proudly retired to the hills;
> Four times he declined offers from the court.
> Few before him had learned the five-dragons method;
> Men after him sought his divine eight trigrams.
> With fluffy white clouds sealing the cliff,
> He lies on his stone bed through the ages.

The Dragon-and-Tiger Reunion of Shi Hongzhao
the Minister and His Friend the King

Tired of the academy, you asked to leave;
Gaily you look for West Lake's red-tailed fish,
As worthy a prefect as the past two or three;
In you Ouyang Xiu would have found his match.
With hoary hair and wide-spread fame,
Did you wear flowers on the Double-Ninth day?
Who arrived first at the Hall of Stars
To hold the gold vessel and the jade jar?[1]

This poem was written by Liu Jisun, a literati official of the Song dynasty, on the occasion of the departure of Su Shi [Su Dongpo] from the Hanlin Academy to assume his post as prefect of Hangzhou.[2] As it happened, Su Dongpo, academician of the Hanlin Academy, had been to Hangzhou twice, the first time as controller general of Hangzhou in the second year of Emperor Shenzong's[3] Xining reign period [1069], and the second time as magistrate of the greater Hangzhou region in the Yuanyou reign period [1086–93]. Hence the many historic sites in Hangzhou with inscriptions of Su Dongpo's poems. Among the multitude of fine scholars converging into the region after the imperial court relocated to the south, there was none but Hong Mai,[4] a member of the Hanlin Academy, whose talent could match that of Su Dongpo. Author of the thirty-two volume *Records of Yijian* [Yijian zhi], he was a leading historian of the time. However, as it was mostly the emperor's protégés who occupied positions of power in the court of Emperor Xiaozong [1163–89], it was not until after Hong Mai repeatedly sent memorials to the emperor from the Hanlin Academy requesting a position outside the capital that the emperor granted him the office of prefect of Shaoxing in Yuezhou. To commemorate the occasion of Hong Mai's assumption of the post one spring during the Chunxi reign period [1174–89], the poet Xiong Yuansu of the Yuan dynasty composed an ingenious poem that could be read both backwards and forwards:

Warm is [the] sun and clear is [the] sky.
Fine is [the] horse, saddle and reins embroidered.
With soft winds and falling flowers, red is [the] ground.
Light is [the] rain, gentle and green are [the] willows.
Lush meadows and winding rivers,
White-tipped branches and jadelike steps.
Alas! Rarely occur reunions, however good is [the] scenery.
Flittingly fly [the] swallows, nimble and swift.

It is another poem if read backwards:

Swift and nimble, [the] swallows fly flittingly.
[The] scenery is good; however, reunions occur rarely. Alas!
Steps jadelike and branches white-tipped,
Rivers winding and meadows lush.
[The] willows are green and gentle, [the] rain is light;
[The] ground is red, flowers falling and winds soft.
With embroidered reins and saddle, [the] horse is fine;
[The] sky is clear and [the] sun is warm.

Hong Mai held a banquet in the Zhenyue Hall in Shaoxing in honor
of the entire assembly of officials. It was a most impressive sight, with all the
runners of the yamen and members of the catering service standing in attendance at the side. The fruits were most fresh and the food most exquisite. After
three rounds of wine, one of the courtesans present, a certain Wang Ying, with
fingers as delicate as spring bamboo shoots and tender buds, played a tune on
a flute inlaid with gold threads and a dragon head. The resounding and melo-
dious music greatly enthralled the audience. Hong Mai ordered his attendants
to bring him the four treasures of the scholar's study[5] and, in the presence
of the officials as well as the courtesans, wrote in a joyous mood, without the
slightest pause in the movement of his brush-pen, a lyric poem to the tune
of "The Beautiful Lady Yu." The poem read,

Suddenly, the flute, on the jade terrace,
A sound rising to heaven on high.
The notes glide up and down the scale,
Stirring the green pond dragon, a wondrous sight.
In sobs it flies up to the sky,
Loath to part from the Liangzhou tune,
Vanishing into clouds with a rock-splitting clap,
Making plum blossoms fall like pieces of jade.

Improvisation of such a poem was no challenge for a talented scholar like Hong Mai, who was capable of the most refined poetry. Upon his presentation of the poem, the delighted assembly of officials were full of praise: "How original! A fine poem indeed!"

Before the words of praise and admiration had subsided, one of the officials present burst into a fit of laughter. "As ingenious as this poem is," said he, "it is a cento whose lines are stolen from eight different ancient poems."

Directing his eyes to the speaker, Hong Mai saw that it was Controller General Kong Deming. Much startled, Hong Mai asked, "May I have the honor of benefiting from your knowledge?" Thereupon Controller Kong launched into a detailed explanation right there from his seat at the banquet table.

As it turned out, the first line of the poem, "Suddenly, the flute, on the jade terrace," was stolen from the fourth line of the poem "The Taoist Hermit" by Zhang Ziwei:[6]

> *Is the room touched by the pale moonlight*
> *That shines upon the land in the frosty sky?*
> *In the Moon Palace, the sounds of the lute;*
> *On the jade terrace, the notes of a flute.*
> *A gold well, a dewy winch—the autumn water is cold;*
> *A thatched hut, a stone bed—the dusk clouds are clear.*
> *Dreaming at night about the jasper pool,[7]*
> *I walk along the twelve-bend balustrade.*

The second line in Hong's poem, "A sound rising to heaven on high," was taken from the third line of "Lyrics of Wang Jiaozi" by Scholar Luo:[8]

> *A sweet voice sang at Xie's feast;[9]*
> *Whose was it behind the screen?*
> *The sound rose to heaven on high*
> *And brought the flying clouds to a halt.*

The third line, "The notes glide up and down the scale," was from the second line of Cao Xiangu's[10] "The Sound of Wind":

> *With shreds of jade floating in the sky,*
> *The notes glide up and down the scale.*
> *Before they settle into a tune,*
> *The wind blows them to join other strains.*

The fourth line, "Stirring the green pond dragon, a wondrous sight," was borrowed from the third and fourth lines of the poem "The Oars" by Su Dongpo:

Surging down the river like arrows,
The waves vanish without a trace.
From afar, a glow on the wondrous sight,
Stirring the dragon of the deep green pond.

The transitional fifth line, "In sobs it flies up to the sky," came from the fourth line of the poem "Wild Geese" by Zhu Shuzhen:[11]

My heart is filled with grief and sorrow;
The south-flying geese have no home of their own.
They wing their way, glum and forlorn;
In sobs they fly up to the sky.

The sixth line, "Loath to part from the Liangzhou tune," was from the fourth line of "Song and Dance" by Qin Shaoyou[12] [of the Northern Song dynasty]:

The lithe waists a-dancing,
The oriole voices a-singing,
With such wonders here in the hall,
I am loath to part from the Liangzhou tune.

The seventh line, "Vanishing into clouds with a rock-splitting clap," was taken from the third line of the poem "Canon at the Bottom of the Water" by General Liu Qi [of the Southern Song dynasty]:

Like roaring thunder boomed the cannon;
Midst the splashing waves, water creatures went quiet.
Into the clouds vanished the rock-splitting clap,
Driving out the evil, bringing back the good.

The last line, "Making plum blossoms fall like pieces of jade," was taken from the fourth line of "Looking South of the River on the Lantern Festival" by literati scholar Liu Gaizhi on the occasion of his meeting with Vice-Director Chen of Wuzhou [of the Southern Song dynasty]:

On the balmy night of the Lantern Festival,
Willows let down their golden threads.
Plum blossoms fall like pieces of jade,
Under the full moon that shines in the sky.
With his people the good prefect shares the joy,
Flutes, drums, and brightly lit streets.
Wheels and hooves wear out the Moon Palace;
The charm of the night, long may it last!

Thus concluded Controller General Kong's explications. Hong Mai was immensely delighted. "Amazing! Amazing!" exclaimed the audience. Hong Mai had his attendants ply the controller general with another cup of wine, after which Hong said to him, "Your commentary was most brilliant. Please do me the favor of writing a poem with the theme 'the dragon-headed flute' for me to cherish for the rest of my life." After acknowledging his gratitude, Controller General Kong accordingly wrote a poem to the tune of "Prelude to Water Music":

> The fair lady displays her smooth wrists;
> Her soft hands set off her ruby lips.
> The dragon flute, with its lonesome tune,
> Gives delight to the listening ear.
> Sing along with the prince of Ning.[13]
> Or play the flute like Huan Yi;[14]
> Enjoy in quiet the ringing notes.
> A discerning eye in olden times
> Landed on the bamboo of Keting.[15]
>
> The night deep, the moon bright, the stars sparse.
> The sky high, the air crisp,
> The water and the hills green and frosty.
> In the midst of the charm,
> The notes of a bamboo flute strike the ear.
> With echoes from rocks, they rise to the clouds,
> Making all ghosts silently fade away.

Indeed,

> It takes one talent to know another;
> Recording the event will not be in vain.

Storyteller, why this prologue on poems about the dragon-headed flute? Well, it is because the story I shall now proceed to tell starts with two travelers who made their way to the Eastern Peak of Mount Tai to make a burnt offering of two Qizhou bamboo sticks—the kind of bamboo that would make the best dragon-headed flutes. This event led to the granting of two titles to a courtesan of the Fengning region of Zhengzhou Prefecture, for she married a worthy man who later rose to be a commander of four regions. Stories about this man, whose name enjoys eternal glory, are still being told today with immense relish. But what is the name of this man who started from humble beginnings? How did he rise to power and wealth?

> His power swept throughout the empire;
> His name struck awe everywhere in the land.

There is a poem on the rise and fall of the Five Dynasties that says,

> *After the fall of the house of Tang,*
> *Misery spread throughout the land.*
> *Upon the army hung the empire's fate;*
> *Frontier generals held the court in fear.*
> *Through the harsh winter, the pines stood tall;*
> *Before dawn, the stars keep on shining.*
> *After five royal houses in fifty-three years,*
> *The land awaits a truly mighty king.*

As the story goes, during the Tang of the Five Dynasties, there were two traveling merchants, Wang Yitai and his brother Wang Ertai, who came into possession of two most extraordinary-looking Qizhou bamboo sticks, each with one end resembling a dragon's head. This was the kind of bamboo that matchless dragon-headed flutes were made of. They then made a special trip to make a burnt offering at Fire Pond at the foot of the temple of the Eastern Peak of Mount Tai in Fengfu County, Yanzhou.

After the offering, the lord of Mount Tai granted the bamboo sticks to Duke Bingling, his third son, who then dispatched the two celestial generals Kang and Zhang to the Fengning region of Zhengzhou to summon the flute-maker Yan Zhaoliang. Shortly thereafter, the two generals were in Zhengzhou and, assuming the shapes of mortal beings, went to see Yan Zhaoliang. The latter was in the very act of making a flute in front of his door when he caught sight of two men approaching with bows of greeting. After saluting him, they said, "There is an official who has come into possession of two bamboo sticks good enough to be made into dragon-headed flutes. He invites you to go and do the job for him. Being rather of an impatient disposition, he wants us to take you to him immediately, but he will reward you handsomely after the job is done." There and then, Yan Zhaoliang collected his tools and followed the two men on their way. In a twinkling, they came upon a place where, upon lifting his eyes, Yan Zhaoliang saw a board with the inscription "Eastern Peak of Mount Tai." Behold:

> *The first of all mountains,*
> *Most revered of the Five Peaks,*
> *Above are thirty-eight twists and turns,*
> *Below are seventy-two chambers of hell.*[16]
> *The cascades glitter in the sun;*
> *The heavenly pillars soar into the skies.*
> *Divine light brightens the nine halls*
> *With tiles blue as frozen smoke.*

> *Over the peaks on all sides,*
> *The golden dragon shines through the mist.*
> *Bamboo Grove Temple floats in the air;*[17]
> *Sunrise Peak shelters the gods.*

Without much understanding of the poem, Yan Zhaoliang was led by
Kang and Zhang into the presence of Duke Bingling and then into a pavilion,
where the bamboo sticks were already laid out on a table. After telling Yan
Zhaoliang to start on the job right away, Kang and Zhang warned him, "This
is the netherworld. Do not wander afar, for if you venture out and lose your
bearings, you will have a hard time finding your way back." With this admonishment, the two generals departed. Before long, Zhaoliang finished the job
and played a few notes, which came out clear and delightful. After waiting
for a considerable time without seeing Kang and Zhang returning, Zhaoliang
thought to himself, "Since I am already here, it would be a pity if I didn't
venture out for a look around," whereupon he walked away from the pavilion
and, before long, saw a palace looming ahead. As he approached the corridor
of the palace, he heard the crack of a whip that was a warning to be silent,
signaling the start of a court session. As he applied his eyes to a crevice in the
window, behold:

> *Tasseled curtains rolled up;*
> *Pheasant-tail fans spread out.*
> *The solemn court began its session,*
> *With one in a king's crown seated in the middle.*
> *Jade tablets of office in hand,*
> *The gods streamed in, right and left.*
> *The gold bell tolled, the jade chimes sounded.*
> *Celestial music filled the colored clouds,*
> *Leading the gods to their lord.*

After the lord of Mount Tai had dismounted his royal carriage and ascended
the throne and the assembly of gods had made their obeisance, the lord ordered
that the prisoners be brought forth. A man with his neck and arms in a long
cangue was pushed into the court. Yan Zhaoliang thought to himself, "This
man surely looks familiar," but for the moment he could not place him.

A second imperial decree followed, ordering that the man be taken out
for the installation of a copper gallbladder[18] and an iron heart, in preparation
for his return to the mortal world to become a commander of four regions.
(*It takes a copper gallbladder and an iron heart to become a dominant figure in
the times of the Five Dynasties.*) He was, at the same time, warned against any
unjust taking of human lives. Zhaoliang was dumbfounded as he listened.

Suddenly, a demon clerk called out, "How can a mortal being eavesdrop on our court?" Thereupon Yan Zhaoliang hastened back to the pavilion where he had been making the flutes. It was not until a long while thereafter that Kang and Zhang returned to the pavilion. Seeing that the work had been done, they made their way, together with Zhaoliang, to present the dragon-headed flutes to Duke Bingling, who was immensely overjoyed at their delightful notes. "I will add to your happiness and longevity," he said to Yan Zhaoliang, who replied, "I have no wish to have my happiness and longevity augmented, but I have a sister, Yan Yueying, who is now a prostitute. My only wish is for her to extricate herself from her present circumstances and settle down in a decent marriage as soon as possible."

Duke Bingling said, "Such a wish can dwell only in the heart of a worthy man, albeit a man of the mortal world. Your sister shall marry a commander of four regions."

After bows of gratitude, Zhaoliang was escorted back by Kang and Zhang. As they were approaching a high point on a precipitous cliff, the two escorts directed Zhaoliang's eyes to a spot to distract his attention while, with one quick movement of the hand, they pushed him over the edge of the cliff.

In shock, Yan Zhaoliang opened his eyes, only to find himself in bed at home, surrounded by his wife and children.

"Why are you weeping over me like this?" he asked his wife.

"You were working in front of the door the other day when you suddenly dropped dead. As your chest still felt a little warm, we carried you to bed, where you have been lying for two days. What did you do down there in the netherworld?"

Everyone in the room was aghast at Zhaoliang's account of what had happened to him. Nothing worthy of note occurred for some time thereafter.

It was winter, with snow falling from the sky. There is a poem titled "Snow" by Shi Xindao[19] that gives a good description of the scene:

> The spinning flakes fall the whole night through,
> Bedecking the city's morning scene.
> Houses are wrapped in white jade,
> Towers in silvery splendor.
> The plum blossoms on Mount Yu, where did they come from?
> The flying catkins on Zhang Terrace, when will they stop?[20]
> My thoughts turn to the silver toad in the blue sky
> And the rider of the green phoenix on the red hills.

With the snow gathering force, it grew too cold for Yan Zhaoliang to work. As he was sitting idly by the door, the sight of a strongly built man passing by in the street struck him dumbfounded. "Isn't this the man who received a copper gallbladder and an iron heart in the netherworld, the very same man who is destined to be a commander of four regions? Now that he is passing by, why don't I go forward and make his acquaintance? What am I waiting for?" (*Master Yan being a man without a single streak of the vulgarity of the mundane world, it certainly makes sense to have the friendship begin before that man's rise to fame and fortune.*) Holding up the lower part of his gown, he hurriedly ventured into the snow and, in a few big strides, caught up with the strongly built man. Taking another step forward, he called out, "Please accept my greetings, sir."

Somehow, the man knew him to be a flute-maker. Returning the greeting with a bow, he said, "How can I be of service to you, flute master?"

"I would like to invite you for a few drinks to warm yourself up in such cold, snowy weather." So saying, he took the man into a wineshop.

It turned out that the man was named Shi Hongzhao, courtesy name Hua-yuan, with the nickname "Simpleton." He was a foot soldier in the Vanguard Battalion. According to *The History of the Five Dynasties,* he was "a native of Xingze, Zhengzhou, and a most courageous man who could walk as fast as a horse." Having downed the wine, the two men went their separate ways home.

The following day, Yan Zhaoliang went to see his sister Yan Yueying and said to her, "I am here to tell you about a man I met yesterday. It was the very man I saw when I was dead to the world for two days, making flutes in the netherworld. With a copper gallbladder and an iron heart installed in him, he is preordained to be a commander of four regions and to be your husband. It's been some time since then, and I had almost forgotten about him when I happened to see him yesterday. I invited him for a few drinks."

"What sort of a man is he?" asked Yan Yueying.

"He is the nice, kind Big Man Shi of the Vanguard Battalion."

Yan Zhaoliang's answer so incensed his sister that she snapped, "I don't believe that I am destined to marry a man of such lowly status!"

From that time on, Yan the flute-maker never failed to treat Shi Hong-zhao to wine every time they met. After being the subject of Yan's hospitality quite a few times, Shi Hongzhao, in his turn, invited Yan into a wineshop when the two ran into each other on the street. After much wine and food, Yan was ready to pay the bill, but Shi Hongzhao would not hear of it. "You must allow me to reciprocate for once." Thereupon Yan Zhaoliang took his leave and stepped out of the wineshop.

Turning to the waiter, Shi Hongzhao said, "I haven't brought any money with me. You can follow me to the camp for the money."

The waiter had no choice but to follow him. Once at the entrance of the camp, Shi said, "I haven't got a penny today. You go back now. I'll return with the money tomorrow to pay your master."

The waiter protested, "He'll surely put the blame on me."

"What if he does?" demanded Shi. "If you know what's best, you'll go. Otherwise, watch out for my fists!" The waiter could only turn back.

Now, Shi Hongzhao proceeded to Mr. Wang, the vender of sweet-rice dumplings, and said to him, "Sir, I owe the wineshop some money, but I have nothing to pay them back with. Guard your door well tonight, for I'll be coming to steal your wok."

Taking this warning as a joke, Mr. Wang, told his wife after he got home, "I've never heard anything more ridiculous in the whole wide world. Simpleton Shi warned me to guard my door well because he's coming tonight to steal my wok." His wife was also tickled.

At about three-fifths of a watch past the second watch in the night, Shi Hongzhao did indeed come to push himself against the door. Being as strong as he was, he broke the bolt and entered the house. The old couple heard the movements. "Let's wait for his next move," said Mrs. Wang. Stirring up a loud noise, Shi Hongzhao walked up to the stove, removed the wok, and put it on the ground, saying, "If it breaks, I'll have nothing to pay the wine bill with." So saying, he struck the wok with a stick to make a clattering sound. (*A real man hides nothing even when stealing.*) Then he picked up the wok, turned it over, and placed it on his head. Little did he know that there was some water in the wok, but this was no time to fuss about a wet face and clothes. Off he went with the wok on his head.

"Stop thief!" cried Mr. Wang, who threw on some clothes and ran after Shi. The local headman, who heard the cry, also rushed to the scene. Panic-stricken, Shi Hongzhao threw down the wok and ran into an alley to hide. How was he to know that it was a blind alley? Terrified, he tried to climb up the wall of someone's yard but slipped and fell down over the wall, as was witnessed by the headman, who had followed him into the alley. "Madam Yan!" he cried. "A thief has just jumped over your back wall!"

Courtesan Yan heard the cry and came out for a look, with her maid-servant holding a candle for her. Instead of any thief, what struck her eyes was an extraordinary animal the color of snow:

> It gleamed like a white silk ribbon
> And dazzled like a pile of silver.
> It shook its fur like shimmering frost
> And wagged its tail like three feet of snow.
> Its eyes flashed forth bolts of lightning;
> Its red mouth was huge as the sea.

Courtesan Yan stood appalled. But upon a second look, what she saw was Big Man Shi crouching against the outhouse. (*Like Lady Liang's first encounter with Han Shizhong.*)²¹ At the sight of her, he rose and, all in a fluster, approached her with a bow of greeting. Having witnessed the extraordinary appearance he had assumed, and recalling her brother's words about her destiny to marry this man who was to rise to eminence some day, she hid him inside the house, safe from the pursuers. After waiting for some time without hearing a sound from the Yan residence, the crowd dispersed. Yan Yueying then let him out through the front door.

The night passed without further ado. The following day, Yan Yueying sent for her brother the flute-maker and said to him, "Brother, you said before that I am destined to marry Big Man Shi, who will rise to be a commander of four regions. I didn't believe you at the time, but last night when I heard cries about a thief having jumped to my side of the wall, my maid and I went out for a look by candlelight and saw a white tiger crouching on the ground. Upon a closer look, it turned out to be Big Man Shi. Such an unusual aura about him convinced me that he is indeed a man with a brilliant career ahead of him. I am willing to marry him. Will you approach him on my behalf?"

"Sure," said Yan Zhaoliang. "I'll fix the match today."

Knowing that Shi Hongzhao was predestined to rise to wealth and power, Yan the flute-maker was in raptures now that his sister was willing to marry the man. He made his way straight to the camp to look for Shi. It so happened that Shi, having tried (as he should not have done) to steal Mr. Wang's wok and with the debt of a wine bill weighing upon him, dared not venture out of the camp. (*Surely a real man doesn't want to be in debt, but when penniless, there's no other alternative.*) Yan easily found him and invited him out, saying, "I am here to make a good match for you."

"What match?"

"A match between you and my sister, Courtesan Yan, who has some property and cash. What do you say?"

"It's a good match all right, but there are three things that make me hesitate to accept."

"What three things? Pray tell me."

"First, whatever she owns must be at my disposal. Second, after I enter her household, she must not entertain clients as before. Third, I have a sworn brother as well as some friends who are constantly on the road. If they come to see me, I want to give them meals and lodging. If you promise me these three things, I'll accept the marriage proposal." (*These words alone show him to be a husband out of the common run.*)

Yan Zhaoliang promised, "Since my sister will be wedded to you, you'll surely be the master in everything."

That very day, the marriage deal was made and duly reported back to Yan Yueying. Now that both sides were willing, an auspicious day was chosen for the wedding. As the Yans did not expect Shi to be able to offer wedding gifts, they provided him with a new outfit for the wedding ceremony, after which the groom moved into Yan Yueying's residence.

Two months later, Shi Hongzhao was sent by an order from above to the town of Filial Piety and Righteousness to deliver a military document. Before he had stayed there for a month, everyone under the rank of sergeant had fallen victim to his bullying. (*It's not that he's a bully, but none of the men was to his liking.*) However, as he was well supplied with money, which he used freely for treats of wine, no one stood up to him.

One day, he went into the officers' barracks to sleep. The sergeant said, "I'm in no mood to have to put up with this troublemaker." Before he had quite finished complaining, a man was seen approaching from the west. With a bow of greeting to the sergeant, the newcomer asked, "Is there a Shi Hongzhao here?"

The sergeant replied, pointing at Shi, "He's right there, asleep." It was this visit that changed the course of Shi Hongzhao's life. Who was the visitor? Indeed,

> All over the land and across the seas,
> Old acquaintances will manage to meet.

The visitor looking for Shi Hongzhao was Guo Wei, courtesy name Zhongwen, a native of Yaoshan County of Yingzhou Prefecture. As he was the firstborn son of the family, he was also known as Big Brother Guo. What did he look like?

> He moves his left leg—a dragon coils in shallow waters.
> He moves his right leg—a phoenix dances on the red terrace.
> A rosy halo over his head,
> A purple mist over his body.
> With the brows and eyes of Yao and Shun,
> The back of Yu, and the shoulders of Tang.[22]
> He is to rise above princes and dukes,
> To be second only to the Son of Heaven.

When under straitened circumstances in the Eastern Capital, Big Brother Guo had stolen hairpins from a courtesan, Pan the Eighth, who was so impressed with his extraordinary appearance that she kept him with her as a brother instead of handing him over to the authorities. After his situation improved, he went to see a show at a fair and ended up killing a young entertainer. That very night, he fled the city and tried to seek refuge with his sworn brother Shi Hongzhao in Zhengzhou. Inquiries at the Vanguard Battalion camp led him to the town of Filial Piety and Righteousness. The sergeant accordingly woke up Shi Hongzhao from his bed in the barracks, saying, "You have a visitor who's been waiting for you for quite some time now."

Shi Hongzhao walked over impatiently. "Who is it?"

Big Brother Guo stepped forward and said, "It's been a long time since I saw you last, my brother. I am glad you look well."

Recognizing the visitor to be his sworn older brother, Shi Hongzhao hastened to drop to his knees in a gesture of obeisance. After the exchange of greetings was over, Shi Hongzhao said, "Brother, don't go anywhere else. Just stay with me for the time being. If you need pocket money, I will get it for you from home." No one dared raise any objections to his keeping Big Brother Guo in the barracks. After a few days there, Big Brother Guo joined Shi Hongzhao in bullying the people around them. Their daily gambling and stealing wreaked such havoc in the neighborhood that no one did not curse them with great spite.

Let us follow another thread of the story and turn our attention to the imperial court, where Emperor Min [934] now ascended the throne as successor to the deceased Emperor Mingzong [926–33] of the Later Tang dynasty. All the ladies of the court were ordered to leave the palace and get married. Among the court ladies dismissed was a Lady Chai, the seal-keeper, who had some knowledge about fortune-telling through signs of nature. Noticing an auspicious aura over the territory of Zhengzhou, she brought along her dowry and headed for the region. After settling down in Granny Wang's house in the town of Filial Piety and Righteousness, she started to search for a marriage candidate of high status. Several days passed, but of all the men walking up and down the streets, there was not one who struck her fancy. "Why is it so quiet around here?" she asked Granny Wang.

"Madam, the streets can be easily brought to life if you send out word to small brokers that you are sponsoring a fair."

"What a good idea!"

Thus, word spread out through Granny Wang that Lady Chai was sponsoring a fair the next day.

As the news reached the ears of the sworn brothers Guo and Shi, they took counsel of each other. "How about making a little money for a drink? What shall we sell tomorrow?"

Shi Hongzhao had this idea: "Why don't we sell dog meat? Let's borrow a plate, a stand, and a cleaver, steal a dog somewhere, beat it to death, cook it, and sell the meat. Wouldn't that be easier than going to the regular market?"

"But there are no more dogs in the neighborhood," remarked Big Brother Guo. "We've stolen and eaten them all, and the neighbors don't keep dogs anymore."

Shi Hongzhao suggested, "Community Headman Wang keeps a big dog.

Let's go and get it." Accordingly, they betook themselves to Headman Wang's house. One of them tried to coax the dog out while the other held a cudgel, waiting for the earliest chance to deal the crushing blow. Seeing what was going on, Headman Wang stepped out with an offer of three hundred in cash: "Spare my dog. Take this, and buy yourselves a drink."

"Mr. Wang!" protested Shi Hongzhao. "What an unreasonable man you are! This big dog of yours is surely worth more than three hundred in cash! You are shortchanging us!"

Big Brother Guo assumed a more conciliatory tone: "Show some respect for the old man, and be satisfied with whatever is offered."

Before the night was out, the two of them went to another place, stole a dog, skinned it, and cooked it until the meat was tender.

On the following day, with Shi Hongzhao carrying a plate on his head and Big Brother Guo a rack on his back, they walked up to Lady Chai's door and cried, "Meat for sale!" The rack was lowered onto the ground and the plate placed on it.

At the sight of Big Brother Guo through the curtain, Lady Chai said to herself, "I've searched high and low, but here he is, standing right in front of my eyes." At her orders, a servant took out a plate and asked Big Brother Guo to fill it with meat.

As Guo was cutting the dog meat, Granny Wang, who happened to be by Lady Chai's side, protested, "This is dog meat! Surely it's not for a lady like you!"

Lady Chai countered, "I am doing this as a sponsor of the fair rather than out of a preference for the meat!" She then had her accountant pay one tael of silver for the meat. The money having exchanged hands, the two men took their leave after acknowledging their gratitude.

The fair was over soon thereafter. Lady Chai turned to Granny Wang and said, "I have a favor to ask of you."

"What is it?"

"Who were the two men selling dog meat here just a moment ago? Where do they live?"

"Those two men are the terror of the town. The one who cut the meat is named Guo. The one who carried the plate is Shi. Both live in the barracks in town. Why do you ask?"

"I want to marry Guo, the one who cut the meat. Would you please be the matchmaker?"

"But a lady of your status will have plenty of decent marriage proposals. Why marry such a man?"

"Don't you worry about that," Lady Chai answered. "I'm positive that he will be a man of distinction. Just approach him and make the proposal for me."

Thus instructed, Granny Wang set off immediately for the barracks to look for Big Brother Guo, but he was nowhere to be seen. The sergeant said, "He's drinking in the wineshop across the street," whereupon Granny Wang crossed over to the wineshop, lifted the blue cotton portiere, and walked in.

"Big Brother Guo!" she called out when she saw the two. "How can you be sitting and drinking away when a tremendous stroke of luck is coming your way!"

"What's with this woman?" said Big Brother Guo. "The moment I get myself some silver, you come to ask for a share. I have nothing for you except a drink, if you want."

"An old woman like me is not after a drink."

"If it isn't wine you're after," said Big Brother Guo, "I have nothing to offer you, not even a penny. Just take a drink if you know what's good for you."

Shi Hongzhao chimed in, "What a cheeky old woman you are! You know all too well that we are not the most sweet-tempered kind of men, and yet you turn down a well-meant offer of wine. A few moments ago, you almost ruined our chances by letting on that it was dog meat we were selling. Luckily, the lady still bought from us. How shameless of you to come for a handout! Mark this: Don't even expect a treat of wine from me. You'll get nothing from me but kicks and blows!"

"I am here not to ask for wine or money, but to tell Big Brother Guo that Lady Chai has taken a liking to him and wants to marry him."

At these words, Big Brother Guo flew into a rage and gave her a slap across the face. Collapsing to the floor, Granny Wang wailed, "Woe is me! What a way to treat a well-meaning matchmaker!"

Big Brother Guo thundered, "Who sent you here to make fun of me? I'll spare you from more blows if you leave here in peace. A lady like that marrying me! What nonsense is this!"

Granny Wang scrambled to her feet, left the wineshop, and went straight to Lady Chai.

"I appreciate what you did for me," said Lady Chai.

"I got slapped for making a matchmaking proposal," complained Granny Wang. "He thought I was there to make fun of him."

"I'm sorry that you were treated so roughly, but I have no other choice than to ask you to make another trip. Take this gold hairpin first. If this works out, I will reward you heavily."

"I dare not go again. If I do, there will be no one to stand up for me even if I'm beaten to death."

"I understand," Lady Chai reassured her. "He thought you were making fun of him because you didn't bring anything. But with a token of faith, he'll hardly turn you down."

"What token?"

When Lady Chai produced the object and showed it to her, Granny Wang stood aghast. What was that thing?

> *Haven't you heard? Zhang Fu married his daughter to Chen Ping,*[23]
> *Who lived in a hut with a mat as door.*
> *Visited by streams of great and wise men,*
> *With grace he stood out above the common run.*
> *Mr. Lü of Shanfu was no less wise,*
> *When he married his daughters to Fan and Liu.*[24]
> *Within the period of ten years of war,*
> *Fan rose to be a duke, and Liu was crowned.*
> *Lü's name thereafter spread far and wide,*
> *Bringing glory to his home.*
> *But men of today, when choosing sons-in-law,*
> *Pick only those with mansions and wealth.*

What Lady Chai showed Granny Wang was a gold belt weighing twenty-five taels. It was to be offered to Big Brother Guo as a token of the lady's good faith. Nothing in this world provides more motivation for human behavior than money. Humiliated though she had been by the young man, Granny Wang, with the gold hairpin in her possession and the gold belt as a gift to offer, found it hard to restrain her feet from going. The gold belt in hand, she lost no time in making a second trip to the wineshop. On the way, she thought to herself, "I shouldn't have gone empty-handed the first time. Otherwise I wouldn't have been slapped. But this time, he won't do anything to me, if only for the sake of the belt."

As she came upon the door of the wineshop and lifted up the blue cotton portiere, she found the two brothers still drinking. Stepping forward, she addressed Big Brother Guo as follows: "I am here to convey to you a message from Lady Chai. Afraid that you might not believe her, she gave me this gold belt weighing twenty-five taels as a token of her good faith, but she is also waiting for something from you in return."

Big Brother Guo thought to himself, "I don't even have a penny to my name. Since she is making the first move, I might just as well take the belt before I decide what to do." He asked Granny Wang to sit down and had the waiter bring another cup for the old woman to join him in the drinking. After having downed three drinks, he said, "Where can I get anything to offer her?"

"Anything that you have on you will be fine," said the woman.

Thereupon, he took down his cap, removed the rim, all greasy and smelly, and handed it to Granny Wang as a token in return. (*Ingenious.*) Granny Wang could not contain her laughter as she took it. "You do know how to take the easy way out!" she said. As she handed it to Lady Chai upon her return, the latter put it away with a smile.

Now that the betrothal procedures were complete, an auspicious day was chosen for the wedding, which was to be held at Granny Wang's home. Invited guests included Shi Hongzhao (now Lady Chai's brother-in-law) and her sister-in-law Yan Yuying, who had come all the way from Zhengzhou. After the wedding in the town of Filial Piety and Righteousness, the new couple, as dictated by custom, went to the bride's home to stay for a few days.

One day, Lady Chai looked at her husband, Big Brother Guo, and said, "You'll miss the chance of your life if you stay on in this place. Let me write a recommendation letter for you. You can go to the Western Capital, in Henan Prefecture, to see my maternal uncle Duke Fu and seek a position as a first step up the ladder of officialdom." Big Brother Guo thanked his wife for her suggestion and, following her advice, packed up and set off on his journey on a chosen auspicious day, equipped with Lady Chai's letter.

> He walks with a red aura over his head
> And sits in a cloud of purple mist.
> On the road during the day,
> His cudgel serves him as a friend.
> In the tavern all through the night,
> He has for company the lamp on the wall.
> In time, he will rise to attain great fame;
> Today, he is but a traveler, unknown.

Stopping only for food and drink when necessary, he traveled by day and rested by night. In a few days' time, he arrived in the Western Capital and found lodging in a tavern. Little did he know that his journey to the Western Capital, motivated by the desire to gain fortune through the help of Duke Fu, would lead to the loss of a life. Truly,

> Before his career soared to heaven,
> He was plunged first into prison.

In the Western Capital in Henan Prefecture, Big Brother Guo saw

> Yujun was the name of the county,
> Henan was the name of the prefecture.
> With over a million residents,
> It was the grandest city there was.
> Within its borders, far and wide,
> The streets teemed with traffic and people.
> Amid the hustle and bustle of the city,

Wheels rumbled and hooves clopped.
Wind-wafted music filled the air;
From which house came the light and clear notes?
Silk clothes gave off the fragrance of flowers
That were in bloom in gardens everywhere.
To the east, the city joined Gong County;
To the west, it abutted Mianchi.
To the south stood the richly endowed Luokou;
To the north thundered the Yellow River.
The city walls stood in a crescent skyline,
The towers soared into the heavens.
The city was full of dukes and lords
Who lived in mansions with vermilion doors.
Speak not of its glory as the old capital;
It is just as splendid even today.
Truly,
In spring, it is a pile of red brocade,
In summer, a tent of green silk gauze.

After spending a night at the tavern, Big Brother Guo was about to set out for Duke Fu's residence the next morning, carrying with him the letter from his wife, when he was suddenly struck with a thought: "A worthy man should establish his name by virtue of his own abilities. How can I start a career through a woman's words?" Putting the letter aside, he went empty-handed to the recruitment office in front of the yamen and waited for Li Bayu, master of martial arts, to see him.

"Did you bring anything?" asked Li Bayu.

"Yes, I did."

"What is it that you brought?"

"I brought with me all eighteen kinds of martial arts."

What Master Li had in mind was a monetary gift. At Guo's irrelevant answer, he said, "I will notify you when the duke calls the court to order." But he did not do as he promised.

From that day onward, Guo waited at the yamen every day for over two months without ever getting a chance to see the duke. The desk clerk at the tavern, knowing that Guo was unsuccessful in his attempts to see the duke, said something he should have known better than to say: "Mr. Guo, you've been wasting your time. Master Li is after money. How can you get to see the duke if you don't give the sergeant some money first?"

Anger flared up in Guo. "So that's what the scoundrel is after!"

Instead of going to the yamen that day, he sat down dejectedly in front of the tavern. At the sight of a man offering a gambling game with fish as the prize, Big Brother Guo stepped forward and, on his first try, won the fish. The man pleaded with Guo, saying, "I went to a lot of trouble last night getting these pennies that I bought the fish with, hoping to make a little money to support my old mother. So far, I haven't made even a penny. And now, with you scooping up the money, I have nothing left to offer to my mother. Please lend me back the fish, so I can win some money at the game, and I'll give back to you what's yours."

Impressed by the man's filial devotion, Guo did as he was asked and told the man, "Let me know when you lose."

As the man approached the wineshop, carrying the fish, he heard a voice call out, "Where is the man with the fish game?" As this newcomer on the scene happened to be predestined to engage in a fistfight with Big Brother Guo, the ground in front of the wineshop became a small battlefield. Who was the man calling out for a gambling game?

> He was a monstrous sinner in the past;
> Heavenly retribution is due today.

The one who stopped the man with the fish was none other than Li Bayu, master of martial arts in the Western Capital in Henan. He was drinking in the wineshop when, catching sight of the man with the fish, he called the man into the wineshop for a game. He lost a few pennies, but he took the fish anyway. The game man dared not protest but came back and told Big Brother Guo, "Someone in the wineshop took my fish, but I did win a few pennies from him. At least I can give you back your money."

Guo exploded, "Who is that man? He should have known better than to take the fish when he loses! Since the fish is now mine, I'll go to take it back." Had he not gone to ask for the fish, all would have been well. But as it was, when he went to the wineshop and saw who it was, his feelings were best described by the following lines:

> When enemies meet,
> Eyes flare with anger.

When he saw that it was none other than Master Li Bayu, his fury grew tenfold. Staring at Li, he said in front of the wineshop door, "Why did you take my fish?"

"I took the fish from the game man. How come it's yours?"

Clapping his hands, Guo exclaimed, "I came to the Western Capital to look for a job, but just because I didn't bribe you, you got me stranded here for about two months without letting me see the duke. Now what do you have to say to me?"

"Come to the yamen tomorrow. I'll let you have what you want."

Guo thundered, "You scoundrel who blocks the advancement of worthy men! I won't set any traps for you. I challenge you to a fight right here to see who's stronger!" As he took off his shirt, a cry was uttered from the crowd. It so happened that in his childhood, Guo had met a Taoist sage who tattooed several small birds on the right side of his neck and a few ears of rice on the left side, saying, "To attain full wealth and power, wait until the birds reach the rice." Henceforth, he was also known as Guo the Bird. Upon his assumption of the throne, the birds and the rice did indeed merge together, but this happened much later. To come back to where we were, when Big Brother Guo bared his arms, revealing his tattooed neck, the crowd burst into cheers. Truly, the tattoo was like

> Sichuan brocade when examined up close,
> A tuft of flowers when seen from afar.

"Do you really want a fight?" said Li Bayu. "Stay here, then!"

Guo shot back, "Don't waste any words. Come on!"

As Li Bayu also bared his arms and revealed his powerful muscles, the crowd again burst into cheers. They were like

> Pig iron cast by a raging fire,
> And hard rocks used for a tombstone.

The two men thus started a fistfight under the eyes of spectators all around them. The blows and kicks became more and more fierce, until one of the two fell to the ground in a pool of blood, amid exclamations from the crowd. Which one lost the fight?

> His malice and all kinds of evil deeds
> Earned him the contempt of one and all.
> He thought he could be hurt by none,
> Little knowing that death was close at hand.

Big Brother Guo rained blows upon Li Bayu until the ground was covered with Li's blood. He was still at it when he heard shouts of guards announcing the approach of the duke and his entourage. From the back of his horse, Duke Fu saw that a man enveloped in red light and purple mist was fighting Li Bayu and that Li was all too evidently the loser. The duke ordered his men, "Don't make a lot of noise, but have the two men come forward to me."

The men went over to the scene of the fighting and said courteously, "Please stop the fight. The duke wants you to see him." Accordingly, the two men followed him to the duke's mansion. Directing his eyes to Big Brother Guo, Duke Fu saw that he had

> *The brows and eyes of Yao and Shun,*
> *And the back and shoulders of Yu and Tang.*

"Where are you from?" the duke asked Big Brother Guo. "Why were you beating Li Bayu?"

"I am Guo Wei, Your Honor, a native of Yaoshan County of Xing Prefecture, here to seek a position in your service. I got stranded in a tavern for over two months because Li Bayu, greedy for a bribe, kept me from entering your august presence. A chance encounter with him led to the fight. This being an offense against Your Honor, I deserve the death penalty."

The duke asked further, "Since you traveled such a great distance to try to enter my service, may I ask what abilities you have?"

"I am skilled in the use of each and every one of the eighteen weapons." Thereupon the duke ordered a staff fight between Li Bayu and Guo Wei right there in the hall.

Knowing that he was no match for Guo after what had occurred, Li Bayu said to the duke, "I am in no condition to fight, because he sneaked up on me just moments ago and gave me bruises all over." But the duke was not to be shaken in his resolve.

Staring squarely at Li Bayu, Guo Wei said, "So I sneaked up on you, did I? Now's the chance to fight it out and see who's better!" Staff in hand, the two men shouted greetings to each other and, at the bidding of an official, started the fight.

> *Blows in the Shandong manner;*
> *Jabs in the Hebei style.*
> *The blows as fierce as a monster turtle,*
> *The jabs as furious as the Kunlun falls.*
> *Three about-turns and two kicks*
> *Sound like whirlwinds and horses' neighs.*
> *Rapid movements to ward off blows*
> *Look like white ribbons flapping in the air.*
> *The thrusts and shoves*
> *Sound like wind and rain driving past the ears.*

Thus the two men fought on in the hall, wielding their staffs high and low, back and forth, winning cheers from Duke Fu Yanqing after just a few rounds.

> *In sickness, Yang Hu recommended Du Yu;* [25]
> *Guan Zhong was saved from prison by Bao Shu.* [26]
> *Of all the heroes within the four seas,*
> *How many know the worth of others?*

Let us come back to the fight between the two men. A poor match for his opponent, Li Bayu fell to the ground at a mighty blow from Big Brother Guo. The duke was immensely delighted. There and then, he appointed Guo grand master of martial arts, a position superior to that of Li Bayu. Big Brother Guo thanked the duke and entered the duke's service in Henan. For some time thereafter, nothing remarkable happened.

One day, Grand Master Guo was taking a leisurely walk in the busy section of town when he saw a man, seated in front of a restaurant, raving in exaggerated agitation and ordering his men to smash the restaurant. Guo asked the waiter, "Why is this man kicking up such a fuss here?"

The waiter pulled him aside before saying, "This man is Mr. Shang, son of an influential local official. About two weeks ago, he saw my master's beautiful eighteen-year-old daughter and sent a messenger to pass the word: 'My mother invites the young lady over for a talk. Should your family be in need of money, please let us know.' My master said, 'I'd rather die than sell my daughter!' Angry at the father's refusal, Mr. Shang is now here to pick a fight." At these words, Big Brother Guo

> Flew into a rage
> And smoldered with anger.
> His phoenix eyes blazed with anger;
> His dragonlike brows rose in wrath.
> Fury shot from his feet to his head;
> The fire in his heart leapt ten thousand feet.

Stepping forward, Master Guo addressed Mr. Shang in these words: "Benevolence is the essential quality in man. Even evil thoughts harbored in the dark do not escape the gods' eyes, which are as bright as lightning. You must not let desire for women make you deviate from the right way. Humble though I am, I ask that you mount your horse and be on your way."

The young man asked gruffly, "Who are you?"

"I am Guo Wei, grand master of martial arts under Duke Fu of Henan."

Mr. Shang shot back, "You have no jurisdiction over me, nor do I over you. Why meddle in my affairs? Come on, men! Beat up this fellow for me!"

Big Brother Guo responded hotly, "How can you treat me like this, when I was offering you advice out of the best intentions! You don't know what kind of a man you are dealing with!" Grabbing the young man with his left hand, he pulled out a small knife with his right hand. As his hand went down, what, you may ask, happened to Mr. Shang?

> To wipe out all wrongs under heaven
> Is the wish of all heroes in the world.

In his attempt to right a wrong, Grand Master Guo killed Mr. Shang. Mr. Shang's followers fled from the scene, whereas Guo himself made his way straight to the yamen of Henan Prefecture to turn himself in to the authorities. To Duke Fu, who held the court session, Guo reported, "I am here to ask for punishment, for I killed a brute of a man who was bullying people."

After learning all the details of the incident, the duke had Guo put in a long cangue and taken to the Office of Criminal Justice to await punishment. How do we know that the Office of Criminal Justice was a terror of a place?

> *Known as the office that punishes,*
> *It is a tightly guarded place of fear.*
> *The wardens with cudgels, fierce as ox-head demons,*
> *The turnkeys with iron chains, brutal as rakshasas.*
> *Which of the three kinds of cangues to wear*
> *Depends on the severity of the case;*
> *Which cell to stay in*
> *Depends on whether one is to die or live.*
> *In chilly winds, crows cry in the Trial Hall.*
> *In mottled sunlight, willows shield Xiao's temple.*[27]
> *Turn your head, you run into the demon lords,*
> *Open your eyes, you see Yama, king of hell.*

On that very day, Guo's case was handled by a clerk named Wang Xiu. Once brought into the hall, the criminal was tied up for questioning. Presently, at an order from Duke Fu, Wang Xiu went into a side hall, where the duke gave him a few words of instruction and wrote something with his brush-pen on the desk. Wang Xiu saw that he had written, "Be lenient with Guo Wei."

"I will act according to the rules of the law," said Wang Xiu. Abruptly, the duke went behind the screen and left. Terrified, Wang Xiu called out, "Yes, sir!" and returned dejectedly to his office, where he laid his head on his arms on the table to go to sleep. As he did so, his eyes fell upon a small red snake wriggling merrily on the table. "How strange!" he muttered to himself. Yet, however hard he tried to drive it away, the snake always managed to stay ahead of him, adjusting its pace with his. Upon reaching a cell on the east side, the snake slithered onto Big Brother Guo's cangue, into his nose, and through all the seven apertures in his head. Wang Xiu found the prisoner covered in red light and purple mist. His mind not yet registering the significance of what he saw, Wang Xiu suddenly woke up and found himself still in his room.

It is a matter of truth that sleep is often a state induced by worry over some thorny problems or anxiety over personal financial difficulties. That is why the written character for sleepiness [*kun*] is associated with poverty and worry rather than with joy and happiness. After the dream, Wang Xiu thought to himself, "No wonder Duke Fu told me to be lenient with the man. It does indeed take one great man to recognize another." After giving much thought to the matter, Wang Xiu was still not able to come up with a plan to let Guo go. The fact was, Big Brother Guo was destined to suffer many hardships before his rise to eminence. He had lost his father when he was small and then followed his mother to Luzhou, where she married into the Chang family. Later, an incident prompted him to leave Hebei. It was after a multitude of setbacks that he became a grand master through the kind intervention of Duke Fu, and yet he got himself into trouble again by meddling in other people's affairs.

As night fell, a local resident's house caught fire. Wang Xiu knitted his brows and came up with a plan that helped Guo escape from prison. What was the plan? Truly,

> From his sleeve he stretched out his magic hand,
> And picked up the man sought by divine law.

When the house caught fire at night, Wang Xiu hastened to report to the duke his intention to let Guo go in the midst of the confusion and to attribute his escape to the fire. The duke was greatly delighted, for he had already written an order to Wang to release Guo on some pretext, an order that he now gave Wang, who accordingly proceeded to the prison, where he took the cangue off Big Brother Guo, gave him a cap to wear, and handed over the duke's letter to him, saying, "The duke wants you to go without the slightest delay to Bianjing to see Mr. Liu, commandant of the palace guards." The fire had still not subsided when Guo was out of the prison. Taking advantage of the commotion, he rushed to his former office to gather together some money and personal belongings before setting out that very night for Bianjing, Kaifeng Prefecture.

In a few days' time, he arrived in Kaifeng and found lodging. The following morning, he betook himself to the office of the Palace Command[28] to wait for an opportunity to present the letter of recommendation. It was a considerable time before Commandant Liu returned from a session in the court. There, for all to see, were

> Blue canopies floating like clouds,
> Red tassels on horse-necks jumping like flames.

This was, then, the procession of Liu Zhiyuan, commandant of the imperial guards. Stepping forward, Big Brother Guo called out some words of salute and said, "Duke Fu of the Western Capital has a letter for you. Would you be kind enough to read it?"

Commandant Liu had one of his men take the letter and follow him into the yamen. Having opened and read the letter, Commandant Liu summoned Guo, the bearer of the letter, into the hall for an exchange of greetings.

Judging by Guo Wei's refined looks, the marshal knew that he was looking at a man destined for a great career. He kept Guo as his aide-de-camp, for which Guo Wei bowed in gratitude.

Some days later, Commandant Liu was returning to the yamen with his troops when he passed by the residence of the Prime Minister Sang Weihan at a moment when Sang and his wife were looking out onto the street from the street-viewing windows installed by the gate. With Liu Zhiyuan leading the way, the procession of three hundred men was indeed an awe-inspiring sight. Looking at her husband, the lady said, "Did you see him?"

"That must be Commandant Liu," said Sang Weihan.

The lady continued, "With such airs, this man must be holding a higher position than you are."

Sang Weihan dismissed her remark with a laugh: "He is but a military man not worthy of any attention. Just watch me summon him and make him bow in deference." (*[Illegible] the beauty herself [illegible] without realizing that she, in turn, may not be to the liking of some others. This is what happens, in most cases, to eminent figures falling from power.*)

"If you can really do that," said the wife, "I will drink a toast to you. If not, you will drink a toast to me," whereupon Sang Weihan ordered his men to summon Commandant Liu.

In the meantime, he had a pair of boots placed behind the curtain. The messenger caught up with the commandant and said, "The prime minister summons you." Immediately, Liu Zhiyuan proceeded to the prime minister's mansion, dismounted from horseback, and entered the hall, where he bowed and called out a greeting. Indeed,

> A general of a mighty army
> Had to bow to a pair of boots.

Commandant Liu waited for a long time in the hall without receiving any further instructions. The fact was that Sang Weihan and his wife were so wrapped up in their drinking that they forgot to give further orders, and no one dared remind them. When evening set in, Commandant Liu could do no more than return to his own yamen. In a fit of anger, he burst out, "A true man who has gained his fame and fortune through his bow and battle-horse is now insulted by a pedantic scholar-official!" At the fifth watch, upon the first light of dawn, he was approaching the imperial court for the morning session when he saw Sang Weihan dismount from horseback and enter the hall. Anger flared up in Liu Zhiyuan. "He insulted me yesterday by making me salute his boots," he seethed. "How can he have the nerve to face me today!" Boiling with rancor, he treated Sang Weihan with disrespect during the court session, as a consequence of which he was sent away by the emperor to serve in Taiyuan as a regional commander. Now all this is less about Liu Zhiyuan's assumption of a post in Taiyuan than about Shi Hongzhao's later rise to eminence and wealth, as dictated by destiny. Truly,

> *Plant flowers with care, and they die on you;*
> *Enjoy your wine, and merrily they bloom.*

Assigned as regional commander for Taiyuan, Liu Zhiyuan left the capital and chose a day to set off on the journey to his new post. He was to lead the way with his close subordinates and attendants, while Aide-de-Camp Guo was to bring up the rear and take care of the women, children, and baggage. And so they set out on the journey.

> *Red flags fluttered in the wind;*
> *Colored banners flapped against the sky.*
> *The soldiers carried swords at their waists;*
> *The commanders held maces in their hands.*
> *At dawn, they left an isolated village;*
> *At sunset, they spurred their horses over hills.*
> *Passing by markets and bridges,*
> *They rested at inns and taverns.*
> *They saw the morning clouds in the blue sky,*
> *And watched the sun set in a red glow.*

Thus they advanced, winding their way over hills and across rivers. As they approached a forest, they saw

> *Trees standing thousands of feet high,*
> *With gnarled roots spreading far and wide.*
> *In their shade grew curious bushes,*
> *With magic mushrooms below and phoenixes above.*
> *Twigs wavered as chilly winds arose.*
> *Buds sprouted, blocking half the sky.*
> *In width, the forest covered ten li of ground;*
> *In height, it reached to the ninth heaven.*

Commandant Liu was about to pass through when a group of men appeared in front of him and blocked the way. Much taken aback, Commandant Liu took them to be robbers and was on the point of ordering his men to charge forward when the group of men spread out in a row and called out a respectful greeting. Their leader said, "The Division of Palace Guards sent me, Sergeant Shi Hongzhao, here to welcome you and escort you to Taiyuan." Impressed with Shi Hongzhao's looks as a man of heroic mettle, Liu Zhiyuan kept him as an aide-de-camp. In a few days, Shi Hongzhao arrived in Taiyuan with the commandant. When the women and children also arrived, Shi Hongzhao saw Aide-de-camp Guo and threw himself upon the ground in salutation. Thus the sworn brothers saw each other again, both as aides-de-camp with Commandant Liu as their patron. Later, after the Khitans[29] conquered the Later [Eastern] Jin dynasty, Commandant Liu led his army into Bian, with Shi and Guo as vanguards. They expelled the Khitans, and Commandant Liu took over the throne from the Later Jin, calling the new dynasty the Later Han. Henceforth, Shi Hongzhao rose in rank until he became commander of the regions of Shan, Hua, Song, and Bian. The riches and glories that he enjoyed defy description:

> Blue-curtained chariots and black-silk banners,
> Mace-carrying guards and fan-holding women.
> Warm in winter in canopies of red brocade,
> Cool in summer behind green-gauze shades.
> Led in front by two rows of maids,
> Supported at the sides by two graceful ladies.

The above story is told as old storytellers in the capital tell it. According to his biography in *The History of the Five Dynasties,* edited by Ouyang Xiu, Shi Hongzhao started as just another soldier chosen from every seventh household, as was the rule toward the end of the Later Liang dynasty. A subordinate of the commander in charge of the Vanguard Battalion, he was later selected for the imperial army. Then he rose to be a sergeant under the command of Liu Zhiyuan (later to become Emperor Gaozu of the Later Han), who, when he was in command of Taiyuan sometime later, promoted him to be a military commander and the prefect of Leizhou. On the strength of his meritorious service, he rose to be military commissioner of the Army of Loyalty and Bravery, and infantry commander-in-chief of the palace guards. From that position he was transferred to be commander-in-chief of the calvary and infantry of the palace guards, commissioner of the Pledged Allegiance Army, and assistant to the director of the Grand Secretariat before he finally became director of the Grand Secretariat. By the time Guo Wei, Emperor Taizu of the Later Zhou dynasty, took the throne, Shi Hongzhao had passed away, but was enfeoffed posthumously as prince of Zheng. There is a poem that says,

> Make friends only with strong and worthy men;
> Keep away from the feeble and the weak.
> The strong rise to fame when their time does come,
> But the weak fail in every endeavor.

風吹殘月夜
三更千里赴
魂飲舊同盟

In the dead of night, windy and moonless,
A ghost travels far to honor a pledge.

16

The Chicken-and-Millet Dinner for Fan Juqing, Friend in Life and Death

When planting trees, plant not weeping willows;
In making friends, avoid the fickle ones.
Willows cannot withstand the autumn wind;
Ties with the fickle easily form and break.
Witness how yesterday's letter speaks of the past,
But today when you meet, you know not each other.
Such friendships live shorter than the willows,
Which at least return with the spring breezes.

The above poem, titled "On Friendship," laments the difficulties in form-ing friendships. I shall now tell of a scholar named Zhang Shao, courtesy name Yuanbo, who lived in Nancheng of Ruzhou at the time of Emperor Ming [r. 58–75] of the Han dynasty. Son of a farmer, he educated himself through assiduous studies but remained unmarried at the age of thirty-five. His mother being nearly sixty-years old, he and his younger brother, Zhang Qin, worked hard in the fields to eke out a living.

At that time, the emperor was recruiting worthy men to enter his service. Zhang Shao took leave of his mother and brother and, a bag of books on his back, set out on a journey to Luoyang, the Eastern Capital, to take the exami-nations. The journey was to take several days.

One evening when he had covered most of the distance to Luoyang, he went to an inn for lodging. During the night, he heard repeated cries from an adjoining room. At last he asked the waiter if he knew who was making the noise on the other side of the wall. The waiter answered, "It's a scholar who's dying from a disease that's going around."

"Since he's a scholar, I owe him a visit," said Zhang Shao.

The clerk objected, "The disease is contagious. Even we keep away from him. You'd better not go, sir."

Shao insisted, "Life or death is a matter of fate. How can a disease be contagious? (*By no means conventional thinking.*) I must go and see him."

Over the waiter's protests, Shao pushed open the door and went in. Lying on his back on an earthen bed was a sallow-faced and emaciated man crying for help. Noticing in the room a bag of books and some articles of clothing, all of which bespoke a candidate on his way to take the examinations, Shao bent down and said into the man's ear, "You have nothing to fear, sir. I, Zhang Shao, am also a candidate for the examinations. I shall do my best to help you in your grave illness and serve you medicine and porridge. You can rest easy now."

The man said, "If you can help me get well, I shall certainly repay you well."

Shao had someone call a doctor, who dispensed some medicine. He himself attended to the patient's needs, serving him medicine and porridge. (*Such devotion is hard to come by.*)

Several days later, the patient broke out in a sweat, and his condition improved. Gradually he was able to breathe normally and regained his ability to stand up and walk. Shao found out that he was called Fan Shi, courtesy name Juqing, and that he was forty years old and a native of Shanyang in Chuzhou. He had been born into a family of merchants but lost his parents at an early age and was now married and had a son. He was there on his way to Luoyang to take the examinations, determined to abandon the life of a merchant. However, by the time Fan Juqing had fully recovered, the examinations were already over. Fan said, "The fact that my illness kept you from your pursuit of a career weighs heavily on my conscience."

Shao rejoined, "A true man values friendship and loyalty above all else. Fame and fortune are too trivial by comparison. Since it is all a matter of fate, how can you talk about having kept me from my pursuit of a career?" (*One who is ready to sacrifice his own chances at fame and fortune for the benefit of a friend is indeed a man with a true sense of loyalty and honor.*)

Henceforth, the two men developed a friendship as close as flesh and blood, and took an oath of brotherhood. As Fan Shi was the older of the two by five years, Zhang Shao honored him as older brother.

After pledging brotherhood, they stayed together day and night, and thus half a year went by before they knew it. As Fan Shi wished to return home, Zhang Shao settled the bill with the innkeeper, and the two men set out on the journey. A few days later, at the point where they were to part company, Zhang Shao offered to go with Fan Shi farther down the road, but Fan Shi objected, saying, "If you do, I will need to walk you back. It's best for us to say good-bye here and set up a time to meet again."

As they went into a wineshop for a drink, their eyes fell upon yellow chrysanthemums and red leaves, a riot of autumn colors that provided a cheerful setting for the scene of farewell. The sight of dogwood petals floating in the wine cups prompted them to ask the shopkeeper what day it was. They were told that it was the Double-Ninth Festival.[1]

Fan Shi said, "Since my parents died when I was young, I have submitted myself to a life as a merchant. However hard I try to apply myself to my studies of the classics, I am hampered by my wife and son. My good brother, you are fortunate that your mother is still with you. Since your mother is also my mother, I will come to your house on this day next year to pay my respects to her in acknowledgement of the family tie."

"But our home in a humble village has hardly anything to offer to you," said Zhang Shao. "Yet, since you will have the goodness to come, I shall prepare some chicken and millet for you. Please do not let me down."

"How could I ever let my good brother down?" said Fan Shi.

After several drinks, they still could not bear to take leave of each other, but Zhang Shao bowed to Fan Shi in a gesture of farewell, and, after Fan had turned away, he tearfully gazed at his back. Fan Shi also looked back, tears in his eyes, and so they sadly took leave of each other, as these lines attest:

> With chrysanthemums floating in their wine,
> They pledge to meet again in one year's time.
> By the forked road they linger, hating to part;
> Hand in hand, they stand with sad tears streaming.

Upon his return, Zhang Yuanbo went to his mother, who said to him, "My son, you sent no message home all the time you were away. I've been waiting for you as the hungry and thirsty wait for food and drink."

"Your unfilial son," said Zhang Shao, "met Fan Juqing of Shanyang on his way to the examination site and pledged brotherhood with him. That is why I was delayed for so long."

"What kind of man is Juqing?"

After Zhang Shao's detailed description, she commented, "Fame and fortune are all a matter of fate. I am pleased that you have made friends with a man who has a true sense of loyalty." (*What a good mother! Like mother, like son.*)

In a short while, Zhang Shao's younger brother came home. Zhang Shao repeated his account, and his brother also was delighted to hear it.

Henceforth Zhang Shao applied himself anew to the study of the classics, and thus time sped by. Soon the Double-Ninth Festival was drawing near. Shao had raised a fat chicken and brewed some wine for the occasion. On the day of the festival, he rose bright and early and swept clean the main hall, in the middle of which he placed a chair for his mother and, to one side, a chair for Fan Juqing. Having filled the vases with chrysanthemums and lit the incense sticks on the table, he called his brother to help him kill the chicken and get the meal ready in Juqing's honor.

"Shanyang is a good thousand li away from here," said his mother. "Juqing might not be able to come on time. It won't be too late to kill the chicken after he arrives."

"Juqing is a man of his word," rejoined Shao. "He will surely be here today to keep the 'chicken-and-millet' appointment. If he sees what I promised to serve for the meal the moment he steps in, he will know that I have indeed been waiting for him. If I kill the chicken after his arrival, my sincerity will be less apparent."

"Any friend of my son's must be a worthy man," said his mother.

Thereupon, preparation of the chicken got under way in anticipation of the guest's arrival.

It was a fine day without a cloud in the vast expanse of clear sky. Shao adjusted his clothes and cap and stood at the farm gate by himself on the lookout for his friend, but the better part of the morning went by without any sign of a visitor. Afraid that farm work would be delayed, his mother told Zhang Qin to reap the crops in the fields. At each dog-bark in the next village, Zhang Shao would go forth expectantly, and thus he went back and forth six or seven times. Meanwhile, the red sun sank below the western horizon, yielding to a new crescent moon. The old lady emerged from the door and told her younger son to relay these words to Shao: "You must be tired from standing so long. It looks like Juqing is not coming today. Why don't you come back for dinner?"

Shao said to his brother, "How do you know Juqing is not coming? I swear not to return until he is here. Now you must be tired from the farm work. You should go ahead and take a rest." And so he turned a deaf ear to repeated pleas from his mother and brother, and waited till night deepened. After everyone had retired for the night, Shao still leaned against the gate as if in a trance. At every rustle of the wind in the trees and grass, he would startle and think to himself, "Might this be him?" But all that could be seen was the dark sky bestrewn with the shining stars of the Milky Way. At almost the third watch of the night, the moonlight faded away. In the engulfing darkness, there appeared indistinctly a human figure approaching along with the wind. A close look convinced Shao that it was Juqing. Shao leapt with joy and said with two bows, "I have been waiting for you since this morning, knowing that you would not fail me, and here you are indeed! The chicken and the millet that I promised you last year have long been ready for serving. It's been a long and tiring journey. Didn't you bring a companion with you? Please go into the hall and meet my mother."

Without a word of reply, Fan Shi headed straight for the hall. Zhang Shao pointed at the seat reserved for him and said, "I put this seat of honor here especially for you." Smiling radiantly, Zhang Shao continued, with two more deep bows, "You must be tired from such a long journey. Before you go to see my mother, please take some of the homemade wine, the chicken that I raised, and the millet to stay your hunger." So saying, he made another bow.

Fan Shi stood rigidly without uttering a word, shielding his face with his sleeve. Shao rushed into the kitchen and came back with the chicken, millet, and wine, which he placed in front of Fan, saying with two more bows, "Humble as the offer is, it comes from my heart. Please don't reproach me."

In the darkness, Fan was seen fanning the aroma toward his nose, without taking any of the food and wine.[2]

Shao asked, "Is it because my mother and brother failed to go out of the house to meet you that you refuse to eat? Please allow me to bring my mother out, and we will apologize together to you."

Fan shook his hand in protest. Shao continued, "Then, shall I call my younger brother forth to greet you?" Fan shook his hand again.

"In that case, said Shao, "would you like to have some chicken and millet before I offer you some wine?"

Fan frowned as if telling Zhang Shao to step back. Shao said, "However inappropriate chicken and millet are for an honored guest, these are what I promised you before. Please do not take offense."

"Please take a step back, my brother," said Fan. "I will tell you everything. I am not a mortal of this world, but a ghost from the netherworld."

Shao was aghast. "How can you say such a thing?"

"After we parted, I was preoccupied with business concerns in order to support my wife and son. I was so deeply entangled in worldly affairs that a whole year went by without my noticing it. It is not that I didn't have our 'chicken-and-millet' appointment at heart, but that worries about puny business profits pushed the date of the appointment out of my mind. I did not know that today was the Double-Ninth Festival until this morning, when my neighbors sent over some dogwood wine. I was heartbroken when I realized I had forgotten about the appointment with you. The thousand-li distance from Shanyang to your place is not to be covered within one day. But should I have failed to keep the appointment, what would my good brother have thought of me? If a promise for such a trivial thing were to be easily broken, what would happen if a matter of greater importance were at stake? (*What can be of greater importance than death? For whatever they do, men of heroic mettle have in mind not what lies immediately under their eyes but what will last for generations to come.*) I was at my wit's end when I recalled a saying by the ancients: 'A man cannot travel a thousand li, but a ghost can in one day.' So I told my wife, 'After I die, do not bury me until my brother Zhang Yuanbo comes.' That said, I cut my own throat, and my spirit rode on a gust of wind from the netherworld to be here for the 'chicken-and-millet' appointment.

Please be compassionate, forgive my negligence, and appreciate my sincerity in committing this act of violence. If you can leave your home and take a thousand-li journey to Shanyang for a look at my body, I shall close my eyes in death without regret." With tears gushing from his eyes, he abruptly left his seat and went down the steps. Shao followed, but a false step landed him on a patch of moss, and he fell to the ground. After a puff of chilly wind blew past, Juqing disappeared from view. There is a poem in evidence:

> *In the dead of night, windy and moonless,*
> *A ghost travels far to honor a pledge.*
> *Vows are broken easily by mortals,*
> *But he laid down his life to prove his worth.*

As if in a trance, Zhang Shao burst into loud wails of grief. In alarm, his mother and brother rose and rushed out for a look, only to see a display of chicken, millet, wine, and fruit in the hall, and Zhang Yuanbo lying unconscious on the ground. They revived him with a splash of water and helped him into the hall. For a considerable time he could not speak a word but kept weeping bitterly.

His mother asked, "Why are you so upset about your brother Juqing not showing up? Is so much crying worth it?"

"Juqing died before his time in order to keep the appointment with me."

"How do you know this?"

"Just a moment ago, I saw Juqing come with my own eyes. I invited him in and offered him the chicken and millet. Because he didn't take any of the food, I pleaded with him time and again until he said that his business concerns had made him forget the appointment until this morning when he woke up. Afraid of breaking his promise, he cut his own throat, and his spirit traveled a thousand li to see me. Mother, please let me go to Shanyang to bury my elder brother's body. I will pack and set out as early as tomorrow morning."

His mother said between sobs, "The ancients said, 'A prisoner dreams about pardon; a thirsty man dreams about water.' My son, what appeared to you was a dream, because you have been thinking about him all the time."

"That was no dream. I did indeed see him. The wine and the food are still here. I fell when I tried to follow him. How could this have been a dream? Juqing is a man of integrity. How could he have told a lie?"

His younger brother said, "I don't believe what I hear. We should ask someone who goes to Shanyang to find out if all this is true."

Shao said in reply, "Human lives are subordinate to the laws of heaven and earth. To match the five elements of heaven and earth—metal, wood, water, fire, and earth—there are, in people, the five virtues of benevolence, righteousness, propriety, wisdom, and fidelity, and among them, the virtue of overriding importance is that of fidelity. Benevolence matches wood because of its life-generating quality. Righteousness matches metal because it shares the quality of firmness. Courtesy matches water because of its humble modesty. Wisdom matches fire because of its brilliance. Fidelity matches earth because of its weightiness. Confucius said, 'If carriages, large or small, lack the means to hold in place the crossbars that yoke oxen or horses to them, what is there to make them go?'³ Also, 'Since time immemorial, people have had to die, but they cannot survive if there is no trust.'⁴ Juqing died for the sake of fidelity. How can I fail to go because of a lack of fidelity? My younger brother's farm work should produce enough to support Mother. After I'm gone, you should be doubly respectful, and serve Mother day and night with never a misstep." (*This trip will mean his death. Surely Juqing's death cannot be unaccompanied by Zhang Shao's death.*)

He turned to his mother and said these words of farewell: "This unfilial son Zhang Shao has to go to mourn his sworn older brother, Fan Juqing, who died for the sake of fidelity. I have repeatedly reminded Zhang Qin to take care of you, Mother. Please try to eat well and free your mind from worries. Take good care of yourself. Having done nothing in the service of the empire or the family, I am living a wasted life, which provides all the more reason for me to go and fulfill at least my obligation of fidelity."

His mother said, "A trip to Shanyang a thousand li away should not take you more than a month. Why did you say such ominous things?"

Shao said, "Life is as fragile as foam. Death may befall us any moment of the day." He broke down in tears and made another bow.

"Shall I go with you?" said his younger brother.

Shao declined his offer: "Mother will have no one to take care of her. You should do your best to serve Mother well so that I will have no worries." Tearfully he bade farewell to his younger brother and, a bag of books on his back, set out on his journey the following morning. There is a poem in evidence:

> To Shanyang he went, leaving kith and kin;
> The long journey gave him much time to dream.
> Not that he valued his flesh and blood less,
> But that he honored fidelity more.

Along the way, he gave no heed to what he ate when hungry or what he wore when cold. While sleeping at inns at night, he wept even in his sleep. Every day he rose early to press on with the journey. How he wished to grow two wings! Several days later, he arrived in Shanyang. After inquiries about Juqing's address, he headed straight for the house, only to find the door under lock and key. The neighbors, when asked, told him, "Juqing has been dead for fourteen days. His wife has left with the coffin for the burial ceremony outside the city wall, and the mourners have not yet come back."

Shao asked where the burial site was and hastened toward the outskirts of the city. There, in front of a wooded hill, was a newly erected earthen wall, by which stood several tens of people staring at each other in amazement. Perspiring all over, Shao drew near and saw a woman in mourning clothes and a boy about seventeen or eighteen years old bent over a coffin, crying. Shao shouted, "Might this be Fan Juqing's coffin?"

"Might you be Zhang Yuanbo?" asked the woman.

"Yes, but I have never been here before. How do you know my name?"

The woman said tearfully, "My husband's last words were all about you. My husband Fan Juqing often talked about your kindness after he came back from Luoyang. At the Double-Ninth Festival, he said to me in a sudden fit of panic, 'I've lost my friend Zhang Yuanbo's trust. What meaning can life have for me now? I have often heard that a thousand-li journey is beyond any living man's ability. I would rather die than fail to keep the 'chicken-and-millet' appointment. Do not bury me after I die until Yuanbo comes to see my corpse.' Today being already the fourteenth day after his death, people urged me, saying, 'Go ahead with the burial, for there is no telling when Yuanbo will come. It will not be out of turn to notify him after the burial.' That's why I escorted the coffin all the way here. The men have been trying to lower the coffin into the pit, but it would not budge. And so here we were standing in astonishment in front of the grave, unable to get anything done. And then you appeared, running from afar in great haste. I guessed it must be you."

Yuanbo threw himself onto the ground in a violent fit of weeping. The woman also broke down in tears in heart-rending agony. There was not a dry eye among all those present.

Shao took some money out of his bag for the purchase of some offerings, incense, candles, and paper money, which were then arranged in a display in front of the coffin. He took out an elegy and, having poured out a libation on the ground, he bowed twice and read the following, between bitter sobs:

> *On this day of the —— month of the —— year, I, Zhang Shao, your younger brother, do hereby offer a chicken roasted in wine and other sacrificial offerings to the spirit of my older brother, Fan Juqing:*
>
> *Your noble spirit soars as high as the rainbow and your sense of loyalty is as exalted as the Milky Way. It was my good fortune to have known you and developed a friendship with you in a deserted roadside inn. It was on a Double Ninth day that we pledged to meet again, and it was on the same day a year later that a sword took your life. Your forlorn spirit in the moonlight reminded me of your loving self in the sun-filled world of the living. I have taken leave of my mother to come and visit your grave. You, my brother, also told your wife to wait for the*

carriage covered in white ribbons of mourning.[5] *Old friends honor their friend-*
ship in life as well as in death. Who would be willing to betray an eternal pledge?
A true man makes light of his life and readily takes up the sword. His sword
never dulls throughout eternity; his promise he never fails to keep. Should my
brother's soul remain, I shall have an eternal companion in the netherworld.
Alas! Please accept these offerings.

Opening the coffin lid for a look, Yuanbo burst into wails of grief that shook
the earth. He turned to Juqing's widow and said, "My elder brother died for
my sake. How can I live without him? In my bag there is enough money for
a coffin. My sister-in-law, if you could show compassion and bury me by his
side, that would be the greatest blessing of my life."

"How can my brother-in-law say such a thing?" said she.

"My mind is made up," said Shao. "Please do not be frightened." So saying, he drew out his sword and cut his own throat. Everyone was appalled.
They made sacrifices to him and buried him, complete with grave clothes and
a coffin, in Juqing's grave.

When word reached the ears of the local prefect, he wrote a memorial to
the emperor to report the matter. Impressed with the expression of such loyalty between two friends, Emperor Ming granted the two men posthumous
titles to provide inspiration for posterity, although they had never gained
office in life. Fan Juqing was granted the title of duke of Shanyang and Zhang
Yuanbo that of duke of Runan. In front of the grave bearing the inscription
"Tomb of Loyalty" was erected a shrine named the Shrine of Loyalty. The
two men's families were given great honor and provided by the government
with food and clothing for the raising of Juqing's son, Fan Chunshou. He later
passed the imperial examinations, became a *jinshi,* and rose to be head of the
Court for Dependencies.[6] Of the multitude of poems inscribed on these ancient
monuments that remain in Shanyang to this day, the best is the lyric poem "Ta
Sha Xing" by an anonymous poet:

> Over a distance of a thousand li,
> Over a span of one long year,
> They kept in their hearts the pledge they had made.
> One had his soul keep his promise;
> The other cooked the chicken and millet in vain.

> By the dim lamp on a moonless night,
> Tears fell in unbroken threads.
> In life, in death, their love knew no border.
> With the coffin waiting for the friend to arrive,
> In the next world, with a smile, they meet again.

Shan Fulang's Happy Marriage in Quanzhou

The gate of Jiaru opens to the skies,
Guarding the city founded in the Zhou.
Claim not that virtue has no lock and key;
The empire was secure for eight hundred years.[1]

What is described in the above quatrain is the Western Capital [Xijing],[2] the seat of government of nine emperors of the Song dynasty and a city of unsurpassed prosperity, with the cities of Chenggao on its left, Mianchi on its right, and Yijue before it and the Yellow River behind it. I shall now tell of a County Magistrate Xing and a Judge Shan, both natives of the Western Capital, who lived next door to each other on Filial Piety Street. As their wives happened to be sisters, the men addressed each other as "Brother-in-law" and, with frequent visits back and forth, were as intimate as one family, though under different family names. Before the two men had gained office, the two sisters made a pledge to each other when they got pregnant at the same time: "Should we have a boy and a girl, we shall make them husband and wife." It turned out that the Shan family had a boy, whom they named Fulang, and the Xing family had a girl, whom they named Chunniang [Spring Girl]. The two sisters thereupon talked their husbands into the idea, and henceforth they treated each other as in-laws. Fulang and Chunniang often played together when they were small and were called the "young couple" by the two families. Later, after they had grown up, Fulang, under the new name of Feiying, with the courtesy name of Tengshi, entered a school to study, and Chunniang remained in the seclusion of her boudoir. The two stopped seeing each other.

In the third month of the seventh year in the reign period of Xuanhe [1125] under Emperor Huizong of the Song dynasty, Mr. Xing was appointed as magistrate of the county of Shunyang in Dengzhou, and Mr. Shan Senior was selected as judge of Yangzhou. Before they left with their families to assume their respective posts, they pledged to return upon completion of their terms of office to the Western Capital to hold the wedding ceremony. Taking his wife and son Fulang with him, Judge Shan went to Yangzhou, and there I shall leave them.

Let us follow Magistrate Xing to the county of Shunyang in Dengzhou, where, in less than six months, Jurchens[3] swept in from different directions and the Jurchen general Wolipu[4] took Shunyang. With the exception of the twelve-year-old Chunniang, the entire family of County Magistrate Xing perished. Some riotous soldiers kidnapped her and sold her to a brothel owned by a certain Yang family in Quanzhou for seventeen thousand in cash. Having studied the classics and a thousand Tang dynasty poems at an early age, Chunniang was quite literate and was especially skilled in the art of conversation. Treasured dearly by the madam of the brothel, she, now named Yang Yu, learned to play musical instruments and to sing and dance, and she became most accomplished in these skills. Truly,

> *In beauty, she outshone all court ladies.*
> *In song and dance she was without equal.*

One thing that distinguished her from the rest of the girls was that, being from a genteel official's family, she was demure and well-mannered. After performing at feasts in a yamen, all the other girls always flirted wantonly with the men, stopping at nothing, while she alone stood by herself in silence, never speaking or laughing improperly, more like a well-bred woman than a courtesan. For this, she won much admiration and respect from all and sundry.

Our story forks at this point. Let me now turn to Judge Shan. In the third year of his term of office, the Jurchens took Bianjing[5] and kidnapped Emperors Huizong and Qinzong. Lü Haowen [1064–1131] persuaded Zhang Bangchang, the puppet emperor, to welcome Prince Kang as the successor to the throne. Prince Kang crossed the river into the south and ascended the throne in Yingtianfu.[6] He became Emperor Gaozong. Out of fear of the Jurchens, Emperor Gaozong dared not return to the Western Capital but moved to Yangzhou. Because of his outstanding service leading the militia in protecting the emperor, Judge Shan was promoted repeatedly until he was appointed a vice minister and followed the emperor [from Yangzhou] to Hangzhou. Enraptured by the beautiful scenery of Hangzhou, Emperor Gaozong settled down there and made Hangzhou the new capital under the name Lin'an [Temporary Peace], as the following poem attests:

> *With hill upon green hill, tower upon tower,*
> *How long can the West Lake songs and dances last?*
> *Intoxicated by the warm breezes,*
> *The sightseer takes Hangzhou for Bianzhou.[7]*

The northwestern regions being overrun by the Jurchens, countless civilians followed Emperor Gaozong to the Wu region in the south. As word about the new capital Lin'an spread around, many moved there and settled down as registered residents.

When going over the registry books in the Census Bureau, Mr. Shan noticed the name of Xing Xiang, a native of the Western Capital. He pondered to himself, "Could this Xing Xiang be a brother of County Magistrate Xing Zhen?" Ever since they parted to take up their respective official posts, he had heard nothing from the Xing family and wondered about their fate. Quietly he sent someone to investigate. It turned out that this man was indeed County Magistrate Xing's younger brother, known as Master Xing the Fourth. Without losing a moment, he invited Mr. Xing over and asked him for news.

"After Dengzhou fell," answered Mr. Xing, "I heard that my older brother and every member of his family died, but I am not sure if this is true." With these words, tears flowed down his cheeks. Nor could Mr. Shan contain his grief. Considering that his son was old enough to marry, he thought of arranging another marriage, but hoping against hope that the rumor was groundless and that his daughter-in-law was still alive, he decided to wait until peace was restored before making inquiries. Henceforth, Mr. Shan and Master Xing the Fourth honored each other as relatives and remained in frequent contact.

Now, when Emperor Gaozong first ascended the throne, he changed the reign title to Jianyan [1127–30], which, four years later, was changed to Shaoxing [1131–62]. In the first year of Shaoxing, in appreciation of Mr. Shan's service in escorting him to the south, the emperor appointed Mr. Shan's son Shan Feiying revenue manager of Quanzhou. After thanking the emperor for the favor, Mr. Shan Junior took leave of his parents on a chosen day and set out on his journey to Quanzhou to assume his post. The handsome eighteen-year-old Revenue Manager Shan, the youngest official in the county, won admiration from all who laid their eyes on him. On the day he took up office, the prefect set out a feast attended by a host of courtesan singers. As a matter of fact, according to custom in the Song dynasty, all registered prostitutes were considered to be at the service of the government. All dinners held at the yamen, for business as well as private reasons, were occasions to summon courtesans. On that day, Yang Yu was among those summoned. Of all the courtesans present, she was the only one whom Revenue Manager Shan found appealing. In fact, he felt himself quite attracted to her. As the poem says,

> A predestined bond ties them wherever they go,
> The gifted youth and the fair maiden.
> When will he, like Zhang the loving husband,
> Lean by the window and paint his wife's eyebrows?[8]

Zheng An, administrator for public order, a talented young man of an old family from Xingyang, had taken a liking to Shan the very first time he saw him. Noticing Shan's glances at Yang Yu, Administrator Zheng guessed what was on his mind. One day, when paying Shan a visit, Zheng asked, "Why did you, a nice young man from a good family, come to assume your post all alone, without bringing your family along?"

Shan answered, "To tell you the truth, I've been engaged ever since childhood, but I have no knowledge whether my betrothed is dead or alive after the turbulence of the Jurchen invasion. That's why I'm still unmarried."

Zheng said with a smile, "Who in the world is exempt from the feeling of loneliness? How would the graceful courtesan-singer Yang Yu do as a 'plum for you to look at to quench your thirst,' so to speak?"

Shan demurred at first, but, after much persuasion by Zheng, who claimed to understand his mind, he stopped trying to hide his true feelings, and laid them bare.

"If the gifted scholar is taken with the beautiful lady," said Zheng An, "I will, of course, offer my help to bring about the union." (*Smart fellow.*)

Henceforth, every time he saw Yang Yu at a dinner, Revenue Manager Shan deliberately avoided throwing glances her way, so as not to arouse suspicions, but his longing for her grew more intense. As eager as he was to bring about the union, Administrator Zheng found himself unable to do anything, out of fear of the strict prefect.

Two years later, the incumbent prefect left upon expiration of his term of office. The new prefect, Chen by name, was a sincere and kind man. The prefect being an old acquaintance of Zheng's from the same native town, Zheng repeatedly recommended to him the talent and the integrity of Revenue Manager Shan. The prefect thus came to hold Shan in high regard.

One day, Zheng set out some wine and invited Shan to his private quarters for a talk, to be waited upon by Yang Yu alone. Unlike the usual feasts swarming with people, this time, with only the host present, Shan was able to look freely at Yang Yu, and he found her truly beautiful. There is a lyric poem to the tune of "Remembering the Lady of Qin" that says,

> She stands before the wine vessel,
> Fragrant and fair as jade,
> Her hair adorned with pins
> Of kingfisher feathers and gold phoenix,
> Her dress in the style of ladies of the court.
> Wearing a demure frown on her brows,
> She sings to people only plaintive songs,
> Full of sorrow over the trials of life.

Zheng started by saying, "Today, there being no other guests, we will dispense with the usual etiquette—we will drink to our hearts' content and have as much fun as possible." Filling a huge wine vessel, he offered it to Shan, who drank while Yang Yu sang songs to add to the pleasure.

When he was well-warmed with wine, Shan fixed his gaze upon Yang Yu in such rapt fascination that he was not able to control himself and feigned drunkenness as an excuse to stop drinking.

Knowing what was on his mind, Zheng suggested, "Why don't you go to the study to take a rest. I'll offer you more wine later."

Shan was in no mood to admire the books, paintings, chess set, musical instruments, and antiques in the room where Zheng did his reading, but flung himself onto the bamboo couch for a nap.

Zheng said, "Rest for a while if the wine is too much for you." Rushing out, he told Yang Yu to make a pot of jasmine tea and take it into the room.

Shan was well aware of Zheng's intentions to bring him and Yang Yu together. Now that Yang Yu came in with the tea all by herself, he knew that Zheng was letting him have his way. With alacrity, he rose from the couch, closed the door, held Yang Yu in his arms, and asked for intimacy. Yang Yu feigned unwillingness, but Shan insisted, "I have long been admiring you, and this is a chance that's hard to come by. The administrator is a good friend of mine. He will not mind, even if he knows about this."

Yang Yu also gained a good idea of what was afoot. She did not firmly resist but had to submit. On the couch, they had a brief game of clouds and rain. There is a poem that bears witness:

> For two years they admired each other;
> Now came the time to fulfill their desire.
> Though it did not last the whole night long,
> It was better than daydreaming in vain.

Shan asked Yang Yu quietly, "With such outstanding talent and elegance that set you apart from all other courtesans, you must be from a good family. Now don't hide anything from me. Tell me the truth. Who *are* you?"

With shame written all over her face, Yang Yu answered, "The truth is that I am indeed from an official's family but got stranded here. I am not Madam Yang's daughter."

Flabbergasted, Shan asked further, "What, then, is the name of your father, and what office did he hold?"

Before she realized it, tears gushed out from her eyes. "My true last name is Xing," said she. "I used to live on Filial Piety Street in the Eastern Capital.[9] In my childhood I was betrothed to my aunt's son. After my father was appointed magistrate of Shunyang County in Dengzhou, the barbarian invaders came and ravaged the land. Both of my parents died from their swords, and I ended up being kidnapped and sold to this place."

Shan pursued his questioning: "What is the name of the family you were to marry into? What office does your father-in-law hold? What is the name of your betrothed?"

"It's the family of Shan I was to marry into. My father-in-law was the judge of Yangzhou. His son is called Fulang, but I have no idea if he is still alive." With these words, she broke down in passionate weeping.

By now Shan already knew that she was none other than Chunniang. But, instead of telling her the truth, he only comforted her by saying, "Now that you have more fine clothes, good food, and romance than you need, and even government officials treat you with respect, who would ever snub you? Moreover, being separated from your family and knowing nothing about the fate of your prospective husband, you can very well spend the rest of your life enjoying whatever your fate offers you. Why all this grief and weeping?"

With a frown, Yang Yu countered, "I have heard that 'all women are born with the desire for a home.' I am where I am because I have no other choice. My fiancé's family being of high status, I cherish no hope of marrying him even if he turns out to be safe and sound. I only wish I could marry some humble commoner and live the life, however simple, of a decent woman with a family. That'll be thousands of times better than entertaining customers in this place." (*Sad words.*)

Shan nodded in agreement. "That's true. If you do indeed mean it, I'll do something to help you."

Yang Yu said with a bow, "If you can deliver me from this misery, you will have accumulated enough credit in the netherworld to last you for thousands of generations."

Before the words were quite out of her mouth, Administrator Zheng pushed open the door and said, stepping in, "Have you woken up from your dreams? If you have nothing pressing, we can drink some more wine."

"No," objected Shan. "I've had too much. I can't drink any more."

"You are ten times more intoxicated from love than from wine," said Zheng.

Shan corrected him: "I am ten times more intoxicated from admiration for virtue than from wine." They all burst out laughing.

The table was laid out anew with clean wine cups and more wine. They did not take leave of each other until after they had enjoyed themselves to the full.

Several days later, Shan prepared some wine, invited Zheng, and summoned Yang Yu for service. Yang Yu having arrived first, Shan said to her gravely, with none of the previous flirtatiousness, "You said the other day that you would be content to marry a humble commoner. Would you be willing to live with me now that my wife has died and I have not yet found a replacement for her?"

Yang Yu answered in tears, "A thorny bush is by no means a resting place for a phoenix. Since you are kind enough to take me, it is indeed my wish to leave this life of sending off and welcoming clients, and to serve you and enjoy ample food and clothing. I am only afraid that your future wife might be of too stern a disposition to tolerate me. I will certainly restrain myself and submit to her, but, should she get too harsh, I will gladly enter the service of the Buddha and stay single for the rest of my life to repay your kindness."

Saddened by these words, Shan now fully realized that she did indeed mean it when she expressed distaste for her life as a courtesan.

In a short while, Zheng arrived. Seeing Yang Yu's tear-stained face, he teased, "The ancients said, 'Extreme joy begets sorrow.' Is that the case?"

Yang Yu replied gravely, "The sorrow comes from the depth of my heart. There is no end to it."

After Shan told Zheng what Yang Yu had said about marrying, Zheng said, "If you indeed wish to do so, I will gladly do what I can to help." They set to drinking, and the rest of the day passed without further ado.

After the dinner was over, Shan wrote a letter to his parents by candlelight, saying, "My father-in-law, County Magistrate Xing, perished with the rest of his family, except Chunniang, who ended up as a courtesan. She detests her life of shame and harbors aspirations that are most admirable. I do not mind her lowly status and would gladly fulfill the old pledge of marriage." Mr. Shan Senior was greatly taken aback upon reading the letter. Without a moment's delay, he asked Master Xing the Fourth over and discussed the matter with him. The two men were overcome with emotion. Mr. Xing offered to go personally to Quanzhou to make arrangements for the wedding and asked Mr. Shan Senior to write a letter to the prefect, asking him to remove Chunniang's name from the register of entertainers. Mr. Shan Senior accordingly wrote the letter and gave it to Mr. Xing, who then took his leave and set off on his journey. In a matter of days, he arrived at Quanzhou, went directly to Shan's yamen, and stated the purpose of his visit.

When consulted by Revenue Manager Shan, Zheng was most encouraging, saying, "There is a proverb that says, 'A man changes friends when he rises to power, and changes wives when he becomes rich.' Your willingness to marry a courtesan and your disregard for her drop in status put you in the same class with the noblest ancients." Thereupon he went with Shan to see the prefect, and told him the whole story.

After reading the letter from Mr. Shan Senior, the prefect said, "This is a wonderful thing. How can I refuse?"

The following day, Master Xing the Fourth handed in a formal request for Chunniang to be released from her registered status as a courtesan so that she could fulfill her pledge of marriage, a request that the prefect approved in Master Xing's presence.

The morning passed without any document coming from the prefect. Growing apprehensive, Shan quietly sent someone to find out if things had taken an unexpected turn. He learned that chefs were busy preparing for a feast. "In whose honor?" he asked himself. "Could it be a farewell dinner for Yang Yu? But since preparations are already under way, there's nothing I can do but wait and see."

Shortly thereafter, Yang Yu was indeed summoned to serve at the feast to which the prefect had invited only one guest, the controller general. After three rounds of wine and two courses of food, the prefect called Yang Yu to his side and told her about Shan's offer to fulfill the old marriage pledge and Xing Xiang's request that she be relieved of her present registered status.

With a bow of gratitude, Yang Yu said, "Sir, I owe you my life and my honor."

The prefect continued, "A courtesan today, but an honorable lady tomorrow. Now, how are you going to repay me?"

Yang Yu replied, "You have accumulated a mountain-high pile of credits in the netherworld by delivering me from misery. The only thing I can do is pray to heaven day and night that your descendants be blessed with wealth and rank."

The prefect said with a sigh, "I will never again see a beauty like you." In spite of himself, he stepped forward, put his arms around Yang Yu, and said, "Repay me now!"

Seeing that the prefect had lost control of himself, the controller general, being a man of honor, stood up and said harshly, "Since she has long been betrothed to the revenue manager, she is no less than a lady to be honored by us as the wife of a colleague. A gentleman should follow proper conduct and refrain from any act that might deviate from the right decorum."

In embarrassment (*He cannot but feel embarrassed, for this is no less than a lecture on morals*) the prefect said thankfully, "I should not have been so carried away. I wouldn't have realized my error had you not reminded me. Now that I have given offense to the revenue manager, I owe him a sincere apology." Thereupon he asked Yang Yu to go to his private quarters to make acquaintance with the women in his family, while he summoned Administrator Zheng and Revenue Manager Shan to the back hall for the feast. They did not part company until daybreak.

Without returning to his private quarters, the prefect went directly to the morning court session and issued an order that the Yang family remove Yang Yu's name from the registry. Caught by surprise, Mr. Yang and his wife came to see the prefect with loud wails, saying, "We have spared no pains taking care of this daughter for over ten years, but we dare not resist your order. Our only wish is to bid her farewell. We'll be content with just another look at her."

The prefect sent Yang Yu the message. Standing in the back hall, Yang Yu said to the couple from the other side of the screen, "It is a good thing that I am reuniting with my husband. I have indeed benefited from your kindness for ten years, yet the money I have earned for you is enough to provide for you in your old age. We shall never meet again. Please put me out of your thoughts."

The madam was still shedding copious tears when the prefect sharply ordered the couple to leave the hall. He then had some attendants carry Yang Yu out from the back hall all the way to Shan's yamen and, out of his private account, gave Shan a hundred thousand in cash for the latter to use toward wedding expenses. The revenue manager repeatedly declined the offer and finally accepted it only at the prefect's adamant insistence. On that day, with Administrator Zheng as the matchmaker and Master Xing the Fourth as the master of ceremonies, the wedding was held in accordance with proper etiquette, complete with decorated candles in the bridal chamber. There is a poem in evidence:

> The man in love was burning with desire;
> The demure lady no less passionate.
> Tonight in their room, they fulfilled their pledge,
> Lest he be labeled a heartless man.

On the following day, the prefect and the entire assembly of officials in the prefecture came to offer their congratulations. The revenue manager set out wine for the guests. Master Xing the Fourth went back to Lin'an to report to Mr. Shan Senior. The love between the new couple does not need further description here.

Time sped by like an arrow. Before they knew it, Shan's three-year term of office came to an end. Chunniang said to her husband, "In my years in the courtesans' quarters, Mr. Yang and his wife treated me kindly and I made close friends with some of my sisters. Now that I am going to a faraway place, I will never get to see them again. Would you allow me to prepare a modest farewell dinner in their honor?"

"Who in the entire prefecture has not heard about your story?" said Shan. "What is there to hide from anyone? There is nothing inappropriate in bidding farewell over a cup of wine." (*Typical of a gallant man. A pedantic scholar would say this is superfluous, like adding feet to the drawing of a snake.*)

Thereupon, Chunniang laid out a feast in Huisheng Monastery and invited Mr. Yang and his wife and over ten of the girls she was friends with. Shan sent a messenger to wait at the monastery for everybody to arrive before notifying him. The Yang couple were the first to arrive, followed one after another by the courtesans. The messenger counted the heads to make sure that everyone had arrived before he reported to the revenue manager. Escorted by a host of attendants, the lady mounted the sedan-chair and proceeded to Huisheng Monastery, where she exchanged greetings with all the guests and, after some amenities, sat down at the feast table. After rounds of wine, Chunniang left her seat to serve wine around the table.

One of the courtesans, Li Ying, a next-door neighbor of the Yang family, used to call Chunniang Elder Sister and had learned from the latter all of her musical skills. The two had been as loving as sisters born of the same parents. Since Chunniang left, Li Ying missed her so much that she often plunged into moods of dejection. Now when Chunniang stopped at her side to pour her more wine, she grabbed her hand and said, "You have lifted yourself out of the mud to soar above the clouds up on high, but I am still bogged down in this filth, with no end in sight. We are now as far apart as heaven and hell. Will you do something to save me?" With these words, she burst into loud sobs.

Overcome with grief, Chunniang also broke down in tears.

Now this Li Ying was most accomplished in the art of sewing, able to sew in the dark without missing one fraction of a stitch. Truly,

> Of old, Lady Zhao[10] wove with wondrous skills,
> But few are women with needles divine.
> Who has the art of the Weaving Maid Star?
> Courtesan Li in the house of pleasure.

Chunniang said, "It just so happens that my husband needs a seamstress. Would you be willing to live with us?"

"If you can get me out of here, you'll be doing a great work of merit. If your husband needs a seamstress anyway, I'd be a better choice than just any stranger." (*This will prove to be a more remarkable predestined marriage bond.*)

"That's true," said the Chunniang, "but you have always been my equal in every way. How can you take a position beneath mine?"

Li Ying objected, "Even in our old days, I was your inferior. Now with you high in heaven and me down on earth in the mud, plus the difference in status in your household, I'd be most content waiting on you day and night. How would I dream of being your equal?"

"In that case, I will talk this matter over with the revenue manager."

After the guests had dispersed, Chunniang returned to her residence and raised the matter with her husband.

"Once is enough," he said with a laugh. "How can I do the same thing a second time!"

Despite Chunniang's urges, the revenue manager remained adamant. Chunniang sulked for days on end.

In the meantime, Li Ying sent someone to pay her respects to the lady by way of reminding her of the matter. Chunniang said to her husband, "Sister Li Ying is of a gentle disposition and unsurpassed in the art of sewing. To have such a helpmate would be a rare blessing. Moreover, it would be one thing if you don't take in any concubine for the rest of your life, but if you will eventually, it would be better to take in Sister Li. I've known her so well since childhood that we wouldn't ever scorn each other. Why don't you ask for the prefect's permission? If he refuses, you won't be worse off than you are, except for having to suffer the humiliation of a rejection. And for my part, I would be able to give her a reason for the refusal. If, by some lucky chance, the prefect approves, wouldn't that be a most wonderful thing?"

Thus repeatedly pressed by his wife, Shan had no choice but to first tell Administrator Zheng about this. Then, he dragged Zheng with him to see the prefect and explained at great length the reason for this request. The prefect said with a smile, "So you wish to shoot down two birds with one arrow? I will certainly do as you wish, so as to atone for my offense that the controller general scolded me about." There and then the prefect issued another order, removing Li Ying from the registry and delivering her to Revenue Manager Shan. Shan used half of the prefect's gift of one hundred thousand in cash to redeem Li Ying and gave the other half to Madam Yang as a reward for having brought up Yang Yu. From then on, Chunniang and Li Ying addressed each other as sisters and lived in great harmony.

Shan Feiying had been a bachelor when he first assumed office, but now, with boundless joy, he found himself blessed, all too unexpectedly, with a wife and a concubine, both as beautiful as they were talented. A later poet had this to say:

> He used to sit sadly alone in his room;
> Now he rejoices in blissful double marriage.
> He did not forget the pledge of old;
> She need not have wished for a next-life reunion.
> An empty hand suddenly had two jade pieces;
> From the mud emerged twin lotus flowers.
> Predestined marriage bonds cut across classes;
> Once fulfilled, the bond lasts five hundred years.

On a chosen auspicious day, Revenue Manager Shan bade farewell to the officials of the yamen and returned to Lin'an with his wife and concubine. When he presented Chunniang to his parents, all present gave way to their emotions and wept bitterly. After they had cried their fill, Shan Feiying brought forth Li Ying. When Mr. Shan Senior asked who she was, the son gave a full account of her background. Mr. Shan Senior flared up in anger: "As for the one who is of our own flesh and blood but was lost and regained, we should, by rights, accept her. We cannot do otherwise. But why do you have to drag in an outsider?" (*Valid point.*)

A frightened Shan Feiying hastened to ask for forgiveness, but his father's anger remained unmollified. The old lady, trying to bring about some kind of a compromise, led Li Ying to her own room and asked her to marry some other man. Li Ying turned a deaf ear but piteously pleaded for permission to stay. Moved by her sincerity, the old lady kept her as a temporary companion. After a few days, she came to appreciate Li Ying's discretion and gentleness as well as her skillful sewing, and persuaded her husband to accept her as their son's concubine. When Shan Feiying was appointed to a new post as a vice-director, his superiors were, to a man, impressed by his chivalrous act of marrying courtesans, and, as the story circulated, no one did not hold him in high esteem. (*The morals of our times being as bad as they are, such an event would instead be considered a crime.*) Through recommendations, he was promoted time and again until he became chamberlain for ceremonials. Chunniang had no issue, but Li Ying gave birth to a son, whom Chunniang loved as if he were her own. The boy applied himself to his studies, passed the imperial examinations, and made quite a name for himself in Lin'an. This has become a much-told story going around, even to this day, among houses of pleasure. There is a poem that bears witness:

> Pledges of love are easily broken.
> Who would claim a bride from a brothel?
> Loyalty has its rightful rewards:
> His career soared, his descendants prospered.

Yang Balao's Extraordinary Family Reunion in the Land of Yue

Did not Wei Qing the slave
Rise to power overnight and marry Princess Pingyang?[1]
Wasn't the melon grower of Xianyang
At one time an enfeoffed duke?[2]
Like spinning balls, fortunes turn round and round;
The winds of change shift all too often.
Those with wisdom and insight stay aloof
And watch puppets dance on the stage of life.

The above ancient-style poem makes the point that fortune or the lack of it is something preordained. Wealth may well come first, only to be followed by a decline into poverty. By the same token, a lowly and humble man may well rise to eminence. The vicissitudes of life are no less capricious than the clouds, and just as unpredictable. A case in point: Scholar Lü Mengzheng of the Song dynasty was in straitened circumstances before his time came. After spending three days without much of a meal, he managed to buy a melon on credit on Tianjin Bridge,[3] but when he tried to knock it open against the bridge railing, he lost his grip. The melon fell into the river and floated downstream, without a single bit ever reaching his mouth. Later in his life, he became *zhuangyuan*, finishing first in the palace examinations. When he rose to be prime minister, he built a pavilion in memory of the lost melon to remind himself of his days of poverty and misfortune. Therefore, we can see that even those destined to be *zhuangyuan* and prime ministers are not even allowed the joy of a melon if their time has not come. If, let us suppose, someone had announced at the time the melon fell, "This man will attain prosperity and high status in the future," goodness knows how many grimaces would have been made and how many hundreds of buckets of saliva would have been spat in contempt, for who would have believed him? That is why there is the saying "The future is shrouded in darkness beyond anyone's reach."

As another example, in the Song dynasty there was a certain Yang Rengao, who, as a lowly soldier, carried stones and earth for the construction of a mansion for Duke Ding of Jin, the prime minister. He said bitterly, while sweating all over under the summer sun, "We all are human beings born of parents, but how happy are the residents of mansions and how hard is the lot of us laborers! Indeed, 'He who is richly blessed by fate is served by those not so blessed.'" His complaints were silenced by the whip of the foreman. In a few years' time, Prime Minister Ding committed an offense and was demoted to the position of revenue manager of Yazhou, whereas Yang Rengao flourished because some close relative of his married into the royal family. Consequently, he rose to be grand commandant. As a member of the imperial family, he was granted the very mansion that had belonged to Prime Minister Ding. As it turned out, Prime Minister Ding had, in fact, unknowingly served as an overseer for the construction of the mansion for the benefit of none other than Yang Rengao. Truly,

> *Mulberry fields change into vast oceans;*
> *Vast oceans change into mulberry fields.*
> *No good fortune stays the same forever,*
> *All changes are dictated by heaven.*

We shall make no more such idle comments but shall get started with our story, titled "Yang Balao's Extraordinary Family Reunion in the Land of Yue." This story takes place in the prefecture of Xi'an, Shaanxi, during the Mongol Yuan dynasty, immediately after the Song but well after the Han and Tang dynasties. The prefecture of Xi'an, being part of Yongzhou, according to "The Great Yu's Laws of the Land" in *The Classic of History* [Shujing], was named Wangji in the Zhou dynasty, Guanzhong in the Qin dynasty, Weinan in the Han dynasty, Guannei in the Tang dynasty, Yongxing in the Song dynasty, and Anxi in the Yuan dynasty. Our story takes place in the Zhida reign period [1308–11] during the Yuan dynasty. There lived in Zhouzhi County in Xi'an Prefecture a man named Yang Fu with the pet name of Balao [the Eighth] because he was born on the day of the Mid-Autumn Festival in the eighth month. His wife, Li-shi, bore a son who was now an extraordinarily intelligent seven-year-old. They named him Shidao, and the couple's love for him goes without saying.

One day, Yang Balao took counsel with his wife, saying, "At nearly thirty years of age, I have failed at making a name for myself as a scholar, and family circumstances have been gradually deteriorating. My forefathers were merchants who plied their trade in Fujian and Guangdong. What do you say if I raise some capital, buy some goods, and sell them in Zhangzhou for some profit to support the family?"

Li-shi replied, "It is said that thrift and hard work are the basic principles in maintaining a household. What good is there in waiting at home for some miracle to happen, like the man who waited by a tree for a hare to run into it?[4] Being in the prime of your life, you are at the right age to travel. Go pack quickly. There is no need to hesitate."

"That's all very well said, but our son is so young and you so frail. How can I not worry if I leave you to yourselves?"

"Fortunately, our son is not a child any more. I can take care of his education all by myself. I wish you would go as soon as possible, so as to return all the sooner." That very day, they made up their minds, and, on a chosen auspicious day, he bade his wife and son farewell and set out on his journey. Taking with him a page boy called Suitong, he took a boat and headed in a southeasterly direction. There is an ancient-style poem describing the trials and tribulations of life as a traveling merchant:

> *A merchant's life is full of woes,*
> *Traveling always away from home.*
> *At the mercy of the wind and the rain,*
> *And shouldering the night stars and the moon.*
> *On water, he is tossed by waves and winds,*
> *On land, chickens and dogs disturb his sleep.*
> *All ambition he once had is now gone,*
> *And he has lost all interest in wine and song.*
> *He either earns too little or works too much*
> *And arouses jealousy once he gains.*
> *When illness confines him to his bed,*
> *Who can send his letter home so far away?*
> *Years pass by with no hope of returning;*
> *His wife and children are sick with worry.*
> *At the sudden good news of his return*
> *They rejoice as though he had gained new life.*
> *Whatever pleasure there is in journeys,*
> *It is better to be with his loved ones.*
> *The bird that stands by the river—*
> *He never leaves home, but does he ever starve?*

To get on with our story, Yang Balao's journey took him to Zhangpu County in Zhangzhou Prefecture, where he lodged with Madam Nie and started his business purchasing Cantonese goods. Madam Nie had no son but only one daughter, a twenty-three-year-old widow whose now-deceased husband had lived with them and helped with the household work until a year before. Impressed with Yang Balao's well-lined pocket, his sincerity and honesty, and his genial manners, Madam Nie grew very fond of him and wanted to have him stay on in the household as a son-in-law to provide for her in her old age. As Yang was reluctant at the beginning, Madam Nie repeatedly offered the following argument: "Master Yang, being a traveler ten thousand miles from home with no kith and kin around, you have no one to take care of you. Now, my daughter is young enough to be a good match for you. Wouldn't it be nice if you could set up two households? When you go back home, you'd have your wife to serve you, and when you come to Zhangzhou, you'd have my daughter. In this way, you'd never get lonely, which would be good for your business, too. I'm not asking that you go to a great deal of expense. My only wish is that my daughter, my only child, marry a good man and have sons and daughters, so that I can have someone to fall back on in my old age. Your wife will not take it amiss even if she hears about this. Goodness knows how many travelers throw away their money in brothels, but what I am proposing is within the bounds of decency. Please consider what course would be best in the long run. Do not decline outright."

Convinced by her reasoning, Yang finally agreed. The wedding ceremony was held on a chosen day, and Yang was thus married into the Nie family. The couple lived in harmony, and the days that went by were uneventful. In less than two months, Nie-shi became pregnant. In due course, she gave birth to a son, to the delight of the entire family. There was much celebration among kith and kin on the third day and again at the end of the first month after the birth of the baby, but of this, we shall speak no further.

In the meantime, Yang Balao missed his wife and child back in Xi'an. He had originally planned to return home for a visit within one year after the wedding. However, he could not very well leave Nie-shi when she was pregnant, and, after the child was born, Nie-shi would not let him go. Time sped by like an arrow. Before they noticed it, three years had gone by since Yang Balao's arrival, and the boy was now two years old. He was named Shide. Though this name was picked to show that he and Yang's older son, Shidao, were brothers,[5] Shide took his mother's surname and was called Nie Shide.

One day, Yang Balao told Nie-shi that he was going away on a short trip back to Shaanxi to visit his first wife, but that he would return soon. No amount of remonstration from her could hold him back. She could not do otherwise than let him have his way. Yang packed his goods, but before he set out on the journey, he took out some account books and spent the following few days trying to collect payments from customers. Suitong took on part of the job and went on a separate route.

Balao's own debt-collecting route took him to the district yamen, where he saw a poster saying, "This yamen has received notice from our superiors that Japanese pirates are looting and plundering along the coast. Patrol is to be intensified throughout the prefecture to forestall any invasion. All those leaving and entering by the city gates shall be subject to interrogation. The city gates shall be opened late and closed early," and so forth. Yang Balao was startled. "I never anticipated that such a warning would be issued just as I was about to leave. If the Japanese pirates do come and the city gates do close, who knows when things will quiet down again? I'd better get out of here before it's too late."

Instead of going to the next customer as he had planned, he turned back home, telling Nie-shi that since payments were not to be easily collected on the spot anyway, he could afford to put the job aside until he came back from the trip. Having heard that pirates were active on his route, he decided not to bring any goods with him. After packing some personal belongings, he was determined to leave the very next day.

Pained at the thought of parting, Nie-shi said to him, carrying their three-year old child in her arms, "My mother married me to you in hopes of having someone to rely on in her old age. Luckily we have this child. For the sake of the child, if not for me, you should by all means come back soon, so as not to make us wait too long." With these words, tears coursed down her cheeks in spite of herself.

Yang Balao said in an effort to comfort her, "Don't worry. We've had three years of life as a loving couple. I wouldn't go away if I had a choice. But it'll be less than a year before we'll meet again." That night, his mother-in-law laid out some wine as a farewell treat.

Early the following morning, Yang Balao rose, washed himself, took leave of his mother-in-law and wife, and set out on his journey with his servant Suitong. Before two days had gone by, what came into view gave him a shock:

> *Boats and carts were squeezed among the crowds;*
> *Men and women ran helter-skelter.*
> *Everyone was scared of the savage pirates;*
> *All hated the useless government troops.*
> *Some led their old and their young, in spite of the trouble;*
> *Some ran for their own lives, leaving children and wives.*
> *The rich, the poor, the mighty, the humble,*
> *All were the same in this moment of crisis.*
> *City market, mountain, forests,*
> *All were sought for a place of shelter.*
> *Truly: Better to be a dog in times of peace*
> *Than a human rendered homeless by war.*

What Yang Balao saw was a swarming crowd of people trying to seek refuge in the city. It was said that the Japanese pirates were killing and burning as they advanced. The government troops having failed to check them, they would arrive any moment. Yang was so stricken with terror that he felt as if his soul had left him. Unable to make up his mind which way to go, he thought it best to follow the crowd into the city of Dingzhou before deciding what to do next.

Four hours later, about three li from the city, earth-shaking battle cries were suddenly heard. Those at the back of the mass of refugees broke out into bitter wails, for the Japanese were upon them. Many of the refugees were so frightened that their legs gave way under them. Catching sight of a thicket by the side of the road, Yang Balao made a dash in that direction, followed by quite a crowd, little knowing that ambush was the cunning pirates' favorite strategy. From among the trees leapt out a Japanese. Thinking he was alone, the refugees were about to take him on when, at a blow on his conch, a host of scimitar-brandishing pirates jumped out from goodness knows where and surrounded them. Several stout-hearted men not untrained in martial arts stepped forward with whatever weapons they had to engage the enemy at the risk of their lives. Like snow thrown into a fire or dust flicked into the wind, they died like chopped melons and vegetables under the enemies' swords. Appalled at the sight, the rest of the refugees dropped to their knees and begged for mercy.

The fact was that the Japanese pirates did not kill every Chinese they saw. They would ravish captured women until they had had enough and then set the women free. The more sentimental among them would even give the women some gifts. However, these women, although spared their lives, would be held up for ridicule until the end of their lives. As for the men, the old and the weak were killed. Able-bodied men, however, had their heads shaved and brushed with paint, after which they were passed off as Japanese and sent to the front lines of battle. The Chinese government troops would claim a reward for every Japanese head they cut off. Therefore, for the sake of the reward, the soldiers would go so far as to kill bald-headed Chinese civilians and offer their heads up for the reward. As for those captured on the battlefields, none was spared, whether they were Japanese or not. Those fake Japanese with shaven heads knew all too well that they were going to die anyway and figured that by acting their part, they might get to live a few days longer. So they fought with all their might. The real Japanese would wait for the fake ones to bear the brunt of the attack before charging forward. The Chinese troops repeatedly fell for this ploy, and victory remained beyond their reach. A poet of those days had this to say about the Japanese military strategies:

> Noiseless the Japanese pirates are,
> Scattered about in no battle array.
> The conch blows, and they come out like butterflies;
> When they march, they zigzag ahead like snakes.

Fanning out, they disappear from view,
But when they attack, their swords are all a blur.
Mixing captives with their own men,
They brought devastation to our land.

Yang Balao and other civilians fell into the pirates' hands. Like turtles in a jar with no hope of escape, they had no choice but to submit to the will of their captors in the hope of being spared their lives. Suitong was nowhere to be seen and could well be dead, for all Yang Balao knew. Reduced to such a plight, anyone would be too concerned with himself to worry about others. Let us leave Yang Balao there in his distress but turn our attention to the Japanese, who were in raptures with the gold and valuables they had looted from the villages. When they heard that the imperial army of the Yuan dynasty was heading their way, they seized a great many ships and drove all the captives on board. Merrily, they set out on their return journey to Japan.

As a matter of fact, the Japanese sovereign more often than not had no knowledge of the incursions into China by pirates who were actually poor island residents banding together for voyages across the sea, much as Chinese pirates would do. When out on looting raids, which, to them, were like regular business trips, they divided themselves into different tribes, calling the chieftains "great kings"—titles that they stopped using after returning home. Most of the valuables that they looted were equally distributed. Sometimes they would offer ten to twenty percent to the chiefs of the islands to keep them quiet. Those killed by the Chinese were written off as business losses. Able-bodied captives were kept as servants. With their heads shaven and their feet bare in the Japanese fashion, they were given swords and taught how to jump according to the Japanese way of fighting. The Chinese had to obey out of fear. Within a year, they would grow accustomed to the climate, learn to speak Japanese, and end up looking no different from the natives.

Time sped by like an arrow. Before he noticed it, Yang Balao had been living in Japan for nineteen years. Every night he prayed secretly to heaven, "May the gods bless me and let me return to my native land to see my family again." Winter or summer, there was not a day that went by without this prayer, as these lines attest:

After nineteen years in a foreign land,
Memories of home faded from his dreams.
Su Wu's staff lost all of its hair;[6]
Hong Hao's head turned pure white with the years.[7]
To the empire they were staunchly loyal,
But what am I here suffering for?

Grieving over the remoteness of home,
I offer pious prayers night by night.

As the story goes, in a lean year in Japan during the Taiding reign period [1324–27] of the Yuan dynasty, pirates again gathered together for an incursion into China, and Yang Balao was brought along. He was filled with mixed feelings, for he rejoiced at the opportunity to go back to China, where he had families in Shaanxi and Fujian. With the blessing of heaven, he might even get to be reunited with his loved ones. At the same time, he was also worried that he looked too much like a Japanese, so much so that his appearance was shocking even to himself at each glimpse into the mirror. How could anyone else recognize him? Moreover, swords and spears knew no mercy. This was an ill-boding voyage that could end with his death. However, there is the saying that it is better to be a ghost in one's native place than to be alive and well in an alien land. Would that heaven be merciful and send him to either Shaanxi or Fujian! Other places would mean nothing to him.

As a matter of fact, when setting out to sea, the Japanese submitted themselves to the will of heaven and allowed themselves to be guided by the direction of the wind. If the wind was out of the north, that dictated an invasion of Guangdong; an easterly wind meant that Fujian was to be the target; a northeasterly wind would take them to Wenzhou, and, with a southeasterly wind, they would be heading for Huaiyang. It was the second month of the year when they set sail. A robust northeasterly wind that lasted for several days in a row blew them all the way to Wenzhou.

The Yuan dynasty had enjoyed peace for so long that coastal defense consisted of nothing more than a few ships with several hundred old, weak soldiers who were so poorly prepared for battle that they fled upon the first sight of the oncoming enemy. Unopposed, the pirates landed and, as usual, went on a burning and killing spree.

However reluctant he was, Yang Balao was obliged to follow. In the period from the second month to the eighth month, the government troops suffered a series of defeats and lost several cities and towns to the pirates, who then descended upon Ningbo, Shaoxing, and Yuhang, all along the way committing atrocities that defy description. Magistrates of various prefectures and counties submitted to the imperial court appeals for emergency assistance. An imperial decree to the Ministry of Defense ordered Grand Marshal Puhua of the Pingjiang region to lead troops forward to expel the invaders. A most wise and resourceful man, with quite a number of crack troops and fine officers under his command, the grand marshal led his well-armed army forward into the Zhejiang region. When his scouts learned that the Japanese were camped around Clear Water Dam, Grand Marshal Puhua arranged to have the local troops join him in pressing ahead by land as well as by water. The Japanese, having never taken Chinese government troops seriously, ignored their advance. Little did they know that Grand Marshal Puhua had under him ten commanders who all had the valor to combat ten thousand men single-handedly. Equipped with an abundance of cannons, part of the Chinese troops lay in ambush. When the Japanese were in the middle of a heated battle with the rest of the Chinese troops, those in ambush charged into the open under cover of the cannons. The path of retreat being thus blocked, the Japanese suffered a bitter defeat. Over a thousand heads were chopped off. More than two hundred men were captured alive. Of those who tried to flee by ship, many were intercepted and killed by the Chinese navy. Others fell into the water and drowned. The victorious grand marshal rewarded his troops. Then, a hunt for any surviving Japanese got under way. Truly,

> *As fierce as wolves and tigers you may be;*
> *You pay when your evil deeds reach the peak.*

Our story forks at this point. At Clear Water Dam there stood a temple known as the Temple of Smooth Sailing, which had been built in honor of a deity named Feng Jun, originally a native of Qiantang. At the age of sixteen, he had dreamt that a deity from heaven appeared to him and, acting upon a decree from the Jade Emperor, cut open his belly and changed all the vital organs in his body. Upon waking up, he still felt the pain in his belly. He was illiterate, for he missed the chance for education when he was small, but, after that dream, his mind suddenly saw the light. Henceforth, there was no book that he did not know. He excelled in writing and could predict the future. One day, he fell asleep at home. No one could wake him up, and when he finally did awake, he said, to his family's disbelief, that he had been at a banquet in the palace of the Dragon King of the Eastern Sea, who forced too much wine on him. It was not until he vomited exotic seafood never seen before that his story came to be believed.

At the age of thirty-six, he declared suddenly one day, "The Jade Emperor appointed me as god of the rivers. I shall take up the post three days from now." Three days later he passed away, a man free from any ailment. That day, furious waves in the river were on the verge of capsizing passing boats when a god emerged from among the clouds on a red-bannered, black-canopied carriage pulled by a white horse with red reins. At his command, the waves died down. Local natives, when asked, said that the god was the very image of Feng Jun. Thereupon, a temple named Smooth Sailing was erected on the site of his residence. During the Shaoding reign period [1228–33], he was granted the title Valiant Prince. The deity he had become was most responsive to prayers.

When the Japanese were occupying Clear Water Dam, Yang Balao secretly offered prayers in the temple, and, to his inward delight, his divination was granted a most auspicious answer. He and twelve other men captured by the Japanese years before got together and agreed to surrender when the Chinese troops arrived, yet they hesitated for fear that the soldiers might take them for Japanese and capture them to claim rewards.

On the twenty-eighth day of the eighth month, the Japanese pirates were put to rout. Yang Balao and the other twelve men hid themselves in the temple without daring to venture out. While they were thus stranded in the temple, they heard loud cries outside. It was Battalion Commandant Wang Guoxiong, who was leading government troops to search the temple. All thirteen men were taken alive. They were tied together and hung by their hands from the eaves. The men protested that they were being wronged and that they were not Japanese, but their cries went unheeded. As evening set in, Commandant Wang decided to spend the night in the temple and take the captives along the following morning to claim his reward from the authorities. As luck would have it, a servant of the commandant's, Wang Xing, rose in the night to relieve himself and heard, amid the wails from the corridor, a voice with a Shaanxi accent. (*A wonderful twist in the plot.*) Intrigued, he quietly lit a lamp and went over for a look. The light happened to fall on Yang Balao's face. Feeling a little apprehensive, Wang Xing said, "If you are not Japanese, where are you from, then? Why are you in their ranks, and why do you look the same as they do?"

Yang Balao explained, "Everyone here is from Fujian except me. I'm a native of Zhouzhi County in Xi'an Prefecture. Nineteen years ago, I was traveling in Zhangpu when I was captured by Japanese pirates. My hair was shaven off and my shoes taken away, and I was made to suffer all manner of hardships. Everyone else here was captured at the same time. When we were brought here, we thought of giving ourselves up to the authorities, but, looking as strange as we do, we were afraid that no one would believe us unless we ran into some old acquaintances. We were trying to make up our minds when, luckily for us, the imperial army defeated the Japanese enemy, bringing us hope for deliverance from our misery. Who would have thought that the old general would hang all of us up like this without even a questioning. If we are brought before the commander in chief tomorrow, we'll all be dead." At these words, the captives all broke out into sobs. Wang Xing hastily shook his hand in admonition and said, "Don't be so loud. You'll only ruin your own chances if you wake up the old general. Now, you from Xi'an Prefecture, what is your name?"

"My surname is Yang. I am Yang Fu, nicknamed Balao. You, sir, also have a slight Shaanxi accent. Might you be from the same county, by any chance?"

Wang Xing was taken aback. "So you are my old master! Do you remember Suitong? It's me!"

"Ah yes, of course!" exclaimed Yang Balao. "But you look different from the old days, and I really couldn't have recognized you face to face. How did you end up here after we were separated in Fujian?"

"Let's not get into details now," said Wang Xing. "Tomorrow morning when the old general rises to take you off under escort, I'll be standing on one side. You can look at me and call my name. I will then step forward and plead for you." So saying, he picked up the lamp and went away. As the others asked Yang what all that was about, Yang gave a brief account, to the delight of one and all. Truly,

> They would escape from the jaws of death,
> For their time of deliverance had come.

Wang Xing had been nineteen years old when he served Yang Balao as a page boy. Now, nineteen years later, he was a man of thirty-eight, changed beyond immediate recognition. After being separated from his master, he had hidden himself in the latrine and, by sheer luck, was not captured by the Japanese. Battalion Commandant Wang, a company commandant stationed there at the time, saw him by chance and, impressed with his smartness, asked him about his background and kept him as a servant. The commandant agreed to inquire about the whereabouts of Suitong's master, but all his efforts were to no avail. Later, Company Commandant Wang was promoted to battalion commandant for his merit and transferred to a position in Zhejiang. Now renamed Wang Xing, Suitong rendered him competent service. Indeed, Yang the Eighth was destined not to perish at this time, nor was his career to be terminated yet. Extreme adversities now gave way to good fortune. It was the will of heaven that he be reunited with his former servant.

Let us digress no more. The following morning, Battalion Commandant Wang did a roll call, found everyone present, and ordered that the thirteen Japanese captives be delivered to the commander in chief so the battalion could claim its reward. At the point of departure, one of the captives stared at Wang Xing and cried at the top of his voice, "Suitong! I am your old master. Come and save me!" Wang Xing feigned surprised recognition and the two fell upon each other's shoulders and wept.

Having no memory of what had happened so many years before, Commandant Wang asked Wang Xing what all this emotion was about. Wang Xing said in explanation, "This is my old master, whom I lost sight of nineteen years ago. I couldn't find him. Little did I know that he was captured by the Japanese. I was looking at him and thinking how familiar his face was when he recognized me and called me by my old name. Should my benefactor look into my old master's case and set him free, I would have no regrets even if I die right here at the foot of these very steps." With these words, he burst into loud sobs. The rest of the captives all joined him in claiming their innocence and pronouncing their names, native places, and the facts of their lives.

Commandant Wang said, "Since this appears to be a case of mistaken identity, I would not presume to pass any judgment on my own. Let me send the captives over to the grand marshal, so he can decide."

Wang Xing pleaded, "Please take me along so that I can testify as to the truth." Commandant Wang refused at first, but finally gave in to Wang Xing's pitiable pleas.

That very day, the thirteen captives plus Wang Xing were brought under guard to the mansion of Grand Marshal Puhua, who declared, "Being Japanese captives, they should be decapitated." All the thirteen plus Wang Xing loudly protested, stating their innocence. Wang Guoxiong dropped to his knees and gave an account of what he had heard from Wang Xing. The grand marshal found the report credible and ordered Wang Guoxiong to escort the captives and Wang Xing to Yang Shidao, the assistant prefect of Shaoxing, for an interrogation.

In those times during the Yuan dynasty, an assistant prefect was the equivalent of a present-day vice-prefect, who, second in rank only to the prefect, worked with the prefect in the management of prefectural affairs. A most powerful position it was. That day, Assistant Prefect Yang presided over the court, and an orderly court it was. How do we know this? There is a poem in evidence:

> The clerks stood as stiff as figures of clay;
> The armed guards as still as statues of wood.
> However cunning the villains may be,
> The laws of the court show mercy to none.

By order of the grand marshal, Commandant Wang himself brought the thirteen Japanese captives to Assistant Prefect Yang's yamen. After the usual exchange of greetings, Commandant Wang explained the purpose of his visit. The assistant prefect then saw the commandant out before returning to his own seat in the hall. Wang Xing was the first to give an account of the case, followed by wails of grief from the captives. Assistant Prefect Yang took down Wang Xing's testimony and summoned Yang Balao for questioning. Yang Balao duly supplied detailed information about his name and native place.

"Since you are from Zhouzhi County," asked the assistant prefect, "what is your wife's family name? Do you have children?"

Yang Balao replied, "My wife is from the Li family of the East Village. We have only one son, named Shidao, who was seven years old when I went to

Zhangpu on a business trip. I lived in Zhangpu for three years, after which I was captured by the Japanese and taken to Japan, where I lived for nineteen years. Since I left home, I never heard from my family, nor do I know if my wife and son are dead or alive. If my son is alive, he would be twenty-nine years old now. If you don't believe me, you can send an order to Zhouzhi County for the local authorities to verify the names of all my kith and kin, however far removed. Then my innocence will be established."

The assistant prefect turned to Wang Xing and got the same answer. The rest of the captives again called out their grievances. The assistant prefect carefully questioned each of them and found that all were civilians from Fujian captured at the same time as Yang Balao. The assistant prefect reflected a long while before he ordered sharply, "Put them in prison for now. They are not to be released until they are cleared by a background check by the local authorities."

After leaving the court, he returned to his private quarters and told his mother that he had encountered the strangest thing. The old lady asked, "What kind of a case was it that you handled today, my son? What is so strange about it?"

"A Commandant Wang brought to me thirteen Japanese captives who turned out to be Chinese who had been captured by the Japanese. One of them, called Yang Fu, is a native of Zhouzhi County in Shaanxi. He said that twenty-one years ago, he took leave of his wife, Li-shi, and went to ply his trade in Zhangpu. Three years later, during one of the Japanese incursions, he was captured and taken to Japan. When he left home, his son was seven years old and should be twenty-nine by now. You often said, Mother, that when I was seven, my father went to Zhangzhou on a business trip and never came back. That man's name is identical with my father's; so is his wife's name with yours, and I happen to be twenty-nine years old. I don't believe such coincidences are possible. What's more, Commandant Wang has a servant, Wang Xing, who is positive that the captive is his former master. Wang Xing says he used to be called Suitong and that he lost sight of his master at Zhangpu amid the onslaught of the pirates. Isn't it strange that Suitong also happens to be the name of my father's former servant?"

The old lady also exclaimed, "A most strange thing indeed! Granted that coincidences do occur, but certainly not to this extent! There must be something to it. Hold another interrogation session tomorrow. I'll listen from behind the screen. The truth can be determined then."

Thus advised, Yang Shidao summoned the thirteen captives again the following day for another interrogation and found no deviation from the story given the day before. The old lady cried out from behind the screen, "Yang Shidao, my son! There is no need to go on. This man from Zhouzhi County is none other than your father! Wang Xing is indeed Suitong."

Yang Shidao the assistant prefect was so startled that he lost his balance and fell down from his seat. Throwing his arms around Yang Balao, he broke out into loud sobs. He then invited his father, followed by Wang Xing, into the back room. There, the family of three fell upon each other's shoulders and shed bitter tears. It was indeed like a dream. Suitong also broke down in passionate weeping. They cried their fill before the son made his bows to the father following proper etiquette. Suitong also kowtowed to pay his respects to his former master and mistress. Yang Balao said to his son, "In Japan, I prayed to heaven every night that I be allowed to return to my native land and to see my wife and son again. Now my wish is granted with the blessings of heaven. It is my great joy to see my son in such a high position. But those twelve other men are all natives of Fujian who were captured at the same time and, like me, were forced into doing what we did. Please set them free as soon as possible. Do not show any partiality to me, for that will arouse resentment."

Thus admonished, Yang Shidao set the other twelve men free and, to their immense gratitude, gave each of them three taels of silver to pay for travel expenses on their way home. While instructing the clerk to write a report to the grand marshal, he also started preparations for a celebration banquet. Yang Balao bathed in perfumed water and changed into a new outfit complete with a cap and a waistband. Yang Shidao's wife, Zhang-shi, also came out to pay her respects to her father-in-law. It was indeed a scene of family reunion filled with boundless joy.

The story spread to the Shaoxing prefectural yamen. At word that Assistant Prefect Yang had found his father, Prefect Nie prepared some wine and lamb, betook himself to Assistant Prefect Yang's yamen to offer him congratulations, and asked with much insistence to see Mr. Yang Senior. Yang Fu was obliged to come out and exchange greetings with Mr. Nie. After the usual amenities, the hosts and the guest took their seats respectively. Prefect Nie was most profuse in his admiration and praise. Assistant Prefect Yang set out wine and kept the prefect for dinner, in the course of which the prefect asked why Mr. Yang had stayed in Fujian for so long before calamity struck.

Yang Balao answered, "I had originally intended to return home within a year's time, but the Nie family, with whom I stayed, wished to have me as a husband for their twenty-three-year-old widowed daughter so that I could be of help to the family. Thus I married into the Nie family and stayed for three years."

"Did you have children in those three years?" asked Mr. Nie.

"It was because Nie-shi got pregnant and gave birth to a son that I could not tear myself away. Otherwise, I would have left much earlier."

Mr. Nie asked further, "Did you name the child?"

Without an inkling as to the prefect's name, Yang Senior replied readily,

"As I had named my older son, now the vice-prefect, Shidao, the one I had by Nie-shi was named Nie Shide, for they are brothers, though with different surnames. Nie-shi's son should be twenty-two years old this year, though I have no idea what has become of the mother and son." So saying, he broke down in tears. Neither did Prefect Nie show much delight. After a few more cups, he took his leave and returned home, where he related to his mother what had happened. "The woman he married in Zhangpu bore your surname, mother, and there is no discrepancy in the dates. Might not he be my father?"

The old lady said, "Why don't you invite him to a banquet tomorrow? I'll watch him from behind the screen. We'll then know the truth."

The following day, Yang came to return the prefect's call and presented his name card. The prefect set out wine and kept him for a feast. What Lady Nie saw from behind the screen was a neatly dressed Yang Balao, easily recognizable because he no longer looked like a Japanese. Before she had heard much, the old lady called out, "Nie Shide, my son! Invite your father into the inner quarters for a proper greeting!" Yang Balao was taken aback, for little did he expect things to take such a turn. The prefect hastily dropped to his knees and said, "Your son failed to recognize you. Please forgive me for such a lack of filial piety." Thereupon Yang Balao was led into the private quarters, where he was greeted by Lady Nie. They fell upon each other's shoulders and wept bitterly. It was indeed a repetition of the scene in Assistant Prefect Yang's residence.

In the midst of the conversation, Suitong came by Assistant Prefect Yang's order to the prefect's yamen to escort Mr. Yang Senior back. Astonished upon learning that Mr. Yang was also the prefect's father, Suitong hurried, uninvited, into the inner quarters and kowtowed to the old lady, who realized, after questioning, that this was Suitong, whereupon Suitong gave an account of how he had met Commandant Wang after his separation from his master. The whole family rejoiced. Prefect Nie's wife, Jiang-shi, also came to pay her respects to her father-in-law. The prefect ordered that a banquet be prepared, to which Assistant Prefect Yang was also invited so that he could be given a full explanation. The prefect and assistant prefect did not know until then that they were, in fact, brothers born of the same father. That day, the assistant prefect's wife, Zhang-shi, was also invited over for the family reunion banquet, to the immense joy of all. (*After years of life as a captive in a foreign land, Mr. Yang suddenly finds himself reunited with two wives and two highly-placed sons, with whose support he is to live in grand style. From the jaws of death to the ninth level of heaven, from separation to reunion, from estrangement to affection, from lowliness to dignity: isn't all this dictated by destiny?*) Indeed,

> *Where bitterness ends, sweetness begins;*
> *Out of the depth of misfortune comes bliss.*

The Fengcheng swords reunite as a pair;[8]
The Hepu pearls return to their native place.[9]
An aged student passes the exam;
A beggar digs up hidden wealth.
Widows regain their husbands, like flowers blooming;
Orphans find their fathers, like grass taking root,
Happier than seeing friends in a distant land,
More welcome than rain after a long drought.
Just as parted duckweeds can join in the sea,
Chance meetings can occur anywhere one goes.

Yang Balao had suffered hardships for nineteen years in Japan, little knowing that Yang Shidao, the son of his first wife, Li-shi, and Nie Shide, the son of his second wife, Nie-shi, had grown up, passed the civil service examinations in the same year, and assumed office in the same county of Shaoxing. It was the will of heaven that brought together Balao, who had survived the shackles, his two wives, and his two worthy sons—an extraordinary reunion rarely witnessed in all of history. By the third day, as the news spread throughout the yamen, the entire assembly of officials came to offer congratulations, and so did Commandant Wang. He did not protest Wang Xing's return to his old master. Wang Xing's wife being with the Wang household, the commandant, as a gesture to please the prefect and the assistant prefect, sent for her with all speed so that she could join the reunion. Prefect Nie and Assistant Prefect Yang jointly wrote a memorial addressed to Grand Marshal Puhua, in which they gave a full account of the events that had led to their reunion with their father. The grand marshal in turn reported the matter to the imperial court, which duly bestowed royal titles and gifts on the entire family. Nie Shide changed his surname to Yang, becoming Yang Shide. Yang Balao enjoyed prosperity until he died at a ripe old age. This story illustrates the adage that life and death are all a matter of fate; wealth and rank are determined by the will of heaven. All rises and falls in human life are preordained by destiny, and all attempts to seek the impossible are futile. There is a poem that bears witness:

Barely out of hell, he rose to heaven.
Reunion with wives and sons brought him wealth and rank.
What is ordained will happen, come what may;
Why complain if things fail to go your way?

317

Yang Qianzhi Meets a Monk Knight-Errant on a Journey by Boat

With sword and zither, he roams the four seas,
Singing with joy, free to follow every whim.
Say not that a true man has no soul mate;
On the moonlit boat, he met the valiant monk.

Yang Yi, courtesy name Qianzhi, was a native of Yongjia of Zhejiang. Ever since childhood, his was a carefree soul that rose above petty concerns. An erudite scholar who wrote in a grand and exuberant style, he was appointed to be magistrate of Anzhuang County in Guizhou. Anzhuang County reached beyond the Five Ridges and shared a border with Sichuan to the south.[1] It teemed with barbarians with a love for poisons and fights rather than decorum and polite letters, who worshipped ghosts and spirits and practiced black magic. It was also a region rich in gold, silver, and treasures of every description.

During the Song dynasty, it was the tradition that the emperor would hold audiences in the front hall for officials about to leave for provincial posts. They would be asked to compose poems for the occasion to let themselves be judged for administrative aptitude. In the third month of the second year of the Jianyan reign period [1128], upon Yang Yi's departure by order of the court, Emperor Gaozong asked him, "What office will you be holding?"

Yang Yi replied, "Magistrate of the county of Anzhuang in Guizhou."

The emperor continued, "Have you made any inquiries about the scenery and local customs there?" Thereupon Yang Yi presented a poem that read,

Strands of miasma swirl in the east wind
Beyond a distance of ten thousand li.
I know little of the local dialect,
But will find the birds' chirping much the same.
Amid the palm trees I will lose my bearings,
In that southern land beyond the reach of mail.
Ashamed of my lack of merit, I shall
Prove my worth by civilizing the land.

Nodding approvingly for a long while after hearing the poem, the emperor, moved to compassion, said, "You do indeed have my sympathy for being appointed to such a faraway place. Go ahead for now. I will have you transferred back before long."

Yang Yi took a tearful leave of the emperor and left the court. Once outside, he ran into Military Commissioner Guo Zhongwei. After an exchange of greetings, Guo Zhongwei said, "I heard that you have been assigned to Anzhuang. What's to be done about it?"

"With diseases spreading in the miasma-filled air," said Yang Yi, "I am nine times more likely to die than to survive. I thought of refusing to go, and yet I have no other choice. But if I go, I will surely die there. What advice do you have?"

"The only thing I can think of," said Zhongwei, "is for the two of us to ask for more information from my benefactor Judge Zhou. He has been demoted to serve in Lianzhou² and is also leaving soon." The two men accordingly went to see Judge Zhou Wang.

Yang Yi bowed twice and said, "I, Yang Yi, having recently been appointed to office in the remote Anzhuang County, am here to ask for your advice."

Hastening to return the greeting, Zhou Wang said, "Anzhuang is a region frequented by barbarians who all know how to use black magic to poison and cast spells over people. If you can subdue them, their treasures will all be yours. If not, you'll have good reason to watch out for yourself. You must not take your wife with you, so as to keep her away from harassment by local officials."

With tears coursing down his cheeks, Yang Yi lamented, "What am I to do?"

Out of sympathy for Yang Yi, Zhou Wang continued, "I have been demoted to a post in Lianzhou, which means I can go with you as far as the Guangdong border. I'll take care of all the travel expenses. You don't have to worry about that."

The two visitors took their leave. Yang Yi waited over half a month for Zhou Wang to start the journey with him. After treating them to wine by way of bidding farewell, Guo Zhongwei went about his own business.

Zhou Wang and Yang Yi then proceeded to Zhenjiang, where they hired a big boat. They occupied several big cabins in the middle, but the boatmen rented out the rest of the cabins to make some money. Among the thirty to forty passengers, there was a traveling monk on his way to Mount Wudang of Huguang on a pilgrimage. Claiming to be from Mount Funiu in Henan Province, the monk was a most rude man, with no regard for manners. None of the twelve or thirteen men in his cabin liked him, but he insisted on their serving him hot tea and meals. His cabinmates said, "Monks are supposed to be compassionate, discreet, and free from desires. But you, on the contrary, are trying to take advantage of us!"

The monk retorted, "You're nothing but a bunch of worthless men. Consider yourselves lucky that I still want your service instead of finding you too filthy." He continued to pour out a stream of curses, which so angered the men that they started cursing him back. Some even hit him. All calm and collected, the monk pointed at those who were cursing him and said, "Stop your curses!" Thereupon they immediately stopped, unable to utter another sound. Then he pointed at those who were hitting him and said, "Stop your blows!" Thereupon they stopped, their hands gone limp. (*An extraordinary man must be in possession of extraordinary abilities. He who judges people with his naked eyes is nothing less than a petty rogue.*) Collapsing on the floor of the cabin, they stared into the air, stupefied. Those who did not curse or hit the monk were terrified at the sight and called out, "Good grief! There's an evil spirit here!"

These desperate cries drew spectators from all the other cabins. Zhou and Yang also emerged from their central cabins to take a look and were alarmed at what they saw. Before they could ask questions of the monk, the latter, seeing that Zhou and Yang were dressed like officials, rose and saluted the two men, saying, "I am a monk from Mount Funiu, on this boat of yours on my way to visit the temple on Mount Wudang. These men have been bullying me. You two honorable gentlemen, please stand up for me."

"They were wrong to curse and hit you," said Zhou Wang, "but you were not behaving like a compassionate monk, either."

"If you two gentlemen are pleading on their behalf," said the monk, "I will readily forgive them." He touched the lips of those who had been struck dumb and said, "Speak!" At his command, the dumb-struck ones regained their speech. Then he pulled at the hands of those who had lost their use and said, "Move!" The men did indeed raise their hands. It was like a stage performance. All the onlookers on the boat burst into laughter.

Zhou Wang whispered to Yang Yi, "This is a monk who practices sorcery. He's the kind of man we are looking for. Why don't you invite him to your cabin to ask for his advice?"

Yang Yi agreed. "Right you are. Since my family is not with me, he can stay in my cabin." Turning to the monk, he said, "Since you don't get along with your cabinmates, why don't you move into my cabin? I'll take care of the tea and meals."

The monk demurred. "I really shouldn't disturb you." So saying, he followed Yang Yi to his cabin.

The two men spent the next three or four days discussing the Buddhist classics as well as affairs of the world. There was nothing that the monk was ignorant of. Yang Yi kept talking about the hardships of the journey to get the monk's attention. When the subject of his assumption of office in Anzhuang County was brought up, the monk said, "If you are going to Anzhuang, you must be fully prepared," whereupon Yang Yi told the monk about his concerns.

The monk said, "My name is Li. I am a native of Yazhou, Sichuan, but I have some relatives who moved to Weiqing County,[3] and I have brothers and sisters there, too. When I go back, I will look for someone skilled in sorcery to accompany you and make sure that you are safe. If I can't find anyone, do not leave too rashly by yourself, because I'll change my plans and go with you as far as Guangli instead of to Mount Wudang." (*Those who help others at the sacrifice of their own interests are heroes, one and all.*)

With profuse thanks, Yang Yi confided in the monk all his worries, sparing no detail. Yang Yi's candor, sincerity, and amiableness increased the monk's respect for him. Aware of Mr. Yang's straitened circumstances, he took out from his shoulder-bag about ten taels of gold of the finest quality and fifty to sixty taels of loose silver and offered them to Mr. Yang for his travel expenses. Yang Yi declined the offer time and again. It was only at the monk's firm insistence that Mr. Yang finally conceded.

Without realizing it, they had spent half a month on the boat, which now came to the region of Guangdong and Qiongzhou.[4] Zhou Wang said to Mr. Yang, "To the east is Lianzhou, my destination. I should keep you company for a while longer, but since you have this kind monk here to take care of you, my services can well be dispensed with. I am leaving now, and, should the will of heaven grant it, I will see you again in future." Turning to the monk, he said, "Everything is now in your hands."

The monk assured him by saying, "Don't worry. I know what to do."

Zhou Wang set out some wine and food and bade farewell to Mr. Yang and the monk. After drinking for quite some time, Zhou Wang asked for a small boat and went on his way.

After traveling for another few days, Mr. Yang and the monk arrived in the county of Pianqiao.[5] The monk said to Yang Yi, "This is where my family lives. Just tie the boat to the pier and wait for me here while I go to look for someone to take up the job. I'll be back soon." Flinging his bag and his staff across his shoulders, he took himself off.

Seven or eight days went by without any news from the monk. Yang Yi grew anxious. However, knowing the monk to be a reliable man incapable of false promises, he continued to wait hopefully. On the ninth day, the monk appeared with seven or eight men carrying two loads of trunks, baskets, and some food. There also came, heading for the boat, a sedan-chair, from which, when curtains were lifted up, emerged a beautiful woman (*How extraordinary!*) of about twenty-four or twenty-five years of age. How did she look? As the poem says,

In her alone dwell all the charms of spring;
Her skirt dyes crimson the clouds in the sky.
Her eyes sparkle like pools of autumn water;
Fairer is she than fairy maids of dreams.

There is another poem that says,

In the moonlight, by the crab apple twigs,
Lady Yang,[6] mellow with wine, stands unrivaled.
Pipa notes from horseback urging her to go[7]
Stirred Aman's[8] rancor against the spring.

After the monk, the woman, and Mr. Yang exchanged greetings, the monk called over a family with a maidservant, his adopted daughter, and two page boys and bade them kowtow to Yang Yi. Pointing at the woman, the monk said, "This is a niece of mine. As she is a widow, I brought her here to serve you. She's capable of sorcery, an art she started learning in childhood. With her taking care of everything, no harm will come to you for the rest of the journey." This said, he ordered that the luggage be brought onto the boat. The evening was too advanced for the monk and the others to spend the night elsewhere than on the boat. The maidservant and the girl went into the kitchen to prepare a meal. After everyone had eaten, Li-shi, the widow, gave to the boatmen a tip of half a tael of silver out of her own purse. Now that he had gained a beautiful woman, some trunks, and helpers, at no expense to himself, Yang Yi bowed to the monk in gratitude, saying, "I will never be able to repay you for your great kindness."

The monk said, "Everything that happens is predestined rather than a result of human effort."

After some wine, the monk and the others retired to their respective cabins, whereas Mr. Yang and Li-shi shared the main cabin and spent a most tender night together.

On the following day, after rising and having breakfast with the rest of the company, the monk took leave of Mr. Yang and Li-shi, reminding her, "As I already told you the other day, be prudent and never put on airs. I will see you again when Mr. Yang gets a reappointment to a better place." The monk watched the boat sail away before he turned around.

Li-shi was as gentle, capable, and intelligent as she was bewitchingly beautiful. The mutual love between her and Mr. Yang was not any less tender than that between a married couple. In about ten more days, they came upon the

Zangke River, which, being confluent with the Chuan River of Sichuan in the east and Dianchi Lake in Yelang Prefecture in the west, was so turbulent that it was hardly navigable even with no wind. Upon approaching the mouth of the river, a boatman had to have a full stomach before he could start the crossing. Once he set sail, there was no way he could stop, because he would be driven forward by the wind and the waves. Worse still, the boatman also had to maneuver his way through the reef that infested the river. A single bump and the boat would be lost. The well-prepared boatmen were just about to blow a horn to announce the start of the crossing when Li-shi hastily admonished Mr. Yang, "We cannot go yet. We need to stay here for another three days before the wind will die down."

Mr. Yang said, "But there is no wind now. Why can't we move ahead?"

Li-shi answered, "A big windstorm is coming any moment now. Believe me and steer the boat into a small harbor to seek shelter from the storm."

Taking this to be a chance to test Li-shi's skills, Yang Yi asked a boatman, "Are there any harbors around here?"

The boatman said, "Yes, there's Stone Bridge Harbor ahead of us. Northwest of the harbor is a town with lots of residents and no lack of anything. That'll be a nice place to steer the boat to."

"In that case, let's go there quickly," said Yang Yi.

The boatmen started the boat, and no sooner had they arrived at the mouth of the harbor than a windstorm came racing in from the northwest, blowing up dust at first, and then uprooting trees and turning the green water into a turbid mass of black. The towering waves, with their eerie howls, struck terror into people's hearts. The storm destroyed goodness knows how many boats, and its fury did not subside until sunset. Li-shi had the girl and the maidservant serve tea and supper, and then, after cleaning up everything, went to bed.

The following day, the storm rose again. After it died down in the afternoon, a few small boats came to sell products from the town's market. Mr. Yang had his men buy some fresh fruit and local products for Li-shi as a token of his appreciation for her knowledge of astronomy and the arts of sorcery. On another boat, a peddler was hawking his betel-pepper paste. How does it taste? There is a poem in evidence:

> In white jade plates lie red betel peppers;
> Bright gold tripods set off their splendor best.
> Ripening in the eighth month of the year,
> Verily they are ambrosia on earth.

"I have heard," said Mr. Yang, "that betel-pepper paste is a delicacy in Yunnan and Sichuan, but I have never tried it. Why don't we buy some for

Madam?" So saying, he had a boatman ask the peddler how much a jar of the paste would cost.

"Five hundred full strings of cash," said the peddler.

"In that case," said Yang Yi, "send a page boy into the cabin and ask Madam for money."

The page boy went in and asked Li-shi for money to buy the paste with.

"Don't buy the paste," said she. "We'll get into trouble if we do."

At the page boy's report, Yang Yi said, "How can a jar of paste get us into any trouble! Madam is saying this only because she hates to spend money on such an expensive thing," whereupon he gave the barbarian peddler some silver out of his own money, bought the jar of paste, and took it into the cabin. When the lid was taken off, the aroma filled the air. The color was as lovely as red agate, and the taste sweet and delicious. With great alacrity, Li-shi put the lid back on, saying, "My lord, you must not eat any of this, because trouble is sure to follow. Betel peppers are not native to this region but are products of Vietnam. The tree resembles the paper mulberry tree in its trunk and the mulberry tree in its leaves. The leaves grow to be two or three inches long, but there aren't many of them. The fruit ripens in the frost of the ninth month and is picked and made into paste by the natives. It is a delicacy offered to the royal court. This jar of paste was stolen, and they are coming after the thief."

It turned out that this jar of betel-pepper paste was bought at great price in Vietnam by a rich man who made the trip there by order of the county magistrate, who in turn was commissioned by the director of the Department of State Affairs. The latter did not dare keep the paste for himself but intended to present the exotic delicacy to the emperor. It was after he had gone through numerous hardships and much expense, to the point of bankruptcy, that he managed to lay his hands on one jar of the paste. Before he could pour the contents into a silver jar to present to the director of the Department of State Affairs through the county magistrate, the jar was stolen by a barbarian. The loss of the jar so alarmed the rich man's entire family that they put up wanted posters everywhere as if this were a murder case. At a tip from an informed source, the rich man took a group of government soldiers and embarked on an express boat, and the whole company of twenty to thirty men, armed with swords and spears, and, amid the clangor of drums and gongs, swept forward to Magistrate Yang's boat to get back the jar of paste.

When the battle boat was within only half an arrow's range from his boat, Magistrate Yang hid himself in the cabin, terrified, and said to Li-shi, "What's to be done?"

She answered, "I told you not to buy from that man, and now look at what has happened. In this land of the barbarians, they kill at the slightest provocation. There is no regard whatsoever for decorum and law!" But she continued, "Don't panic." So saying, she had a page boy bring in a basin of water. Chanting some incantations, she drew a line in the water and the battle boat got stuck, unable to budge so much as an inch however hard the men rowed. There it was, transfixed in the midst of the water, unable to move back or forth. The men on the battle boat were seized with fear. "There must be some sorcerer on that boat," they exclaimed. "Get a better sorcerer, quick!"

Li-shi, meanwhile, sent over a boatman, who, using the local dialect, addressed the other side in these words: "Please do not be angry. Our boat happens to be here to seek shelter from the windstorm. When a peddler came to sell a jar of betel-pepper paste, we bought it from him, knowing nothing about how he had come by that jar. The jar has not been touched. We are more than willing to return it to you without asking for our money back."

At this sensible explanation, now knowing that the jar of paste remained intact, the soldiers said, "As long as you return it, we'll give you back your silver."

After reporting to Magistrate Yang, the boatman took the jar over to the other side and got back the silver in return. Neither side resorted to force. After Li-shi drew her finger back and forth a few times in the water-filled basin, the battle boat glided away smoothly, taking the thief to the county court for indictment. Magistrate Yang said to Li-shi, "Luckily, you were here to save me from trouble."

"Just do as I say in the future," said Li-shi, "and I can guarantee that nothing will happen to you." (*It's not a bad deal at all for a henpecked husband to have such a woman for wife.*)

The following day, the windstorm died down. Truly,

> Fish and dragons stay still under calm gold ripples;
> Sparrows and birds perch on noiseless jade tree branches.

After breakfast, the boat started on its way across the river.

They moved ahead or stopped for a rest as they wished and gradually drew near Anzhuang. All of the employees of the local yamen were there to greet them. Assistant Magistrate Xu, the only other official in the county apart from his superior, the magistrate, also came to exchange greetings and was the first one to return to the county seat. When they entered the county, they were met by sedan-chair carriers, who took the baggage and carried Li-shi in a sedan-chair big enough for four people. The attendants and maids were provided with two small sedan-chairs and several horses and escorted to their destination. Next to go was Magistrate Yang. Accompanied by a native drum band, the procession of the new county magistrate attracted many spectators from far and near. Upon arrival in his yamen, Magistrate Yang went directly into the back quarters to make sure that Li-shi and the rest of his entourage were all settled down before he came out to meet the assistant magistrate. After mutual greetings, they sat down for wine and food.

While drinking, Magistrate Yang said to Mr. Xu, "Having but just arrived, I know nothing about local customs. I will need your advice."

"I wouldn't presume to offer any! It is I who need your guidance." Mr. Xu then continued, "In our neighboring region, Malong, there is a Pacification Commissioner Xue. Being a descendant of Xue Rengui [614–83] of the Tang dynasty, his wealth rivals that of a kingdom. The local native tribes listen only to him. Though our posts are of a different order than his,[9] it is a custom at the yamen for any new magistrate to pay him a visit right after offering incense at the temple. He will then return the courtesy as the beginning of a friendly relationship. I hope you will keep that in mind."

Magistrate Yang assured him, "I will." He went on to ask, "How far is Malong from here?"

"About forty li."

Their conversation then drifted to other county matters.

After they finished drinking, they went to their own quarters of the yamen. When Magistrate Yang told Li-shi about Pacification Commissioner Xue, she said, "Mr. Xue may be young, but he is a most cunning man. Yet, if you go out of your way to befriend him, he'll even let you share some of his wealth. We'll still be in his power even after we leave here. The last thing to do is to show him contempt because of his status as a local official. Do not slight him in any way." She continued, "Within the next three days, a sorcerer dressed in red will come to see you. Don't be coaxed into standing up. Just ignore him, however rude and insulting he is." Magistrate Yang made a mental note of this.

Three days later, after the ceremony of incense-burning in the temple of the local deities, Magistrate Yang held his court and all his subordinates came to pay their respects. At the end of the disposal of official business, a local native wearing a square cap and a red robe with a round neckline walked up to the magistrate from below the steps and said, without falling to his knees, "Please rise. Here is an old man greeting you."

The magistrate asked, "Which county are you from? Are you related in any way to this yamen?"

Instead of answering the questions, the old man repeated, "Please rise. An old man is greeting you."

Though he tried to ignore the provocations, the magistrate thought that his dignity was at stake, for the scene was attracting more attention. Fearing that he would become a laughing stock, he ended up letting his anger get the better of him, though he did remember the part of Li-shi's admonitions about not standing up. "Take the old man away and beat him hard!" he called out to the lictors. Two of them ran up to take the old man away for a beating, but the latter was too strong for them, standing defiantly with squared shoulders while exclaiming, "You can't beat me!" At the insistence of the county magistrate, all the lictors present swarmed up, overpowered the old man, and gave him ten strokes with a heavy rod. As the clerks came forward to ask for mercy on behalf of the old man, Mr. Yang thundered, "Drive him out!"

The old man said on his way out, "You take it easy!"

The magistrate had expected this first court session to mark an auspicious beginning of a successful term of office. Now that his day was ruined by that brute of an old man, he pulled himself together with an effort and disposed of some official business before he dismissed the gathering and returned dejectedly to his private quarters. Li-shi said upon seeing him, "I told you not to pay any attention to a man in red, and yet you had to have a showdown with him."

Magistrate Yang was quick to defend himself: "I did follow your advice by remaining seated, and he was given only ten strokes."

"He is the very man here to beat me in a contest of magic power. Had you stood up, he would have changed into a demon to haunt you at night. Had you yielded to him like a coward, you might as well have given up your office to him. All the clerks and lictors are his men. You and I have no power over them. After this beating, instead of coming to haunt you, he will come at night to kill you."

"What's to be done?"

"Don't worry. Just set your mind at ease. I know how to deal with him when night comes."

Yang Yi said, "I am totally in your hands."

When evening set in, they ate supper and cleared away the table. In all four corners of the room, Li-shi drew four magic figures with white powder and added one in the empty space in the middle. Then she made Mr. Yang sit on the figure in the middle and told him, "When a monster appears at night to frighten you, you must remain absolutely still. Just sit here and don't be afraid." Then she dressed herself up, took out a big gold brooch three to four inches in length, placed some incense candles and a vermilion magic talisman in front of the gods' images, and sat waiting outside the white circle.

Around the second watch of the night, the sounds of a rainstorm began to draw near, becoming louder and louder until, upon reaching the eaves, a sinister-looking thing flew into the house with a tremendous bang. The size of a tea saucer, the thing charged at Mr. Yang, who could see not much more than a blur. But it stopped at the border of the white circle. All it could do was fly around the circle without being able to get in. Mr. Yang trembled with fear. Li-shi began to chant some incantations and burned a magic figure in the air, a move so effective that the evil thing's movements slowed down. In less time than it takes to describe in words, Li-shi mustered up all her strength, fixed her eyes upon the evil thing, and shouted, "Stop!" At the same time, she raised her right hand to grab at the evil thing, which dodged by diving down toward the ground. Taking advantage of the dive, Lishi bent down and pressed it with her hands against the ground. When she picked it up with both hands, there for them to see was a most hideous batlike thing with black and white stripes all over its body and a long, blood-red beak.

Petrified with fear, Mr. Yang did not get up until quite some time later. Li-shi said to him, "This evil thing is, in fact, that old man in a changed form. If it's beaten to death here and now, the old man would be dead, too, but then we'd have a problem on our hands because his numerous descendants would certainly come to seek revenge. Let me keep him here for the time being." So saying, she lifted the two wings, joined them together, and pinned them down with a gold needle on the magic figure in the white circle. The evil thing could not make the slightest movement. After covering it with an inverted basket to prevent cats and mice from hurting it, Li-shi retired to her room with the magistrate.

The following morning when the court began its session, about twenty neatly dressed old men came and knelt down in front of the magistrate, saying, "We are all relatives and neighbors of Old Man Pang, who is now held by you after his impudent affront against you last night. Please be so kind as to forgive him this time and only this time. We will surely bring him with us to show our allegiance to you."

The magistrate said, "You should have known that I would not have dared to hold office in this place if I did not know some sorcery. I am not going to kill him. I'll just wait and see if he can get himself out alive."

The old men pleaded again, "We will not hide anything from you. The affairs of this county have always been in his hands as well as ours. The officials have never been in control. But now that we are convinced of your power, we dare not offend you again. If you let Old Man Pang go, the entire county will be yours."

The magistrate continued, "You may all rise. I will do as I see fit."

The old men withdrew in eager deference.

After dismissing the court session, Yang Yi went back to Li-shi and told her about the old men's pleas for mercy. Li-shi said, "He is not to be released until tomorrow when they come again to ask for clemency."

One more night went by. The following day, when the county magistrate sat in court, the same group of old men came again to plead on their knees. So piteous did they sound that the magistrate said, "For your sake, I will forgive him this time, but I will show absolutely no clemency if he gives offense again."

The old men bowed in gratitude and left. When the magistrate retired to his private quarters, Li-shi said, "Now we can let him go."

That night, Li-shi walked into the white circle and pulled out the gold needle. The evil thing immediately flew away.

When the thing reached home, Old Man Pang rose from his bed and thanked the other old men, saying, "I thought I would never get to see you again. The county magistrate is all right. It's the mistress who's the one to fear. I don't know where she learned her art, but it's different from ours. In a couple of days, I'll go with you to pay our respects to him and offer gifts. Let's not provoke him ever again."

After being treated to some wine and food, the old men took leave of each other, saying, "We'll gather together someday and go to pay him our respects."

In the meantime, Mr. Yang retired into his private quarters and thanked Li-shi.

"Today is the day to see Commissioner Xue," she reminded him.

"But we'll have to put together some gifts first."

"The gifts are ready," said Li-shi. "Satin with flowers embroidered in gold thread, two bolts of patterned ko-hemp cloth, a scroll by a famous calligrapher, and an antique ink slab." (*Nice gifts.*) The gifts, all prepared, were ready to be brought out. Yang Yi did not have to worry about a thing. He now went out to get some sedan-chairs, carriers, and horses, and started on his way before the night was out. He arrived in Malong at daybreak.

The pacification commissioner's yamen was a large, imposing compound protected on all sides by a brick wall. Within the walled compound of about twenty li in circumference were halls, terraces, ponds, and towers, with every appearance of a royal palace. The county magistrate sent someone in to announce his arrival. In a short while, he was invited in. Commissioner Xue himself came out to greet him. At the entrance of the main hall, the two men, after much demurring, crossed the threshold at the same time. After more salutations in the hall, County Magistrate Yang was invited to the back hall for some tea. After some polite small conversation, the magistrate was invited to the garden terrace for dinner.

Though of small stature, Magistrate Yang made a favorable impression on Mr. Xue by the breadth of his knowledge, his style of conversation, his poetic inclinations, and his capacity for wine. As a test of the magistrate's literary talent, Commissioner Xue had his men bring out a purple-gold antique mirror and said, "This mirror made of purple gold is most smooth and shiny. On the back of the mirror are four divination trigrams, each of which, when tapped, gives a different sound. The middle area, when tapped, sounds like a musical stone. Emperor Cheng of the Han held this mirror for Empress Feiyan[10] when she painted her eyebrows. Under the influence of an aphrodisiac, the emperor was murmuring tender words in front of this mirror when he died."

Holding the mirror in his hand, Yang Yi saw that it was indeed an antique of great value. Then and there, he wrote a poem that said,

> What a wondrous mirror I am,
> Made in the Yellow Emperor's times
> By the master artisan with his mold,
> In the pose of the Yan Emperor with his axe.
> After the chaos was cut through,
> The universe was suffused with light.
> Fu Xi's divination trigrams
> Were complete with all four seasons.
> Music then came into being,[11]
> With Shikuang as the master.
> Clear and dulcet,
> The melodies delight the ear.
> Perfect in shape and color,
> I function just as well.
> Men see in me their dignified selves;
> Women delight in the reflections.
> The fair and the ugly are told the truth;
> A smile, a scowl, the mirror shows them all.

Without even bothering to add punctuation marks, Mr. Yang handed the poem over to Mr. Xue, who read it carefully over and over again and praised it profusely, saying that it showed literary talent seen only in the Han and calligraphy worthy of the Jin, and that he was a rare genius of the likes of Wang Bo, Yang Jiong, Lu Zhaolin, and Luo Binwang of the Tang dynasty. He took out an even more curious small antique mirror and asked for one more poem, whereupon Mr. Yang wrote,

> Able to penetrate dark secrets,
> I find out the ominous in life.
> With no ears to hear or eyes to see,
> I give back but nature's light.
> In me is reflected everything,
> Making one forget what's in and what's out.

After reading it, Xue exclaimed, "What a fascinating poem!" His respect and admiration for Mr. Yang grew even further. He kept him for five days, treating him each day to fine feasts. At Mr. Xue's inquiry about the Old Man Pang incident, Mr. Yang gave him a full account, and both men laughed. Yang

Yi insisted on taking his leave to return to his county, but Xue would not hear of it. "May I ask how old you are?" he said,

Mr. Yang replied, "I have frittered away thirty-six years."

"I am twenty-six years old, ten years your junior." Thereupon he honored Yang as his older brother. Joyfully, they pledged brotherhood. A farewell feast was laid out, in the course of which wine vessels worth over two thousand taels of gold and silver were offered to Mr. Yang. The latter repeatedly declined, but Mr. Xue said, "Since we are brothers now, we don't have to stand on ceremony. I have quite enough to live on, whereas you are a newcomer who can do with some help. In the future, I will often send gifts your way. Do not reject them."

Mr. Yang bowed in gratitude, took leave of Mr. Xue, and returned to the county yamen, where he saw Old Man Pang, accompanied by that group of old men, coming to him with sheep, wine, bolts of silk and satin, and a hundred taels of silver each, totaling over two thousand taels. At the sight of such an abundance of gifts, Magistrate Yang said, "You shouldn't have gone to such trouble. I cannot very well take this."

The old men said, "This is just a slight token of our sentiments. You are different from all of your predecessors. Though the local people are not easy to rule, they are most simple and honest. If we have pledged allegiance to you, no one in this county would dare stir up any trouble. In the future, we will be offering you more tokens of our allegiance."

Impressed with their eagerness to please him, Mr. Yang kept them in his residence for some wine and food. They then took their leave with bows of gratitude.

According to an old local custom, anyone filing an official complaint had to pay an advance of three-tenths of a tael of silver, regardless of which way the verdict might turn out. If an official received a good many such complaints during his term of office, his income would be greatly supplemented. In murder cases, if a more lenient settlement was wished for, the plaintiff would, along with neighbors and witnesses, assess the financial status of the murderer and request that the county magistrate divide the defendant's property into three portions—one for the magistrate himself to keep, one for the plaintiff, and one for the defendant. This was a way to win favor with the magistrate. Another custom prevalent among the natives was to send gifts, from far and near, to the magistrate upon every festive occasion.

During over three years' time in Anzhuang, County Magistrate Yang amassed quite a fortune. Every time he received a gift, he deposited it with Commissioner Xue, and in due course, the magistrate found himself quite a rich man. One day, he said to Mr. Xue, "It is said that contentment is a virtue. What with your kind and generous gifts and my own income, I now have enough to live on. I have already handed in my resignation. My only worry is how to get my possessions home. Please help me, my brother."

Mr. Xue replied, "Since you have already resigned, there is no way I can keep you any longer. As for the possessions you've collected over time, I will have them loaded onto boats. Don't you worry."

After Yang Yi took his leave, Mr. Xue laid out a farewell feast and loaded on Yang's boat, ahead of time, farewell gifts worth a thousand taels of gold. Upon returning to the county yamen, Yang Yi summoned the old men and addressed them as follows: "I am much obliged for your kindness to me in my three years' stay here. I have retired, and while bidding farewell to you, I would like to present you with some parting gifts. I am leaving with the very same few pieces of luggage that I came here with. You will see for yourselves in the hall."

The old men protested, "Having nothing to present you with, how can we dream of accepting gifts from you?" Each of them ended up receiving a small gift and went cheerfully back.

On the day of the magistrate's departure, the local people turned out with flowers and candles to see him off and noticed that the magistrate had few pieces of luggage. Little did they know that Commissioner Xue had already made previous arrangements for the shipping of his possessions, so as to make Mr. Yang look as if he were carrying nothing away with him. After embarking on the boat, Mr. Yang and Li-shi set out on the journey back to where they had come from.

It was an uneventful journey. More than a month later, they came upon the place near Li-shi's home where they had moored their boat the last time they passed by. As they approached the bank, there for all to see were the monk and several other men waiting for them. They got on the boat and exchanged joyous greetings with Mr. Yang. Li-shi also came to pay her respects to the monk. Mr. Yang had some wine set out so they could talk to catch up on what each had gone through since they last met.

When Mr. Yang acquainted the monk with his experience in Anzhuang County, the monk replied, "I know everything. You don't have to tell me. I'm here today on account of my niece. She is married. I brought her to you against all sense of propriety, because I saw that you could not go to your appointed office without her help. Thank heavens, you are now back, safe and sound. My niece cannot follow you any farther because she has to return to her husband. The material possessions are all at your disposal."

At these words, Mr. Yang burst into tears. With loud wails, he threw himself at the feet of Li-shi and the monk, saying, "Woe is me! I'd be better off dead." He drew out a knife and aimed it at his throat, but before he could plunge it down, Li-shi held him in her arms, snatched away the knife, and also broke down in sobs. The monk tried to pacify them by saying, "Don't feel so bad. Parting is inevitable. I promised to return her to her husband, and a monk keeps his word." (*What kind of man is this husband, to make the monk abide by his word?*)

With tears in his eyes, County Magistrate Yang said, "You two can take away all my possessions. It's only the pain of parting with her that I cannot stand."

Moved by such sincerity, the monk said, "I have a solution. We can all retire for the night now and take leave of each other tomorrow."

Mr. Yang and Li-shi talked away the whole night without so much as closing their tear-filled eyes for a moment. The following morning, after toilette and breakfast, the monk suggested that Yang's wealth accumulated while at his post be divided into ten portions, saying, "Six-tenths will go to the Honorable Mr. Yang, three-tenths to my niece, and one-tenth to me." No one raised any objections. Li-shi and Mr. Yang held on to each other desperately, as if the parting were a matter of life and death.

After Li-shi had gone ashore and Mr. Yang's boat started moving away, the monk said, "You're going to have a most perilous journey by water. I will accompany you all the way to Lin'an before I turn back. We will surely not be doing any robbing, but at least we shouldn't be robbed by others." The monk accompanied Magistrate Yang all the way to Lin'an, where the latter kept him at his home over his protests for two months and showered him with gifts. Mr. Yang also wrote a letter to Li-shi to send her his greetings and thus started an unending stream of correspondence. There is a poem in evidence:

> *Alone at his post in an alien land,*
> *He owed to the monk the joys of his life.*
> *Do not snub anyone you meet,*
> *For he might turn out to be your savior.*

Chen Congshan Loses His Wife on Mei Ridge

You ride a white horse on high mountain roads;
I row a lonesome boat through rocky shoals.
Tease not each other—the whip and the oar;
Neither has a life free from trials.

Our story takes place in early spring of the third year of the Xuanhe reign period [1121] under Emperor Huizong of the Song dynasty, when imperial examinations were widely held to recruit worthy men. In the Huyiying district in the city of Bianliang, the Eastern Capital, there lived a twenty-year-old scholar, Chen Xin, courtesy name Congshan, whose father, now deceased, had been the commander of the palace army. Both of his parents having died early, he lived all by himself. An eager learner ever since childhood, he was accomplished in both the military and civil arts. Indeed, he outshone Confucius and Mencius in literature and surpassed Sun Wu and Wu Qi in the art of war. He knew everything there was to know about the Five Classics, the Three Histories, the *Six Strategies,* and the *Three Tactics.* His newly wedded wife, with the pet name Ruchun [Like Spring], was the daughter of Hanlin Academy Editor Zhang of the Gold Beam Bridge neighborhood in the Eastern Capital. At "double eight," or sixteen years of age, she was as fresh as a flower and as fair as jade—a flower that understood human speech and jade that gave forth fragrance. They were a most loving couple, as inseparable as fish and water, so much so that they wished they could die on the same day, even though they were not born on the same day. Being a man given to good deeds, Chen Xin often donated alms to monks and Taoist priests.

One day, Chen Xin said to his wife, "An imperial examination is coming up. I would like to go and take it. How nice it would be if I could gain some office and bring a change to the family fortune!"

"I'm only afraid that it's not in your fate to pass the imperial examination at the provincial level," said his wife.

"But I'm one of those who are 'ready to serve the royal family with their literary talent and military skills.'"

Several days later, he went to the examination hall and then waited, as all other candidates did, for the results of the examination. Within ten days, the results were posted, announcing that he had been awarded a *jinshi* degree. After the royal feast given in honor of the successful candidates, he thanked the emperor, who then appointed him military inspector of the town of Shajiao in Nanxiong, Guangdong.

Back at home, he said to his wife, Ruchun, "The emperor has graciously appointed me military inspector of Nanxiong. I need to be on my way very soon to assume the post. I've been told that it will be an arduous journey because the hilly region of Guangdong is infested with robbers and thieves, and the air is filled with poisonous miasma. Now that I should be packing for the journey, what am I to do?"

"Being your wife, I have the obligation to share hardships, if not comforts, in your life. I'll certainly follow you to your new post, however formidable the journey. Why worry about anything?" These words made him feel more reassured. Indeed,

> *When a green dragon and a white tiger go together,*[1]
> *There's no knowing if what follows is joy or sorrow.*

Later that very day, Inspector Chen called his servant Wang Ji and told him, "I have been appointed military inspector of Nanxiong in Guangdong. However, as the journey will be an arduous one, I need you to find me another servant to go with us." Thus instructed, Wang Ji went on a search in the busy sections of town, but this is no concern of ours here.

In the meantime, Inspector Chen told the maids in the kitchen, "Tomorrow being the third day of the fourth month, prepare a lot of vegetarian food to offer to priests. All traveling priests of the Quanzhen order[2] shall be served without exception."

We shall leave them to their preparations and turn our attention to a certain Sage Purple Sun in the Divine Realm of Daluo.[3] From there the sage witnessed Chen Xin's devotion to Taoism and Taoist priests. He also foresaw that on Chen Xin's way to Nanxiong to assume his post, his wife would come under misfortune that was to last a thousand days. He turned to the Sage of Great Wisdom and ordered him, "Change yourself into a Taoist youth and mark this: You are to call yourself Luo Tong and escort Chen Xin and his wife on their journey. If his wife meets with some monster, it will be your job to protect her."

The Taoist youth accordingly followed Sage Purple Sun to Chen Xin's house, where, after an exchange of greetings, they partook of a vegetarian meal. Then the sage asked Chen Xin, "You were always happy when treating priests to meals. Why do you look worried today?"

With his hands joined together in front of him in a gesture of deference,

Chen Xin said, "To tell you the truth, the emperor has graciously appointed me military inspector of Nanxiong. However, it takes a long and difficult journey to get there, and I have no brother to go with me. That is what worries me."

The sage said, "Young as he is, this page boy of mine, called Luo Tong, will be of help to you. You may keep him until you get to the town of Shajiao in Nanxiong and then send him back."

The husband and wife thanked him with a bow, saying, "We can never repay your kindness in honoring us with your presence and giving us a companion for the journey."

"This poor monk," said the sage, "is above material and vainglorious concerns. I ask for nothing in return." With a flick of his sleeves, he turned and went away.

Chen Xin said, "I am so delighted to have Luo Tong as a companion."

Having packed Chen's zither, sword, and bookcases and bade farewell to the relatives and neighbors, they locked and sealed the doors and left the Eastern Capital. They stopped for a rest after each five or ten li and thus wended their way ahead. Along the way, they saw

> Thatched cottages and bamboo fences
> Strewn throughout the villages;
> Earthen jars and jugs filled with fragrant wine;
> On the rack, a hemp gown
> Pawned by a herdboy the day before;
> On the wineshop banner, bold writing
> By a drunken village scholar.
> Patrons stop by, putting down their loads;
> Wayfarers in a hurry pass by
> Without getting off their horses.

With the inspector on horseback, Ruchun in the sedan-chair, and Wang Ji and Luo Tong carrying the bookcases and baggage, the four of them ate when hungry, drank when thirsty, halted at night, and set off again at dawn.

Luo Tong thought to himself, "Being the Sage of Great Wisdom in the Divine Realm of Daluo now accompanying Inspector Chen to Shajiao in Nanxiong by order of Sage Purple Sun, I'd better play the part of a fool so that they'll never guess who I really am." Thereupon he slowed down his pace and fell behind.

Annoyed at Luo Tong's slowness, Ruchun repeatedly urged her husband to send him back, but the inspector declined for fear of betraying the sage's kindness. When lighting a fire on the road to cook a meal, Luo Tong tearfully refused to eat. Even the inspector was irritated. As Ruchun insisted on sending him back, Luo Tong threw a tantrum, crying, "I can't walk another step!" Wang Ji helped him along, supporting him by his arms, but before they had gone five more li, he screamed again, "My back hurts!"

In the midst of his unending wails, Ruchun said to her husband, "In the beginning, I hoped he would be of some use, but since he hasn't done the slightest bit of work, why don't we send him back?"

The inspector should not have done as she wished, for Ruchun almost lost her life in that strange land. Truly,

> The case of the deer baffled the counselor of Zheng; [4]
> Zhuang Zhou thought himself a butterfly in a dream. [5]

Having regained peace after sending Luo Tong back that day, the Chen couple and Wang Ji continued their journey.

Now, to the north of Plum Ridge was a cave called Shenyang Cave, in which dwelt a demon called the Master of Shenyang, who was really a monkey spirit. Also known as the Great Sage Equal to Heaven, he had two brothers: Great Sage Leading to Heaven and Great Sage Filling Up Heaven. Their younger sister was called the Holy Mother of Sizhou. The Great Sage Equal to Heaven was a monkey capable of many bodily transformations and had enough magic power to subdue the mandrills in the various caves and to rule the fierce beasts of the various mountains. He could conjure up demons and use his black magic to steal any woman who struck his fancy. Whistling to the moon and singing to the wind, he would drink the finest wine to his heart's content. He was to enjoy the same age as the sky and earth, the sun and the moon.

From his cave, he saw, carried in a sedan-chair at the foot of the mountain, a woman as fresh as a flower and as fair as jade. Seized with the desire to take this woman, he summoned the mountain deity and told him, "Do as I say. Conjure up an inn. You change yourself into the waiter, and I'll be the innkeeper. They will certainly come for lodging. In the quiet of the night, I'll take the woman into my cave."

The mountain deity accordingly conjured up an inn with the Master of Shenyang sitting inside as the innkeeper. When dusk set in, Inspector Chen, Ruchun, and Wang Ji found themselves at the foot of Plum Ridge. As the hour was getting late, Wang Ji went forward and knocked at the door of the roadside inn, which was advertising for patrons.

The waiter asked, "What can I do for you, sir?"

"My master is on his way to Shajiao in Nanxiong to take up office as military inspector. There being no other inns, we would like to stay for the night here and be on our way early tomorrow morning."

The Master of Shenyang led the Chen couple into the best room of the inn. "I am over eighty years old," he told the inspector. "Let me say something that might be out of turn, but I want to warn you that Plum Ridge, ahead of you, is quite wild and is infested with tigers, wolves, and robbers. You'd be better off leaving your wife here with me while you go on ahead to assume your post. You may then send some government soldiers here to pick her up."

Inspector Chen rejoined, "This humble official is from a family of three generations of generals. Being thoroughly competent in the martial arts, I am most eager to render service to the empire. How can a few tigers, wolves, and robbers scare me?"

Realizing that the man was not to be easily persuaded, the Master of Shenyang did not venture more advice but withdrew from the room.

While the Chen couple were eating some supper in their guestroom, the first watch of night passed and the second watch approached. The inspector was the first to get into bed. He had barely taken off his clothes and lain down when a gust of wind rose right in the middle of the room. Truly,

> Its force felled the trees in front of Hades
> And blew up dust over the underworld.

When the wind subsided, the lamp, almost extinguished, flickered back into a steady flame. In great alarm, Inspector Chen threw some clothes on and rose to take a look around. His wife was nowhere to be seen. He opened the door and called Wang Ji, who, awakened from his sleep, had no idea what had happened. To the confused Wang Ji, the inspector said, "A violent gust of wind rose in the room, and now my wife is nowhere to be seen."

Master and servant hastened to call the innkeeper, but they heard no response. Upon a closer look, they realized, to their consternation, that the whole inn was gone. They found themselves standing in the wilderness, with no lights or inn or innkeeper but only the bookcases, baggage, and horse in front of them. From that night on, three years were to pass by before the inspector saw his wife again. What happened later? Truly,

> In the village shrouded in rain and fog,
> They lost their bearings, north or south.
> Perplexed, they consulted Zhang's work[6]
> And rolled up the scroll of colored ink.

Inspector Chen and Wang Ji heard the strike of the fourth watch from a watchtower. By the light of the moon and the stars, the two of them were frightened out of their wits as they found themselves in the middle of nowhere, with no inn before them or house behind them. The only thing for the inspector to do was to have Wang Ji carry the load of baggage while he himself mounted the horse and moved ahead along the moonlit path. On horseback, he thought to himself, "It must have been some evil magic power that made an inn appear out of thin air and then snatched away my wife. I have never heard of such a bizarre thing happening in all of history." As he went, he moaned between sobs, "Where am I to find my wife?" They wended their way forward until dawn broke.

Wang Ji suggested to him, "Put your worries aside for the moment, and think about what should be done next. Plum Ridge ahead of us looks dangerous and rugged. Yet we have no choice but to cross it. You can take up your post in Shajiao town first before coming back to search for Madam." The inspector could not do otherwise but follow his advice and reluctantly continued the journey.

In the meantime, Zhang Ruchun, snatched away by the Master of Shenyang to his cave, was stupefied with horror. When, after some time, she regained consciousness, her tears flowed like rain. It so happened that in the cave was another woman, called Peony, who had been kidnapped quite some time ago. She stepped forward to pacify Ruchun. The Master of Shenyang said to the latter, "You and I have a predestined bond. This cave is a different world from the one you know. After eating my magic peaches, magic wine, and peppered rice, you will achieve immortality. The immortal maidens in this cave of mine were all brought here by me from the mortal world. Don't be upset. We'll have some clouds and rain in the bedchamber."7

At these words, Ruchun burst into sobs. "I don't want to live happily as an immortal in this cave," said she. "My only wish is to die an early death. Clouds and rain are out of the question."

The Master of Shenyang thought to himself, "I am in raptures over her, but she is so bitter and unyielding. Such a stubborn woman will take her own life if pushed too hard. Wouldn't it be a shame to lose such a beauty?" So thinking, he summoned a woman named Golden Lotus, whom he had kidnapped years before, and told her, "Talk to Ruchun gently. Be nice to her, and try to coax her with kind words until she comes around."

Thereupon, Golden Lotus took Ruchun into her room and treated her to wine and food, but Ruchun refused all such offers and remained as resentful as before. Time and again, Golden Lotus and Peony tried to pacify her by saying, "Now that you are already here, there's nothing you can do. As the ancients say, 'If the eaves of the house are low, you might as well lower your head.'"

Turning to Golden Lotus, Ruchun said, "You don't know that I am a married woman, snatched away from my husband in the middle of the night by this old demon. I will never yield to his demands for clouds and rain. My only wish is to die soon to prove my chastity. The ancients said, 'A virtuous woman does not change husbands.' I would rather die than endure such a dishonor."

Golden Lotus rejoined, "As the saying goes, 'If you want to know what happened at the foot of the mountain, please ask those who have passed through there.' I've had the same experience. I used to live in Nanxiong. My husband had wealth and status. It's been five years since the Master of Shenyang snatched me away and brought me here. You are put off by his ugliness. I was, too, at first, but later I got used to him and felt better. Now that you are already here, there's nothing you can do. Why don't you just yield to him?"

Ruchun lashed out in a rush of indignation, "I'm not a lewd and cheap woman like you, who hang on to a life of humiliation. What are you living for? You worthless slut!"

Golden Lotus shot back, "If you turn a deaf ear to good advice, you're only asking for trouble."

She then turned around and told the master how the newcomer, instead of giving in to her persuasion, had called them vicious names. The master exploded with rage, "What an insolent slut! I should have beaten her to death with a copper mallet, but at the sight of her matchless beauty, I couldn't bring myself to do it. Yet here she is, as stubborn as ever."

Turning to Peony, he continued, "Let me put her in your custody. Cut that slut's hair short and make her go barefoot to the hilltop to fetch water for the flowers and trees. Feed her only simple meals three times a day."

Thus instructed, Peony had Zhang Ruchun's hair cut short, took away her shoes, and handed her a pair of water buckets. Ruchun contemplated throwing herself over a cliff but changed her mind, for she thought to herself, "If, by any chance, heaven takes pity on me and delivers me from this misery, I might still get to see my husband." With these thoughts, she went ahead with the chores, tears in her eyes. Truly,

> She'd rather go through hardships and remain chaste
> Than stoop to greed and lust.

We shall leave Zhang Ruchun in her misery in the cave and come back to Inspector Chen and Wang Ji, who had been on the road for over two months since leaving the Eastern Capital. Since the inspector's wife, having been snatched away by the Master of Shenyang north of Plum Ridge, was nowhere to be found, Wang Ji urged his master to go to take up his post before doing anything else, and so the inspector did. Catching sight of a wineshop right ahead of them, the inspector rode up to the door, dismounted the horse, and went into the shop with Wang Ji for some wine and food. After paying their bill, they resumed their journey.

At the foot of Plum Ridge there came into view a fortune-teller's thatched hut, where a sign said, "Yang Diangan, assisted by immortal beings, never errs in predicting the future." Inspector Chen dismounted at the door and went in. After an exchange of greetings, Diangan asked, "Where are you from, sir?" Thereupon the inspector recounted in detail the whole story about his wife's disappearance the previous night. While Yang Diangan burned incense to request assistance from an immortal being, inspector Chen prayed on his knees. An immortal did come, and wrote the following quatrain as an oracle:

> The mishap is to last a thousand days,
> But unyielding the lady remains.
> Wait till the day Purple Sun appears;
> The broken mirror will be made whole again.

Yang Diangan interpreted the quatrain in these words: "Put your worries aside. Your wife is to suffer for a thousand days, but in three years' time, you will be reunited with her when you meet with Purple Sun again."

Inspector Chen thought to himself, "I met Sage Purple Sun in the Eastern Capital and got Luo Tong as a companion but sent him back because of his temper tantrums. Now that I am a thousand li away, how do I get Purple Sun to come here?" Feeling slightly relieved, he paid the fortune-teller, mounted his horse, and went on his way with Wang Ji to Plum Ridge. It was indeed a precipitous ridge:

> Of all perilous roads in this world,
> None strikes more terror than Plum Ridge.
> Fierce, teeth-grinding tigers prowl in hordes;
> Giant, hissing snakes wriggle around.

Inspector Chen crossed the ridge and, at a point twenty li to the south, came upon a small pavilion used for greeting new officials. The inspector got down from his horse and went into the pavilion for a brief rest. Suddenly, Wang Ji approached to report that guards from the inspector's yamen in Shajiao Town, Nanxiong, still quite a distance away, were here to greet him. Inspector Chen summoned them in, and they exchanged greetings. The following day the whole company proceeded to the yamen, where, upon arrival, the new inspector held court for an exchange of greetings with all present. Thus started Inspector Chen's career in Shajiao Town, and he proved to be an honest and upright official. Time sped by like an arrow. Indeed,

> Outside the window, the sun flits by in a finger-snap.
> Around the table, the flowers' shadow moves as you sit.

Before he knew it, he had been in office for over a year. The men he sent out to look for his wife found no trace of her. Truly, it was as if

> The rock had sunk to the bottom of the sea;
> The paper kite had broken free from its string.

Knowing nothing about the fate of his wife, Inspector Chen was sick at heart. Thinking of his wife, he spent whole days in tears. His thoughts were again with Ruchun when a guard came in and reported, "Sir! There's trouble! The magistrate of Nanxiong sent a written message about an emergency. A bandit called Yang Guang, with the nickname Tiger of the Mountain, has gathered five to seven hundred men and occupied South Grove Village, where they are robbing, killing, burning, and wreaking havoc on the people. The magistrate wants the inspector to take one thousand armed cavalry and go immediately to subdue and arrest the bandits. This matter allows no delay." The inspector lost no time in readying weapons and horses. He led a thousand cavalry in full battle array at top speed toward South Grove Village.

In the meantime, Tiger of the Mountain was drinking in his camp in the village. At the report of the arrival of government troops, he took up his sword, hastily mounted his horse, and, at the clang of gongs, went forward to engage the enemy, followed by five hundred of his men. Without the exchange of a single word, Inspector Chen charged at Tiger of the Mountain, who, nothing more than an untrained local bandit, was no match for the inspector. In fewer than ten rounds, the inspector brought him down off his horse with a stab of the lance, cut off his head, and drove away his followers. The inspector then brought the head back to Nanxiong and presented it to the prefect, who was greatly delighted and gave out handsome rewards. Upon returning to his own yamen, the inspector held a banquet to celebrate the victory. With the slaying of Tiger of the Mountain, indeed,

> His fame spread throughout the Nanxiong region;
> His skills in the martial arts won praise from all.

Soon Inspector Chen's three-year term of office expired, and a new inspector came to replace him. He gathered together his personal belongings and left Shajiao Town with Wang Ji. They pressed hastily ahead. Before long, the westering sun sank below the horizon, and dusk set in. They caught sight of a monastery in the midst of pine trees far in the distance. Wang Ji suggested, "Let's go there and put up for the night."

Reining in his horse, the inspector went forward and saw that the horizontal tablet over the monastery door bore three big characters in gold: "Red Lotus Monastery." He dismounted and entered the temple with his retinue.

As a matter of fact, the abbot of this monastery, known as Chan [Zen] Master Zhandahui, was well-versed in the Buddhist dharma and was also a man of high morals and a reincarnation of Buddha. An acolyte reported to him, "A gentleman passing by is asking for lodging tonight." The abbot accordingly sent the monk to invite him in. After an exchange of greetings in the abbot's cell, the abbot asked, "Where are you from, sir?" Consequently,

Inspector Chen acquainted him with what had happened before and said, "I would never forget your great benevolence if you could be so kind as to show me how to find my wife."

The abbot said, "Listen. That monster is a white monkey spirit who, having attained his present status through a thousand years of cultivation, is capable of the most clever bodily transformations. Being firmly determined to preserve her virtue, your wife refuses to yield to him and, with her hair cut short and her feet bare, is leading a miserable life carrying water buckets to water flowers. Known as the Master of Shenyang, that fellow often comes to this monastery to listen to lectures on Chan and the Buddhist dharma. If you want to see your wife, you may stay in the monastery for some time until the Master of Shenyang comes again, for I will persuade him to change his ways and give you back your wife. What do you say?"

Most pleased at these words, the inspector accepted the offer of a longer stay in the monastery. Truly,

> *A small hill whose top takes a five-li climb to reach*
> *Has paths that lead north, south, east, and west.*
> *Many of those losing their bearings*
> *Have regained the right path with the point of a finger.*

Inspector Chen's stay in Red Lotus Monastery stretched to over ten days. One day, the acolyte reported to the abbot, "The Master of Shenyang is here." Hearing this announcement, Inspector Chen hid himself behind the screen in the abbot's cell. The abbot went to receive him, and, after an exchange of greetings, the abbot and the Master of Shenyang sat down as host and guest, and the acolyte served tea. After tea, the Master of Shenyang said to the abbot, "I have been unable to eradicate the desire for love. My natural disposition is possessed by lust. Who can 'untie the golden bell from the tiger's neck,' so to speak?"

The abbot answered, "If you want to have the golden bell untied from the tiger's neck, you must relieve yourself of lust. Form is emptiness and emptiness is form. By staying free of even a speck of dust of this mortal world, you will gain enlightenment into all the laws of the dharma. Don't blame me for speaking out of turn, but I've heard that you've been keeping a woman called Ruchun in your cave for three years. She is a woman of virtue. If you let her return to her native place, you will be cleansed of lust."

The Master of Shenyang rejoined, "Your Reverence, I hate this woman and made her carry water for three years as a punishment, but she still refuses to come around. I will never let go easily of such a stubborn woman!"

At these words Inspector Chen, listening behind the screen, fumed with rage. Truly,

His heart burned with fire;
His teeth gnashed in wrath.

In a rage, Inspector Chen whipped out his sword from his side and hacked right at the Master of Shenyang's head. With a lift of his finger, the Master of Shenyang made the sword go back to the inspector himself. "If it hadn't been for the sake of the abbot," said he, "I would have crushed you to powder, but I will not let this insult go unavenged." So saying, the Master of Shenyang bade the abbot adieu and left. Back in his cave, he summoned Zhang Ruchun and was going to kill her by cutting her heart out of her chest when Peony and Golden Lotus rescued her. She continued to carry water buckets to water the flowers, and we shall leave her there for the moment.

It would have been better if Inspector Chen had remained in the dark about his wife's whereabouts, but now that he knew she was in Shenyang's cave, he found himself in greater distress than before. In the abbot's cell in Red Lotus Monastery he beseeched the abbot to tell him how to find a way to see his wife. The abbot said, "That can be easily done. I'll show you a path up the mountain. You can go on your own to look for her." The abbot told the acolyte to lead the way up the mountain. The acolyte then returned to the temple and left the inspector there to a search by himself. Would Chen Xin be able to find his wife? Truly,

Cicadas on the trees aren't heard till the wind dies;
The moon outside the window isn't seen till the lamp goes out.

That day, Inspector Chen brought Wang Ji along and followed the acolyte up to the very top of Plum Ridge. In spite of the ruggedness of the path, they pressed their way ahead until they came to a pond by the rocks, where they caught sight of a barefoot woman carrying water. Hastily stepping forward to take a better look, they saw that it was none other than Ruchun. Husband and wife weepingly fell upon each other's shoulders and related to each other what had happened to them, wondering if they were seeing each other in a dream. Ruchun said, "I almost died yesterday when the master came back to the cave."

The inspector said, "We meet thanks to the abbot of Red Lotus Monastery, who pointed out the way for me. Why don't we just run away?"

Ruchun objected, "We can't do that. The master is infinitely resourceful with his immense magic power. If he knows I've gone, he will catch up with us, and both of us will be dead. I've heard that he fears only Sage Purple Sun. Only the sage can deliver us out of this misfortune. Now you must hurry back to the monastery, for if the master knows about this, we'll be in deep trouble."

The inspector could do no more than leave his wife and return to the monastery, where he thanked the abbot for having made it possible for him to see his dear wife. "The master fears only Sage Purple Sun, whom I once met in the Eastern Capital. But he is so far away from here. How can I reach him to get him to come to the rescue?"

At this earnest plea, the abbot said, "I must enter into meditation to take a look before I can know what to do." Having bidden the acolyte to burn incense, the abbot entered into meditation. After some time, he told Inspector Chen, upon coming out of the meditative state, "Sage Purple Sun gave you a Taoist youth, whom you dismissed when you had gone only part of the way. You may now go in that direction and travel for three days with all speed. Something is bound to happen to reward you." Thus instructed, Inspector Chen walked on foot out of the temple with all the speed he could muster and pressed ahead for two days. But nothing came to pass.

In the meantime, in the Divine Realm of Daluo, Sage Purple Sun remarked to Luo Tong, "Three years ago when that Inspector Chen set out on his way to assume new office, his wife was up for a thousand-day ordeal that will soon draw to an end. Considering his devotion to Taoism, I shall go down to the mortal world today with you to deliver his wife from Plum Ridge and send them back to their native place." Accordingly, Luo Tong descended with the sage into the world of mortals and headed for Guangdong.

As he caught sight of the sage and Luo Tong approaching from afar, Inspector Chen fell on his knees and implored, "Please save us! My wife Zhang Ruchun has been kept by the Master of Shenyang in his cave for three years. Please deliver her from her misery!"

The sage said with a laugh, "Chen Xin, you may go first to Red Lotus Monastery to wait for me. I'll be there in a moment." Chen Xin bowed as he took leave of the sage. Upon returning to the monastery, he laid out an altar in preparation for the sage's delivery of his wife from her distress. Truly,

> A divine master of the Tao,
> He has gone through no lack of trials.
> An iron tree may burst into blossom,
> But those sent to hell can hardly regain life.

Inspector Chen waited one day before Sage Purple Sun came to the monastery. He was indeed of a saintly appearance. The abbot went outside to receive him. After an exchange of greetings in the abbot's cell, they sat down as host and guest. The abbot was most impressed by the sage's sublime grace and dignified air.

Prostrating himself before the sage, Inspector Chen pleaded, "In your compassion, please save my wife Ruchun's life and let her return home. I will greatly appreciate your kindness."

Planting himself in front of the altar, the sage mumbled something, and, the next moment, a gust of wind sprang up in the room. The following quatrain is a description of the wind:

> *Shapeless, traceless, it makes itself felt*
> *And blows open the peach blossoms of spring.*
> *Sweeping withered leaves all along the way,*
> *It enters mountains and brings out white clouds.*

When the wind had blown away, two ferocious-looking, red-scarfed celestial generals came into view. Chanting a greeting to the sage, they asked, "What order do you have for us, master?"

"Go quickly to Shenyang Cave and bring to me the Great Sage Equal to Heaven. Do not fail me."

Before long, the two celestial generals came back to the sage with the Master of Shenyang tied with an iron chain. With the latter on his knees, Sage Purple Sun passed his judgment and had the celestial generals escort the Master of Shenyang to prison in the underworld to face charges. Luo Tong was told to go into Shenyang Cave, release all of the women kept there, and send them back to their homes.

Reunited with each other, Zhang Ruchun and Chen Xin bowed to Sage Purple Sun in gratitude.

Having bidden farewell to the abbot and Chen Xin, the sage rose slowly into the sky with Luo Tong.

Inspector Chen presented the abbot with some gifts as a token of his gratitude, took leave of the monks in the monastery, gathered together his personal belongings, got ready his carriage and horse, and left Red Lotus Monastery with Wang Ji and other attendants. Wending their way ahead, they arrived in their native town, the Eastern Capital, in a matter of days. The husband and wife never left each other again until they died at a venerable old age. There is a poem in evidence:

> *For three years she suffered in Shenyang Cave,*
> *To the loving couple's heartbreaking grief.*
> *Evil lost to good in the end;*
> *Her virtuous name is praised to this day.*

Qian Liu in a gambling game with the Zhong brothers.

Qian Poliu Begins His Career in Lin'an

Fame and name came to you against your will;
For years you had a hard life on the hills.
Now three thousand retainers fill your grand halls.
Fourteen prefectures you rule with your sword.
For Laizi clothes you exhaust your palace silk.[1]
Your poems, like Xie's,[2] put to shame sunset's rosy clouds.
When your name appears in the Hall of Fame,[3]
Why envy the noble lords of old times?

These eight lines were written by Guanxiu [832–912], a famous poet-monk who lived late in the Tang dynasty. He fled from the chaos wrought by Huang Chao's rebellion[4] and made his way to the Yue region south of the Yangzi River. When he dedicated this poem to King Qian[5] to ask for an audience, the latter showed much delight upon reading it, but the line "Fourteen prefectures you rule with your sword" struck him as lacking in grandeur,[6] whereupon he sent a messenger to Guanxiu, saying that only if he changed "fourteen prefectures" to "forty prefectures" would the monk be granted an audience. The messenger had barely finished when Guanxiu started intoning a quatrain:

I desire no glory and fear no kings,
Nor will I change numbers at someone's will.
A crane in the clouds stays not in one place,
But flies over all rivers and the skies.

After this, he left with ethereal grace for the Sichuan region. King Qian was stricken with remorse, but attempts to bring him back were too late. What a remarkable monk he was! A later poet had this to say in derision of the king:

Scholars have always sneered at lords and dukes,
But oceans never turn away small streams.
He who tolerates not even a monk,
Can never add prefectures to his rule.

The above lines make the point that King Qian was too narrow-minded to realize his ambition and remained a ruler of no more than fourteen prefectures. Even so, his was a life of no small achievement. Born in troubled times, he made himself a king of that part of the empire. Who, you may ask, was King Qian and what was his background? There is a poem that bears witness:

> The Xiangs declined, the Lius rose from poverty;[7]
> Through a battle their fight came to an end.
> Of all those observing the contention,
> Who spotted the mighty hero in the dust?

Here begins our story. King Qian, named Liu, with the courtesy name of Jumei and the nickname of Poliu, was a native of the county of Lin'an in Hangzhou Prefecture. During his mother's pregnancy, fire often broke out around the house, only to vanish when people came to put it out. The entire family was much bewildered.

One day, toward dusk, Mr. Qian was approaching the house from outside when he caught sight of a giant lizard about ten feet long climbing down from the roof, its eyes bright and sparkling, its head almost reaching the ground. Mr. Qian stood aghast. He was about to scream for help when the lizard disappeared. A glow of fire suddenly illuminated the sky from both the front and back of the house. Alarmed at what he thought was a fire, Mr. Qian cried to neighbors for help. All the neighbors, including those already gone to sleep, rushed to the scene with long hooks and water buckets, but there was no fire to be seen. Instead, they heard a newborn baby's cries coming out of Mrs. Qian's room. A shamefaced Mr. Qian apologized to the neighbors for having disturbed them with a false alarm. The sight of the giant lizard and the strange happenings prompted Mr. Qian to decide to drown the newborn baby because he thought it must be some kind of demon that would only bring calamity if left to live. But the baby was not destined to die yet.

There was a Granny Wang who lived in a house east of the Qians. A devout Buddhist, she was given to kind deeds and was a close friend of Mrs. Qian's. That night, at Mr. Qian's cries of fire, she also hastened to take a look. Upon hearing that Mrs. Qian was giving birth, she went in to offer help and was beside herself with joy at the sight of the baby. As she was carrying the baby to the basin for a bath, Mr. Qian tore the baby from her arms. He was about to push the baby into the basin and drown it when Granny Wang bent down and firmly protected the baby from him, crying out in great agitation, "What a sin! What a sin! It is by redeeming himself through many sufferings that he has found reincarnation as a boy. What has he done to deserve a drowning death! As the ancients put it, 'Even tigers and wolves feel the bond between father and son.' What's wrong with you?" Mrs. Qian in her bed also cried out in protest.

"Many strange things happened around the house before the birth," said Mr. Qian. "I'd hate to keep a devil that'll only grow up to bring ruin upon us."

Granny Wang shot back, "How can you know for sure what kind of man this tiny lump of flesh and blood will grow up to be? What's more, strange things also happen before the birth of great men. How do you know that what you saw were not auspicious signs? If you don't want to keep this baby, let me take him and give him up for adoption to a childless couple. A life will be spared, and you'll be saved from sin." (*Granny Wang is right.*)

It was Granny Wang's pleas that made Mr. Qian agree to keep the baby. The baby was thus given the nickname Poliu [Kept by Granny]. There is a poem in evidence of this:

> *Born in the fifth month, just as was Lord Mengchang,[8]*
> *King Qian almost died because of strange omens.*
> *Consider the cases of Dou Wen and Houji:[9]*
> *Those meant to be kings will live to be kings.*

In ancient times, Jiang Yuan conceived a child by standing on the footprints of a giant. Out of fear, she abandoned the newborn baby boy in the fields, only to take him back after three days when he was found to be still alive, protected by the wings of a hundred birds. He was thus named Qi [The Abandoned]. His innate saintly virtues became evident as he grew up. Skilled in the growing of crops, he was appointed by King Yao to take charge of agricultural matters and came to be known as Houji. Later, he became the patriarch of the Zhou dynasty, which began with King Wu and lasted eight hundred years.

During the Spring and Autumn period, a minister of the state of Chu named Dou Bobi had an affair with Master Yun's daughter, who gave birth to a son.[10] Fearful of a scandal, Lady Yun, Master Yun's wife, secretly abandoned him in the Meng Marshes. As Master Yun passed by the marshes on one of his hunting expeditions, he saw a tigress breastfeeding a human baby. After the tigress had finished with the feeding and left, Master Yun, who marveled at the sight, had someone bring the child home and told his wife that the boy would grow up to be no ordinary man. As his wife recognized the baby to be none other than her own grandchild, she told her husband the truth. He thereupon married his daughter to Dou Bobi and put the boy into Dou's care. In the Chu dialect, "breast" was called *gu* and "tiger" was called *wutu*. Therefore, he was given the name of Guwutu. Later in his life, he became prime minister of the state of Chu, known in our times as Prime Minister

Ziwen of Chu. This bears out the sayings "Great men never die before their time" and "A narrow escape from death is a guarantee of good fortune." To come back to our story, isn't it a matter of fate that Mr. Qian's attempt to drown the baby was thwarted by Granny Wang?

Let us not encumber our story with further idle comments. Qian Poliu was now an extraordinarily well-grown five- or six-year-old boy whose strength found no match in the other children of the neighborhood. Even teenage boys could not beat him at wrestling or fighting and had to accept him as their leader.

There was in Lin'an a hill called Stone Mirror Hill with a rock, all round and shiny, that reflected images like a mirror. In his daily frolics on the hill with his playmates, Qian Poliu was seen, as reflected in the stone mirror, wearing an emperor's robe with a jade belt, and a crown on his head. The awestruck boys said with one voice that this must have been the work of some divine being. With total composure, Poliu announced to the boys, "The divine being in the mirror is me! All of you, get down on your knees and bow to me," and so they did. Poliu accepted the bows in all complacency, and the practice continued.

One day, back from the hill, he told his father about this. In disbelief, his father went with him to the stone mirror and did indeed see what the others had seen. Much startled, Mr. Qian prayed silently to the mirror, "If it is indeed the destiny of my son Poliu to rise to wealth and eminence and to bring honor to the Qian clan, may the gods make his royal apparel disappear from the mirror, for, should others see this, disaster could follow." After the prayer, he bade Poliu take another look in the mirror. Now the image was that of an ordinary child without any royal apparel. Mr. Qian said in a deliberately severe tone, "Your eyes saw something that was not there. Don't ever tell such lies again!"

The following day, Poliu went again to play by the stone mirror. The boys refused to bow to him because the divine being had disappeared. But a plan came to Poliu's mind. By the side of the stone mirror stood a huge tree with a trunk that took a hundred men to join hands around it. Its abundant foliage cast a shade over several *mu*[11] of land. Under the tree was a big rock seven or eight feet high. Poliu said, "Let's pretend that this tree is an emperor's palace and this rock the emperor's chair. Whoever is the first to climb onto the rock can claim the throne. All the others will bow to him in congratulation." The boys all agreed heartily.

As they attempted the climb, they found the rock much too high, too steep, and too slippery. Being as smart as he was nimble, Poliu first took stock of the situation and saw that the gnarls on the tree trunk could serve as footholds. So he jumped onto the roots at the base of the trunk and climbed up step by step. At about ten feet above the ground, he looked well and hard at the rock before he let go and jumped. As he landed neatly on the rock in a sitting posture, the boys let out a cry and prostrated themselves on the ground.

"Now, are you quite convinced?" said Poliu.

The boys all said, "Yes."

Poliu continued, "In that case, you will do whatever I say." Right away, he commanded that tree branches be snapped off to serve as banners. Then he made the boys form two orderly lines. Henceforth, every morning the boys would stand in lines just as officials did in court sessions and make bows to him. He also divided them into armies fighting each other, flying green and red paper flags. He himself, in the meantime, sat on the rock and commanded the troops to advance or to retreat as he saw fit. Anyone who disobeyed was beaten up. As the boys could win no fights with him, they had no choice but to follow his orders. No one did not stand in fear of him. (*Deng Ai*[12] *played with battle formations, Zhu Xi with the stratagem of the Eight Trigrams,*[13] *and now Poliu is playing the commander.*) Truly,

> *He was a born leader of heroic mettle;*
> *Do not ignore what seem to be childish acts.*
> *Before he rises to rule the land,*
> *He shows his power to shake heaven and earth.*

By the time he reached the age of seventeen or eighteen, with his hair tied into a circlet, he was a tall and handsome young man with a powerful physique and a self-learned mastery of the skills necessary for each and every one of the eighteen weapons. He had obtained a rudimentary education during his brief school attendance but gave up further studies, refusing to devote his mind to the books, nor was he willing to take up business as a broker of agricultural products. Instead, he was given to dishonorable conduct—stealing chickens, beating dogs, drinking, and gambling, losing most of the few valuables his parents had. (*A true hero with all befitting qualities!*) His parents' attempts to reproach him only made him so resentful that he would leave the house and not return for days on end. Unable to control him, they could only let him have his way. He was now known in the neighborhood as Big Brother Qian. No one dared call him by his nickname anymore.

One day, he found himself out of money. An idea flashed upon him: "Gu Sanlang and his gang once tried to have me join them in smuggling salt. For lack of anything better to do, why don't I go seek him out?" On his way to see Gu, he passed by the house of Old Man Qi near a Buddhist temple. Now this Old Man Qi had been the first to open a gambling house in Qiantang County. Prostitutes were kept in the house to attract gambling patrons, and Poliu had often stayed overnight there on his gambling sprees. At that moment, as he was passing by the house, he ran into none other than Old Man Qi, with a steelyard in his left hand and a rooster and a pig's head hanging from his right. Seeing Poliu, he said, "Big Brother, I haven't seen you for some time."

"Any good patrons today?" asked Poliu.

"I won't keep anything from you. The county administrative director has two sons who are fond of gambling and spending money on wine. Some busy-body told them about my place, and now they are here demanding game partners, but because of their government connections, no one dares to show up. If you have enough cash to put down as ante, won't you join them for a game? They play with cash and not on credit, not even for a penny."

Poliu thought to himself, "I happen to be short of money. Why not go and make off with a few strings of cash?" So he said to Old Man Qi, "Others may fear them for their government connections, but I couldn't care less. One little game won't hurt. The only thing is that these rich men will laugh at me for not having enough money to put down as ante. When the game starts in a little while, I'll just say that my money is with you. If you cover for me, I'll give you half of my earnings if I win. If I lose, I'll give you back whatever I owe you."

Knowing Poliu as a man who had never played tricks on him at the gambling table, the old man agreed. He led Poliu into the house and brought him to Zhong Ming and Zhong Liang, sons of Zhong Qi, the administrative director of the county.

The old man said by way of introduction, "This is Big Brother Qian. He may be young, but he is most skilled in the martial arts and gambling. He heard that you are at my place and is here to make your acquaintance."

It so happened that the Zhong brothers also took delight in the martial arts, so they were greatly pleased that this young man with impressive physique had the same interest. After an exchange of greetings, they spent a few moments comparing notes on martial arts before Zhong Ming asked that the table be set for gambling. Placing on the table a ten-tael ingot of silver, he declared, "Since this is the first time we meet Brother Qian, we'll just put down this ingot of silver as ante."

Poliu made a feint of searching in his sleeves and said, "I didn't bring any cash with me, because I was on my way to see a friend and dropped in only when I heard from Mr. Qi that you were here." Turning to the old man, he said, "Won't you please put down some money for me, since you're keeping some of my money anyway?"

The old man agreed and took out ten taels of silver. Gathering the pieces together on the table, he said, "I happen to have on hand only these ten taels, enough for you to have two games."

As the saying goes, "The bigger the ante, the more daring the gambler."

Without a penny of his own, Poliu could not afford to be daring with what was the old man's possession. In his anxiety, he lost both games. Zhong Ming swept up his winnings with some words of apology and had a page boy give the old man one tael of silver as his share.

Though he had more silver at home, the old man was afraid that Big Brother Qian would only lose it all, and so he resignedly took the tael of silver and pushed the game board aside to make room for some food and wine, but Poliu was by no means in a drinking mood. "Please wait while I go back home to get some more money for a final game," he said.

Zhong Ming agreed, "That's a good idea." But Zhong Liang objected, "If you want to do that, come here early tomorrow so that we can have a whole day of fun. But, for the rest of today, let's just drink in celebration of making each other's acquaintance."

Poliu had to oblige. Two prostitutes came forward to offer their singing for the young men's added pleasure. Truly,

> With prostitutes in the gambling house,
> The patrons throw away silver like bricks.
> They end up dying under the peonies
> To repay their debt of romance.

In the midst of the carousing, there came knocks at the door. It was the officer on duty in the administrative director's tribunal. "His Honor the administrative director wishes to see the two young gentlemen," he announced. "I've been everywhere looking for you. I never thought you'd be here!"

The Zhong brothers rose and said, "Our father has to be obeyed. Brother Qian, we'll see you here early tomorrow morning." With a few words of thanks to the old man, they left with the officer. Poliu was about to step out the door when the old man held him back with both hands. "When are you going to give me back my ten taels of silver?" he demanded.

With a single swipe of his hand, Poliu freed himself from the old man's grasp and walked away, promising to return the money the very next day. Out on the street, he muttered to himself, "I lost because I had no money. Before I can come tomorrow to win back the money I lost, I'll still have to go to see Gu Sanlang to borrow some money." In his slightly inebriated state, he headed straight for South Gate Street.

He was relieving himself at the entrance of a deserted lane when someone slapped the back of his head. "Big Brother Qian, what wind has blown you here?"

Poliu turned around, only to see none other than Gu Sanlang, head of the salt-smuggling gang. "I have something to say to you, Sanlang," said Poliu.

"What is it?"

"To tell you the truth," confessed Poliu, "I've been losing at the gambling table for the last couple of days and would like to borrow about a hundred strings of cash to win back what I've lost."

"No problem," said Gu Sanlang. "Just follow me tonight to get the money."

"Where are you going?"

"Don't ask. If you follow me to the outskirts of the city, you'll find out."

As the two of them walked out the city gate, the sun was just sinking in the west behind the hills, and dusk fell. About two li later, they came upon a harbor where a small boat could be seen in the darkness, tied at the end of a rope stretching several feet offshore. The boat was covered tightly with reed mats. No one was in sight. Gu Sanlang picked up a clod of dirt and threw it onto the reed mats. At the thud, the mats opened. Two men emerged from inside the boat and coughed. Gu Sanlang coughed back, whereupon the two men poled the boat over. As Gu Sanlang and Poliu stepped down onto the boat, which had four more men hidden in the cabin, the two men asked, "Sanlang, who's that with you?"

"I have enlisted a most capable man. Don't waste words. Get the boat going! Quick!"

Working hard at the scull and the poles, the men started on their way down the river, fast as a shuttle.

"What are you up to tonight?" asked Poliu.

Gu Sanlang explained, "To tell you the truth, we are hard pressed for cash because no business has come our way in the last couple of days. We heard that Regional Commander Wang's family boat is anchored at the foot of the Tianmu Mountains, waiting for the incense-offering trip tomorrow morning. Wang is an immensely rich man. The boat must be laden with gold and silk, which would come in quite handy for us. But his two guards, Zhang the Dragon and Zhao the Tiger, are so fierce that none of us can overpower them. I was just thinking about your extraordinary fighting skills when I ran into you by a stroke of good luck. You are indeed a godsend. That's why I made bold to invite you here."

Poliu said, "There's nothing wrong in taking ill-gotten goods from corrupt officials."

As they were talking, their ears caught the sound of oars. Another small boat arrived on the scene with five strong men on board. The men on both boats coughed by way of signal. Knowing that the newcomers were part of the gang, Poliu held back from asking further questions. As the two boats drew near each other, Gu Sanlang asked in a whisper, "Where is it?"

A man in the second boat answered, "Within view, about one li ahead." Thereupon they maneuvred the boats into a dense growth of reeds and made a fire by striking stones. All the men exchanged greetings with Poliu. As big bowls of wine and thick slabs of meat were set out, the men fell to with voracious appetites. Each equipped with the weapon assigned to him, the thirteen men sallied forth in the two boats.

From afar, they could see that the big boat still had its lights on. As they drew near, they let out a formidable cry and jumped onto the prow, with Poliu at the head of the assault, an iron cudgel in hand. Zhang the Dragon ran up, only to fall into the water at one blow of Poliu's cudgel. Zhao the Tiger fled in the direction of the stern. None on the boat dared put up further resistance. Frightened out of their wits, all fell to their knees, asking for mercy. Poliu said, "Brothers, listen to me. Take no lives, but only the valuables." (*Clearly a man who rises above mundane concerns.*) Thus admonished, the men took as many things as they could lay their hands upon. At a whistle, they disembarked in two teams as before and sped away in their small boats.

It so happened that Regional Commander Wang arrived the following day on another boat. Upon being told that his wife and children had been robbed, he made a detailed list of all the missing objects and filed a complaint at the Hangzhou Prefectural Tribunal. The prefect of Hangzhou, Dong Chang, signed an order that was issued to all counties for the arrest of the robbers and recovery of the goods. When the prefectural order reached Lin'an County, the county magistrate set a deadline for the county sheriff and his officers to accomplish the mission.

Let us return to Gu Sanlang and his gang. They moored the boat again in the depth of the reeds and divided the booty into thirteen equal shares. But, as Poliu had done more work than anyone else, it came to be generally agreed that he should receive two shares, which amounted to three big ingots of silver, some loose pieces of silver worth about a hundred taels, and about a dozen gold and silver wine vessels and pieces of jewelry. By this time, day had broken and the city gates were open. Carrying the load of valuables in his arms, Poliu jumped onto the bow of the boat and said to Gu Sanlang, "Thank you for letting me do this job. I will surely serve you again next time." He then made his way straight to Old Man Qi's house.

The old man was tossing on his bed when he was woken up by Poliu. Rubbing his eyes with his hands, he asked, "What brings you here so early?"

"Why aren't the Zhong brothers here yet?" said Poliu. "I've come to win back the money." Handing over to the old man all the silver, wine vessels, and jewelry, he said, "I'll have to trouble you again with putting down antes for me. These things are all yours to keep. Deduct from this the ten taels I borrowed from you yesterday. (*Action befitting a hero.*) When the Zhong brothers come, take a few taels of loose silver and set out a feast for me in their honor."

Overjoyed at the sight of so many valuables, Old Man Qi promised eagerly, "That's but a trifle. I'm at your service."

Poliu continued, "I got up too early this morning. Since they're not here yet, I'd like to take a nap in a quiet place." The old man led him into a small room with a white wooden bed and said, "Make yourself comfortable. I'll go wash up."

After breakfast in the tribunal, Zhong Ming and Zhong Liang stuffed several ingots of silver in their sleeves and wended their way to Old Man Qi's house. The old man was doing some shopping nearby when he saw them approaching. "Big Brother Qian is treating you today," he said. "He waited for you for so long that he's now taking a nap in a small room. Please go ahead. I'll join you in a moment."

The Zhong brothers secretly marveled, "A man so true to his word is hard to come by." As they entered the hall, they were startled by the sound of snoring as loud as peals of thunder. As they found their way into the side room, they suddenly saw a two-horned giant lizard over ten feet long lying on the bed amid multicolored clouds and mist. "How strange!" exclaimed the Zhong brothers. Their cry dispelled the clouds and mist and, instead of the lizard, what they saw now, upon a closer look, was none other than Big Brother Qian, fast asleep. The two brothers thought to themselves, "It is often said that some extraordinary men can appear in extraordinary shapes. We saw the lizard only too clearly, but it turned out to be Big Brother Qian. This man will surely amount to something. Wouldn't it be nice if we pledge brotherhood with him before he rises to eminence?" After some discussion, they made up their minds.

When Poliu woke up, they said, without any mention of what had led to their decision, "Being admirers of men of good faith, we would be more than happy to make a Peach Garden pledge of brotherhood[14] with you. What do you say?"

As Poliu had also taken a liking to the Zhong brothers for their frankness and generosity, there and then he performed with them the eightfold obeisances and completed the ritual of the pledge of brotherhood. (*"Sworn brothers of old had true sense of honor; / Sworn brothers today have nothing but rancor. / Sworn brothers of old were better than real ones; / Sworn brothers today dump each other half way. / They pour out their hearts over wine and meat, / But act like strangers when there's need for help. / Even real brothers fall out all too often, / Let alone those who have taken but an oath!" However unrefined this song may be, it aptly captures the ills of the day.*) Being the youngest of the three, Poliu became Third Brother. That day, instead of gambling, they drank to their hearts' content. Before they took leave of each other, Zhong Ming handed back to Poliu the ten taels he had won the day before, but Poliu flatly turned down the offer. "I have paid back Old Man Qi," he said. "Keep the silver for yourself until the day I need to borrow from you." Zhong Ming had to take back the money.

Henceforth, the three of them often gathered together, and, through their drinking and fighting, they built a reputation for themselves in gambling circles as the Three Tigers of Qiantang. Most displeased as he got wind of this, Zhong Qi forbade his two sons to loaf about on the streets and confined them to their home. Not having seen the Zhong brothers for days, Poliu went to the tribunal for some news and heard about what had happened. He took fright and dared not go to see the brothers again for quite some time. Truly,

> Choosing the right friends is a matter
> Not to be taken lightly.
> Good discipline produces good children;
> Filial sons bring the father peace of mind.

Now that Qian Poliu was estranged from the Zhong brothers, he naturally resumed his relationship with Gu Sanlang and his gang. Dozens of times he joined them in their illegal operations of salt smuggling and robbery. First timers in the smuggling business might be faint-hearted, but the second time around, they grow more daring. By the third or fourth time, they become positively dauntless. This business costs them no capital but brings in silver and cash galore for their reckless spending. As long as they are lucky enough not to be found out, they are free to enjoy the good days. Once found out, they will get ready to put up a hard fight. But, as it has always been said, "If you don't want others to know about it, don't do it." Chen Xiaoyi, a member of Gu Sanlang's gang, was exchanging a pair of pure gold lotus-shaped cups for silver at a silversmith's when the silversmith recognized the cups as the property of Squire Li Shijiu and reported as much to the police, who in turn reported to the county sheriff and obtained a list of the gang members' names. Action was to be taken soon.

One day, the sheriff invited Director Zhong and his sons for a drink in his residence. As Zhong Ming was a good calligrapher, the sheriff invited him into the study and asked him to write a scroll. Zhong Ming accordingly wrote Li Bai's [also spelled Li Po, 701–762] poem "Ballad of Youth." The sheriff was spreading the scroll to its full length and admiring the calligraphy when Zhong Ming's eyes happened to rest upon some paper under the ink-stone. Pushing away the ink-stone, he saw that it was a list of names. Being the shrewd man that he was, Zhong Ming took the list when he was unobserved and hid it in his sleeve. When he stole a look at it, he was startled to see a list of salt smugglers' names, Qian Poliu's name among them. At the dinner table, he feigned a stomachache after only a few cups of wine and said he had to go home. The sheriff thought he was truly ill and let him go. Little did the sheriff know that the illness was but a ploy.

Instead of returning home as he had claimed, Zhong Ming rushed to Old

Man Qi's house and asked him to look for Poliu and bring Poliu to him. It so happened that Poliu was right there in the house, gambling away. At the sight of Poliu, Zhong Ming grabbed him by the arm, dispensing with the usual ceremony of greeting under the pressure of time, led him outside to a secluded place, and told him everything. "Luckily I saw and stole the arrest list. It's here. Hide yourself quickly, because the police will be coming soon. By that time, I won't be able to save you. But in the meantime, I'll bribe the sheriff and his men. If things stay quiet for the next three months, you can then come out of hiding. Do take care!"

"The many people on the list are all my trusted friends," said Poliu. "Since you'll be maneuvering on my behalf, please also let each of them off the hook. If one is brought before the authorities, all of us will be implicated."

Zhong Ming promised, "I'll come up with something." With this, Zhong Ming took himself off.

Poliu was so alarmed at the news that he ran frantically all the way to the south gate to tell Gu Sanlang about it. He added that the gang should quickly leave the place, so as not to get themselves into trouble.

Gu Sanlang agreed, saying, "We'll get off the salt boat and spread out among different towns. Nobody will notice anything. But you have no place to go other than your parents' house. What's to be done?"

Poliu said, "Don't worry about me. Take care of yourself." With these words, he took leave of Gu. From that day on, Poliu feigned illness and stayed at home for three whole months. He spent his days practicing martial arts and dared not set foot out of the house. Even his parents were surprised, but they had no clue as to the real reason. There is a poem that bears witness:

> Zhong tried to save him in his hour of need;
> He, in his turn, alerted his partners.
> Loyal comrades share their joys and sorrows;
> Men of honor betray not their true friends.

The following day, the county sheriff made ready for the arrest operation, but he could not find the list of names that he thought was under the inkstone. All hell broke loose. He strung up and whipped the page boy whose job it was to take care of the study, but the boy confessed nothing.

The chaos lasted for three days, but no clue was found. The sheriff was at his wits' end. In the meantime, Zhong Ming and Zhong Liang were bribing high and low. All of the officers had been bought. And now, two hundred taels of fine silver were sent through an officer to the sheriff, along with the request that he put the case to rest. Fortunately, the sheriff was a greedy man. When he was told that the administrative director's tribunal would also be taken care of for him, it occurred to him that the director might actually have been bribed first. In that case, he thought it wise for him to do the director a favor and let go of the case. Consequently, he accepted the silver and made a show of setting a deadline for the officers to arrest the smugglers. Two months went by without anything being done. Truly, this bears out the sayings "No official business remains urgent after three days" and "Money makes even ghosts grind the mill." But we shall digress no more.

Our story branches at this point. Let me now tell of a soothsayer from Hongzhou, Jiangxi:

> *Well-versed in astronomy,*
> *He was a master fortune-teller.*
> *The white rainbow that stretched across the sky*
> *Revealed to him the plot at Yishui.*[15]
> *He recognized the Fengcheng swords*[16]
> *By their divine aura in the air.*
> *He foresaw Ban Chao's*[17] *rise to power*
> *And Deng Tong's*[18] *death from hunger.*
> *Divinely accurate he was,*
> *A true master of the art.*

This soothsayer by the name of Liao Sheng, knowing that the Tang dynasty was to experience great chaos, chose to live the life of a recluse on Pine Gate Mountain. One night, as he was sitting, he saw under the Dipper and Altair stars a faint aura of many colors that suggested to him the presence of a future sovereign in the region of Qiantang. Thereupon he packed for a journey there. Another look at the clouds convinced him that the scope should be narrowed to Lin'an. Consequently, he took up residence in the city of Lin'an as a physiognomist. Although he had throngs of clients every day, none was out of the common run. A thought suddenly came to him: "Director Zhong Qi is an old acquaintance of mine. Why don't I go to see him?" Hurriedly he went to the director's tribunal and had his name announced.

Hearing that Liao Sheng, an old friend, was there, Zhong Qi rushed out in great haste. After the exchange of greetings and some amenities, Zhong Qi asked him about the purpose of his visit, whereupon Liao Sheng dismissed the attendants and whispered to Zhong Qi, "I was looking at the night sky when I detected the presence of an extraordinary man in your county. I have spent several days in town trying to meet that man, but so far without success. Your physiognomy is indeed distinguished, but not enough to warrant such an aura in the sky."

Zhong Qi summoned his two sons for Liao to take a look at. Liao Sheng said, "I do see from their bones a prominent future, but they will be no more than ministers. By 'extraordinary man,' I mean no less a person than a sovereign, someone whose status is exalted enough to emanate an aura under the stars of the Dipper and Altair. He should be at least a powerful lord." Zhong Qi kept him for the night in the tribunal.

The following day, claiming that there were some thorny problems in the county to be discussed, Zhong Qi held a feast at Wushan Monastery for the best-known men in the county and had Liao Sheng look secretly at every one of them. Some looked more distinguished than others, but none had the physiognomical features of a sovereign. After the feast, Zhong Qi invited Liao Sheng to spend another night in the tribunal so that he could look at more men of distinction in the villages the following day. After night had fallen, the two of them returned on horseback, riding shoulder to shoulder.

Now let me come back to Qian Poliu. He was immensely relieved at being able to remain at home in peace for three months. Remembering the Zhong brothers' kindness in saving his life, he mustered his courage and betook himself to the director's tribunal. Upon learning that Zhong Qi was away at a feast at Wushan Monastery, he slipped into the tribunal and asked to see the Zhong brothers to express his gratitude. Zhong Ming and Zhong Liang rushed out upon hearing that Poliu had arrived and, taking advantage of their father's absence, greeted Poliu and kept him for some conversation. All of a sudden, horse-bells were heard, announcing Zhong Qi's return. Poliu was so frightened at the sight of Zhong Qi that, his heart pounding, he hung his head and ran out. Zhong Qi asked who he was and ordered that he be seized. With alacrity, Liao Sheng admonished Zhong Qi, "Do not be rude to this man. Amazingly enough, this is the extraordinary man I have been talking about."

Always a believer in Liao Sheng's soothsaying, Zhong Qi changed his tone and ordered his men to invite Poliu, in all politeness, to come to him. Poliu had no choice but to return. To Zhong Qi's request for his name, he remained as silent as a clay or wooden statue. Zhong Qi grew impatient and asked his sons, "What is this man's name? Where does he live? How did you come to know him?"

Realizing that they could no longer conceal the fact from their father, Zhong Ming was obliged to come out with the truth: "His surname is Qian, nicknamed Poliu, a native of Lin'an."

Zhong Qi burst into laughter. Pulling Liao Sheng aside, he said to him under his breath, "How wrong you are! This is a local bum lucky enough to be out of the reach of the law for the moment. How can such a man gain wealth and rank?"

Liao Sheng said, "I am not mistaken. You and your sons will owe your eminence to him." He turned to Poliu and said, "Your bone structure is extraordinary. You will, without fail, rise to great fame and shining glory. I hope you will conduct yourself well." Then he turned to Zhong Qi: "I go in search of extraordinary men not in the hope of sharing their future wealth and eminence, but just to test if my predictions are accurate. Ten years from now, what I said will come true, as you shall see. Now I am bidding farewell to you, probably never to meet again." With these words, he took himself off with light and airy steps.

By now, Zhong Qi was convinced that Poliu was no common sort. He was all the more struck with awe when Zhong Ming and Zhong Liang told him about the horned lizard that they saw in Old Man Qi's house. That night, he had his sons ask Poliu to stay over and to relay to Poliu his advice: "Apply yourself to martial arts. Don't do anything unlawful and hurt your reputation. I will attend to any need for money." Henceforth, the Zhong brothers and Poliu resumed their constant mutual visits. Indeed, the bond of friendship grew deeper than before. There is a poem in evidence:

> Great heroes are hidden among common men;
> But who ever seeks them among the poor?
> Only Liao Sheng saw him for what he was
> And inspired Zhong Qi's respect for the man.

In the second year of the Qianfu reign period [875] under Emperor Xizong of the Tang dynasty, Huang Chao raised an army and ravaged the eastern part of Zhejiang. Dong Chang, the prefect of Hangzhou, issued an order to recruit soldiers. When Zhong Qi learned of the news, he told his sons, "With that rebel Huang wreaking havoc and heading in our direction, the prefect is recruiting men to crush the bandits. This is the moment for the brave to prove their worth. Why don't you talk Poliu into it?"

Zhong Ming and Zhong Liang said, "We'll be happy to go with him and prove our worth." Overjoyed, Zhang Qi sent for Poliu right away and explained the situation. Poliu rubbed his fists and wiped his palms in great eagerness to go. Zhong Qi paid for all the armor and weapons he needed and gave him another twenty taels of silver for his family. He changed his name to Qian Liu, courtesy name Jumei, Liu being of the same pronunciation as the second syllable in his childhood name, Poliu. The three young men took leave of their parents and set out on their journey. Once in Hangzhou, they presented themselves to Prefect Dong Chang. Much impressed by Qian Liu's powerful physique, the prefect tested him in the martial arts and was so pleased by his remarkable skills that he made them all adjutants with orders to serve in the front ranks.

A few days later, a spy reported, "Tens of thousands of Huang Chao's forces are approaching Lin'an. Please send reinforcements." Dong Chang appointed Qian Liu as Deputy Commander to lead the rescue mission. He asked Qian, "How many men do you need?"

Qian Liu answered, "A general wins by his wits rather than his valor; an army wins by the quality of its men rather than by sheer numbers. If I could have the Zhong brothers' help, I'd be content with only three hundred men," whereupon Dong Chang gave him permission to select three hundred men from the prefectural army. With Zhong Ming and Zhong Liang as co-commanders, the men set out for Lin'an.

Upon reaching the town of Shijian, they found out that the enemy troops were only fifteen li away. Qian Liu consulted the Zhong brothers: "Since we are few and they are many, our only chance of winning is not by force but by strategy. Let's give them a surprise attack." (*Since ancient times, a good commander has been one who wins battles with an army outnumbered by the enemy. His advantage lies in preparedness rather than in reckless ventures.*) He sent two cannoneers to hide themselves along the road that the enemy troops would take. Then he selected twenty archers with crossbows and led them, armed with good arrows, to strategic positions in the valley, where they lay in ambush. As soon as the enemy troops walked into their ambush, the cannoneers were to fire a signal for the twenty archers to unleash their arrows. Zhong Ming and Zhong Liang each led a hundred men and lay in ambush on either side to provide reinforcement. The rest of the men were dispersed throughout the valley, ready to wave flags and shout battle cries so as to add terror to the scene. (*These three hundred were a match for any tens of thousands of men.*)

Hardly had the men taken their positions before Huang Chao's forces arrived. The mountain paths of the region were so narrow that only a single rider could enter at a time. The enemy advance team led by their vanguard was on one such path in single file when a cannon boomed out, immediately followed by arrows flying from twenty strong bows. The much-startled enemies had no idea how many men they had encountered. The enemy vanguard officer, wearing a red brocade robe and carrying a halberd in his hand with a command flag inserted on his back, was advancing jauntily on his yellow battle-horse when an arrow hit him right in his neck, and down he tumbled. The enemy troops were thrown into disarray. Leading their two hundred men, Zhong Ming and Zhong Liang charged fiercely forward from both ends of the path, striking terror into the hearts of their enemies, who, fooled by all the battle-cries around them into believing they were outnumbered, trampled each other in great confusion. Five hundred heads were cut off. The rest of the enemy was put to flight.

Now that he had won a complete victory, Qian Liu thought to himself, "This is but a trick that worked by a stroke of good luck. It can't be used more than once. (*Never do again the same thing that brought you luck. Never visit again the same place where you once thrived.*) Should the main forces of the enemy bear down upon us, the three hundred of us will be reduced to powder. About thirty li away, there is a village called Eight Hundred Li. Let me lead my men to camp there." He said to an old woman by the roadside, "If anyone asks you about the Lin'an troops, just say that Eight Hundred Li is where they are camped."

Now, having heard that his advance team was beaten at the town of Shijian, Huang Chao led the main forces of his troops in that direction. Indeed, so numerous were his men that as they swept along, they darkened the mountains and the fields. As not even one government soldier was in sight by the time they arrived in the town, they searched for residents to question. In a short while, the old woman was brought before them.

"Where are the Lin'an troops?"

The old woman replied, "Eight Hundred Li is where they're camped." She stuck to the same answer when asked time and again.

Without knowing that Eight Hundred Li was the name of a place, Huang Chao thought that the government troops' camps covered a distance of eight hundred li. With a sigh, he said, "We were no match for only twenty archers, let alone an army that needs eight hundred li to accommodate their camps. It's impossible to take Hangzhou." Thereupon, he decided not to keep his troops in town any longer but pressed ahead to Yuezhou. And thus it was that Lin'an was spared from ravages, as these lines attest:

> He outwitted the many with a few,
> A fine general with strategies divine.
> With three hundred men camped at Eight Hundred Li,
> He scared off the enemy and regained peace.

Liu Hanhong, the surveillance commissioner of Yuezhou, was not prepared for any enemy advance. When word got to him that Huang Chao's army was approaching, he sent a messenger out to say that he would be willing to give them liberal amounts of gold and silk, if only they would spare the city from attack and looting. Accepting the offer of gold and silk, Huang Chao passed by Yuezhou and went on ahead. Now, this Liu Hanhong used to be the prefect of Hangzhou, with Dong Chang in the subordinate position of adjutant in charge of recruitment. As a reward for having crushed Wang Ying's rebellion some time before, Dong Chang was promoted to the post of prefect of Hangzhou, whereas Liu Hanhong rose to be surveillance commissioner of Yuezhou. Many a time did Liu Hanhong seek ways to bully his former subordinate Dong Chang. As Dong Chang found it too hard to swallow the insult, the animosity between the two men grew deeper.

Now, though Yuezhou was spared from killing and looting, bribing Huang Chao cost Liu Hanhong a fortune. His chagrin increased when he learned that Dong Chang of Hangzhou was claiming credit for having defeated the enemy in battle. One of his retainers, a certain Shen Ke, offered him this advice: "It was Commander Qian Liu who defeated the enemy at Lin'an by strategy. I've heard that Qian Liu is a man of wisdom as well as courage. I suggest that you send Dong Chang a letter along with some handsome gifts, saying that as Yuezhou is still in turmoil, you need to borrow Qian Liu from him to wipe out the bandits. Once Qian Liu is here, you can either treat him nicely to win him over, or find an excuse to kill him. For Dong Chang, losing him will be as incapacitating as losing his right arm. As things stand now, the imperial court is at sixes and sevens with eunuchs abusing power. Official decrees have lost all authority. Men of heroic aspirations throughout the empire all have their minds set on establishing their own separate regional bases. Crushing Dong Chang would mean having both Hangzhou and Yuezhou under your power, and that would be an impressive achievement indeed." (*Not a bad plan to listen to, but Hanhong is not meant to be a king.*)

Being a man of high aspirations but little talent, Liu Hanhong found the suggestion much to his liking. Stroking Shen Ke's back with his hand, he said, "What a brilliant idea from my trusted confidant!" There and then, he wrote a letter that said,

> *To my old friend Mr. Dong from Hanhong with repeated bows:*
>
> *With few generals and a small army, Yuezhou is ill prepared for the ravages of Huang Chao's bandit army. I hear that you have a Commander Qian Liu who is as great a strategist as he is a brave warrior. Now that peace has been restored in your prefecture, I humbly plead that you send Qian Liu to assist me in repelling the enemy, for ours are neighboring cities as closely related to each other as lips and teeth. After the mission is accomplished, all credit will go to your name. I am sending herewith a suit of golden armor and two prize horses, hoping in all humility that you will accept this small token of my sincerity.*

As a matter of fact, Dong Chang, out of his mistrust for Liu Hanhong, had sent spies to find out about the situation at Yuezhou and, therefore, knew that Huang Chao had already left. Wondering about the reason behind the reference in the letter to the ravages of the bandit troops, he took counsel with Qian Liu.

Qian Liu said, "Let us acknowledge the fact that your discord with Commissioner Liu is already beyond reconciliation. It is said that Commissioner Liu, calling himself a descendant of the royal house, harbors inordinate ambitions. Instead of fighting the bandits, he sought peace by bribery, and his real intentions are quite unclear. If you give me two thousand of your finest men for me to bring over to him as a gesture of assistance, Liu Hanhong, being the unimaginative man that he is, will be most happy to take us. We will then

look for an opportunity to wipe him out, and Yuezhou can be had for the taking. A memorial can then be presented to the emperor, charging Hanhong
with the crimes of appeasing the bandits and of sedition. The emperor, in trying to put the matter to rest, will certainly reward you heavily. Wouldn't this
plan bring honor to your name and security to your position? You have nothing to lose."

Dong Chang readily consented and wrote a letter of reply for the messenger to take back. After the messenger had left, he gave Qian Liu two thousand
of his crack troops and reminded him before bidding him goodbye, "Use caution, and act only when the opportunity presents itself."

Now, Liu Hanhong was beside himself with joy upon receiving the reply
from Dong Chang assuring him that Qian Liu was on his way. Again, he
turned to Shen Ke the retainer for consultation.

Shen Ke said, "The two thousand men Qian Liu is bringing are all the
best soldiers. They'll be difficult to control once they are let into the city. I
suggest that they be greeted before they arrive, and made to camp outside the
city. Summon no one else but Qian Liu. With no wings of support, he will
have to succumb to us. Then we can send another general to lead the Hangzhou troops, handsomely shower them with bounty, and make them turn
around and attack Hangzhou with the speed of lightning. Caught unawares,
Dong Chang can surely be wiped out." (*This all sounds very good, but what
if Qian Liu does not fall into the trap?*)

Again, Liu Hanhong was full of praise: "What a brilliant idea from my
trusted confidant!" That he ordered Shen Ke to go out the city gate to welcome
Qian Liu needs no description here.

Let us turn to Qian Liu, who was now approaching Yuezhou with his two
thousand men. Shen Ke came forward to stop the advance and exchanged greetings with Qian Liu. "By order of the commissioner," announced Shen Ke, "I
invite you alone into the city because the city is too small for the accommoda-
tion of so many soldiers. They will have to be camped outside the city."

Qian Liu was aware of Liu Hanhong's trick, and in an attempt to turn the
trick against Liu himself, he feigned indignation, saying, "I am but a worthless
man, but the commissioner overlooks my humbleness and calls for my service
with a generous offer of gifts. I am more than willing to repay his kindness with
my life. Though outwardly cordial with the commissioner, Prefect Dong in
fact bears a grudge against him and at first refused to let me come. Then he
relented but would give me only five hundred men. It was at my insistence
that he agreed to two thousand. I handpicked the finest soldiers, each the match
of a hundred men. And here we are to assist the commissioner in achieving
eternal fame. Little did I know that the commissioner would summon me like
a slave to his tribunal in the city instead of coming out in person to reward

the tired soldiers with food and drink. This is by no means the proper way to treat worthy men. I will now turn back with my men, for I have lost all wish to see the commissioner." Then, with his face turned to the sky, he heaved a sigh, saying, "Such high aspirations I had. What a pity! What a pity!"

Mistaking the show of regret to be sincere, Shen Ke changed his line with alacrity. "Please don't take offense," he pleaded. "The commissioner was unaware that you feel this way. Let me go into the city to tell him about this. He will certainly come out in person to reward your troops and to greet you." With these words, he galloped back on his horse. Qian Liu instructed his trusted subordinates to make preparations in secret.

In the meantime, Liu Hanhong, believing what Shen Ke reported to be true, ordered that fodder be prepared and oxen and horses slaughtered to be offered to the Hangzhou troops. Preceded by drummers and a team bearing banners, he set out for an inn outside the north gate and sat down to wait for Qian Liu to be introduced to him as an adjutant would be to his commander in chief. To his astonishment, in marched Qian Liu jauntily, followed by twenty of his trusted men. With hands joined in front of his chest, Qian Liu said to Liu Hanhong, "Please forgive me for not kneeling down, encumbered as I am by my suit of armor." (*By this time, Qian Liu already has more than enough power to wipe out Hanhong.*) Liu Hanhong's anger left him drained of all color.

Feeling guilty for having let the commissioner down, Shen Ke stepped forward and, with a flushed face, said in a burst of rage, "The general is quite mistaken! As the saying goes, 'An army follows the general. The generals follow the commander in chief.' Ranks and classes have been well defined since ancient times. Prefect Dong sent you to assist the commissioner, so you are a subordinate of the commissioner. What's more, even Prefect Dong, who used to be under the commissioner, dares not defy him. What ground do you have to be so arrogant? Do you think we have no army of our own in Yuezhou?"

Before he had quite finished, Qian Liu thundered, "How dare a miserable nobody like you lecture me!" At a tip of his cap, he and his twenty men acted faster than it takes to describe. With one quick draw of his sword out of its sheath, Qian Liu swung it upon the unsuspecting Shen Ke and cut off his head. Liu Hanhong ran toward the back of the inn while about a hundred of Liu's men pressed forward to take Qian Liu, but they were no match for him. Fighting with supernatural strength, he wielded his sword as if cutting gourds and vegetables and battled his way to the backyard of the inn to look for Liu Hanhong but found no trace of him. As his eyes fell upon a breach in the earthen wall, he realized, to his great chagrin, that the man had escaped. With two thousand men at his command, he had a mind to take Yuezhou by force, but, seeing that the city was well prepared for an attack and afraid that he would not be able to achieve anything without troop reinforcements, he was left with no choice but to turn around and return the way they had come. When word got to Liu Hanhong in the city that Qian Liu's troops were turning back, the commissioner immediately mustered five thousand crack troops and gave chase with the brave Lu Cui as the vanguard and himself as the commander.

Well aware that Yuezhou troops would be hot upon their trail, Qian Liu led his men forward, never stopping night or day. As they approached White Dragon Mountain, a peal of gongs burst out and there emerged from the mountain more than two hundred men, who formed themselves into a neat row. How did their leader at the front look? What was he wearing?

> *A cap woven of golden threads,*
> *A coat made of green brocade.*
> *A girdle around his waist,*
> *Leather boots on his feet.*
> *A quiver of arrows on his shoulders,*
> *A sharp sword in his hand.*
> *Heavy brows and big eyes,*
> *A ruddy face and a curly beard.*
> *He was well known on smugglers' boats*
> *And matchless on the battleground.*

At the sight of Qian Liu, who rode forward to take a closer look, the man threw down his sword, dropped to his knees, and made a bow. Qian Liu recognized him to be none other than Gu Quanwu, nicknamed Gu Sanlang, the salt smuggler and robber. Qian Liu got down from his horse saddle and raised Gu to his feet. "It's been a long time since I saw you last, Sanlang!" he exclaimed. "Why are you here?"

Gu Quanwu said, "Ever since you saved my life, I've been looking for ways to repay you for your kindness. Hearing that Huang Chao's forces were arriving, I planned to raise a volunteer army to protect the region so as to have a chance to see you. Then I learned that you crushed the enemy and won an appointment from the imperial court. Later, when I got word that you were going to help Commissioner Liu of Yuezhou, I gathered together over two hundred men in the salt business to offer our service to you. (*Who says salt smugglers are of no use?*) I didn't expect to run into you here. But why are you on your way back so soon?"

After recounting in detail what had occurred between himself and Liu Hanhong, Qian Liu said, "You are indeed a godsend. I need to ask a favor of you. We are pushing on night and day because I expect Liu Hanhong to be pursuing us. As he used to be Prefect Dong's superior, he has no respect for the prefect, and he was formerly the prefect of Hangzhou. So, if he can't catch us, he will surely go directly to Hangzhou to challenge Prefect Dong. You can put two hundred men at the foot of White Dragon Mountain and wait until his troops pass by to come out and pretend that you are surrendering to him. When you reach Hangzhou, I will lead my men out for a battle. You will then rise and kill Liu Hanhong, whose life will be the stepping stone in your career. I will do my best to recommend you to Prefect Dong. You have a bright future in front of you. Do not let anything go wrong."

Gu Quanwu assured him, "I will do whatever you say," whereupon they took leave of each other and went their separate ways. Indeed,

> *In times of peace, life thrives everywhere;*
> *In times of war, death lurks every moment.*
> *With men always at one another's throat,*
> *From the battlefields how many return?*

In the meantime, Liu Hanhong led his troops to the boundary of Yuezhou. Being told that Qian Liu had gone back in great haste, Lu Cui the vanguard reported as much to Liu Hanhong and asked for permission to give up the pursuit. Hanhong responded hotly, "Now that I am insulted by a nobody like Qian Liu, how can I return and face the people of this prefecture? Hangzhou used to be under my rule, and Dong Chang owes his promotion to my recommendation. I shall now personally lead my troops there and demand that Dong Chang kill Qian Liu. I will not forgive him until he admits his guilt. Otherwise, I swear not to live a moment longer!" Having thus dismissed Lu Cui with these words, he gave the order for the army to march toward Hangzhou.

They were approaching White Dragon Mountain in Fuyang when, at the sound of a gong, there emerged over two hundred men, who formed themselves into a neat line. At the head of the line stood their leader, a most ferocious-looking man with a sword in hand. Startled at the sight, Liu Hanhong was about to engage the enemy when the man pushed back his sword and demanded in a harsh voice, "Are you Commissioner Liu of Yuezhou?"

Hanhong answered, "I am."

The man hastily threw down his sword and flung himself on the ground in front of the commissioner's horse, saying, "I have been waiting here a long time for you."

To Liu Hanhong's question about his intentions, he replied, "I am Gu Quanwu, a native of Lin'an County. I have long since been on the move, running for my life, because I am wanted by the county magistrate for smuggling salt. Recently, as I heard that my former partner and pledged brother Qian Liu had made his way in the world and got himself an official post, I went to him for help, but how was I to know that he would turn out to be a man jealous of other capable men? Now that he is somebody, he has no sympathy for friends of his humble old days. Since he refuses to take me on, I have no other choice but to take temporary shelter on White Dragon Mountain. Yesterday when Qian Liu passed by, I would have killed him if not for fear of being outnumbered. As I've heard that he has offended the commissioner, I will be happy to be your vanguard and render you what little service I can."

Liu Hanhong was greatly delighted and bade Gu Quanwu take over Lu Cui's duties. A thousand men were assigned to Gu to lead the way, whereas Lu Cui was ordered to bring up the rear.

In a matter of days, they found themselves at the city wall of Hangzhou. By this time, Qian Liu had seen Dong Chang and made the necessary preparations. As word got to him that the Yuezhou army was there, Dong Chang mounted the wall and shouted, "The commissioner and I, both being officials appointed by the imperial court, owe it to our duty to keep guard over our own dominions. I would never dream of giving you any offense. What, may I ask, are you here for?"

Liu Hanhong thundered, "You despicable ingrate! If you knew better, you would kill Qian Liu and offer me his head to avoid my resorting to force."

Dong Chang said, "Please don't be angry, Commissioner. Qian Liu is coming out to offer his apologies."

The city gate opened, and out galloped an army headed by none other than Qian Liu, flanked by Zhong Ming on his left and Zhong Liang on his right. Forward they charged at the enemy ranks to capture Liu Hanhong, who cried out in panic, "Where is my vanguard?"

A man by his side answered, "Here I am!" With a single lunge of his sword, he cut Liu Hanhong down from his horse. Waving his sword, Qian Liu charged into the enemy ranks, shouting, "Surrender and live!"

The five-thousand-man army surrendered without a single attempt to put up a fight. Lu Cui died by his own sword. The man who killed Liu Hanhong was none other than Gu Quanwu. Truly,

> Cunning without courage still has its value;
> But courage without cunning easily costs lives.
> Only when cunning is coupled with courage
> Can every battle be a victory.

Seeing that Liu Hanhong was dead, Dong Chang opened wide the city gates and recalled the troops. Qian Liu introduced Gu Quanwu to an overjoyed Dong Chang, who then composed a memorial to the imperial court charging Liu Hanhong with crimes and listing the merits of Qian Liu and other officers under him. The imperial court, too preoccupied with other concerns to conduct a thorough investigation of this case, promoted Dong Chang to the post of surveillance commissioner of Yuezhou to replace Liu Hanhong. Qian Liu replaced Dong Chang as prefect of Hangzhou. Zhong Ming, Zhong Liang, and Gu Quanwu were all granted titles. Zhong Qi married his daughter to Qian Liu. After Dong Chang had left for Yuezhou, leaving Hangzhou to Qian Liu, the latter's parents moved to live with him in Hangzhou. That the whole family enjoyed a life of glory and prosperity need not be described here.

Now, a peasant in Lin'an County was tilling a field in the foothills of the Tianmu Mountains when he dug up a small stone tablet with a few lines of characters engraved on it. Being illiterate, the peasant showed the tablet to the village schoolteacher, Luo Ping, who wiped away the dirt and saw that the four lines were a prophecy:

> *The Tianmu Mountains have two long breasts;*
> *Dragons and phoenixes fly to Qiantang.*[19]
> *At Sea Gate*[20] *where the Kan and Zhe Hills rise,*
> *A king will be born in five hundred years.*

On the back of the tablet was engraved, "Guo Pu of the Jin dynasty." Scholar Luo kept the tablet at home as a priceless treasure. The following day, he went to the tribunal of the prefect of Hangzhou and offered the tablet to Prefect Qian Liu with a few confidential words about the mandate of heaven.

After reading the inscriptions on the tablet, Qian Liu flew into a rage. "How dare this scoundrel try to make up such lies to me!" he exploded. "This is a crime punishable by death!"

It was only after Scholar Luo's piteous pleading that Qian Liu relented and had his men just beat the scholar with their cudgels all the way out of the tribunal. The tablet was smashed to pieces in the courtyard. The truth of the matter was that Qian Liu realized that it was an auspicious prophecy that would be fulfilled by him, but, being the cautious man that he was, he decided to pretend not to believe, for fear that rumors might spread far and wide to his disadvantage.

Let us go back to Scholar Luo. The beating left him in deep hatred of the prefect for his lack of graciousness. Good will had now turned into malice. An idea occurred to him. Why not offer the tablet to Commissioner Dong of Yuezhou? Surely he would have something to gain from this. Though the tablet was smashed, the pieces could still be put together. Therefore, he bribed the gatekeeper of the tribunal and had the pieces of the tablet picked up and returned to him. It turned out that the tablet had broken into only three pieces. When put back together again, the characters were still as legible as before. Luo Ping's heart overflowed with joy. He wrapped up the stone tablet as before and set out on his journey to Yuezhou.

He had been two days on the road when he saw a crowd gathered around a twelve- or thirteen-year-old boy carrying a cloth-covered bamboo cage, inside which was a tiny kingfisher. Luo Ping drew near and asked what was going on. He was told that the bird, though not a parrot, could talk. They were offering one full string of cash for the bird, but the boy refused to sell it. Before the explanation was quite finished, the little bird chirped with two nods of its head, "Emperor Dong! Emperor Dong!" (*Gao Jidi [Gao Qi, 1336–74] had a song that goes, "At the first cry of Luo Ping's evil bird, / Three thousand bows shoot at the tidewater." Luo Ping is most probably a place name but is here taken as a man's name. This could have been a mistake passed on from story writer to story writer.*)

Luo Ping asked, "Has this bird been trained to talk or was it born that way?"

The boy answered, "My father was chopping firewood when he heard a voice speaking from the top of a tree. It was this bird. He caught it with a glued stick. It's never been trained."

"I'll give you two full strings of cash for it," said Luo Ping.

The two strings of cash in hand, the boy left happily. Luo Ping took over the birdcage and continued hurriedly on his way.

Before long, he arrived in Yuezhou. His claims of having confidential matters for the ears of the commissioner obtained him an audience with Dong Chang. Dismissing all attendants, Dong Chang was about to question him when the little bird chirped again in its cage, "Emperor Dong! Emperor Dong!" Dong Chang was agape with astonishment. "What bird is this?" he asked.

Luo Ping answered, "This bird is of an unknown type. For its innate ability to talk, it can be called the Wonder Bird." Then he took out the stone tablet from his bosom and explained, "It has been five hundred years from the beginning of the Jin dynasty to the present moment. That accounts for the 'five hundred years' as inscribed on the tablet. As things stand now, the emperor is weak, and the Tang dynasty is doomed. The two princes of Liang and Jin are locked in fierce rivalry. All men of aspirations throughout the empire have the intention of setting up their own separate regimes. It is not by accident that the tablet appeared in Qiantang, where you started your career. Moreover, the Wonder Bird is a good omen and a revelation of the mandate of heaven. By crushing Huang Chao and killing Liu Hanhong, you have already built a name for yourself, a name that inspires awe far and near. If you seize the opportunity and take over Zhejiang with your Yuezhou and Hangzhou troops, you will be able to impinge upon the Central Plains to the north and enjoy as much power in the south as Sun Quan did in the Three Kingdoms period." (*Too bad Dong Chang is not the man so destined.*)

As it turned out, Dong Chang had long been harboring ambitions of taking advantage of the chaos throughout the land to gain power for himself. Luo Ping's words pleased him immensely. "Your coming over such a great distance," said he, "is a sign from heaven that I will succeed. When victory is mine, I will reward you with the office of commissioner of this prefecture." He engaged Luo Ping as his military adviser and started building up his army while taxing civilians to raise provisions and funds for the troops. He had a skilled craftsman make a birdcage of gold wire for the Wonder Bird and a layer of Sichuan brocade for the cage. He also wrote a confidential letter and had a messenger take it to Qian Liu in Hangzhou, instructing him to recruit more soldiers in case of need.

Qian Liu was aghast after reading the letter. "Dong Chang is getting ready for a rebellion!" he said to himself. Thereupon, he wrote a secret memorial to the imperial court. As a result, he was promoted to the post of commissioner for the prefectures of Suzhou and Hangzhou. Qian Liu then started expanding Hangzhou to cover an area of seventy li from the Qinwang Mountains to Yufanpu. After another memorial, he was further promoted to the position of regional commander of Zhenhai and was granted the title of Kaiguo Duke.

At the news that the imperial court was showering promotions and titles upon Qian Liu, Dong Chang flew into a rage. "That worthless scoundrel!" he cursed. "How dare he betray me to get promotions! I will first take Hangzhou to vent my anger."

Luo Ping offered this advice: "Qian Liu's ambition has not yet been exposed. Moreover, since he has been newly favored with promotions, there is no good excuse to send a punitive expedition against him. The best thing to do would be to claim that the court has conferred upon you the title of prince. With that authority, you can first conquer Muzhou. With your army expanded, you can then head for Huzhou by way of Hangzhou. If Qian Liu refuses to submit himself to you, kill him at the first opportunity; if he sends forth troops to assist you, then Hangzhou will be yours without a fight. What more can you ask for?"

Dong Chang followed his advice. Falsely claiming that the imperial court had issued a decree conferring upon him the title of prince of Yue and giving him command over all troops in the Zhejiang region, he had the insignia of the prince of Yue put on all army flags. At the same time, he showed the stone tablet and the Wonder Bird to all residents of the prefecture to make known to them the will of heaven. By conscripting one man out of three into his army, he raised an army fifty thousand strong, and, claiming to be one hundred thousand strong, the mighty army swept onward to Muzhou. Caught off guard, Muzhou fell. A spell of peace followed that lasted for over a month, during which time new officials were assigned to replace the incumbents. His military power now at a great height with another thirty thousand experienced soldiers added to his army, Dong Chang thought himself invincible and planned to have himself proclaimed king of Yue. He moved forward to Hangzhou, with an eye on Huzhou.

Qian Liu said, "It is not wise to resist the Yue troops at this moment when they are at their strongest. It is best for us to welcome them now and attack only after they have settled in Huzhou and shown signs of weakness. At that point, victory will surely be ours." Thereupon he sent Zhong Ming to treat the Yue troops to food and drink in all humility and then personally led five thousand cavalry soldiers forward and, much to Dong Chang's delight, volunteered to lead the way for Dong Chang's army. After marching for several days, Qian Liu feigned illness and stayed behind, allegedly to regain his health. Dong Chang was as unsuspecting as ever and urged the troops to march ahead. (*Dong Chang is a fool.*) There is a poem in testimony:

> Gou Jian,[21] with designs on the Wu region
> Humbly sent gifts before his conquest.
> Dong Chang, failing to see through Qian Liu's plans,
> Pushed on to Lake Tai, assured of his might.

In the meantime, having learned through inquiries that the Yuezhou army was by this time far in the distance, Qian Liu led his troops back. Then he selected a thousand of his finest men and, under banners carrying fake Yuezhou army insignias, went to attack Yuezhou, with Gu Quanwu as the vanguard. He also instructed Zhong Ming and Zhong Liang to lead five hundred experienced men each and lie in ambush in Yuhang, where they were not to move from their positions (*So as to mislead the enemy*) until Dong Chang's army passed by on their way back to rescue Yuezhou. Only then were they to attack from behind. Dong Chang would be in no mood to engage them, and total victory would be a certainty. After assigning these tasks, he said to his guest Zhong Qi, "Now I entrust you with the job of guarding the city. Yuezhou is Dong's bastion. I will surely go there personally to see how the situation develops. If his final bastion falls, there is no doubt that Dong Chang will perish." Thereupon he led two thousand of his finest soldiers forward as a reinforcement for Gu Quanwu and his men.

Let us now turn to Gu Quanwu. Flying banners with the Yuezhou army insignia, he proceeded unimpeded all the way to the city walls of Yuezhou. Saying that they were there to get firearms to force open enemy city gates, Gu Quanwu and his men were admitted into the city. Once inside, Gu Quanwu shouted, "Dong Chang made false claims and rebelled against the imperial court. By the authority of an imperial decree, Regional Commander Qian is here on a punitive expedition. A mighty army one hundred thousand strong is already at the city walls."

Dong Chang had taken all the military men in the city with him. All who remained were the elderly and the weak. Who dared to resist? Gu Quanwu proceeded straight into the commissioner's tribunal, captured the fake prince's eldest son, Dong Rong, and all members of the Dong clan, totaling over three hundred, including the old and the young, and threw them into one single room guarded by his soldiers. At this juncture, the main Hangzhou troops arrived. Knowing that Gu Quanwu had taken the city, the army marched in without committing the slightest offense against the city residents. Gu Quanwu welcomed Qian Liu into the tribunal. After posters were put up to reassure the public, Qian Liu wrote a letter and had it sent to Dong Chang's army. The letter read,

> *I have heard that just as there are not two suns in the sky, there should not be two sovereigns on earth. Weakened though the Tang dynasty is, the mandate of heaven remains unchanged. Your arrogant pretensions to the title of prince and the military build-up arouse the indignation of all Tang officials. It is for the sake of justice that I, Qian Liu, with Gu Quanwu as my aide-de-camp, am leading my troops on a punitive expedition. Yue soldiers surrender wherever we go. Your family members are now all under arrest. If, under such circumstances, you plead guilty to your crimes, they will all be spared their lives. I entreat you to succumb in time to save your family.*

Dong Chang was brooding in his tent over not being able to conquer Huzhou when he heard the Wonder Bird chirp again, "Emperor Dong! Emperor Dong!" He lifted the brocade cover to take a look. His vision blurred. What he saw was not the Wonder Bird, but a blood-smeared human head hanging in the gold wire cage. Recognizing the features to be those of Liu Hanhong, he stood aghast with horror. With a loud cry, he fell to the ground. A bevy of his subordinates rushed over to revive him. As he came to, he waited until he regained his vision before he turned his eyes to the cage again and saw that it was covered with spots of blood. The Wonder Bird had indeed disappeared.

In great vexation, Dong Chang summoned his military adviser Luo for an emergency consultation and gave him an account of the incident. "Is this an omen of fortune or disaster?" he asked.

Aware as he was that this was a bad omen, Luo Ping dared not speak the truth. Instead, he said, "As the killing of Liu Hanhong marked the beginning of your rule over the greater Yue region, the appearance of Liu Hanhong's head today is an indication of victory over your enemies." He had not quite finished speaking when an announcement came that a letter had arrived from

Hangzhou. Dong Chang was mortified to learn, upon reading the letter, that Yuezhou had fallen.

Luo Ping said, "In waging wars, there are too many tricks to believe every claim. Qian Liu must have had some wicked scheme in mind when he stayed behind under the excuse of illness. Now that he is spreading rumors to shake army morale, please do not lose your presence of mind."

"Even though there is no way of establishing the truth of the claim," said Dong Chang, "we still would do well to turn back to save our home base."

To avoid any leakage of their plans, Luo Ping ordered that the messenger be killed. Then he gave instructions to spread the word that no effort should be spared in attacking the city, so that the enemy in the city would have no suspicion that they would be leaving under the cover of night. That day they did keep up the attack on Huzhou before night fell, and broke camp when it was at last the second watch of the night. Xue Ming and Xu Fu, two of his valiant generals, led ten thousand cavalry each as the advance detachments, followed by Dong Chang and the main forces. Luo Ping and the thirty thousand cavalry from Muzhou brought up the rear. Witnessing the retreat, the Huzhou army in the city dared not give chase, for fear of falling into some trap.

Now, Generals Xu and Xue led their men in marching day and night. Stopping at the foot of Yuhang Mountain, they were about to lay out cooking utensils to cook a meal when there burst out from the valleys a series of bombardments and the sounds of drums and horns. Zhong Ming and Zhong Liang led two groups and galloped out from both sides. Xue Ming went forward and engaged Zhong Ming. Xu Fu engaged Zhong Liang. Brave as Xu and Xue were, the panic-stricken soldiers were in no mood to fight, for they were already exhausted after days and nights of marching. How were they able to resist those two groups of soldiers as fierce as tigers and wolves? As the ancients put it, "If the soldiers desert, the general loses." Seeing that his troops were thrown into disarray, Xue Ming took fright and, caught unprepared, was cut down by Zhong Ming from his horse. Zhong Ming then spurred his horse on to join the fight against Xu Fu. Being no match for the two, Xu Fu was cut down by Zhong Liang. All the soldiers discarded their armor and surrendered.

The Zhong brothers took counsel together, saying, "Though we have beaten the advance detachment of the Yue army, Dong Chang and the main forces will be here any moment now. We will be outnumbered. The best course would be to break into several groups, lie in ambush, and, when they have passed by, attack from behind. When they know what has happened to their advance detachment, they will panic and think of escape. Victory will then be total." Having thus made up their minds, they released the soldiers who had surrendered and told them to report the news to Dong Chang.

Dong Chang and his mighty army were pressing ahead when the defeated soldiers approached in a continuous stream, reporting, "Generals Xu and Xue both died on the battlefield." Dong Chang was appalled, but he had to pull himself together and urge his army to move on. They passed Yuhang Mountain without encountering the enemy. Before his apprehensions had subsided, Dong Chang heard from behind a series of bombardments. The soldiers in ambush on both sides charged out in numbers unknown. The Yuezhou soldiers vied with one another in running for their lives, trampling upon one another and dying in countless numbers. Those who survived did so by running over fifty li. When they were gathered together, it was found that one-third of the entire army had perished. Now all hope was pinned upon Luo Ping and his detachment, which brought up the rear. As it happened, the Muzhou soldiers had never been happy under Dong Chang, even though they had been following his orders. Now that the army was turning back, several minor officers consulted each other and killed Luo Ping. After offering Luo Ping's head to the Zhong brothers as a gesture of surrender, they came in search of Dong Chang, who, having got word of this, dared not take the major thoroughfares of Hangzhou but made a big detour and turned to the roads of Lin'an and Tonglu.

Qian Liu, however, had foreseen what route Dong Chang would take. He bade Zhong Qi guard Yuezhou, while he himself returned with his troops to Hangzhou to wait for Dong Chang. In the meantime, Gu Quanwu, by Qian Liu's instructions, led one thousand cavalry to lie in ambush in strategic positions on Lin'an Mountain to block any chance of Dong Chang's escape. When Dong Chang arrived in Lin'an, his troops, in total disarray, were climbing the mountain and passing the strategic positions when Gu Quanwu's group charged out. In the forefront was Gu Quanwu, who, wielding his sword, rode furiously in all directions and killed every man he saw while shouting, "Surrender and live!" All the enemy soldiers, to a man, flung themselves onto the ground. Who would be so reckless as to engage him in a fight! Seeing that things had taken an ugly turn, Dong Chang took off his gold helmet and armor and fled to a villager's home to seek refuge but was trussed up by the villagers and brought forward. Gu Quanwu thought, "Even though the Yue troops have surrendered, their numbers are still impressive. It would be best to forestall anything untoward." With a swish of his sword, he cut off Dong Chang's head to put to rest any illusions that the Yue troops might still have. The villagers were heavily rewarded.

Before he could pitch camp for some rest, Gu heard from the valleys of the mountain earth-shaking sounds of drums and bugles. Kicking up clouds of dust, a mighty army was moving in his direction. Gu Quanwu said, "This must be the rear detachment of the Yuezhou troops." He grabbed his sword and mounted his horse, ready for battle. When the army drew near, he saw that the two commanders were none other than Zhong Ming and Zhong Liang on their way to pursue Dong Chang. The three men dismounted and exchanged stories of their accomplishments. That night, they pitched camp together in Lin'an. The following day, they broke camp and were on the road for two days when they ran into Qian Liu and his men. It so happened that Qian Liu's spies had learned that Dong Chang was making a detour by way of Lin'an. Afraid that Gu Quanwu might not be able to deal with Dong, Qianliu led the main forces and came to offer reinforcement, only to be told that both detachments had won victory. Consequently, they joined forces and returned to the city of Hangzhou. Truly,

> *Cheerfully they tap their stirrups with whips;*
> *Joyfully they return with songs of triumph.*

Gu Quanwu presented Qian Liu with Dong Chang's head, and the Zhong brothers presented him with the heads of Xue Ming, Xu Fu, and Luo Ping. Qian Liu gave the order to kill all of the three hundred members of Dong Chang's clan now imprisoned in Yuezhou and composed a memorial to the emperor to report the victory. That happened in the fourth year of the Qianning reign period [897] under Emperor Zhaozong of the Tang dynasty.

At the time, the Central Plains were beset with hostilities, and the Wu and Yue regions were geographically beyond the reach of the imperial court. Therefore, upon learning through the memorial that Qian Liu had successfully quelled a rebellion, the court was most appreciative and awarded him certificates of redemption.[22] He was also granted the titles of Supreme Pillar of State, prince of Pengcheng, and secretariat director. Soon thereafter, he was made king of Yue and, later, king of Wu, with the privilege of granting officials titles in Run, Yue, and twelve other prefectures. In all complacency, Qian Liu built himself a palace in Hangzhou. With his father already dead, it goes without saying that he supported his mother in the palace in the finest luxury. His wife, Zhong Qi's daughter, was granted the title of royal consort. Zhong Qi rose to be prime minister and joined him in the administration of the land. Zhong Ming, Zhong Liang, and Gu Quanwu each obtained the post of surveillance commissioner of one of the various prefectures.

One year, there was a great flood. Its surging tides reached as far as the city walls. A dike construction project was begun. Numerous laborers worked for months without being able to finish it. Qian Liu went in person to the construction site for an inspection and saw that the job was made difficult by the raging waves. In a towering rage, he thundered, "What river god dares defy my wishes!" By his order, hundreds of strong archers shot their arrows into the tide, and, just as soon, the waves quieted down. (*This event alone proves that he did not rise to be a king by chance but was born to be one.*) In another few days, the dike was finished. Its gate was named Tide-Watching Gate.

Qian Liu said with a sigh, "The ancients had a saying: 'He who has attained wealth and power but fails to make a return trip to his hometown is like one who flaunts his splendid silk robe in pitch darkness.'"[23] Consequently, he selected a day and set out for Lin'an, where he paid his respects to his grandfather's grave, offered sacrifices of oxen, sheep, and pigs, and raised a great fanfare on the mountain, complete with banners, drums, and horns. He changed the name of the county from Lin'an to Silk Robe County, and the mountain from Stone Mirror to Silk Robe, covered the Stone Mirror in brocade, and had the stone guarded by soldiers to prevent people from stealing looks into it. The big rock that he had sat on was now named the Silk Robe Rock. The big tree was named the Silk Robe General and was also covered in brocade. New pieces of brocade were to replace the old should they be damaged by wind and rain. He called the house where he used to live the Silk Robe Residence and had a memorial gateway erected. The carrying pole that he had used when selling salt, now covered in a tailor-made brocade case, was enshrined in the hall of his old residence as a reminder of his humble beginnings. Oxen and horses were slaughtered for a grand feast, to which all old acquaintances in the neighborhood, male and female, were invited.

A neighbor woman over ninety years of age, carrying a pot of white wine and a plate of dumplings, approached Qian Liu and said laughingly, "What a joy it is to see that you, Qian Poliu, have indeed made your way in the world!"

Qian's attendants were about to call out in reproach when Qian Liu checked them, saying, "Don't frighten her." With alacrity, he dropped to his knees and thanked the woman: "If it were not for you, Granny Wang, who saved my life in the beginning, I would not be where I am today!"

Granny Wang raised him to his feet, filled a cup to the brim with the white wine, and offered it to him. In one gulp, he finished the wine to the last drop. Granny Wang extended the plate of dumplings to him. While eating from the plate, he said, "I, Qian Poliu, have plenty to eat. Don't you worry about me. Enjoy your own life now." He ordered the county magistrate to allocate a hundred *mu* of fertile land to Granny Wang as her means of support for the rest of her life. She left after saying many words of thanks. The assembly of men and women in the neighborhood knelt down, one and all, at the sight of Qian Liu's royal attire of a python-patterned robe and a jade belt. Qian Liu raised them to their feet, bade them take their seats, and personally served them wine. Octogenarians were offered gold cups. Centenarians, about a dozen in all, used jade cups. (*Qian Liu well deserves full credit for the peace that pre-vailed throughout the land.*) After serving a round of wine, Qian Liu stood and intoned the following lines:

> *With grand titles, I return in silk robe;*
> *King of Wu and Yue, I come back in style.*
> *Under the winter sun in a bright sky,*
> *Rare are such occasions as time goes by.*

Being uneducated rustics, the audience looked at one another in puzzle-ment. None uttered a sound. Not content at the reaction, Qian Liu started chanting in the local Wu dialect,

> *So happy are you all to see me,*
> *A unique feeling it is indeed.*
> *You will live on in the depth of my heart.*
> *None of you shall I ever forget.*

The song was met with general applause amid happy laughter. Having thoroughly enjoyed themselves, they came back on the following day for another gathering. Three days passed in this way. Everyone received gifts of silk and brocade. The owner of the gambling house, Old Man Qi, having died, members of his household were summoned and heavily rewarded. This done, Qian Liu returned to Hangzhou.

Later, the emperor of the Tang abdicated to the Liang, whereupon Zhu Quanzhong, emperor of the Liang [r. 907–14], changed the reign period to Kaiping and made Qian Liu king of Wu and Yue and, soon thereafter, supreme national commander in chief. Though a king in title only, Qian Liu enjoyed privileges no different from those of an emperor. There was just as much fanfare on his leaving from and returning to his palace, and his sub-jects greeted him with the same three shouts of "Ten thousand years to you!" According to *The History of the Five Dynasties* by Ouyang Xiu, the Wu and Yue regions had been proclaimed an empire. The reign titles of Tianbao, Baoda, and Baozheng—still seen inscribed in temples throughout Hangzhou—were, in fact, Wu-Yue reign titles. From the time Qian Liu became the king of Wu and Yue until he died at the advanced age of eighty-one, the region suffered no harassment from neighboring states. He was granted the posthumous title of Wu Su [Valiance and Solemnity]. His throne passed on to his son Yuanguan, and later from Yuanguan to his son Zuo and from Zuo to his younger brother Chu. After the first emperor of the Song dynasty assumed the throne subse-quent to the Chen Bridge incident [960], Qian Chu served in the new Song court. Upon Emperor Taizong's succession [in 976], Qian Chu donated his land to the imperial court, whereupon his title was changed to king of Deng. The Qian clan dominated the Wu and Yue regions for ninety-eight years, thus fulfilling the prophecy of the stone tablet unearthed in the Tianmu Mountains. A later poet had these lines of praise:

> *Generals and ministers may not be so,*
> *But kings and princes are born to rule.*
> *A smuggler of salt in days gone by*
> *Now wears a silk robe of glory.*
> *A stone mirror revealed his true self,*
> *A Liao Sheng predicted his success.*
> *Laughable was that "Emperor Dong,"*
> *Who died in vain, misled by prophecy.*

Zheng Huchen Seeks Revenge in Mumian Temple

> *The lotus and cassia buds by the bank*
> *Mourn memories of the glorious past.*
> *A phoenix rested by the Tianmu Mountains;[1]*
> *Six dragons at Sea Gate[2] flew with the tide.*
> *Jia Chong was proved wrong for lack of vision.[3]*
> *Yu Xin in his grief found solace in poems.[4]*
> *Praise not this landscape to the Central Plains;*
> *Xishi[5] of West Lake caused eternal regret.*

The above poem is by Zhang Zhiyuan.[6] After the Song dynasty moved its capital to the south, the years of the Shaoxing [1131–62] and Chunxi [1174–89] reign periods knew no warfare. Hence, the emperor and the ministers considered themselves to be in the midst of peaceful times and indulged in every pleasure to their hearts' content. Literati scholars toured the scenic lakes and hills, with never a thought of recovering the Central Plains. That is why the last two lines of the above poem read, "Praise not this landscape to the Central Plains; / Xishi of West Lake caused eternal regret." At that time, West Lake was graced with cassia buds all through the autumn, and the fragrance of flowering lotus filled the air for a distance of ten li. Fringed by wooded hills, the lake, with its green water and reflections of gilded towers and terraces, was indeed a most beautiful resort. Academician Su Dongpo [Su Shi][7] had a poem that contained these lines: "Shall I compare the West Lake to Xishi, / Just as charming with makeup heavy or light?" Therefore, the emperor and the ministers were so deeply lost in the pleasures of the scenery that they cast aside all worries about the troubles besetting the empire, just as the state of Wu had fallen under the spell of Xishi.

Xishi was a favorite concubine of Fu Chai, the king of Wu, who spent his days with her enjoying the sights of Hundred Flowers Islet, the Brocade Sail River, and Gusu Terrace. There was an evil minister, Bo Pi, who abetted the king and encouraged him in his dissipated ways while, at the same time, advising him to kill ministers of moral integrity. As a result, when the Yue troops descended upon them, the kingdom fell and the king lost his life.

Now, after the Song dynasty moved its court to the south, it was still possible, for all the rampant power of the barbarians, to recover the Central Plains, because the people there still pledged their loyalty to the house of Zhao. It was by similarly letting some evil ministers hold power that the Song dynasty perished, a victim of its own extravagance and inertia. Who were the evil ministers? They were Qin Hui [1090–1155], Han Tuozhou [1151–1207], Shi Miyuan [d. 1232], and Jia Sidao [1213–75]. During his nineteen years of office as prime minister, Qin Hui assiduously advocated appeasement, murdered Yue Fei, and removed Generals Zhang Jun, Han Shizhong, and Liu Qi from military power. Prime minister for fourteen years, Han Tuozhou ruined Prime Minister Zhao Ruyu, deposed upright ministers, rashly caused disputes at the border, and brought humiliation to the empire and calamity to the people. In his twenty-six years as prime minister, Shi Miyuan murdered Zhao Hong, prince of Ji, and appointed none but the evil to posts in the Censorate and the Bureau of Remonstrance. Almost all men of honor were either demoted or expelled from power.

At the time, with a strong Mongol empire in the north and with the frequent occurrence of strange natural phenomena, the Song dynasty was already well on its way to final collapse. A certain Jia Sidao appeared on the scene as if to accelerate the preordained doom of the dynasty. In his fifteen years as prime minister, he did nothing but deceive the imperial court and seek comfort and pleasure for himself. Even though he was later demoted and deprived of all his titles, and died in Mumian Temple, the damage he had done to the empire was already beyond repair. There is a poem in evidence:

> All too many are ruined by villains
> Who, alas, easily gain monarchs' trust.
> If the court knows the good from the evil,
> Peace and harmony will forever reign.

Here begins our story. During the Jiading reign period [1208–24] under Emperor Ningzong of the Southern Song dynasty, there lived in Taizhou, Zhejiang, a man by the name of Jia She. He set out with his page boy on a journey to Lin'an to await appointment for office. On their way, they passed by a place in Qiantang called Phoenix's Mouth, and, hungry and thirsty after much walking, they stopped at a cottage to ask for lunch. Surrounded by a bamboo fence, the thatched cottage appeared to be quite deserted. Jia She said loudly, "Anybody home?" Thereupon a reed curtain was raised, and out stepped a woman. How did she look?

> Her face as fair as the full moon,
> Her black hair flowing like the clouds.

A slight touch of powder and rouge
Added to her beauty and charm.
Artless in her manners,
She was blessed with natural grace.
With bright eyes and jade-smooth arms,
She had about her an auspicious air.
Cotton skirt and crude hairpins she might wear,
But her refinement shone through,
Like a piece of jade buried in a rock,
Or a shining pearl fallen into an abyss.
Even oafs would be smitten at the sight,
Much less a lonely traveler on the road.

Seeing Jia She, the woman greeted him calmly with a deep bow. Impressed with her gracefulness, Jia She thought to himself, "Being in the prime of life yet without a son, I would ask for no more than to have this woman for a concubine!" So thinking, he said to her, "I am on my way to the capital to wait for appointment and happened to pass by your house. Would you be so kind as to cook a meal for me? I will certainly pay you for it."

The woman replied, "Since it is my duty to take care of the kitchen, I will gladly cook for you. What's more, how could I presume to disobey a distinguished gentleman like you! However, since my husband is away, please do not blame me if I turn out to be a poor hostess." Her articulateness further pleased Jia She.

Before long, she reemerged from the interior of the house, holding in her hands two bowls of bean soup, saying, "There being no tea in our humble home, please have some of this soup instead, to allay your thirst." Shortly afterward, she set out a meal for the honored guest and his page boy. Jia She took out some beef jerky and preserved vegetables that he had with him to go with the rice.

The woman placed on the table a big porcelain pot filled with hot water and said, "This is for you to rinse your mouth with."

Observing her attentiveness, Jia She asked, "What is your name? Why are you living here alone?"

"My surname is Hu. My husband is called Wang Xiaosi. For the last few years, our farm has been doing badly. We are now so poor that he wants us to enter the household of some rich man, but I vowed never to do that. Unable to talk me into it, he has no choice but to find odd jobs for neighboring families to eke out a living while I look after the house all by myself."

Jia She ventured to remark, "May I say something that might be out of turn?"

"Go ahead, please," said the woman.

Jia She continued, "I have a good knowledge of physiognomy. Judging from your looks, I don't think you are destined for a lowly life. Aren't you ruining your future by staying with a peasant unworthy of you? Moreover, he is too poor to be concerned with your pride. I am a man in the prime of life but still without a son. I am looking for a concubine. Should you be willing, I'd be happy to give your good husband much gold and silk for him to take another wife. Wouldn't that suit all of us well?"

The woman said, "My husband did indeed want to sell me, but each time I refused. Since you are kind enough to show such compassion, please tell him so yourself when he returns. I dare not take it upon myself to make promises."

Before she had quite finished, she pointed at the door and said, "My husband is back."

Wang Xiaosi came into view wearing a tattered cap and a worn-out white shirt, and barged into the house in an inebriated state. Jia She rose and said to him, "I am on my way to the capital to await appointment for office. I happened to pass by and stopped to ask for lunch. I'm sorry for the disturbance."

"That's all right," said Wang Xiaosi. Then he turned to his wife. "My master needs a sewing woman. I've seen how good your sewing is, so I told him about you. He wants you to teach his maids and gave me two full strings of cash. This time, you have to do as I say, and go." (*Coincidences lead to matches.*)

Standing near the half-raised reed curtain, Hu-shi replied, "I'm too embarrassed to live off other people. No, I won't go."

Wang Xiaosi was annoyed. "If you don't go, I can find no way of supporting you."

Seeing this as a good moment to put forward his proposition, Jia She feigned a need to relieve himself and left the room but instructed his page boy to lead the man on with hints.

"Sir," said the page boy, "How can you let your pretty wife live in another man's house?" (*Clever page boy.*)

"My little brother," replied Wang Xiaosi, "you know nothing about the poor. Drop all sense of shame for one day, and you'll have a full stomach for three days. We can't afford to sit around idly drinking and eating as the rich do. If she wants to put on airs, she shouldn't be living with me."

The page boy pressed his point further. "If there were a rich man ready to pay you and take your wife, would you be willing to let her go?"

Wang Xiaosi exclaimed, "Why wouldn't I be!"

"As a matter of fact, my master is looking for a concubine. Should you be willing, I'll try to convince him to give you some extra strings of cash." Wang Xiaosi consented.

After the page boy's report, Jia She instructed him to pull off the deal with

Wang at forty taels of silver. Wang asked a village schoolmaster to write for him a statement agreeing to the selling of his wife and drew a cross as his signature. The silver having been weighed out, Wang Xiaosi took it, and Jia She took the statement. Afraid that his wife would be unwilling, Wang Xiaosi coaxed her with sweet words. Little did he know that the woman had already taken a fancy to Jia. The attraction being mutual, it was indeed a match made in heaven.

That same night, Jia She and his page boy were lodged in Wang Xiaosi's house. Wang also took his bedding out to keep the guests company, leaving the woman to sleep alone in the inner room. The following morning, Jia She rose and urged the woman to speed up her toilette. Breakfast over, Wang Xiaosi rented a draft animal from a villager, and, with the woman sitting on its back, they set off on their way to Lin'an. There is a poem in evidence:

> *Matches are brought about through predestined bonds;*
> *The unseen red thread ties the couple together.*
> *Wealth and royal titles were hers to enjoy;*
> *A peasant's wife for life she was not to be.*

About six months after he took Hu-shi into his temporary quarters in Lin'an, Jia She was appointed vice-magistrate of Wannian County in Jiujiang. He returned to his native town to meet his wife, Tang-shi, before he went, with wife and concubine, to assume his new office.

Tang-shi was a jealous woman with a violent temper, and Jia She quite a hen-pecked husband. Now that she saw a concubine in the house, she seethed with indignation and threw temper tantrums at home every day. When she got word that Hu-shi was three-months pregnant, she thought to herself, "My husband has never had a son. If this cheap little woman bears him a son, she'll naturally be even more favored by him. By that time, she'll be too well established for me to do anything. Even if I do get a child of my own in the future, her son will still be the first-born and old enough to bully mine. I'd be better off if I could get rid of this root of all troubles as soon as possible." Accordingly, she found an excuse and gave Hu-shi a sound beating. Taking off Hu-shi's nice clothes, she made her do menial jobs with maidservants of the house such as boiling tea, cooking meals, sweeping the floor, wiping tables, and making the beds. She also forbade her husband to sleep with her. Not a day passed without her finding some excuse to beat and scold Hu-shi. All this was done to make her lose the baby in a miscarriage. Jia She was choked with fury, but there was nothing he could do.

One day, Chen Lüchang, the county magistrate, invited Jia She for a drink. As they came from the same prefecture, the two families were on very friendly terms. In the midst of the drinking in the magistrate's tribunal, Chen noticed that Jia She looked troubled and asked him why. Jia She could not very well deny the facts but gave him a detailed account of his wife's jealousy of the concubine. "The continuation of my family line," said he, "depends entirely on her. Do you have any suggestion as to how to protect my concubine? Should she be blessed with good fortune and give birth to a son, my ancestors in the underworld will all be grateful to you."

After a moment of reflection, Chen said, "It's not hard to protect her, but my only fear is that you'd hate to part with her."

"I am not allowed to be intimate with her anyway," said Jia She. "It's as if we're worlds apart, even though she may be right by my side. Why wouldn't I bear parting with her!"

Chen whispered into his ear, "If you want to protect her until she reaches full term, just do thus-and-thus." He took out a red silk flower and handed it surreptitiously to Jia She, bidding him to give the flower to Hu-shi as a secret mark that the whole plan would depend upon, as was proved by later developments. There is a poem that attests to this:

> *Jealousy is a sentiment as old as time;*
> *She risked scandal to stop the family line.*
> *The magistrate conceived the red flower plan;*
> *How could a clever woman outwit a man?*

One day, word got to Magistrate Chen that the vice-magistrate had engaged a doctor to treat his wife, Tang-shi, for a slight illness. After she had recovered, Magistrate Chen had his wife visit her with a gift of four boxes of tea and fruit. (*Good chance for a social call.*) Tang-shi kept the visitor for a snack, with a row of maids attending on the side. In the midst of the conversation, the visitor said, "It is so nice that you have many maids to attend to you. But our household is short of hands. It's so annoying to have no one to wait on you when you are in need. Since we can't find anyone at the moment, could we borrow one of your maids to help us out? We'll give her back to you when we find someone capable."

Tang-shi said, "How can you say 'borrow'? I'm afraid that our maids are too clumsy to be of any use to you, but feel free to pick anyone you like. I'll give her to you as a present."

After thanking her, the magistrate's wife saw, standing among the maids, a pretty girl with the red silk flower in her hair. Realizing that this was none other than Hu-shi, she pointed to her and said, "I would like to borrow this girl."

Tang-shi, being consumed with jealousy, was only too happy to be rid of her. This request accorded exactly with her wishes. She knew her husband would not object, for how could a vice-magistrate dare turn down his superior, the magistrate? Readily she gave her consent, saying, "This maid's surname is Hu. She has not been with us long. Since you would like to have her, I'll have her follow you home right away."

After the table was cleared, the magistrate's wife took her leave. Hu-shi made four bows to Tang-shi, put together a few pieces of clothing, and followed Madam Chen's sedan-chair to the county tribunal. It was only then that Tang-shi told Jia She about it, whereupon Jia She sighed in mock regret. Truly,

> Well designed and well carried out,
> The plan kept her in the dark.
> A safe haven the tribunal was,
> Safer than where Zhao-shi hid her son.[8]

Upon Hu-shi's arrival at the tribunal, the magistrate's wife gave her a full account of what had happened and prepared a separate room for her to stay in. Time flew by like an arrow. Before anyone knew it, she had reached full term. On the eighth day of the eighth month, after spasms of pain, Hu-shi gave birth to a son. The magistrate's wife kept the fact from the family, claiming to all that the baby was the son of one of her maids. It so happened that Jia She went to another prefecture to check upon a case, and, before his return in the ninth month, he got to see the magistrate quite often. Chen quietly sent him the good news. Overwhelmed with gratitude, Jia She told Chen of his wish to see the newborn baby, whereupon Chen had a maid ask Hu-shi to stand behind a curtain while the maid carried the baby out and handed him to Jia She. Happy as he was with the baby in his arms, Jia She kept his eyes upon the curtain and could not restrain his tears from flowing. Separated by the curtain, Jia She and Hu-shi exchanged a few tender words. Hu-shi then bade the maid take the baby back. Jia She returned by himself. From then on, he often sent money secretly to Hu-shi for her expenses. The entire family except Tang-shi learned about this.

Time sped by, and, before they knew it, two years had elapsed. The magistrate, having served his full term of office, received a promotion and was about to leave Lin'an. Jia She was left with no choice but to acquaint Tang-shi with the facts, for the mother and the son needed to be brought back home. Upon hearing this, Tang-shi became hysterical and started ranting and raving. Not even the magistrate's wife was spared from her curses. She ended up demanding that the child not return unless her husband marry off Hu-shi to some other man. If marrying off Hu-shi were the only condition, Jia She would have accepted it, but he hesitated for fear that if the baby were brought home, Tang-shi would stop feeding him or murder him by some other means.

In the midst of Jia She's debates with himself, a visitor from Taizhou was announced. Jia She hastened to greet the visitor, who turned out to be his older brother Jia Ru. Jia Ru was in charge of picking girls from good families to send to the imperial palace for possible selection as concubines for the crown prince. His daughter Jia Yuhua was already among those selected. (*This is where Imperial Consort Jia started.*) He was here to take his brother's counsel about how best to bribe the grand commandant Liu Ba into helping his daughter rise in status. Jia She was on friendly terms with the commandant because it was the commandant's house that he had rented during his sojourn in Lin'an. At the sight of his brother, Jia She thought to himself, "He couldn't have come at a better time." He related to Jia Ru the whole story in detail, from his taking a concubine to the birth of the son and the jealousy of Tang-shi. "As Mr. Chen is about to leave his post," he continued, "I have no one to send the child to. If, for the sake of the Jia family line, you would take him with you and raise him, I would be deeply grateful."

Jia Ru said, "I have no son so far. As we're of the same branch of the clan, who else can you entrust the child to but me?"

Immensely delighted, Jia She quietly hired a wet nurse, took the child back from the magistrate, and handed the boy to the wet nurse. Reminding his brother to take good care of the boy, he wrote a letter to Liu Ba and also gave Jia Ru some travel money. He then asked Mr. Chen the magistrate to take Hu-shi with him and let her remarry.

However reluctant Jia She and Hu-shi were to part with each other, there was nothing they could do. Tang-shi was, on the other hand, greatly satisfied to hear from her husband that both mother and son were to be out of her sight. The really miserable one was Hu-shi. Deprived of her baby, away from her husband, she followed Magistrate Chen on his journey, so heartbroken that in spite of Mrs. Chen's efforts to placate her, she wept bitterly every step of the way. Chen was annoyed. When approaching Yangzhou, he told the boatmen to find a local matchmaker to marry her off. As long as the man was honest and trustworthy, no wedding gift would be necessary. Now, who would not jump at the offer of a wife who costs nothing?

Before long, a matchmaker brought forth a man, claiming that he was a fine stonemason and greatly praising his sincerity and honesty. You may well say that there could hardly have been only this stonemason for a candidate in a city as big as Yangzhou. Let me tell you why. It is often said, "A greedy lot are the women of the nine professions."[9] A promise of extra strings of cash reward was enough to buy over the money-grabbing matchmaker. The stonemason bowed four times to Magistrate Chen and stepped back to stand to one side. Learning that the cleanly dressed young man of strong physique in front of him had never married before and could afford to support a wife with his skilled craftsman's hands, Chen gave Hu-shi away to him. At no expense whatever to himself, the stonemason led Hu-shi away as his wife. But of them, for the time being, no more.

Since his separation from Hu-shi and his son, Jia She spent his days in misery. One day, Tang-shi suddenly fell ill and lay down on her bed. Failing to respond to medicine, she died. Jia She bought a coffin, resigned from his post, and escorted the coffin with her body to his native town, where he was as pleased to see his son growing up well as he was saddened to learn that he was not to see Hu-shi, for she had remarried. Indeed,

> *The flower bloomed, only to be ravaged by rain;*
> *The rain stopped, but the flower withered.*
> *Nothing is perfect in this world;*
> *Few flower watchers have unmarred pleasure.*

Jia's son was now a seven-year-old boy of unusual intelligence. He needed to read a text only once before he could recite it from memory. His father gave him the name Sidao and the courtesy name Shixian. At fifteen, Jia Sidao had read all the books he could get his hands on and was able to write improvised essays as fast as his brush-pen could go. As bad luck would have it, his father, Jia She, and his Uncle Jia Ru died of illness one after the other. The funerals and the burials over, he found himself free of disciplinary restraints and plunged right into gambling, cock-fighting, horse-racing, drinking, and whoring. In four or five years, he squandered away all of his inheritance from both families. He had once heard in family circles that his biological mother, Hu-shi, was married to a stonemason in Yangzhou and that his sister Jia Yuhua[10] was an imperial consort living in the palace. He thought to himself, "Yangzhou is too far from here, and a stonemason living off his trade can't be a rich man. I know that my sister was selected to be a consort for their prince of Yi, but now that the prince is the emperor, I wonder if his favorite consort Jia is my sister. Why don't I go to the capital and find out?" It was the first year of the Duanping reign period [1234] under Emperor Lizong of the Song dynasty and the year that Jia Sidao was predestined to start his rise in the world. He sold what was left of the household effects for a few strings of cash, packed up his baggage, and set out for Lin'an.

Lin'an, the capital of the empire, was a bustling place swarming with people, but Jia Sidao, being a newcomer, had no acquaintances from whom to get information. He spent his days roaming around the lake and venturing into the gambling houses and prostitutes' quarters. Not many days passed by before he found himself penniless and in rags, sponging meals off rich households in the West Lake area.

One day, groggy with wine, he was taking a nap at the foot of Qixia Hill when a cotton-robed Taoist with a feather fan passed by. At the sight of Jia

Sidao, he stopped in his tracks and stared at Jia for a considerable time before saying, "Have some self-respect for yourself. You will have a career as illustrious as the great general Han." Who was this Han? Well, he was Han Shizhong, lord of Qi [1089–51].¹¹ Being the prime minister as well as a general, he was held in admiration by the Chinese as well as by foreigners. How many men have there ever been whose fame could match his? Jia Sidao dismissed the prediction as nothing more than words of jest not to be taken seriously. (*This was indeed said in jest. But, as it turned out, Sidao, in his later years, was to take these words of jest all too seriously.*) The Taoist left.

A few days later, a drunken Jia Sidao fell down the steps in the midst of a gambling brawl at the house of Madam Zhao in the prostitutes' quarters. His forehead hit the ground and there was blood all over his face. Though he was in no danger, he ended up with a scar on his forehead. One day, he ran into the Taoist again in a wineshop. Stamping his foot, the Taoist sighed, saying, "What a shame! What a shame! Now that your forehead is marred by a scar, even though you will attain immense fame, you will die a violent death." (*Such is the will of heaven.*)

Grabbing the Taoist by his clothes, Jia Sidao asked, "If there is indeed fame and fortune in store for me, I don't mind dying after enjoying even one day of fulfillment. (*So that's the full extent of his ambition!*) But, as things are now, how can you talk about wealth and power when I'm such a penniless wanderer, with no one to turn to for help?"

The Taoist took another close look at his complexion and said, "Your bad luck is over. Within three days, you will meet someone who will miraculously start you on a meteoric rise in the world. But mark this: In your days of glory, on no account should you set yourself against scholars." With this admonition, the Taoist took himself off, leaving Jia Sidao unsure whether or not to believe what he had heard.

The days dragged by. On the third day after the encounter with the Taoist, Chen Erlang of the gambling house came to Jia Sidao and said, "Recently, the emperor granted the title of imperial consort to a favorite concubine of his named Jia, whose every wish he indulges. Claiming that Taizhou is her native town, she has sent Grand Commandant Liu Ba to visit her relatives there. (*Good plot.*) Could she be the sister you often mention? I am telling you about this so that if you are truly related to her, you can go and see Commandant Liu. You'll surely have something to gain."

These words had the effect of awakening Jia Sidao from a dream. He thought to himself, "While Father was alive, he did often say that he had rented a house from Commandant Liu, with whom he developed quite a friendship. It was also through the commandant's help that Sister got to serve the emperor. I should have gone to him the moment I arrived in Lin'an instead of foolishly wasting time wandering around! But I'm all in rags. How can I go to see the commandant like this?" An idea came to him. From a pawnshop he rented a nice robe and a new cap. Jauntily he betook himself to the residence of Commandant Liu and, announcing himself as the son of an old friend, Mr. Jia of Taizhou, asked to see the commandant.

Commandant Liu was, at this point, packing for his trip to Taizhou to visit Consort Jia's relatives. Afraid that the visitor might be another pretender, he sent a trusted valet to check his background before letting him in. In a short while, his valet reported back, "It is indeed Jia She's son, Jia Sidao."

"Quickly invite him in!" said the commandant.

The commandant's residence was known for its strict rules. In ordinary circumstances, visitors were just "let" in. The word "invite" was rarely heard. Such courtesy on this occasion was due to the imperial consort's exalted status.

At the sight of the commandant, Jia Sidao sank to his knees and kowtowed. Though the commandant returned the greeting, doubts still remained in his mind about the visitor's identity. Only after a detailed questioning was he reassured that this was no pretender. He kept the visitor for some tea and a meal and put him up in the study for the night.

The following morning, he reported the visit to Consort Jia, who, in turn, told Emperor Lizong about it. The emperor then summoned Jia Sidao into the palace to greet the imperial consort. As they chatted about family matters, sister and brother fell upon each other's shoulders in a flood of tears.

Leading Jia Sidao into the presence of the emperor, the imperial consort said between sobs, "This is the only brother I have. In your august benevolence, please do something for this homeless bachelor."

The emperor took up his brush-pen and appointed him director of the Sacred Fields, a position entitled to a mansion in the city of Lin'an, ten court ladies for wife and concubines, three thousand taels of gold, and a hundred thousand taels of silver for household expenses—all to be claimed from Commandant Liu.

After thanking the emperor for his grace, Jia Sidao followed Commandant Liu out of the palace and said to him, "The house that the emperor is bestowing upon me must be near West Lake to suit my taste." (*He is going to enjoy the best time of his life there.*)

Only too eager to ingratiate himself with Jia Sidao for the sake of the imperial consort, the commandant picked a huge mansion by the side of the lake, and paid double the amount allowed by the government, using his own money to make up the difference. He then presented the house, complete with servants, furniture, and housewares of every description, to Jia. On the following day, the ten court ladies arrived along with more than ten carriages loaded with valuables sent as a personal gift from the imperial consort. With all this wealth attained overnight, Sidao rewarded Chen Erlang with a hundred taels of gold for his information. Another hundred taels of gold was sent to the pawnshop to thank the owner for having rented him the clothes. But how could the pawnshop owner dare accept the money? On the contrary, the owner came with lavish gifts to offer his congratulations.

From then on, Consort Jia often summoned Jia Sidao to the palace. The emperor himself, while on his outings to the lake, also visited him at his residence and played games and drank with him as with a family member. Matchless indeed were the favors showered upon him. Taking full advantage of his royal connections, Jia Sidao cast all appearances of decency to the winds and visited celebrated courtesans in his sedan-chair or horse-carriage day in and day out. When he met one who struck his fancy, regardless of all rules of propriety, he would take her on his boat to keep company with guests touring West Lake. When there were too many guests, the whole company would be accommodated by several boats that sailed side to side. There was also a never-ending flow of small boats that carried wine and food. You may well ask, how could a man of humble origins such as Jia Sidao have any guests to entertain? As the ancients put it so well, "A poor man is deserted by kith and kin; a rich man attracts friends galore." Now that Jia Sidao was a royal kinsman wallowing in ever-increasing imperial favors, who would not fawn upon him? If one got in, he would bring in others, and it was no surprise that the house became as crowded as a marketplace. Of men of letters, there were Liao Yingzhong, Weng Yinglong, and Zhao Fenru; of military officers, there were Xia Gui and Sun Huchen, just to mention a few of the more famous of the guests. The rest we shall not list one by one.

One day, Emperor Lizong was on Phoenix Hill on one of his excursions when he saw bright candles lightening up the night sky over West Lake. "That must be Jia Sidao," he said to his followers. He ordered a man to go posthaste on horseback to investigate. It was indeed Sidao touring the lake. The emperor told the imperial consort about this and sent over another carriageful of gold and silk for Jia Sidao's wine expenses. Henceforth, Sidao became even more unscrupulous in his dissipated ways, as these lines attest:

> Lulled by the peace, the emperor lacked any plans,
> But indulged his kinsman in wanton pleasure.
> Was the matchless beauty of West Lake
> The best weapon of the empire's defense?

At the time, the Song dynasty had just wiped out the Jurchens with the aid of the Mongolian army. However, following the advice of Zhao Fan and Zhao Kui, the court engaged the Mongols in hostilities over control of the Yellow River and Yougu Pass and demanded to recover the three cities of

Kaifeng, Luoyang, and Yingtian. It was a move that triggered a Mongolian invasion in retaliation against the Song breach of their agreement. The Huai and Han River valleys were thrown into turmoil, and the emperor took alarm.

Having undeservingly won the favor of the emperor, Jia Sidao knew that he could not very well further seek royal titles without incurring reprobation. High position was not possible unless he won top honors by driving the invaders away from the borders, which was the very first priority of the empire. (*It's all right to treat something as a first priority, as long as no fuss is made over a trifle.*) Therefore, claiming that he was well-versed in military strategies, he offered his services and volunteered to go to Yangzhou to raise an army and crush the enemy for the protection of the southeastern region in the name of the emperor. Immensely delighted, Emperor Lizong appointed him military commissioner of the Huai region,[12] to be stationed in Yangzhou. Sidao thanked the emperor, left the court, and, with his wife, concubines, and retainers, went to Yangzhou to assume his post.

Three days later, he quietly sent a trusted retainer to visit his biological mother, Hu-shi. The man found out that she was indeed living at the east end of Guanglingyi with a stonemason. Having ascertained the fact, he reported as much to Sidao, who immediately dispatched a sedan-chair procession to bring her to him. When an official of the tribunal led the sedan-chair carriers in bowing to Hu-shi, the woman was so frightened she almost fainted and did not pull herself together until the official explained his mission entrusted to him by the commissioner.

"Since I am married," said she, "I cannot do anything without my husband's knowledge." Right away, she sent someone to bring the stonemason back and told him about the situation. As the stonemason wanted to follow her, she could not very well refuse him and had to take him along. With Hu-shi riding in front in the sedan-chair and the stonemason on a horse following behind, the procession made its way to the commissioner's residence. Sidao invited his mother into his private quarters. Mother and son fell upon each other's shoulders and wept. When they were separated, Sidao was only three years old and Hu-shi in her twenties. More than thirty years had passed before this reunion. How could they not have been filled with emotion?

Hearing that the stonemason was also there, Sidao was ill-disposed toward meeting him. He took out three hundred taels of silver and sent a trusted follower to accompany the stonemason on a business trip down the river. Acting on Sidao's secret instructions, the man got the stonemason drunk when they were half-way down the river and pushed him into the water. At the report of the stonemason's death from some illness, Hu-shi felt sorrowful. Henceforth, never an obstacle came between mother and son.

By a stroke of luck, during the six years that Sidao served as commissioner in Yangzhou, all was peaceful and well in the southeastern region of the empire. To please the imperial consort, who missed her brother, the emperor summoned Sidao back to the court and appointed him vice-director of the Bureau of Military Affairs, an appointment that coincided with Wu Qian's replacement of Ding Daquan as vice–prime minister. With the courtesy name Lüzhai, Wu Qian was a self-assured man of bold spirit and got all of his brothers important positions in the court. Jealous of Wu Qian for being higher than himself in the echelons of officialdom, Jia Sidao made up a song and told a young court valet to sing it to the emperor. This is how the song went:

> Centipedes, centipedes, big and small;
> They're curses of the earth that poison all.
> Currying favor with pests of all kinds,
> They will eat the dragon if made to fly.

The emperor asked Sidao, "What kind of omen is implied in this song, which I understand is circulating among children of the city?"

Sidao replied, "All such songs are taught to children by the god of the planet Mars in the disguise of a child. Since this is a portent from heaven, we cannot but analyze it carefully. Since *wu* is the same as the surname Wu, as I see it, the centipedes [*wugong*] refer to the power-abusing Wu brothers. Should their ambition be further nurtured, they will certainly bring ruin upon the imperial court. Your Majesty being the dragon in the sky, it is by heaven's will that the song warns about the dragon being eaten. The best course to avoid calamity is to dismiss Wu Qian from the office of prime minister and replace him with a worthier man."

The emperor believed him and immediately ordered a member of the Hanlin Academy to draft an edict sending Wu Qian into exile in Xunzhou and stripping his brothers of all official posts. Replacing Wu Qian as the vice–prime minister, Sidao sent a trusted follower to order Liu Zongshen, the prefect of Xunzhou, to rake up incriminating evidence against Wu. Unable to endure the persecution, Wu Qian took poison and died. (*Having already stripped them of their official posts, how can he have the heart to go further and take their lives? What a vicious man!*) This is how vicious Sidao could be.

Meanwhile, Mongke [1209–59], the Mongol Khan, had stationed his troops outside the city wall of Hezhou and sent his brother Kublai [1215–94] to lay siege to Ezhou and Xiangyang. The menacing situation struck terror into people's hearts. In one day, the Bureau of Military Affairs received three emergency appeals, to the great consternation of the imperial court. Jia Sidao was then named director of the Bureau of Military Affairs and concurrently the Jing-Hu pacification commissioner, and was to lead the army to Hanyang to lift the siege against Ezhou. Sidao dared not refuse but had to accept the appointment with all due deference. He tried to recruit Zheng Long, a student at the National University who was, as he was told, accomplished in both the military and civil arts. Well aware of Sidao's treachery, Zheng Long was afraid of working with him and instead sent him a name card with the following poem written on it:

> *The load of affairs of the universe*
> *Is easier put on than taken off.*
> *May you hold high your hands that support the sky,*
> *For looking on are many a critical eye.*

This poem makes the explicit point that, being in an exalted position, Jia Sidao should, in all modesty, exercise caution in going about his business. Should Jia gladly follow this advice after reading the poem, it would be worthwhile for Zheng Long to enter his service, if only briefly. Who would have expected that Jia Sidao would be so irritated at the admonishing tone of the poem that he would tear it to pieces, calling Zheng Long a deranged bookworm? Of this, no more need be said.

Supported by his retainers, among whom were Liao Yingzhong and Zhao Fenru, distinguished for their scholarly merits, and Xia Gui and Sun Huchen, distinguished for their military accomplishments, Jia Sidao carefully selected two hundred thousand experienced soldiers of the imperial army and spared no expense in equipping them with weapons and armor. On a chosen day, the mighty army left the capital. It was an awe-inspiring sight indeed.

Not many days passed before they arrived in Hanyang, where they pitched camp. The Mongolian troops' attack was so vehement that Ezhou was moments away from falling. Sidao was petrified with fear. How could he dare charge forward? After consulting Liao Yingzhong and others, he wrote a letter and had it sent by a trusted follower, Song Jing, to the Mongolian side, asking for their withdrawal in exchange for the Southern Song's humble subordination and tributes of money. Kublai declined the offer, but Sidao insisted and sent his messengers back and forth three or four more times. At this juncture, Mongke, khan of Mongolia, died at the foot of Mount Diaoyu in Hezhou. With his heart set upon taking over the throne, Kublai lost all interest in the battle and accepted Sidao's peace offer to pay annual tribute money as a subordinate of the khan. Both parties having sworn to the settlement, Kublai broke camp and left to attend the funeral and succeed to the throne.

Now that the Mongol troops had gone north and Ezhou was out of danger, Jia Sidao submitted a memorial to the emperor, exaggerating his accomplishments while suppressing the truth about his offer to pay tribute in exchange for peace. The memorial claimed only that the Mongol army had fled out of fear of his awe-inspiring name. He bade Liao Yingzhong write a victory report and a "chronicle of achievements" to record his accomplishments at Ezhou. When Mongolia sent a messenger to discuss the matter of the annual tribute, Sidao ordered that the man be put under house arrest in Zhenzhou, out of fear that Sidao's lies would be exposed. As long as the imperial court could be fooled, what did he care if he broke his promise to the barbarians? To reward Jia Sidao for what was thought to be his great merit, Emperor Lizong issued an edict in praise of him, added to his titles that of junior preceptor, and bestowed upon him an untold amount of gold and silk and more land in the Ge Hills to enlarge his residence. His mother, Hu-shi, was also granted the title Lady Liangguo.

In all complacency, Jia Sidao gave himself the airs of a true hero who had rendered the empire great service. Day and night, he caroused on the lake with his concubines and took pleasure from their singing and dancing. Tribute flowed to him from all directions in a steady and endless stream. All of his retainers, to a man, were granted important offices, including positions wielding military power. Truly, he was under only one man, but above all the rest of the empire. Every year on his birthday, on the eighth day of the eighth month, thousands of lyric poems of praise poured in. Sidao read each one of them to evaluate the quality. For a time, those poems were on everyone's lips and were copied so widely that paper became a rare commodity. The masterpiece that emerged was one by Lu Jingsi to the tune of "Eight Beats of a Ganzhou Song":

> *In the midst of peace throughout the empire*
> *Comes the autumn bumper harvest of rice.*
> *Never a greater service to the land,*
> *Never a more abundant year in the fields.*
> *Well content are the people with their lives;*
> *In cheerful leisure they while away their time.*
> *The plan that defeated the Mongols*
> *Was so ingenious as to defy words.*
> *(Defy words it does!)*
> *Should the Jade Emperor invite you up,*
> *Send to his garden a part of the lake,*
> *Complete with tea stoves and fishing boats.*
> *Before the autumn wind rises, your thoughts*
> *Go to your mother's flowered terrace.*
> *A million years to you,*
> *Magnate in heaven, immortal on earth.*

Poems of a like nature were too many to be enumerated here. One day, Sidao was amusing himself with his concubines on a tower overlooking the lake when there came approaching the bank in a small boat two well-dressed and refined-looking young scholars carrying feather fans. One concubine in the company said under her breath, "What handsome young men they are!" Sidao heard the remark and said, "If you wish to marry those two, I will certainly make them send you a betrothal letter." In consternation, the woman asked for forgiveness. Before long, Sidao assembled the concubines and had a maid step forward with a box in her hands. Sidao said, "There was among you one who just expressed admiration for some young scholars touring the lake. I have already accepted a betrothal request for her." The concubines did not believe what they heard. When the box was opened, what confronted their eyes was that woman's head. No one present did not tremble with fear. This was how ruthless Sidao could be with his concubines.

Many a time he also ordered his followers to smuggle hundreds of boats of salt into Lin'an for sale. A poem by a student at the National University had this to say of him:

> Last night on the green waves of the river
> Rode salt-laden boats of the minister.
> Granted that he needs salt for seasoning,[13]
> Surely he has no use for all that much.

Sidao now wished for a plan to build up the economic and military power of the empire. Censor Chen Yaodao suggested that the best way to raise army provisions and promote the interests of the empire as well as those of the people would be to limit the possession of land. How would this plan work? As things stood at the time, the rich possessed huge tracts of land, whereas the poor did not even have a speck of land of their own in which to stick an awl. Those with land did not do the tilling, whereas those willing to till had no land. Therefore, the plan was to limit the amount of land owned by officials according to their ranks. Officials of a certain rank were to be allowed only a certain amount of land, whereas farmers under their rule were also to be allowed a certain amount of land. Extra land could be either bought back by the original owner with no time limit or bought through designation by those rich households whose quota for land had not yet been reached, or be bought by the government as "public land" to be tilled by hired hands, with the land rent collected therefrom to be used for army provisions. The plan was to be tried first in western Zhejiang and then, if successful, to be carried out throughout the empire. (*There does appear to be good sense in what he does. But if the sophistry of fame-seeking villains is taken as good sense, evil is being bred without anyone's realizing it.*) Most of the land bought by private households had poor soil but was taxed at the regular rate, whereas good land was bought by the government at a price lower than the actual cost. This resulted in chaos and bankruptcies throughout the Zhejiang region. (*This is only to be expected. If justice prevails and the people are given freedom of action, even Wang Anshi's Green Seedling Method*[14] *would be a good policy, and nothing bad could come of it.*) Resentment was widespread. That student of the National University now had this to say:

> *Dust kicked up by the invaders' horses*
> *Darkens the sky midst the sound of war drums.*
> *But he hangs on to the lake and the hills*
> *And refuses to go out to battle.*
> *Not knowing where the real problems lie,*
> *He brings ruin with his policy on land.*

Seeing that his policy was not working, Jia Sidao contributed to the government more than ten thousand *mu*[15] of his own land in Zhejiang. As word of this spread around, all court officials, to a man, contributed some of theirs in their eagerness to please the prime minister. (*Doing disservice to himself as well as to others.*) Xu Jingsun, a member of the Hanlin Academy, wrote a memorial enumerating the harms wrought by the public land policy but was removed from office through impeachment by Censor Shu Youkai at Sidao's bidding. Editorial Director Chen Zhu also submitted a memorial accusing Sidao of deceiving the emperor and impoverishing the people, only to be dismissed from office upon some false charge from Sidao. Chen Maolian, the official in charge of public land, who witnessed all the wrongdoings, handed in his resignation and left. There was also a certain Ye Li, courtesy name Taibai, a native of Qiantang and an old acquaintance of Sidao, who wrote a letter of remonstration that so incensed Sidao that Ye ended up exiled in Zhangzhou with his face tattooed with ink, as was done to criminals. Henceforth, no one at the imperial court dared breathe a word of dissent.

Sidao then proceeded to establish the policies of "history-checking" and "land-measuring." What did this mean? Well, an owner of land would be ordered to produce deeds and the history of all past transactions of his land. If investigations found discrepancies in his account, he would be charged with perjury and his land would be confiscated. This was the policy of history-checking. There was also the measuring of land. If it turned out that there was actually more land than was reported, the owner would be charged with the crime of failure to report the exact amount of land, which would, as a result, also be confiscated. This was the land-measuring policy. With these policies in place, an untold amount of private land was lost through confiscation. That National University student wrote another poem that said,

> *With two-thirds of the empire already gone,*
> *He still busily measures inches of land.*

Even if he wrests some acres here and there,
The empire will not regain its former size.

There was also someone who wrote a lyric poem to the tune of "Spring in Qin's Garden":

A journey south of the Yangzi
Finds posters on whitewashed walls everywhere,
Announcing who rents from whom in what village.
The desolation that meets the eye
Is worse than the region has ever known.
Why do officials think only of themselves,
With no compassion to spare for the people?

For a hundred years,
An immense empire remains torn apart.
On the Sichuan cliffs,
Clouds block the birds' way.
On the fields of the Huai region,
Beacon fires warn of war.
With the minister abusing power
And villains deceiving the emperor,
Who'd worry about wars at the borders?
To rule is nothing but to tithe the land.

As repeated reports of the National University student's satires reached his ears, Sidao burned with rage. After taking counsel with Censor Chen Boda, he proposed a new system of registration for the examinations. All examinees, including those exempted from examinations at the local levels, were issued a form for personal information. They were to describe on the form, in their own handwriting, their appearance, age, family background, and schooling and present the form to examiners at the prefectural level, who would then check the handwriting as a preventive measure against fraud. Meanwhile, spies were sent out for secret investigation. All those talented in the writing of poems were suspected as possible sources of slander and, consequently, were disqualified, for one reason or another, when their handwriting was subjected to examination. As a result, sycophants moved up whereas the truly talented felt only frustration. A contemporary had this to say:

Invaders sweep in, shaking earth and sky.
Throughout Jingxiang[16] resound grief-stricken cries.
The prime minister knows not what to do,
But torments the examinees instead.

There was also a lyric poem to the tune of "Spring in Qin's Garden":

> *One after another are listed*
> *Questions for the examinees.*
> *What do your children study?*
> *What do your father and brothers do?*
> *What's the field of your scholarly interest?*
> *No detail is spared,*
> *Not even the name of your wife.*
> *But how relevant are the names of wives?*
> *Tired of the endless checking,*
> *The sponsors ask for money.*
>
> *With laws well-established by ancestors,*
> *Why the need for the thousands of changes?*
> *With new bills*[17] *and the land and rice policies,*
> *The people live in dire poverty,*
> *Fleeced of whatever they had.*
> *Only scholars still had a breath left,*
> *But are now in the deepest woe.*
> (Well put.)
> *Who started it all?*
> *Chen Boda, the power-hungry sycophant!*

When Chen Boda got hold of the poem, he showed it to Jia Sidao, who then sent spies to find out who had written it, but to no avail. Knowing that it must have been the work of a scholar, he took advantage of the death of Emperor Lizong and declared cancellation of the imperial examinations for that year, thus incurring the deep anger of all potential examinees at the National University, the Military School, and the School for the Imperial Family. There were, however, some shameless scholars who led a campaign to sing the praises of Jia Sidao, who, in a bid to befriend the academics, showered them with handsome rewards. Those grateful for the favors were more than willing to enter into his service. As the scholars were by no means of one mind, nothing was done to redress the injustices, but of this, no more need be said. (*Detestable.*)

With the succession of Emperor Duzong to the throne, the reign title was changed to Xianchun [1265–74]. When Emperor Duzong was still living in the east wing of the palace, Sidao had done him a favor by instating him as crown prince. Now that he had ascended the throne, he granted Sidao the titles of grand preceptor and duke of Wei. At every session of the court, the

Son of Heaven invariably returned Sidao's bows and addressed him not by his name but as "Prime Minister." Moreover, Sidao was allowed to report to the court only once every ten days, with the rest of the time at his own disposal. All affairs of the empire, big or small, were dealt with in his private residence. A two-line song began to spread around:

> There is no prime minister at the court;
> He is to be found only on the lake.

One day, Sidao summoned Vice–Prime Minister Ma Tingluan and Military Affairs Commissioner Ye Mengding for a drink on the lake. As a drinking game, Sidao suggested that each make up a story about presenting a gift to an ancient historical figure, who would then respond with a couplet. He started off the game by saying, "I have a chess game that I gave to Qiu the chess master, who responded with this couplet:

> 'I have met no match since I took up the game;
> Well can I afford concessions with good grace.'"

Ma said, "I have a bamboo pole that I gave to Lü Wang the angler,[18] who responded with this couplet:

> 'The night still, the water cold, the fish not eating;
> The empty boat goes back, laden with moonlight.'"

Ye Mengding came up with these lines: "I had a plow that I gave to Yi Yin the venerable ancient,[19] who responded with this couplet:

> 'May you keep a corner of your land
> For your offspring to till and farm.'"

Sidao detected sarcasm in both men's words. The following day, at his suggestion, the emperor dismissed the two men from office on some made-up charges.

In the meantime, the Mongols had become powerful under the new dynastic name of Yuan. That the Mongol troops had kept Xiangyang and Fancheng under siege for three years was a fact known to all in the imperial court except the emperor himself. Well aware that the empire was in imminent danger, Sidao wallowed in pleasures nonetheless. On the day of the Clear and Bright Festival,[20] he composed the following poem while touring the lake:

> On the eve of the festival, willows adorn every house;
> Not much longer can spring be kept behind.
> Drink to your fill while the wine still lasts!

> *Your offspring at your grave—how many will be sad?*
> (This poem sheds light on Sidao's innermost thoughts. So he has no
> other plans than to live from day to day.)

On the Ge Hills, he built a most elegant mansion—complete with exquisite towers, terraces, and pavilions—that came to be filled with beautiful women (prostitutes and nuns included) selected from among the commoners. Hearing about the beauty of Ye-shi, a court lady, he bribed a eunuch with access to the private chambers of the palace and brought her out to be his concubine. Day or night, his dissipation knew no bounds. Halls were erected to store his mountain-high collections of rare works of art, which he had acquired by every conceivable means. His daily visits to the halls to admire his possessions grew into a habit. Anyone who so much as mentioned the trouble at the borders met with immediate punishment.

One day, Emperor Duzong asked him, "I heard that Xiangyang has been under siege for a long time. What is to be done?" (*It's not that Emperor Duzong cares nothing about border defense, but, had he appointed some competent man to be prime minister, how could the empire have ended up in such a wretched state?*)

Sidao replied, "The northern troops have long since retreated. Why do you ask?"

The emperor said, "A consort of mine told me about it just now. The prime minister should know if that is the truth."

"It is a lie. Do not believe a word of it. If there is any trouble, I will certainly take it upon myself to lead a mighty army and wipe out the enemy for Your Majesty." (*Boastful words to fool the emperor.*) With these words, court was dismissed. Sidao had the eunuch in charge of the inner chambers of the palace quietly find out the name of that consort and upon some made-up charge, ordered her to take her own life within the palace grounds. Indeed,

> *A word too many leads to misfortune;*
> *To stand out from the crowd brings on trouble.*
> *How absurd that none of the many advisers*
> *Had as much courage as this court lady.*

After the death of the court lady, no one inside or outside the palace ever brought up the subject of war again. It was not overnight that the empire found itself in such peril.

Sidao started another construction project. This time, it was the Half-Leisure Hall, with his own statue in the main hall, which was flanked by hundreds of side rooms to accommodate necromancers and traveling Taoists. On a day of leisure, Sidao would sit in meditation in the central hall and converse with the necromancers and Taoists. Many a man among his retainers wrote lyric poems in praise of the Half-Leisure Hall. Sidao's favorite was one to the tune of "Tangduoling":

> *Fairies from heaven*
> *Crossed the Pass riding green oxen.*[21]
> *A new mansion is added to the fairyland*
> *With bamboo, flowers, and hills.*
> *Fame and high office are of no account;*
> *Leisure is what should be sought after in life;*
> *But true leisure visits not the world of men.*
> *Half of the hall is for fairies to enjoy,*
> *The rest for you to find your true leisure.*
> (Ingenious poem.)

There was a necromancer called Fuchunzi who excelled in using the sound of wind and the cries of birds to prophesy events. Jia Sidao summoned him to test his art. When asked what would happen on the next day, Fuchunzi wrote something secretly on a piece of paper, sealed it, and said, "Do not open it until late at night."

The following day, Sidao gave a banquet on the lake by the hills. He was standing on the bow of the boat, sending off the guests, when the bright moon in the sky inspired him to intone a couplet by Cao Cao:[22] "By the light of the bright moon and sparse stars, / The crows are flying south." At this, Liao Yingzhong, who was standing by his side, advised him, "Now is the time for you to open the seal and look at the prophecy."

It turned out that the piece of paper contained nothing but this couplet: "By the light of the bright moon and sparse stars, / The crows are flying south." Sidao was astounded. Thus convinced of the man's uncanny powers, Sidao took his counsel again about what lay in his future. Fuchunzi offered him this advice: "Your wealth and eminence are unparalleled in history, but you are incompatible with the surname Zheng. Keep yourself at a safe distance from any man named Zheng."

Long ago in his childhood, Sidao had once dreamed that he was rising to heaven on the back of a dragon, only to fall down into a ditch at the blow of a fierce warrior wearing a vest on which were embroidered the characters "Xingyang," and Xingyang County was the home base of the Zheng clan. How could he not believe in Fuchunzi now that the warning against Zheng tallied with his own dream?

Henceforth, Sidao kept a close watch over the roster of court officials and did everything he could to oust any man with the surname Zheng. Sure enough, the court was soon cleared of all Zhengs. Having guessed what Sidao was after, a retainer of his said, "Zheng Long, a student at the National

University, must be got rid of on account of all those poems he's written that mock the court."

Remembering the insult he had suffered from the poems of criticism some time ago, Sidao ordered the National University to banish the man, on some framed-up charge, to Enzhou as a tattooed criminal. (*How abhorrent! How pitiful!*) Zheng Long had gone only part of the way when he died of anguish.

There was a man skilled in the art of glyphomancy who could foretell the future with miraculous accuracy. Now that Sidao had attained as much wealth and eminence as any man could ever hope for, he gradually developed the ambition of taking over the throne. However, afraid that the secret deal he had made with the Mongols would come to light, in which case he would not be able to escape the censure of the court, he was tempted to follow the examples of Dong Zhuo and Cao Cao.[23] In his indecision, he summoned the glyphomancer and traced with his cane the character *qi* on the ground for the man to analyze. After a moment of thought, the glyphomancer said, "Whatever plan you have will not go through, because the upper part of this character would have been the character 'to establish' [*li*] if it didn't share its bottom horizontal line with the lower part of the character, which means 'permitted' [*ke*]. As it is, if you want to 'establish,' it is not 'permitted.' If you wish to go by the lower part of the character and get 'permission,' you will be breaking up the upper part, which means 'to establish,' and therefore fail in your endeavor." (*Clever.*)

Sidao fell silent and sent the glyphomancer away with a generous reward of gold and silk. Afraid that the man would reveal the secret, Sidao ordered to have him murdered half-way on his journey. From then on, his ambition for the throne declined. Noticing that Sidao was acting strangely, Fuchunzi fled elsewhere, afraid that some calamity might befall him. He was, indeed, a man who knew what was best for himself.

Now let us return to Lady Hu, Sidao's mother, who, supported by her son for about forty years, died in her eighties one day in the third month of the tenth year of the Xianchun reign period [1274]. (*After her death, the Jia family went into decline, and so did the House of Song. Contemporaries said that the woman had her worth, for all appearances to the contrary. That is a valid comment.*) We need hardly say that the burial clothes, coffin, and funeral services were of the most extravagant kind. After observing the forty-nine days of mourning, Jia Sidao escorted the coffin to Taizhou to be buried in the same grave as Jia She. On the day of the burial, the imperial court dispatched the emperor's guards of honor. Imperial relatives and court officials of all ranks under the empress dowager vied with each other in laying out sacrificial altars all along the route of the procession. Some altars were piled up so high that just decking them out with sacrificial items claimed a number of lives. All in mourning clothes, the assembly of court officials accompanied the coffin for a hundred li. The emperor cancelled his court sessions. In a downpour of torrential rain, the ground was submerged in water three feet deep. (*Heaven is disgusted with him.*) Drenched in rain and splattered with mud, all in the procession plodded through waist-high water, but no one dared take a step back. After the burial, thirty thousand monks were fed because their blessings were needed for the deceased in the netherworld. One monk put his alms bowl upside down on the ground after the meal and went away. As no one was able to lift the bowl, (*Remarkable*) Sidao was informed of the matter. In disbelief, Sidao arrived at the spot to take a look for himself. To his great astonishment, as he gently lifted the bowl, he saw written inside it with white sand two lines of characters in an exquisite style:

> *Relinquish your ways while there is still time;*
> *At Mian will flowers bloom and fruit be borne.*

He was still wondering about the meaning when the characters suddenly disappeared. Sidao asked all his retainers about the meaning of the couplet, but no one could come up with an explanation. It was not until he later died in Mumian Temple that the meaning was revealed. Generally speaking, the rich and the powerful had by no means been of any common sort in their previous lives. That was why a holy monk had come along to caution Sidao to relinquish his evil ways and avoid disaster. As it turned out, Jia Sidao was so blinded by his avarice that he failed to come to his senses. Such, indeed, is the case since ancient times with most powerful men who do not end up well.

Let us digress no more. The burial service over, Jia Sidao wrote a memorial to the emperor in acknowledgment of his gratitude. As the emperor issued an edict summoning him back to the imperial court, Sidao requested an extension of his leave, ostensibly to observe the full term of the mourning period, but, at the same time, he enjoined the censors to suggest that the emperor not fill the office of prime minister during his absence but keep the position for him until his return. (*Sidao does know how to maneuver the censors.*) There poured in a stream of imperial edicts urging him to return to the court. It was not until the beginning of the seventh month that he went to see the emperor and resumed his post.

Toward the end of the same month, Emperor Duzong died. The crown prince acceded to the throne, to be known in history as Emperor Gongzong. Shi Tianze and Bo Yan, the two co–prime ministers of the Yuan, led troops in a southward expedition, striking out in different directions. Xiangyang, Dengzhou, and the Huai and Yangzhou regions all sent in emergency appeals. Knowing full well that young Emperor Gongzong was a faint-hearted sort, Jia Sidao deliberately exaggerated the desperateness of the situation and asked to be allowed to lead troops to engage the enemy at the borders. (*Boastful words to fool the emperor.*) At the same time, he privately instructed the censors to advise the emperor to keep him at court. And this is what the censors said to the emperor: "The prime minister is the only one to fall back on. If he is appointed to lead the troops, he will be hard put to take care of the Xiang-Han and Yangzhou regions all at the same time. (*How abominable the censors' words are!*) The best alternative is to have him remain in the heart of the empire and devise strategies that will assure victories a thousand li away. Should he leave your presence, who would be left for you to consult?" (*What use is there in consulting Sidao?*) The emperor agreed. "How can I manage without the prime minister for even one day?" he said.

Within several months, the city of Fancheng fell, followed by Ezhou. Lü Wenhuan, having guarded Xiangyang for five years against heavy odds, now found himself without reinforcements and the food supply for the city exhausted. Unable to hold out any longer, he could do no better than surrender to the Yuan army (*A fine man Lü Wenhuan is! What a pity!*), which then pushed farther south. This time, Jia Sidao knew that he could not hide the truth any longer from the emperor. The emperor was appalled at his report. "With the Yuan troops bearing down so closely upon us," he said, "there is no better person to lead the troops than you, Prime Minister."

Sidao replied, "I did ask for the appointment early on, but Your Majesty turned me down. If you had listened to me earlier, the barbarians would not have gotten this far." (*The temerity!*) Thereupon the emperor issued an edict authorizing Jia Sidao to be the commander in chief. Sidao, in his turn, recommended that Lü Shikui be his military consultant. And so it was that in the first year of Deyou [1275] under Emperor Gongzong, Sidao led his troops on their way by land and by water. It was a grand sight, with banners and flags blocking out the sky and boats and ships stretching out for a thousand li. Sidao himself, his two sons, his wife and concubines, and their supplies and household effects took up over a hundred boats. His retainers also went along, bringing their families. (*Sidao is not planning on returning.*) The military consultant preceded him and arrived in Jiangzhou to surrender the city to the Yuan troops, who then went ahead and took Chizhou as well. When word got to Sidao, he dared not venture forward, but stopped at Lugang. Both Bandit-Suppression Commissioner of the Infantry Sun Huchen and his naval counterpart, Xia Gui, were Jia Sidao's retainers. They had impressed Sidao with their eloquence in daily conversation, but neither had the mettle of Zhang Jun, Han Shizhong, Liu Qi, or Yue Fei.[24] How could they expect to win a major battle by sheer luck? (*Sidao fools the Son of Heaven. His retainers, in turn, fool him.*)

After Sun Huchen had stationed his troops in Dingjiazhou, the Yuan troops, led by Commander Ashu [Bayan, 1227–1280], descended in an attack. Overpowered by the enemy, Sun Huchen mounted his horse and fled for his life. The infantrymen all took to their heels and ran pellmell in all directions. Bayan set men to shout at the boats of the Song army, "The Song infantry is finished! What are you navy men waiting for? Surrender now!" The men were so terrified at the words that they lost all will to fight. The only thought on their minds was to make their escape. In the ensuing chaos, the boats tossed about and bumped into one another. Numerous men were drowned. Unable to put a stop to the confusion, Sidao summoned Xia Gui for an emergency consultation. Xia said, "With our troops already put to rout, fighting would serve no purpose. In my opinion, our best course is to go to Yangzhou, where we shall recruit survivors and ride to the sea. Unworthy as I am, I am more than willing to defend the Huaixi region to my death." With these words, he took himself off.

In a short while, Sun Huchen stepped off a boat and said tearfully, with his hand beating his chest, "It is not that I didn't want to put up a hard fight, but what more could I do when I had no one willing to risk his life?" Before Sidao could answer, a sentry boat approached to report that Commissioner Xia had already departed by boat, destination unknown. (*A nice try at "defending the region to my death!"*)

At the strike of the fourth watch, the sentry boat came back and reported to Sidao, who was at his wits' end, "The Yuan troops are coming from all directions!" Sidao's face turned the color of dirt. With all the haste he could muster, he ordered gongs to be struck to announce the retreat. His troops were put to total defeat. Supported by Sun Huchen, Sidao fled to Yangzhou in a small boat. A runner named Weng Yinglong retrieved the commander in chief's seal and went to Lin'an with all speed.

The following day, the river was filled with boats carrying the defeated men. Sidao ordered Sun Huchen to step onto the bank and wave a flag to rally the men together, but there was no response other than curses. "That crook Jia Sidao pulled the wool over the emperor's eyes! It's his fault that the enemy has grown so strong. What a scourge he is to the empire and the people! Look at what he brought us to now!" There were also voices saying, "Why don't we kill those crooks to avenge the tens of thousands of people out there!" Before the voices had died down, arrows flew into the boat, knocking Sun Huchen to the ground. Realizing that a rebellion was on his hands, Sidao hurriedly ordered the boatmen to dodge the arrows and fled all the way to the city of Yangzhou, where he hid himself from the public, pleading illness.

Let us now leave him and come to the vice–prime minister, Chen Yizhong, who had gained his office through ingratiating himself to Sidao in every way. Seeing Weng Yinglong running back in great haste, Chen Yizhong asked, "Where is the prime minister?" Weng said that he did not know. Assuming that Sidao had died in the chaos, Yizhong composed a memorial to the emperor, charging Jia Sidao with the crime of treason and defeat at war, and requesting the eradication of the entire Jia clan to atone for the damages done to the empire. Consequently, the censors, in their haste to please Yizhong, relayed the vice–prime minister's memorial to the emperor. (*What better example than this of the treachery of officialdom!*) It was not until then that Emperor Gongzong realized Sidao's treachery and issued an edict enumerating his crimes. The gist of the edict was as follows:

> *For a court minister commanding respect all over the four seas, there is no greater crime than that of treason. For a commander in chief who holds military power, there is no greater punishment than that for the defeat of his army. In his two consecutive terms as prime minister, Jia Sidao, with no talent or great morals to his credit, accomplished nothing of benefit to the empire. Instead, he undermined the very foundation of the empire by changing the land policy, suppressed talent by changing the registration system for the imperial examinations, withheld information about the situation at the borders, and failed to build up military strength. It was not until the enemy was closing in that he proposed to lead the troops to counter the enemy. When he should have charged forth with all speed, he took to his heels, causing the disintegration of the armies and the disloyalty of the generals. The empire has fallen into peril and the people's resentment runs high. By way of a moderate punishment, he should be demoted to the position of director of ceremonies. Alas! In regaining territories, we are beyond hope of achieving the accomplishments of the duke of Zhou. In punishing the culprits, we shall be more lenient than "The Canon of Shun." The prime minister should be divested of all civil as well as military power and removed from the office of commander in chief.*

Upon hearing of Sidao's demotion, Liao Yingzhong, who was also in Yangzhou with his entire family, went to Sidao's residence to extend his sympathy. When the two men met, both were too overcome with emotion for words. Liao asked for wine, and until the striking of the fifth watch of the night, they downed cup after cup while tearfully singing in grief.

Back in his own residence, instead of going to bed, Yingzhong asked his favorite concubine to brew some tea for him. When the tea was served, he sent her away for some wine and then secretly swallowed a handful of borneol. Now, borneol is a most poisonous substance, which, if swallowed, brings certain death. As it would take a few moments for the borneol to take effect, Yingzhong began to fear that he might not die after all, and frantically asked for the heated wine, with which, when it was brought to him, he swallowed several more handfuls of borneol that he had hidden in his sleeves. It was only then that the concubine realized what he was doing. She rushed forth and snatched away the poison, but it was already too late. As she held him in her arms, weeping, Yingzhong said, fighting back his tears, "There, there, don't cry. Throughout my twenty years of service for the prime minister, I enjoyed much wealth and luxury. Now that disaster has struck, I consider myself fortunate to be able to die at home." His words were still in the air when he died, with blood flowing from all the nine apertures of his head and body. Woeful it is that such a brilliant and learned man, a master of prose and verse, should serve as a lackey for the powerful and end with such a violent death! As the poem says (*However unworthy, Yingzhong was, at least, loyal to Sidao, and superior to Chen Yizhong on that score*),

> *Instead of being a contented earthworm,*
> *He chose to be a fly chasing rotten meat.*
> *When the winds knock the tree down to the ground,*
> *No branch can ever thrive again.*

Meanwhile, Jia Sidao's demotion caused a flurry of talk at the imperial court, and the consensus was that his crimes were worse than this. The court ministers submitted another memorial, requesting that Sidao be decapitated by axe. The emperor, however, could not bear the thought of subjecting a senior official of the court to such violence. Instead, Sidao was further demoted to the position of military training commissioner of Gaozhou, with the freedom of settling down in Xunzhou. All of his estate was confiscated for the benefit of the military. The notice of demotion was issued on the eighth day of the eighth month, which happened to be Sidao's birthday. The speech that Sidao wrote himself to mark his birthday is summarized here as follows:

> *What does the public have against this old minister innocent of any crime? The Lord on High loves life, but mine is now drawing to an end. Let me make a few remarks on this birthday of mine before I depart this life. I, Jia Sidao, have served three emperors with unswerving loyalty, through many trials and tribulations. To crush the arrogance of the invaders, I led an army composed of weak men to offer resistance. However, as the soldiers failed to fight with courage, victory was beyond reach.* (Good excuse.) *Never will I be able to clear myself of the onslaught of unjust denunciations levied against me. After forty years of devoted service, I now regret that I did not retire earlier, as Zhang Liang*[25] *of the Han dynasty did. Instead, I am reduced to the status of an exile, banished to a place three thousand li away, my entire clan subject to extermination, as Huo Guang's was.*[26] (This fellow doesn't write badly.) *Raising my eyes to heaven, I am filled with mortification. Looking down, I feel unworthy of my parents. May heaven and earth witness a return to the wise ways of Emperors Lizong and Duzong.*

May the emperor, the Queen Mother, and the empress retract their wrath and
allow a proper burial for my bones in my place of exile. May the gods in the
nine imperial ancestral temples exercise their power and drive the demons out
of the empire.

As stipulated by law in Song times, any court minister banished to a
faraway place had to be escorted by a guardian whose job was more to keep
watch over the prisoner than to provide protection, as the name might suggest.
In the case of Sidao's banishment to Xunzhou, the court deliberated upon the
choice of a guardian, who had to be a capable, sharp, and resourceful man
with a grudge against Jia Sidao. But Xunzhou was too far away to attract any
volunteers.

There was only one official who willingly offered to go. You may ask,
who was this official? He was Zheng Huchen, marshal of Kuaiji, who had just
arrived in the capital upon expiration of his term of office. He was none other
than the son of Zheng Long, the National University student who was banished as a branded criminal by Jia Sidao and died on his way to exile. Huchen
volunteered so as to give vent to his pent-up resentment. (*In this life, you never*
know whom you'll meet again somewhere. That's why you should, on no account,
make an enemy of anyone.) Upon learning the facts, the court gave its consent
and duly appointed him as the guardian.

Though unaware that Huchen was Zheng Long's son, Jia Sidao did
remember the dream he had when he was a boy as well as the admonition
of Fuchunzi the fortune-teller. Now that a man named Zheng was coming
his way, his consternation could be well imagined. Before setting out on his
journey into exile, Sidao prepared a feast for Huchen, who readily took the
seat of honor. Calling Huchen the emperor's messenger and himself a criminal, Sidao offered him gifts of exquisite curios worth tens of thousands of
taels of gold. With tears in his eyes, he sobbed out an account of his childhood
dream. "May the emperor's messenger show the compassion of a bodhisattva,"
he implored, "and preserve my worthless life. I shall never dare to forget to
repay you for your kindness in this life and thereafter." This said, he dropped
to his knees.

With a dry smile on his lips, Zheng Huchen said, "Please rise. These
curios bring nothing but disasters. How can you expect me to accept them?
Let us get on our way first before we talk about anything else." To Sidao's
repeated supplications for mercy, Huchen responded with only a smile. Sidao
was seized with even greater fear.

The following day, they set out on the journey at Huchen's urging,
with more than ten carriages of gold, silver, and other valuables and nearly

a hundred maidservants and page boys. Huchen did not protest at the beginning, but several days later, he grew impatient at the way the cumbersome entourage was slowing down the journey and gradually drove away the servants. At every temple they passed by, he forced Sidao to give away gold and treasure as donations. Sidao dared not object. (*Hurrah!*) In half a month, all that remained were three carriages and fewer than ten servants, old and young, who dared not get near Sidao for fear of Huchen's constant beatings and scoldings. On the carriage where Sidao sat stood a bamboo pole with a silk banner, on which was written, "Escorting by imperial decree Jia Sidao, the scourge of the empire, to Xunzhou for his banishment." Overcome with shame, Sidao covered up his face with his sleeves all day long. (*Hurrah!*) Other abuses from Huchen throughout the journey were too numerous to be listed here.

Many more days passed before they came upon Luoyang Bridge in Quanzhou.[27] There came into view a traveler hurrying along in their direction. At the sight of the inscription on the banner, he shouted, "It's been a long time since I saw you last, Prime Minister! Who would have expected us to meet here after twenty years!" Taking him to be an old friend, Sidao lowered his arm, and who do you suppose it was? (*Fated enemies are bound to run into each other on a narrow road.*) It was Ye Li, courtesy name Taibai, a native of Qiantang, whom Sidao had banished to Zhangzhou as a branded criminal because of his remonstrations against Sidao's ways. After the downfall of Sidao, all those who were persecuted by him were rehabilitated and allowed to return to their native places. Having received his pardon, Ye Li was on his way back to Qiantang by way of Quanzhou when he ran into Sidao and deliberately called out a greeting. A shame-faced Jia Sidao dismounted and saluted him, offering profuse apologies. Ye Li asked for a piece of paper and a pen from Zheng Huchen and wrote a lyric poem for Sidao. The poem read,

> *You are going where I am coming from;*
> *This route is never devoid of traffic.*
> *Are the land and money policies still in place?*
> *Who brought ruin to the empire?*
> *Wherever we are, Leizhou or Yazhou,*
> *Our paths are sure to cross some day.*
> *I regret having no steamed lamb to offer,*
> *But just a lyric with lines of varying length.*

Back in the days of Emperor Renzong[28] of the Northern Song dynasty, Prime Minister Kou Zhun repelled the Liao invaders from the north at Chanyuan,[29] but the evil court minister Ding Wei cast aspersions on him and contrived to have him demoted to the post of comptroller of revenue of Leizhou.

Before long, Ding Wei was exposed for his treachery and ended up being banished to Yazhou. When he was passing through Leizhou on his way to his destination, Kou Zhun had a messenger send him a steamed lamb as a gift from himself as a local resident. Ashamed, Ding Wei dared not stay in Leizhou, but quietly stole away in the night. Ye Li used this story in his lyric poem to make the point that, as the ways of heaven are by no means immutable, one would do well not to bring total destruction to one's enemy. Overcome with shame upon receiving the poem, Sidao offered Ye Li a package of valuables to use for travel expenses. Ye Li refused to take it and continued on his way. Zheng Huchen thundered, "Who wants those ill-gotten goods of yours? Even dogs and pigs would turn up their noses at such things!" So saying, he snatched the package from Sidao's hands and tossed the contents on the ground. This done, he ordered the driver to start quickly moving and unleashed another torrent of angry curses at Sidao, whose eyes had not a dry moment.

Zheng Huchen's plan was to bully Jia Sidao into committing suicide. Little did he expect Sidao to cling so desperately to life. By the time they reached Zhangzhou, the servants had all slipped away, leaving Sidao and his two sons to fend for themselves. With no decent clothes or good food, they found themselves as lowly as slaves and as poor as beggars. Their misery indeed defies description.

Zhao Fenru, the prefect of Zhengzhou, happened to be a former retainer of Jia Sidao's. Hearing that his former patron was arriving, he went outside the city gate to welcome him. Saddened though he was at the sight of the pitiable state Sidao was in, he dared not show much hospitality, for fear of incurring the anger of the scowling Zheng Huchen. That very day, Zhao Fenru prepared a feast at their inn in honor of Zheng Huchen. When he asked that Sidao be seated at the same table as Zheng Huchen and himself, Huchen declined the request. Sidao himself also said in all humility, "How dare I, a criminal, sit at the same table with the emperor's messenger?" An apologetic Zhao Fenru could do nothing more than set another table in a separate room for Sidao attended by the controller general, whereas he himself sat with Huchen.

In the midst of the drinking, Fenru found out through the conversation that Huchen had a deep hatred of Sidao. He asked purposefully, "With the emperor's messenger escorting him here over such a distance, I assume that he does not have long to live. Why don't you make him die sooner? Wouldn't that save you some trouble?"

Huchen replied with a laugh, "That's because that wretch would rather suffer than die a more honorable death."

Zhao Fenru knew better than to venture further remarks. At the fifth watch of the night, Huchen urged the men to be on their way before the prefect could come to bid them farewell.

At the first light of dawn they came upon a temple five li away from the city. Huchen ordered that they take a rest in the temple, where they could wash and eat breakfast. At the sight of the characters "Mumian Temple" inscribed on the horizontal board of the monastery, Jia Sidao was dumb-founded. "Two years ago," he said, "a monk with supernatural powers left me a poem in his alms bowl, saying, 'At Mian will flowers bloom and fruit be borne.' Could it be that the prophecy is to be fulfilled today? In that case, I'll be dead!"

Once inside the temple, he hastened to summon his two sons for a few words, but Huchen had already put them in a separate room. Sidao knew that death was imminent. While washing his face, he took out a package of bor-neol that he had hidden on himself and swallowed it with water. Stung with sharp pains in the stomach, he asked for a nightstool and sat down, looking more dead than alive.

Guessing that he had taken poison, Huchen lashed out, "You mean wretch! Millions of people died at your hands. You slowed down the journey a good many days, and now you want to take your own life, but I won't let you!" With that, he swung his heavy cudgel and struck twenty to thirty blows against Sidao's head, smashing it to a pulp. After it was all over, he sent word to Sidao's two sons, saying, "Your father has taken poison. Come quickly to take a look." At the sight of their father's dead body, the sons broke into wails of grief. In a rage, Huchen finished them off with one blow each. He then had his men drag the bodies to one side and spread word that the two sons had taken flight.

Throwing the cudgel onto the ground, Huchen said with a sigh, "Now that I have avenged my father and rid the people of a scourge, I can leave this world without regrets." He wrapped up Sidao with a straw mat and buried the body, together with the articles of clothing of the deceased, at the side of the temple. This done, he wrote a report to Prefect Zhao Fenru, claiming that Jia Sidao had died of illness. Knowing only too well that this was the work of Huchen, Zhao Fenru dared not question him, out of fear for his violent tem-per. There was no alternative for the prefect but to pass on the report to related bureaus for settlement of the case. It was only after Zheng Huchen had left that he prepared a coffin, dug up Sidao's body, and buried it properly in a grave. He composed an elegy that included these lines: "Alas! Wu Qian per-ished in Sichuan at the hands of Zongshen. My master perished in Fujian at the hands of Huchen. How tragic!" (*Short as it is, the elegy makes clear the author's feelings. The work of a master.*)

Wu Qian was the prime minister at Emperor Lizong's court. Coveting his office, Jia Sidao charged him with false crimes and had him banished to Xunzhou, where Liu Zongshen, the prefect, forced him to take poison. As for Jia Sidao himself, he died an even more tragic death in Mumian Temple without even reaching Xunzhou, his destination. In a subtle way, the elegy was a reminder of the law of heavenly retribution. Even though he had lived under Jia Sidao's patronage, Zhao Fenru still retained some conscience, after all.

But enough of such idle comments. After Sidao's banishment, his landed estates were confiscated by the government, but the huge mansion in the Ge Hills with the high terraces and winding ponds was left unattended. As the days went by, the walls crumbled and the estate was reduced to a scene of bleak desolation. Visitors to the area, one and all, sighed with emotion. Following are two of the many poems written on the doors and the walls:

> The deserted yards are overgrown with weeds,
> But the gleam of gold on the screens still remains.
> Who'd have foreseen that with him went all glory;
> When this one man fell, so did the whole empire.
> Under Emperor Lizong he rose to power;
> At the hands of a Zheng he died, as foretold.
> The dragon refused to stay in the ditch,
> Leaving only its bright glow on the walls.

And

> With no tricks to pull in an hour of peril,
> He could hardly repeat his Ezhou "glory."
> Mumian Temple reeks of a thousand years' rancor;
> Autumn Valley Pavilion[30] is but a dream.
> On stones with thick moss, monkeys wail in moonlight.
> By dead leaves at Pine Pavilion, birds call in the wind.
> Let not grief overwhelm you, visitor,
> But, from Wu Hill, look toward the palace.

Zhang Shunmei Finds a Fair Lady during the Lantern Festival

On Lantern Festivals in times of peace,
Lanterns everywhere brighten up the moon.
So many young men and women of good birth
In their finery look for romance in the crowds.[1]

In Bianliang, the Eastern Capital, Lantern Festivals were celebrated in grand style under the aegis of Emperor Huizong [r. 1101–25] of the Song dynasty. As our story goes, there lived in the city a certain Zhang Sheng, son of an eminent official. At eighteen years of age, he was a most handsome and bright young man and not yet betrothed. When at Qianming Temple viewing lanterns during the Lantern Festival, he picked up in the hall a red silk handkerchief with a sachet tied to one corner. Upon a closer look, he found a poem inscribed on it:

The sachet seals my innermost feelings;
The red handkerchief is dotted with tears.
Keep this as a token of my love
And put it in your sleeves, my dear one.

The poem was followed by a line written in fine script: "To him who picks up this handkerchief: Forget not to come and meet me at the next Lantern Festival on the fifteenth night of the first month of next year at the rear gate of Great State Councilor Monastery. Look for mandarin-duck lanterns at the front of my carriage." Zhang Sheng read the poem several times, heaved many sighs in admiration, and then wrote a poem in reply:

The scent is from the hands that sealed the bag,
The color darker than rosy cheeks.
Though a long way off from the date of the tryst,
I am in raptures as if in a dream.

Henceforth, Zhang Sheng lived his life counting the hours, the days, and the months, until the old year yielded to the new one. With the Lantern

Festival drawing near, Zhang Sheng betook himself to the rear gate of Great State Councilor Monastery on the eve of the festival to keep the appointment. There did indeed come into view a well-guarded carriage with a pair of mandarin-duck lanterns. Zhang Sheng was beside himself with astonishment and joy. There being no other way to find out who was in the carriage, he composed a poem and, with hesitating steps, approached the carriage, intoning,

> *Who left behind a red silk handkerchief*
> *Imbued with meaning that inspires passion?*
> *When its absence was first felt,*
> *Her soft hands must have searched around her waist.*

These lines having stirred her memory about a lost sachet, the woman in the carriage drew aside the curtain, and the sight of a handsome man with graceful bearing stirred up her desire. She ordered her maid, Golden Flower, to convey her feelings. Zhang Sheng understood the message. In a moment, the carriage drove away and disappeared into the distance.

The following night, Zhang Sheng waited at the same spot. An old carriage with a blue canopy and a pair of mandarin-duck lanterns in front drew near with no retinue of followers. Looking into the carriage, Zhang Sheng found a nun, not the young woman he had seen the night before. The carriage driver said repeatedly, "I am driving the nun back to the temple." Before he could decide what to do, Zhang Sheng saw the nun beckon him with her hand. Quietly, he followed behind the carriage.

Upon arriving at Qianming Temple, an old nun came to the door to greet them, saying, "Why are you so late?"

Zhang Sheng followed the nun into a well-lit small room, where a table had been laid out for dinner. The nun took off her outfit, revealing brightly colored clothes and an elaborate coiffure. Zhang Sheng and the woman sat down together while the old nun remained at one side. The dinner over, the woman said, "I would like to see the things that made our date possible," whereupon Zhang Sheng took out the sachet and the red silk handkerchief for her to see. With a laugh, she said, "Of the multitudes of people coming and going in the capital, you are the one who chanced upon it. Isn't this a sign that heaven has granted a marriage bond between the two of us?"

"I wrote a poem in reply when I first came upon it." So saying, he presented her with the poem.

The woman exclaimed happily, "You are indeed meant to be my husband." Thereupon, the two of them went to bed and fulfilled their desire to the utmost. Shortly thereafter, at the first crows of roosters, she said to Zhang Sheng, "I am the eighth concubine of Squire Huo. Being old and sickly, he never comes into my room. Every night, I burn incense and wish to heaven that I can meet a good man and marry him. Luckily, you came along, bringing me enough happiness to last a lifetime. It is with a trick that I slipped out today. I cannot go back. Now that I belong to you, I will be more than willing to be with you, dead or alive. Otherwise, what will become of me?"

"I am not made of unfeeling wood or stone," said Zhang Sheng. "How can I bear parting with you? But no good plan comes to mind. If we are caught, I would rather die with you at the end of a rope and become ghost lovers." With these words, they threw themselves into each other's arms and broke into bitter sobs.

Coming in from the outside, the old nun said, "If you want to be husband and wife, all that's necessary is the will to do so. You don't have to end up miserably like that!"

Zhang Sheng and the woman fell upon their knees and begged for advice. The old nun continued, "If you can go away to a far place a thousand li away, beyond rivers and lakes, and live under changed names, you'll be able to enjoy each other to the end of your lives."

With their heads bowed, the woman and Zhang Sheng accepted this advice. The old nun took out a packet of gold and silver and handed it to Zhang Sheng, saying, "This is the young lady's savings. I now give it to you for your travel expenses."

Zhang Sheng returned home and gathered up his valuables into a parcel. That very night, they took leave of the old nun and set out on their way. After spending the night at an inn by Tongjin Gate, they hired a boat the following morning and traveled across the Huai River all the way to Suzhou, where they settled down and lived to a venerable old age as loving to each other as ever. Truly,

> Loving as a pair of mandarin ducks,
> The couple enjoyed a blissful marriage.

Why did I bring up this story? It is because the fair lady of our main story also ran into a romantically inclined young scholar on a Lantern Festival night and the encounter led to a series of strange happenings. If you wish to know whether they also ended up as a married couple, please listen to my account in the next storytelling session. Truly,

> They first met when the lanterns were first lit,
> The moon waxing full, plum blossoms in bloom.

Whom did the woman meet? It was Zhang Shunmei, a native of Yuezhou. At twenty years of age, he was a graceful young man and a fine scholar whose talent was yet unrecognized. He had come to Hangzhou to take the provincial examinations but stayed on after having failed them. He had been in the city for over half a year when the Lantern Festival came around. Shutting his door behind him, he went out for some amusement. Hangzhou was a city filled with hustle and bustle. How do we know that Hangzhou was such a good place? There is a lyric poem to the tune of "Watching the Sea Tide" by Liu Yong[2] that speaks particularly of the attractions of Hangzhou:

> The leading city in the Southeast
> And the lower reaches of the Yangzi,
> Qiantang has been a bustling place since times of old.
> Amid the misty willows and bridges,
> Behind the fine jade curtains,
> Live ten thousand households.
> Tall trees line the winding dike;
> Choppy waves toss up frost and snow;
> The natural moat of the tower stretches afar.
> The markets display pearls and gems;
> Houses overflow with silks and satins,
> Vying in displays of luxury.
>
> The lakes and hills offer a scene of beauty,
> With cassia buds throughout the autumn
> And miles of flowering lotus.
> String and wind music on sunny days;
> Songs at night while picking water caltrops.
> Happy are the hoary anglers
> And the lotus-picking children.
> A thousand riders rally around the banners;
> Tipsy with wine, they listen to the flute and drums
> While admiring the clouds of sunset.
> This fine scenery should be sketched some day
> For the imperial court to enjoy.

While viewing the sights of the city, Shunmei waxed poetic and indulged himself by verbally improvising a lyric poem to the tune of "As in a Dream: A Song":

> The bright moon filters through the willow trees;
> The spring is as mellow as wine.
> On the first night the lanterns are lit,
> I walk on the six bridges with my friends.
> Turning my head back, I wonder
> If the lady upstairs sees me.

Intoning the poem as he went along, he noticed, far away in the shadow of lantern light, a maid carrying a colored phoenix lantern across her shoulders, followed by a young lady walking slowly in his direction. With cloud-like hair and eyebrows shaped like silkworms, she had a most seductive look. The sight shook Shunmei from his inebriated state. He adjusted his cap and started swaggering and strutting toward her. Why did he put on such an act? As a matter of fact, all those about to start a courtship do some such trick at the first encounter. For strangers meeting each other by chance, there are several ways to test the other party. Let me now quote a few lines from "The Code of Flirtation" for the benefit of our playboys:

> Play the coquette with a pretty face;
> Show off wealth with fancy clothes.
> At a distance or close at hand,
> Convey love with your eyes.
> Rubbing shoulders, or brushing the back,
> Follow her with nimble feet.
> If she strikes your fancy, let her know;
> If like-minded, she will smile and respond.
> A nod will suffice;
> A cough will do.
> Never relax when things are going well.
> Create some fun when things quiet down.
> When flirting with words, watch well what you say.
> When leading her on, do not shy away.
> Play demure to test her true feelings.
> Take action to see if she was willing.
> There is no limit to the ways of testing.
> Resort to wiles to make it happen.
> Even if she has a heart of iron,
> You can turn her soft as candy.

The young woman was so aroused by Shunmei's captivating ways that she found it hard to contain herself. Her vision blurred, her heart fluttered, her legs felt weak, her feet grew numb. For a good while, she stood stupefied, her eyes gazing into his, expressions of love written on both their faces. When she started to walk fast, Shunmei quickened his pace and followed right at her heels. When she slowed down, he did so too, but no word could be exchanged. Before they knew it, they found themselves on Zhong'an Bridge, where traffic was so congested with peddlers, buyers, and pedestrians that it was hard to elbow one's way through. After crossing the bridge, Shunmei lost track of the woman. He could do nothing but return home, dejected. As he opened the door, he found the room dimly lit and chilly with drafts. How was he to sleep with such cold pillows and quilts? His mind was still on the woman. How nice it would be to spend some more time with her! Isn't it absurd that a man can be so infatuated with a woman? Indeed,

> With flowers by the window and a hazy moon,
> He is sick with longing for love.

When day broke at long last, he rose, washed, and dressed. After the three meals of the day, preparations started in the streets for another evening of lantern-viewing. Unable to restrain himself, Shunmei hastily closed his door and headed straight for the spot where he had met the woman the night before. He stood, paced to and fro, searched around, and leaned against various supports as he waited, but the woman failed to show up. To kill time, he composed a lyric poem to the tune of "As in a Dream: A Song":

> I slept not a wink all through the blissful night;
> I smile to the east wind, tipsy with wine.
> The lady, my sweetheart—
> Where is she amusing herself tonight?
> On the lookout for her,
> I'd fain return but choose to stay.

After intoning the poem, he waited a good while longer. He was about to turn back when he saw a maid carrying colored mandarin-duck lanterns emerge out of the crowd with the young lady. At the sight of Shunmei, the woman broke into a brilliant smile. Shunmei knew that about half of the battle was won. The woman headed for Salt Bridge, went into Vast Happiness Temple to offer incense, and then turned into the back hall, with Shunmei following right behind. As the woman suddenly turned around, a giggle escaped her. Shunmei responded with an awkward laugh. The two now began to rub against each other without any scruples. Bending down, the woman pulled out from her sleeves a symbol of love made of paper folded into the shape of two overlapping diamonds. When she threw it to the ground, Shunmei took the hint and picked it up. Unfolding it under the lantern light, he found it to be a sheet of flowered notepaper. All would have been well if he had not read it, but as it was, the scholar read it and suffered from such severe lovesickness for one to two years that he almost died. You may well ask, what on earth was written on the paper? It turned out to be another lyric poem to the tune of "As in a Dream: A Song":

> Meeting you by chance
> Yet drawn to you like an old friend,

> *I have lost my heart to you.*
> *Where mandarin-duck lanterns hang high,*
> *Is the residence where I live.*
> *Come, come, and visit me tomorrow night.*

Following the poem were written these lines:

> *I live in the eighth house facing south in Shiguanzi Lane. Tomorrow my parents,*
> *brother, and sister-in-law are leaving for a Lantern Festival gathering at my*
> *uncle's house by the river and will not be back until the seventeenth of the month.*
> *My maid Xiaoying and I will be the only ones left at home. I make bold to invite*
> *you to come for a visit to console my feelings. I shall burn incense, clean the*
> *house, and wait for you in eager expectation.*

> *Respectfully yours,*
> *Liu Suxiang*

Shunmei read the passage over and over again, beside himself with joy. In the meantime, the woman took herself off. He walked back to his room and spent a wakeful night without a wink of sleep.

The following day was the fifteenth of the month. When night fell at last, Shunmei went to the house as directed but dared not go in of his own accord. Instead, he composed another poem to the tune of "As in a Dream: A Song" and intoned,

> *The water-clock drips as if sobbing;*
> *The wind spreads the fragrance of incense.*
> *The sight of the colored mandarin-duck lanterns*
> *Sends my heart racing.*
> *I should have spoken, I should have spoken,*
> *Last night when we met.*

Having heard these lines, the woman lifted the curtain and stepped out. Indeed, it was the man dear to her heart whom she had met under the light of the lanterns. She led him into her room and, blowing out the silver lamp, undressed and lay down in bed. Both craving love, they were as eager as hungry tigers pouncing upon lambs or as flies swooping down upon drops of blood. In their hurry to have that business done, they had no time to spare for asking names and exchanging amenities. There is a lyric poem to the tune of "Song of the Southern Country" describing the scene of love:

> *Her gown soaked in scented sweat,*
> *They play at clouds and rain.*

Her feet on his shoulders,
Her brows knit in rapture.

Wild to the extreme, she cries out in delight.
Her tongue, at first taste,
Like honey or sugar,
Its flavor lingers long.

After they had fulfilled their desire, Shunmei said, "I was but a stranger to you. Your great kindness to me made me feel as if I were being favored by a fairy. Being but a young student, I regret having nothing to repay you with."

Stroking his back, Suxiang said, "I love you for your talent, not out of designs for money."

While Shunmei was pouring out words of gratitude, Suxiang suddenly heaved a long sigh and said tearfully, "Now that this day is over, my parents will be home tomorrow, and it will be impossible for us to meet again. What's to be done?"

Both fell silent. After some moments of thinking, a plan came up. Suxiang suggested, "The best course is for us to elope so as to spare ourselves the pain of separation. How does the idea strike you?"

Shunmei was greatly delighted. "I have a distant relative who keeps an inn on Wutiao Street in Zhenjiang. We can go to him for help." Suxiang agreed.

That night, Suxiang put together a package of valuables and, dressed as a man, started on the journey, hand in hand with Shunmei. At the second watch of the night, they found themselves only at the north gate of the city. You may well ask, why did they cover only three or four li in so much time? It was because of Suxiang's small feet, which were fit only for taking a few graceful steps under embroidered skirts on balconies and flowery paths. Accustomed to being carried in a sedan-chair from hall to hall in a magnificent mansion, she was now wearing a pair of large boots for a long journey to a distant place. How could she make it, as nervous as she was? Worse still, amid crowds pushing their way out of the city and crowds outside the city jostling their way in, the two of them let go of each other's hand. Walking single file, they made their way through the outer gate, but, swept along by the crowd, they lost sight of each other.

After leaving the gate, the woman wandered off in the direction of Bantang-heng. (*Shunmei is to blame.*) Shunmei thought that such a frail woman, being too weak to push her way out, might still be inside the city gate. He hurriedly turned back to ask the soldier guarding the gate. The soldier said, "Just now, there was a scholarly looking young man asking about his friend. At this moment, he shouldn't be more than half a li away on his way back." (*Had there not been such trials and tribulations, life would have been too easy for them, and there would have been no story to tell.*) Now, of the three roads that led respectively to Qiantang Gate, Shigu Bridge, and Chujiatang, Shunmei pondered which road to take. After much hesitation, he chose to turn back the way he had come. By the time he reached Shiguanzi Lane, where the woman's home was, the gate of the house was closed and all was quiet. With all speed he rushed to the north gate, only to find it closed as well. He spent the whole night looking for her.

When daybreak came at last, he made his way out the gate. At New Wharf, he came upon a crowd of people gathered tightly around an embroidered shoe. (*The plot thickens.*) Recognizing it to be a woman's shoe, Shunmei dared not utter a sound. Someone in the crowd was saying, "I wonder why a girl would leave her family and drown herself here, leaving a shoe behind?" At these words, Shunmei broke into a cold sweat. He returned to the city to make inquiries, only to hear rumors all over town that the daughter of the Liu family on Shiguanzi Lane had been kidnapped. In another version, she had drowned herself, and the constables had taken up the case. What with a restless night, an empty stomach, and grief over the woman's untimely death, Shunmei fell ill upon returning to his inn. Confined to his bed, he ran a high fever, with rushes of heat alternating with shivers of cold. His condition grew so grave that he found himself on the verge of death. (*Shunmei could have died this time.*) Truly,

> *When is he to see again his loved one?*
> *Sickness and worry wear away his youth.*

Let us leave Shunmei in his sickbed for now and return to Liu Suxiang, who, having lost sight of Shunmei at the north gate, walked from the second watch until the fifth watch before she reached New Wharf. She thought to herself, "Since Shunmei was unable to find me, he must have gone before me to Zhenjiang." So thinking, she quietly took off one embroidered shoe and threw it on the ground. Why did she do this? She was afraid that her family would track her down, and the shoe would convince her parents of the futility of further search. (*Unwise though this move may have been, Suxiang is shown to have plenty of brains. With her talent and good sense, she is far superior to Shunmei in getting things done.*) Under cover of predawn darkness, Suxiang rented a boat and went down the river. For the next several days, she was so cautious every time she relieved herself that the boatman had no inkling that she was a woman. Upon arrival in Zhenjiang, she paid the boatman and went ashore. As she pressed ahead, she made inquiries all along the way about Zhang Shunmei's relative, but, as she had forgotten his name and address, her inquiries were all to no avail. By sunset, she still had no place to stay.

When she found herself passing by a pavilion on the riverbank, she went in for a rest. It being the twenty-second day of the first month, the moon was late in rising. In the darkness not much relieved by fishermen's dim lights, she could not see beyond one foot ahead. She pondered her fate. Now that she had abandoned her parents and brothers for Zhang Shunmei's sake and he was nowhere to be seen, her best course would be to drown herself in the river. After she had cried for a considerable time over regrets that the man would not even know where she died, night set in before she knew it, and the moon shed its light into the pavilion. She moved along the balustrade and gazed into the vast expanse of water. Truly,

> The river glides under the midnight moon;
> Green hills surround the city of Nanjing.

While Suxiang was sobbing and talking sadly to herself, a nun emerged from a dark corner of the pavilion and asked her, "Are you a human or a ghost? How did you land yourself in such misery?"

Suxiang replied, "Since you are good enough to ask me, I will not keep anything from you. I am a native of Zhejiang. I was on my way with my husband to Xinfeng, where he was to assume a post, when, all too unexpectedly, disaster struck. My husband's money and my looks stirred the evil mind of the boatman, who killed my husband and our maids, sparing only my life. He tried to force himself upon me, but I would rather have died than submit myself to him. The following day, when the boatman was drunk, I put on my husband's clothes and escaped. And that's how I ended up here." Suxiang could not very well tell the nun about her elopement, and so came up with this story instead.

The nun said with deep emotion, "I was at the home of a benefactor, and so I was late in crossing the river on my way back. Heaven sent me here to this pavilion to meet you. There is indeed a predestined bond between us. Will you be willing to follow me?"

Suxiang said, "I was looking in the direction of my hometown, but it lies beyond a thousand mountains and rivers. Your help will give me a new life."

"Mercy being a guiding principle for us nuns, I do only what I should. Don't mention it."

Suxiang kowtowed in gratitude.

At the break of day, Suxiang followed the nun to Great Compassion Convent. Taking off her worldly clothes, she tied up her hair with pins into a circlet and stayed in a room of her own. After just one reading, she could recite any scripture or incantation. From morning to night, she attended services to worship the Buddhas, prayed to the bodhisattva Guanyin, and pleaded for more readings of the Buddhist scriptures. Seeing such devotion, the nun congratulated herself on having come upon the right person. Of this, we shall speak no further.

In the meantime, Shunmei gradually regained his health under medical care at the inn. Unwilling to return to his native town, he stayed on at the inn, reviewing the classics and histories. Time sped by, and the Lantern Festival rolled around again. With memories of last year's events, Shunmei betook himself to Shiguanzi Lane and saw that everything remained as before except, alas, that she was missing. With a heavy heart, he returned to his room and recited the lyric poem to the tune of "Mountain Hawthorns" by Scholar Qin Guan of the Song dynasty:

> *On the night of last year's Lantern Festival,*
> *The lantern-filled streets were as bright as day.*
> *With the moon atop the willow branches,*
> *We arranged for a date after sunset.*
> *On the night of this year's Lantern Festival,*
> *The moon and the lanterns shine as before,*
> *But with her gone,*
> *Tears wet my sleeves.*

In a dejected mood, Shunmei returned, shedding copious tears. Lamenting the vicissitudes of human fate in an otherwise unchanging world, he lost all hope and, to prove himself worthy of Suxiang's love, vowed never to marry. (*A creditable effort he makes.*)

Three years of life in Hangzhou soon elapsed. In the new round of imperial examinations, Shunmei ranked first at the provincial level. After the banquet for the successful candidates, he immediately wrote a letter to his parents. Relatives and friends filled their house to offer congratulations. Several days later, he took his zither, sword, and cases of books and started off on a journey to the capital for the national examination. Braving the wind, he pressed ahead and slept in the open air all along the way. At the mouth of the Zhenjiang River, his boat was about to cross when a fierce wind sprang up. The boat moved close to the bank to wait out the storm. As the wind blew relentlessly for days on end, there was nothing he could do but stay on the anchored boat.

In the meantime, Liu Suxiang, who had lived in Great Compassion Convent for three years, saw in a dream that night the bodhisattva Guanyin, who said to her, "Your husband is coming tomorrow." (*The bodhisattva acts kindly.*) She woke up with a start and found herself covered with sweat. She thought to herself, "I've never had such a dream before. How strange!" She kept the dream a secret.

Shunmei waited for days on end. Feeling down in spirits, he took a walk by himself along the river, looking around idly as he went. His steps took him to a grove of pine trees and bamboo, in the midst of which stood a small but elegant-looking convent bearing a board with the inscription "Great Compassion Convent." As he went inside, the abbess walked out to greet him and invited him into the main hall for some tea. The will of heaven made Liu Suxiang throw a casual glance through a window into the hall. Her eyes opened wide and she stood agape with astonishment, as if she had just woken from a wine-induced dream.

As the abbess stepped out for some fresh tea, Suxiang told her about all that had happened. Returning to the hall, the abbess asked, "Might you be Scholar Zhang of Yuezhou?"

Shunmei was shocked. "I have never seen you before. How did you know?"

The abbess pursued further, "Are you married?"

With tears coursing down his cheeks, Shunmei said, "My wife Liu Suxiang disappeared from sight when we were watching lanterns during the Lantern Festival three years ago. I still don't know where she is. Unworthy as I am, I came out first in the provincial examinations. I vow never to marry again, even if I get the degree of *jinshi* in the examination in the capital."

At that moment, the abbess called Suxiang to come forth. The couple fell upon each other's shoulders and wept bitterly. After a considerable time, they held back their tears and said, "I never thought I would see you again in this life!" With mixed feelings of grief and joy, they bowed to the abbess in gratitude. Then they bathed and changed clothes and, with offerings of incense to the bodhisattva, bowed a hundred times. With gifts of a hundred taels of silver and two bolts of silk to the abbess for her birthday, they took leave of her and embarked on a boat. It was indeed an occasion for great joy, reunited as they were like a moon waxing full again or a broken string rejoined on a musical instrument.

They made their way to the capital, where Shunmei later achieved honors in successive examinations, became a *jinshi,* and was appointed county magistrate of Putian, in Xinghua Prefecture, Fujian. After offering thanks for the appointment, he returned to his native place. Passing by Great Compassion Convent in Zhenjiang, the couple went in and presented the abbess with a gift of fifty taels of silver. Back in Hangzhou, they headed straight for Shiguanzi Lane and presented a name card with a request to see Suxiang's parents. At the words "Your humble son-in-law Zhang Shunmei" on the red name card, Mr. Liu thought the horse carriage was at the wrong door and was about to turn the visitors away when the young couple, dressed as an official and his wife, started making obeisances in the hall. The sight greatly astonished Suxiang's parents, brother, and sister-in-law. Their grief and joy intermingled. The mother said, "After we lost our daughter on the Lantern Festival, we almost died when we heard that she had drowned herself. We never thought that we would see her again. And it is the good fortune of the Liu family to have gained such a good son-in-law."

A grand banquet was laid out, and the celebration lasted several days. Xiao-ying the maidservant was assigned to follow the couple. The two took leave of Suxiang's parents and went to Shunmei's parents' home.

With an explanation from Shunmei, Suxiang stepped forward and kow-towed to her parents-in-law. Their joy exceeding their expectations, Zhang Shunmei's parents laid out a banquet to celebrate. A few days later, Shunmei and his wife took leave of his parents and went on their way to assume Shun-mei's new post. Later in his life, he rose to be vice-minister of personnel. His descendants enjoyed prosperity and high status. There is a poem that bears witness:

> *Parted for three years, she rose from the dead,*
> *With the town of Zhenjiang witnessing their love.*
> *By the light of candles tonight,*
> *Their smiling eyes take on greater brightness.*

Yang Siwen Meets an Old Acquaintance in Yanshan

> *One night of the east wind*
> *Swept the willow twigs clean of snow.*
> *By the palace amid the warm mist,*
> *Stands the colorful hill of lanterns.*
> *The flutes and drums bring in the dusk;*
> *The phoenix carriage returns to the palace.*
> *A thousand doors are brightly lit;*
> *The roads are filled with lovers.*
> *Into the boudoirs the ladies retire*
> *To rest after the fun and frolic.*
> *Trying out new dresses,*
> *They raise the bead curtains halfway.*
> *Softly they speak, demure and shy,*
> *Playing with silk flowers in their hands.*
> *An occasion for reunions,*
> *The Lantern Festival is here.*

The above lyric poem to the tune of "The Jade Maiden Messenger" was written by Hu Haoran.[1] Lantern Festivals were celebrated with the most jubilation during the Xuanhe reign period [1119–25] under Emperor Huizong of the Song dynasty. Every year on the fourteenth of the first month, the eve of the Lantern Festival, the emperor would drive in his carriage between two hundred pairs of gold-trimmed red-gauze lanterns to Felicity Pool at Five Peaks Temple.[2]

By night, palm-shaped fans with long, glazed jade handles would be added on to the carriage, which was preceded by fleet-footed runners equipped with pearl-lined red-gauze lanterns. When evening set in, the emperor would return to his palace past the hill of lanterns. Members of the Office of Imperial Transportation would gather in front of the carriage and sing "Charm Follows the Poles." The carriage would turn around in a circle and then go backward all around the hill of lanterns. It was a feat, known as "Turn of the Dove" or "Stepping around Five Flowers," that invariably earned the driver a reward.

The emperor himself would then ascend Extolling Virtue Tower while spectators flocked to the open-air stage shows.

On the fifteenth day of the month, the emperor would visit the Temple of Exalted Purity and remain until dusk before returning to his palace. On the day after the festival, the royal carriage would proceed again to the tower after breakfast. With the curtains drawn up, the emperor would have pedestrians summoned to his presence. Those who arrived early could thus see the Son of Heaven with their own eyes. Wearing a small cap and a red robe, the emperor would be flanked on both sides by attendants; in front of the curtains stood attendants holding golden fans. In a short while, the curtains would be let down and music struck up for all to enjoy. The resplendent light of the lanterns and candles, blended with the moonlight, shone far and wide. At the third watch of the night, a small red-gauze lamp would be lowered halfway down the tower on a rope, a signal that the imperial carriage was to return to the palace. Following is a lyric poem written by the emperor to the tune of "Jiazhong Palace: Xiaochong Hills":

> Midst the fragrance of the silks and satins,
> Gold lotuses bloom on dry land
> While my carriage goes around the city.
> In all directions stretch green wooded hills.
> The east wind, in its haste,
> Sweeps down half the stars from heaven.
>
> Ten thousand households rejoice in the peace,
> Songs fill the air on flower-strewn paths
> Where moonbeams follow at the heels.
> The royal gauze lanterns add light to the scene.
> The strains of flutes travel afar
> To the banquet in the immortal realm.

I shall now tell of a man who had always enjoyed the festivities in the Eastern Capital but, with the unexpected changing of times, came to be stranded in Yanshan Prefecture[3] and observed the Lantern Festival celebrations there. And how was the festival celebrated in Yanshan?

> Northerners though they are,
> They take joy in the festival as well.
> But instead of flutes and drums,
> Only the shrill Hun reeds are heard.
> Though every door is lit,
> No gold lotus is to be seen on the ground.
> Though nothing is left unadorned,

> *No silk flowers embellish the hair.*
> *The Hun men wear garlic at their temples;*
> *The Jurchen⁴ women wear chives in their hair.*
> *The men all carry lutes;*
> *The women beat flower drums.*

Every year, the Lantern Festival in Yanshan was celebrated in imitation of the festivities in the Eastern Capital. It was not until the third year of the Jianyan period [1129] under Emperor Gaozong of the Southern Song dynasty that the festivities reached a grand scale. That year, a hill of lanterns was put up in Yanshan, an event enjoyed by officials and commoners alike.

Now, the young man of our story used to be employed in Prince Su's⁵ mansion as a herald and a correspondence clerk for the imperial consort. He was named Yang Siwen but also known as Fifth Master Yang, for he was the fifth son in the family. In the Jingkang reign period,⁶ he came to be stranded in Yanshan, where, luckily, he met his uncle Zhang Er, an innkeeper, who took him in as a lodger. With no other means of subsistence, Yang Siwen eked out a living by doing some copying work every day in the marketplace. As the Lantern Festival rolled around, he saw that the streets were teeming with people out to view the lanterns. His uncle came to take him along to join the festivities. In a dejected mood, Siwen declined the offer. "As familiar as I am with the Lantern Festival in the Eastern Capital, how can I be expected to settle for anything less? (*How sad!*) You go ahead, Uncle. I'll catch up with you later." Consequently, Zhang Er set off alone.

By the time dusk set in, the noise on the streets had risen to such a level that, finding it hard to sit quietly, Yang Siwen could not do otherwise than go out to see the lanterns. Behold:

> *So bright were the lotus lanterns,*
> *Could they be stars blown down from heaven?*
> *Men and women thronged the streets,*
> *Like parades of celestial fairies.*
> *On the crowds the moon shed its light;*
> *Half are refugees from the old capital.*

The streets were filled with people coming and going. As he approached Blue Heaven Monastery, there came into view the golden statues of the fifty-three bodhisattvas and a hundred-foot-high bronze flagpole with an inscription in gold: "Blue Heaven Monastery of Compassion and Loyalty, constructed by imperial order." Entering the monastery, Siwen saw that both hallways were brightly lit. His leisurely steps took him to the Hall of Arhats, where he saw five hundred arhat statues in pure gold. An acolyte stood in front of the shrine asking for alms, saying, "Benefactors, please make a donation for some oil for our lamps. We shall pray for your fortune and longevity."

Detecting an Eastern Capital accent (*[Illegible] The reference to the Eastern Capital calls attention to the man's nostalgia for his hometown*), Yang Siwen said, "May I ask the honorable monk where he is from?"

"I used to be an acolyte in River Sand Hall of Great State Councilor Monastery in the Eastern Capital. I'm now an acolyte here. Please sit down for a chat."

Seated on a stool, Siwen was watching the pedestrians passing by when a group of women keeping closely to themselves entered the Hall of Arhats. One of the women threw a glance at Siwen. As their four eyes met, Siwen noticed that the woman was dressed in the fashion of an Eastern Capital resident. She was

> *Lissome and graceful,*
> *With eyes sparkling like autumn water.*
> *She wore her jewelry like a court lady,*
> *And her headgear in the palace style.*
> *Still the fashion of the Xuanhe reign,*
> *Still the charm of the capital of old.*

The sight of someone from his native town stirred up such nostalgic emotions in Yang Siwen that he sank into dejection. As fatigue stole up on him, he drifted off to sleep. By the time he was awakened by the acolyte, the woman was nowhere to be seen. Yang Siwen sighed, "I was hoping to wait until they came out, so I could see if there might be relatives of mine among them, and now I've missed the chance."

Turning to the acolyte, he asked, "Where are the women who just came into the monastery?"

The acolyte replied, "They made a donation and left, saying that they would return tomorrow to hold a memorial service for some kinsmen. Don't feel bad, sir. You can come back to wait for them tomorrow."

Thus advised, Yang Siwen also donated some alms and took leave of the monk. After leaving the Hall of Arhats, he went around the monastery and had been looking around for some time when he suddenly noticed a lyric poem to the tune of "Ripples Sifting Sand" inscribed on the wall of the prayer hall:

> *I lean against the railings till sunset,*
> *With nothing around me but woeful sights.*
> *The frontier can be seen from up on high.*
> *In pain I hear the bugle on the tower,*
> *While the plains are under a layer of snow.*

The years speed by but my thoughts go back south,
To Meridian Gate,
Where the emperor rejoiced with his people.
The temple keeps records from the days gone by,
But the hill of lanterns is nowhere in sight.

The poem further saddened Yang Siwen. He returned to the inn, where he spent a sleepless night. He rose upon the long-awaited first light of dawn, and the day passed without further ado.

When evening fell, he told his uncle that he was going to Blue Heaven Monastery to look for the woman he had seen the night before. Soon he found himself in the midst of the hustle and bustle of the streets. He was still walking along when he heard a peal of thunder. Afraid that it was going to rain, Siwen was about to turn back when he raised his eyes and saw

A bright moon shining over the Milky Way,
The streets of heaven ablaze with lights.
The precious candles glowing in the air,
While fragrant winds caress the ground.

Upon a closer look, he saw a large carriage approaching from the west. Several dozens of Jurchen officers followed behind as the carriage rumbled along. Behold:

The shouts of the guards rise to the sky,
While the procession blocks the streets.
In front, fifteen pairs of red-gauze lanterns,
With candle flames ablaze.
On both sides, twenty golden spears,
Shining in dazzling splendor.
The scented carriage goes by like an arrow,
The attendants press ahead like a cloud.

Behind the carriage followed several waiting women, one of whom was dressed in purple with a fish-shaped silver badge[7] at her waist, a white handkerchief in her hand, and a silk scarf around her neck. Yang Siwen took a closer look by the light of the moon and saw that she bore a striking resemblance to Lady Zheng Yiniang, wife of his sworn brother Han Sihou, protocol officer in the Diplomacy Section of the Bureau of Military Affairs.[8] She was also the adopted daughter of Imperial Consort Qiao. As her husband, Officer Han, was Siwen's fellow townsman, the two men had pledged brotherhood. Siwen used to address her as sister-in-law. Since separating, they had not heard from each other for quite some time. When their four eyes met, neither the woman in purple nor Siwen dared speak up. Instead, Siwen followed the carriage all the way to the Qin Tower in the city. The carriage drove in and the noble lady went upstairs, whereas the Jurchen officers took their seats downstairs. The Qin Tower was an impressively large tavern, about the same size as the Baifan Tower in the Eastern Capital. There were sixty rooms upstairs and between seventy and eighty tables with stools downstairs. That night, much wine was sold amid buoyant revelry.

After the noble lady entered the tavern, Yang Siwen also went in and summoned a waiter. At the sight of Siwen, the waiter made a deep bow, but Siwen raised him up and said, "Please dispense with such ceremony." A closer look revealed him to be Chen San'er, formerly a waiter at the Baifan Tower in the Eastern Capital. Much delighted, Siwen asked him to sit, but San'er insisted that he would not presume to. Siwen said, "Both of us being from the old capital, for us to meet in a distant place is enough cause for sitting down together." The waiter sat down with an apology. Siwen handed San'er five taels of silver and told him to bring out some fine wine and dishes of meat and vegetables.

In the course of their conversation over the meal, San'er said, "When I first came here in the second year of the Jingkang reign period, I was given to a military officer as a slave. Later, when the Qin Tower opened, I thought of my days at the Baifan Tower as a waiter, and so I redeemed myself by paying the officer eighty in cash each day and came to work here. I'm so happy to see you, sir." As they conversed, a band somewhere struck up music. Siwen asked, "Where does all this music come from?"

"The music is played by the maids of the Lady of Han, who just went upstairs."

Upon Siwen's further inquiries about the lady, San'er said, "She is a most kind lady who often brings her maids and waiting women here for a cup of wine. I have often gone upstairs to serve them and she always gives nice tips."

"I ran into her entourage just now by the roadside and saw, among the maids behind the carriage, a woman who looked like my sister-in-law, Lady Zheng. I could be mistaken, though."

"I was also going to tell you that every time I went upstairs to serve them, I saw her, too, but I never dared to greet her for fear of making a mistake."

"I have a favor to ask of you. Would you go up now to serve them? Look for Lady Zheng and tell her that I am waiting for her downstairs to ask her about my brother."

Thus instructed, San'er went upstairs, while Siwen remained where he was, waiting. In a moment, San'er came down with a finger pressed against his lower lip, a gesture that Siwen knew was used by Eastern Capital residents to signal completion of a job.

"How did it go?" Siwen asked.

"I said to Lady Zheng, 'Fifth Master Yang is waiting for you to go down so that he can ask you about your husband.' The lady said tearfully, 'So my brother-in-law is here, too. Please tell him that I'll be down in a moment to speak to him.'"

Siwen thanked San'er, paid his bill, and stood waiting outside the door. Before long, he saw the attendants go in, and, a moment later, the Jurchen officers came out, escorting the carriage. After the carriage went past, Siwen saw, among the maids, his sister-in-law in a purple dress with a silver fish badge and a silk scarf around her neck. He stepped forward and asked, after some initial amenities, "Why are you not with my brother?"

Lady Zheng answered, wiping away her tears, "In the winter of the Jingkang year [1126], your brother and I went down the Huai River on a hired boat. We were at Xuyi when the boatman was hit by an arrow and the helmsman was cut down by a sword blow. I was then separated from my husband, who was captured by the barbarians. The barbarian chief, Marshal Saba, tried to take advantage of me, but I refused to submit and was brought here as a captive to Yanshan. Exasperated at my stubbornness and disgusted with my emaciated body, the marshal sold me to a family named Zu, which I later learned was in fact a brothel. Being the wife and daughter of court officials, I could not bear the humiliation of living like Su Xiaoqing.[9] I chose to die like Mengjiangnü.[10] So, when unobserved, I tried to hang myself with my girdle from a house beam, but I was found and saved from death. The Lady of Han, wife of Marshal Saba, heard about this and took pity on me. She ordered that I be taken care of and kept me as her maid. The scars on my neck have not yet healed. That's why I wear a silk scarf around it. I didn't know what had become of my husband after we parted during the confusion. Only recently did I hear that he escaped in disguise. He is now in Jinling.[11] He has taken up his old post and has been there for four years without having had the heart to remarry. I have burned incense, going as far as to burn some on the top of my head. I have also consulted fortune-tellers and prayed to the gods, hoping to escape to Jinling, but I have not yet found a way. Since I am nothing more than a slave waiting on the Lady of Han at the banquet table, I dare not talk with you for too long. Please ask every southerner you meet to send a message for me." (*This story told at the reunion could well have happened in a dream.*)

Before Yang Siwen could ask more questions, a Jurchen officer with a mace in his hand came over and yelled, "How dare you seduce one of our slaves in the middle of the night?" He raised the mace and was about to strike right at Siwen's face when Siwen ran away with all speed. The officer, being slow of foot, failed to catch up with him. Now out of the officer's reach, Siwen hastily returned in a cold sweat to his uncle's inn.

Surprised at Siwen's agitated state, Zhang Er asked, "Why do you look so flustered?" At Siwen's account of what had happened, Zhang Er heaved many a sigh. He set out some wine to drink with Siwen to cheer him up, but the latter was in no mood for wine, so disturbed was he by his thoughts of his brother Protocol Officer Han and sister-in-law Lady Zheng.

Thus it was that he spent the Lantern Festival in low spirits. When the third month came, Zhang Er said to him, "I'll be going away for a couple of days. Will you take care of the inn while I'm away?"

"Why are you going away?" asked Siwen.

"Now that the two states are at peace, I'm going to Weiyang to make some purchases. I'll be back soon."

With his uncle gone, Yang Siwen felt bored, left all alone by himself, and the long days of spring made him drowsy. He went out and took a leisurely walk to the Qin Tower. After he looked around for a while, a waiter approached him and called out with a salute, "Fifth Master Yang!" It was not Chen San'er, but his face looked familiar. Who could he be?

The waiter introduced himself: "I am Little Wang. I used to work at the Yuxian Tavern in the Eastern Capital. Chen San'er was summoned by his master, the military officer, a few days ago, and he is not allowed to come out."

Now that Chen San'er was gone, Yang Siwen sank into deeper gloom. He ordered some appetizers, without really caring what they were, and asked Little Wang, "The Lady of Han who came here for a drink on the night of the Lantern Festival—do you happen to know where she lives?"

"I asked her attendants and was told that she lives behind Lord of Heaven Monastery." Before the words were quite out of Wang's mouth, Siwen raised his head and saw a poem written on the wall, its ink still wet. A closer look revealed a line of explanation that said, "This poem was written by Han Sihou of Changli when passing Lake Huangtian on a boat trip from Jinling, to mourn his deceased wife, Zheng-shi." The poem, to the tune of "Walking on Palace Steps," is as follows:

> *Mix a thousand taels of powder and rouge,*
> *And mold a statue of Guanyin.*
> *The resemblance is slight, at most,*
> *For it lacks her wit and charm.*
> *I wait till dusk for dreams to begin,*
> *But throughout the night, I seek her in vain.*
>
> *Where has her sweet spirit gone?*
> *It may well be here on the boat.*
> *Without a word, I lean against the door,*

Facing the white-capped surging waves.
Should my tears be measured as water,
They would fill several lakes.

Yang Siwen was aghast after reading the poem. "This is my brother Han Sihou's handwriting. So he believes his wife is dead, but I saw her with my own eyes in the Qin Tower on the fifteenth of the first month. She spoke with me and said she was a maid for the Lady of Han. But he says she is dead. How strange!" In disbelief, he asked Little Wang, "Where is the man who wrote this poem? The ink is still wet."

"I have no idea. Now that the two states are at peace, envoys from the south have come here and lodged at the government inn. A group of four or five of them were here for a drink just a short while ago, and one of them must have written the poem."

Storyteller, this could not be true! How can envoys on a mission to another state go out freely to buy drinks? Well, according to *The Records of Yijian,*[12] at that time there was as yet no prohibition on official envoys' free association with local people.

To continue with our story, on that day, which was the fifteenth of the third month, Yang Siwen asked where the government inn was located. Little Wang said, "It's in the southern part of town." Thereupon, Siwen paid his bill, went downstairs, and hurriedly proceeded to the inn to look for Han Sihou. Upon arrival, he saw Su and Xu, two protocol officers, at the door, looking around idly. Being old acquaintances of Yang's, they recognized him and came over to exchange greetings.

"What brought you here, Mr. Yang?" they asked.

"I am here to look for my brother, Protocol Officer Han."

"He's inside in a discussion session. Let's go in and bring him out." So saying, they went inside and brought Han to the door.

At the sight of Protocol Officer Han, Siwen hastened to make a bow, overwhelmed by mixed feelings of joy and sadness at the reunion in Yanshan with a beloved friend far away from home.

"Is my sister-in-law well?" asked Siwen.

Tears coursed down Sihou's cheeks as he replied, "In the winter of the year of Jingkang, I hired a boat and was going down the Huai River with her when, at Xuyi, the boatman was hit by an arrow and the helmsman was cut down by a sword blow. Your sister-in-law was taken away, while I was captured and taken to an enemy camp in the wilds. At the third watch of the night, I pleaded my way out, without knowing if my wife was dead or alive. Later, while lying low in the grass, a servant of mine, Zhou Yi, saw her reject advances from the barbarian Marshal Saba and cut her own throat to end the humiliation. I made my way back to where the emperor was and regained my old post."

"Did you see what happened to her with your own eyes?"

"No. It was Zhou Yi who told me about it."

Siwen continued, "I believe she is alive. During the last Lantern Festival, I saw her with the Lady of Han on an outing to the Qin Tower. I asked Chen San'er the waiter to send a message upstairs for her to come down and see me. The first part of her account tallied with yours. She also said that you have regained your old post but have not had the heart to remarry in the last four years."

Sihou found these words hard to believe. Siwen went on, "It's easy to find out if she's dead or alive. Why don't you go with me to the residence of the Lady of Han, behind Lord of Heaven Monastery, to ask what really happened?"

Sihou agreed, "That's a good idea." He went back into the inn to notify his colleagues and then set off with Siwen, bringing a valet with him.

In a short while, they reached the area behind the monastery. It was a deserted place without a soul in sight. All that met their eyes was an abandoned house, its locked front gate covered with cobwebs, its windows laden with dust, its doorsteps overgrown with weeds, and the ground green with moss. Yang Siwen said, "We might have to use the back gate."

They walked along the wall and, dozens of steps later, came upon a house in which an old man was plaiting silk cords. They stepped forward and greeted him with a bow, saying, "Could you tell us where the entrance to the residence of the Lady of Han is?"

The old man, short in temper and rude in manners, paid them no attention. Upon further questioning, he said only that he did not know. Soon, there came along an old woman carrying a hamper and mumbling complaints against the old man. The two visitors greeted her and she returned the greeting in an Eastern Capital accent. The two men asked where the house of the Lady of Han was. The old woman was about to answer when the old man grumbled something, trying to quiet her. Ignoring him, the old woman said to the two visitors, "I am from the Eastern Capital, but this old man is from the uncivilized province of Shandong. It is my bad luck to be married to this brute who has not a grain of sense. I serve him meals and tea everyday, but he's still full of complaints. What a disgusting man! What do you have against my answering the gentlemen's questions?"

The old man started mumbling again. Paying him no attention, the old woman told the two visitors, "It is the locked empty house ahead."

Much startled, the two men asked, "But where is the lady?"

"She died the year before last. The family moved away. She was buried in the garden. If you don't believe this, would you care to go with me for a look?"

The old man objected, "Don't go! If the authorities hear about this, I'll be getting into trouble as well."

The old woman turned a deaf ear to his protests and took the visitors along. On the way, they asked, "There's a Zheng Yiniang in the lady's household. Is she still around?"

The old woman said, "Might you be Protocol Officer Han Sihou? Is the other gentleman Fifth Master Yang?"

In astonishment, the two men exclaimed, "How do you know?"

"I've heard Lady Zheng talk about you."

Sihou asked further, "How did you know her? Where is my wife now?"

The old woman replied, "Two years ago, there was a Marshal Saba who established a household here. His wife, the Lady of Han from the Cui family, was a most compassionate woman of a kind hard to come by. She often asked me into the house, and I heard her talk about a woman called Zheng Yiniang who was captured by the Marshal at Xuyi. The marshal took quite a fancy to her, but she swore never to be humiliated, and cut her own throat. Respectful of her chastity, the Lady of Han had her cremated and her ashes stored in a box. Later, after the Lady of Han died, the ash box was buried with her in this yard. Lady Zheng is dead, but she certainly looked no different than a live human being in flesh and blood. When I went into the yard, I often saw her come out. I was scared at first, but she said, 'Don't be afraid, Granny, I won't hurt you. I just want to tell you my misfortunes.' She said she was Zheng Yiniang from the Eastern Capital. She was adopted at an early age by Imperial Consort Qiao and, later in her life, married court officer Han Sihou. She also told me that he had a sworn brother, Yang Siwen, otherwise known as Fifth Master Yang. I also learned about what happened at Xuyi. She said, 'My husband, for whom I died to preserve my chastity, is now an official in Jinling.' On rainy days, I would go into the garden to chat with her. If you want more details, you will be able to see for yourselves."

When the company of three arrived at the big locked house, the old woman climbed over the wall, followed by the two men. What came into their view was a deserted garden that had been left to run wild. They walked through the grass and the withered flowers as they searched without avail for the woman. In one of the three large rooms facing south stood a screen with a landscape by Guo Xi.[13] Sihou was looking at the painting when his eyes strayed to a few lines of writing on the wall. A closer inspection revealed a gentle and delicate penmanship that was just like that of Lady Zheng Yiniang. Overjoyed, he said, "Fifth brother, your sister-in-law is indeed here!"

"How do you know?" asked Siwen.

Sihou showed him the poem. It was a lyric poem to the tune of "Happy Events Approaching":

With whom can I speak of the past?
In silence, I shed tears of blood.
When is the saddest moment of all?
The hour when dusk sets in.

I gaze from the tower and pace around.
Who knows the pain in my heart?
Would that I fly with the wild geese home
While south of the Yangzi spring is in bloom!

At the end of the poem was a line that said, "Written the day after the third full moon of the year." The two men were taken aback: "So she wrote it today! Isn't this amazing!" As they moved farther along to another side, a tower came into sight. Holding on to the railings, the two men helped the old woman mount the stairs. Up there was another large screen inscribed in the same handwriting with a song titled "In Memory of My Love":

At sunset under a lonesome spring cloud,
I long for my love at the ends of the earth.
Butterflies in pairs flutter in the wind,
A sight that adds to the pain in my heart.
All day long, I wait for him in vain;
My youthful beauty slowly fades away.
Spring is in full splendor, mellow as wine;
Flowers fall on the steps amid birds' chirping.
By my lonely bed through the endless night,
The lamp burns out, the incense is gone.
The swings in the yard are long out of use;
The colored ropes sway for none to enjoy.
My brows always knitted,
My tears always flowing.
In silence I mount the tower
And lean against the railing.
Time flies by like a weaver's shuttle;
The waves surge forth, never to return.
My love is gone, never to return;
My looks are fading, what should I do?

Having read the poem, Han Sihou said, his hand stroking the wall, "How tragic that my wife was taken captive!"

His eyes were still on the poem when he heard Yang Siwen cry out, "My sister-in-law is here!" Turning around, Sihou saw a woman with a silk scarf around her neck approaching. Upon a closer look, Siwen recognized her as the very same woman he had met at the Qin Tower. (*As in a dream.*) The old woman also cried, "The lady is here!" In amazement, the three of them rushed downstairs, only to see her turn into the left corridor at the back, heading toward a pavilion. The two men were seized with fear, but the old woman said, "Since we are already here, why don't we go into the pavilion for a look?" She led them there and found the door closed. A board on the door bore this inscription: "Memorial Hall of the Lady of Han." The old woman pushed open the latticed door and they stepped in. In the middle, set up to receive offerings, was a spirit tablet with the words "My deceased wife, the Lady of Han." To one side were a portrait of Yiniang and another spirit tablet with the inscription "Maid Zheng Yiniang." The altar in front was covered with a thick layer of dust. At the sight of the portrait, which, in clothing and appearance, differed not in the least from Siwen's description, Han Sihou broke down in passionate weeping.

The old woman said, "The box with Lady Zheng's ashes is under the table. She often spoke of it and showed it to me. It's a black lacquer box with two copper rings. Every time she mentioned the box, she would cry and say to me, 'I died with no regrets, for I died out of loyalty to my husband.'"

At these words, Sihou asked the old woman, with a promise of a handsome reward, to help him pry up the floor bricks and take out the box for a burial in Jinling. She agreed. The three of them moved aside the altar, pried up the bricks, and reached for the box. However hard they tried, the box would not budge. The harder they tried, the firmer it stuck to the ground.

"Stop! Stop!" cried Siwen. "She is showing her power, my brother. If the box is to be taken away, there must be a proper ceremony. Let's leave this place for now to prepare for a sacrificial ceremony complete with an elegy in her honor. Only then can the box be taken away."

Han Sihou agreed, "There is much sense in what you say." The three of them climbed over the wall again and went to the old woman's house, where they told the servant Zhang Jin to buy some wine, meat, incense, and candles and composed an elegy right there in the old woman's house. When daylight came, they carried the offerings with the help of the old woman and the servant, climbed over the wall, and laid everything out in the memorial hall.

By the third watch of the night, the incense and the candle had almost burned out, and the cups and plates were found to be in disarray. As the constellations crossed the Milky Way, Sihou poured out three libations and, standing by the altar table, read the elegy aloud, shedding copious tears. When the elegy was burned together with paper money, there sprang up a gust of strong wind. The candlelight flickered in a way that sent chills down their spines. As the wind blew past, a fit of weeping became audible. (*Very much like a dream.*) After the wind died down, the flicker steadied itself into a flame, bringing into view a woman with a face as fresh as a flower and with skin as smooth as jade. A silk scarf around her neck, she straightened her sleeves, moved forward in mincing steps, and greeted Yang Siwen. In astonishment, the two men returned the greeting. Han Sihou stepped forward tearfully and reached for her hand.

After much weeping, Lady Zheng said to Sihou, "By now, you should have learned what happened at Xuyi. At the Qin Tower on the night of the Lantern Festival when I met my brother-in-law, I did not have the chance to say all I wanted to say. If I had clung to life, I would have brought disgrace to my husband. Luckily, I treasured your good name like jade and treated my own life as dust. That is how we came to be parted by death, to my eternal sorrow." With these words, she broke down in another fit of weeping.

The old woman tried to comfort her, saying, "Don't cry now. Let's talk about moving your remains away from here."

Holding back her tears, Lady Zheng sat down. While the other three partook of food and wine, she did nothing more than sniff at the aroma.

"When I saw you at the Qin Tower on the night of the Lantern Festival," said Siwen, "you were waiting on the Lady of Han. Were the many attendants behind the carriage ghosts or humans?"

"In times of peace," she replied, "humans and ghosts live in separate worlds, but in these current times, humans and ghosts mix. None of those in the entourage was a living being."

Sihou said, "Since my good wife died for my sake, if only to show my gratitude, I shall never remarry. What do you say if we move your remains back to Jinling?"

The lady objected: "Please listen to me, while both Granny and Brother-in-law are here. Since you have been so kind as to take pity on my lonely soul, how would I be loath to return home with you? But you should visit me often so that our love can be kept alive across the two worlds. Should you remarry, you will certainly forget me. If it turns out that way, I would rather stay here."

No amount of persuasion from the three of them could shake her from her resolve. Turning to Siwen, she said, "My brother-in-law, how can you not know my brother! When I was alive, his weakness for women was such that it was hard to keep him in check. Now that I am dead, it is a matter of course that he will, if he is to have his way, abandon the old in favor of the new." (*Her repeated refusals are meant to strengthen her husband's resolve. But why should a ghost be jealous?*)

Siwen tried again to plead with her: "Please listen to me, my sister-in-law. My brother is now a different man. Out of gratitude for your honorable death, he will never take another woman for a wife. Now that he is here to take you back, how can you have the heart to refuse him? Please take my advice."

"I thank my brother-in-law for taking such pains to offer me words of counsel. If my husband is indeed to remain true and will take an oath now, I will gladly follow him."

At these words, Sihou poured wine on the ground and said, as an oath, "In the event that I break my promise, may I be killed by bandits when traveling on land or, if I travel on water, may my boat capsize in huge waves."

The lady protested in haste, "Stop, stop. You don't have to swear like that. Since you are determined not to remarry, my brother-in-law will be a witness." This said, a gust of fragrant wind sprang up. She disappeared as the wind blew past. Astounded, the three of them relit the candles, lifted up the brick under the altar, and took out the box without the least effort. Having gathered the things together, they climbed over the wall and went to the home of the old woman. The following evening, they thanked the old woman with three taels of silver, and Sihou presented Siwen with ten taels of gold over the latter's repeated protests. After bidding farewell to Siwen, Sihou returned to the inn, accompanied by his servant Zhang Jin, who carried the box. It was about a month later that he received his commission to return to the south. Siwen set out wine for a farewell dinner, reminding him over and over again, "Brother, don't forget my sister-in-law's words."

Carrying the box of the lady's remains, Sihou and his party left the city of Yanshan by Fengyi Gate to return south. About a month later, they reached Xuyi and found lodging in an inn. There, a man came up to Sihou with a bow of greeting. Sihou recognized him to be Zhou Yi, his former servant, who now worked at the inn. He led Sihou into a room containing a portrait of a woman on the wall and a spirit tablet, on which was written, "Lady Zheng, my master's deceased wife." To queries from a surprised Sihou, Zhou Yi answered, "Having witnessed how the lady died for you to preserve her chastity, how could I not set up a shrine in her honor?" Thereupon Sihou gave Zhou Yi a full account of everything that had happened in the house of the Lady of Han in Yanshan and showed him the box of remains. Zhou Yi kowtowed in bitter sobs. That night, Sihou and Zhou shared the same bed, head to foot and foot to head.

At the first light of dawn the following day, Zhou Yi said to Sihou, "In the old days, there were more than twenty people in your household, but now I have only my own shadow to look at. I would much rather follow you to Jinling and serve you again." Sihou agreed and brought Zhou Yi back to Jinling. Sihou returned to the tribunal and presented his superiors with the letter of reply. Zhou Yi then followed Sihou to the hills, where they selected a burial site and buried the remains with the proper rites. Beside himself with grief, Sihou went to the grave every three days with sacrificial offerings and returned only when dusk had set in. Zhou Yi was given the task of watching over the grave.

One day, Protocol Officers Su and Xu said to Sihou, "Liu Jintan, abbess of Saturn Convent here in Jinling, though a woman, is most virtuous and noble. Why don't we go to her convent for a memorial service in honor of your deceased wife?" Sihou agreed. On a selected day, he went to the convent with Su and Xu to visit Liu Jintan. You may well ask, how was she dressed?

> *A sky-blue cap on her head,*
> *An ivory tablet in her hand.*
> *On her body a white silk robe,*
> *On her feet emerald shoes.*
> *Without aid of rouge or powder,*
> *She looked like a plum blossom in the frost.*
> *Elegant and pure,*
> *She stood like a lotus above water.*
> *Matchless her beauty,*
> *Unrivaled her grace.*

The moment Han Sihou laid eyes on the abbess, his soul took flight, and he stood there stupefied, eyes unblinking and mouth agape. After the exchange of greetings, Jintan gave instructions for holding a service and invited the visitors to go inside for a look at a magic mushroom. The three of them walked past Double Purity Hall and Emerald Flower Pavilion and turned from Eight Trigram Altar into Crimson Silk Hall, where the magic mushroom was kept. While the others were gathered around the magic mushroom, Sihou slipped into the abbess's cell and looked around. His eyes swept from the bright windows and clean tables to the objects of art placed throughout the room. On the desk was an array of stationery items. From under a paperweight, he drew out a piece of paper on which was inscribed a lyric poem to the tune of "Sand of the Silk-Washing Stream" (*Very much like Chen Miaochang.*[14] *This must be the way with all nuns and monks*):

> *My beauty is untouched by worldly dust,*
> *In my star cap, cloud cape, and purple skirt.*
> *With the door shutting out the slanting sun,*
> *I strum idly my zither of jade.*
>
> *Flowers in this lonesome convent pain my heart.*
> *The moon by the window fills me with longing.*
> *To return to the secular world,*
> *What a blessing that would be!*

Han Sihou's desires had already been stirred up at the first sight of Jintan's beauty. These words plunged him deeper into yearning. He wrote a lyric poem to the tune of "The Moon over the West River":

> *Such beauty needs no rouge and powder.*
> *Such a plum is no common flower.*
> *All day long, she ponders the Taoist truth,*
> *To the neglect of the world of romance.*
>
> *On her cap are the stars of the Big Dipper,*
> *From her staff hangs the Taoist canon.*
> *When shall I enter this fairyland*
> *And ride the colored phoenix with her?*

Clapping his hands, he chanted the poem at the top of his voice. Jintan's expression hardened. In rage, she lashed out, "What is the meaning of this? How dare you take advantage of my helplessness to sully the name of my convent! Get me my sedan-chair! I'm going to the authorities. They will know what to do with you."

However hard Su and Xu tried to stop her, she turned a deaf ear. Han Sihou took out from his bosom the poem she had written and showed it to them, saying, "Don't be so upset, my good abbess. Who is the author of these lines?"

Jintan was so consternated that she wished she could hide herself. Her scowl softened to a radiant smile. She laid out a banquet in honor of the guests. Amid the drinking and the carousing, everything about the memorial service was forgotten. Both being amorously disposed toward each other, they did not part company until well intoxicated with wine.

Now this Liu Jintan was a native of the Eastern Capital. Her husband, Feng the Sixth, had been the recipient of edicts in the Bureau of Military Affairs. During the Jingkang reign period, the couple had fled to Jinling on a hired boat. When on the Huai River, Feng the Sixth was shot by an arrow and fell into the water to his death. His wife, Liu-shi, vowed to enter the Taoist order in Saturn Convent in honor of her late husband's memory. Her fame having thus spread to the court and through the public, she was appointed to be its abbess. After this visit, Han Sihou began to frequent the convent.

One day, Su and Xu pooled their money, prepared some gifts, and treated Liu Jintan and Han Sihou to dinner at the convent. After several rounds of wine, Su and Xu held up their cups and made this suggestion to Sihou and Jintan: "Your love for each other is due to a predestined marriage bond. With all the rumors floating around, you can't very well go on like this. Why don't you, Jintan, return to secular life and marry our brother with proper ceremonies, complete with wedding gifts and a matchmaker? Wouldn't that be nice!"

Sihou and Jintan accepted their counsel. Jintan paid a fee for permission to return to secular life. Sihou selected a day, and the wedding ceremony duly took place. She ceased to mourn her deceased husband, nor did he continue to visit his wife's grave. Hand in hand, they leaned against the window and exchanged tender words of love.

Some days after the wedding, Zhou Yi, whose job it was to watch the grave, went to the Han residence to find out why Mr. Han had stopped visiting the grave. He asked the gatekeeper, "Why has the master not been seen at the grave for some days?"

The gatekeeper replied, "Mr. Han is newly married to Liu Jintan of Saturn Convent and has no time to go to the grave anymore."

Being a tactless northerner, Zhou Yi smoldered with indignation at these words. As coincidence would have it, he ran straight into Sihou, who was on his way out. After the greeting, Zhou Yi exploded, "Master, what a heartless man you are! Lady Zheng died for your sake. How could you have taken another wife?" While lashing out at him, Zhou Yi also wept for Lady Zheng.

Afraid that the commotion would not reflect well on his newly wedded status, Han Sihou sharply ordered the gatekeeper to drive Zhou Yi out. A dispirited Zhou Yi returned to his hut by the grave. That day being the Clear and Bright Festival,[15] Zhou Yi tearfully complained to the grave about what had happened. At the third watch of the night, Lady Zheng called out to Zhou Yi, "Where does your master live now?"

Zhou Yi told her all he knew about how Sihou had broken faith and remarried. "He now lives on Sanshiliuzhang Street. Why don't you go and settle things with him?"

The lady answered, "That's exactly what I'm going to do."

Zhou Yi woke up with a start from the dream. A cold sweat broke out all over his body.

In the meantime, the newly wedded happy couple were enjoying the moonlight at a table laid out with wine. In the midst of the drinking, Liu-shi suddenly grabbed Sihou and, with her willowlike eyebrows knit in an angry frown and her starry eyes wide open, she cried, "You owe me too much! Pay me back with your life!" The voice was that of Lady Zheng.

Seized with fear and at a loss what to do, Sihou pleaded, "My good wife, please forgive me." But the grip remained firm. While he was struggling, Su and Xu, out on a walk in the moonlight to visit Sihou, appeared on the scene. At the sight of Liu-shi keeping a tight grip on Sihou, the two men came forward and released him. Sihou scurried away and, after taking counsel with Su and Xu, decided to have Priest Zhu of Iron Chain Temple of Bamboo Bridge perform an exorcism. Zhang Jin the servant was sent immediately to bring the priest over.

When he saw Liu-shi, Priest Zhu said, "The injustice done to her was so great that this case is beyond me. The only thing left for me to do is to offer her some soothing words."

Slapping her own face and mouth, Liu-shi gave the priest a tearful account of what had happened in Yanshan, adding, "Please be compassionate in your judgment, Your Honor."

The priest tried to placate her by saying repeatedly, "There will surely be a memorial service for you to redeem your soul. If you refuse to stop this behavior, you will be violating the laws of heaven."

At these words, Liu-shi thanked the priest with a sob and said, "I will go now."

It was some moments before Liu-shi regained consciousness. The priest drew a magic charm for her to eat[16] and posted some ghost-expelling signs on the door before he left. That night passed without further ado.

The following day, Sihou brought some incense and paper to Bamboo Bridge to thank the priest. Barely had he sat down when a servant of his came to report that his wife was possessed again. To Sihou's pleas to go to his house for another exorcism, the priest replied, "If this thing is to be put to an end once and for all, you will need to dig up the grave and dump the box of remains into the Yangzi River. Only then will you never be bothered again." Sihou had no better choice than to do as the priest said. He hired laborers, went with them to the grave, dug it open, took out the box, and threw it into the Yangzi River. From then on, Liu-shi was herself again. How preposterous that such ingrates were not met with retribution from heaven!

So Sihou betrayed Zheng Yiniang and Liu Jintan betrayed Feng the Sixth, the recipient of edicts. In the eleventh year of the Shaoxing reign period [1141], the emperor moved to Qiantang,[17] followed by officials and civilians. Sihou also left Jinling and took his family farther south. When they reached Zhenjiang, Sihou wished to revisit the scenic Jin Mountain. He hired a boat and went on board with his wife, Liu-shi. When they were in midstream, the boatman burst into a song to the tune of "Happy Events Approaching":

> With whom can I speak of the past?
> In silence, I shed tears of blood.
> When is the saddest moment of all?
> The hour when dusk sets in.
>
> I gaze from the tower and pace around.
> Who knows the pain in my heart?

Would that I fly with the wild geese home
While south of the Yangzi spring is in bloom!

Sihou was appalled, for it was the very poem that was written on the screen by Zheng Yiniang, maid of the Lady of Han in Yanshan. "Where did you learn this poem?"

The boatman answered, "Recently, an envoy went up north to Yanshan and heard this song all over the city. The lyrics were originally on a screen in the house of the Lady of Han and were recorded by an old woman who plaits cords for a living. (*Picking up an earlier thread.*) The story is that there was a Zheng Yiniang, wife of an official south of the Yangzi, who died to preserve her chastity. Later, her husband took her remains back to the south, and the poem came to be spread throughout the empire and beyond."

These words were like ten thousand knives stabbing at Sihou's heart. Tears coursed down his face. In a trice, a storm sprang up. Waves surged furiously, sending up sheets of spray and mist. Strange-looking fish appeared and vanished, and river monsters threw the waves higher. There emerged from the waves a man wearing a square cap, who grabbed Liu-shi by her hair and threw her into the river. "Madam fell into the water!" The maid shouted at the top of her voice and called Sihou for help, but Liu-shi was already far beyond any hope of rescue. The next moment, a woman appeared. A silk-scarf around her neck, her eyes blazing with anger, she seized Sihou and dragged him into the depths of the waters, and there he drowned. There was nothing the boatman could do, much as he wished to help. In low spirits, he went back home. Alas! Such has been the fate of all heartless ingrates of times old and new, and therefore I pass this story on. As the poem says,

She betrayed her husband and drowned to death,
He wronged his wife and perished in the waves,
Dying as did Cao E,[18] the filial daughter,
If not like Qu Yuan the loyal minister.[19]

Yan Pingzhong Kills Three Men with Two Peaches

On Tu Mountain when the great Yu held court,
The dukes hurried along with silk and jade.
Fangfeng's bones were cast in the wilderness.
What could have kept him from coming on time?

The above quatrain is by Hu Zeng.[1] In olden times, the Three Sovereigns and Five Emperors[2] yielded their thrones to their successors. In the time of Shun, a great flood wreaked havoc on people's livelihood. Shun charged Gun with the task of controlling the flood, but Gun failed at the job. The flood surged on. In a rage, Shun killed Gun in the Feather Mountains. Later, Gun's son Yu was appointed to control the flood. Yu dredged the nine rivers, thus draining the floodwaters out to sea. In executing his duty, Yu passed by his home three times without going in. He assembled all the dukes of the land in the Tu Mountains in Kuaiji, saying that all those late to arrive were to be beheaded. Fangfeng, the only one who arrived late, evoked Yu's anger and was killed. His corpse was abandoned in the wilderness. Later, during the Spring and Autumn period, a cart that was filled up with one bone and one bone only, so it was said, was found in the wilderness in the state of Yue. As no one knew what bone it was, they turned to Confucius, who told them, "This is Fangfeng's bone. Killed by King Yu, his bones still remain. He was a giant of a man." Fangfeng was indeed a giant. Among the ancients were many men big in stature and kindly in disposition. There was an abundance of humans as ugly as beasts. Shennong, for example, had two horns of flesh on top of his head. Haven't you heard the old saying "The ancients looked like beasts but possessed great virtue. The moderns look like humans but have hearts as wicked as those of beasts"?

I shall now tell how three big men died at the hands of a dwarf less than three feet tall who used nothing more than a few tiny objects for the purpose.

In the Spring and Autumn period, there was, in the court of King Jing of the state of Qi, a man named Tian Kaijiang. Standing fifteen feet tall, this man had a complexion as ruddy as blood, eyes as shiny as stars, a vulture's mouth, fish's jowls, and front teeth that had no cracks in between. Once, when he was following the king on a hunting expedition in the Tong Mountains, a fierce tiger suddenly sprang out from the western hills and charged at the king's horse. The terrified horse collapsed, bringing the king to the ground. Tian Kaijiang, who was by the king's side at the moment, pounced upon the tiger with nothing but his bare hands. Grabbing its neck with his left hand, he hit it with his right fist while kicking its face with his feet until he killed the tiger and rescued the king. The assembly of civil as well as military officials were awestruck, to a man. Upon returning to the court, King Jing granted him the title Lord Shouning. Thus he became the greatest terror in the state of Qi.

The second man in our story is Gu Yizi. Thirteen feet tall, he was a man with a complexion as dark as ink, jaws that bristled with a brown beard, hands shaped like copper hooks, and teeth as sharp as those on a saw. Once when he was crossing the Yellow River with King Jing, a rainstorm came upon them, stirring up surging waves that shook the boat almost to the point of capsizing it. The king, greatly alarmed, saw a fiery thing glistening merrily in the mist on top of the water. Gu Yizi said, "This must be the flood dragon of the Yellow River." The king said, "What is to be done?" Gu Yizi assured him, saying, "Don't worry, sire. Let me cut it with my sword." So saying, he took his sword and got into the water, naked. A few moments later, the storm died down, the waves subsided, and there for all to see was Gu Yizi, leaping out of the water with the head of the flood dragon in his hand. The king was aghast. Gu was accordingly granted the title Lord Wu'an and became the second terror of the state.

The third man of our story is Gongsun, with the given name Jie. Standing twelve feet tall, his head like a tiered pagoda, his eyes the shape of triangles, and his back as strong as that of an ape, he could lift an object weighing a thousand catties. One day, when the Qin army crossed over the state border, King Jing led his troops forward to engage the enemy but was defeated. The Qin army swept in and besieged the king in the region of Phoenix Cry Mountain. Armed with a one-hundred-fifty-catty iron halberd, Gongsun Jie fought his way into unsuspecting enemy ranks one hundred thousand strong and rescued the king. Granted the title Lord Weiyuan, he became the third terror of the land. The three men pledged brotherhood, vowing to stand by each other until death. Ignoring all codes of courtesy, the three of them tyrannized the court, treating the king and the ministers as if they were nothing but grass and trees. The king found the threesome as irritating as thorns in his flesh. (*Should these three men who vowed to stand by each other until death have worked as one for their master, even Yanzi would have had to admit defeat. What a pity that they instead sought their own death by insulting the king.*)

One day, the state of Chu sent Ordinary Grand Master Jin Shang over to negotiate peace. The neighboring states of Qi and Chu had been engaged in warfare for over twenty years without respite. Having been appointed as the envoy by the king of Chu, Jin Shang was brought into the presence of King Jing.

"The long-standing enmity and war between the states of Qi and Chu," said Jin, "have brought much suffering to the people. I am therefore charged with the task of negotiating peace with you, so that our weapons can be laid down forever. The state of Chu, with its three rivers and five lakes, with thousands of li in area and enough storage of crops to last us for several years, has the economic and military power to be the suzerain state. Should you decide to accept the proposal, sir, you will be in for both fame and gain."

Tian, Gu, and Gongsun were furious. "What's so mighty about your puny state of Chu?" they roared. "The three of us shall lead our powerful army and level the state of Chu to the ground! No Chu person will be left to live!" They ordered Jin Shang to leave the court and sent a guard with a gold bludgeon to follow him out, kill him, and come back with a report.

At this moment, a man only three feet eight inches tall emerged from one side of the hall. With dark eyebrows, refined-looking eyes, white teeth, and red lips, he was Yan Ying, courtesy name Pingzhong, prime minister of the state of Qi. Stepping forward, he stopped the guard and asked for a full account of what had happened. After hearing Jin Shang's account, Yan Ying had him released, saying that Jin Shang could return to his state and that Yan Ying would follow for a peace talk. Then he ascended the steps of the hall to report to the king. The three men exploded with rage. "We were going to have him killed. Why did you let him go back?"

Yan Ying said, "Haven't you heard the saying 'Two states engaged in war do not kill each other's envoys'? He came here all by himself. Should our neighboring states hear that we had him taken captive and killed, we would become a laughingstock for thousands of generations to come. Unworthy as I am, I am willing to go to the state of Chu and, with my three-inch tongue, talk the king of Chu and his ministers into bowing their heads to Qi to ask for forgiveness and honor Qi as their suzerain state. I need no weapon or soldier. What do you say to the plan?"

Bristling with anger, the three men lashed out, "What do you know? You dwarf! How stupid the people of this state were when they let you be prime minister! How dare you talk so big! Each of the three of us has the power to kill dragons and tigers and to battle ten thousand men. With us to lead an elite army to wipe out the state of Chu, what need is there for you?"

The king intervened: "The prime minister must have good reasons for his ambitious proposal. Let's wait until his mission is over. If he does succeed, it will be a better option than going to war."

The three men said, "If this dwarf brings shame to our state on this mission of his, we'll chop him into mince meat when he comes back!" With that, they left the court.

The king admonished the prime minister, "Do not take your mission lightly."

Yan Ying replied, "Rest assured, Your Majesty. Once in the state of Chu, I will see their king and his ministers as nothing but dirt." Thereupon, he took his leave, followed by a retinue of about ten people.

When it was announced to the Chu court that his carriage had arrived in Yingdu, the capital, the Chu king took counsel with his ministers and came to this conclusion: "Yan Ying of Qi being the eloquent speaker that he is, our policy should be to take the initiative so that he won't even have the courage to start his speech." Having thus decided upon their course of action, the king and the ministers summoned Yan Ying to enter the court. Upon arrival at the entrance of the hall, Yan saw that the golden gate was closed, with only the lock board underneath left ajar. The intention was to humiliate the short Yan by making him bend low and go through the low opening. Without a moment of hesitation, he bent over and was about to stick his head into the opening (*Wonderful!*) when his followers hastily stopped him, saying, "They are throwing an insult at you because of your shortness. How can you play into their hands?"

He replied with a hearty laugh. "Don't you know anything? Doors are for human beings, whereas doghouses have only holes. If I am an envoy to a state of human beings, I will naturally use a door, whereas if I am among dogs, I will naturally go through a dog's hole. Isn't this clear enough?"

At these words, the Chu ministers hurried to open the golden gate to greet him. Seemingly oblivious to all the people around him, Yan Ying jauntily stepped in.

In the hall, after the customary salutations, the king of Chu asked, "Is it true that Qi is but a sparsely populated small state?"

Yan Ying rejoined, "The state of Qi extends to the sea islands in the east, to the states of Wei and Qin in the west, the states of Zhao and Yan to the north, and the states of Wu and Chu in the south. The crows of roosters and the barking of dogs reverberate through thousands of li. How can you say the state is small?"

The Chu king pressed his point further: "The land may be vast, but the population is sparse and resources are scarce."

"My countrymen's breath rises like clouds; their sweat falls like rain. When they walk, they rub shoulders; when they stand still, their toes touch others' heels. Gold, silver, pearls, and jade pile up like mountains. How can you say that the population is sparse and resources are scarce?"

"If the land is so vast and the population so dense, why is such a short man sent to my state as an envoy?"

"Great men are sent to great states, whereas lesser men are sent to lesser states. That is why I, Yan Ying, am ordered to come to you."

The king of Chu looked at his ministers, but they were at a loss for a reply. He invited Yan to mount the steps and offered him a seat. As the attending ministers served wine, Yan Ying drank to his heart's content as if nothing had happened.

In a short while, guards with gold bludgeons brought to the banquet a man protesting against an injustice. Upon a closer look, Yan Ying recognized him to be one of his followers, whom he had brought from Qi. When asked what crime he was charged with, the Chu ministers said, "This man is a thief. He was trying to leave with some stolen wine vessels when our guards stopped him. This is a clear case of theft fully supported by evidence."

The man said, "I did no such thing. The guards are trying to frame me."

"Since the evidence is here," said Yan Ying, "the theft must have been committed. How dare you deny the crime! Quickly take him out to the marketplace for execution!"

The Chu ministers said, "Why didn't the prime minister bring along some honest men on this mission? Wouldn't a follower's theft bring shame upon his master?"

"This man," said Yan Ying, "has been a follower of mine ever since childhood. I know him inside out. What's so surprising that he became a thief today? He had always been a gentleman in the state of Qi but degenerated into a thief once he was in Chu territory because of the change in local customs. I have heard that in Dongting, south of the Yangzi River, there is a kind of tree that bears golden oranges with a sweet smell and a delicious taste. If replanted in the north, instead of oranges, it bears green citrons with a stinking smell and a sour and bitter taste. The reason that the same tree bears different fruit when moved from the south to the north is the change in local climate. (*Good analogy.*) Thus, it can be deduced that a man who never steals in Qi will naturally be reduced to a thief once he finds himself in Chu. Is that not so?"

Overcome with shame, the king of Chu hastily left his throne and, with his hands folded across his chest, said to Yan Ying, "You are indeed a great man, more than a match for even ten thousand dukes of all sorts in my state. I will be happy to follow whatever advice you offer me."

"Please sit down, Your Majesty, and listen to this. There are, in the state of Qi, three mighty men, each of whom can battle more than ten thousand men. They have long had the wish to annex Chu by force, but I have been trying my best to dissuade them from such a course of action, for how can we bear to subject the people of the two states to the misery of war? That is why I am here today to negotiate peace. Your Majesty may issue a decree to the state of Qi, stating the wish to form a fraternal alliance with it. Should other neighboring states use force against us, we shall come to each other's assistance. Free from all wars, both states will live for ten thousand years. If you ignore my advice, you are inviting calamity upon yourself. I am not trying to scare you. Please mark my words."

The king said, "I would be more than willing to form alliances with people of your ability. But I dare not go to Qi for fear of the three treacherous strong men."

Yan Ying assured him, "Please do not worry. I'll be with you. With a little trick, I shall make the three men die in front of your eyes so that our two states can be rid of a source of peril."

The king promised, "If the three men die, I will be content with being a subordinate of Qi. We shall make annual tributes with no complaint."

Yan Ying accepted the offer. The king laid out a grand banquet in honor of Yan Ying who subsequently returned, while the king gathered together some gifts as tribute in preparation for his upcoming visit to Qi.

Yan Ying sent a messenger to announce his arrival. Immensely delighted, King Jing of Qi ordered his dukes to follow him out the city gate to welcome the prime minister back. When the three men heard about this, they seethed with anger. Upon Yan Ying's arrival, King Jing alighted from his carriage in greeting and, after some words of appreciation for Yan Ying's service, the king and the prime minister returned in the same carriage. Spectators filled up the streets. Yan Ying then took leave of the king and went back to his residence. The following day when he entered the palace, he saw the three men diverting themselves with a game in front of the hall. To Yan Ying's salutations they paid no attention, as if he did not exist—such was their arrogance. (*By believing that, with their physical power, they can well afford to slight able men, the threesome are actually bringing an early death upon themselves.*) Yan Ying remained standing for a considerable time before he turned away.

Once in the presence of the king, he told him about the insolence of the three men. King Jing said, "These three men always bring their swords with them into the court and treat me like a child. If this goes on, I'm sure they will usurp the throne. I've long wished to have them put out of the way, only I don't have the means to do so."

"Rest assured, Your Majesty," said Yan. "Tomorrow when the king of Chu and his ministers are here, a grand banquet can be laid out. I shall play a small trick during the course of the banquet and make the threesome take their own lives. What do you say to that?"

"What is the trick?"

"These three are long on courage but short on intelligence. If we do this and that, we can rid ourselves of these pests." The king was overjoyed.

On the following day, equipped with carriages of valuables and treasures of every kind, the king of Chu led about a hundred officials, civil as well as military, to the Qi court. King Jing invited them in. The king of Chu was the first one to drop to his knees in paying homage to the king of Qi, who hastened to return the salute, and then the two kings sat down as host and guest. At the order of the king of Chu, his ministers made their obeisance at the foot of the steps of the dais. With folded hands, the king of Chu begged for forgiveness: "I have given you much offense within the last twenty years. I am now here to ask for forgiveness, as is advised by your prime minister. Please accept these modest gifts as tribute." With thanks, King Jing of Qi accepted the gifts and laid out a banquet, in the course of which the kings and the ministers of the two states toasted one another. The threesome, in the meantime, stood at the foot of the steps, looking formidable with their swords strapped to their waists. When he moved around as courtesy required of him, Yan Ying paid no particular attention to the three men.

When they were well warmed with wine, King Jing said, "The peaches in the royal garden are ripe enough to be picked for dinner." In a trice, a court attendant came up carrying five of them on a gold plate. The king of Qi said, "The peach tree in the yard bore only five peaches this year. Their sweet taste and smell make them distinct from peaches of other trees. The prime minister will now serve wine to mark the occasion."

In those ancient times, peach trees were hard to come by. Five peaches in the same garden were quite a rare sight. Holding a jade wine vessel, Yan Ying served wine first to the king of Chu, who, after downing it, ate one of the peaches. Next was the turn of the king of Qi, who also ate one peach after finishing his cup of wine. The king of Qi said, "Such peaches are hard to come by. The prime minister deserves one for his most valuable service in promoting peace between the two states." On his knees, Yan Ying ate one and was granted a cup of wine. The king of Qi continued, "Among the high officials of the states of Qi and Chu, those who have rendered valuable service have the right to the remaining peaches." (*Good stratagem.*)

Tian Kaijiang stepped forward brazenly onto the banquet platform and said while standing, "When following you, Master, on a hunting expedition in the Tong Mountains, I killed a fierce tiger. Wasn't that valuable service?"

The king of Qi said, "There is no service more valuable than rescuing the sovereign."

Yan Ying was quick to serve him a cup of wine and a peach.

Now Gu Yizi sallied forth jauntily, saying, "What's so remarkable about killing a tiger? I killed a flood dragon of the Yellow River, rescued the master, and escorted him back home. I trod on the surging waves as if walking on level ground. Wasn't that valuable service?"

The king said, "Indeed, it was a service unparalleled anywhere in the world. Wine and peach are in order!"

With alacrity, Yan Ying served him as he was bid, whereupon Gongsun Jie came forward and said, holding up the lower part of his robe, "With an iron halberd, I saved the master from an army of a hundred thousand, while none of their soldiers dared come near me. Wasn't that valuable service?"

The king of Qi said, "Your meritorious service was indeed matchless anywhere between heaven and earth. However, there is no peach left. You will be offered just a cup of wine. You may wait another year."

"Your merit was the greatest of all," said Yan Ying. "It is a pity that you spoke too late. There is no peach left to reward you with for your worthy deed."

With his hand resting on the handle of his sword, Gongsun Jie said, "Killing dragons and tigers is nothing compared to what I did, sweeping through the enemy ranks to rescue the master as if I were in no-man's-land. For such a great service, I gain no share of the peaches. Thus humiliated in the presence of the kings and ministers of both states, I will be scorned by thousands of future generations. I won't be able to live down the shame." So saying, he drew out his sword and killed himself.

Appalled at the sight, Tian Kaijiang also drew out his sword and declared, "The two of us got to eat the peaches for our insignificant service, whereas my brother was given none, though what he did deserves more. How can I live down this shame!" With these words, he also took his own life, whereupon Gu Yuzi shouted at the top of his voice, "The three of us are as dear to one another as if we were born brothers. We have vowed to perish together. Since two of us have already died, how can I go on living by myself?" Turning his sword on himself, he also slit his own throat.

Yan Ying said with a laugh, "They would not have died without the two peaches. Now that a source of trouble has been removed, what do you think of my plan?"

The king of Chu left his seat and, with a deep bow, said in admiration, "The prime minister's divine foresight does command respect. From now on, I shall forever honor your state as our suzerain state, and I hereby take an oath never to invade your land."

The king of Qi had the threesome buried outside the east gate.

Henceforth, Qi and Chu established peace between them and put an end to all use of force. The state of Qi rose to be a dominant power of the times.

Yan Ying's name lived on through history. Even Confucius had good words for him. Later, Zhuge Liang[3] wrote a poem to the tune of "Liang Fu Yin" about the incidents that we have related above. The poem says,

> *Stepping out through the Qi city gate,*
> *I gaze at Tangyinli in the distance.*
> *There lie three graves.*
> *They look much the same.*
> *Whose graves are these?*
> *In them lie Tian, Gu, and their brother.*
> *Their strength could push back the southern mountains*
> *And cut the ropes that tie the four corners of the earth.*
> *Victims of slander at the court,*
> *They perished over two peaches.*
> *Who was capable of such a scheme?*
> *Yan Ying, prime minister of Qi.*

There is also a lyric poem to the tune of "Full River Red" by a poet of ancient times about the same story:

> *The valiant King Jing of Qi*
> *Was fond of hunting by the sea.*
> *In the midst of his chase came a fierce beast,*
> *Much to the terror of all at the scene.*
> *Kaijiang the mighty one came to the rescue*
> *And killed the tiger with his bare fists.*
> *His wounds dripping blood, he saved the king's life;*
> *Great his glory, the newly enfeoffed duke!*
> *To slay the dragon, there was Gu Yizi;*
> *To defeat the Qin, there was Gongsun Jie.*
> *Foolishly they rode roughshod over Qi.*
> *Yan Ying's little scheme of peaches*
> *Tricked them into taking their own lives.*
> *In the wilderness by the east gate of Qi*
> *Lie three graves under the moonlit sky.*

Shen Yu sees the thrush in the Imperial Aviary.

26

Shen Xiu Causes Seven Deaths with One Bird

A bird it was that was the root of it all;
Seven lives lost, how appalling!
May all parents take warning:
Do not let your children stay idle.

As the story goes, in the third year of the Xuanhe reign period [1121] under Emperor Huizong of the Song dynasty, there lived, by New North Bridge outside Wulin Gate in the prefecture of Ninghai,[1] a weaver named Shen Yu, courtesy name Bixian. A man of quite some means, he took himself a wife whose maiden name was Yan. The loving couple had an only son, whom they named Shen Xiu. At the time of which I speak, Shen Xiu was eighteen years old and not yet married. The father made his living by weaving fabrics, whereas his romantically inclined son, ignoring all proper pursuits, did little more than take care of his birds. (*The root of all trouble.*) As he was the only son, his parents were too doting to apply any discipline to him. The neighbors gave him a nickname: Birdie Shen. Every dawn at the fifth watch, he would take one of his thrushes to the willow grove in the city for fresh air, and so the days went by.

On one of those colorful days toward the end of spring when summer was already in the air, a day that was neither cold nor hot, Shen Xiu rose at the first light of dawn and, having washed and eaten his breakfast, made ready a cage into which he put a thrush. It was indeed a divine bird with no match on earth. Never had it lost a fight anywhere Shen Xiu took it, nor did it fail to bring in piles of money. Therefore, Shen Xiu loved it no less than he did his own dear life, and he made it a gold lacquer cage with brass hooks, water and food bowls of the finest Geyao[2] porcelain, and a green-gauze cage-cover. Cage in hand, he swaggered his way into the city, heading straight for the willow grove. Little did he know that he was to die a violent death in much the same way as

Pigs and sheep on their way to the butcher's,
With each step, drawing nearer to their death.

So Shen Xiu took his thrush to the willow grove, but he was too late. Those who usually gathered there to give their birds fresh air were already gone. The whole place was now dark and deserted, with not a soul left. All alone, he hung the cage on a willow branch. After the thrush sang for a while, Shen Xiu felt bored. He took down the cage and was about to turn back when a sharp pain shot through his belly and he sank into a squatting position.

As a matter of fact, Shen Xiu suffered from a chronic hernia, each attack of which left him more dead than alive. That morning, because he had risen earlier than usual but arrived too late for the gathering, he felt low-spirited, and so the attack was more severe than usual. With a thump, he collapsed by a willow tree and lost consciousness for a good four hours.

As coincidence would have it, the bucket-cooper Mr. Zhang was walking through the willow grove, a load on his shoulders, on his way to the Chu residence for a job. From afar, he saw a man lying under a tree. Taking what would be the space of three ordinary steps in two, he rushed forward and put down his load. What he saw was a young man in a coma, his face drained of all color. There was nothing of any value about him other than the birdcage, in which the cursed bird was, at that very moment, singing more beautifully than ever. Indeed, as the saying goes, the sight of money stirs up one's greed, and the direst poverty leads to action. Zhang thought to himself, "How can I ever get to have some fun with the pittance I make?"

Shen Xiu was meant to die at that moment, for the thrush began to sing exceptionally well at the sight of Zhang. "This thrush alone," said Zhang to himself, "would be worth two or three taels of silver at least, not to mention anything else." So saying, he picked up the cage, but before he got away, Shen Xiu came to. When he saw Zhang carrying the birdcage, he tried in vain to get up. "Old jerk!" he cried out. "Where do you think you're taking my bird?" (*What good does cursing do? He brings death upon himself for lack of self-restraint in a trifling matter.*)[3]

"So this little bastard has a sharp tongue!" Zhang thought to himself. "If I walk away with the thing, he'll get up and catch up with me, and I'll end up the loser. If I am to get a bad name anyway, I might as well finish him off." From his bucket he drew out a paring knife, held Shen Xiu to the ground, and struck with one blow of the knife. It being a sharp, curved knife struck down with mighty force, the young man's head rolled to one side. (*There goes the first one.*)

Panic overtook Zhang. He looked around in all directions, afraid that he might have been seen. Raising his eyes, he saw a hollow willow tree. With great haste, he picked up the head and tossed it into the hollow trunk. He then put the knife back into the bucket, hung the cage from his carrying pole, and pressed ahead, not to the Chu household for the job but, through streets and alleys, to a place where what he was to do would cause more lives to perish on account of the bird. Truly,

> *A soft whisper uttered on earth*
> *Is heard in heaven as loud as thunder.*
> *An evil deed done in a dark room*
> *Is seen by gods' eyes as clear as lightning.*

Zhang thought to himself as he went along, "I've noticed that in an inn at Huzhoushu, there is a traveling merchant who is interested in buying pets. Why don't I go and sell him this bird?" And he headed straight for this inn outside Wulin Gate.

This merchant's allotted span of life was destined to draw to an end. When going through the gate, Zhang ran into three travelers, followed by two young attendants, who had packed up their merchandise. All of the men were from the city of Bianliang, the Eastern Capital. One of them, a trader in herbal medicine by the name of Li Ji, was also fond of thrushes. (*Root of trouble.*) At the sight of the fine bird in the cage hanging from the pole, he asked Zhang if he could take a look. Zhang put down his load. Much impressed with the thrush's fine feathers, eyes, and voice, the traveler asked Old Zhang, "Would you be willing to sell it?"

All too eager to rid himself of this source of trouble, Zhang said, "How much will you pay, sir?"

The more Li Ji looked at the bird, the more he liked it. "One tael of silver," said he.

Zhang was well pleased over this good deal. "I shouldn't haggle," he said, "but, as the saying goes, anything that truly strikes one's fancy is worth any amount of money. Add a little more and you'll have it."

Li Ji took out three pieces of silver that weighed one and a fifth taels. "All right," he said and handed over the silver to Zhang.

The pieces of silver now in his hand, Zhang examined them and put them in his bag. He gave the bird to the traveler and, with a few words of farewell, took himself off. "It's a good thing that I have now rid myself of that root of all trouble," he muttered to himself. Instead of going to work, he headed straight home, not in an altogether carefree frame of mind. Truly,

> *The evil fear punishment from heaven and earth;*
> *The wicked fear knowledge by gods and demons.*

Zhang lived with his wife by Yongjin Gate. They had no children. Upon his return, his wife said, "You haven't used any of the rattan strips. Why are you back so early? What do you have in mind?"

Without a word of reply, Old Zhang carried his load into the house, put it down, turned around, and closed the door before he spoke up. "Wife, come here. I have something to tell you. Just now . . . " He went on to give an account of what had happened. "With the one and a fifth taels of silver," he continued, "you and I are going to have a good time." The couple were beside themselves with joy, but of this, we shall speak no further.

Let us come back to the deserted willow grove. It was not until about nine in the morning that two men carrying loads of manure passed by. Appalled at the sight of a headless corpse blocking the way, they cried out and caused quite a stir among the residents and headmen of the nearby neighborhood. The neighborhood headmen reported the murder to the county authorities, who, in their turn, reported it to the prefect. The following day, some officers and coroners were sent to the willow grove to investigate. No wounds were found on the headless body, nor did any family members of the deceased come forward to identify the corpse. After the officers reported back to the prefect, inspectors were sent out to search for the murderer. Commotion broke out throughout the city and beyond.

In the meantime, Shen Xiu's parents waited in vain for their son until evening came. They then sent someone out to search everywhere for him, but to no avail. At daybreak, as another search party went to the city, they heard in Huzhoushu much excited talk about a murdered headless corpse in the willow grove. When she heard this, Shen Xiu's mother thought to herself, "My son took the bird to the city yesterday and is still missing. Might it be him?" She turned to her husband and urged, "You must go there yourself to find out what happened."

Shen Yu gave a start and, in alarm, hurried into the willow grove. There he saw the headless corpse. A close examination of the clothes convinced him that it was indeed his son. He broke down in bitter weeping. The neighborhood headman remarked, "Now we've got the family, but there's still no clue as to the murderer."

Shen Yu went to the prefect of Lin'an and pleaded, "My son took his thrush into the city early yesterday morning and for whatever reason was murdered. Please, Your Honor, make sure that justice is done!"

The prefect issued orders to inspectors throughout the prefecture, demanding that the murderer be arrested within ten days.

Shen Yu put the corpse in a coffin, left it in the willow grove, and returned home. "It is indeed our son," he said to his wife. "He was murdered, but his head is still nowhere to be found. I have appealed to the prefect, who then sent orders all over the prefecture to arrest the murderer. I bought a coffin for the body. Now what should be done next?"

At this account, his wife burst into loud wails and collapsed to the ground.

The condition of her five vital organs was not readily apparent, but her four limbs visibly went limp. Truly,

> *Her body feeble as the waning moon;*
> *Her breath as weak as a dying candle.*

When she came to after bystanders forced some warm water down her throat, she lamented between sobs, "My son always turned a deaf ear to good advice, and now he has died without even a burial place. What a tragic death for such a young man! I never expected that I would have no son to support me in my old age!" So saying, she broke down in another flood of tears. Then she resumed her laments, refusing all offers of tea and food. Her husband tried desperately to console her, and at last she calmed down. Half a month went by with no more news about the case. The couple took counsel with each other and decided that since it was their son's waywardness that brought this calamity upon himself, there was nothing much they could do if the murderer could not be found, but at least the corpse should be made whole. It would be best if they wrote a poster to let it be known to all that a reward would be given to anyone who could find the head so as to have the corpse made whole.

Having thus decided, the couple promptly wrote several posters and put them up in various places throughout the city. On the posters were written these words:

To all and sundry:

A reward of a thousand strings of cash will be given to anyone who finds Shen Xiu's head. Two thousand strings of cash will be the reward of anyone who captures the murderer.

The matter was reported to the prefect, who, while again charging inspectors with the task of arresting the murderer, also put up posters that said,

The prefecture offers a reward of five hundred strings of cash to anyone who finds Shen Xiu's head and one thousand strings of cash to anyone who captures the murderer.

The posters caused quite a stir throughout the city.

Now, at the foot of Southern Peak there lived an old man, with the surname Huang, who was as poor as could be. Nicknamed Old Dog Huang, he was not a man known for his good sense. In his younger days, he had made a living by carrying sedan-chairs, but now, in his declining years, having lost his sight, he could do no better than allow himself to be supported by his two sons, Big Bao and Little Bao. This family of three could hardly scrape together enough food to fill their bellies nor enough clothes to cover their bodies. One day, Old Dog Huang called together Big Bao and Little Bao and addressed them as follows: "I have heard that a rich man, Shen Xiu, was murdered, and his head is still missing. For anyone who can come up with the head, there'll be a reward of one thousand strings in cash from the family and another five hundred strings in cash from the prefect. Now, I've called you together just to say that, being a useless and sightless old man with no source of income, I'd be better off dead if, in exchange, you two could live it up. Tonight, the two of you can cut off my head and hide it by West Lake. Wait for a few days for it to rot beyond recognition, and then take it to the prefectural yamen to claim the reward of fifteen hundred strings of cash. Wouldn't that be better than suffering in such misery here? This is a wonderful plan that needs to be carried out without delay, for if someone else does it before us, I'll have died for nothing." Such was the folly of Old Dog Huang. To make matters worse, the two sons were also densely ignorant imbeciles who knew nothing about the law. (*The law is only of secondary importance.*) Truly,

> *The mouth is the door that leads to disaster;*
> *The tongue is the sword that gives the fatal blow.*
> *Shut your mouth and hide your tongue,*
> *And you shall have peace everywhere you go.*

The two brothers went outside to talk it over. Little Bao said, "Father's plan is indeed more ingenious than what any general or commander could have come up with. But, however ingenious it might be, it's too bad that we'll be losing our father."

Big Bao, being as stupid as he was ruthless, rejoined, "He's going to die soon anyway. Wouldn't it be better to finish him off now? Let's dig a pit at the foot of the mountain and bury him. With no trace left behind, how would we be found out? What we'll be doing is but giving the whole thing a push and a finishing touch, so to speak. In all conscience, it's he who wants us to do this, not the other way around."

"It's a good idea all right," said Little Bao, "but let's wait until he's fast asleep before we do it."

Having thus decided upon the course they were to follow, they went out and, after much running around, bought two bottles of wine on credit. The father and the sons drank until they tumbled every which way. Upon waking up at the third watch of the night, the two brothers rose and saw that the old man was sound asleep. Big Bao took a kitchen knife from the stove and, with one strike, cut his father's head off. (*There goes the second one.*) In great haste, they wrapped it up in a ragged piece of clothing, put it by the bedside, and proceeded to the foot of the mountain, where they dug a deep pit. They then carried the body there and buried it. Before the night was out, they took the head to the lake near Lotus House by South Screen Mountain and buried it in a shallow spot by the water's edge.

Half a month later, they went into the city, read the posters, and made their way to Shen Yu's house. "Yesterday," they reported, "the two of us were catching shrimp and fish in the lake near Lotus House when we saw a human head. We thought it might be your son's."

"If it is," said Shen Yu, "you shall get your reward of a thousand strings of cash, not a penny less."

After treating them to wine and food, Shen followed them to the lake. A human head could be seen thinly concealed under a layer of soil. When lifted up for a look, it turned out to be a head so bloated from all those days in the water as to be beyond all hope of recognition. But this must be it because, if not, how could there be another unclaimed human head? Shen Yu wrapped it up in a handkerchief and went with the two brothers to the prefectural yamen to report, "Shen Xiu's head has been found."

To the prefect's repeated queries, the two brothers answered, "We saw it while we were catching shrimp and fish. That's the full extent of our knowledge."

The prefect believed their story and handed out the reward of five hundred strings of cash. The money now in their possession, they carried the head and followed Shen Yu to the willow grove, where they opened the coffin, fit the head onto the neck, nailed the coffin up again, and returned with Shen Yu to his house. Pleased at hearing that her son's head had been found, Yan-shi set out wine and food in honor of the two brothers and gave them the reward of one thousand strings of cash. The two men took the money, bade the couple farewell, and returned home to build a new house and buy farming implements. The two men said, "Now we don't have to carry sedan-chairs as before. We can very well make a living by hard work at farming and selling firewood." But of them, for the time being, no more.

Indeed, time flew like an arrow, and the days and months passed by as fast as a weaver's shuttle. Quite unnoticeably, several months elapsed. The prefectural yamen's attention was diverted elsewhere, and the case gradually ceased to be a topic of conversation.

Now let us return to Shen Yu. Being a weaver for the Eastern Capital, it was now his turn to escort a shipment of silk to the capital. When all the other weavers had finished their work, Shen Yu went to the prefectural yamen to get the permit for delivery of the goods. Upon returning home, he gave instructions for the arrangement of household affairs and set off on his journey. He was to see the bird again, an encounter that was to lead to another death. Truly,

Never take what is not rightfully yours;
Never do what should not rightfully be done.
Justice on earth goes wherever you go,
And though unseen, the gods follow you, too.

To resume our story, Shen Yu went on the road, eating and drinking whenever necessary, resting by night and traveling by day. Some days later, he arrived in the Eastern Capital. After delivering the bolts of silk and taking his receipt, he thought to himself, "The sights of the capital are said to be quite different from other places. Why don't I take a look around? It's only once in a long while that I get to visit the capital." And so he made a tour of all the famous hills, scenic spots, temples, monasteries, and historic sites. Chance took his steps past the Imperial Aviary. Being a lover of pets, Shen Yu wished to go in for a look. After paying about a dozen cash at the gate, he was allowed in. He heard a thrush singing beautifully. A closer look revealed it to be none other than the missing thrush that had belonged to his son. Upon recognizing Shen Yu, the bird sang with more gusto. It hopped about, stretching its neck toward him. The sight of the thrush reminded Shen Yu of his son. Tears gushed out, and a pain shot through his heart. In spite of himself, he cried out in anguish, "How can there be such a thing!"

The guard of the aviary sharply reprimanded him, saying, "This brute has no idea of regulations! This is no place for you to kick up such a fuss!"

Feeling wronged, Shen Yu cried even louder.

Afraid of being blamed by the authorities, the guard saw no alternative but to apprehend Shen Yu and take him to the Court of Judicial Review. The court judge thundered, "Who do you think you are, making such a noise in a royal place? How were you wronged? Speak the truth, and I'll let you off." Shen Yu thereupon gave a full account of how his son was murdered while on an outing with the bird. The court judge was astounded and fell silent, for this bird had been offered as tribute to the aviary by Li Ji, a resident of the capital. How could he have known the story behind it? Accordingly, he sent runners to bring Li Ji with all speed to the court.

The interrogator asked, "Why did you murder his son in Ninghai and offer the thrush here as tribute? Confess, and you shall be spared from torture."

"I was on my way to Hangzhou on business," said Li Ji, "when at Wulin Gate I ran into a bucket-cooper, who had this thrush in a cage hanging from his carrying pole. The bird was so beautiful and was singing so well that I bought it for one and a fifth taels of silver. It is such a fine bird that I dared not keep it for myself but offered it in tribute to the emperor. I know nothing about any foul play."

"Don't try to shift the blame onto someone else," said the interrogator. "We have this thrush as physical evidence. Out with the truth!"

Li Ji pleaded time and again, "I did indeed buy it from the old bucket-cooper. I know nothing about any murder. I can't confess to something I didn't do."

The interrogator pressed further: "If you bought it from an old man, what is his name? And where is he from? If you make a clean breast of everything, I will have him brought in. Then we'll establish all the facts and let you go."

"I bought it from him when I ran into him on the road. I know nothing about his name or where he lives."

The interrogator lashed out, "Don't try to get by with evasive answers! You can't make someone else pay for the murder! This thrush is conclusive evidence against you. (*The judges go only by whatever evidence they happen to see under their noses. A big flaw in the system.*) The brute has to be beaten before he'll confess!"

After he was beaten till his skin split and his flesh ripped, the pain was too much for Li Ji to stand. He had no choice but to confess to having "killed Shen Xiu and discarded his head for the sake of the beautiful thrush." Consequently, he was thrown into jail to await sentence. In the meantime, as a response to the judge's report, an imperial decree came saying that Li Ji, being the murderer of Shen Xiu, as evidenced by the surviving thrush, was to be executed in accordance with the law. The bird was given back to Shen Yu, who was permitted to return home, whereas Li Ji was taken under guard to the marketplace to be decapitated. (*There goes the third one.*) Truly,

> When the old turtle's meat won't cook tender,
> Innocent mulberries are cut down to feed the fire.

The two merchants who had traveled with Li Ji to Ninghai to ply their trade were angered by the news. "What an injustice! We saw him buy the bird! We would have defended him, only we don't know the seller's name, either, though we do remember how he looked. Moreover, it all happened in Hangzhou. What if we were to be incriminated too, without being able to clear his name? A human life was unjustly taken for the sake of a mere bird! If ever we find ourselves in Hangzhou, we will surely try to get the truth out of that man." We shall leave them for the moment and come back to Shen Yu.

Having packed his belongings, Shen Yu took the bird and hastened on his way home, without waiting for the night to be over. Upon arriving home, he said to his wife, "I got our son avenged in the Eastern Capital."

"How did it all happen?" asked his wife, whereupon Shen Yu gave her a full account of the story, beginning with his sighting of the bird in the

Imperial Aviary. When she saw the thrush, Yan-shi broke down in a flood of tears, for it reminded her of her son, but this is no concern of ours here.

The following day, Shen Yu took the bird to the prefectural yamen to have his permit canceled, and he gave a report of everything that had happened. Greatly pleased at the account, the prefect exclaimed, "What a remarkable coincidence that was!" Truly,

> Do nothing that will trouble your conscience;
> No one has ever been spared from justice.

It goes without saying that cases involving human lives, being matters of concern to heaven, are by no means child's play. The prefect ordered, "Since the murderer has been brought to justice and executed, the coffin of Shen Xiu may now be cremated." Accordingly, Shen Yu had the coffin cremated and the ashes scattered into a temple pond, but of this, no more.

In the meantime, the two merchants, He and Zhu, who had traveled with Li Ji to Hangzhou to sell medicinal herbs, were now in Hangzhou again. They stayed in the inn at Huzhoushu and disposed of all the herbs left in their stock. Still indignant at the injustice done to Li Ji, the two of them went into the city to look for the bucket-cooper. They searched a whole day without finding a clue. In low spirits, the two men returned to the inn. The following day, they went into the city again and ran into a man carrying a cooper's load. They stopped him and said, "May we ask you something, brother? We are trying to find a cooper, an old man," and they proceeded to give a description of the old man's looks. "Would you happen to know his name?"

The man said, "In my line of business, there are only two old men, a Li who lives on Pomegranate Lane and a Zhang who lives by the western city wall. I don't know which of them you might be asking about."

The two men thanked him and proceeded to Pomegranate Lane, where they saw Mr. Li there cutting rattan strips. They looked him over, but he was not the man they were after. They then headed toward the house by the western wall and asked, upon arrival, "Is Mr. Zhang in?" His wife said, "No, he's out on a job."

The two men turned back without another word. In the early afternoon, when they had covered hardly half a li on their way back, they saw a cooper with his load coming in their direction from afar. This man was to pay for Shen Xiu's life and clear Li Ji's name. Truly,

> Do good deeds far and wide,
> For you never know whom you'll run into.
> Never make an enemy,
> For you're bound to meet him on a narrow road.

Zhang was heading south while the two travelers were heading north, and so they met face to face. Zhang did not recognize the two men, but they recognized him. Stopping him, they said, "May we ask your name, sir?"

"My surname is Zhang."

"Might you be the Mr. Zhang who lives by the western wall?"

"Yes," replied Zhang. "Why are you asking me these questions?"

"We have a lot of work at the inn for an experienced cooper. Where are you heading?"

"I'm on my way home."

The three men chatted as they went along, until they came to Zhang's door. "Please come in for some tea," said Zhang.

"It's too late. We'll come back tomorrow."

"In that case, I'll stay at home tomorrow to wait for you."

After parting company with Zhang, the two men did not return to the inn. Instead, they went straight to the prefectural yamen to make their report while the court was in its evening session. They got down on their knees in the hall and gave a detailed account of how Shen Yu had recognized the thrush, how Li Ji had ended up being executed, and how they had witnessed Zhang selling the thrush. "Believing that an injustice was done, we are here to make sure that Li Ji is avenged. (*Good men. Good men.*) Please apprehend Zhang for interrogation, Your Honor, and find out how he came by the thrush."

The prefect said, "Shen Xiu's case is closed. The murderer has already been executed. What more is there to talk about?"

The two men pleaded, "The judge of the Court of Judicial Review made a poor judgment when he unjustly sentenced Li Ji to death on the evidence of the thrush alone, without any investigation. In the face of such injustice, we ask that Li Ji's life be paid back. We wouldn't have dared to make this report if what we say is anything less than the truth. Please stand by us in your mercy." The sincerity of their pleading made the prefect decide to dispatch runners to arrest Zhang that very night, in much the same way as

> Black vultures chasing a purple swallow,
> Fierce tigers pouncing on a little lamb.

That night, the runners hurried to the western wall and trussed Mr. Zhang up with ropes. They then brought him to the prefectural yamen and threw him into jail. The following day when the prefect called the court session to order, the runners took Zhang out of jail and made him kneel down. The prefect said, "How could you have murdered Shen Xiu and let Li Ji die in your place? Now that the truth has come to light, the will of heaven will not spare you." He sharply ordered that the man be given a sound beating.

After thirty strokes, his skin split, his flesh ripped open, and blood ran all over the place, but he still refused to confess.

The two merchants and their two companions said in unison, "Li Ji is dead, but the four of us all saw with our own eyes how he bought the thrush from you for one and a fifth taels of silver. Now who are you going to shift the blame to? If you didn't do it, tell the court where you got the bird. Hard facts cannot be denied. Lying won't get you anywhere!"

As Zhang insisted on his innocence, the prefect roared, "With the bird as evidence of your theft and the four men here as eyewitnesses, I will order that the ankle-squeezers be used on you if you don't confess!"

A terrified Zhang had no choice but to confess how he had stolen the bird and cut off Shen Xiu's head.

"Where did you put the head?" asked the prefect.

"In a moment of panic, I tossed the head into a hollow willow tree by the roadside. Then I took the bird, walked out Wulin Gate, and ran into three traveling merchants with two attendants, who bought the bird from me for one and a fifth taels of silver. I took the money home and spent it. All this is true."

The prefect made Zhang sign his confession and sent runners to bring Shen Yu. With Zhang under guard, they went to the willow grove to find the head. The news caused an uproar throughout the city. Countless people swarmed to the willow grove to watch the spectacle. There, for all to see, was indeed a hollow willow tree. As the tree fell to a saw, the crowd gave a shout because, lo and behold, there was indeed a human head that, when lifted up, was found to be as fresh as when alive. (*The aggrieved soul of the dead man refused to go away.*) A closer look convinced Shen Yu that it was his son's head. He broke out into loud wails of grief and fell to the ground unconscious. When he came to after a considerable while, he wrapped up the head with a kerchief. Zhang was then taken under guard to the prefectural yamen.

"Now that the head has been found," said the prefect, "guilt is established beyond a doubt." With a big cangue put on his neck and shackles on his hands and feet, Zhang was taken to the cell for those condemned to death, where he was kept under close guard. (*The fourth one.*)

The prefect said to Shen Yu, "It is questionable where the Huang brothers, Big Bao and Small Bao, got the head for which they claimed a reward. Now that Shen Xiu's head has been found, whose head could the other one be?" Immediately he sent runners to bring the Huang brothers to him for interrogation. Shen Yu went with them all the way to the Huangs' house on Southern Peak, and they took the brothers to the prefectural yamen, where they were made to kneel down in the hall.

"Shen Xiu's murderer has been brought to justice," said the prefect. "Shen Xiu's head has also been found. Whom did you brothers murder in order to claim a reward for the head? Confess everything and you will be spared from torture."

Disconcerted by the question, Big Bao and Little Bao found themselves tongue-tied and unable to come up with any answer. The prefect flew into a rage. At his order, the two men were hung up and beaten. As they still refused to confess after a good deal of flogging, red-hot irons were applied to them. The pain was so overwhelming that they fainted. When splashes of water brought them back to consciousness, they had no recourse but to come out with the truth (*The fifth and sixth*): "Our father being old, sick, and lonely, we got him drunk and cut off his head, something we shouldn't have done. We buried the head by the side of West Lake near Lotus House. We then came to claim the reward, passing off his head as the one wanted."

"Where did you bury your father's body?" asked the prefect.

"At the foot of Southern Peak," was the reply. The two men were immediately taken there and some digging did indeed reveal a headless corpse buried in the ground. The two men were brought back to the prefectural yamen to await further instructions.

At the report that there was indeed a headless corpse buried in the shallow soil at the foot of Southern Peak, the prefect exploded, "What an atrocity! This is an outrageous violation of all laws of heaven. How can there be such monsters among men! I have no wish to talk, hear, or write about them. They'd better be beaten to death right on the spot. How else is the crime to be vindicated?" On his order, the lictors did not bother about counting, but beat the two men through several rounds of losing and regaining consciousness. They were then locked up in huge cangues and thrown into the cell for prisoners condemned to death. There, they were put under close guard. Shen Yu and the plaintiffs waited at home for further instructions.

A memorial on the unjust death of Li Ji was promptly submitted to the imperial court. Acting on an imperial decree, the Ministry of Justice and the Censorate cross-examined the judge who had sentenced Li Ji to death, stripped him of all official posts, and banished him to Lingnan, in the south. To compensate for the unjust death of Li Ji, the court granted the family of the deceased a thousand strings of cash and exempted his descendants from corvée labor. Zhang was sentenced to death for having committed a murder for monetary gain and causing the unjust death of an innocent man. For this double crime, he was to be cut by knife two hundred forty times and his body dismembered into five pieces. The Huang brothers, for their crime of patricide for monetary gain, were given the same sentence, with no attempt to distinguish one of them as the main culprit and the other as his accessory. They too were to be sliced by knife two hundred forty times, their bodies cut into five pieces, and their heads hung high for the public to see. Truly,

> Heaven is not to be deceived;
> Evil designs are seen before they're hatched.
> Do nothing that will trouble your conscience;
> No one has ever been spared from justice.

When the documents arrived, officers and coroners put the three men on wooden "mules" and publicized the event throughout the city for three days, after which their corpses were dismembered and their heads hung up for public exposure, as was dictated by the law.

Having heard that her old man was to be executed, Zhang's wife betook herself to the marketplace, hoping to see her husband once more. However, when the executioners started slicing at the signal to begin, the gruesome sight frightened the wits out of her. As she turned away to flee from the scene, she tripped and fell with a heavy thump to the ground, injuring her five internal organs. She died soon after arriving home. (*The seventh.*) Indeed,

> Good deeds beget good fortune;
> Evil acts bring evil upon oneself.
> Think this over carefully, and you'll find
> Heaven and earth never make a mistake.

Jin Yunu Beats the Heartless Man

Branch on one side of the wall, flowers on the other;
The flowers fall, adrift at the mercy of the wind.
The branch, though bare, will blossom again,
But the fallen flowers can never regain the branch.

The above quatrain, titled "The Abandoned Wife," was written by a poet of olden times. It compares married women to flowers on branches. Branches bereft of flowers will blossom again in the spring, but once off the branches, the flowers will never be able to make their way back. Every woman is thereby admonished to serve her husband as best she can, share with him all the joys and sorrows of life, and remain faithful to him and him alone, to the end of her life. Never should a woman covet the wealth of other men and despise her own husband's poverty, for such lack of devotion will cause her regret later in life.

I shall now tell of a famous minister at the court of the Han dynasty. His wife, who failed to recognize in him the makings of a great man, left him before his rise in the world, an act that she regretted, to no avail, in later years. Now you might well ask, where was that man from and what was his name? He was Zhu Maichen, courtesy name Wengzi, a native of the region of Kuaiji.[1] Before his time came, he and his wife lived in poverty in a humble hut. Every day he went into the mountains and chopped firewood to sell in the marketplace to eke out a living. Much given to scholarly pursuits, he was never seen without a book in his hand. Carrying a load of firewood across his shoulders, he would hold a book and chant the lines as he walked. At the familiar sound of his chanting, the local residents would know that Maichen was here with his firewood and, out of pity for this scholar-peddler, they would all buy from him. Maichen, on his part, never haggled over price, but just let the customers pay whatever they thought fit. Therefore, he disposed of his firewood more quickly than did other peddlers. But there were also the usual lot of children and frivolous young men who often gathered in threes and fives to make fun of this firewood peddler with scholarly interests. Maichen, however, did not mind their taunts in the least.

One day, his wife went out to draw water and saw a group of children following Maichen about, clapping their hands and laughing. Deeply humiliated, she offered this advice to Maichen upon his return: "If you want to study, give up selling firewood. If you want to sell firewood, give up your studies. You should be old enough and sensible enough not to do things that make children laugh at you. Don't you see how humiliating it is?"

"I sell firewood to save us from poverty, and I study to try to attain wealth and rank. The two things are not mutually exclusive. Let them laugh at me, for all I care."

His wife sneered, "If you're really after wealth and rank, you shouldn't be selling firewood. Who ever heard of a firewood peddler turning into an official? What nonsense!"

"Wealth and rank or poverty and lowliness are all destined to occur in one's life at the appointed time. A fortune-teller told me that I will surely rise in the world by the age of fifty. As the saying goes, 'The ocean cannot be measured with a scoop.' Don't take me for a hopeless case yet."

"The fortune-teller was kidding you because you looked like a lunatic. He can't be taken seriously. By the time you're fifty, the firewood load will be too heavy for you (*Not a bad guess*), and what follows is death from starvation, not an official post—unless Yama, king of hell, needs you to fill up a vacancy as a judge there!"

Maichen retorted, "Jiang Taigong[2] at age eighty was still fishing by the Wei River when King Wen [11th century B.C.E.] of the Zhou dynasty invited him into his chariot and honored him as adviser. The incumbent prime minister Gongsun Hong was still herding swine by the Eastern Sea at age fifty-nine. He was sixty when he was finally presented to the emperor and was granted titles. If I start to rise at fifty, I'll be behind Gan Luo[3] but ahead of those two. You'll just have to wait patiently."

"Don't go over all of history with me," snapped his wife. "The angler and the swineherd were truly learned scholars, but you, with what little useless knowledge you have, will never amount to anything even if you go on studying until you're a hundred! I really lost out when I married you! With children making fun of you, you're bringing shame on me, too. If you don't do as I say and throw away your books, I will leave you. We can go our separate ways and not ruin each other's chances."

"I'm now forty-three. I'll be fifty in seven years. The better part of the waiting is now behind us. You'll just have to be patient for a little while longer. If you're so heartless as to leave me, you'll surely regret it later!"

"Are there so few woodcutters in the world that I shall ever have regrets? If I stay with you for another seven hungry years, I don't know where my dead bones will end up. Please do me a favor and let me go. You'll be saving my life, you know."

Maichen saw that his wife was not to be shaken in her determination to go. With a sigh, he said, "All right, all right. I hope your next husband will be better than Zhu Maichen."

"No matter what, he'll be better than you if only by the least bit." So saying, she took two bows and merrily went out the door without so much as a look back. Overcome with emotion, Maichen wrote four lines on the wall:

> *Marry a dog, follow the dog;*
> *Marry a rooster, follow the rooster.*
> *It was my wife who deserted me,*
> *Not I who abandoned her.*

When Maichen reached fifty, Emperor Wudi [r. 140–87 B.C.E.] of the Han dynasty issued a decree to recruit worthy men to assume office. Maichen betook himself to the Western Capital,[4] where he submitted his proposals to the court and stayed on to wait for news. A fellow townsman named Yan Zhu[5] recommended Maicheng's abilities to the emperor. Maichen being a native of Kuaiji (*Luckily the wise ruler sets great store by talent. That's why scholars' words carry weight.*) with full knowledge of the local way of life, the emperor appointed him prefect of Kuaiji, and off he rode on horseback to assume his post.

Having heard that the new prefect would soon arrive, the magistrate of Kuaiji hired a great many laborers to repair the roads. Among them was the second husband of Maichen's wife. Her hair disheveled and her feet bare, she was serving her husband a meal when she caught sight of the prefect and his entourage approaching. Looking on from the roadside, she recognized the prefect to be her former husband, Zhu Maichen. From his seat in the carriage, Maichen also recognized her at the first glance and had her put in a carriage at the rear of the procession.

Upon arrival at the prefect's residence, the woman was so overcome with shame that she wished she could find a place to hide herself. She kowtowed and pleaded for forgiveness. Maichen summoned her second husband. Shortly thereafter, the man arrived and prostrated himself on the floor without daring to raise his eyes. Laughing heartily, Maichen said to his former wife, "I fail to see how a man like this is better than Zhu Maichen."

The woman went on kowtowing and apologizing. In bitter remorse over her lack of faith in Maichen, she offered to be reduced to the status of a maidservant or concubine so as to serve him for the rest of her life. Maichen ordered a bucketful of water poured down the steps. "If this spilt water can be put back

into the bucket," he said to her, "you can come back to me. Out of consideration for our marriage tie committed at an early age, I give you the vacant land
in my backyard for you and your husband to cultivate and support yourselves
with."

As the woman followed her new husband out of the prefect's residence,
passersby pointed at her and said, "That's the new prefect's wife." The humiliation so overwhelmed her that when she reached the backyard, she threw
herself into the river and drowned. There is a poem in evidence:

> *A washerwoman fed a hungry stranger;[6]*
> *A wife left her poor scholar husband.*
> *Had she known that spilt water can't be recovered,*
> *She would have yielded to his love of books.*

There is another poem that says snobbery is all too common and is by no
means limited just to Maichen's wife:

> *Merit is judged only by success;*
> *Who can recognize a dragon in the mud?*
> *Blame her not for lacking a discerning eye;*
> *How many women are like Fuji's[7] wife?*

The above story is about a wife deserting her husband. I shall now tell of
a husband abandoning his wife out of the same ungratefulness, love of riches,
and contempt for poverty. But all that he gained in the end was notoriety as a
heartless man in a much-told story.

The story took place in Lin'an during the Shaoxing reign period [1131–62]
of the Song dynasty. Though it was the capital of the empire and a prosperous
city, there was still no lack of beggars. The beggars had a chief to look after
them. Known as Beggar Chief, he demanded a daily tribute out of whatever
alms they received. On days of rain and snow when they could hardly go out
to beg, the chief would cook some thin gruel to feed them. Whatever tattered
clothes they had were also in his care. Therefore the beggars were as submis-
sive to him as slaves were to their master, always careful not to give him any
offense.

With his pretty regular income, the beggar chief would lend out money
among the beggars and charge them interest. If he was not given to gambling and whoring, he could easily build up for himself a sizable enterprise.
With such a means of livelihood, he would have no wish to change professions. The only drawback was the title Beggar Chief. He might have acquired
acres upon acres of land and inherited wealth from several generations back,
but he would still be a beggar chief with a status lower than that of decent
ordinary folks. As he could command no respect from outside his family, he

had to content himself with being the master of his own house behind closed doors.

Be that as it may, when it comes to the distinction between the decent and the lowly, the four kinds of people belonging to the latter category are prostitutes, entertainers, yamen runners, and soldiers. Beggars are not among them. Hence it appears that beggars are considered to be poor but not base. As a case in point, Wu Zixu, a minister of the Spring and Autumn period, had, as a fugitive, begged for food by playing a vertical flute in the marketplace in the state of Wu. Zheng Yuanhe of the Tang dynasty had sung "The Lotus Petals Fall," a beggar's song, as a hired mourner. When they gained fame and fortune later in their lives, they were able to cover up their humble past with a "brocade quilt." These are examples of successful men who had been beggars. Thus it can be seen that however looked down upon, beggars are above prostitutes, entertainers, runners, and soldiers in social status.

Let us get on with our story. In the city of Hangzhou, there lived a beggar chief called Jin Laoda. Being a seventh-generation beggar chief, he was in possession of a considerable family business, with fine houses and fertile lands, nice clothes and good food. His barns were filled with surplus grain and his pockets well lined with extra money. He gave out loans and kept maid servants. Though not the richest of the rich, his was a household that easily came to mind when one counted off the wealthy. Being a man who rose above mundane concerns, Jin Laoda yielded his position as beggar chief to a kinsman called Scabby Jin so that he himself could fully enjoy what he had without having to deal with the beggars. Even so, the neighbors still called him Beggar Chief out of sheer habit. His wife having died without giving him a son, Jin Laoda, now in his fifties, had only a daughter called Yunu, a most beautiful girl. How do we know this? There is a poem that testifies to her beauty:

> As fair as flawless jade,
> Her grace put flowers to shame.
> Had she put on palace dress,
> Another Lihua[8] she would be.

Jin Laoda cherished his daughter as a jewel and taught her from an early age to read and write. By fifteen or sixteen, she was already accomplished in prose as well as verse and wrote with the greatest ease. She was equally skilled at needlework and playing the zither and flute. Indeed, she excelled in everything she did. Considering her talent and her beauty, Jin Laoda was determined to find her a scholar for a husband. In fact, such a girl would be difficult to find even among old families of distinction, but, being the daughter of a beggar chief, she received no proposals of marriage. On the other hand, Jin Laoda had no wish to give her away to some petty trader without a future. Thus, unable to claim kinship with those of higher social status but refusing to go lower, Jin Laoda let the years go by, and the girl was now eighteen but still unbetrothed.

One day, an old man of the neighborhood came and addressed him as follows: "At the foot of Peace Bridge there lives a student named Mo Ji. He is a handsome and well-learned young man of twenty years of age, unmarried because his parents died, leaving him no money. Recently, he passed the examination qualifying him to be a student at the National University. He's willing to be a live-in son-in-law. Your daughter would be just right for him. Why don't you take him in as son-in-law?"

"In that case," said Jin Laoda, "would you be kind enough to act as the matchmaker?"

And so the old man went straight to Peace Bridge, sought out Scholar Mo, and said to him, "In all honesty, I must tell you that the girl comes from a family of generations of beggar chiefs, but that profession was given up long ago. And what a fine girl she is! The family is well off, too. If you are not disdainful of the match, I'll be happy to bring it off for you."

Without saying anything aloud, Mo Ji thought to himself, "Being short of food and clothing, I am in no position to afford the expenses of taking a wife. Why not stoop a little and marry into that family? Wouldn't I be killing two birds with one stone? I can't afford to concern myself with what people will say in ridicule." He then announced to the old man, "Uncle, that is indeed a nice offer, but I am too poor to buy the wedding gifts. What's to be done?"

"As long as you give your consent, you won't have to pay for even a sheet of paper. Just leave everything to me."

After he reported back to Jin Laoda, an auspicious day was chosen for the wedding ceremony, and the Jin family presented Mo with a new outfit. And so Scholar Mo entered the Jin family as a son-in-law. Yunu's talents and beauty threw Mo Ji into raptures over his unexpected good fortune. Having thus been blessed with a lovely wife at no cost to himself, not to speak of ample food and clothing, he was content in every possible way. Well aware of Mo Ji's straitened circumstances, his friends all understood his decision and no one laughed at him.

When they had been married for a month, Jin Laoda prepared a banquet to celebrate the occasion and had Mo Ji invite his schoolmates so as to bring honor to the house. The wining and dining lasted six to seven days. It turned out, in a way no one would have expected, that Scabby Jin, Jin Laoda's kinsman, took offense, and his anger was not unjustified. "You may well be a chief, but I am one, too," he thought. "Granted that your family has been in this line of business for generations and is loaded with money, we are in fact descendants of the same clan. By rights, I should have been invited to my niece's wedding banquet, and now, to celebrate the first month, a banquet has been going on for a week without my having received even a one-by-three-inch invitation card. Your son-in-law may well be a scholar, but even if he were a head of a ministry or a prime minister, wouldn't I still be an uncle worthy of a seat at the table? How arrogant can you be! Let me give them some trouble and spoil the fun!" He gathered together fifty to sixty beggars and took them to Jin Laoda's residence. Behold:

> *Tattered hats, ragged clothes,*
> *Strips of old mats, matched with strands of frayed rugs,*
> *Short bamboo sticks paired with chipped coarse bowls.*
> *Crying "Father!" "Mother!" "Benefactor!"*
> *They stirred up a commotion at the gate.*
> *Putting on shows with snakes, dogs, and monkeys,*
> *They displayed an assortment of oral skills.*
> *Beating clappers, they sang beggarly tunes;*
> *The ugly sounds jarred on the ears.*
> *Striking bricks, they powdered their faces;*
> *The hideous sight offended the eyes.*
> *When such rowdy demons gather together,*
> *Even Zhong Kui⁹ can't make them submit.*

As the noise reached his ears, Jin Laoda opened the gate to take a look, and in swarmed the beggars, with Scabby Jin leading the way. All hell broke loose. Scabby ran straight up to the banquet tables and stuffed himself with the best food and wine. "Tell the newly wedded couple, my niece and her husband, to come and make bows to their uncle!" he demanded.

The scholars present were so frightened that they took to their heels, with Mo Ji following them. Jin Laoda could do nothing but repeatedly plead with Scabby, "My son-in-law is the host today. I have nothing to do with it. I'll invite you as a special guest another day to apologize." He distributed a good deal of cash among the beggars and took out two jars of fine wine and some live chickens and geese for them to carry over to Scabby's house as compensation. The noisy crowd did not depart until late at night, leaving a mortified Yunu shedding tears in her room.

That night Mo Ji stayed with a friend and did not return until the following morning. The sight of his son-in-law sharply reminded Jin Laoda of the disgrace, and his face burned with shame. Mo Ji could not help experiencing some rancor, but none of them brought their feelings into the open. Truly,

> *A mute tasting bitter cork-tree bark*
> *Cannot express his disgust through words.*

Now let us come back to Jin Yunu. Regretting her lowly family connections, she urged her husband to apply himself assiduously to his studies so as to attain a higher status. She would go to any expense to buy books, classical as well as contemporary, for her husband to read. She engaged tutors for discussions and lectures, never begrudging the cost. She also provided money for him to make his name better known by enlarging his circle of acquaintances. (*Of first importance.*) As a result, Mo Ji made steady progress in his studies and began to build a name for himself.

At the age of twenty-three, he passed a series of examinations all the way up to the highest level. That day, after the celebration banquet in honor of the successful candidates, he rode on horseback to his father-in-law's home, wearing a black hat and an official's robe. Before he had gained the door of the house, some neighboring children rushed over for a look. Pointing at him, they cried out, "Beggar Chief Jin's son-in-law is now an official!" (*It may be shameful for an official's son-in-law to be a beggar chief, but how can it be shameful for a beggar-chief's son-in-law to be an official?*)

On horseback, Mo Ji heard these words, but, as he could not very well make a scene, all he could do was put up with it. Though he was not remiss in observing proper etiquette on greeting his father-in-law, he was boiling with rage inside. He thought to himself, "Had I known earlier that I would be this successful, I could well have waited for some noble family to take me in as a son-in-law. Instead I've got a beggar chief for a father-in-law. Isn't this a lifelong disgrace? My children will be laughed at as a beggar chief's grandchildren. But since things have come to this and my wife is a virtuous woman who has not committed any of the seven offenses,[10] I cannot very well break with her. Truly, as the saying goes, 'Acting before you think thrice is to invite regrets in a trice.'"

He sank into despondency. To Yunu's repeated questions about his low spirits, he remained silent, much to her bewilderment. How ludicrous it is that while reveling in his newly gained eminence, Mo Ji forgot his humble, poverty-stricken past and what his wife had done to help him achieve fame. Indeed, his heart was not in the right place.

Shortly thereafter, Mo Ji was appointed comptroller of revenue of Wuwei County.[11] His father-in-law laid out a farewell feast. This time the beggars, as one would expect, dared not barge in to stir up trouble again.

Luckily, Wuwei County could be easily reached from Lin'an by water. Mo Ji took along his wife and embarked on a boat to make the journey to his new post. A few days later, they arrived at Caishi Cliff and moored off the north bank. That night, the moonlight was as bright as day. Unable to sleep, Mo Ji rose, put on his clothes, and sat down at the prow to enjoy the moon. He looked around without seeing anyone about. The thought of being connected with a beggar chief again plunged him into melancholy. All of a sudden, an evil idea came to his mind: "The only way to rid myself of this otherwise life-long shame is for this woman to die, so that I can marry another."

He quickly devised a plan. He entered the cabin and tried to coax Yunu into rising from the bed to watch the moon in its splendor. She was asleep, but he insisted that she get up, and she did not want to resist her husband's wishes. She threw on some clothes and walked to the cabin door. As she unsuspectingly craned her neck to look at the moon, Mo Ji dragged her out onto the prow and pushed her into the river. Quietly, he woke up the boatmen and told them to get under way immediately, for which they would get a handsome reward. Without knowing why they were to do so, the boatmen made haste and punted and rowed their way ahead.

It was not until the boat had covered a good ten li that Mo Ji said, after they had moored again, "The mistress fell into the water while looking at the moon. It was too late to save her." So saying, he handed out three taels of silver to the boatmen for them to buy wine with. The boatmen now knew what was afoot, but who dared say anything? The stupid maidservants on board believed his story about the mistress having accidentally fallen into the river and cried bitterly before they gave it up, but of them, no more. There is a poem in evidence:

> Because the name Beggar Chief lacked grace,
> He abandoned his wife when his luck changed.
> Ties made in heaven are not to be broken;
> All he gained was the name Heartless Man.

As coincidence would have it, no sooner had Mo Ji's boat moved away than a certain Xu Dehou, on his way to his new post as commissioner of transportation in Huaixi, moored his boat off the north bank of Caishi Cliff at the very spot where Mo Ji had pushed his wife into the water. Xu Dehou and his wife, not yet retired for the night, were looking at the moon through the open window over a cup of wine. All of a sudden, they heard from the bank a woman's bitter sobs, heartrending to hear. Anxiously, they asked the boatmen to look around, and, indeed, there was a woman sitting all by herself on the shore. They invited her aboard and asked her who she was. It turned out that she was none other than Jin Yunu, wife of the comptroller of revenue of Wuwei County.

When she first fell into the water, she was frightened out of her wits and gave herself up for dead. Suddenly she felt something in the water supporting her feet, enabling her to float on the water until she came to the bank. When she struggled ashore and took a look around, all that met her eyes was a vast expanse of water. The comptroller's boat was nowhere in sight. It was not until that moment that she realized that her husband, having achieved higher status, had turned his back on his humble past and determined to drown her in order to get himself another wife. Though she had now escaped death, she had nowhere to go for support and was therefore reduced to bitter tears.

Mr. Xu's questions prompted her to give a detailed account of everything that had happened. As she finished, she broke down in another torrent of weeping. The Xu couple were also moved to tears. They said in an attempt to placate her, "Don't grieve so. If you would agree to become our adopted daughter, we'll think of what to do next."

Yunu bowed in thanks. Mr. Xu told his wife to get some dry clothes for Yunu to change into and gave the latter the exclusive use of the back cabin. The servants, male and female, were told to call her the Young Mistress. The boatmen were instructed not to say anything about what had happened.

In a couple of days, Mr. Xu arrived at his post. Wuwei County being under Mr. Xu's jurisdiction, Comptroller Mo naturally joined the other officials to pay his respects to Mr. Xu, his superior. At the sight of Mo Ji, Mr. Xu thought to himself, "What a shame that such a fine-looking young man is capable of such treachery!" (*Mr. Xu is a marvelous man.*)

Several months later, Mr. Xu announced to his subordinates, "I have a beautiful and talented daughter, now of marriageable age. I would like to select a son-in-law to live in our household. Can you think of anyone?"

Having heard before that young Comptroller Mo had lost his wife, the officials, in unison, recommended Mo to Mr. Xu, saying that with his outstanding attributes, he would qualify as a good candidate.

"I have had my mind set on that young man also for quite some time," said Mr. Xu. "However, having achieved success so young, he must have higher aspirations than to marry into our household."

His subordinates objected, "Being of humble origin, he should be only too grateful for your help in advancing his status, for he will be like a creeper that attaches itself to a jade tree. Far be it from him to object to living with his wife's family."

Mr. Xu said, "Since you believe this can be done, would you convey the message to him? To find out what he thinks, just say that you're approaching him on your own initiative. Don't mention my name, for he might be embarrassed."

Thus instructed, the officials told Mo Ji about this and offered to serve as matchmakers. Eager as he was to seek connections in high places, Mo Ji was only too happy to form a marriage alliance with his superior. Joyfully, he said, "I am in your hands. I will surely repay you for your kindness in making the match."

"Just leave everything to us," said the officials, who then reported back to Mr. Xu.

"Though the comptroller of revenue was kind enough to accept the proposal," said Mr. Xu, "my wife and I have always so doted on our daughter that I'm afraid she is quite spoiled. That is why we wish that she remain with us after she marries. But the comptroller, being the young man he is, might not be as obliging, and the slightest trouble in the marriage would be painful to my wife and me. I will agree to take him into the family only if he is prepared to be forbearing in every way."

The officials again conveyed the words to Mo Ji, who readily agreed to everything. Having come a long way from his humble days as a poor scholar, he offered gold flowers and fine silk as wedding gifts and selected an auspicious date for the wedding ceremony. Eagerly, he made the preparations for the event, his bones itching and his pores oozing with the desire to be the transportation commissioner's son-in-law.

In the meantime, Mr. Xu told his wife to say to Jin Yunu, "My old man hates to see you live like a widow and wishes to get you another young man with a *jinshi* degree for a husband. You must not object."

"I may be from a humble family," replied Yunu, "but I know very well what constitutes proper decorum. I married Mo Ji, and so I should stay married to him till I die. For all his snobbery and ill will, I shall still do my best to fulfill my obligations. How can I remarry at the expense of womanly virtue?" With these words, she broke down in a flood of tears. (*A woman hard to come by.*)

Convinced of her sincerity, Mrs. Xu told her the truth: "The young *jinshi* is none other than Mo Ji. My old man is angry at Mo's heartlessness but is determined to save the marriage. He spread the word that he would like to take in a son-in-law for his daughter. At his instruction, his subordinates made the proposal to Mo Ji, who readily agreed and will be joining our household tonight. The moment he steps into the bridal chamber, this is what you must do to avenge yourself . . . "

Only then did Yunu stop weeping. She redid her toilette, changed into new clothes, and started busying herself with preparations for the wedding.

When evening came, the immaculately dressed Comptroller Mo, wearing a red brocade cape and a hat with a gold flower, rode on a fine horse with a decorated saddle to the Xu residence, led by two drum bands. All of Mr. Xu's subordinates came to join the wedding procession, which drew enthusiastic applause all along the way. (*What a moment of joy!*) Truly,

> Amid the drum music came the white horse;
> A dashing, wondrous son-in-law he was!

Rejoicing at the exchange of in-laws,
For what happened at Caishi he felt no grief.

That night, the transportation commissioner had carpets spread out and colorful festoons hung up. A band struck up joyous music in anticipation of the bridegroom. When Comptroller Mo arrived and dismounted from his horse, the formally dressed Mr. Xu went out to receive him. After the officials in the entourage took their leave, Mo Ji headed straight for the private quarters. The bride, her face covered with a red kerchief, emerged from inside, supported by two waiting women. With the master of ceremonies shouting instructions from beyond the balustrade, the bride and the bridegroom bowed to heaven and earth, to the bride's parents, and to each other. They were then escorted into the nuptial chamber for the wedding feast. Mo Ji was on cloud nine with joy that defied description. His chin way up, he jauntily entered the chamber.

Hardly had he crossed the threshold than seven or eight maidservants, old and young, emerged from both sides of the door. Armed with thin bamboo staffs, they pounced upon him, knocking off his black gauze hat. As the blows landed on his shoulders and his back like rain, the terrified comptroller of revenue yelled unceasingly, not knowing what to do. (*It wouldn't be as interesting just to have the couple reunite. The beating is what affords gratification.*) He crouched on the floor and cried out in desperation, "Father-in-law! Mother-in-law! Help!"

At this juncture, a sweet voice from inside the chamber was heard saying, "Don't beat that heartless man to death. Bring him to me."

The blows stopped. The maidservants pulled him by his ears and arms in the same way that the six senses had tormented Amita Buddha,[12] and carried him to the bride, his feet barely touching the floor. "What did I do wrong to deserve this?" demanded Mo Ji. (*Vivid description.*) When he opened his eyes, whom did he see by the light of the many candles but his deceased wife, seated solemnly in bridal attire. Frightened out of his wits, he screamed, "A ghost! A ghost!"

The maidservants giggled with amusement. At this moment, Mr. Xu stepped into the chamber, exclaiming, "My good son-in-law, have no fear. This is no ghost but my daughter, whom I adopted at Caishi Cliff."

It was only at these words that Mo Ji's heartbeat returned to normal. Getting down on his knees with alacrity, he said with both hands folded in front of him, "I now realize what wrong I did. I beg your forgiveness."

"This has nothing to do with me," said Mr. Xu. "If my daughter has nothing to say about it, well and good."

Spitting in Mo Ji's face, Yunu lashed out, "You heartless scoundrel! Don't you remember Song Hong's lines 'Forget not friends you made in poverty; / Abandon not the wife who shared your hard lot'?[13] After you married empty-handed into my family, it was all thanks to our money that you were able to further your studies, build a name for yourself, and rise as high as you have. I was hoping for the honor that a successful husband brings to his wife. I never expected that you would be so ungrateful and so unmindful of our bond as husband and wife that you would repay kindness with evil and push me into the river. Fortunately, heaven took pity on me and had me rescued by Mr. Xu, who then adopted me as his daughter. If I had died in the belly of some fish and you had taken a new wife, how could you live with your conscience? How can I so abase myself as to be reunited with you!" With these words, she burst into wails of grief, calling him a heartless ingrate amid an unceasing stream of curses. With shame written all over his face, Mo Ji uttered not a word but busily kowtowed and begged for forgiveness.

Believing that Mo Ji had been scolded enough, Mr. Xu raised him to his feet and said to Yunu, "My child, please restrain your anger. Since my good son-in-law has repented, I trust that he will not hurt you again. Though you were husband and wife in the past, you are now a newly wedded couple in this house of mine. For my sake, let bygones be bygones." He turned to Mo Ji and said, "My good son-in-law, it was all your own fault. Do not blame it on any-one else. Tonight, all you need to do is to exercise patience. I will have your mother-in-law come to intercede." So saying, he left the bridal chamber.

In a short while, his wife arrived. It was only after many more mediation efforts that reconciliation was brought about between the two.

The following day, Mr. Xu laid out a banquet in honor of the new son-in-law. In the course of the banquet, he returned the wedding gifts to Mo Ji, saying, "One bride is not to receive wedding gifts twice. You already offered wedding gifts to the Jin family. Therefore, I will not presume to accept any this time."

As Mo Ji remained silent with his head lowered, Mr. Xu continued, "You despised your father-in-law so much for his lowly status that you ceased to love your wife and nearly brought an end to her life. Now what do you think of my rank? I hope it's not so low as to cause you discontent?"

Mo Ji's face went crimson. He left his seat and begged once more for forgiveness. There is a poem in evidence:

> Full of hopes to climb high through marriage,
> He little expects to meet his wife again.
> Beaten, lectured, and shamed,
> Why does he bother to seek new in-laws?

Henceforth, Mo Ji and Yunu lived twice as amicably as ever before. Mr. Xu and his wife treated Yunu as their own daughter and Mo Ji as their own son-in-law. Yunu, on her part, also honored them as she would her own parents. Even Mo Ji was moved. He invited Jin Laoda the beggar chief into their house and supported him to the end of his days. Later, when Mr. Xu and his wife died, Jin Yunu mourned them as a daughter out of gratitude for their kindness. For generations thereafter, the descendants of the Mo clan and the Xu clan claimed kinship and saw a great deal of each other's company. As the poem says,

> *Song Hong is praised for his noble spirit;*
> *Huang Yun[14] is despised for spurning his wife.*
> *Witness Mo Ji, who remarried the same bride;*
> *Such destined bonds are not to be broken.*

Li Xiuqing Marries the Virgin Huang with Honor

On a day of leisure,
I think on the past and present.
How many men in times of peril
Have sidestepped traps through wisdom divine?

Men make wrong moves in moments of panic;
It is women who make wonders happen.
Only a man wiser than a woman
Is worthy of the cap that rests on his head.

It is often said that intelligent women are worthier than men. Since ancient times, there has been no lack of such women. I propose not to speak of the Empress Dowager Lü [d. 180 B.C.E.] of the Han dynasty, the Tang empress Wu Zetian, and others like them whose viciousness led to momentous consequences; nor shall I tell of Zhuang Jiang of Wei, Cao Lingnü, and other women of nonpareil virtue. In the same vein, I shall not speak of Ban Zhao, Ban Jieyu, Su Ruolan, Shen Manyuan, Li Qingzhao, Zhu Shuzhen, and other literary figures of prominence any more than I will speak of Lady Feng of the Former Han dynasty, Lady Ren, Lady Xi, Princess Pingyang, Madam Liu (*See* The History of the Han Dynasty *[Han shu] for more on Feng-shi, with the given name of Liao, and Ren-shi, wife of Cui Ning. See* The Comprehensive Mirror for Aid in Government *[Zi zhi tong jian] for more on Xi-shi, wife of Feng Bao, and Princess Pingyang, wife of Chai Shao. For more on Madam Liu, see* The History of the Jin Dynasty *[Jin shi].*) and other courageous heroines and masterminds of ingenious strategies.[1] I shall tell only of bizarre, enigmatic pretenders to masculinity who lack the yang element—or, rather, true women who are in men's disguise. The stories of their lives, while kindling admiration and affection, also provide entertainment and inspire tributes of praise. Verily,

Tales about women cheer the heart;
Words about men take away the delight.

According to stories from Tang times, there lived in Suiyang of Henan Prefecture a young woman by the name of Mulan [Magnolia], whose father was called into military service at the frontier. Feeling sorry for her ailing father, she donned men's clothing and went in her father's stead. Clad in armor, with a helmet on her head, lance and dagger-axe in hand, and bow and arrows hanging from her waistband, she fulfilled her night patrol duties, ate her meals in the full force of the winds, slept on grass, and endured hardships of every description. When she returned home ten years later upon the expiration of her term of service, she remained a virgin. Not one of the tens of thousands of soldiers at the frontier had any inkling of her true identity as a woman. A poet of later times had these words of praise for her:

> Remarkable as was Tiying of the Han,[2]
> More wondrous were the deeds of Mulan.
> More filial, loyal, and chaste was she
> Than most men could aspire to be.

I shall now tell of another woman, by the name of Zhu Yingtai, who was a native of Yixing in Changzhou. From an early age, she was given to the pursuit of learning. When she heard that Yuhang was where civil arts flourished the most, she expressed her wish to pursue her lessons there. But her brother and sister-in-law objected: "In the old days, upon reaching the age of seven, boys and girls were no longer allowed to share the same seat and the same dining table. How preposterous for a sixteen-year-old like you to travel around and get mixed up with men!" (*Point well taken.*)

Yingtai replied, "I have a better idea." Putting a cap on her head and a belt around her waist, she dressed herself up as a man. Even her brother and sister-in-law failed to recognize her when she walked up to them in her new attire.

It was the beginning of summer when Yingtai was ready to set out on her journey. She plucked a branch of blooming pomegranate flowers and, planting it in a flowerbed, prayed to heaven in these words: "As I, Zhu Yingtai, am about to go on a journey for the pursuit of my studies, I pray that this branch will take root and grow leaves every year as long as my good name and chastity remain unsullied. Should anything dishonorable happen to tarnish the family reputation, may this branch wither and die." With this prayer, she crossed the threshold and went on her way, calling herself Master Zhu the Ninth.

She came to cultivate a friendship with a man by the name of Liang Shanbo, a native of Suzhou. The two studied at the same school and, out of mutual affection and respect, swore an oath of brotherhood. For three years thereafter, they ate together during the day and slept in the same bed at night, without Zhu Yingtai's ever taking off her clothes. There were several times when the puzzled Shanbo asked her a few questions, but each time she got by with evasive answers. Their studies completed by the end of three years, they took leave of each other and went their separate ways home, but not before Yingtai made Liang Shanbo promise to visit her in two months' time.

As it was again the beginning of summer upon her return, the pomegranate branch in the flower bed was heavy with flowers and foliage, which convinced her brother and sister-in-law of her unbesmirched purity. An immensely rich man named Ma in the Village of Peace and Happiness heard about the virtues of the ninth daughter of the Zhu family and asked a matchmaker to approach Yingtai's brother, who readily gave his consent. The preliminaries were completed[3] and the wedding ceremony was scheduled for the second month of the following year. The truth of the matter was that Yingtai was in love with Shanbo and was biding her time until his visit to reveal her plans. Little did she know that Shanbo was detained by some business at home. She did not presume to suggest postponement of the wedding, for fear that her brother and sister-in-law would suspect her motives.

It was not until the tenth month that Shanbo set out on his journey, six months late. Upon his arrival at the Zhu manor, he was told by a tenant upon his inquiry about Master Zhu the Ninth that there was no one by that name in the manor unless he meant Zhu the Ninth Daughter. Suspecting that something was amiss, Shanbo nonetheless submitted his visiting card, whereupon a maid appeared and led him into the main hall, where whom did Shanbo see but Zhu Yingtai herself in full womanly attire. Shanbo was astounded. Only then did he realize that Yingtai was a woman who had been disguised all along as a man. He reproached himself for not having been discerning enough to guess the truth. After an exchange of conventional amenities, he raised the subject of marriage. Yingtai declined, saying she had already been betrothed to Mr. Ma by her brother and sister-in-law. Bitter remorse swept over Shanbo for having come too late.

After Shanbo returned home, he pined away till he died in his sick bed as the year drew to a close. His parents buried him at the intersection leading to the Village of Peace and Happiness, as he had requested. The following year, as Yingtai's wedding procession approached that intersection on its way to the Ma residence, there sprang up a savage blast of wind that darkened the sky, preventing the procession from moving on. As Yingtai raised her eyes, there wafted into her view Liang Shanbo himself, saying, "I died of lovesickness for you and am buried at this very spot. For old time's sake, please step out of the sedan-chair and take a look." As Yingtai did so, the ground split open with a loud bang, leaving a ten-feet wide gap, into which she threw herself. Her clothes, which followers in the procession tried to grab, flew off in pieces, like skin sloughed off by a cicada. The next moment, the sky cleared. The crack in the ground was found to be no wider than a thread, and the sedan-chair was seen resting right by Liang Shanbo's tomb. Now the realization came that the two sworn brothers in life were now husband and wife in death. Eyes then turned to the floating pieces of Yingtai's clothing, which changed into a pair of colorful butterflies. As legend has it, it was the spirits of the couple that had changed into the butterflies, the red one being Liang Shanbo, the black one Zhu Yingtai. The species multiplied and spread throughout the land and are, to this day, still called Liang Shanbo and Zhu Yingtai. A later poet left behind these words of praise:

> For three years they shared their days and nights;
> The marriage bond was fulfilled only after death.
> Blame not Shanbo for overlooking the truth;
> Praise Yingtai instead for her unflinching virtue.

There was another woman by the name of Huang Chonggu, a native of Lingqiong of Sichuan, who was as beautiful as she was clever and well versed in poetry. Both of her parents had died, leaving her with no relatives to turn to. When Prime Minister Zhou Xiang was inspecting the area, Chonggu disguised herself as a male scholar and presented to the prime minister the poems she had written. Zhou Xiang was so impressed with every poem and every single word in them that he appointed her assistant prefect. She proved to be a wise administrator and solved beyond a shadow of a doubt all the long-pending thorny court cases as soon as they were brought to her attention. She was appointed acting prefect and county magistrate many times. Her name having spread far and wide, she was held in awe by petty court clerks and in reverence by the common people. Zhou Xiang recommended her to the imperial court for an important appointment befitting her remarkable ability. Wishing to have Chonggu as his son-in-law, Zhou Xiang even asked the prefect to act as the matchmaker. To these offers, Chonggu smiled but held back any answer. While she was having an audience with him, Zhou Xiang made the offers again, whereupon Chonggu asked for paper and a pen and composed a poem, which she handed to the prime minister. The poem is as follows:

> No longer frolicking by the green river,
> In poverty I lived in a hut and wrote poems.
> Upon donning the blue robe of office,
> I bade farewell to my mirror and eyebrow brush.
> My integrity stands tall like a pine tree;
> My virtue is as unblemished as white jade.
> If you want me for a son-in-law,
> May heaven first change me into a man.

The prime minister was aghast. Further questioning left him with no doubt as to her gender. It being an offense against decency for a woman to pose as a man, the whole matter could hardly be publicized. Chonggu resigned from her post as she was told to do, lived in seclusion outside the city wall, and married a scholar chosen for her from the same district. Later, the scholar attained the *jinshi* degree through examinations and gained exalted office, and Chonggu was repeatedly granted noble titles. However, according to the play "The Story of Spring Peach"[4] currently being staged, Huang Chonggu won the honor of becoming a woman *zhuangyuan,* but that is sheer exaggeration. A poet of later times had this to say of her:

> *A gem of a poet with a graceful style,*
> *In governing she also proved her might.*
> *If born in Empress Wu's times,*
> *They would have made a pair of female heroes.*

The stories you have just heard are, without exception, about women of previous dynasties. I shall now tell a story that took place in recent times during the Hongzhi reign period [1488–1505] of the great Ming dynasty. There lived in Shangyuan County of Yingtian Prefecture, Nanjing, a man by the name of Huang, who made a living by selling incense sticks and other miscellaneous items, traveling around in the region north of the Yangzi River. Observing his fairness in doing business, the local people called him Honest Huang. His household consisted of a wife and two daughters, the elder of whom was named Daocong, the younger one Shancong. Daocong having been married to Zhang the Second of the Green Creek Bridge district in the same city, only Shancong, twelve years of age, stayed at home. Their mother was seized with a sudden illness and died. The funeral over, it was necessary for Honest Huang to set out on another business trip north.

He thought to himself, "I fear for my unbetrothed young daughter's safety if she is left alone in the house with no company. It would not be proper to leave her with her brother-in-law, either. On the other hand, if I give up the business that I have come to know well, where can I find the money to support us?" Turning his mind this way and that, he could not decide whether to leave or stay. Orders for his merchandise had already been made, but he was still at a loss what to do about his daughter. After giving much thought to this problem for days, he hit upon an idea: "That's it! Since I'll have no company on my journey, why don't I dress her up as a boy and take her with me? I'll think of another way out after she grows up. There is one catch, though. My patrons up north all know that I do not have a son. If I take the child along and then give way under their questions, wouldn't I be held up to ridicule? I'll just say that she is a nephew of the Zhang family, out on the journey as an apprentice. That shouldn't stir up any suspicion." His mind thus made up, he got his daughter's consent and made a boy's robe and socks, which he then put on her. In this outfit, complete with a cap on her head, she became indeed a fine boy to look upon. Truly,

> Her eyes and brows bespoke refinement;
> Her mind by nature was quick and clever.
> Nine out of ten of those without male issue
> Would gladly adopt her to be their son.

Honest Huang and his daughter, selling merchandise along the way, arrived by boat in Luzhou Prefecture north of the [Yangzi] river and lodged in an inn. Impressed with Shancong's refined looks, the innkeeper was full of praise for the youngster and asked Huang, "How is this child related to you?"

"He is called Zhang Sheng and is a nephew of mine. Since I have no son, I am taking him along to let him get to know the patrons so that he can take over the business in the future." No one took the explanation amiss. Every day, Honest Huang went out to attend to his business, dispatching goods and collecting debts, leaving Shancong behind to watch over the single guest room that he had booked. In his absence, Shancong did not cast one undue glance around, nor did she walk one step too many. Her good behavior won her the hearts of all and sundry, and they all said Young Master Zhang was even more honest than his grandfather.[5]

As the proverb has it, "There are unexpected storms in nature, just as there are unforeseen vicissitudes in life." Less than two years had gone by when Honest Huang fell ill in Luzhou and died after all attempts at treatment failed. With bitter tears, Shancong bought a coffin, put her father's body in it, and placed the coffin, for the time being, in an old temple outside the city wall.

After much thought, she decided that as a young orphan girl, she could not very well wander from place to place. Now, staying in the guest room next to hers was a traveler, also in the incense trade, from her home prefecture. Convinced by her observations that he was a trustworthy young man, she asked him about his name and background. The young man replied, "I am Li Ying, courtesy name Xiuqing. Since childhood, I have been following my father on his business travels. Now that my father is too advanced in years to bear the hardships of a traveling life, he gave me the capital and made me take over the business."

Shancong said, "I am Zhang Sheng. I came here with my grandfather. To my great sorrow, he died, leaving me with no one to turn to. If it is agreeable to you, I will gladly pledge brotherhood with you and enter into a business partnership so that we can have each other to fall back on."

Li Ying agreed: "I could hope for nothing better."

As Li Ying was eighteen years of age, Zhang Sheng's senior by four years,

Zhang Sheng honored him as elder brother. The two got along amicably. In their discussion a few days later, the brothers came up with the idea that it would be more efficient for the business if one of them went to Nanjing to sell goods while the other stayed in Luzhou to take care of dispatching goods and collecting debts. Shancong said, "I am too young. Moreover, I am too ashamed to return to my native town without being able to afford to escort my grandfather's coffin back. It would be better if you do the traveling to Nanjing." Thereupon Zhang Sheng gathered together the capital and handed the money to Li Ying, who, in turn, entrusted Zhang Sheng with the ledgers and what was left of the inventory. On both sides of the business, they were fair and honest to the last penny.

Henceforth, all their luggage was stored together in one room. Every time Li Ying came to Luzhou, the two shared the same room, just as they shared the same dining table and the same bed at night. Much to Li Ying's amazement, Zhang Sheng never took off any piece of clothing when he slept, not even his shoes and socks. Zhang Sheng's explanation for this oddity was "I've had an ailment since childhood that makes me sensitive to cold. The moment I unbutton my underwear, I become violently ill. I've grown quite used to sleeping in my clothes like this."

Li Ying shot another question at her: "Why is there a hole in each of your earlobes?"

"When I was a child, the fortune-teller my parents consulted said I was threatened by a predestined disaster. That is why they had my earlobes pierced [to pass me off as a girl]."

Being the trusting person that he was (*He was indeed!*), Li Ying took her word for the truth. Not a doubt entered his mind. Zhang Sheng, for her part, exercised great caution to hide her identity. She never failed to wait until dark to use the lavatory, unobserved. Therefore, she did not betray herself in all the years she lived in this place, as these lines attest:

> *Though physically different men and women are,*
> *Her caution hid all telltale signs.*
> *But one detail might give her away:*
> *Her three-inch feet that made her steps sway.*

Thus, Huang Shancong plied her trade in Luzhou Prefecture under the pseudonym of Zhang Sheng. From the time she came to this place at the tender age of twelve, nine years sped by like an arrow, and, quite unnoticeably, she reached the age of twenty. Through her assiduous work in the last few years, she was now in possession of a goodly amount of cash. In these changed circumstances, her thoughts turned to her father's coffin, which remained unburied in a town other than his native place, and to her sister, whom she had not seen in all these years. Moreover, her own future was by no means settled. With these considerations in mind, she told Brother Li Xiuqing about her wish to take her grandfather's coffin back home for a proper burial. Li agreed, "This is an act of filial piety. But a coffin, unlike anything else, is too much for you to take care of by yourself. Let me go with you so that, as older brother, I won't have to worry in your absence. We'll come back together after the funeral is over." Zhang Sheng thanked her brother for his kind offer.

That very night, they chose an auspicious day to start on the journey. When that day arrived, they engaged several monks for a sutra-chanting service to remove the spirit tablet that had been set up for the deceased. The coffin with the body of Honest Huang was then carried onto a hired boat. The boat set sail when the wind was favorable and stopped when the wind blew in the wrong direction, and arrived in Nanjing before many days had passed. They found a vacant house outside Chaoyang Gate and deposited the coffin there to await an auspicious day for the burial.

Let us skip unnecessary descriptions but come to the moment when Li Ying and Zhang Sheng were about to go their separate ways once inside the city gate. "Where is my brother's home located?" asked Li. "I wish to pay you a visit sometime."

"My family's house is right by Green Creek Bridge on the Qinhuai River. I'll be waiting for you to come have a cup of tea." Thereupon they took leave of each other.

Being of the Huang family, how was she to know the way to her brother-in-law's house? Fortunately, the Qinhuai River was not some obscure place but a well-known name that proved to be of great assistance in her quest for direction there. When she found herself by Green Creek Bridge, she asked again for the Zhang residence and stepped right into the house after a knock or two at the door.

It happened that her brother-in-law was not at home that day. As she walked straight in, her sister, Daocong, lashed out, "Every decent household has its inner quarters off limits to outsiders. What shameless rascal is this, charging straight into the inner quarters! Should the man of the house see you, you'll be in for a hundred raps on your anklebone! Get out of my sight this minute!"

With great composure, Zhang Sheng made a bow and exclaimed with a broad grin, "Elder sister! Don't you recognize your own brother?"

Her sister snapped back, "Glib-tongued scoundrel! I have no brother!"

Zhang Sheng continued, "Try to remember what happened nine years ago."

"I don't have to try!" retorted her sister. "My memory goes as far back as another nine years before that! My father had no son but just two daughters.

My younger sister Shancong was taken by my father on a business trip north of the river to sell incense. They never came back, nor have they been heard of ever since. I don't even know if they are dead or alive. Who are you to lay false claim to being my brother!"

"If you want to know about your sister Shancong, I am none other than she." With these words, Zhang Sheng burst into loud sobs.

Her sister was still incredulous. "If you are, why are you dressed like this?"

"Before we set out, Father disguised me as a boy and claimed that I was Zhang Sheng, his nephew, following him on the trip to learn the business. All too unexpectedly, Father died of a sudden illness two years later. Though I did encoffin the body, I regret to say that I was too poor to escort it back home. There is an honest and upright man named Li Xiuqing who comes from the same place we do, with whom I vowed an oath of brotherhood and entered into a business partnership for lack of alternatives. Another six or seven years in the same place went by. I couldn't make plans for a return journey until this year. And now here I am, back to visit you, my sister."

"I see. Since you've been in business with a man for so many years, you must already be man and wife. As the proverb has it, 'Honest people do nothing under the table.' Why don't you tie up your hair into a chignon with a circlet? You'll look better that way. How shameful you look now, neither like a man nor a woman!"

Zhang Sheng defended herself: "I won't hold the truth back from you, my sister. I'm still a virgin. How could I dream of bringing disgrace to the family by doing dishonorable things!"

Unconvinced, Daocong led her into a secluded room for a test behind closed doors. What, you may well ask, is this test like? This is how such a test is conducted: Put some fine dry ashes into a chamber pot. Have the woman to be tested pull down her lower garments and sit on the pot. Roll a sheet of tissue paper into a stick and poke it into the woman's nose to induce a sneeze. The woman who has lost her virginity will have air pass through her lower body at the same time that air passes through the nose with the sneeze, thereby blowing the ashes in the pot. If still a virgin, the ashes will remain undisturbed. This is a test used in the imperial court in the selection of consorts for the emperors. Being born and raised in the capital, Daocong surely was not ignorant of the method. The test proved Shancong to be a virgin, just as she claimed. The two sisters fell on each other's shoulders and wept. With all the haste she could muster, Daocong opened the family chest, from which she took out her own clothes for her sister to change into, after a bath in perfumed water. Shancong said, "To tell you the truth, my sister, during all these years since I left home, I have never taken off my clothes and bared my body. Only now, in your presence, do I feel at ease."

That night Zhang Er, after returning home, slept in another room at his wife's bidding, leaving the sisters under the same quilt on the same bed, where they poured out their hearts and talked away the whole night, without so much as sleeping a wink.

The following morning, after she rose and did her toilette, Huang Shancong presented herself in her new attire to her sister and brother-in-law, to whom she extended greetings anew. Daocong was full of praise to her husband of her sister's chastity. Her enthusiasm even extended to Li Xiuqing: "If he were not an honest man, how could my sister have maintained so many years of friendship with him?" Before these words were quite out of her lips, a cough was heard from outside the door, followed by the question "Anybody home?"

Huang Shancong recognized Li Xiuqing's voice. "Please have my brother-in-law go out to meet him," she implored of her sister. "I can't very well see him in my present state."

Daocong objected, "Since you've pledged brotherhood with him, and he is such a good man at that, there's nothing wrong in your meeting him." But Shancong turned bashful and refused to go to the door. Daocong was obliged to bid her husband to greet the visitor and to judge by the way he spoke if he was aware of the truth about Shancong. Without a moment's delay, Zhang Er went out to receive the visitor. After the customary salutations, the two took seats—one as the host, the other as the guest of honor.

"I am Li Ying," the visitor started by identifying himself. "I am here to visit my brother Zhang Sheng. May I ask how you are related to him?"

Zhang Er said, beaming with smiles, "I am a close relative of his. I'm afraid that you made a trip for nothing, because Zhang Sheng may not wish to see you today."

"How is that possible? We are loving, sworn brothers, even though we don't share the same surname. How can he refuse to see me when I am here today for the very purpose of fulfilling a mutual agreement?"

Zhang Er hastened to pacify him: "Please allow me some time to explain the reason behind this." But Li Xiuqing would not listen and was in such a state of vexation that he was on the verge of an outburst of rage. A consternated Zhang Er scurried into the inner quarters and beseeched his wife to urge her sister to go forth to meet Li Xiuqing, but Shancong refused to budge, whereupon Zhang Er and his wife slipped away, but they sent someone to lead Li Xiuqing into the inner part of the house.

No sooner had Xiuqing caught sight of Huang Shancong than he recoiled several steps before even getting a clear view of her. Shancong said loudly, "Brother, do not hesitate. Please come forward for a talk."

The voice reassured Xiuqing that he was looking at Zhang Sheng himself.

He stepped forward and asked with a bow, "My brother, why are you in these clothes?"

"It's a long story," said Shancong. "Please take a seat, and let me tell you everything." With Li seated facing her, she gave a full account of the circumstances leading to her departure from home with her father at the age of twelve. "My heart overflows with gratitude for your help and support," she continued. "However, as sworn brothers in the past, we are likely to come under suspicion for misdemeanor as man and woman. Therefore, this will be the last time we see each other."

Xiuqing was struck speechless for a considerable time, all the while reproaching himself for being so blind as not to have known earlier that it was with a woman that he was sharing every moment of his life—day and night—for all those five or six years.

"Please listen, my sister," he said. "We both know that we were greatly attached to each other during all these years. Let's say no more about what has gone by. Now, since both of us are unbetrothed and of the right age, why don't we put our brotherhood behind us and get married? Wouldn't it be perfect for us to grow old together in a blissful matrimony without ever having to leave each other?"

Shancong flushed crimson with embarrassment and rose to her feet. "I took the liberty of seeing you today at the risk of incurring suspicion only because I thought you were an honorable man. But what you said is a violation of proper etiquette. Such a thought could not be further from my mind." While heading for the inner quarters of the house, she continued, "Please go away now to avoid gossip."

Dispirited by this lecture, Li Xiuqing returned home in a trance. Unable to bear the thought of losing Shancong, he asked a matchmaker to intercede for him with the Zhang family. Zhang Er and his wife were by no means averse to the marriage proposal, but Shancong was not to be shaken in her resolve. She said, "I cannot but try to hold myself above suspicion in a delicate situation like this. If I were to marry him, I'd be held up to ridicule and all my efforts at preserving my chastity during those seven years would be cast to the winds, even though no impropriety was ever committed." (*A woman moralist indeed! Truly respectable! Truly respectable!*) No amount of dissuasion from the matchmaker and her sister could change her mind, but Mr. Li, on the other hand, was determined to have Shancong as his wife and pestered the matchmaker every day with requests to pass on his messages. This insistence annoyed Shancong greatly, but she firmly held her ground without even yielding so much as half an inch. In such circumstances, you may ask, could it be that the marriage was not to take place? Please read what unfolds in the next installment. Truly,

> *Loving brothers for seven years,*
> *From the past they now turn away.*
> *To her virtuous name she adheres*
> *And opts to lose a brother rather than marry.*

There are in this world three kinds of mouths that are more of a terror than all others: a scholar's mouth in which there is a bitter tongue that lashes out at all and sundry; a monk's mouth that takes in food everywhere he goes; and a matchmaker's mouth that spreads gossip to all four corners of the earth. (*Well said.*) How, you may ask, does a matchmaker spread gossip? Listen to this song:

> *Flitting about from one house to another,*
> *She is swift of foot and short of breath.*
> *Seen in companies of three or four,*
> *She need not fear the dogs at the door.*
> *She finds friends in every house, on every street.*
> *To whoever happens to come her way,*
> *She flashes smiles sweet and happy,*
> *And without being asked, gives you the gossip.*
> *Babbling and gabbing she carries on;*
> *At others' expense she wags her tongue.*
> *One household has scandal; soon a hundred will know.*
> *When did she ever let gossip sit till the morrow?*
> *Tea and wine she spares none;*
> *Cheek and brass she has both.*
> *Should a word of praise fall her way,*
> *She'll drool saliva, buckets at a time.*

The extraordinary story about the virtuous Huang Shancong disguising herself as a man was spread through the matchmakers' lips, house by house. One person would pass it on to ten and the ten to a hundred. In no time at all, there was no one in the capital who had not heard of it. Words of praise and admiration were on everyone's lips. Even officials of exalted status, when their conversation turned to this story, would comment, "How remarkable!"

There was a eunuch, Grand Commandant Li, who did not believe what he heard. However, when investigations done at his orders bore out the story, he summoned Li Xiuqing, whose answers were all in accord with what had been told. He asked Xiuqing why he had set his mind upon Miss Huang while there was no lack of beautiful women in the whole wide world, to which Xiuqing replied, "I cannot bear the thought of abandoning those seven years of loving relationship. I have no desire for any other woman."

Out of compassion for the young man, Commandant Li hid him in his tribunal. The following day, he summoned the matchmaker who had served Li Xiuqing and gave her the following instructions: "Go to Miss Huang, whose virtue, as I hear, commands respect, and seek her agreement for marriage to a nephew of mine. You will be rewarded if successful." (*There are no such well-disposed eunuchs, not even one out of ten.*)

In those days, a grand commandant was a most influential official in the imperial court. Who would dare not comply with his wishes? The matchmaker returned to report that Miss Huang had given consent. Using his own money, Mr. Li paid for Xiuqing's betrothal gifts and rented a vacant house, which he had Xiuqing move into quietly before he personally made his appearance and hosted the wedding ceremony, complete with bridal candles and a musical band.

When the bridal veil was lifted after the ceremony was over, the bride and groom could hardly contain their mirth upon recognizing each other. Knowing full well by now that she had fallen victim to Commandant Li's trap, Shancong could not very well reverse the situation.

Mr. Li adopted Xiuqing as his nephew and bought lavish gifts for Shancong as her dowry. (*Who else would be willing to do this?*) He also notified the local authorities, in consequence of which all of the various government branches and the prefects sent contributions, partly in deference to Mr. Li, partly out of genuine good wishes for the remarkable couple. Xiuqing was thus made one of the wealthiest men in the city. (*What a good deal! This is far better than selling incense.*) The loving couple had two sons, one following closely upon the other, who grew up to be eminent scholar-officials. Some prying busybody composed out of all this a ballad titled "The Story of the Incense Seller." There is a poem that bears witness:

> *After seven years in a man's disguise,*
> *Unmarried she resolved to remain.*
> *The tale is told as a lesson for all maidens,*
> *To wipe away all longing for unapproved love.*

There is another poem that specifically praises the fine qualities of Mr. Li the eunuch:

> *He helped preserve virtue and love;*
> *Who among eunuchs is as worthy as he was?*
> *Though not fated for romance in this life,*
> *He sowed the seeds for an alliance in his next one.*

Monk Moon Bright Redeems Willow Green

Newly dug graves are filled with the young;
Practice Chan [Zen] before your hair grows white.
Dark and fraught with danger the road ahead;
Waste no hours of the day seeking wisdom.

The above quatrain makes the point that it is by no account easy for Chan Buddhist monks to attain enlightenment through meditation. Goodness knows how many monks have tried to do so through good works before turning to spiritual devotion, or practiced spiritual cultivation before turning to good works.

In this story I propose to tell of a young man named Liu¹ Xuanjiao, a native of Chongyang in Yongjia County of Wenzhou Prefecture, in the Shaoxing reign period [1131–62] under Emperor Gaozong of the Song dynasty after the imperial court moved to the south. At twenty-five years of age, he was already an erudite scholar well-versed in ancient history. The books he had read could easily fill up five carriages. The death of both of his parents when he was a child had left him an impoverished orphan with neither kith nor kin to turn to. All by himself, he labored at his studies and joined Comptroller Gao's household as a son-in-law. Later, he passed the imperial examinations at the first attempt and assumed, by imperial decree, the post of prefect of Lin'an² in the Ninghai District. His wife, Lady Gao, twenty years of age, was as intelligent as she was graceful in appearance.

And so, less than a year into the marriage, Liu Xuanjiao, now a prefect, having moved into the house of his wife's family, bade farewell to his parents-in-law and, bringing a servant named Sai'er, set out for Lin'an Prefecture to take up his office. Stopping only for food and drink when necessary, they traveled by day and rested by night, and soon arrived in Lin'an, where in and around the Pavilion to Welcome New Officials were already assembled all the subordinate officials, town elders, monks, headmen, archers, foot soldiers, and sedan-chair carriers, all waiting to bid him welcome.

After having unpacked and settled down in his residence, Prefect Liu went to the yamen and exchanged greetings with all of his subordinates. When checking the names against the roster one by one, he found that Monk Yutong was the only person who had failed to make an appearance. A native of Sichuan, the monk resided at Water and Moon Monastery on Bamboo Grove Peak, south of the city. The prefect thundered in a rage, "How can that bald man be so impudent!" He turned to the Chan masters of other temples: "Why is that monk not here to greet me? Bring him here! He shall be called to account!"

The head monks of various temples pleaded, "That monk is a reincarnation of Buddha. He has never left Bamboo Grove Peak, where he has been living for the last fifty-two years. For every obligation to welcome or see off officials, his disciples represent him. (*Nowadays, if there is indeed a monk who has practiced the Buddhist virtues for fifty-two years, a prefect should go and pay him homage. How could the monk be blamed for failing to come and greet him? The prefect is too worldly.*) Please forgive him."

Though the prefect gave in and dropped the idea of apprehending the monk, his mind was still seething. The company dispersed.

On that very day, at the prefect's mansion, a feast was held in the course of which a sixteen-year-old courtesan-singer so impressed the prefect with her beauty and her voice that he asked for her name. She replied, "I am Red Lotus Wu, serving exclusively in the hall for guests of honor."

Before the feast was over, Prefect Liu summoned her and instructed her under his breath in these words: "Tomorrow, go to Water and Moon Monastery and devise some means to coax Monk Yutong into having relations with you. If you succeed, bring me some evidence (*There goes the poison*) and I will give you a handsome reward in addition to releasing you from a courtesan's life. Should you fail, you will suffer for it."

Red Lotus replied, "I will do as you bid, sir." On her way home, she racked her brains for a plan, and, with a knit of her brows, a plan did come to her mind. After she arrived home, she gave her mother a full account of Prefect Liu's talk with her. The mother and daughter spent the whole night discussing the plan.

The following day was overcast, as was typical in the twelfth lunar month, with winter drawing to a close. At noontime, there being no rain, Red Lotus Wu left the city gate, dressed in white mourning clothes and carrying a meal box in her hand. By about three o'clock in the afternoon, when she had almost reached Water and Moon Monastery after covering several li, there sprang up a strong wind with driving rain. She walked up to the monastery gate and leaned against it. Without anyone coming out, she could not very well go in.

It was not until evening had set in that an old monk came out to lock the gate. Red Lotus stepped forward with a bow of greeting. The monk returned the greeting and said, "It is getting dark. Please go back. I need to lock the gate."

With tears streaming down her cheeks, Red Lotus pleaded with another bow, "Please take pity on me. Today being the one hundredth day after my husband's death, I came from the city, where I live by myself, to make some offerings of food at my husband's grave. I was there crying when the rain began and evening set in. With the city gate closed at this late hour, I cannot go home but must spend the night in the monastery. Please have mercy on me, and make the abbot let me stay in the monastery until tomorrow morning, so that I won't fall prey to a tiger on the way back."

Shedding copious tears, she prostrated herself on the ground and did not rise until the monk said, "Please rise. I will do something for you."

Having closed the gate, the old monk led Red Lotus into a small room—his own bedroom—at one end of the monks' quarters, and told her to sit down. Without a moment's pause, he hurried to the abbot's meditation room and reported to him, "There is at the gate a young woman in mourning who says that she was offering food at her husband's grave when she was caught in the rainstorm, and, because the city gate is now closed, wants to be put up for the night here in the monastery before returning to the city tomorrow morning."

The abbot said, "That would be a kind thing to do. Since it's getting late, just have her spend the night in your room, and send her on her way tomorrow morning at the fifth watch."

Thus instructed, the monk went to tell Red Lotus. She made another bow of gratitude, saying, "Dead or alive, I will never forget your great kindness in saving my life." With these words, she sat down on the bench in the monk's room while the monk himself went around the monastery putting everything in order and closing all the windows and doors before returning to the room and lying down on the earthen bed with his clothes on. Having worked hard during the day, he fell asleep immediately.

Situated in the midst of vegetable fields, with no farm houses in sight, Water and Moon Monastery was a most quiet and undisturbed place, especially that night, with the two novices away begging alms. As the night watch drum announced the second watch, Red Lotus began to fret. "What's to be done?" she thought to herself. Much disconcerted, she tiptoed to the abbot's room. The door was closed, but the big latticed window on one side was still brightly lit by a lamp with a glazed shade. The abbot, sitting in meditation on his chair, also saw Red Lotus through the window.

Eyeing the abbot, Red Lotus said in an undertone, "Please have mercy and help me, Abbot."

"Go to the monk's room and leave here tomorrow morning. Do not disturb me in my meditation room. Go quickly!"

Red Lotus took a dozen deep bows outside the window, saying, "Isn't it true, Abbot, that for a monk, mercy is the guiding principle, and kind deeds are the means to enlightenment? My clothes are too thin for the cold night. Please open the door and lend me some clothes. I will be most thankful to you for saving my life." So saying, she broke into sobs. (*Women are full of tears. The abbot should not have let her in.*)

Being the kind-hearted man that he was, the abbot thought to himself, "It would not look appropriate to have someone die of cold right at my door. The ancients said, 'Saving a human life gets you more credit than building seven stupas.'" Thereupon, he got down from his seat of meditation and opened the door to let her in. He gave her an old, worn-out robe of his and returned to his seat of meditation. She walked up to him and, with about a dozen deep bows, said tearfully, "My stomachache is killing me!"

Totally oblivious to her pleas, the abbot remained in his seat with his eyes closed. But the bitterly sobbing young woman leaned her body against him, letting out moans as if in pain. Then she lay down across his lap one moment, sat up to press against him the next, then stood up uttering cries of pain. By the third watch, the abbot's endurance failed him. "Young lady," he said, "why are you crying so hard? Where is the pain?"

"When my husband was still alive, every time I had a stomachache like this, he would take off his clothes and hold me in his arms. With his warm belly against my cold one, the pain would go away. And now my stomach is acting up again, but this time, the night being so cold, I'll surely die. If you'd be kind enough to save my life by pressing your warm belly against me, I'll be cured. If so, I'll owe my second life to your great kindness."

Unable to bear her pleading any longer, the abbot resignedly unbuttoned his patchwork robe and held her to him. (*So he found himself aroused. He must have seen through her designs, but just could not contain himself.*)

Now that she saw her plan was working, she promptly undressed from the waist down and, throwing herself into his arms, said, "Please also take off your underwear and press your warm belly against mine to save my life." He refused. But after urging him repeatedly, she untied his pants, held his member with her delicate fingers, and worked at it until it stood up hard. Then she moved to meet it with her own private parts. The abbot's peace of mind could not but be disturbed. (*At this point in the narration, it becomes clear that the abbot should not have failed to go and greet the prefect.*) His desire stirring at the sight of her alluring body, the two made merry on that very bed of meditation. Truly,

> Tathagata's teachings were cast aside;
> Buddha's last words were thrown to the winds.

Eyes glazed with lust, he panted and moaned,
Like an oriole flitting among willows.
In passion, she let out bewitching cries,
Like a flower being taunted by a butterfly.
By the pillow, the monk muttered sweet words of love,
While Red Lotus swore vows of fidelity.
The abbot's cell became a scene of joy,
And Water and Moon Monastery a land of bliss.

Holding Red Lotus in his arms, the abbot asked, "What is your name? Where do you live? Why are you here?"

"I dare not hide anything from you. I am a courtesan serving the prefectural yamen. My name is Red Lotus Wu. I live by New South Bridge in the city."

Possessed by the Evil One at that moment, he said cheerfully, "Do not let on to others what happened between you and me."

Shortly afterward, when the cavorting was over, Red Lotus tore off with her teeth a sleeve from a white cotton garment, wiped off his fluid with it, and stuffed it into her own sleeve. Though too exhausted to take much notice of what she was doing, the abbot grew a little apprehensive. "There must be a reason why you are here, sister," said he. "Tell me the truth."

He pressed so hard for an answer that Red Lotus saw no other way but to tell him the truth: "The new prefect was so annoyed by your failure to show up to greet him that he sent me here to seduce you."

The abbot was aghast. Bitter remorse swept over him. "The Evil One is upon me. You tricked me and made me break the commandment against lust. I will fall into hell." As the day had already dawned, the abbot had the monk open the gate. Red Lotus bade the abbot farewell and went back as fast as her legs could carry her.

In the meantime, the abbot sent the old monk away to the kitchen to boil some bath water for him, while he himself rubbed his ink stick against the inkstone and, with his brush-pen, composed a poem, "On Departing from This World":

As a monk, my thoughts never strayed;
For fifty-two years, I enjoyed peace of mind.
In a fleeting weak moment,
I broke my vow against lust.
You sent Red Lotus to ruin me,
For I owe her a debt from an earlier life.
You smeared my name as a man of virtue,
The same will I do to your family line.
(He has made up his mind before leaving this world.)

He folded the piece of paper that bore the poem and slipped it under the incense-burner. The monk brought in the hot water and attended to the abbot until he finished his bath and put on a new robe. The abbot then gave the old monk these instructions: "When Prefect Liu of Lin'an sends for me, give the messenger the piece of paper under the incense-burner and have him take it back to the prefect. Do not fail me."

Thus instructed, the monk went away to his daily chores of burning incense and sweeping the ground, without any inkling that Abbot Yutong had already willed himself to death.

Let us follow another thread of the story and come back to Red Lotus. Having eaten breakfast and changed into colorful clothes, she went to Lin'an to see Prefect Liu, carrying with her the sleeve she had torn off. At the sight of Red Lotus, the prefect hurriedly left his seat in the main hall and withdrew into his study, where he questioned the girl about her mission. While supplying a full account of her nocturnal adventure, she showed him the sleeve as evidence. Immensely delighted, the prefect had a small black lacquer box brought from the main hall, put the white cotton sleeve in it, and sealed the box. A brush-pen in hand, he wrote the following quatrain:

> *Monk Yutong of Water and Moon Monastery*
> *Seldom left Bamboo Grove Peak.*
> *How sad that drops of bodhi water*
> *Fell into two red lotus petals.*

He put the poem into an envelope, sealed it, and sent a runner to deliver it to the abbot and to come back immediately with a reply from the latter. The runner left. Prefect Liu rewarded Red Lotus with five hundred strings of cash and released her from her singing duties for one year. Gratefully she returned home with the money, but of her, for the time being, no more.

Now the runner, carrying the letter and the box containing the torn sleeve, went to Water and Moon Monastery and saw only the old monk burning incense in the hall. Asked where the abbot was, the monk led him to the abbot's meditation room, only to find the abbot dead on his meditation chair. The monk said, "The abbot said, 'When Prefect Liu sends for me, give the messenger the letter under the incense-burner by way of reply.'"

Much startled, the runner said, "Only someone who is a reincarnation of Buddha would have predictions as accurate as that." Without a moment's delay, he brought the letter of reply and the small box back to the prefectural yamen, presented the prefect with the letter of reply as well as the prefect's own, and told of the abbot's death.

Upon opening the letter of reply, Liu Xuanjiao was astonished to see that it was a poem on departing from the mortal world. "What a monk! I shouldn't have marred his otherwise perfectly good name." But remorse was now too late. He sent word for a carpenter to make a coffin for the abbot and invited Abbot Fakong of the famous Pure Mercy Monastery of Southern Mountain to direct the cremation ceremony.

Abbot Fakong went first to Prefect Liu's yamen for an explanation. After learning about Abbot Yutong's encounter with Red Lotus, he lamented, "What a pity! In a moment of weakness, that monk deviated from the right path. What you did ruined his virtuous record. I shall go to his cremation ceremony and point out to him the right path to follow, so that he will not stray into the crowd of those condemned to be reincarnated as animals." With these words, he took leave of the prefect and betook himself to Water and Moon Monastery, where he ordered that the coffin be carried into the vacant lot behind the temple. A torch in hand, Abbot Fakong drew a circle in the air and said,

> For decades since he first came here,
> He practiced Buddhism with devotion.
> He wished to have Zhaozhou's[3] enlightened mind,
> But his good fate turned into an evil one.
> By peach blossoms and willows fresh as before
> A creek flows gently past the stones.
> Let me lead you to the road of bodhi;
> Never again covet red lotus.

I hereby respectfully submit to the soul of the deceased Great Monk Yutong:

For fifty years of your simple life, your soul was as clear and bright in all its purity as the shining moon that sheds its unsullied lustre upon the universe. What a pity it was that for all your sagacity, you made a slip; instead of joining the Buddha on Holy Vulture Peak,[4] you succumbed to the charms of Red Lotus. Form should have been emptiness, but who would have known that emptiness has come to be form! You are destined not to enjoy the leisure of a life in heaven bathed in the light of Buddha, but to plunge into the drudgery of the transient mortal world. Though you were on the right road, you went all too quickly. Do not laugh at him, everyone. I will put him on the right path. Behold!

> A point of holy light brightens the sky;
> Into a grand house is born a new life.

So saying, Abbot Fakong threw the torch onto the coffin, which was soon totally consumed. The huge crowd of onlookers saw a golden ray rise from the flames up to the sky. After Abbot Fakong had gathered the ashes and taken them into the pagoda, the crowd dispersed.

That very night, Prefect Liu's wife, Lady Gao, dreamt of a heavily built monk with a face shaped like a full moon walking into her bedchamber. She was so startled that she woke up in a cold sweat. At that very moment, she conceived a child without being aware of it. Time sped by like an arrow. When the pregnancy came to full term, a baby girl was born, whereupon a waiting woman reported the good news to Liu Xuanjiao. When the baby was one month old, she was named Cuicui [Green]. Many a feast was laid to mark the one hundredth day after her birth as well as her first birthday. Truly,

Outside the window, the sun flits by in a finger-snap;
Around the table, the flowers' shadow moves as you sit.

When Liu Cuicui [Willow Green] was eight years old, Liu Xuanjiao completed his term of office and packed up for the journey back to his hometown. However,

Good things in this world do not last;
Pretty clouds disperse, colored tiles break.

Liu Xuanjiao fell victim to an epidemic and died within a few days. Honest and incorrupt while in office as prefect, he left his family with little means. Having encoffined the body, put on mourning clothes, read the scriptures, and deposited the coffin in Liuzhou Temple, his widow wished to return to her hometown, Wenzhou, with her maid Sai'er and daughter Cuicui, but she had no relatives to turn to and too little money for the long journey. Instead, she rented for the three of them a room in front of White Horse Temple in the city. With no regular income, what little savings she had dwindled away in eight years' time. The maid ran away. (*I have often wondered whether the heavenly principles are flawed when children are not granted to officials of integrity. But, as is said often, "Officials of integrity have no issue because they are too harsh to people." The case of Liu Xuanjiao convinces me of the truth of this saying.*)

By this time, Liu Cuicui had grown into a beautiful sixteen-year-old girl. Daily existence for the mother and daughter became so uncertain that they were reduced to asking for loans through the mediation of their next-door neighbor, Mrs. Wang, who obtained for them three thousand strings of public tax money from Chief Clerk Yang of the Yangbatou District of Lin'an. Six months later, the lender pressed them harshly for repayment. Unable to stand the harassment any longer, Mrs. Liu had no alternative but to offer her daughter, through Mrs. Wang, as a concubine to Mr. Yang (*The poison is breaking out*), who, in turn, was to provide for Mrs. Liu in her old age. Within a few days, Mr. Yang came to live with them as the son-in-law, saying, "With me to provide for the two of you in this second home of mine, you will have enough food and clothing."

Before they knew it, two months sped by. Inconvenienced as he was by his obligations, both in terms of time and money, toward two households, Mr. Yang returned one day and consulted with his wife about his intentions of moving back permanently. Subsequent to his father-in-law's filing of a complaint accusing him of taking on a concubine to the neglect of his wife, the Lin'an prefectural yamen had Mrs. Liu and her daughter apprehended. Upon being pressed to return the betrothal gifts, Mrs. Liu, desperate for money, offered Cuicui for sale to the yamen. However, there was a Director Zou in the Ministry of Works who, hearing that Liu Cuicui was a beautiful and clever girl, obtained her release from the yamen and installed her as his concubine, along with her mother, in a house bought for their use on Swordsman Camp Street. In addition, he bought a maid and a serving boy to attend to their needs. Henceforth, Liu Cuicui changed her name to Liu Cui.

At that time, when the imperial court of the Song dynasty had moved south, Lin'an was a most prosperous city. On Tonghe Street under Golden Waves Bridge, there was Flower and Moon House. To the east, there were Bright Spring House and Southern Marketplace. To the south were streets and lanes called Swordsman Camp, Lacquerware Wall, Sandpaper, and Harmony, where marketplaces abounded just as they did in streets to the west with names like Peace, Towels, and Lions.

Being a reincarnation of Monk Yutong, Liu Cui was gifted in the skills of reading and writing. There was nothing she did not know about poems and songs, just as there was nothing she could not do in the arts of sewing and embroidery. As Director Zou did not visit her more than once in ten days or half a month, he should by all accounts have chosen any other location for the house than Swordsman Camp Street, which was most notorious as a brothel-infested place. In her idleness, Liu Cui watched clients of the brothels come and go in the neighborhood and, merrily following the examples set by prostitutes all around her, also took to parading her charms at her door. Ogling men soon began to follow her into the house and stay overnight. Her mother, having protested to no avail, was resigned to becoming her procuress. Many young men from wealthy families fell for her, and not a day was not spent in drinking and carousing. Disgusted at the unruliness, Director Zou severed all ties with her and resolved never to have anything to do with her again. Liu Cui was only too happy to be released from any control he had over her and, casting all scruples to the winds, came out into the open. Her degeneration, in fact, was an act of retribution upon her father, Liu Xuanjiao, for his unkindness; such is the justice of the ways of heaven. People of later generations should by all means take warning from this story. There is a poem in evidence:

> *He who uses tricks shall end up the victim;*
> *He who loves small gains shall end up the loser.*

If by sheer luck he gets away,
His children will surely have to pay.

Later, it was a Buddha who redeemed Liu Cui and brought her back onto
the right path so that she could resume her former identity as a Buddha. Who,
you may ask, is this Buddha who came for the girl's redemption? It was Monk
Moon Bright. Having renounced the world at an early age, he truly observed
the five Buddhist commandments[5] without the slightest deviation. Now the
abbot of Piety Monastery on Mount Gaoting,[6] he had known Abbot Yutong
well in their studies of Buddhism. Upon learning about Yutong's death, he
had laughed heartily, saying, "So, the mother-in-law is not firmly established
in her status, but has to relive the life of a daughter-in-law."[7] Later, when he
got word of Liu Cui's fame as the accomplished beauty of Swordsman Camp
Street, he knew instinctively that she was a reincarnation of Abbot Yutong and
his compassion was aroused.

One day, while Abbot Fakong of Pure Mercy Monastery was paying him
a visit at Piety Monastery, he confided in Fakong, "It has been some time since
old Yutong fell into the company of less than honorable women. My fear is
that he might come to enjoy it and lose his natural qualities. He should be
redeemed and pulled out of that place at the first opportunity."

It so happened that however lowly her status as a prostitute was, Liu Cui
had this to be said about her: she was well-versed, since childhood, in the
teachings of Buddhism. Of the gold and silk and other payments that she
received, she gave much away freely, with never so much as a flinch. Being
Mrs. Liu's own daughter, she was not to be stopped from doing whatever she
had set her mind to. Under the Hill of Ten Thousand Pines, a stone bridge
was built and named Liu Cui Bridge. A well was dug along Swordsman Camp
Street and named Liu Cui Well. Her other deeds of generosity were too many
to enumerate here. She made a rule of removing her makeup, putting on a
plain cotton outfit that had been made for the purpose, and, within closed
doors, offering prayers to Buddha on the first and the fifteenth days of every
month. All visitors, throngs of them, were flatly declined admission on these
days, and this came to be a rule. This was precisely what prompted Monk
Moon Bright to see in the depth of her soul enough innate goodness to be
worthy of redemption. Truly,

Those free from stinginess and greed
Will in the end head for the West.[8]

Abbot Fakong, as enjoined by Monk Moon Bright the previous day, proceeded accordingly to Liu Cui's door on Swordsman Camp Street as if to beg
for alms. Knocking at his wooden fish,[9] he chanted in a loud voice,

In the sea of desire life after life,
Is a perdition that lasts forever.
The glamour and wealth of the moment
All too quickly fade away.
After the end of this life,
All four elements exist no more.[10]
Repent when there is still time;
Renounce the world and embrace the dharma.

Liu Cui, just back from an outing to West Lake, was much impressed by the refined voice and diction of the alms-seeking monk and sent her maid to bring him into the main hall. "Your Reverence," she said, "what ability do you have, that you come here to beg for alms?"

"This poor monk can do nothing more than say a few things about the operations of karma."

"What is karma?"

Abbot Fakong explained, "What went before is the cause and what follows is the effect. The doing is the cause, the results are the effect. In the saying 'Plant melons and you get melons; sow beans and you get beans,' the planting and sowing is the cause and what you get is the effect. If you don't sow, whence can you reap? Good causes beget good effects; evil causes beget evil effects. Therefore, if you want to know the cause in your previous life, look at the effect in this life. If you want to know the effect in your next life, look at what you've done in this life."

Much delighted with this clear explanation, Liu Cui offered him a meal. "Of the multitudes of Buddhas," she continued, "are there any who rose to that status from my lowly world of prostitution?"

"Well, once, troubled by the excessive lust of the beings of this world, the great bodhisattva Guanyin incarnated herself as a most attractive prostitute in a brothel. All men—even of noble birth—who laid eyes on her, were, to a man, overwhelmed by her beauty. But their lust subsided upon the first encounter with her. Evil forces were no match for her immense power. When she died, free of any disease, neighbors bought a coffin and made arrangements for burial. At the sight of her grave, a foreign monk joined his palms in a salute, exclaiming, 'How wondrous!' The neighbors said, 'This is the grave of a prostitute. You are mistaken.' The monk insisted, 'She was no prostitute but a reincarnation of Bodhisattva Guanyin, who had come to redeem the lustful men of the mortal world and to bring them back onto the right path. If you don't believe me, just dig into the grave and see for yourselves. The remains must be most extraordinary.' The neighbors did not believe him. They promptly set about digging into the grave to break open the coffin. Much to their amazement, what they saw was an unbroken chain of bones the color of gold. Consequently, upon that very grave was erected a temple named Temple of the Bodhisattva of Golden-Chain Bones. This is what is known as the 'purity of a lotus untarnished by the silt it grows in.' Your life of sin in this house of ill repute is a corollary to the seed of lust that was sown in a previous existence. If you remain unrepentant and go on selling your charms for the rest of your life, you will be condemned to the sea of desire life after life, with no hope of ever achieving exemption from samsara."

Liu Cui was struck cold by these words. Her jubilant mood plummeted. In a sudden wave of remorse, she said (*Touched by the sincerity of these words*), "What you said about the laws of karma is very enlightening. If you would deign to accept my humble company, I will be most happy to provide you with food and lodging here so that I may profit from your teachings from morning to night. Would you kindly consent?"

"I am not worthy enough to teach you, but there is an Abbot Moon Bright at Piety Monastery on Mount Gaoting in this region who, being a reincarnation of the living Buddha, knows all about everyone's past and future. If you are truly resolved to seek salvation, I will introduce you to him. His words of wisdom will make you see the cause of your present fate, enlighten your mind, and allow you to see your true nature."

"I have long heard of his celebrated name. I will certainly pay him a call tomorrow if you will kindly take me there."

"I will, with pleasure. Just wait for me early tomorrow morning in front of Piety Monastery. Do come without fail."

With her delicate and soft hands, Liu Cui took from her hair a pair of gold hairpins shaped like phoenixes' heads and handed them to the abbot, saying, "This is but a small token of my sincerity. Please do not refuse."

The abbot objected, "Though I do beg for alms, I need nothing other than food. What would a monk do with jewelry?"

Liu Cui insisted, "You may not need it yourself, but this token of my faith can contribute toward repair and maintenance of the monastery."

Turning a deaf ear to her pleas, the abbot joined his palms together in a gesture of gratitude and went away. There is a poem that bears witness:

> *In seeking pleasure and selling charms,*
> *She was the first in Swordsman Camp.*
> *Hearing her fate in her previous life,*
> *She marveled at the laws of karma.*

After the monk's departure, Liu Cui gave herself up to thoughts that kept her awake all night. The following morning, after her toilette was done, she changed into a new outfit and claimed that she was going to Mount Tianzhu to offer incense. Who, including her mother, would dare hold her back? Thus, carried in a sedan-chair that a maidservant called for her, she headed straight for Piety Monastery on Mount Gaoting, where Abbot Fakong was already waiting at the gate.

As Liu Cui alighted from the sedan-chair, the abbot led her past the gate and into Great Hero Treasure Hall, where they kowtowed to the statue of Tathagata before presenting themselves to Monk Moon Bright in his abbot's cell. At the sight of the meditating monk, Liu Cui prostrated herself on the ground, saying, "Your disciple Liu Cui is here requesting an audience."

Instead of returning the greeting, Monk Moon Bright thundered, "Your twenty-eight years of prostitution have already more than repaid your debt. What more do you want to accomplish?"

Liu Cui was so taken aback that she broke into a cold sweat. Something in her stirred as if she were awakening to some truth. Before she could ask further, the monk roared again, "Love has its bounds; rancor will run its course. Only a mind enlightened by Buddhism remains constant. Now that you have evened the score with Prefect Liu, it is time you gathered up your things and went back."

Beginning to see some light now, Liu Cui kowtowed again, saying, "I have heard that in all your wisdom, you know the operations of karma for three lifetimes. Please enlighten me in my ignorance."

Another shout came from the monk: "To know what you were, go to Water and Moon Monastery, ask for Abbot Yutong, and you'll get your proof. (*It's better to do it yourself than to ask for help.*) Be gone this very moment! Go! A moment's delay and I will crush your delicate bones with this ruthless cane of mine!"

This episode is known as "Three Outbursts from the Abbot of the Piety Monastery." Truly,

> *To know the karma of three lifetimes,*
> *Three outbursts of the abbot will suffice.*

After three outbursts from Master Moon Bright, Liu Cui dared not utter another word but rose with alacrity, went out the gate and into the sedan-chair and, with a few words of instructions to the carriers, went straight to Water and Moon Monastery in search of Abbot Yutong for proof.

In the meantime, the acolyte of the monastery, catching sight of a woman's sedan-chair approaching the monastery gate, immediately called caretakers of the monastery to stop her from getting down. To Liu Cui's question as to the reason, the acolyte replied, "The former abbot of this monastery died at the hands of a woman. Therefore, I've been instructed not to let women in."

"What woman? How did it all happen?"

"Twenty-eight years ago, a woman came here and asked to be put up for the night. She sounded so piteous that the old master took her in out of compassion. It turned out that the woman was not a decent sort but a prostitute called Red Lotus Wu, who had been ordered by Prefect Liu to seduce the master. That night, she feigned a stomachache and contrived to have the master press himself against her, thus breaking his vow against lust. Stricken with shame, the master willed himself to death after writing an eight-line farewell poem."

Liu Cui asked again, "Do you remember the poem?"

"Yes, I do." He then recited all eight lines of the poem. When he came to the lines "You smeared my name as a man of virtue; / The same will I do to your family line," Liu Cui suddenly gained a clear idea of what had happened, just as if it had been her personal experience. She asked again, "What was the Buddhist name of the master?"

"Abbot Yutong."

Liu Cui nodded in understanding and, without the slightest delay, had the sedan-carriers carry her back to Swordsman Camp, where she told the maid to boil some water for her bath. After the bath, with the maid attending, Liu Cui tied up her hair, put on her cotton robe, and closed the chamber door. On a table laid out with the four treasures[11] of a scholar's study, she spread out a sheet of white paper and composed two farewell poems. The first one said,

> *A vow against lust gave rise to lust;*
> *The monk's black robe gave in to a red skirt.*
> *Today I have been truly stripped bare;*
> *Nothing is left of the willow and lotus.*

The second one ran as follows:

> *Smearing your name, I too bear the shame;*
> *The cycle of vengeance, when will it end?*
> *I now dispose of all old scores*
> *And return to the temple of twenty-eight years ago.*

She added, "After I'm gone, encoffin me in my everyday clothes, send the coffin to the foot of Mount Gaoting, and ask Master Moon Bright to light the merciless fire of cremation." With this instruction, she threw down her pen and died.

On pushing open the door, the maid noticed no movement, but, upon a closer look, she saw Liu Cui sitting in a chair with her legs crossed in lotus position. Liu Cui's failure to respond to her calls convinced her that she had passed away. (*A free spirit comes and goes readily.*) With all the haste she could muster, she went to report to Madam Liu. Much startled, Madam Liu burst into loud wails, calling her daughter over and over by her pet names. After the initial shock wore off, she read the two farewell poems and the will attached thereon and asked the maid about what had happened on the trip to offer incense at Mount Tianzhu.

Upon learning about the talks with the abbot at Piety Monastery and the acolyte at Water and Moon Monastery, she realized that this was all the fault of her husband, Liu Xuanjiao, who had destroyed Abbot Yutong's ascetic record, an act that led to Yutong's reincarnation into the Liu family to tarnish the family name in justifiable retaliation for the wrong inflicted on him. Now that Monk Moon Bright had laid bare the connections, her daughter had found it an opportune moment to slip away from this life. Liu Cui's wish to be sent to the foot of Mount Gaoting could not be denied, but Madam Liu could not bear the thought of complying with the part of her will concerning her cremation. There were enough clothes and jewelry left behind to pay for a grave. Without letting a moment slip by, Madam Liu bought a coffin and, as instructed, put the body into it with none of the usual brocades, silks, and gold, but only the clothes that the body was found in. This done, all the men in town who had known her came to offer their condolences. There was many a sigh when the way Liu Cui died became known. Madam Liu sent a messenger to Piety Monastery to apprise Monk Moon Bright of the death and to take his counsel on matters relating to the burial. The monk gave Madam Liu a vacant lot at the foot of Mount Gaoting for the burial site. On the propitious day chosen for the ceremony, all of the people in town turned out for what they believed was the funeral of someone who was nothing less than the manifestation of a buddha, as evidenced by the strange death. After the grave was completed, Monk Moon Bright pressed his palms together in salutation and intoned a quatrain that said,

> *Twenty-eight years' debt of lust*
> *Was paid off at long last.*
> *Gone are Willow Green and Red Lotus,*
> *And Yutong enjoys eternal peace.*

The site of Liu Cui's tomb at the foot of Mount Gaoting still exists to this day, as these lines attest:

> *In the end, Liu was hurt by his own scheme;*
> *Lust led Yutong into a life of lust.*
> *With three shouts at Piety Monastery,*
> *All came to light on Mount Gaoting.*

Abbot Mingwu Redeems Abbot Wujie

Once a dweller in the mortal world,
He now joins the Buddhist assembly in heaven.
In the Pure Land, a willow twig in hand,
He looks back upon his previous life.

Our tale begins in the days of Li Yuan [566–635], first emperor of the Tang dynasty, who, taking over the empire from the Sui dynasty, made Chang'an, Shaanxi, capital of the new dynasty and promulgated a new set of laws. With his second son, Li Shimin, leading the troops, he crushed all enemies at the seventy-two border posts and wiped out eighteen barbarian strongholds. During the new Wude reign period [618–26], he founded the Institute of Education, with its eighteen leading scholars; built the Pavilion Reaching into Mists to honor twenty-three men who had rendered him outstanding service; and appointed as successive prime ministers Wei Zheng [580–643], Du Ruhui [585–630], and Fang Xuanling [578–648] so as to bring order to the empire. The years during the reign periods Zhenguan [627–49], Zhiping [1064–67, Song dynasty],[1] and Kaiyuan [713–41] went by in peace and prosperity. It was only toward the end of Emperor Xuanzong's reign [712–55] that the emperor's exclusive shower of favors upon the treacherous court ministers Li Linfu [d. 752], Lu Qi [d. ca. 784], and Yang Guozhong [d. 756] incurred the An Lushan rebellion. Though the insurgence was put down, the dynasty thereafter knew no peace, with border posts breaking away from central rule and eunuchs abusing power in a court where villains replaced worthy men.

Let me now tell of a man in Luoyang by the name of Li Yuan, with the courtesy name Zicheng, an erudite scholar who had learned by heart enough books to fill five carriages and who knew everything there was to know about history from time immemorial. Disgusted at the vice-ridden court, he resigned from office and developed a close friendship with Abbot Yuanze of the local Huilin Monastery. Yuanze, a reincarnation of Buddha, was held in high esteem by all the worthy men in Luoyang of the time for his renown as a poet as well as for his many deeds of compassion. On many a day, the two men would visit scenic spots and historic sites and wax poetic under the inspiration of the moon, wind, mountains, and rivers.

One day, they left on a journey by river for Qutang of the Three Gorges to visit Skyscape Temple. There were four of them in the boat: Li Yuan with his servant and Yuanze with a disciple. Upon arrival in less than two weeks' time, they anchored the boat along the shore and were standing up and straightening their clothes when they caught sight of a pregnant woman about thirty years of age wearing old, worn out clothes over her brocade vest. She carried a jar of baked clay on her back and was drawing water from a clear spring. Yuanze was annoyed. Pointing at the woman, he said to Li Yuan, "This pregnant woman is the one to give me rebirth. I will be on my way to the West² early tomorrow morning."

A startled Li Yuan asked, "What makes you say this?"

Yuanze replied, "I have some farewell words for you before I will my death." Thereupon, the four men entered the monastery, where they were greeted by a monk. After tea, Yuanze explained about his imminent death, much to the astonishment of everyone present. He then took a bath in perfumed water and, after leaving instructions with his disciple, bade farewell to Li Yuan in these words: "It is my good fortune, in my forty years of life, to have enjoyed a close friendship with you, but my time is up and there is nothing I can do but part with you. Three days after my rebirth, please pay a visit to that woman's house, where, while being washed, I will give you a smile as evidence of my identity. I will then die that very night, but will see you again twelve years later, in Tianzhu Monastery in Hangzhou." So saying, he took a pen and a sheet of paper and composed these lines bidding farewell to the earthly world:

> *In forty years of self-cultivation,*
> *Poems and wine kept me merry company.*
> *Bidding you farewell as I am today,*
> *I shall see you again on Mount Tianzhu.*
> *Behold!*
> *Back into the mortal world I shall come,*
> *So as to meet with you once more.*

With these words, he sat down in lotus position and breathed his last. The monks of the monastery carried his coffin behind the mountain, where Abbot Moon Peak was to light the cremation fire. After the monks had chanted a sutra, the abbot ascended the sedan-chair and, joining his palms in a salute, intoned these lines, torch in hand:

> *The three teachings rise from the same source;*
> *My master is enlightened in all three.*

As he embarks on his way to the West,
Listen to this account of his life.

He continued, "This is dedicated to the enlightened soul of the distinguished monk, the deceased Abbot Yuanze:

"He was born in Henan and brought up in Luoyang. Ever since he entered the Buddhist order, his mind has been free of worldly concerns. His capacity for wine could drain rivers and oceans; his poems moved demons and gods to tears. A lover of nature, he was content with coarse clothes and simple food. While touring Qutang of the Three Gorges with his bosom friend Li Yuan, he saw a pregnant woman carrying a jar, a sight that inspired him with the thought of transmigration. In his next life, he will meet his friend in Hangzhou, but now he is sent to heaven for enlightenment by a recluse monk. Hark!

"On Mount Tianzhu they shall meet again.
By Ge Hong Well³ he shall search for signs."

With these words, the abbot lit the cremation fire. In the ensuing columns of smoke that rose to the clouds, Yuanze emerged with his palms pressed together, wafting upward toward heaven. Shortly thereafter, beadlike drops of his bones fell from the sky like a torrent of rain. As the monks put his bones into the stupa, Li Yuan was beside himself with grief.

The abbot kept Li Yuan at the monastery as a guest. On the third day of his stay, he went out of the monastery to visit the local inhabitants. Less than half a mile from the monastery there lived a family by the name of Zhang, to whom a baby son had been born three days before. The newborn was having a bath when Li Yuan requested but was denied permission to see him. It was only after much explanation and bribery with gold and silk that he was led into the main hall, where a woman was bathing the baby. At the sight of Li Yuan, the baby did flash a smile. After an elated Li Yuan went back, the baby died that very night, just as was foretold. Li Yuan took leave of the abbot and returned home, but we shall say no more of him for the moment.

Days and months passed, the constellations changed their positions, and more than ten years slipped by quite unnoticeably. It was now the third year of the Qianfu reign period [876], under Emperor Xizong. The insurgence led by Huang Chao⁴ had wreaked havoc in the empire. Tens of thousands of people were rendered homeless. The emperor fled to Shu,⁵ and ordinary peoples' homes as well as the royal palaces were all burnt down by the rebels. Fortunately, Li Keyong, king of Jin, raised an army and wiped out Huang Chao's forces. When Emperor Xizong returned to the capital, the empire began to stabilize and thoroughfares started to open up for traffic.

A business trip took Li Yuan to Hangzhou in the Zhejiang region. It happened to be around the Clear and Bright Festival, that time of the year when the scenery at West Lake and North Hill was at its best, attracting throngs of tourists. Keeping in mind Yuanze's promise twelve years ago about seeing him on Mount Tianzhu, Li Yuan walked at a leisurely pace with the crowds down the road, admiring the crystal-clear stream that flowed between the hills. Before he knew it, he was in the western corridor of Tianzhu Monastery, looking at the well where Ge Hong had allegedly concocted elixirs of immortality. When he found himself behind the monastery, there came into view a giant rock with a stream flowing by. Enraptured at the sight, he sat down.

While seated there, he heard singing coming from across the stream. Then he became aware of a herdboy about twelve or thirteen years of age on the other side, singing with gusto on the back of a buffalo. Marveling at the sight, Li Yuan pricked up his ears, and this was what he heard:

> *The spirit of yore on the three-life rock*
> *Finds delight in the moon and the wind.*
> *From afar a friend comes to visit me,*
> *In a new body but the same soul.*

And

> *A myriad things happen beyond one lifetime.*
> *I wish for a chat but I fear the pain.*
> *Having toured all the scenic spots of Wu and Yue,*
> *I instead seek a boat to ascend to Qutang.*

The song over, the herdboy looked at Li Yuan across the water and, clapping his hands, indulged in hearty laughter. Much taken aback, Li Yuan tried in vain to cross the stream to question him. Helplessly he watched the boy disappear into a willow grove. In low spirits, Li Yuan remained on the rock for a good while. When he asked a monk about the place, he was told that this was the stone of Ge Hong. Li Yuan knew only too well Monk Yuanze's farewell poem twelve years ago and the cremation words of Abbot Moon Peak. This meeting here on Mount Tianzhu would be precisely during the monk's third life. As inquiries about the herdboy's whereabouts led to nothing, a disheartened Li Yuan went on his way back home. The rock that Li Yuan sat on came to be known as the Rock of Three Lifetimes and remains intact to this day. Qu Zongji of later times [the Ming dynasty] had these lines to say:

> *With purple clothes reflected in green waves,*
> *They met by chance on a riverboat.*

So many things happen life after life,
The Rock of Three Lifetimes proved their predestined bond.

Wang Yuanhan [late Ming dynasty] had this to say:

Life on earth being nothing but a dream,
Why talk about things beyond one lifetime?
The Rock of Three Lifetimes by the sunset hills
Reminds one of the absurdity of it all.

The above story is about a reunion in the third lifetime. Now I shall propose to tell of another reunion across lifetimes known as "Abbot Mingwu Redeems Abbot Wujie" or "Abbot Foyin Redeems Su Dongpo."[6]

During the years of the Zhiping reign period [1064–67] under Emperor Yingzong of the Song dynasty, there was, on the famous South Mountain, beyond Qiantang Gate in the Ninghai District, Zhejiang, a Cleansing Mercy Filial Piety Light Monastery of long standing. There were in the temple two eminent monks who had studied together. One was Abbot Wujie [Five Commandments], the other Abbot Mingwu [Bright Enlightenment]. Abbot Wujie, thirty-one years of age, with his left eye blind and his height less than five feet, was most odd in appearance. A native of Luoyang, the Western Capital, he was endowed with prodigious intelligence and literary facility. He was a virtuoso in the arts of the zither, chess, calligraphy, and painting. After entering the Buddhist order upon reaching adulthood, he had become well versed in the teachings of the Chan sect of Buddhism through meditation and visits to senior monks. His original surname was Jin, his Buddhist name Wujie. What are the five commandments? They are

1. Thou shalt not kill.
2. Thou shalt not steal or rob.
3. Thou shalt not engage in sensual indulgence.
4. Thou shalt not touch alcohol and meat.
5. Thou shalt not make false claims and misstatements.

One day, one of his study tours took him to this temple, where the abbot was so impressed with his Buddhist scholarship that he kept him there as his chief disciple. After the abbot's death in a few years' time, the monks of the monastery made him the abbot. Henceforth, he spent his days in meditation.

Abbot Mingwu, on the other hand, was a man with a round head, big ears, a broad face, a well-shaped mouth, neat eyebrows, bright eyes, and a graceful bearing. At twenty-nine years of age, he stood seven feet tall, the very image of an arhat. A native of Taiyuan Prefecture, Henan, with the original surname of

Wang, he also had possessed great intelligence since his youth and was a formidable calligrapher. After he took to Buddhism and engaged in meditating and visits to senior monks, he became a monk at the local Shatuo Temple and adopted the Buddhist name of Mingwu. On one of his study tours, he came to Cleansing Mercy Monastery in the Ninghai District to visit Abbot Wujie. Impressed with his brilliance, the abbot kept him at the temple as a junior companion in his studies. The two came to be as close as brothers born of the same mother. When a lecture was to be made, the two would mount the platform together to explicate the Buddhist dharma, but we need say no more of this.

It was a cold day at the time of the year when winter gives way to spring. It snowed for two days under an overcast sky. On the third day, the snow stopped and the sky cleared up. Abbot Wujie was seated in his meditation chair early in the morning when he heard a baby's cries in the distance (*It is predestined that he should hear a baby's cries from afar, just as when Kumarajiva heard two babies crying over his eyebrows*),[7] whereupon he said to the trusted acolyte Qingyi, who was by his side, "Go for a look outside the temple gate and report to me if there is anything amiss."

Qingyi assured him, "It just cleared up after two days of snow. There shouldn't be anything amiss."

The abbot urged, "Go quickly, take a look, and report to me." Unable to fend off the abbot's insistence, Qingyi had no choice but to head for the gate, which was still closed, as it was still not yet bright daylight. He asked the gatekeeper to unbolt the gate. No sooner had he opened it than he gave a violent start at what he saw. "My goodness!" he cried. Truly,

> *Every day he extends a helping hand;*
> *Every moment he shows a kind heart.*
> *To such good deeds he devotes himself*
> *With never a question about his own future.*

What Qingyi saw was a baby lying on a tattered mat on the snow-covered ground underneath a pine tree. "Good grief!" he exclaimed. "Who left this child here? It'll surely die either of cold or of hunger." A closer look revealed the child to be a five- or six-month-old baby girl, wrapped up in rags. At the baby's bosom was a slip of paper with her date and hour of birth written on it. Without saying anything out loud, Qingyi thought to himself, "As the ancients say, 'To save a human life is better than building a seven-tiered stupa.'" Thereupon, he hurried back into the temple and reported to the abbot, "Someone abandoned a five- to seven-month-old [sic] baby girl and left her, wrapped up in rags, under the pine tree outside the gate. There being no passersby on such a cold day, let us do a good deed and save the baby!"

The abbot said, "Good! You are indeed a man of compassion. Why don't you carry the baby to your room and feed her some porridge or rice. You can take care of her until she is old enough to be put up for adoption. Saving a life gives you more credit than does becoming a monk."

Qingyi rushed out the gate and carried the baby into the abbot's cell. While looking the baby over, the abbot said, "Qingyi, show me the slip of paper." Qingyi did so accordingly. On the slip of paper were written these words: "Born around noon on the fifteenth day of the sixth month of this year. Pet name: Red Lotus." The abbot told Qingyi to carry the baby to his room and, as an act of charity, to raise her until she reached five to seven years of age, when she could be put up for adoption. (*Good solution.*) Thus admonished, Qingyi carried the baby to his quarters in a single-story house with three rooms and four rafters behind the Hall of a Thousand Buddhas. He started a fire to warm the baby and fed her some porridge. As the days and the months went by, the girl remained hidden in the empty house, with no one any the wiser. Even the abbot forgot about her presence. Before anyone knew it, Red Lotus had grown to be a girl of ten, with refined looks and a sharp mind. Qingyi continued to hide her in the house, locking the door every time he left and closing it every time he returned, such was his caution.

Time shot by like an arrow, and the days and months sped as quickly as the shuttle on a loom. Red Lotus was now sixteen. Qingyi treated her as if she were his own daughter. Even though clad in men's clothing and wearing men's shoes and socks, with her chin-length hair and bangs reaching her eyebrows in the fashion of a young monk, she still looked the pretty girl that she was. (*The first mistake in the Buddhist order is to have women dressed like men passed off as monks, and monks passed off as nuns.*) She cooked meals, boiled tea, and did needlework. Qingyi, for his part, was hoping to find a son-in-law to support him in his old age and to take care of his burial.

On a hot summer day in the sixth month, the memory of what had happened more than ten years before suddenly flashed back to Abbot Wujie. Having taken a bath and eaten his porridge for supper, he headed straight for Qingyi's quarters behind the Hall of a Thousand Buddhas. Qingyi said, "It's so seldom that you come here."

The abbot came straight to the point: "Let me ask you something. Where is the girl Red Lotus whom you found?"

Qingyi dared not hide anything from the abbot but led him to his quarters. The abbot was so struck by the sight of the girl that

> The eight pieces of his skull bones opened up,
> And half a bucket of ice and snow poured in.

The sight of Red Lotus awakened the abbot's lust. He said with a chuckle to Qingyi, "Send her to my bedroom tonight. Do so without fail. If you do what I say, I will certainly also do something for you. On no account is this to be let on to anyone else. Have her come as a young monk. Make sure that no one can tell she is a girl." Qingyi voiced his consent, but to himself, he thought, "I can't very well fail to do as he says, but if I do obey him and let her go into his room tonight, she'll lose her virginity. What a spot I'm in!"

Noticing Qingyi's hesitation, the abbot said, "Qingyi, lock the door and follow me into my room." And so Qingyi did. The abbot took out ten taels of silver from his clothes trunk and, handing it to Qingyi, said, "Take this for your expenses. Tomorrow, I'll get you your ordainment papers, shave your head, and take you on as a disciple. What do you say to that?"

"I am much obliged." He had no choice but to accept the silver before taking leave of the abbot. Back in his quarters, he told Red Lotus under his breath, "My child, the man who just came is the abbot of this monastery. He has taken a fancy to you. After night falls, I'll send you over to serve him. Be careful. Don't make any mistakes." Red Lotus promised to do as her father advised.

When evening set in, the two ate their supper. At around the second watch, Qingyi led Red Lotus straight to the abbot's room and went in, unimpeded, through the open door. As it happened, the abbot had told the two acolytes who served him not to close the door and the windows that night because he wished to take a walk in the cool air. That was why they had no barriers to deal with. The abbot had been waiting in the room for Qingyi to bring Red Lotus to him. At the sight of a young man escorted by Qingyi, he stepped forward and led them in. "At this time tomorrow," he told Qingyi, "come again and take her back." Qingyi went back alone.

The abbot closed the door, put out the lamp with a glazed shade and, taking Red Lotus by her hand, pulled her to his bed, where he had her take off her clothes. Then he held her in his arms and lifted her onto the bed. They were like

> *Mandarin ducks playing in the water,*
> *Phoenixes flitting among the flowers.*
> *Merrily they were intertwined like vines;*
> *In rapture their hearts were tied up as one.*
> *The oriole's warbles never left his ears;*
> *Her tongue tip delivered sweet saliva.*
> *Her willowlike waist was filled with passion;*
> *Her cherrylike lips let out gasps of breath.*
> *Eyes glazed, beads of sweat coursed down her fragrant body;*
> *Soft breasts swayed, dew trickled into the peony's heart.*
> *He, at this first taste of woman,*

Was like a hungry tiger pouncing on a lamb.
She, at this first encounter with a man,
Was like a thirsty dragon in the water.
How sad that drops of bodhi water
Fell into two red lotus petals.

By the time their game of clouds and rain was over, it was already the fifth watch, and dawn was approaching. The abbot had to think of a way to hide her. There being a big wardrobe in the room, he unlocked it, put to order the things in it, made her sit down inside, and said, "I'll bring you food. Don't you worry. Just be patient." The girl, all too delighted at her first sexual experience, readily went into the wardrobe, which was then locked up. In a short while, having finished his sutra-intoning ritual in the hall, the abbot returned to the room, closed the door, and unlocked the wardrobe so that Red Lotus could come out for her meal. Then he put some fruit in the wardrobe and locked her in again. At night, Qingyi came and took Red Lotus back.

That very night, after finishing a meditation session in his chair, Abbot Mingwu, as perceptive as he was, knew that in a moment of weakness Abbot Wujie had been intimate with Red Lotus, thus breaking his oath against lust and throwing away so many years of abstinence. He thought, "I should give him some advice and gently urge him to mend his ways."

The following day was the last day of the sixth month, with red and white lotus flowers in full bloom in the bone-ash pond outside the temple. Abbot Mingwu had an acolyte pick a white lotus and put it in a vase in his own room. While another acolyte was preparing tea, the abbot asked him to go and, with the following words, invite Abbot Wujie over for a talk: "Let us admire the lotus and compose poems while we talk."

In a short while, Abbot Wujie was brought in. The two abbots sat down. Mingwu said, "My brother, with lotus flowers in full bloom, I had one picked and put in a vase for you to compose a poem on such beauty."

Wujie said, "I am very obliged for a such a favor." At this point, the acolyte came in and served tea. After the tea, Abbot Mingwu said to the acolyte, "Go and get me the four treasures of the study." And so the acolyte did.

"What shall I write about?" asked Wujie.

"About the lotus."

Wujie took up the brush-pen and wrote this quatrain:

A lotus bud with petals just opening,
By summer blossoms at the height of fragrance.
The fire-red pomegranate may be lovely,
But how can it be as fragrant as the green-leaved lotus?

Thereupon Mingwu said, "How can I have nothing to say in response to your poem?" With a brush-pen he wrote these four lines:

> *With spring come peach and apricot blossoms,*
> *Vying for beauty in a blaze of color.*
> *Lovely indeed is the summer lotus,*
> *But how can red ones be as fragrant as the white?*

Upon finishing the quatrain, Abbot Mingwu roared with laughter.

When the meaning of the quatrain suddenly dawned on Wujie, his face turned red and then paled again. There and then, he took leave of Mingwu, returned to his room, and told an acolyte to boil some bath water. The acolyte hastened to do his bidding. After his bath, he put on a new outfit, took his meditation chair into the room, and, brush-pen in hand, wrote a farewell poem on a piece of white paper:

> *At forty-seven years of age,*
> *All dharma should return to the source.*
> *A moment of weakness*
> *Makes me bid this hasty farewell.*
> *Pass this on to Abbot Mingwu.*
> *Why should he press me like this?*
> *In a flash I will be gone,*
> *But blue as ever heaven will be.*
>
> (There seems to be a trace of bitterness in his tone. This is what gives
> rise to his propensity for vilifying Buddha in his next life.)

Then he had some incense burnt in front of him in a censer. With his feet pressed against each other and his palms joined together, he passed away on his meditation chair.

The acolyte promptly reported the death to Abbot Mingwu. Appalled at the news, the abbot went to Wujie's room to take a look for himself, only to find his friend dead and gone. Having read the farewell poem, he said, "A good monk you were, except for this misdemeanor. Though you'll be born in a man's body, if you have no faith in the Three Precious Ones of Buddha, dharma, and *sangha*,[8] you will certainly end up vilifying Buddha. For that, you'll be thrown into the sea of bitterness in your afterlives, never to regain the Buddhist path. Alas, what a pity! You said yours was a hasty farewell, but I'm sure I'll be able to overtake you!" (*The freedom to come and go between this world and the other is what goes beyond dharma.*) He had an acolyte boil some bath water for him. After a change of clothes, he went into his room and assumed the lotus position on his meditation chair.

"I will be on my way to overtake Abbot Wujie," he declared to the assembly of his disciples. "You can put the two corpses into two separate caskets and burn them in the same cremation fire after three days." With these words, he willed his death. All the monks present were amazed at such an extraordinary event. News about the two abbots of the temple dying on the same day so shook the town that the local people as well as men and women from out of town swarmed in untold numbers to the temple to burn incense and make offerings. After three hectic days, the corpses were carried to Golden Ox Temple for cremation, and the ashes were then disposed of.

Qingyi then sought a matchmaker and married his daughter, Red Lotus, to a Master Liu, a fan maker, who supported Qingyi for the rest of his life, but this is of no bearing to our story.

In the meantime, Mingwu, freed from his body, sped to the town of Meishan in Meizhou, Sichuan, where Wujie had already been reborn to Su Xun, courtesy name Mingyun, a poet known as the Resident of the Old Spring. His wife, Wang-shi, had dreamt that a one-eyed monk entered her room, much to her astonishment. The following morning, she gave birth to a baby boy with refined features. The parents were delighted and spared no festivities in celebration of the boy's third day of his life and, thereafter, the thirtieth day, the hundredth day, and the first birthday a year later, but this is of no concern to us.

Mingwu was also reborn in the same area, to a man named Xie Yuan, courtesy name Daoqing. His wife Zhang-shi had dreamt of an arhat who, a seal in hand, came to her asking for alms. She woke up with a start and gave birth to a son who was later given the name Xie Ruiqing. From childhood on, he stayed away from meat and wine, and had his heart set on becoming a monk. Being descendants of generations upon generations of officials, his parents would not hear of his renouncing the world but instead sent him to school, much against his will. He proved to be a most gifted pupil, with a memory that could retain lines of text after no more than a cursory glance. He also excelled in the writing of prose and verse. His favorite reading materials were the classics, which he understood upon the first reading. His eloquence was unsurpassed by any eminent monk. What a pity it was that, as learned as he was, he disdained to take the imperial examinations, nor was he interested in seeking office. Any mention of fame and fortune brought only a smile from him, but no comment. This, however, is of no immediate concern to us either.

Let us go back to the son of Su the Resident of the Old Spring. When taught to read and write at the age of seven, he turned out to be so brilliant that he could take in five lines at one glance. By the age of ten, he had learned everything there was to learn in the Five Classics and the Three Histories.[9] He was named Su Shi,[10] courtesy name Zizhan. So beautiful were his writings that they came to be rated the best in the empire.

From early childhood on, Su Shi cultivated a close friendship with Xie

Ruiqing in their studies together, though they had different aims in life. Su Shi had his mind set on taking the imperial examinations. Rejecting Buddhism, he had the greatest contempt for monks. He often said, "No shave, no knave; no knave, no shave; if knave, then shave; if shave, then knave. Someday when I rise to power, I shall have no peace until I do away with all monks." Xie Ruiqing's abstinence provoked these amused remarks from him: "Wine and meat provide nutrition to the human body. If you were to have your way and no life was to be killed for meat, then our streets and alleys would be filled to overflowing with sheep, pigs, chickens, and geese, with no space left for human beings. Moreover, wine is made of rice. What harm is there in drinking something that does no injury to life?" Every time they met, Ruiqing would try to convert Su Shi to Buddhism, whereas Su Shi would press Ruiqing to seek office.

"Holding office," said Ruiqing, "is by no means a worthy undertaking. I advise you to attain enlightenment through Buddhism."

Su Shi objected, "Your Buddhism is all too intangible. I advise you to become an official; that's a solid career." However endlessly the arguments dragged on, neither could convince the other.

In the first year of the Jiayou reign period [1056] under Emperor Renzong, Su Shi tried in vain to have Xie Ruiqing go with him to the Eastern Capital to sit for the imperial examinations. Su Shi achieved fame overnight and was appointed by imperial decree as a Hanlin academician entitled to a life of extravagant riches, with clothes of brocade, food of the finest quality, and an impressive entourage on his outings. His thoughts went back to his friend Xie Ruiqing, who refused to take the road to officialdom: "I will invite him to the capital. My wealth and exalted status will surely change his mind." Consequently he wrote a letter of invitation and sent a messenger to Meishan to escort Xie Ruiqing to the capital. Xie Ruiqing, afraid that Su Shi might, if he did become rich and prominent, indeed defame Buddhism and do away with all monks, agreed to go, in order to convince him to change his mind. Therefore, he followed the messenger to the capital. When they met, they resumed their old ways of preaching to each other without either side yielding an inch.

Won't you agree that events happen through coincidence? Well, it so happened that the region was hit by a severe drought that left thousands of acres of land dry and parched. By Emperor Renzong's decree, an altar was set up on the palace grounds for a seven-day rite to pray for rain. The emperor himself made offerings of incense twice a day while the entire assembly of court officials ran about attending to their business in white clothes of mourning. As speech writing was the responsibility of officials of the Hanlin Academy, Su Shi was charged by imperial decree to write the speeches for this occasion. He urged

Ruiqing to join in the event, but Ruiqing had no desire to go. (*That's where his origin lies. He does not wish to go, but cannot very well put Zizhan to blame.*) Su Shi argued, "You normally find the greatest delight in Buddhist rituals. How can you miss the grand occasion when the imperial court has engaged celebrated monks from thirty-six places to pray by the altar built specially for the purpose?"

Ruijing countered, "A prayer service arranged by the imperial court will be nothing but a pageant with a lot of meaningless fanfare. I'm sure there won't be any revered monks with lectures worth listening to!" However, the occasion proved to be an opportunity for the fulfillment of Su Shi's predestined bond with Buddhism.

On the day in question, Su Shi insisted on taking Ruiqing with him to the service, and, unable to resist any longer, Ruiqing yielded and went along. Upon arrival at the site, Su Shi joined the other officials in providing services for the occasion, whereas Ruiqing, dressed as an acolyte, walked to and fro, observing the ceremony.

All of a sudden, Emperor Renzong arrived. As the assembly of officials greeted the emperor, prostrated themselves, and offered incense before the statues of the Buddha, Ruiqing stepped forward to take a closer look at the emperor, but the emperor noticed that furtive move. Seeing that the man had distinguished features and a refined bearing, the emperor asked, "Who is this man?"

A consternated Su Shi suddenly hit upon an idea and, falling on his knees, said, "This is an acolyte who recently came to Great State Councilor Monastery. Being most knowledgeable about the Buddhist classics, he has been brought here to help out at the service."

"What a distinguished look he has!" said the emperor. "Since you are so knowledgeable about the Buddhist classics, I shall make you an ordained monk."

Xie Ruiqing had, ever since an early age, wanted to be a Buddhist monk. The imperial decree fit in exactly with his wishes. After expressing his gratitude, he said, "Since Your Majesty has kindly conferred upon me the status of a monk, please also grant me a Buddhist name."

Thereupon, Emperor Renzong, the Son of Heaven, obtained a sheet of ordainment paper from the Ministry of Rites and, with a flourish of his royal brush-pen, wrote "Foyin [Buddha Seal]." Ruiqing respectfully took the document and kowtowed again in gratitude. He waited for the emperor to withdraw before shaving his head in front of the statues of Buddha by the altar. Henceforth he called himself Foyin instead of Xie Ruiqing. None of the monks of Great State Councilor Monastery dared cold-shoulder such an erudite scholar of the dharma, a monk ordained by the emperor himself and a close friend of Academician Su. He came to be known to all and sundry as Chan Master, but of this, no more need be said.

Now, Su Shi felt laden with guilt because it was for the sole purpose of persuading Ruiqing to seek office that he had made the latter travel all the way to the capital. The last thing he had expected was to have Ruiqing shaved and ordained as a monk just because of an innocuous tour of the prayer service. He had always resisted Ruiqing's attempts to press the tenets of Buddhism upon him, but now he ended up being the cause of Ruiqing's renouncement of the world. Wasn't it all attributable to a predestined fate?

However much he secretly liked the life of a monk, Foyin feigned such anger at Su Shi that the latter, haunted by his own guilt, was full of humble apologies and dared not utter another unkind word against monks. However endlessly Foyin lectured about the Buddhist scriptures and dharma, Su Shi had to listen with all his patience if he had no wish to provoke Foyin into another burst of rage. (*One thing leads to another. Ingenious.*) With more exposure to such lectures, Su Shi gradually became attuned to Buddhist teachings, and his enmity began to wear off. He gave in to Foyin's insistence that he pay homage to the Buddha and partake of a vegetarian meal in State Councilor Monastery on the first and fifteenth days of each month. Since he had always enjoyed conversing with Foyin, Su Shi often visited him in the monastery in his leisure time for an idle talk or for a poetry reading. As Foyin touched no meat or wine, Su Shi also followed a vegetarian diet. The Buddha-defaming and monk-bashing Academician Su was now a defender of the dharma with full respect for monks. Foyin went a step further and tried to talk Su Shi into abandoning his post in favor of the practice of Buddhism. Su Shi promised, "After I attain the height of my career and fame, I will build a house to the east of your monastery and join you in a life of seclusion." Therefore, he called himself Su the Resident of the Eastern Slope and came to be known to all and sundry as Su Dongpo [Eastern Slope Su].

After several years at the Hanlin Academy, Su Dongpo was appointed as examination administrator in the first year of the Xining reign period [1068] under Emperor Shenzong. In assigning examination topics, he satirized the incumbent prime minister, Wang Anshi, who in turn vilified him in front of the emperor, saying that such an impudent and flamboyant fellow did not belong in the Institute of Historiography. Consequently Su Shi was demoted to the position of controller-general of Hangzhou. He took leave of Foyin and went to Hangzhou to assume his new post.

One day, when he was sitting idly in his yamen, a gatekeeper came in to report that a monk calling himself the abbot of the local Lingyin Temple was requesting an audience with him. Su Dongpo had a runner go out and inquire about the monk's business, whereupon Foyin asked for some paper and ink from the gatekeeper and wrote the words "The poet monk is here to see you." When the note was brought to Su Shi, he also took up his pen and wrote, "How dare a poet monk request an audience with an eminent official!" When the gatekeeper showed the note to the monk, the latter wrote a quatrain:

> *Great oceans shelter flood dragons;*
> *High hills let phoenixes roam free.*
> (Standing on high ground.)
> *What a petty, small-minded knave you are*
> *To deny the request of a poet monk!*

It was only then that Su Dongpo recognized the handwriting. He marveled, "Why is he also here? Quickly invite him in!" Who do you suppose the monk was? He was none other than Abbot Foyin. He had resigned from Great State Councilor Monastery upon learning of Academician Su's demotion and had traveled to Lingyin Temple in Hangzhou to be the abbot there. Thus, they resumed their daily visits. Later, Su Dongpo relocated from Hangzhou to Xuzhou and from there to Huzhou, and Foyin followed him all along.

In the second year of the reign period Yuanfeng [1079], under Emperor Shenzong, Su Dongpo was the prefect of Huzhou when he wrote several poems with a satirical sting against current events. Censors Li Ding, Wang Gui, and others submitted memorials to the emperor, accusing Su Shi of slandering the imperial court. In a rage, the Son of Heaven sent officers to arrest Su. He was thus brought to the capital and thrown into jail to be interrogated by none other than his enemy Li Ding, a student of Wang Anshi's. He was charged with treason and sentenced to death. Sitting in prison, he pondered over why, as a scholar-official, he should lose his life over a few lines of verse. He lamented his fate with another poem:

> *Others wish their sons to be smart,*
> *But I will be dying for being so.*
> *May all sons be weak-minded imbeciles,*
> *And rise to dukedom without a mishap.*

Tears gushed from his eyes as he thought to himself sadly, "The way things are, I'm no better than a chicken or a duck in the hands of a butcher. Come to think of it, what crimes did the chickens and ducks commit that they deserve to be killed to fill the dinner plate? They are slaughtered only because they cannot speak and defend themselves. But I, Su Shi, with my glib tongue, am no more able to speak for myself. Woe is me! Foyin did try to talk me into keeping away from any meat of slaughtered creatures, giving up office, and becoming a monk. I see now how true his words were. I should have followed his advice."

Before the sighs were quite out of his mouth, he heard the click of a prayer bead and an exclamation of "Amitabha." Much startled, Dongpo opened his eyes and saw Abbot Foyin in front of him. Forgetting that he was in a prison cell, Dongpo scrambled to his feet to greet him, saying, "Why are you here, my brother?"

Foyin said, "I am here to take you to Cleansing Mercy Filial Piety Light Monastery on South Mountain to view the blooming red lotus flowers." Dongpo found himself following his friend until they came to the monastery. Once past the gate, Dongpo was seized by a sense of déjà vu as they wound their way through the halls. Much to his amazement, all the clocks, chimes, and volumes of scriptures displayed in the halls looked as familiar to him as if they were his very own. As no lotus flowers had come into view during the entire tour of the monastery, he asked Abbot Foyin, "Where are the red lotus flowers?"

Foyin replied, pointing in the direction behind him, "Here she comes."

Turning around, Dongpo saw a young woman approaching with mincing and delicate steps from behind the Hall of a Thousand Buddhas. (*A vivid scene.*) She stopped in front of him and made a deep bow. Dongpo had a vague feeling of having known her before. The woman took out from her sleeve a sheet of flowered notepaper and requested the inscription of a poem from the academician. With brush-pen and ink slab provided by Foyin, Dongpo wrote the following quatrain without any hesitation:

> *In one moment of weakness in his forty-seven years,*
> *He abased himself for a red lotus.*
> *At the toll of the morning temple bell,*
> *This time he will hold on to Buddha's feet.*

The woman had no sooner finished reading the poem than she tore the sheet into small pieces and, putting her arms firmly around Dongpo, said, "The academician must not be so ungrateful!" Dongpo was at a loss what to do, but Foyin cut her off with a single slap of his hand. As he woke up in a cold sweat, he realized that it was nothing but a dream. It was the fifth watch by the prison watch drum. Dongpo marveled at the extraordinary dream and wondered why he could recall every word of the quatrain. Suddenly, his ears caught the distant tolls of the monastery bell, announcing the coming of dawn. A flash of understanding lit up his mind: "So I was a monk at Filial Piety Light Monastery in my previous life and succumbed to the temptation of lust. That explains the misery in this life of mine. Should Buddha kindly forgive me and spare my life, I will, without fail, defend the dharma with my whole heart and devote myself to the practice of Buddhism."

In a short while, at the break of day, a prison warden came in to congratulate him for having been pardoned by an imperial decree and only demoted to the position of deputy military training commissioner of Huangzhou. He was barely out the prison gate when he saw Abbot Foyin approaching him, saying, "How fares the academician? This poor monk has been waiting a long time!"

As it happened, on the very day Dongpo was taken away, Foyin also left Huzhou and came to Great State Councilor Monastery in the Eastern Capital to wait for news about Dongpo. When he got word of Dongpo's death sentence, he made every effort to defend Dongpo and, seeking high and low for help (*Such a good friend is hard to come by. I'm on the verge of tears and ready to drop down on my knees to pay him homage*), secured the assistance of Wu Chong and Wang Anli [Wang Anshi's brother], two righteous men who did their best to convince the emperor of his innocence. Empress Dowager Caoshi, impressed with Su Shi's fame as a talented scholar ever since the reign of Emperor Renzong, also intervened on his behalf. (*Women are more appreciative of talent than men. But it's lamentable that a scholar in distress should incur the sympathy of a woman.*) The emperor did come around and issue the pardon. Having regained the life that he had given up for lost, Dongpo was doubly happy to see Foyin. After acknowledging his gratitude to the emperor at the Gate of Five Phoenixes, Dongpo proceeded to Great State Councilor Monastery to tell Foyin about his dream. He was halfway through when Foyin interrupted him, saying, "I had the same dream last night," whereupon Foyin related the latter half of his dream, which, much to their amazement, tallied exactly with Dongpo's in every detail.

The following day, the imperial decree came, demoting Su Shi to Huangzhou. By a prior agreement with Foyin, Dongpo made a detour on his way to his post in order to visit Filial Piety Light Monastery outside Qiantang Gate in the Ninghai District. Upon arrival, he found every path, door, and window the same as in his dream. The monks he talked with all told him about Abbot Wujie's furtive encounter with Red Lotus. They still kept the farewell poem that Wujie wrote before he died. Dongpo asked for the poem and found it a veritable companion piece to the quatrain he had composed in his dream. Now he was convinced that reincarnation was by no means a false Buddhist claim. Not a doubt remained in his mind that Foyin was a reincarnation of Abbot Mingwu. At that moment, Dongpo wanted to shave his head, put on a monk's robe, and become Foyin's disciple, a request that Foyin denied. "You are not to renounce the world until twenty years from now, for your ties to fame and fortune are not yet broken, but in the meantime, keep your faith firmly and unalterably." Thus admonished, Dongpo did indeed, after his assumption of office in Huangzhou, refrain from eating anything that was a victim of killing, limited his drinking, and, wearing cotton from head to toe and inside out, he made it a daily habit to read Buddhist scriptures and pay homage to the Buddha. Throughout his three years in Huangzhou, Foyin stayed at his side, morning and night, day in and day out.

With the change of the reign title to Yuanyou [1086–93] under Emperor Zhezong, Dongpo was summoned to the capital and rehabilitated as academician of the Hanlin Academy, where his duty was to explicate the classics to the emperor. In another few years' time, he was promoted to the position of secretary of the Ministry of Rites and chief academician of Duanming Hall. Foyin, for his part, resumed his position at Great State Councilor Monastery and they kept up a steady stream of mutual visits.

During the reign period of Shaosheng [1094–97], the new prime minister, Zhang Chun, reinstated Wang Anshi's policy and banished Dongpo to Dingzhou. As Dongpo bade farewell to Foyin at the monastery, Foyin said, "The karma of your previous existence has not come to an end. There are more hardships in store for you."

Dongpo asked, "When will I be released?"

> *"You will return when you encounter the word* yong.
> *Your life will end when you come across the word* yu.*"

He continued, "Mark this: Your journeys will take you too far for me to follow you. I will therefore just wait for you in the capital."

Dongpo glumly took his leave. Less than six months after he arrived in Dingzhou, he was further demoted to an assignment in Yingzhou. Shortly afterward, he was again demoted to one in Huizhou, and, after a little more than a year, was transferred to Danzhou, and from there to Lianzhou and later to Yongzhou.[11] Such a vagrant life fully bore out what Foyin had predicted about his journeys "taking him far."

He was not long in Yongzhou before an imperial pardon was issued, granting him the post of supervisor of Yuju Temple. He thought to himself, "What Foyin said about my returning upon the encounter of the word *yong* has already been born out. Now, here comes the word *yu*, which means the end of my life." So thinking, he hastened back to the capital to see Abbot Foyin. "I have long wished to go home," said the abbot, "but I have been waiting for you to go with me." By this time, Dongpo had gained a thorough knowledge of the dharma and readily understood what Foyin meant. That very night, the two of them took a bath at Great State Councilor Monastery and talked until the fifth watch before they took leave of each other. Foyin willed his death in that very monastery, whereas Dongpo, upon returning to his own quarters, also passed away without any ailment.

In the time of Emperor Huizong [r. 1101–25], there was a necromancer who remarked, "Dongpo is already an arhat. It was Foyin, a reincarnation of Buddha, who followed him throughout his life and saved him from perdition." A relationship that lasted for two lifetimes is so rarely heard of since ancient times that the story is still being told and elaborated by storytellers. There is a poem in evidence:

> *Chan is indeed a remarkable sect,*
> *Brought by Buddha into the world of men.*
> *It is easier for an iron tree to blossom*
> *Than for the condemned to get out of Avichi Hell.*

開合司司馬貌
斷獄

Sima Mao disrupts order in the underworld and sits in judgment.

Sima Mao Disrupts Order in the Underworld
and Sits in Judgment

Mundane earthlings as we are,
When will we ever be content?
Only one who accepts his lot,
Be it for rich or for poor,
Can bear the hardships of adversity.
In success, push not your luck,
For the tide will turn soon enough.
In vain will your hair have turned white,
Leaving nothing to your name.
Who'd not fain have a house of gold?
Or barns overflowing with grain?
If such is not your lot,
To no avail will be your plotting.
Leave the children to their own fate.
Why seek elixirs of life?
Just let your desires be few.

This lyric to the tune of "Full River Red," written by Monk Hui'an,[1] exhorts people to be content with their lot. Everything that ever happens to every mortal being is determined by fate. What is predestined comes to you of its own accord. What is not meant for you cannot be had, do what you may. You are not Scholar Sima Chongxiang. Do you think you can argue with Yama, king of hell, over your fate?

Storyteller, as for that Sima, how did he argue with Yama? Which of them had justice on his side? Please read on, and you will find out. As the poem says,

Injustices abound in this world;
Let me find a long ladder to ask heaven.
But blame not heaven for being unjust;
How one fares from life to life is all in one's stars.

It is said that during the reign of Emperor Ling [168–89] of the Eastern Han dynasty, there lived in Yizhou Prefecture of the Shu District a scholar by the name of Sima Mao, courtesy name Chongxiang. Endowed with a most quick mind, he was such a good reader that he could take in ten lines at a single glance. At the age of eight, capable of composing essays as fast as he could write, he was sent as a child prodigy to take the imperial examinations in the capital, only to be disqualified by the examiner for his impertinent remarks.

When he was older and wiser, he deeply regretted his indiscretion and did his best to cultivate prudence and modesty. He immersed himself in his studies behind closed doors, totally oblivious to happenings in the outside world. After his parents died, he moved into a hut, where he lived for six years in mourning and won a reputation as a filial son. He was recommended several times for official posts on the grounds of filial piety, virtue, and breadth of knowledge, but each time the position was seized by someone with political backing, leaving him bitterly disappointed.

In the first year of the Guanghe reign period [178], Emperor Ling started the construction of his Western Palace. To raise money for the project, he put official positions and titles up for sale, with prices varying with the rank of the position. The title of duke was sold for ten million and that of minister for five million. There was one Cui Lie, who, through the emperor's nurse, bought with five million the title of minister of education. On the day of Cui's inauguration and the offering of thanks, the emperor regretted the deal. With a stamp of his foot, he said, "I was shortchanged for such a nice title. I could have got ten million if only I had made things a little harder for him."

The emperor then founded the School at the Gate of the Great Capital and ordered the magistrates, prefects, and the three highest offices to recommend sons of rich families to enter the school. Those offering enough money were made inspectors for a provincial appointment and imperial secretaries for a metropolitan one. Scholar-officials regarded association with these people as a disgrace.

The poverty-stricken Sima Chongxiang had no one to recommend him, and so, by the time he reached fifty years of age, his circumstances had seen no change, however talented and erudite he was. A member of the common folk he remained, much to his seething resentment. In a state of inebriety, he took up the four treasures of the study[2] and composed a lyric poem to the tune of "Grievances," intoning the words as he wrote them. The poem said,

> *Are my heaven-bestowed talents*
> *Not to be given use?*
> *A great man I aspire to be,*

But with fate I find no favor.
Unrecognized I remain at fifty,
Suffering from dire poverty.
Honors and glories—
To whom have they gone?
To those with nothing in their heads
But too much in their pockets.
The rich rise to the clouds;
The poor fall into the mud.
The worthy and the lowly change places;
The strong are written off as the weak.
As morals of the time fall low;
I remain standing tall.
The ways of heaven are not to be known.
Might they be unfair?
I would like to find out all the details,
But instead, my tears of grief fall like rain.

Having finished the poem, he intoned it over and over again. However, as this outburst still did not give full vent to his bitterness, he wrote another eight lines:

Gains and losses, poverty and wealth
Are all destined before one's birth.
When passing judgments,
Why, I ask, do you ignore one's worth?
Men of merit are cast aside
While knaves flaunt their triumph.
If I were the king of hell,
All wrongs would be set right.

Before he knew it, evening had set in. He lit the lamp and chanted the poems several times. Rage suddenly seized him. He threw the poems into the lamp's flame, exclaiming, "Heaven! Oh Heaven! If there is still any good sense left in you, what can you say for an answer? I, Sima Mao, have never in my life been guilty of anything that would compromise my integrity. Even if you take me before Yama, I wouldn't flinch a bit. What do I have to fear?" After this outburst, he felt a weariness steal over him, and he fell asleep by the table.

Then there emerged from under the table seven or eight of Yama's demon runners, standing only three feet tall, with green faces, and long teeth sticking out of their mouths. Teasing Chongxiang, they said, "Scholar, what talents do you have to make you speak so bitterly of heaven and earth and to throw such libel at the netherworld! We are here to take you to Yama, king of hell. We'll see if you still can find your tongue!"

Chongxiang shot back, "What logic is this, to accuse me of libel when Yama's injustice is a fact!"

Without bothering to hear him out, the demons sprang upon him, dragged him by hand and by foot down from his seat, and threw a black noose around his neck. With a loud cry, he woke up in a cold sweat. What met his eyes was the sadly flickering flame of the lamp.

Shivers of cold ran through him. Feeling indisposed, he had his wife, Wang-shi, bring him a warm cup of tea. The tea made him dizzy, as if his legs were giving way under the weight of his head. Wang-shi helped him to bed. The following day, he fell into a coma and failed to respond to her calls. She wondered what he could be ill with. When the day drew to a close, he breathed his last, lying stiff in bed. Wang-shi broke down in a flood of passionate weeping. As his hands and feet were found to be still soft and his chest still slightly warm, she dared not move his body but stayed by the bedside, sobbing bitterly.

Let us follow another thread of the story and describe how the god on night patrol saw Chongxiang burn his poem "Grievances" and duly reported the event to the Jade Emperor. The latter flew into a rage. "Fame and fortune are a matter of fate. Should human status be determined by worth and talent, as he would have it, the world would know nothing but eternal peace, nor would there be any change of dynasties. How preposterous! (*Subtle words that give food for thought.*) What does this petty scholar know? Yet he accuses me of being unfair! He needs some punishment, the sooner the better, as a warning to all those given to false accusations."

At this point, the Gold Star of Venus remarked, "Imprudent though he was, he said those bitter words because, for all his talents, his is a hard life. If we go by the rule of rewarding the good and punishing the evil, his remarks did not overstep the bounds of reason. In view of the circumstances, I plead that he be forgiven."

The emperor said, "It was most presumptuous of him to claim that he would set all wrongs to right if he were Yama. What mortal, I ask you, can be Yama? With case files piled up mountain-high, the ten kings of the netherworld are so overwhelmed with work that they have no time for meals. And this Sima Mao, of all people, comes along and claims that he can set all the cases straight!"

The Gold Star of Venus spoke again: "If he has the arrogance, he probably has the competence. As far as the netherworld is concerned, it is indeed true that injustice has been done. There still remain cases that should have been tried hundreds of years ago. The bitterness of those souls that are thus confined to hell can be felt even in heaven. In my humble view, the best course is to take him to the netherworld and let him take over Yama's duties for half a day. Let him settle cases that have been mishandled. If his judgments are wise and fair, it will be a credit to offset his offense. If not, that will be the time for punishment, and only under those circumstances will he accept the justice of it." (*A unique ruling that does justice to the wisdom of that old man, the Star of Venus.*) The Jade Emperor approved the suggestion. Thereupon, the Gold Star of Venus, with authorization from the Jade Emperor, descended to the Palace of Darkness in the netherworld and ordered Yama to summon Sima Mao and give him the royal seat for twelve hours that night so that he could accept petitions and try cases. If his judgments were found to be wise and fair, he was to enjoy immense fame and wealth in his next life, as compensation for his misery in this one. Should his judgments lack wisdom, he was to be condemned to hell, never to be reincarnated as a human being again. Thus instructed, Yama sent the Demon of Impermanence to bring Chongxiang down to hell.

Chongxiang did not show the slightest fear at the sight of the demon and followed him all the way to the Palace of Darkness, where the demon yelled a command for him to drop to his knees. Chongxiang protested, "Why should I? Who's the man sitting up there?"

"That's Yama himself."

Chongxiang was overjoyed. "Oh, Yama! Yama! I, Sima Mao, have long been looking forward to seeing you to unburden myself of all my complaints. (*The audacity!*) How happy am I to be in your presence! In your exalted status as king, you have the judges, the Ox-Heads, the Horse-Faces, and tens of thousands of demon runners to help you, whereas I, Sima Mao, am but a lonely and penniless scholar whose life and death are in your hands. Don't try to intimidate me with your power. Let's have a debate in all fairness. The one with the most convincing argument will be the winner." (*In the world of the living, who would allow you to have a debate in all fairness?*)

"Being master of the netherworld, I follow the mandate of heaven in everything I do. What virtue and ability do you have that qualify you to take my place? What records do you want to set straight?"

"Yama, you said you follow the mandate of heaven, but the mandate of heaven is based on the love for humanity. It exhorts people to virtue and calls for punishing the wicked. Yet, as things are, the greedy wallow in wealth, whereas the generous find themselves impoverished. The wicked attain fame and fortune to do evil with impunity, whereas the kindhearted are humbled, brought to grief, and denied every wish. The virtuous are often duped by the treacherous and the talented bullied by the benighted. (*He says everything I wanted to say to unburden myself of all my complaints.*) The wronged have no one to turn to for vindication. All this, Yama, is attributable to the lack of justice in your judgments. Take me for an example: All my life, I, Sima Mao, have labored at my studies with unflinching diligence and made every effort to practice filial piety. What did I do in violation of the will of heaven that I should suffer one setback after another and be unjustly reduced to a status inferior to that of the merely mediocre? What good are you if you turn right and wrong upside down like this? If I were the king of hell, such injustices would never occur."

Yama laughed. "Retribution is only a matter of time, and may not be readily apparent. It may happen in this lifetime for something one did in a previous existence, or it may be visited upon one's offspring. In the case of a stingy rich man, he is blessed with wealth because he mortified his flesh in his previous life, but his stinginess in this life will make him die of hunger in his next one. A poor man is poor because, in his previous life, he sinned or lived in wanton extravagance off some ill-gotten gains. Should he devote himself to good deeds, he will still be able to live a life of plenty in his next existence. Thus, it can be seen that the mean and treacherous will find it hard not to lose the fame and fortune they have in this life, and that the honest and kind will eventually attain prosperity without fail, however grievous their life may be at the moment. This immutable law brooks no doubt. Mortal beings do not see what lies beyond their noses, but heaven has a vision that reaches far and wide. As it is beyond their capacity to understand the workings of heaven, humans cry out in protest but only because they do not know better."

Chongxiang challenged, "If you are thorough in meting out retribution, as you say, don't tell me there aren't souls of victims of injustice here in the netherworld. I challenge you to let me check your past records. If every case was fairly handled to the satisfaction of one and all, I, Sima Mao, will be content to plead guilty to libel."

Yama replied, "I have a decree from the Lord on High to yield my throne to you for twelve hours so that you can review my records. If your judgments are fair and wise, you will enjoy fame and fortune in your next life. If not, you will be condemned to perdition, never to be reincarnated as a human being again."

Chongxiang was delighted: "So, the Jade Emperor did grant my wish."

Yama rose from his throne and called him into a back hall. There, Chongxiang put on a crown, a robe embroidered with patterns of pythons, and a jade belt. And the very image of Yama he was!

Demon runners struck the tribunal drum, announcing, "The new Yama now calls the court to order!" There formed against the wall in neat order two lines of judges and runners from the Departments of Virtue and Evil and from the six bureaus. A jade tablet in hand, Chongxiang marched jauntily into the tribunal hall and mounted the throne. After the customary salutations, the assembly of officials inquired if notices should be posted to announce that the court was ready to hear cases. Chongxiang thought to himself, "Goodness only knows how many people there are throughout the five mountains and the four seas of the empire,[3] but the Lord on High grants me only twelve hours. If I fail to finish my job on time, I'll be accused of incompetence, and the consequences of such an offense won't be pleasant."

At this point, a plan sprang to mind. He addressed the judge as follows: "As I am allotted only twelve hours by the Jade Emperor, there is no time to go over all cases. Just bring me some past records. To show you the right way to handle cases, I will settle a few of the most difficult ones that have remained unsolved for hundreds of years."

The judge reported, "Your Majesty, there are, for your examination, only four files containing cases that have remained unresolved for more than three hundred fifty years, since the beginning of the Han dynasty."

"Bring them to me."

The judge did so accordingly.

Turning over the pages, Chongxiang saw that they were the cases of

> Murder of Loyal Officials
> > *Plaintiffs: Han Xin, Peng Yue, and Ying Bu*
> > *Defendants: Liu Bang and Empress Lü-shi [d. 180 B.C.E.]*
> Requiting Kindness with Enmity
> > *Plaintiff: Ding Gong*
> > *Defendant: Liu Bang*
> Abusing Power and Usurping the Throne
> > *Plaintiff: Qi-shi*
> > *Defendant: Lü-shi*
> Taking Advantage of the Victim's Desperate Situation to Force Him
> > to Commit Suicide
> > *Plaintiff: Xiang Yu*
> > *Defendants: Wang Yi, Yang Xi, Xia Guang, Lü Matong, Lü Sheng, and*
> > *Yang Wu.[4]*

After he finished reading the files, Chongxiang gave a great guffaw. "What makes these cases so difficult to solve? All of you in the six bureaus should be reprimanded, and it's all because Yama has been dragging his feet. (*Dragging one's feet is better than making an arbitrary judgment.*) Tonight, I will bring these cases to a close." Thereupon, he had the demon scribe on duty copy down all the names of the plaintiffs and the defendants as they appeared in the four files and summoned them for a hearing. The news sent waves of shock throughout the netherworld, as these lines attest:

Knotty cases are put aside,
In hell just as in this world.
With Chongxiang comes a breath of fresh air
That dispels rancor centuries-old.

The demon scribe on duty reported, "The prisoners are here awaiting instructions from Your Honor."

"Bring forward the parties involved in the first case," commanded Chongxiang.

The judge shouted at the top of his voice, "Roll call for the parties to the first case!" The roll call found the plaintiffs Han Xin, Peng Yue, and Ying Bu and the defendants Liu Bang and Lü-shi all present.

Han Xin was the first one called forward.

"When you were first in the service of Xiang Yu," said Chongxiang, "you were nothing more than a gentleman of the interior whose suggestions were invariably brushed aside. Once you turned to Liu Bang, you rose to eminence and glory. You were even granted a title of nobility as a reward for your meritorious service. How could you have turned against him later in a conspiracy that ended rightfully in your death? What grounds do you have for lodging a complaint against your lord?"

Han Xin replied, "Your Majesty, please allow me to explain. Out of gratitude for the emperor of Han's recognition of my ability and his kindness in building a platform for a grand ceremony honoring me as grand marshal, I took pains to acquit myself well. I devised the strategy of building a plank pathway on a cliff to divert Xiang Yu's attention while quietly slipping our forces past Chencang. I helped my master conquer the region of the three Qins. I saved his life at Xingyang, captured Bao, the king of Wei, crushed the army of the state of Dai, and took Xie, the king of Zhao, prisoner. To the north, I swept up the territory of Yan; to the east, I annexed the state of Qi, taking over seventy cities in total; to the south, I put to rout a two-hundred-thousand-man Chu army and killed the celebrated general Long Qie; at Nine-Li Mountain, I laid ten ambushes and killed Chu soldiers to the last man; I dispatched six generals to pursue Xiang Yu until he took his own life in desperation at the Wu River ferry. Ten great achievements I have to my name, and content I was in the thought that my descendants could enjoy fame and fortune for generations to come. Then to my great dismay, once he won the empire, the emperor demoted me, in total disregard for my good service. Empress Lü, in a plot with Xiao He, induced me to go to the Palace of Eternal Happiness, where, before I could protest, some armed men bound me up and killed me. In falsely charging me with attempted insurrection, they also wiped out everyone within three degrees of kinship in my family. In all of these three hundred fifty years, this cruel injustice done to me has not been vindicated. Innocent as I am of any wrongdoing, I humbly appeal to Your Majesty's judiciousness in the settlement of this case."

Chongxiang snapped, "As a grand marshal, how could you have been so foolhardy as to have been coaxed into a trap and bound up like a child? Didn't you have anyone to consult? Who can you blame now?"

Han Xin replied, "I did have a military counselor by the name of Kuai Tong, who began well but left me halfway."

Chongxiang called out to the demon scribe, "Bring Kuai Tong immediately for questioning."

Kuai Tong was brought forward in a trice.

"Why did you, as Han Xin alleged, abandon your duties as his military counselor?" Chongxiang demanded.

Kuang Tong said in defense of himself, "I was not at fault. I left because Han Xin rejected my advice. At the time when Han Xin defeated Tian Guang, king of Qi, it was I who submitted a memorial to Liu Bang in Luoyang to request conferral of a temporary title of king for Han Xin so as to pacify the Qi people. The king of Han sneered, 'That lowly rascal who crawled between someone's legs!⁵ How can he covet a title before the state of Chu is conquered!' At this point, Zhang Liang quietly stepped on the king's foot from behind and whispered into his ear, 'This is a time when you need capable men. Do not let a trivial concern bring you a major loss.' Thereupon the king changed his tone and said, 'When a man of honor seeks a position, he seeks not to be a temporary king but a real king.' So saying, he ordered that the royal seal be brought to him and granted Han Xin the title King of the Three Qis. My observations led me to believe that the king of Han still held Han Xin in distrust and would eventually discard him. Therefore, I advised Han Xin to rise against the king of Han, seek alliance with the state of Chu, and then, with the empire thus divided into three powers, wait for the right opportunity to present itself. But Han Xin said, 'When the prince built a platform and made me a marshal, I took a vow to be loyal to him as long as he treated me with equal honor. How could I betray him then?' My repeated attempts to make him see the advantages of such a move failed to shake his resolve. On the contrary, he reproached me for instigating treason. Out of fear of punishment, I feigned madness and fled to the village I came from. Just as I had expected, he was murdered at the Palace of Eternal Happiness after he had helped the king of Han conquer Chu. By then, it was too late for him to regret."

Chongxiang turned to Han Xin: "What made you turn a deaf ear to Kuai Tong's advice?"

Han Xin replied, "A fortune-teller by the name of Xu Fu said that I was not to die until the age of seventy-two, at the height of my fame and fortune.

That was why I chose not to betray the king of Han. As it turned out, I died way before my time, at the age of thirty-two."

Chongxiang thereupon had Xu Fu the fortune-teller brought under guard for questioning: "How could you have promised Han Xin seventy-two years of life when he was allotted only thirty-two? How can a fortune-teller throw around phony predictions? In your eagerness to relieve your clients of their purse, you had total disregard for the grief your words might bring them. How despicable!"

Xu Fu protested, "Please listen to me, Your Majesty. It is often said that 'The allotted span of life can be shortened just as it can be extended.' Therefore, the length of one's span of life can well baffle a fortune-teller. That Han Xin should have lived to be seventy-two was what I derived from my calculations. Little did I know that his excessive killing and squandering of his store of merit would bring about his untimely death. I, for my part, did not predict wrong."

Chongxiang asked, "What exactly did he do in the way of excessive killing and squandering of merit? Tell the court and spare no details."

Xu Fu said, "Having abandoned the state of Chu, Han Xin was on his way to enter into the service of the king of Han when he lost his bearings. Fortunately for him, he came upon two woodcutters who showed him a path that led to southern Zheng. Fearful that the king of Chu would send men in pursuit of him and learn of his whereabouts from the woodcutters, he went back with his sword drawn and killed the two men. Insignificant as they were, the woodcutters had done him a favor, and heaven punishes the ungrateful most severely. As the poem says,

> *Fleeing like an arrow leaving the bow,*
> *Only when shown the way could he press ahead.*
> *By killing the men for their kind act,*
> *He lost ten years from his lifespan.'"*

Chongxiang pressed further: "What about the other thirty years?" To this Xu Fu answered, "In a fanfare to show his high regard for Han Xin, the man recommended three times by his prime minister, Xiao He, the emperor of Han built a thirty-foot-high platform where he put Han Xin on the seat of honor, while he himself, with a gold seal in hand, bowed to Han Xin and acknowledged him as grand marshal. Han Xin accepted the salutation in all complacence. As the poem says,

> *'The marshal's power reached far and wide;*
> *His words prevailed over royal decrees.*

> *For him to take these bows from his lord*
> *Was enough to cost him another ten years.'"*

Chongxiang said, "A subject who accepts bows from his sovereign is indeed bound to suffer the consequences. But what about the remaining twenty years?"

Xu Fu replied, "There was a Scholar Li, counselor by profession, who persuaded Tian Guang, king of Qi, to surrender himself to the state of Han. Tian Guang then spent his days reveling in wine in Li's company. Taking advantage of Tian Guang's lack of preparedness, Han Xin crushed Qi in a surprise attack. Tian Guang attributed the defeat to Li's double-dealing and killed him in boiling water. And so Han Xin scored a great victory to his credit, but only because he betrayed a state that was ready to surrender and took credit that rightfully belonged to Li. As the poem says,

> *'Li won over the king of Qi and gained merit first,*
> *But Han Xin seized the chance and wiped out the Qi.*
> *For stealing Li's credit and causing his death,*
> *Han Xin lost ten more years of his own lifespan.'"*

Chongxiang remarked, "There is indeed much sense in what you say. But how do you account for the remaining ten years?"

"That was due to another misdeed. When pursuing Xiang Yu to Guling, the troops of the state of Han were vastly outnumbered by those of the state of Chu. Moreover, Xiang Yu was a man with enough strength to uproot mountains and raise cauldrons. In such a desperate situation, when the Han troops were too few and too weak to gain the upper hand, Han Xin laid out a surefire battle formation with ambushes on all sides at Nine-Li Mountain. All one million Chu soldiers and one thousand generals were killed to the last man; Xiang Yu, the king of Chu, was forced to make his escape, all alone, to the Wu River ferry, where he slit his throat and died. As the poem says,

> *'Rancor congeals at the foot of Nine-Li Mountain;*
> *One million fierce soldiers lost their lives.*
> *His plots and killings broke divine laws*
> *And cost him forty years in all.'"*

Han Xin was at a loss for an answer after Xu Fu finished speaking. Chongxiang asked, "Han Xin, what do you have to say in your own defense?"

Han Xin replied, "It was through Xiao He's recommendation that I was made grand marshal. It was the selfsame Xiao He [d. 193 B.C.E.] who later masterminded the plot that lured me into the Palace of Eternal Happiness, where I was arrested and murdered. Xiao was as responsible for my destruction as he was to be credited for my success. It is a grievance that I bear even to this day."

"Oh, very well," said Chongxiang, "I will summon Xiao He and get the truth out of him."

Before long, Xiao He was brought before him. Chongxiang asked, "Xiao He, why were you so erratic as to change from recommending Han Xin to destroying him?"

"There is a reason for this," said Xiao He. "I recommended him because he, for all his talent, did not win any recognition, while the king of Han, later the emperor, needed a competent grand marshal. Thus they fitted each other's purposes perfectly. Who would have known that the emperor would change his mind and grow jealous of Han Xin for his abilities? Before setting out on an expedition to quell a rebellion by Chen Xi, the emperor reminded the empress to be on guard against Han Xin. After he had departed, the empress acted upon his instructions and took counsel with me, stating her intention to kill Han Xin for conspiring against the throne. I said, 'Han Xin is the number one worthy subject of the emperor. If he is guilty of conspiracy, no signs of it are evident. I dare not carry out your order.' The empress flew into a rage. 'May I presume,' she said, 'that you are an accomplice? If you fail to come up with a plan to do away with Han Xin, you will also be punished upon the emperor's return.' Fearing the power of the empress, I was obliged to present her with a plan whereby Han Xin was summoned into the palace to join in celebrating the crushing of Chen Xi by the emperor's troops, and then, at a sharp order, he was seized and executed by armed men. I never had any intention of harming him."

Chongxiang said, "It seems that Liu Bang alone was responsible for Han Xin's death." Thereupon, he instructed the demon judge to present him with copies of all of the depositions. "This court finds that the rise of the Han dynasty was largely the work of Han Xin, a man who was not rewarded for his merit. Such an unprecedentedly cruel injustice must be redressed in his next life." With these comments, he put aside the file for the time being.

Next, he summoned Peng Yue, prince of Daliang, for a hearing: "What crime did you commit that made Empress Lü order your death?"

Peng Yue replied, "I am not guilty of any wrongdoing. Instead, I have rendered the emperor meritorious service. I was put to death because while the emperor was away on an expedition to the border regions, Empress Lü, being the wanton woman that she was, asked a eunuch to name a handsome minister in the Han court. Upon being told that Chen Ping was the most handsome man in the imperial court, the empress asked where he was. The eunuch replied, 'He is with the emperor on the expedition.' 'Name another one,' said the empress. The eunuch said, 'There is Peng Yue, prince of Daliang, a handsome man of heroic mettle.' Thereupon, Empress Lü issued a secret decree, summoning me into the court. I proceeded to the Hall of the Golden Bell, but the empress was not there. The eunuch said, 'Her Majesty wishes to discuss a secret matter with you in the Hall of Eternal Faith.' Scarcely had I stepped into the hall than the gate was locked and bolted. The empress descended the flight of steps to greet me and invited me to a feast inside the hall. After three cups of wine, her lust aroused, she asked me for intimacy, but I refused out of fear of breaking the ethical codes of behavior. In a towering rage, she ordered her men to kill me with stabs of bronze sledgehammers. My body was cooked and chopped into mincemeat, and my head hung in the street with orders that it not be buried. The emperor, upon his return, was told only that I had sought to rise against him. What a gross injustice!"

The empress, listening to this at one side, burst into tears and protested, "Your Majesty, don't listen to his lies. It is always men who harass women. Who has heard of a woman taking liberties with a man? When I summoned Peng Yue into the palace for a consultation, he was so impressed by my wealth that he made advances toward me. A minister who flirts with the sovereign's wife should, by rights, be executed."

Peng Yue broke in, "When in the Chu army, Empress Lü had a long-lasting affair with Shen Yiji. I, Peng Yue, a man of integrity for all my life, am the last one to harbor any indecent thoughts!"

Chongxiang remarked, "Peng Yue's words ring true, whereas the empress is deceitful. There is no need to go into this further. This court finds Peng Yue a most worthy minister of moral fortitude and matchless loyalty. He will again be a man of honor in his next life, when the wrongs inflicted upon him will be redressed, just as in the case of Han Xin." With these comments, the file was put aside.

Ying Bu, prince of Jiujiang, was the next one to be called forth. This was how Ying Bu stated his case: "Han Xin, Peng Yue, and I worked together as one. It was through the three of us that the Han empire came into being. I did not have in me the slightest trace of rebellious thought. One day, when I was relaxing by the riverside, there came the announcement of the arrival of an imperial messenger, who, upon a decree from the empress, gave me a jar of mincemeat. After thanking the envoy for this gift, I set the table, had a taste of it, and found it delicious. Then I came upon a human fingernail. I was filled with apprehensions. Upon questioning, the messenger denied all knowledge of the contents of the jar. In a fit of anger, I had him beaten, and the truth came out: It was the flesh of Peng Yue, prince of Daliang. Sickened at hearing this, I induced vomiting by inserting my fingers into my throat, and the meat spurted out in the shape of tiny crabs. To this day, there still exist such 'Peng Yue' crabs, which embody Peng Yue's grievance. Looking for someone to vent my anger on, I killed the messenger then and there. When the empress learned this, she dispatched men carrying a double-edged sword, drugged wine, and three yards of red silk to kill me and return to the palace with my severed head. It is my humble wish that Your Majesty will, in your wisdom, vindicate me for my unjustified death."

"The three worthy men did indeed die all too miserably," said Chongxiang. "I, as Yama, do hereby divide the Han empire into three portions and bestow to each of the three of you one portion as a reward for the significant contributions you made when you were alive. (*Wise judgment.*) Your case is closed." All parties signed their depositions and left.

As the first group of prisoners withdrew, the second group was called in. This was the case of requiting kindness with enmity. After the names of both the plaintiff, Ding Gong, and the defendant, Liu Bang, were called and they were found to be present, Ding Gong began stating his case: "When I had the Han emperor encircled on the battlefield, I released him only after he promised to share the empire with me. It turned out, in a way no one would have expected, that he had me murdered after he claimed the throne. I resent such injustice and hope that Your Majesty will judge in my favor."

Chongxiang turned to Liu Bang: "What do you have to say for yourself?"

The emperor of Han replied, "Being Xiang Yu's favorite general, Ding Gong was guilty of disloyalty when he failed to capture me, Xiang Yu's enemy, when I was in his hands. Therefore, I killed him as a warning to all who are lacking in loyalty. It is not a case of wanton killing of the innocent."

Ding Gong protested, "If so, what did you do for Ji Xin, your loyal subject, who laid down his life for you at Xingyang? You did not even confer a title upon him. How ungrateful of you! Xiang Bo, being a kinsman of Xiang Yu, was the first one to be guilty of disloyalty when he drew his sword and, with Fan Kuai, came to your rescue at the Hongmen Banquet. How is it that he was granted a royal surname and a title instead of being killed? There was also Yong Chi, another of Xiang's favored generals, whom you loathed most. Yet later, you made him a lord. Why did you bear me, of all people, such malice?" (*Admirable! What a clever tongue Ding Gong has!*)

The emperor was struck dumb. Chongxiang said, "My verdict for this case is ready. Summon Xiang Bo and Yong Chi, who will be judged along with Ding Gong. Both the plaintiff and the defendant may now withdraw."

Parties involved in the third case, that of abusing power and usurping the throne, were now brought forward. After confirming the presence of Lady Qi, the plaintiff, and Empress Lü, the defendant, Chongxiang addressed Lady Qi in these words: "Lü being the empress, you were but a favored consort. How could you go against all common sense by accusing her of abusing power and usurping the throne, when her son was all too clearly the rightful heir to the throne of the Han dynasty?"

Lady Qi poured out her woes: "During the battle at River Sui before he gained the throne, the emperor, fleeing desperately with Ding Gong and Yong Chi in close pursuit, stumbled all by himself into our Qi village, where my father hid him. I was playing the zither in my room when the emperor heard the music. He asked to see me and, pleased with my looks, he wanted to have me as a concubine, a request that I declined. He said, 'If things turn out the way I wish and I do gain the empire, I will set up your son as the crown prince.' With that, he tore off a part of his battle robe and gave it to me as a token of his sincerity. Only then did I give my consent. Thus, my son, when he was born, was named Ruyi [As One Wishes]. The emperor had promised that after his death, Ruyi would succeed to the throne, but nothing came of the promise because all the ministers of the court stood much in fear of the empress.

"After the emperor's death, Empress Lü set up her own son as the successor to the throne and made Ruyi a mere prince of Zhao, but my son and I dared not object. As it turned out, Empress Lü was still not satisfied. She cajoled us into her quarters for a feast, in the course of which she gave Ruyi some poisoned wine that killed him instantly. Blood flowed out from all of the nine apertures of his head and body. The empress made a feint of being too inebriated to notice anything amiss. With all the hatred burning in my heart, I dared not break down in tears but just threw her a sidelong glance. Claiming that it was precisely my phoenix eyes that enamored the emperor, she had a palace maid blind me by stabbing gold needles into my eyes. Then, a stream of molten bronze was poured down my throat. My four limbs cut off, I was left abandoned in the latrine. What crime did I and my son commit to deserve such cruelty? The wrongs we suffered remain unvindicated to this day. Please do right by us, Your Majesty." With these words, she burst into heartrending sobs.

Chongxiang comforted her: "Don't weep so. I will see that justice is done. You will be a queen mother and your son a sovereign in your next lives, and both mother and son will live together to a ripe old age."

She signed her deposition and left.

Next came the fourth case, that of taking advantage of the victim's desperate situation to force him to commit suicide. After a rollcall found all parties involved in the case present, Chongxiang asked Xiang Yu, the plaintiff, "It was Han Xin who eliminated you and fostered Liu Bang. Why did you sue the six generals instead of Han Xin?"

Xiang Yu said, "Han Xin is not to blame for having abandoned me. It was my fault that I did not recognize his abilities, even though, with two pupils in each of my eyes, I should have been more perceptive. Defeated at Gaixia, I broke through the enemy siege and was on the run when I saw a farmer and asked him which of the two roads lying on both sides of me was a thorough-fare that would lead me out of the area. He told me to take the one on the left, which turned out to be the wrong one, and I was overtaken by Liu Bang's forces. The farmer was, in fact, Xia Guang, a general of the state of Han, in disguise. I fought as best I could with all the force and skills I could muster and broke out of the tight siege. At the Wu River ferry, I came upon an old acquaintance, Lü Matong. I was counting on him to let me go for old time's sake, but he and four other commanders forced me to take my own life. They then cut me apart and each took one piece of my body so as to claim a reward. That accounts for my resentment."

Chongxiang nodded in agreement: "The court finds that the six comman-ders did not deserve the titles and territories conferred upon them because they accomplished nothing in the battlefield but, by sheer good luck, took advantage of Xiang Yu's desperate situation and forced him to commit suicide. In their next lives, they will be generals again but will be slain by Xiang Yu in vindication for the injustice done to him." With this judgment, the case was put aside.

Then, Chongxiang had the judge present him with the registration book and issued his sentences, without the slightest unfairness, requiting kindness with kindness and meting out punishment for wrongdoings. While Chong-xiang was speaking, the judge sat by his side writing down his words with a brush-pen, filling in information on birthplaces, given names and surnames, and times of birth and death. All the plaintiffs and defendants were called into Chongxiang's presence for a lecture before being sent away for reincarnation.

"Han Xin," said Chongxiang, "you dedicated yourself to the service of your country and won most of the land for the Han empire. It is a shame that you died of a cruel wrong. I will now reincarnate you as Cao Cao,[6] courtesy name Mengde, to be born in the house of Cao Song of the town of Qiao-xiang. You will be prime minister in the Han court and, later, king of the state of Wei, with Xudu as your seat of power and having under your control half of the land of the Han empire. You will hold such sway as to be able to seek retaliation for all the injustices inflicted upon you in your previous life. You are not to lay any claim to the throne in your lifetime, so as to rise above any suspicion of disloyalty to the Han empire. Your son, to whom the throne of the Han will be yielded, will confer upon you posthumously the title of Emperor Wu of Wei, an honor that should compensate you for the ten meri-torious deeds you accomplished for founding the Han."

Next he called forth Liu Bang, the first Han emperor: "You will again be reborn into the Han royal family as Emperor Xian [r. 189–220], to tremble with fear under the bullying of Cao Cao for your whole life and to enjoy no peace of mind whether sitting or lying down. Each day of your life will drag on as painfully as if it were a year. In your previous existence, you as a sovereign wronged your subject. As a retribution, your subject will get even with you in your next life."

To Empress Lü, he said, "You will be reincarnated into the Fu family to be married to Emperor Xian and suffer from all kinds of cruel mistreatment from Cao Cao until you are strangled to death in the palace with a piece of red silk as retribution for the murder of Han Xin in the Palace of Eternal Happiness."

Han Xin asked, "What is the judgment for Xiao He?"

Chongxiang replied, "Xiao He was your benefactor before he did you wrong." So saying, he called forth Xiao He: "You will be reborn into a Yang family to be named Xiu, courtesy name Dezu. When Liu Bang took over the heartland of Qin, all other commanders scrambled for gold and silk, but you were the only one who was after files and documents. In your next life, you will be a man of matchless intelligence and insight. As master of records for Cao Cao, with the generous emoluments that come with such an important position, you will be amply rewarded for having strongly recommended Han Xin three times to the king of Han. But you will be killed by Cao Cao for having rightly guessed and exposed his secret military strategy. You will thus pay with your life for having cajoled Han Xin into the Palace of Eternal Happiness to meet his death." The judge took due note of everything.

Ying Bu, Prince of Jiujiang, was the next one to be called forth. "You will be reborn as the son of Sun Jian of the region to the east of the river. You will be named Sun Quan, with the courtesy name Zhongmou.[7] You will rise to be the lord of Wu, and later, the emperor of Wu, with reign over the entire region east of the Yangzi River, where you will enjoy the riches of the land."

Next, he called forth Peng Yue: "Being a man of integrity, you will be reborn as Liu Bei, courtesy name Xuande, son of Liu Hong of Lousang Village of Zhuojun County.[8] Your name as a man of honor and benevolence will spread far and wide. Later in your life, you will be the emperor of Shu and reign over the Sichuan region. The empire will be split among you, Cao Cao, and Sun Quan. It is the Cao family that will wipe out the Han dynasty, but your succession to the Han throne is a testament to your loyalty."

Peng Yue said, "With the empire split among three powers, that surely will be a time of chaos. How is Shu, with only a small territory, to be a match for the states of Wu and Wei?"

"I'll provide you with several aides," said Chongxiang, whereupon he summoned Kuai Tong: "Being a wise and resourceful man, you will be reborn in Nanyang as Zhuge Liang, courtesy name Kongming, also known as the Sleeping Dragon.[9] You will be Liu Bei's military adviser and help him with his cause."

Next, Xu Fu the fortune-teller was summoned. "You said that Han Xin was to live to be seventy-two years old, but actually he died at thirty-two, a death that, for all its untimeliness, was predestined. You will be reborn in Xiangyang as Pang Tong [179–214], with the courtesy name Shiyuan, nicknamed the Young Phoenix, to help Liu Bei take Sichuan. You are preordained to die at the age of thirty-two at the foot of Phoenix Fall Hill. Dying at the same age when Han Xin did is a retribution for your quackery as a fortune-teller. (*Fortune-tellers, watch out!*) All future fortune-tellers will learn from your early death not to mislead people with their nonsense."

Peng Yue said, "Military advisers need good generals to support them."

"You will have them," said Chongxiang. He called forth Fan Kuai: "You will be reborn into a Zhang family in Zhuozhou Prefecture, Fanyang, as Zhang Fei, courtesy name Yide."[10]

Next, he had Xiang Yu step forward: "You will be reborn in a Guan family in Xieliang, Puzhou Prefecture. Your surname will be changed but not your given name: You will be Guan Yu [d. 220], with the courtesy name Yunchang. The two of you [Xiang Yu and Fan Kuai], both fearless warriors who easily push back ten thousand men, will pledge brotherhood with Liu Bei in the Peach Garden and join hands in laying the foundation of a great career. Fan Kuai did wrong in letting his wife Lü Xu aid Empress Lü in her tyranny. The wife's sin will be visited upon the husband. Xiang Yu did wrong in killing Ziying, king of Qin, and in burning the city of Xianyang. Both of you, therefore, are preordained to die unnatural deaths. However, Fan Kuai, you were a loyal and valiant subject who never resorted to flattery. Xiang Yu, you have the three virtues of not killing Liu Bang's father, not sullying Empress Lü, and not trying to ambush Liu Bang when he was a guest at your table. Both of you are predestined in your next lives to be men of honor, courage, and candor and will assume the stature of gods after you die."[11]

He then called Ji Xin over: "For all your dedication to the Liu family in your previous life, you did not enjoy wealth for a single day. You will now be reborn into a Zhao family of Changshan as Zhao Yun [d. 229], courtesy name Zilong, a famous general of the kingdom of Shu. Your prestige will spread far and wide for rescuing the future emperor[12] from the million-strong enemy troops in Changban, Dangyang. You will be spared all ailments and die of natural causes at the advanced age of eighty-two."

Lady Qi was the next one to be called forth. "You will be reborn into the Gan family," said Chongxiang, "to be married to Liu Bei as his head wife. Empress Lü had admired the good looks of Prince Peng and failed in her attempt to seduce him. She was also jealous of you for enjoying the emperor's love. That is why I make you Peng Yue's wife so that Empress Lü will have no legitimate reason for jealousy. (*Brilliant and full of humor.*) Ruyi, Prince of Zhao, will still be your son, to be named Liu Shan [207–271], with the nickname of Adou, and will succeed to the throne. He will enjoy wealth and eminence for forty-two peaceful years in compensation for his sufferings in his previous life."

Ding Gong was the next in line. "You will be reborn," said Chongxiang, "into the Zhou family as Zhou Yu [175–210], with the courtesy name Gongjin, to serve Sun Quan as his commander. You will be driven to death by frustration at the hands of Zhuge Liang at the age of thirty-five. In your previous life, your service to Xiang Yu did not last long, nor will your service to Sun Quan in your next life be maintained to the end."

To Xiang Bo and Yong Chi, he said, "Xiang Bo betrayed his kinsman and entered the service of the enemy to seek riches and fame. Yong Chi was granted noble titles by the enemy. The two of you, being guilty of offenses against Xiang Yu, will be reborn as Yan Liang and Wen Chou respectively, both to be killed by Guan Yu in revenge for the grievances from his previous life." (*Brilliant.*)

Xiang Yu asked, "What will be done to the six commanders?"

Chongxiang ruled that they were to be subordinates of Cao Cao and would be given the duty of guarding border passes. Yang Xi would be reborn as Bian Xi, Wang Yi as Wang Zhi, Xia Guang as Kong Xiu, Lü Sheng as Han Fu, Yang Wu as Qin Qi, and Lü Matong as Cai Yang. All six of them were to be killed by Guan Yu as he charged through the five passes in retaliation for their forcing him to take his own life at the Wu River in his previous existence. (*Brilliant again.*) All those present found Chongxiang's sentences to be fair and just.

Chongxiang then asked all the soldiers and officers who died unjustly when Chu and Han were contending for power, all whose talents were not put to full use, and all those who had debts of gratitude to pay and injustices to vindicate—indeed, he asked all who had cases to plead to come to him, and all of them were reborn in the time of the Three Kingdoms. The mean and cruel who refused to pay their debts of gratitude were reincarnated as warhorses to serve officers and commanders. Instances of this nature will not be described in detail here. The judge made meticulous notes of all the cases and, before they noticed it, roosters' crows announced the arrival of the fifth watch.

Having left the court and removed his official robe, Chongxiang resumed his identity as a scholar. He handed his files over to Yama for his inspection. After many a gasp of admiration, the latter forwarded the documents to heaven for a celestial judgment. (*Yama is a worthy king who appreciates talent and righteousness.*) The Jade Emperor was full of praise: "I am impressed by his efficiency in settling within twelve hours cases that have been pending for over three hundred years—and settling them in a way that manifests the impartiality of the universe and the infallibility of the law of retribution. What a rare talent he is! All his judgments on the complaints shall be acted upon accordingly. For a man of such inestimable ability, Sima Mao is, indeed, short-changed in this life. He should be granted a royal title in his next life and be reborn into a Sima family so that his surname will remain the same. His given name will be changed into Yi [178–251], with the courtesy name Zhongda. He will lead a life of distinction as a commander, then as prime minister. He will pass down his title to his descendants, who will merge the three kingdoms and name the dynasty Jin. (*The Jade Emperor has a bolder vision.*) Though Cao Cao as a reincarnation of Han Xin will be out to seek vindication for the injustices he suffered, his insults to the emperor and his killing of the empress as spelled out in Chongxiang's sentence are by no means exemplary conduct. Lest future generations emulate such evil behavior without knowing the underlying causes, it is advisable to have Sima Yi humiliate Cao Cao's descendants as retribution for Cao Cao's humiliation of Emperor Xian. This will serve as a warning to posterity against evil deeds." (*Getting more and more interesting.*)

The Jade Emperor thus issued his imperial decree, which was duly read with much ceremony by Yama, who then laid out a farewell feast in Chongxiang's honor. Chongxiang made a request of Yama: "My wife Wang-shi, since marrying me at an early age, has known nothing but hardships all her life. Please be so kind as to intercede on my behalf with heaven and make us husband and wife again in our next lives so that she can share riches and distinction with me." Yama gave his consent.

While bidding farewell to Yama in the netherworld, Chongxiang suddenly turned over in his bed and, opening his eyes, saw his wife Wang-shi sitting by his side, weeping bitterly. "How strange!" he exclaimed over and over again and gave his wife a detailed account of how he had disrupted the normal conduct of affairs in the netherworld. "Having received the Jade Emperor's decree, I dare not linger on. Luckily, I will be joined with you again in my next life." With these words, he closed his eyes and died. Now that Wang-shi knew what lay ahead, her grief subsided and she busied herself with arrangements for Chongxiang's funeral, after which she, too, died. Sima Yi and his wife of the later period of the Three Kingdoms were none other than Chongxiang and his wife reincarnated. This extraordinary story is still being told to this day, as attested by a poem of later times:

> Yama for half a day, he set wrongs right,
> With all injustices redressed, rancor dissolved.
> Do nothing that will trouble your conscience,
> For you will get whatever you deserve.

Humu Di Intones Poems and Visits the Netherworld

Vice has never failed to come home to roost;
Do nothing evil to gain wealth and fame.
Just as sure as water drips from the eaves,
Retribution never misses the mark.

It is said that the most treacherous court minister of the Song dynasty was Qin Hui [1090–1155],[1] courtesy name Huizi, a native of Jiangning. He was born with a peculiarity: his feet measured one foot four inches from heel to toe. He was therefore nicknamed the Long-Foot Scholar when he was a student in the National University. Later, he passed the imperial examinations and rose to the post of vice–censor in chief in the reign period of Jingkang [1126], when the capital fell under attack by the Jurchen [Jin] army and the two emperors, Huizong and Qinzong, were carried off to the north. Qin Hui, too, found himself stranded among the Jurchens. He cultivated a friendship with Wanyan Chang,[2] a Jurchen tribal chief, and said to him, "If you let me go back to the south, I'll be willing to spy for the Jurchen state. If, by any luck, I rise to power, I will certainly initiate a peace negotiation out of my gratitude for the great Jurchen state, and have the Southern Song dynasty cede territory and subjugate itself to the Jurchen state." Wanyan Chang reported accordingly to the Jurchen ruler, who instructed his fourth son, Wuzhu [Wanyan Zongbi, d. 1148], to enter into a secret pact with Qin Hui. Qin Hui was then released to the south.

Qin Hui and his wife, Wang-shi, journeyed south by sea. On arriving at Lin'an, the capital of the Southern Song dynasty, they claimed that they had gotten away by killing their Jurchen prison wardens. Emperor Gaozong believed their story and asked Qin Hui about the situation in the north. Qin Hui extolled in glowing terms the prowess of the Jurchen troops and claimed that the Southern Song dynasty was no match for them. Not surprisingly, Emperor Gaozong took fright and asked Qin Hui for a good plan. Qin Hui said, "Since the house of Shi of the Later Jin dynasty submitted itself to Liao, the central plains have been on the decline and there is little chance of revitalizing in a short period of time. That the empire was nearly wiped out in the

Jingkang crisis was more the will of heaven than the work of humans. Your Majesty just started the southern dynasty, with the populace still apprehensive and the generals away from court, in command of massive forces. Should any one of them betray you, the game will be as good as lost. (*A foreshadowing of the murder of Yue Fei.*) The best course of action for now is to hold back the troops and make peace. Draw a demarcation line separating north and south so that both sides will not invade each other. Remove military power from the generals, and Your Majesty can sit back and enjoy your riches in ease, while the people of the empire will be free from misery and suffering. Wouldn't that be most desirable?"

The emperor replied, "I do wish to make peace. My only fear is that the Jurchens will not agree."

"When I was among the Jurchens," said Qin Hui, "I came to be respected by the Jurchen chieftains. If Your Majesty entrusts me with the mission, I will find a way to guarantee success of the peace talks. Nothing will go wrong."

Overjoyed, the emperor then and there conferred upon Qin Hui the title of vice-director of the Department of State Affairs. Promoted soon thereafter to the post of deputy prime minister, Qin Hui took on the sole responsibility for peace talks and appointed Goulong Ruyuan as his vice–censor in chief. All court ministers who advised against the peace talks were removed from their posts at Qin Hui's insistence. (*How efficient!*) Among those demoted and banished were Zhao Ding, Zhang Jun, Hu Quan, Yan Dunfu, Liu Dazhong, Yin Tun, Wang Juzheng, Wu Shigu, Zhang Jiucheng, and Yu Chu.

In the meantime, Yue Fei [1103–42] was putting the Jurchen forces to rout in battle after battle. Wuzhu, the fourth son of the Jurchen ruler, was driven into such desperation that he sent his trusted subordinate Wang Jin to Qin Hui with a note stuffed into a wax ball. On the note was written, "If there is a will for peace, why all this show of force at the border? The prime minister is insincere. Nothing less than the death of Yue Fei will make the peace talks a success." Thereupon, Qin Hui had Wang Jin take back a letter of reply promising that he would kill Yue Fei as a token of his good faith.

In the course of a single day, he issued twelve golden plaques ordering Yue Fei to withdraw his forces from the front, much to the indignation of all the soldiers. There was not a dry eye among the villagers, old and young, in the Henan region. Yue Fei duly returned, only to be demoted to the position of supervisor of Longevity Temple. Bent upon the total destruction of Yue Fei, Qin Hui took counsel with his trusted man Zhang Jun and found out that Wang Jun, commander in chief under Yue Fei, had a grudge against vice–supreme commandant Zhang Xian, whereupon they heavily bribed Wang Jun into falsely accusing Zhang Xian of conspiring to seize the town of Xiangyang in order to restore military power to Yue Fei. Wang Jun did as he was told to do. Qin Hui threw Zhang Xian into prison and, with a counterfeit imperial decree, summoned Yue Fei and his son to confront Zhang Xian. Vice–censor in chief He Zhu, who was in charge of the trial, found the accused innocent of the charges and informed Qin Hui accordingly. Qin Hui flew into a rage and replaced He Zhu with Moqi Xie [1083–1157]. Now this Moqi Xie, having long harbored ill feelings toward Yue Fei, fabricated a case against him and his son and sent them to prison on charges of planning a rebellion with his subordinates Zhang Xian and Wang Gui. Xue Renfu, director of the Court of Judicial Review, and others appealed on Yue Fei's behalf. Zhao Shiniao, director of the Office of Imperial Clan Affairs, vouched for Yue Fei's loyalty by pledging the lives of a hundred members of his clan. The military affairs com-missioner, Han Shizhong, indignant at the injustice, made a personal call to Qin Hui's residence to challenge him. But all who spoke up were either repri-manded or deposed.

With Yue Fei now in prison, Qin Hui sat alone by the east window and pondered over the matter: "If Yue Fei is spared his life, he might obstruct the peace talks, and I'll lose credibility in the eyes of the Jurchens. Should the emperor come to his senses, the blame will be upon me. But, to kill Yue Fei would be to risk public outcry." And so he debated with himself, unable to come to a decision. (*Qin Hui still has a trace of goodness in him at this time. If he had had a virtuous wife, the evil deed might not have been done.*) His wife, Wang-shi the tongue-wagger, happened to walk up to him and ask, "What is it that you are undecided about?" When Qin Hui took her counsel, she pro-duced a mandarin orange from her sleeve and split it apart. She handed one half to her husband. "What is so difficult about splitting this orange in half? Haven't you heard the ancient proverb 'It is easier to capture the tiger than to release it'?" It was these remarks that made up Qin Hui's mind. Thereupon, he sent to the prison warden a sealed letter containing a note with several characters on it. And thus it was that Yue Fei was hanged in his prison cell that very night. His son Yue Yun was taken under guard, along with Zhang Xian and Wang Gui, to the marketplace for execution.

As news of Yue Fei's death reached the Jurchens, there was not a person among them who did not celebrate with wine. Peace was established, with the middle course of the Huai River and Tang and Deng Prefectures as the border. The Jurchen dynasty in the north, being the bigger country, claimed to be the "uncle," whereas the Southern Song dynasty, smaller in territory, was the "nephew." Qin Hui was granted the titles of grand preceptor and duke of Wei, later changed to duke of Yiguo, and was given a mansion near Wangxian Bridge, a mansion not any less grandiose than the imperial palace itself. His son Qin Xi received the honor of *zhuangyuan* at the age of sixteen, later to be promoted to the position of Hanlin academician in charge of the Institute of

Historiography. (*With a trusted subordinate as the imperial censor, he makes sure that all criticisms against him in his lifetime are under control. With his offspring as historians, he makes sure that records after his death will be in his favor. He leaves nothing unplanned for. But how is one to know what Yama's books say?*)[3] Qin Xi's son Xun was assigned in his infancy a position in the Hanlin Academy. At the moment of her birth, Qin Xi's daughter was granted the title Lady Chongguo. The family's power and influence had no match in all history.

When Lady Chongguo was six or seven years old, she had a pet cat. One day, the cat disappeared. The prefect of Lin'an was ordered to find it before a deadline. Cao Yong, the prefect, dispatched runners everywhere who brought back hundreds of cats. Cases where owners found themselves accused and had to buy themselves out of trouble were too numerous to be mentioned here. Yet, as none of the cats sent under guard to the prime minister's mansion was found to be the right one, thousands of drawings of the cat were posted in tea-houses and wineshops, with the prefectural reward set at one thousand strings of cash. The uproar throughout Lin'an lasted for over a month, but the cat was still nowhere to be seen. Under pressure from an official sent by the prime minister to see that the job was done, a frightened Cao Yong had a cat cast of gold and sent it, through heavily bribed waiting women, to Lady Chongguo. Only then was the case laid to rest. (*Even his seven-year-old daughter loves bribery. It is indeed something that runs in the family.*) This incident alone is enough to demonstrate the extent of the traitor Qin Hui's formidable power.

Later in his life, he began to have designs on the throne but feared those court ministers who had survived his purges. In an attempt to send all of them to prison, he accused Zhao Ding, Zhang Jun, Hu Quan, and fifty others of rebellion. His secretary wrote the memorial to the emperor. That very day when the memorial was ready for his signature, Qin Hui went on an outing to West Lake. (*These men's lives are now hanging by a thread.*) In the midst of the drinking, there came into view a man with disheveled hair. A closer look revealed him to be none other than Yue Fei, who said, his voice loud and harsh, "I am instructed by the Lord on High to take your life as punishment for your destruction of the loyal and the virtuous and for bringing calamity to the empire and the people."

Agape with astonishment, Qin Hui turned to the people around him, but none of them had seen anything. Then and there, he fell ill and returned to his residence. The following day, when his secretary presented him with the memorial for his signature, his attendants helped him sit down in Getian Pavilion. When he tried to sign his name with a brush-pen, his hand started trembling and the memorial was all smeared with ink blots. Another copy was promptly brought to him, but the same thing happened, so that not even one character could be attempted. His wife, Lady Wang the tongue-wagger, shook her hand from her position behind the screen, saying, "Don't make him too tired!" The next moment, Qin Hui fell forward upon the tea table. By the time he was brought into his bedchamber, he was already unconscious and unable to utter a single word. He died shortly thereafter. The fifty-three ministers were not destined to perish at his hands after all. Fair and just indeed are the ways of heaven, as these lines attest:

> *He exiled Zhao Ding, murdered Yue Fei,*
> *And destroyed the kind and the worthy.*
> *But his failed attempt to sign his name*
> *Proves that good men are secretly blessed.*

Soon after Qin Hui's death, his son Qin Xi also died. At the funeral ceremony arranged by Lady Wang the tongue-wagger, the necromancer was in the midst of a prayer by the altar when he saw Qin Xi standing in the netherworld with an iron cangue on his neck. The necromancer asked, "Where is His Excellency your father?" Qin Xi replied, "He is here in the netherworld." The necromancer went there, and whom did he see but Qin Hui, Moqi Xie, and Wang Jun, with disheveled hair and dirty faces, moving ahead in iron cangues in great anguish, under the promptings of cudgel-wielding demon guards.

Qin Hui said to the necromancer, "Please be kind enough to convey a message to Lady Wang and tell her that what she said to me by the east window has been disclosed." Unaware of what this was about, the necromancer duly relayed the message to Lady Wang, who knew all too well its underlying meaning. She was stunned. How true it is that human whispers ring as loud as thunder in the ears of heaven, and evil deeds done in a dark room are as clear as lightning in the eyes of heaven. She died thereafter of an illness brought on by the shock. Soon after her death, Qin Xun also died. In a matter of a few years, the Qin family's fortunes went on the decline. Later, when construction of a canal got under way by order of the imperial court, loads of earth and dirt were piled up right in front of the Qin residence. At this grim sight, a poet passing by Wangxian Bridge wrote these lines on the wall:

> *The mansion remains, but where are the Qins?*
> *The Yanyue Hall[4] is deep, but so is the wrath.*
> *Instead of seeking a peaceful old age,*
> *He abused power for his own profit.*
> *Without a qualm, he leveled false charges,*
> *Oblivious of heaven watching above.*

A forlorn and woeful sight is his grave;
His house a dumping ground for earth and dirt.

After Qin Hui appeased the Jurchens, the Song dynasty lost its chance and ended up serving its enemies. While the emperor and his ministers were indulging in wanton dissipation, Temujin [Genghis Khan], Emperor Taizu of the Yuan dynasty, raised an army from the desert steppes. His grandson Kublai, Emperor Shizu of the Yuan, wiped out both the Jurchen and the Song dynasties. Song prime minister Wen Tianxiang [1236–83], courtesy name Wenshan, who was a man of honor and integrity, mustered troops to render service to the emperor. However, for all his aspirations, he was captured by Zhang Hongfan, a Yuan general, but he adamantly refused to surrender in spite of all efforts to win him over, and was executed at Chaishi, Yanjing, in the nineteenth year of the Zhiyuan reign period [1264–94] of the Yuan dynasty. His sons Daosheng, Fosheng, and Huansheng all died before him. His younger brother Wen Bi, also called Wenxi, and Wen Bi's son Wen Sheng, who was made Tianxiang's heir, both ended up ingratiating themselves to the powerful and the eminent in the Yuan court, as these lines by a contemporary poet attest:

Their names spread south of the river;
Fine brothers they were indeed.
How sad that plum blossoms grow apart,
The south branch warm with sun, the north one cold with frost.

In the reign period of Huangqing [1312–13] under Emperor Renzong of the Yuan dynasty, Wen Sheng rose to be grand academician of the Academy of Scholarly Worthies.

Our story forks at this point. Let me now tell of a scholar by the name of Humu Di, who lived in the town of Jincheng in the beginning years of the Zhiyuan reign period [1335–40] under Yuan emperor Shunzong. An upright and outspoken man, he often said, "Should I some day rise to power, I shall not rest until the imperial court is swept clean of all insidiousness and peopled by none but the virtuous." But his time had not yet come. He sat for ten imperial examinations in succession but failed each time. He became a recluse on Weifeng Mountain, where he continued with his studies and, at the same time, planted a vegetable garden as a way of supporting himself. However, he was still prone to occasional eruptions of wrath at the injustices of the world.

One day, he sat drinking all by himself in a small room. When he had drunk himself into a state of semi-intoxication, he reached into his bag for a book to read. The book he laid hands on happened to be *A Biography of Qin Hui the Conspirator by the East Window*. Before he had quite finished the book, a seething rage seized him and out came an endless stream of indignant words against Qin Hui's treachery. The second book he extracted from the bag was *The Posthumous Transcripts of Prime Minister Wen Tianxiang*. After he had read the text aloud from beginning to end, his anger at the injustice mounted. With a slap on the table, he cried at the top of his voice, "How blind heaven is to let such a loyal and righteous man be killed and left heirless!" In a rush of indignation, he poured himself more wine and drank until he was tipsy. He prepared some ink and wrote a quatrain on the book about Qin Hui:

> *The long-foot villain and his long-tongued wife*
> *Destroyed the good who resisted the Jin.*
> *Should I someday sit in Yama's seat,*
> *I would peel off that knave's skin ten thousand times!*

After intoning these lines over and over again, he pushed the book aside and wrote another quatrain on the transcripts of Prime Minister Wen:

> *He failed to hold up the sky with one hand,*
> *But his integrity shines like the sun.*
> *How sad that without an heir to his name,*
> *His soul has to drift from place to place.*

Still in a poetic mood, he added another quatrain:

> *In peace did the villain Qin die;*
> *His sons also led enviable lives.*
> *But Wenshan died in pain, without an heir.*
> *When did heaven ever know good from evil?*

With this, he threw down his brush-pen and read the poems aloud several times over again. Overwhelmed by the effect of the wine, he went to bed without even bothering to take off his clothes.

Presently, there came approaching him two runners in black, who said with a bow, "We are sent by King Yama to invite you. Please follow us without delay."

The name Yama meant nothing to Humu Di in his groggy state. He said, "I don't know anybody by that name. Why is he inviting me?"

The runners in black laughed. "You will know the moment you get there. There's no need for more questions." Humu Di was about to say something more in protest when the two grabbed him and dragged him off. Several li out of the city limits, there was nothing but desolate wilderness shrouded in a late-autumn misty rain. Several li later, there loomed into view the walls of a city that appeared to be teeming with inhabitants and traders. It was only when they drew near the city gate that Humu Di realized, from the characters inscribed on the board across the gate, "Fengdu," that this was no other place than the netherworld. Now that he had gotten this far, there was no turning back.

After passing through the gate, they came upon a magnificent palace with the words "Palace of the Sun" inscribed above the tall vermilion gate. One of the runners in black stayed with Humu Di, while the other went in and emerged quickly again to lead him to King Yama. They stopped in front of a hall labeled "Hall of Darkness," where Yama presented an imposing appearance in his royal robe and crown, looking just like a statue of a deity in a temple of the mortal world. To his left and right stood six runners in green robes and black boots, tall caps, and wide belts, each carrying a register. At the foot of the dais stood about a hundred attendants, among whom were the fearsome Ox-Heads and Horse-Faces, with their long muzzles and red hair.

As Humu Di kowtowed from his position at the foot of the steps, Yama asked, "Are you Humu Di?"

"Yes, sire."

In an outburst of rage, Yama thundered, "As a scholar well-versed in the classics, you should know better than to harbor such bitterness against the ways of heaven and to speak of deities in such disparaging terms!"

Humu Di rejoined, "I am but a humble young man who started learning the ways of the former sages and worthies from an early age, and, poor as I am, I have been content with my lot and cultivate myself morally. I harbor bitterness to none, man or heaven."

"You did say, 'When did heaven ever know good from evil?' If that is not bitter slander, what is?"

It now dawned upon Humu Di that he had indeed written such a line in a drunken state. He bowed twice in apology: "When I was reading the biographies of a good man and a villain, wine got the better of my customary caution and prompted me to utter those bitter words. I beg for Your Majesty's forgiveness."

"Explain yourself," said King Yama. "How is it that heaven does not distinguish good from evil?"

"Qin Hui betrayed the country, sought peace with the Jurchens, and murdered the emperor's loyal subjects, yet he himself enjoyed a life of wealth and fame, his son Qin Xi became a *zhuangyuan,* and his grandson Qin Xun a Hanlin academician. All three generations had the honor of being members of the Institute of Historiography. On the other hand, Yue Fei, a most loyal subject who dedicated himself to the service of the empire, was slain, as was his son. Wen Tianxiang, the minister of the greatest integrity toward the end of the Song dynasty, died without an heir, his three sons having died before him of hardships of a life constantly on the run. His brother surrendered to the enemy and yet both father and son rose to prominence. Where is the way of heaven that should reward the good and punish the evil? That is what puzzles me and where I need your enlightenment."

King Yama gave a hearty guffaw and said, "What do you, a petty scholar of the mundane world, know about the subtle workings of heaven? Emperor Gaozong was, in fact, a reincarnation of the third son of King Qian Liu,[5] ruler of the states of Wu and Yue. For a hundred years of their reign, the Qian family did nothing to tarnish their good name. Later, when Qian Liu entered the imperial court, he was detained by Emperor Taizong, who pressed him for territorial concessions. During the reign of Emperor Huizong, the pregnant Empress Xianren dreamt that a god in a golden cuirass said to her with a fierce glare, 'I am the king of Wu and Yue. Because you wrested territory from me for no justifiable reason, I am now sending my third son to be reborn to you to claim back our land.' No sooner had the empress woken up than she gave birth to a son, later named Gou, also known as Emperor Gaozong. His hopes were to regain his territories in the south, so he had no ambition to recover the central plains. It therefore fits into the scheme of the workings of heaven to have Qin Hui seek peace with the Jurchens. (*This is the account given in* Past Events of the Xuanhe Reign Period *[Xuanhe yishi] and repeated in* The West Lake Records *[Xihu zhi].*)

"However, as Qin Hui should not have ruined the innocent, the Lord on High put an end to his family line. Qin Xi was not the issue of Qin Hui, but was adopted by Qin's wife from her brother Wang Huan. Granted that the subsequent generations did live in grandeur, how is it possible for Qin's soul to receive offerings made by descendants of another clan?

"Yue Fei is a reincarnation of Zhang Fei [d. 221] of the period of the Three Kingdoms, whose integrity and loyalty remained every bit as firm as a thousand years before. Zhang Fei was first reborn as Zhang Xun with the same surname, and again as Yue Fei with the same given name. However unjustly both Yue Fei and his son died, their descendants from generation to generation have been thriving and will continue to thrive. As for Wen Tianxiang, the reputation of his loyalty and righteousness and the same qualities of his sons and his wife will go down to posterity through the ages. Wen Sheng, his nephew, inherited the family line and, by being an upright official, preserved the family's good name. How can you call Wen Tianxiang heirless? (*This convinces me that nephews are indeed like sons.*) Retribution from heaven can occur during or after one's lifetime. A blessing may turn out to be a calamity; a calamity may turn out to be a blessing. Only by seeing the larger picture—in the mortal world as well as in the netherworld—from a historical perspective can one realize the perfection of the workings of the ways of heaven. You are looking at the sky through a narrow tube, which explains your limited view."

Humu Di nodded vigorously and said, "Your words of wisdom have enlightened me in my ignorance in much the same way as the sun dispels clouds. I am much obliged. However, the average man, in his ignorance, cares only about the pleasures and hardships of this life. How is he to know about the retribution that will be visited upon him after his death? To urge people to adopt virtuous ways and shun evil is to ask them to do something as intangible as to grasp the sound of the wind or the reflection of the moon in the water. There is no deterrent to hold them back. That is why bad people far outnumber the good. However unworthy I am, I would like to visit the netherworld from one end to the other and witness all the retribution for evil deeds, so that I can relate what I have seen to inhabitants of the mortal world to motivate them to cultivate themselves. Will you let me?"

Yama nodded and, handing a letter to a runner in green, instructed him in these words: "Tell the warden of the Prison for the Condemned to open the gate and show this scholar how retribution is done in the netherworld. Tell the warden not to be remiss in his duty."

Thus instructed, the runner led Humu Di into a western corridor. About three li after passing the hall, they came upon a stone wall several tens of feet high, with an iron gate bearing the inscription "Prison for the Condemned." The runner rapped the knocker three times before the gate opened, and out came several *yakshas*,[6] who charged at Humu Di. The runner checked them with a shout: "This scholar is an innocent man." When he showed the *yakshas* the letter from Yama, they said, "We thought it was another condemned soul. We had no idea a scholar would be visiting. Please don't take offense." With that, they bowed and let Humu Di in. There was a square stretching for over fifty li in width as well as in length. It was a chilly and bleak place, with tablets hanging on all four sides. The one to the east said "Prison of Wind and Thunder," the one to the south "Prison of Fire Vehicles," the one to the west "Vajra Prison," and the one to the north "Prison of Coldness." Scattered all about were more than a thousand men and women in iron cangues.

When they came to a small door, they saw about twenty naked men with disheveled hair confined to iron beds by enormous nails driven through their hands and feet. With iron cangues on their necks, they were covered with scars and weals from swords and canes. The stench from the pus and blood was most repulsive. By their side was a woman in an iron cage, stripped to the waist. A *yaksha* was pouring boiling water on her. Her skin and flesh all festering, she gave out wails of pain. The runner in green said, pointing at three men on the iron bed, "These are Qin Hui, Moqi Xie, and Wang Jun. The woman in the cage is Qin Hui's wife, Lady Wang the tongue-wagger. The others are Zhang Dun, Cai Jing and his sons, Wang Fu, Zhu Mian, Geng Nanzhong, Ding Daquan, Han Tuozhou, Shi Miyuan, Jia Sidao, and other depraved villains.[7]

I am instructed by King Yama to inflict torture upon them in your presence." This said, he drove Qin Hui and others into the Prison of Wind and Thunder, where they were tied to a copper column. Each time a *yaksha* struck a ring on the column with his whip, a bevy of daggers emerged from the wind and stabbed the men's bodies, which in no time looked just like sieves. After what seemed like an eternity, a thunderbolt struck their bodies and reduced them to powder. Their blood gushed out and curdled on the ground. Before long, in a gust of sinister whirling wind, they reassumed their human shape. The runner said to Humu Di, "What you saw was the thunder and wind of the netherworld at work."

He then called upon *yakshas* to drive them to the Prisons of Vajra, Fire Vehicles, and Coldness and subjected Qin Hui and others to further torture. They were fed iron balls to stay their hunger and molten copper to quench their thirst. The runner explained, "In three days, they are made to go through all of the prisons for tortures of every description. After three years, they will be reborn into the mortal world as oxen, sheep, dogs, and pigs to be slaughtered, skinned, and eaten. Their wives will be reborn as sows to eat human filth and to be knifed and cooked. Those that you see have already been reborn as beasts over fifty times."

Humu Di asked, "When will they be absolved of their sins?"

"Only when the universe reverts to its original state of swirling chaos."

Humu was then led in a westerly direction to a small gate bearing the inscription "Prison for the Evil." In the prison were over a hundred prisoners in cangues who looked like hedgehogs, with their bodies covered from head to toe with daggers. To Humu Di's question about their identities, the runner replied, "These are generals and court ministers of past dynasties—Liang Ji [d. 159], Dong Zhuo [d. 192], Lu Qi, Li Linfu [d. 752] among them—known for their wickedness in deceiving the emperor and plaguing the people. Once every three days, they are put to the same tortures as Qin Hui and others, and in three years' time, they will be reborn as beasts, just as Qin Hui will be."

They then directed their steps to a small gate to the south with the inscription "Prison for Disloyal Eunuchs." Tied to iron columns with iron chains piercing through their noses, hundreds of cows were being slowly roasted by a fire blazing on all sides. Humu Di asked, "What did the cows do to deserve this?"

The runner put up a hand in admonition: "Say nothing. Just watch."

At his bidding, a *yaksha* fanned the fire with a huge fan. As the raging flames roared and leaped high, the insufferable pain made the cows bellow and move about as their skin and flesh burned. A good while later, the skin of each cow split open with a tremendous crackling sound and out emerged men who, upon a closer look, turned out to be beardless eunuchs. As the *yaksha* threw the eunuchs into a cauldron of boiling water at the bidding of the runner, the skin and the flesh disappeared, leaving only heaps of white bones. Shortly thereafter, cold water was poured in, whereupon the bones gathered themselves into human forms again.

Pointing at the eunuchs, the runner said, "These are eunuchs of past dynasties, including Zhao Gao [d. 207 B.C.E.] of the Qin dynasty; the ten eunuch directors of the Han dynasty; Li Fuguo [704–62], Qiu Shiliang [781–843], Wang Shoucheng, and Tian Lingzi of the Tang dynasty; and Tong Guan [1054–1126] of the Song dynasty. Raised in royal style in palaces, they learned to cheat their masters and bring about the downfall of the loyal and the virtuous, wreaking havoc throughout the empire. The retribution meted out upon them here will last for *kalpas* and *kalpas*."

When they went to the prison to the east, they saw thousands of men and women, naked and barefoot, some of whom were having their hearts boiled, peeled, or gouged and some of whom were being cut, seared, pestled, or ground. Their wails and lamentations could be heard several li away. Pointing at them, the runner said, "In their lifetime, they were all greedy, corrupt, and lawbreaking officials who brought affliction to others and betrayed their teachers and elders, in total defiance of all norms of loyalty and filial piety. It was their iniquity that brought such retribution upon themselves."

Humu Di was enraptured. He said with a happy sigh, "Now I know how fair and how discerning heaven and the gods are. The bitterness pent up in me for my whole life is now all gone."

The runner pointed to the north and said, "That's the prison for monks and nuns guilty of extortion and debauchery. There's another prison for dissolute women, jealous women, rebellious women, and fierce women."

Humu Di said, "I now know well enough about the operations of karma and need not see more."

The runner, with a smile on his face, led Humu Di by hand back into the Hall of Darkness, where Humu Di bowed twice and, after some words of gratitude, presented Yama with a quatrain:

> The wicked may well abuse their power,
> But retribution will not pass them by.
> Be warned of the tortures in the netherworld,
> Or regrets for your sins will be too late.

Humu Di said again, "I fully accept the evidence of my eyes about the retribution visited upon the wicked. But where are the loyal ministers and other men of honor? I would be delighted beyond measure if my wish to see them could be granted."

With his head lowered, Yama thought long and hard before he replied,

"They are all reborn as human beings destined for greatness and heaven's bounties. After living out their natural spans of life, they return here to wait for the next reincarnation. Since you wish to see them, I will take you there."

King Yama ascended his chariot and bade his valets to escort Humu Di and follow closely behind. Before they had traveled quite five li, there came into view a richly decorated jade palace with a green-tiled roof and a vermilion tablet inscribed in gold "Court of the Underworld." Inside, there were hundreds of celestial youths dressed in purple silk, wearing bright jade pendants, and carrying colored streamers, a bird-feather canopy, and flower banners amid wisps of ephemeral mist and spinning flower petals. Celestial music filled the air, with dragons and phoenixes joining in the band. An exotic fragrance assailed the nostrils. Sitting on the raised dais were over a hundred people, wearing crowns, robes of brocade, and vermilion shoes. The jade ornaments they wore shone in dazzling splendor. Around the dais, over five hundred jade maidens in red silk stood in a ring, some carrying tall fans, some holding decorated jars. At the sight of Yama, they descended the steps to greet him. The exchange of greetings over, guest and hosts took their respective seats. After tea was served, King Yama explained the reason for Humu Di's visit and bade the latter to make another bow. The men returned the bow and said in unison in a praising tone, "This gentleman is indeed 'a man of true worth who loves as well as hates.'" A seat of honor was set aside for Humu Di, who demurred and repeatedly declined the offer. Yama said, "This extra honor is done in recognition of your righteousness. Why insist on declining the honor?" Thus admonished, Humu Di took the seat with a bow of gratitude.

Yama said, cupping one hand before the other in front of his chest in a gesture of respect, "These gentlemen on the dais were all loyal ministers and honorable men whose names are passed down to posterity in the mortal world and who enjoy bliss and beatitude in the netherworld. Every time a sagacious sovereign appears on the scene, they are reborn as members of the nobility to support the sovereign in his rule, for the benefit of the empire. Today marks another of these changes in the cycle of destiny, because every several decades, there will emerge a great man to bring order to chaos. Thus, the gentlemen here will be reborn one after another to become famous court ministers who will assist in the establishment of a new dynasty." (*The good officials in the imperial court of the current dynasty are all reincarnations of these men.*)

Humu Di, as before, presented the company with a quatrain:

> *In my reading of history,*
> *It grieved me that the virtuous should suffer.*
> *I have now seen how they are rewarded;*
> *Heaven forsakes not the true and worthy.*

The gentlemen all raised folded hands in a gesture of gratitude. Yama said, "You have now seen how retribution for both good and evil never errs. If you were made King Yama, I am afraid that you would not be able to do better than this." At these words, Humu Di left his seat, made a deep bow, and asked for forgiveness, but with one voice, the gentlemen said in his defense, "This scholar is not to blame. His complaints were prompted by his sense of righteousness."

Yama laughed, "How right you are!"

Humu Di asked with another bow, "I still have a question that I humbly ask you all to shed light on. I have been most assiduous in my studies from childhood on and have never been guilty of major aberrations. Why have I never attained any academic honors? Am I to understand that this is a retribution for my sins in a previous life?"

Yama said, "At present, the empire is ruled by the Mongol Yuan dynasty, which has turned the world upside down. You, being the honest and outspoken man that you are, should not hold office in such a court, because you have no predestined bond with the Mongols. As my term of office is due to expire soon, I have been weighing your strengths and weaknesses and find you to be the right man for my current position. I shall report to the celestial court and recommend you as my successor. (*This is much better than passing the imperial examinations.*) For now, you may return to the mortal world and live out the rest of your preordained span of life. I will come to greet you after ten years' time." So saying, he ordered two runners in red to escort Humu Di back home. An overjoyed Humu Di bowed twice in gratitude and bade farewell to the assembly.

After he walked for over ten li, dawn began to break. The runners told Humu Di, "Your house is where the sun is rising." Humu grabbed them by their clothes in an attempt to offer them a token of his gratitude, but the two firmly refused. For all his insistence, his hand slipped without his realizing it, and, in that very moment, the two runners vanished from view. The next moment, Humu Di was asleep with arms stretched out. His lamp was still flickering feebly against the sunlight that was showing through the window paper.

Henceforth, Humu Di gave up all thoughts of obtaining office but assiduously applied himself to self-cultivation. Another twenty-three years elapsed. He was sixty-six years old when, one afternoon, runners from the netherworld appeared to him with orders to escort him to his new post. Behind the runners was a procession of chariots and attendants, a procession grand enough for a king. Humu Di died that very evening. In another ten years came the fall of the Yuan dynasty, and China regained control of the empire.

The gentlemen in the Court of the Underworld were notified of their rebirths for important positions in the imperial court. A later poet had this to say:

Laws of the land may have loopholes;
Retribution from hell spares not a soul.
You need not see the underworld itself;
Reading Humu's poems will suffice.

Old Man Zhang Grows Melons and Marries Wennü

> *Dark clouds gather in the vast sky;*
> *Houses are suffused with auspicious light.*
> *Before willow catkins dance in the air,*
> *Plum blossoms bloom hither and yon.*
> *With a rustle, the flakes land on curtains;*
> *Noiseless, they fall into water.*
> *Overnight they gather on ancient pines,*
> *Unperturbed by the north wind of the dawn.*

The above eight lines describe falling snow, which resembles three things: salt, willow catkins, and pear blossoms. Why do I say snow is like salt? Xie Lingyun[1] had a line about snow that says, "Could it be salt sprinkling down from the sky?" There is a lyric poem by Su Dongpo[2] to the tune of "River God":

> *At dusk it was still a steady drizzle.*
> *At dawn when the curtain is raised,*
> *The eaves are seen to be laden with jade.*
> *The sky hanging low over the vast river,*
> *Blue wineshop flags are nowhere to be seen.*
> *I chant poems, sitting idly alone.*
> *I breathe on my frozen hands*
> *And stroke my thinning beard.*
>
> *Let us get drunk, host and guest!*
> *This crystal salt, for whom is it sweet?*
> *Plum twigs in hand, I look east and think of Tao Qian.[3]*
> *Snowfalls, though lovable, like the ancients,*
> *Are detested by some.*

Why do I say the snow resembles willow catkins? Xie Daoyun[4] had a line about snow that says, "Like willow catkins blown about by wind." Huang Luzhi[5] had a lyric poem to the tune of "Treading on Grass":

Jade flowers pile up, willow catkins float around.
By dawn all paths are lost to sight.
In the vast sky, dark clouds linger,
Dancing with every return of the wind.

I drink to the scene and try to write a line.
Turning back, I laugh at my lack of words.
A whole day has gone by, but why does no poem come?
On yonder hills, a patch of green remains.

Why do I say snow is like pear blossoms? Li Qingzhao[6] said, "Pear blossoms fall off travelers' dancing sleeves." There is also a lyric poem by Zhao Shuyong[7] to the tune of "Immortal by the River":

Masses of dark clouds for ten thousand li,
The color of jade suffusing the sky.
Flying like catkins, the flakes land on mud.
Along the road to the village ahead,
Pear blossoms fall off the dancing sleeves.

What scene best to capture at this moment?
Rivers, lakes, boats, and fishermen's houses.
The splendor of the season calls for wine.
A cape on my back, a hat on my head,
I set cheerfully out across the streams.

Just as snow resembles three things, it is also administered by three gods. Which three? They are Sage Guye and the fairy maidens Zhou Qiongji and Dong Shuangcheng. Zhou Qiongji's responsibility is Hibiscus Town.[8] Dong Shuangcheng is in charge of the glazed vase that contains flakes of snow. Every time dark clouds gather, Sage Guye taps at the vase with gold chopsticks until one flake comes out, causing a timely one-foot fall of snow. (*Similar to the way Li Jing[9] makes rain on behalf of the Dragon King.*) One day, the Sage of the Purple Palace invited Sage Guye and Dong Shuangcheng to a banquet, at which they got drunk and tapped at the vase with their gold chopsticks to beat time for a song. Unfortunately, the vase broke. As the snowflakes fell out, an unusually heavy snowfall followed. (*How absurd! Traditional stories tend to offer such absurdities as their best features.*) There is a lyric poem to the tune of "Remembering the Fairy Maiden":

When Sage Guye gave a feast in the Purple Palace,
Shuangcheng broke the snow vase.
The flower fairy tossed in the air
The white pearls and jade morsels.

The sky glows with their brilliance,
Adding to the moon's luster on the sea.
By dawn, bamboos are coated with snow;
Branches droop with glistening whips of jade.

Along the bends of the mountains,
Over the curves of the green waters,
Birds fly home in the evening chill,
Only to find that their nests are gone.
For love of the icicles on the eaves,
Don't let the children knock at them with sticks.
Imitate Yuan An[10] and Xie Daoyun of old,
And write inspired lines in praise of the snow.

Just as Sage Guye was the snow god, there was also a snow spirit in the shape of a white mule. Each hair shaken from its body would bring ten feet of snow. The mule was kept in a gourd watched over by a fairy called Hong Ya. After a banquet hosted by the Sage of the Purple Palace, Hong Ya, in an inebriated state, failed to put the stopper in tightly enough. The white mule escaped and wandered into the alien lands, where it shed many hairs, bringing on another snowstorm.

Now I shall tell of a man who, because he lost a white horse in the snow, mysteriously achieved immortality and rose to heaven with his entire family in broad daylight. The site of his ascension remains to this day.

In the wintry twelfth month of the sixth year of the Putong reign period [525] under Xiao Yan, Emperor Wudi of the Liang, an imperial counselor named Wei Shu was demoted to the position of director of the imperial horse stable for having remonstrated against Emperor Wudi's enthusiasm for Buddhism. This official was

Loyal and upright,
Honest and unyielding.
He gave advice to set the world to rights
And rid the court of the evil and vile.

This Mr. Wei was now put in charge of the royal stable located in Luhe County of Zhenzhou Prefecture. Emperor Wudi had a white horse named the Jade Lion, Star of the Palace.

Its hooves as if carved of jade,
Its body as if covered with jasper.
Its chest white as face powder,
Its tail ten thousand silver threads.
Able to gallop, able to carry,

> *It covered a thousand li at a stretch.*
> *Never gasping, never neighing,*
> *It could leap over any broad ravine.*
> *A heavenly lion incarnated on earth,*
> *A Whitemarsh[11] descended from heaven.*

For its errors at Changlu when carrying Emperor Wudi of Liang in his pursuit of Bodhidharma,[12] the white horse was sent to the royal stable as punishment. After a heavy snowfall, the stable-boy came to report to Counselor Wei the following morning, "I bring you bad news. Last night, the Jade Lion left its stall."

A panic-stricken Counselor Wei immediately summoned his men for a consultation about a solution. A stable-boy stepped forth and said, "It should be easy to find this horse, because its hoofprints in the snow will lead us to wherever it is."

"Right you are," said Wei. Without a moment's delay, the stable-boy was sent off with a few followers to look for the horse's hoofprints. They wended their way across the fields for several li and came upon a snow-covered garden. Behold:

> *The house was coated with white powder;*
> *The pavilion was covered with jade.*
> *The jasper railings sagged under the snow,*
> *Flanking a silver ribbon of a path.*
> *The Taihu rocks the shapes of salt tigers;*
> *The tall pine trees like winding jade dragons.*
> *The withered grass gained new color;*
> *The plum blossoms sent forth their aroma.*

It was a fenced farm house. Turning to his followers, the stable-boy said, "The horse is here." At their knocks on the gate, an old man came out. The stable-boy saluted him and said, "Please allow me to ask you something. Last night in the snow, we lost a white horse from the royal stable. It is called the Jade Lion, Star of the Palace, and serves the Liang emperor himself. Judging from its hoofprints, we believe that it has jumped over the fence into your garden. If it's still here, we will tell the counselor, and he will reward you with wine and money."

"Yes," said the old man, "the horse is indeed here. Please sit down. I'll get you something to eat."

The visitors sat down and watched the old man go to the back of the garden, where, with his fingers, he dug out a sweet melon from under the snow. It was indeed a melon

With green leaves, a tender stalk,
And yellow flowers blooming at the top.
From its pungent source rose its fragrance;
From bitterness came its sweet taste.

At the sight of the vine and leaves that were still attached to this fresh-looking melon, the visitors thought to themselves, "The old man can't have just picked it off the vine." The old man took a knife and peeled the melon and cut off the top, letting out an extraordinary fragrance. After offering it to the visitors, he went back into the snow and brought back three more melons. "Please give Counselor Wei these melons with the compliments of Mr. Zhang." (*The man's surname is not revealed until now.*)

The men accepted the melons. From somewhere at the back of the garden, the old man led out the white horse and returned it to the stable-boy, who took the bridle and thanked the old man. They then returned to the stable and reported to Counselor Wei. "How very strange!" they exclaimed. "How could he have grown such sweet melons in such heavy snow?" Without delay, Wei Shu called forth his wife and his eighteen-year-old daughter, and the melons were shared among the family.

His wife said, "We are much obliged to that old man. How shall we thank him for having kept the horse and sent us these melons?"

Two months went by with the snap of a finger. On a clear day in mid-spring of the following year, Lady Wei said, "This is perfect weather for us to go and thank Mr. Zhang for his melons as well as for the horse."

Counselor Wei asked for a jar of wine, some boxes of food, a pot for warming wine, and some delicacies. He called forth his eighteen-year-old daughter and said to her, "I am going today to see Mr. Zhang to offer him thanks. I'm taking you and your mother along so you can have some fun."

With the counselor on horseback and his wife and daughter following behind in two sedan-chairs, they arrived at Mr. Zhang's gate and asked for Mr. Zhang. Promptly, the old man came out and greeted them. Lady Wei said, "You looked after our horse some time ago. My husband has brought some wine to thank you for your kindness."

In the hall, wine vessels, bowls, and plates were set out, and Mr. Zhang was invited to sit with the Wei family, an offer that he repeatedly declined. (*Failure to marry off a daughter now already eighteen years old—this is mistake number one. Taking her along on an excursion—mistake number two. Letting her sit with Mr. Zhang—mistake number three.*) Instead, he took a bench and sat down on one side. After three rounds of wine, Lady Wei asked Mr. Zhang, "May I ask your age, sir?"

"I am eighty years old," he replied.

"How large is your family?" asked the lady again.

"I live all by myself."

"Don't you need a wife to keep you company?" said the lady.

"A good match is not that easy to come by," was the reply.

"How about a wife of about seventy years old?"

The old man said, "Too old! Don't people say that

> 'A hundred years go by in a finger snap;
> All too few live to be past seventy'?"

"In that case, what about sixty or so," said the lady.

"Too old!" He continued,

> "Once past the fifteenth day of the month,
> The moon loses its luster.
> On reaching middle age,
> Life loses all its glow."

Lady Wei insisted, "What about fifty or so?"

"Too old!

> "No glory at thirty, no money at forty,
> You'd be better off dead at fifty."

Lady Wei's patience was wearing thin. She thought to herself, "Let me tease him a bit." "In that case," she said, "get yourself a thirty-year-old."

"Too old."

"Now what age do you have in mind?"

Rising from his seat, he said, pointing at the eighteen-year-old girl, "I will be content if I can have her for wife." (*The audacity!*)

At these words, Counselor Wei flared up with rage. Instead of listening to anything more, he ordered his men to come forward and beat the old man. But his wife protested, "This can't be done. We are here to thank him. How can we end up beating him? It's his old age that makes him say such preposterous things. Just ignore him." They put together their wine utensils and left.

The story continues. For three days thereafter, Zhang stayed within closed doors. Two flower sellers from Luhe County called Wang San and Zhao Si came with large baskets to his house to ask for flowers. Finding the door closed, they knocked and called out his name. The old man came out coughing as he talked and panting for breath like someone suffering from either tuberculosis or lovesickness. (*How extraordinary for an eighty-year-old to be lovesick!*) How do I know this? There is a lyric poem to the tune of "A Night Stroll in the Palace":

Of all illnesses one may ever have,
Lovesickness torments the most.
The heart might have neither aches nor pains.
But while unnoticed, the body wastes away.

Flowers and moonlight evoke misery.
Dusk is the most feared moment of the day.
An itchy feeling in the chest
Brings on one cough after another.
(Vivid description.)

So the old man came out and said to them in a hoarse voice (Comic touch), "I am much obliged to you for coming, but I am not feeling well these last couple of days. You can take some flowers for free, but I do have a favor to ask of you. Find me two matchmakers. If you do, I will give you two hundred cash, not a penny less, for you to buy some wine with."

The two men picked some flowers and left. Shortly afterward, they brought back two matchmakers. Now those matchmakers—

Their eloquence makes marriages happen;
Their words ensure conjugal harmony.
They tend to solitary phoenixes;
They take care of all who sleep alone.
They recoil at no triple gates,
Nor do twelve-story towers stop their advance.
In men, even Liuxia would be stirred with desire;
In women, even Magu would be spurred to passion.
The Jade Maiden would seduce with her charms;
The Golden Boy would flirt midst tender words.
They lead the Wushan Goddess on to bewitch men,
And make the Weaving Maiden sick with longing.[13]

The two matchmakers were brought in to greet the old man. "I have a job for you," he said. "I've seen the one I have in mind, but it'll be hard to talk her into marrying me. Here are three taels of silver for each of you. If you manage to bring back a reply, I'll add another five taels each. If the reply is favorable, I'll help you make a small fortune for yourselves."

"Which family's girl do you have in mind?"

"It's the eighteen-year-old daughter of Counselor Wei of the imperial horse stable. Please go there on my behalf."

The two women smiled discreetly and left with their three taels of silver each. When they reached an earth mound half a li away, Madam Zhang looked at Madam Li and said, "How are we going to put this to Counselor Wei?"

"Easy," said Madam Li. "We'll first buy ourselves some wine and drink it up so as to make our faces flushed. Then we'll walk as far as Counselor Wei's gate before we go back to Mr. Zhang and say that we gave them the message, but there's no reply yet."

Before the words were quite out of her mouth, they heard a cry: "Don't go yet!" Turning around, they saw that it was Zhang hurrying up to them. "I guessed that the two of you were going to buy yourselves some wine and drink it to make your faces flushed, walk by Counselor Wei's gate, and then come back to tell me that there's no reply yet. Did I guess right? If you want your reward, go quickly now and be sure to get a reply."

After this speech by Old Zhang, the two matchmakers were obliged to go and do as he wished.

Arriving at the imperial stable, the two women asked to have their visit announced to Counselor Wei. "Have them come in," said Wei. After the greetings, he asked them, "You are here to make a match, I presume?"

The two matchmakers smiled without venturing a reply.

Counselor Wei said, "I have a twenty-two year old son who is away on an expedition with Wang Sengbian.[14] I also have an eighteen-year-old daughter, whom I, being an incorrupt official, am too poor to marry off."

The two matchmakers made bow after bow at the foot of the steps without daring to utter a word.

"You don't have to bow so hard," said Mr. Wei. "Just say what you came here to say."

Matchmaker Zhang said, "We do indeed have something in mind. We don't want to say it but we are obligated to do so for the sake of the six taels of silver, and yet, if we say it, we are afraid it would be so ridiculous as to offend you."

Mr. Wei asked what it was. Matchmaker Zhang continued, "Oddly enough, Old Man Zhang the melon-grower sent for us today, telling us to make a match between him and your daughter. I'll show you the six taels of silver that he gave us." She took out the silver from her bosom, showed it to Mr. Wei, and went on, "With your help, we'll be able to keep the silver. Otherwise, we'll have to give it back to him."

"Is the old man in his right mind?" said Mr. Wei. "My daughter is only eighteen years old, and I have as yet no intention of marrying her off. Now what can I do to help you keep the six taels of silver?" (*Strange.*)

"He said," replied Matchmaker Zhang, "that as long as we get a reply from you, we'll be able to keep the six taels of silver."

Pointing a finger at the matchmakers, Mr. Wei said, "Tell that old idiot from me that for the marriage to take place, he needs to offer, no later than tomorrow, a betrothal gift of a hundred thousand strings of cash all in copper coins with no gold coins thrown in." He then treated the matchmakers to some wine before letting them go.

The two bowed their thanks and went back to Mr. Zhang's house, where he had been waiting for them in eager expectation, like a goose with a craned neck. (*Comic touch.*) Upon the return of the two women, he said, "Please sit down! It was a tough job for you!" He took out ten taels of silver, laid the silver on the table, and said, "Thank you for having brought off the match for me."

"How did we do that?" asked Matchmaker Zhang.

"My father-in-law wants me to offer a betrothal gift of a hundred thousand strings of cash all in copper coins before the marriage is to take place."

"Right you are," exclaimed the matchmakers. "The counselor did indeed say that, just as you guessed. But what are you going to do?"

The old man took out a jar of wine, opened it, put it on the table, and offered the matchmakers four cups each. He then took them around to look under the eaves at the side of the house and said, "Look!" Following his pointing finger, they saw with the left and right pupils of their matchmakers' all-seeing eyes a pile of copper coins in the amount of a hundred thousand strings.

"You see," he said, "I've got everything ready." The two matchmakers were instructed to return that very day to report the matter to the counselor before the money was to be sent over. The matchmakers went off.

In the meantime, Zhang made arrangements for transportation. He called forth from the house several men wearing gold flowers in their hats and purple robes adorned with red silk and silver ornaments. As they pushed along the carts, it was like

> Thunder rumbling down the open road,
> A tidal wave sweeping through the wilderness.
> Could the earth be shaking and the sky trembling?
> Could the stars be spinning and the sun turning?
> At first glance,
> It was like the Qin emperor driving stones into the sea.
> On first sight,
> It was like Xia'ao moving ships across dry land.[15]
> All along the river were heard
> The cries of wild geese and golden pheasants.

With streamers that bore the inscription "Mr. Zhang's betrothal gifts for Counselor Wei's family," the carts were pushed all the way to the gate of the

Wei residence. The men shouted three times in salutation, and, after the carts were arranged in two rows, they sent someone in to announce their arrival. When Mr. Wei came out and saw the carts, he stood agape with astonishment. He sent for his wife and asked her what was to be done.

"You should not have asked him for a hundred thousand strings of cash," said his wife. "I wonder where the old man got all this money? If we reject him, we'll be going back on our word, but if we accept the marriage, how can a girl from a decent family marry an old gardener?"

As the husband and wife pondered over this dilemma, unable to come to a decision, Lady Wei said, "Let's call out our daughter and hear what she has to say about the matter." (*Good decision.*) The girl took out a brocade purse from her bosom. As a matter of fact, this girl had been a mute until one day, when she was seven years old, she suddenly uttered a quatrain:

> *Heaven's will can hardly be known to men.*
> *My fate is tied to the Yangzhou area.*
> *Cold embers will again turn hot as fire;*
> *Withered willows will put forth leaves anew.*

From that moment on, she was able to write, and her name was changed to Wennü [Maiden of Letters]. The poem was put in a brocade purse and kept there for twelve years. Now she showed the poem to her father and said, "Mr. Zhang may be old, but I'm afraid this might be the will of heaven."

Seeing that her daughter was willing, and wondering if the old man, with his gift of one hundred thousand strings of cash, might not be a supernatural being, Lady Wei relented and gave her consent to the marriage. An auspicious day was chosen for the wedding, to the delight of Mr. Zhang. Truly,

> *The dried-up lotus grows fresh roots after the rain;*
> *The withered tree gains new life with the coming of spring.*

After the wedding, Zhang took his bride, along with her personal belongings, to his home. Counselor Wei forbade all other members of the household to visit Zhang's house.

In the sixth month of the seventh year of the Putong reign period [526], the counselor's son Wei Yifang, who was as accomplished in letters as he was in the military arts, returned home to Luhe County from the northern expedition with Wang Sengbian. It was a hot day. How do we know this?

> *The six dragons had no clouds to ride;*
> *Over the trees no birds flew.*
> *The ground burned, stones cracked, rivers and lakes boiled,*
> *But still no breath of wind came to the south.*

As he drew near home, he caught sight of a woman with disheveled hair in front of a farmhouse by the road. Wearing a simple blue skirt and straw sandals on her feet, she was selling melons at her door. Indeed,

Picked from the west garden, fragrant and dewy,
The melon cools down the south-facing room.
You may wonder why no flies fly around;
The icy jade ball is too cold to get near.

With green melon in a gold basin filled with well water,
One wakes up from a midday dream.
The venerable poet will not return;
Where else but by Blue Gate[16] could they be grown?

Thirsty after much walking, Wei Yifang went up to buy a melon. As he looked up, a cry escaped his lips: "Wennü, what are you doing here?"

"My brother," exclaimed the girl, "Father married me off here."

"I heard on my way here that Father married you off to Zhang the melon-peddler for a hundred thousand strings of cash. How did that happen?"

After Wennü told him the whole story, he asked, "May I see him?"

"If you wish to see him," said Wennü, "wait a moment. Let me tell him first." She promptly went into the house and told Mr. Zhang about the visit. She then reemerged to say, "Mr. Zhang says he does not wish to see you because you have a temperament as hot as fire and a will as changeable as the wind. But, my brother, it will be all right if you go to see him with no ill will." With these words, she took him into the house.

When the old man stepped out of his room, his back bent down, Wei Yifang exclaimed, "Good grief! How could such a man have a hundred thousand strings of cash with which to get my sister for a wife! He must be a sorcerer." In a trice, he drew out his precious Tai'e[17] sword and struck right at Zhang's head. Lo and behold! The hilt remained in his grip but the blade broke into fragments.

"What a shame!" said Zhang. "We've lost another immortal!"

Wennü pushed her brother out and scolded him: "I told you not to bear him any ill will. Why did you have to try to cut him down!"

Wei Yifang returned home and, after greeting his parents, demanded that they explain how they could have married off Wennü to Old Man Zhang.

Counselor Wei said, "The old man is a sorcerer."

Wei Yifang agreed, "That's what I believe, too. I drew my sword against him, but instead of hurting him, I got my sword ruined."

The following morning, Wei Yifang rose, and, after washing himself, rinsing his mouth, and preparing for a journey, he announced to his parents,

"I am determined to bring my sister back today. Should I fail to do so, I will never return to see you again." He bade farewell and brought two followers to Zhang's house. But all that stretched before their eyes was an empty expanse of land with no signs of human habitation. A local resident to whom he directed inquiries said, "Yes, there was a melon-grower named Zhang who had lived here for about twenty years, but last night there came a severe windstorm, and since then he has not been seen."

In astonishment, Wei Yifang raised his head, only to see a quatrain carved on a tree trunk, saying,

> *Two baskets of a kind unseen on earth:*
> *The garden in one, the house in the other.*
> *As for where I now make my abode,*
> *It's Peach Blossom Manor in heaven.*

Having read these lines, Wei Yifang told his men to search for Zhang in all directions. When they came back, they reported, "Mr. Zhang and his wife are on their way to Zhenzhou, each riding a donkey carrying two baskets."

Wei Yifang and the two other men gave chase. They heard people on the road say, "We saw an old man and a young girl each riding a donkey. The girl didn't want to go and pleaded tearfully with the old man for permission to let her go home to bid farewell to her parents, but the old man beat her with a stick all along the way. It was a pitiful sight, heartrending to see."

At these words, a wave of indignation swept over Wei Yifang from head to toe, while flames of indescribable anger rose in his heart thirty thousand feet high. Unable to contain himself, he took his men and pressed ahead. However, several tens of li later, they were still far behind. By the time they came to the ferry at Guazhou [Melon Port], they were told that the couple had just crossed the river.

Wei Yifang got himself a boat, crossed the river, and, when he came to the foot of Mount Mao,[18] he was told upon inquiry that the couple had already gone up the mountain. Wei Yifang gave some words of instruction to his men, deposited their luggage in an inn, and hurried up the mountain all by himself.

Half a day went by, but Peach Blossom Manor was still nowhere in sight. His steps took him to a wide stream that blocked his way. Behold:

> *The babbling water was cool and clear,*
> *Its icy surface smooth as a mirror,*
> *Its faraway waves capped as if with snow.*
> *Willow branches shade the riverbank*
> *Where mortals find themselves denied access.*

Wei Yifang stood by the stream thinking, "I have been in pursuit for so long without being able to get hold of my sister and bring her back. How am I to face my parents? I might as well jump into the water and die." While hesitating, he noticed a waterfall flowing from the top of the rock cliff by the water's edge, bringing down some peach petals. Wei Yifang wondered to himself, "It is now the sixth month. How can there be peach blossoms at this time of the year? Might Peach Blossom Manor, where my brother-in-law Mr. Chang has taken up residence, be up there?" At the sound of a flute, Yifang saw a herdboy on the back of a donkey playing a flute on the other side of the stream. Behold:

> *Shielded by deep green at the ancient ferry,*
> *A herdboy riding backwards playing a flute.*
> *The tune "Ode to Peace" that came from the flute*
> *Evoked much anguish in the traveler's heart.*

The herdboy drew nearer to the water's edge and shouted, "Might you be Wei Yifang?"

"Yes, I am."

"By Sage Zhang's orders, I am here to invite you over." The herdboy drove the donkey across the stream and carried Wei back across it. With the herdboy leading the way, they came to a farmhouse. What was it like? There is a lyric poem to the tune of "Immortal by the River" that bears witness:

> *A farmer's life is the happiest of all,*
> *With his bamboo fence and quiet farmhouse.*
> *He plows in spring, sows in summer, reaps in fall;*
> *In winter, he watches the welcome snow*
> *And lies abed in wine-induced slumber.*
>
> *Elms and willows abound outside his door;*
> *Flying catkins land all over the creek.*
> *Free from all boredom and sorrows,*
> *He laughs at those obsessed with fame and gain,*
> *Bogged down in affairs of the mundane world.*

Upon arrival, the herdboy entered the house, and two attendants in red robes emerged from the garden to greet Wei Yifang, saying, "Sage Zhang is attending to some official business and is unable to see you, but he told us to entertain you." So saying, they led him to a large pavilion with a panoramic view. A tablet bore the inscription "Green Bamboo Pavilion." Behold:

> *The dense foliage of trees and bamboos*
> *Embowers the hills and the windows.*

Fog locks in the pavilion but not the red-crowned cranes' cries;
Clouds obscure the deep valleys but not the wild monkeys' calls.

With a display of wine vessels inside, the pavilion was surrounded on all sides by beautiful peaches, apricots, and exotic flowers and plants. The red-robed attendants sat down with Yifang at the richly spread table. Before Yifang could ask what kind of man Zhang was, the attendants forced cup after cup of wine upon him so that he did not have a chance to ask the question. When the meal was over, the attendants took leave of him and told him to wait a little while by himself in the pavilion.

After waiting for a considerable time without further news, Wei Yifang stepped down out of the pavilion. As he was walking along, he caught sight of a magnificent palace through the trees and flowers. Hearing voices within, he used his tongue to moisten and then poke a hole in the paper pane of the red latticework window, and this was what he saw:

Red railings, jade steps;
Tall eaves, carved walls.
Mica screens and pearl curtains side by side,
Magnificent halls face to face.
By magic mushrooms, green and red phoenixes flew about.
In jade trees' shadows, white deer and black apes stood.
Jade Maiden and Golden Boy on the right and left,
Amid the auspicious mist and vapor.

There, on the dais, sat Mr. Zhang in full royal attire complete with headdress, boots, sword, and scepter. At the foot of the steps stood two rows of attendants in red robes, some of them deities, some demons. Two iron cangues were in view. The one nearer Zhang held a man in a purple robe and golden waistband who claimed to be the city god of a certain prefecture and was there on trial for his failure to take measures against the ravages brought about by tigers and wolves in his region. The other cangue held a man in helmet and armor. He was the mountain god of a certain county in a certain prefecture, on trial for his subordinates' failure to act against tigers and wolves that were preying upon the local residents.

As Mr. Zhang passed verdicts on the two men on the basis of their offenses, a cry escaped the lips of Wei Yifang as he watched through the window: "How very strange! How very strange!"

Hearing this exclamation, the lictors in the hall dispatched two strong men in yellow turbans to bring Wei Yifang to the foot of the steps. At their accusation that he had committed a crime by partaking of divine secrets, Wei Yifang frantically kowtowed in apology.

Before the sage could say anything, there emerged from behind a screen a woman wearing a phoenix circlet and a rosy cape over her long skirt and pearl shoes. She was none other than Wennü, Yifang's younger sister.

Dropping to her knees, she pleaded to Zhang, "Please forgive him, Sage, for he is my own elder brother."

Zhang said, "Wei Yifang was destined to be an immortal. He should not have tried to cut me down with a sword, but I forgave him because he is my brother-in-law. Now here he is again, stealing looks at my palace and planning to divulge divine secrets. For his sister's sake, I will spare his life. I will give him a token with which to claim a hundred thousand in cash."

Zhang turned around and went to the interior of the palace. In a short while, he reemerged with an old rattan hat, which he handed to Wei Yifang, and told him to look for Mr. Shen, owner of an herb store by Kaiming Bridge in Yangzhou, to claim a hundred thousand in cash, using the hat to prove his identity. "Immortals and mortals move in different worlds," said Zhang. "This place is not for you to stay for long." At his order, the boy with the flute took Wei out of Peach Blossom Manor on the back of a donkey. Upon reaching the creek, the boy pushed Wei Yifang down from the back of the donkey and he fell, head first.

Upon waking up from a sleep that was as deep as if induced by wine, Yifang found himself sitting on the ground by the stream. He looked down and found a hat on his chest. Unsure whether it had been a dream or not, he brought along the rattan hat and made his way down the hill.

By the time he returned to the inn where he had deposited his luggage the day before, his two followers were nowhere to be seen. The innkeeper came out with this explanation: "Twenty years ago, there was a Mr. Wei who left his luggage here and went up Mount Mao and got detained there. The two officers did not wish to wait any longer and went back to where they came from. It was exactly twenty years ago. It's now the second year of the reign period Daye [606] of Emperor Yang of the Sui dynasty." (*Like the story about the rotten axe-handle.*[19] *Twenty years in this world is only one day for a celestial being. That's one of the wonders about celestial beings.*)

"It's been but one day," said Wei. "How did a day become twenty years! Let me go back to the imperial stable at Luhe County to look for my parents." He bade farewell to the innkeeper and went back to Luhe County. Upon inquiry, he was told that twenty years before, a Counselor Wei of the imperial stable had ascended to heaven with twelve other members of his family in broad daylight and that the Ascending to Heaven Platform where this had happened was still there to be seen. They also said the counselor had a son who went away and never came back. At these words, Wei Yifang threw back his head and wept bitterly, for, during the twenty years that had passed by as one day for him, his parents had gone, and now he himself had nowhere to go to. At the end of his wits, he set off to find Mr. Shen to claim the one hundred thousand strings of cash.

From Luhe County he wound his way to Yangzhou and, upon inquiry, was directed to Kaiming Bridge, where there was indeed a Mr. Shen running an herb shop. Upon entering the shop, Wei Yifang saw an old man:

> *With the oddest looks and attire,*
> *A gray beard and snowy white hair,*
> *Hawk shoulders, and a turtle back,*
> *He looked like a star descended from heaven.*
> *With crane bones and a pine-tree frame,*
> *He resembled Lao Zi, who changed into Buddha.*[20]
> *Could he be a Qin hermit on Shang Hill?*
> *Or Lü Shang the angler at Pan Creek?*

To this old man seated in the shop, Wei Yifang said, "Greetings to you, sir! Might this be Mr. Shen's herb shop?"

The old man said, "Yes."

Running his eyes over the stock in the shop, Wei Yifang found

> *Of four baskets, three were empty,*
> *And the fourth was filled with the northwest wind.*

Wei Yifang thought to himself, "But how can he afford to have one hundred thousand strings of cash for me?" He said to the old man that he wanted to buy three coppers' worth of mint.

"Good choice!" exclaimed the old man. "*The Materia Medica*[21] says it cools the head and clears vision. How much do you want?"

"Three coppers' worth," was the answer.

"Too bad. I'm out of it," said the old man.

"How about some hundred-herb mixture?"

"Hundred-herb mixture helps the wine-induced flush in the face subside and lubricates the throat. How much do you want?"

"Three coppers' worth."

"Too bad. Sold out."

"Give me some licorice root, then," said Wei Yifang.

"Good choice! Licorice root is mild and nonpoisonous. It goes well with other herbs in cleansing the body of poison from metal, stone, herbs, and wood. It's also known in the trade as the 'king of herbs.' How much do you want?"

"Five coppers' worth."

"I beg to inform you, too bad. I'm out of it also."

Wei Yifang then said to the old man, "I am here not to buy herbs but to convey a message from Zhang the melon-grower."

"What message can he have for me?"

"He told me to come here and claim a hundred thousand strings of cash."

"I do have the money," said Mr. Shen, "but what proof do you have?"

Wei Yifang fumbled in his robe and produced the rattan hat. Mr. Shen turned to the blue cloth portiere and called for his wife to come out and take a look. As the portiere was raised, a seventeen- or eighteen-year-old girl emerged, saying, "What is it, husband?"

Wei Yifang thought to himself, "So he shares Mr. Zhang's preference for young wives."

Mr. Shen asked his wife to check if the hat was the right one. The girl said, "The other day, Mr. Zhang passed by our door on his donkey and asked me to sew up his torn hat. As I was out of black thread at the time, I used red thread instead on the inner side of the crown." When the hat was turned inside out, there, for all to see, were indeed stitches in the crown made with red thread. Then and there, Mr. Shen took Wei Yifang inside the house and gave him the one hundred thousand strings of cash. Wei Yifang used the money to build bridges and roads and for distribution among the poor. (*Doing justice to Mr. Zhang's rattan hat.*)

One day, when passing by a wineshop, Wei Yifang saw a boy riding a donkey. Recognizing the boy to be the one who had taken him across the stream, he asked, "Where is Mr. Zhang?"

"He is now upstairs in the wineshop having a cup of wine with Mr. Shen."

Wei Yifang mounted the stairs and, finding Mr. Shen and Mr. Zhang seated facing each other, he bowed in greeting.

Mr. Zhang said, "I am, in fact, Zhang Gulao [Ancient Zhang], elder immortal of the Eternal Happiness Palace. Wennü is the Jade Maiden from Upper Heaven, who chose to live in the mortal world. Afraid that she would be sullied by mortal men, the Lord on High sent me in this shape to bring her back to heaven. You, Wei Yifang, were destined to be an immortal, but, with such a propensity to kill, you shall be no more than a local deity for the city of Yangzhou." Having said this, he waved his hand and there appeared two red-crowned cranes. Mr. Shen and Zhang Gulao each got on the back of one and rose in air. From the sky fluttered down a scroll of paper which, when spread out, revealed these lines:

Twenty years away from eternal joy,
I grew melons and lived hidden on earth.
Alas! Who among mortal beings
Could recognize an immortal in their midst?
Yifang will be made a local god,
Wennü returned to heaven on a phoenix.
Henceforth the Crane-Riding Tower
Will be an impressive sight in Yangzhou.

李元闇遊救
朱蛇

Li Yuan, on a leisurely tour, saves a red snake.

34

Mr. Li Saves a Snake and Wins Chenxin

Read no more sutras,
Chant no more mantras.
Filled with mercy though they are,
They cannot save you from your karma.
Sow hemp, and you shall get hemp;
Sow beans, and you shall get beans.
Retribution in all its fairness
Visits all those guilty of vice.

The above eight lines, written by Xu the Divine Taoist of the Song dynasty, mean that good deeds will be duly rewarded and evildoing will be punished. The ancients said, "If you amass wealth for your offspring, they might not be able to keep it; if you collect books for your offspring, they might not be able to read them. The best course is to do good deeds to accumulate moral credit in the netherworld, for the benefit of your descendants generation after generation."

In olden times, there was a man named Sun Shu'ao, who, when leaving home early one morning, saw a two-headed snake blocking his way. He killed it with a brick and buried it in the ground. After returning home, he told his mother, "I am going to die."

His mother said, "How do you know that?"

"I've heard that anyone who sees a two-headed snake is bound to die, and I saw one today."

"Why didn't you kill it?"

"I did, and I buried it so that no one else will see it and die. I'd rather die myself than jeopardize more lives."

"My son, your wish to save lives will earn you moral credit. You are not going to die."

Later, Shu'ao rose to be prime minister of the state of Chu [in the Spring and Autumn period]. Now we shall tell of a scholar who was rewarded for having saved a snake.

In the Xining reign period [1068–77] under Emperor Shenzong of the

Song dynasty, there lived in Bianliang a man named Li Yi, a native of Chenzhou, who was reappointed from his position as magistrate of Qi County to that of assistant prefect of Hangzhou. He had a wife with the surname Han and a son, Li Yuan, courtesy name Boyuan, who was devoted to the study of the Confucian classics. Li Yi went home to pack up his personal belongings and, bringing only two servants, set out on his journey to Hangzhou to assume the new post, leaving his wife and son behind.

One year went quickly by. Suddenly seized by concerns about his son Li Yuan's progress in his studies at home, he wrote a letter for his servant Wang An to take to Chenzhou. Wang An was then to bring Li Yuan to Hangzhou to be a companion for his father and to buy books along the way. Wang An took leave of his master and, in a few days, arrived in Chenzhou, where he presented himself to Li Yi's wife and showed her the letter. The son was called forth from his study to read his father's letter and to pack for the journey. Having failed in the imperial examinations, Li Yuan was in no mood for books or musical practice but had been amusing himself by touring scenic spots. Now that his father was sending for him, he gathered together his zither, sword, and books, took leave of his mother, and set out on the journey with Wang An. Changing boats all along the way, they came to the Yangzi River in a few days. Fascinated by the landscape, Li Yuan composed a poem:

> *From the Kunlun Mountains to the Eastern Sea,*
> *The thundering waves burst over the cliffs.*
> *In moonlight, the roar of wind fills the ears;*
> *The sound of the river escorts the boats.*

They crossed the river to Runzhou and wended their way to the Wu River via Changzhou and Suzhou.

Toward dusk on the day they arrived, Li Yuan saw from his boat that the scenery along the Wu River was no less beautiful than the landscape paintings of Song Di, an artist of the Song dynasty. Greatly delighted, he told the boatman to moor the boat by Long Bridge. He went ashore and walked up the bridge to the Pavilion of the Hanging Rainbow, where he sat by the balustrade to enjoy the evening scene on Lake Tai. While admiring the view, he saw a house behind a whitewashed wall to the east of the bridge and wondered what it was. As a fisherman happened to draw near with his rolled-up net, Li Yuan asked him with a bow, "Whose house is that—the one behind the whitewashed wall to the east of the bridge?"

The fisherman replied, "That's the Shrine of the Three Worthy Men."

"Who are the Three Worthy Men?"

"They are Fan Li, Zhang Han, and Lu Guimeng."

Overjoyed, Li Yuan pressed ahead and found his way over a bridge to the shrine. He entered by a side door and looked at the stelae. As he went up the hall, he saw three statues in a row, with Fan Li in the middle, flanked by Zhang Han on the left and Lu Guimeng on the right. In the midst of his reflections, an old man with a walking cane approached him. When asked, the old man identified himself as the caretaker of the shrine. Li Yuan asked further, "How long has the shrine been here?"

The old man replied, "For nearly a thousand years."

Li Yuan said, "As far as I know, Zhang Han was a prominent official in the imperial court [of the Jin dynasty] before he resigned and returned to his native place out of nostalgia for its delicious perch and watercress. He never resumed office again. He was a truly wise man who had the vision to retire at the height of his career. Lu Guimeng [d. 881], a first-rate poet of his time, was also a most wise man, living as a recluse on the Wusong River, enjoying the pleasure of raising ducks. Building a temple in honor of these two men is all too justifiable. Fan Li, a senior minister of the state of Yue [during the Spring and Autumn period], conquered the state of Wu by offering the beautiful Xishi to King Fuchai of Wu to slacken his vigilance. Later, disgruntled at the perfidy of the king of Yue, he left the king's service and toured the five lakes on a flat boat, calling himself Leather Bag. Though a worthy man, he was, nevertheless, an enemy of the state of Wu. How can he be honored like this here in the land of Wu?"

The old man said, "The shrine was built long ago. I have no idea as to the reason for that."

Li Yuan borrowed a brush-pen and an ink slab and wrote a poem on the wall to say that Leather Bag did not deserve a place in the shrine. The poem was as follows:

> *Zhang and Lu are praised by all and sundry;*
> *They well deserve their places in the shrine.*
> *Memory of the end of Wu still rankles;*
> *Leather Bag does not merit such honor.*

He then returned the brush-pen and the ink slab to the old man, took leave of him, and continued on his way. There came into his view several children in the midst of tall grass beating a small snake with bamboo sticks. Upon taking a closer look, Li Yuan saw that it was a most unusual snake with golden eyes, a yellow mouth, a foot-long reddish brown body as thin as bamboo but shaped like corals covered with shiny scales, and a tuft of inch-long green hair under the chin. Seeing that it still had breath left in it, Li Yuan hastily stopped the children, saying, "I'll give you a hundred in cash for this little snake." As the children gathered around him to get the money, he wrapped up the red snake in his sleeves. Then he took the children to the boat and gave them the money. After they had gone, he had Wang An open the book trunks to get some mugwort leaves to make soup with. Kept warm in a bowl, the soup was then used to wash the bloodstains off the snake. He ordered the boatman to set off. Looking ahead of him, he saw a stretch of land overgrown with dense grass and trees. Believing that no one would be coming to that place any time soon, he set the red snake free then and there.

The snake looked back at Li Yuan several times. Li Yuan said, "I, Li Yuan, am setting you free. Go hide yourself in some deserted place safe from human eyes."

The red snake dived into the water and swam away. Li Yuan ordered the boat to change its course and head in the direction of Hangzhou.

He arrived three days later. Respectfully he greeted his father, and, in the middle of their conversation about family matters, his father asked him about his studies and was much pleased with his answers. After spending several days in his father's official residence, he said to his father, "There being no one at home to take care of mother, I would like to go back. Besides, I will need to take the spring examinations." Accordingly, the father bought some presents with his savings from his salary and had Wang An accompany Li Yuan back home. With the luggage already on the boat, Li Yuan bade his father farewell and left Hangzhou with Wang An via the Guantang thoroughfare near Dongxin Bridge. They passed the Dam of Eternal Peace and the prefecture of Jiaxing. When they came to the Wu River, he was, now as before, so taken with the beauty of the hills and lakes that he could hardly tear himself away from the place.

By the time they reached the Long Bridge, the sun had sunk below the horizon in the west. Li Yuan told the boatman to stop there for the night and resume the journey the following morning. In the meantime, he could enjoy the sights. The boat having moored under the bridge, he went ashore and took a walk by himself. Once on the bridge, he went to the Pavilion of the Hanging Rainbow and, leaning forward against the balustrade, gazed at the sparkling lake and the mist-shrouded hills. The wind having subsided, what rose instead was the singing of fishermen's songs. Ripples in the water shook the reflections of the wild geese.

While he was thus enjoying the scene, a green-robed boy suddenly came into his view. Taking a few steps forward, the boy bowed and said, with a name card in his hand, "This is the name card of my master, who wishes to see you but dares not do so without your permission."

"Where is your master?"

"There, standing at the left side of this bridge, awaiting your call."

Li Yuan took a look at the card, on which was written, "Your student Zhu Wei."

"Your master must have mistaken me for someone else."

"He is very eager to see you. There is no mistake."

"Being from the other side of the Yangzi River, I have no acquaintances here, nor is there a Mr. Zhu among my friends. Maybe he is looking for someone with the same surname as mine?"

"It's Li Boyuan, son of Controller-General Li, whom he wishes to see. There is no mistake whatsoever."

"In that case, he must be a scholar of some kind. I will see him."

The green-robed boy went off and, in a short while, brought back a scholar with refined features and white teeth set off by red lips. There was about him a graceful air that set him above the average worldly man. At the sight of Li Yuan, the scholar made a deep bow, whereupon Li Yuan returned the greeting with haste. Scholar Zhu said, "My father was a good friend of your father's. Having heard that you are on your way back from Hangzhou, he told me to wait here for you. Would you be so kind as to go to our home and talk with him about the old days?"

"I am too young to know anything about the friendship between my father and your father," said Li Yuan. "Please forgive me for not having paid my respects earlier to your father."

Scholar Zhu said, "Our humble residence is close by. Please do not deny us the honor."

At Scholar Zhu's insistence, Li Yuan followed him out of the Pavilion of the Hanging Rainbow to one end of Long Bridge, where, in the shadow of willow trees, was moored a painted pleasure-boat on which were several brightly dressed men of imposing stature. When he was invited onto the boat, Li Yuan was amazed to see colorful decorations and luxurious furniture. At the bidding of Scholar Zhu, the oars were set to work and the boat shot away as if flying, sending up white spray that whirled about like snowflakes.

In a trice, the boat reached the shore. Scholar Zhu asked Li Yuan to go ashore. What met Li Yuan's eyes was a stretch of spreading pine trees and about twenty men in purple robes and silver waistbands standing on the sandy beach, guarding two wisteria sedan-chairs. Li Yuan asked, "What yamen do these constables come from?"

Scholar Zhu replied, "They are my father's servants. Please get in the sedan-chair. The residence is close by."

Much puzzled and confused, Li Yuan mounted the sedan-chair and was escorted through the pine trees until, less than a li later, there came into view a palace with wooded hills at the back and green water in front. Across the water was a bridge with granite balustrades. Under the glazed-tile roof of the palace were walls of red clay. Above the three vermilion doors was a placard bearing the gold characters "Jade Flower Palace." Upon reaching the palace gate, Li Yuan was asked to alight from the sedan-chair. Without daring to move one step, Li Yuan trembled uncontrollably with fear. From inside the palace came two men wearing coronets decorated with sable tails and cicada wings, purple brocade robes, and gold belts around their waists, with patterned tablets in their hands. Stepping forward, they greeted Li Yuan with a bow, saying, "His Majesty wishes to see you, sir." For a considerable time, Li Yuan was at a loss for words. Scholar Zhu cut in from the side, "My father wishes to see you. Please do not be alarmed."

"What place is this?"

The scholar answered, "You will know when you go into the hall."

Reluctantly, Li Yuan followed the two court ministers up the steps of the eastern corridor. Once in the hall, he saw an elderly man being escorted in by dozens of palace guards. Wearing a cicada-wing hat, wide sleeves, vermilion boots, and a long robe and carrying a jade tablet in his hand, he approached Li Yuan to greet him. With great alacrity, Li Yuan dropped to his knees in a gesture of obeisance but was raised to his feet by the valets at the king's order. The king said, "I thank you for having graced us with your presence even though the invitation was all too abrupt. Please forgive us." Li Yuan could do no better than manage a few hardly audible syllables by way of reply.

After having been escorted into the hall, the king ascended his throne and invited Li Yuan to sit down on a stool with embroidered upholstery set to the left of the throne. Li Yuan threw himself onto the ground and said after two bows, "I am but a humble student. How dare I sit in the presence of a king?"

"You did my family a great kindness," said the king. "That is why I had my oldest son invite you here today. There is nothing improper in taking a seat."

The two ministers proclaimed, "Please do not decline the king's gesture of good will."

After repeated attempts at turning down the offer, Li Yuan had no choice but to lower his head and sit down on the stool, leaning forward. The king then summoned his younger son to come forth and pay homage to his savior.

In a short while, several palace maids led a young man into the hall from behind a screen. Wearing a small coronet on his head, a crimson robe, a jade waistband, and embroidered boots, the young man stood by the king's side, his face as fair as if powdered, his lips as red as if rouged. The king pronounced, "My son was playing by the riverside the other day when he was unfortunately captured by some urchins. He would have perished were it not for you. Our entire clan owes you a debt of gratitude. Now that you are here, please accept a bow from my son." The young man stepped forward and dropped on his knees. Hurriedly Li Yuan returned the greeting. The king said, "My son owes a great deal to you. Please accept his bows." So saying, he had the attendants hold Li Yuan upright while the young prince made the bows.

Looking up to the throne, Li Yuan noticed that the king, with whiskers all over his face, had eyes that shone with divine brilliance and that all others present looked as if they were beings out of this world. Realization now came to him that he was looking at the Dragon King in his palace under the river, and that the young man was none other than the small snake that he had rescued the other day behind the Shrine of the Three Worthy Men. With alacrity he fell on his knees at the foot of the steps and touched the ground with his head. The king rose and said, "This is hardly the right place to pay respects to a savior. Please come to the inner quarters of the palace, where we will offer you some wine."

Li Yuan followed the king past the jade screen. The patterned floor tiles were covered by embroidered rugs. On both sides of the hallway stood embroidered screens. After they left the hall, they turned into a corridor and came upon a side hall brightly lit by dragon lanterns and phoenix candles. A jade stove gave off the aroma of musk. The walls were lined with embroidered curtains with flowing tassels. In the middle were two seats decorated with flood dragons. Li Yuan was too scared to sit down. The king ordered his men to help Li Yuan take the seat of honor.

Heavenly music rose on both sides, and there filed in tens of beautiful maidens with musical instruments in hand. Those leading the processions serving wine and fruit in exquisite cups and plates were women of unparalleled beauty. The ravishing fragrance and the auspicious vapor that permeated the hall so intoxicated Li Yuan that he was at a loss what to do. At the king's order, the two princes bowed repeatedly and served wine. Looking at the table with a fine spread of treats, Li Yuan saw that all the vessels were made of glass, crystal, amber, and agate of an exquisiteness unseen in the human world. The king rose to toast Li Yuan, who found the taste of the wine most delicious. There was also an abundance of dishes that he could not name. As the king ordered the ministers to take turns raising their cups to toast Li Yuan, the latter soon felt the effects of the wine. With a bow to the king, he pleaded, "Your subject has indeed already taken too much wine." So saying, he fell to the ground without being able to rise again. The king had some attendants help him out of the hall to the guesthouse so that he could take a rest there.

When he woke from his inebriated state, the red sun was already shining through the window. With a start, he rose and looked around and found the bed, canopy, and curtains all decorated in patterns of flood dragons. After he had washed himself and rinsed his mouth, Scholar Zhu, whom he had seen the previous evening, came into the room, attended by servants, to issue an invitation. Instead of dressing himself as a scholar in the mortal world, he had on a court official's cap, a crimson silk robe, a jade waistband, and black boots. His followers were all armed with battle axes.

Li Yuan said apologetically, "It was most rude of me to have gotten drunk last night."

"Please forgive us," said Zhu Wei, "for having nothing to offer you. My father is waiting for you for breakfast in the side hall."

Once led into the king's presence, Li Yuan was told to relax and stay for a few more days, whereupon Li Yuan bowed twice and declined the offer: "I am grateful for Your Majesty's kind offer, but my father wants me to return home to take care of my mother as well as to take the spring examinations, and the examination date is drawing near. Moreover, my servant who has been waiting for me all this time must be concerned over my disappearance. If he goes back to Hangzhou and reports to my father, my father will be worried. That is why I dare not stay longer but would like to leave right away."

The king replied, "If that is your wish, I will not try to detain you any longer. The modest gifts we have for you will not be enough to repay our debt to you, but I shall offer you whatever you may wish for."

"I entertain no excessive hopes. My only wish for the rest of my life is to be granted gratification [*chenxin*]." (*Slightly similar to the story about Qinghong getting his wish.*)[1]

The king laughed, "If it is your wish to have my daughter for your wife, I will be happy to comply. But you must return her in three years' time." Thereupon, the king ordered that his daughter Chenxin [Gratification] be called forth.

In a trice, maidservants escorted a beautiful girl into the hall. Casting a furtive glance at her, Li Yuan saw that, with cloudlike hair, delicate eyebrows, and sparkling eyes, she was a striking beauty lovely enough to cause the fall of a city or a state and to shame fish and geese into hiding themselves from view. The king said, pointing to the girl, "This is my daughter Chenxin. Since it is your wish to have her, I am happy to offer her to you as your wife."

Prostrating himself on the ground, Li Yuan said, "What I meant was gratification at passing the imperial examinations at the first attempt. How could I dream of having a heavenly princess as my wife?"

The king said, "Chenxin is my daughter's pet name. Since I have already promised her to you, I cannot go back on this. If you wish to succeed in the examination, my daughter will also be able to make that happen for you." At the king's bidding, Zhu Wei escorted his sister and Li Yuan out. Li Yuan bowed repeatedly in gratitude.

Zhu Wei led Li Yuan out of the palace to the side of the boat. The girl had changed into everyday clothes and was already in the boat. Zhu Wei said,

"I cannot accompany you any farther because you are crossing into the mortal world. Please take good care of yourselves."

"May I ask the name of your worthy father His Majesty?"

"My father is the king of all dragons in the Western Sea. His many merits made the Jade Emperor give him the honor of guarding this region. Luckily, the water is clean and the waves crystal clear, something that brings honor to our offspring. You must never reveal any information about us, lest a calamity should follow. Nor should you get too inquisitive with my sister."

With hands folded in front of him, Li Yuan heard him out and then took leave of him. When Li Yuan embarked on the boat, Zhu Wei handed over a package of valuables as a present. Amid the sounds of a rainstorm that filled his ears, Li Yuan soon found himself by Long Bridge. The valets escorted the girl and Li Yuan up onto the shore, gave them the package of valuables, and left without a moment's delay. The oars flew through the air, and in the twinkling of an eye, the boat disappeared from view.

Li Yuan felt as if he had just woken up from a dream. Turning his head, he found, much to his surprise and delight, that the girl was still with him. He said to her, "Your father made you my wife. Are you willing to follow me?"

The girl replied, "By the king's order, I shall serve you as your wife. But you must not reveal my identity to your family. If anything leaks out, I will not be able to stay long with you." When Li Yuan led the girl to his boat, Wang An the servant was astounded. He led Li Yuan onto the boat and said, "Master, I looked everywhere for you. Where were you all night?"

"I met a friend who invited me for a cup of wine on the lake and gave me this girl as my wife."

Wang An refrained from pressing for details, but invited the girl into the boat, hid the valuables in the baggage, and prepared for departure.

Crossing rivers and dams, they arrived in Chenzhou soon enough. Li Yuan greeted his mother in the main hall. After talking about his father, he went down on his knees and said, "On my way home, I got myself a wife, but I dare not present her to you, because father and you did not so instruct."

His mother said, "Marriage is a ritual that has been in existence since ancient times. You have already taken a wife—why don't you bring her home?" His mother ordered that Chenxin be led in to be introduced to her. It was a joyous occasion for the entire family.

A few days after his return home, the examination date drew near. Li Yuan noticed that Chenxin was an intelligent girl who knew all there was to know, and said to her, "Your father advised me to consult you if I wish to be successful in the examinations. Since the exam is scheduled for tomorrow, do you have anything to teach me?"

"I'll get the essay question of the exam for you tonight, so that you can write the essay at home before the exam. Tomorrow, all you have to do is to copy your draft."

"This does sound like a wonderful idea, but how are you going to get hold of the essay question?"

"I will need to close my eyes while making the effort. Be sure not to look at me while I'm at it."

Li Yuan was not convinced. Chenxin returned to her room and closed the door tightly. There arose a gust of wind that blew up the curtains. A couple of hours later, she opened her door and emerged with a sheet of paper that contained an essay question and handed it over to Li Yuan, to his great delight. Freely consulting various books, he finished writing his essay. The following day when he sat for the examination, the essay question turned out to be the very one he had worked on. His essay was thus finished without the least effort. The same thing happened the day after. The woman stole the essay questions for all three sessions of the examination by flying through the air into the examination grounds. When the results of the examination were announced, it was found that Li Yuan had indeed scored high marks. He was appointed to be a notary of the assistant prefect of Jiangzhou. After receiving congratulations from relatives and friends, he set out on his journey to assume his post. In one year, he was reappointed to the Office of Memorials. Upon expiration of his three-year-term, he was promoted to the position of magistrate of Wujiang County, south of the Yangzi River. Leading his wife and five servants, he took leave of his parents and went to assume his new post.

A few days after he assumed office, Chenxin bade farewell to him, saying, "Three years ago, my parents made me serve you as a wife in repayment of a debt of gratitude to you for having saved my brother's life. Now that the three years have passed, I should be leaving you. Take good care of yourself."

Unwilling to see her go, Li Yuan tried to embrace her, but before he could do so, a gust of strong wind had already blown her out the door. A cloud appeared under her feet, and she rose slowly into the sky. To Li Yuan, who was wailing bitterly with his face turned upwards, she said, "Do not waste your youth. Find yourself another wife. When you are promoted to be a minister, you should retire. If I don't go back now, I will be subject to severe punishment. I've written a short poem for you to keep as a souvenir." From the sky was tossed down a piece of flowered notepaper on which was written a poem:

> In three years Chenxin's debt was paid in full;
> After I am gone, heave no sigh of grief.
> The jade palace where snow is buried by the waves
> Is nowhere to be found under the moonlit sky.

Li Yuan was plunged into despair. Later, upon expiration of his three-year term of office, he returned to Chenzhou. He was then appointed assistant in the Palace Library, and Prime Minister Wang made him his son-in-law. He rose further up the ladder of officialdom until he became the minister of personnel. To this day, there still stands, outside the west gate by the Wu River, a temple to the Dragon King, built years ago by Li Yuan. There is a poem that bears witness:

> *Of old, Liu Yi married the Dragon King's daughter;*
> *Now, there is Li Yuan who met Chenxin.*
> *Be compassionate and do good deeds;*
> *Heaven will surely give you much blessing.*

The Monk with a Note Cleverly Tricks Huangfu's Wife

Light clothes of white linen feel soothingly cool.
Sounds of silkworms eating leaves fill the corridor.
By Yu Gate,¹ peach blossoms bloom in waves.
In the moon palace, cassia flowers smell sweet.²
A North Sea roc, a phoenix turning to the sun,
The scholar leaves home with his books and sword.
Knowing that he is heading for the clouds,
He scorns the studious who stay on earth.

Forty-five li to the north of the capital at Chang'an was a certain Xianyang County, in which lived a man with the two-character surname Yuwen and the given name Shou. He left Xianyang for the imperial examinations in Chang'an but failed time and again. Upon his return bearing no news of success, his wife, Wang-shi, wrote a lyric poem to the tune of "Gazing at the South," using two-character [two-syllable] surnames³ to mock him:

Gongsun [the prince] was filled with sorrow
Brush-pens made of Duanmu [straight wood] were put away.
Remember where we parted at Ximen [West Gate]?
Wenren [heard that someone] wrote to set a date in the fall;
Tuoba [pitter-patter] shed copious tears.

Yuwen [literature of the land] forsaken,
He left sadly on a Dugu [fornlorn lonesome] boat
With no wish to gain Goulong [the highest honor].
Murong [admired beauty] and good looks put to rest,
He is content with his life at Lüqiu [hometown].

Feeling she had not yet said everything on her mind, Wang-shi looked at her husband and made up another four lines:

My good man prides himself on his talent,
But why is he let go year after year?

Henceforth he'll be so ashamed to face his wife
That he'll return only under cover of night.

Yuwen was shamed into making a firm resolve: "Should I fail again, I will never come back." The following year he achieved instant fame but chose to stay on in Chang'an instead of returning home.

Knowing full well why her husband chose not to return, Wang-shi said to herself, "I wrote a poem to mock him. That's why he's not coming back." Thereupon, she wrote a letter and summoned Wang Ji the servant, saying, "Deliver this letter for me to my husband forty-five li away." The letter started with some usual words of greeting, which were followed by a lyric poem to the tune of "A Southern Song":

Magpies chirp gaily on the morning trees;
Flowers blossom under the midnight lamp.
Sure enough, news reached the ends of the earth
Telling of my worthy husband's success.

Past rancor fades from my painted eyebrows;
New delight brightens my flushed rosy cheeks.
I shouldn't have doubted him in the past;
He'll henceforth enjoy life away from home.

After the lyric poem, she added a quatrain:

Chang'an, a city not too far away,
Is filled with an aura of romance.
In your triumphant youthful pride,
Tipsy with wine, where will you sleep tonight?

Yuwen spread out the letter and read the lyric poem as well as the quatrain. "You once wrote to tell me not to return unless under the cover of night," said he. "Now that I have made it, you want me back!" In his lodgings, he took out the four treasures of the scholar's studio and composed a lyric to the tune of "Treading on Grass":

My feet on the ladder leading to the clouds,
My hands grasping the divine cassia boughs,
I found my name high on the honor roll.
Roads are cleared for the zhuangyuan on horseback;
Gold saddles and jade reins line up in rows.

Returning from the imperial banquet,
I wallow amid pleasures of the flowers,

Fulfilling my lifelong wishes.
This letter is to her on the phoenix tower;
What a dashing husband she is blessed with!

Having finished the poem, he took a piece of paper with a floral pattern and folded it letter-size so as to copy the poem onto it to be delivered to his wife. As he was grinding the ink, his hand clumsily knocked over the ink slab and wetted the paper. He took another piece of paper, folded it, wrote on it, and gave it to Wang Ji the servant, saying, "Tell my wife that I have passed the examinations and will return under the cover of night. Go quickly and tell her not to expect me until after night falls." Wang Ji took the letter and, with a salute, returned home over a distance of forty-five li.

Now, having sent the letter and finding nothing to occupy himself with in the inn that evening, Yuwen Shou went to bed. He had hardly drifted off to sleep than he dreamed that he had returned to his home in Xianyang County and saw Wang Ji take off his straw sandals and wash his feet by one side of the door. Yuwen Shou asked, "So you've been back for quite some time, Wang Ji?" No answer came to his repeated queries. Just when his patience was running out, Yuwen Shou raised his eyes and caught sight of his wife, Wang-shi, entering her chamber with a lit candle in her hands. He ran up to her and announced in a loud voice, "Wife, I am back!" But she took no notice of him. He said it again, but still got no response. Without realizing that he was in a dream, he followed his wife into the chamber and watched her put the candle on the table and take out the letter he had sent. She then took down her gold hairpin, with which she broke the seal of the envelope, only to find that it contained a blank piece of paper. With a smile, his wife wrote four lines by candlelight on the paper:

I opened the letter by the green-gauze window,
Only to find a blank piece of paper.
So you do wish to come home early,
For the blank is eloquent with your feelings.

Having finished writing, she took another envelope and sealed it. As she used the hairpin to scrape away the candle drippings, Yuwen Shou felt a prick on his face and woke up with a start, only to find himself abed in an inn. By the remaining light of the candle, he saw that he had indeed sent home by mistake the blank sheet of paper. He took another sheet and wrote down that quatrain. After breakfast the following morning, Wang Ji brought back his wife's reply, which, when opened, turned out to contain four lines identical to the ones he had dreamed about. Then and there, he put his things together and set out for home.

This story, then, is called "The Wrongly Sealed Letter." Next, I shall tell you "The Wrongly Delivered Letter." A husband and wife were sitting peacefully in their home when a man delivered a letter to the wife, a letter that led to a most strange story. Truly,

> *When will there be no more dust on horses' hooves?*
> *When will there be an end to affairs that pain the heart?*

There is a lyric poem to the tune of "Partridge Sky" that describes a beautiful woman:

> *Eyebrows lightly painted, hairpin askew,*
> *She has no passion for needlework.*
> *Deep in her boudoir behind misty clouds,*
> *She spreads out paper to practice her brush.*
>
> *In her dazzling ethereal beauty,*
> *She has no earthly match.*
> *Plum blossoms are said to resemble her,*
> *But are not as pretty upon a closer look.*

In Zaoshuo Lane in Kaifeng, the Eastern Capital, there lived a man with the two-character surname of Huangfu and the given name of Song. A guard at the imperial court, he was twenty-six years of age, and his wife, Yang-shi, was twenty-four. They had no relatives but lived in a household of three with a thirteen-year-old maidservant called Ying'er. Huangfu was sent to deliver winter clothes for the garrison stationed at the frontier and did not return until New Year's Day came around.

There was, at the mouth of the lane, a small teahouse, the owner of which was known as Wang the Second. On the day of which I speak, a man stepped into the teahouse at noontime, when the tea hours had come to an end. He had

> *Thick brows, big eyes, a snub nose, a large mouth;*
> *Above, a tall bucket-shaped hat;*
> *A lined robe with wide collar and big sleeves;*
> *Below, matching pants and neat shoes and socks.*

He entered the teahouse and sat down. Teapot in hand, Wang the Second the shopkeeper stepped forward with some words of greeting and served tea. After drinking his tea, the patron said, looking at Wang the Second, "Please allow me to stay here for a while. I am expecting someone."

"Certainly," said Wang the Second.

A considerable while later, a boy called Seng'er appeared with a tray in his hand, peddling dumplings with quail filling. Beckoning the boy over with his hand, the man called out, "Give me some!" Thereupon Seng'er came into the teahouse and put his tray down on the table. He used a bamboo stick to skewer some dumplings and laid them, along with a pinch of salt, in front of the man, saying, "Enjoy the dumplings, sir."

"Yes, I will," said the man, "but first do me a favor."

"What is it?"

Pointing at the fourth house in Zaoshuo Lane, the man asked, "Do you know that family?"

"Yes, it's the home of Mr. Huangfu, who has just come back from delivering clothes up to the frontier."

"How many people are there in the household?"

"There's just Mr. Huangfu himself, his young wife, and a maid."

"Do you know his wife?"

"His wife," said Seng'er, "rarely shows her face outside of the portiere. She sometimes calls me in to buy some dumplings. That's how I got to know her. Why do you ask?"

The man took a gold-threaded bag from his waist and, to Seng'er's great delight, spilled down from it onto the boy's tray about fifty in cash. With much reverence, he asked, "How may I be of service to you, sir?"

"Do this for me," said the man, while he produced from his sleeve a white paper packet containing a pair of clustered rings, two short gold hairpins, and a letter. "Deliver these three things to the wife," he continued. "Don't give them to her husband. When you see the wife, just say that a man insisted that she accept these three things. Go now. I'll wait here for you to report back."

Seng'er took the packet, left his tray on the counter of the teahouse, and headed for Zaoshuo Lane. As he came to Huangfu's door, he lifted the green bamboo portiere and stuck his head in for a quick look. It so happened that Huangfu was seated in an armchair right by the door. At the sight of the young dumpling peddler lifting the portiere and then trying to slip away after taking a surreptitious peek, Huangfu gave a thunderous shout that truly made him resemble

> Brave Zhang Fei[4] on Dangyang Bridge,
> With one shout halting Cao Cao's million-man army.

With that shout, he asked, "What are you doing here?" Without a look back, the boy took to his heels, but Huangfu caught up with him in two strides and brought him back. "What is the meaning of this?" he said. "Why did you slip away after one look at me?"

"A gentleman told me to deliver these three things to your wife, not to you."

"What things?"

"Don't ask," said the boy. "I'm not giving them to you."

With his tightly clenched fist, Huangfu hit the boy on the head and said, "Show them to me!"

Reeling from the blow to his head, the boy had to produce the paper package from his chest. "I was told to deliver them to your wife," he mumbled, "not to you. What did you hit me for?"

With one swift movement of the hand, Huangfu snatched away the paper package and opened it to find a pair of rings, two short gold hairpins, and a letter. Huangfu opened the letter and read,

> In reverence I repeatedly bow to you, my lady. Please accept my greetings in this early spring season. I had the good fortune of drinking with you the other day, and, since then, you have never been absent from my thoughts. Some trivial business prevents me from coming to visit you in person. Therefore, I have written a little lyric poem instead. It is titled "Words from the Depth of My Heart." Please give it your kind attention.

The poem was as follows:

> Now that your husband has returned,
> My heart is broken to pieces.
> A pair of rings, a letter, gold hairpins.
>
> Take these, doubt me not, and be of good cheer.
> Since we parted, I've been lonely in bed,
> Wretched and forsaken in my study.

After he read the letter, Huangfu's eyes blazed with anger. Gnashing his teeth, he turned to Seng'er: "Who gave you these things?"

Seng'er replied, pointing at Wang the Second's teahouse at the mouth of the lane, "It was a gentleman with thick eyebrows, big eyes, a snub nose, and a large mouth who told me to give them to your wife but not to you."

Grabbing Seng'er by the hair with one hand, Huangfu left the lane and headed straight for Wang the Second's teahouse. Pointing at the teahouse, Seng'er said, "The gentleman who was just now sitting on the makeshift bed there told me to give the packet to your wife, not you, and yet you beat me up!"

Finding no one in the teahouse, Huangfu cursed, "What a liar!" Before Wang the Second could say anything in protest, he dragged Seng'er out of the teahouse and back to his home.

Upon arriving at home, he bolted the door, sending shudders of fear down Seng'er's spine. He called forth from the interior of the house his wife who, at twenty-four years of age, was as pretty as a flower. "Look at these!" he snapped.

Unaware of what had happened, the young woman sat down in an armchair. Huangfu showed her the letter and the jewelry. She read the letter in bewilderment. (*There is no lack of people of honor and loyalty who are wrongly accused, just as Yang-shi is. Pitiable.*) Huangfu demanded, "In the three months while I was away at the frontier, whom did you drink with here at home?"

"I was betrothed to you early in childhood," rejoined his wife. "How could I have been drinking with any man in your absence?"

"If not," shot back Huangfu, "where did these things come from?"

"How should I know?"

His left hand pointing at her, he gave her a slap on the face with his right. Uttering a cry, the woman covered up her face and weepingly went back into the inner quarters of the house. Huangfu then called the thirteen-year-old maid Ying'er. He took down a bamboo stick from the wall, laid it on the ground, and demanded that she step forward. Ying'er was a girl with

> Short arms and bow legs,
> Strong enough to chop wood and fetch water,
> Healthy enough to eat and shit.

Huangfu Song then took down a rope from a clothing shelf, tied up the girl's hands with one end, and tossed the other end over a rafter. With a downward pull at the rope, the girl rose in mid-air. A bamboo stick in hand, he demanded, "In the three months that I was away, who's been drinking here with my wife?"

"No one," said the girl, whereupon Huangfu hit her legs with the stick until she screamed like a pig in a slaughterhouse. Unable to withstand any more of the questioning and the beating, the girl allowed herself to say, "While you were away those three months, the mistress slept with someone every night."

"Now you're talking!" said Huangfu. He let the girl down, untied her, and pressed further: "And whom did she sleep with?"

Wiping away her tears, the girl said, "I won't hide anything from you. While you were away, the mistress slept with none other than me!"

"Don't you try to get smart with me!" With that, he dismissed her, took a lock, stormed out the gate, and locked it. He then went to the mouth of the lane and called four men. They were local constables, known today as "connect-hands" or "watch troops." Zhang Qian, Li Wan, Dong Chao, and Xue Ba duly went to his house, unlocked the door with a key, and pushed the door open. Huangfu dragged out Seng'er the dumpling peddler and said, "Please be kind enough to take this boy into custody."

"At your service, sir," said the men.

"Don't go yet," continued Huangfu. "There's more." Calling forth the thirteen-year-old Ying'er and his pretty twenty-four-year-old wife, Huangfu said, "Take them along as well."

The four men protested, "How dare we take away your wife?"

Huangfu flew into a rage. "You dare not take her?" said he. "Don't you know that someone's life is at stake?"

These words frightened the four men into leading Huangfu's wife, Ying'er, and Seng'er the dumpling peddler all the way to Magistrate Qian's⁵ yamen in Kaifeng.

At the foot of the steps in the main hall, Huangfu saluted the magistrate and handed in the letter. After reading it, Magistrate Qian ordered that the accused be taken away. He then summoned Officer Shan Ding, who took on the case and called forth Seng'er for interrogation. To Officer Shan's questions, Seng'er answered, "It was a man with thick eyebrows, big eyes, a snub nose, and a large mouth who gave me this letter in the teahouse for me to deliver to the lady. This is all I know, even if you beat me to death."

When the officer turned to Ying'er, her answer was "No one came to drink with the mistress, nor do I have any idea who sent the letter. This is all I know, even if you beat me to death."

Before he could turn to the young woman, Huangfu's wife said, "Ever since we were betrothed in childhood, we haven't even had any contact with relatives. There's been only the two of us, husband and wife. I don't know who could have sent this letter."

Looking at the young woman's thin frame, Officer Shan Ding wondered how she was to withstand torture and the rigors of interrogation. From the interior of the yamen he summoned a prisoner, who was escorted by two prison wardens. This is how the prisoner looked:

> *His facial bones were gnarled;*
> *His cheeks were grotesque.*
> *He looked like the demon of disease,*
> *Spreading misfortune wherever he went.*

The prisoner, nicknamed the Lord of Mount Jing, was a ringleader of outlaws. At the sight of such a man, the young woman covered her face with both hands without daring to open her eyes. Officer Shan turned to the wardens with a sharp order: "Work on him!"

Pulling the cangue so that the prisoner's head was forced down, the wardens picked up a thorny staff and beat him until he screamed like a pig in a slaughterhouse.

"Have you killed?" asked Officer Shan.

"Yes, I have!" the Lord of Mount Jing readily conceded.

"Have you committed arson?"

"Yes, I have!" Thereupon the wardens were ordered to take him back into his cell.

Turning now to the young woman, Shan said, "You just witnessed how a few strokes made the Lord of Mount Jing confess to crimes of killing and arson. If you are guilty, you would do well to confess, because the beating will be too much for you."

Tears gushed out of her eyes as she replied, "Since nothing is to be kept from you, please give me paper and a brush-pen so I can write my confession."

Her confession ran as follows:

> In all the years since I was betrothed in childhood, I have never had any contact with any relatives, nor do I have any knowledge as to who sent the letter. It will be up to the magistrate to determine if I am guilty.

However many times she was pressed to confess, her answer remained the same.

Three days passed by in like fashion. Officer Shan was standing in front of the yamen, undecided as to what to do, when he raised his head abruptly, and whom did he see in front of him but Huangfu, bowing and asking, "Why has the case been under consideration for three days without a verdict? Could it be that some bribery from the sender of the letter made you hold up the case?"

At this accusation, Shan asked, "What is it you want, sir?"

"I want a divorce."

That very day, Officer Shan betook himself to the prefectural yamen and presented the case to Magistrate Qian during the evening session of the court. The magistrate summoned Huangfu into the hall and said, "To convict a thief, you need to find the stolen goods. To convict adulterers, you need to catch the two in the act. In this case, how are you going to establish guilt without any evidence?"

Huangfu Song rejoined, "I would rather divorce my wife than have to return home with her."

The magistrate's judgment was for the husband to do as he wished. Huangfu set off on his journey home, whereas Seng'er and Ying'er were ordered out of the yamen and went their separate ways. The abandoned woman wept her way out, muttering to herself, "My husband doesn't want me, and I have no relatives to turn to. Where can I go? I'd be better off dead." (*Pitiable.*)

Upon coming to Tianhanzhou Bridge, she stared at the Bian River, with its shiny waters and silvery bank. She was about to throw herself in when someone grabbed her clothing from behind. Turning around, she found that it was an old woman (*A frightening trap*), who had

Eyebrows like two piles of snow,
A chignon like a skein of silk.
Eyes as hazy as autumn waters,
Hair as hoary as mountain clouds.

"My child," said the old woman, "why are you trying to kill yourself? Do you know me?"

"No, Granny," said the young woman.

"I am your aunt. After you married, I lost touch with you because my family is too humble to be associated with you. The other day I heard that there is a lawsuit between you and your husband. Since then, I have been waiting here for you. Today I heard that a divorce has come through, but why did you try to jump into the water?"

"With not a tile over my head or enough land to stick an awl into, abandoned by my husband, and left with no relatives to turn to for help, I'd be better off dead, and now is as good a time as any!"

"Why don't you follow me to my home," said her aunt, "and we'll see what to do next."

The young woman thought to herself, "I have no way of knowing if she is indeed any aunt of mine, but having no place to go, why don't I just follow her and see what will happen?" So she followed the old woman home. The woman was in possession of a nice though sparsely furnished house with light blue curtains, armchairs, tables, and benches.

A couple of days later, they had just finished their meal when a man was heard shouting at the top of his voice outside the door, "Hey, old woman! You sold my things, but how come I still don't see the money?" At this, the old woman rushed out, all flustered, to greet the man. When he was invited in for a seat, the young woman saw that the man had

Thick brows, big eyes, a snub nose, a large mouth;
Above, a tall bucket-shaped hat;
A lined robe with wide collar and big sleeves;
Below, matching pants and neat shoes and socks.

The young woman said to herself, "How he fits Seng'er's description of the man who sent the letter!"

The man stepped in, took a seat, and addressed the old woman with exaggerated severity: "You sold goods belonging to me worth three hundred strings of cash, but it's been more than a month now, and I have yet to receive the money."

The old woman explained, "I have found a patron, but the money hasn't been paid yet. As soon as I get it, I'll bring it to you."

"It shouldn't take so many days for money and merchandise to exchange hands. Be sure to bring me the money as soon as you get it." With that, he walked off.

The old woman came back into the house and, with tears coursing down her cheeks, said to the young woman, "What am I to do now?"

"What is it?"

"That gentleman named Hong used to be the controller general of Cai-zhou, but now he no longer holds any official post and is in the jewelry business. The other day, he gave me an item to sell, but I came off badly in the deal and have no money to pay him. I don't blame him for being impatient. A couple of days ago, he gave me another job and I failed again."

"What was it that he asked you to do?"

"He wanted me to find him a beautiful concubine. He would surely be pleased to get someone with your looks. Now, your husband having abandoned you, you are not going to live like this for the rest of your life, are you? Wouldn't it be best if you marry this man, with me as the matchmaker, so that your future is not compromised and I can also have someone to fall back on? What do you say?" (*The saying "Abhor the evil ones, for they confuse what is right and what is wrong" is of much relevance here.*)

The young woman mused a long while before she finally consented, for lack of a better way out. The old woman duly apprised the man of the news. A couple of days later, the man brought the young woman to his home as his wife.

Another year went by quickly. It was now New Year's Day again. Since divorcing his wife, Huangfu had been living a miserable life. Truly,

> *Time is like a fire that, aided by wind,*
> *Melts away the coldness of the heart.*

He thought to himself, "Each New Year's Day, my wife and I used to go together to the prefectural Great State Councilor Monastery to make offerings of incense, but this year, I am all alone. I wonder where she might be?" Tears fell from his eyes as he sank into silent melancholy. With an effort, he put on a purple silk gown and, a silver incense box in hand, went to the monastery to make offerings of incense.

Having made his offerings, he was about to step out of the monastery when his eyes fell upon a man and a woman. The man had thick eyebrows, big eyes, a snub nose, and a large mouth, and the woman following him was none other than Huangfu's wife. The woman returned his gaze. The four eyes met, but neither he nor she ventured to speak. The man then took her into the monastery.

Huangfu Song was in the middle of his thoughts at the monastery gate when he noticed an acolyte collecting alms. At the sight of the couple stepping into the monastery, the acolyte said, "So, he's here, that man who ruined me!" With great strides, he stormed into the monastery.

While the acolyte was trying to catch up with them, Huangfu stopped him in his tracks. "Are you trying to catch up with those two?"

"So I am," replied the acolyte. "It's all because of that man that I'm in such a fix today. I can't even hold up my head!"

"Do you know the woman?" asked Huangfu.

"No."

"She was my wife," said Huangfu.

"Why is she with him?"

Whereupon Huangfu gave him a full account of the divorce and the incident of the letter that had led to it.

"So that's what happened!" said the acolyte who then asked Huangfu, "Do you know that man?"

"No."

"Well, that man was a monk in Potai Monastery in the eastern section of the capital. I was an acolyte in the same monastery. My master the abbot, who had over a hundred in cash, took that man on as an assistant. About a year ago, that scoundrel fled with some of the master's silverware worth about two hundred taels of silver. I was blamed for the theft. I was beaten up hard and driven out of the monastery, with no place to turn to for a living. Luckily the head monk of Great State Councilor Monastery let me stay here to collect alms. Now that he's here, I will certainly not let him get away!" He had hardly finished speaking before the monk and Huangfu's wife came out from the corridor. Pulling up his robe, the acolyte was about to charge forward to seize the man when Huangfu stopped him and pulled him aside to hide behind the monastery gate. "Don't confront him yet," he said. "Let's follow this bastard and see where he lives before we bring any charges against him." (*Meticulous.*) So they followed him.

To pick up another thread of our story, let us turn our attention to the woman, who had burst into tears at the sight of her ex-husband. On their way back after having burned incense at the monastery, the man asked her, "Why did you cry when you saw your former husband? I went to much trouble to get you. When I first passed your door before all this happened and saw you standing by the portiere, I was struck by your beauty and had my heart set on having you. It was by no means easy to get you as my wife." (*Volunteering a confession. It's the rock god of Yellow Stone Cliff speaking out, manifesting the will of heaven.*)

While conversing, they arrived at home. Once inside the house, the woman asked, "Who sent the letter, anyway?"

"If you want to know, it was I who made Seng'er the dumpling peddler deliver the letter to you. Your husband fell into my trap and did indeed divorce you."

At this revelation, she grabbed him and screamed in grief. Her cries so alarmed him that he seized her by the throat to choke her to death. Outside, Huangfu and the acolyte had followed them to the door and watched them enter. As the commotion inside reached their ears, they rushed in and found the man strangling Huangfu's wife to within an inch of her life. Huangfu and the acolyte overpowered him and sent him to the court of Magistrate Qian in Kaifeng. And who was this Magistrate Qian?

> When traveling, his men with whips cleared the way;
> When indoors, he had women support his arms.
> He came from a long line of officials;
> His offspring were to enjoy high status.
> Son of King Qian of Zhejiang,
> Grandson of the king of Wu and Yue.

When the magistrate called his court to order and brought up this case, Huangfu and his wife gave him a full account of everything that had happened. In a towering rage, the magistrate ordered the monk put in a big cangue. After a hundred thrashings on the legs right there in the courtroom, the man was brought under guard to the Court of Judicial Review for a thorough investigation.

After all the facts had been established, Huangfu Song was told to take his wife back. The acolyte was given a reward. The monk admitted to all wrongdoings, including his scheme of deception and, later, his murder attempt. In accordance with the Criminal Code, he was sentenced to be beaten to death. The old woman, for posing as the victim's aunt and failing to inform the authorities against the man, was banished to a neighboring prefecture. That day, when the monk was taken to the execution ground, a writer of popular stories witnessed the scene and composed this impromptu poem to the tune of "Song of the Southern Country":

> A monk guilty of foul deeds
> Receives a sentence of death.
> With the case firmly proven against him,
> He dies by the cudgel as a lesson to all.
>
> When the onlookers listen,
> They find him chanting the sutra.
> Guardian gods join their palms and murmur:
> An indestructible body he has!

Tightwad Zhang is unjustly convicted of crime in the Kaifeng court.

Song the Fourth Greatly Torments Tightwad Zhang

Money comes and goes like a flowing stream.
Don't grudge giving to the widowed and poor.
Witness how Shi Chong's grand Golden Valley
Is now overgrown with thistles and thorns.

Our story relates that during the Jin dynasty there lived a man named Shi Chong, courtesy name Jilun. Before he gained fame and fortune, he made a living by plying his small boat up and down the Yangzi River, catching fish with a bow and arrows.

One night, at about the third watch, he heard knocks on the boat and a voice saying, "Jilun! Help!" Shi Chong pushed open the mat door, stuck out his head, and saw that on the sparkling moonlit surface of the water stood an old man.

"What could have happened to make you seek help at this time of the night?" Shi Chong asked.

The old man repeated, "Please help me!"

Shi Chong invited the old man to step into the boat and asked him again what had brought him there.

"I am not a mortal human being," replied the old man. "I am the old Dragon King of the upper course of the river. Old and weak as I am, I have been challenged to fight by the young dragon of the lower course of the river who takes advantage of my age. I have lost to him so often that I don't even have a place to go to. Now he has challenged me to another big fight tomorrow. I will surely be beaten again. That's why I am here to ask for your help. At noontime tomorrow, please get your bow ready. When you see two fish fighting each other in the river, the one running ahead will be me. The one giving chase will be the young dragon. Please help me by shooting to death the big fish in pursuit. I will certainly repay you handsomely for your great kindness."

Shi Chong respectfully gave his consent. The old man took leave of him and leaped into the water.

When noon approached the following day, Shi Chong got his bow and

arrows ready. When the hour of noon came, behold! Two big fish appeared
on the surface of the river, one chasing the other. Shi Chong put his arrow on
his bow and, aiming at the one giving chase, shot the arrow right into its belly.
The river was dyed red as the big fish died. The wind and the storm subsided
and nothing else happened. At the third watch of the night, the old man came
knocking at the boat again, this time to thank him: "It is thanks to your great
kindness that I have regained a peaceful life. At noon tomorrow, you may
bring your boat to the seventh willow tree on the southern bank at the foot
of Mount Jiang¹ and wait for me there. I have a big reward for you." Having
said that, he took himself off.

Shi Chong did as he was told and went by boat to the designated willow
tree at the foot of Mount Jiang to wait for the old man. Behold: three ghostly
messengers rose to the surface of the water and pushed the boat away. Before
long, the boat came back, laden with gold, silver, pearls, and jade. The old
man himself also emerged from the water and said to Shi Chong, "Should
you want more of these, just come back on an empty boat and wait here for
it to be filled." (*Absurd.*) He then took his leave and went away.

Thereafter, every time Shi Chong came on his boat to wait by the willow
tree, he was given a boatload of treasures, and thus he accumulated enough
wealth to match that of the whole empire. He used his treasures to buy the
favor of the powerful and received repeated promotions until he became a
grand commandant. Now he had both wealth and position. He bought a big
house in the city and built behind it Gold Valley Garden, with pavilions, terraces, towers, and halls. With thirty pecks of large gleaming pearls, he bought
a concubine named Green Pearl. With a host of other concubines, waiting
women, and maids, he wallowed in pleasures day and night. He cultivated
the friendship of court officials and the emperor's kith and kin. His wealth
was such that he was able to erect on his estate a brocade wall over ten li in
length. Indeed, he enjoyed luxury matchless in heaven and on earth.

One day, he laid out a feast in honor of Wang Kai, brother of the empress.
No other guests were invited. When the two men were well warmed with
wine, Shi Chong called forth Green Pearl to ply the guest with more wine.
The sight of her beauty threw Wang Kai into raptures. His lust was stirred.
After the feast was over, Wang Kai said his thanks and returned home, regretting the lack of a chance to fulfill his desire for Green Pearl. As a matter of
fact, Wang Kai already harbored evil designs against Shi Chong because the
latter always beat him in their frequent games of showing off their collections
of treasures. He had not yet found an excuse to do anything, since Shi Chong
never failed to treat him with the utmost hospitality.

One day, the empress invited Wang Kai to dinner in her private quarters
in the palace. Once in his sister's presence, Wang Kai wept and said, "In this

city there is an immensely rich man who has an unlimited collection of the most exquisite treasures. He often invites me to dinner to compare our precious possessions, but even one or two of his items are worth more than a hundred of mine. Please take pity on me, sister, and lend me something extraordinary from your treasury so as to let me beat him and win back some honor."

Thus appealed to, the empress ordered the eunuch in charge of the imperial treasury to get Wang Kai the most prized possession of the palace— a big coral tree standing three feet eight inches high. Without reporting the matter to the emperor, she had some men carry it over to Wang Kai's residence. Wang Kai thanked his sister and returned home, where he had the coral tree covered with layers of Sichuan brocade.

The following day, he had the coral tree carried into an empty pavilion in Gold Valley Garden before inviting Shi Chong to a sumptuous feast there. When half tipsy with wine, Wang Kai said, "I have a treasure to show you. Please don't laugh."

Shi Chong asked to have the brocade cover taken off, looked at the coral tree with a smile, and, with a swing of his cane, smashed it to smithereens.

Wang Kai was appalled. "This is the most prized piece in the imperial treasury," he moaned. "How could you destroy it out of spite just because you can't beat me this time? What's to be done now?"

Shi replied with a hearty laugh, "Don't you worry, brother of the empress! You haven't seen the best there is." Thereupon he took Wang Kai to a rear garden, where there stood more than thirty coral trees of various sizes, with some as tall as seven to eight feet. One that was three feet eight inches tall, the same height as Wang Kai's, was presented to Wang Kai for him to return to the treasury. A taller and larger one was given to him as a gift. In shame, Wang Kai took his departure, consumed with jealousy at the thought that even the imperial treasury was no match for Shi Chong's wealth. He devised a wicked plan.

One day, in an audience with the emperor, Wang Kai said, "There is in this city an immensely rich man named Shi Chong who holds the post of grand commandant. With more wealth than there is in the whole empire, he lives in greater luxury than Your Majesty. If he is not removed as soon as possible, I am afraid something untoward might happen."

The emperor agreed and issued a verbal decree for the imperial guards to arrest Commandant Shi Chong and throw him into prison. All of his possessions were confiscated. Determined to have Green Pearl as a concubine, Wang Kai ordered soldiers to surround the house and seize her. Green Pearl, in the meantime, thought to herself, "My husband's life is in danger because of this man's false accusations. Now that he is after me, how can I ever submit? I'd rather die than suffer such humiliation!" She threw herself down the belvedere into Gold Valley Garden. How pitiable!

Wang Kai flew into a rage upon hearing this and had Shi Chong executed in the marketplace. Before the execution, Shi said with a sigh, "It's all because you people are jealous of my wealth."

The executioner replied, "Since you knew that too much money would bring you trouble, why didn't you give it away before it was too late?" (*This executioner is a wise man.*)

At a loss for an answer, Shi stretched out his neck for the axe. Hu Zeng[2] wrote a poem that says,

> *Since the beauty fell from the jade tower,*
> *Sorrow began to haunt the house of Jin.*
> *The trees left in Gold Valley Garden*
> *Mourn their old age under the setting sun.*

What I related above is about how Shi Chong showed off his wealth and his beautiful concubine, incurred the animosity of Wang Kai, brother of the empress, and brought disaster upon himself. I shall now tell of another rich man, who kept a low profile and did nothing to stir up trouble. However, a lingering trait of miserliness brought on some extraordinary events that have come to serve as the material for an entertaining story. What, you may ask, is the name of the rich man? Well, as I was going to say, he was called Zhang Fu [Wealth], addressed as Squire Zhang, who lived in Kaifeng, the Eastern Capital, and was owner of a pawnshop that he had inherited from his ancestors. This Squire Zhang had one weakness, which was a propensity to

> *Pluck a tendon from the back of a flea*
> *And cut meat from the legs of an egret;*
> *Peel gold off the face of a Buddha statue*
> *And scrape lacquer from the skin of a black bean;*
> *Save phlegm to use as lamp oil,*
> *And use pine needles to cook meals with.*

His four major wishes in life were

> *First, that clothes would never wear out;*
> *Second, that food would remain undigested;*
> *Third, that he would pick up valuables all around;*
> *Fourth, that he would make love with ghosts in his sleep.*

He was indeed a skinflint who hated to part with a single penny. If he picked up a penny from the ground, he would rub it until it shone like a mirror, knead it into the shape of a chime-stone, take nips from it so it looked like a saw, call it "my baby," kiss it, and put it in his bag. His miserliness won him the nickname Tightwad Zhang.

One day around noontime, the squire was in the back of his shop, eating a bowl of cold cooked rice soaked in hot water while his two managers counted money by the front door. There appeared a man wearing nothing over his much tatooed upper body. He had on trousers of white gauze tied up around his waist. A bamboo ladle in hand, he peeped into the house and made a deep bow, saying, "Please spare some change for this beggar." The squire not being within view, one of the managers tossed two pennies into the ladle, an act that happened to have been witnessed by Squire Zhang from behind the portiere. Out he came and said, "A fine thing you did, manager! Why did you have to give him two pennies? Two pennies a day means two whole strings in a thousand days!" In great strides, he rushed forward, caught up with the man with the ladle and, with a single swipe of his hand, emptied all the coins in the ladle onto the shop's pile of cash. He then had his men beat up the beggar. (*How could he!*) Even passersby were incensed at the sight. The man with the ladle took the blows without daring to protest. He just stood at the door, pointing with his finger and mouthing some angry words.

A man said loudly, "Brother, come over here. I have something to tell you."

The beggar looked around and saw that it was an old man dressed like a prison warden. After an exchange of greetings, the old man said, "Brother, this Tightwad Zhang is a man who doesn't listen to reason. Don't even bother to argue with him. Here are two taels of silver. Even if you sell turnips at only one penny a piece, you'll at least be a businessman." With the silver, the man made a bow and went away, but, of him, no more for the time being.

The old man was a native of Fengning District in Zhengzhou. Being the fourth son of the Song family, he was called Song the Fourth, an idler without a proper occupation.

On Gold Beam Bridge around the third watch of the night, he bought, for four pennies, two fried buns with vegetable filling, tucked them inside his shirt, and walked over to Tightwad Zhang's door. There being no other pedestrians in the moonless night, he took out a strange-looking object, hooked it up to the eaves, climbed up onto the roof, and jumped down into the yard, which was flanked on both sides by rows of chambers. As he drew near a lit window on one side, he heard a woman's voice saying, "It's so late now, but Third Brother still hasn't shown up."

Song said to himself, "Oh, this woman must be having an illicit affair." He looked at the woman and saw that she had

> *Black silky hair, a white, lovely forehead,*
> *Curving eyebrows and coquettish eyes,*
> *A straight nose and rosy cheeks,*
> *A fragrant mouth and a smooth chest,*

Creamy breasts and delicate hands,
A narrow waist and arched feet.

Song walked up to her and covered her face with his sleeves. "Third Brother," said the woman, "why scare me like that?" With a quick movement, Song held her tight by the waist and took out his knife, saying, "Be quiet. If you raise your voice, I'll kill you!"

Trembling all over, the woman said, "Please spare my life."

"Young woman," said Song, "I am a burglar. Let me ask you something. How many traps are there from here to the storehouse?"

"About ten steps from my room, there's a pit watched over by two ferocious dogs. Pass that and you'll come across five guards drinking and gambling. Each of them will be on duty for one watch. When you enter the storehouse, you'll see a paper man with a silver ball in his hand and a trap underneath. If you step on the trap, the silver ball will drop and roll along a groove all the way to the squire's bed to wake him up so that he can have you arrested."

"So that's how it is," said Song. "Young woman, who's that coming up behind you?"

Without realizing that it was a trick, the woman turned around, only to be cut down from the shoulder by Song with his knife. With blood spurting, she fell down dead. Song left the room and, after about ten steps, kept to the west side of the path, passing the pit. As he did so, he heard two dogs barking. He took out the buns, added a drug to them, and, upon drawing nearer, tossed them to the dogs. The buns smelled so delicious that the dogs gobbled them up and soon collapsed to the ground. Song went further ahead and heard five or six people noisily engaged in a game of dice-throwing. He took out a small container from his bosom, put in some mischievous stuff, and lit it with a flintstone, producing an aroma that assailed the nostrils. The five men exclaimed, "What a nice smell! The squire is always burning incense, day and night." While busily sniffing the aroma this way and that, they tumbled head over heels, one after another. In a trice, all five men lost consciousness. Song the Fourth walked up to them and finished what was left of the wine and food. Their eyes wide open, the five men lay there, unable to utter a sound.

He then went up to the storehouse and saw on the door an arm-length triple padlock. He took out from his bosom a skeleton key called "open-all" that could be applied to all locks, big or small. With one turn, he opened the padlock and entered the storehouse. At the sight of the paper man holding a silver ball, he took away the ball and threaded his way through many a trap before he found some valuables of the finest quality worth fifty thousand strings of cash. After wrapping them up into one package, he took out a brush-pen and, moistening it with his saliva, wrote a quatrain on the wall:

A carefree wanderer from Song
Leaves his marks over the four seas.
His name has been carved on memorials of fame.
His fame spreads far and wide, here and everywhere.

Having written the quatrain on the wall, he made his way out without even bothering to close the door of the storehouse. "The Eastern Capital may be a nice place," he thought to himself, "but it's not where I should linger for too long." That very night, he set out on a journey back to Zhengzhou.

Now, let us come back to Squire Zhang's house. When the five guards woke up at the break of day, they found the door of the storehouse open, the two dogs dead of poison, and a woman murdered. Upon their report, the squire informed the authorities, whereupon Magistrate Teng sent Inspector Wang Zun to track down the thief. At the sight of the quatrain on the wall, one of the more experienced runners, a certain Zhou Xuan the Fifth, said to the inspector, "Sir, this is the work of Song the Fourth."

"How do you know? asked Inspector Wang.

"In the first line, 'A carefree wanderer from Song,' there is the word 'Song.' In the second line, 'Leaves his marks over the four seas,' there is the word 'four.' In the third line, 'His name has been carved on memorials of fame,' there is 'has been,' and in the last line, 'His fame spreads far and wide, here and everywhere,' there is the word 'here.' Strung together, they form the sentence 'Song the Fourth has been here.'"

Inspector Wang said, "I have long heard that there is a most skilled thief called Song the Fourth, a native of Zhengzhou. This must be him." Consequently, Zhou the Fifth, Zhou Xuan, was ordered to take some runners with him to Zhengzhou to arrest Song the Fourth.

Eating when hungry, drinking when thirsty, resting by night, and off again next dawn, in due time they arrived in Zhengzhou, where they asked their way to Song's house. They stepped into the little shop in front of his house for some tea, and an old man went to the stove to make tea for them. The visitors said, "Why don't you also invite Song the Fourth out to have a cup of tea with us?"

"The master is in bed not feeling well," said the old man. "Let me go in and give him the message."

With the old man gone, Song was heard to yell from inside, "When this headache of mine first came on, I told you to buy me three pennies' worth of porridge, but you refused. I'm spending all this money every day on you without getting anything in return. What good are you?" With that, he gave the old man a few loud slaps.

Soon the old man reappeared, carrying a porridge bowl in his hand, and said, "Please wait a little while. The master wants me to go and buy some porridge. He'll be coming out after he eats it."

The visitors waited for what seemed like an eternity, but neither the old man nor Song the Fourth showed up. Their patience exhausted, the men went into the inner chambers and saw an old man all trussed up. Taking him to be Song the Fourth, the men came over to arrest him, but the old man said, "I am Mr. Song's servant. The one who went out with a bowl to buy porridge is Mr. Song."

Much taken aback, the men said with a sigh, "What a cunning man! Slipping through our hands like that when we weren't looking closely enough!" They had no choice but to run out after him, but since he was already far beyond their reach by this time, they had to split up and go separately to track him down. But of them, for the time being, no more.

What had happened was that when Song listened from his room, he detected the runners' Eastern Capital accent when they were talking over their tea. He took a peek and saw that they looked like men from the yamen. Growing apprehensive, he deliberately started shouting abuses and complaints. He then exchanged clothes with the old servant and walked out, with his head lowered, pretending to be on an errand to buy porridge. The men did not suspect a thing.

Once out of the house, Song thought to himself, "Now, where should I go? I do have an apprentice, Zhao Zheng, a native of Pingjiang Prefecture, who is now in Mo County, as he said in his last letter. Why don't I go to him for help?" He changed his clothes and made himself look like a prison warden. Covering up his face with a fan, he feigned blindness and slowly made his way to Mo County. As he drew near the county border, there came into view a small wineshop. Behold:

> Banners flutter amid the clouds and mist;
> The days pass slowly in these times of peace.
> Wine can make heroes take on more courage
> And help drown the sorrows of the beauties.
> Over the weeping willows on the banks,
> Midst the plum blossoms hangs the tavern sign.
> Men who failed to achieve their ambition
> Sing and drink till lost in the joy of wine.

Feeling the pangs of hunger, Song stepped into the wineshop and placed an order for wine. The waiter served the wine, and Song was into his third cup when a handsome young man entered the wineshop. What was the newcomer wearing?

A brick-shaped cap tied at the back,
A black satin gown with a double belt,
Wide-bottomed trousers underneath,
And shoes of silk on his feet.

When the young man said, "Greetings to you, sir," Song raised his head and saw that it was none other than his apprentice Zhao Zheng. As he thought it best not to make their relationship known to people around them, Song said simply in reply, "Please take a seat." Zhao Zheng did so, and after they had expressed polite concern for each other, he had the waiter bring another wine cup. After a drink, Zhao Zheng said in a lowered voice, "I haven't heard from you for a long time, my master."

"Second Brother," said Song, "how's your business going?"

"Business does come my way, but I have spent everything I made on pleasures of all sorts. I heard that you went to the Eastern Capital and had quite a windfall."

"Nothing much, just forty to fifty thousand in cash." He then asked Zhao Zheng, "Where are you planning to go, Second Brother?"

"I was thinking of going to the Eastern Capital to tour the city so that I have something to brag about when I get back to Pingjiang."

"You can't go, Second Brother."

"Why not?"

"For three reasons. First, you are from western Zhejiang. You know little about the Eastern Capital, and few in our profession there know you. Who are you going to turn to for help? Second, the outer wall of the Eastern Capital, one hundred eighty li in length, is known as Buffalo Wall, and we in our line of business are known as 'bandits in the grass.' As the proverb says, 'Once in the buffalo's mouth, the grass won't have long to live.' Third, in the Eastern Capital, there are five thousand sharp-eyed and swift-handed government runners and three hundred inspectors."

"None of these three things scares me," said Zhao Zheng. "Don't you worry, Master. I don't get caught easily."

"If you ignore what I say and insist on going, let's strike a deal. I have a package of valuables from Tightwad Zhang. I will now go back to my inn and put the package next to my pillow. If you can steal it from me, you may go to the Eastern Capital as you wish."

"Agreed!" said Zhao Zheng.

Having thus settled on the deal, Song paid the bill and returned with Zhao Zheng to his inn. The clerk greeted him and his friend, and the two men went into Song's room, where Zhao Zheng took a look around, said good-bye, and went off. Evening set in. Behold:

A dark mist veils the distant hills.
A thin fog spreads across the clear sky.
The stars try to outshine the moon;
The waters and hills vie to show off their green.
The peaceful chimes from the ancient temples
Echo through the depth of the woods.
On small boats by the winding river's edge
Flicker points of light from fishermen's lamps.
Birds on the branches sing to the moon;
Butterflies nestle midst fragrant flowers.

Seeing that the evening was advanced, Song thought to himself, "Zhao Zheng is a master of the game. Being his teacher, I would become a laughing stock if I end up losing the package to him. I'd better get to bed early."

Afraid that Zhao Zheng might sneak in on him while he was asleep, he put the package by his head and lay down. There came into his hearing some squeaking sounds from the rafters. "How strange!" he said to himself. "It's not even the first watch yet, and the mice are already out to do their mischief." As he raised his head and looked up at the beams, some dust fell. He sneezed a couple of times. The mice quieted down, but a moment later two cats were heard meowing and fighting each other. A stream of urine trickled down into his mouth. What a foul smell! Gradually, he felt himself succumb to drowsiness and fell asleep.

When he rose at the break of day, the package of valuables was nowhere to be seen. He was at a loss what to do when the inn clerk came in to say, "Sir, the gentleman who came with you last night is here to see you."

Song stepped out and, sure enough, it was Zhao Zheng. After an exchange of greetings, Song invited him in and closed the door. Zhao Zheng took out a package from his bosom and handed it to him. "My brother," said Song, "let me ask you something. Neither the door nor the windows have been touched. How did you manage to get the package?"

"I won't keep anything from you," said Zhao Zheng. "As a matter of fact, the blackened barred windows by your bed are covered with rice paper. First, I climbed onto the roof and imitated mice squeaking. The dustlike stuff that fell from the roof into your eyes and nose and made you sneeze was a drug. The cat urine actually came from me."

"You swine! You didn't have to do that!"

Zhao Zheng continued, "Then I made my way to your window, peeled off the paper, removed two bars with my small saw, and sidled my way in. I got to your bed, stole the package, climbed out through the window, nailed the bars back into place, and replaced the paper, leaving no trace at all."

"All right! All right!" said Song. "You may have done it this time, but that doesn't mean you are a true master. If you can get the package from me again tonight, I'll believe you can really do it."

"All right. That's easy." Zhao Zheng returned the package to Song and said, "My master, I'm going now. I'll see you tomorrow." With a fling of his arms, he went off.

Without saying anything out loud, Song thought to himself, "Zhao Zheng is better at this game than me. If he gets the package again, I'll look even worse. I'd better get out of here!" He called the clerk and said to him, "I am leaving. Here's two hundred in cash. Please use a hundred of it to buy me some roast pork well seasoned with extra salt and pepper, fifty of it to buy me some steamed pancakes, and keep the remaining fifty to buy yourself a drink."

The clerk thanked him, went downtown, and bought the roast pork and steamed pancakes. On his way back, a man called out to him from a teahouse about ten houses away from the inn, "Hello! Where are you going?"

The clerk raised his eyes and saw that it was Song's friend. "Mr. Song is leaving, and he asked me to buy some roast pork and steamed pancakes."

"Show me," said Zhao Zheng. He opened the packet wrapped up in lotus leaves and asked, "How much did you pay for the roast pork?"

"One hundred in cash."

Zhao Zheng took out two hundred in cash and said, "Brother, leave the stuff here. Here's another two hundred. Please buy me the same things, and keep the remaining fifty to buy yourself a drink."

"Thank you, sir." The clerk went off and came back some moments later with the food. Zhao Zheng said, "Please be kind enough to wrap up the pork again for Mr. Song. When you see him, tell him from me to be on his guard tonight." The clerk promised and went on his way.

When he reached the inn, he handed the meat and the pancakes to Song. "Thank you very much for all the trouble," said Song.

"The gentleman who came this morning," said the clerk, "asked me to tell you to be on your guard tonight."

Having gathered together his baggage and paid his bill, Song left the inn, carrying his bedding on his back and the package of Squire Zhang's valuables in his hand. More than a li later, he took the road leading to Bajiao Town, to the southwest of Kaifeng. At the ferry, while waiting in vain for the ferryboat, which was in view by the opposite shore, he felt hungry and sat down on the ground, putting the package of valuables in front of him. He opened the packet with the roast pork and pancakes, split open a steamed pancake, dipped four or five pieces of the fatty pork deep in the pepper and salt, and rolled them up in the pancake. But hardly had he chewed two mouthfuls before the sky and earth changed places and he collapsed to the ground. A man dressed like a runner came up to him and, before his wide-open eyes, took away the package of valuables. As any attempt to cry out or to run after the man was beyond him, Song had to watch him cross the river with the package.

Upon regaining the use of his limbs after a considerable while, Song thought to himself, "Who was that runner who took away my package? There must have been something funny about the roast pork that the inn clerk bought for me!" Swallowing the humiliation, Song called the ferryboat over, crossed the river, and went ashore, all the while wondering where he was to go to look for the man. Hungry and thirsty and in low spirits, he saw a village wineshop ahead of him:

> The firewood gate was left ajar;
> The tattered banner was hanging low.
> The tavern waiter, a country bumpkin,
> Knew nothing of the dishwashing Xiangru.[3]
> The uncouth maid, keeper of silkworms,
> Was a poor match for Wenjun.
> On the walls, poems by the drunken village scholar.
> On the rack, a farmer's hemp clothes left as a pledge.
> Cracked jars of coarse brew stood by the clay beds;
> Paintings of drunken immortals were dark with dust.[4]

Song the Fourth went into the wineshop for some wine to drown his sorrows with. The waiter said, "Yes, sir!" to his request and brought him wine. He drank in moody silence and was into his third cup when he saw a woman come in from outside.

> With sleek hair and a powdered face,
> White teeth and ruby lips.
> A brocade hat that reached down to her brows,
> A silk skirt that trailed on the ground,
> With flowers adorning her temples,
> She wore a coy smile on her face.
> Though not a beauty of the gentry class,
> She had her charms as a wineshop maid.

Having entered the wineshop, the woman bowed in greeting to Song and started singing a song, clapping her hands to the rhythm. Upon a closer look, Song found her face slightly familiar. Assuming that she was a singing-girl making a living in wineshops, he asked her to sit down. The woman accordingly took a seat by his side, had another wine cup brought to her, and downed one cupful. Song gave her a hug, a pinch, and a few pats. Saying, "Sweetheart!" he reached for her breasts but found none. Then he reached down to touch her private parts but felt only a dangling member. "Damn!" said he. "Who are you, anyway?" (*Song the Fourth is not a decent fellow, either.*)

The one in woman's attire replied with composure, arms akimbo, "Sir, I am not a prostitute singing in wineshops for a living. I am Zhao Zheng from Suzhou in Pingjiang Prefecture."

"What a crafty scoundrel! I am your teacher, and you made me touch that thing of yours! So the runner was you."

"Yes, it was me all right."

"My brother, where did you put my package of valuables?"

Zhao Zheng called out to the waiter, "Give back to Mr. Song the package that I deposited with you."

The waiter brought the package over. Song took it and asked, "My brother, how did you do it?"

"I was sitting in a teahouse a few doors away from the inn when I saw the inn clerk walk by with a package of roast pork. I asked to look at it and made him buy another package for me. I put a drug in the pork, wrapped it up again, and had him take it to you. I disguised myself as a runner and followed you until you fell. Then I got hold of the package and came here to wait for you."

"What a true master you are! You are ready for the Eastern Capital."

After paying the bill, the two men went out of the wineshop together. In a deserted place, Zhao Zheng took off the flowers, washed his face in a stream, and changed back into male attire complete with a blue gauze cap.

"Now that you are going to the capital, I'll give you a letter of introduction to another apprentice of mine. He lives by the Bian River and makes a living by selling buns with fillings of human flesh. His name is Hou Xing. Being the second child of the family, he is known as Second Brother Hou."

"Thank you, master," said Zhao Zheng. In a teahouse farther down the road, Song wrote the letter and gave Zhao Zheng some words of advice before they parted company. Song remained in Mo County.

That night, Zhao Zheng went to an inn to spend the night. When he opened Song's letter, he saw that it read,

My good brother and sister-in-law:

How have you been since I saw you last? The bearer of this letter, Zhao Zheng, is a thief from Suzhou, wishing to do business in the capital. I told him to come to you, because this man is no friend of our profession. The abundant flesh on his body will be useful for your business. I was humiliated by him three times. Be sure to bump off this man, so as to remove a potential danger to our profession.

Zhao Zheng was so shocked that his tongue hung out and refused to be drawn back in. "Another man in a similar situation might be frightened into giving up the trip, but I'll see what they can do to me! I'll know the right thing to do." He folded the letter up and sealed it as before.

At daybreak, he left the inn and headed for Bajiao Town. After passing the town, he made his way to Chenliu County via Ban Bridge and continued walking along the Bian River. Around noontime, he saw a bun shop on the bank. A woman in front of the shop with a checkered scarf around her waist shouted, "Please have some buns before you go on, sir!" On the sign at the door was written, "Hou Family Restaurant. The finest buns and pastries."

Zhao Zheng said to himself, "So this is Hou Xing's house." As he stepped in, the woman greeted him and asked, "Refreshments, sir?"

"One moment, please." So saying, he took down his backpack and revealed a packet of gold and silver hairpins he had picked up along the way, of which some bore elaborate ornaments, some were linked together, and some were undecorated.

The sight of the hairpins stirred up the greed in Hou Xing's wife. "This client has two to three hundred hairpins!" she said to herself. "I with my human-flesh bun business and my husband with his thefts don't have as much as that man does. In a few moments when he orders buns, I'll give him a big dose of the drug, and the hairpins will all be mine."

"Sister," said Zhao Zheng, "please bring me five buns."

"Yes, sir!" said Hou Xing's wife. She took a dish, put five buns on it, and liberally sprinkled on them some stuff from a container on the stove.

Zhao Zheng said to himself, "So that's the container for the drug." From his bosom, he took out a packet of medicine and said, "Sister, I need some cold water to help my medicine go down." When Hou Xing's wife put half a bowl of water on the table, Zhao Zheng said, "I'll eat the buns after I take the medicine." Having taken the medicine, Zhao Zheng used two chopsticks to pry open a bun. He took a look at the filling and said, "Sister, my father said to me, 'Don't buy buns from the shop by the Bian River, for they use human flesh for the filling.' Sister, look! Here's a piece of fingernail, which means this is a human finger. The many short hairs on that piece of skin mean it's the private parts."

"Don't be ridiculous!" shot back Hou Xing's wife. "What kind of talk is this!"

When Zhao Zheng finished the buns, the woman said in front of the stove, hoping that Zhao Zheng would collapse, "Fall!" But nothing happened. "Sister," called out Zhao Zheng. "Give me another five."

Hou Xing's wife thought to herself, "The dose must have been too small. Let me add more this time." Zhao Zheng took out another packet and took some more medicine.

"What medicine are your taking, sir?" asked Hou Xing's wife.

"This is called Cure for a Hundred Illnesses. It's dispensed by the judicial commissioner of Pingjiang Prefecture. It works well on all women's ailments, including headaches, pregnancy, childbirth, troubles with the spleen, and gastric pains."

"Would you please give me a packet?" said Hou Xing's wife.

Zhao Zheng took out a different packet from his bosom and gave her about a hundred tiny pills. She took them all and collapsed in front of the stove. "This woman tried to work on me," thought Zhao Zheng to himself, "but ended up being tricked by me. Another man would have slipped away, but I'm going to stay." Defiantly, he loosened his belt and began to look for fleas. (*Funny.*)

Before long, a man came in, carrying a load. "This must be Hou Xing," Zhao Zheng thought to himself. "I'll see what he's going to do."

After an exchange of greetings, Hou Xing said, "Have you been served any refreshments, sir?"

"Yes," said Zhao Zheng.

"Wife!" called out Hou Xing. "Have you settled the bill with the gentleman?" A search for his wife led him to the stove, where he saw her lying on the ground, foaming at the mouth and mumbling none too clearly, "I've been drugged."

"I see," said Hou Xing. "This woman must have failed to recognize some old hand at the profession and got tricked. It must be the customer outside." To Zhao Zheng he said, "Sir, my stupid wife failed to recognize a brother in the same profession. Please forgive the offense."

"May I ask your name, honorable brother?" said Zhao Zheng.

"I am Hou Xing."

"I am Zhao Zheng from Suzhou."

After an exchange of greetings, Hou Xing gave his wife an antidote.

"Brother," said Zhao Zheng, "Master Song the Fourth has a letter for you."

After opening it, Hou Xing saw that it was a long letter, at the end of which were the words, "Bump off this man." Rage seized him. "Even my master was humiliated by him three times. Tonight, I'll surely finish him off!"

Turning to Zhao Zheng, he said, "I have long heard about your outstanding qualities. How fortunate for me to get to meet you!" He set out wine in honor of the guest. After dinner, he put Zhao Zheng in a guest room; then he and his wife continued to work by the front door.

The offensive smell in his room started Zhao Zheng on a search. When he came upon a big jar underneath the bed, his groping hand touched a human head. He reached out again and found a hand and a foot. He carried them out the back door, strung them up with a rope, and hung them up on the eaves over the door. Then he closed the door and went back to his room, just in time to overhear the woman say, "Husband, it's time!"

"Not yet!" admonished Hou Xing. "Let's wait till he's more soundly asleep."

"Husband," said the woman. "I saw him take out two to three hundred gold and silver hairpins. After we do away with him tonight, I'll put them all over my head tomorrow to win some applause."

Zhao Zheng said to himself, "So! They're indeed out to get me! But that's all right."

Hou Xing had a ten-year-old son called Ban'ge, who was in bed, sick with malaria. Zhao Zheng went into his room, carried the boy over to his own bed, covered him up with the quilt, and went out the back door. (*Good foresight.*) Before long, Hou Xing's wife, carrying a lamp, and Hou Xing, armed with a big firewood axe, pushed open Zhao Zheng's door. At the sight of a human figure beneath the quilt, he swung down the axe twice and cut him, quilt and all, into three pieces. As he lifted up the quilt to take a look, he cried out, "Woe is me! It's our son, Ban'ge!" While the husband and wife were seized with violent fits of weeping, Zhao Zheng shouted from behind the back door, "Why did you have to kill your son for lack of a better thing to do? Zhao Zheng is right here!"

A furious Hou Xing took up the axe and ran after Zhao, but, as he rushed out the back door, he hit his forehead against something, which, when he paused to take a look, turned out to be a human head, a hand, and a foot strung together like decorations on a bamboo pole. Hou Xing told his wife to move them into the house, while he himself continued to charge forward. Seeing that Hou Xing was upon his heels, Zhao threw himself into the stream ahead of him because, being a native of Pingjiang, he was a good swimmer. Hou Xing also jumped into the water. Zhao Zheng's kicks and strokes in the water got him to the other bank in no time. Hou Xing also knew how to swim but was slower. Zhao reached land first and took off his clothes to wring them dry. And so Hou Xing gave chase from around the fourth watch of the night to a little past the fifth watch over a distance of eleven to twelve li, until they came to a public bathhouse by Shuntian Gate, also known as Xinzhen Gate. Zhao was inside the bathhouse washing his face and drying his clothes by the fire when a man came up, pulled at his legs with both hands, and toppled him over. Seeing it was Hou Xing, Zhao brought up his knees sharply, knocked the latter to the ground, and landed his fists on him.

At this juncture, an old man dressed like a prison warden stepped forward and said, "Cut it out for my sake." Both men raised their heads and saw that it was none other than their master, Song the Fourth. Each of them called out a respectful greeting and bowed to him. Song said something to reconcile the two and took them to an herb shop for a cup of tea. When Hou Xing told his master about everything that had gone before, Song said, "Don't bring up the past any more. Tomorrow, Brother Zhao will go to the Eastern Capital to see Wang Xiu, also a man in our line of work. He sells buns with vegetable fillings under Gold Beam Bridge. He is the best roof-walker there is, and is nick-named Sick Cat. He lives behind Great State Councilor Monastery. On his peddler's stand, there is a large porcelain jar adorned with gold threads. He loves the jar as much as he does his life because it was made in the kiln of Dingzhou.⁵ Will you be able to steal it?"

"No problem," said Zhao Zheng. He promised to meet his master at Hou Xing's place around noon, after the city gate was opened. He then put on a brick-shaped cap tied at the back and his double-belted black satin gown and made his way to Gold Beam Bridge, where he saw an old man behind a stand, on which was a large jar adorned with gold threads.

> A Yunzhou-style blue gauze cap,
> A cotton shirt with willow patterns,
> And a checkered scarf around his waist,
> The old man stood with arms akimbo.

Zhao Zheng thought to himself, "So this must be Wang Xiu." He crossed over the bridge, pinched a few grains of red rice in front of a rice shop, picked some leaves from a vegetable stand, and chewed the rice and vegetable in his mouth before he walked up to Wang Xiu's stand. He took out six pennies to buy two buns and deliberately dropped one penny to the ground. When Wang Xiu bent down to pick up that penny, Zhao Zheng spit the rice and leaves onto Wang's cap and went off with the buns. He was standing on top of Gold Beam Bridge when a small boy hopped his way along. "Little boy," said Zhao Zheng. "Here's five pennies for you. Go tell Mr. Wang, the bun seller, that there is a heap of bug droppings on his cap, but don't say I told you to say so."

The boy did as he was told. "Mr. Wang," he said, "Look what's on your cap!"

Wang Xiu took off his cap and went into a teahouse to wipe off what he thought were bug droppings. By the time he went back to his stand, he realized that the jar was not there. What happened was that Zhao Zheng had taken advantage of Wang Xiu's brief absence to snatch away the jar. He then hid it in his sleeves and went straight to Hou Xing's home.

Song and Hou Xing were agape with astonishment. Zhao said, "I don't want this thing. I'll give it back to his wife."

He returned to his room, changed into an old and tattered cap, a pair of worn hemp shoes, and a ragged shirt, and headed for the rear of the monastery. Upon seeing Wang Xiu's wife, he called out a greeting and said, "Mr. Wang sent me here to get from you a new cotton shirt, an undershirt, a pair of pants, and new shoes and socks. I have here the gold-threaded jar to prove that I'm telling the truth."

Without knowing that she was falling into a trap, she took the jar and brought out the clothes for Zhao Zheng. He took them and went again to see Song and Hou, saying, "I exchanged the jar for so many pieces of clothing from his home. Let the three of us go together in a short while to give them back to him and have a laugh. In the meantime, let me put them on and go have some fun."

Zhao Zheng put on Wang Xiu's clothes and went to town again, where he toured the Sang Family Pleasure Grounds and had some wine and refreshments before he left the grounds. He was about to cross Gold Beam Bridge when someone called out, "Mr. Zhao!" He turned around and saw that it was his master Song the Fourth and Hou Xing. The three of them crossed the bridge together and saw Wang Xiu selling his buns. Song said, "Mr. Wang, shall we have a cup of tea with you?"

Wang Xiu greeted his teacher and Hou and, looking at Zhao Zheng, asked Song, "Who is this gentleman?" Song was about to tell him when Zhao Zheng dragged him to one side and said, "Don't give out my name. Just say that I'm a relative of yours. I have a good reason for that."

Wang Xiu asked again, "What is this gentleman's name?"

"He's a relative of mine," said Song. "I invited him over to tour the capital."

Believing his story, Wang Xiu deposited his stand with the teahouse, and the four of them went together to a quiet wineshop outside Shuntian Gate. When they got there, the waiter served them wine. After three rounds of drinking, Wang Xiu said, "Master, I'm in bad luck today. I had barely set up my stand when a man came up to buy buns and dropped a penny on the ground. When I bent down to pick up the penny, my cap became soiled by some bug droppings. I went into the teahouse to wipe it clean, but, by the time I returned, my gold-threaded jar was nowhere to be seen. I've been feeling wretched the whole day."

"What an impudent man, whoever it was!" said Song. "But isn't he something? To be able to pull off tricks like that on you, of all people! Don't feel bad. Tomorrow when we have time, we'll help you look for the jar. It's the only jar of its kind. Whatever happens, we'll be able to find out its whereabouts. It can't have just disappeared." Zhao Zheng, in the meantime, laughed in his sleeves. The foursome continued drinking. It was not until night set in that they parted company in a state of drunkenness.

When Wang Xiu arrived home, his wife asked him, "Brother, did you just tell someone to bring the jar back home?"

"No, I didn't."

"But it's here," said his wife, bringing it to her husband. "That man also took away some clothing."

Wang Xiu had no idea who that man could have been, but all of a sudden, he remembered that Song's relative was wearing clothes that looked like his. Feeling dejected, he poured himself some wine and, putting aside all his worries, drank with his wife until he was tipsy. Having taken off his clothes and gone to bed, he said to his wife, "We haven't been together for a long time."

"You are too old for such naughty thoughts!" snapped his wife.

"Haven't you heard the saying 'The young can take it easy, but the old burn like fire'?" While so saying, he had already moved over to his wife's side of the bed and was at it when a bang was heard on the door. What had happened was that Zhao Zheng, seeing the couple drunk, had sneaked in through the door and hid himself under the bed. When he heard them in the act, he flung the chamber pot against the door. Much taken aback, Wang Xiu and his wife took a look and saw a man crawl out from under the bed, carrying a package in his hand. Upon a closer look by the lamplight, Wang Xiu recognized him to be the companion of Song and Hou at the wine table. "What are you doing here?" demanded Wang Xiu.

"Song the Fourth told me to return this package to you."

Wang took the package and saw that it contained his clothes. "Who are you?" he asked again.

"I am Zhao Zheng from Suzhou, Pingjiang Prefecture."

"Oh, I have long heard your name."

Now that they had made their acquaintance, Wang Xiu kept Zhao Zheng for the night.

The following day, Wang Xiu took Zhao Zheng around for a walk. "That large mansion at the foot of White Tiger Bridge," said Wang Xiu, "is Prince Qian's residence. There's a lot to be had!"

"Let's do something later tonight," said Zhao.

Wang Xiu agreed.

At around the third watch of the night, Zhao Zheng dug a tunnel to the Qian family storehouse and stole thirty thousand strings of cash and a white jade belt with a veiled design of a coiling dragon. Wang Xiu stood guard outside and escorted him back to his house to hide.

The following day, Prince Qian wrote a letter to Magistrate Teng, who, after reading it, flared into wrath. "How can there be such accursed burglars in the capital!" Then and there, he ordered Inspector Ma Han to arrest the burglar within three days.

Thus ordered, Inspector Ma Han told his men to take turns working around the clock. When passing by Great State Councilor Monastery, he saw a man with a brick-shaped cap tied at the back and a purple shirt. "Shall we have a cup of tea, Inspector?" said the man. The two of them went into the teahouse, where a waiter served them tea. The man in purple took out from his bosom a packet of pine nuts and walnut kernels and put them into the two cups of tea.

"May I ask your name?" inquired the inspector.

"I am Zhao Zheng, the very one who robbed the Qian residence last night."

At these words, Inspector Ma broke into a sweat, but he had to wait for his men to come and help arrest Zhao. After drinking a cup of tea, heaven and earth changed places, and he collapsed. "The inspector is drunk," said Zhao Zheng. He caught the inspector from falling and, with a pair of his burglar's scissors, cut off half of each of the inspector's sleeves, which he then stuffed into his own sleeves. When paying the bill, he said to the waiter, "I'll send someone over to attend to the inspector." With that, he took himself off.

In about the time it took to eat two bowls of rice, the effect of the drug in Inspector Ma's stomach wore off. After he came to and did not see Zhao Zheng anywhere in sight, Inspector Ma went back. After a night's sleep, he followed the magistrate to the morning session at the imperial court. On horseback, the magistrate was about to enter Xuande Gate when a man wearing a black shirt and a hat with curved corners blocked his way. Chanting a respectful greeting, the man said, "Prince Qian has an official letter for you." Magistrate Teng accepted the letter. After the man had gone with another salute, the magistrate noticed that the buckle on his goldfish waistband had disappeared.

The letter read as follows:

From Zhao Zheng, thief of Suzhou, to the Honorable Magistrate:

I am responsible for the burglary at the Qian residence. Should the magistrate wish to find me, my home is as far as beyond one hundred eight thousand li or as near as right in front of your eyes.

Even more vexed, the magistrate called his own court to order upon returning from the imperial court session, and started to read complaints from citizens who had deposited their letters of complaint in special boxes. When he got to about the tenth one, he noticed that the letter, instead of being written in accordance with any established format, contained only a lyric poem to the tune of "The Moon over the West River":

Just as all waters return to the sea,
Idle men all flock to the capital.

Inspector Ma, his sleeves cut off,
Finds his authority also missing.
As for the one who stole the prince's belt
And cut off the magistrate's gold buckle,
If you wish to know his surname,
It's a small moon beside an earthly bolt of cloth.[6]

The magistrate said, "This again is the work of the artful Zhao Zheng." He summoned Inspector Ma Han for a progress report.

"I saw that thief Zhao Zheng face to face yesterday," said Ma Han, "but I let him get away because I didn't recognize him. He is truly a master in his line of work. I have learned that he was an apprentice of Song the Fourth of Zhengzhou. If we can get hold of Song, we can get Zhao as well."

Magistrate Teng suddenly remembered that Song was still at large after his burglary of Squire Zhang's storehouse. He summoned Officer Wang Zun and told him to help Ma Han arrest both criminals.

Officer Wang said, "The criminals being very elusive, I wish we could be given more time. If the authorities could announce a reward and put up posters, those greedy for the money would come forward with information, and the case could be easily solved."

Magistrate Teng accordingly gave them one month and, following the inspector's advice, wrote a poster promising a thousand strings of cash from the authorities for anyone with information about the stolen goods. Equipped with the poster, Ma Han and Wang Zun headed straight for the Qian residence and requested that Prince Qian match the reward by another thousand strings, and so the prince did. Then the two men went to Tightwad Zhang to make the same request. Having already lost valuables worth fifty-thousand strings of cash, Squire Zhang was not to be persuaded.

"Please don't try to save a little only to lose a lot," said the inspectors. "If the burglar is caught, you'll get all your stolen goods back. The magistrate has promised a reward for your sake. Prince Qian also matched it with a thousand strings. If you refuse, the magistrate won't think much of you."

Finding himself losing the argument, Squire Zhang also wrote a reward poster, reluctantly pledging five hundred strings. Inspector Ma went to the yamen to put up the posters, and, in the meantime, he made arrangements with Officer Wang to search along different routes.

Among the huge crowd of people gathered in front of the prefectural yamen to read the posters was Song the Fourth. He then went to consult Zhao Zheng. "That Wang Zun and Ma Han be cursed!" said Zhao Zheng. "They never had any grudges against us, and yet they had to come up with the idea of increasing the rewards to get us! And damn Squire Zhang! He's so stingy and thinks us so cheap that he offers only five hundred strings, when the others offer a thousand! Let's play some tricks on him to get even."

Song was also resentful of Officer Wang for having led men to arrest him and of Inspector Ma for having found out that Zhao Zheng used to be his apprentice. The two of them put their heads together and decided upon a plan. With one accord, they exclaimed, "What a wonderful plan it is!" Zhao gave Song the white jade belt that he had stolen from the Qian residence, and Song gave Zhao a few of the more precious items from the package of valuables he had stolen from Tightwad Zhang. The two men then went their separate ways to carry out their plan.

Song had just turned around when he ran into the man with the bamboo ladle who had begged at Squire Zhang's door. With one grab of his hand, Song dragged the man out Shuntian Gate and all the way to Hou Xing's house. "I have a favor to ask of you," he said.

The man with the ladle replied, "What can I do for you, my benefactor? I'll do whatever you say."

"I will help you make a thousand strings of cash for you to support your family with."

The man cried out in astonishment, "What a thought! Such luck is not in my stars."

"Just do as I say. It'll be good for you."

He took out the white jade belt with the veiled designs of a coiling dragon and told Hou Xing to dress himself up as a palace officer, saying, "Take this belt to Tightwad Zhang and pawn it. This belt is priceless, but take no more than three hundred strings of cash, and say to him, 'I'll come back to redeem it in three days. If I don't, you can add two hundred strings and buy it. Keep the belt in the house for the moment, and put it away in a safe place.'"

Thus instructed, Hou Xing went off. Being the greedy man he was, Squire Zhang was elated at the offer of the jade belt plus the prospect of making some money out of it. Without bothering to ask how Hou Xing had come by the jade belt, Squire Zhang paid the three hundred strings. (*Misers are invariably a greedy lot, and therefore they bring trouble upon themselves.*) After Hou Xing brought the money to Song, the latter made the beggar go to Prince Qian's door to take down the poster and claim the reward. At word that the stolen item had been found, Prince Qian summoned the beggar for questioning. The man said, "I was on my way to the pawnshop when I saw the manager trying to sell a white jade belt to a traveler from the north at the price of one thousand five hundred taels. I heard that the belt is from your residence. That's why I've come to report the matter."

Prince Qian dispatched about a hundred guards, who, guided by the beggar, ran to Squire Zhang's house with the speed of wind. Without pausing to hear any explanations, they searched the storehouse and found the white jade belt. When Squire Zhang came out to defend himself, the guards put a noose around his neck without bothering to listen to him and brought him, along with the two managers of his pawnshop, into the presence of Prince Qian.

The sight of the belt convinced Prince Qian that the informant had told the truth. He thereupon gave the beggar a note, asking the treasurer to give the man the thousand-string cash reward. Then, the prince personally went to Kaifeng in a sedan-chair to see Magistrate Teng, bringing along with him the jade belt as well as Squire Zhang and others for an interrogation. Having failed in his attempt to find the criminals, the magistrate was greatly embarrassed that Prince Qian had beaten him on this, and he lashed out at Squire Zhang, "You reported a burglary at your house to me the other day, listing a great many valuables. I've been wondering how a commoner like you could have come into possession of so much wealth. Now I know that you have been enlisting the service of thieves! Out with the truth now! Who stole the belt for you?"

"What I have I inherited from my ancestors. My possessions are no stolen goods. As for this belt, a palace officer brought it to me late yesterday afternoon, and I paid three hundred strings of cash for it."

The magistrate pursued further, "Didn't you know that Prince Qian lost a white jade belt with veiled designs of a coiled dragon? Why did you give the man money on the spot without asking him how he had come by it? Where is that palace officer now? You are talking nothing but nonsense!" (*Those wearing officials' gauze caps can say anything.*) He ordered prison wardens to flog Zhang Fu and the two managers until their skin was torn, their flesh ripped open, and blood squirted out. Unable to bear the pain any more, Zhang Fu asked to be given three days to find the man who had pawned the belt, adding that he would be willing to plead guilty if he failed. Magistrate Teng was not without apprehensions as to Squire Zhang's guilt. Therefore, only the two managers were kept behind under guard, whereas Zhang Fu was escorted out by prison wardens but ordered to report back within three days.

His eyes brimming with tears, Zhang Fu went out of the yamen into a wineshop and sat down to treat the guards to wine. The wine cups had barely been raised before an old man entered the wineshop at a leisurely pace and asked, "Which one of you is Squire Zhang?"

Zhang Fu kept his head down without venturing an answer. The guards asked, "Who might you be? Why do you wish to see Squire Zhang?"

"I have good news for him," said the old man. "I went to his pawnshop but was told that he was at the yamen for a trial. That's why I came all the way here."

It was not until that moment that Zhang Fu stood up to say, "I am Zhang Fu. What good news do you have for me? Please take a seat and tell me."

The old man sat down by Squire Zhang's side and asked, "Have you found the things stolen from your storehouse?"

"No."

"Well, I know something. That's why I'm here to tell you about it. If you don't believe me, I'll be happy to go with you on a search. I'll claim the reward only when you actually see the stolen goods."

Squire Zhang was greatly delighted. "If the fifty thousand strings worth of goods can really be recovered, I'll have more than enough to repay Prince Qian for his loss. The rest I can use to bribe high and low to get myself out of this mess." He asked, "Since you sound sure about this, can you tell me the name of the thief?"

The old man whispered something in his ear. In astonishment, Squire Zhang said, "I don't believe this."

The old man insisted, "I'll be more than willing to write a report to submit to the yamen. If the stolen goods are not there, I'll plead guilty."

Squire Zhang said with immense delight, "Please be kind enough to have a few drinks with me here. We'll go together when the magistrate opens his evening court session."

The four men drank themselves into a state of semi-intoxication. When the magistrate's court was called in session, Squire Zhang bought a piece of paper, had the old man write an accusation, and the foursome went to the prefectural yamen to submit a report.

After reading the report from the old man, who called himself Wang Bao, accusing Inspector Ma and Officer Wang of being responsible for the burglary at Zhang Fu's residence, Magistrate Teng thought to himself, "With their years of experience in catching thieves, they can't be guilty." He asked Wang Bao, "Aren't you trying to frame them out of some personal grudge? What evidence do you have?"

Old Man Wang Bao said, "I am a broker from Zhengzhou. I saw two men selling a great deal of jewelry there. They said they had more at home and could bring it to exchange for money. I knew them to be prefectural officers and wondered how they could have come by so many treasures. Then I saw Zhang Fu's list of stolen goods, which is very similar to what I saw. I'm willing to go with Zhang Fu to their houses for a search. If nothing can be found, I'll plead guilty."

Not quite convinced, Magistrate Teng dispatched Inspector Li Shun and some able runners to escort Wang Bao and Zhang Fu.

In the meantime, Inspector Ma Han and Officer Wang Zun were still away from home, working on the two cases. With a shout, the group [Li Shun and the runners] barged straight into Officer Wang's house. Wang's wife, with her three-year-old child in her arms, was eating a date cake in front of the window and playing with the child when the commotion broke out. Much startled, she wondered what could be causing all the excitement. Afraid that the child might be frightened, she covered up his ears with her sleeves and went to another room, but the crowd followed upon her heels and, surrounding her, demanded, "Where are Squire Zhang's possessions hidden?"

Her eyes wide open, the woman found herself tongue-tied. Since she had nothing to say, the men set about ransacking the trunks and chests, producing no stolen goods but only a few silver hairpins and some clothes. Inspector Li was just about to scold Wang Bao when the latter, with his head bent down, dived under the bed and smilingly emerged with a package that he had untied from a leg of the bed next to the wall. It was opened to reveal a pair of gold cups in floral designs inlaid with various kinds of gems, ten gold-rimmed tortoiseshell cups, and a string of prayer beads made of pearls from the North Sea. Recognizing these to be his property, Squire Zhang broke down in loud sobs of pain.

Without the slightest idea where the things were from, the woman trembled all over in panic. Her jaw dropped open, and her arms hung limp. Allowing no word of explanation, the men threw a rope around her neck. Sobbingly, she left her child with a neighbor and could not do otherwise than follow the men.

The group then went to Inspector Ma's house, and the same scenario of commotion followed. Again, Wang Bao poked here and there and produced from the eaves a packet of pearls as well as some gold bracelets inlaid with gems (*Why doesn't anyone wonder why Wang Bao always knows exactly where the stolen goods are hidden?*)—things that Squire Zhang also recognized as his own.

When the wives and children of both families were brought to the yamen, Magistrate Teng was sitting in the hall, waiting for news. As the crowd swarmed in and laid down many recovered goods in an array at the foot of the steps, claiming that they had been found under the bed and under the eaves, and that Zhang Fu had recognized them as his possessions, the magistrate said in great astonishment, "I have often heard that those whose job it is to catch thieves end up being thieves themselves, but I never expected that Wang Zun and Ma Han would go as far as this!" He sharply ordered that the two men's wives and children be put in jail to await a verdict. He then set a time limit for the prompt arrest of the culprits and ruled that the recovered goods be deposited, for the time being, in the prefectural treasury. The informant was to wait outside and claim his rewards, as announced in the posters, after the recovered goods had been properly identified.

Zhang Fu kowtowed and said, "I am a man of sufficient means. I have no knowledge whatsoever about the jade belt stolen from the Qian residence, but

I am resigned to my bad luck and, having recovered my own possessions, I am willing to pay a compensation to the Qian family. Please release me and my two managers. Your kindness in doing so will get you enough credit in the netherworld to last for thousands of generations."

Knowing that Zhang Fu had been wronged, Magistrate Teng allowed him to leave on bail. Wang Bao followed Squire Zhang home, claimed his five-hundred-string reward, and left.

As a matter of fact, Wang Bao was none other than Wang Xiu, who had the nickname Sick Cat for his matchless skill in roof-walking. It had been Song's idea to have Wang Xiu hide the stolen goods from Squire Zhang's house under the bed and under the eaves of the two inspectors' houses and, under the assumed name Wang Bao, present himself as an informant. How was the magistrate to guess at the truth?

Now, Wang Zun and Ma Han were away working on their cases when they heard that their wives and children had been arrested. They hurried back to see Magistrate Teng, only to be beaten to a pulp at the order of the magistrate, who allowed no word of explanation. How were they to confess to having stolen from Zhang Fu? When the two wives were led out from prison, they could do no more than stare at each other without being able to come up with any words of defense. Even the magistrate found it hard to come to a decision. All of them were put in jail to await a verdict.

The following day, Zhang Fu was again brought under guard to the yamen, where he was persuaded to use whatever money he had on hand to pay back Prince Qian, for the return of his recovered goods was to take some time. Under coercion, Zhang Fu had no choice but to consent. Back at home, he sank into such depression at the thought of having to part with his money that he hanged himself in his storehouse. How tragic that miserliness cost the famous Tightwad Zhang his life! Inspector Wang Zun and Officer Ma Han both died in jail, whereas the band of thieves ran amuck in the Eastern Capital and lived in high style, drinking fine wine and visiting famous courtesans, and no one could do anything to them. In those times, no household was spared from the havoc they wreaked in the city. It was not until the Honorable Judge Bao became magistrate that these thieves dispersed in fear and the city regained its peace. There is a poem in evidence:

> Greed and miserliness brought disaster;
> Robbers wreaked havoc in the capital.
> Only when Judge Bao arrived on the scene
> Was it shown that good officials bring people peace.

Emperor Wudi of the Liang Dynasty Goes to the Land of Extreme Bliss through Ceaseless Cultivation

I heard not the morning orioles,
Nor the rain in the temple garden.
When I woke, the peppered rice was ready.[1]
And the moon still shining over the hills.

This poem was written by an acolyte by the surname of Fan, with the Buddhist name Puneng, who cultivated his inner nature in Guanghua Monastery in Xuyi County during the reign of Emperor Ming [r. 494–98] of the Qi dynasty [479–502]. In his previous existence, he was a white-necked earthworm born in the front yard of the cell of Abbot Datong of Thousand Buddhas Monastery. In his hours of meditation, Abbot Datong intoned only the Lotus Sutra. The earthworm happened to be one endowed with intelligence. Every time it heard the chanting of the sutra, it stretched out its head and listened. For three years, the abbot intoned the sutra and the earthworm listened.

One day, the abbot emerged from his meditation room to partake of a vegetarian meal and to pay homage to the Buddha. As his eyes happened to rest on the excessively overgrown weeds in front of his cell, he called a young novice to hoe up the weeds. Having weeded the middle section of the yard, the novice moved to one corner of the wall. With a mighty wave of the arm, he struck his hoe several inches deep into the ground. He realized too late that the earthworm was right there and had been cut in two. "Amitabha!" exclaimed the novice. "How sinful it was of me to have killed a life!" He dug up some earth and buried the earthworm. We shall speak no further of this.

With the strength he had gained while listening to the sutras, the earthworm gained human form and was born into the Fan family. After the loss of his parents when he had grown into adulthood, he left secular life to live in Guanghua Monastery, serving Abbot Empty Valley as kitchen attendant. An honest man, he lived near the kitchen, boiled tea, and cooked meals, attending to the needs of the abbot as best he could. He treated all other monks in exactly the same way. Though illiterate, Puneng had learned some sutras by heart, but the Lotus Sutra was the one text that he could recite from beginning to end without the least effort. Whenever he had a moment to himself during the day, he would intone the sutras to cultivate his soul. After living for over thirty years in the monastery, he heard that Abbot Datong of Thousand Buddhas Monastery had willed his own death. Full of admiration for the blissful way the abbot died, he thought of an idea and said to Abbot Empty Valley, "I have lived in this monastery for many years. For all my life, I have observed a vegetarian diet. Never have I entertained the least bit of greed, nor have I ever wasted any of nature's resources. Today, I would like to leave you and depart from this life. Would you please kindly pray for a good place of reincarnation for me?" With these words, he fell on his knees.

"Rise and listen to me," said the abbot. "Though you have cultivated your inner nature, you have not yet gained enlightenment. If you choose to go, be sure to live a quiet life and avoid the trap of wealth and rank. (*The trap of wealth and rank is where all evil comes from.*) Should you fall victim to a moment of weakness, you will not even be granted transmigration." Thus admonished, Acolyte Fan bade farewell to the abbot and went to the kitchen, where he took a bath and changed into clean clothes. After paying homage to the Buddha, heaven and earth, and his parents, he took leave of the other monks and, stepping into a monk's coffin, sat down with his legs folded in lotus position, closed his eyes, and was gone.

The monks chanted sutras for him and asked some laborers to carry the coffin to a vacant lot. They were about to get the abbot for the cremation ceremony when a bell was heard pealing from the hall. Hastily the abbot sent someone to say, "Do not light the fire." Immediately thereafter, the abbot arrived at the scene in a sedan-chair and had the lid of the coffin opened. There, for all to see, was Acolyte Fan, back to life again with his eyes wide open. Unable to stand up, he said to the abbot with his palms joined together, "I went to a nice place just a moment ago. I was lying comfortably under a red canopy of brocade when I heard a bell toll. A golden arhat pushed me into a big pool of white lotus flowers. I woke up with a start. What instructions do you have for me?"

The abbot said, "You were reincarnated into the animal world because of some impure thought in your mind. It was I who woke you up so that you might start the reincarnation process over again." Turning to the rest of the monks, he said, "Dig up the green rock under the ginkgo tree outside the monastery gate and take a look."

The monks all proceeded to the tree, dug up the stone, and revealed a small, newborn red snake, lying there dead. In astonishment, the monks returned to report what they had witnessed to the abbot, who then had his most senior disciple tell Acolyte Fan, "Keep your mind clean from impure thoughts and you will find yourself in a good place. After cycles of transmigration, you will achieve the rank of kings and dukes, but you still need to devote yourself ceaselessly to spiritual cultivation in order to enter the land of extreme bliss." At this prediction, Acolyte Fan shouted, "Namah Amitabha!" and closed his eyes. Invited by the monks to light the cremation fire, the abbot put on his Tathagata robe and went in a sedan-chair to Acolyte Fan's coffin. And this is what he said about Acolyte Fan:

> *Acolyte Fan, Acolyte Fan,*
> *At the kitchen stove every day.*
> *He saw gold lotuses in the fire,*
> *Upside down, upside down.*

After intoning these lines, the abbot had someone light the fire, which soon crackled into flames. As the monks chanted Buddha's name, a wisp of blue smoke curled up from the top of the coffin to reach a height of several tens of feet before it spiraled away toward the east.

Now, to the east of Xuyi County lay the Village of Happiness and Peace, where there lived an immensely rich man named Huang Qi. Instead of resorting to chicanery to cheat and squeeze money out of people, he accumulated much moral credit in the netherworld by doing good deeds far and wide. His wife, Meng-shi, well advanced in pregnancy, was on the verge of childbirth. Acolyte Fan, bearing in mind the abbot's instructions, threw himself with a flash of divine light into Meng-shi's belly. Therefore, Acolyte Fan had no sooner passed away than Meng-shi gave birth to a handsome and well-shaped baby. In his forties, Squire Huang had never had a son. This baby brought as much delight to the entire family as would acquisition of a rare treasure. A happy occasion it was, all right, but the baby cried day and night and refused to be fed. Consumed with worry, the couple prayed to gods and Buddha, but to no avail.

Their steward, a Mr. Li, suggested to the squire, "There might be a reason for the baby's ceaseless crying. Twenty li from here, in the mountains, is Guanghua Monastery, where Abbot Empty Valley is a living Buddha with knowledge about the past and future. Why don't you go to him for help? He will surely have an answer for you." Without a moment's delay, Squire Huang prepared some boxes of gifts and offerings of incense, and set out for the monastery. What did the monastery look like? As the poem says,

> *To the west of the valley with bells chiming,*
> *It stands in a mist by brooks gently streaming.*

Over fields strewn with wildflowers,
Sightseers stroll idly down the stone dike.

Barely had he been greeted by Abbot Empty Valley in his cell than Squire Huang fell on his knees and said, "My newborn baby cries day and night, refusing to be fed. His life is hanging by a thread now. I will never forget your kindness if Your Reverence will show compassion."

The abbot knew that Acolyte Fan was crying day and night in an attempt to seek his blessings. Without letting on any of this, the abbot said to Squire Huang, "I will have to go myself to see him. He'll be all right." He kept Squire Wang for a vegetarian meal in his cell. Then the two of them together mounted sedan-chairs and went to the squire's house before the night was out. After being offered a seat in the hall, the abbot asked to have the baby brought in, which the squire did.

Caressing the baby's head, the abbot whispered a few words into the baby's ear out of everyone else's earshot. With another stroke of the baby's head, the abbot proclaimed, "You shall encounter no disasters. You shall bring benefits to your parents, and there shall be no change in your Buddhist nature."

At these words, the baby stopped crying, much to everyone's amazement. "Never have we seen such a strange thing before!" exclaimed the onlookers. "This is indeed the work of a reincarnated Buddha!"

Squire Huang said, "When he is one year old, I will send him to your monastery to register his name as a monk."

"That would be best," said the abbot. With that, he took leave of Squire Huang and returned to the monastery. Happy that the baby was made well again, the Huang family raised him with much love.

Time sped by. Before they knew it, the baby's first birthday came around. Squire Huang declared, "I promised that the baby will be registered as a monk in the monastery." He prepared some boxes of fabrics, had the baby carried by a waiting woman, and they proceeded in two sedan-chairs to the monastery. Once in the abbot's cell, Squire Huang bowed in gratitude to the abbot and presented him with the gifts. The abbot gave the baby the religious name Huang Furen [Restore Benevolence] and gave the boy a small monk's robe and a monk's cap. After a vegetarian meal, Squire Huang returned home with his boy. And thus the comings and goings continued. Quite unnoticeably, Furen reached six years of age. The squire hired a tutor for him. Being, after all, of uncommon background, the boy proved to be most intelligent. It was widely known among the villagers that he was a reincarnation of Acolyte Fan of Guanghua Monastery and was destined to achieve fame and fortune later in his life.

In the same county was a Grand Commandant Tong, who, considering

Furen's smartness and good looks as well as the Huang family's wealth numbered in the millions, sent a matchmaker to the Huangs to offer his daughter, of the same age as Furen, to the latter in marriage. At first, Squire Huang was noncommittal, but, yielding under persistent pressure from Commandant Tong, he had no alternative but to grant the betrothal. Three hundred boxes, two hundred taels worth of gold jewelry, a thousand taels of silver, and several bolts of colored silk were promised as betrothal gifts. It was indeed a predestined union, for the girl was exceedingly intelligent and had learned to read without ever having gone to school. She also had a passion for intoning Buddhist scriptures. How did this come about? In fact, she had been a maid serving Mahakasyapa, disciple of Sakyamuni, and was reincarnated to fulfill her preordained destiny. The boy and the girl knew nothing of the ways of the world. By the time they had grown to be fifteen or sixteen, both had their hearts set on offering themselves to the service of Buddha. Neither would consent to marriage. Because Furen had now reached an appropriate age, Squire Huang chose a day for the wedding. When Miss Tong got word of the wedding date, she took fright and quickly wrote a letter, which she then had a waiting woman present to her mother. The letter said,

> Well aware am I that marriages are endorsed by The Book of Songs and The Book of Rites. However, rules can hardly be uniformly applied to different situations. My heart is set on the order of Buddha rather than the position of a wife. My thoughts are with the attainment of enlightenment rather than with marital bliss. Without a single worldly concern, I have broken all ties with the mortal life. With the monastery lights on, what need is there for bridal candles? With the monastery bells chiming, what need is there for sweet notes of music? I will be content with a life with chipped bowls and tattered clothes. Form and material matters I put out of my mind; life and death I take no account of. I entreat you, my mother, to show compassion and be tolerant of my aspirations. I would much prefer following Chang'e to the moon than living the romantic life of the Wu Mountain fairy maiden. Should I attain enlightenment, my debt to your parental love will be repaid. Ask not about the flute that attracted the phoenix[2] nor about the jade pestle that led to a marriage.[3] Appealing to your kindness, I beg for your understanding and pity.

Having received the young lady's letter transmitted by the waiting woman, Mrs. Tong said to the latter, "I haven't sent anyone over to visit my daughter these days, because I've been preoccupied with the Huang family's marriage proposal. Why did my daughter have you bring this letter over?" The waiting woman thereupon told her about the young lady's wish to enter the order of Buddha rather than marry and about her assiduous reading of Buddhist scriptures. Mrs. Tong was displeased. She sent for her husband to read the letter.

After reading it, Commandant Tong exploded, "What an imbecile! It is only proper that men and women should marry. Only filial piety and fraternal love move the gods. What can Buddhist practices accomplish?" Tearing the letter to shreds, he cursed, "What crap!" The commandant went ahead and married his daughter off on the day chosen by the Huang family.

Though Huang Furen and Miss Tong occupied the same room after the wedding, they slept in separate beds. This went on for over half a year. The couple remained as deferential toward each other as they would be to guests. To Huang Furen's announcement that he was going away as a traveling monk, she replied, "In that case, I will join you and enter the service of Buddha. As the ancients put it, 'A married woman follows her husband for the rest of her life.' I'll never compromise my chastity."

Seeing that she was adamant about entering the Buddhist order and rejecting the idea of remarriage, Furen said to her, "If so, why don't we pledge to be brother and sister and practice religion together?"

The young lady was delighted. The two bowed in front of the Buddha's image, and, after the vows were taken, they changed into clothes made of coarse cloth and, maintaining a simple diet, started their cultivation of the spirit at home, much to the annoyance of Squire Huang. Afraid of being laughed at, the squire sent the young couple off, together with a waiting woman and two maids, to a deserted place in West Village in the mountains, where the couple continued to do nothing but read the sutras, pray to Buddha, and meditate.

More than three years later, the couple were seated in meditation under the eternal light in front of the Buddha's image when a beautiful woman suddenly came into Huang Furen's view. Walking in swaying, seductive steps, she stopped in front of Furen and said with a bow, "I am Rucui, a singing girl in Commandant Tong's residence. Mrs. Tong is afraid that since you do not share the same bed with the young mistress, the Huang family line will come to an end. Besides, this will not affect your spiritual cultivation, and nobody will know about it." So saying, she started making advances to Furen. With such a beauty using her charms on him and talking about the Huang family line, Furen found that his desire was slightly stirred in spite of himself. A second thought struck him: "Miss Tong is a much greater beauty. I have never even touched her. How can I let this woman soil my thoughts?" In the midst of these thoughts, he heard a loud bang. In the next moment, ten thousand flames blazed up and whirled around. Furen woke with a start, only to find that the young lady was also taking a recess from her meditation. Furen hurriedly got up to make bows to the Buddha and, turning his bows to the young lady, said, "I was not firm enough in my resolution and almost fell under an evil spell. Please point out the way for me."

The young lady, with her remarkable intelligence, had a better understanding of things than did Furen. "My brother," she said, "you had a hallucination while under the spell of the demon of lust. I will go with you to see Abbot Empty Valley to ask for delivery from this evil influence."

The following day, they went to Guanghua Monastery to see the abbot. Empty Valley had this to say: "Once desire raises its head, there is no hope of attaining enlightenment. Only by another transmigration will you be delivered." He then intoned for them these lines:

> Leap out of the abyss of lust;
> Drink from the Vulture Peak⁴ to allay your thirst.
> The husband will find salvation;
> The wife will tread on the fields of blessing.
> In the Temple of Shared Felicity,
> They will reach the land of extreme bliss.

The couple took leave of the abbot and returned to West Village. To the waiting woman and the maids, they said, "We two, brother and sister, are leaving you tonight for another world."

The waiting woman objected, "I have also been engaged in cultivation of the spirit all these years while serving you. Why don't you bring me along?"

"I'm afraid this is not something that can be done forcibly when you're not ready for it," said Furen.

The waiting woman rejoined, "I know what to do."

Having taken a bath, the couple bowed to the image of the Buddha, sat down, and willed their deaths. Somehow, the waiting woman also managed to pass away in her room. When word of this got to Squire Huang, he came to take care of the remains. Of this, no more need be said.

Now Young Master Huang's soul found reincarnation in the Xiao family, whereas the young lady found herself in the Zhi family. In the region of Yu Lake, there lived a Second Master Xiao, a descendant of an old family well known during the Qi dynasty, belonging to the same clan as Xiao Yi⁵ and Xiao Tanzhi. Second Master Xiao's wife, Shan-shi, a most compassionate woman who had done a good many kind deeds, had been pregnant for nine months and was on the point of delivery when Furen willed his own death. In the middle of the night, Shan-shi saw in her dream a man of gold over ten feet tall in royal attire and a crown, surrounded by a spectacular parade of banners and flags. A procession of pink-clothed men escorted by carriages and valets came to the Xiao residence and rested in the main hall. The man of gold, all by himself, entered Shan-shi's room and bowed deeply to her. Much startled, she was about to ask him questions when she woke up and gave birth to a boy, whose loud wails were quite different from those of ordinary babies.

He was given the name Xiao Yan. When he was eight or nine, he had about him an extraordinary fragrance that would not go away. A most brilliant boy, he outdid all others in letters and scholarship. He also showed in his conversation great knowledge of military strategy. His accurate predictions about enemy movements and his stratagems were flawless. He had been born on the fifth day of the fifth month. Children born on such a day were, in the Qi dynasty, believed to be a peril to their own parents, and, in most cases, the parents would refuse to raise them. Xiao Yan's mother, however, brought him up in secrecy, without the knowledge of her husband. Now, when the boy was nine, she took him into the presence of his father. "A child born in the fifth month," said his father, "is a peril to his parents. What's the good of raising him?"

Yan replied, "If it is as you say, have I ever brought any harm to my parents during all these nine years of my life? If not, how can I harm you after I am nine? Please put your mind at rest."

Surprised at the argument, his father felt slightly relieved. When his uncle Xiao Yi heard about this, he said, "A boy of such wisdom will surely surpass our ancestors in status." Recognizing from this incident the boy's unusual qualities, Xiao Yi henceforth sought the opinion of the boy on every matter of concern.

At the time, a certain Prefect Li Ben conspired against the emperor and claimed to be the emperor of Yue, with his own separate government structure.[6] The imperial court ordered General Yang Piao to lead a punitive expedition against Li Ben. Afraid that he might not be able to prevail over the powerful Li Ben, Yang Piao consulted Xiao Yi from time to time. Xiao Yi said, "I have a nephew, Xiao Yan, who, young as he is, has enough intelligence to rule an empire. I will send for him. I am sure that he will come up with a good plan."

With all speed, Xiao Yi sent a message for Xiao Yan to come and meet Yang Piao. Impressed with Yan's unusual deportment, Yang saluted the boy and consulted him in all modesty on ways to defeat Li Ben. The following, then, was Yan's advice: "Li Ben has been planning this rebellion for a long time. His is a mighty army with high morale. If you put a small army against him, you'll be throwing a piece of meat to a tiger. Defeat will be instantaneous. I have heard that Li Ben, occupying the Huainan region, is poised for a descent upon Guangzhou. Sun Jiong was charged with crime for having tarried. Lu Zixiong was ordered to kill himself for his defeat. Feeling high and mighty, Li Ben has cast all caution to the winds. You can lead a massive army to the Huainan region, pitch camp there, and have Chen Baxian[7] lead one division to take a shortcut to the rear of the enemy. Send out just a couple thousand men to engage Li Ben in battle, but do not try to win. Instead, fake defeat and flee so as to lure the enemy all the way to Huainan, where the main army is. In the Huainan region, overgrown with rank reeds, the ground is too wet and muddy for riding. You will do well to sit tight in your well-defended camps and, instead of engaging the enemy in battle, wait until their fighting spirit wears off. When the wind starts to blow in the right direction, light a fire while Chen Baxian's men block the enemy's path of retreat. They can then pretend to be Li Ben's men in flight and capture the enemy stronghold. Caught in between with nowhere to retreat, Li Ben will be easily captured." (*He sees the enemy's defeat in his mind's eye.*)

Yang Piao was agape with astonishment and admiration at the speech. He made a bow and left. Following Xiao Yan's plan, he did put Li Ben's troops to rout. Thus, Xiao Yan's fame spread far and wide and captured the hearts of the populace.

Yan had high aspirations. Emperor Ming of the Qi had a mind to use his army to conquer the state of Wei but dared not act rashly, for fear of Gao Huan's powerful contingent. One day, he sent a eunuch to summon Xiao for a consultation. Xiao Yan followed the messenger into the court and made obeisance to the emperor. Well aware though he was of Xiao Yan's reputation, the emperor saw that Yan was no more than a boy and said, "What is so remarkable about your talent that you have gained such reputation in such youth?"

Xiao Yan replied, "The realm of knowledge is boundless, but human intelligence is limited. I make no claims to possessing enough talent to serve Your Majesty."

These words filled Emperor Ming's heart with respect. He did not treat Yan as a child but asked for Yan's advice, saying, "I wish to attack the state of Wei and wipe out Erzhu Rong, but Gao Huan is in command of a large, strong army. That's why I am seeking your opinion."

Yan had this to say: "Having a large army means nothing more than having a large number of deaths in the end. But a strong army is one that wins the hearts of the rank and file. (*Well-known dictum.*) Now, Erzhu Rong is a vicious and cunning man given to the most flagrantly evil deeds. Gao Huan is known for his treachery, blackmailing, and other devious actions. They may possess a large army but not the hearts of the soldiers. Moreover, with the ministers and their sovereign harboring different plans and forming their own cliques, they will not be able to hold out for long in any endeavor. What Your Majesty should do is select generals, train troops, and claim that you will strike north while you actually hit east. Should they be prepared for any attack in the east, we will just call the expedition off. By dispatching one division there this year and another brigade the next, we will keep harassing and annoying them until they are exhausted. What is more, the rulers being at variance with their subordinates, internal turmoil is bound to erupt. If Your Majesty can take advantage of the turmoil, victory will be yours."

Much pleased, Emperor Ming kept Xiao Yan in his court. Yan was then led into the inner quarters of the palace, where the empress and the ladies of the court saw him frequently and came to enjoy his company. Over time, his significant advisory role and his hard work gained him promotions until he became the prefect of Yongzhou.

Later, Xiao Baojuan [r. 499–501] succeeded to the Qi throne and indulged himself in dissolute pleasures, granting no audiences to his court ministers and trusting only the eunuchs. Aware of such a state of affairs, Xiao Yan offered this advice to Zhang Hongce: "Now that the Great Six, including Xiao Yaoguang and Xu Xiaosi, are dominating the court, there will certainly be turmoil. Moreover, with our sovereign abetting evil and Prince Lun of Zhao showing signs of a rebellion, we cannot afford not to prepare ourselves for an eventual calamity of earth-shaking magnitude." Consequently, he started quietly building up arms and raised an army of tens of thousands of brave men. A large number of bamboos and trees were felled and thrown into Tanxi Creek. Great stacks of hay were piled up mountain-high.

Realizing Xiao Yan's ambition, the Qi emperor consulted Zheng Zhi about a punitive expedition against Yan. Zheng Zhi said, "Xiao Yan has been preparing for this move for a long time. With an army of such power, he is not to be subdued easily. I would venture to suggest that you send him a nicely worded decree and grant him the title of duke. He will surely receive me, which will be a good time to have him assassinated. That will be only one man's work, saving you a good deal of money, fodder, and troop movements."

The Qi emperor was immensely delighted. He sent Zheng Zhi to Yongzhou with the mission of assassinating Xiao Yan.

Much alarmed when he learned about the plan, Abbot Empty Valley of Guanghua Monastery appeared in Xiao Yan's dream and handed over to him a book from heaven with a sharp knife placed between the pages. Upon waking up, Yan thought to himself, "Wasn't it a monk I saw? Why did he give me a book from heaven with a knife in it? Is it because someone is coming to assassinate me? I'll see what happens tomorrow."

The following day, a man came to announce that Zheng Zhi had been sent from the imperial court to deliver the emperor's decree granting Yan a royal title. "So this is it," said Xiao Yan. Instead of greeting Zheng Zhi, he ordered a feast set out in the residence of Zheng Shaoshu,[8] pacification administrator. It was only after an ambush had been laid that he called in Zheng Zhi. "Since the imperial court has sent you here to kill me, there must be a decree to that effect."

Zheng Zhi denied. "There is no such thing!"

Xiao Yan called out, "Search him for me!" In an instant, thirty to forty men emerged from behind the curtains and held Zheng Zhi. A body search produced a sharp knife and a secret edict ordering Yan's death.

Xiao Yan boiled with anger. "What harm have I done to the imperial court to warrant assassination?" Before the night was out, he summoned Zhang Hongce for counsel and, with banners leading the way, the contingent of twenty thousand selected men, a thousand horses, and about thirty boats moved out from Tanxi. The bamboo, wood, and hay that they had been storing were now immediately put to use. With Wang Mao and Cao Jingzong as the vanguards, the army marched to Hankou and, taking the high tide, sailed downstream and took the Jiahu region.

Now the two cities of Yingcheng and Lucheng were the gateways to Jiahu and Jiankang.[9] When Jiahu fell to Vanguard Wang, the officials guarding the two cities were frightened out of their wits. Knowing that they would surely lose the fight, they agreed with each other that they would surrender. Thus the defenseless city of Jiankang fell to the sweeping forces of the enemy. When Xiao Yan's army pushed to the suburbs, the Qi emperor, still wallowing in a life of pleasure, sent forth General Wang Zhenguo and others, who deployed a hundred thousand crack troops at Red Sparrow Gate along the Qinhuai River, but Lü Sengzhen set their camps on fire. Cao Jingzong then swept along with the main force of Xiao Yan's army. The officers and the soldiers fought valiantly amid earth-shaking beatings of drums. Zhenguo and his men were subdued. Their entire army was put to rout. Xiao Yan's troops pushed deep into the city until they came to Xuanyang Gate. All of Xiao Yan's brothers and nephews assembled together. General Xu Yuanyu surrendered, offering up the city of Dongfu, whereas Li Jushi yielded the city of Xinting. In the twelfth month of the year, Xiao Baojuan, the emperor of Qi, perished at the hands of Qi men.

By a decree issued in the name of the empress dowager, Xiao Yan demoted Baojuan posthumously to the position of duke of Donghun, declared himself to be minister of war, and invited into the court Empress Dowager Xuan De to take over all affairs of state. Xiao Yan then made himself counselor-delegate and was granted the title of duke of Liang along with all the nine dignities that an emperor could bestow upon distinguished ministers.[10]

It so happened that at the time when Huang Furen was reincarnated, the waiting woman was reincarnated as Fan Yun and the two maids as Shen Yue and Ren Fang respectively. All were now officials serving the prince of Jingling, son of Emperor Wudi, as was the duke of Liang. With such a predestined bond among them, they had a natural rapport with each other. The duke of Liang made Fan Yun his counselor, Shen Yue his palace attendant, and Ren Fang his military advisor. In the fourth month of the following year Xiao Yan, the duke of Liang, took over the throne and further demoted the former Qi emperor to the position of prince of Baling. The empress dowager was moved into another palace.

Although the Liang emperor gained the empire by military force, his predestined bond with Buddhism was not severed, for he did not ignore the element of benevolence in the midst of the killing and still set his heart on spiritual cultivation. To end the ceaseless warfare, he struck a peace deal with the state of Wei. One day, Eastern Wei sent an adviser named Li Xie over for peace negotiations. After a long talk with Li Xie, the Liang emperor dismissed him, but, as it was too far into the night for the emperor to return to his own quarters, he decided to spend the night in the study in a side hall. Having dismissed all company and the palace maids, he sat quietly by himself by the open window, viewing the moon. At about the third watch, there emerged from a narrow lane thirty to fifty blue-robed men who walked up to where he was. One of them was singing a song:

> Our life in the cages is full of woes,
> Though we have had moments of joy before.
> Alas! Tomorrow we die by the cleaver,
> Never to sing again "Song of the White Trotters."

The Liang emperor was bewildered. The men drew near and kowtowed to him, saying, "Your Majesty is full of love and compassion for people and things. We are all animals to be offered as sacrifice in the temple. There are a million of us to be slaughtered first thing tomorrow morning. We beseech Your Majesty to show compassion and deliver us from our sufferings. That will be an act of boundless munificence."

The Liang emperor said to the blue-robed men, "I had no idea that so many animals were to be slaughtered for sacrifice at the temple. This is indeed a disturbing thought. I will do something about it tomorrow."

The blue-robed men, one and all, kowtowed, made piteous pleas, and left with tears on their faces.

The following day, the Liang emperor related the incident to the civil and military officials during the morning court session. "Granted that homage must be paid in the temple to the gods, yet I find it hard to bear the thought of slaughtering animals. Henceforth, only food items made of flour and rice shall be offered as sacrifice. In this manner, the sacrificial tradition will be maintained at no peril to benevolence and compassion. No harm is done on either account."

The new system was thus established to last for an eternity. Who would dare to violate it?

Every day, the Liang emperor observed a vegetarian diet and made obeisance to the Buddha. One night, he saw in a dream a group of crimson-robed gods who, tablets in hand and riding on divine unicorns and phoenixes under the escort of guardsmen, invited him to visit the netherworld. When the tour took him to a grand hall, a deity wearing a gold crown and a Buddhist robe served as his guide. In every hall that he set foot in, he was greeted by the deity in charge. Those who had been virtuous human beings were enjoying the peace and leisure of paradise without the least hindrance, whereas the treacherous were put through tortures of every description, such as the mountain of swords and the sea of blood, the pulling out of tongues, frying in cauldrons filled with oil, the biting of snakes and tigers, and so forth. A group of men in rags, with disheveled hair and bare feet with sores all over them, poured out their sufferings to the Liang emperor, supplicating to him in piteous tones, "Please show compassion and deliver us from this place! We are all starving, solitary souls with no offspring, and have been stranded in hell for a long time."

The Liang emperor replied, "All right. After I go back to my court, I will try to deliver you from hell."

The sinners thanked him in their mournful tones.

Last, he came to a big mountain with a cave opening, from which protruded a giant python's head the size of a room. The sight of the python's head, which rose higher as he approached, so startled him that he turned upon his heels, but before he could get away, the python opened its blood-red pool of a mouth and said, "Don't be alarmed, Your Majesty. I am your deceased wife. By way of retribution, I was changed into a python after my death because I used to be a jealous and malicious woman. My unwieldy size makes me hungry all the time, for I can hardly get myself any food. If you still care for your wife for old time's sake, I beg you to do kind deeds far and wide so as to deliver me from my misery. You will accumulate boundless merit."

Empress Xi had been his first wife. A most jealous woman, she resorted to all means to persecute every court lady whom her husband took a liking to. An untold number of them died at her hands. There being nothing else he could do to contain her, the Liang emperor had hunters capture a hundred black-naped orioles every month, made soup with the birds, and served it to her daily for he had heard that black-naped oriole soup had a curing effect on jealousy. Her jealousy did indeed subside slightly. Later, when she learned about this, the empress threw away the soup and her jealousy resumed as before. Now that she had been changed into a python after her death, her soul was begging her husband for help.

He promised, "After I return to my court, I will certainly try to offer penitence for your sins."

"Many thanks for Your Majesty's kindness," said the python. "I will now escort you back to your court. Do not be alarmed." So saying, it slithered out of the cave, revealing a body hundreds of arm spans around and goodness knows how many thousands of feet in length. The Liang emperor broke into a cold sweat. Upon waking up, he realized it was all but a dream. He stayed awake until dawn, heaving sigh upon sigh.

After the morning session of the court, he consulted the monks about initiating an Avalamba Festival.[11] He also wrote *The Liang Emperor's Repentance*.[12] The Avalamba Festival, not unlike a grand feast in the traditional sense, was for the benefit of the hungry ghosts with no offspring. *The Liang Emperor's Repentance* was written to win forgiveness on behalf of Empress Xi for her evil deeds and, at the same time, to absolve the rest of the souls of their sins. As a consequence of the festival and the scripture, all sinners in the netherworld were delivered from all of their sins until not a single soul was left in hell. In a dream, he saw Empress Xi, who, dressed as she had been before her death, happily acknowledged her thanks: "Your Majesty's book on penitence has extricated me from the body of a python and landed me in heaven. Please accept my gratitude." In another of his dreams, a million former prisoners in hell bowed to him in gratitude, saying in unison, "It was only through your beneficence that we had the good fortune of leaving hell."

Henceforth all the more dedicated to the worship of Buddha, the Liang emperor repeatedly issued decrees seeking monks of great learning to enlighten him on the religion, but none came forth. When he heard that there was a Monk Kowtow, an expert in interpreting the sutras, he issued another order and sent an attendant to bring the monk to him. The monk did indeed follow the messenger into the palace. Emperor Wudi, at the time, happened to be in a side hall playing a game of chess with Shen Yue. When the attendant announced, "The monk sought by imperial decree is now at Wu Gate awaiting further instructions," Emperor Wudi's mind was totally absorbed in planning to capture some chess pieces. The announcement was repeated three times, but he heard not a word. Placing a chess piece down on the board, he said, "I'll do away with this one!"

The emperor was referring to the chess piece, but the attendant took what he said to mean killing the monk. "Yes, sire!" he called out. He then passed on the order all the way to Wu Gate, and the monk was executed then and there.

After the chess game was over, Shen Yue reminded the emperor, "The monk is here, awaiting your further orders." Immediately, Emperor Wudi called the attendant and asked him to invite the monk into the hall. The attendant reported, "He has been executed, as was ordered."

Agape with astonishment, Emperor Wudi realized that what he had said about doing away with a chess piece had been misunderstood. "What did the monk say before the execution?" he asked the attendant.

"The monk said that when he was a young novice in his previous existence, he once weeded with a hoe and, by accident, killed an earthworm, which was none other than Your Majesty. He also said that thus it was only right for him to repay the debt with his life in this existence."

The emperor grieved for a considerable time and grew all the more convinced of the theory of transmigration and retribution. He then ordered that the monk be buried with honor. For days on end, he remained in low spirits.

Perceptive enough to have guessed what was on the emperor's mind, Shen Yue sent men out to visit eminent monks all over the land. When word came to him that there was a holy monk known by the Buddhist name Abbot Zhi Daolin[13] practicing austerities in a thatched hut ten li from Jiankang, he reported the news to the emperor, who immediately sent him to visit the monk. And so Shen Yue made his way there in an impressive entourage complete with banners, horse-drawn carriages, and a great many attendants. The pomposity of it all caused quite a stir far and near. In spite of all the clamor and the announcements, Daolin remained seated in meditation, not the least perturbed. Shen Yue walked up to his couch and said, "Does the monk know that the palace attendant is here?"

Opening his eyes, Daolin said, "Does the palace attendant know that the monk is in the midst of his meditations?"

Shen asked again, "How did the monk come by this house?"

Daolin rejoined, "Those in the service of Buddha are free to move from place to place." With this remark, the temple and the monk disappeared from view, leaving behind nothing but a stretch of bare land. Shen Yue was shocked in no small measure. As realization came to him that this was indeed nothing less than a holy monk, he promptly made a deep bow and addressed the air, "Please forgive me, Your Reverence, for being a mundane mortal being with imperceptive eyes. I am not by nature arrogant, but I had to follow the imperial court's orders."

Monk Zhi appeared again out of thin air to greet Shen Yue and kept him for a vegetarian meal. To Shen Yue's pleas for some words of enlightenment, the monk gave him this quatrain:

> You covered him in the chestnut affair;
> What was the cutting of tongue all about?
> To lay aside your secret worries,
> Offer to heaven your prayers.

On the back of the paper, he wrote the character *yin* [to conceal] about ten times. What gave rise to this quatrain from Monk Zhi? Well, one day, when a giant chestnut measuring about two and a half inches was presented to the imperial court as a gift from Yuzhou, the emperor and Shen Yue each wrote from memory stories about chestnuts. Shen Yue deliberately wrote three stories fewer than the emperor, saying, "I am no match for Your Majesty." Once out of the court, he said to others, "That man never admits a fault," referring to the emperor's reluctance to acknowledge his weaknesses. Later, the emperor learned of this remark and bore a grudge against Yue.

As for the reference to the "cutting of tongue," Shen Yue and Fan Yun once tried to persuade Emperor Wudi to take over the throne. On his sick bed, Yue dreamed that Emperor Hedi of the Qi cut off his tongue with a sword. In great fear, Yue secretly asked a Taoist priest to offer a prayer to heaven to atone for his sin. These two incidents that preyed on Shen Yue's mind were known only to himself. Now that Monk Zhi was making reference to them, Shen Yue broke into a cold sweat. So frightened was he that it seemed as if his soul had left his body. After some moments of stupefied silence, he pressed the monk for an explanation of the word *yin*.

Why did Monk Zhi write this character about ten times in succession? Well, after Shen Yue's death, the imperial court proposed enfeoffing him posthumously as duke of Wen. Out of spite for him, the Liang emperor refused to do so, saying, "Not revealing all is to conceal." Consequently, the title was changed to duke of Yin [Conceal].

The first two incidents that Monk Zhi referred to occurred in the past, but that concerning the posthumous title had yet to take place. How was Shen Yue to have any inkling as to what lay in store for him in the future? To his repeated pleas for the monk to explain, the monk replied, "Heaven's design is not to be freely divulged. Future happenings will bear out what I said." With these words, he closed his eyes as before and remained in his seat.

Disappointed, Shen Yue returned to see Emperor Wudi and acquainted him with all the details about the honorable Monk Zhi's magic power. Emperor Wudi said, "There do exist divine Buddhas in this world, but mundane humans are kept from that knowledge." By the emperor's order, the royal carriage set out the following day to the temple, escorted by an assembly of civil and military ministers, twenty thousand guards and attendants, drummers, and banners.

Well aware that the procession was on its way to pick him up, Monk Zhi gathered his things together as if ready for a journey. Emperor Wudi and Shen Yue greeted the monk upon arrival at the temple. In spite of his exalted status, the emperor fell on his knees and honored Monk Zhi as his mentor. The salutations over, the monk said, "Please be seated, Your Majesty, and accept a bow from this monk."

"Who has ever seen a teacher bow to a pupil?" asked the emperor.

"Nor has anyone seen a wife resisting her husband," rejoined the monk.

These remarks were like a bucketful of cold water pouring down on the very crown of the emperor's head. A numb weakness spread throughout his body. In an instant, the emperor somehow gained enlightenment and recalled what had happened in a previous existence between Huang Furen and Miss Tong. The two men nodded in understanding, feeling at the same time a growing attachment toward each other.

The emperor invited the monk to go to his court in the same carriage and put the monk in the study along a side hall. Every day after his court session was over, Emperor Wudi would retire to the room to discuss with the monk the ways of Chan, in order to seek enlightenment. The monk said to the emperor, "My living here is not, after all, the best arrangement. I would like to take leave of Your Majesty and return to the monastery."

Emperor Wudi said, "About thirty li away, there is a White Crane Mountain, which is a most quiet and secluded place. I will build a monastery there for you to live in." The monk consented.

Emperor Wudi charged an official with the task of supervising the construction of this monastery. It was a grand project that consumed a million in cash and produced thousands of halls and meditation rooms. The new building was named the Monastery of Shared Felicity, a name that meant that the husband and wife were to reach the land of the Buddha together. Thousands of monks came from far and near to partake of the meals. In the Monastery of Shared Felicity, Monk Zhi lived for more than a year.

The Liang emperor had a son, Prince Zhaoming, who, a most intelligent, kind, and filial son now six years old, could already recite the Five Classics. One day, he suddenly lost the use of his four limbs and fell unconscious, his eyes and mouth tightly shut. The entire palace was thrown into panic and the emperor was made aware of the situation. Physicians from all over the land were summoned, but none could come up with a cure. The emperor said, "My son is a most brilliant boy. Should he not survive, Id have no wish to live on, either."

Alarm spread throughout the palace. A group of court ladies residing in the east wing of the palace suggested, "Unconscious as the prince is, his body is still warm. Why doesn't Your Majesty go to see Monk Zhi and ask for his advice?" Promptly, the emperor mounted his carriage, went to the Monastery of Shared Felicity, and told the monk about the prince's death.

The monk said, "There is no cause for alarm, Your Majesty. The prince is not dead. He is just in a coma. In olden times, Duke Mu of Qin took a tour of heaven, where the celestial joys kept him for seven days before he woke up. Zhao Jianzi of the state of Jin [toward the end of the Spring and Autumn period] also toured heaven for five days and killed a bear there before he regained consciousness, just as Bianque the physician had said. By Zhao's order, the event was duly recorded by Dong Anyu in the palace. Now your son has been in heaven for four days. On the thirty-third level of heaven, the god of the Ganges is holding festivities. The prince was so enraptured by the celestial music that he was pecked by the Three-Legged Divine Bird. The Queen Mother of the West has already killed the bird, but the prince is still up there. I'll go and bring him down for you."

The Liang emperor fell on his knees. "Should my son live again, I would be more than willing to move into the monastery with my son and devote ourselves to Buddhism."

"Your Majesty may now return to the palace," said the monk, "for the prince has come to."

The emperor went back with all speed and saw that his son had indeed come back to life. He held his son in his arms, and father and son broke down in bitter weeping. The emperor said, "My son, your comatose state in the last few days so frightened me that I could hardly live or die. What a miserable time I had!"

The prince said, "I was watching a festival in heaven when a divine bird pecked my hand. The Lord on High had a divine physician apply some ointment to the wound. I was still playing when a monk held me and brought me down."

"That monk," said the emperor, "is Abbot Zhi, whom I will take you to see tomorrow." He then went on to explain about the pledge of devotion to Buddhism. For three days the Liang emperor held a vegetarian banquet catered by the imperial kitchen staff for the benefit of the whole populace as an acknowledgement of his gratitude to heaven and earth. The Liang emperor and the prince did move into the monastery for spiritual devotion. The prince had a poem that said,

> From the palace to the front gate,
> The thoroughfare extends farther beyond.
> With carriage bells sounding like phoenix cries,
> The banners fly into the winding paths.
> The calm valley stream leads to the gorges;
> The deep forest trees rustle with rhythm.
> The fire trees shine with the sunlight;
> The golden temple leads to the sky.
> The moon shines on the pagoda afar;
> Wisps of mist hide half the tower.
> The dharma rain moistens the fragrant groves;
> The good wind sings praises of the emperor.
> For those who enter the Buddhist order,
> Mahayana is the path to take.

For those who pursue traditional learning,
The way of the sage kings is the best of all.
The aroma of the peppered rice
Joins the fragrance of the mountain flowers.
Longevity may have been an exception,
But all other blessings reach far and near.

The Liang emperor and the prince had stayed in the monastery for over twenty days when civil and military officials as well as commoners came to the monastery with pleas that the emperor return to the court—pleas that the emperor turned down. The empress dowager sent eunuchs to ask for his return, but also to no avail. At night, Monk Zhi said to the emperor, "The sin of only one moment of amorous desire will come back to haunt you time and again. Your Majesty will need to pay several more years of the debt before you can be redeemed. Your Majesty must now return to the court and come back here only after the predestined allotment of time has run its course. By that time, there will be nothing to pull you back."

The emperor gave his consent.

The following day, various officials came again to invite the emperor back. He addressed them as follows, "I have vowed to devote myself to the service of Buddha. If I return to the court without a valid reason, my vow would be tantamount to a lie. However, I have an idea. If you want me back, you all must pay a ransom. (*This is more a child's game than a religious practice.*) I myself will contribute ten thousand taels. Every official's household will contribute ten thousand taels each. The empress dowager will also pay ten thousand taels. All of the money will be sent to this monastery to be offered to Buddha and the monks. Only then will I and the prince return to the court."

The various officials and the empress dowager duly sent their silver to the monastery. The emperor himself also had ten thousand taels of silver delivered to the monastery before he returned to his court.

Something happened not long thereafter. To the west of the sea was a land called the Roman Empire, under whose jurisdiction was a state named Tiaozhi,[14] whose ruler, eight to nine feet tall, ate raw food and was as ferocious and savage as a beast. Also in possession of some magic powers, he was capable of swallowing swords, belching fire, and slaughtering humans and horses. As word got to his ears about the Liang emperor's ascension to the throne, he mobilized all the forces of the state for an attack against Liang. No sooner had the officials guarding the sea border learned of the news than they reported the news posthaste to the Liang emperor, who then took the counsel of the assembly of officials, civil as well as military. "It wouldn't have mattered if the challenge had come from any other source," said he. "But how can we stand up to the forces of the state of Tiaozhi? What is to be done? Any one of you who can lead the troops to fight them for me will be generously promoted."

At these words, the various officials looked at each other in dismay. No one had the courage to engage the enemy.

Palace Attendant Fan Yun suggested, "I will go to the Monastery of Shared Felicity to ask Abbot Daolin for advice."

"I will go myself," said the emperor. With all speed, the emperor headed for the monastery, where, upon arrival, he greeted the abbot and gave him to understand the situation. The monk said, "Don't worry. In order to come here from Tiaozhi, they will need to cross the Western Sea before reaching the ocean. It's one thousand seven hundred li to Mingzhou[15] and another two or three rivers from Mingzhou to Jiankang. In Mingzhou there is the Sarira stupa, built by King Aśoka of India. The stupa contains Sakyamuni's fingernails and hair. It was built for the express purpose of protecting the mouth of the Western Sea from attacks against China, and a great deal of good it has done indeed. The pagoda now is badly in need of repair. If Your Majesty could restore it to its former state so that it can provide a protecting influence over the area, I will pray for the divine protective power of Sakyamuni and King Aśoka. How will it then be possible for the Tiaozhi troops to cross the sea?"

Thus advised, the Liang emperor promptly ordered that the stupa be reconstructed to attain a height of nine hundred feet, with the spire as high as one hundred feet, like the Changgan Pagoda of Jinling. A tremendous amount of money, grain, and manpower was lavished upon the project.

While the construction was going on, Tiaozhi's mighty army of one hundred thousand men and horses, under the urging of the emperor of the Roman Empire, set sail in one thousand ships across the ocean for a major onslaught. Abbot Daolin saw the scene in his meditation. The following day, he invited the Liang emperor to the monastery for a prayer session devoted to Sakyamuni and King Aśoka. While the abbot was paying homage to Buddha and offering penitence, the emperor took off his royal robe, put on a Buddhist monk's gown, and went to a quiet hall furnished with nothing but a simple couch and some earthenware. There he personally delivered a lecture, explicating the scriptures.

Great indeed was the power of Buddha, for while the prayer ceremony was going on, the Tiaozhi troops were caught in a hurricane less than three or four days after they had set sail on the sea. Almost every ship was capsized. They took refuge on an island in the middle of the sea and waited more than ten days until the wind subsided before continuing on their way. Soon the wind rose again. With surging waves spouting sky-high, they had no hope of crossing over, so they turned back to their shelter on the island. The wind died down when they decided not to set sail but rose again when they were ready to go. Grand General Qiandu of Tiaozhi said, "This is all too strange! There's no wind when we stay put, but there it blows whenever we're ready to set sail. This is indeed a blessing for the Chinese emperor. Even if heaven lets us cross over for a battle, we may not be able to prevail, judging from what is happening now. The best course is to withdraw."

When the boats turned back, the wind stopped altogether, to let them return in peace. Followed by a group of various chieftains, Qiandu went to see the emperor of the Roman Empire and acquainted him with the previous happenings. The emperor said, "The Chinese emperor is immensely blessed. We are but a small state. Let us not try to pit ourselves against a big empire." He ordered Qiandu and several other chieftains to write a statement of surrender, and so this group of foreign officials went to the Chinese imperial court with tribute offerings of lions, rhinoceroses, peacocks, three-legged pheasants, and long-crowing roosters. At Qiandu's account of how the wind had prevented them from crossing the sea, the Liang emperor knew that this was the work of Buddha as a response to his reconstruction of the pagoda. Henceforth, he was even more devoted to Buddhism and more ardent in serving the Buddha.

Emboldened by China's wealth and power, the Liang emperor wanted to annex the two Wei states and make Hou Jing surrender. Hou Jing was in the service of Gao Huan of Eastern Wei. With his left leg shorter than the right one, Hou Jing was by no means skilled in archery or horsemanship, but was unsurpassed by other commanders in astuteness and sagacity. He had once suggested to Gao Huan, "If I could have thirty thousand of your best soldiers, I would have them sweep all over the land and capture Old Man Xiao on the other side of the river so that you could have the whole empire."

Greatly delighted, Gao Huan gave him one hundred thousand generals and soldiers for control over Henan. After Gao Huan's death, the Liang emperor, aware of the strained relationship between Gao Huan's son Gao Cheng and Hou Jing, set the two men against each other. Gao Cheng did indeed suspect Hou Jing of wrongdoing and summoned Jing with an order issued in the name of Gao Huan. Knowing that it was a trap, Hou Jing used Henan as his base and rose against Wei. Hou Jing then made Commandant Ding Hefeng submit to the Liang emperor a statement of surrender, offering him all of the thirteen prefectures of Henan.

One night in the first month of the year, the Liang emperor saw in a dream various prefects coming to surrender to him with offerings of land. The following day, he gave Zhu Yi an account of his dream. "This is an omen," said Zhu Yi, "of the unification of the land." When Ding Hefeng came to the Liang emperor with the statement of surrender, it became known that it was in fact that very night that Hou Jing made up the plan to surrender.

Marveling at the coincidence, the Liang emperor accepted Hou Jing's surrender, made him duke of Henan, and provided him with reinforcements of soldiers and horses. Little did he know that Hou Jing was a treacherous man. Knowing that Xiao Zhengde, the prince of Linghe, had repeatedly offended the Liang emperor by his greed and ruthlessness and was maintaining an army of dare-to-die soldiers while awaiting a chance for an insurgence, Hou Jing wrote Xiao Zhengde a letter that said,

> With the Son of Heaven at a venerable old age, the evil court ministers are wreaking havoc in the empire, but you who should be the rightful crown prince have been deposed. Unworthy though I am, I gladly offer my services to you.

Enraptured at this letter, Zhengde wrote back to Hou Jing in an attempt to form a secret alliance with him. The letter said,

> I shall work from the inside and you from the outside. What better arrangement than that? Speed being the key to success, now is the time to act.

Thus it came to pass that Hou Jing and Xiao Zhengde, by a secret pact, set the troops in motion, falsely claiming that they were on a hunting expedition. In the tenth month, they took Qiaozhou and captured Prefect Xiao Tai. Liyang was the next city to fall. Zhuang Tie the prefect surrendered, offering up the city as well as these words of advice to Hou Jing: "The empire has enjoyed peace for so long that people are no longer used to war. Your military action shocked all of the empire and beyond. You would do well to seize the opportunity and descend upon Jiankang with all speed, for victory will be yours without even a bloodstain on the edge of the sword. If the imperial court is given time to prepare and dispatch a thousand crack troops to guard Caishi, even a million of your best armed soldiers will not be able to resist." Much pleased at the advice, Jing made Zhuang Tie the vanguard.

Knowing nothing about Zhengde's secret alliance with Hou Jing, the Liang emperor appointed Zhengde, of all people, as the commander in chief of the troops stationed in Danyang. Zhengde dispatched several tens of big boats as reinforcements for Jing, claiming that the boats were laden with reeds. As soon as he crossed over, Hou Jing laid siege to Jiankang. The assault lasted night and day until Dong Xun led Jing's men up the city walls, and so the city fell. The Liang emperor was confined to the East Hall of Ultimate Bliss under the heavy guard of five hundred armored men posted both inside and outside the hall.

Taking up residence in the palace, Hou Jing grabbed every treasure and antique in the palace that struck his fancy and appropriated for himself hundreds upon hundreds of beautiful court ladies. Of powerful physique, Hou Jing was a man of unsatiable lust. Several tens of women a night still could

not satisfy him. Hearing that Princess Liyang was a ravishing beauty with
a remarkable talent for music, he wanted to take her as a concubine. By his
order, a young eunuch, Tian Xiang'er prepared a gilded decorative box with
heart-shaped bows made of soft purple silk threads and some matched pairs
of fruits, and quietly sent it over to the princess. When she opened it for a
look, those in attendance by her side exploded with rage and advised her to
destroy it and reject the gifts. "No," said the princess. "This is something
beyond your ken. Hou Jing is a mighty hero. My father had dreamed of a rhe-
sus monkey[16] ascending the imperial throne. This is indeed happening today.
If I do not yield myself to Emperor Hou, all in the Xiao clan will be exterminated." (*A woman of such good sense is superior to pedantic scholars. Similar cases
are Chen Shi's[17] mourning the death of Zhang Rang[18] and Di Renjie's [607–700]
serving Empress Wu as a court minister.*) Thereupon she sent to Hou Jing a pair
of coral pillows inlaid with gold and a brocade quilt embroidered with a pair
of phoenixes.

Immensely delighted at Tian Xiang'er's reply, Hou Jing dispatched several
tens of close attendants to bring the princess to him. That night, the princess
swallowed her pride and endured all sorts of debauchery on the part of Hou
Jing. Remaining unshaken in her devotion to him, she gradually gained his
favor, was able to have her way, and interfered in the affairs of the court. It
was thanks to her that no harm came to the royal family. Later, Wang Wei
advised Hou Jing to depose Emperor Jianwen [Xiao Yan's successor] and
enthrone a new emperor and to wipe out all members of Xiao Yan's clan, but
the princess raised objections against Wang Wei and, as a consequence, lost
favor with Hou Jing.

Confined as he was by Hou Jing, the Liang emperor was not able to see
Monk Zhi again. (*If Monk Zhi had magic powers, he wouldn't have to wait for
the Liang emperor to come over. It's just that the will of heaven is not to be defied.*)
His requests were mostly denied. His daily food portions were also reduced.
Grief and indignation wore him down. His requests for honey to sweeten the
bitter taste in his mouth were ignored, and he died, bitter and rancorous, at
the age of eighty-six. (*This tragic death, being attributable to a revenge by Xiao
Baojuan, will not prevent him from attaining salvation.*) Though Hou Jing did
not announce his death, Abbot Zhi knew full well what had happened. As his
time had now come, an event that brooked no delay, he sat in the monastery
and willed his death.

Aggrieved over the tragic death of the Liang emperor at the hands of Hou
Jing, Prince Xiao Yi of Xiangdong of the Liang claimed himself to be the court-
appointed commander in chief of various armies and led the men on an expedition against Hou Jing. Wang Sengbian, prefect of Jingling, was sent to head
an advance party of five thousand men and horses to recover Jiankang. When

the troops marched to Xiangzhou, Sengbian quietly ordered Zhao Bochao to find out about Hou Jing's strength. Considering the perilous nature of the mission, Bochao disguised himself as an ordinary merchant and set out on his way. When he was passing through the forest by Baitong Peak, he caught sight in the distance of the Liang emperor and Monk Zhi slowly approaching him, each leaning on a staff. Upon drawing nearer, Bochao realized with a start that it was indeed the Liang emperor. Falling on his knees, he said, "What brings Your Majesty and the abbot here? Where are you heading?"

The Liang emperor replied, "I have fulfilled my destiny and am on my way west with the abbot to the Land of Ultimate Bliss. I have here a letter for the prince of Xiangdong. I was just wondering whom to ask to deliver the letter. Put the letter carefully in a safe place and deliver it for me." With these words, the Liang emperor took out the letter from his sleeve and handed it over to Zhao Bochao. The letter had barely exchanged hands when the Liang emperor and Monk Zhi disappeared. Later, when giving Wang Sengbian a report on what he had found out about Hou Jing, Bochao produced the letter, with an account of how he had met the Liang emperor. Upon opening the letter, the prince of Xiangdong found it to be a poem written in an ancient style:

> The villain stole the divine throne;
> The scourge spread over the four seas.
> Alas! How sad that Xiao Zhengde
> Should have fallen into Jing's snare.
> To the one who betrayed the sovereign,
> No more support should be given.
> The prince of Xiangdong is the only one
> Who shows loyalty and righteous anger.
> Baxian's battle plan at Luoxing Town
> Will bring Hou Jing to defeat.
> He will flee to Xie Daren,
> But only to be killed by Yang Chi.
> His head will roll from his body;
> His five sons will all die in a foreign land.
> His corpse will be shown in the marketplace,
> To be fought over for food and revenge.
> Today, I take off my humble shoes;
> Nothing will hamper my movements.
> I shall enjoy honor and leisure
> In Tusita and the land of ultimate bliss.
> But how will the usurper fare?
> A violent death and a notorious name.

After reading the poem, the prince of Xiangdong burst into sobs in spite of himself, with tears gushing from his eyes. Later, Wang Sengbian and Chen Baxian did put Hou Jing to rout, and Hou Jing did flee to the Wu region to seek shelter from Xie Daren. Yang Kan's second son, Yang Chi, killed Hou Jing and exposed the corpse in the marketplace, where the local residents fought over it for the flesh. Even the bones all disappeared. Princess Liyang also ate some of the flesh in order to vindicate herself in the eyes of heaven. She then took her own life. (*The princess is not fully understood until now. A true heroine.*) All of Hou Jing's five sons were killed by Northern Qi [550–577] people. Every prediction in the poem was born out. There is a poem that says,

> *How absurd that men are so shortsighted*
> *And think only of immediate concerns!*
> *From Jiankang a road leads to the Western Paradise,*
> *Where empty valleys have been proved to exist.*

She tells him, "Be sure to come early tomorrow morning."

Ren the Filial Son with a Fiery Disposition Becomes a God

Know well the meaning of the word "romance,"
For good marriage destinies may go awry.
A fool falls for every woman he sees;
An impassive eye finds fault with them all.
Never pick idle flowers and wild grass
For the sake of peace of body and mind.
However humble your wife might be,
She gives you no lovesickness, nor costs you money.

The point of this lyric poem is that lust and desire make you forget who you are, and, therefore, one should be always on guard against such lapses.

The story goes that in the first year of the Shaoxi reign period [1190] under Emperor Guangzong of the Southern Song dynasty, there lived, in front of a government wine storage house at the southern end of Clear River District in the prefectural city of Lin'an, an immensely rich man named Squire Zhang, who owned an herbal medicine store specializing in products of Sichuan and Guangdong. The store was located in the front of his residence. His mother had passed away. Now in his sixties, he had only one son, who was called First Master Zhang Xiu. At age twenty, he was a clever and handsome young man. The family business kept him in the store every day. Believing that the thriving business was too much responsibility for their young son, the couple hired a general manager for the store, twenty-five-year-old Mr. Ren Gui.

Ren Gui's mother had died when he was very young, leaving him with only his father, who was blind and could do no more than sit at home all day long. Every day, Ren Gui the filial son said good-bye to his father before he left home and greeted him when returning at night. He lived, as had his ancestors, on Ox-Skin Street in Jianggan. That winter, he got married, through a matchmaker, to a twenty-year-old woman of remarkable charm called

Shengjin, daughter of the umbrella-maker Mr. Liang, who lived in the same city, near Rixin Bridge by the river.

After marrying Ren Gui, the woman never stopped secretly blaming her parents, for she felt wretched married to such a down-to-earth and unromantic man. "Of all places," she thought to herself, "my parents sent me off here, so far away from home that I cannot easily go back any time I want." Every day, she pulled a long face and wore a frown, nor was she in any mood for dolling herself up as before. Ren Gui's busy schedule, leaving home early and returning late, added to her discontent.

The fact of the matter was that the woman had had an illicit relationship, before her marriage, with Zhou De, son of Editorial Assistant Zhou, who lived across from her parents' house. This Zhou De was a handsome man with graceful manners and was given to indulge in wine and women. Much favored by women, this thirty-year-old man wanted no wife but only illicit love affairs. That he had clandestine dates with Sister Liang was common knowledge to all the neighbors. That was why her parents, although they had no male issue,[1] had no choice but to marry her off to Jianggan to avoid further gossip. Being an unsophisticated man, Ren Gui took her in without any investigation into her background. However, although she was now Ren Gui's wife, her heart was still with Zhou De, and their passion for each other was by no means at an end.

Time sped by. Indeed,

> *The weeping willows have just turned green*
> *When, in a trice, the wheat crops have ripened.*
> *The cicadas have barely stopped chirping*
> *When wild geese are already on their wings.*

It was now the eighteenth day of the eighth month, when the Qiantang River was at its highest tide of the year. All the fashionable men and women of the city turned out to watch the tide. Zhou De and his two brothers also preened themselves and went out of the city through Tide-Watching Gate. It was a busy scene with carriages and horses coming and going, and crowds of people milling around like ants. Instead of watching the tide with the crowd, Zhou De shook himself free of his two brothers and made his way straight to Ren Gui's home on Ox-Skin Street. As it happened, Ren Gui's father had the habit of sitting under the eaves behind the closed gate, intoning Buddha's name. When Zhou De knocked at the gate with the handle of a fan, Mr. Ren Senior thought it was his son coming back and groped his way out to open the gate. Knowing that this must be Mr. Ren Senior, Zhou De said, "Sir, please accept a bow from me."

Realizing that this was not his son's voice, the old man asked, "Who might you be? What brings you here?"

"Sir, I am Umbrella-Maker Liang's sister's son. My cousin is married to your son. I'm here to see her on my way to watch the tide. Is your son, my brother-in-law, at home?"

Since the visitor claimed to be his daughter-in-law's kinsman, the sightless Mr. Ren Senior invited him in and called out toward the inner quarters of the house, "Daughter-in-law, your cousin is here to see you."

The woman was sulking upstairs when she heard the call. In great haste, she liberally applied rouge and powder and put on hairpins and bracelets and, donning some brightly colored clothes, rushed downstairs, taking three steps in two. A peek through the cotton curtain assured her that it was none other than her sorely missed dear lover. Emerging from behind the curtain, she stepped forward to greet him, a radiant smile on her lips. At the sight of her, Zhou De felt

> Relieved by sweet rain after a long drought,
> Happier than seeing old friends in a distant land.
> Thinking only of the joys of the bedchamber,
> How was he to foresee that death was near?

The two sat down, shoulder to shoulder. The sight of Zhou De sent the woman into raptures. Unable to control herself, she lifted the curtain while holding Zhou De's hand, saying without meaning what she said, "Cousin, let's go upstairs for a chat." Mr. Ren Senior remained sitting on the bench under the eaves, intoning Buddha's name.

Barely were the two upstairs than they fell into each other's arms. The woman cursed, "You won't live long, you scoundrel! You made me miss you so much that I got sick! Why didn't you come to see me for so long? You heartless rascal!"

With a laugh, Zhou De said, "Sister, after you got married and left for the upper reaches of the river, I missed you so much that I almost died. I often wanted to come, but I didn't dare to because your husband might have found out." While uttering these words, he carried her to the bed. Loosening their belts and taking off their clothes, they renewed their pledges of love and fulfilled their desire to the utmost. Truly,

> At the height of their passion,
> He held her tight, cheek to jowl.
> His hands on her soft creamy breasts—
> What a wonderful feeling!
> Trousers and shoes taken off,

Her body pressed against his,
The mouths open with tongues touching.
The storm over, she said to him,
"Don't fail to come earlier tomorrow!"

The above lyric poem to the tune of "Song of the Southern Country" is a description of this love scene in broad daylight. After the game of clouds and rain was over, they adjusted their clothes. Holding Zhou De in her arms, the woman said, "My husband leaves home early and comes back late. If you do indeed care for me, come here often and just say you are visiting. The old man is blind. What will he know! We'll just enjoy ourselves upstairs. Don't you ever let me down."

"My good sister, my darling, I will never let you down. If I do, may I fall into Avichi Hell and suffer for ten thousand *kalpas* without ever regaining human form."

At Zhou De's curse upon himself, the woman turned his face toward her, stuck her tongue into his mouth, and said, "My darling, I didn't love you in vain. From now on, come often to see me. Don't ever make me wait for you at the door." Much as they hated to take leave of each other, they could do no better than go downstairs for Zhou De to bid Mr. Ren Senior goodbye and leave the house. The woman told her father-in-law, "He's my aunt's son. He's a kind and honest man, so simple-minded that he never has much to say." (*An honest man indeed! As the proverb puts it, "No three hundred taels of silver buried here."*)[2]

Mr. Ren Senior said, "Good, good."

The woman went to the kitchen and served the old man lunch before she went back upstairs and slept until evening set in. Ren Gui came home and mounted the stairs after first greeting his father. Husband and wife, having nothing to say to each other, slept until day broke. Ren Gui took leave of his father and went back into the city.

From that time on, Zhou De became restless, his thoughts constantly with the woman. Barely had two days gone by than he would go again for a tryst to quench his fiery passion. In those days, Ox-Skin Street was sparsely inhabited. Therefore, the few neighboring families the Rens were friends with knew nothing about the affair.

However, quite unexpectedly, Zhou De got involved in a lawsuit and failed to show up for two months. Consumed with lust and dashed hopes, the woman became feverishly ill. Indeed,

The sun and moon move by all too quickly.
When will they ever stop for a rest?
Nü Wa smelted rocks to patch up the sky,[3]
But knew not how to glue the sun and moon in place.

Soon enough, the Lantern Festival rolled around again, and residents of Lin'an erected frames at their doors to display colorful lanterns in celebration. It so happened that Zhou De's lawsuit had been brought to a close. Putting on nice clothes, he set out on his way at around nine in the morning for a visit.

With a salute to Mr. Ren, who was intoning Buddha's name at the gate, he walked upstairs. The two partook of the roast goose meat that he produced from his sleeves, loosened their clothes, and went to bed. As sweet to each other as sugar and honey and as inseparable as lacquer and glue, they experienced the very height and fulfillment of love, enjoying each other more than ever before. After such a long separation, they could hardly tear themselves away from each other's tight embrace. At such considerable length did they sport with each other that they were still upstairs at three in the afternoon. Hungry and resentful, Mr. Ren Senior thought to himself, "How come that cousin of hers spent a whole day up there?" He called out from downstairs, "I'm hungry! I want something to eat!"

The woman replied, "I have a stomachache. Wait for me. I'll be down shortly."

Swallowing his anger, Mr. Ren went to the door and sat down again. "There must be something fishy going on," he thought to himself. "I'll ask my son tonight when he returns."

The lovers now had to let go of each other. They softly descended the stairs and slowly opened the door. Zhou De took himself off. Feigning a stomachache, the woman served Mr. Ren some food and went back upstairs to think about her lover, and there we shall leave her.

When Ren Gui returned home in the evening and greeted his father, the latter said to him, "My son, don't go upstairs right away. I have something to ask you about."

Ren Gui stopped to listen.

"There is a certain cousin in your parents-in-law's family who came here on the eighteenth day of the eighth month last year on his way to watch the tide and since then has been frequently coming for visits. I don't mind if he always goes directly upstairs to talk, but this morning he came again, and they stayed up there until afternoon without serving me lunch. I couldn't help calling your wife. The cousin heard me and left in a hurry. I am much puzzled. I've been meaning to ask you about this, but I always forget because you leave home early and return late. To my thinking, if a man and a woman spend a whole day upstairs, an affair must be going on. There's nothing a blind old man like me can do. You'll have to find out about this yourself, but take your time." Ren Gui seethed with anger at these words and stormed up the stairs. Indeed,

The mouth leads to disasters;
The tongue is the sword that kills.
Shut your mouth and hide your tongue,
And live in peace wherever you are.

Ren Gui stormed up the stairs in a rage. Without voicing his thoughts, he told himself, "I'll control myself for the moment and see what this woman has to say for herself." At the sight of his wife sitting there, he asked, "Has father had his supper yet?"

"Yes," came the reply. She lit the lamp, spread out the bedding, took off her clothes, and lay down. Ren Gui followed her onto the bed, but, instead of lying down, he sat by the pillow and said, "Let me ask you something. Why does a cousin often come to visit you? Tell me which one he is."

At these words, the woman sat up and put on her clothes. Her willowlike brows tightly knit, her eyes opening wide, she declared, "He is the son of my father's sworn sister. Out of their concern for me, my parents tell him to visit me often. What's there to be so suspicious about?" She demanded in a tantrum, "Who's been tongue-wagging? I'm not to be easily bullied like some defenseless old granny! Every brick you throw needs to land somewhere. Tell me who's been throwing rumors around. I'll go with you for some good questioning."

Ren Gui said, "Not so loud! Father told me just a moment ago that a cousin of yours spent a whole day today upstairs. That's why I asked you. If there's nothing to it, that'll be that. You don't have to get so worked up." So saying, he took off his clothes and went to sleep, but the woman continued with her show of hysteria, saying between sobs and gasps for breath, "My parents should have known better than to marry me off to this place. Then they wouldn't have to send someone to visit me and set tongues wagging."

And so her raving and ranting went on. Unable to go to sleep, Ren Gui could not do otherwise than sit up, move to her side, embrace her, and say soothingly (*The word "soothingly"* [fuxu] *is nicely chosen*), "Oh well, it's my fault. For the sake of our marriage, I apologize." The woman threw herself into Ren Gui's arms and conjured up a game of clouds and rain that lasted half the night. We shall speak no more of this.

Ren Gui rose at daybreak and went into the city after taking leave of his father. Every day he worked assiduously, leaving home early and returning late. The lust-crazed woman, however, had her mind set on meeting her lover. She thought to herself, "I'll have to come up with some trick to get out of here. I won't be able to get together with Zhou De and have a good time unless I find an excuse to go back to my parents' house." Day and night she turned the idea over and over in her mind. In the meantime, another half month passed by.

One day after mealtime, Zhou De came again. He opened the gate and charged straight into the house and up the stairs without a word of greeting to Mr. Ren Senior. The woman put her arms around him and said under her breath, "That blind old donkey told his son that you often come to sit and talk with me upstairs. I defended myself until my lips cracked before I got myself off the hook. I can't bear the thought of not seeing you ever again. We need to come up with a plan for me to go home so that we can enjoy ourselves to the full."

Zhou De knitted his brows in thought and came up with a plan. "The cats are crying like crazy on the roof," he said. "If you get hold of one and hold it to your chest, it'll surely scratch you. You can then let it go, lie down in bed, and weep until your husband comes back. When he asks you, which he will certainly do, say to him, 'Your good father has been making passes at me. I resisted, so he scratched my chest.' You can then burst into loud sobs. Your husband will surely send you back home. In that way, we'll get to enjoy ourselves every day. Won't that be better than stealing an occasional tryst? Stay at home for three months to half a year before we think about what to do next. What a brilliant plan!"

The woman exclaimed in admiration, "I didn't love you in vain! You have a good heart and a sharp mind, too!"

Without even taking off their clothes, they fell back on the bed for another game of clouds and rain. After it was over, Zhou De scurried downstairs in haste. Indeed,

> When the old turtle's meat won't cook tender,
> Innocent mulberries are cut down to feed the fire.

The woman bade her time for a few more days before she caught a cat, bared her chest, and put the cat under her clothes. Finding itself all covered up, the cat kicked and scratched with all its might. In spite of the pain, the woman waited until her breasts were all lacerated before she loosened her clothes and let it go. It was already past three in the afternoon. Instead of preparing supper, she threw herself on her bed with her clothes on and rubbed her eyes till they were fiery red. She then wept and screamed by turns until dusk fell and Ren Gui returned home. After greeting his father, Ren Gui proceeded to the inner quarters of the house. Failing to find his wife, he called out, "Wife, why aren't you downstairs?" At this, the woman broke into louder wails, whereupon Ren Gui went up, asking, without an inkling as to the cause, "Have you had supper? Why are you crying?"

It was only after he repeated his questions several times that the glib-tongued slut started screaming between sobs, "You'd better not ask, for you'll only be bringing out the shame I've suffered! Write a statement of divorce and send me back to my parents. I can't put up with such humiliation. If you don't send me back, I'll kill myself tomorrow!" And she started wailing again.

"Stop crying. Tell me what's bothering you."

The woman got up, dried her tears, and showed him her lacerated breasts criss-crossed with seven or eight welts. "A fine thing your dear father did to me!" she said. "This morning, after I saw you off at the door, I came back upstairs. Little did I know that the beastly old donkey noiselessly followed me up. With one sweep, he gathered me into his arms, fondled my breasts, and tried to force himself on me. As I resisted, he wildly scratched my breasts without letting go of me. It was only when I screamed that he gave up and groped his way downstairs. I've been waiting anxiously for your return." So saying, she broke into loud sobs and continued, "Such filthy, beastly things don't ever happen in *my* family."

"Don't be so loud!" admonished Ren Gui. "If the neighbors hear this, we won't look too good."

"If you're afraid of gossip, get me a sedan-chair tomorrow, let me go home, and I'll call it quits."

A filial son though Ren Gui was, when he heard the trumped-up story, a smoldering rage burned his heart. (*How can a filial son not know his father's character? How wrong Ren Gui is! He should have known better.*) He said, "This truly bears out the saying. 'It's easy to draw a tiger's skin but not its bones. It's easy to know a person's face but not his heart.' So this is what happened! Now I know there's no truth whatsoever to all those things he made up about some affair between you and your cousin. From this day on, I will not so much as look at that old beast! Stop crying, wife. Go prepare supper and then go to bed."

Secretly delighted that her husband believed her story, the woman went downstairs, cooked supper, ate, and went to bed. Truly,

> A lovely wife who shares the husband's bed
> Can get her way nine times out of ten.

Ren Gui was so enamored by the charms of that woman that he did not bother to verify the facts with his father. The following morning, after he rose and ate breakfast, he called a sedan-chair and sent the woman back to her home with a roast goose and two bottles of fine wine. The woman gathered her clothes together into a parcel and mounted the sedan-chair, without a word of goodbye to Mr. Ren Senior. As soon as she reached her home, she went upstairs. Zhou De came over at news of her arrival. The two fell into a tight embrace and laid themselves down on her mother's bed for fulfillment of their desires. Zhou De said, "Wasn't that a wonderful plan?"

"Yes, indeed! Let's have some fun the whole night through to make up for what we've lost."

After their intimacy, Zhou De wanted to go down to buy some wine and food. The woman said, "I've brought some roast goose and fine wine to share with you. If you want to buy anything, some fish, vegetables, and fruit will be enough." (*They do know how to live it up.*)

In a short while, Zhou De came back with a fish, a pig's trotter, fresh fruits of all colors, and a big bottle of Wujiapi liquor. By the time the maid Spring Plum had finished preparing the meal, it was already about three in the afternoon. The woman set the table. With her parents taking the seats of honor, Zhou De and the woman sitting opposite each other, and the maid serving the wine, the company of four drank until the first watch of the night. Dinner over, Mr. Liang and his wife went downstairs to retire for the night. The younger couple remained upstairs. Indeed, never before had their joy been so complete. They had just decided to go on with their sporting for the rest of the night when they heard knocks at the door. Indeed,

> Those who have done nothing shameful by day
> Need not fear a knock at the door at night.

As I was saying, the two of them were determined to enjoy the whole night when, all too unexpectedly, there came knocks at the door. Spring Plum was cleaning up the kitchen range when she heard the knocks and went with a lamp to answer the door. It was Ren Gui. Petrified with alarm, she screamed from where she was standing, "Mr. Ren Gui is here!"

Zhou De hurriedly put on his clothes and rushed downstairs. As he desperately tried to think of a place to hide, the privy in the empty lot came to his mind, and there he went. The woman slowly walked downstairs and said, "Why are you here at this late hour?"

Ren Gui replied, "The city gate was closed by the time I was ready to leave. I thought of spending the night with Squire Zhang, but it's too late. That's why I came here to stay for the night."

"Have you had supper?"

"Yes. I just want some warm water to wash my feet with."

With alacrity, Spring Plum brought over a washbowl so he could wash his feet. The woman went upstairs first, while Ren Gui made his way to the privy. All would have been well if there had been someone to stop him from going, but as it was, he almost died a violent death because of this visit to the privy. Indeed,

> Do good deeds far and wide,
> For you never know whom you might meet.
> Never make any enemies,
> For enemies' paths are bound to cross.

677

Ren Gui had barely stepped into the lavatory than Zhou De suddenly emerged and grabbed him tight, yelling, "Stop thief!" Mr. Liang and his wife, the woman, and the maid all brought sticks of firewood and showered him with blows. "It's me, not some thief!" cried Ren Gui. They would not listen but gave him a good thrashing. Zhou De took advantage of the commotion and slipped away. The beating did not stop until Ren Gui cried himself hoarse. When a lamp was brought over, the crowd stood agape with astonishment as they saw it was Ren Gui. Ren Gui said, "I was grabbed by a real thief but you beat me while the real thief got away."

They grumbled with feigned regret, "Why didn't you say so sooner! We thought you were the thief, and in the meantime, the real one got away." So saying, they went their separate ways.

Swallowing the humiliation, Ren Gui said to himself, "Could it be that they hid someone there and beat me up only because I stumbled upon their secret? Let me not rush things but carefully try to find out about this."

As it was already the third watch by the night-watch drum, he retired to Mr. Liang's bed. But his troubled thoughts kept him awake. When the fifth watch was struck at last, he rose, dressed, and made for the door, even though it was not yet quite light.

Mr. Liang said, "Wait until daybreak, and have some breakfast before you go."

Still aching all over from the beating, Ren Gui was in no mood to answer him. He opened the front gate, closed it after himself, and, under the starlight, headed straight for Tide Watching Gate.

It was too early. The gate was not yet open. (*Good plot.*) Numerous brokers and peddlers with loads of salt across their shoulders were seated by the gate, waiting for it to open. Some people were singing, some chatting, some engaged in small business transactions. Ren Gui sat down among the crowd and retired into his own thoughts. You may very well say that coincidences do happen. Indeed,

> *Be sparing with spices in your food.*
> *Do not go where you do not belong.*
> *Try hard to learn things that call for respect.*
> *Never do what you fear others might know.*

Ren Gui was brooding over his own troubles when a man said, all of a sudden, "A funny thing happened to a neighbor of mine, Liang the umbrella-maker."

"What was it?" asked another man.

"Well, the Liang family has a daughter, now in her twenties, with the pet name of Shengjin. Before she married, she had an affair with Zhou De, son of

Editorial Assistant Zhou, opposite their house. Last year, she married a certain Ren Gui, manager of a medicine store, living on Ox-Skin Street outside the city. That Zhou De still kept up his visits but was exposed by the blind father-in-law and could not go any more. Yesterday, the daughter returned home. Last night, Zhou De bought food and fine wine and feasted until late at night. The two were enjoying themselves upstairs when the least expected thing happened. As it was too late for the son-in-law to get out of the city, he went to his parents-in-law's house to spend the night. Zhou De the adulterer was so shocked that, for lack of a place to hide, he took refuge in the lavatory. But it so happened that Ren Gui also went there to relieve himself. Now wasn't that a funny thing? That Zhou De was indeed a smart one. He grabbed Ren Gui and yelled, 'Stop thief!' The parents-in-law and the daughter went up and beat Ren Gui to a pulp while the adulterer got away. Now that's an extraordinary thing, if ever there is one in this world!"

The audience clapped their hands and said laughingly, "That man is a real pushover! Didn't he know he was being cheated by the adulterous couple?"

The man continued, "If that happened to me, I would cut them in half with a sharp cleaver! That man is no hero, all right. Must be a faint-hearted sort."

Another man commented, "Maybe he didn't know his wife was having an affair. That's why things got so far." This remark was followed by another burst of laughter. Indeed,

> Remember that words are hooks and lines
> That draw up nothing but trouble.

Ren Gui overheard every word of the conversation. The gate opened at this juncture. The crowd poured out of the city and dispersed in various directions. Ren Gui, however, instead of going out the gate, turned back to Squire Zhang's house, where he took three to five taels of silver, with which he bought a knife at an ironsmith's shop, slipped it into its sheath, and strapped it to his waist. Recalling that the temple of the duke of Yan the Water God by Qiantang Gate was most responsive to prayers, he bought a white rooster, incense, candles, and paper horses and took them to the temple. There he lit the incense sticks and prayed, "Gods, please show your power! I, Ren Gui, am married to a woman of the Liang family. She has an adulterous relationship with her neighbor Zhou and, at night . . . "

After the prayer was over, he drew the knife from its hilt, picked up the rooster, and asked for a sign from heaven: "If I am to kill one person, make the chicken jump once on the ground. If I am to kill two people, make it jump twice." With a single plunge of his knife, he chopped off the rooster's head. The rooster jumped on the ground four times in a row before it gave a mighty leap all the way from the ground over the beam and fell down again, making altogether five jumps. Ren Gui slipped the knife back into the sheath and bowed repeatedly, wishing that the gods would lend him their divine power for his revenge. Having burned the paper, he walked out of the temple and onto the street. Hither and thither he wandered, but, unable to think up a plan, he returned by night to Squire Zhang's house. He was in no mood to attend to any business matters.

The following morning, he rose early and strapped the knife to his waist but was not at all sure what to do. He would have gone to the Liang house to have it out with them if not for fear that Zhou De might not be there. Killing the woman alone would not mean much. Turning these thoughts over and over in his mind made him wish he could sink his teeth into that man. His steps took him to a place where he was to throw all his usual caution and kindness to the winds. Indeed, he wreaked havoc on Rixin Bridge and caused quite a stir throughout the city of Lin'an. Truly,

> If a green dragon and a white tiger go together,
> There is no telling if joy or sorrow will follow.[4]

Ren Gui went wherever his steps took him until he found himself in his older sister's house by Meizheng Bridge. He said to his sister, "I have some things to take care of in the next couple of days. There'll be no one to take care of father. So do not refuse if he has to stay with you for a while."

His sister replied, "He can stay as long as he wants." She did indeed send her son to get her father and bring him to her house.

That day, Ren Gui again wandered aimlessly in the streets before returning to his sister's house, where he saw his father and gave him to understand the situation. "That evil woman," he said, "fooled me with her wicked stories about you, Father. I almost fell into her trap. How am I to avenge myself?"

"Throwing her out is enough," said his father. "Why do you have to be so bitter?"

Ren Gui continued, "If ever she should run into me, I won't let her get away!"

"Don't do anything reckless. Why don't you just keep away from her house, divorce her, get yourself a good wife, and be done with it?"

"I know what to do," said Ren Gui. He took leave of his father and sister and went to the city in none too amiable a mood.

Dusk had set in by this time. He went to Squire Zhang's house and acquainted the squire with all the details. "Now that my father is with my sister, I have no more worries."

Squire Zhang offered him this counsel: "Be patient. Think well before you do anything. The ancients say, 'To convict an adulterous couple, catch them in the act. To convict a thief, produce the stolen goods.' If you make a mess of it, you'll suffer, and all for nothing. If you are thrown into a prison cell to await execution, no one will be there to help you. It's better to take my advice than to kill. Make no enemies but only friends." At these words of admonishment, Ren Gui hung his head without saying a word.

The squire had a waiting woman set out some wine and food for Ren Gui and told him to retire to his room for the night and not to decide upon anything until the following day. Ren Gui thanked the squire.

Once in his own room, he threw himself onto the bed without bothering to take off his clothes, his heart in as much pain as if stabbed by a knife. He tossed and turned through four watches of the night, his rage mounting higher and higher, until, unable to control himself any longer, he rose, quickly got dressed, strapped his knife to his waist, groped his way to the kitchen, quietly opened the door, and leaned himself against the rear wall. The wall being not overly high, one stride took him to the top. The late summer and early autumn moon was shining as brightly as daylight. In one leap, he landed on the ground with the exclamation "So be it!" And so he headed straight for his parents-in-law's house.

When he was about ten houses away from his destination, he stood still under the eaves in the darkness, thinking to himself, "I'm going to do it, all right, but how do I get the door open?" It was at this moment of indecision that Mr. Wang, peddler of sesame-seed cakes, was seen walking along, carrying a load of cakes across his shoulders and striking a small bamboo tube in his hand. All of a sudden, Ren Gui's parents-in-law's door swung open. Out came Spring Plum, who stopped Mr. Wang and bought some cakes from him. Ren Gui said to himself, "That fellow is indeed meant to die!"

Taking three steps in one, he ran into the house and headed straight for Mr. Liang's room by the stairs. Knife in hand, he opened the door and saw his parents-in-law both asleep. "So, that rascal Zhou De must be upstairs," he thought. Pinning the old couple down, he cut off their heads with two swings of his knife and threw the heads down to the foot of the bed. He was on the point of taking the stairs when Spring Plum, having closed the door, appeared by the side of the stairs. Ren Gui grabbed her and warned, "Don't scream! If you do, I'll kill you. Tell me, where's Zhou De?"

Recognizing Ren Gui's voice, the woman knew that things had gone wrong. Seeing a knife in his hand, she screamed, "Mr. Ren is here!" In a rage, Ren Gui cut off her head with one swing of his knife. With the girl's head now on the ground, Ren Gui stormed up the stairs in great strides to kill the adulterous couple. Truly,

As you sow, so will you reap.
Nothing slips through the net of heaven.

Before Ren Gui ran up the stairs, the man and the woman had been cavorting in bed. At Mr. Wang's strikes of the bamboo tube, they had awakened Spring Plum and told her to buy some sesame-seed cakes. The bedroom door was left open, and the lamp on the table still on. By the time Ren Gui approached the bed, the woman already knew, for she had heard Spring Plum's screams and was pretending to be asleep. Pinning down her head with one hand, Ren Gui slit her throat with the other hand, cut off her head, and threw it on the floor. "Now I feel avenged on this score," he said aloud, "but I won't be fully satisfied until I do away with that scoundrel Zhou De." He suddenly recalled that the rooster he killed in the temple had jumped five times. Now that he had killed his father-in-law, mother-in-law, his wife, and the maid, the four killings accounted for only four of the jumps. "That the chicken gave a final jump from the beam must foreshadow something." So thinking, he raised his head, and whom did he see but Zhou De, naked, lying on the beam on his stomach.

"Come down quick!" shouted Re Gui. "I'll spare your life if you do!"

Zhou De had climbed up in a moment of desperate haste. The sight of Ren Gui threw him into such jitters that he lost the use of his four limbs and remained transfixed as if in a spell.

In a moment of blinding rage, Ren Gui climbed up the beam from the bed and stabbed Zhou De indiscriminately with his knife. How pitiful! Zhou De fell down from the beam, head first. Ren Gui jumped down and, with a foot planted on his chest, stabbed him another ten times or so. Then Ren Gui cut off the man's head, loosened his hair, and tied his head to that of the woman. Slipping the knife back into its sheath, he walked downstairs, the two heads in hand. He picked up the maid's head at the foot of the stairs and went searching for the heads of the parents-in-law. He then loosened the hair, tied all five heads together, and put them on the ground.

It was now broad daylight. "I have killed to my heart's content," he thought to himself. "To get caught fleeing from the scene is by no means a heroic thing to do. I'd be better off surrendering myself to the authorities so that, even if I am cut to pieces, my name will go down to posterity." So thinking, he opened the door, summoned the neighbors, and announced to them, "As you all know, my wife was a loose woman. I have killed her and the entire family plus the adulterer Zhou De. I'm afraid that if I leave the scene, you the neighbors might be implicated in a lawsuit. Therefore, I ask that you take me to the authorities."

The neighbors did not believe what they had heard. As they hurried into Mr. Liang's room for a look, what confronted their eyes were the old couple's headless bodies. At the foot of the stairs was lying the corpse of the maid. As they ascended the stairs, they found Zhou De dead in a pool of blood, with stab wounds all over his body, and the woman dead in bed. (*Good recapitulation, much like the style of the Grand Historian [Sima Qian].*) Appalled at the sight, the neighbors walked down the stairs, only to see the five heads tied together in a cluster. "What a man!" they exclaimed. "We'll go to the authorities and tell them what happened." They called in more neighbors, who came with the neighborhood headman and the police to arrest Ren Gui. As they were trying to bind him up with ropes, Ren Gui said, "Don't bother. I'm quite ready to pay for what I did. I will not cause you any trouble." So saying, he picked up the five heads and strode out the door. The crowd of neighbors followed him out. The street was filled with countless men and women eager to take a look at the scene. Having caused such a stir throughout the city, Ren Gui became indeed

> *A filial son of a fiery nature when alive,*
> *A revered god with a respected name after death.*

Followed by the neighbors, Ren Gui arrived in the yamen of the magistrate of Lin'an. Hearing that it was a case of murder, the much appalled magistrate quickly called his court to order. With lictors standing in rows flanking both sides of the hall, Ren Gui put down the five heads and the knife and dropped to his knees.

"My name is Ren Gui," he said. "Twenty-eight years of age, I am a native of this prefecture, where my ancestors established their residence on Ox-Skin Street by the mouth of the river. My mother having died early, I used to live with only my blind father. In the winter of the year before last, I married, through a matchmaker, the daughter of Mr. Liang, who lived near Rixin Bridge by the river, and the marriage lasted until today. Without any business of my own, I have been working as a manager for Squire Zhang's store. My long work day displeased the woman who was my wife. On the eighteenth day of the eighth month last year, my father was sitting downstairs intoning Buddha's name when Zhou De came. Claiming himself to be a cousin of the woman's, while actually he was a neighbor who had begun an illicit affair with her before she married me, he went upstairs to talk with her. From then on, he came frequently. But my father, being blind, had no idea what was going on.

"One day, my father told me, 'There is a cousin who often comes to sit upstairs. There must be an affair going on.' Thus warned, I lashed out at the woman, but, in a moment of credulousness, I believed her lies about my father's advances to her. Therefore, I sent her back to her parents' home three days ago. That same day, as I left my work late after the closure of the city gate, I went instead to my wife's home to stay for the night, much to the surprise of the adulterer, who then fled to the privy. Before I retired for the night, I also went to the privy, only to be grabbed by him and accused as a thief. At his cries, my parents-in-law, the woman, and the maid all came out and gave me a sound beating with sticks of firewood while the adulterer slipped away. I went back home in pain, upset that I didn't even have a way to avenge myself. However, when night came, I took a knife and went into their house, killing first my parents-in-law and the maid before I went upstairs and killed that slut. As I suddenly raised my head, I saw Zhou De lying on the beam on his stomach. So I climbed up and stabbed him to death with the knife. I am now turning myself in with the five heads in the hope of getting a fair judgement from Your Honor."

The magistrate was struck speechless. After he recovered a considerable time later, he questioned the neighbors to verify the truth of Ren Gui's words and, having established the facts, ordered Ren Gui to commit the confession to paper in his own handwriting. He then sent a county marshal and several lictors to take Ren Gui back to the house to verify the identity of the corpses. A heaving mass of spectators swarmed to the scene.

The trail-blazing god has shed his robe;
An unusual event this was indeed.

That day, they went together to Mr. Liang's house. All of the five corpses were identified and examined and the gate of the house sealed up. The county marshal brought his charge back to the magistrate's court, reporting, "Five corpses have been found and identified, just as the murderer confessed."

The magistrate said, "Even though he did confess everything, he is not to be exempted from punishment." By order of the magistrate, Ren Gui was beaten twenty strokes before he was put in a big cangue, iron shackles, and manacles and brought under guard to the prison cell designated for those under death sentence. The neighbors all returned home. The local authorities were instructed to sell all of the Liang family assets. The proceeds were used to buy five coffins. The bodies were laid in the coffins, which were then put aside to await further orders from the authorities.

In prison, Ren Gui won general respect for his character. His meals were well taken care of. No more need be said of this.

The magistrate of Lin'an took counsel with the officer on duty about Ren Gui's case. While it was agreed that Ren Gui was a man of real character, it was a pity that he had been so ruthless. There was very little room for any maneuvering in his favor. They had no alternative but to submit a report to the Ministry of Punishment, which, in turn, reported to the emperor, at whose orders the chief judge gave the verdict, after investigation, that the killing of the adulterous couple was justifiable but that of the parents-in-law and the maid was not. The local authorities were ordered to execute the prisoner within sixty days by dismembering his body in a local public place. The bodies of Mr. Liang and the others were to be cremated and all their property confiscated by the government.

Several days after the decree reached the yamen, the magistrate had the county marshal lead lictors and soldiers into the prison to bring Ren Gui out. When the magistrate showed Ren Gui the verdict from the imperial court, Ren Gui realized the extent of his crime and lowered his head in submission to the death sentence. By the magistrate's order, Ren Gui was freed from the cangue and chains and put on the wooden donkey. There, for all to see, were

> Four long nails that held him in place;
> Three hemp ropes that bound him tight.
> Two blades that were raised over him;
> One paper flower⁵ that fluttered in the air.

With two rounds of drum-beating and a bang of the gongs, the county marshal and his men pushed Ren Gui along to Ox-Skin Street to show him to the public. Headed by a poster displaying all the charges against him, the procession moved ahead. Men armed with clubs and sticks brought up the rear. They reached Ox-Skin Street and formed a circle around the execution ground to wait for the execution to take place at the scheduled time of a quarter to noon. Spectators filled up the street. As the time drew near, a most extraordinary thing happened. All too unexpectedly, the sky darkened. As the sunlight faded away, a fierce gust of wind sprang up. It blew up sand and stones, soil and dust with blinding force, driving the panic-stricken onlookers scurrying away in all directions.

In a short while, when the storm died down and the sky cleared up, the county marshal, the executioner, and onlookers found Ren Gui dead in an upright sitting position on the wooden donkey, freed from the ropes and the long nails. "Never has such an extraordinary thing happened in all of history!" exclaimed the crowd in unison. Numbed with awe, the overseer of executions hastily ordered the lictors to watch over Ren Gui's corpse, while he himself rode to Lin'an on a horse to report the matter to the magistrate, who, astounded by the news, promptly mounted his sedan-chair and, together with the overseer, rushed to the scene. Ren Gui had indeed willed his death. The magistrate went to the minister of punishment to make his report and ordered that the local residents keep a night vigil by the corpse.

The following morning, the matter was reported to the imperial court to be settled by imperial decree. The next day, at about nine in the morning, an order from the Ministry of Punishment was delivered to the magistrate, directing that convict Ren Gui's body be immediately cremated instead of dismembered. Consequently, the county marshal lit the cremation fire right there on the street. Tens of thousands of local residents as well as people from out of town swarmed to the scene, exclaiming, "Who has ever seen such an extraordinary thing?"

Upon learning about Ren Gui's death, Mr. Ren Senior and his daughter prepared some food, and, with the grandson supporting the blind old man and the daughter carrying the sedan-chair, they went to the execution ground and tearfully offered sacrifices. Then, Ren Gui's sister had her son help his grandfather back home, where they went on with their life, supporting the old man in his old age.

Let us not encumber our story with trivialities. Two months later, Ren Gui's ghost began to come out often at dusk. Those passersby who saw him would fall ill upon returning home, but all ailment went away upon the offering of food and paper money right there on the street. One day, Ren Gui attached himself to the body of a little boy who came to Ox-Skin Street to play and announced to the crowd of spectators, "The Jade Emperor loves me for the honest, upright, filial, and loyal man I was and, upon recommendations from the local deities and guardian spirits of various places, has ordered me to be the guardian spirit of Ox-Skin Street. All good people may build a temple where my house used to be and make offerings to me every spring and autumn so that I will protect the nation and the people." Having said these words, the boy regained consciousness. Who among the local residents would dare to be incredulous when witnessing such a display of superhuman power?

That very day, they pooled their resources and bought some timber, with which they built a temple where Ren Gui's house had stood. Without any delay, they hired a skilled sculptor of Buddhist images to make a holy image of Ren Gui, placed the statue in the middle of the hall, and reverently provided sacrificial animals and other offerings to him. Henceforth, the temple was never short of worshippers making offerings, nor was Ren Gui ever remiss in responding to their prayers. The temple still stands to this day. A later poet inscribed a poem on the wall of the temple in praise of Ren Gui's willing himself to death and rising to the status of a deity. The poem says,

> Iron will erode, rocks will decay;
> Only the spirit never wears away.
> In fighting debauchery he perished,
> As unflinching as King Yama of hell.

Wang Xinzhi Dies to Save the Entire Family

The white-haired dame by the Su Dike,
One wonders when she was born.¹
She followed the court to the south,
With tales to tell of old Bianjing.²
On an outing came the emperor,
Who grieved when reminded of the past.
Her fish soup, most savory in taste,
She offered to him, with both hands raised.

Our story takes place in the Qiandao [1165–73] and Chunxi [1174–89] reign periods of the great Song dynasty. After ascending the throne, Emperor Xiaozong honored his father, Emperor Gaozong, as the Imperial Patriarch. Good relations with the Jurchen state had been restored, and all was calm on the four frontiers. Military activities gave way to pursuit of the civil arts, and the emperor shared with the populace the joys of those halcyon days. Every now and then, Emperor Xiaozong escorted his father on excursions by dragon boat on West Lake, where no restrictions whatsoever were imposed on the merchants. Consequently, there was no lack of commoners taking advantage of the emperor's outing to make a profit. Wine sellers alone numbered over a hundred.

Now, among them was a wine seller with the surname of Song, who, being the fifth born in her family, was known as Fifth Aunt Song. She was famous in the old capital for her delicious fresh fish soup. During the Jianyan reign period [1127–30], she had followed the migratory flow as the emperor moved to the south and by now had established her residence, along with many others, by the Su Dike, to ply her trade.

One day the Imperial Patriarch's boat was moored by the Su Dike in the middle of a tour of the lake when conversation in the Eastern Capital dialect came into the old emperor's hearing. He sent an attendant to bring over whoever was talking. It turned out to be an old woman. An old eunuch recognized her to be Fifth Aunt Song of Fanlou in Bianjing, who was known for her delicious fish soup, and reported as much to the emperor's father, who, overcome with nostalgia at the mention of days gone by, ordered her to bring forward some of her fish soup. Upon finding the taste indeed exquisite, he rewarded her with one hundred in cash. As the story spread all over Lin'an, the rich, the influential, and the royal kith and kin all descended upon her shop to buy her fish soup, bringing the old woman enormous wealth. There is a poem that bears witness:

> *How much for a bowl of fish soup*
> *That reminds the emperor of old Bianjing?*
> *Buyers fought for it at double the price,*
> *Partly for his sake, partly for its taste.*

On another occasion, the imperial boat was passing by the Broken Bridge when the emperor's father went on shore and took a leisurely walk. His eyes came to rest upon an elegant wineshop. After he sat down, he noticed a white screen on which was written a lyric poem to the tune of "Wind through the Pine Trees":

> *Spring is a time I spend on flowers,*
> *Tipsy with wine by the lake every day.*
> *My horse knows well the way to the lake*
> *And goes by the wineshop with a proud neigh.*
> *There's song and dance midst the sweet red blossoms,*
> *And swinging in the green willow's shade.*
>
> *On a sunny day with a gentle breeze,*
> *Maidens find their hair flattened by flowers.*
> *The painted boat goes back, laden with spring,*
> *Leaving tender feelings on the misty lake.*
> *Tomorrow I return with leftover wine,*
> *To seek the scattered hairpins down the road.*
> (Good poem.)

The Imperial Patriarch read through the poem and was full of praise. To his inquiry as to the author, the shopkeeper answered, "The poem was written in a moment of drunkenness by Yu Guobao, student at the National University."

The former emperor said with a smile, "A good poem though it is, the line with 'leftover wine' lacks grace." Thereupon he asked for a brush-pen and amended the line on the screen to read, "Tomorrow I return on the last strength of the wine." That very day, Yu Guobao was summoned to his presence and made editorial assistant in the Hanlin Academy. Now that the screen in the wineshop had been touched by an imperial brush-pen, visitors flocked to the shop for a look, and, consequently, its sales of wine boomed, making the owner a very rich man. A later poet had this to say about Yu Guobao's fortunate encounter with the emperor's father:

He wrote on the white screen, tipsy with wine,
Not meaning to be seen by royal eyes.
Who, you may ask, offered up his name?
The wineshop keeper, a real Wei Wuzhi.³

There is another poem in praise of the wineshop keeper:

Before the royal ink was dry,
All the town flocked to see the sight.
The sudden success of the humble shop
Bore witness to the royal grace.

During those peaceful times in the Southern Song dynasty, goodness knows how many people unexpectedly benefited from imperial grace. In the same period, however, there was also a famous man of heroic mettle accomplished in both the military and civil arts who, instead of chancing upon imperial favor, was falsely accused by some vile characters. These false charges led to a great misfortune, however absurd it may sound. This was indeed the work of fate, timing, and luck. Truly,

When your time comes, good luck falls in your lap.⁴
When your time goes, ill luck follows your heels.⁵

Our story takes place in the Qiandao reign period. In Sui'an County of Yanzhou, there lived a rich man named Wang Fu, courtesy name Shizhong, who had passed the local examinations. With his wealth and power, he ran the affairs of the region with an iron hand and held the officials under his influence. A true local despot he was. However, he killed someone and, because he came up against a powerful adversary, was banished to Jiyang District⁶ in the far south. However, on the strength of his connections with Zhang Jun, the duke of Wei, he managed to secure a pardon, using the pretext that he would render service to the empire by recruiting for the army. Thus he returned home and managed his assets so efficiently that he regained his prodigious wealth.

This Wang Fu had a younger brother, born of the same parents, named Wang Ge, courtesy name Xinzhi, who had lived with him since childhood. Wang Xinzhi was a man as erudite in learning as he was skilled in martial arts. One day, the brothers got into a dispute while drinking. In a fit of rage, Wang Xinzhi stormed out of the house, saying, "I swear never to return unless I make myself richer by a thousand pieces of gold!" With nothing of value about him other than an umbrella (*A hint of his impulsiveness*), he thought to himself, "Where to go? I've heard that in the region of Huaiqing, farmers and blacksmiths do well. Why don't I go there and see what will happen?"

With no traveling money for the journey, he hit upon a plan. As he had studied since childhood some martial arts using spears, staffs, and fists, he could well roll up his sleeves and make himself look like a martial arts master. Thus, wherever there was a crowd, he would put on a show either with or without his umbrella to function as a spear or a staff. Usually some people would applaud and give money. By not being picky, he was able to scrape a living and buy himself food and wine.

Not many days later, he crossed the Yangzi River, observing the terrain all along the way until he reached Anqing Prefecture. At a place called Madi Slope, about thirty li past Susong, he saw a dilapidated temple standing all by itself in the midst of a stretch of uninhabited hills covered with wood for charcoal. He said to himself, "If I set up a foundry here with a ready supply of charcoal, I'll be able to corner the market."

Taking the old temple as his home, he gathered together some local vagrants and had them make charcoal on the hills. With the money from selling the charcoal, he bought iron and set up a foundry. The ironware that they produced was then sold in the marketplace. Each of his employees had a well-defined job, and his combination of kindness and discipline won admiration and respect from all. In a few years, his foundry grew into a prosperous and sizable enterprise. He had his wife brought over from Yanzhou to Madi Slope, where he built a magnificent mansion with a thousand halls and chambers. He also came into ownership of a local wineshop, which yielded him decent profits each year. He learned that in Wangjiang County there was a Tianhuang Lake, about seventy li in circumference, that was teeming with fish and rushes. He acquired the lake as part of his estate and collected fish tax from the hundreds of fishermen who followed his orders.

With his wealth continually growing, he became quite a local tyrant, using his power to make rulings on all matters in the region. When he went out, he would wear a sword or a sabre and was followed by a large retinue, in much the same grand style as would be displayed by an eminent official. Poor people from far and wide flocked to him as to a marketplace. His generosity made them willing to lay down their lives for him. (*Such people, with their quickness of action, will be of use.*) He also used his wealth to befriend local officials of the county. With those who treated him well, he shared a cup of wine. As for those who set themselves against him, he would ferret out evidence of their misdemeanors. In less serious cases, he would bring them to court to tarnish their names. For greater offenses against him, he would have ruffians do away with them by the roadside and wipe out all traces of the crime. Therefore, all and sundry stood in fear of him and vied with each other to gain his favor. Indeed, he was

A Guo Xie born again,
A Zhu Jia given new life.[7]
His power felt all over the region,
His name known throughout the land.

Our story forks at this point. Huangfu Ti, the pacification commissioner[8] for the Yangzi-Huai region, a most generous man much to the liking of the gentry, was recruiting men of bold spirit from all over the land. He grouped the bravest among the recruited into his Army of Loyalty and Justice. They were well supplied with money and provisions and given intensive training from morning till night. Tang Situi, the prime minister, envious of his reputation, wanted to have his protégé Liu Guangzu take over the commander's post. (*Putting personal concerns over and above the interests of the empire is a corrupt practice common among court ministers past and present.*) Secretly he bade a trusted subordinate, a censor, to report to the imperial court, accusing Huangfu Ti of wasting money and grain on good-for-nothing hooligans less likely to fight a war than to become a scourge to plague the region. (*He does have a way with words.*) Consequently, the imperial court removed Huangfu from his post and replaced him with Liu Guangzu. Now Liu Guangzu was a mean and cowardly man bent on ingratiating himself with the prime minister. To bring to naught what Huangfu had done, he dissolved the Army of Loyalty and Justice and sent the men back to the fields, to prevent them from stirring up trouble in the region. What a pity that years of work by Huangfu in training the men into soldiers was now all gone in one day. Some of the soldiers returned to their native villages; others banded together and became outlaws.

Among the dismissed men, I shall now tell of two brothers, Cheng Biao and Cheng Hu, natives of Jingzhou. Both were skilled in the martial arts. The all-too-unexpected discharge order from Liu Guangzu set them discussing whom to go to for help, for they had spent all their pay and had no means of subsistence. Suddenly they recalled Hong Gong the martial arts master, who now ran a teahouse on Granary Lane at the south gate of Taihu County. Formerly also an aide-de-camp in the army, he had been on good terms with them. Why not seek him out and take his counsel about future plans? The two brothers gathered their belongings and made their way to Taihu County to look for Hong Gong. He happened to be in his teahouse when they arrived. After an exchange of greetings and amenities, the visitors explained what they had come for. Hong Gong treated them to a chicken dinner and put them up for the night in a nearby temple, for he thought his own house too small to accommodate guests.

The following day, Hong Gong invited the two men home for breakfast and, producing a letter, said, "I am honored that you came so far to see me.

I would keep you longer if I were richer and a better host, but I am recommending you to someone you can go to. I assure you that not only will you find the man to your liking, but you will also gain some modest wealth."

The two men took their leave with words of gratitude. On the envelope they read, "To be opened by Twelfth Master Wang Xinzhi of Madi Slope, Susong County." Following the instructions, they went to Madi Slope and presented Wang Xinzhi with Hong Gong's letter. Wang Xinzhi opened it and read:

> *I, Hong Gong, respectfully submit the following to Your Excellency Twelfth Master Wang Ge:*
>
> *Since I saw you last, you have been constantly in my thoughts. This letter is to introduce to you the brothers Cheng Biao and Cheng Hu, former members of the Army of Loyalty and Justice, who are exceptionally skilled in the martial arts. Now that they have been discharged by the new commander in chief, I recommend them to you in the hope of their obtaining posts in your household for the benefit of your son.*
>
> *Also, in my humble county, there are several productive lakes. Your Excellency has already postponed several appointments to inspect them. Please postpone no more. I will be eagerly awaiting your visit, for these will be valuable additions to your estate.*

Greatly delighted with the letter, Wang Xinzhi immediately called forth his son Wang Shixiong to greet the visitors. Wine was set out, and a room was prepared for their use. Henceforth, Cheng Biao and Cheng Hu lived in the Wang residence, teaching Wang Shixiong archery, horsemanship, and the use of spears and staffs.

Quite unnoticeably, three months passed by. Wang Xinzhi was to go to Lin'an on business. When the Cheng brothers heard that he was going away, they also stated their intention to leave.

"Where are you going?" asked Wang Xinzhi.

"Back to Taihu to see Master Hong."

Wang Xinzhi wrote a letter for them to take to Hong Gong and was about to see the Cheng brothers on their way when Wang Shixiong appeared and said to his father, "I haven't yet mastered the art of using spears and staffs. I would like them to stay a little longer so that they can teach me some more."

Wang Xinzhi yielded to his son's wish and said to the Cheng brothers, "My son needs more of your teaching. Please be so kind as to stay for another month or two until I come back to give you a proper send-off." The sincerity of the request made the Cheng brothers agree to stay.

Wang Xinzhi went to Lin'an and finished his business. Alarmed by rumors that the Jurchens had broken the peace treaty, the emperor was soliciting suggestions of ways to defend the empire. Wang Xinzhi submitted directly to the emperor a memorial in which he strongly criticized all peace initiatives: "Even at a time of peace, the empire will find itself in danger once it relaxes its readiness for war. The Yangzi-Huai region being of great strategic importance in the southeast, dissolving the Army of Loyalty and Justice could not have been a graver mistake." In conclusion, he said, "Unworthy though I am, I would fain lead all the loyal and brave men throughout the Huai River region in a vanguard contingent to regain the central plains and settle accounts left over for generations. Only in so doing can this humble subject make known his devotion."

After reading the memorial, the emperor convened a meeting of the Bureau of Military Affairs. Now the members of this bureau were a cowardly lot who knew no better than to dig a well only when already assailed by thirst. How could such men have enough vision to remove firewood before the danger of a fire arises? Moreover, who would be willing to break the rules and recommend a commoner? Besides, rumors about the Jurchen onslaught were by no means confirmed. Therefore, they gave the emperor no reply but politely invited Wang Xinzhi to stay in the city to await an opportunity to enter into service. Consequently, instead of hurrying home as planned, Wang Xinzhi stayed on in Lin'an. Truly,

> No court officials rise to save the land;
> A commoner offers service in vain.
> His gold spent, his furs in tatters,
> He regrets having written to the throne.

To pick up another thread of our story, having stayed for almost a year in the Wang household, Cheng Biao and Cheng Hu had taught Wang Shixiong everything they knew about martial arts and expected in return handsome gifts of gratitude. Wang Shixiong did indeed wish to offer generous gifts, but his father had not returned. Growing impatient with waiting, the Cheng brothers were determined to go. Wang Shixiong did the best he could to keep them, but in the end, his attempts failed. Caught at a moment when he was out of cash, he scraped together fifty taels of silver and gave each man twenty-five taels and a suit of clothes.

At the farewell dinner table, Wang Shixiong said, "I am greatly indebted to you for your instructions. I should be more generous in my thanks, but my father is still in Lin'an and you insist on leaving. With no access to the family account, I have only my small private savings to offer to you as traveling money. Please come by here again to give me another chance to express my gratitude."

Greatly disappointed at the meager amount of silver, the Cheng brothers thought to themselves without saying anything out loud, "Master Hong gave us to understand that we were to gain some measure of wealth because the Wang father and son value friendship much more than money. And so we came and stayed for a year. But for us to leave like this is not any better than if we had stayed with the Army of Loyalty and Justice. Had we known earlier, we would have left while Wang Xinzhi was at home, for he at least would have been more generous with traveling money. Now that he is still away and we've already had the farewell dinner, we can't very well stay on even if we want to." They could do no better than sullenly take their leave.

Before they set out, they asked Wang Shixiong for a letter to Master Hong. Not being much of a scholar, Wang Shixiong handed to them the letter that his father had written before and asked them to send Hong his regards. Wang Shixiong accompanied them part of the way before turning back.

The Cheng brothers walked till they were exhausted. When night fell, they found an inn and poured out their grievances to each other over a cup of wine.

"Wang Shixiong is not a three-year-old child," said Cheng Hu. "Don't tell me he can't take responsibility for a couple hundred in cash! He was just pretending to be poor so as to shortchange us!"

Cheng Biao said, "Granted he shortchanged us, but the boy is at least nice enough. The one to blame is Wang Xinzhi, for he thought nothing of us. In several months' time, he didn't even write us a letter. He did leave word that he would compensate us upon his return. But if he chooses to stay there for ten years, are we supposed to wait for that long?"

"These rich local despots are not at all like Lord Mengchang,[9] who valued friendship more than money. To think that the son has no control over money in his father's absence! How small-minded!"

"Nor is Master Hong a good judge of character," said Cheng Biao. "How could he have no other acquaintances to refer us to? Why did he have to send us off to that miserable place in the middle of nowhere?"

And so the complaints went on until late into the night, when, quite tipsy with wine, Cheng Hu suggested, "Why don't we open the letter from Wang Xinzhi to Master Hong and see what it says?" Thereupon Cheng Biao took out the letter from a bundle, wetted the seal, and opened it. It said,

> *Your humble student Wang Ge respectfully submits this letter to my honored mentor:*
>
> *It has been a long time since we met last, but you are often in my thoughts. You can well imagine how your letter brought me as much pleasure as if I were in your presence. I thank you for your recommendation of the Cheng brothers, whom I have kept for my son. However, they are now anxious to leave, and I,*

with an upcoming journey to Lin'an, find myself unable to offer them a hand-some reward. I feel quite ashamed for being so disappointing.

At the end of the letter was another line in smaller script:

As to that other matter, I will do what I promised upon returning from Lin'an, which should be sometime in the fall.

Respectfully yours, Wang Ge

Cheng Hu flared up with rage after reading the letter: "Being such a rich man, he could well have made friends with us by being generous with his gold and silk. After all, we did go to him for help, and, in the future, his path might again cross ours. We were not his hired laborers. What difference does it make how long we stay? All that talk about not being able to come up with handsome presents because we were anxious to leave was but an excuse. He never intended to give us much!" (*A valid point.*)

Cheng Hu would have ripped up and burned the letter if Cheng Biao had not stopped him and put the letter back.

"Master Hong did us the favor of recommendation," he said. "We need to show him the letter to let him know that it wasn't much of a deal for us."

Cheng Hu agreed, "Right you are."

They retired for the night without further ado.

The following morning, they rose and traveled for another day. On the third day, they arrived in Taihu County and saw Master Hong in his teahouse, where they sat down and exchanged amenities. Hong Gong had a concubine named Xiyi, who was a hard-working woman always busy with weaving, rais-ing silkworms, and other chores for the family. Hong Gong loved her dearly. However, she was so thrifty in managing the household that she would even grudge offering a cup of water to a guest. During the Cheng brothers' last visit, she nagged Hong Gong for quite a few days about his having treated them to supper and breakfast even though he had sent them away to a temple for the night. Now that the Cheng brothers were back again, Hong Gong dared not keep them for meals, but, there being no money to give them, he got it into his head to give them some of the few bolts of good silk in the house. Knowing full well that Xiyi would not let him do that, he went without her knowledge to his room and took four bolts. (*Being henpecked can be a cause of calamity, as will be shown in this case.*) He had barely stepped out the door with the silk in his arms when he ran into Xiyi, who blocked his way and demanded, "Old fool, where do you think you are taking these bolts of silk?"

Realizing he was not to get away with this, Hong Gong had no choice but to plead, "The Cheng brothers are good friends of mine. They came all the way here to say goodbye to me on their way home, and I have nothing to give them as a token of friendship. Just consider this a loan to me. Don't contradict me."

Xiyi shot back, "I didn't work my fingers to the bone weaving those bolts of silk just for them to be given away. If you've got silk of your own, go ahead and give it away as favors, but don't you touch what's mine!"

Hong Gong insisted, "They came all the way to see me out of the best intentions. I haven't even treated them to a little wine. How can I grudge them these four bolts of silk? Please, my good woman, let me have my way for once. As soon as they are gone, I'll give you a decent apology." With these words, he turned away.

Grabbing his sleeves, Xiyi said, "They may well have come a long way, as you say, but for what purpose? Last time they ate two free meals and this time they are expecting something again. I can't even bear the thought of using that silk for making clothes for myself. What do you owe them that you have to give it to them? If they want silk, let them come to me!"

Seeing that the woman was unyielding and afraid that the Cheng brothers had been waiting too long, Hong Gong hardened his heart, tore his sleeve free from her grip, and ran into the teahouse.

In desperation, Xiyi screamed, "Shameless scoundrels! They are no relations of ours, and yet they never cease harassing us! They should have known better than to expect much of petty teahouse owners like us! As the proverb says, 'To pay someone else's bills doesn't make him rich but only makes yourself poorer.' This old thing is too stupid to know what's good for him. All he does is bring home good-for-nothings to stir up trouble! If there's nothing left in your pot, would any of those friends of yours help you out with a handful of rice?" She deliberately stationed herself behind the screen and launched into a torrent of curses.

The Cheng brothers had heard every word she said when she was inside arguing with Hong Gong. Already greatly vexed, they grew more restless upon hearing the renewed tirade. Picking up their luggage, they headed for the door without waiting for a parting word with Hong Gong. Running up to them from behind, Hong Gong said, "My woman has been angry with me these last couple of days. That's why she's not too civil in her use of words. Do not take it amiss. Please do accept these four bolts of coarse silk as substitutes for a meal, and don't reject them for being too humble." The Cheng brothers turned a deaf ear and adamantly declined the offer. Hong Gong could do no more than turn back with the silk. It was not until Xiyi saw the bolts of silk that she stopped hurling abuse. Indeed,

> *The woman was a miserly sort*
> *Who hated to part with a penny.*

She brought shame to her man
And drove away kinsmen and friends.

Granted that it is a virtue for a woman to be hardworking and frugal, she should also show good sense in dealing with people. For example, Xiyi's stinginess made her husband lose face. It was all very well for her, because she did not have to emerge from her own house, whereas the man had to go out and face the world. How was he to conduct himself? There is no lack of instances where friendship would thus turn into enmity and, eventually, calamity. As the ancients put it so well, "A good wife brings peace to a man's life; a filial son brings solace to the father's mind."

Not to encumber our story with further idle comments, I will now come back to the Cheng brothers. They had expected Master Hong to offer them hospitality as before, so that they could confide in him and ask him to recommend them to a better place before they could work out a plan for themselves. Little did they expect to be given such a tongue-lashing. Thinking of a way to avenge themselves, they remembered Wang Xinzhi's undelivered letter and wondered about the reference in the letter to fulfilling some promise in the fall. "Wang Xinzhi being the scoundrel that he is, why don't we make him out to be a conspirator against the empire so as to get even with both of them at the same time? (*Too malicious.*) What an ingenious plan! Only no fact can very well be established from the letter, unless . . . " They left Taihu County and went to Jiangzhou, where they found an inn outside the city gate and put away their luggage.

The following day, the two brothers changed their clothes and hung around the gate of the pacification commissioner's yamen for a while before they returned to have breakfast. "It's been a long time since we went up Xunyang Tower," they said. "Why don't we go there today?" They locked the door and, equipped with some loose pieces of silver, made their way to Xunyang Tower. Atop the tower was a swarming crowd of sightseers. The two of them leaned against the balustrade and admired the view. Suddenly, a man tugged at Cheng Biao's clothes and exclaimed, "Big Brother Cheng, when did you get here?"

Turning around, Cheng Biao recognized the man to be a detective in the yamen with the nickname Bald Head Zhang. Cheng Biao promptly called forth his brother, Cheng Hu, and, together, the two saluted the officer, saying, "It's a long story. Let's sit down together and we'll tell you over a couple of drinks."

The three of them sat down around a table and ordered wine.

"I've heard," said Bald Head Zhang, "that you are teaching in the Wang household in Anqing. What great luck!"

Cheng Biao rejoined, "What luck is there to speak of? We almost got ourselves into big trouble!" He lowered his voice to a whisper and continued, "Wang Ge has been a local despot for so long that he has come to plot rebellion. He engaged us to teach archery and the skills of battle to thousands of his followers. Now that they have been well trained, he is planning a rebellion in the fall in alliance with Master Hong Gong of Taihu and asked the two of us to contact former members of the Army of Loyalty and Justice to join the rebellion. We turned him down and fled here."

Bald Head Zhang asked, "What proof do you have?"

"We have a letter from him addressed to Hong Gong, but we didn't deliver it," answered Cheng Hu.

"Where is the letter? Let me see it."

"It's at the inn," said Cheng Biao.

After paying the bill for their round of drinks, the three men went to the inn. Bald Head Zhang read the letter and said, "This is important confidential information not to be divulged to anyone else. I will immediately report the matter to the pacification commissioner. You two will surely be handsomely rewarded." With these words, he took his leave.

The following day, Bald Head Zhang reported the matter in great secrecy to Liu Guangzu, the pacification commissioner, who promptly brought the Cheng brothers to jail to obtain their depositions, which were then dispatched secretly with all speed to the Bureau of Military Affairs along with Wang Xinzhi's letter of reply to Hong Gong. The members of the bureau were appalled.

"Since Wang Xinzhi is still in the city waiting for an appointment," they said, "why don't we arrest him and bring him over for questioning?"

By the time they sent runners to arrest him, he was already gone. Being a man who valued friendship more than money, Wang Xinzhi had made friends with employees in the Bureau of Military Affairs who tipped him off as soon as they heard that things had gone wrong. Therefore, he escaped before the night was out. Having failed to seize Wang Xinzhi, the bureau officials became even more nervous and wrote a memorial to the emperor, who then issued a decree for the pacification commissioner to arrest Wang Xinzhi, Hong Gong, and their accomplices. The pacification commissioner, in his turn, passed the decree to arrest the rebels on to Prefect Li of Anqing and, from there, to the counties of Taihu and Susong.

Now Hong Gong, with a good many informants in Taihu County, got wind of the arrest warrant and took flight. But Wang Ge could hardly get away on short notice, encumbered as he was by his enormous assets. At the time, the post of Susong County magistrate was vacant. Temporarily in charge was He Neng, the county sheriff. Upon receipt of the order, he led more than two hundred locally recruited men and headed in the direction of Madi Slope.

Before he had covered ten li on horse, Sheriff He thought to himself, "I've heard that the Wang father and son are valiant fighters, with as many as a thousand foundry workers and fishermen in their employment. Am I not risking my life for nothing?" So thinking, he consulted his officers and led the men to a secluded place in the valley, where they stayed for several days before returning to report to Prefect Li, "Wang Xinzhi is indeed plotting a rebellion. His manor is heavily armed in preparation for resisting arrest. Being greatly outnumbered, we had to withdraw. I plead that a more competent commander be sent so that the operation can be successful." Prefect Li believed his story and summoned Commander Guo Ze for a consultation.

"Wang Xinzhi has indeed been playing the local despot for quite some time in defiance of the authorities," said Guo Ze. "But as for the charges of rebellion, the facts have not yet been established. If he resisted arrest, why did the troops not suffer casualties? In my humble opinion, there is no need to resort to force. Unworthy as I am, I would be willing to go there to see how things are. If no incriminating evidence is found, I will ask him to come to the yamen to defend himself. If he refuses to come, we will still have time to get rid of him."

"That is indeed a most sensible suggestion," said Prefect Li. "Please be good enough to take on this mission. Be sure to take note of every detail. Let nothing escape your eyes."

"I understand."

Prefect Li continued, "How many men do you need?"

"About ten of my men will be enough."

Prefect Li offered, "I will also give you someone to assist you." So saying, he summoned Constable Wang Li, who came in, called out a greeting, and stood to one side. Pointing at him, Prefect Li said, "This is a brave man. You will find him useful in all situations."

As a matter of fact, Guo and Wang Xinzhi were old friends. He had meant to go by himself to offer some advice to Wang Xinzhi to help him out. Little did he expect that the prefect would send Wang Li along. If Wang Li, emboldened by the prefect's trust in him, tried to make a show of his abilities, Guo Ze would not have much of a chance to do as he pleased. Yet, afraid that rejecting the man would incur the prefect's suspicions, he could do no better than accept the offer. Disheartened, he took his leave.

The following morning, as soon as he was ready to be on his way, Wang Li went to press Guo Ze to set out on the journey. "We need to bring along the arrest warrant. If Wang Xinzhi comes to us, fine. If not, I have with me a hemp rope to put around his neck. The law is the law. We'll get him even if he flies into the sky!"

Already much vexed, Guo Ze rejoined, "Though I do have the warrant with me, we needn't produce it right off. We'd better tailor our strategy to the actual circumstances."

Under Wang Li's insistence on seeing the warrant, Guo Ze had no choice but to show it to him. When Wang Li tried to grab it, Guo Ze withdrew his hand and slipped it into his own sleeve. That very day, Guo Ze and Wang Li mounted their horses, left the city with a retinue of fewer than twenty men, and headed for Susong.

In the meantime, Wang Xinzhi, back at home from Lin'an, had learned about the arrest order from the Bureau of Military Affairs. Wondering how all this commotion could have arisen, he remained undisturbed, believing that there was no evidence of rebellion against him. When County Sheriff He led soldiers to arrest him, he was warned in detail ahead of time, though they never actually came. Surely, his spies were put to work this time as well. When he learned that Commander Guo had been sent from the prefecture with a retinue of fewer than twenty men, he warned himself that this could be a ruse to trap him. He alerted his retainers, and preparations got under way. At the same time, he ordered his son Wang Shixiong to lie in ambush with some able-bodied men to be ready for a fight the moment the government troops arrived.

Now, Shixiong's wife, who was the daughter of Zhang Silang, a salt merchant of Taihu, was a most wise woman. Seeing her husband in battle attire, she asked him what was going on. Upon learning the truth, she went out of her room and said to Wang Xinzhi, "Father-in-law, your reputation as a chivalrous hero has incurred the displeasure of the authorities over the years. If you have no intentions of rebelling, the authorities should know. The best course now is for you to go out and explain yourself. Charges against you will be largely dismissed, and the whole family may be left unharmed. If you are guilty of resisting arrest, what were false charges could become substantiated, and you will never be able to talk yourself out of them. Regrets will be too late by then." (*What happens later bears out her prediction.*)

Wang Xinzhi dismissed her by saying, "Commander Guo is an old friend of mine. He will surely have an idea for me." His daughter-in-law's advice was thus brushed aside.

In the meantime, Guo Ze arrived at Madi Slope. He headed straight for Wang Xinzhi's house, only to find Wang Xinzhi already at the gate, waiting for him.

"I did not know earlier that the commander was coming to this remote place," said he, "or I would have gone forward a long way to meet you."

Guo Ze said, "I have indeed no other choice but to pay you this visit. You will surely forgive me."

After an exchange of greetings, they stepped into the main hall and took their seats as host and guest. While engaged in conversation, Guo Ze noticed a constant stream of men coming and going in the hallways amid a conspicuous display of shining swords and spears. Terrified as he was, he refrained from speaking his mind, because Wang Li had planted himself firmly by his side.

"Who is this?" asked Wang Xinzhi.

Guo Ze answered, "This is Constable Wang, sent by the prefect."

Wang Xinzhi rose and saluted Wang Li, saying, "Please forgive me for any lack of respect." Wang Li was forthwith invited to sit down in a small chamber on one side of the hall, attended to by a steward. The rest of the men in Guo Ze's retinue were led to an empty room by the gate. In a short while, a rich banquet was laid out on three tables, one for Guo Ze as the guest of honor, one for Wang Xinzhi as the host, and another one for Wang Li. The rest of the followers enjoyed the banquet to the full, eating meat by the plate and drinking wine by the jar.

In the course of the banquet, Wang Xinzhi drew Guo Ze into his study and asked him about the purpose of the visit. Making no mention of the arresting order, Guo Ze said, "The prefect is convinced that the case against you is all trumped up and therefore sent me here to offer you some advice. If you refuse to come with us, you would be inviting suspicion. But if you are willing to go to the prefect's yamen to defend yourself, I will do everything I can to clear your name."

"Please enjoy the wine for now," said Wang Xinzhi. "We'll talk about this later."

Guo Ze was sincere in his desire to help Wang Xinzhi. Now that Wang Li was out of earshot, he pressed Wang Xinzhi to come to a decision, but the urgency in his tone made the latter grow even more apprehensive. As it was a steaming hot day in the sixth month, Wang Xinzhi asked Guo Ze to take off his robe and drink to his heart's content, but Guo declined. Wang Xinzhi did not let him go, despite his repeated attempts to extricate himself, but kept filling the wine vessels and plying the guest with wine. It was already three in the afternoon, but the banquet, which had started at nine in the morning, still showed no signs of coming to an end. Afraid that Wang Xinzhi might keep him for the night because evening would soon be setting in, Guo Ze made up his mind and, rising from his seat, said, "Every word I said was utterly sincere, without the slightest intention to deceive you. Make a decision as soon as possible whether you are following my advice or not, so as not to cause any undue delay for either side."

In a slightly inebriated state, Wang Xinzhi said, calling Guo Ze by his courtesy name, "Xiyan, you are an old friend. I will not hide anything from you. I am innocent. I am being falsely accused for reasons beyond my imagination. I would willingly go to pay my respects to the prefect, but I fear that he would try to ingratiate himself to his superiors and convict me anyway, without bothering to find out the truth. Even mice and sparrows love life. How can human beings not cherish their lives? I have here four hundred in paper currency. Please use it to get me two or three more months' time. I will also appeal to some powerful people in Lin'an to ask a favor from the Bureau of Military Affairs on my behalf. Only after this has been settled by the highest authorities will I dare to venture out. Please don't turn me down, if only for our old friendship's sake."

Guo Ze had no intention of accepting the money, but, afraid that Wang Xinzhi would suspect something and change his mind, he put on a smile and said, "Being a friend, I am naturally in your service. Why bother with gifts? I will accept this for the moment, but I'll return it intact to you later."

He held out his hand to take the bills, little knowing that Constable Wang was standing outside the window and had heard Wang Xinzhi offering money to Guo Ze. Angry that he was not offered any bribe, he banged at the window and roared in his drunken state, "A fine commander you are! The Bureau of Military Affairs acted on the imperial decree and ordered our yamen to arrest the rebel, but you are taking a bribe to grant him more time! Who else would dare do such a thing?"

It turned out that Wang Shixiong and his men were lying in ambush right behind the wall. At these words, they leapt out and bound Guo Ze with a rope.

"My father was such a good friend of yours," Wang Shixiong shouted angrily. "How could you try to coax my father into the yamen to his death while the imperial decree is hidden on you all this time! Why?"

Wang Li, on the other side of the window, was aware that things had gone wrong and took to his heels, only to be stopped by a big man with a sword. Named Liu Qing but better known as Thousand Catty Liu, the man was Wang Xinzhi's most trusted retainer. "Where do you think you're going, you scum?" he thundered.

Wang Li pulled out his sword from his waist and tried to fight his way through, but Liu Qing struck him on his left arm. He ran away in pain, with Liu Qing following close on his heels. Loud cries were heard from outside the manor, for Wang Xinzhi's retainers were cutting down Guo Ze's men, killing all of them. Struck a second time on his shoulder, Wang Li knew that he could not possibly make his way out. He threw himself upon the ground at the blow and feigned death. He was then dragged away with a hook and thrown onto the pile of corpses by the wall. In the main hall, with Wang Xinzhi in his seat, Wang Shixiong brought forth Guo Ze, and a body search produced the warrant from his sleeve. Wang Xinzhi read the documents and fumed with anger. As he gave the order to decapitate Guo Ze, the latter kowtowed and begged for his life, saying, "This has nothing to do with me. It was County Sheriff He's false report of your resisting arrest that stirred the prefect's anger. I came here on orders from above, not out of my own free will. If I can be allowed to verify the truth with County Sheriff He face to face, I will have no regrets if I die."

"All right then," said Wang Xinzhi. "I'll save your donkey head, if only to provide a witness against that dog of a county sheriff." He ordered that Guo Ze be locked up temporarily in a side room and that Wang Shixiong go to the charcoal hill and the foundry to assemble all able-bodied men to await further orders.

Now, the charcoal hill was inhabited mostly by timid peasants. At word of the Wang family's rebellion, they fled to less accessible regions of the mountain. But, most of the men in the foundry being ruffians, about three hundred of them gathered at the first call and went to the Wang manor, where oxen and horses were slaughtered in preparation for a feast for the new army. The Wang family was in possession of three fine horses capable of covering hundreds of li daily and worth a thousand pieces of gold each. Each had its own name. They were called

Smarty, Piebald Girl, and Barbarian Lady

Wang Ge also had a long-standing friendship with four remarkably valiant men. Who were they?

Gong Four-Eight, Dong Three, Dong Four, and Qian Four-Two

The foursome had also come to the manor and ate and drank to their hearts' content until the fifth watch struck. When the men were all well warmed with wine and food, Wang Xinzhi dressed himself up in battle attire. How dashing he looked!

His hair in a knot tied up on his head,
On his body a robe of white brocade.
Tight boots on his legs,
A girdle around his waist.
His quiver filled with arrows,
His sword held high.
How awe-inspiring he was indeed,
A hero from Madi Slope.

Wang Xinzhi mounted Barbarian Lady, led by Liu Qing, another none-too-gentle type. How did he look?

Whiskers hard as steel, eyes round as rings,
Eight feet tall in a brocade robe.

His iron arms, a thousand catties strong
Made the bravest shiver with fear.

Wang Xinzhi led a hundred men as the vanguard. Dong Three, Dong Four, and Qian Four-Two led three hundred as the main force, whereas Wang Shixiong, riding Piebald Girl, followed by Gong Four-Eight on Smarty with Commander Guo under his guard, brought up the rear with over one hundred men. After all the tasks and responsibilities had been properly assigned, three shots were fired, and the regiment set out to Susong to capture County Sheriff He. Indeed,

Men mean no harm to tigers,
But tigers make men their prey.

By the time they were about five li from the city, the sky had become suffused with light. Qian Four-Two ran up to Wang Xinzhi and said, "Why all this fanfare if we're only after a county sheriff? It would suffice to have several men charge in, tie him up, and bring him over."

"That's a good idea."

Therefore Wang Xinzhi called the procession to a halt, and, leaving Qian Four-Two with the troops to pitch camp, he himself led Dong Three, Dong Four, Liu Qing, and about twenty other men to press ahead. Approaching the city, they saw a group of children by the moat singing, with their arms locked together:

There is a Wang of two times six,
Who crossed the river in a stolen boat.
How many days to go after that?
A cup of warm wine will mark his end.

And so the singing went on. When Wang Xinzhi whipped his horse forward to yell at them, they suddenly disappeared from view. Misgivings began to cross his mind. It was already time for the morning court session when they arrived at the county yamen, but all was quiet, with nothing astir. Wang Xinzhi was about to dismount, when an old gatekeeper on night duty emerged, humming a tune. With one sweep of his arm, Liu Qing grabbed him and asked, "Where is County Sheriff He?"

"He went to East Village yesterday on some official business and has not returned."

Wang Xinzhi made the old man lead them out through the east gate. About twenty li later, they came upon a big temple called the Temple of Lord Fuying. Services at the temple, the largest of its kind in the entire county, were most devout and prayers most effective.

The old gatekeeper pointed at the temple and said, "Officials on business trips always stay here. You can go in and ask about the sheriff."

Wang Xinzhi dismounted and entered the temple. The caretaker was scared out of his wits at the awe-inspiring sight of heavily armed men on strong horses. He fell on his knees to greet the men. At Wang Xinzhi's inquiry about the sheriff, he said, "The sheriff did indeed spend the night here, but he left on his horse this morning at the fifth watch. I have no idea where he went." Only then did Wang Xinzhi believe the gatekeeper. He released the old man and had lunch in the temple. His men were sent out to search for the sheriff, but to no avail. At about three in the afternoon, his patience wore out. At his order, the temple was burned down to the ground. (*What does this have to do with the temple god?*)

On the way back, Liu Qing suggested, "Even though the sheriff can't be found, his wife and children are in the yamen. If we take them as hostages, surely the sheriff will show up."

Wang Xinzhi nodded his approval.

When they came up to the east gate, evening had not set in, but the city gate was closed. The fact was that Constable Wang Li had not died, but fled back in pain to the city and reported everything to the military inspector. The inspector was so mortified that all color drained from his face. On the one hand he ordered that the city gate be closed against a possible attack, and on the other, he reported the matter to the prefect, requesting that troops be dispatched to capture Wang Xinzhi the rebel and murderer. Seeing that the city gate was closed, Wang Xinzhi was about to set the gate on fire, when a gust of eerie wind swept down from the top of the city gate. It was a hair-raising terror of a wind. Even the horse Barbarian Lady reared and, neighing in fright, recoiled a few steps. With a loud cry, Wang Xinzhi fell from the horse to the ground. Truly,

> Dead or alive, no one could be sure,
> But his limbs were not moving at all.

With alacrity, Liu Qing raised him up, but he was found to be in a speechless, unconscious state, as if a spell had been cast over him. The best Liu Qing could do was to lift him onto the saddle and lead the horse onward, with Dong Three and Dong Four guarding him left and right. When they reached the south gate, they joined Wang Shixiong and twenty to thirty men with lit torches. They went another two li before Wang Xinzhi came to.

"How strange!" he said. "I saw all too clearly a god tens of feet in height with a head like a wheel and dressed in a white robe over a gold cuirass. He was sitting on the city wall with his feet reaching the ground. Numerous celestial soldiers were gathered around him. On the banners was written 'Lord Fuying.' With his left foot, this god kicked me off my horse. He was probably blaming me for having burned down his temple. Let's bring our main force here tomorrow and attack the city during broad daylight. We'll see what happens."

Wang Shixiong said, "Father, you may not know that Qian Four-Two was afraid that he might be implicated and left us after some kind of an agreement with the men, for, after his departure, many of the men also went away one after another. Two-thirds of the men are gone. It would be best if we return home before deciding what to do next." Wang Xinzhi's heart sank at the news.

When they arrived at their main camp, Gong Four-Eight gave the same report. As Guo Ze was still in chains, Wang Xinzhi pulled out his sword in a moment of blinding rage and cut Guo Ze in half. He led the men back to Madi Slope, but along the way many more of them deserted. Upon arrival at his residence, a count showed that only sixty men were left.

With a sigh, he said, "I have always been a man of loyal devotion, and yet I've been framed for reasons quite unknown to me. My plan was to capture the county sheriff to find out the truth behind all this and to avenge myself. Then I would have used money from the treasury to recruit brave men to wipe out all those corrupt officials in the Yangzi-Huai region and establish a name for myself throughout the land. After that I would have submitted myself to the grace of the imperial court and entered into the service of the empire to establish a career of eternal glory. It is a matter of fate that I have ended up in failure like this."

He turned to Gong Four-Eight and the others and continued, "I am grateful to you, my brothers, for having followed me all the way, but I cannot bear the thought of implicating you. Since a death sentence awaits a criminal like me anyway, I am already as good as dead. Why don't you all bind me up and deliver me to the authorities? At least you'll get yourselves out of trouble."

In unison, Gong and the other men said, "What kind of talk is this, Older Brother! You have taken good care of us. How can we turn our backs on you now that disaster has struck? We are together in life or in death. Please do not take us for Qian Four-Two."

Wang insisted, "Though it is as you say, staying at Madi Slope means certain death, for there is no retreat once government troops are here. Most government operations fade away after a brave beginning. Let us flee from here. Should heaven take pity on me and allow my family line to continue, this region will still belong to my offspring. Otherwise, my soul will never get to revisit this place."

With these words, tears gushed from his eyes. Wang Shixiong burst into loud sobs. Gong and the others also wept so bitterly that they could not raise their eyes.

"I'm afraid," said Wang Xinzhi, "that government troops will arrive by dawn. We must lose no time. There are some fishermen by Tianhuang Lake who can be counted upon to give us refuge for the time being." So saying, he took out all the valuables he had with him and gave half to the Dong brothers, telling them to go to Lin'an as merchants under assumed names to spread the word that Sheriff He had wronged Wang Xinzhi, who was by no means a rebel against the empire. The two of them were to explain the case to everyone they encountered and lament the injustice. The other half of the valuables he gave to Gong Four-Eight, telling him to take his three-year-old grandson into hiding in Wu Prefecture. (*Preserving the family line. Sensible.*)

"The authorities," he continued, "will only expect me to go north to contact the Jurchens. They would never suspect that I'm still around. When the hue and cry is over, go to Sui'an County in Yanzhou and look for my older brother, Wang Shizhong, who will surely keep my son." He then gave the three fine horses to the three men. Gong objected, saying, "These horses are so unusual in their coat and color that they'll easily give us away. We can't ride them."

"If they are left to other people," said Wang Xinzhi, "no good will come out of it." Raising his sword, he killed the three horses in three sweeping strokes. Then he set fire all around the manor. As the merciless flames roared and leapt with fury, he bade a tearful farewell to Gong and the Dong brothers by the light of the fire. Seeing that her three-year-old son had been taken from her, Shixiong's wife, Zhang-shi, broke into wails of grief and threw herself into the fire. Had Wang Xinzhi followed her advice, things would not have come to this. Truly,

> *Good medicine tastes bitter;*
> *Good advice jars the ear.*
> *Women of wisdom*
> *Are worthier than men.*

Wang Xinzhi was consumed with grief, but nothing could be done. As daybreak was drawing near, he told the men that those not wishing to follow him were free to do whatever they wished. Taking his wife, his son, Liu Qing, and about thirty of his most trusted men, he headed straight for Tianhuang Lake, Wangjiang County. Once there, they boarded five fishing boats and rowed their way into the depths of the reeds for shelter.

To follow another thread of our story, Prefect Li of Anqing was greatly alarmed at the report from Susong County and promptly reported the matter to his superiors. At the same time, he issued to the various counties orders that they recruit militia to wipe out the rebels. Liu Guangzu, pacification commissioner of the Yangzi-Huai region, gave the matter more importance than it warranted in his report to the imperial court. The emperor accordingly issued a decree to the Bureau of Military Affairs to assemble troops from various counties so that the joint effort would stop the rebellion from spreading. Liu Guangzu thus gathered together four to five thousand men from various counties. Having learned that Wang Xinzhi had burned down his estate and fled to Tianhuang Lake, Liu Guangzu ordered his troops to advance by land as well as water. The Pingjiang region also received orders to use military force to stop the rebels from escaping. The commanders, being no more than petty officers such as sheriffs, were a fainthearted lot, for they had all heard of Wang Xinzhi's legendary bravery and the large size of his forces. The ground troops pitched camp outside Wangjiang City and the marines stationed themselves in a cove on the lake. They looted the local residents' homes and whiled away their time consuming the provisions. Not one of them dared venture out to capture the rebels.

More than twenty days elapsed without any sign of movement on the lake. Several of the more courageous men went out on a reconnaissance mission in a small boat. They saw continuous smoke rising from amid the reeds and heard the dull thunder of drums from afar. They dared not draw near for a closer look but turned back the way they had come. Several days later, the smoke stopped and so did the drumming. At the report of the scouts, the commanders ordered the boats out of the cove, and, with a great fanfare of gongs and drums, the soldiers advanced into the lake, waving banners and uttering loud battle cries. All small fishing boats had moved out of their way. As the men searched among the reeds where smoke had been seen, not even the trace of a footprint was to be found. All that could be seen were a few broken boats with the wooden planks charred black by piles of smoldering wood chips and grass roots. On the islet were two or three big drums with half-starved sheep tied to them. It was, in fact, the sheep's hooves that had been hitting the drums and the smoldering wood chips that had been giving off the smoke. Wang Xinzhi had gone east down the river quite some time before. (*Wang Ge being such an able military strategist, the imperial court would have been able to benefit considerably from his service. What a pity!*)

Afraid of being held accountable for Wang's escape, the officers had to give chase. As they came to the mouth of the river, they saw five fishing boats moored by the riverbank, with a man standing on one of them. The boats were recognized as ones from Tianhuang Lake. As they drew near for some questioning, the man on the boat said with tears in his eyes, "I am Fan Su, a native of Sichuan. I came here to do some peddling. After my business was done, I took a big boat with a fellow villager. We came here three days ago and ran into these five fishing boats. There were many strong men on the boats, saying that Twelfth Master Wang wanted to exchange the five small boats for our big ones for his men. I refused, but they pulled their flashing swords on me. So I had to let them have their way. Now, you tell me, how can I cross the river in such a tiny boat? I'll have a hard time trying to find another boat!"

The two officers took each other's counsel and said, "That Twelfth Master Wang must have been Wang Xinzhi. So his troops have already dispersed. Since all who remain with him are on those two boats, he will be easily taken. Let's go ahead with no fear."

When they came to Caishi Cliff, they saw an array of numerous battle-ships on the river. It turned out that Taiping Prefecture had sent out officers, who led their soldiers in blocking all the waterways out of Caishi and questioning all boats passing by so as to intercept Wang Xinzhi the rebel in flight. Having ascertained each other's identity, commanders from both sides met.

The commander from Anqing said, "Wang Xinzhi has fled from the lake onto the river and taken two big boats by force so as to accommodate his family. He must have come this way, but why haven't we seen him, though we are on his trail?"

The commander at Caishi stamped his feet in alarm and exclaimed, "I've been taken in by that cunning scoundrel! Two days ago, at about eight in the morning, two big boats carrying a family did indeed pass by. A man, all dressed up, complete with an official's cap and waistband, approached me, calling himself Wang Zhongyi, an official from Sichuan, and said that he was on his way to the capital for reappointment, as his previous term of office had expired. Now that I think about it, the characters for the name Wang Zhong-yi, with a few strokes added, can be rearranged into those for Wang Ge. That man was indeed none other than the rebel himself! But he's gone now, and I have no idea where."

The commanders consulted each other and, realizing that there was no way they could hide the fact that they had lost Wang Xinzhi, could come up with no better plan than to report the facts to their superiors. Growing even more suspicious at Wang's elusiveness, their superiors requested that the Bureau of Military Affairs offer a reward for his capture and put up portraits of Wang Xinzhi everywhere. Whoever captured Wang Xinzhi would be rewarded with ten thousand strings of cash and a promotion of three grades. Whoever captured one of his family members would be rewarded with three thousand strings of cash and a promotion of one grade.

In the meantime, the two boats carrying Wang Xinzhi sailed down to Lake Tai. A few days later, as word reached him that government troops were hot on his trail, he knew he could not hide there any longer and had the boats scuttled and sunk to the bottom of the lake. He then entrusted his family to the care of a fisherman to whom he gave a sizable amount of gold and silk, and promised to come back for them in a year. At the same time, he told Liu Qing and his son Wang Shixiong to take less-traveled roads to Wuwei Prefecture and give themselves up to the transport commissioner. Wang Shixiong was to explain that his father had no intention of rebelling but was the victim of a frame-up by County Sheriff He Neng. He was also to plead that the authorities take him under guard to get his father in his hiding place in the capital, so as to avoid dispatching troops and incurring much expense. Having been told firmly by his father to go without delay, for the sake of protecting the entire family, Wang Shixiong had no alternative but to do as he was bidden. After reading Wang Shixiong's confession and questioning him on details, the transport commissioner had him taken under guard to Lin'an to arrest Wang Xinzhi while, at the same time, notifying the Bureau of Military Affairs and other yamen.

Wang Xinzhi, all by himself now that he had made arrangements for his family, changed clothes and headed straight for Lin'an. After staying for several days outside the city without hearing anything about his son, Shixiong, he remembered that Bai Zheng, magistrate of the north district, was an old acquaintance of his. So he went to Bai Zheng's residence at night and knocked on the door for an audience. The sight of Wang Ge so frightened Bai Zheng that he tried to slip away, but before he could do so, Wang grabbed him and said, "Please have no fear. I am here to surrender myself, not to implicate you."

Only then did Bai Zheng calm down. "The authorities are after you," he said. "Why are you here?"

After giving him a full account of the false charges against him, Wang Xinzhi said that if Bai Zheng were to assist him in clearing his name with the emperor, he would leave the world without regrets. Bai Zheng kept him for the night. The following morning, Bai Zheng made a report to the Bureau of Military Affairs, and Wang Xinzhi was imprisoned at the Court of Judicial Review. To questions from the prison officials as to his family's whereabouts and his collaborators' names, he answered, "My wife and children all perished in the fire. The only one spared was my son Shixiong, who knows nothing about all this, for he has been traveling on business for many years. My followers are all local residents and have fled for their lives, and I do not remember their names." No more information was obtained from him despite severe torture. (*Brave man.*)

Now Bai Zheng, instead of claiming a reward and a promotion, took pity on Wang Xinzhi and helped him in every way to make his life in prison easier. The most extraordinary news of Wang the Rebel's surrender spread throughout the city of Lin'an. As word reached the Dong brothers, they also came to secretly offer bribes on his behalf. (*Important.*) By the time all officials high and low throughout the yamen had been bribed, Wang Xinzhi began to find himself treated a little better. While in prison he wrote a memorial to the emperor to the following effect:

> *Your subject Wang Ge had once, in a certain month of a certain year, offered to lead the righteous and the loyal in the Huai region in repelling the attacks of the barbarians and recovering the central plains for the empire. As sincere as I was in aspiring to serve the empire, how could I harbor any thoughts of betrayal? I have no knowledge as to who falsely accused me as a rebel, nor do I have any inkling as to what gave rise to the charges. It is my hope that I can confront the accuser so as to clear my name. If so, I will find peace even in death.*

After reading the memorial, the emperor ordered the prefecture of Jiujiang to send Cheng Biao and Cheng Hu under guard to the capital for questioning at the Court of Judicial Review. (*Fair.*) The report from the transport commissioner of Wuwei Prefecture arrived at the same time as Wang Shixiong. The day of the joint trial witnessed quite some activity. We hardly need say how grief-stricken the Wang father and son were at their reunion. The all-too-unexpected sight of the Cheng brothers as the accusers staggered them and revealed to them the cause of all the trouble they had gone through.

During the trial, the Cheng brothers said nothing, referring only to Wang Xinzhi's letter to Hong Gong as evidence.

In defense of himself, Wang Xinzhi said, "The reference in the letter to the meeting in the fall was about my plans to buy lakes in Taihu County. There was nothing more than that."

"Hong Gong is at large," said the judge. "How are you going to produce a witness?"

"I have heard that Hong Gong is now living in Xuancheng. If he can be brought here, everything will be clarified."

Not in a position to make a ruling on the spot, the judge ordered that the four men be placed under separate supervision. At the same time, he issued a subpoena to Ningguo Prefecture. In a couple of days, Hong Gong was brought to the capital under guard. Liu Qing bribed the guard and told Hong Gong how Cheng Biao and Cheng Hu had been the cause of everything. Confident that he was not to be convicted, Hong Gong entered the court with great composure. He related everything in order, starting from his recommendation of the Cheng brothers, to his invitation to Wang Xinzhi to see the lakes. He also gave an account of how the Cheng brothers were sour at the meagerness of the compensation they received from the Wang family and how they refused his offer of silk. He went on to say that the Cheng brothers kept Wang Xinzhi's letter of reply to him and, out of spite rather than anything else, devised this scheme to lay false accusations against innocent men. His deposition in court was duly recorded, and the Wang father and son and the Cheng brothers were brought out from jail to testify. Cheng Biao and Cheng Hu had nothing to say for themselves to contest the veracity of Hong Gong's statement. Wang Xinzhi, for his part, related how County Sheriff He had stopped midway and enraged the authorities by falsely charging him with resisting arrest. Since repeated questioning failed to produce any discrepancies in the accounts, the judge, having already accepted bribes, was determined to give a lenient sentence. The verdict read,

> This court finds the accused, Wang Ge, with a reputation as a knight-errant, not guilty of rebellion.
>
> The case against the said Wang Ge started when Cheng Biao and Cheng Hu deliberately misinterpreted Wang Ge's letter out of a personal grudge against him. Thereafter, Sheriff He's misrepresentation of facts marked the beginning of the use of force. A review of the facts has convinced the court that the accused was left with no other alternative.
>
> However, he was wrong not to have come forward with an explanation, nor should he have assembled thugs and killed government official Guo Ze and several soldiers. The motive is pardonable, but not the crimes.
>
> Consideration is also taken of the fact that the accused willingly surrendered himself to the authorities without the least attempt at resisting arrest.
>
> More than one man was involved in the killings, but according to Wang Ge's deposition, all of his men have fled, and he recalls no other names. However, the prefect's report made mention of a certain Liu Qing, whom it behooves the court to bring to justice so as not to let anyone go unpunished.
>
> With regard to Wang Shixiong, son of the accused, his involvement is difficult to establish, but his confessions taken in Wuwei Prefecture reveal no relationship to the crimes. Therefore, it is the judgment of this court that he be granted leniency on the grounds that he voluntarily surrendered himself to the authorities.
>
> Wang Ge is hereby sentenced to death and is to be executed without delay. His body shall be dismembered and his head exposed to the public.
>
> Wang Shixiong shall be flogged and banished to a distance of two thousand li.
>
> Cheng Biao and Cheng Hu shall also be flogged and banished to a distance of one thousand li for having pressed false charges.
>
> The above sentences are to take effect as soon as Liu Qing and other accomplices are brought to court. Hong Gong is to be acquitted on the basis of the fullness of his deposition. County Sheriff He Neng shall be removed from his post for his lack of competence in arresting the rebels.
>
> (The verdict sounds reasonable enough.)

The verdict was submitted to the emperor, who gave his approval. As soon as he got wind of it, Liu Qing sent word to Wang Ge in prison before the news was announced, advising the latter to commit suicide by taking poison.

Wang Xinzhi's death bore out the rhyme chanted by the children at the Susong city gate. Wang Ge was the twelfth child in the family, a fact hinted at by the line "There is a Wang of two times six." The line "Who crossed the river in a stolen boat" was a reference to his taking the two boats by force. As for "How many days to go after that? A cup of warm wine will mark his end," Wang Xinzhi did indeed wash the poison down with warm wine, bearing out the prediction. According to the ancients, children's rhymes are, in fact, prophecies by the heavenly god of the planet Mars, who assumes a child's shape. Even though Wang Xinzhi did not accomplish great deeds, the authorities made a mountain out of a molehill by moving troops through several prefectures, thus making Wang's name known throughout the capital and even to the emperor. It was not by accident that children's rhymes emerged to make prophecies about his end.

Let us not digress but come back to the story. After Wang Xinzhi's body was examined by the coroner of the Court of Judicial Review, the head was cut off and hung up on the city gate. Liu Qing hid the body, stole the head in the middle of the night, and buried them about ten li away from the north gate of Lin'an. The following day, he told Dong Three about the site before he turned himself in to the Court of Judicial Review. Not only did he confess to having been responsible for all the killings, but also to having quietly buried his master. (*Had he not done so, the case would never have been closed.*) No amount of torture could make him reveal the site of the burial place. Unable to take any more torture, he died that very night in jail. A later poet had this to say in praise of him:

> *Calmly he gave himself up to the law*
> *And for his master laid down his life.*
> *Of all those paid by the court,*
> *How many would die as Liu Qing did?*

With Liu Qing's death, the Court of Judicial Review brought the case to a close. Wang Shixiong and the Cheng brothers were released from prison and sent on their way into exile. The Dong brothers having already bribed the floggers, Wang Shixiong suffered not even a scratch on his skin. Cheng Biao and Cheng Hu, however, suffered a severe beating. The escorting guards were also bribed into tormenting the Chengs all along the journey. (*Hurrah!*) They had covered only half the distance when Cheng Biao died of illness. Cheng Hu was taken farther and was never heard from again. The heavily bribed guard escorting Wang Shixiong released him when they had gone only three to four hundred li. Wang Shixiong thus began the life of an anonymous itinerant performer of martial arts and peddler of medicine, but of this, no more need be said.

In the meantime, the Dong brothers put together their money and went to Suzhou, where they found Gong Four-Eight and took the child. Then they proceeded to Lake Tai, where they found the fisherman who was sheltering the other members of the Wang family. Dressed as servants, Dong Three, Dong Four, and Gong Four-Eight escorted the family all the way to Wang Ge's brother's residence in Sui'an County, Yanzhou Prefecture. (*Wang Ge is surrounded by men willing to die for him, as is shown throughout the story.*) Upon learning the details of the case, the brother, Wang Fu, was overcome with emotion and arranged housing for the newcomers. Gong Four-Eight and the Dong brothers relocated their families to live nearby. With Wang Fu as their patron, no one in the region dared raise any objections.

Six months later, when the excitement about the whole affair had died down, Wang Fu sent Gong and Dong Four to Madi Slope to dispose of Wang Xinzhi's estates. They discovered that the foundry was operating as before and were told, upon inquiries, that Qian Four-Two had taken over Wang Xinzhi's business. Of the local residents, only the fishermen on Tianhuang Lake refused to obey.

Dong Four said in indignation, "That traitor does know how to take advantage of people! How does he reconcile that with his conscience? I am going to avenge my brother Wang Xinzhi even if I have to die for it." So saying, he took up his sword and was on his way out to kill Qian when Gong Four-Eight stopped him.

"Don't do this," he admonished. "Since he is quite established here, the local people will be on his side. You'll be outnumbered and laughed at. It's best for us to report to Wang Fu before deciding on the next step."

The two men went to Susong. Little did they realize that they were passing by the residence of the late Commander Guo Ze. A man who recognized Dong Four wagged his tongue and commented to Guo Xing, servant of Commander Guo, "That short, fat man is Dong Xue, otherwise known as Dong Four, a trusted henchman of Wang Xinzhi's."

At these words, Guo Xing thought to himself, "How can I not avenge my master?" He waited till the unsuspecting Dong Four passed by before he struck a mighty blow against Dong's back. As Dong fell to the ground, Guo Xing yelled, "I have caught a murderer in the service of rebel Wang Xinzhi!"

Four or five men ran out of the house, and neighbors also swarmed to the scene. Gong was so scared he dared not try to rescue Dong Four but took to his heels. Guo Xing had the local headman tie up Dong's hands behind his back and shave his head clean. Beaten with a cudgel every step of the way, he was brought to the Susong County yamen. As the new county magistrate had not assumed office and Sheriff He was already dismissed, sitting in office was the chief clerk, who dared not make decisions on his own but sent the men to Prefect Li in Anqing. Prefect Li was still bitterly upset at having been reprimanded by his superiors for his exaggeration of Wang Xinzhi's case. Now that Wang's name was brought up again, he was so vexed that his head started to ache. Angry at the local headman for being so meddlesome, he said, "Wang's murder case was already settled according to imperial decree. Guo Ze's death has already been avenged. Why stir up all this trouble again? The chief clerk and the escort guard should have known better than to send the man here!" And so he ordered the release of Dong Four. Guo Xing and the others, thus rebuffed, went their separate ways. Dong Four, injured by the beatings, went back in pain to Sui'an County.

Let us turn now to Gong Four-Eight, who returned before Dong Four and gave Wang Fu a detailed report on how Qian had taken over the enterprise and how Dong Four was captured by Guo. Anticipating that Dong Four would be sent to the prefect, Wang Fu was about to send a messenger to Anqing to use bribery on his behalf (*It takes money to use bribery. This has always been so. What are the poor to do?*) when all of a sudden, a hairless Dong Four ran in and told his story, saying that if it had not been for Prefect Li's clemency, he would not be alive.

"Judging from the prefect's tone," said Wang Fu, "I believe that the case is closed. Though Brother Dong Four had a rough time, he brought us good news."

A few days later, Wang Fu led about twenty household servants to Madi Slope and asked to see Qian Four-Two. How would Qian dare to show his face when he heard that Wang Fu himself was here? He took his wife and children and fled before the night was out, leaving behind all the estates.

"These ill-gotten goods are not to be used," said Wang Fu. He gave all that was left behind to the local residents, who were free to take whatever they wanted. Even the houses were torn down. Then he bought timber, baked bricks, and made tiles for building another house. An inventory was taken of the foundry, and the whole business was returned to the Wang clan. Then Wang Fu went to Tianhuang Lake and distributed cotton cloth and money among the fishermen to win their hearts. Thus, Tianhuang Lake, with a circumference of seventy li, remained the property of the Wang family. Through some acquaintances, he bribed high and low throughout the prefectural yamen and got himself a business license in his name. After a ten-month stay in Madi Slope, during which he settled everything (*Wang Fu is also an able man*), he returned to Sui'an, leaving behind two servants in charge of the business.

Soon thereafter, Emperor Zhezong died. Upon assuming the throne, the new emperor issued a decree for a general amnesty. It was only then that

Wang Shixiong gathered enough courage to return home. He paid a tearful visit to his uncle Wang Fu in Sui'an, from whom he learned that members of the family were all well. He saw his mother again. His son, now quite grown up, had been named Wang Qianyi by Wang Fu. Joy and grief intermingled in Wang Shixiong's heart. Several days later, he asked for his uncle's permission to go with Dong Three to Lin'an to bring back his father's remains for a proper burial.

"This is an act of filial piety," said Wang Fu. "Of course I will not stop you from going. But if you go, go soon and come back early. There are vacant lots on Wujiang Mountain nearby with good locations for graves. I'll make arrangements for the burial for you ahead of time."

Wang Shixiong and Dong Three left. The journey was uneventful. In a couple of days, they were back with Wang Xinzhi's remains, which were then encoffined, and a day was chosen for the funeral.

After the ceremony, Wang Fu said to his nephew, "Even though the business in Madi Slope is doing well, it was there that your father met his misfortunes, and many of your father's enemies live there, too. Gong and the Dong brothers are easily recognized there. That's not the place for you. A long time ago, your father took offense at an idle remark of mine and resentfully went off to Madi Slope, and that led to this series of fateful events. Now I am going to give over to you all my business here, partly because it has been quite established, and partly because you can look after your father's grave here so that down in the Nine Springs your father may lay aside his grievances. As for the business in Madi Slope, I will move there with my family, for no one can do any harm to me there."

Wang Shixiong thanked his uncle, and that very day, Wang Fu handed over to Wang Shixiong all of the account books of the estates in Sui'an. Leaving half of the servants behind, he took his family to Madi Slope. Henceforth, the Wang family split into two branches, one based in Sui'an and one in Susong, which stayed in close contact with each other. Through his uncle's wealth, Wang Shixiong won the admiration and esteem of all. His wife having died by throwing herself into a fire, he stayed a widower for the rest of his life and devoted himself to the education of his son. Later, Wang Qianyi passed the imperial examination for military officers at the provincial level and rose to be commander of the imperial guards. The family line after him thrived. Thus this story is called "Wang Xinzhi Dies to Save the Entire Family." A later poet had these lines in praise of him:

> *An upright and awe-inspiring hero,*
> *He left home barehanded but made his fortune.*

A man of honor, he never lacked help,
Yet small-minded villains brought him to ruin.
Sword in hand, he was forced into revenge;
Bravely he surrendered to save his family.
Nobly, his brother yielded his home;
Who would malign his eternal name?

Shen Xiaoxia Encounters the Expedition Memorials

At leisure in my study, I read tales old and new,
And marvel at this amazing story.
Good officials are crushed by evil ones;
In helpless wrath I weep for the hero.
But do not hasten to resign office yet,
For the sun and moon cannot stay darkened for long.
Retribution is bound to come in the end,
For heaven still marks off good from evil.

As the story goes, with a saintly emperor on the throne in the Jiajing reign period [1522–66] in the present dynasty [Ming], crops thrived in favorable weather and the empire and its people enjoyed peace and prosperity. However, the unfortunate appointment of an evil minister compromised the integrity of imperial rule and brought the empire to the brink of chaos. Who was this evil minister? He was Yan Song, courtesy name Jiexi, a native of Fenyi in Jiangxi. He had won favor by playing the sycophant, ingratiating himself with eunuchs, setting up Taoist altars, and writing invocations to please the emperor.[1] So he rose rapidly to prominence. For all his feigned humbleness and modesty, he had, in fact, a suspicious and evil mind. His calumnies ruined the grand academician Xia Yan, whereas he himself took over as prime minister, with full power over the imperial court as well as the general public. His son Yan Shifan, who rose from the status of an official student to become vice-minister of the Ministry of Works, was an even more ruthless man, but he was not without such talents as a malicious mind might possess, for he had wide learning, a good memory, and a quick, calculating brain. Jiexi, his father, had the greatest trust in his advice and invariably sought his counsel on all thorny problems. Hence the father and the son came to be known in the court as the Elder Prime Minister and the Younger Prime Minister.

In collusion, father and son seized power, solicited bribes, and sold titles and government posts for profit. Those wishing to attain wealth and status needed only to bribe the father and son generously and honor them as godfathers to be appointed to eminent posts. As a consequence, unsavory characters flocked to them until all government offices were filled with their trusted lackeys. All those who stood out against them were immediately crushed. Less serious offenders were subject to beatings and exile. Graver offenses were punishable by death. What a terror they were! Only those prepared to die dared venture remarks on the side of justice. Anyone other than such passionately loyal and patriotic men as Guan Longfeng[2] and Bi Gan[3] would rather sacrifice the interests of the empire than offend the prime minister. Such a state of affairs prompted an anonymous poet of the time to change the poem "On Prodigies"[4] into this quatrain:

> You need not study hard while you are young;
> For money will buy you a fine career.
> Consider how Prime Minister Yan Song
> Appoints to high office none but the rich.
> (This poem was incorporated in the play *Story of the Crying Phoenix*.)

Changes to another poem produced the following:

> The Son of Heaven favors the powerful;
> To open one's mouth is to invite trouble.
> All other pursuits are of little worth;
> Flattery is the noblest of them all.[5]

Secure in the knowledge that they were favored by the emperor, Yan Song and his son wallowed in vice. Their mountain-high record of evildoings prompted a loyal subject to stand up against them. His remarkable deeds have been kept alive in an extraordinary story. He died, but it was a death that brought him eternal fame. Verily,

> A family with filial sons finds happiness;
> An empire with loyal officials enjoys peace.

The man, a native of Shaoxing in Zhejiang, was named Shen Lian, courtesy name Qingxia. Endowed with outstanding talent in the military as well as civil arts, he aspired to bring peace to the land and the people. From an early age, he greatly admired Zhuge Liang[6] for his integrity and loved to recite the two memorials contained in the collection of Zhuge Liang's works—memorials to the throne requesting permission for an expedition against the enemy. Hundreds of times he copied these petition memorials by hand and posted them all over his walls. Each time he had drunk a lot, he would recite them aloud, and, when he came to the line "Devote my life to my duty till I die," he would heave deep sighs and burst into passionate weeping. Accustomed to his ways, people called him "the mad man."

In the cyclical year of *wuxu* [1538] during the Jiajing reign period, Shen

Lian passed the imperial examinations and, as a scholar with a *jinshi* degree, was appointed as a county magistrate, a post that he served for three terms in the counties of Liyang, Chiping, and Qingfeng consecutively, and a fine magistrate he turned out to be. Indeed,

> *His subordinates observed the law;*
> *Incorrupt, he had no love for money.*
> *The local despots were held in check,*
> *And the common folk slept in peace.*

Being an outspoken man loath to fawn on his superiors, he was transferred to the position of registrar of the imperial guards. Soon after arriving in the capital, he boiled with indignation when he discovered that the Yan family was laden with ill-gotten goods. One day, at an official banquet, he was disgusted by the arrogance of Yan Shifan. In the midst of the drinking, Yan Shifan ranted and raved as if no one else were present and asked for a huge wine vessel. Those unable to finish the wine were subject to punishment. The vessel was big enough for over two gallons of wine, but none of those present dared refuse, for fear of Yan Shifan's power. There was only a Censor Ma who, having no capacity for wine, pleaded to be excused when Shifan deliberately set the vessel before him. As Shifan turned a deaf ear to his pleas, Censor Ma had to comply, but no sooner had his lips touched the wine than his face flushed red and his eyebrows knitted together in an expression of crushing misery. Shifan went down the table, grabbed Censor Ma by one ear, and forced the wine down his throat. The censor could do no better than hold his breath and swallow the wine in successive gulps. It would have been all right if he did not take in the wine, but, as it was, he felt as if the sky and the earth had changed places and the walls were all revolving around him. Feeling weak and unsteady on his feet, he could hardly manage to keep himself from falling.

While Shifan clapped his hands and roared with laughter, Shen Lian's anger flared. All of a sudden, he stood up, rolled up his sleeves, seized the wine vessel, filled it to the brim, and walked up to Shifan. "Censor Ma is too drunk to return the courtesy that you did him," said he. "So let me do the honor for him."

A stunned Shifan was about to raise his hand to decline the offer when Shen Lian continued harshly with a stern look, "If others can drink it, so can you. Others may fear you, but not I, Shen Lian!"

Grabbing Shifan by one ear, he forced the wine down Shifan's throat, doing just what Shifan had done to Censor Ma. As Shifan finished up in one gulp, Shen Lian tossed the vessel on the table, clapped his hands, and roared with laughter, just as Shifan had done. (*Hurrah! Guan Fu[7] was no hero, because he fawned on the prime minister before turning against him.*

Guan Fu was a brave man at best, but Shen Lian here is a man of honor and loyalty.) All of the other officials present were so frightened that their faces were drained of all color. They hung their heads and dared not make a sound. When Shifan feigned drunkenness and left the banquet, Shen Lian did not rise to see him off.

Remaining seated in his chair, he sighed, "The Han dynasty and the traitor can never coexist!" He repeated this quotation from Zhuge Liang's second petition memorial seven or eight times, comparing the Yans to Cao Cao and his son.[8] Though the others were breathless with fear that Yan Shifan might hear him, Shen Lian himself took no notice of them but continued to drink cup after cup and did not leave until he had drunk himself to a stupor.

When he woke up at the fifth watch, he thought to himself, "In an outburst, I forced wine down that scoundrel Yan Shifan's throat. He will certainly seek revenge out of spite. Since I've done it, I might as well carry it through and get ahead of him. The vices of the Yan father and son have stirred the anger of humans as well as gods. But with the emperor so firmly on their side and my position so humble that my words carry no weight, I need to bide my time until the right moment before I strike. However, I cannot afford to wait. Let me imitate Zhang Liang, who attacked the First Qin Emperor at Bolangsha. Even though he missed, he served as an example for all."

Resting his head on the pillow, he mentally composed a memorial to the emperor. By daylight, when he had the words ready in his head, he rose, burned some incense, washed his hands, and wrote the memorial, which enumerated ten major crimes of Yan Song and his son, ranging from their seizure of power and acceptance of bribes to their acts of deceiving the emperor and endangering the empire. He pleaded that the Yan father and son be executed in the interests of the empire.

The emperor responded by a decree that said, "For his calumny against court ministers and his attempt to seek fame for himself, it is hereby ordered that Shen Lian be given a hundred heavy strokes by the imperial guards and exiled, as a civilian without official rank, to the northern frontier."

Yan Shifan sent a messenger to instruct the imperial guards to make sure that Shen Lian was beaten to death. Fortunately, the captain, Lu Bing, was a man with a mind of his own. He had great respect for Shen Lian's integrity and, moreover, as his subordinate, was on quite good terms with him. Therefore, he went out of his way to protect Shen Lian and used, for the beating, only the middle portion of the rod instead of the tip, thus inflicting less pain. (*Lu Bing is a henchman of the Yans. The fact that he went out of his way to protect Shen shows that there is still some goodness in him.*) Thereafter, Shen Lian registered at the Ministry of Revenue as a citizen of Bao'an Prefecture. With his wounds still unhealed, he gathered together his belongings that very day and, with his wife and children, hired a carriage and rode out through the city gate in the direction of Bao'an.

Shen Lian's wife, originally of the Xu clan, had given him four sons. The oldest son, Shen Xiang, a prefectural student with a stipend, had remained in Shaoxing. The second and third sons, Shen Gun and Shen Bao, had followed their parents to the capital to pursue their studies. The youngest son, Shen Zhi, was only one year old. As the family of five set out on their journey, not a single person from the entire assembly of civil and military officials ventured to come and see them off, for fear of the Yans' power, as this poem testifies:

> A piece of paper angered the mighty;
> Sadly he set off for the wilderness.
> Acquaintances dared not see him off,
> Lest they offend that evil man and come to grief.

Let us pass over the hardships of the journey. Fortunately, the family made it to Bao'an Prefecture. Being part of Xuanfu Military Region, Bao'an was a remote place with none of the glamour of cities closer to the center of the empire. This alien land was nothing but desolation wherever you looked. Moreover, days upon days of dismal rain had so darkened the sky and the earth that the place looked doubly heartrending. They wished to rent a house, but, there being no acquaintances to guide them, they were at a loss as to where to find lodging. As they were wondering what to do, a man with a small umbrella came into view. Noticing the baggage by the roadside and impressed by Shen Lian's refined looks, the man stopped and asked, after a closer look, "May I ask your name, sir? And where are you from?"

"My surname is Shen," replied Shen Lian. "I just came from the capital."

"I've heard that there is a Registrar Shen in the capital who wrote a memorial to the emperor, asking that Yan Song and his son be executed. Might you be he?"

"Yes, I am."

"I have long admired you. I am so happy to meet you. This is not a place to talk. My humble home being not far from here, allow me to take you and your family there before you decide what to do next."

The man's sincerity made Shen Lian decide to oblige him. They soon arrived. Though not an imposing mansion, it was nevertheless a fine house. In the main hall, the man saluted Shen Lian with folded hands and dropped to his knees in a deep bow. In great haste, Shen Lian returned the salutation and asked, "Who might you be? Why are you so kind to us?"

"I am Jia Shi," replied the man. "I have the title of battalion commander of the local garrison, a title that I inherited from my older brother, who died recently without leaving a son. But, with the treacherous Yans in power, all those who inherit ranks must pay heavy bribes. I have no wish to hold office. Thanks to my ancestors, I have a few *mu* of land to make a living with. The other day, I heard about your attempt to impeach the Yans. You are truly a most loyal official and a most righteous man. Then I heard that you were in this area. I was dying to see you but never expected that my path would, by heaven's will, cross yours. This is the luck of three lifetimes!" With these words, he dropped to his knees again, only to rise after Shen Lian insisted on raising him to his feet. He was then introduced to Shen Gun and Shen Bao. Jia Shi told his wife to take Shen Lian's wife to the interior of the house to arrange for their lodging. After the luggage had all been unloaded, the carriage driver was sent away. Jia Shi then had his men kill a pig and buy wine for the guests.

"On such a rainy day," said Jia Shi, "I don't think you would have a chance of finding lodging anywhere else. Please put your mind at ease and feel free to have some cups of wine to refresh yourselves after the hardships of the journey."

Shen Lian said in gratitude, "We just met by chance. How can I deserve such hospitality?"

Jia Shi rejoined, "Mine is but a humble farmer's cottage with nothing more to offer than coarse food. I hope you won't mind." The host and the guest fell into a conversation deploring current events and found each other's company so congenial that they wished they had met earlier.

After having spent the night, Shen Lian rose the following morning and said to Jia Shi, "I would like to look for a house for my family. Would you please give me some guidance?"

"What kind of house?" asked Jia Shi.

"I would be most happy to have one like yours. As for rent, I'll follow whatever advice you give me."

"That can be easily done." So saying, Jia Shi went off but returned after a short while. "There is no lack of houses for rent," said he, "but they are all dirty and damp. A decent house is hard to come by on such short notice. Why don't you just stay here a while? I'll take my family to live with my wife's parents until you return to the capital. Wouldn't that be nice?"

Shen Lian objected, "I am grateful for your kindness, but how can I take over your house? I will never hear of it."

Jia Shi rejoined, "I may be nothing more than a farmer, but I do know right from wrong. Much as I admire you for being a man of honor and integrity, I have not been able to serve you. Now that heaven grants me the opportunity to offer these humble rooms to you as a temporary residence, please do accept my goodwill." He had hardly finished speaking before he instructed his men to bring out the cart, the horse, and the donkey to carry off his valuables and personal belongings. Furniture and housewares were left in the house for Shen to use. Overwhelmed by such generosity, Shen Lian expressed willingness to pledge brotherhood with him. (*To have such a sworn brother is by no means a bad deal.*)

"I am but a village farmer," said Jia Shi. "How would I dream of aligning myself with an eminent official?"

Shen Lian protested, "It is the mind and sentiment that true men value. What does social status matter?"

Jia Shi, being the younger of the two by five years, honored Shen Lian as his older brother. Shen Lian, in his turn, made his two sons honor Jia Shi as their uncle. Jia Shi also called forth his wife to greet the new relatives. After having partaken of the dinner with Shen Lian, Jia led his wife away to live with his parents-in-law, while Shen Lian stayed on in Jia Shi's house. A contemporary poet had this to say about Jia Shi's offering his house:

> Out of true friendship from a chance encounter,
> He moved away and offered his house.
> While all too many kinsmen and friends
> Shamefully fight for estate and money.

As news spread throughout Bao'an that Registrar Shen had been banished to this region for having made accusations against Prime Minister Yan, all the local elders came to pay their respects to him. Some brought along firewood and rice, some brought wine and food, and some sent their sons and brothers to him to be his students. Every day, Shen Lian gave talks to local residents about loyalty, filial piety, and the deeds of men of honor and justice in history. At rousing moments in his speeches, he would pound the table and shout at the top of his voice, his hair standing on end. At other times he would heave long sighs of grief and let tears freely course down his cheeks. The audience, old and young alike, was held spellbound. When he contemptuously cursed the Yans, they would join in. Anyone who did not do so would be accused by the rest of the audience of being lacking in their sense of justice and loyalty. This spontaneous reaction later became a tradition. (*Source of trouble.*) As word spread that Registrar Shen was as skilled in the military arts as he was in letters, they also asked him to join them in archery practice.

He ordered that three effigies be made of straw and wrapped up in cloth. On one of them was written "Li Linfu, evil prime minister of the Tang dynasty." On another was written "Qin Hui, evil prime minister of the Song dynasty." And on the third one was written "Yan Song, evil prime minister of the Ming dynasty." The three effigies were used as targets. Those wishing to shoot at Li Linfu were to cry out, "Villain! Here comes my arrow!" The same thing was done to the other two effigies.

Shen Lian got the unsophisticated and outspoken Northerners so excited that they never worried that the Yan family might hear about what they were doing. As the old proverb says, "The only way to prevent people from knowing is not to do it." (*Do not do something just for the sake of gratification. This is a case in point.*) Families with power and influence never lack informers. What Shen Lian was doing was promptly reported to Yan Song and his son. Deeply angered, Yan Song and his son planned to find some excuse to kill Shen Lian so that he could not pose a threat to them any more.

As the post of military governor of Xuanfu and Datong happened to be vacant at the time, Prime Minister Yan ordered the Ministry of Personnel to give the post to his godson Yang Shun. The Ministry of Personnel complied. As Yang Shun went to the Yan residence to bid the Yans farewell, Yan Shifan set out wine in his honor. In the midst of the drinking, Yan Shifan dismissed all others present and told Yang Shun to find out Shen Lian's misdemeanors. Yang Shun left with profuse promises to carry out the order. Truly,

> *The poison was ready to mix with the wine;*
> *The sword was made, awaiting the hand to strike.*
> *Pity the honorable Mr. Shen,*
> *Boasting before the men of straw.*

Soon after Yang Shun assumed office, Altan Khan, the Tartar chief at Datong, invaded the Yingzhou[9] region. Over forty strongholds were taken and numerous men and women were captured. Yang Shun dared not send forth his troops to the rescue. Instead, he waited until the Tartars were gone before ordering his men to give chase. Just as in a real battle, gongs and drums were beaten, banners were unfurled, and cannonballs were shot, but all this was done just for show, because not even the shadow of half a Tartar was anywhere in sight. Knowing fully well that he would be held accountable for having missed the opportunity to strike, Yang Shun secretly ordered the commanders and soldiers to capture civilians who were in hiding from the troops, shave and cut off their heads, and present them as Tartars' heads to the Ministry of War to claim credit. Goodness knows how many innocent civilians were slaughtered as a result.

Shen Lian flew into a rage when he heard of this. He wrote a letter and asked a lieutenant to deliver it to Yang Shun, but the lieutenant, knowing all too well that Shen was a troublemaker prone to making offensive remarks, refused to deliver the letter. Thereupon Shen Lian donned a blue robe and a small cap and stood outside the yamen waiting for Yang Shun to come out so he could deliver the letter himself.

Yang Shun took the letter, only to find that it said, roughly,

One man's fame is all too trivial a matter in comparison with the overriding importance of human lives. To kill civilians for the sake of claiming undeserved credit is absolutely unconscionable. Moreover, the Tartars did nothing more than loot and capture our people, whereas our own troops killed. The officers thus committed crimes worse than those of the Tartars.

At the end of the letter was a poem that ran as follows:

He resorts to killing to claim credit;
Behind his glory lie ten thousand bones.
On stormy nights in the battlefields,
The aggrieved ghosts call out for their severed heads.

The letter so angered Yang Shun that he tore it into pieces.

Having also written an essay in memory of the dead, Shen Lian and his followers prepared offerings and made bows heavenward in a memorial service to honor those who died so unjustly. He also wrote this poem titled "Lament at the Frontier":

The Tartars' beacons rise high at Datong;
How the Chinese general does his job!
He kills not the Tartars but our own men
Whose blood, alas, dyes red the frosty swords.

He also wrote another poem:

They fled from the Tartars to save their lives,
Only to meet greater peril.
Had they known their heads were to pass as Tartars',
They would have joined the Tartars' ranks.

Governor Yang had under him a trusted commander named Luo Kai who copied the poems and the memorial essay and secretly presented them to Yang Shun. Stirred into even greater rage, Yang Shun changed the first poem to read,

The Tartars' beacons rise high at Datong;
The Chinese general does his job in vain.
If the Tartars could kill that villain,
He need not die from the emperor's sword.

He also wrote a secret letter, which he sealed tightly with the poems, and made Luo Kai deliver it to Yan Shifan. The letter said, "Out of spite against the prime minister and his son, Shen Lian is taking advantage of the situation to seek revenge by engaging knights-errant and assassins. During the Tartar invasion, he wrote these quatrains, urging the Tartars to 'kill that villain.' His sinister intentions are all too clear."

Appalled at the letter, Shifan took counsel of Lu Kai, his trusted censor, who said, "Unworthy as I am, I can relieve you of this major source of worry if I am sent to that region."

Greatly delighted, Shifan ordered that the Censorate dispatch Lu Kai to the region as an inspector. (*Treating official titles as his own private property to be given out freely by the Censorate at his order alone, as if there's no one else in the imperial court.*) Before Lu set off on his journey, Shifan set out wine in a farewell feast and said, "Please convey this message to Yang Shun: 'If you work as a team and remove this thorn from my flesh, I will reward you with royal titles. I'll surely keep the promise to both you and Mr. Yang.'"

Lu Kai promised to do as he was told. He arrived in Xuanfu a few days later, equipped with his credentials, and met with Governor Yang. After Lu Kai gave Yang Shun a full report of Shifan's message, Yang Shun said, "I have been turning this matter over in my mind from morning to night, forgetting food and sleep. But I still haven't come up with a good plan to do away with that man."

"Let's work on this together," said Lu Kai, "partly to live up to the Yans' expectations of us and partly in order not to miss the opportunity of advancement."

"Right you are," Yang Shun agreed. "We'll let each other know when the right moment comes."

After they parted, Lu Kai's words kept Yang Shun awake the whole night through. The following morning, as he sat in court session, his adjutant reported, "The Weizhou guards have captured two rebels. They are now outside the gate, awaiting your orders."

"Bring them in," said Yang Shun.

The escorting guard kowtowed and presented Yang Shun with a letter that, when opened and read, made Yang Shun burst into laughter. The two men, Yan Hao and Yang Yinkui, were followers of the sorcerer Xiao Qin, ringleader of the White Lotus Cult. A frequent visitor to the Tartar regions, Xiao Qin skillfully deceived the locals by offering incense and coaxed Altan Khan into believing that he was in possession of such magic that a curse from him would bring instant death to men and a cry from him would bring instant ruin to a city. The khan, being a densely ignorant man, believed him and honored him as Grand Master Xiao Qin. His several hundred followers, forming a separate battalion, served as guides for the Tartars' incursions across the border, bringing much harm to China. Yang's predecessor, Governor Shi, had sent generous bribes through interpreters to Tuotuo, the Tartar chief, with this message:

The celestial court is well inclined to establish a friendly relationship with you. We are willing to exchange our grain and clothing for your horses at a "horse market." A cessation of warfare and the establishment of peace would benefit both sides. Our only concern is that Xiao Qin and his followers might try to block the peace process. Xiao Qin is nothing more than a Chinese hooligan with no magical powers whatsoever. All he has is cunning, which he uses to lure you into looting for his own advantage. If you doubt me, ask Xiao Qin to try his magic. If he can indeed reduce cities to ruins by his cries and bring death to men by cursing, he can then be put to good use. If his curses and shouts do not work, he will thus be exposed as an imposter to be bound up and handed over to the celestial court. Out of gratitude for your help, we will reward you handsomely. Once the barter system is in place, you will enjoy boundless profits year after year, which will be immensely more beneficial than pillage.

Tuotuo nodded in approval and reported as much to Altan Khan, much to the latter's delight. The khan then summoned Xiao Qin and ordered him to lead a thousand horsemen and approach the city to try out his magic. Knowing that he would surely fail the test, Xiao Qin changed clothes and tried to escape under cover of night, but was stopped and questioned by guards at Juyong Pass. His followers Qiao Yuan, Zhang Panlong, and others were also captured and brought before Governor Shi. Upon their confession that there were numerous followers of their cult scattered in the western and southern regions, arrests were made in various places. Yan Hao and Yang Yinkui, who were now brought before Governor Yang, were also well-known followers of Xiao Qin. Governor Yang was overjoyed at the capture of the two men, partly because this would be an achievement to his credit since his assumption of the post and partly because it was an opportunity to do away with Shen Lian. That very evening, he asked Censor Lu to his private chamber for a consultation.

"There being no other way to get Shen Lian," said Yang, "the White Lotus Cult's collusion with the Tartars will do it, because this is what angers the emperor most. Let us add Shen Lian's name to the confession by cult members Yan Hao and Yang Yinkui, presenting him as their mentor, saying that Shen Lian, disgruntled at his loss of office, taught them sorcery and colluded with the Tartars in a conspiracy of rebellion against the empire. We will then plead that since he has been captured, thanks to heaven, he should be executed to put an end to this potential threat once and for all. Let us first send a secret message to the Yan family so that they can urge the Ministry of Justice to give its approval promptly. I can guarantee that Shen Lian will not give us the slip this time!"

Lu Kai clapped his hands and exclaimed, "How ingenious! How ingenious!"

Then and there, the two of them decided on what they were going to write and arranged to send the report and the secret message that same day. Yan Song, being the first to read them, instructed Yan Shifan to send word to the Ministry of Justice. Minister Xu Lun was an incompetent old man. At the order from the Yans, he dutifully gave a speedy approval that fully granted Yang and Lu's request. Then, there followed the emperor's decree that the cult members were to be executed without delay by the local authorities. Yang Shun's son was appointed battalion commander of the imperial guards. Lu Kai, for his service, was promoted three ranks and was put on the waiting list for vacancies in the capital.

Let us now follow another thread of the story. After sending in the reports, Yang Shun secretly had Shen Lian thrown into jail. At a loss what to do, the panic-stricken Lady Xu, Shen Gun, and Shen Bao sought the counsel of Jia Shi, Shen Lian's sworn brother.

"This must be the work of the two villains Yang and Lu in revenge on behalf of the Yan family," said Jia Shi. "Imprisonment means they have falsely charged him with some serious crime. The two young men would do well to escape to some faraway place, not to return until the Yan family's power subsides. If you remain here, Yang and Lu will not leave you in peace."

"How can we leave before knowing what will happen to Father?" said Shen Gun.

Jia Shi replied, "Your father offended the wrong man. His case is already beyond all hope. Your first concern should be to continue the family line. How can you court your own death for the sake of a minor act of filial piety? You also need to advise your mother to make plans to ensure her own safety. As for your father, I will surely see to it that he is well taken care of. Don't worry."

When the two sons repeated Jia Shi's words to their mother, she said, "How can you abandon your father when he is in jail on a framed-up charge? However well-intentioned Uncle Jia may be, he is, after all, an outsider. I believe that the scoundrels Yang and Lu, in trying to curry favor with the Yans, are only out to get your father, not his wife and sons. Your escape will be an admission of guilt, and if, after you have left, your father dies with no one to bury his bones, you will be cursed forever as unfilial sons. How will you be able to face the world?" (*Valid point, morally speaking.*) So saying, she broke down into a flood of tears. Shen Gun and Shen Bao also wailed in grief. When word came to him that Lady Xu would not hear of his advice, Jia Shi heaved a sigh and left.

A few days later, Jia Shi found out the truth. Shen Lian had indeed been sentenced to death for his alleged involvement with the White Lotus cult. In jail, Shen Lian kept up a stream of curses. Knowing that he was in the wrong, Yang Shun feared that he would look bad if Shen denounced him in public at the execution. So he ordered the jailers to produce a note testifying to Shen Lian's illness and then had him murdered.

When Jia Shi told Lady Xu about this, it goes without saying that the mother and sons wept bitterly. Luckily Jia Shi bought the corpse from one of his many acquaintances and told the jailers to produce another corpse if there was an order that Shen's head was to be cut off and hung up for public display. Then he arranged, without the knowledge of the Shen brothers, to have the body buried in a coffin in a vacant lot. It was not until after the burial that he told Shen Gun, "Your father's remains are in a safe place. But the location is a secret not to be divulged yet. I will show you where it is after all the commotion subsides."

The Shen brothers were overwhelmed with gratitude. To Jia Shi's renewed attempts to talk them into fleeing, Shen Gun said, "We feel very bad for having occupied your house for so long, but it is our mother's wish that we wait until the injustice has been redressed before we carry the coffin home. That's why we are still here."

Jia Shi said in irritation, "All my life, I have devoted myself to the well-being of other people. What I said just now was for the good of your family. How could I have tried to talk you into leaving because you have been occupying my house? However, since your mother is so determined, I won't insist. Now, I'll be away for a year or so to attend to some minor business. Stay here by all means, but take care."

As his eyes happened to rest on the two petition memorials by Zhuge Liang in Shen Lian's handwriting on the wall, Jia Shi continued, "I'd like to have these two scrolls as a souvenir while I'm on the road. Should we meet in future, they'll serve as a token of faith."

Shen Gun accordingly took down the scrolls, rolled them up, and handed them to Jia Shi. Tucking them away in his sleeves, Jia Shi bade them a tearful farewell. The fact of the matter was that Jia Shi had premonitions that, as Shen Lian's good friend, he would surely be implicated because Yang and Lu, being the wicked men they were, would not stop at the death of Shen Lian alone. Therefore, before any action could be taken against him, he fled to stay with his relatives in Henan, but of him, for the time being, no more.

Let us come back to Lu Kai, who, emboldened by the reply from the Ministry of Justice and the imperial decree, brought Yan Hao and Yang Yin-kui out of jail for execution. Shen Lian's head was to be cut off and displayed in public together with theirs. Little did the authorities know that Shen Lian's real body had already been bought and taken out by Jia Shi, nor were they able to tell the difference, but this is of no concern to us.

In the meantime, Yang Shun was disgruntled that he was rewarded with no more than a post for his son. He complained to Lu Kai, "Yan Shifan promised that he would reward me with a royal title upon completion of the job. I wonder why he went back on his word."

After reflecting for a while, Lu Kai said in reply, "Shen Lian was the Yan family's archenemy. He is dead all right, but his sons are untouched. Weeds will grow back if they are not pulled out by the roots. I believe that's the reason why the prime minister is discontented with us."

"If so," said Yang, "that can be easily taken care of. We'll write another memorial to say that though Shen Lian has been done away with, his sons should also be brought to justice for their involvement, and their property should be confiscated, for laws of the empire are to be enforced so as to strike fear in the heart of the populace. We'll also arrest and punish all those ruffians who shot at the straw men with him and the man who gave him lodging. After the Yans are thus fully avenged, we will claim rewards by reminding them of their promise. By then, what excuse can they have to go back on their word?" (*Ingenious.*)

"How ingenious!" exclaimed Lu Kai. "This matter brooks no delay. We'd better act while his family is still here, so that we can get them one and all. My only fear is that his sons might hear of this and give us the slip. That'll mean more work for us."

Yang Shun agreed. They wrote a memorial to the throne and a note to the Yans, pledging their loyalty. In the meantime, they also notified the prefect of Bao'an, asking him to have the Shen family kept under tight watch to prevent them from running away. Action was to be taken as soon as the imperial decree arrived. As the poem says,

> When the nest is broken, eggs rarely survive;
> When weeds are cut, the roots are also removed.
> Families of good men unjustly killed
> Are also ruined to please those in power.

A few days later, the imperial decree arrived. Carrying arrest warrants, constables from the yamen went for Shen Lian's family. All who had associated with Shen Lian were identified and arrested, with the exception of Jia Shi, who, having fled, was reported to be in hiding. Such was Jia Shi's foresight. A contemporary poet had this to say in praise of him:

> Hard to come by are loyal friends like Jia,
> Who proved his foresight when he took to flight.
> However wide the net may spread,
> Divine birds find a way to fly.

Yang Shun personally interrogated the Shen brothers about how they had colluded with the Tartars. The brothers cried in protest. How could they have anything to confess! At Governor Yang's orders, they were beaten to a pulp. Their constitution unable to withstand the torture, Shen Gun and Shen Bao both died under the rod. How sad it was that these two young men ended up in the City of the Unjustly Dead in the underworld! All the others arrested with them were convicted as accomplices. The dead numbered in the dozens. The infant son, Shen Zhi, was exempted from charges but, forbidden to live in Bao'an, was banished with his mother Lady Xu to the remote town of Yunzhou.

Lu Kai again took counsel with Yang Shun and said, "Shen Lian's oldest son Shen Xiang is a famous scholar in Shaoxing. Should he rise to power someday, he will surely be hostile to us. The best thing to do is to eliminate him as well, to stamp out all sources of future trouble as well as to impress the prime minister with our thoroughness."

Yang Shun agreed and sent documents to Zhejiang designating Shen Xiang as a criminal sought by the imperial government to be delivered under guard for trial. He also ordered a trusted subordinate, Registrar Jin Shao, to select competent yamen runners to deliver the letter and murder Shen Xiang at a convenient point on the way back. They were also to obtain an official statement from the local area testifying that the man had died of sickness. When the job was done, they would be rewarded handsomely, and Jin Shao would be recommended for a promotion of more than one grade. With this last assurance, Jin Shao hurried back to his yamen and carefully selected two experienced runners, Zhang Qian and Li Wan, invited them to the private quarters of the yamen for wine and food, and presented them with twenty taels of silver from his own pocket.

Zhang Qian and Li Wan said in protest, "How could we dream of accepting a reward without having done anything to deserve it?"

Jin Shao said in explanation, "This silver is not from me but from Governor Yang, who wants you to carry an order to Shaoxing to arrest Shen Xiang. Keep a tight watch over him all along the way. You must do such and such . . . [10] When you come back, you will be handsomely rewarded. If you fail, be advised that the governor's yamen is no place for joking. You'll have to go there yourselves to make your report."

Zhang Qian and Li Wan exclaimed, "Even if it's just an order from Your Honor rather than the governor, how would we dare say no?" They put away the silver, thanked Jin, and, equipped with the prefect's summons, hastened on their way south.

Now let us come to Shen Xiang, courtesy name Xiaoxia, a prefectural stipendiary scholar in Shaoxing. He had heard some time ago with great concern that his father had been convicted of a crime over some verbal remarks and was banished, deprived of all official rank, to regions beyond the border.

He wished to make a trip to Bao'an but hesitated because the affairs of his household would be unattended to. One day, there suddenly came to him runners from the prefecture of Bao'an who, without stopping for a word of explanation, tied him up in chains and took him to the prefectural yamen. Having let Shen Xiang read the summons carefully, the prefect handed him over to the runners along with a letter of reply and told them to be careful along the way. Only then did Shen Xiang learn that his father and two younger brothers had died untimely deaths and that his mother had been exiled to a remote region. He burst into loud sobs.

Weeping as he went out the yamen gate, he saw his entire family, old and young, huddled together there crying their hearts out. What had happened was that because the document contained the phrase "confiscated by imperial decree," the prefect had ordered the county marshal to seal up the house and drive out all the members of the household. At this added blow, Shen Xiaoxia wept until he choked. A moment or two later, relatives of the family came to bid him farewell. Knowing full well that his departure boded ill, they felt obliged to offer some words of comfort. Meng Chunyuan, his father-in-law, offered the two runners a packet of silver and begged that they take good care of his son-in-law, but the runners thought the offer insufficient and refused to take it. It was not until Shen's wife Meng-shi added a pair of gold hairpins that they accepted.

Between sobs, Shen Xiaoxia told his wife, "This journey bodes ill. Don't worry about me. Just consider me dead, and go back to live with your parents. Being from a genteel family, you are not likely to remarry. I won't have to worry on that score." He continued, while pointing to his concubine Wen Shunü, "However, she, being young and without a place to go, should remarry. I am thirty years old and still without a son. She is now two and a half months pregnant, and if, by any chance, she gives birth to a boy, the Shen family ancestral sacrifices can be carried on. For my sake, my wife, please take her to your parents' home and let her stay there until the pregnancy comes to full term. Whatever the sex of the baby, she will then be ready to be sent away wherever you want."

His voice was still in the air when Wen-shi said, "What kind of talk is this? You're going thousands of li away. How can you manage without some family member looking after you! The mistress can return to the Meng family, but I will be happy to follow you and serve you, however hard life may be, so that you will have company and the mistress won't have to worry too much."

Shen Xiaoxia objected, "I don't object to having a family member with me, but this journey is not a happy one. What good will it do to have you die with me in a remote place?"

Wen-shi rejoined, "Everyone knows that while your father held office in the capital, you were here at home. Even though he was falsely accused of wrongdoings, how could you have been an accomplice when you were so far away? I will help you appeal to the authorities and defend yourself. I am sure you will not be sentenced to death. If you are imprisoned, I would still be free to look after you."

Meng-shi was just as worried about her husband, and, impressed by the concubine's reasoning, she also urged her husband to take Wen Shunü along. Shen Xiaoxia had always loved Shunü for her talent and wisdom. Now that Meng-shi was also supportive, he felt obliged to comply.

That night, they all stayed with Meng Chunyuan, his father-in-law. The following morning, with the two runners Zhang Qian and Li Wan urging them to set out on the journey, Wen-shi changed into cotton clothes, wrapped up her hair in a blue kerchief, took leave of Meng-shi, and, baggage on her back, set off with Shen Xiaoxia. The sorrow of parting need not be described here.

All along the way, Wen-shi stayed by Shen Xiaoxia's side and personally served him food and tea. At the outset, Zhang Qian and Li Wan treated them fairly well, but, assured after crossing the Yangzi River and switching to over-land travel in Xuzhou that they were by now far from Shen's home base, they gradually grew mean, yelling at them and making things difficult for them. Noticing the change in Zhang and Li's behavior, Wen-shi said quietly to her husband, "I think these two thugs are up to something. Being a woman, I don't know the roads we are traveling, but if we find ourselves in some deserted wilderness, we'd better watch out for ourselves." Shen Xiaoxia nodded, though without much conviction.

A few days later, however, he noticed that the two runners frequently whispered to each other in private. As his eyes happened to rest upon a shining Japanese sword in their baggage, his heart gave a jump. In fear, he said to Wen-shi, "You said that the thugs were up to something. I can feel it, too. Tomorrow, we'll be in the prefecture of Jining. Beyond Jining are the Taihang and Liangshan Mountains. If the two of them strike in such bandit-infested places, you won't be able to help me, and I won't be able to help you either. What's to be done?"

"Things being the way they are," said Wen-shi, "if you can think of any way to escape, please go. I'll stay here. They can't swallow me alive!" (*What a woman! With such courage, she should be of service to the empire.*)

"By the east gate of Jining, there is a Secretary Feng who is at home in mourning for his father. He is a most chivalrous man and a close friend of my father's. They passed the examinations in the same year. Tomorrow I'll go to him for help. He'll surely take me in. My only concern is that you, being a woman, can't deal with the two thugs. How can I have a clear conscience if you suffer on my account? If you feel you can handle them, I'll be more ready to go. Otherwise, we shall share life and death together to meet our destiny, and I'll have no regrets if I die."

"Don't hesitate to escape when there is a chance," said Wen-shi. "I will know what to do. Don't worry about me."

Their muffled conversation went undetected, for, having had a long day, Zhang Qian and Li Wan were snoring away in a deep, wine-induced sleep.

The following morning, Shen Xiaoxia asked Zhang Qian when they set out again, "How far are we from Jining?"

"Only forty li. We'll be there at around noon."

"By the east gate of Jining lives a Secretary Feng who is a friend of my father's," said Shen Xiaoxia. "When he was in the capital, he borrowed two hundred taels of silver from my father. I still have with me the receipt of the loan. He has since been in charge of Beixin Customs and should have lots of silver at home. If I go in my present wretched circumstances to claim back the loan, he will surely pay me back. This money should be more than enough to cover the traveling expenses and make the journey more comfortable."

Zhang Qian hesitated, but Li Wan readily granted the request. He said in Zhang Qian's ear, "He looks like an honest man to me. What's more, if his beloved concubine and his baggage are here, I don't think there's anything fishy. If he comes back with the silver, the two of us will be in luck. Why not let him go?"

"What you said may be very true," said Zhang. "But still, let's pick an inn and put down the luggage. I'll keep watch over the woman there while you follow him. Nothing can go wrong that way."

Let me skip unimportant details. By nine in the morning, they had reached the outskirts of Jining and put their baggage in a clean inn.

"Why don't the two of you follow me to the east gate?" suggested Shen Xiaoxia. "We'll still be in good time for lunch back here."

"I'll go with you," said Li Wan. "They might even keep us for lunch and some wine."

At this point, Wen-shi said purposefully to her husband, "As the proverb says, 'Relationships change with shifts in status.' Secretary Feng may have owed your father money, but now that your father is dead and you are in trouble, who would be willing to pay up? You'll only be asking for humiliation. It would be better for us to eat lunch now and get on with the journey."

Shen Xiaoxia insisted, "It's not much of a walk from here to the east gate. It won't hurt to call on him."

With designs on the two hundred taels of silver, Li Wan eagerly urged Shen to go.

Shen Xiaoxia said to Wen-shi, "Sit here and be patient. If we come back too soon, that means nothing came of it. If he is kind enough to keep us for lunch, he will surely give me back the money. In that case, I will hire a sedan-chair for you tomorrow. I can tell that riding on that donkey has been hard for you all these days."

While the two runners were not looking, Wen-shi gave her husband a meaningful look and said, "Come back soon. Don't make me wait too long." (*The affectionate words between husband and wife cannot make the runners suspicious.*)

Li Wan commented with a sneer, "How long is the trip anyway? Why do they have to be as long-winded as old folks?"

Seeing that her husband had stepped out, Wen-shi deliberately called Li Wan back and said to him, "If Mr. Feng keeps you for lunch and makes you stay long, be sure to remind him that you need to be on your way."

"Of course," promised Li Wan. By the time Li Wan walked down the steps, Shen Xiaoxia was already quite a distance away. Li Wan, not being alert enough, did not suspect anything, for he knew his way around Jining and knew how to get to Secretary Feng's house by the east gate. A few steps farther down the road, he felt the need to relieve himself, found a latrine pit, and took his time doing what he needed to do before he got up and slowly made his way toward the east gate.

When Shen Xiaoxia turned around and found Li Wan nowhere in sight, he ran all the way to Secretary Feng's home. Xiaoxia was predestined to be saved, for it so happened that Secretary Feng was all by himself in the hall. They had got to know each other well when they lived in the capital, and Feng was startled upon seeing the young man. Without bothering to make bows, Shen Xiang grabbed Feng by his clothes and said, "I need a place to talk."

Feng realized what was afoot and led him into the study. As Shen Xiaoxia broke down in tears, Feng said, "My boy, tell me quickly what is the matter. Don't let grief make you neglect what you need to do."

Shen Xiaoxia said between sobs, "I won't repeat how my father died un-justly at Yan's hands, but my two younger brothers, who followed my father to his post, were also murdered by Yang Shun and Lu Kai. That left only me still alive at home. Then orders came to the prefect to have me escorted under guard for interrogation. The family line is coming to an end any moment now. The two runners escorting me are up to some mischief. I suspect that they have been ordered by the villains Yang and Lu to murder me when we reach the Taihang and Liangshan Mountains. I thought of a plan, got away from them, and came to you for help. If you could come up with a way to shelter me, my deceased father's spirit in heaven would be most grateful. If you, my uncle, can't shelter me, I shall bang my head against these steps till I die. To die in front of you is better than at the hands of those thugs."

"My good boy, don't worry. At the back of my bedchamber, there is a double wall. You may well hide yourself there. You won't be found, however hard anyone may search. I will now take you there, where you may stay for several days. I'll think of a plan in the meantime."

With a bow, Shen Xiang said gratefully, "You, my uncle, are the father of my rebirth!"

Taking Shen Xiang by the hand, Feng led him to the back of his bedchamber, where he pried up a piece of the floor to reveal a secret passageway that led, after fifty to sixty steps, to three small lit rooms surrounded on all four sides by walls. It was indeed a well-hidden place. Every day, Mr. Feng personally brought in tea and food. His household rules being as strict as they were, who dared to leak out half a word? Truly,

> Deep mountains shelter leopards;
> Dense willow leaves hide ravens.
> You needn't be sad for this Ji Bu,
> For he found his own Zhu Jia.[11]

Let us now come back to Li Wan, who, having relieved himself at the latrine pit, made his way to the Feng residence by the east gate.

"Is the Honorable Secretary Feng at home?" he asked the old doorkeeper.

"Yes, he is."

"Did your master admit a visitor in a white robe?"

"Yes, they are having lunch in the study."

These words made Li Wan feel even more relaxed. He waited until about one in the afternoon when, indeed, a man in white came out. Li Wan stepped forward eagerly, only to find that the man was not Shen Xiang. The man headed straight for the door and went out. Li Wan waited till his patience wore out. Feeling the pangs of hunger, he couldn't help but ask the old doorkeeper, "The visitor whom you said your master was keeping for lunch—why is he still inside?"

"Didn't you see him leave just a moment ago?"

"Aren't there other visitors in your master's study?"

"Not that I know of."

"Who was that man in white?"

"He is the master's brother-in-law. He comes often."

"Where is your master?"

"The master always takes a nap after lunch. He must be sound asleep now."

Realizing that they were not talking about the same man, Li Wan started to panic. "I'll be frank with you," said he. "I am sent by the governor of Xuanfu and Datong. I have been escorting a Shen Xiang of Shaoxing with the courtesy name Xiaoxia, a wanted criminal. He said that he wished to pay a visit to his father's friend, your master. I followed him to your house. He went in, but

I have been waiting all this time for him without seeing him come out. You may not know it, but he might still be in the study. Please go in and remind him to come out quickly because we need to be on our way."

"What are you talking about?" demanded the old man with calculated bewilderment. "I don't understand a thing you say." (*Wonderful acting.*)

In spite of his irritation, Li Wan patiently repeated every word. The old doorkeeper spit into his face and cursed, "You've been seeing ghosts! When was there ever a Mr. Shen here? The master is in mourning and is receiving no one from outside the family. This door is my responsibility. All visitors are announced by me. And here you are, talking such nonsense! Might you be a house burglar pretending to be some kind of government runner? Get out of my sight and stop pestering me like this!" (*He has been instructed by Mr. Feng to do this.*)

Li Wan grew frantic. In a burst of rage, he said, "This Shen Xiang is a major criminal wanted by the imperial court. This is not a joke. Call your master out. I need to speak to him."

"The master is asleep. How would I dare to disturb him for nothing? What a barbarian!" So saying, he walked off with a swagger.

"What an incompetent old croaker!" said Li Wan to himself. "I simply asked him to make an announcement, and he had to make it so difficult! Shen Xiang must be inside. I have a warrant from the military authorities. I am here not for some private matter. What do I have to fear even if I go straight in?" Recklessly he stormed into the hall, banged on the screen, and shouted, "Mr. Shen, it's time to go!"

No answer came. He kept shouting until a young servant-boy emerged from within.

"Where is the doorkeeper?" asked the boy. "Whom did he let in, to make so much noise in the hall?"

Before Li Wan could stop him for a word, the boy took a look behind the screen and headed west.

Li Wan said to himself, "Maybe the study is in the west wing. Let me go and take a look. What do I have to fear?"

From the hall he turned west and saw a long corridor stretching ahead of him. There being no one around, he pressed ahead and came to what looked like women's quarters, where quite a few women were moving about. Intimidated at the sight, Li Wan retraced his steps. As he found his way back to the hall, he heard a commotion outside and went out to see what it was. It turned out that Zhang Qian was there looking for him and, failing to see him, was quarreling with the doorkeeper. At the sight of Li Wan, Zhang Qian lashed out before Li Wan could say anything in explanation, "A fine partner you are! Thinking of nothing but wine and food instead of doing a stroke of useful work! You left for the town at nine in the morning. It's now almost five in the afternoon and you are still here idling about! Why haven't you taken the prisoner away? What are you waiting for?" (*Bravo!*)

Li Wan said, "Phooey! What wine and food are you talking about? I haven't even seen the shadow of the man!"

"Didn't you come here with him?"

"While I was at the latrine, that damn Southerner hurried ahead and got a start on me. I wasn't able to catch up with him. By the time I arrived here, the doorkeeper said there was a visitor in a white robe eating lunch in the study. I thought it must be him, but he hasn't come out yet, and the door-keeper refused to announce me. I haven't been able to get myself even a cup of water. My brother, would you please do me a favor and stay here for a moment while I go back to the inn to grab a bite?"

"You idiot!" said Zhang. "Don't you know what an important prisoner he is? How could you have let him walk alone? You should have at least fol-lowed him into the study. How do you know if he is really in the study at this moment? I am amazed that you still talk as if nothing has happened. You made this mess. It has nothing to do with me!" So saying, he turned around as if to go. Li Wan darted forward and stopped him.

"I'm sure he's inside," said Li Wan. "Where else could he go? Why don't you help me say something to get him out. You have a full stomach. Why are you in such a rush?"

"His concubine is still at the inn," explained Zhang. "I did ask the inn-keeper to keep an eye on her, but I'm still worried because she is the rope with which we can lead Shen Xiang by the nose. As long as we keep her with us, Shen Xiang will surely return."

Li Wan agreed, "You are right." So Zhang Qian left.

Suffering from the pangs of hunger, Li Wan waited until dark, but still there was no sign of Shen. As evening was setting in, Li Wan's hunger got the better of him. Catching sight of a refreshment shop nearby, he took off his shirt and pawned it for a few pennies' worth of pastries. Before long, he heard the sound of a door being bolted. By the time he rushed back, the door of the Feng house was already closed. Li Wan said to himself, "I have never been so humiliated before in all my years as a runner! How highly placed must a secre-tary be for his doorkeeper to put on such airs? Shen Xiang is also a man who doesn't know any better. With his wife and baggage at the inn, he should have at least sent word out if he is staying here for the night. Well, things being the way they are, I'll have to make do tonight under the eaves and wait until day-break for a smarter servant to talk to." It being the tenth month of the year, the weather was not overly cold, but in the middle of the night, a wind sprang up and brought on a drizzle that drenched his clothes. A miserable night it was.

By daybreak, the rain stopped. Who appeared but Zhang Qian again, at the persistent urging of Wen-shi. With official documents with him, Zhang Qian consulted with Li Wan about what to do. As soon as the door opened, they barged into the hall and yelled at the top of their voices, over the protests of the old doorkeeper. In a moment, the commotion attracted all the members of the family, young and old, who swarmed into the hall. With everybody talking at once, the noise could be heard from the streets. A crowd of spectators gathered at the door for a peek inside. All this bustle got the attention of Mr. Feng, who, being a righteous and benevolent man, was staying at home mourning the death of his father. From the interior of the house he emerged in leisurely steps. Let me now describe how he looked. He was wearing

> *A white cap of mourning,*
> *A coarse hemp shirt sewn inside out,*
> *A hemp rope tied around his waist,*
> *And a pair of straw sandals on his feet.*

Hearing a cough, the servants cried, "The master is here!" As they withdrew to stand on both sides of the hall, Feng entered and asked, "What is all this noise about?"

Zhang Qian and Li Wan stepped forward and said with a salute, "Master Feng, by order of the governor of Xuanfu and Datong, we went to Shaoxing to arrest Shen Xiang, a criminal wanted by the imperial court, and were passing through this area on our way back when Shen Xiang claimed that, his father being a friend of yours, he wished to pay you a visit. We did not dare to object, but let him have his wish. Since he came to your house yesterday morning, he has not yet come out. Our journey is being delayed, yet your servants refuse to announce us. We beg that you do us the kindness of urging him to be on his way as soon as possible." Zhang Qian took out from his bosom the arrest warrant and other official documents. After reading them, Feng asked, "Is Shen Xiang the son of Registrar Shen Lian?"

"Yes," said Li Wan.

Covering up his ears and sticking out his tongue, Feng said, "How insensible you runners are! For Shen Xiang to be a criminal wanted by the imperial court is not as bad as his being an enemy of Prime Minister Yan, and who would dare shelter an enemy of the prime minister! (*How clever to change the subject to the Yans!*) He didn't come to my house yesterday as you claim. Should your lies get spread to the authorities and should they report to the Yan family, how am I to shoulder the blame? The two of you were too careless, or you may have taken bribery and set a major prisoner free. And now you are here to put the blame on me!" He ordered the servants to throw the two men out, to close the door, and not to get involved, for it would be no laughing matter if the Yans heard of this.

With some more angry words, Feng turned back into the interior of the house. Thus ordered by the master, the servants pushed and shoved, and, in a trice, the two runners found themselves on the other side of the door, which then swung closed. Curses could still be heard from inside. Zhang Qian and Li Wan stared at each other in shock, with mouths agape and tongues sticking out. Zhang Qian grumbled, "Yesterday, it was you who urged that he be allowed to go into town. Now you go ahead and find him."

"Don't start blaming me yet. Let's go back to ask his wife. She might know where he is. Then we'll come back to get him."

Zhang Qian agreed, "You are right. They are a loving couple. Last night when he didn't come back, the woman sat alone for four to six hours quietly shedding tears. She should know where her husband is." While talking, the two men hurried out of the city and back to the inn.

Hearing the runners' voices, Wen-shi rushed out from her room and asked, "Why isn't my husband here?"

Zhang Qian replied, pointing at Li Wan, "Ask him." Whereupon Li Wan gave a full account of the happenings of the day before, complete with details of his stop at the latrine, which slowed him down, and everything that had occurred at the Feng residence.

"I went to town this morning on an empty stomach," said Zhang, "and now I'm fully loaded with humiliation. Your husband does seem to have left Feng's house. He must have told you where he would go. Tell us before it's too late, so that we can go and look for him."

Before he had quite finished, Wen-shi grabbed the two men and cried with tears in her eyes, "A fine thing you did! Give me back my husband!"

"Your husband wanted to pay a visit to some friend of his father's, and we let him go out of the goodness of our hearts. Now that he has disappeared, we are the ones to be held accountable. That's why we are so anxious to get him back, if only we knew how. Now, here you are, demanding that we give you back your husband. Are you saying we hid him? How ridiculous!" Loosening their shirts, they sat down in anger.

Wen-shi stepped outside, blocked the entrance, and, stamping her feet, called out her grievances in loud wails. As the old innkeeper rushed over to pacify her, she said, "Grandpa, let me tell you what happened. My husband took me in as a concubine when he was thirty years old and without a son. I've been with him for two years now. As I am more than three months pregnant, he couldn't bring himself to send me away. That's why I am with him every step of the way on this thousand-li journey. Yesterday, he went to see a friend of his father's because we were running out of traveling money. That runner, Li, went with him. I got suspicious when they did not return last night. This morning, the two runners came back without him. They must have murdered him. Please help me get back my husband, or I won't call it quits."

"Don't jump to conclusions, young lady," said the innkeeper. "They have no grudge against your husband. Why would they kill him for no reason at all?"

Wen-shi explained in sobs, "Grandpa, you may not know that Prime Minister Yan hates my husband. These two runners must have received some order from the Yans, or they are trying to claim credit for themselves from the Yans. (*Brilliant.*) Now, does it stand to reason that my husband would suddenly disappear without a word to me after having brought me so far from home? Even if he tried to escape, how could Li, who went with him, let him go? To please the Yans, they have killed my husband and left me, a helpless woman, to face the world alone. Please help me appeal to the authorities to bring the two murderers to justice." She poured her words out in such a torrent that Zhang Qian and Li Wan were not able to get a word in, much as they tried to. The innkeeper found Wen-shi's reasoning quite convincing. He, too, became suspicious of the runners. Out of pity for the woman, he tried to console her by saying, "What you said may all be very true, but your husband may not be dead yet. Why don't you wait for one more day?"

"One more day may not do any harm, but whose responsibility will it be if the two murderers get away in the meantime?"

"If we wanted to escape after murdering your husband," said Zhang, "why did we come back here?"

Wen-shi countered, "You thought I, being a woman, would not know what to do, so you came back to kidnap me. Now, out with it! Where's my husband's corpse? You'll have to tell anyway when we are in court!"

Overwhelmed by her sharp tongue, the innkeeper did not utter another word. The forty to fifty onlookers who had gathered in the meantime were all moved by the woman's sad story. Indignant at the two runners, they said to her, "If you want to appeal to the authorities, we'll take you to the military commissioner."

With a deep bow, Wen-shi said tearfully, "I am so grateful to you all for your readiness to help a poor woman in distress. Please take the two murderers with you. Don't let them escape!"

"Don't worry. We'll make sure of that."

Before Zhang Qian and Li Wan could say a word, the onlookers continued, "You two don't have to explain. Lies will be lies; the truth will be the truth. If you are not guilty of anything, why don't you just go with her to the authorities? What do you have to fear?"

As Wen-shi sobbed her way ahead, the crowd pushed Zhang Qian and Li Wan all the way to the military commissioner's yamen, but the gate was still closed.

It so happened that it was the day on which the yamen was to hear cases of complaint. With a white apron tied to her waist, Wen-shi ran past the gate. Seeing a big drum on a stand by the entrance, she grabbed the drumstick hanging from the stand and started beating the drum frantically. Frightened out of their wits at the earthshaking sound, the captain and gatekeeper rushed over and tied her up with a rope, shouting, "How dare you!"

Wen-shi threw herself to the ground in a fit of passionate weeping while, at the same time, crying that a gross injustice had been done to her. At a sharp order from inside, the gate was opened. Military Commissioner Wang took his seat in the court and asked who had been beating the drum.

After the captain brought Wen-shi in, she tearfully gave a detailed account of how the family had been struck with misfortune, how the father and two sons had died untimely deaths, leaving behind only her husband Shen Xiang, and how Shen Xiang had been murdered on the road by the two runners the day before. The commissioner called forth Zhang Qian and Li Wan for questioning. To everything Zhang Qian and Li Wan said, she offered a rebuttal. So convincing was she that Zhang Qian and Li Wan found themselves unable to fault her reasoning.

"The Yans being as powerful as they are, such cases of secret murder do take place from time to time," the commissioner thought to himself. "I can't say this case is not one of them." Thereupon, he ordered the captain to take Wen-shi and the two men to the prefectural yamen for further questioning.

Charged now with the responsibility for this case, Prefect He promptly summoned the innkeeper so as to hear the testimony of all four of them. The woman was adamant in accusing the two men of murdering her husband. Li Wan confessed that his stop at the latrine made him lose track of his man. Zhang Qian and the innkeeper also made depositions to the best of their knowledge. The prefect was unable to make up his mind. The woman looked so heart-stricken that her story seemed quite believable, but on the other hand, Zhang Qian and Li Wan refused to admit that they had done what they were accused of. After some reflection, the prefect detained the four of them while he himself got into a sedan chair to visit Secretary Feng and find out what he had to say.

At the announcement of the prefect's visit, Feng hastened to greet him and ushered him into the main hall. After some tea, Prefect He brought up the subject of Shen Xiang. No sooner had the name of Shen Xiang been mentioned than Feng covered up his ears and said, "That man is the prime minister's enemy. Although I may have passed the examinations the same year he did, we were not really friends. Please don't ask me about him, Your Honor. I'm afraid that should the Yan family hear about this, I might be implicated." So saying, he stood up and continued, "Since Your Honor is busy with official business, I would not presume to keep you longer."

A disappointed Prefect He could not do more than take his leave. Riding in his sedan-chair, he thought to himself, "Judging from Feng's fear of the Yan family, I don't think Shen Xiang is in his house. Shen may indeed have been murdered by the runners. Or he may have gone to someone else he knew after being rejected by Feng."

Back in his yamen, he again called forth the four people in the case. "Apart from Secretary Feng," he asked Wen-shi, "what other acquaintances did your husband have in the prefecture?"

"None, Your Honor."

"When did your husband leave? When did Zhang Qian and Li Wan tell you they had lost him?"

"My husband left the inn with Li Wan before lunch yesterday. In late afternoon, Zhang Qian also went to town under the excuse of urging them to get on with the journey. When he returned at night, he said to me, 'My brother Li Wan is staying for the night with your husband in the Feng residence. I will go again early tomorrow morning to urge them to be on their way.' Today, Zhang Qian was away all morning and returned with Li Wan but not my husband. If those two didn't kill my husband, who did? If my husband was not in the Feng residence, Li Wan should have looked for him yesterday, and Zhang Qian should have been worried, too. Why did he try to pacify me with nice words? It's all very obvious. Zhang Qian and Li Wan must have arranged on the road for Li Wan to strike under the cover of night. This morning, Zhang Qian went to town to help him bury the corpse before they came back to give me a reply. Your Honor, I look forward to your wise judgment."

Prefect He said, "What you say does make sense."

Before Zhang and Li could say anything in defense of themselves, the prefect thundered, "What kind of runners are you? If you didn't murder him, you must have taken bribes and set him free. What do you have to say for yourselves?" At his order, Zhang and Li were given thirty thrashings. Their skin ripped open and blood spurted out (*Hurrah!*), but still they did not confess. Out of pity for the woman, who kept weeping bitterly at one side, the prefect ordered that ankle-squeezers be applied to the two runners. (*Hurrah!*) The fact was, the two men had not committed murder. However sharp the pain, what did they have to confess? The ankle-squeezers were applied twice, but still no confession came. When the prefect ordered that the squeezers be applied a third time, Zhang and Li, unable to withstand any more torture, pleaded, "Shen Xiang is not dead. Please set a deadline, Your Honor, and we will, under guard, find Shen Xiang and give him back to his wife."

For lack of a definitive plan of his own, the prefect reluctantly gave his consent. Wen-shi was sent to stay in a nunnery. Four militiamen were dispatched to put Zhang Qian and Li Wan in chains, escort them in their search for Shen Xiang, and report at the yamen every five days. They would be subject to a beating if unsuccessful. (*Good!*) The innkeeper was released. The case was duly reported to the military commissioner, who approved of the prefect's decision.

With Zhang and Li tied to the same chain, the four militiamen took turns watching them. The few taels of traveling money they had were taken away by the four men to pay for food and wine. Their Japanese sword was also exchanged for wine. (*Good!*) Linqing[12] was a huge place teeming with travelers. Where were they to look for Shen? To search there was just an excuse to buy some time.

As soon as the first five days were over, Wen-shi left the nunnery and went to the yamen, where, amid her wails of grief, she threatened to kill herself. The prefect was thus obliged to have Zhang and Li beaten up for having failed to accomplish their mission. The deadline was extended over ten times, and goodness knows how many bamboo rods were broken in the thrashings until the two men could not move a step. Zhang Qian at last fell ill and died. Li Wan, left alone (*Good!*), went to the nunnery to plead with Wen-shi.

"I am so desperate now that I'm going to tell you everything. When we first undertook the job, there was indeed a verbal message from Registrar Jin Shao saying that Governor Yang had ordered us to murder your husband at some point along the journey and get a death certificate from the local authorities to close the case. We gave our promise all right, but how could we bring ourselves to do such an evil thing? For some unknown reason, your husband suddenly escaped, which truly and honestly had nothing to do with us. With heaven above as my witness, if I've said a word that is not true, let my whole family perish! (*So be it!*) Now that my brother Zhang Qian has been beaten to death for having failed to meet the prefect's five-day deadline, it would be another injustice for me to die also. Your husband is indeed alive. You will, someday, be reunited with him. I beg only that you stop weeping at the yamen. You will accumulate credit in the underworld if you can help extend the deadline and spare my unworthy life."

"It's hard to believe that you are not guilty of murdering my husband, but, since you say so, I'll stop going to the yamen and give you more time to search. But you need to work hard at it. Don't waste your time."

Li Wan humbly voiced agreement as he left. There is a poem in evidence:

Murder was plotted for twenty taels of silver,
But the prisoner escaped halfway down the road.
Unable to withstand all the torture,
He pleaded hard with her in the convent.

The prefect had set up and strictly observed the deadlines for the capture of Shen Xiang partly because Shen was wanted by the governor and partly because of the woman's daily entreaties. But Li Wan was not destined to die yet, for something happened that spared his life. Governor Yang Shun and Censor Lu Kai consulted each other day and night on plans to ingratiate themselves with the Yan family in hopes of obtaining royal titles. All too unexpectedly, a Secretary Wu Shilai of the Office of War heard about Yang Shun's killing of innocent civilians to claim credit and wrote a memorial denouncing him and also accusing Lu Kai of abetting him in his evil deeds. The memorial reached Emperor Jiajing just when he was making preparations for a prayer service. The report about the massacre so enraged the emperor for its disruption of universal harmony that he dispatched imperial guards to bring Yang Shun to face charges. Awed by the emperor's towering rage, Yan Song was not able to come to the rescue in time. However, Yan Song's mediation lightened the sentence to the deprivation of all official titles. How laughable that Yang Shun and Lu Kai killed to please their superiors, only to end up becoming objects of ridicule! What purpose did all their scheming serve? (*Good!*)

When word reached Prefect He that Governor Yang had been removed from office, the importance that the prefect attached to the case began to diminish. Now that Wen-shi stopped coming to make her tearful appeals and one of the two runners had died, leaving only Li Wan with his piteous pleas for mercy, Prefect He ordered that he be freed from his iron chains and try hard to bring Shen Xiang to the authorities. These were all too obviously signs that he was now a free man. Li Wan kowtowed again and again as if he had received an amnesty and, once out of the yamen, ran as fast as his legs could carry him. With no traveling money on him, he could do no better than beg his way home, but, of him, no more.

Now Shen Xiaoxia had been hiding in the double wall of Mr. Feng's house for months and learned everything that had happened through the inquiries of his host. News about Wen-shi finding shelter in a nunnery brought Shen Xiaoxia great inward joy. About a year later, he learned that Zhang Qian and Li Wan were no longer on his trail and that the case had cooled off. Feng had three inner rooms cleaned up for Shen Xiang to do his studies in, but would not allow him to venture out, nor was Shen's presence known to anyone outside. Though Mr Feng's three years of mourning had come to an end, for Mr. Shen's sake, he did not resume office.

Time sped by like an arrow. Shen Xiang had been staying with Mr. Feng for eight years now. Yan Song's wife Ouyang-shi died. Yan Shifan, the son, refused to accompany her coffin back to her native village but instead, urged his father to write a memorial requesting that he remain in the capital to "serve his father." In fact, during the mourning period, he drank and caroused day and night in the company of his concubines. Emperor Jiajing, being a most filial son, was displeased upon learning of such behavior. There was a priest called Lan Daoxing who could commune with the gods. The Son of Heaven summoned him and asked him to invoke some gods to answer questions about the virtue of the court ministers.

"The gods I invoke," said Lan Daoxing, "are true gods who dwell in heaven. Being of the highest integrity and not prone to flattery, they might say things offensive to Your Majesty. Please forgive me if this happens."

"It is indeed the divine words of truth that I wish to hear," said the emperor. "Why would I blame you for something that has nothing to do with you?"

Lan drew magic figures and chanted incantations, upon which the following lines appeared on his sand tray:[13]

> A high hill and foreign grass;
> The father and son are ministers of state.
> The sun and moon lose their brightness;
> The sky and earth are turned upside down.

Emperor Jiajing read the lines and said, "Please explain."

"But I am too ignorant to understand," said the priest. (*What a subtle way of offering advice! A clever man of the olden times.*)

"I do," said the emperor. "A high hill refers to the character *Song*, for it is made up of the components 'high' and 'hill.' 'Foreign grass' refers to the character *fan*, for it consists of the components 'foreign' and 'grass.' This is a reference to Yan Song and his son Yan Shifan. I have long heard that they have been abusing their power to the detriment of the interests of the empire. Now that the gods have revealed the truth to me, I will immediately take action, but you must not tell anyone about this."

With kowtows and assurances that he would not say a word about this, Lan Daoxing took his reward and departed.

Henceforth, Emperor Jiajing gradually distanced himself from Yan Song. A censor named Zou Yinglong took the opportunity and wrote a memorial to the emperor, accusing Yan Shifan of relying on his father's power to sell government posts and titles and commit many other evil deeds, and urging that he be executed. The memorial also requested that Yan Song, who doted on his evil son and formed a clique to bring down the worthy and the virtuous, be removed from his post so as to clean up the court. Immensely pleased with the memorial, Emperor Jiajing promoted Yinglong to the position of commissioner of the Bureau of Transmission. Yan Shifan was brought before the Judicial Office and charged with crimes punishable by banishment. Yan Song was sent back to his native village.

Soon thereafter, Lin Run, regional inspector of Jiangxi, reported that instead of performing military service, Yan Shifan stayed at home and became more of a despot, seizing fields from local residents, sheltering unsavory characters at home, establishing illicit communications with Japanese pirates, and engaging in other conspiratorial activities. By an imperial order, he was brought to the three judicial offices[14] for interrogation. After the investigators reported back to the imperial court confirming the charges, Yan Shifan was executed and his property confiscated. Yan Song was sent to a poorhouse, where he was to spend the rest of his days. All officials who had been wronged were rehabilitated.

As soon as he learned the good news, Feng hastened to repeat it to Shen Xiang, who was then let out of the study to go to the nunnery to see Wen Shunü. At the reunion, the husband and wife fell upon each other's shoulders and wept. Wen-shi had been three months pregnant when she left home. Now, her son, born in the nunnery, was already ten years old. Under Wen-shi's personal tutoring, the boy could already read the Five Classics,[15] to Shen Xiang's immense delight.

Feng decided to go to the capital for reappointment and asked Shen Xiang to go with him to clear his father's name. In the meantime, Wen-shi could stay with the Feng family. Shen Xiang took the advice and went with Feng to Beijing. As a first step, Mr. Feng paid a visit to Censor Zou of the Bureau of Transmission. Before showing him Shen Xiang's written complaint, he explained to Censor Zou the injustice done to Shen Lian and his sons. Zou Yinglong promised to do his utmost to have the case settled. The following day, Shen Xiang sent his memorial to the imperial court through the Bureau of Transmission. Thereafter, the emperor issued a decree that granted Shen Lian a posthumous promotion of one rank to redress the wrong done to a loyal subject. His wife and youngest son were to return to their native place. All their confiscated property was to be returned in full by the county and prefectural authorities. Having been a student on government stipend for many years, Shen Xiang was now made a tribute student[16] and a county magistrate.

Shen Xiang wrote another memorial to express his gratitude:

My father, Lian, intoned poems in indignation upon witnessing in Bao'an how Yang Shun, governor of Xuanfu and Datong, slaughtered civilians to claim false credit for himself. Imperial Censor Lu Kai, while inspecting the area, conspired

*with Yang Shun under secret orders from Yan Shifan and inflicted the death
penalty on my father and killed my two brothers. I myself had a narrow escape
from death. With the unjustly dead still unburied and the family line almost
discontinued, the sufferings my family has gone through are unsurpassed.
Although Yan Shifan has been executed, Yang Shun and Lu Kai are still safe
and secure in their native places. The grievances of the tens of thousands of the
unjustly killed at the frontier remain unaddressed and the three aggrieved souls
in my family remain unavenged. To satisfy popular feelings, anything less than
capital punishment will not suffice.*

The emperor approved the request. Yang Shun and Lu Kai were summoned again to Beijing and convicted of crimes punishable by death.

While Yang Shun and Lu Kai were in jail awaiting execution, Shen Xiang went to bid farewell to Mr. Feng, for he needed to go personally to Yunzhou to escort his mother and youngest brother Shen Zhi to Beijing to live somewhere near the Feng residence there. He would then proceed to Bao'an to search for his father's remains and bring them back for a proper burial.

Mr. Feng said, "I've just received an answer to my inquiries about your mother in Yunzhou. She is well. Your brother Shen Zhi is already a scholar. I will send someone to escort them here. Your most important task is to find your father's remains. You'd better go quickly. You can join your mother here later."

Thus instructed, Shen Xiang headed straight for Bao'an. Two days of searching produced nothing. On the third day, he was sitting tired in front of a house when an old man came out to invite him into the hall for a cup of tea. Shen Xiang's eyes fell upon a calligraphy scroll hanging on the wall. It was Zhuge Liang's two petition memorials, bearing a date but no signature. Shen Xiaoxia examined the scroll with such fixed intensity that the old man asked, "Why are you looking at that scroll?"

"May I ask who wrote it?"

"My deceased friend Shen Lian."

"Why is it in your house?"

"My name is Jia Shi," replied the old man. "When Shen Lian was sent to this region, he stayed with me in my house. We became sworn brothers. Who would have thought that later, a most extraordinary disaster was to strike him. Afraid that I would be implicated, I fled to Henan to be out of harm's way. I took with me two scrolls of calligraphy, which I remounted on one scroll and often look at it as if looking at his face. It wasn't until after Governor Yang was removed from office that I dared return here. Lady Xu and her youngest son Shen Zhi moved to Yunzhou. I often go there to visit them. Recently, when I heard that the Yan family was on the decline, I thought that my brother could now be rehabilitated, and sent a messenger to Yunzhou to report the news. I believe Mr. Shen Junior will come for his father's remains. I hung up the scroll in the main hall so that he could recognize his deceased father's handwriting."

At these words, Shen Xiaoxia threw himself to the ground, crying, "My most kind uncle!"

Jia Shi hastened to raise him to his feet, saying, "Who might you be?"

"I am Shen Xiang. It's my father's writing on that scroll."

"I heard that Yang Shun had summoned you in order to finish off the entire family. I thought he had killed you. How did you manage to survive?"

Shen Xiaoxia's detailed account of what had taken place at Linqing drew amazed exclamations from Jia Shi, who then told the servants to set out dinner in honor of the visitor.

"You must know where my father's remains are. Please show me the place."

"Your father died unjustly in prison. I stole his corpse and buried it without daring to breathe a word about it to anyone. Now that you are here to carry the remains back to your native place, my pains were not taken in vain."

They were heading for the door when a young man on horseback came up.

"What a coincidence!" Jia Shi said, pointing at the newcomer. "This is your youngest brother."

The young man was none other than Shen Zhi. As Shen Zhi got down from the horse to greet them, Jia Shi pointed at Shen Xiaoxia and said, "This is your oldest brother Shen Xiang."

This being the first time the brothers had ever laid eyes on each other, they embraced tearfully, not quite believing that this was not a dream. With Jia Shi leading the way, the three of them repaired to Shen Lian's grave, which was found to be so overgrown with weeds that the mound was hardly discernible. As Jia Shi led the Shen brothers in kowtowing to the tomb, the two brothers shed such bitter tears that they collapsed to the ground. "There are important matters I need to consult you about," said Jia Shi, trying to pacify them. "Don't let yourselves be consumed with grief."

Only then did they dry their tears. Jia Shi continued, "Your two brothers also died untimely deaths. It was the kindhearted jailer Mao, who, out of sympathy for them, secretly buried them three miles west of the city. Mao has passed away, but I know where he buried them. Since you are escorting your father's coffin back, why don't you also take your two brothers' remains back so that the spirits of the father and sons may stay together? What do you say?"

The Shen brothers agreed, "We could hope for nothing more."

That very day, they followed Jia Shi west of the city to look at the site and were overwhelmed with grief.

The following day, they prepared coffins and chose an auspicious day for digging up the graves for reburial. The three bodies remained as fresh as if they were alive. It was their righteous spirit that spared them from the least decomposition. That Shen Xiang and his brother shed more tears of grief need not be described here. When the carriages for the three coffins were ready, they went to take their leave of Jia Shi.

Before departing, Shen Xiang said to Jia Shi, "I would like to have the scroll for display in the memorial hall. I hope you will not turn me down."

Jia Shi readily gave consent, took down the scroll, and gave it to them as a gift. The Shen brothers bowed in gratitude and bade him a tearful farewell. Shen Xiang escorted the coffins first to Zhangjiawan,[17] where he had them loaded on a boat. Then he returned to Beijing, where he reported to his mother Lady Xu and thanked Mr. Feng before he got ready to leave.

Out of respect for Shen Lian's virtues and admiration for the Shen brothers for undertaking the journey with the coffins, all the officials in the capital sent gifts, money, and travel documents. Shen Xiaoxia accepted only one travel document and turned down all the others. Back at Zhangjiawan again, the party was transferred onto a government-owned boat. With a hundred men pulling and towing, the boat moved ahead at great speed. In a few days they arrived at Linqing. Shen Xiang ordered that the boat be moored while he himself went unaccompanied into town, delivered to the Feng residence a letter from Mr. Feng assuring his family of his well-being, and then took Wen-shi and their ten-year-old son to the boat. They paid their respects to the coffins before going to greet Lady Xu. The sight of her grown-up grandson filled the old lady with unspeakable joy. There was a time when the family line was thought to have been extinguished, but, in fact, it was now continuing well into the next generation, whereas the enemies of the family had all perished miserably as a retribution from heaven. The will of heaven indeed prevailed. Clearly, the wicked will come to grief, whereas virtue pays in the end.

Let us get back to our story. When the ship arrived in Shaoxing in Zhejiang, Meng Chunyuan, leading his daughter and Shen Xiang's wife, Mengshi, went twenty li from home to greet the Shen family. Sorrow and joy mingled at the family reunion. The boat bearing the coffins was moored in the harbor. All the local officials went there for mourning. Confiscated family possessions were all checked and returned. The Shen brothers buried the coffins in their ancestral graveyard and strictly observed three years of mourning. No one failed to praise them for their outstanding filial piety. The local magistrate also had a memorial hall erected in honor of Shen Lian, where memorial services were held each spring and autumn. The scroll in Shen Lian's handwriting is, to this day, hung in an honored place in the memorial hall.

On the day the mourning period ended, Shen Xiang went to the capital, where he was appointed a county magistrate. Being honest and incorrupt, he rose to be a prefect. Wen-shi's son passed the imperial examinations at an early age and became a *jinshi* in the same year as his uncle Shen Zhi. The family never ran short of scholars from generation to generation.

For his efforts to save Shen Xiang, Mr. Feng won great prestige in the capital for his loyalty and rose through the official ranks until he became secretary of the Ministry of Personnel. One day, Shen Lian appeared to him in a dream and said to him, "The Lord on High, impressed by my honesty and integrity, has made me the city god of Beijing. You are to be the city god of Nanjing. We shall be assuming our posts at the hour of noon tomorrow."

Feng woke up in amazement. When noon came, he saw a horse-drawn carriage approaching to receive him, and he passed away without any illness. Both men became gods. There is a poem in evidence:

> *Their integrity preserved their remains;*
> *Their spirits became immortal gods.*
> *The evil sank to perdition in hell;*
> *Divine justice was clear for all to see.*

Notes

Sources included in the Bibliography
are listed here in abbreviated form.

Introduction

1. Lu Shulun, "Feng Menglong," in his
Feng Menglong sanlun, 7.

2. See Pi-ching Hsu, "Celebrating the
Emotional Self," 41; Lu Shulun, *Feng Menglong
yanjiu,* 17–18.

3. See the Qing vernacular story "Jue
xinkeng qiangui cheng caizhu," *Zhao shi
bei,* in *Zhongguo gudai zhenxi ben xiaoshuo*
(Shenyang: Chunfeng Wenyi, 1994), 9:283.

4. *Guazhir, juan* 5:21a, in Wei Tongxian,
ed., *Feng Menglong quanji* (Shanghai: Shanghai
Guji, 1993), 42:145.

5. Hanan, *The Chinese Vernacular Story,*
80–81.

6. Lu Shulun, *Feng Menglong yanjiu,* 14.

7. Pi-ching Hsu, "Celebrating the Emotional Self," 57.

8. Hanan, *The Chinese Vernacular
Story,* 95.

9. Lu Shulun, "Feng Menglong," 76.

10. Hanan, *The Chinese Vernacular
Story,* 89.

11. *Guazhir, juan* 4:2b.

12. See Feng Mengxiong, "Fengshi *Linzhi
xiaoxu,"* in Feng Menglong, *Linjing zhiyue,* 1b,
in Wei Tongxian, ed., *Feng Menglong quanji,*
1:2.

13. Lu Shulun, "Feng Menglong," 85.

14. On the two titles of *Chunqiu hengku,*
see Wei Tongxian, "*Chunqiu hengku* yingyin
shuoming," in Wei Tongxian, ed., *Feng
Menglong quanji,* 3:1.

15. Pi-ching Hsu, "Celebrating the
Emotional Self," 46.

16. Hanan, *The Chinese Vernacular Story,*
82–83.

17. Ibid., 98–99.

18. Pi-ching Hsu, "Celebrating the
Emotional Self," 48.

19. Quoted in Lu Shulun, "Feng
Menglong," 92.

20. See Xu Shuofang, "Feng Menglong
nianpu," in *Xu Shuofang ji,* 2:433.

21. Hanan, *The Chinese Vernacular Story,*
86.

22. The facsimile edition of *Feng
Menglong quanji* (Complete works of Feng
Menglong), published by Shanghai Guji
Chubanshe in 1993, contains forty-three
volumes that, when stacked together, are
more than six feet tall.

23. Hanan, *The Chinese Vernacular Story,*
80–81.

24. Hanan, *The Chinese Vernacular
Story,* 81.

25. Rawski, "Economic and Social
Foundations of Late Imperial Culture," 3.

26. Hegel, *The Novel in Seventeenth-
Century China,* 11.

27. Ibid.

28. Rawski, "Economic and Social
Foundations of Late Imperial Culture," 9.

29. Hegel, *The Novel in Seventeenth-
Century China,* 14–15.

30. Ichisada Miyazaki, *China's Examination Hell,* 121.

31. Miyazaki, *China's Examination
Hell,* 118.

32. Hegel, *The Novel in Seventeenth-
Century China,* 15.

33. The moralistic and didactic tone
of the three *Sanyan* titles (*Illustrious Words
to Instruct the World, Comprehensive Words
to Warn the World,* and *Constant Words to*

Awaken the World) can probably also be understood in the same light.

34. Y. W. Ma, "Feng Meng-lung," in Nienhauser, ed., *The Indiana Companion to Traditional Chinese Literature*, 381.

35. Hanan, *The Chinese Vernacular Story*, 104; and *The Chinese Short Story*, 76–86.

36. In his "Preface to *Art Song Prosody*" (Qulü xu), Feng complains that "the most abused literary genres today are classical poetry and prose." In his preface to *Hill Songs*, he also says that "although there is an abundance of false poetry and prose, there are no false folk songs." See Guo Shaoyu, *Zhongguo lidai wenlun xuan*, 3:194, 231.

37. Birch, "Feng Meng-lung and the *Ku Chin Hsiao Shuo*," 82.

38. See Margaret L. John, "Parallelism in the Vernacular Short Story: Reading 'Yang Jiao'ai sheming quanjia' and 'Wu Bao'an qijia shuyou' as Pair Stories" (unpublished paper, University of Michigan, 1992), 1, 2, 13, 15.

39. Wong, "Morality as Entertainment," 59.

40. Jaroslav Průšek, "The Beginnings of Popular Chinese Literature; Urban Centers—the Cradle of Popular Fiction," in his *Chinese History and Literature*, 413.

41. See Shuhui Yang, *Appropriation and Representation: Feng Menglong and the Chinese Vernacular Story*, chap. 3.

42. Hanan, "The Nature of Ling Meng-ch'u's Fiction," 87.

43. See Hanan, "The Early Chinese Short Story," 304–6; and Rolston, *Traditional Chinese Fiction and Fiction Commentary*, 231.

44. Rolston, *Traditional Chinese Fiction and Fiction Commentary*, 231.

45. Hanan, "The Nature of Ling Meng-ch'u's Fiction," 87.

46. Rolston, *Traditional Chinese Fiction and Fiction Commentary*, 232. Rolston also says that the simulated storyteller can be seen "as a functional attempt to deal with the absence of the 'author' in early vernacular fiction."

47. The word *huaben* was adopted as the regular term for the traditional Chinese vernacular short story only in this century. On its early usage as simply "story," rather than "prompt-book," see Wivell, "The Term 'Hua-pen,'" 295–306. The "prompt-book" theory has been criticized from another angle: because professional storytellers were more likely to have relied on abstracts or notes in the classical language, the earliest extant *huaben* texts were perhaps also meant for reading, rather than reciting, as were their later imitations; see André Lévy, "*Hua-pen*," in Nienhauser, ed., *The Indiana Companion to Traditional Chinese Literature*, 443.

48. See Idema, "Storytelling and the Short Story in China," 3, 35–39.

49. Idema, "Some Remarks and Speculations Concerning *P'ing-hua*," rpt. in his *Chinese Vernacular Fiction*, 72.

50. Y. W. Ma, "Feng Meng-lung," in Nienhauser, ed., *The Indiana Companion to Traditional Chinese Literature*, 381.

51. See, e.g., Yang Xianyi and Gladys Yang, trans., *The Courtesan's Jewel Box*.

52. See Hu Wanchuan, "*Sanyan* xu ji meipi de zuozhe wenti," rpt. in his *Huaben yu caizi jiaren xiaoshuo zhi yanjiu*, 123–38.

53. Ling, "*Pai'an jingqi* xu," in *Chuke Pai'an jingqi*, 1; translation from Liu Wu-chi, *An Introduction to Chinese Literature*, 224, with some modifications.

54. Hanan, *The Chinese Vernacular Story*, 150.

55. This does not mean that he did not make plays out of his *own* stories; see Liu Hongjun, "Li Yu xiaoshuo chuangzuo tong xiju chuangzuo de guanxi," *Xinyang shifan xueyuan xuebao*, 1996. 2:57–58; reprinted in *Zhongguo gudai jindai wenxue yanjiu*, 7:98–99.

56. Patrick Hanan, "Introduction," in Hanan, trans., *Silent Operas*, vii.

57. Rolston, *Traditional Chinese Fiction and Fiction Commentary*, 232.

58. For Ling Mengchu's negative com-

ment on the arrangement of paired stories, see item 1 of his "General Principles" (Fan li), in his *Pai'an jingqi*, 3. Ling was the first to use parallel couplets for vernacular stories. Li Yu paired stories in his first two collections (see Rolston, review of Hanan, *The Invention of Li Yu*, 62–63). But a few years later he chose to use a parallel couplet for the title of each of the stories in his *Priceless Jade* (Liancheng bi), an expanded and modified edition of his previous two collections. In his last collection, *Twelve Towers*, couplets are used not for story titles, but for chapter titles. See Xiao Xinqiao, "Jiaodian shuoming," in *Li Yu quanji*, 8:i.

59. This phrase is from Huang, "Dehistoricization and Intertextualization," 45.

Title Page and Preface to the 1620 Edition

1. *Zaju* (lit., "variety show" or "miscellaneous entertainment") is a four-act musical drama, now commonly translated as "Yuan drama"; *chuanqi* (romance drama, lit., "transmission of the remarkable") is the designation used for several hundred "southern-style" plays of the Ming and Qing periods. Compared with *zaju*, a *chuanqi* play is much longer, usually comprising thirty to forty scenes.

2. The legendary ruler Fuxi was reputed to have invented the Eight Trigrams and writing.

3. Later texts have the variant "from one's childhood days" (*xiaosong*) for "every day" (*risong*). See Liu Wu-chi, *An Introduction to Chinese Literature*, 216 n. 3.

4. Generally believed to be Feng Menglong himself.

5. See note 4.

1. Jiang Xingge Reencounters His Pearl Shirt

Story 1 has been translated as "The Pearl-Sewn Shirt" by Cyril Birch, in Feng, trans. Birch, *Stories from a Ming Collection*, 39–96;

and as "The Pearl Shirt Reencountered" by Jeanne Kelly, in Ma and Lau, eds., *Traditional Chinese Stories*, 264–92.

1. In the Ming dynasty, Huguang consisted of what are now Hubei and Hunan Provinces. Xiangyang Prefecture was located in the northern part of what is now Hubei.

2. The six preliminaries are: giving presents to the prospective bride's family, providing written documentation of the prospective bride's name and date of birth, securing through divination by the groom's family of a good omen endorsing the marriage, sending a letter and wedding gifts to the bride's family (whose letter of acceptance confirms the marriage), requesting approval by the bride's family of an auspicious date for the wedding, and the groom's going in person to bring the bride home.

3. "Clouds and rain" is a metaphor for sexual encounters. It was first used in the prose poem "Gao tang fu," attributed to Song Yu (c. 290–c. 223 B.C.E.).

4. The seventh day of the seventh month of the lunar calendar is a festival that celebrates the annual meeting across the Milky Way of the stars Herdboy and Weaving Maiden. On the day of the festival, women set out fruit offerings to Weaving Maiden and prayed that they would be blessed with better skills in sewing and embroidery. As the festival was known as Qiqiao (Praying for Skills), the third (*san*) daughter of the Wang family, born on that date, was thus called Sanqiao (The Third Blessed).

5. Xishi, also known as Xizi, was a legendary beauty of the state of Yue in the Warring States period (475–221 B.C.E.).

6. Nanwei was a famous beauty in the court of Duke Wen of Jin (636–628 B.C.E.) in the Spring and Autumn period (770–476 B.C.E.).

7. The bodhisattva Guanyin, the embodiment of compassion, was popularly conceived in late imperial China as a beautiful young woman.

8. A mace in the Ming dynasty equalled 3.69 grams.

9. Song Yu was a disciple of the great poet Qu Yuan (ca. 340–278 B.C.E.). See also note 3 of this story.

10. Pan Yue (265–419), courtesy name Anren, but more often known as Pan An, personifies male beauty.

11. *Hejian fu,* "debauched woman," was a term first used by Liu Zongyuan (773–819) in his "Story of Hejian." It was later used to refer to Pan Jinlian (Gold Lily), a debauched woman in the Ming novel *The Plum in the Golden Vase.*

12. Liu Bang (256–195 B.C.E.) was the founder of the Han dynasty. Xiang Yu (232–202 B.C.E.), king of Chu, was his major rival in contending for the throne. Before he became emperor, Liu Bang enlisted the service of Han Xin (d. 196 B.C.E.) and built a platform for a grand ceremony honoring him as grand marshal. Later, Han Xin proved to be instrumental in the defeat of Xiang Yu.

13. Linqing is in present-day Shandong Province.

14. Sima Xiangru (179–117 B.C.E.), one of the most celebrated *fu* (prose poem) writers in the history of Chinese literature, is also known for his romance with Zhuo Wenjun. The two eloped after their first meeting.

15. According to Song dynasty folklore, Pan Bizheng, a native of Henan, fell in love with the Taoist priestess Chen Miaochang. The two were later joined in matrimony.

16. The Lantern Festival falls on the fifteenth day of the first month. For the Clear and Bright (Qingming) Festival in April, people visit the graves of their ancestors.

17. The seven offenses by a wife that warranted divorce were: failure to produce a son, adultery, failure to serve the parents-in-law, verbal viciousness, theft, jealousy, and affliction with foul disease.

18. Jingkou is present-day Zhenjiang, Jiangsu.

19. Hepu is a pearl-producing area in present-day Guangxi Autonomous Region.

20. According to a legend from the Eastern (or Later) Han dynasty (25–220), the pearl-bearing oysters that abounded in the sea off the coast of Hepu County gradually migrated away because successive prefects were insatiably avaricious. When Meng Chang became prefect and put an end to all corruption, the oysters returned.

21. According to a legend from the Jin dynasty (265–420), Zhang Hua (232–300) saw that there was an aura over Fengcheng that bespoke of hidden precious swords. After he appointed Lei Huan as prefect of Fengcheng, Lei Huan dug up a pair of swords and presented one to Zhang Hua, keeping the other for himself. After both men died, the swords were seen at Yanping Ferry, where they joined together and changed into two dragons.

2. Censor Chen Ingeniously Solves the Case of the Gold Hairpins and Brooches

Story 2 has been partially translated as "The Clever Judgment of Censor Chen Lien" by E. C. Chu, in *China Journal* 10:59–66 (1929); and partially translated as "The Case of the Gold Hairpins" by P. C. Yao, in *Renditions* 118–36 (Autumn, 1975).

1. Pei Du (765–839) of the Tang dynasty was, before his rise to power, touring the Fragrant Temple one day when he found two jade belts and a belt made of rhinoceros horn that a woman had obtained as a loan with which to redeem her father from prison. Pei Du returned the belts to her, an act that was believed to have earned him merit in the otherworld and accounted for his attaining the post of prime minister later in his life.

2. See note 2 of story 1 in this collection.

3. Legend has it that in the Song dynasty, Qian Yulian entered into a betrothal with Wang Shipeng against the wishes of her stepmother. Later, when Wang Shipeng was

demoted and sent away, her stepmother forced her to marry her rich nephew Sun Ruquan, whereupon Qian Yulian tied a rock to herself and jumped into the Ou River, but was rescued.

4. A tribute student was one who was admitted into the National University as a nominee of local Confucian schools for advanced study and subsequent admission to the civil service.

5. Burning incense was a way of expressing gratitude to a deity, a spirit, or a benefactor to whom one had no other means of offering thanks.

3. Han the Fifth Sells Her Charms in New Bridge Town

Story 3 has been translated as "Han Wuniang Sells Her Charms at the New Bridge Market" by Robert C. Miller, in Ma and Lau, eds., *Traditional Chinese Stories*, 312–24.

1. *Poems on Historical Events* is a collection of poems by Hu Zeng (fl. 860). An otherwise obscure poet, he is most frequently cited for poems on historical sites in the earliest historical narratives in the vernacular, the *pinghua*.

2. It was in a horse stable that the above-mentioned Duke Ling of Chen was killed by Xia Zhengshu, the son of his mistress.

3. This is a reference to King Chen and his two concubines' hiding themselves in a dry well.

4. This was part of the Grand Canal project that linked the Yellow and Yangzi Rivers.

5. Yuwen Huaji was a subordinate of Emperor Yang.

6. The two capitals were Chang'an and Luoyang.

7. See note 8 of story 1.

8. Mount Gen Gate was the northeast gate of the city of Lin'an.

9. According to traditional Chinese medical knowledge, there are three pulses in each wrist.

4. Ruan San Redeems His Debt in Leisurely Clouds Nunnery

1. Xiang Chang (courtesy name, Ziping) of the Eastern Han dynasty was a recluse who refused to accept appointments for office, abandoned all family duties after his children were married, and spent the rest of his life touring scenic mountains. Hence, to marry off a child is to "fulfill the wish of Xiang Ziping."

2. The Song Western Capital, Xijing, is present-day Luoyang, Henan.

3. The Song Eastern Capital is present-day Kaifeng, Henan.

4. The *xiao* is a vertical bamboo flute.

5. The *sheng* is a reed-pipe wind instrument.

6. Song Yu (see also notes 3 and 9 of story 1) said in one of his prose poems (*fu*) that a beautiful girl stole furtive glances at him from over the neighbor's wall for a period of three years.

7. Zhuo Wenjun, daughter of an immensely rich family in the Han dynasty, eloped with Sima Xiangru after the latter played the lute to her in covert courtship. See also note 14 of story 1.

8. See note 15 of story 1.

9. Zongruan means "a descendant or a member of the Ruan family."

10. The caves in Big You Mountain and Small You Mountain in Hunan were said to be full of books left there by people of the Qin dynasty.

5. Penniless Ma Zhou Meets His Opportunity through a Woman Selling Pancakes

Story 5 has been translated as "Wine and Dumplings" by Cyril Birch, in Feng, trans. Birch, *Stories from a Ming Collection*, 103–15.

1. The academicians Du Ruhui, Fang Xuanling, et al. constituted the Institute of Education (Wenxueguan), founded by Emperor Taizong.

2. It was actually not until the Song dynasty that there came to be eighteen regional military commanders in the empire.

3. This is a metaphor for a sovereign (dragon) meeting his minister (tiger).

4. This refers to Tao Yuanming (Tao Qian, 365–427) who, in refusing to "stoop low for the sake of five piculs of rice," resigned from his post and spent the rest of his life as a recluse, farming in his native village. See also note 3 of story 8.

5. Han prime minister Xiao He (d. 193 B.C.E.) recommended to Liu Bang the services of Han Xin, who was instrumental in helping Liu Bang (256–195 B.C.E.) found the Han dynasty.

6. Wei Wuzhi recommended to Liu Bang (see note 5 above) the services of Chen Ping, who later became prime minister.

7. On Liu Bang (Emperor Gaozu's name), see notes 5 and 6 above.

8. This refers to the story that Han Xin (d. 196 B.C.E.), before he became commander in chief under Liu Bang (see notes 5, 6, and 7 above), was fishing when an old woman washing clothes by the river noticed that he looked hungry and gave him some food. After he rose to power, Han Xin sought out the old woman and gave her a reward of a thousand pieces of gold. See also note 12 of story 1.

9. Persian merchants trading with China were known as connoisseurs of jewelry and antiques.

6. Lord Ge Gives Away Pearl Maiden

1. On King You's beacon fires on Mount Li, see the first paragraph of story 3.

2. *Ge* also means "kudzu vine."

3. See note 5 of story 5.

4. On Han Xin, see note 12 of story 1 and note 8 of story 5.

5. On the Clear and Bright Festival, see note 16 of story 1.

6. Yang Yuhuan (Yang Guifei; 719–56)

was a favorite consort of Emperor Xuanzong (Minghuang; r. 712–55) of the Tang dynasty.

7. Zhao Feiyan (d. 1 B.C.E.) was a court lady in the service of Emperor Cheng (r. 32–6 B.C.E.) of the Han dynasty and was later made empress.

8. On Xishi, see note 5 of story 1.

9. On Nanwei, see note 6 of story 1.

10. Ma Zhou is the main character in story 5.

11. A green dragon symbolizes luck, and a white tiger misfortune.

12. In 911, the king of Jin put the Later Liang army to rout at Baixiang (in present-day Hebei) in a major battle with Li Cunzhang as the commander of the Jin army.

13. During the Warring States period, Prince Zhao of Yan had a stage erected southeast of Yishui and piled a thousand pieces of gold upon the platform in a bid to recruit men of worth. The stage thus came to be called the "platform of gold."

7. Yang Jiao'ai Lays Down His Life for the Sake of Friendship

Story 7 has been translated as "Yang Jiao Throws Away His Life in Fulfillment of a Friendship" by William Dolby in *The Perfect Lady by Mistake and Other Stories by Feng Menglong*, 144–58. In the original text, there is a note appended to the title: "One text reads: 'Yang Jiao'ai Dies to Fight Jing Ke.'"

1. The Qiang tribes lived mostly in areas that are now in the provinces of Gansu, Qinghai, and Sichuan.

2. The Liang Mountains are in present-day Shaanxi.

3. *Guang Yu Ji* is possibly a variant title of *Guang yu tu*, an official Ming Dynasty atlas of the empire.

4. In the Spring and Autumn period, ordinary grand master (*zhong da fu*) was around the middle of the nine official ranks.

5. Jing Ke (d. 227 B.C.E.) is famous for

his failed assassination attempt against the First Emperor of Qin (r. 221–210 B.C.E.). He took on the ill-fated mission for Prince Dan of Yan (d. ca. 222 B.C.E.).

8. Wu Bao'an Abandons His Family to Ransom His Friend

Story 8 has been translated as "The Journey of the Corpse" by Cyril Birch in Feng, trans. Birch, *Stories from a Ming Collection*, 129–49; and as "Wu Pao-an Ransoms His Friend" by John Kwan-Terry, in Ma and Lau eds., *Traditional Chinese Stories*, 4–18.

1. According to traditional decorum, a host does not introduce his wife to ordinary guests.

2. Yang Jiao'ai and Zuo Botao are the heroes of story 7.

3. Tao Yuanming expressed such a wish in his prose poem (*fu*) "The Return" (Gui qu lai ci). See also note 4 of story 5.

4. Ji Kang (courtesy name Shuye, 223–62), severed his friendship with Shan Tao, who recommended him to office against his wishes.

5. Liu Xiaobiao was the courtesy name of Liu Jun (462–521).

6. Gong Yu, in the reign of Emperor Yuandi (48–33 B.C.E.) of the Han dynasty, had such a close friendship with Wang Ji that they would assume or leave office at about the same time. Contemporaries said of them, "When Wang takes office, Gong Yu dusts his cap, ready for his own appointment."

7. On Jing Ke, see note 5 of story 7.

8. Ban Chao (C.E. 33–103) of the Eastern Han dynasty was sent by Emperor Ming to regions to the west of China and established alliances with over fifty states. See also note 17 of story 21.

9. Fu Jiezi was an imperial envoy to the Western Regions under Emperor Zhao (86–74 B.C.E.) of the Western Han dynasty.

10. Empress Wu Zetian (r. 684–704) was the only female sovereign in Chinese history.

11. Zhuge Liang (courtesy name Kongming, 181–234), was adviser to Liu Bei (162–223), founder of the kingdom of Shu in the Three Kingdoms period (220–265). Meng Huo was chieftain of the tribes living in what is now Yunnan.

12. The Jian Mountains are in present-day Sichuan.

13. The Wuman tribes lived in what is now Yunnan.

14. Ma Yuan (14 B.C.E.–C.E. 49) was a general who set up bronze pillars at the border of Jiaozhi (in what is now Vietnam) to commemorate the success of his military expedition.

15. The duke of Ji of the Shang dynasty (ca. 1600–ca. 1028 B.C.E.) remonstrated with the cruel King Zhou (d. 1027 B.C.E.) to no avail and, feigning madness, ran away as a slave.

16. Su Wu (140–60 B.C.E.), as envoy from the Han emperor to the Huns, was detained by the Huns and made to herd sheep near Lake Baikal in Siberia. He returned to China nineteen years later.

17. Yu Fan (courtesy name Zhongxiang, 164–226) was a subject of Sun Ce and Sun Quan of the state of Wu during the Three Kingdoms period.

18. The central plains are the regions along the middle and lower reaches of the Yellow River.

19. Yangping, also known as Wuyang County, was in what is now Shandong.

20. See note 19.

21. A line from "Mugua," in *The Book of Songs*.

22. See note 16. When the Chinese asked for Su Wu's release, the Huns said he was already dead. It was not until after the Chinese side claimed that the emperor had shot down a wild goose carrying a letter from Su Wu, proving that he was alive, that the Huns relented and set Su Wu free.

9. Duke Pei of Jin Returns a Concubine to Her Rightful Husband

1. Heng and Ji are in present-day Hebei.

2. Zi and Qing are in present-day Shandong.

3. Kuaiji is now pronounced Guiji.

4. See note 16 of story 1.

5. According to "The Biography of Zhu Fu," in *The History of the Later [Eastern] Han Dynasty* (Hou Han shu), a pig in Liaodong was very proud of the whiteness of its offspring, but, once it crossed the river, it was astounded to see that all the pigs there were white.

6. Literally, "When your time goes, a thunderbolt will smash the stone tablet of the Jianfu Temple." This is from a Song dynasty (960–1279) story: When the famous essayist and poet Fan Zhongyan (989–1052) was prefect of Raozhou, a poverty-stricken scholar went to seek his help. Fan Zhongyan offered to make him one thousand rubbings of a Jianfu Temple stone tablet with inscriptions by the most popular calligrapher of the day, Ouyang Xun, for each would be worth a thousand in cash. On the very night before the rubbings were to be done, the stone tablet was destroyed by a thunderbolt.

7. Literally, "When your time comes, the wind will send you to the Pavilion of Prince Teng." This is from a Tang dynasty legend about Wang Bo (640–676), a famous poet and master of prose. He was on his way to visit his father in Jiangxi when a gust of wind blew him to the prefect's banquet in the Pavilion of Prince Teng in the city of Nanchang by the West River, and that was how he came to write his best-known piece, "A Preface to the Poem 'Pavilion of Prince Teng.'"

10. Magistrate Teng Settles the Case of Inheritance with Ghostly Cleverness

Story 10 has been translated as "The Hidden Will" by Yang Xianyi and Gladys Yang, in *The Courtesan's Jewel Box,* 89–116; and as "Magistrate T'eng and the Case of Inheritance" by Susan Arnold Zonana, in Ma and Lau, eds., *Traditional Chinese Stories,* 485–501.

1. Xie An (320–385) once asked his sons and nephews why parents would wish their sons success in life. A nephew, Xie Xuan, answered, "It is just as one would wish to have orchids and jade trees grow in his own yard." Hence, "orchids and jade trees" has become a metaphor for children who bring their parents honor.

As legend has it, in the Han dynasty there lived three brothers—Tian Zhen, Tian Qing, and Tian Guang—who, in the process of dividing up their deceased parents' property, talked about cutting up the redbud tree in the yard. Suddenly, the tree withered and died. Awed by the sight, the three brothers decided not to divide their inheritance, whereupon the tree came back to life again.

2. In imperial China, the lunar calendar prepared by the Directorate of Astronomy had to be approved by the emperor before it was put to use, hence the term "imperial calendar." It was also called the "yellow calendar" because its cover was yellow.

3. On the first birthday of a boy, parents, as dictated by tradition, put various objects on a tray for the boy to choose from. The first thing he laid his hands on was understood to indicate his future aspirations.

4. Chinese families often give children of the same generation names with one character in common as a mark of their generational identity within the family or clan.

5. One *mu* is equivalent to roughly one-sixth of an acre.

6. It is believed that on the night the soul of the deceased is to return home to wreak havoc, family members should leave the house to keep themselves out of harm's way.

7. Lord Guan (Guan Yu; d. 220), a sworn brother of Liu Bei (see note 11 of story 8) in the Three Kingdoms period, is, to this

day, revered as a central figure in the folk pantheon and is the embodiment of fidelity to commitments.

8. Master Guigu was a leading political strategist of the Warring States period (475–221 B.C.E.).

11. Zhao Bosheng Meets with Emperor Renzong in a Teahouse

1. Blue clouds are a metaphor for high office.

2. The rivers' high tide in the second and third months of the year, when peach blossoms are in bloom, is often referred to as the "peach blossom tide." It is also a time when carp are believed to gather at Dragon Gate Hill by the Yellow River near Hejin County, Shanxi. Legend has it that those carp that could jump over Dragon Gate Hill became dragons, hence the analogy of candidates passing the imperial examinations to carp jumping over the Dragon Gate.

3. "Weicheng" is a poem by the famous poet Wang Wei (701–61) on the sorrow of separation between friends.

4. In ancient times, willow branches were broken to be given as parting gifts because the words "willow" (*liu*) and "to stay" (*liu*) are homophones.

5. Feasts customarily were given by the emperor in honor of those who passed the imperial civil service examinations at the metropolitan level and became *jinshi*.

6. "Phoenix tower" refers to a woman's living quarters. It may also imply an eligible daughter of a rich and eminent family.

7. The four treasures of the scholar's study are brush-pen, ink slab, ink-stone, and paper.

8. The poem "Nine Arguments," attributed to Song Yu, starts with a line describing his melancholy. See also notes 3 and 9 of story 1, and note 6 of story 4.

9. Jiang Yan (444–505) wrote a prose

poem titled "On Resentment" (Hen fu).

10. Han Yu (768–824), a major figure in the history of Chinese literature, was once exiled to the far south for having criticized Emperor Xianzong.

11. Su Qin (d. 317 B.C.E.), of the Warring States period, was shunned by his kinsmen for having returned home impoverished after a prolonged journey to find employment.

12. A thin fabric made of yellow grass was specific to the region of Suzhou in the Song dynasty.

13. This is the character *xu* 旭 in Zhao Xu's name.

14. Wind and clouds are a metaphor for a scholar's receiving recognition from the imperial government. The expression appears in the original text as "wind and rain," but the word "rain" must be a misprint.

15. Zhao was the surname of the imperial family during the Song dynasty.

16. Sent as imperial envoy to the peoples of the southwest, Sima Xiangru passed by his hometown, where he had lived in poverty, and was honored by all local officials and his father-in-law. See also note 14 of story 1, and note 7 of story 4.

17. Su Qin, a native of Luoyang of the period of the Warring States, had been humiliated by his kith and kin. Later, when he passed by his hometown after his rise to power, his relatives did not even dare to look at him because, in his sister-in-law's words, "You're now a powerful man loaded with gold." See also note 11 above.

12. The Courtesans Mourn Liu the Seventh in the Spring Breeze

1. The character for "poems" (*shi*) in this text appears in *Quan Tang shi* (A complete collection of Tang poems) as *shu* (letter, book, document). South Mountain is located about three miles south of Xiangyang in modern north-central Hubei.

2. In the Chinese lunar calendar, spring marks the beginning of a year.

3. Meng Haoran (689–740) spent most of his life on South Mountain.

4. The Eastern Capital (Dongjing) in the Tang dynasty is now Luoyang, Henan, but this prologue story most probably took place in Chang'an, the Tang Western Capital.

5. According to *Quan Tang shi,* this line should be "Faint clouds bedim the Milky Way."

6. These lines refer to the huge Dongting Lake outside of the city of Yueyang, Hunan. Opinions differ as to whether Yun and Meng were separate marshes or a single one.

7. It is "Emperor Shenzong" in the original text, but as Emperor Shenzong's reign did not begin until 1068, fifteen years after Liu's death, the author must have had Emperor Renzong in mind, the words *ren* and *shen* being pronounced the same way in his native Wu dialect. Later in the story when the emperor is mentioned again, he is referred to as "Emperor Renzong."

8. The character *jian,* "adultery," consists of three identical component parts, each being the character *nü,* "woman."

9. Qin Guan (1049–1100), courtesy name Shaoyou, was a famous *ci* poet.

10. "Chang'an" was sometimes used to refer, in general, to the capital and, in this case, to the Song Eastern Capital, Bianliang.

11. See note 3 of story 1.

12. In the original poem as it appears in *Quan Song ci* (The complete collection of Song *ci* poems), this line is "In letters of late, there is nothing but empty talk." The author changed it to suit the story line.

13. Zhang Youyu probably is Zhang Chou (1577–1643), a native of Wu, five years younger than Feng Menglong.

14. Lü Wang, popularly known as Taigong Wang, Jiang Taigong, or Jiang Ziya,

was a miliary strategist who did not rise to eminence until, while fishing by the Wei River when he was about eighty years old, he was accosted by King Wen of the Zhou dynasty (ca. 1027–256 B.C.E.).

15. Literally, "He shall supervise the rating of officials in the Imperial Secretariat twenty-four times," an allusion to the fact that Guo Ziyi (697–781), prime minister in the Tang dynasty, supervised the rating of Imperial Secretariat officials twenty-four times in his long career.

16. Pei Du was granted the title of duke of Jin by Emperor Xianzong of the Tang dynasty. See also note 1 of story 2.

17. On Guo Ziyi, see note 15.

18. Wen Tianxiang (1236–83) is remembered for his courage in facing death after being captured by the Mongols.

19. The Bureau of Remonstrance was an agency of the central government, first established in 1020, charged with scrutinizing and criticizing policy decisions.

20. "In moonlight and breeze" (*feng qian yue xia*) also means "in love."

21. In Chinese mythology, the Jade Emperor is the supreme sovereign of heaven.

22. See note 16 of story 1.

13. Zhang Daoling Tests Zhao Sheng Seven Times

1. Tang Yin (courtesy name, Bohu; 1470–1524) was a painter and calligrapher, and appears as a romantic figure in popular literature.

2. Zhang Liang (courtesy name Zifang; d. 189 B.C.E.) is known for his failed attempt to assassinate the First Emperor of Qin. Later he served as advisor to Liu Bang, the founder of the Han dynasty. On Liu Bang, see also note 12 of story 1, and notes 5 and 6 of story 5.

3. Also romanized *Tao-te Ching,* the *Daode jing* is a short text attributed to the philosopher Lao Zi. It is the best-known text in classical Taoist philosophy and the book

that has most frequently been translated from Chinese to English.

4. Fuxi is one of the legendary Three Sovereigns who ruled in antiquity. See also note 2 of the title page and preface to the 1620 edition, and note 2 of story 25.

5. Physiognomists believe that the forehead ridge and long arms indicate potential wealth and high social status.

6. As legend has it, Prince Hui of Qin of the Warring States period wanted to wage war against the state of Shu (present-day Sichuan) but, unable to find any thoroughfare leading to Shu, had five bulls carved of stone and hid gold under their tails, claiming that the bulls excreted gold droppings. Fu Li, the prince of Shu, was taken in and sent five strong men to pull the stone bulls to Shu, thus revealing the secret passage.

7. The Red Terrace, in folk tradition, is a residence of gods.

8. Sala is probably a fictitious kingdom, but it could refer to the ancient kingdom of Sravasti in northwest India.

9. Taoist alchemists believed that the longer the firing process was and the more frequently the elixir was returned to the crucibles, the more powerful the elixir would be.

10. Liuxia Hui, a court official of the state of Lu in the Spring and Autumn period, was known for his stoic indifference to sexual temptation.

11. Master Lü Chunyang, also known as Lü Dongbin, is one of the Eight Immortals in Taoist legends.

14. Chen Xiyi Rejects Four Appointments from the Imperial Court

1. Chen Tuan (d. 989) was a famous scholar recluse.

2. Peng Zu was a legendary figure in the time of the sage king Yao (before 2100 B.C.E.) who was said to have lived for eight hundred years.

3. *The Yellow Court Canon* and *Lao Zi* are central texts of "inner alchemy" and Taoist philosophy.

4. The seven emotions are joy, anger, sorrow, fear, love, hate, and desire.

5. In Buddhist terms, the six desires are the six sexual attractions arising from color, form, carriage, voice, softness, and features. The expression has come to mean human desires in general.

6. Zhenwu or Xuanwu was a legendary figure of the Han dynasty who was said to have crossed the Eastern Sea and received a double-edged sword from a god. Then he went into the mountains, from which he later ascended to heaven. Because he watched over the northern region by the order of the Lord on High, the title Xuanwu became identified with the serpent-entwined tortoise that symbolizes the north.

7. This is a reference to Xuanwu. See note 6.

8. Zhao Kuangyin was the founder of the Song dynasty.

9. The Khitans were a Tatar people who dominated north China from the tenth to the twelfth century and established the Liao dynasty (916–1125).

10. The Duangong reign period lasted for only two years. There could not have been a fifth year.

15. The Dragon-and-Tiger Reunion of Shi Hongzhao the Minister and His Friend the King

Title: The dragon represents a sovereign, and the tiger his minister.

1. "Red-tailed fish" is a metaphor for assiduous workers, for the ancients believed that when tired, fish would turn red in the tail. The prefects referred to probably are previous distinguished prefects of Yingzhou: Yan Shu (991–1055), Ouyang Xiu (1007–72), and Lu Gongzhu (1018–89). Ouyang Xiu, also a historian, epigrapher, statesman, and

leading personality of his time, was prefect of Yingzhou before Su Shi (see note 2 below) was. The Double-Ninth Festival, on the ninth day of the ninth lunar month, is celebrated by climbing hills and drinking chrysanthemum wine. The Hall of Stars was where Ouyang Xiu, while prefect of Yingzhou, met with his literati friends.

2. Su Shi (Su Dongpo, 1037–1101), one of the greatest men of letters in the history of Chinese literature, requested in 1091 to leave the Hanlin Academy and was assigned a few months later as prefect not of Hangzhou but of Yingzhou (present-day Fuyang, Anhui). There was in Yingzhou a West Lake (referred to in the poem), which the author apparently mistook for West Lake in Hangzhou, hence the confusion.

3. It was actually in the fourth year of the Xining reign period (1071) that Su Shi assumed the post of controller general of Hangzhou.

4. Hong Mai (1123–1202) was the author of *The Records of Yijian,* a collection of nearly 2,700 stories that deal with dreams, relations between the human and supernatural worlds, the origins of poems, etc.

5. See note 7 of story 11.

6. Zhang Ziwei or Zhang Nie (1096–1148). His literary works are collected in *Ziwei ji.*

7. The "jasper pool" is a metaphor for the abode of the gods in heaven.

8. As yet unidentified.

9. Wang Tanshou of Song (420–79) of the Southern Dynasties, a good singer, was told about Xie An's wish to hear him sing. One day, when Xie An was giving a feast in the East Earth Mountains, Wang Tanshou rode there on horseback, sang a song, and left.

10. Cao Xiangu was a female Taoist of the Song dynasty.

11. Zhu Shuzhen was a native of Qiantang (Hangzhou) in the Song dynasty. Unhappy in her marriage, she wrote *ci* poems of a mostly melancholy nature.

12. On Qin Shaoyou, see note 9 of story 12.

13. The prince of Ning was the brother of Li Longji, Emperor Xuanzong of the Tang dynasty, and a skilled flute player.

14. Huan Yi, prefect of Jiangzhou in the Jin dynasty, was also an accomplished flute player.

15. Cai Yi of the Han dynasty was passing through a place called Keting when he noticed that a piece of bamboo used as a house rafter could be made into a wonderful flute.

16. Yan Zhaoliang is being taken to the netherworld, as the story goes on to tell.

17. The Bamboo Grove Temple, located near Mount Tai, is often reflected in the clouds like a mirage after a rainfall.

18. It was believed that the size of one's gallbladder determined one's degree of courage.

19. Shi Xindao is as yet unidentified.

20. In classical poetry, plum blossoms and willow catkins are often used as metaphors for snowflakes. Mount Yu, on the border of Jiangxi and Guangdong, is famous for its abundance of plum blossoms. Zhang Terrace was a feature in the king of Qin's palace in the Warring States period.

21. Han Shizhong (1089–1151) was a famous general who successfully repelled attacks by invading Jurchen troops.

22. Yao (pre-Xia era), Shun (pre-Xia era), Yu (Xia dynasty), and Tang (Shang dynasty) are all revered as sage kings.

23. Chen Ping, a prime minister in the Han dynasty, suffered from poverty before his rise to prominence.

24. Mr. Lü of Shanfu married his daughter Lü Si to Liu Bang, who later became the first emperor of the Han dynasty, and his daughter Lü Xu to Fan Kuai, Liu Bang's subordinate.

25. Yang Hu, a military commander of the Western (Former) Jin dynasty (265–316),

recommended that Du Yu replace him after his death to carry out his plan to expand the empire.

26. Bao Shu and Guan Zhong, of the state of Qi in the Spring and Autumn period, were good friends, one serving Prince Xiaobai, the other serving Prince Jiu. Later, when Xiaobai assumed the throne as King Huan of Qi, Prince Jiu died in defeat, and Guan was thrown into prison. It was through the recommendation of Bao Shu that King Huan appointed Guan Zhong to office. For more on these two, see story 7.

27. Xiao He, prime minister under the first emperor of the Han dynasty, formulated the larger part of the Han penal code. See also note 5 of story 5.

28. The Palace Command (Diansi or Dianqiansi) was the administrative headquarters that controlled the imperial armies.

29. See note 9 of story 14.

16. The Chicken-and-Millet Dinner for Fan Juqing, Friend in Life and Death

Story 16 has been translated as "Fan Chu Ching's Eternal Friendship" by John Lyman Bishop in his *The Colloquial Short Story in China*, 88–103.

1. The Double Ninth Festival falls on the ninth day of the ninth month. On this day, it is a Chinese tradition to drink chrysanthemum wine, climb up mountains, and deck the hair with dogwood sprays. Wang Wei's famous poem "Thinking of My Brothers in Shandong on the Ninth Day of the Ninth Month" mentions dogwood as a reminder of a brother's absence.

2. It was believed that ghosts, unable to partake of food, could only consume the aroma.

3. *The Analects*, 2:22. This sentence refers to the virtue of fidelity.

4. *The Analects*, 12:7. This does not fit the notion of fidelity in this context but

refers to the trust that people place in their government, although the Chinese character for both concepts, out of context, is the same (*xin*).

5. According to the biography of Fan Shi in Fan Ye's *History of the Later Han Dynasty*, it was Fan Shi who went to the funeral of Zhang Shao, who had died of an illness. Zhang Shao's mother saw Fan Juqing "approaching with loud wails of grief in a white carriage drawn by a white horse."

6. In the Han dynasty, the Court for Dependencies was responsible for receiving tributary envoys at court.

17. Shan Fulang's Happy Marriage in Quanzhou

1. Jiaru, in what is now Luoyang, was the capital of the Eastern Zhou dynasty (770–256 B.C.E.). The dynasty is divided, according to the location of the capital, into Western Zhou and Eastern Zhou, and altogether lasted about eight hundred years.

2. In the Song dynasty, Luoyang was also known as the Western Capital.

3. The Jurchen people established their own dynasty, the Jin, between 1115 and 1122 and drove the Song dynasty south of the Huai River. The Jin was destroyed in 1234 by the Mongols.

4. Wolipu (d. 1127), the second son of Aguda (Ogda), Emperor Taizu (r. 1115–22) of the Jin (Jurchen) dynasty. (See note 3 above.)

5. Bianjing (or Bianliang), the "Capital on the Bian [River]" from which the Song ruling house fled, is present-day Kaifeng, Henan.

6. Yingtianfu was in what is now Henan.

7. Bianzhou is another name for Bianjing.

8. Zhang Chang of the Han dynasty often painted his wife's eyebrows for her.

9. Luoyang was known as the Western Capital in the Song dynasty, as is explained

in note 2, but much earlier, in the Zhou dynasty, it was called the Eastern Capital, while Chang'an was the Western Capital.

10. Lady Zhao was the wife of Sun Quan (182–252), King of Wu, who reigned over the entire region southeast of the Yangzi River. She was said to have woven hair into bed curtains.

18. Yang Balao's Extraordinary Family Reunion in the Land of Yue

Story 18 has been translated as "The Strange Adventures of Yang Balao" by Yang Xianyi and Gladys Yang, in *Lazy Dragon*, 25–44.

1. Wei Qing (d. 106 B.C.E.) was a slave who later rose to prominence and married Princess Pingyang, sister of Emperor Wu of the Han dynasty.

2. Duke Shao Ping was reduced to poverty after the fall of the Qin dynasty.

3. Tianjin Bridge was southwest of Luoyang.

4. A story in the "Five Vermin" (Wu du) chapter of *Han Fei Zi*, by the philosopher Hen Fei (ca. 280–233 B.C.E.), tells of a peasant who saw a hare run into a tree trunk and die, whereupon he gave up farming and sat beside the tree, waiting for another hare to do the same.

5. On customs for naming children, see note 4 of story 10.

6. On Su Wu, see note 16 of story 8. When Su Wu herded sheep during his years as a captive of the Huns, he used his staff denoting his official status to show his loyalty to the imperial court of the Han dynasty. After nineteen years, all of the ox-hair on the staff had worn off.

7. Hong Hao (1088–1115) was sent on a mission as secretary of the Ministry of Rites to the Jurchens and was kept captive by them for fifteen years.

8. On Fengcheng swords, see note 21 of story 1.

9. On Hepu pearls, see note 20 of story 1.

19. Yang Qianzhi Meets a Monk Knight-Errant on a Journey by Boate

1. Sichuan actually is north of Anzhuang.

2. Lianzhou is now Lian County, Guangdong.

3. Weiqing County is in present-day Qingzhen County, Guizhou.

4. Qiongzhou is now Hainan Province.

5. Pianqiao County is in present-day Shibing County, Guizhou.

6. On Lady Yang, see note 6 of story 6.

7. Soldiers accompanying Emperor Minghuang on his flight from Chang'an blamed Lady Yang for the disaster that befell the empire and demanded her death. See also note 6 of story 6.

8. Aman was a court lady well liked by Lady Yang.

9. The magistrate and assistant magistrate were appointed by the imperial court, whereas the post of pacification commissioner was a hereditary one assumed by natives. The pacification commissioner was responsible for controlling bandits and disruptive aboriginal tribes.

10. On Empress Feiyan, see note 7 of story 6.

11. The twelve notes of ancient Chinese music were believed to correspond to the number of months in a year.

20. Chen Congshan Loses His Wife on Mei Ridge

1. On the green dragon and white tiger, see note 11 of story 6.

2. The Quanzhen order of Taoism, founded by Wang Chongyang, was the most important of the three new Taoist sects in north China during the Jurchen (Jin) dynasty.

3. This is, in Taoist belief, the uppermost of the thirty-six levels of heaven.

4. A woodsman in the state of Zheng

forgot where he hid the deer that he had killed and thought he had dreamt about it. Another man heard about this, found the deer, and took it home. Then the woodsman remembered in a dream the place where he had hidden the deer and, in the same dream, also saw the man who got the deer. The two men brought the case to court. When asked for his judgment, the state counselor said, "I can't tell what is dream and what is not."

5. Zhuang Zhou or Zhuang Zi (ca. 369–286 B.C.E.) was a Taoist philosopher. According to the book that bears his name, he once dreamed that he was a butterfly, which did not know that it was Zhuang Zhou. When he awoke suddenly, he found himself Zhuang Zhou again, but he did not know whether he was Zhuang Zhou who had dreamed that he was a butterfly, or a butterfly dreaming that it was Zhuang Zhou.

6. Zhang Sengyao of the Southern Liang dynasty (502–557) was adept at painting landscapes and Buddha images.

7. On "clouds and rain," see note 3 of story 1.

21. Qian Poliu Begins His Career in Lin'an

1. Laizi, or Laolaizi, a hermit in the state of Chu in the Spring and Autumn period, was said to have worn clothing colored like that of a child when he was seventy to please his aged parents. This line is meant to praise Qian Liu (see note 5) for his filial piety.

2. Xie Tiao (464–499) was a famous poet.

3. The Hall of Fame was Lingyan Pavilion in Chang'an, where Tang emperor Taizong (r. 627–49) had the portraits of twenty-four men of great merit painted on the walls.

4. Huang Chao (d. 884) was leader of a major peasant rebellion toward the end of the Tang dynasty.

5. Qian Liu (852–932), king of the Wu and Yue regions in the period of the Five Dynasties, is the title character of this story.

6. In fact, Qian Liu had but thirteen prefectures under his rule.

7. Xiang Yu (232–202 B.C.E.), major rival of Liu Bang (see also note 12 of story 1, and notes 5–7 of story 5) in contending for the throne, was from an aristocratic family, whereas Liu Bang, who defeated Xiang Yu and became the first emperor of the Han dynasty, was of humble background.

8. Lord Mengchang (Tian Wen; d. 297 B.C.E.) of the period of the Warring States was born on the fifth day of the fifth month. Children born in that month were believed to be potential dangers to their parents, but his mother kept him in spite of his father's wishes to the contrary.

9. The stories of Dou Wen and Houji follow in the text.

10. The son was Dou Wen of the poem above.

11. See note 5 of story 10.

12. Deng Ai (197–264) was a general of the state of Wei.

13. This refers to *Essence of the Yijing [The book of changes]* of Zhou by Zhu Xi (1130–1200), one of the most influential philosophers in Chinese history. The Confucian classics he annotated and edited were standard textbooks for literati education for almost six centuries until 1905, when the civil service examination system was abolished.

14. The Peach Garden pledge of brotherhood was that among Liu Bei (162–223), Guan Yu (see also note 7 of story 10), and Zhang Fei (d. 221). There is a reference to this pledge in story 31. See *Three Kingdoms: A Historical Novel*, trans. Moss Roberts, (Berkeley: University of California Press, 1991), chap. 1.

15. On Jing Ke, see note 5 of story 7. It was said that Jing Ke's noble spirit so moved the heavens that a white rainbow appeared in

the sky. It was by the Yishui River that Prince Dan of Yan saw Jing Ke off on his mission to assassinate the First Emperor of Qin.

16. On Fengcheng swords, see note 21 of story 1.

17. Of humble origin, Ban Chao was enfeoffed as a noble lord later in life. See also note 8 of story 8.

18. Deng Tong of the Han dynasty was an immensely rich court favorite with the authority to mint his own money. But he lost favor with the new emperor and later died of hunger in prison. See story 9.

19. The Tianmu Mountain chain extends to the county of Qiantang.

20. Sea Gate (Haimen), in Zhejiang, is where the Qiantang River flows into the sea.

21. Gou Jian (d. 465 B.C.E.), king of Yue, was defeated by the king of Wu, but by acting humble to fool his enemies, he eventually wiped out the kingdom of Wu.

22. The certificates of redemption were in the form of iron tablets issued by the imperial court of those who had rendered meritorious service to exempt them and their descendants from charges of crime.

23. Quoted from the biography of Xiang Yu in Sima Qian's (ca. 145–ca. 85 B.C.E.) *Records of the Grand Historian* (Shi ji).

22. Zheng Huchen Seeks Revenge in Mumian Temple

1. This is a reference to Phoenix Hill in Hangzhou.

2. On Sea Gate, see note 20 of story 21.

3. Emperor Wu (r. 265–90) of the Jin dynasty ordered Jia Chong to be the commander in chief in the campaign against the state of Wu. Afraid that he might lose, Jia Chong advised against the operation. Later, when the Jin army did crush Wu, Jia Chong was overcome with shame and fear.

4. Yu Xin, a poet of the Wu region, was sent as emissary to Western Wei during the

reign of Emperor Yuan (r. 552–54) of the Liang dynasty and was never allowed to return. He wrote a number of nostalgic poems.

5. On Xishi, see note 5 of story 1.

6. This poem actually was written not by Zhang Zhiyuan, but by Zhang Yining (courtesy name Zhidao, 1301–70).

7. On Su Dongpo, see note 2 of story 15.

8. In the famous story "Orphan of the Zhao Clan," set during the reign of Duke Jing of the state of Jin in the Spring and Autumn period, Tu'an Gu killed the entire Zhao clan except Zhao Shuo's wife, who fled to the depths of the palace, where she gave birth to a son, Zhao Wu. Cheng Ying and Gongsun Chujiu, retainers of the Zhao family, saved the orphan, who later sought revenge against Tu'an Gu.

9. The nine women's professions are Buddhist nun, Taoist priestess, fortune-teller, dealer in human traffic, matchmaker, witch, procuress, doctor, and midwife.

10. Jia Sidao and Jia Yuhua were, in fact, cousins.

11. On Han Shizhong, see note 21 of story 15.

12. The Huai region is between the Huai River in the north and the Yangzi River in the south, in present-day Anhui and Jiangsu.

13. In a common metaphor, a minister's ruling of the state was referred to as cooking.

14. The Green Seedling Method was a law promulgated by Chief Councilor Wang Anshi (1021–86) whereby the state lent farmers funds at planting time and was paid back at harvest at an interest rate much lower than the usurious rate in the private market. For all its good intentions, the policy in the end aggravated rather than alleviated the farmers' debts.

15. See note 5 of story 10.

16. Jingxiang is in present-day Hubei.

17. Jia Sidao issued a new paper currency

called Guanzi to replace Huizi, which the Ministry of Revenue had issued since 1160.

18. See note 14 of story 12.

19. Yi Yin was a prime minister in the Shang dynasty.

20. On the Clear and Bright Festival, see note 16 of story 1.

21. Lao Zi, the founder of Taoism, was said to have crossed Yougu Pass on the back of a green buffalo to live the life of a recluse.

22. Cao Cao (courtesy name Mengde; 155–220), prime minister in the Han dynasty and later king of the state of Wei, was a military strategist as well as a famous poet. See also note 6 of story 31.

23. Neither Dong Zhuo (d. 192) nor Cao Cao (see note 22 above) took the throne himself, but each had an emperor under his control.

24. Zhang Jun (1068–1154), Han Shizhong (1089–1154), Liu Qi (1098–1162), and Yue Fei (1103–42) are remembered for their accomplishments in repelling the advances of Jurchen invaders.

25. On Zhang Liang, see note 2 of story 13.

26. Huo Guang (d. 68 B.C.E.) effectively controlled the court for twenty years, but only three years after he died, his entire clan was exterminated.

27. Quanzhou is present-day Fujian.

28. The event described here occurred during the reign of Emperor Zhenzong (r. 998–1022), not Renzong (r. 1023–63).

29. In the first year of the Jingde reign period (1004–7) under Emperor Zhenzong, the Liao swept south in an invasion against the Song. Kou Zhun (961–1023), the prime minister, led an expedition to Chanyuan (in present-day Henan) and killed the leading Liao general. However, the advocates of appeasement prevailed and negotiated peace in a treaty historically known as the Treaty of Chanyuan.

30. Autumn Valley Pavilion was built by Jia Sidao for his sumptuous garden.

23. Zhang Shunmei Finds a Fair Lady during the Lantern Festival

1. See note 16 of story 1.

2. Story 12 is about Liu Yong (Liu the Seventh).

24. Yang Siwen Meets an Old Acquaintance in Yanshan

Story 24 has been translated as "Strange Encounter in Yanshan" by Yang Xianyi and Gladys Yang, in *Chinese Literature* (December, 1961): 46–68.

1. Hu Haoran was an obscure poet of the Song dynasty. The editors of *Quan Song ci* (The complete collection of Song *ci* poems) (Beijing: Zhonghua Shuju, 1965) attribute this poem to Chao Chongzhi.

2. Felicity Pool and Five Peaks Temple were in Bianliang (present-day Kaifeng), the Eastern Capital of the Northern Song dynasty.

3. Yanshan Prefecture is in present-day Beijing.

4. On the Jurchens, see note 3 of story 17.

5. Prince Su was Zhao Shu, son of Emperor Huizong.

6. During the Jingkang period (1126) Emperors Huizong and Qinzong were captured by the Jurchens, the Northern Song dynasty perished, and many residents of Kaifeng, the capital, fled to Yanshan.

7. The badge was a pass for access to the palace grounds.

8. In the Song dynasty, the Diplomacy Section was a unit in the Bureau of Military Affairs that handled correspondence and diplomatic exchanges between the imperial court and foreign peoples.

9. Su Xiaoqing was a famous courtesan from Luzhou who figured in a popular love story during the Song dynasty.

10. Mengjiangnü was a legendary figure.

Her husband, Fan Xiliang, being one of the conscripted laborers building the Great Wall, she undertook a long journey to deliver winter clothes to him, but by the time she arrived there, he had already died. Her bitter wails caused the Great Wall to collapse, revealing her husband's remains. She later threw herself into the sea and drowned.

11. Jinling is present-day Nanjing.

12. On *The Records of Yijian,* see note 4 of story 15.

13. Guo Xi was a famous landscape painter of the Northern Song dynasty.

14. On Chen Miaochang, see note 15 of story 1.

15. On the Clear and Bright Festival, see note 16 of story 1.

16. When performing exorcism, a Taoist priest would draw a magic charm, burn it, and have the ashes eaten by the person believed to be possessed by a ghost.

17. Qiantang was another name for Hangzhou.

18. According to legend, Cao E, of Shangyu County in the Eastern Han dynasty, wailed with grief for seventeen days as she went along the river to find her father's drowned corpse. She then threw herself into the river. Five days later, she reemerged with her father's body.

19. Qu Yuan (ca. 340–278 B.C.E.), one of the best known figures in traditional Chinese culture, drowned himself in the Milo River.

25. Yan Pingzhong Kills Three Men with Two Peaches

1. See note 1 of story 3.

2. The Three Sovereigns and Five Emperors were legendary rulers in antiquity. According to the most common belief, the Three Sovereigns are Fuxi, whose reign supposedly began around 2800 B.C.E., Shennong (Divine Farmer); and Huangdi (Yellow Emperor). The Five Emperors, according

to *Records of the Grand Historian* by Sima Qian, are Huangdi, Zhuanxu, Diku, Yao, and Shun.

3. On Zhuge Liang, see note 11 of story 8.

26. Shen Xiu Causes Seven Deaths with One Bird

Story 26 has been translated as "The Canary Murders" by Cyril Birch, in Feng, trans. Birch, *Stories from a Ming Collection,* 155–171.

1. Ninghai is present-day Hangzhou.

2. Geyao (lit., "Older Brother's kiln") refers to the work of Zhang Shengyi, the famous potter of Dragon Spring Country of Song times. The porcelain of his younger brother was called Diyao (Younger Brother's kiln).

3. This is borrowed from a line in *The Analects of Confucius:* "The lack of self-restraint in small matters will bring ruin to great plans" (*The Analects:* 15:27; trans. D. C. Lau. [Harmondsworth, Eng.: Penguin Books, 1979]).

27. Jin Yunu Beats the Heartless Man

Story 27 has been translated as "The Beggar Chief's Daughter" by Yang Xianyi and Gladys Yang, in *The Courtesan's Jewel Box,* 141–53; and as "The Lady Who Was a Beggar" by Cyril Birch, in Feng, trans. Birch, *Stories from a Ming Collection,* 19–36.

1. In the Qin dynasty, Kuaiji Prefecture was in Wu County (present-day Suzhou). In the Eastern Han dynasty, the boundaries of the prefecture were redrawn and it became Shanyin County (present-day Shaoxing County). Zhu Maicheng was a native of Wu County.

2. On Jiang Taigong, see note 14 of story 12.

3. Gan Luo was a native of the state of Qin during the Warring States period. He was granted a royal title at the age of twelve for his meritorious service to the state.

4. Present-day Xi'an is the site of the Han Western Capital.

5. Yan Zhu was a native of Kuaiji and filled the post of ordinary grand master under Emperor Wudi.

6. On the washer woman and Han Xin, see note 8 of story 5.

7. Xi Fuji was a minister of the state of Cao in the Spring and Autumn period. When Chong'er, prince of the state of Jin, fled to the state of Cao, his wife had a premonition that Chong'er would return home later and rise to power. She advised her husband to receive the Prince. Later, after becoming the duke of Jin, Chong'er led an invasion into the state of Cao but granted amnesty to the entire Xi clan.

8. Zhang Lihua, a great beauty, was a concubine of the last ruler of the Chen dynasty (583–89).

9. Zhong Kui is, in folklore, a fighter of demons.

10. On the seven offenses, see note 17 of story 1.

11. Wuwei County is in present-day Anhui Province.

12. The six senses are sight, sound, smell, taste, touch, and thought. In Buddhist legend, the six senses assumed shapes and tormented Amita Buddha to distract him from his spiritual devotions.

13. Song Hong, of the Eastern Han dynasty, declined Emperor Guangwu's offer of marriage to an imperial princess, Guangwu's sister, with these words.

14. When Yuan Wei of the Eastern Han dynasty was seeking a husband for his niece, he saw Huang Yun and said, "If only I could find such a nephew-in-law." When these words reached him, Huang Yun promptly divorced his wife.

28. Li Xiuqing Marries the Virgin Huang with Honor

1. On Empress Wu Zetian, see note 10 of story 8. Zhuang Jiang was the wife of Duke Zhuang of the state of Wei in the Spring and Autumn period. She was viewed traditionally as a less than virtuous woman who, upon the advice of her tutoress, later made every effort to cultivate her character. Cao Lingnü, née Xiahou Lingnü, was the wife of Cao Wenshu of the Wei dynasty (220–65). When pressed to remarry after Cao Wenshu's death, she protested by cutting off her nose and an ear. Ban Zhao was the daughter of Ban Biao of the Eastern Han dynasty, sister of Ban Gu, and the wife of Cao Shishu. A learned and talented scholar, she helped finish Ban Gu's *History of the Han Dynasty*. Ban Jieyu, a poetically inclined imperial consort of Emperor Cheng of the Eastern Han dynasty, was later demoted to the position of maid to the empress dowager. Su Ruolan was the wife of Dou Tao of the Jin dynasty, prefect of Qinzhou, who distanced himself from her after he took a second wife. Su wove into pieces of brocade melancholy poems addressed to Dou that could be read a great number of ways. Shen Manyuan was a woman poet of the Southern Liang dynasty who is believed to have written five volumes of poetry, all of which have been lost. Li Qingzhao (1084–1151) was China's greatest woman poet. On Zhu Shuzhen, see note 11 of story 15. Feng Liao was the wife of the regent marshall of the state of Wusun. She was also an imperial envoy to that state. Lady Ren was the concubine of Cui Ning, a regional commander in the Tang dynasty. When the city of Chengdu came under attack while Cui Ning was away at the capital, she contributed family assets for financing the recruitment of thousands of soldiers and led the troops in pushing back the invaders. Lady Xi was the wife of Feng Bao, prefect of Gaoliang in the Northern and Southern Dynasties (420–589). After his death, Lady Xi ruled the region south of the Wuling Mountains. Princess Pingyang was the daughter of Li Yuan, Emperor Gaozu (r. 618–26) of the Tang dynasty, and the wife of Chai Shao. When Chai Shao rose in arms to follow Li

Yuan, Princess Pingyang raised an army of women to join the campaign. Madam Liu was otherwise known as the Banner-Bearing Woman Warrior of the Jin dynasty. In the thirteenth year of the reign period Jiading (1208–24) under Emperor Ningzong of the Song dynasty, Li Quan was driving Jin troops into a valley when Madam Liu appeared on her horse and repelled his forces.

2. Tiying was the daughter of Chunyu Yi of the Han dynasty. When her father was condemned to corporal punishment, she followed him to the capital, Chang'an, and submitted a request to the imperial court that she be allowed to work as a maidservant in a government institution to redeem her father. Emperor Wen eventually pardoned him.

3. On engagement preliminaries, see note 2 of story 1.

4. There was a rather obscure play titled "The Story of Spring Peach" that was perhaps written in the early Ming dynasty, but the reference here might be to a better-known play based on it by Xu Wei (1521–93) titled "The Female *Zhuangyuan*."

5. The relationship between Honest Huang and Zhang Sheng is confusing here. Huang introduced his daughter as Zhang Sheng, his nephew. The words "nephew" and "grandson" share the same pronunciation in the Wu dialect, which was the editor's mother tongue, but the characters are written differently. It is unclear whether the mistaking of their relationship as that of grandson and grandfather is a matter of confusion on the part of those making the comment or an error on the part of the author or editor. In any case, the "mistake" is perpetuated by Shancong below.

29. Monk Moon Bright Redeems Willow Green

1. The surname Liu means "willow."

2. Lin'an is present-day Hangzhou.

3. The eminent monk Hao Congshen

of the Tang dynasty, abbot of Bodhisattva Monastery in Zhaozhou (in present-day Zhao County, Hebei), was known as the Monk of Zhaozhou.

4. Sakyamuni preached his sermons at Holy Vulture Peak, Grdhrakuta, in ancient India.

5. The five Buddhist commandments are against killing, stealing, engaging in sensual indulgence, lying, and consuming liquor and meat.

6. Mount Gaoting is northeast of Hangzhou.

7. This means that Abbot Yutong's status has been greatly reduced.

8. "The West" refers to the Western Pure Land in Buddhist belief.

9. A round carved wooden fish is used by monks to keep time in chanting; a long one is used to summon monks to meals in the monastery.

10. In Buddhism, it is believed that the world consists of the four elements of earth, water, fire, and wind.

11. On the four treasures, see note 7 of story 11.

30. Abbot Mingwu Redeems Abbot Wujie

1. Logic would require one of the Tang reign titles, not one from the Song. However, the fact that the main part of this narrative begins in this reign period might somewhat account for its otherwise inexplicable appearance here.

2. In Buddhist terms, to "go to the West" is to die.

3. Ge Hong (courtesy name, Zhichuan; 281–341) was a Taoist scholar who allegedly achieved enlightenment by a well on Mount Tianzhu.

4. On Huang Chao, see note 4 of story 21.

5. Shu is present-day Sichuan.

6. On Su Dongpo (Su Shi), see note 2 of story 15.

7. Kumarajiva (344–413) was an eminent Indian monk and a great translator of Buddhist scriptures into Chinese. In a state of drunkenness one night, he was forcibly locked in a room with a girl. Like Abbot Wujie in this story, he broke the monastic prohibition against sex.

8. *Sangha* is a Buddhist religious community.

9. The five Classics are: *The Book of Songs, The Book of History, The Book of Changes, The Book of Rites* and *The Spring and Autumn Annals.* The Three Histories are: *Records of the Grand Historian, History of the Han Dynasty* and *History of the Later Han Dynasty.*

10. On Su Shi, see note 2 of story 15.

11. Huizhou being in present-day Guangdong, Danzhou in present-day Hai'nan, Lianzhou in present-day Guangdong, and Yongzhou in present-day Guizhou, Dongpo was being sent, for all practical purposes, to the ends of the earth.

31. Sima Mao Disrupts Order in the Underworld and Sits in Judgment

1. Monk Hui'an lived during the Southern Song dynasty.

2. On the four treasures of the study, see note 7 of story 11.

3. The five mountains are Mount Tai in Shandong, Mount Heng in Hunan, the Hua Mountains in Shaanxi, the Heng Mountains in Shanxi, and the Song Mountains in Henan. The four seas were believed in ancient times to be the Eastern, Southern, Western, and Northern Seas.

4. Han Xin, Peng Yue (d. 196 B.C.E.), and Ying Bu (d. 195 B.C.E.) were advisers to Liu Bang, the first emperor of the Han dynasty. On Han Xin, see also note 12 of story 1 and note 8 of story 5. On Liu Bang, see also note 12 of story 1, notes 5–7 of story 5, and note 7 of story 21. Ding Gong, also

known as Ding Gu, was a general under Xiang Yu (232–202 B.C.E.), Liu Bang's major opponent in contending for the throne. When Ding Gong laid a siege against Liu Bang, the latter talked him into withdrawing his troops. After Liu Bang became emperor, Ding Gong went for an audience, and Liu Bang killed him. Qi-shi was a concubine of Liu Bang.

5. In his youth, Han Xin was once challenged by a bully to crawl between his legs. Han Xin swallowed his pride and did as he was told.

6. For stories about Cao Cao and the following reincarnated characters, see *Three Kingdoms: A Historical Novel,* trans. Moss Roberts. See also note 22 of story 22.

7. On Sun Quan, see note 10 of story 17.

8. On Liu Bei, see note 11 of story 8.

9. On Zhuge Liang, see note 11 of story 8.

10. On Zhang Fei, see note 14 of story 21.

11. Guan Yu is, to this day, revered as a central figure in the folk pantheon and is the embodiment of fidelity to commitments. There are also temples to Zhang Fei.

12. The future emperor is Liu Bei's son Liu Shan, nicknamed Adou.

32. Humu Di Intones Poems and Visits the Netherworld

1. "Hui" here can be and often is pronounced "Kuai" or even "Gui." "Hui" is the most modern pronunciation.

2. Wanyan Chang was a cousin of Emperor Taizu of the Jin. On Taizu, see note 4 of story 17.

3. On Yama, king of hell, see story 31.

4. The Yanyue Hall is where Li Linfu (d. 752), prime minister in the Tang dynasty, drew up his schemes to bring about the downfall of other court ministers.

5. See story 21, which is about the life of Qian Liu (Qian Poliu).

6. A *yaksha* is a malevolent spirit in Buddhist belief.

7. Zhang Dun was a court minister of the Northern Song dynasty known for his persecution of other officials. Cai Jing (1045–1126) was another notorious evil minister. Wang Fu was a collaborator of Cai Jing. Zhu Mian (1075–1126) a collaborator of Cai Jing, was known for his notorious project transporting ornamental rocks from the south to please Emperor Huizong. Geng Nanzhong, a court official in the reign of Emperor Qinzong of the Song dynasty, advocated making territorial concessions to the Jin invaders. Ding Daquan was a greedy and evil court minister of the Southern Song period who died in exile. Han Tuozhou (1151–1207) was a powerful minister in the reign of Emperor Ningzong of the Song dynasty. Shi Miyuan (d. 1232) murdered Han Tuozhou and replaced him as prime minister. Story 22 is a story about Jia Sidao.

33. Old Man Zhang Grows Melons and Marries Wennü

Story 33 has been translated as "The Fairy's Rescue" by Cyril Birch, in Feng, trans. Birch, *Stories from a Ming Collection*, 175–198.

1. Xie Lingyun (385–433) was a famous poet in the Six Dynasties period.

2. On Su Dongpo (Su Shi), see note 2 of story 15.

3. On Tao Qian (Tao Yuanming), see note 4 of story 5, and note 3 of story 8.

4. Xie Daoyun was Xie Lingyun's sister. See note 1 above.

5. Huang Tingjian (courtesy name, Luzhi; 1045–1105) was a famous poet, but this poem is believed to have been written by the author of the story.

6. On Li Qingzhao, see note 1 of story 28.

7. Zhao Chongzhi (Zhao Shuyong) was a Northern Dynasties poet. This poem too is believed to have been written by the author of the story.

8. Hibiscus Town is a legendary fairyland.

9. Li Jing, or Devaraja Li, is the mythological Pagoda Bearer.

10. Yuan An (courtesy name, Shaogong; d. 92) was once found lying in bed half frozen during a snowstorm. When asked why he chose to stay indoors, he explained that although he was hungry, he did not wish to go out and beg from people.

11. The Whitemarsh is a mythical beast.

12. Bodhidharma is reputed to have been the first patriarch of the Chan School of Buddhism in China.

13. On Liuxia Hui, see note 10 of story 13. Magu is the only female among the eight sages of popular Taoism. The Jade Maiden and the Golden Boy are a maid and a page in the service of Taoist immortals. The Wushan Goddess is the mythical figure that gave rise to the expression "clouds and rain" as a metaphor for sexual encounters. See also note 3 of story 1. On the Weaving Maiden, see note 4 of story 1.

14. Wang Sengbian (d. 555) was a general of the Liang dynasty who quelled a rebellion by Hou Jing.

15. According to one legend, the First Emperor of Qin (r. 221–209 B.C.E.) wanted to construct a stone pier at the seashore so that he could watch the sunrise. An immortal used his powers to drive the stones into the sea with his whip. Xia'ao, son of Hanzhuo of the Xia dynasty (ca. 2100–ca. 1600 B.C.E.), was a master in naval warfare and could maneuver ships over dry land.

16. The Blue Gate refers to the blue southeast city gate of Chang'an, where Zhao Ping, duke of Dongling, grew his famous melons when he was reduced to poverty after the fall of the Qin dynasty.

17. The legendary precious Tai'e sword was made in the Spring and Autumn period by Ouyezi and Ganjiang.

18. Mount Mao, located in present-day Jiangsu, was traditionally associated with Taoist legends.

19. According to *Accounts of Extraordinary*

Happenings (Shu yi ji) by Ren Fang of the Later Liang dynasty, a man named Wang Zhi was chopping firewood when he saw some children singing. One of the children gave Wang Zhi an object that resembled the pit of a date. Zhi put it in his mouth and felt instantly relieved of hunger. When the children said after a little while, "Why are you still here?" Wang Zhi saw that the handle of his axe had rotted away. Upon his return, none of his contemporaries was to be found.

20. According to a belief popular at the end of the Eastern Han dynasty, Lao Zi left China and turned himself into Buddha.

21. *The Materia Medica* (Ben cao) is a compendium on herbs and medicines dating from the Han dynasty.

34. Mr. Li Saves a Snake and Wins Chenxin

1. Source unidentified.

35. The Monk with a Note Cleverly Tricks Huangfu's Wife

Story 35 has been partially translated by Yang Xianyi and Gladys Yang as "The Monk's Billet-doux," in *The Courtesan's Jewel Box*, 52–64.

1. Yu Gate, also called the Dragon Gate, allegedly was built by the Great Yu. See note 2 of story 11.

2. To break off branches from cassia trees growing on the moon is a metaphor for passing the imperial examinations.

3. The two-character (two-syllable) surnames used in the poem are Gongsun, Duanmu, Ximen, Wenren, Tuoba, Yuwen, Dugu, Goulong, Murong, and Lüqiu. The meaning of each of the surnames is given within brackets.

4. Zhang Fei (d. 221) was a brave warrior and a sworn brother of Liu Bei.

5. Magistrate Qian was a great grandson of Qian Liu (Qian Poliu), the title character of story 21.

36. Song the Fourth Greatly Torments Tightwad Zhang

Story 36 has been translated as "Sung the Fourth Raises Hell with Tightwad Chang" by Timothy C. Wong, in Ma and Lau, eds., *Traditional Chinese Stories*, 535–54.

1. Mount Jiang, also known as Mount Zhong, is east of the present-day city of Nanjing.

2. On Hu Zeng, see note 1 of story 3.

3. Sima Xiangru and Zhuo Wenjun (see note 14 of story 1) ran a small wineshop for a time.

4. The walls of wineshops were often decorated with paintings of drunken immortals or poets.

5. Dingzhou was upgraded to Zhongshan Prefecture in the third year of the Zhenghe reign period under Emperor Huizong of the Song dynasty. Located in present-day Hebei Province, it was famous in the Song times for its production of porcelain.

6. This describes the character "Zhao."

37. Emperor Wudi of the Liang Dynasty Goes to the Land of Extreme Bliss through Ceaseless Cultivation

1. Legend has it that in the Eastern Han dynasty, Liu Chen and Ruan Zhao were in the Tiantai Mountains collecting medicinal herbs when two immortal maidens offered them some peppered rice and kept them for half a year. By the time they went back, their descendants were already into the seventh generation.

2. Legend has it that during the Spring and Autumn period, the daughter of Prince Mu of Qin was married to Xiao Shi, who with a flute could imitate the sound of a phoenix. When a phoenix came in response, the couple got on its back and flew away.

3. According to legend, Pei Hang of the Tang dynasty was crossing Blue Bridge

when he asked for some soy milk from an old woman, who called forth her daughter Yunying to give it to him. Pei Hang asked for Yunying's hand in marriage, but the old woman said, "You must produce a jade pestle as a betrothal gift." Later, when Pei Hang obtained a jade pestle, he married Yunying, and the couple passed over into the immortal world.

4. On Vulture Peak, see note 4 of story 29.

5. Xiao Yi, in fact, was the older brother of Xiao Yan, Emperor Wudi of the Liang (r. 502–49) who, in this story, is Young Master Huang Furen reincarnated.

6. This in fact happened after, not before, Xiao Yan became Emperor Wudi of the Liang.

7. Chen Baxian [r. 557–59], founder of the Chen dynasty, was in fact not born until 503, one year after Xiao Yan became emperor.

8. Zheng Shaoshu was Zheng Zhi's brother. The name appears erroneously in the text as "Zheng Shaoji."

9. Jiankang (now Nanjing) was the capital of the Qi dynasty.

10. The nine dignities are chariot and horse, royal raiment, musical chimes for audiences with the emperor, vermilion doors, the right of access through an inner staircase to the emperor, palace guards, battle-axes, bows and arrows, and instruments for sacrificial rituals.

11. The Avalamba Festival, or the Festival of All Souls, first observed in the time of Emperor Wudi of the Liang, is a Buddhist festival held on the fifteenth day of the seventh month for the purpose of releasing souls of the dead from purgatory and feeding "hungry ghosts."

12. *The Liang Emperor's Repentance*, a ten-volume work, came to be used for the prayer services at Avalamba Festivals.

13. Zhi Dun (courtesy name, Daolin) died in 366. The monk who had a close relationship with Emperor Wudi of the Liang was Bao Zhi (418–514).

14. According to *Records of the Grand Historian* by Sima Qian, the state of Tiaozhi was located between the Tigris and Euphrates Rivers.

15. Mingzhou is present-day Ningbo, Zhejiang.

16. The surname Hou shares the same pronunciation as the word for "monkey."

17. Chen Shi (104–187) was considered a man of great integrity. See his biography in Fan Ye's *History of the Later Han Dynasty* (Hou Han shu).

18. Zhang Rang (d. 189) was a notorious eunuch in the Han court. See his biography in *The History of the Later Han Dynasty.*

38. Ren the Filial Son with a Fiery Disposition Becomes a God

1. Parents with only a daughter would often have her and their son-in-law live with them rather than with his parents, as was customary.

2. These are said to be words on a sign put up over a spot where money was hidden. The saying is used to refer to people guilty of some wrongdoing who give themselves away by overly protesting their innocence.

3. Nü Wa, a principal character in Chinese mythology, is a goddess who smelted stones of five colors to patch up the sky after it had been damaged.

4. On the green dragon and white tiger, see note 11 of story 6.

5. In the Song dynasty, convicts sentenced to death wore paper flowers in their hair on their way to the execution ground.

39. Wang Xinzhi Dies to Save the Entire Family

Story 39 has been translated as "Wang Xinshi's Death, and It Saved His Whole Family" by John Page and C. T. Hsia, in *Renditions:* 6–30 (Spring 1985).

1. The famous Su Dike is on West Lake in the city of Lin'an (present day Hangzhou), capital of the Southern Song dynasty.

2. Bianjing, present-day Kaifeng, was the Song capital before the court moved south. Also see note 5 of story 17.

3. On Wei Wuzhi, see note 6 of story 5.

4. On "When your time comes," see note 7 of story 9.

5. On "When your time goes," see note 6 of story 9.

6. Jiyang District is in present-day Hainan Province.

7. Guo Xie and Zhu Jia were knights-errant of the Han dynasty.

8. On the position of pacification commissioner, see note 9 of story 19.

9. Tian Wen (d. 297 B.C.E.), with the title Lord Mengchang, was known for his generosity and maintained more than three thousand retainers in his household. See also note 8 of story 21.

40. Shen Xiaoxia Encounters the Expedition Memorials

Story 40 has been translated as "A Just Man Avenged" by Yang Xianyi and Gladys Yang, in *The Courtesan's Jewel Box*, 154–96.

1. The Jiajing emperor of the Ming dynasty was inclined toward Taoism.

2. Guan Longfeng, a legendary court minister during the last years of the Xia dynasty (ca. 2100–ca. 1600 B.C.E.), was put to death for his remonstrations against the tyrant King Jie.

3. Bi Gan, uncle of King Zhou of the Shang dynasty, was killed for his remonstrations against the King.

4. Wang Zhu of the Song dynasty wrote a number of "Poems on Prodigies" that were later compiled into a popular children's primer. The original four lines are as follows:

Study hard while you are young;
Your writing will bring you a fine career.

Those in court officials' robes, one and all,
Have gained office through nothing
  but books.

5. The original four lines are:

The Son of Heaven favors the worthy;
Your writing gains you recognition.
All other pursuits are of little worth;
To study is the noblest of them all.

6. On Zhuge Liang, see note 11 of story 8.

7. Guan Fu of the Western Han dynasty was known for his wine-induced outbursts against Prime Minister Tian Fen. He was later killed by the latter.

8. Although Cao Cao held the Han emperor hostage, he never took the step of usurping the dynasty, but his son Cao Pi (187–226) did, after Cao Cao's death. See also note 22 of story 22, and note 6 of story 31.

9. Yingzhou is in present-day Shanxi Province.

10. A narrative that trails off is a convention used in vernacular stories to create suspense until the action alluded to takes place.

11. After the death of Xiang Yu, his rival Liu Bang ordered the arrest of Xiang Yu's aide Ji Bu. He was given shelter by a man named Zhu of the state of Lu.

12. The Linqing in the text is apparently located in the vicinity of Jining, where Secretary Feng lives, and is not the present-day Linqing at the Shandong border, about one hundred miles northwest of Jining.

13. This is a method of divination. The writing in the sand is supposed to be a revelation from the gods.

14. The three judicial offices were the Censorate, the Ministry of Justice, and the Court of Judicial Review.

15. On the Five Classics, see note 9 of story 30.

16. On tribute students, see note 4 of story 2.

17. Zhangjiawan was a major port during the Ming dynasty.

Bibliography

English-Language Works

Andres, Mark F. "Ch'an Symbolism in *Hsi-yu pu:* The Enlightenment of Monkey." *Tamkang Review* 20, no. 1 (1989): 23–44.

Bantly, Francisca Cho. "Buddhist Allegory in *The Journey to the West*." *Journal of Asian Studies* 48, no. 3 (1989): 512–25.

Birch, Cyril, ed. "Feng Meng-lung and the *Ku Chin Hsiao Shuo*." *Bulletin of the School of Oriental and African Studies* 18, no. 1 (1956): 64–83.

———. "Some Formal Characteristics of the *Hua-pen* Story." *Bulletin of the School of Oriental and African Studies* 17, no. 2 (1955): 346–64.

Bishop, John Lyman. *The Colloquial Short Story in China*. Cambridge: Harvard University Press, 1956.

Brandauer, Frederick P. *Tung Yüeh*. Boston: Twayne, 1978.

Brokaw, Cynthia J. *The Ledgers of Merit and Demerit: Social Change and Moral Order in Late Imperial China*. Princeton: Princeton University Press, 1991.

Brook, Timothy. *The Confusions of Pleasure: Commerce and Culture in Ming China*. Berkeley and Los Angeles: University of California Press, 1998.

Cahill, James. *The Compelling Image: Nature and Style in Seventeenth-Century Chinese Painting*. Cambridge: Harvard University Press, 1982.

Campany, Robert. "Cosmogony and Self-Cultivation: The Demonic and the Ethical in Two Chinese Novels." *Journal of Religious Ethics* 14 (1986): 81–112.

———. "Demons, Gods, and Pilgrims: The Demonology in the *Hsi-yu chi*." *Chinese Literature: Essays, Articles, Reviews* 7, no. 1–2 (1985): 95–115.

Cao Xueqin. Trans. David Hawkes, and John Minford. *The Story of the Stone*. 5 vols. Harmondsworth, Eng.: Penguin Books, 1973–86.

Carlitz, Katherine. "Desire, Danger, and the Body: Stories of Women's Virtue in Late Ming China." In Christina K. Gilmartin et al., eds., *Engendering China: Women, Culture and the State*, 101–24. Cambridge: Harvard University Press, 1994.

———. *The Rhetoric of Chin p'ing mei*. Bloomington: Indiana University Press, 1986.

———. "The Social Uses of Female Virtue in Late Ming Editions of *Lienü zhuan*." *Late Imperial China* 12, no. 2 (1991): 117–48.

Chan, Albert. *The Glory and the Fall of the Ming Dynasty*. Norman: University of Oklahoma Press, 1982.

Chang, Chun-shu, and Shelley Hsüeh-lun Chang. *Crisis and Transformation in Seventeenth-Century China: Society, Culture, and Modernity in Li Yu's World*. Ann Arbor: University of Michigan Press, 1990.

Chang, H. C., trans. *Chinese Literature: Popular Fiction and Drama*. Edinburgh: Edinburgh University Press, 1973.

Chang, Kang-i Sun. *The Late-Ming Poet Ch'en Tzu-lung: Crises of Love and Loyalism*. New Haven: Yale University Press, 1990.

Chaves, Jonathan, trans. *See* Yuan Hongdao et al.

Cheung, Samuel H. N. "Structural Cyclicity in *Shuihu zhuan*: From Self to Sworn Brotherhood." *CHINOPERL Papers* 15 (1990): 1–16.

Chou, Chih-p'ing. *Yüan Hung-tao and the Kung-an School*. Cambridge: Cambridge University Press, 1988.

Clunas, Craig. *Superfluous Things: Material Culture and Social Status in Early Modern China*. Urbana: University of Illinois Press, 1991.

Crawford, William Bruce. "'The Oil Vendor and the Courtesan' and the *Ts'ai-tzu chia-jen* Novels." In Nienhauser, ed., *Critical Essays on Chinese Literature*, 31–42.

de Bary, Wm. Theodore, et al., eds. *The Unfolding of Neo-Confucianism*. New York: Columbia University Press, 1975.

———et al., eds. *Self and Society in Ming Thought*. New York: Columbia University Press, 1970.

Dolby, William, trans. *See* Feng Menglong.

Dolezelova-Velingerova, Milena. "Pre-Modern Chinese Fiction and Drama Theory." In Michael Groedon and Martin Kreisworth, eds., *The Johns*

Hopkins Guide to Literary Theory and Criticism, 132–39. Baltimore: Johns Hopkins University Press, 1994.

Eberhard, Wolfram. *Guilt and Sin in Traditional China.* Berkeley: University of California Press, 1967.

———. "Notes on Chinese Storytellers." *Fabula* 11 (1970): 1–31.

Edwards, Louise P. *Men and Women in Qing China: Gender in* The Red Chamber Dream. Leiden: E. J. Brill, 1994.

Elvin, Mark. "Female Virtue and the State in China." *Past and Present* 104 (1984): 111–52.

Eoyang, Eugene. "The Immediate Audience: Oral Narration in Chinese Fiction." In Nienhauser, *Critical Essays on Chinese Literature,* 43–57.

Epstein, Maram. "The Beauty Is the Beast: The Dual Face of Woman in Four Ch'ing Novels." Ph.D. diss., Princeton University, 1992.

Fan, Ning. "Early Vernacular Tales. " *Chinese Literature,* 1955, no. 3 (March 1955), 86–89.

Feng Menglong. Trans. Cyril Birch. *Stories from a Ming Collection: Translations of Chinese Short Stories Published in the Seventeenth Century.* New York: Grove Weidenfeld, 1958.

———. Trans. William Dolby. *The Perfect Lady by Mistake and Other Stories by Feng Menglong.* London: Paul Elek, 1976.

Fitzgerald, John. "Continuity and Discontinuity: The Case *Water Margin* Mythology." *Modern China* 12, no. 3 (1986): 361–400.

Furth, Charlotte. "Androgynous Males and Deficient Females: Biology and Gender Boundaries in Sixteenth- and Seventeenth-Century China." *Late Imperial China* 9, no. 2 (Dec. 1988): 1–31.

Gimm, Martin. "Bibliographic Survey: Manchu Translations of Chinese Novels and Short Stories. An Attempt at an Inventory." *Asia Major* 1, no. 2 (1989): 77–114.

Goodrich, Carrington, ed. *Dictionary of Ming Biography, 1368–1644.* New York: Columbia University Press, 1976.

Gulik, R. H. van. *Sexual Life in Ancient China: A Preliminary Survey of Chinese Sex and Society from ca. 1500 B.C. till 1644 A.D.* Leiden: E. J. Brill, 1961.

Hanan, Patrick. "The Authorship of Some *Ku-chin hsiao-shuo* Stories." *Harvard Journal of Asiatic Studies* 29 (1969): 190–200.

———. *The Chinese Short Story: Studies in Dating, Authorship, and Composition.* Cambridge: Harvard University Press, 1973.

———. *The Chinese Vernacular Story.* Cambridge: Harvard University Press, 1981.

———. "The Composition of the *P'ing Yao Chuan.*" *Harvard Journal of Asiatic Studies* 31 (1971): 201–19.

———. "The Development of Fiction and Drama." In Raymond Dawson, ed., *The Legacy of China,* 115–43. Oxford: Clarendon Press, 1964.

———. "The Early Chinese Short Story: A Critical Theory in Outline." *Harvard Journal of Asiatic Studies* 27 (1967): 168–207.

———. *The Invention of Li Yu.* Cambridge: Harvard University Press, 1988.

———. "The Making of 'The Pearl-sewn Shirt' and 'The Courtesan's Jewel Box.'" *Harvard Journal of Asiatic Studies* 33 (1973): 124–53.

———. "The Nature of Ling Meng-ch'u's Fiction." In Plaks, ed., *Chinese Narrative,* 85–114.

———, trans. *Silent Operas.* Hong Kong: The Chinese University Press, 1990.

———. "Sources of the *Chin p'ing Mei.*" *Asia Major* 10, no. 2 (1963): 23–67.

Hegel, Robert E. "Distinguishing Levels of Audiences for Ming-Ch'ing Vernacular Literature." In Johnson et al., eds., *Popular Culture in Late Imperial China,* 112–42.

———. *The Novel in Seventeenth-Century China.* New York: Columbia University Press, 1981.

———. *Reading Illustrated Fiction in Late Imperial China.* Stanford: Stanford University Press, 1998.

———. "*Sui T'ang yen-i* and the Aesthetics of the Seventeenth-Century Suchou Elite." In Plaks, ed., *Chinese Narrative,* 124–59.

———. "*Sui T'ang yen-i:* The Sources and Narrative Techniques of a Traditional Chinese Novel." Ph.D. diss., Columbia University, 1973.

———. "Unpredictability and Meaning in Ming-Qing Literati Novels." In Hung, ed., *Paradoxes in Chinese Literature,* 147–66.

————and Richard C. Hessney, eds. *Expressions of Self in Chinese Literature.* New York: Columbia University Press, 1985.

Henry, Eric. *Chinese Amusements: The Lively Plays of Li Yu.* Hamden, Conn.: Archon Books, 1980.

————. "The Motif of Recognition in Early China." *Harvard Journal of Asiatic Studies* 47 (1987): 5–30.

Hessney, Richard C. "Beautiful, Talented, and Brave: Seventeenth-Century Chinese Scholar-Beauty Romances." Ph.D. diss., Columbia University, 1979.

Ho, Ping-ti. *The Ladder of Success in Imperial China: Aspects of Social Mobility, 1368–1911.* New York: Columbia University Press, 1962.

Hsia, C. T. *The Classic Chinese Novel: A Critical Introduction.* New York: Columbia University Press, 1968.

————. "The Scholar-Novelist and Chinese Culture: A Reappraisal of *Ching-hua yüan.*" In Plaks, ed., *Chinese Narrative,* 266–305.

Hsu, Pi-ching. "Celebrating the Emotional Self: Feng Meng-lung and Late Ming Ethics and Aesthetics." Ph.D. diss., University of Minnesota, 1994.

Hsu, Wen-hung. "The Evolution of the Legend of the White Snake." *Tamkang Review* 4, no. 1 (April 1973): 109–27; 4, no. 2 (Oct. 1973): 121–56.

Huang, Martin Weizong. "Author(ity) and Reader in Traditional Chinese Xiaoshuo Commentary." *Chinese Literature: Essays, Articles, Reviews* 16 (1994): 41–67.

————. "Dehistoricization and Intertextualization: The Anxiety of Precedents in the Evolution of the Traditional Chinese Novel." *Chinese Literature: Essays, Articles, Reviews* 12 (1990): 45–68.

————. *Literati and Self-Re/Presentation: Autobiographical Sensibility in the Eighteenth-Century Chinese Novel.* Stanford: Stanford University Press, 1995.

————. "Notes Toward a Poetics of Characterization in the Traditional Chinese Novel: *Hung-lou meng* as Paradigm." *Tamkang Review* 21, no. 1 (Autumn 1990): 1–27.

Hummel, Arthur W., ed. *Eminent Chinese of the Ch'ing Period (1644–1912).* 2 vols. Washington, D. C.: Government Printing Office, 1943, 1944. Rpt., Taipei: Ch'eng Wen, 1976.

Hung, Eva, ed. *Paradoxes of Traditional Chinese Literature.* Hong Kong: The Chinese University Press, 1994.

Idema, W. L. *Chinese Vernacular Fiction: The Formative Period.* Leiden: E. J. Brill, 1974.

———. "Storytelling and the Short Story in China." *T'oung Pao* 59 (1973): 1–67.

Johnson, David, Andrew J. Nathan, and Evelyn S. Rawski, eds. *Popular Culture in Late Imperial China.* Berkeley & Los Angeles: University of California Press, 1985.

Kao, Karl S. Y. "An Archetypal Approach to the *Hsi-yu chi.*" *Tamkang Review* 5, no. 2 (1974): 63–97.

———. "Aspects of Derivation in Chinese Narrative." *Chinese Literature: Essays, Articles, Reviews* 7 (1985): 1–36.

Ko, Dorothy. *Teachers of the Inner Chamber: Women and Culture in Seventeenth-Century China.* Stanford: Stanford University Press, 1994.

Kral, Oldrich. "Several Artistic Methods in the Classic Chinese Novel *Ju-lin wai-shi.*" *Archiv Orientalni* 32 (1964): 16–43.

Lau, Joseph S. M. "The Saint as Sinner: Paradox of Love and Virtue in 'The Predestined Couple.'" *Tamkang Review* 1, no. 1 (April 1970), 183–91.

Lee, Yun Phin. "Art and World in the Chinese Short Story: *San-yen* Collections in the Light of Western Critical Method." Ph.D. diss., Washington University, 1982.

Lévy, André. *Inventaire analytique et critique du conte chinois en langue vulgaire.* 4 vols. to date. Paris: Presses Universitaires de France, 1978–.

———. "On the Question of Authorship in Chinese Traditional Fiction." *Hanxue yanjiu* 6, no. 1 (June 1978): 249–68.

Li, Wai-yee. *Enchantment and Disenchantment: Love and Illusion in Chinese Literature.* Princeton: Princeton University Press, 1993.

Li Yu. Trans. Patrick Hanan. *The Carnal Prayer Mat.* New York: Available Press, 1990.

———. Trans. Nathan Mao. *Twelve Towers.* 2d rev. ed. Hong Kong: Chinese University Press, 1979.

Lin, Shuen-fu. "Ritual and Narrative Structure in *Rulin waishi.*" In Plaks, ed., *Chinese Narrative,* 244–65.

Liu, James J. Y. *The Chinese Knight-Errant*. Chicago: University of Chicago Press, 1967.

———. *Chinese Theories of Literature*. Chicago: The University of Chicago Press, 1975.

———. *Language—Paradox—Poetics: A Chinese Perspective*. Princeton: Princeton University Press, 1988.

Liu, Xiaolian. "A Journey of the Mind: The Basic Allegory of *Hou Xiyou ji*." *Chinese Literature: Essays, Articles, Reviews* 13 (Dec. 1991): 35–55.

———. *The Odyssey of the Buddhist Mind: The Allegory of "The Later Journey to the West."* Lanham, Md.: University Press of America, 1994.

Liu Wu-chi. *An Introduction to Chinese Literature*. Bloomington: Indiana University Press, 1966.

Lo, Andrew Hing-bun. "*San-kuo yen-i* and *Shui-hu chuan* in the Context of Historiography: An Interpretive Study." Ph.D. diss., Princeton University, 1981.

Lowry, Kathryn. "Excess and Restraint: Feng Menglong's Prefaces on Current Songs." *Papers on Chinese History* (Fairbank Center for East Asian Research, Harvard University) 2 (Spring 1993): 94–119.

Lu, Sheldon Hsiao-peng. *From Historicity to Fictionality: The Chinese Poetics of Narrative*. Stanford: Stanford University Press, 1994.

Lu, Tonglin. *Rose and Lotus: Narrative Desire in France and China*. Albany: State University of New York Press, 1991.

Luo Guanzhong. Trans. Moss Roberts. *Three Kingdoms: A Historical Novel*. Berkeley: University of California Press, 1991.

Ma, Y. W. "The Knight-Errant in *Hua-pen* Stories." *T'oung Pao* 61: 4–5 (1975): 266–300.

———. "The Textual Tradition of Ming *Kung-an* Fiction: A Study of the *Lung-t'u kung-an*." *Harvard Journal of Asiatic Studies* 35 (1975): 190–220.

———, and Joseph S. M. Lau, eds. *Traditional Chinese Stories: Themes and Variations*. New York: Columbia University Press, 1978.

Mann, Susan. *Precious Records: Women in China's Long Eighteenth Century*. Stanford: Stanford University Press, 1997.

Mao, Nathan, and Liu Ts'un-yan. *Li Yü*. Boston: Twayne, 1977.

McLaren, Anne E. "Chantefables and the Textual Evolution of the *San-kuo chih yen-i.*" *T'oung Pao* 71, no. 4–5 (1985): 159–227.

———, trans. *The Chinese Femme Fatale: Stories from the Ming Period.* University of Sydney, 1994.

———. "Ming Chantefables and the Early Chinese Novel: A Study of the Chenghua Period *cihua.*" Ph.D. diss., Australian National University, 1983.

McMahon, Keith. "A Case for Confucian Sexuality: The Eighteenth-Century Novel *Yesou puyan.*" *Late Imperial China* 9, no. 2 (Dec. 1988): 32–55.

———. *Causality and Containment in Seventeenth-Century Chinese Fiction.* Leiden: E. J. Brill, 1988.

———. *Misers, Shrews, and Polygamists: Sexuality and Male-Female Relations in Eighteenth-Century Chinese Fiction.* Durham, N. C.: Duke University Press, 1995.

Miller, Lucien. *Masks of Fiction in Dream of the Red Chamber: Myth, Mimesis, and Persona.* Tuscon: University of Arizona Press, 1975.

———. "Sequels to *The Red Chamber Dream:* Observations on Plagiarism, Imitation and Originality in Chinese Vernacular Literature." *Tamkang Review* 5, no. 2 (1974): 187–215.

Miyazaki, Ichisada. *China's Examination Hell.* New York: Weatherhill, 1976.

Mowry, Hua-yuan Li. *Chinese Love Stories from "Ch'ing-shih."* Hamden, Conn.: Archon Books, 1983.

Naquin, Susan, and Evelyn Rawski. *Chinese Society in the Eighteenth Century.* New Haven: Yale University Press, 1987.

Nienhauser, William H., ed. *Critical Essays on Chinese Literature.* Hong Kong: The Chinese University of Hong Kong, 1976.

———, ed. and comp. *The Indiana Companion to Traditional Chinese Literature.* Bloomington: Indiana University Press, 1986.

Plaks, Andrew H. "After the Fall: *Hsing-shih yin-yuan chuan* and the Seventeenth-Century Chinese Novel." *Harvard Journal of Asiatic Studies* 45, no. 2 (1985): 543–80.

———. *Archetype and Allegory in the Dream of the Red Chamber.* Princeton: Princeton University Press, 1976.

————, ed. *Chinese Narrative: Critical and Theoretical Essays.* Princeton: Princeton University Press, 1977.

————. "The Chongzhen Commentary on the *Jin Ping Mei:* Gems Amidst the Dross." *Chinese Literature: Essays, Articles, Reviews* 8, no. 1–2 (1986): 19–30.

————. *The Four Masterworks of the Ming Novel.* Princeton: Princeton University Press, 1987.

————. "Full-length *Hsiao-shuo* and the Western Novel: A Generic Reappraisal." In William Tay et al., eds., *China and West: Comparative Literature Studies,* 163–76. Hong Kong: The Chinese University Press, 1980.

————. "*Shui-hu chuan* and the Sixteenth-Century Novel Form: An Interpretive Analysis." *Chinese Literature: Essays, Articles, Reviews* 2.1 (1980): 3–54.

————. "Towards a Critical Theory of Chinese Narrative." In Plaks, ed., *Chinese Narrative,* 309–52.

Průšek, Jaroslav. *Chinese History and Literature: Collection of Studies.* Dordrecht, Holland: Reidel, 1970.

————. "Urban Centers: The Cradle of Popular Fiction." In Cyril Birch, ed., *Studies in Chinese Literary Genres,* 259–98. Berkeley: University of California Press, 1974.

Rawski, Evelyn S. "Economic and Social Foundations of Late Imperial Culture." In Johnson et al., eds., *Popular Culture in Late Imperial China,* 3–33.

Rickett, Adele Austin, ed. *Chinese Approaches to Literature from Confucius to Liang Ch'i-ch'ao.* Princeton: Princeton University Press, 1978.

Roddy, Stephen John. *Literate Identity and Its Fictional Representations in Late Imperial China.* Stanford: Stanford University Press, 1998.

Rolston, David L., ed. *How to Read the Chinese Novel.* Princeton: Princeton University Press, 1990.

————. "Oral Performing Literature in Traditional Chinese Fiction: Nonrealistic Usages in the *Jin Ping Mei cihua* and Their Influence." *CHINOPERL Papers* 17 (1994): 1–110.

————. "'Point of View' in the Writings of Traditional Chinese Fiction Critics." *Chinese Literature: Essays, Articles, Reviews* 15 (1993): 113–42.

———. Review of Patrick Hanan, *The Invention of Li Yu. Ming Studies* 29 (Spring 1990): 56–64.

———. *Traditional Chinese Fiction and Fiction Commentary.* Stanford: Stanford University Press, 1997.

Ropp, Paul S. *Dissent in Early Modern China: "Ju-lin wai-shih" and Ch'ing Social Criticism.* Ann Arbor: University of Michigan Press, 1981.

Roy, David T., trans. *The Plum in the Golden Vase, or Chin P'ing Mei,* vol. 1, *The Gathering.* Princeton: Princeton University Press, 1993.

Salmon, Claudine, ed. *Literary Migrations: Traditional Chinese Fiction in Asia (17th–20th Centuries).* Beijing: International Publishing Corp., 1987.

Scott, Mary Elizabeth. "Azure from Indigo: *Honglou Meng*'s Debt to *Jin Ping Mei.*" Ph.D. diss., Princeton University, 1989.

Shi Nai'an and Luo Guanzhong. Trans. Sidney Shapiro. *Outlaws of the Marsh.* Beijing: Foreign Languages Press; Bloomington: Indiana University Press, 1981.

Spence, Jonathan D. *Ts'ao Yin and the K'ang-hsi Emperor.* New Haven: Yale University Press, 1966.

Strassberg, Richard E. *The World of K'ung Shang-jen.* New York: Columbia University Press, 1983.

Swatek, Catherine C. "Feng Menglong's 'Romantic Dream': Strategies of Containment in His Revision of 'The Peony Pavilion.'" Ph.D. diss., Columbia University, 1990.

———. "Plum and Portrait: Feng Meng-lung's Revision of The Peony Pavilion." *Asia Major* 3rd series, 6, no. 1 (1993): 127–60.

Swihart, De-an Wu. "The Evolution of Chinese Novel Form." Ph.D. diss., Princeton University, 1990.

Tien, Ju-k'ang. *Male Anxiety and Female Chastity: A Comparative Study of Chinese Ethical Values in Ming-Ch'ing Times.* Leiden: E. J. Brill, 1988.

Wang, Jing. *The Story of Stone: Intertextuality, Ancient Chinese Stone Lore, and the Stone Symbolism in "Dream of the Red Chamber," "Water Margin," and "The Journey to the West."* Durham, N.C.: Duke University Press, 1992.

Wang, John C. Y. *Chin Sheng-t'an.* New York: Twayne, 1972.

Widmer, Ellen. "*Hsi-yu cheng-tao shu* in the Context of Wang Ch'i's Publishing Enterprise." *Chinese Studies* 6, no. 1 (1988): 37–64.

———. *The Margins of Utopia:* Shui-hu hou-chuan *and the Literature of Ming Loyalism.* Cambridge: Harvard University Press, 1987.

———. "Xiaoqing's Literary Legacy and the Place of the Woman Writer in Late Imperial China." *Late Imperial China* 13, no. 1 (June 1992): 111–55.

———, and Kang-I Sun Chang, eds. *Writing Women in Late Imperial China.* Stanford: Stanford University Press, 1997.

Wivell, Charles. "The Chinese Oral and Pseudo-Oral Narrative Traditions." *Transactions of the International Conference of Orientalists in Japan* 16 (1971): 53–65.

———. "The Term 'Hua-pen.'" In David Buxbaum and Frederick W. Mote, eds., *Transition and Permanence: Chinese History and Culture,* 295–306. Hong Kong: Cathay Press, 1972.

Wong, Timothy C. "Entertainment as Art: An Approach to the *Ku-Chin Hsiao-Shuo.*" *Chinese Literature: Essays, Articles, Reviews* 3, no. 2 (July 1981): 235–50.

———. "Morality as Entertainment: Altruistic Friendship in the *Ku-chin hsiao-shuo.*" *Tamkang Review* 13, no. 1 (Fall 1982): 55–69.

Wu Cheng'en. Trans. Anthony C. Yu. *The Journey to the West.* 4 vols. Chicago: University of Chicago Press, 1977–83.

Wu, Hua Laura. "Jin Shengtan (1608–1661): Founder of a Chinese Theory of the Novel." Ph.D. diss., University of Toronto, 1993.

Wu Jingzi. Trans. Yang Xianyi and Gladys Yang. *The Scholars.* Beijing: Foreign Languages Press, 1957.

Wu, Pei-yi. *The Confucian's Progress.* Princeton: Princeton University Press, 1990.

Wu, Yenna. *The Chinese Virago: A Literary Theme.* Cambridge: Council on East Asian Studies, Harvard University, 1995.

———. "The Inversion of Marital Hierarchy: Shrewish Wives and Henpecked Husbands in Seventeenth-Century Chinese Literature." *Harvard Journal of Asiatic Studies* 48, no. 2 (Dec. 1988): 363–82.

———. "Repetition in *Xingshi yinyuan zhuan.*" *Harvard Journal of Asiatic Studies* 51, no. 1 (1991): 55–87.

Yang, Lien-sheng. "The Concept of *Pao* as a Basis for Social Relations in China." In John K. Fairbank, ed., *Chinese Thought and Institutions,* 291–309. Chicago: University of Chicago Press, 1957.

Yang, Shuhui. *Appropriation and Representation: Feng Menglong and the Chinese Vernacular Story.* Ann Arbor: Center for Chinese Studies, University of Michigan, 1998.

Yang Xianyi and Gladys Yang, trans. *The Courtesan's Jewel Box: Chinese Stories of the Xth–XVIIth Centuries.* Beijing: Foreign Languages Press, 1981.

———, trans. *Lazy Dragon: Chinese Stories from the Ming Dynasty.* Hong Kong: Joint Publishing Co., 1981.

Yen, Yüan-shu. "Biography of the White Serpent: A Keatsian Interpretation." *Tamkang Review* I, no. 2 (Oct. 1970): 227–43.

Yu, Anthony C. "History, Fiction, and Reading Chinese Narrative." *Chinese Literature: Essays, Articles, Reviews* 10, no. 1–2 (1988): 1–19.

Yuan Hongdao et al. Trans. Jonathan Chaves. *Pilgrim of the Clouds: Poems and Essays by Yüan Hung-tao and His Brothers.* New York: Weatherhill, 1978.

Zeitlin, Judith T. *Historian of the Strange: Pu Songling and the Chinese Classical Tale.* Stanford: Stanford University Press, 1993.

———. "Shared Dreams: The Story of the Three Wives' Commentary on *The Peony Pavilion.*" *Harvard Journal of Asiatic Studies* 54, no. 1 (1994): 127–79.

Zhao Yiheng. "The Uneasy Narrator: Fiction and Culture in Early Twentieth-Century China." Ph.D. diss., University of California at Berkeley, 1988.

Zhou, Zuyan. "Carnivalization in *The Journey to the West:* Cultural Dialogism in Fictional Festivity." *Chinese Literature: Essays Articles, Reviews,* 16 (1994), 69–92.

Chinese-Language Works

Chen Dakang 陳大康. *Tongsu xiaoshuo de lishi guiji* 通俗小説的歷史軌跡. Changsha: Hunan Chubanshe, 1993.

Chen Hong 陳洪. *Zhongguo xiaoshuo lilun shi* 中國小説理論史. Hefei, Anhui: Anhui Wenyi, 1992.

Chen Wanyi 陳萬益. "Feng Menglong 'qingjiao shuo' shilun" 馮夢龍『情教説』試論. *Hanxue yanjiu* 6.1 (June 1988): 297–307.

———. *Wan-Ming xiaopin yu Mingji wenren shenghuo* 晚明小品與明季文人生活. Taipei: Da'an, 1988.

Cheng Hong 程弘. "*Jingshi tongyan* zhong de aiqing gushi" 警世通言中的愛情故事. In *Ming-Qing xiaoshuo yanjiu lunwenji*, 1–7. Beijing: Renmin Wenxue, 1959.

Dai Bufan 戴不凡. *Xiaoshuo jianwen lu* 小説見聞錄. Hangzhou: Zhejiang Renmin, 1982.

Dong Guoyan 董國炎. *Dangzi, rouging, tongxin: Mingdai xiaoshuo si chao* 蕩子，柔情，童心：明代小説思潮. Taiyuan: Beiyue Wenyi, 1992.

Fang Zhengyao 方正耀. *Ming Qing renqing xiaoshuo yanjiu* 明清人情小説研究. Shanghai: Huadong Shifan Daxue, 1986.

Feng Menglong 馮夢龍. *Feng Menglong quanji* 馮夢龍全集. Ed. Wei Tongxian 魏同賢. 43 vols. Shanghai: Shanghai Guji, 1993.

———. *Gujin xiaoshuo* 古今小説. Shanghai: Shanghai Guji, 1987.

———. *Jingshi tongyan* 警世通言. Ed. Wu Shuyin 吳書蔭. Beijing: Beijing Shiyue Wenyi, 1994.

———. *Jingshi tongyan* 警世通言. Ed. Yan Dunyi 嚴敦易. 2 vols. Beijing: Renmin Wenxue, 1987.

———. *Xingshi hengyan* 醒世恆言. Ed. Gu Xuejie 顧學頡. 2 vols. Beijing: Renmin Wenxue, 1987.

———. *Xingshi hengyan* 醒世恆言. Ed. Zhang Minggao 張明高. Beijing: Beijing Shiyue Wenyi, 1994.

———. *Yushi mingyan* 喻世明言. Ed. Chen Xizhong 陳曦鐘. Beijing: Beijing Shiyue Wenyi, 1994.

———. *Yushi mingyan* 喻世明言. Ed. Xu Zhengyang 許政揚. 2 vols. Beijing: Renmin Wenxue, 1987.

Gao Hongjun 高洪鈞. "*Guazhir* chengshu kao ji Feng Menglong Hou Huiqing lianli yuanwei" 『掛枝兒』成書考及馮夢龍侯慧卿戀離原委. *Zhongguo gudai jindai wenxue yanjiu* (July 1992): 195–200.

Guo Shaoyu 郭紹虞. *Zhongguo wenxue piping shi* 中國文學批評史. Rev. ed. Shanghai: Shanghai Guji, 1979.

———, comp. *Zhongguo lidai wenlun xuan* 中國歷代文論選. 4 vols. Shanghai: Shanghai Guji, 1979.

Guo Yushi 郭豫適. *Zhongguo gudai xiaoshuo lunji* 中國古代小說論集 Shanghai: Huadong Shifan Daxue, 1985.

He Guli 何谷理 [Hegel, Robert E.]. "Zhanghui xiaoshuo fazhan zhong sheji dao de jingji jishu yinsu" 章回小說發展中涉及到的經濟因素. *Hanxue yanjiu* 6.1 (1988):191–97.

Hong Pian. 洪楩. *Qingpingshan tang huaben* 清平山堂話本. Reprint, Shanghai: Shanghai Guji, 1992.

Hu Shiying 胡士瑩. *Huaben xiaoshuo gailun* 話本小說概論. 2 vols. Beijing: Zhonghua Shuju, 1980.

Hu Wanchuan 胡萬川. "*Sanyan* xu ji meipi de zuozhe wenti." 『三言』敘及眉批的作者問題. Reprinted in his *Huaben yu caizi jiaren xiaoshuo zhi yanjiu,* 123–38. Taipei: Da'an, 1994.

Huang Lin 黃霖 and Han Tongwen 韓同文. *Zhongguo lidai xiaoshuo lunzhu xuan* 中國歷代小說論著選. Nanchang: Jiangxi Renmin, 1990.

Jiang Ruizao 蔣瑞藻. *Xiaoshuo kaozheng* 小說考證. 2 vols. Shanghai: Shanghai Guji, 1984.

Li Huiwu 李悔吾. *Zhongguo xiaoshuo shi mangao* 中國小說史漫稿. Wuhan: Hubei Jiaoyu, 1992.

Li Mengsheng 李夢生. *Zhongguo jinhui xiaoshuo baihua* 中國禁毀小說百話. Shanghai: Shanghai Guji, 1994.

Li Yu 李漁. *Li Yu quanji* 李漁全集. 20 vols. Hangzhou: Zhejiang Guji, 1991.

Liao Kebin 廖可斌. *Mingdai wenxue fugu yundong yanjiu* 明代文學復古運動研究. Shanghai: Shanghai Guji, 1994.

Ling Mengchu 凌濛初. *Chuke Pai'an jingqi* 初刻拍案驚奇. Ed. Zhang Peiheng 張培衡 and Wang Gulu 王古魯. 2 vols. Shanghai: Shanghai Guji, 1982.

———. *Erke Pai'an jingqi* 二刻拍案驚奇. Ed. Zhang Peiheng 張培衡 and Wang Gulu 王古魯. 2 vols. Shanghai: Shanghai Guji, 1983.

Liu Hongjun 劉紅軍. "Li Yu xiaoshuo chuangzuo tong xiju chuangzuo de guanxi 李漁小說創作同戲劇創作的關係," *Xinyang shifan xueyuan xuebao: Zheshe ban* 信陽師範學院報：哲社版, 1996. 2:57–61. Reprinted in *Zhongguo gudai jindai wenxue yanjiu* (Beijing: Renmin Daxue Fuyin Ziliao) 1996. 7:98–103.

Lu Shulun 陸樹侖. *Feng Menglong yanjiu* 馮夢龍研究. Shanghai: Fudan Daxue, 1987.

———. *Feng Menglong sanlun* 馮夢龍散論. Shanghai: Shanghai Guji, 1993.

Lu Xun 魯迅. *Gu xiaoshuo gouchen* 古小說鉤沈. 2 vols. Reprint, Hong Kong: Xinyi, 1976.

Ouyang Daifa 歐陽代發. *Huaben xiaoshuo shi* 話本小說史. Wuhan: Wuhan Chubanshe, 1994.

Qi Yukun 齊裕焜. *Mingdai xiaoshuo shi* 明代小說史. Hangzhou: Zhejiang Guji, 1997.

Qian Mingzi 潛明茲. "*Sanyan* de meixue lixiang" 『三言』的美學理想. *Zhongguo gudai jindai wenxue yanjiu* (May 1992): 237–44.

Shi Changyu 石昌渝. *Zhongguo xiaoshuo yuanliu lun* 中國小說源流論. Beijing: Sanlian, 1994.

Sun Kaidi 孫楷第. *Zhongguo tongsu xiaoshuo shumu* 中國通俗小說書目. Beijing: Renmin Wenxue, 1982.

Sun Xun 孫遜 and Sun Juyuan 孫菊園. *Zhongguo gudian xiaoshuo meixue ziliao huicui* 中國古典小說美學資料匯粹. Shanghai: Shanghai Guji, 1991.

Tan Zhengbi 譚正璧. *Huaben yu guju* 話本與古劇. Rev. ed. Shanghai: Shanghai Guji, 1985.

———, ed. *Qingpingshan tang huaben* 清平山堂話本. Shanghai: Gudian Wenxue, 1957.

———, ed. *Sanyan Liangpai ziliao* 三言兩拍資料. 2 vols. Shanghai: Shanghai Guji, 1980.

———— and Tan Xun 譚尋. *Guben xijian xiaoshuo huikao* 古本稀見小說匯考. Hangzhou: Zhejiang Wenyi, 1984.

Wang Ling 王凌. *Jiren, qingzhong, qipinguan: Feng Menglong tanyou* 畸人，情種，七品官：馮夢龍探幽. Fuzhou: Haixia Wenyi, 1992.

Wang Yunxi 王運熙 and Gu Yisheng 顧易生, eds. *Zhongguo wenxue piping shi* 中國文學批評史. 3 vols. Shanghai: Shanghai Guji, 1981.

Wang Zhizhong 王枝忠. *Gudian xiaoshuo kaolun* 古典小說考論. Yinchuan: Ningxia Renmin, 1992.

Wu Shiyu 吳士余. *Zhongguo xiaoshuo siwei de wenhua jizhi* 中國小說思維的文化機制. Shanghai: Huadong Shifan Daxue, 1990.

Xia Xianchun 夏咸淳. *Wan Ming shifeng yu wenxue* 晚明士風與文學. Beijing: Zhongguo Shehui Kexue, 1994.

Xiao Xiangkai 蕭相愷. *Song Yuan xiaoshuo shi* 宋元小說史 Hangzhou: Zhejiang Guji, 1997.

———— and Zhang Hong 張虹. *Zhongguo gudian tongsu xiaoshuo shilun* 中國古典通俗小說史論. Nanjing: Nanjing Chubanshe, 1994.

Xiao Xinqiao 蕭欣橋. "Dianjiao shuoming" 點校說明. In *Li Yu quanji* 李漁全集, 8: i–ii. Hangzhou: Zhejiang Guji, 1991.

Xu Shuofang 徐朔方. *Xu Shuofang ji* 徐朔方集. 5 vols. Hangzhou: Zhejiang Guji, 1993.

Yang Jialuo 楊家駱, ed. *Quan Ming zaju* 全明雜劇. Taipei: Dingwen, 1979.

Yang Jun 楊雋. "Chenqie yishi yu nüxing renge: Gudai shidafu wenren xintai yanjiu zhiyi" 臣妾意識與女性人格——古代士大夫人心態研究之一. *Zhongguo gudai jindai wenxue yanjiu* (November 1991): 20–29.

Yang Yi 楊義. *Zhongguo gudian xiaoshuo shilun* 中國古典小說史論. Beijing: Zhongguo Shehui Kexue, 1996.

Ye Ru 野儒. "Guanyu Feng Menglong de shenshi" 關於馮夢龍的身世. In *Ming-Qing xiaoshuo yanjiu lunwen ji* 明清小說論文集, 34–38. Beijing: Renmin Wenxue, 1959.

————. "Guanyu *Sanyan* de zuanjizhe" 關於三言的纂集者. In *Ming-Qing xiaoshuo yanjiu lunwen ji*, 29–33. Beijing: Renmin Wenxue, 1959.

Zhang Jigao 張季皋. *Ming Qing xiaoshuo cidian* 明清小說辭典. Shijiazhuang: Huashan Wenyi, 1992.

Zhang Jun 張俊. *Qingdai xiaoshuo shi* 清代小説史. Beijing: Zhongguo Renmin Daxue, 1989.

Zhang Tingyu 張廷玉 et al., eds. *Ming shi* 明史. Beijing: Zhonghua Shuju, 1974.

Zhang Zhenjun 張振軍. *Chuantong xiaoshuo yu Zhongguo wenhua* 傳統小説與中國文化. Guilin: Guangxi Shifan Daxue, 1996.

Zhao Xingqin 趙興勤. "Cai yu mei: Ming-Qing xiaoshuo chutan" 才與美：明清小説初探. *Ming Qing xiao shuo luncong* 明清小説論叢 4 (1986): 14–23.

Zheng Zhenduo 鄭振鐸. *Zhongguo su wenxue shi* 中國俗文學史. Reprint, Beijing: Dongfang, 1996.

Zhongguo tongsu xiaoshuo zongmu tiyao 中國通俗小説總目提要. Ed. Jiangsu Shehui Kexue Yuan Ming-Qing Xiaoshuo Yanjiu Zhongxin Wenxue Yanjiusuo 江蘇社會科學院明清小説研究中心文學研究所. Beijing: Zhongguo Wenlian, 1990.

Zhou Qizhi 周啓志, Yang Lierong 羊列容, and Xie Xin 謝昕. *Zhongguo tongsu xiaoshuo lilun gangyao* 中國通俗小説理論綱要. Taipei: Wenjin, 1992.

Zhou Weipei 周維培. *Gudian xiaoshuo lansheng* 古典小説攬勝. Zhengzhou: Zhongzhou Guji, 1994

Zhu Yixuan 朱一玄. *Ming Qing xiaoshuo ziliao xuanbian* 明清小説資料選編. 2 vols. Jinan: Qilu Shushe, 1989.